AF238138

Diccionario de Contabilidad Inglés-Español

Colección
Derecho de la A a la Z

Centre for Lexicography
(ASB, Universidad de Aarhus)

Escuela de Empresariales
(Universidad de Valladolid)

DICCIONARIO DE CONTABILIDAD INGLÉS-ESPAÑOL

ARANZADI

Primera edición, 2010

Editorial Aranzadi, SA
Camino de Galar, 15
31190 Cizur Menor (Navarra)

Imprime: Rodona Industria Gráfica, SL
Polígono Agustinos, Calle A, Nave D-11
31013 - Pamplona

Depósito Legal: NA 1301/2010

ISBN: 978-84-9903-459-1
Printed in Spain. Impreso en España

Autores

Pedro A. Fuertes Olivera
Profesor Titular de Filología Inglesa. E.U.E. Empresariales de la Universidad de Valladolid.

Pablo Gordo Gómez
Profesor Titular de Economía Aplicada. E.U.E. Empresariales de la Universidad de Valladolid.

Marta Niño Amo
Profesora Titular de Economía Financiera y Contabilidad. E.U.E. Empresariales de la Universidad de Valladolid.

Ángel de los Ríos Rodicio
Profesor Titular de Economía Aplicada. E.U.E. Empresariales de la Universidad de Valladolid.

Mª Ángeles Sastre Ruano
Profesora Titular de Lengua Española. Facultad de Filosofía y Letras de la Universidad de Valladolid.

Sven Tarp
Catedrático de Lexicografía, Centre for Lexicography, Aarhus School of Business, Universidad de Aarhus.

María Sol Velasco Sacristán
Profesora Titular de Filología Inglesa. E.U.E. Empresariales de la Universidad de Valladolid.

Sandro Nielsen
Profesor Titular de Lexicografía, Inglés y Traducción. Centre for Lexicography, Aarhus School of Business, Universidad de Aarhus.

Lise Mourier
Profesora Titular de Inglés y Traducción. Copenhagen Business School.

Henning Bergenholtz
Catedrático de Lexicografía, Centre for Lexicography, Aarhus School of Business, Universidad de Aarhus.

Base de datos y Diseño

Richard Almind
Ayudante de Investigación. Centre for Lexicography, Aarhus School of Business. Universidad de Aarhus.

PRÓLOGO

El *Diccionario de Contabilidad Inglés-Español* se ha elaborado en el marco de los Proyectos de Investigación "El Inglés y el Español en Internet: Construcción de Diccionarios de Economía" (Ref. FFI2008-01703/FILO), financiado por el Ministerio de Ciencia e Innovación, y "Lexicografía Pedagógica Especializada: La construcción de Introducciones Sistemáticas Bilingües (Inglés-Español) en el Campo de la Economía", (Ref. VA039A09), financiado por la Junta de Castilla y León.

Forma parte de un conjunto de diccionarios desarrollados originariamente en el Centre for Lexicography, Aarhus School of Business, Universidad de Aarhus (Dinamarca). Desde el año 2008 diversos investigadores de la Universidad de Valladolid se han sumado a los trabajos del Centre for Lexicography con objeto de continuar la labor investigadora llevada a cabo en Dinamarca, lo que ha permitido acceder al conocimiento y la tecnología lexicográfica creados en Dinamarca en los últimos 20 años. En un futuro próximo está prevista la publicación de otros dos diccionarios hermanos: el *Diccionario de Contabilidad Español-Inglés y el Diccionario de Contabilidad Español.* Aunque cada diccionario es independiente, fundamentalmente porque incorpora una selección de palabras propias, debemos resaltar que todos ellos se basan en los principios de la *teoría funcional de la lexicografía* elaborada en el Centre for Lexicography.

Un mismo planteamiento teórico facilita la construcción de diccionarios con una misma idea. Para nosotros un diccionario como éste es una herramienta de uso que debe tener el objetivo de ayudar al usuario a llevar a cabo todas o algunas de estas funciones: leer, escribir y traducir textos de contabilidad desde el inglés al español. Por este motivo, los usuarios del diccionario encontrarán datos gramaticales de la palabra inglesa y su definición en inglés, una palabra equivalente en español, frases, ejemplos, y diversas notas sobre aspectos importantes de la contabilidad. Esta estructura lexicográfica es muy similar al diccionario fuente del que surge: *Den Engelske Regnskabsordbog (The English Dictionary of Accounting)* desarrollado por Sandro Nielsen, Lise Mourier y Henning Bergenholtz, y por Richard Almind (diseño de la base de datos y del formato).

En especial el diccionario puede ser de gran utilidad para cuatro tipos de usuarios definidos: (I) traductores; (II) profesionales de la contabilidad y la auditoría; (III) estudiantes de Económicas/Empresariales; (IV) legos interesados en la materia. Como se verá en la Guía de Uso, cada uno de estos usuarios potenciales puede encontrar en los artículos del diccionario datos suficientes y lexicográficamente relevantes sobre la terminología de la contabilidad y sus características. Por ejemplo, hemos prestado una gran atención a la terminología española empleada en los manuales de contabilidad, finanzas, gestión y economía. También está presente la terminología de las Normas Internacionales de Contabilidad (NICs), las Normas Internacionales de Información Financiera (NIIFs), y el Nuevo Plan General Contable (NPGC). Teniendo en cuenta que las necesidades de los usuarios son diferentes, que existen tradiciones contables específicas, y que estamos asistiendo a un proceso de armonización contable, el diccionario incluye notas explicativas de hechos lexicográficamente relevantes. Por ejemplo, en aquellos casos en los que la terminología "oficial" nueva –es decir, la que aparece por vez primera en las Normas y en el NPGC– no concuerda con la terminología tradicional (por ejemplo, **coste incremental y coste marginal**), el diccionario recoge este hecho en una nota de uso (*usage note*) como la siguiente:
Although traditional Spanish accounting texts have used 'coste marginal', the Nuevo Plan General Contable has adopted the IAS/IFRS term 'coste incremental'.

Finalmente, debemos indicar que el *Diccionario Inglés-Español de Contabilidad* es el resultado de un trabajo de cooperación internacional que se ha beneficiado de las sinergias conseguidas gracias a los fondos aportados por las administraciones españolas mencionadas en el párrafo inicial y por diversas instituciones danesas: FRS's Studie -& Understøttelsesfond, Kraks Fond, Generalkonsulinde Anna Hedorf og Generalkonsul Frode Hedorfs Fond, y Mads Clausens Fond. Queremos mostrar nuestro agradecimiento a todos los patrocinadores daneses y españoles y destacar la importancia de la cooperación internacional, que ha hecho posible el desarrollo de un proyecto tan importante y ambicioso.

GUÍA DE USO DEL DICCIONARIO

Un diccionario es una obra de referencia y una herramienta de consulta que puede tener una o varias funciones. El *Diccionario de Contabilidad Inglés-Español* tiene varias funciones. *Puede ayudarte a solucionar problemas comunicativos* (por ejemplo, cuando quieras traducir al español un texto de contabilidad escrito en inglés, o cuando quieras leer un texto de contabilidad escrito en inglés, o cuando quieras escribir un texto de contabilidad). También puede *ayudarte a aumentar tus conocimientos sobre la contabilidad.*

Los artículos del diccionario tienen una estructura típica que te mostramos a continuación. Utilizamos como ejemplo la entrada **abandoned operation**. Es importante que tengas una visión general de la estructura de los artículos, teniendo en cuenta que la misma responde a las funciones del diccionario. El ejemplo que te ofrecemos a continuación te indica también los diferentes tipos de información que puedes encontrar en las entradas del diccionario:

abandoned operation UK/IAS/IFRS	entrada
= abandoned activity	sinónimo de la entrada
An abandoned operation is a non-current asset or an activity that is held, but not in continuing use. Abandoned operations may not be intended sold, but rather used to the end of their economic lives - during which period the operation will recover its carrying amount - or closed down, and therefore they are not classified as held for sale. Abandoned operations may be seen as discontinued operations at the date when they are not used anymore and closed down.	definición de la entrada en inglés
operación interrumpida	palabra equivalente en español
= actividad interrumpida	sinónimo de la palabra equivalente en español
revenue from abandoned operations ingreso procedente de operaciones interrumpidas	*frase en inglés* traducida al español
SOURCE IFRS 5	SOURCE te lleva a un sitio de Internet donde puedes consultar textos en los que aparece la entrada
⇒ discontinued operation	referencia cruzada a otro artículo del diccionario relacionado con la entrada

En este diccionario se usan los siguientes términos gramaticales:

adjective	adjetivo
adverb	adverbio
noun	nombre / sustantivo
preposition	preposición
verb	verbo

En situaciones comunicativas, el diccionario puede ayudarte a solucionar los problemas que tengas a la hora de **traducir**, **escribir** o **leer** un texto de contabilidad.

Ayuda para traducir al español textos de contabilidad escritos en inglés

A la hora de traducir al español textos de contabilidad pueden surgirte dudas sobre la palabra española equivalente o sobre la forma correcta de escribirla. Te ofrecemos información sobre estos dos aspectos en la presentación de la palabra española. Por regla general, ofrecemos una **sola** palabra equivalente en español para cada entrada inglesa. La palabra equivalente en español es la que recomendamos. En caso de que existan otra u otras palabras posibles las ofrecemos como sinónimos, precedidas por el símbolo =, y las colocamos debajo de la palabra española, como vemos en la entrada de **insurance contract**.

insurance contract
contrato de seguro
= contrato de seguros
póliza de seguro
póliza de seguros

En algunos casos el artículo del diccionario sólo contiene una referencia precedida por el símbolo →. Este símbolo te dirige a la entrada indicada a continuación del mismo y te indica que no debes usar la primera entrada, o bien porque está escrita de forma incorrecta o bien porque no la recomienda el diccionario:

break-even analysis
→ breakeven analysis

Si consultas la entrada que hay después del símbolo, que es la entrada recomendada por el diccionario, puedes encontrar la información que el diccionario ofrece:

breakeven analysis
A breakeven analysis is an analysis that makes it possible to calculate the breakeven point and constitutes the first step in a cost-volume-profit analysis.
análisis del punto muerto
= análisis del umbral de rentabilidad
an expanded breakeven analysis un análisis del punto muerto ampliado
do a breakeven analysis llevar a cabo un análisis del punto muerto
⇒ breakeven chart, breakeven point, cost-volume-profit-analysis

La definición que te ofrecemos en la mayoría de las entradas es de gran ayuda: te permite confirmar o desmentir la idea inicial que puedas tener sobre el significado de la palabra inglesa que quieres traducir. Si no estás seguro de que el significado de la palabra inglesa que quieres traducir es el mismo que tú crees, el diccionario te permite confirmar o desmentir tus suposiciones con la definición. Las definiciones son completamente necesarias en todos los casos y son especialmente útiles cuando la palabra inglesa tiene más de un significado. En estos casos en los que la misma palabra inglesa tiene más de un significado, el diccionario te informa sobre dos "tipos de significados diferentes" posibles. Uno de ellos procede de la existencia de di-

ferencias gramaticales entre las dos palabras (por ejemplo una es un verbo y la otra es un nombre). En estos casos la diferencia se indica con un número superíndice, como vemos a continuación:
benchmark[1] *noun*
A benchmark is a standard or measurement by which an enterprise measures its organisational performance and practices …

benchmark[2] *verb*
To benchmark means to use as a reference standard for comparison, e.g. the organisational performance and practices of an …

El otro caso ocurre cuando la diferencia de significados de la misma palabra no se debe a razones gramaticales (es decir, las dos palabras son nombres, o adjetivos, o verbos); en este segundo caso la diferencia de significados se indica colocando un número delante de la definición. Por ejemplo, **depreciation** tiene dos significados:

depreciation
1. Depreciation is the systematic allocation of the cost of an asset over its useful life. Several depreciation methods exist. Depreciation for accounting purposes is differentiated from depreciation for tax purposes, as different rules apply. The term 'amortisation' is generally used when referring to intangible assets, whereas the term 'depreciation' applies to tangible assets.
amortización
2. Depreciation means a reduction in value, e.g. a currency's fall in value.
depreciación

Estas dos formas de separar los significados diferentes te permiten seleccionar con facilidad la palabra española más adecuada y correcta para el texto que estás traduciendo. El diccionario te ofrece todavía más: en algunos casos también puede ser muy útil la información adicional que el diccionario te ofrece en las NOTES. Por ejemplo, en la entrada **incremental cost**, la NOTE precisa el uso de la palabra española tradicional **coste marginal** y el de la nueva palabra **coste incremental** que se usa en el Nuevo Plan General Contable y que procede de una traducción al español de las Normas Internacionales de Contabilidad:

incremental cost
Incremental cost is the differential cost resulting from a decision, i.e. the difference in total cost between two alternatives, where the alternative includes the total cost plus additional costs.
coste marginal
NOTE Although traditional Spanish accounting texts used 'coste marginal' the Nuevo Plan General Contable has adopted the IAS/IFRS term 'coste incremental'.

Como sabemos que las frases son difíciles de traducir, el diccionario quiere ayudarte ofreciéndote más de 27.000 frases inglesas ('collocations') traducidas al español, como las que aparecen en la entrada de **deemed cost**:

deemed cost
…
fair value or reevaluation as deemed cost valor razonable o revalorización como coste atribuido *have a deemed cost of zero in the opening IFRS balance sheet* tener cero como coste atribuido en el balance de apertura basado en la NIIF *the deemed cost of goodwill* el coste…

Ayuda para escribir textos de contabilidad en inglés

El diccionario también puede ayudarte a escribir textos de contabilidad en inglés. En primer lugar, puede ayudarte a resolver las dudas que puedas tener sobre la ortografía exacta de la palabra inglesa que estás escribiendo. Cuando sea relevante, el diccionario te ayuda informándote en la presentación de la entrada si la palabra inglesa es propia del inglés británico (UK), del inglés norteamericano (US), o del inglés internacional (IAS/IFRS). Por ejemplo, las entradas que presentamos a continuación incluyen las etiquetas IAS/IFRS, US y UK, que nos indican que las palabras inglesas correspondientes a la palabra española **cuenta de pérdidas y ganancias** se usan en inglés internacional e inglés norteamericano, y en inglés británico, respectivamente:

income statement IAS/IFRS, US
profit ands loss account[1] UK

En aquellos casos en los que no aparecen las etiquetas UK, US, o IAS/IFRS al lado de la entrada, la palabra inglesa puede usarse en cualquier texto. Esta información no solo es válida para la entrada; también puede aparecer junto a las frases (collocations) y definiciones que pueden identificarse como propias del inglés internacional IAS/IFRS, siglas con las que hacemos referencia, respectivamente, a las Normas Internacionales de Contabilidad (NIC), y a las Normas Internacionales de Información Financiera (NIIF).

El diccionario también te ofrece ayuda cuando estás escribiendo un texto y quieres usar una palabra diferente a la que estás buscando, pero con el mismo significado. Por esta razón el diccionario te ofrece sinónimos, que van precedidos por el símbolo = , y que son las palabras que puedes usar en lugar de la entrada, como por ejemplo:

subsequent event IAS/IFRS, US
= event after the balance sheet date (IAS/IFRS, US), post balance sheet event (UK, US)

El resto de la información ofrecida se puede usar de la misma forma que cuando estás traduciendo (ver la sección anterior sobre traducción). Tiene especial relevancia lo siguiente:

Referencia gramatical: Cuando buscas una palabra o una variante ortográfica que este diccionario no recomienda, la presencia del símbolo → te dirige a la entrada en la que se presenta la palabra recomendada.

Definition: Te permite confirmar o rechazar el significado de una palabra que te ofrece dudas.

Frases (collocations): Aunque las palabras tienden a aparecer juntas sabemos que no todas ellas pueden combinarse. Por esta razón usamos el símbolo ▲ para informarte de la existencia de una serie de frases relevantes en los textos de contabilidad.

Ayuda para leer textos de contabilidad escritos en inglés

Cuando estás leyendo un texto de contabilidad escrito en inglés puedes tener dudas sobre el significado de una palabra. Una solución fácil a este problema te la ofrecen los sinónimos, que siguen al símbolo =, y los antónimos, que van precedidos por el símbolo ≠. Por ejemplo:

control[1] *noun*
1 = dominant influence
≠ significant influence

Normalmente las definiciones te dan la información necesaria. En el diccionario diferenciamos entre las palabras que sólo tienen un solo significado y las que tienen más de uno. La mayoría de las palabras que aparecen en los textos contables sólo tienen un significado, como es el caso de **balance sheet**:

balance sheet
...

The balance sheet is a statement of the enterprise's assets, equity and liabilities at the balance sheet date. The statement is a status report estimating the enterprise's assets, equity and liabilities as a snapshot at a certain date.
balance

En aquellos casos en los que la palabra tiene más de un significado es necesario que establezcas una comparación entre los diferentes significados ofrecidos y el texto que estás leyendo. Los diferentes significados se enumeran mediante una de estas dos formas. Primero, se coloca un número delante de la definición. Segundo, se utiliza un superíndice que indica que cada significado diferente corresponde a palabras gramaticalmente diferentes. En ambos casos la definición va delante de la palabra española equivalente. Por ejemplo:

authority[1] *noun* <no indefinite article, the, no plural>
Authority is the power delegated to a person or body, usually called the agent, to act in a particular way on behalf of someone else, called the principal, thereby creating rights and obligations binding on the principal.
autorización
...
authority[2] *noun* <an, the, authorities>
An authority is an official
organisation with the power or right to direct, control or judge the actions of other people.
autoridad

A veces las palabras se usan en contextos en los que puedes tener dudas sobre su significado concreto en un texto concreto. En esta situación te puede ser de gran ayuda comparar las frases del texto que estás leyendo con las del artículo del diccionario. En este caso las traducciones en español te pueden ayudar a entender el texto.

Ayuda para adquirir algún conocimiento sobre la contabilidad

Las funciones que hemos descrito en las secciones anteriores están relacionadas con funciones comunicativas específicas. Además, el diccionario también te puede ayudar si quieres ampliar tus conocimientos, es decir, *si quieres adquirir algún conocimiento sobre la contabilidad.* Es verdad que un diccionario no es el sustituto de un manual o de un libro de texto. Sin embargo, la información sobre sinónimos, antónimos y las referencias cruzadas precedidas del símbolo ⇒ te permiten ir de un artículo del diccionario a otro y de esta forma aprender algo relacionado con la contabilidad.

En algunos artículos se incluye también la expresión SOURCE seguida de una referencia a una Norma Internacional de Contabilidad o Norma Internacional de Información Financiera (IAS/IFRS). Esta referencia te indica una fuente en la que puedes aumentar el grado de conocimiento sobre alguno de los aspectos contables tratados en el artículo del diccionario. Por ejemplo:

policyholder
...
SOURCE IFRS 4, Appendix A

Apéndices
Al final del libro puedes encontrar 11 ejemplos dedicados a ilustrar algunos formatos contables ingleses con sus traducciones al español. Están divididos en tres conjuntos. El primero contiene ejemplos de documentos contables en inglés internacional: cuentas de pérdidas y ganancias divididas por función y por naturaleza; un balance consolidado; y un flujo de efectivo consolidado. El segundo contiene ejemplos de dos cuentas de pérdidas y ganancias y un balance en inglés británico. El tercero contiene ejemplos de documentos contables en inglés norteamericano: una cuenta de pérdidas y ganancias consolidada; un balance consolidado; un flujo de efectivo consolidado. Estos apéndices te permiten observar la colocación de los conceptos contables centrales en los estados financieros y la terminología contable relevante en inglés y en español.

A

A

1 The letter 'A' is applied by the credit rating agencies Moody's and Standard & Poor's at the credit rating of the creditworthiness of an enterprise. An obligation rated A is somewhat more susceptible to the adverse effects of changes in circumstances and economic conditions than obligations in higher rated categories. However, the capacity to meet financial commitment on the obligation is still strong. A rating between Aaa and Baa3 (Moody's), and AAA and BBB- (Standard & Poor's) is an investment-grade rating. S&P ratings from AA to CCC may be modified by the addition of a plus or a minus sign to show relative standing within the major rating categories, while Moody's applies the figures 1, 2 or 3 for Aa to B ratings.

A

▲ *rated A with Stable Outlook* clasificado A con Stable Outlook

2 The letter 'A' is applied for differentiation between shares in share classes.

A

▲ *share class A* acción de clase A

A rating

An A rating is an assessment of credit risk and investment quality made by a credit agency placing the investment (typically a bond) in the upper medium grade of a rating system. This means that the investment is fairly safe, but suggests that it is susceptible to impairment in future.

rating A

= calificación A, índice A, tipo A

▲ *businesses with an A rating* empresas con un rating A ▲ *give an A rating* calificar con un rating A ▲ *lose one's A rating* perder su rating A

A share US

= class A share

An A share is an ordinary share carrying other rights than B shares. Usually, A shares have more voting rights, e.g. 10 times more votes per share than B shares.

NOTE In some countries, A shares may be non-voting ordinary shares. Whether A shares are voting or non-voting shares will appear from a company's articles of association.

acción de clase A

= acción privilegiada

NOTE In Spanish law shares can have different economic benefits but all of them have the same voting rights.

▲ *A share trading* cotización de la acción de clase A ▲ *acquire A shares* comprar acciones de clase A

⇛ B share, share class

A share capital US

A share capital is the part of share capital that consists of A shares or ordinary shares carrying full voting rights compared with B shares, and A shares typically carry 10 times more votes per share than B shares.

NOTE In some UK companies, A shares have limited voting rights compared with B shares.

capital en acciones de clase A

▲ *the A share capital is held by x* el capital en acciones de clase A pertenece a x

A1

A1 is a notch on the credit rating agency Moody's rating scale for long-term debt ratings classified as upper-medium grade. The lowest investment-grade rating is Baa3, and the highest speculative-grade rating is Ba1.

A1

▲ *a long-term rating of A1* un rating A1 a largo plazo ▲ *an issuer rating of A1* un rating de emisor A1 ▲ *assign a rating of A1* calificar con un rating A1

A2

A2 is a notch on the credit rating agency Moody's rating scale for long-term debt ratings classified as upper medium-grade. The lowest investment-grade rating is Baa3, and the highest speculative-grade rating is Ba1.

A2

▲ *a long-term rating of A2* un rating A2 a largo plazo ▲ *an issuer rating of A2* un rating de emisor A2 ▲ *assign a rating of A2* calificar con un rating A2

A3

A3 is a notch on the credit rating agency Moody's rating scale for long-term debt ratings classified as upper medium-grade. The lowest investment-grade rating is Baa3, and the highest speculative-grade rating is Ba1.

A3

▲ *assign an A3 rating* calificar con un rating A3

AA

AA is a long-term credit rating used by the credit rating agency Standard & Poor's stating that the enterprise has a sound economy and a very strong ability to meet its financial commitment. A rating between AAA and BBB is an investment-grade rating. The ratings from AA to CCC may be modified by the addition of a plus or a minus sign to show relative standing within the major rating categories.

AA

▲ *achieve an AA rating* obtener un rating AA ▲ *award an AA rating* adjudicar un rating AA

Aa

Aa signifies investment-grade rating and is used by the credit rating agency Moody's. The lowest investment-grade rating is Baa3, and the highest speculative-grade rating is Ba1.

Aa

▲ *achieve an Aa rating* obtener un rating Aa ▲ *award an Aa rating* adjudicar un rating Aa

AA rating

An AA rating is an assessment of credit risk and investment quality made by a credit agency (e.g. Standard & Poor's) placing the investment (typically a bond) in the superior grade of a rating system. Although rated as high-grade, the investment still entails a somewhat larger long-term risk than the AAA rated investments.

rating AA

= calificación AA, índice AA, tipo AA

AA

▲ *achieve an AA rating* obtener un rating AA ▲ *assign an AA rating* calificar con un rating AA ▲ *award an AA rating* adjudicar un rating AA

Aa1

Aa1 is a notch on the credit rating agency Moody's rating scale for long-term debt ratings classified as high-grade. The lowest investment-grade rating is Baa3, and the highest speculative-grade rating is Ba1.

Aa1

▲ *achieve an Aa1 rating* obtener un rating Aa1 ▲ *award an Aa1 rating* adjudicar un rating de Aa1 ▲ *long-term debt rating Aa1* deuda a largo plazo con rating Aa1

Aa2

Aa2 is a notch on the credit rating agency Moody's rating scale for long-term debt ratings classified as high-grade. The lowest investment-grade rating is Baa3, and the highest speculative-grade rating is Ba1.

Aa2

▲ *a long-term debt rating of Aa2* una deuda a largo plazo con rating Aa2 ▲ *achieve an Aa2 rating* obtener un rating Aa2 ▲ *award an Aa2 rating* adjudicar un rating Aa2

Aa3

Aa3 is a notch on the credit rating agency Moody's rating scale for long-term debt ratings classified as high-grade. The lowest investment-grade rating is Baa3, and the highest speculative-grade rating is Ba1.

Aa3

▲ *assign an Aa3 rating to a company* calificar una empresa con un rating Aa3 ▲ *award an Aa3 rating* adjudicar un rating Aa3

AAA

AAA is a long-term credit rating used by the credit rating agency Standard & Poor's stating that the enterprise has a high equity ratio and extremely strong ability to meet current liabilities. A rating between AAA and BBB is an investment-grade rating.

AAA

▲ *award an AAA rating* adjudicar un rating AAA ▲ *be rated AAA* estar calificada AAA

Aaa

Aaa is the highest notch on the credit rating agency Moody's

rating scale for long-term debt, also referred to as 'gilt-edged'.
Aaa
▲ *award an Aaa rating* adjudicar un rating Aaa ▲ *with a credit rating of Aaa* con una calificación crediticia Aaa

AAA rating
AAA is a long-term credit rating used by the credit rating agency Standard & Poor's stating that the enterprise has a high equity ratio and extremely strong ability to meet current liabilities. A rating between AAA and BBB is an investment-grade rating.
rating AAA
= calificación AAA, índice AAA, tipo AAA
▲ *assign an AAA rating* calificar con rating AAA ▲ *award an AAA rating* adjudicar un rating AAA

abandoned activity
= abandoned operation
An abandoned activity is a major, separate business segment or other operating activity of an entity that is discontinued because of planned sale, sale or other disposal.
actividad interrumpida
= operación interrumpida
▲ *a scaled-down or abandoned activity* una actividad recortada o interrumpida
⇛ discontinued operation

abandoned asset
Abandoned assets are assets that an enterprise does not hold for sale but for use until the end of the assets' economic lives at which time they are closed and disposed of.
activo abandonado
▲ *a provision for abandoned assets* una provisión para activos abandonados
SOURCE IFRS 5

abandoned operation UK, IAS/IFRS
= abandoned activity
An abandoned operation is a non-current asset or an activity that is held, but not in continuing use. Abandoned operations may not be intended sold, but rather used to the end of their economic lives –during which period the operation will recover its carrying amount– or closed down, and therefore they are not classified as held for sale. Abandoned operations may be seen as discontinued operations at the date when they are not used anymore and closed down.
operación interrumpida
= actividad interrumpida
▲ *revenue from abandoned operations* ingreso procedente de operaciones interrumpidas
SOURCE IFRS 5
⇛ discontinued operation

ABC system US
= activity-based costing system US
The ABC system refers to the activity-based costing system by which costing and resource-consuming activities can be identified and monitored. Under the ABC system, overhead costs are recognised by each function or activity, allowing them to be assigned to individual cost objects (products or services) through the use of cost drivers.
sistema ABC
= método ABC
▲ *an effective ABC system* un sistema ABC eficiente ▲ *implement an ABC system* implementar un sistema ABC

ability to pay
Ability to pay means the capacity to meet demands of payment at the date of maturity.
capacidad de pago
= solvencia de pago
▲ *the customer's ability to pay* la capacidad de pago del cliente ▲ *the debtor's ability to pay* la capacidad de pago del deudor ▲ *the debtor's ability to pay all amounts due* la capacidad del deudor para pagar todas las cantidades vencidas ▲ *the enterprise's ability to pay ongoing pension benefits* la capacidad de la empresa para pagar los planes de pensiones vigentes

ABM US
= activity-based management US
ABM is the abbreviation for activity-based management, i.e. a management accounting system focusing on the use of activity-based costing for operating, marketing, competitive and strategic decision-making. Costs are collected by functions or activities and reduced by analysing cost drivers.
ABM
= sistema de costes ABM, sistema de costes por actividades ABM
▲ *introduce ABM* poner en marcha un sistema ABM ▲ *use ABM* utilizar un sistema ABM

abnormal spoilage

Abnormal spoilage refers to spoilage that does not derive from the daily operations or production processes of an enterprise but which is the result of e.g. machine breakdowns, faulty production processes or unexpected power failures.

deterioro anormal

= desperfecto anómalo

▲ *abnormal spoilage costs* costes por deterioro anormal ▲ *calculate abnormal spoilage* valorar el deterioro anormal

⇛ normal spoilage, spoilage

absence

1 Absence means that something or somebody is not present.

ausencia

= baja

▲ *at the time of the absence* en el momento de la ausencia ▲ *compensate employees for absence for various reasons* compensar a los empleados por baja por varias razones ▲ *in the absence of* en ausencia de ▲ *in the absence of evidence to the contrary* en ausencia de pruebas en contra ▲ *in the absence of explicit guidance* en ausencia de una directriz explícita

2 Absence means that somebody is unable to attend something.

ausencia

▲ *the absence of the chairman of the supervisory board* la ausencia del presidente del comité de supervisión

absence due to sickness

= absence from work due to sickness

Absence due to sickness is an employee's failure to attend work for the reason of bad health.

baja por enfermedad

▲ *a drop in absence due to sickness* un descenso en las bajas por enfermedad ▲ *an increase in absence due to sickness* un aumento en las bajas por enfermedad ▲ *numbers of absence due to sickness by sector* cifras de baja por enfermedad por sectores ▲ *prevent absence due to sickness* prevenir las bajas por enfermedad ▲ *reduce absence due to sickness* reducir las bajas por enfermedad ▲ *targets for absence due to sickness* objetivos en relación con las bajas por enfermedad ▲ *the employees' absence due to sickness* las bajas por enfermedad de los empleados ▲ *total absence due to sickness* total bajas por enfermedad

absenteeism

≠ leave, leave of absence

Absenteeism refers to a period of time during which an employee stays away from work without permission and without legitimate reason.

absentismo

= excedencia, licencia sin sueldo

▲ *employee absenteeism* absentismo laboral ▲ *reduce absenteeism* reducir el absentismo

absorption approach

= absorption costing, allocation costing, full absorption

The absorption approach is a costing method which seeks to estimate the value of an inventory by assigning all variable manufacturing costs and all fixed manufacturing costs to each production unit. The fixed costs are typically allocated to output units based on direct labour hours, machine hours or material costs.

criterio de coste integral

= absorption approach, criterio del coste completo

NOTE Spanish accountants typically maintain English terms for referring to some cost accounting methods.

▲ *based on a full absorption approach* basado en un criterio de coste integral ▲ *use the absorption approach* utilizar el criterio de coste completo

⇛ full costing method, overhead absorption rate

absorption costing

= absorption costing approach, allocation costing

≠ variable costing

Absorption costing is a costing method which seeks to estimate the value of an inventory by assigning all variable manufacturing costs and all fixed manufacturing costs to each production unit. The fixed costs are typically allocated to output units based on direct labour hours, machine hours or material costs.

sistema de coste completo

= coste absorbente, sistema de coste integral

▲ *an alternative to absorption costing* una alternativa al sistema de coste completo ▲ *total*

absorption costing total sistema de coste completo
⇛ full costing, overhead absorption rate

absorption costing approach
= absorption costing, allocation costing
The absorption costing approach is a costing method which seeks to estimate the value of an inventory by assigning all variable manufacturing costs and all fixed manufacturing costs to each production unit. The fixed costs are typically allocated to output units based on direct labour hours, machine hours or material costs.
criterio de coste completo
= criterio de coste integral, método de coste completo
▲ *an alternative to the absorption costing approach* una alternativa al criterio de coste completo ▲ *total absorption costing approach* total criterio de coste completo
⇛ full costing, overhead absorption rate

absorption standard costing
Absorption standard costing is a costing method where all costs related to the production of a unit are calculated by assigning all variable costs and all fixed costs to each production unit according to a set standard. The fixed costs are typically allocated to output units based on direct labour hours, machine hours or material costs.
sistema estándar de coste completo
= sistema estándar de coste integral
▲ *use absorption standard costing* utilizar el sistema estándar de coste completo
⇛ absorption costing

accelerated depreciation
≠ straight-line depreciation
The accelerated depreciation method recognises higher amounts of depreciation in the earlier years and lower amounts in the later years of a fixed asset's life.
amortización acelerada
▲ *accelerated depreciation allowances* deducciones por amortización acelerada ▲ *accelerated depreciation for tax purposes* amortización acelerada por motivos fiscales ▲ *accelerated depreciation on fixed assets traded within the group* amortización acelerada de activos fijos negociados dentro del grupo ▲ *cumulative accelerated depreciation* amortización acelerada acumulada ▲ *eliminate accelerated depreciation in the acquirer* eliminar la amortización acelerada en el adquirente
⇛ declining-balance method, reducing-balance method

accept
To accept is to decide that there is nothing you can do to change a situation or fact or to agree that what someone says is right or true.
aceptar
▲ *accept a note receivable* aceptar un efecto a cobrar ▲ *accept or assume responsibility* aceptar o asumir la responsabilidad ▲ *an employee's decision to accept voluntary redundancy* la decisión de un empleado de aceptar la baja incentivada

acceptance
Acceptance is an affirmative reply provided orally or in writing.
aceptación
= conforme
▲ *acceptance of new contracts* aceptación de nuevos contratos ▲ *acceptance of the group's dispositions* aceptación de los acuerdos de un grupo ▲ *the market's acceptance of price increases* la aceptación por el mercado de las subidas de precios

accepted
Accepted means that something is widely used or approved of.
aceptado
= admitido
▲ *a generally accepted procedure* un procedimiento generalmente aceptado ▲ *accepted industry practices* prácticas aceptadas del sector ▲ *generally accepted accounting principles* principios contables generalmente aceptados ▲ *it is accepted practice* es una práctica aceptada

accessory
Accessory means that something is supplementary, i.e. not an integral part of the main feature.
adicional
▲ *accessory contract* contrato adicional ▲ *accessory revenues* ingresos adicionales

accordance

Accordance means conformity or compliance.

acuerdo

▲ *in accordance with* de acuerdo con ▲ *in accordance with the contingent ordinary share provisions* de acuerdo con las provisiones para acciones ordinarias contingentes ▲ *in accordance with the entity's expected requirements* de acuerdo con los requisitos estimados por la entidad

account[1] *noun* <an, the, -s>

1 An account is a record in monetary terms of accounting transactions listing items of a similar type on a debit or credit basis. Accounts are part of an accounting system and usually classified according to a specific category, e.g. cash account, ledger account, nominal account, contra account, deposit account etc.

cuenta

▲ *a chart of accounts* un plan de cuentas ▲ *a frozen account* una cuenta congelada ▲ *a revenue account* una cuenta de ingresos ▲ *a special account* una cuenta especial ▲ *a T account* una cuenta en T ▲ *a trade receivable account* una cuenta deudora comercial ▲ *an account due* una cuenta vencida ▲ *an account with a securities depositary* una cuenta de títulos ▲ *an asset account* una cuenta de activo ▲ *an equity and liabilities account* una cuenta de pasivo y neto ▲ *an expense account* una cuenta de gastos ▲ *make a deposit on an account* hacer un depósito en una cuenta ▲ *open account* cuenta abierta ▲ *overdraw an account* girar a una cuenta en descubierto ▲ *to balance an account* cuadrar una cuenta ▲ *to charge an account with an amount* cargar una cantidad en un cuenta ▲ *to close an account* cerrar una cuenta ▲ *to credit an account with an amount* abonar una cantidad en una cuenta ▲ *to credit an amount to an account* ingresar una cantidad en una cuenta ▲ *to debit an amount to an account* adeudar una cantidad en una cuenta ▲ *transfer an amount to an account* transferir una cantidad a una cuenta

⇛ accounts

2 An account is an arrangement with a firm allowing credit and deferring payments to a later date, usually the end of the month, or a statement of money paid or due for goods or services.

cuenta

= cuenta abierta

▲ *dealing on own account* girar con cargo a nuestra cuenta ▲ *for the enterprise's own account* para la propia cuenta de la empresa ▲ *safekeeping and administration of financial instruments for the account of clients* custodia y administración de valores de la cuenta de clientes

3 An account is an expression for a regular client or customer who does a large amount of business and has an account with a particular supplier or other enterprise.

cuentas

NOTE Always plural in Spanish.

▲ *account director* director de cuentas ▲ *account executive* ejecutivo de cuentas ▲ *account manager* gestor de cuentas ▲ *key accounts* cuentas clave ▲ *substantial accounts* cuentas representativas

account[2] *noun* <no inflections>

Account means consideration, e.g. to give consideration to something when you plan.

cuenta

= consideración

▲ *not take something into account* no tener algo en cuenta ▲ *take into account* tener en cuenta ▲ *take risks and uncertainties into account* tener en cuenta riesgos e incertidumbres ▲ *taking into account* teniendo en cuenta ▲ *taking into account that* teniendo en cuenta que ▲ *taking into account the loss of capacity resulting from planned maintenance* teniendo en cuenta la pérdida de capacidad resultante del plan de mantenimiento previsto ▲ *when adjustments have been taken into account* cuando se hayan tenido en cuenta los ajustes

account[3] *verb* <-s, -ed, has -ed, -ing> *passive* <is -ed, was -ed>

To account means to show in the enterprise's financial statements or bookkeeping records, usually according to specific rules or methods.

contabilizar
= anotar
▲ *account for* contabilizar ▲ *account for deferred tax in full* contabilizar la totalidad de impuestos diferidos ▲ *account for each component separately* contabilizar cada componente por separado ▲ *account for under an accruals basis* contabilizar según criterio del devengo ▲ *the method used to account for subsidiaries* el método utilizado para contabilizar las filiales

account analysis US
An account analysis measures cost behavior by looking at data in the accounting records. For the analysis, a cost driver is selected, and each account is classified as a variable or fixed cost. Each account balance is then analysed by the cost accountant who estimates the variable cost per unit of cost-driver activity or the periodic fixed cost.
análisis contable
= análisis de cuentas
▲ *based on an account analysis* basado en un análisis contable ▲ *prepare an account analysis* preparar un análisis contable
⇛ engineering analysis

account analysis method
The account analysis method is a method applied for estimating a cost function and identifies whether an account in the accounting system contains variable costs, fixed costs (capacity costs) or a mix of such costs, in relation to the activity.
método de análisis contable
= método de análisis de cuentas
▲ *according to the account analysis method* de acuerdo con el método de análisis contable ▲ *use the account analysis method* utilizar el método de análisis contable
⇛ capacity cost, conference method, fixed cost, variable cost

account for
To account for means to show in the enterprise's financial statements or bookkeeping records, usually according to specific rules of accounting treatment.
contabilizar
= anotar
▲ *account for a lease of land and buildings* contabilizar un arrendamiento financiero de terrenos y construcciones ▲ *account for an error correction retrospectively* contabilizar una corrección de error de forma retrospectiva ▲ *account for impairment losses recognised before the end of the first annual accounting period* contabilizar el reconocimiento de las pérdidas por deterioro antes del fin del primer periodo contable anual

account form
= horizontal format
≠ narrative form US, report form, vertical format
The account form is one of two formats allowed for presenting the balance sheet in the annual report of an enterprise. This format shows assets on the left, liabilities and equity on the right. The alternative form, called the report form, positions assets above liabilities and equity.
forma de cuenta
= formato de cuenta
≠ forma vertical, formato vertical
▲ *format for balance sheet in account form* formato del balance en forma de cuenta ▲ *present a balance sheet in account form* presentar un balance en forma de cuenta

account payable US, IAS/IFRS
= creditor, amount falling due within one year UK, short-term creditor, short-term debt IFRS/IAS, US
≠ account receivable
An account payable is an amount owed by an enterprise to its creditors, e.g. for supplying goods and services. Accounts payable are recognised as current liabilities in the balance sheet.
cuenta acreedora
= cuenta a pagar
≠cuentas a cobrar, cuentas deudoras
▲ *accounts payable* cuentas acreedoras ▲ *accounts payable, total* cuentas acreedoras, total ▲ *accounts payable turnover* rotación de acreedores ▲ *change in trade accounts payable* cambios en las cuentas acreedoras comerciales ▲ *other accounts payable* otras cuentas acreedoras ▲ *trade accounts payable* cuentas acreedoras comerciales

account receivable US, IAS/IFRS

= amount receivable IAS/IFRS, US, debtor UK, receivable IAS/IFRS, US, trade receivable IAS/IFRS, US

≠ account payable, creditor

An account receivable is an amount owed to an enterprise, generally by a customer, as a result of usual extension of credit.

cuenta deudora

= cuenta a cobrar

≠ cuenta a pagar, cuenta acreedora

NOTE Spanish accountants prefer 'cuenta deudora' to the IAS/IFRS term 'cuenta a cobrar'.

▲ *a current account receivable* una cuenta deudora corriente ▲ *accounts receivable turnover* rotación de cuentas a cobrar ▲ *change in trade accounts receivable* cambio en las cuentas deudoras ▲ *measure accounts receivable at amortised cost* medir las cuentas deudoras a valor neto ▲ *other accounts receivable* otras cuentas deudoras ▲ *total accounts receivable* total cuentas deudoras ▲ *write-down for anticipated losses on other accounts receivable* amortizar los gastos anticipados en otras cuentas deudoras

account-holding

= custodian

Account-holding means keeping an account for a customer. The expression refers to a bank or other financial institution that is responsible for the registration of e.g. deposits, payments and funds transfers or securities portfolios on behalf of its customers.

depositario

▲ *account-holding institution* institución depositaria

accountancy UK

= accounting IAS/IFRS, US

Accountancy refers to the professional activities carried out by accountants such as the preparation and audit of financial statements, the keeping of financial records and consultancy on tax and other financial matters.

contabilidad

▲ *competence in accountancy and/or auditing* competencia en contabilidad y/o auditoría

accountant

An accountant is a person who has professional qualifications in accountancy. Accountants perform accountancy services such as the preparation and auditing of financial statements as well as consultancy on e.g. tax matters.

experto contable

NOTE Spanish law only requires special trainings or degrees for auditors but not for accountants.

▲ *a certified public accountant* un censor jurado de cuentas ▲ *a chartered accountant* un experto contable forense ▲ *a registered public accountant* un experto contable colegiado ▲ *a state-authorised public accountant* un experto contable de contabilidad pública ▲ *professional fees paid to accountants* honorarios profesionales de los expertos contables ▲ *the Institute of State Authorised Public Accountants in Denmark* el Instituto de Contabilidad y Auditoria de Cuentas (ICAC)

⇛ auditor, bookkeeper

accounting[1] *noun* **1**

1 = accountancy UK

Accounting refers to the professional activities carried out by accountants such as the preparation and audit of financial statements, the keeping of financial records and consultancy on tax and other financial matters.

contabilidad

▲ *competence in accounting and/or auditing* competencia en contabilidad y/o auditoria ▲ *financial accounting* contabilidad financiera ▲ *financial and management accounting* contabilidad financiera y de gestión ▲ *management accounting* contabilidad de gestión

2 Accounting is the process procedures activities including identification, measurement and recognition of an enterprise's transactions and includes financial and management accounting. For financial accounting, i.e. the communication to external users, the financial data are prepared in monetary units and presented in financial statements such as a balance sheet, an income statement, and a cash flow statement. Management accounting applies to the internal use of financial data by managers.

contabilidad

= contabilización, reflejo contable

▲ *accounting for construction contracts* la contabilidad de las empresas constructoras ▲ *the initial accounting for goodwill* la contabilización inicial del fondo de comercio ▲ *the primary basis of accounting* los principios básicos de la contabilidad

⇛ financial accounting, management accounting

accounting[2] *adjective*

Accounting refers to accountancy, i.e. the professional activities carried out by accountants such as the preparation and audit of financial statements, the keeping of financial records and consultancy on tax and other financial matters.

contable

▲ *accounting amortisation* amortización contable ▲ *accounting assets* activos contables ▲ *accounting assumption* supuesto contable ▲ *accounting changes* cambios contables ▲ *accounting depreciation* depreciación contable ▲ *accounting fraud* fraude contable ▲ *accounting liabilities* pasivos contables ▲ *accounting performance measures* medidas de actuación contable ▲ *accounting rate of return* tasa de retorno contable ▲ *accounting requirements* requisitos contables ▲ *accounting revaluation* revalorización contable ▲ *accounting treatment* tratamiento contable ▲ *classification for accounting purposes* clasificación a efectos contables ▲ *equity accounting adjustments* ajustes contables de los títulos

⇛ accountancy

accounting amortisation UK, IAS/IFRS

= accounting amortization US, amortisation for accounting purposes IAS/IFRS, UK

Accounting amortisation is the systematic allocation of the cost of an intangible asset over its economic life in the financial statements.

amortización contable

▲ *accounting amortisation, depreciation and write-downs* amortización, depreciación y bajas contables

⇛ accounting depreciation

accounting assumption

= underlying assumption

Accounting assumptions are the basic accounting conventions underlying generally accepted accounting principles, such as the going concern assumption that the enterprise will continue in operation for the foreseeable future, the separate entity assumption that the activities and financial statements of an enterprise are separate from those of the owners, the monetary unit assumption that financial disclosures are made and transactions measured in money terms in the financial statements, and the time period assumption that financial reporting is made periodically and on a timely basis.

principio contable

▲ *the fundamental accounting assumptions underlying the preparation of financial statements* los principios contables fundamentales subyacentes en la preparación de los estados financieros ▲ *the underlying accounting assumptions* los principios contables subyacentes

⇛ going concern convention, monetary unit, separate entity

accounting consolidation

= consolidation

Accounting consolidation is the presentation of a parent company and its subsidiaries as one entity. The financial statements of the group enterprises are combined in consolidated financial statements where intra-group balances are eliminated.

consolidación contable

= consolidación

▲ *a need for accounting consolidation* una necesidad de consolidación contable ▲ *use accounting consolidation as a starting point* utilizar la consolidación contable como punto de partida

⇛ consolidated accounts, consolidated financial statements

accounting convention

An accounting convention is a customary practice and standardised approach adopted in an accounting context such as placing debits on the left side and credits on the right side of an account.

convencionalismo contable

▲ *accounting convention and basis of consolidation* convencionalismo contable y base de consolidación ▲ *comply with an accounting convention* cumplir con el convencionalismo contable ▲ *in accordance with an accounting convention* de acuerdo con el convencionalismo contable

accounting council

An accounting council is a consultancy body of accounting professionals and financial experts addressing issues related to accountancy, such as the Danish Accounting Council set up by the Danish Commerce and Companies Agency under the Danish Financial Statements Act.

organismo profesional de contabilidad

▲ *the Accounting Council's Report of 1996 on Revision of the Danish Annual Accounts Act* el Informe de 1996 del Organismo Profesional de Contabilidad sobre la Legislación relativa a las cuentas anuales danesas ▲ *the recommendation of the Accounting Council* la recomendación del Organismo Profesional de Contabilidad

SOURCE Danish Financial Statements Act s. 137(2)

accounting depreciation

= book depreciation, depreciation for accounting purposes

≠ depreciation for tax purposes, tax depreciation

Accounting depreciation is the systematic allocation of the cost of a tangible asset over its useful life in the financial statements.

depreciación contable

= depreciación con criterios contables

≠ depreciación con criterios fiscales

▲ *accounting depreciation, amortisation and write-downs* amortización, depreciación y bajas contables

⇛ accounting amortisation

accounting directive

An accounting directive is a legal act adopted by the EU governing financial reporting and accounting and is implemented in the EU member states through national legislation or administrative acts.

directiva contable

▲ *changes in the accounting directives* cambios en las directivas contables ▲ *examination of the conformity between SIC 1 to SIC 25 and the European Accounting Directives* examen de conformidad entre la interpretación de la SIC 21 a la SIC 25 y las directivas contables europeas ▲ *in accordance with the EU's accounting directives* de acuerdo con las directivas contables de la UE ▲ *the Commission's programme of modernisation of the accounting directives* el programa de modernización de las directivas contables de la Comisión ▲ *the EU's accounting directives* las directivas contables de la UE ▲ *the European accounting directives* las directivas contables europeas

Accounting Directive *proper noun*

→ accounting directive

accounting document

An accounting document is a record of an accounting transaction or a statement containing financial data and disclosures about an enterprise such as a balance sheet or a profit and loss account.

documento contable

▲ *create an accounting document* crear un documento contable ▲ *the whole accounting document* el documento contable completo

accounting entity

An accounting entity is a separate, independent, economic unit subject to the preparation of financial statements. Examples of accounting entities are business organisations, such as sole proprietorships, partnerships or companies, and not-for-profit organisations.

entidad contable

▲ *a separate accounting entity* una entidad contable diferente ▲ *consider the group an accounting entity* considerar al grupo una entidad contable ▲ *treat as one accounting entity* tratar como una entidad contable única

⇛ reporting entity

accounting estimate

An accounting estimate is an assessment of the impact of future financial events on financial results or an approximation of financial data pending precise measurement.

estimación contable

▲ *account for as a revision to an accounting estimate* contabilizar como una revisión a una estimación contable ▲ *accounting treatment of changes in accounting estimates* tratamiento contable de los cambios en las estimaciones contables ▲ *as a result of a changed accounting estimate* como resultado de una estimación contable cambiada ▲ *changes in accounting estimates* cambios en las estimaciones contables ▲ *income resulting from changes in accounting estimates* ingresos resultantes de cambios en las estimaciones contables ▲ *the effects of changes in accounting estimates* los efectos de los cambios en las estimaciones contables ▲ *the monetary effect of a change in an accounting estimate* el efecto monetario de un cambio en la estimación contable ▲ *the nature of a change in an accounting estimate* la naturaleza de un cambio en una estimación contable

accounting expense

1 Accounting expenses constitute an enterprise's expenditure to accountants for auditing and other professional accounting services such as tax consultancy.

honorario profesional contable

▲ *legal and accounting expenses* honorarios profesionales por asesoramiento legal y contable ▲ *the accounting expenses incurred* los honorarios profesionales contables incurridos

2 An accounting expense is an expense recognised in the financial statements that is not a real or actual expense that involves a cash outflow from the enterprise. Depreciation is an example of an accounting expense.

gasto contable

▲ *determine the accounting expense* determinar el gasto contable

accounting figure

An accounting figure is a number representing an amount recorded in the financial statements under a particular item such as revenue, earnings, equity, total assets or total liabilities.

importe contable

= cifra contable

▲ *adjusted accounting figures* importes contables ajustados ▲ *analyses of accounting figures* análisis de los importes contables ▲ *central accounting figures* importes contables principales ▲ *comparable accounting figures* importes contables comparables ▲ *historical accounting figures* importes contables históricos ▲ *summary accounting figures* resumen de los importes contables

accounting income US

Accounting income is the net profit of an accounting entity for a period as reported in the profit and loss account, before deducting related payments of tax.

ingreso contable bruto

= ingreso contable antes de impuestos

▲ *give rise to differences between taxable income and accounting income* da lugar a diferencias entre ingresos fiscales y contables brutos

accounting information

Accounting information is information that directly or indirectly relates to the financial reporting of an entity.

información contable

▲ *fair accounting information* información contable fiable ▲ *forward-looking accounting information* información contable prospectiva ▲ *historical accounting information* información contable histórica ▲ *include accounting information in the decision-making process* incluir la información contable en el proceso de toma de decisiones ▲ *publication of accounting information* la publicación de la información contable ▲ *quality requirements for accounting information* exigencias de calidad para la información contable ▲ *relevant accounting information* información contable relevante ▲ *transparent accounting information* información contable transparente ▲ *use of accounting information* uso de información contable ▲ *value-based accounting information* información contable basada en el valor

accounting legislation

Accounting legislation is made up of statutes, regulations etc. that contain rules governing the preparation and contents of the accounts and financial reporting documents of enterprises.

legislación contable

▲ *Danish accounting legislation* legislación contable danesa ▲ *European accounting legislation* legislación contable europea ▲ *prepare and present financial statements in accordance with Danish accounting legislation* preparar y presentar los estados financieros de acuerdo con la legislación contable danesa ▲ *the accounting legislation in force* la legislación contable vigente

accounting loss

The accounting loss constitutes the negative results for the period calculated by using generally accepted accounting principles instead of tax rules.

pérdida contable

▲ *an accounting loss of USD 3 million* una pérdida contable de 3 millones de dólares norteamericanos ▲ *carry forward an accounting loss* repercutir la pérdida contable en un ejercicio posterior

accounting method

= method of accounting

An accounting method is the accounting principles, procedures or tools applied to treat and recognise financial data in the preparation of financial statements, such as methods of depreciation, inventory pricing, income and asset measurement, revenue recognition and accrual accounting.

método contable

▲ *apply a specific accounting method* aplicar un método contable específico ▲ *the accounting method adopted* el método contable adoptado

accounting mismatch IAS/IFRS

≠ economic mismatch IAS/IFRS

Accounting mismatch is where assets and liabilities are measured on different bases, or where gains and losses are recognised on different bases, e.g. when financial liabilities are measured on a basis different from that used for the assets funded by the liabilities.

asimetría contable

▲ *eliminate an accounting mismatch* eliminar una asimetría contable ▲ *significantly reduce an accounting mismatch* reducir de forma significativa una asimetría contable

accounting model

An accounting model is a plan for applying accounting concepts and procedures in connection with the measurement and recording of transactions. Accounting models may also prescribe the layout of financial statements.

modelo contable

▲ *development of new accounting models* desarrollo de nuevos modelos contables ▲ *in accordance with an accounting model* de acuerdo con un modelo contable ▲ *introduce a fair value accounting model for non-financial assets* introducir un modelo contable de valor razonable para los activos no-financieros ▲ *the accounting model used in the preparation of the financial statements* el modelo contable utilizado en la preparación de los estados financieros ▲ *the transaction-based accounting model* el modelo contable del precio de adquisición ▲ *the value-based accounting model* el modelo económico del valor

accounting oversight body

An accounting oversight body is an independent supervisory body with members from outside the accounting profession that is set up to oversee accounting practices of auditing firms and prevent accounting scandals. In the US, foreign audit firms have to register with the Public Company Accounting Oversight Body (PCAOB), which is the US accounting supervisory body established in 2002 by the Securities and Exchange Commission.

organismo de supervisión de la práctica contable

NOTE The Spanish accounting oversight body is the 'Instituto de Contabilidad y Auditoria de Cuentas '(ICAC).

▲ *an independent accounting oversight body* un organismo de supervisión de la práctica contable independiente ▲ *the creation of a public accounting oversight body* la creación de un organismo público de supervisión de la práctica contable

accounting period

An accounting period is the period for which the financial statements are prepared by an enterprise, e.g. a quarter of a year, half a year or a whole year.

periodo contable

NOTE The Spanish accounting period cannot exceed 12 months.

▲ *a subsequent accounting period* un periodo contable subsiguiente ▲ *increases in economic benefits during the accounting period* incrementos en los beneficios económicos durante el periodo contable ▲ *starting from the earliest accounting period forming part of the financial statements* comenzando con el periodo contable más antiguo que forma parte de las cuentas anuales ▲ *the accounting period under review* el periodo contable en revisión ▲ *the beginning of the accounting period* el inicio del periodo contable ▲ *the current accounting period* el periodo contable actual ▲ *the end of the accounting period* el final del periodo contable ▲ *the previous accounting period* el periodo contable anterior ▲ *within the same accounting period* dentro del mismo periodo contable

accounting policies

Accounting policies are the criteria and methods applied for the recognition, measurement and presentation, including classification, of the individual items of the financial statements in a particular enterprise whose management have found them appropriate to present fairly the results and financial position of that enterprise.

criterios contables

= políticas contables

▲ *a material change in segment accounting policies* un cambio material en los criterios contables del sector ▲ *a single uniform set of accounting policies* un conjunto de criterios contables uniforme y único ▲ *a statement of accounting policies* una declaración de los criterios contables ▲ *a summary of accounting policies* un resumen de los criterios contables ▲ *accounting policies are unchanged from* los criterios contables no se modifican ▲ *accrual-based accounting policies* criterios contables basados en el devengo ▲ *adjustment relating to changes in accounting policies* ajuste relacionado con cambios en los criterios contables ▲ *appropriate accounting policies* criterios contables adecuados ▲ *changes in accounting policies* cambios en los criterios contables ▲ *disclose accounting policies* dar a conocer los criterios contables ▲ *disclosure of accounting policies* publicación de los criterios contables ▲ *selection of accounting policies* selección de los criterios contables ▲ *significant changes in accounting policies* cambios significativos en los criterios contables ▲ *the specification of accounting policies* la especificación de los criterios contables ▲ *transitional accounting policies* criterios contables transnacionales

accounting principle

An accounting principle is a fundamental rule, convention or idea governing current accounting practice. Accounting principles are used to determine the appropriate procedure when preparing financial statements and include e.g. revenue recognition, measurement of assets and accrual of expenses.

principio contable

▲ *changes in accounting principles* cambios en los principios contables ▲ *generally accepted accounting principles* principios contables generalmente aceptados ▲ *the accruals-based accounting principle* el principio contable del devengo ▲ *the transaction-based accounting principle* el principio contable del precio de acquisición

⇛ accounting policies, accruals concept, consistency concept, going concern concept, prudence concept

Accounting Principles Board US

= APB

The Accounting Principles Board was founded by AICPA in 1959 and has issued pronouncements on accounting principles (referred to as APB opinions) until it was replaced by the Financial Accounting Standards Board in 1973. Many APB opinions still remain part of US Generally Accepted Accounting Principles.

Órgano Rector de los Principios Contables

⇛ Financial Accounting Standards Board

accounting profit IAS/IFRS, UK

The accounting profit is the net profit for a period before deducting tax expense as reported in accordance with accounting legislation and generally accepted accounting principles rather than tax legislation.

beneficio contable

= ganancia contable

NOTE Spanish accountants prefer 'beneficio contable' to the IAS term 'ganancia contable'.

▲ *affect neither accounting profit nor taxable profit* no se ve afectado ni por el beneficio contable ni por el beneficio fiscal ▲ *determine the accounting profit* determinar el beneficio contable ▲ *differences between taxable profit and accounting profit* diferencias entre beneficio fiscal y contable ▲ *included in accounting profit* incluido en el beneficio contable ▲ *the relationship between tax expense and accounting profit* la relación entre gasto fiscal y beneficio contable

⇛ taxable profit

accounting provision

Accounting provisions are statutory rules for the preparation and presentation of financial statements laid down in legislation and executive orders, e.g. in the Danish Financial Statements Act.

norma contable

▲ *a set of accounting provisions* un conjunto de normas contables ▲ *be subject to compulsory accounting provisions* estar sujeto a normas contables obligatorias ▲ *compulsory accounting provisions* normas contables obligatorias ▲ *sporadic accounting provisions* normas contables esporádicas ▲ *supplementary accounting provisions* normas contables subsidiarias

accounting rate of return

= ARR

The accounting rate of return is applied to forecast return on an investment as it measures the profitability of an enterprise, expressed as a ratio between the profit including or excluding interest and tax and the capital employed, i.e. the capital invested in the enterprise at the end of an accounting period. Discounted-cash-flow models are often preferred instead of the accounting rate of return.

tasa de retorno contable

= TRC

▲ *calculate the accounting rate of return* calcular la tasa de retorno contable ▲ *the average accounting rate of return* la tasa de retorno contable media

⇛ capital employed, return on invested capital

accounting ratio

→ financial ratio

accounting records

Accounting records are those documents that evidence or support the entries made in the internal accounts of an enterprise as well as its financial information.

libros auxiliares

▲ *external accounting records* libros auxiliares externos ▲ *filing requirements for accounting records* requisitos de mantenimiento de los libros auxiliares ▲ *internal accounting records* libros auxiliares internos ▲ *the published accounting records* los libros auxiliares publicados

Accounting Regulatory Committee IAS/IFRS

= ARC IAS/IFRS

The Accounting Regulatory Committee (ARC) has been set up by the European Commission under the IAS Regulation. The Committee has a regulatory function and gives opinions on proposals made by the EU Commission for the adoption of international financial reporting standards (IFRS). The ARC is chaired by the European Commission, and ARC members are representatives from EU Member States.

Comité Regulador de Normas Contables

NOTE The Spanish accounting oversight body is the 'Instituto de Contabilidad y Auditorias de Cuentas' (ICAC).

▲ *set up the Accounting Regulatory Committee* nombrar el Comité Regulador de Normas Contables ▲ *the opinion of the Accounting Regulatory Commit-*

tee la opinión del Comité Regulador de Normas Contables
⇛ IAS Regulation, International Accounting Standard, International Financial Reporting Standard

accounting rule

Accounting rules are authoritative statements or guidelines on the preparation of financial statements and include accounting legislation, accounting standards and generally accepted accounting principles.

norma contable

▲ *accounting rules issued by the Danish Financial Supervisory Authority* normas contables publicadas por la Autoridad Supervisora Financiera Danesa ▲ *change existing accounting rules* cambios en las normas contables existentes ▲ *global accounting rules* normas contables globales ▲ *international accounting rules* normas contables internacionales ▲ *introduce new accounting rules* introducir nuevas normas contables ▲ *national accounting rules* normas contables nacionales ▲ *transition to the new accounting rules* transición a nuevas normas contables

accounting standard UK

Accounting standards are official accounting rules for financial reporting that must be followed for financial statements to achieve a true and fair view. The standards are issued by authoritative accountancy bodies such as the UK Accounting Standards Board, the US Financial Accounting Standards Board and the International Accounting Standards Board.

norma contable

▲ *an exposure draft of an accounting standard* un proyecto de norma contable ▲ *convergence of accounting standards* convergencia de las normas contables ▲ *Danish accounting standards* normas contables danesas ▲ *in accordance with Danish Accounting Standard 9* de acuerdo con la Norma Contable danesa 9 ▲ *in accordance with the accounting standards* de acuerdo con las normas contables ▲ *International Accounting Standards* Normas Internacionales de Contabilidad (NIC)

⇛ Financial Accounting Standard, Financial Reporting Standard, International Accounting Standard, International Financial Reporting Standard

Accounting Standards Board UK

= ASB UK

The Accounting Standards Board (ASB) develops, issues and withdraws accounting standards in the UK. The ASB replaced the Accounting Standards Committee in 1990.

Accounting Standard Board

NOTE The Spanish accounting oversight body is the 'Instituto de Contabilidad y Auditoria de Cuentas' (ICAC).

▲ *accounting standards issued by the Accounting Standards Board* normas contables publicadas por el Accounting Standard Board

⇛ Financial Reporting Standard

Accounting Standards Committee UK

= ASC

The Accounting Standards Committee (ASC) was the former UK accounting standards setting body. In 1990, the ASC was replaced by the Accounting Standards Board (ASB) following a review of its operations.

Accounting Standard Committee

NOTE The Spanish accounting oversight body is the 'Instituto de Contabilidad y Auditoria de Cuentas' (ICAC).

⇛ Accounting Standards Board

accounting system

An accounting system is the records and procedures used to collect and process financial data in an enterprise.

sistema contable

▲ *a common accounting system* un sistema contable común ▲ *a hedge accounting system* un sistema contable de protección ▲ *the value-based accounting system* el sistema contable basado en el valor

accounting technical committee

An accounting technical committee is a body set up by a professional organisation of accountants with a particular objective such as the formulation of accounting standards, the issuing of pronouncements on accounting principles etc.

comité de expertos contables

= comité técnico contable

NOTE The Spanish accounting oversight body is the 'Instituto de Contabilidad y Auditoria de Cuentas' (ICAC).

▲ *support and expertise provided by an accounting technical committee* apoyo y experiencia ofrecida por un comité de expertos contables ▲ *the Accounting Technical Committee of the Institute of State Authorised Public Accountants in Denmark* el Comité de Expertos Contables del ICAC ▲ *the technical work of the accounting technical committee* el trabajo técnico del comité de expertos contables

accounting treatment

Accounting treatment is the recognition, measurement and other processing of financial data for reporting purposes under generally accepted accounting principles, accounting standards and legislation.

tratamiento contable

▲ *alternative accounting treatments permitted by IAS* tratamientos contables alternativos permitidos por la NIC ▲ *disclosure of the accounting treatments used* publicación de los tratamientos contables utilizados ▲ *divergence of opinions on accounting treatments* divergencia de opiniones en los tratamientos contables

accounting year UK

= financial year UK, IAS/IFRS, fiscal year US

An accounting year is the accounting period for twelve consecutive months, i.e. the reporting period for which an enterprise prepares its financial statements. Typically, an accounting year follows the calendar year, but may also run in an alternative twelve-month period, e.g. from April 1 to March 31.

año contable

= ejercicio económico

▲ *after the end of the accounting year* después del final del año contable ▲ *at the end of the accounting year* al finalizar el año contable ▲ *beyond the current accounting year* más allá del año contable en curso ▲ *during the accounting year* durante el año contable ▲ *in the course of the accounting year* en el transcurso del año contable ▲ *in two consecutive accounting years* dos años contables consecutivos ▲ *income concerning the accounting year* ingresos concernientes al año contable ▲ *the accounting year in question* el año contable en cuestión ▲ *the previous accounting year* el año contable anterior

⇛ accounting period

accounts UK

= financial statements IAS/IFRS, US

The accounts are the detailed records of an enterprise's financial affairs showing the income and expenses for a period as well as the financial position at a particular date.

cuentas anuales

= estados financieros

▲ *annual accounts* cuentas anuales ▲ *audit the accounts* auditar las cuentas anuales ▲ *audited accounts* cuentas anuales auditadas ▲ *balance the accounts* saldar las cuentas anuales ▲ *close the accounts* cerrar las cuentas anuales ▲ *consolidated accounts* cuentas anuales consolidadas ▲ *keep accounts* registrar las cuentas anuales ▲ *prepare accounts* preparar las cuentas anuales ▲ *preparers of accounts* preparadores de las cuentas anuales ▲ *present the accounts* presentar las cuentas anuales ▲ *report and accounts* informe y cuentas anuales ▲ *the reliability of the accounts* la fiabilidad de las cuentas anuales ▲ *users of accounts* usuarios de las cuentas anuales

⇛ account

accrete

1 To accrete means to increase something gradually.

incrementar

= acrecentar

▲ *accreted at a rate of 8.5%* incrementado a una tasa del 8.5% ▲ *the cumulative interest accreted on the liability component* el interés acumulado incrementado en el componente de pasivo

2 To accrete means to be increased gradually.

acrecentarse

▲ *accrete in value* acrecentarse en valor ▲ *accrete over time* acrecentarse a lo largo del tiempo

accretion US

Accretion means gradual growth or increase in value, amount or level, i.e. growth in assets through mergers and acquisitions.

revalorización

= acumulación contable

▲ *accretion on earnings per share* revalorización de los beneficios por acción

⇛ accretive

accretive US

To be accretive to something means to add to something and make something grow in size by gradual addition, typically used about growth in earnings, EPS and operating results e.g. in connection with an acquisition.

revalorizado

▲ *accretive to* revalorizado hasta ▲ *the acquisition of the company is accretive to EBITDA* la adquisición de la compañía se revaloriza hasta el EBITDA

accrual

An accrual is an increase in something usually over a period of time.

acumulación

▲ *an accrual of £10,000* una acumulación de 10.000£

accrual accounting

≠ cash accounting, cash basis

Accrual accounting means accounting for revenue and expenses in the financial statements on an accrual basis, i.e. recognising revenue when earned and expenses as incurred.

principio del devengo

≠ contabilidad de caja

▲ *prepare financial statements on an accrual accounting basis* preparar los estados financieros de acuerdo con el principio del devengo

⇛ accrual basis of accounting

accrual accounting convention

→ accruals concept

accrual basis of accounting

= accruals concept

The accrual basis of accounting is one of the basic assumptions for the preparation of the annual report and implies that transactions, events and changes in value must be recognised when occurring irrespective of the time of payment.

principio del devengo

= hipótesis contable del devengo

▲ *under the accrual basis of accounting* de acuerdo con el principio del devengo ▲ *use the accrual basis of accounting* utilizar el principio del devengo

accruals

= accrued liabilities

Accruals are expenses accrued but not paid. Accruals appear under liabilities in the balance sheet and may be of two types: long-term accruals such as depreciation and changes in long-term provisions, or short-term accruals such as changes in trade receivables and payables or inventories.

pagos diferidos

▲ *accounts and notes payable, long-term debt, liabilities, accruals and other claims payable* acreedores y pagarés, deuda a largo plazo, pasivos, pagos diferidos y otros efectos a pagar ▲ *deferrals or accruals of past or future operating cash receipts or payments* pagos anticipados o diferidos correspondientes a pagos o tickets de caja pasados o futuros ▲ *undisclosed accruals* pagos diferidos desconocidos

⇛ accrued charge

accruals and deferred income UK, IAS/IFRS

Accruals and deferred income is an item under short-term and/or long-term liabilities in the balance sheet consisting of accrued expenses and income received and recognised before deemed earned.

pagos y cobros diferidos

▲ *an increase in accruals and deferred income* un aumento en los pagos y cobros diferidos ▲ *other accruals and deferred income* otros pagos y cobros diferidos

⇛ accrued expense, prepaid expense, prepayments and accrued income

accruals concept

= accrual basis of accounting, accruals convention, matching principle

The accruals concept is a fundamental accounting concept implying that transactions, events and changes in value must be recognised when occurring irrespective of the time of payment.

principio del devengo
▲ *apply the accruals concept* aplicar el principio del devengo ▲ *recognise under the accruals concept* reconocer de acuerdo con el principio del devengo ▲ *under the accruals concept* de acuerdo con el principio del devengo ▲ *use the accruals concept* utilizar el principio del devengo

accruals principle
= accruals concept
The accruals concept is a fundamental accounting concept implying that transactions, events and changes in value must be recognised when occurring irrespective of the time of payment.
principio del devengo
▲ *apply the accruals principle* aplicar el principio del devengo ▲ *conform with the accruals principle* atenerse al principio del devengo ▲ *in accordance with the accruals principle* de acuerdo con el principio del devengo ▲ *under the accruals principle* según el principio del devengo

accrue
1 To accrue is to recognise revenue when earned and expenses when incurred irrespective of whether cash has been received or paid. In this way, revenue and expenses are matched in a particular accounting period.
devengar
▲ *accrue income and expenses over the terms of the transactions* devengar ingresos y gastos atendiendo a los términos de la transacción ▲ *amounts already accrued* cantidades ya devengadas ▲ *include accrued expenses* incluir los gastos devengados
2 To accrue means to gradually accumulate or increase over a given period of time.
acumular
= acumularse
▲ *accrued interest* interés acumulado

accrue to
To accrue to is to be added to something or be allotted to somebody.
imputar
▲ *a gain or loss accruing to the shareholders* una ganancia o pérdida que se imputa a los accionistas ▲ *accrue to the acquirer* imputar al adquirente ▲ *accrue to the group* imputar al grupo ▲ *any unguaranteed residual value accruing to the lessor* cualquier valor residual no garantizado que se imputa al arrendador ▲ *the present value of the minimum lease payments accruing to the lessor* el valor actual de los pagos mínimos por arrendamiento que se imputan al arrendador

accrued charge
= accrued expense
Accrued charges are expenses incurred during the accounting period and recognised in the profit and loss account, but which have not been paid at the balance sheet date. Examples of accrued expenses are rent, wages and salaries.
pago diferido
= gasto diferido
▲ *accrued charges due under the agreement* pagos diferidos exigibles según el contrato ▲ *calculate accrued charges* calcular los pagos diferidos ▲ *the payment of all accrued charges* el abono de todos los pagos diferidos
⇛ accruals, accruals and deferred income

accrued expense
= accrued charge, accrued liability
Accrued expenses are expenses incurred during the accounting period but which have not been paid at the balance sheet date. Examples of accrued expenses are rent, wages and salaries.
gasto diferido
= gasto devengado, pago diferido
▲ *total accrued expenses incurred this period* total gastos diferidos devengados en este periodo
⇛ accruals, accruals and deferred income

accrued income UK, IAS/IFRS
= accrued revenue US
Accrued income is income which is recognised when it is earned irrespective of whether cash has been received or paid.
NOTE Accrued income constitutes part of the item "prepayments and accrued income" recognised under current assets in the balance sheet according to the accruals concept.

cobro diferido

= ingreso diferido

▲ *other accrued income* otro cobro diferido ▲ *the most significant accrued income amounts* las cantidades por cobros diferidos más significativas ▲ *the treatment of accrued income recognised at year-end* el tratamiento del cobro diferido reconocido a final de año

⇛ prepayments and accrued income

accrued liability

= accrued charge, accrued expense

Accrued liabilities are expenses incurred during the accounting period and recognised in the profit and loss account, but which have not been paid at the balance sheet date. Examples of accrued liabilities are rent, wages and salaries.

pago diferido

= gasto diferido

▲ *a decrease in accrued liabilities* una reducción en el pago diferido ▲ *an accrued liability arising as a result of work performed* un pago diferido resultante del trabajo realizado ▲ *an increase in accrued liabilities* un incremento en el pago diferido ▲ *the unfunded accrued liability* el pago diferido no dotado

⇛ accruals and deferred income

accrued revenue US

= accrued income UK, IAS/IFRS

Accrued revenue is income which is recognised when it is earned irrespective of whether cash has been received or paid. NOTE Accrued revenue constitutes part of the item "prepaid expenses and accrued revenue" recognised under current assets in the balance sheet according to the accruals concept.

cobro diferido

= ingreso diferido

▲ *accrued revenue for interest* cobro diferido por intereses ▲ *other accrued revenue* otro ingreso diferido

accumulate

To accumulate means to increase or grow over a period of time because of periodical additions.

acumular

▲ *accumulate cash and other monetary items* acumular dinero y otros tipos de efectivo ▲ *accumulate costs* costes acumulados ▲ *accumulate experience* acumular experiencia

accumulated

= cumulative

Accumulated means that something has increased or grown over a period of time because of periodical additions.

acumulado

▲ *accumulated amortisation* amortización acumulada ▲ *accumulated depreciation* depreciación acumulada ▲ *accumulated effect* efecto acumulado ▲ *accumulated exchange differences arising from translation* diferencias en el tipo de cambio acumuladas resultantes de la conversión ▲ *accumulated goodwill amortisation* amortización acumulada del fondo de comercio ▲ *accumulated impairment losses* pérdidas acumuladas por deterioro patrimonial ▲ *accumulated net profits* beneficios netos acumulados ▲ *an accumulated non-vesting entitlement* un derecho no ejercitado acumulado ▲ *the accumulated amount of negative goodwill* la cantidad acumulada del fondo de comercio negativo ▲ *the balance of accumulated profit or loss at the beginning of the financial year* el saldo de los beneficios o pérdidas acumulados al inicio del año financiero ▲ *unused entitlement that has accumulated at the balance sheet date* un derecho no utilizado que se ha acumulado a fecha de balance

accumulated amortisation UK, IAS/IFRS

= cumulative amortisation

Accumulated amortisation is the total amortisation charges recognised since the acquisition of an intangible asset.

amortización acumulada

▲ *determine the accumulated amortisation of the goodwill* determinar la amortización acumulada del fondo de comercio ▲ *less any accumulated amortisation* menos cualquier amortización acumulada ▲ *less any subsequent accumulated amortisation* menos cualquier amortización acumulada posterior ▲ *result in a lower amount of accumulated amortisation* resulta en una cantidad menor de amortización acumulada ▲ *the accumulated amortisation at the beginning of the financial year* la amortización acumulada al comienzo del año ▲ *the related accumulated amortisation* la amortización acumulada relacionada

⇛ accumulated depreciation

accumulated amortization US

= accumulated amortisation UK, IAS/IFRS

Accumulated amortization is the total amortization charges recognized since the acquisition of an intangible asset.

amortización acumulada

▲ *determine the accumulated amortization of the goodwill* determinar la amortización acumulada del fondo de comercio ▲ *less any accumulated amortization* menos cualquier amortización acumulada ▲ *less any subsequent accumulated amortization* menos cualquier amortización acumulada posterior ▲ *result in a lower amount of accumulated amortization* resulta en una cantidad menor de amortización acumulada ▲ *the accumulated amortization at the beginning of the fiscal year* la amortización acumulada al principio del año fiscal ▲ *the related accumulated amortization* la amortización acumulada relacionada

accumulated benefit

Accumulated benefit is the total accrued amount of benefits contributed to a pension fund over the contribution period to date.

beneficio acumulado

▲ *the present value of accumulated benefits* el valor actual de los beneficios acumulados ▲ *the value of accumulated benefits* el valor de los beneficios acumulados

accumulated benefit obligation US

= ABO US

The accumulated benefit obligation expresses the pension plan liability as the actuarial present value of vested or nonvested benefits, computed under the pension benefit formula, to employee services provided before a particular date, based on current salary levels.

obligación por beneficio acumulado

▲ *plan with accumulated benefit obligations in excess of plan assets* plan con obligaciones por beneficio acumulado superior a los activos del plan

⇛ projected benefit obligation

accumulated depreciation

Accumulated depreciation is the total depreciation charges recognised since the acquisition of a tangible asset up to a particular time.

depreciación acumulada

▲ *accumulated depreciation at the date of the revaluation* depreciación acumulada a fecha de actualización ▲ *after deducting any accumulated depreciation* después de deducir cualquier depreciación acumulada ▲ *any accumulated depreciation* cualquier depreciación acumulada ▲ *any subsequent accumulated depreciation* cualquier depreciación acumulada posterior ▲ *calculate the accumulated depreciation* calcular la depreciación acumulada ▲ *the accumulated depreciation at the beginning and end of the period* la depreciación acumulada al inicio y fin del periodo ▲ *the amount of the adjustment arising on the restatement or elimination of accumulated depreciation* la cantidad del ajuste resultante por regularización o eliminación de la amortización acumulada

⇛ accumulated amortisation

accumulated impairment loss

An accumulated impairment loss is the total amount by which the value of a fixed asset has been impaired at the beginning or end of an accounting period.

pérdida por deterioro acumulada

= deterioro acumulado, pérdida por deterioro del valor acumulado

NOTE Spanish accountants prefer 'pérdida por deterioro acumulada' to the IAS/IFRS term 'pérdida por deterioro del valor acumulada'.

▲ *accumulated impairment losses at the beginning of the period* deterioros acumulados al principio del periodo ▲ *accumulated impairment losses at the end of the period* deterioros acumulados al final del periodo ▲ *aggregated with accumulated im-*

pairment losses agregado a pérdidas por deterioro acumuladas ▲ *less any accumulated depreciation and any accumulated impairment losses* menos cualquier depreciación acumulada y cualesquiera otras pérdidas por deterioro acumuladas ▲ *subsequent accumulated impairment losses* pérdidas por deterioro acumuladas posteriores
⇛ impairment, impairment loss

accumulated loss US
The accumulated loss shows losses carried forward as a result of the excess of expenses over revenue.
pérdida acumulada
▲ *accumulated loss at the end of the financial year* pérdida acumulada al final del año económico

accumulating preference share
→ cumulative preference share

acid test
→ acid test ratio

acid test ratio
= liquid ratio, quick ratio
The acid test ratio is a financial ratio measuring the liquidity of an enterprise at very short term, defined as current assets excluding stocks less current liabilities, and is a more stringent measure than the current ratio. The ratio should preferably be at least 1:1.
ratio de liquidez
= ratio acid test
▲ *calculate the acid test ratio* calcular el ratio de liquidez ▲ *the average acid test ratio* el ratio de liquidez medio
⇛ current ratio, liquidity test

acid-test ratio *noun* <an, the, -s>
→ acid test ratio

acquire
= buy, take over
≠ dispose of
To acquire is to buy, take possession of or take over something.
adquirir
▲ *acquire at market price* adquirir a precio de mercado ▲ *acquire equity or debt instruments of other enterprises* adquirir títulos o deuda de otras empresas ▲ *acquire in stages* adquirir por etapas ▲ *acquire in the financial year* adquirir durante el año ▲ *acquire liabilities* adquirir obligaciones ▲ *acquire property, plant and equipment* adquirir edificios, instalaciones y equipos ▲ *acquire securities* adquirir títulos ▲ *acquire shares* adquirir acciones ▲ *acquire the majority interest* adquirir la participación mayoritaria ▲ *an intangible asset acquired externally or generated internally* un activo intangible adquirido externamente o generado internamente ▲ *inventory acquired specifically for resale* activos adquiridos específicamente para su venta posterior

acquired company UK
An acquired company is a company over which the acquirer obtains control over the net assets and operations in connection with an acquisition.
empresa adquirida
▲ *goodwill arising from acquired companies* fondo de comercio resultante de las empresas adquiridas ▲ *restructuring costs relating to the acquired company* reestructuración de los costes relacionados con la empresa adquirida ▲ *the acquired company's balance sheet* el balance de la empresa adquirida
⇛ acquiree

acquired goodwill
= goodwill on acquisition, purchased goodwill
Acquired goodwill is the goodwill arising from the acquisition of an enterprise or activity, representing the excess price paid over the net assets' fair value. Acquired goodwill is initially recognised at cost less impairment losses and must be tested for impairment regularly, where formerly it used to be capitalised and amortised over the expected economic life, usually a maximum of 20 years.
fondo de comercio adquirido
▲ *adjustments to acquired goodwill* ajustes al fondo de comercio adquirido

acquiree
= acquired enterprise
≠ acquirer
The acquiree is the enterprise over whose assets and operations another enterprise, the acquirer, on acquisition obtains control in exchange for the transfer of assets, incurrence of a liability or issue of equity.

empresa adquirida
= entidad adquirida
≠ adquiriente
▲ *acquire shares in the acquiree* adquirir acciones en la empresa adquirida ▲ *closing of the facilities of the acquiree* cierre de las instalaciones de la empresa adquirida ▲ *elimination of the product lines of the acquiree* eliminación de las líneas de producción de la empresa adquirida ▲ *exchange the shares of the acquiree for shares of the acquirer* cambiar acciones de la empresa adquirida por acciones de la empresa adquirente ▲ *gain on shares of the acquiree* ganancia en las acciones de la empresa adquirida ▲ *hold voting power in the acquiree* poseer el derecho de voto en la empresa adquirida ▲ *identifiable assets and liabilities of the acquirees* activos y pasivos identificables de las empresas adquiridas ▲ *incorporate into the income statement the results of operations of the acquiree* incorporar en el balance los resultados de las operaciones de la empresa adquirida ▲ *recognise a deferred tax asset of the acquiree* reconocer un impuesto diferido de la empresa adquirida ▲ *restructuring provisions relating to the acquiree* reestructuración de las provisiones relacionadas con la empresa adquirida ▲ *revaluation of assets and liabilities of the acquiree* actualización de los activos y pasivos de la empresa adquirida ▲ *termination or reduction of the activities of the acquiree* finalización o reducción de las actividades de la empresa adquirida ▲ *the acquiree's assets and liabilities* los activos y pasivos de la empresa adquirida ▲ *the board of directors of the acquiree* el consejo de administración de la empresa adquirida ▲ *the employees of the acquiree* los trabajadores de la empresa adquirida ▲ *the shareholders of the acquiree* los accionistas de la empresa adquirida
⇛ acquired company

acquirer
≠ acquiror
An acquirer is the enterprise that in connection with an acquisition obtains control over the net assets and operations of another enterprise, the acquiree, in exchange for the transfer of assets, incurrence of liabilities or issue of equity.
adquirente
≠ adquirida, empresa adquirida
▲ *identify a party as the acquirer* identificar una parte como adquirente ▲ *marketable securities issued by the acquirer* títulos negociables emitidos por la adquirente ▲ *restate to the accounting policies adopted by the acquirer* pasar a los principios contables adoptados por la adquirente ▲ *restructuring provisions relating to the acquirer* reestructurando las provisiones relacionadas con la adquirente ▲ *the acquirer for accounting purposes* el adquirente por motivos contables ▲ *the acquirer's consolidated financial statements* los estados financieros consolidados de la adquirente ▲ *the acquirer's interest in the fair values of the identifiable assets and liabilities acquired* el interés del adquirente por el valor razonable de los activos y pasivos identificables adquiridos ▲ *the legal acquirer* el adquirente legal
⇛ acquisition

acquisition
1 = takeover
An acquisition is a business combination in which one of the enterprises, the acquirer, obtains control over the net assets and operations of another enterprise, the acquiree, in exchange for the transfer of assets, incurrence of liabilities or issue of equity.
adquisición
▲ *acquisition in stages* adquisición por etapas ▲ *additions relating to acquisitions* incrementos relacionados con adquisiciones ▲ *an acquisition achieved by successive purchases* una adquisición realizada mediante compras sucesivas ▲ *deferred tax arising from an acquisition* impuesto diferido resultante de una adquisición ▲ *disclosure requirements for acquisitions* publicación de los requisitos para adquisiciones ▲ *goodwill arising on acquisition* fondo de comercio resultante de la adquisición ▲ *mergers and acquisitions* fusiones y adquisiciones ▲ *purchase as part of an acquisi-*

tion compra como parte de una adquisición ▲ *purchase consideration on acquisition* estudio de la compra a la hora de la adquisición ▲ *restructuring provision on acquisition* reestructuración de las provisiones en la adquisición ▲ *reverse acquisition* deshacer la adquisición ▲ *shares issued in connection with acquisitions* acciones emitidas en relación con adquisiciones ▲ *the acquirer's plan for the acquisition* el plan del adquirente para la adquisición ▲ *the terms of the acquisition* las condiciones de la adquisición ▲ *the transaction underlying the acquisition* la transacción subyacente a la adquisición

2 Acquisition means getting possession or control of something.
adquisición
▲ *the acquisition of an investment in an associate* la adquisición de una inversión en una empresa asociada

3 An acquisition is something that has been taken over, bought or obtained, e.g. a company.
adquisición
▲ *a recent acquisition* una adquisición reciente ▲ *a significant acquisition or disposal* una adquisición o enajenación significativa ▲ *acquisition as part of the transaction to effect the acquisition* adquisición como parte de la transacción para llevar a cabo la adquisición ▲ *acquisitions through business combinations* adquisiciones mediante acuerdos comerciales ▲ *borrowing costs that are directly attributable to the acquisition* costes de endeudamiento atribuidos directamente a la adquisición ▲ *the acquisition of finished goods, materials and services* la adquisición de productos finales, bienes y servicios ▲ *the acquisition of materials* la adquisición de los materiales

acquisition accounting UK
= purchase accounting US, IAS/IFRS
≠ merger accounting UK, pooling of interests US, uniting of interests IAS/IFRS
Acquisition accounting is the application of an accounting method used for business combinations where the identifiable assets and liabilities of the acquired business are recognised in the balance sheet of the acquirer at their fair value at the acquisition date. If the value of the acquired business' net assets is lower than the acquisition cost, this difference is recognised as goodwill.
método de adquisición
▲ *reverse acquisition accounting* no
aplicar el método de adquisición

acquisition accounting method UK
→ acquisition method

acquisition cost[1] *noun* <an, the, -s>
The acquisition cost is the price paid to buy goods, services, or assets. It equals the list price plus normal incidental costs to acquire the item including preparation, transportation and installation.
coste de adquisición
= precio de adquisición
▲ *changes in the acquisition cost of the leased property* cambios en el coste de adquisición de la propiedad arrendada ▲ *less related deferred acquisition costs* menos costes de adquisición diferidos relacionados

acquisition cost[2] *noun* <an, the, no plural>
= cost, original cost
Acquisition cost is the amount recognised in the balance sheet relating to the price paid to buy an asset and obtain title to that asset, i.e. the purchase price including the costs of transaction.
precio de adquisición
= coste de adquisición
▲ *acquisition cost for tax purposes* precio de adquisición a efectos fiscales ▲ *calculation of the acquisition cost* cálculo del precio de adquisición ▲ *nominal acquisition cost* precio de adquisición nominal ▲ *original acquisition cost* precio de adquisición original ▲ *total acquisition cost* total precio de adquisición
⇛ original cost

acquisition date IAS/IFRS
= date of acquisition
≠ date of exchange IAS/IFRS
The acquisition date in a business combination is the date when one enterprise (the

acquirer) obtains control over the acquired enterprise (the acquiree).

fecha de adquisición

▲ *actuarial losses that arose before the acquisition date* pérdidas actuariales resultantes antes de la fecha de adquisición ▲ *allocation of the cost of the business combination as at the acquisition date* asignar el coste del acuerdo comercial a fecha de adquisición ▲ *at the acquisition date* a fecha de adquisición ▲ *the basic earnings per share disclosed for each comparative period before the acquisition date* los beneficios por acción publicados para cada periodo comparado antes de la fecha de adquisición ▲ *the end of the first annual period beginning after the acquisition date* el final del primer periodo anual que empieza después de la fecha de adquisición ▲ *the number of ordinary shares outstanding from the acquisition date* el número de acciones ordinarias pendientes de pago a fecha de adquisición

SOURCE IFRS 3, Appendix A

⇛ business combination

acquisition method UK

= acquisition accounting method UK, purchase method US, IAS/IFRS

≠ merger method UK, pooling-of-interests method US, uniting-of-interests method IAS/IFRS

The acquisition method is an accounting method used for business combinations in which the acquirer obtains control over the acquired enterprise. The assets of the acquired enterprise are recorded at fair value at the date of acquisition giving rise to goodwill on consolidation.

método de adquisición

▲ *account for a business combination using the acquisition method* contabilizar una combinación de negocios usando el método de adquisición ▲ *apply the acquisition method* aplicar el método de adquisición ▲ *the acquisition method of accounting* el método de adquisición ▲ *the date when the application of the acquisition method commences* la fecha al que se aplica el método de adquisición

acquisition of a right

An acquisition of a right is the taking-over of a right previously belonging to someone else.

adquisición de un derecho

▲ *the final acquisition of a right* la adquisición de un derecho pleno

acquisition of shares

Acquisition of shares is the purchase of one or more shares in an enterprise.

adquisición de acciones

▲ *secret acquisitions of shares* adquisiciones secretas de acciones

acquisition year

= year of acquisition

The acquisition year is the accounting period, i.e. the financial year, in which an asset was obtained by an enterprise. In a business combination it is the year when one enterprise (the acquirer) obtains control over the acquired enterprise (the acquiree).

fecha de adquisición

▲ *be expensed in the acquisition year* se contabilizó en la fecha de adquisición ▲ *in the acquisition year* en la fecha de adquisición ▲ *one year after the acquisition year* un año posterior a la fecha de adquisición

act

An act is an official document passed by a legislative body that lays down specific rules applying within a specific country or area.

ley

= norma legislativa

▲ *according to the act* de acuerdo con la ley ▲ *Danish Act on Banks and Saving Banks* Ley danesa de Bancos y Cajas de Ahorros ▲ *Danish Act on Certain Commercial Enterprises* Ley danesa de Empresas Comerciales ▲ *Danish Act on Commercial Enterprises' Presentation of Financial Statements* Ley danesa de Presentación de Estados Financieros por parte de las Empresas Comerciales ▲ *Danish Act on Commercial Foundations* Ley danesa de Fundaciones Comerciales ▲ *Danish Act on Copenhagen Stock Exchange* Ley danesa del Mercado de Valores de Copenague ▲ *Danish Act on Local Government Management* Ley danesa de Gestión de las Administraciones Locales ▲ *Danish Act on Registered Public Accountants* Ley danesa de Expertos Contables ▲ *Danish Act on State-Authorised Public Accountants* Ley danesa de Expertos Contables Públicos ▲ *Danish Copyright Act* Ley danesa de Derechos de Autor ▲ *Danish Financial Business Act* Ley de Empresas Financieras danesas ▲ *Danish Insurance Business Act* Ley de Empresas de Seguros danesas ▲ *pass an act* aprobar una ley ▲ *repeal an act* derogar una ley ▲ *the 2002 Sarbanes-Oxley Act* la Ley Sarbanes-Oxley de 2002 ▲ *the Act mandates a number of reforms* la Ley obliga a un número de reformas ▲ *the Act provides that* la Ley establece que ▲ *the Companies Act 1985* la Ley de Sociedades Mercantiles de 1985 ▲ *the Competition Act 1998* la Ley de la Competencia de 1998 ▲ *the provisions of the Act* el articulado de la Ley

active

When someone or something is active, he or it is doing something.

activo

▲ *a period in which active development is interrupted* un periodo en el que se interrumpe el desarrollo activo ▲ *active employees* trabajadores activos ▲ *an active investor* un inversor activo ▲ *property, plant and equipment that is retired from active use* edificios, instalaciones y equipos que se retiran del uso activo ▲ *take an active interest in* tener un interés activo por

active market

An active market is a market with a high trading volume of homogenous products.

mercado activo

▲ *an active market for an asset* un mercado activo para un valor ▲ *assets traded in an active market* valores negociados en un mercado activo ▲ *by reference to an active market* por referencia a un mercado activo ▲ *current prices on an active market* precios corrientes en un mercado activo ▲ *current prices on an active market for properties* precios corrientes en un mercado inmobiliario activo ▲ *quoted market prices in an active market* precios cotizados en un mercado activo ▲ *sell the output on an active market* vender la producción en un mercado activo ▲ *trade in an active market* operar en un mercado activo ▲ *trade on an active market* explotar un mercado activo

activity

Activity includes the processes, transactions, functions and other actions of an enterprise aimed at achieving its objectives.

actividad empresarial

▲ *a detailed plan for the discontinuance of the activity* un plan detallado para interrumpir la actividad empresarial ▲ *a high level of activity* un alto nivel de actividad empresarial ▲ *a revenue earning activity* una actividad empresarial rentable ▲ *activity ratio* ratio de actividad empresarial ▲ *cash flows from financing activities* flujos de caja por financiación de actividades empresariales ▲ *cash flows from investing activities* flujos de caja por inversión en actividades empresariales ▲ *cash flows from operating activities* flujos de caja procedentes de actividades empresariales en curso ▲ *classification by activity* clasificación por actividad empresarial ▲ *costs identified as directly attributable to activities performed by the lessee* costes identificados como directamente imputables a las actividades empresariales desarrolladas por el arrendatario ▲ *downstream activities* actividades empresariales en los procesos finales ▲ *liabilities for terminating or reducing the activities of the acquiree* obligaciones por finalizar o reducir las actividades empresariales de la empresa adquirida ▲ *ongoing activities* actividades empresariales en marcha ▲ *the activities encompassed by the segment* las actividades empresariales realizadas por el sector ▲ *the nature of the activity* la naturaleza de la actividad empresarial ▲ *the principal revenue-producing activity of the enterprise* la actividad de la empresa que proporciona la principal fuente de ingresos ▲ *undertake an economic activity* llevar a cabo una actividad empresarial ▲ *upstream activities* actividades empresariales en los procesos iniciales ▲ *vertically integrated activities* actividades empresariales integradas verticalmente

activity analysis US, UK

An activity analysis is the determination and assessment of cost drivers and their effects on the cost of making a product or providing a service.

coste de producción

▲ *the preliminary phase of the activity analysis* la fase preliminar del coste de producción ▲ *undertake an activity analysis* determinar un coste de producción ▲ *use activity analysis* utilizar el coste de producción

activity driver UK, US

An activity driver is a factor that measures how frequent an activity is used by a cost object.

medida de actividad

▲ *select an activity driver* seleccionar una medida de actividad

⇛ cost driver, cost object

activity driver analysis

An activity driver analysis identifies and assesses activity drivers by focusing on the resources and activities consumed per product or other cost object, how costs are distributed on various cost objects, and the structural factors affecting costs. Activity driver analyses are typically used as a cost management tool to reduce costs.

análisis de la medida de actividad

▲ *carry out an activity driver analysis* desarrollar un análisis de la medida de actividad ▲ *perform an activity driver analysis* ejecutar un análisis de la medida de actividad

⇛ activity driver, cost object

activity-based budget

An activity-based budget concentrates on expenses incurred by a business in connection with producing and selling products and services.

presupuesto basado en la actividad

▲ *approve an activity-based budget* aprobar un presupuesto basado en la actividad ▲ *prepare an activity-based budget* preparar un presupuesto basado en la actividad

activity-based costing

= sistema de coste basado en la actividad

Activity-based costing (ABC) is a system by which costing and resource-consuming activities can be identified and monitored. Under the ABC system, overhead costs are recognised by each function or activity, allowing them to be assigned to individual cost objects (products or services) through the use of cost drivers.

sistema ABC

= sistema de coste basado en la actividad

▲ *introduce activity-based costing* introducir un sistema de coste basado en la actividad

⇛ activity-based costing system, refined costing system

activity-based costing system US

= ABC system US

The activity-based costing system (ABC system) is a system by which costing and resource-consuming activities can be identified and monitored. Under the ABC system, overhead costs are recognised by each function or activity, allowing them to be assigned to individual cost objects (products or services) through the use of cost drivers.

sistema ABC

▲ *develop an activity-based costing system* desarrollar un sistema ABC ▲ *implement an activity-based costing system* implementar un sistema de coste basado en la actividad

⇛ refined costing system

activity-based flexible budget

An activity-based flexible budget is a budget that assigns various types of costs and expenses on an individual activity or cost driver rather than on a particular department in an enterprise. The budget is flexible in that it recognises changes in cost behaviour and volume of activity.

presupuesto flexible basado en la actividad

▲ *prepare an activity-based flexible budget* preparar un presupuesto flexible basado en la actividad

activity-based management US

= ABM US

Activity-based management is a management accounting system focusing on the use of activity-based costing for operating, marketing, competitive and strategic decision-making. Costs are collected by functions or activities and reduced by analysing cost drivers.

gestión de costes basada en la actividad

= ABM

▲ *consolidated activity-based management tools for planning, monitoring and reporting* herramientas del sistema de gestión de costes basada en actividades consolidadas para llevar a cabo la planificación, la supervisión y la presentación del informe ▲ *implementation of activity-based management* implementación de un sistema de gestión de costes basada en la actividad ▲ *use consolidated activity-based management and budgeting tools* utilizar el sistema de gestión de costes basada en actividades consolidadas y técnicas presupuestarias

activity-level variance

Activity-level variance is the difference between the amounts stated in the master budget and the amounts stated in the flexible budget.

desviación del nivel de actividad

▲ *account for 25% of total activity-level variance* representa el 25% del total de desviaciones del nivel de actividad ▲ *an activity-level variance of 0.5* una desviación del nivel de actividad de 0,5

actual consistency

Actual consistency is one of the basic assumptions of the Danish Financial Statements Act for the presentation of the annual report and implies that financial year, presentation and classification, methods of consolidation and recognition, measurement basis as well as the monetary unit applied must not be changed from accounting period to the next. However, changes may be made if resulting in a truer and fairer view being given or if new rules or standards must be complied with.

uniformidad temporal

▲ *comply with the requirement of actual consistency* cumplir con la obligación de la uniformidad temporal

actual cost

≠ budgeted cost

An actual cost is a cost that is determined on the basis of costs incurred, such as direct material, direct labour and factory overhead, and not on estimated or budgeted costs or averages.

coste real

= coste actual

≠ coste estimado, coste presupuestado

▲ *actual costs capitalised* costes reales capitalizados ▲ *the actual costs incurred* los costes reales incurridos ▲ *the actual costs of the aquisition* los costes reales de la adquisición

actual costing

Actual costing is a costing method according to which real prices and rates are used when direct and indirect costs are assigned to a cost object.

método de coste real

= método del coste real

▲ *use actual costing* utilizar el método de coste real

actual price

The actual price is the real or current price paid contrary to the estimated, budgeted or previously quoted price.

precio real

▲ *reflect actual prices* reflejar los precios reales ▲ *the actual prices paid* los precios reales pagados ▲ *the actual prices paid for similar assets* los precios reales pagados por activos similares

actuarial

Actuarial means calculated by an actuary. When insurance calculations are actuarial they were made by an actuary.

actuarial

▲ *a separate actuarial report* un informe actuarial separado ▲ *actuarial assumptions* supuestos actuariales ▲ *actuarial gains* ganancias actuariales ▲ *actuarial gains and losses* ganancias y pérdidas actuariales ▲ *actuarial hedging* cobertura actuarial ▲ *actuarial information* información actuarial ▲ *actuarial losses* pérdidas actuariales ▲ *actuarial principles* principios actuariales ▲ *actuarial risk* riesgo actuarial ▲ *actuarial techniques* técnicas actuariales ▲ *actuarial valuation* valoración actuarial ▲ *actuarial valuation method* método de valoración actuarial ▲ *actuarial value* valor actuarial

▲ *an actuarial calculation* un cálculo actuarial ▲ *an actuarial measurement* una medición actuarial ▲ *an actuarially determined pension cost rate* valoración del coste de la pensión determinado actuarialmente ▲ *disclose in an accompanying actuarial report* hacer público en un informe actuarial que acompaña ▲ *net actuarial losses* pérdidas netas actuariales ▲ *net cumulative actuarial losses* pérdidas netas actuariales acumuladas ▲ *prepare an actuarial valuation* preparar una valoración actuarial ▲ *the actuarial present value* el valor actuarial presente ▲ *the actuarial present value of promised retirement benefits* el valor actuarial presente de las prestaciones de jubilación prometidas ▲ *the principal actuarial assumptions* los supuestos actuariales relevantes ▲ *the weighted average actuarial assumptions* los supuestos actuariales medios ponderados ▲ *unrecognised actuarial losses* pérdidas actuariales no reconocidas

actuarial assumption

Actuarial assumptions are independent actuaries' best estimates of demographic and financial variables that will affect the cost of benefits provided under a pension plan.

supuesto actuarial

= hipótesis actuarial

NOTE Spanish accountants prefer 'supuesto actuarial' to the IAS/IFRS term 'hipótesis actuarial'.

▲ *changes in the actuarial assumptions* cambios en los supuestos actuariales ▲ *current actuarial assumptions* supuestos actuariales corrientes ▲ *make actuarial assumptions* hacer supuestos actuariales ▲ *material actuarial assumptions* supuestos actuariales materiales ▲ *mutually compatible actuarial assumptions* supuestos actuariales compatibles mutuamente ▲ *previous actuarial assumptions* supuestos actuariales previos ▲ *significant actuarial assumptions* supuestos actuariales significativos ▲ *supportable actuarial assumptions* supuestos actuariales aceptables ▲ *the principal actuarial assumptions* los supuestos actuariales relevantes ▲ *the principal actuarial assumptions used* los supuestos actuariales relevantes usados ▲ *the weighted average actuarial assumptions* los supuestos actuariales medios ponderados ▲ *unbiased actuarial assumptions* supuestos actuariales sin sesgo

actuarial gain

An actuarial gain arises when the actual costs of the post-employment benefits are lower than previously assumed as a consequence of a favourable development in the actuarial assumptions seen on the part of the enterprise.

ganancia actuarial

▲ *causes of actuarial gains* causas de las ganancias actuariales ▲ *cumulative unrecognised actuarial gains* ganancias actuariales no reconocidas acumuladas ▲ *determine the total amount of actuarial gains* determinar la cantidad total de ganancias actuariales ▲ *immediate recognition of all actuarial gains* reconocimiento inmediato de todas las ganancias actuariales ▲ *net actuarial gains* ganancias actuariales netas ▲ *net cumulative actuarial gains* ganancias actuariales acumuladas netas ▲ *recognised actuarial gains* ganancias actuariales reconocidas ▲ *recognition of actuarial gains* reconocimiento de ganancias actuariales ▲ *subsequent actuarial gains* ganancias actuariales posteriores ▲ *the enterprise's accounting policy for recognising actuarial gains* la política contable de la empresa para reconocer las ganancias actuariales ▲ *unrecognised (deferred) actuarial gains* ganancias actuariales no reconocidas (diferidas)

actuarial loss

An actuarial loss arises when the actual costs of the post-employment benefits exceed those immediately assumed because of an unfavourable development in the actuarial assumptions seen on the part of the enterprise.

pérdida actuarial

▲ *cumulative unrecognised actuarial losses* pérdidas actuariales no reconocidas acumuladas ▲ *cumulative unrecognised net actuarial losses* pérdidas actuariales netas no reconocidas acumuladas ▲ *less any actuarial losses* menos cualesquiera pérdidas actuariales ▲ *recognised actuarial losses* pérdidas actuariales reconocidas ▲ *recognition of actuarial losses* reconocimiento de pérdidas actuariales ▲ *the enterprise's accounting policy for recognising actuarial losses* la política contable de la empresa para reconocer las pérdidas actuariales ▲ *unrecognised (deferred) actuarial losses* pérdidas actuariales no reconocidas (diferidas)

actuarial present value

The actuarial present value is the current value of a benefit obligation calculated on the basis of actuarial factors such as the probability of contribution considering retirement age, life expectancy and discounts for interest, between the specified date and the expected payment date.

valor actuarial presente

= valor actual actuarial

NOTE Although Spanish accountants used 'valor actuarial presente' the Nuevo Plan General Contable uses the IAS/IFRS term 'valor actual actuarial'.

▲ *changes in the actuarial present value* cambios en el valor actuarial presente ▲ *the actuarial present value of promised retirement benefits* el valor actuarial presente de las prestaciones por jubilación prometidas ▲ *the amount of the actuarial present value* la cantidad del valor actuarial presente

actuarial risk

Actuarial risk is the risk that an enterprise's actual pension benefit costs will exceed the expected costs because of an adverse development in the actuarial assumptions.

riesgo actuarial

▲ *actuarial risks associated with the current and former employees* riesgos actuariales asociados con los trabajadores actuales y anteriores ▲ *create actuarial risk for the enterprise* generar riesgo actuarial para la empresa

⇛ actuarial loss

actuary

An actuary is a person who calculates risks in order to give advice to pension funds and insurance companies.

actuario

▲ *included in the actuary's report* incluido en el informe del actuario ▲ *independent qualified actuaries* actuarios habilitados independientes ▲ *reflect the actuary's overall assessment* reflejar la valoración global del actuario

addition

1 ≠ disposal

Additions are the resources acquired by the enterprise within a specific period and which the enterprise now owns and controls.

incremento

= sumas

≠ restas

▲ *addition not subject to tax* incremento no sujeto a impuesto ▲ *addition of assets* incremento de activos ▲ *addition of goodwill* incremento del fondo de comercio ▲ *addition of net assets* incremento de activos netos ▲ *additions and disposals* sumas y restas ▲ *additions during the year* incrementos durante el año ▲ *additions from internal development* incrementos causados por el desarrollo interno ▲ *additions resulting from capitalised subsequent expenditure* incrementos que resultan del gasto posterior capitalizado ▲ *additions through business combinations* incrementos mediante combinaciones de negocios ▲ *additions to reserves* incrementos a reservas ▲ *capital additions* incrementos de capital ▲ *result in additions to the cost of the intangible asset* originar incrementos en el coste del activo intangible

2 ≠ subtraction

An addition is something that complements or extends something.

suma

≠ resta

▲ *with addition of expenses* con la suma de los gastos ▲ *with the addition of* con la suma de

additional cost

= additional expense

Additional cost refers to an increase in costs in relation to the budgeted costs or the costs incurred in prior accounting periods, e.g. if an enterprise chooses another way of transporting its goods, it may incur additional costs.

coste adicional

▲ *a modest additional cost* un coste adicional moderado

additional expense

= additional cost

Additional expense refers to an increase in expenses in relation to the budgeted expenses or the expenses incurred in prior accounting periods, e.g. if an enterprise chooses another way of transporting its goods, it may incur additional expenses.

gasto adicional

= coste excepcional

▲ *additional expenses as a result of the assignment of guarantee commitments to a third party* los gastos adicionales resultantes del traspaso de los compromisos de garantía a un tercero ▲ *recognise an additional expense for the excess value given* reconocer un gasto adicional por el exceso de valor dado

additional income

Additional income refers to an unexpected increase in income in relation to the budgeted income or in relation to the income already earned.

ingreso adicional

▲ *result in additional income* resultar en un ingreso adicional

additional paid-in capital US

= capital surplus US, contributed capital in excess of par, paid-in surplus US, share premium UK

Additional paid-in capital is a type of reserves under equity representing additional capital contributed in the form of a premium on issued shares, i.e. amounts contributed in excess of the nominal or stated value to a company.

prima de emisión

=cuenta de prima de emisión

▲ *additional paid-in capital as at January 1* cuenta de prima de emisión a partir del 1 de enero ▲ *appropriation to additional paid-in capital* dotaciones a la cuenta de la prima de emisión

additional payment

= deferred payment

Additional payment is extra payment by way of addition at a later date.

pago extraordinario

= atraso

▲ *additional payments from and repayments to members* pagos extraordinarios procedentes de y devoluciones a los miembros ▲ *the accounting treatment of additional payments* el tratamiento contable de los pagos extraordinarios ▲ *the total additional payment* los pagos extraordinarios totales

adjust

To adjust is to change something slightly or to correct something.

ajustar

▲ *adjust a budget* ajustar un presupuesto ▲ *adjust a previously recognised provision* ajustar una provisión reconocida previamente ▲ *adjust against equity* ajustar contra patrimonio ▲ *adjust against the opening balance of retained earnings* ajustar contra el saldo de apertura de las reservas ▲ *adjust exceptations for something* ajustar salvedades para algo ▲ *adjust expenses to earnings* ajustar los gastos a los ingresos ▲ *adjust for deferred tax* ajustar por impuestos diferidos ▲ *adjust for inflation* ajustar por inflación ▲ *adjust for the effects of transactions of a non-cash nature* ajustar por los efectos de las transacciones no monetarias ▲ *adjust on a continuing basis* ajustar en una base continuada ▲ *adjust retrospectively* ajustar retrospectivamente ▲ *adjust revenue* ajustar el ingreso ▲ *adjust the depreciation charge* ajustar el coste de amortización ▲ *adjust the depreciation rate* ajustar la tasa de amortización ▲ *adjust the expected result* ajustar el resultado esperado ▲ *adjust the financial statements for events after the balance sheet date* ajustar los estados financieros por hechos posteriores a la fecha de cierre del balance ▲ *adjust the gross carrying amount of goodwill* ajustar el valor contable bruto del fondo de comercio ▲ *by adjusting net profit or loss for the year* ajustando el resultado neto del año

adjust downwards

To adjust downwards means to reduce expectations, needs etc.

as compared to pre-set or previous targets and needs.

ajustar a la baja

▲ *adjust downwards the expectations for next financial year* ajustar a la baja las expectativas para el próximo ejercicio ▲ *adjust one's expectations for the coming year downwards* ajustar a la baja nuestras expectativas para el año próximo

adjust the value

= revalue

To adjust the value is to revalue or change the value. Depreciation, amortisation and write-downs for impairment losses contribute to adjusting the value of an asset.

ajustar el valor

▲ *adjust the value on an ongoing basis* ajustar el valor de forma continua ▲ *adjust the value to fair value* ajustar el valor al valor razonable

adjust upwards

≠ issue a profit warning

To adjust upwards means to increase expectations, needs etc. as compared to pre-set or previous targets and needs.

ajustar al alza

▲ *adjust expectations upwards* ajustar al alza las expectativas

adjustable-rate mortgage

= adjustable-rate loan, ARM

An adjustable-rate mortgage is a loan secured on real property, and the interet rate payable is reset at fixed intervals during the term of the loan. The interest rates fixed for the intervals vary according to changes in the market rates of interest, and the interest rate is therefore adjusted regularly.

hipoteca de tipo variable

= hipoteca a tipo variable, préstamo hipotecario a tipo variable, préstamo hipotecario de tipo variable

▲ *the refinancing of adjustable-rate mortgage loans* la refinanciación de préstamos hipotecarios de tipo variable

adjusted

When something, e.g. an amount, has been adjusted, it has been restated, changed or corrected.

ajustado

▲ *adjusted deferred tax* impuestos diferidos ajustados ▲ *adjusted earnings per share* beneficios por acción ajustados ▲ *adjusted equity* patrimonio ajustado ▲ *adjusted financial ratio calculations* cálculos de ratios financieros ajustados ▲ *adjusted for one-time items* ajustado por partidas excepcionales ▲ *an adjusted balance sheet* un balance ajustado ▲ *an adjusted income statement* una cuenta de resultados ajustada ▲ *the adjusted amount of cost of sales* la cantidad ajustada del coste de las ventas ▲ *the adjusted amount of depreciation of property, plant and equipment* la cantidad ajustada por depreciación de edificios, instalaciones y equipos ▲ *the adjusted carrying amount* el valor contable ajustado

adjusted earnings

= normalised earnings

Adjusted earnings refer to the earnings from operations seen in isolation, i.e. excluding unusual and one-off items, i.e. non-recurring items, such as the acquisition and disposal of assets that would otherwise distort the trend.

beneficios corrientes

= ganancias corrientes

▲ *growth in adjusted earnings* crecimiento de los beneficios corrientes ▲ *principles for adjusted earnings* principios para beneficios corrientes

adjusting event

≠ non-adjusting event

Adjusting events are events that provide further confirmation of conditions existing at the balance sheet date. Adjusting events may result in the recognition of assets or liabilities at a different value, that contingent liabilities must be recognised as provisions or ordinary liabilities etc.

acontecimiento de ajuste

= hecho que implica ajuste

NOTE Spanish accountants prefer 'acontecimiento de ajuste' to the IAS/IFRS/ term 'hecho que implica ajuste'.

▲ *adjusting events after the balance sheet date* los acontecimientos de ajuste después de la fecha de cierre ▲ *significant adjusting events* acontecimientos de ajuste significativos ▲ *the effect of adjusting events* el efecto de los acontecimientos de ajuste

⇛ event after the balance sheet date, post balance sheet date event

adjustment

An adjustment is a change or correction to something such as a figure or an accounting entry.

ajuste

▲ *a strategic adjustment* un ajuste estratégico ▲ *adjustment due to change of accounting policies* ajuste debido a cambios de las políticas contables ▲ *adjustment of an acquisition strategy* ajuste de una estrategia de adquisición ▲ *adjustment of return* ajuste del retorno ▲ *adjustment to fair value* ajuste a valor razonable ▲ *adjustment to market price* ajuste a precio de mercado ▲ *adjustment to price contingent on future events* ajuste al precio contingente en los sucesos futuros ▲ *adjustments to the line items* ajustes a las partidas presupuestarias ▲ *an adjustment arising from* un ajuste procedente de ▲ *an adjustment to an amount* un ajuste a una cantidad ▲ *budget adjustment* ajuste presupuestario ▲ *calculate an adjustment* calcular un ajuste ▲ *determine before any adjustments for minority interest* determinar antes cualesquiera ajustes por intereses devengados y abonados a las filiales ▲ *make an adjustment for tax purposes* hacer un ajuste por motivos fiscales ▲ *make an equivalent adjustment* hacer un ajuste equivalente ▲ *subsequent adjustment of fair values and goodwill initially reported* ajuste posterior de los valores razonables y del fondo de comercio inicialmente calculado ▲ *the amount of the adjustments* el importe de los ajustes ▲ *the nature of the adjustments to the comparative figures* la naturaleza de los ajustes a las cifras comparativas

adjustment amount

= amount of the adjustment

An amount that adjusts, i.e. changes or restates another amount is referred to as the adjustment amount.

cuenta de ajuste

▲ *measure the adjustment amount reliability* medir la fiabilidad de la cuenta de ajuste ▲ *the actual adjustment amount* la cuenta de ajuste actual

adjustment factor

= dilution adjustment factor

The adjustment factor compensates for the dilution of the per-share values of earnings, cash flow etc. that results when additional shares are issued by a company at prices lower than market prices with the effect that the proceeds of the company will be comparatively lower than the value of the new shares. The adjustment factor is applied to adjust financial ratios prior to the share issue, making year-on-year comparisons possible.

factor de ajuste

▲ *adjustment factor by increases in share capital* el factor de ajuste por incrementos del capital social ▲ *calculate an adjustment factor* calcular un factor de ajuste ▲ *computation of adjustment factor* cálculo del factor de ajuste

administration

Administration is a term referring to the activities associated with the management, organisation and systematisation of functions within an enterprise.

administración

▲ *a group administration pension plan* un plan de pensiones con administración conjunta ▲ *administration and other general overhead costs* la administración y otros costes de gestión generales ▲ *the cost of factory management and administration* el coste de gestión y administración de la fábrica

administration building

An administration building is the building where the activities associated with managing, organising and systematising the functions within an enterprise are performed.

edificio de administración

= oficina

▲ *aqcuire a new administration building* comprar un nuevo edificio de administración ▲ *construct a new administration building* construir un nuevo edificio de administración ▲ *dispose of an administration building* deshacerse de un edificio de administración

administration co-operation
→ administration cooperation

administration cooperation
Administration cooperation constitutes the combined efforts and coordination between two or more parties concerning the management and organisation of an enterprise, a business project or other particular activities.
cooperación administrativa
▲ *the advantages of administration cooperation* las ventajas de la cooperación administrativa ▲ *the synergies of administration cooperation* las sinergias de la cooperación administrativa

administration facility
Administration facilities are the buildings and equipment provided for the administration of the business activities of an enterprise.
instalación administrativa
▲ *service and administration facilities* instalaciones administrativas y de servicio

administrative expense
= administrative overhead
Administrative expenses are expenses attributable to the administrative functions of an enterprise, i.e. management, organisation and clerical work, rather than expenses attributable to sales, marketing or production.
gasto de administración
▲ *administrative expenses that contribute to bringing inventories to their present location and condition* gastos de administración que contribuyen a ubicar los inventarios en su estado y condición actual ▲ *deduct expected administrative expenses* deducir los gastos de administración esperados ▲ *expenses incurred are recognised as administrative expenses* los gastos incurridos se reconocen como gastos de administración ▲ *general administrative expenses* gastos de administración generales ▲ *include in administrative expenses* incluir en los gastos de administración

admission
Admission means permission of access to or incorporation into something.
admisión
▲ *admission for trading in an authorised market place* la admisión para actuar en un mercado autorizado ▲ *admission of financial instruments to trading* la admisión de los instrumentos financieros a cotización

admission for listing on the stock exchange UK
= flotation UK, initial public offering US, IPO US
Admission for listing on the stock exchange means that a company's shares or debt securities are offered for sale to the public on the stock market for the first time. This ensures the issuing company the advantage of access to a market where additional capital can be raised and where the securities are publicly traded and quoted, which provides them with a fair market value. To be listed, issuing companies must comply with the listing rules of the stock exchange in question.
admisión a cotización en bolsa
= salida a bolsa
▲ *at the time of admission for listing on the stock exchange* en la salida a bolsa ▲ *since the admission for listing on the stock exchange in 2003* desde la admisión a cotización en bolsa en el 2003

adopt
To adopt means to decide, accept or agree on something.
adoptar
= aprobar
▲ *adopt a change* adoptar un cambio ▲ *adopt a policy for the company's relation to its stakeholders* adoptar una política para la relación de la empresa con sus stakeholders ▲ *adopt a proposal* adoptar una propuesta ▲ *adopt a proposal for delisting at a general meeting* adoptar una propuesta en la junta general para retirarse de bolsa ▲ *adopt this IFRS for an earlier period* adoptar esta NIIF para un periodo anterior ▲ *apply IFRS as adopted by the European Union* aplicar la NIIF tal y como adoptó la Unión Europea ▲ *Standards and Interpretations adopted by the International Accounting Standards Board* Normas e Interpretaciones adoptadas por el Comité Internacional de Normas Contables ▲ *the accounting policies adopted*

in measuring inventories las políticas contables adoptadas para valorar inventarios

adoption

Adoption means the resolution of a proposal or election of a particular person as agreed by a group of people, e.g. by vote.

adopción

= aprobación

▲ *adoption at a general meeting* adopción en una junta general ▲ *adoption of a strategy* adopción de una estrategia ▲ *first-time adoption of International Financial Reporting Standards* la adopción por vez primera de las Normas Internacionales de Información Financiera ▲ *technical criteria for adoption* criterios técnicos para la adopción

ADR US

= American Depositary Receipt US

ADR is the abbreviation for American Depositary Receipt, a negotiable receipt denominated in US dollars that is issued by an American depositary bank and represents ownership of a specified number of shares in a non-US company listed on an American stock exchange that are held in trust by the depositary bank.

ADR

▲ *ADR holders* tenedores de ADR ▲ *ADR issuers* emisores de ADR

⇛ depositary bank

ADS US

= American Depositary Share US

ADS is the abbreviation for American Depositary Share, a negotiable certificate denominated in US dollars that is issued by an American depositary bank for trading on an American stock exchange, representing the underlying original share in a non-US company held in trust by the depositary bank. American Depositary Shares may be issued in the form of American Depositary Receipts representing a specified number of ADSs.

acción subyacente de ADS

▲ *dividends paid per ADS* dividendos pagados por acción subyacente de ADS ▲ *earnings per ADS* ganancias por acción subyacente de ADS ▲ *issue an ADS* emitir una acción subyacente de ADS

⇛ depositary bank

advance[1] *noun*

1 = loan

≠ deposit

An advance is money lent by a bank to a customer.

anticipo

= adelanto

NOTE Spanish banks do not usually make advances.

▲ *any amounts set aside in respect of losses on loans and advances in addition to impairment losses* cualesquiera cantidades reservadas por pérdidas en préstamos y anticipos y quebrantos ▲ *loans and advances written off* préstamos y anticipos cancelados ▲ *repay loans or advances* devolver préstamos o anticipos ▲ *short-term advances with the right of full recovery of the amount lent* anticipos a corto con derecho a recuperación de la cantidad prestada ▲ *the amount credited in the financial year for loans and advances previously written off that have been recovered* la cantidad adeuda en el ejercicio por préstamos y anticipos provisionada previamente se ha recuperado ▲ *the basis for the determination of impairment losses on loans and advances* la base de cálculo por quebrantos en préstamos o anticipos ▲ *write off uncollectible loans and advances* cancelar los préstamos y anticipos incobrables

2 An advance is an amount of money paid earlier than expected or agreed, or for a job before it has been completed.

anticipado

= adelantado

▲ *exceed the revenue received in advance* exceder al ingreso recibido por anticipado ▲ *in advance* por anticipado ▲ *payment in advance* pago por anticipado

3 = increase

≠ decrease

An advance means progress or an increase in something, e.g. amount, price or level.

aumento

= incremento

≠ decremento, disminución

▲ *an advance in prices* un aumento en los precios

advance[2] *verb*

1 = lend
≠ deposit
To advance is to lend money to a person or enterprise.
anticipar
= adelantar
▲ *advance money* anticipar dinero

2 = increase
To advance means to progress or increase, e.g. an amount, a price or level.
crecer
▲ *the company advanced* la empresa creció

advance payment bond
An advance payment bond is a guarantee that prepayment of monetary amounts will be effected at commencement of contract work, e.g. for buying materials. The advance payment is subject to repayment, if the contractual obligations are not fulfilled.
justificante de la entrada
= señal de la entrada
▲ *issue an advance payment bond* emitir un justificante de la entrada ▲ *performance and advance payment bonds* factura y justificante de la entrada

advance payment guarantee
→ advance payment bond

advance receipts US
Advance receipts concern payments received at the balance sheet date concerning income that relate to the following year(s), presented as a balance sheet item under liabilities since the enterprise has received the payment before earned and has to deliver the products or services underlying the payment, e.g. in connection with construction contracts.
cobros anticipados
= ingreso diferido
▲ *classify as advance receipts* clasificar como ingreso diferido
⇛ deferred revenue

adverse opinion
An adverse opinion is a modified audit report where the auditor is not able to issue a qualified audit opinion because the effect of disagreement with management is so deep and material that the incompleteness of or misstatements in the financial statements cannot adequately be disclosed through a qualification to the audit report.
informe desfavorable
▲ *express an adverse opinion* expresar un informe desfavorable ▲ *issue an adverse opinion* emitir un informe desfavorable
⇛ audit report, qualified audit report

advertising cost
= cost of advertising activities
Advertising costs refer to the costs incurred by an enterprise in relation to advertising for itself or its products or services.
coste publicitario
▲ *increasing advertising costs* incrementando los costes publicitarios ▲ *the actual advertising costs* los costes publicitarios reales ▲ *the advertising costs incurred* los costes publicitarios incurridos ▲ *the budgeted advertising costs* los costes publicitarios presupuestados

advertising expense US
Advertising expenses refer to the expenses incurred by an enterprise in relation to advertising for itself or its products or services.
gasto publicitario
▲ *increasing advertising expenses* incrementando los gastos publicitarios ▲ *the actual advertising expenses* los gastos publicitarios reales ▲ *the advertising expenses incurred* los gastos publicitarios incurridos ▲ *the budgeted advertising expenses* los gastos publicitarios presupuestados

affiliate[1] US *noun* <an, the, -s>
= affiliated company, related company
An affiliate is an enterprise that is linked to another enterprise in the same group in some way. Depending on how it is controlled, an affiliate may be either a subsidiary or an associate. Two subsidiaries in the same group can be said to be affiliates.
NOTE According to US definition, an affiliate is usually a company in which another enterprise exercises significant influence, or a related company, i.e. sister company to another company in the same group.
empresa del grupo
= filial

▲ *a parent organization and its affiliates* una matriz y sus filiales ▲ *transactions between affiliates* transacciones entre empresas del grupo
⇛ group, group enterprise

affiliate[2] *verb* <-s, -d, has -d, affiliating> *passive* <is -d, was -d>
To affiliate is to become or make a person or an enterprise connected with and related to e.g. a group or an organisation.
incorporarse
= afiliarse
▲ *be affiliated to the company* incoporarse a la empresa

affiliated company US
= affiliate, related company
An affiliated company is a company that is linked to another company in the same group in some way. Depending on the parent company interests in it, an affiliated company may be either a subsidiary or an associated company. Two subsidiaries in the same group are affiliated companies.
NOTE According to US definition, an affiliate is usually a company in which another enterprise exercises significant influence, or a related company, i.e. sister company to another company in the same group.
empresa del grupo
= filial
▲ *merger of affiliated companies* la fusión de las empresas del grupo
⇛ group enterprise

affiliated enterprise
= affiliate, related enterprise
An affiliated enterprise is an enterprise that is linked to another enterprise in the same group in some way. Depending on the parent company interests in it, an affiliated enterprise may be either a subsidiary or an associate. Two subsidiaries in the same group are affiliated enterprises.
NOTE According to US definition, an affiliate is usually a company in which another enterprise exercises significant influence, or a related company, i.e. sister company to another company in the same group.
empresa del grupo
= filial
▲ *the company and its affiliated enterprises* la empresa y sus filiales ▲ *transactions with affiliated enterprises* transacciones con empresas del grupo
⇛ affiliated company, group enterprise, related company

affiliated undertaking UK
= affiliated enterprise
An affiliated undertaking is an undertaking that is linked to another undertaking in the same group in some way. Depending on the parent company's interests in it, an affiliated undertaking may be either a subsidiary undertaking or an associated undertaking. Two subsidiaries in the same group are affiliated undertakings.
empresa del grupo
= filial
▲ *losses realised by the affiliated undertakings* pérdidas realizadas por las empresas del grupo
⇛ affiliated company, group enterprise, related company

affiliation
Affiliation means a relationship and is typically used about the connection between enterprises within the same group that may be interconnected as either associates or subsidiaries to the same parent company.
asociación
= afiliación
▲ *industry affiliation* asociación del sector industrial ▲ *irrespective of affiliation* con independencia de la asociación
⇛ connection

ageing
→ aging

agency theory
The agency theory is the study of the relationship between an agent and the principal on whose behalf the agent interacts with a third party. An example is the contracting between an enterprise and the managers being hired to make decisions on behalf of the enterprise.
teoría de la agencia
▲ *a model using agency theory* un modelo que utiliza la teoría de la agencia

aggregate[1] *verb*
= combine
To aggregate means adding together different parts or figures.

agregar
= incorporar
▲ *aggregate current period figures with budgeted figures for the future* cifras agregadas del periodo actual con cifras presupuestadas para el futuro ▲ *aggregate expenses in the income statement according to their nature* agregar gastos a la cuenta de resultados de acuerdo con su naturaleza ▲ *aggregate immaterial amounts with amounts of a similar nature or function* agregar las cuentas intangibles con cuentas de naturaleza o función similar ▲ *aggregated with accumulated impairment losses* agregado con pérdidas patrimoniales acumuladas ▲ *to aggregate individually insignificant items* agregar las partidas importantes de forma individual ▲ *to aggregate into groups* agregar en grupos ▲ *to aggregate items* agregar partidas

aggregate[2] *adjective*
When something is referred to as aggregate, it is a combination of several parts or a total of several figures.
agregado
▲ *net of the aggregate related tax expense* neto del gasto fiscal agregado relacionado ▲ *provide information at a more aggregate level* ofrecer información a nivel más agregado ▲ *the aggregate amount of* la cantidad agregada de ▲ *the aggregate amount of the cash paid or received as purchase or sale consideration* la cantidad agregada de efectivo pagado o recibido en concepto de compra o venta ▲ *the aggregate carrying amount* el valor contable agregado ▲ *the aggregate cash flows* los flujos de caja agregados ▲ *the aggregate current and deferred tax* impuesto corriente y diferido agregado ▲ *the aggregate fair value* el valor razonable agregado ▲ *the aggregate gains or losses* las ganancias o pérdidas agregadas ▲ *the aggregate information* la información agregada ▲ *the aggregate minimum lease payments* los pagos por alquiler mínimos agregados ▲ *the aggregate present value* el valor actual agregado ▲ *the aggregate share of the net profit or loss of associates* la participación agregada del resultado neto de las asociadas ▲ *the aggregate value* el valor agregado

aggregate[3] *noun*
An aggregate is a total arrived at after adding something together such as figures or parts.
suma total
▲ *an aggregate of items* una suma total de partidas ▲ *disclosed in the aggregate* visto en la suma total ▲ *in aggregate* en suma total ▲ *in the aggregate* en la suma total ▲ *the aggregate adjustment to the carrying amounts reported under previous GAAP* el ajuste de la suma total al valor contable reconocido según los principios contables generalmente aceptados anteriores ▲ *the aggregate of* la suma total de ▲ *the aggregate of the enterprise's share of the net profit or loss of associates, joint ventures, or other investments* la suma total de la participación de la empresa en los resultados netos de asociadas, joint ventures, u otras inversiones ▲ *the aggregate of the fair values* la suma total de los valores razonables

aggregation
An aggregation arises when e.g. amounts, items or data have been combined or added together.
agregación
▲ *aggregation of items* agregación de partidas ▲ *lowest aggregation of assets that generate largely independent cash inflows* la agregación más pequeña de activos que producen flujos de caja independientes más grandes ▲ *the final stage in the process of aggregation* la etapa final en el proceso de agregación

aggregation level
= level of aggregation
The aggregation level is the level at which the record(s) is/are being described and controlled.
nivel de agregación
▲ *at an appropriate aggregation level* a un nivel de agregación apropiado ▲ *at the aggregation level specified in the test* al nivel de agregación especificado en la prueba ▲ *the correct aggregation level* el nivel de agregación correcto

aging
= age analysis, aging analysis

Aging is the age analysis and classification of debtors and creditors by outstanding period of time.

análisis por antigüedad

▲ *aging of accounts* análisis por antigüedad de las cuentas ▲ *aging of accounts receivable* análisis por antigüedad de las cuentas a cobrar ▲ *disclose an aging of financial assets past due* publicación del análisis por antigüedad de los activos financieros ya vencidos

AGM

AGM is the abbreviation for annual general meeting and refers to a formal meeting of the shareholders of a company and its directors. An AGM is statutorily required to be held each calendar year. The main business at the meeting is the presentation of the financial statements, the appointment of auditors and the proposal for dividends.

junta general de accionistas

▲ *at the AGM* en la junta general de accionistas ▲ *present the Annual Report at the AGM* presentar el Informe Anual a la junta general de accionistas

agree

To agree means to decide something together with someone else after a negotiaion or discussion.

acordar

▲ *agree mutually* acordar mutuamente ▲ *agree on something* acordar algo ▲ *agree on something* acordar algo ▲ *agree to a fixed contract price* acordar un precio fijo de contrato ▲ *agree to a fixed rate per unit of output* acordar a un tipo fijo por unidad de producto ▲ *agree to change the provisions of the lease* acordar cambios en las condiciones del arrendamiento ▲ *agree variations or claims that increase or decrease contract revenue* acordar las variaciones o reclamaciones que aumentan o disminuyen el ingreso del contrato

agreement

An agreement is an arrangement or contract made by concord of understanding between two parties on a particular purpose or proposition. An agreement may or may not be legally binding.

acuerdo

▲ *a binding sale agreement* un acuerdo de venta vinculante ▲ *a contractual agreement* un acuerdo contractual ▲ *a fixed-term agreement* un acuerdo a término fijo ▲ *a legally binding agreement* un acuerdo legalmente vinculante ▲ *a separate agreement to repurchase the goods at a later date* un acuerdo por separado para recomprar los bienes en una fecha posterior ▲ *a sub-letting agreement* un acuerdo de subarrendamiento ▲ *based on a long-term agreement* basado en un acuerdo a largo plazo ▲ *by agreement* por acuerdo ▲ *contingent share agreement* acuerdo de acciones contingentes ▲ *enter into an agreement* entrar en un acuerdo ▲ *having regard to the substance of the agreement* respetando la sustancia del acuerdo ▲ *requirements provided for by articles of association or by agreement* requisitos reflejados en los estatutos o en el acuerdo ▲ *strategic partnership and business cooperation agreement* un contrato de sociedad estratégica y de cooperación empresarial ▲ *the intention is supported by an agreement to refinance or to reschedule payments* la intención se apoya en un acuerdo destinado a refinanciar o reestructurar los pagos ▲ *under the agreement* según el acuerdo ▲ *voluntary audit agreement* acuerdo voluntario de auditoria

agreement date IAS/IFRS

The agreement date is the date when a business combination is substantively agreed by the combining entities, and the date of public announcement if the entities are listed. Where the business combination is a result of a hostile takeover, the agreement date is the date when a sufficient number of the acquiree's owners have accepted the offer from the acquirer to obtain control.

fecha del acuerdo

▲ *business combinations for which the agreement date is on or after 31 March 2004* las combinaciones de negocios para las que la fecha del acuerdo es el 31 de marzo de 2004 o poste-

rior ▲ *the agreement date for a business combination* la fecha del acuerdo para una combinación de negocios
SOURCE IFRS 3, Appendix A
⇛ acquiree, acquirer, business combination

agricultural activity IAS/IFRS
Agricultural activities are the actions taken by an enterprise to control the biological transformation of its biological assets into agricultural produce.
actividad agrícola
▲ *a logical and natural extension of agricultural activity* una extensión lógica y natural de la actividad agrícola ▲ *biological assets related to agricultural activity* activos biológicos relacionados con la actividad agrícola ▲ *disclosures related to agricultural activity* divulgaciones relacionadas con la actividad agrícola ▲ *distinguish agricultural activity from other activities* distinguir la actividad agrícola de otras actividades ▲ *financial reporting for agricultural activity* registro financiero de la actividad agrícola ▲ *financial risk management strategies related to agricultural activity* las estrategias de gestión del riesgo financiero relacionadas con la actividad agrícola ▲ *intangible assets related to agricultural activity* activos intangibles relacionadas con la actividad agrícola ▲ *land related to agricultural activity* suelo rústico relacionado con la actividad agrícola ▲ *specified agricultural activity* actividad agrícola especificada ▲ *to engage in an agricultural activity* dedicarse a la actividad agrícola

agricultural produce IAS/IFRS
Agricultural produce is the products enterprises harvest from their biological assets.
producción agrícola
= producto agrícola
NOTE Spanish accountants prefer 'producción agrícola' to the IAS/IFRS' term 'producto agrícola'. A 'producto agrícola' is an individual element whereas 'producción agrícola' refers to the whole process of harvesting the land.
▲ *agricultural produce harvested from the enterprise's biological assets* la producción agrícola obtenida de los activos biológicos de la empresa ▲ *an active market for agricultural produce* un mercado dinámico para la producción agrícola ▲ *each group of agricultural produce* cada grupo de producción agrícola ▲ *estimated point-of-sale costs of agricultural produce* costes estimados en el punto de venta de la producción agrícola ▲ *measure agricultural produce at its fair value* cuantificar la producción agrícola a su valor razonable ▲ *on initial measurement of agricultural produce at the point of harvest* en la valoración inicial de la producción agrícola en origen ▲ *on initial recognition of agricultural produce at fair value* en el reconocimeito inicial de la producción agrícola a valor razonable ▲ *output of agricultural produce during the financial year* salida de la producción agrícola durante el ejercicio fiscal ▲ *processing of agricultural produce after harvest* procesamiento de la producción agrícola después de la cosecha ▲ *production of agricultural produce* producción de productos agrícolas ▲ *sale of agricultural produce* venta de la producción agrícola

AICPA US
= American Institute of Certified Public Accountants US
AICPA is the abbreviation for the American Institute of Certified Public Accountants which is the main US professional organisation of practising certified public accountants. The AICPA is responsible for the accounting profession's ethical rules and for setting the Statements on Auditing Standards. Since 1973, the setting of accounting standards rests with the Financial Accounting Standards Board.
AICPA
= Instituto Norteamericano de Auditores de Cuentas
NOTE The Spanish equivalent body is called ICAC.
▲ *a standard revised by AICPA* una norma revisada por el AICPA ▲ *the technical committee authorized to speak on behalf of the AICPA* el comité técnico autorizado para hablar en nombre del AICPA

all-inclusive income

→ comprehensive income

allocate

To allocate is to systematically distribute e.g. resources over various time periods, products, operations or investments, shares to investors, or to spread e.g. cost over two or more accounting periods.

asignar

= imputar

▲ *allocate a sum of money for a purpose* asignar una suma de dinero a un fin ▲ *allocate according to an appropriate method* asignar de acuerdo con un método adecuado ▲ *allocate capital* asignar capital ▲ *allocate part of a grant on one basis and part on another* asignar parte de una subvención en base a una parte y otra parte en base a otra ▲ *allocate pro rata* prorratear ▲ *allocate the amount of fixed overhead to each unit of production* asignar la cantidad de costes indirectos fijos a cada unidad de producción ▲ *allocated on a reasonable and consistent basis* asignado de acuerdo a una base consistente y razonable ▲ *allocated over more than one class of activity* asignado a más de una clase de actividad ▲ *costs allocated to specific contracts* costes asignados a contratos específicos

allocated

= distributed

When something has been allocated, it has been distributed on several areas or segments.

asignado

= imputado

▲ *allocated capital* capital asignado ▲ *the carrying amount of allocated goodwill* el valor contable del fondo de comercio asignado

allocation

= distribution

Allocation is the systematic distribution of e.g. resources over various time periods, products, operations or investments.

asignación

= imputación

▲ *a systematic allocation of fixed and variable production overheads* una asignación sistemática de la producción fija y variable ▲ *allocation based on taxable income* asignación basada en la renta imponible ▲ *allocation for income taxes* asignación para tributación ▲ *partial allocation* asignación parcial

⇛ breakdown

allocation costing

= absorption costing, absorption costing approach UK, full absorption

Allocation costing is a costing method which seeks to estimate the value of an inventory by assigning all variable manufacturing costs and all fixed manufacturing costs to each production unit. The fixed costs are typically allocated to output units based on direct labour hours, machine hours or material costs.

sistema de coste por asignación

= sistema de coste completo, sistema de coste integral

▲ *an alternative to allocation costing* una alternativa al sistema de coste por asignación ▲ *total allocation costing* total sistema de coste por asignación

⇛ full costing, overhead absorption rate

allocation method

= method of allocation

An allocation method is a method for distributing profits, costs, taxes etc. on accounting elements or separate entities, e.g. in a group.

método de asignación

▲ *allocate according to the full allocation method* imputar de acuerdo con el método de asignación completo ▲ *allocation method for accounting purposes* método de asignación por motivos contables ▲ *allocation method for tax purposes* método de asignación por motivos fiscales ▲ *full allocation method* método de asignación completo

allocation of resources

= resource allocation

The allocation of resources is an investor's diversification of money on investments, based on the weighing of risks and rewards.

asignación de recursos

▲ *decide on the allocation of resources* decidir la asignación de recursos ▲ *the user's allocation of resources* la asignación de recursos del usuario

allotment price

The allotment price is the price set at the grant date of a share option at which the recipient of the option may buy the shares allotted by the granting company at the exercise date. The recipient may keep the shares, but if the allotment price is higher than the market price at the exercise date, a sale of the shares represents a profit.

precio de adjudicación

▲ *a market price exceeding the allotment price* un precio de mercado que excede al precio de adjudicación

allowable cost

Allowable costs are costs which two contractual parties have accepted as costs included in the amount which is payable by one party to the other.

coste aceptado

▲ *actual allowable costs* costes aceptados reales ▲ *adjust the allowable costs* ajustar los costes aceptados ▲ *the allowable costs incurred* los costes aceptados incurridos

allowance US, IAS/IFRS

1 An allowance is an amount given to an employee as compensation for costs and expenses incurred for a specific purpose such as a travelling allowance, or for services rendered such as a car allowance.

compensación

= asignación, dieta

▲ *a reasonable profit allowance for the selling effort* una compensación adecuada por el esfuerzo vendedor

2 An allowance represents an amount that is deducted from another such as a tax allowance or a depreciation allowance.

deducción

▲ *allowances against tax* deducciones contra impuesto ▲ *less allowances for uncollectibility and collection costs* menos deducciones de costes por efectos a cobrar y por gestión de cobro ▲ *obsolescence allowances on inventories* deducción por obsolescencia de inventarios ▲ *personal allowance* deducción personal ▲ *the accumulated allowance for uncollectible minimum lease payments receivable* la deducción acumulada por anticipos por alquiler mínimo no cobrados

3 = provision IAS/IFRS, UK

Allowances are provisions against the value of assets such as allowances for doubtful accounts. Allowances are expensed in anticipation of the resulting reduction in value.

provisión

▲ *allowance for deferred tax* provisión por impuestos diferidos ▲ *establish an allowance* registrar una provisión ▲ *recognize an allowance* reconocer una provisión

⇛ allowance for uncollectibles

allowance account US

= provisions account UK

An allowance account is an account under liabilities in the balance sheet where allowances for bad and doubtful debts are recognised.

cuenta de provisión

= provisión

▲ *adjust an allowance account* ajustar una cuenta de provisión ▲ *details of the movements in any allowance account for impairment losses on loans and advances* detalles de los movimientos en cualquier cuenta de provisión para pérdidas patrimoniales en créditos y anticipos ▲ *the amount of any allowance account at the balance sheet date* la cantidad de cualquier cuenta de provisión a fecha de cierre del balance ▲ *the movements in the allowance account* los movimientos en la cuenta de provisión ▲ *through the use of an allowance account* mediante el uso de una cuenta de provisión

allowance for bad debts

→ allowance for uncollectibles

allowance for doubtful accounts

→ allowance for uncollectibles

allowance for uncollectibles US

= allowance for bad debts US, allowance for doubtful accounts US, provision for bad and doubtful debts UK

Allowance for uncollectibles is a provision recognised in the balance sheet because of expected default concerning amounts receivable.

provisión para insolvencias

= deterioro por insolvencias, provisión por insolvencias

▲ *estimated allowances for uncol-*

lectibles provisiones estimadas para insolvencias ▲ *less allowance for uncollectibles* menos la provisión para insolvencias ▲ *net of allowances for uncollectibles* neto de provisiones para insolvencias

allowed alternative treatment IAS/IFRS

≠ benchmark treatment IAS/IFRS

The allowed alternative treatment is one of two possible accounting treatments allowed in some limited cases in the International Financial Reporting Standards. The other policy is referred to as the benchmark treatment. However, no preference is suggested between the two treatments, and financial statements will meet the IFRS presentation requirements irrespective of which treatment is chosen.

tratamiento alternativo permitido

▲ *in accordance with the allowed alternative treatment* de acuerdo con el tratamiento alternativo permitido

alternate

An alternate is a person who has been appointed to be a substitute for one or more other persons to carry out their duties in particular situations, e.g. during their absence.

suplente

= sustituto

▲ *act as alternate for* actuar como suplente de ▲ *alternate director* director suplente ▲ *alternate for the employee board member* suplente del representante de los trabajadores en el consejo ▲ *nominate as alternate* elegir como suplente

alternative[1] *noun* <an, the, -s>

An alternative is one of several possible solutions to a task or problem.

alternativa

▲ *a chosen alternative for new or improved materials* una alternativa elegida para los materiales nuevos o mejorados ▲ *a realistic alternative* una alternativa realista ▲ *an allowed alternative* una alternativa permitida ▲ *as an alternative* como una alternativa

alternative[2] *adjective*

Alternative means available instead of something else.

alternativo

▲ *a range of reasonably possible alternative assumptions* una serie de supuestos alternativos razonablemente posibles ▲ *alternative reliable estimates of fair value* estimaciones fiables alternativas de valor razonable ▲ *permit an alternative treatment* permitir un tratamiento alternativo ▲ *the alternative method* el método alternativo ▲ *the yield on alternative investments* el rendimiento de las inversiones alternativas

amendment

An alteration or correction of something, especially a written document, is called an amendment.

corrección

= rectificación

▲ *amendment to IAS 16* correcciones a la NIC16 ▲ *following an amendment of a pronouncement* siguiendo una corrección de un dictamen

American Depositary Receipt US

= ADR US

An American Depositary Receipt (ADR) is a negotiable receipt denominated in US dollars that is issued by an American depositary bank and represents ownership of a specified number of shares in a non-US company listed on an American stock exchange that are held in trust by the depositary bank.

American Depositary Receipt

= recibo de depósito americano

▲ *shares traded as American Depositary Receipts* acciones negociadas como American Depositary Receipts ▲ *the acquisition of American Depositary Receipts* la adquisición de American Depositary Receipts

⇛ American Depositary Share

American Depositary Share US

= ADS US

An American Depositary Share (ADS) is a negotiable certificate denominated in US dollars that is issued by an American depositary bank for trading on an American stock exchange, representing the underlying original share in a non-US company held in trust by the depositary bank. American Depositary Shares may be issued in the form of American Depositary Receipts representing a specified number of ADSs.

American Depostary Share
= acción de depósito americana
▲ *acquire American Depositary Shares* comprar American Depositary Shares
⇛ American Depositary Receipt

American Institute of Certified Public Accountants US
= AICPA US
The American Institute of Certified Public Accountants (AICPA) is the main US professional organisation of practising certified public accountants. The AICPA is responsible for the accounting profession's ethical rules and for setting the Statements on Auditing Standards. Since 1973, the setting of accounting standards rests with the Financial Accounting Standards Board.

American Institute of Certified Public Accountants
= Instituto Norteamericano de Auditores de Cuentas
NOTE The Spanish equivalent body is ICAC ('Instituto de Contabilidad y Auditoría de Cuentas').
▲ *be a member of the American Institute of Certified Public Accountants* ser un miembro del American Institute of Certified Public Accountants
⇛ Financial Accounting Standards Board

amortisable UK, IAS/IFRS, UK
When an asset is amortisable, the enterprise may amortise that asset's value over time instead of recognising it as an expense on acquisition.

amortizable
▲ *amortisable assets* activos amortizables ▲ *amortisable non-monetary assets* activos no monetarios amortizables
⇛ depreciable

amortisable amount IAS/IFRS, UK
= amortizable amount US
The amortisable amount is the value of an intangible fixed asset constituting the basis of amortisation represented by the cost of the asset, or other revalued amount substituted for cost, less the residual value and any write-downs.

cantidad amortizable
▲ *10% of the amortisable amount* el 10% de la cantidad amortizable
⇛ depreciable amount

amortisable asset IAS/IFRS, UK
= amortizable asset US
When an asset is depreciable or amortisable, the enterprise may depreciate or amortise that asset's value over time instead of recognising it as an expense on acquisition.
NOTE The term amortisable applies to intangible assets and depreciable applies to tangible assets.

activo amortizable
▲ *the expected pattern of consumption of economic benefits of an amortisable asset* el patrón esperado de agotamiento de beneficios económicos de un activo amortizable
⇛ depreciable asset

amortisation UK, IAS/IFRS
1 = amortization US
Amortisation is the gradual reduction of an intangible asset's cost by systematically allocating the asset's amortisable amount over its definite economic life.
NOTE For tangible assets, the term 'depreciation' is generally used.

amortización
▲ *accelerated amortisation* amortización acelerada ▲ *accumulated amortisation* amortización acumulada ▲ *amortisation based on the asset's revalued carrying amount* amortización basada en el valor contable revalorizado del activo ▲ *amortisation for the year* amortización anual ▲ *amortisation for which separate disclosure is required* amortización para la que se requiere información detallada ▲ *amortisation not deductible for tax purposes* amortización no deducible por motivos fiscales ▲ *amortisation of goodwill* amortización del fondo de comercio ▲ *amortisation of intangible assets* amortización de activos intangibles ▲ *amortisation of patents and licences* amortización de patentes y licencias ▲ *amortisation recognised during the financial year* amortización reconocida durante el año financiero ▲ *commence amortisation* iniciar la amortización ▲ *depreciation and amortisation expense* depreciación y gasto de amortización

▲ *net of amortisation or depreciation* neto de amortización o depreciación ▲ *the effect of amortisation* el efecto de amortización
⇛ depreciation

2 = amortization US, repayment
Amortisation means the regular repayment of instalments and interest on a loan.
reembolso
= amortización financiera
▲ *amortisation of financial assets* reembolso de los activos financieros

amortisation account IAS/IFRS, UK
= amortization account US

1 = amortization account US
An amortisation account is an account in the accounting system recording the periodic accumulated amortisation amount of an enterprise's intangible assets.
cuenta de amortización
= amortización acumulada
▲ *the balance of the amortisation account* el saldo de la cuenta de amortización
⇛ depreciation account

2 = amortization account US
An amortisation account is an account recording and accumulating funds needed to repay a loan.
cuenta de amortización
▲ *amortisation account for cash loans* cuenta de amortización para los préstamos en efectivo
▲ *the balance of the amortisation account* el saldo de la cuenta de amortización

amortisation amount UK, IAS/IFRS
= amortization amount US
The amortisation amount or charge is the amount calculated on the basis of the systematic allocation of the amortisable amount over the useful life of an intangible asset.
cuota de amortización
= gasto de amortización
▲ *a fictitious amortisation amount* una cuota de amortización ficticia ▲ *a fixed amortisation amount* una cuota de amortización fija ▲ *an annual amortisation amount of EUR 250,000* una cuota de amortización anual por valor de 250.000 euros ▲ *the accumulated amortisation amount* la cuota de amortización acumulada
▲ *the total amortisation amount* la cuota de amortización total
⇛ depreciation amount

amortisation balance UK, IAS/IFRS
= amortization balance US
The amortisation balance shows the net book value of an intangible asset less amortisation for the period.
NOTE The term amortisation balance applies to intangible assets.
saldo de depreciación
▲ *a negative amortisation balance* un saldo de depreciación negativo ▲ *increase in the amortisation balance* aumento en el saldo de depreciación
⇛ depreciation balance

amortisation basis for tax purposes UK
= amortization basis for tax purposes US
The amortisation basis for tax purposes is the amount of an intangible fixed asset subject to amortisation allowed under tax rules. This amount constitutes the cost of that asset, or other revalued amount substituted for cost, less the residual value and any write-downs.
base amortizable por motivos fiscales
= base de amortización por motivos fiscales
▲ *amortisation basis for tax purposes according to assessed cash value* base de amortización por motivos fiscales de acuerdo al valor en efectivo estimado
▲ *difference between nominal purchase sum and amortisation basis for tax purposes* diferencia entre el valor de compra nominal y la base de amortización por motivos fiscales ▲ *the amortisation basis for tax purposes of an asset* la base de amortización por motivos fiscales de un activo
⇛ depreciation basis for tax purposes

amortisation charge IAS/IFRS, UK
The amortisation charge is the amortised cost or amount charged to the profit and loss account for a particular accounting period calculated on the basis of the systematic allocation of the amortisable amount over the useful life of an intangible asset.
cuota de amortización
= cargo por amortización, gasto por amortización

▲ *the amortisation charge for each period* la cuota de amortización para cada periodo ▲ *the amortisation charge for the asset* la cuota de amortización para el activo ▲ *the asset's amortisation charge* la cuota de amortización del activo

amortisation expense IAS/IFRS

= amortization expense US

The amortisation expense is the amortised cost or amount charged to the profit and loss account for a particular accounting period calculated on the basis of the systematic allocation of the amortisable amount over the useful life of an intangible asset.

cuota de amortización

= gasto de amortización

▲ *depreciation and amortisation expense* depreciación y cuota de amortización ▲ *including depreciation and amortisation expense* incluyendo depreciación y cuota de amortización

amortisation for tax purposes IAS/IFRS, UK

= amortization for tax purposes US, tax amortisation

Amortisation for tax purposes is the amortisation allowed of an intangible asset.

amortización por motivos fiscales

▲ *cumulative amortisation for tax purposes* amortización acumulada por motivos fiscales ▲ *provide for amortisation for tax purposes* provisionar la amortización por motivos fiscales

⇛ depreciation for tax purposes

amortisation method UK, IAS/IFRS

= basis of amortisation, method of amortisation

The amortisation method is the policy applied by an enterprise for gradually writing down an intangible asset over its economic life. Usually, the straight-line method is chosen.

metodo de amortización

= criterio de amortización

▲ *a variety of amortisation methods* una diversidad de métodos de amortización ▲ *amortisation method for goodwill* el método de amortización para el fondo de comercio ▲ *apply the amortisation method consistently from period to period* aplicar de manera consistente el método de amortización periodo por periodo ▲ *review the amortisation period* revisar el periodo de amortización ▲ *the amortisation method used* el método de amortización utilizado

⇛ depreciation method, straight-line method

amortisation of goodwill UK, IAS/IFRS

= amortization of goodwill US, goodwill amortisation IAS/IFRS, UK

Amortisation of goodwill is the systematic allocation of the amortisable amount of goodwill over its economic life.

amortización del fondo de comercio

NOTE Spanish accounting rules have already been adapted to a recent European directive that mandates eliminating the systematic amortisation of goodwill.

▲ *book amortisation of goodwill disallowed for tax purposes* la amortización contable del fondo de comercio rechazada por motivos fiscales ▲ *related amortisation of goodwill* amortización del fondo de comercio relacionada ▲ *reversal of amortisation of goodwill* anulación de la amortización del fondo de comercio

amortisation period UK, IAS/IFRS

= amortization period US

The amortisation period is the expected useful life of the asset, i.e. the period over which that asset is expected to be used by the enterprise.

NOTE The term amortisation period applies to intangible assets.

plazo de amortización

= periodo de amortización

▲ *a long amortisation period* un periodo de amortización largo ▲ *a short amortisation period* un periodo de amortización corto ▲ *change the amortisation period* cambiar el plazo de amortización ▲ *review the amortisation period* revisar el plazo de amortización ▲ *the amortisation period adopted* el plazo de amortización adoptado ▲ *the remaining amortisation period* el plazo de amortización pendiente

⇛ depreciation period

amortisation policy IAS/IFRS, UK

= amortization policy US

The amortisation policy is the method applied by an enterprise for allocating the costs of intangible assets over their economic lives.
NOTE The term amortisation policy applies to intangible assets.
método de amortización
= criterio de amortización, política de amortización
▲ *amortise in accordance with the group's amortisation policy* amortizar de acuerdo con el método de amortización del grupo ▲ *normal amortisation policy* política de amortización corriente
⇛ depreciation policy

amortisation profile IAS/IFRS, UK
= amortization profile US
The amortisation profile shows the allocation of the amortisation amounts on an asset over the useful life.
NOTE The term amortisation profile applies to intangible assets.
perfil de amortización
▲ *expectations to the amortisation profile of an investment* previsiones con respecto al perfil de amortización de una inversión ▲ *the buyer's amortisation profile* el perfil de amortización del comprador ▲ *the discounted value of an amortisation profile* la bonificación por consumo de un perfil de amortización
⇛ depreciation profile

amortisation rate UK, IAS/IFRS
= amortization rate US
The amortisation rate is the percentage rate at which intangible fixed assets are amortised under a chosen amortisation method to determine the amount for amortisation written off for an accounting period.
porcentaje de amortización
▲ *a wrong amortisation rate* un porcentaje de amortización erróneo ▲ *change of the amortisation rate* cambio del porcentaje de amortización ▲ *the amortisation rates used* los porcentajes de amortización utilizados ▲ *the annual amortisation rate* el porcentaje de amortización anual ▲ *the maximum amortisation rate* el porcentaje de amortización máximo
⇛ depreciation rate, reducing-balance amortisation, straight-line amortisation

amortisation rule IAS/IFRS, UK
= amortization rule US
Amortisation rules are official instructions for amortisation for financial reporting purposes and for tax purposes as provided by accounting standards and tax legislation respectively.
NOTE The term amortisation rule applies to intangible assets.
norma de amortización
▲ *a generous amortisation rule* una norma de amortización amplia ▲ *the revised amortisation rule* la norma de amortización revisada
⇛ depreciation rule

amortisation schedule UK
1 An amortisation schedule is a plan or table for the regular repayment of interest and instalments on a loan over the life of the loan.
cuadro de amortización
= plan de amortización, programa de amortización, tabla de amortización
▲ *a 25 years' amortisation schedule* un cuadro de amortización de 25 años
2 The amortisation schedule shows the allocation of the amortization amounts on an intangible asset over its useful life.
cuadro de amortización
= plan de amortización, programa de amortización, tabla de amortización
▲ *amend the amortisation schedule* modificar el cuadro de amortización ▲ *changes in the amortisation schedule* cambios en el cuadro de amortización ▲ *the amortisation schedule for past service cost* el cuadro de amortización por el coste de los trabajadores anteriores
⇛ amortisation profile

amortise UK, IAS/IFRS
1 = amortize US
To amortise is to allocate the amortisable amount systematically over the useful life of an intangible asset.
amortizar
▲ *amortise a development project over a period of 3 to 5 years* amortizar un proyecto de desarrollo durante un periodo de 3 a 5 años ▲ *amortise any carrying amount of the goodwill* amortizar cualquier valor contable del fondo de comercio

▲ *amortise goodwill* amortizar el fondo de comercio ▲ *amortise goodwill prospectively over its remaining useful life* amortizar el fondo de comercio anticipadamente durante su vida útil restante ▲ *amortise goodwill using the straight-line method* amortizar el fondo de comercio utilizando el método lineal ▲ *amortise in the income statement* amortizar en la cuenta de resultados ▲ *amortise on a systematic basis* amortizar de una manera sistemática ▲ *amortise over a maximum period of 20 years* amortizar en un plazo máximo de 20 años ▲ *amortise over the lease term* amortizar durante el periodo de arrendamiento ▲ *amortise prospectively over the remaining useful life* amortizar prospectivamente durante la vida útil restante ▲ *amortise the asset on a straight-line basis over its estimated useful life* amortizar el activo usando un método lineal durante el periodo estimado de vida útil ▲ *amortise the goodwill over the best estimate of its useful life* amortizar el fondo de comercio en la mejor estimación de su vida útil ▲ *fully amortised intangible assets that are still in use* los activos intangibles totalmente amortizados que están todavía en uso ▲ *previously amortised* amortizado previamente

⇛ depreciate

2 = amortize US

To amortise is to make repayments on a loan by regular payments of instalments and interest.

amortizar

▲ *amortise debts* amortizar deudas ▲ *amortise over the lease term* amortizar durante el periodo de arrendamiento

amortised IAS/IFRS

= amortized US

Amortised means that the amortisable amount has been allocated systematically over the useful life of an intangible asset.

amortizado

▲ *a description of any fully amortised intangible asset that is still in use* una descripción de cualquier activo intangible totalmente amortizado que esté todavía en uso ▲ *amortised cost* coste amortizado

amortised cost UK, IAS/IFRS

= amortized cost US

Amortised cost is the amount at which a financial asset or liability is initially recognised in the financial statements after deducting principal repayments, adding or deducting the total amount amortised on the difference between the amount initially recognised and the amount falling due on maturity, and, for assets, after deducting impairment losses.

coste amortizado

▲ *amortised cost of a financial liability* coste amortizado de un pasivo financiero ▲ *carry at amortised cost* trasladar a coste amortizado ▲ *measure at amortised cost* medir a coste amortizado ▲ *present on the amortised cost basis* presentar en base al coste amortizado ▲ *recognise at amortised cost* reconocer a coste amortizado ▲ *the amortised cost of the host debt instrument* el coste amortizado de un instrumento de deuda anfitrión

amortizable US

= amortisable UK

When an asset is amortizable, the enterprise may amortize that asset's value over time instead of recognizing it as an expense on acquisition.

amortizable

▲ *amortizable assets* activos amortizables ▲ *amortizable non-monetary assets* activos no monetarios amortizables

⇛ depreciable

amortizable amount US

= amortisable amount UK

The amortizable amount is the value of an intangible fixed asset constituting the basis of amortization represented by the cost of the asset, or other revalued amount substituted for cost, less the residual value and any write-downs.

cantidad amortizable

= importe amortizable

▲ *10% of the amortizable amount* 10% de la cantidad amortizable

⇛ depreciable amount

amortizable asset US

= amortisable asset UK

When an asset is depreciable or amortizable, the enterprise may depreciate or amortize that asset's value over time instead of recognizing it as an expense on acquisition.

activo amortizable

▲ *the expected pattern of consumption of economic benefits of an amortizable asset* el modelo esperado de agotamiento de los beneficios económicos de un activo amortizable

amortization US

1 = amortisation IAS/IFRS, UK

Amortization is the gradual reduction of an intangible asset's cost by systematically allocating the asset's amortizable amount over its definite economic life.

NOTE For tangible assets, the term 'depreciation' is generally used.

amortización

▲ *accelerated amortization* amortización acelerada ▲ *accumulated amortization* amortización acumulada ▲ *amortization based on the asset's revalued carrying value* amortización basada en el valor contable revalorizado del activo ▲ *amortization for the year* amortización anual ▲ *amortization for which separate disclosure is required* amortización para la que se requiere información detallada ▲ *amortization not deductible for tax purposes* amortización no deducible por motivos fiscales ▲ *amortization of goodwill* amortización del fondo de comercio ▲ *amortization of intangible assets* amortización de activos intangibles ▲ *amortization of patents and licences* amortización de patentes y licencias ▲ *amortization recognised during the fiscal year* amortización reconocida durante el año fiscal ▲ *commence amortization* iniciar la amortización ▲ *depreciation and amortization expense* depreciación y gasto de amortización ▲ *net of amortization or depreciation* neto de amortización o depreciación ▲ *the effect of amortization* el efecto de la amortización

⇛ depreciation

2 = amortisation UK, repayment

Amortization means the regular repayment of instalments and interest on a loan.

reembolso

= amortización

▲ *amortization of financial assets* amortización de los activos financieros

amortization account US

1 = amortisation account UK

An amortization account is an account in the accounting system recording the periodic accumulated amortization amount of an enterprise's intangible assets.

cuenta de amortización

= amortización acumulada

▲ *the balance of the amortization account* el saldo de la cuenta de amortización

⇛ depreciation account

2 = amortisation account UK

An amortization account is an account recording and accumulating funds needed to repay a loan.

cuenta de amortización

= amortización acumulada

▲ *amortization account for cash loans* cuenta de amortización para los préstamos en efectivo ▲ *the balance of the amortization account* el saldo de la cuenta de amortización

amortization balance US

= amortisation balance UK

The amortization balance shows the net book value of an intangible asset less amortization for the period.

NOTE The term amortization balance applies to intangible assets.

amortización acumulada

▲ *a negative amortization balance* una amortización acumulada negativa ▲ *increase in the amortization balance* aumento en la amortización acumulada

⇛ depreciation balance

amortization base US

1 = amortisable amount IAS/IFRS, basis of amortisation UK

The amortization base means the historical cost of an amortizable asset or other revalued amount substituted for historical cost less in either case the net amount expected to be recovered on disposal of the asset at the end of its useful life.

NOTE The term "amortization base" applies to intangible assets.

base de amortización

= base de depreciación

▲ *amortization base for tax purposes* base de amortización a efectos fiscales ▲ *determination*

of the amortization base determinación de la base de amortización ▲ *measurement of the amortization base* cálculo de la base de amortización ▲ *the amortization base of the asset* la base de amortización del activo ▲ *the buyer's amortization base* la base de amortización del adquirente ▲ *the enterprise's amortization base* la base de amortización de la empresa ▲ *the future amortization base* la base de amortización futura
⇛ depreciation base

2 = amortisation basis UK, amortisation method UK, method of amortisation UK
The basis of amortization is the method of amortization chosen to reflect the depletion of an intangible asset over its estimated economic life in the financial statements. Normally, the straight-line method is the most appropriate for intangible assets.
método de amortización
= criterio de amortización
▲ *a systematic amortization base* un método de amortización sistemático

amortization basis for tax purposes US
= amortisation basis for tax purposes UK, IAS/IFRS
The amortization basis for tax purposes is the amount of an intangible fixed asset subject to amortization allowed under tax rules. This amount constitutes the cost of that asset, or other revalued amount substituted for cost, less the residual value and any write-downs.
base amortizable por motivos fiscales
= base de amortización por motivos fiscales
▲ *amortization basis for tax purposes according to assessed cash value* base amortizable por motivos fiscales de acuerdo al valor en efectivo estimado ▲ *difference between nominal purchase sum and amortization basis for tax purposes* diferencia entre el valor de compra nominal y la base amortizable por motivos fiscales ▲ *the amortization basis for tax purposes of an asset* la base amortizable por motivos fiscales de un activo
⇛ depreciation basis for tax purposes

amortization charge US
= amortisation charge UK
The amortization charge is the amortized cost or amount charged to the profit and loss account for a particular accounting period calculated on the basis of the systematic allocation of the amortizable amount over the useful life of an intangible asset.
cuota de amortización
= gasto de amortización
▲ *the amortization charge for each period* la cuota de amortización para cada periodo ▲ *the amortization charge for the asset* la cuota de amortización para el activo ▲ *the asset's amortization charge* la cuota de amortización del activo

amortization expense US
= amortisation expense UK, IAS/IFRS
The amortization expense is the amortised cost or amount charged to the income statement for a particular accounting period calculated on the basis of the systematic allocation of the amortizable amount over the useful life of an intangible asset.
cuota de amortización
= gasto de amortización
▲ *a fictitious amortization expense* una cuota de amortización ficticia ▲ *a fixed amortization expense* una cuota de amortización fija ▲ *an annual amortization expense of USD 250,000* una cuota de amortización anual por valor de 250.000 euros ▲ *the accumulated amortization expense* la cuota de amortización acumulada ▲ *the total amortization expense* la cuota de amortización total

amortization for tax purposes US
= amortisation for tax purposes UK, IAS/IFRS
Amortization for tax purposes is the amortization allowed of an intangible asset.
amortización por motivos fiscales
▲ *cumulative amortization for tax purposes* amortización acumulada por motivos fiscales ▲ *provide for amortization for tax purposes* provisionar la amortización por motivos fiscales
⇛ depreciation for tax purposes

amortization method US
= amortisation method UK, IAS/IFRS
The amortization method is the policy applied by an enterprise for gradually writing down an intangible asset over its economic life. Usually, the straight-line method is chosen.
método de amortización
= criterio de amortización
▲ *a variety of amortization methods* una diversidad de métodos de amortización ▲ *amortization method for goodwill* el método de amortización para el fondo de comercio ▲ *apply the amortization method consistently from period to period* aplicar de manera consistente el método de amortización periodo por periodo ▲ *review the amortization method* revisar el método de amortización ▲ *the amortization method used* el método de amortización utilizado
⇛ depreciation method

amortization period US
= amortisation period UK, IAS/IFRS
The amortization period is the expected useful life of the asset, i.e. the period over which that asset is expected to be used by the enterprise.
NOTE The term amortization period applies to intangible assets.
plazo de amortización
= periodo de amortización
▲ *a long amortization period* un plazo de amortización largo ▲ *a short amortization period* un plazo de amortización corto ▲ *change the amortization period* cambiar el plazo de amortización ▲ *review the amortization period* revisar el plazo de amortización ▲ *the amortization period adopted* el plazo de amortización adoptado ▲ *the remaining amortization period* el plazo de amortización pendiente
⇛ depreciation period

amortization policy US
= amortisation policy UK, IAS/IFRS
The amortization policy is the method applied by an enterprise for allocating the costs of intangible assets over their economic lives.
NOTE The term amortization policy applies to intangible assets.
método de amortización
= criterio de amortización, política de amortización
▲ *amortize in accordance with the group's amortization policy* amortizar de acuerdo con el método de amortización del grupo ▲ *normal amortization policy* método de amortización normal
⇛ depreciation policy

amortization profile US
= amortisation profile UK, IAS/IFRS
The amortization profile shows the allocation of the amortization amounts on an asset over the useful life.
NOTE The term amortization profile applies to intangible assets.
perfil de amortización
▲ *expectations to the amortization profile of an investment* previsiones con respecto al perfil de la amortización de la inversión ▲ *the buyer's amortization profile* el perfil de la amortización del comprador ▲ *the discounted value of an amortization profile* el valor descontado de un perfil de la amortización
⇛ depreciation profile

amortization rate US
= amortisation rate UK, IAS/IFRS
The amortization rate is the percentage rate at which intangible fixed assets are amortized under a chosen amortization method to determine the amount for amortization written off for an accounting period.
porcentaje de amortización
▲ *a wrong amortization rate* un porcentaje de amortización erróneo ▲ *change of the amortization rate* cambio del porcentaje de amortización ▲ *the amortization rate used* el porcentaje de amortización utilizado ▲ *the annual amortization rate* el porcentaje de amortización anual ▲ *the maximum amortization rate* el porcentaje de amortización máximo
⇛ depreciation rate

amortization rule US
= amortisation rule UK
Amortization rules are official instructions for amortization

for financial reporting purposes and for tax purposes as provided by accounting standards and tax legislation respectively.
NOTE The term amortization rule applies to intangible assets.
norma de amortización
▲ *a generous amortization rule* una norma de amortización generosa

amortization schedule US
1 = amortisation schedule UK
An amortization schedule is a plan or table for the regular repayment of interest and instalments on a loan over the life of the loan.
cuadro de amortización
= plan de amortización, programa de amortización, tabla de amortización
▲ *a 25 years' amortization schedule* un cuadro de amortización de 25 años
2 = amortisation schedule UK
An amortization schedule shows the allocation of the amortization amounts on an intangible asset over its useful life.
cuadro de amortización
= plan de amortización, programa de amortización, tabla de amortización
▲ *amend the amortization schedule* modificar el cuadro de amortización ▲ *changes in the amortization schedule* cambios en el cuadro de amortización ▲ *the amortization schedule for past service cost* el cuadro de amortización por el coste de los trabajadores anteriores

amortize US
1 = amortise IAS/IFRS, UK
To amortize is to allocate the amortizable amount systematically over the useful life of an intangible asset.
amortizar
▲ *amortize a development project over a period of 3 to 5 years* amortizar un proyecto de desarrollo durante un periodo de 3 a 5 años ▲ *amortize any carrying value of the goodwill* amortizar cualquier valor contable del fondo de comercio ▲ *amortize goodwill* amortizar el fondo de comercio ▲ *amortize goodwill using the straight-line method* amortizar el fondo de comercio utilizando el método lineal ▲ *amortize in the income statement* amortizar en la cuenta de resultados ▲ *amortize on a systematic basis* amortizar de una manera sistemática ▲ *amortize over a maximum period of 20 years* amortizar en un plazo máximo de 20 años ▲ *amortize over the lease term* amortizar durante el periodo de arrendamiento ▲ *amortize prospectively over the remaining useful life* amortizar anticipadamente durante la vida útil restante ▲ *amortize the asset on a straight-line basis over its estimated useful life* amortizar el activo usando un método lineal durante el periodo estimado de vida útil ▲ *amortize the goodwill over the best estimate of its useful life* amortizar el fondo de comercio en la mejor estimación de su vida útil ▲ *fully amortized intangible assets that are still in use* los activos intangibles totalmente amortizados que están todavía en uso ▲ *previously amortized* amortizar previamente
⇛ depreciate
2 = amortise UK
To amortize is to make repayments on a loan by regular payments of instalments and interest.
amortizar
▲ *amortize debts* amortizar deudas ▲ *amortize over the lease term* amortizar durante el periodo de arrendamiento

amortized US
= amortised UK, IAS/IFRS
Amortized means that the amortizable amount has been allocated systematically over the useful life of an intangible asset.
amortizado
▲ *a description of any fully amortized intangible asset that is still in use* una descripción de cualquier activo intangible totalmente amortizado que esté todavía en uso ▲ *amortized cost* coste amortizado

amortized cost US
Amortized cost is the amount at which financial assets or liabilities are initially recognised in the financial statements after deducting principal repayments, adding or deducting

the total amount amortised on the difference between the amount initially recognised and the amount falling due on maturity, and, for assets, after deducting impairment losses.

coste amortizado

▲ *amortized cost of a financial liability* coste amortizado de un pasivo financiero ▲ *carry at amortized cost* trasladar a coste amortizado ▲ *measure at amortized cost* medir a coste amortizado ▲ *present on the amortized cost basis* presentar en base a coste amortizado ▲ *recognize at amortized cost* reconocer a coste amortizado ▲ *the amortized cost of the host debt instrument* el coste amortizado de un instrumento de deuda anfitrión

⇛ amortised cost

amount

An amount is the value or quantity of something, e.g. a sum of money.

cantidad

= cuantía, importe

▲ *all amounts in GBPm* todas las cantidades en millones de libras esterlinas ▲ *amounts of local currency* cantidades en divisa local ▲ *amounts owed by affiliated undertakings* las cantidades debidas por las empresas filiales ▲ *amounts owed by undertakings with which the company is linked by virtue of participating interests* las cantidades debidas por las empresas con las que la compañía está relacionada a través de participaciones ▲ *amounts owed to credit institutions* cantidades debidas a las instituciones de crédito ▲ *amounts payable to and receivable from the parent enterprise* deudas a y créditos de la empresa matriz ▲ *an amount equivalent to* una cantidad equivalente a ▲ *an amount in excess of* una cantidad superior a ▲ *ascertain the amount outstanding at the balance sheet date* comprobar la cantidad pendiente a fecha de cierre del balance ▲ *at an amount of* en la cuantía de ▲ *carry at cost or at a revalued amount* trasladar al coste o a una cantidad revalorizada ▲ *deduct an amount* deducir una cantidad ▲ *disclose an amount* revelar una cantidad ▲ *immaterial amounts* cantidades no significativas ▲ *monetary amounts* cantidades monetarias ▲ *recognise an amount* reconocer una cantidad ▲ *reverse an amount* cancelar una cantidad ▲ *the aggregate amount of temporary differences* la cantidad agregada por desfases temporales ▲ *the amount booked* la cantidad asentada ▲ *the amount of any cumulative preference dividends not recognised* la cantidad de cualesquiera dividendos preferenciales acumulados no reconocidos ▲ *the amount of dividends that were proposed or declared after the balance sheet date* la cantidad de dividendos que se propusieron o se anunciaron después de la fecha de cierre de balance ▲ *the amount of the write-down* la cuantía de la pérdida de valor ▲ *the amounts expected to be recovered or settled after more than 12 months* las cantidades que se esperaban recuperar o pagar pasados 12 meses ▲ *the amounts, nature and timing of liabilities* las cantidades, naturaleza y periodificación de los pasivos ▲ *the most likely amount* la cuantía más probable ▲ *the size, nature and function of the amounts* el tamaño, la naturaleza y la función de las cantidades

⇛ recoverable amount, sum

amount due

An amount due is a sum of money that has to be paid.

cantidad debida

= importe a pagar

▲ *exceed the amount due* exceder la cantidad debida ▲ *other amounts due* otros importes a pagar

amount of damages

= compensation

The amount of damages is the pecuniary compensation payable, often by a court order, to the claimant. Payment is made by the tortfeasor or person causing the loss or from the claimant's or the tortfeasor's insurance.

indemnización

= cuantía de los daños

▲ *assess the amount of damages* evaluar la indemnización

amount of depreciation US

= depreciation amount

The amount of depreciation is the amount calculated on the

basis of the systematic allocation of the depreciable amount over the useful life of the asset that is written off each accounting period.

NOTE The term amount of depreciation applies to tangible assets.

cuota de amortización

▲ *a fictitious amount of depreciation* una cuota de amortización ficticia ▲ *a fixed amount of depreciation* una cuota de amortización fija ▲ *an annual amount of depreciation of EUR 250,000* una cuota de amortización anual por valor de 250.000 euros ▲ *the accumulated amount of depreciation* la cuota de amortización acumulada ▲ *the adjusted amount of depreciation of property, plant and equipment* la cuota ajustada de amortización de inmuebles, terrenos y equipos ▲ *the total amount of depreciation* la cuota de amortización total

⇛ amortisation amount

amount of goodwill

The amount of goodwill can be defined as (1) the amount assigned to goodwill and recognised at the date of acquisition or (2) the carrying amount of goodwill less any accumulated amortisation and any impairment losses.

cuantía del fondo de comercio

= importe del fondo de comercio

▲ *calculate the amount of goodwill* calcular la cuantía del fondo de comercio ▲ *determination of the amount of goodwill* determinación de la cuantía del fondo de comercio ▲ *the amount of goodwill arising in the business combination* la cuantía del fondo de comercio procedente de una combinación de negocios

amount of reimbursement

The amount of reimbursement is the sum of money paid as compensation for expenditure.

cuantía del reembolso

= reembolso

▲ *calculate the amount of reimbursement* calcular la cuantía del reembolso ▲ *offsetting of amounts of reimbursement* compensar las cuantías del reembolso

amount paid on account

= part payment

An amount paid on account is a part payment of or an instalment on the total amount payable.

cantidad pagada a cuenta

= abono a cuenta

▲ *insignificant amounts paid on account* cantidades insignificantes pagadas a cuenta ▲ *substantial amounts paid on account* cantidades sustanciales pagadas a cuenta

amount provided

Amounts provided are the financial amounts recognised under provisions in the balance sheet to cover future liabilities.

cantidad provisionada

▲ *a significant adjustment to the amount provided* un ajuste significativo a la cantidad provisionada ▲ *the gross amount provided* la cantidad provisionada bruta ▲ *total amount provided annually* total cantidad provisionada anualmente

amount specification

An amount specification is a statement of a particular amount in a specified accounting unit and currency.

anotación de la cantidad

▲ *dollar amount specifications* anotaciones de la cantidad en dólares ▲ *post-tax amount specifications* anotaciones de la cantidad después de impuestos ▲ *pre-tax amount specifications* anotaciones de la cantidad antes de impuestos

amount to

To amount to means to be equal to and aggregate a certain amount or sum, usually stated in money terms.

totalizar

= ascender a, equivaler a

▲ *amount to a defined contribution arrangement* equivaler a un acuerdo contributivo acordado

amounts owed by group undertakings UK

'Amounts owed by group undertakings' is an item under current assets in the balance sheet according to the Companies Act 1985 required report format. Receivables from subsidiaries or other parents within the same group are recognised in this item.

créditos con empresas del grupo

▲ *include a sum in amounts owed by group undertakings* incluir una suma en créditos con empresas del grupo

amounts owed by undertakings in which the company has a participating interest UK
'Amounts owed by undertakings in which the company has a participating interest' is an item under current assets in the balance sheet according to the Companies Act 1985 required report format. This item represents receivables from associated undertakings.
créditos con empresas asociadas
▲ *a sum included in amounts owed by undertakings in which the company has a participating interest* una suma incluida en créditos con empresas asociadas

amounts owed to group undertakings UK
'Amounts owed to group undertakings' is an item under creditors: amounts falling due within one year or under creditors: amounts falling due after more than one year –depending on whether short-or long-term– in the balance sheet according to the Companies Act 1985 required report format. Payables to subsidiaries and any other parents within the same group are recognised in this item.
deudas con el grupo de empresas
▲ *a sum included in amounts owed to group undertakings* una suma incluida en deudas con el grupo de empresas

amounts owed to undertakings in which the company has a participating interest UK
'Amounts owed to undertakings in which the company has a participating interest' is an item under creditors: amounts falling due within one year or under creditors: amounts falling due after more than one year –depending on whether short-or long-term– in the balance sheet according to the Companies Act 1985 required report format. This item represents payables to associated undertakings.
deudas con empresas asociadas
▲ *a sum included in amounts owed to undertakings in which the company has a participating interest* una suma incluida en deudas con empresas asociadas

amounts written off investments UK
= asset write-offs US, impairment of financial assets IAS/IFRS
'Amounts written off investments' is an item in the profit and loss account.
pérdida por inversiones
▲ *profit or loss before exceptionals and amounts written off investments* resultado antes de contabilizar excepciones y pérdidas por inversiones

analyse
= review
To analyse is to study and consider in detail in order to discover essential features.
analizar
▲ *analyse the transaction as a retention of a fully proportionate retained interest* analizar la transacción como una retención de un interés retenido totalmente proporcionado ▲ *whether analysed as one lease or as two leases* si analizado como uno o dos alquileres

analysis
An analysis is a careful examination or study of something in order to understand it better.
análisis
▲ *a comprehensive analysis of related party balances* un análisis comprensivo de las partidas de balance relacionadas ▲ *a detailed analysis* un análisis detallado ▲ *a direct analysis of the cash flows in question* un análisis directo de los flujos de efectivo en cuestión ▲ *a previous analysis* un análisis previo ▲ *an analysis of earnings and investment* un análisis de ganancias e inversiones ▲ *an analysis of events that have occurred* un análisis de los sucesos que han ocurrido ▲ *an analysis of expenses using a classification based on the nature of expenses* un análisis de los gastos utilizando una clasificación basada en la naturaleza del gasto ▲ *analysis of variances* un análisis de las desviaciones ▲ *complete an analysis* completar un anális ▲ *conduct an analysis* dirigir un análisis ▲ *disclose an analysis of liabilities into relevant maturity group-*

ings publicar un análisis de los pasivos agrupándolos por periodos de vencimiento relevantes ▲ *financial statement analysis* análisis de los estados financieros ▲ *ratio analysis* análisis de ratios

analyst

An analyst is a person who makes analyses, i.e. careful examinations or studies of something in order to understand it better.

analista

▲ *conferences for existing and potential investors and analysts* conferencias para inversores y analistas existentes y potenciales ▲ *contact with analysts* contactar con analistas ▲ *dialogue with analysts* diálogo con analistas ▲ *equity analyst* analista de titulos ▲ *financial analyst* analistas financieros ▲ *independent analysts* analistas independientes

analytical purpose

The analytical purpose sets out the focus of an investigation and explains the intention of making it.

motivo analítico

▲ *equity for analytical purposes* títulos por motivos analíticos ▲ *results for analytical purposes* resultados por motivos analíticos

analytical survey

An analytical survey is an examination based on an analysis of the available data.

estudio analítico

▲ *prepare an analytical survey* preparar un estudio analítico ▲ *publish an analytical survey* publicar un estudio analítico

announce

To announce is to express something clearly and publicly, esp. officially.

anunciar

▲ *announce profit and selected other financial information* anunciar el beneficio y otra información financiera seleccionada ▲ *announce the main features of the restructuring plan* anunciar los rasgos fundamentales del plan de reestructuración ▲ *announce the planned discontinuance* anunciar la interrupción de la planificación ▲ *changes in tax rates or tax laws enacted or announced after the balance sheet date* cambios en los tipos impositivos o en las legislaciones tributarias en vigor o anunciadas para después de la fecha de cierre del balance ▲ *measure tax assets and liabilities using the announced tax rate* medir activos y pasivos fiscales utilizando el tipo impositivo anunciado ▲ *when a detailed formal plan for disposal has been adopted and announced* cuando se ha adoptado y anunciado un plan formal detallado de venta

announcement

An announcement is a statement that has been made clearly to the public to express something, esp. officially.

publicación

= anuncio

▲ *after the announcement of the terms of the acquisition* después de la publicación de las condiciones de la adquisición ▲ *after the publication of a profit announcement* después de la publicación de un anuncio de beneficios ▲ *announcement of tax rates* publicación de los tipos impositivos ▲ *make an announcement of a plan* hacer un anuncio de un plan ▲ *public announcement of a detailed plan* anuncio público de un plan detallado ▲ *public announcement of the main features of the plan* anuncio público de los rasgos principales del plan ▲ *the public announcement of profit* el anuncio público de beneficios

annual

The adjective 'annual' is used about something that is done, happens or occurs within a year.

anual

▲ *an annual appraisal interview* una entrevista de evaluación anual ▲ *an annual audit* una auditoría anual ▲ *an annual budget* un presupuesto anual ▲ *an annual change in the net operating profit* un cambio anual en el beneficio operativo neto ▲ *an annual conversion factor* un factor de conversión anual ▲ *an annual cost saving* un ahorro anual de costes ▲ *an annual growth rate* una tasa de crecimiento anual ▲ *an annual impairment test* un test de deterioro anual ▲ *an annual increase of 6%* un incremento anual del 6% ▲ *an annual interest expense* un pago de intereses anual ▲ *an annual interest rate* un tipo de interés anual ▲ *an annual listing fee* una comisión de cotización anual ▲ *an annual provision* una provisión anual ▲ *an annual reassessment* una reconsideración anual ▲ *an annual return* un rendimiento anual ▲ *an average annual growth rate* una tasa media de crecimiento anual ▲ *an average annual lease payment* un pago medio por alquiler anual ▲ *an average annual price reduction* una reducción media de precio anual ▲ *annual cost of rental and lease commitments* coste anual de las obligaciones de alquiler y arrendamiento ▲ *annual depreciation* depreciación anual ▲ *annual financial reporting* información financiera anual ▲ *annual financial statements* estados financieros anuales ▲ *annual rent* renta anual ▲ *annual revaluation* revalorización anual ▲ *annual revenue of USD 59m* ingreso anual por valor de 59 millones de USD ▲ *annual sales* ventas anuales ▲ *annual turnover* facturación anual ▲ *annual volatility* volatilidad anual ▲ *charge an annual fee* cargar un honorario anual ▲ *expected annual earnings growth* crecimiento de los beneficios anuales esperados ▲ *paid annual leave* licencia anual pagada ▲ *the first annual accounting period* el primer periodo contable anual

annual accounts UK

= financial statements US, IAS/IFRS

The annual accounts constitute an enterprise's financial information for the financial year and include the balance sheet, the profit and loss account, a statement showing changes in equity, a cash flow statement, the accounting policies and explanatory notes.

cuentas anuales

▲ *a full set of annual accounts* un conjunto completo de estados financieros ▲ *annual accounts for previous periods* cuentas anuales de los periodos anteriores ▲ *approval of the annual accounts* aprobación de las cuentas anuales ▲ *consolidated annual accounts* cuentas anuales consolidadas ▲ *consolidated annual accounts of a group controlled by the enterprise* cuentas anuales consolidadas de un grupo controlado por la empresa ▲ *include a cash flow statement in the annual accounts* incluir un estado de efectivo en las cuentas anuales ▲ *net profit or loss according to the last annual accounts* resultado neto de acuerdo con las últimas cuentas anuales ▲ *preparation of annual accounts* preparación de las cuentas anuales ▲ *prepare annual accounts in accordance with the Danish Financial Statements Act* preparar las cuentas anuales de acuerdo con la Ley danesa de Estados Financieros ▲ *prepare annual accounts in conformity with the International Accounting Standards* preparar las cuentas anuales conforme a las Normas Internacionales de Información Financiera ▲ *presentation of annual accounts* presentación de las cuentas anuales ▲ *publication of the annual accounts* publicación de las cuentas anuales ▲ *reading of the annual accounts* lectura de las cuentas anuales ▲ *submission of the annual accounts* rendición de las cuentas anuales ▲ *the annual accounts presented by the management* las cuentas anuales presentadas por la dirección ▲ *the component parts of the annual accounts* los componentes de las cuentas anuales ▲ *the latest annual accounts* las últimas cuentas anuales ▲ *the next annual accounts* las próximas cuentas anuales ▲ *the qualitative characteristics of the annual accounts* las características cualitativas de las cuenta anuales ▲ *the reliability of the annual accounts* la fiabilidad de las cuentas anuales

annual basis

On an annual basis means within a year, however not necessarily the calendar or the financial (reporting) year.

anualidad

▲ *on an annual basis* anualmente

annual general meeting

= AGM, annual meeting of stockholders US, ordinary general meeting

The annual general meeting is a formal meeting of the shareholders of a company and its directors and is statutorily required to be held each calendar year. The main business at the meeting is the presentation of the financial statements, the appointment of auditors and the proposal for dividends.

junta general anual

= junta general de accionistas

▲ *approve amendments to the articles of association at the annual general meeting* aprobar enmiendas al articulado de la asociación en la junta general anual ▲ *approve the annual report at an annual general meeting* aprobar el informe anual en la junta general anual ▲ *at the annual general meeting* en la junta general anual ▲ *convene an annual general meeting* convocar una junta general anual ▲ *decide something at an annual general meeting* decidir algo en la junta general anual ▲ *declare dividends at the annual general meeting* fijar dividendos en la junta general anual ▲ *hold an annual general meeting* celebrar una junta general anual ▲ *present the annual report at the annual general meeting* presentar el informe anual en la junta general anual ▲ *the annual meeting of shareholders* la junta anual de accionistas

⇛ extraordinary general meeting

annual meeting of stockholders US

= annual general meeting, annual shareholders' meeting UK

The annual meeting of stockholders is a formal meeting of the stockholders of a company and its directors and is statutorily required to be held each calendar year. The main business at the meeting is the presentation of the financial statements, the appointment of auditors and the proposal for dividends.

junta anual de accionistas

= junta general anual

▲ *approve amendments to the bylaws at the annual meeting of stockholders* aprobar enmiendas a los estatutos en la junta anual de accionistas ▲ *approve the annual report at an annual meeting of stockholders* aprobar el informe anual en la junta anual de accionistas ▲ *at the annual meeting of stockholders* en la junta anual de accionistas ▲ *convene an annual meeting of stockholders* convocar una junta anual de accionistas ▲ *decide something at an annual meeting of stockholders* decidir algo en la junta anual de accionistas

annual report

The annual report is the document that contains the financial statements, the management's review, a statement by the executive and supervisory boards on the annual report, an auditors' report and any supplementary reports, and the purpose is to disclose information to external users and stakeholders with a view to economic decisions.

informe anual

▲ *add supplementary reports to the annual report* añadir informes adicionales al informe anual ▲ *an auditor's declaration on the annual report* una declaración del auditor en el informe anual ▲ *approve the annual report* aprobar el informe anual ▲ *audit the annual report* auditar el informe anual ▲ *basic requirements for the annual report* requisitos básicos del informe anual ▲ *be included in the annual report* estar incluido en el informe anual ▲ *disagree with an annual report in whole or in part* estar en desacuerdo con el informe anual en todo o en parte ▲ *evaluation of the overall annual report presentation* evaluación de la presentación del informe anual completo ▲ *examine an annual report* examinar un informe anual ▲ *express an opinion on the annual report* expresar una opinión en el informe anual ▲ *joint annual report* informe anual conjunto ▲ *prepare the annual report* preparar el informe anual ▲ *present an annual report* presentar un informe anual ▲ *publish the annual report* publicar el informe anual ▲ *recommend the annual report for approval by the annual general meeting* recomendar el informe anual para su aprobación en la junta general anual ▲ *sign the annual report* firmar el informe anual ▲ *statutory annual report* informe anual estatutario ▲ *submit the annual report* remitir el informe anual ▲ *the approved annual report* el informe anual aprobado ▲ *the audited annual report* el informe anual auditado ▲ *the compulsory parts of an annual report* las partes obligatorias del informe anual ▲ *the elements of the annual report* los componentes del informe anual ▲ *the last approved annual report* el último informe anual ▲ *the next annual report* el próximo informe anual ▲ *the submitted annual report* el informe anual remitido

annual results

The difference between total income and total expenses recognised for a financial year is called the annual results.

resultados anuales

▲ *affect the measurement of the annual results* influir en el cálculo de los resultados anuales ▲ *annual results before tax* resultados anuales antes de impuestos

annual review

= management's review, operating review

The annual review is a narrative statement in the annual report of an enterprise containing management's analysis and information about the enterprise's performance and financial position in the accounting period, outlook, risk management etc.

informe de gesión

▲ *annual review by the executive and supervisory boards* informe de gestión por los órganos de gestión ejecutivos y de supervisión ▲ *disclosure of risks in the annual review* desglose de riesgos en el informe de gestión ▲ *requirements as to the annual review* requisitos en cuanto al informe de gestión ▲ *the disclosures in the annual review* los desgloses en el informe de gestión

annual shareholders' meeting

→ annual general meeting

annualised UK, IAS/IFRS

= annualized US, on an annual basis

To state annualised or on an annual basis is to state e.g. a change which would occur if the movement observed in any period were to continue for exactly 12 months.

anualizado

▲ *the annualised standard deviation of the continuously compounded rates of return on the share over a period of time* la desviación estándar anualizada de las tasas de rendimiento continuamente compuestas de la acción por un periodo de tiempo ▲ *the expected annualised volatility of a share* la volatilidad anualizada esperada de una acción

annualized US

= annualised IAS/IFRS, UK

To state annualized or on an annual basis is to state e.g. a change which would occur if the movement observed in any period were to continue for exactly 12 months.

anualizado

▲ *the annualized standard deviation of the continuously compounded rates of return on the share over a period of time* la desviación estándar anualizada de las tasas de rendimiento continuamente compuestas de la acción por un periodo de tiempo ▲ *the expected annualized volatility of a share* la volatilidad anualizada esperada de una acción

annually

The term 'annually' means that something is done, happens or occurs every year.

anual

▲ *an enterprise that reports only annually* una empresa que informa solo de forma anual ▲ *at least annually* anual al menos ▲ *equivalent to 8.7% annually* equivalente al 8,7% anual ▲ *estimate annually* estimar de forma anual ▲ *test goodwill acquired in a business combination for impairment annually* el examen anual por deterioro del fondo de comercio adquirido en una combinación de negocios

annuity

An annuity is a fixed annual payment made once a year or paid in instalments.

anualidad

▲ *a life-contingent annuity linked to a cost-of-living index* una anualidad por vida contingente unida al índice del coste de la vida ▲ *annual annuity amount* cuantía de la anualidad anual ▲ *ordinary annuity* anualidad ordinaria ▲ *the discounting of annuities included in insurance provisions* el descuento de las anualidades incluidas en las cláusulas del seguro ▲ *the future value of an annuity* el valor futuro de una anualidad ▲ *the present value of an annuity* el valor actual de una anualidad

annuity basis of amortisation

The annuity basis of amortisation is an instalment plan based on the principle of annuity. An annuity is a fixed payment that falls due at fixed intervals of equal length. The annuity basis of amortisation is a method of amortisation (repayment) of a loan according to which a calculation is made as to the number of equal payments required to settle interest on and repayments of the principal amount.

método de amortización mediante anualidad

▲ *use the annuity basis of amortisation* utilizar el método de amortización mediante anualidad

annuity contract

= allocated contract US

An annuity contract is a legal document in which a financial institution, such as an insurance company, unconditionally undertakes to provide fixed or variable payments to an annuitant either immediately or at a future date, e.g. upon retirement. The payments are usually made in exchange for a lump sum investment and once entered, the contract is irrevocable.

contrato de pensión mediante anualidad

▲ *an annuity contract that pays out regular sums* un contrato de pensión mediante anualidad que paga cantidades regulares ▲ *exchange an annuity contract for a life insurance contract* cambiar un contrato de pensión mediante anualidad por un contrato de seguro de vida

annuity loan

An annuity loan is a fixed-rate loan that is repaid by instalments of fixed service amounts over its life. As the loan is repaid the interest part of the service amount decreases while the principal part increases.

préstamo con anualidad constante

▲ *a callable annuity loan* un préstamo con anualidad constante rescatable ▲ *a fixed-interest annuity loan* un préstamo con anualidad constante a tipo de interés fijo ▲ *annuity loan with annual service* préstamo con anualidad constante con pago anual ▲ *annuity loan with monthly service* préstamo con anualidad constante con pago mensual ▲ *annuity loan with quarterly service* préstamo con anualidad constante con pago trimestral ▲ *annuity loan with semiannual service* préstamo con anualidad constante con pago semestrall

annuity principle

The annuity principle is a method of repaying a fixed-rate loan by instalments of fixed service amounts over its life. As the loan is repaid, the interest part of the service amount decreases while the principal part increases.

método de amortización por anualidad constante

▲ *repay according to the annuity principle* amortizar de acuerdo al método de amortización por anualidad constante ▲ *repayment according to the annuity principle* amortización de acuerdo al método de amortización por anualidad constante

anticipatory item

An anticipatory item is an item in the financial statements that concerns an accounting period prior to the period under review.

partida anticipada

▲ *recognise an anticipatory item* reconocer una partida anticipada

antidilution

Antidilution is a protection allowing investors to maintain the percentage of ownership in an enterprise's equity through the purchase of a proportional number of shares of a future share issue.

antidilución

▲ *antidilution protection* protección antidilución ▲ *antidilution provisions* cláusulas antidilución

APB

1 = Accounting Principles Board
APB is the abbreviation for the Accounting Principles Board

that issued pronouncements on American accounting principles until 1973. It has been replaced by the Financial Accounting Standards Board (FASB).

APB

⇛ Accounting Principles Board, FASB

2 = Auditing Practices Board

APB is an abbreviation for the Auditing Practices Board. The APB was established in 2002 and is committed to leading the development of auditing practice in the United Kingdom and the Republic of Ireland.

APB

▲ *auditing standards issued by the APB* normas de auditoría dictadas por la APB ▲ *guidance issued by APB* guía dictada por la APB

⇛ Auditing Practices Board

APB opinion US

APB opinions are pronouncements on accounting principles issued by the US Accounting Principles Board (APB) until 1973 when the APB was replaced by the Financial Accounting Standards Board. Many APB opinions still remain part of US Generally Accepted Accounting Principles.

circular de la APB

▲ *a new interpretation of APB Opinion No. 25* una nueva interpretación de la Circular Nº 25 de la APB ▲ *amendments of APB Opinion No. 18* enmiendas a la Circular Nº 18 de la APB ▲ *the provisions of APB Opinion No. 20* las cláusulas de la Circular Nº 20 de la APB

appendix

= enclosure, schedule

An appendix is additional information accompanying main text, i.e. a collection of separate material at the end of a book or document.

anexo

= adenda, apéndice

▲ *an illustrative appendix* un anexo ilustrativo ▲ *Appendix B to this Standard* el Apéndice B a esta Norma ▲ *appendix to the earnings release* anexo a la publicación de beneficios ▲ *appendix to the interim report* anexo al informe provisional ▲ *see Appendix C* ver Anexo C

⇛ schedule

applicable

An applicable rule, statute or standard etc. is one that governs a particular issue, act or transaction etc. at a particular point in time.

aplicable

▲ *adjust in accordance with the International Accounting Standard applicable to the asset* ajustar de acuerdo con las Normas Internacionales de Contabilidad aplicables al activo ▲ *applicable law* legislación aplicable ▲ *comply with applicable standards* cumplir con las normas aplicables ▲ *if applicable* si es aplicable ▲ *measure at the tax rate applicable to undistributed profits* calcular al tipo impositivo aplicable a los beneficios no distribuidos ▲ *the applicable tax rate* el tipo impositivo aplicable ▲ *the operating costs applicable to revenues* los costes operativos aplicables a los ingresos ▲ *the standard is not applicable to* la norma no es aplicable a ▲ *where applicable* donde sea aplicable

application

1 = use

Application means the use of something for a specific purpose.

aplicación

▲ *application of research findings* aplicación de los resultados de la investigación ▲ *application of the equity method* aplicación del método del patrimonio ▲ *application supplement* suplemento de aplicación ▲ *appropriate application of International Financial Reporting Standards* aplicación adecuada de las Normas Internacionales de Información Financiera ▲ *at the time of the first application* en el momento de la aplicación inicial ▲ *consistent application* aplicación consistente ▲ *first-time application* aplicación inicial ▲ *limited retrospective application* aplicación retrospectiva limitada ▲ *prospective application* aplicación prospectiva ▲ *retrospective application* aplicación retrospectiva ▲ *the application of the matching concept* la aplicación del concepto de equilibrio ▲ *the application of the principle of substance over form* la aplicación del principio del fondo en vez de la forma

2 = scope

Application is the scope of use and specifies when something must be used and to what extent.

solicitud

▲ *range of application* ámbito de la solicitud ▲ *scope of application* alcance de la solicitud ▲ *specific applications* solicitudes específicas ▲ *the practical application* la solicitud práctica

application guidance

Application guidances to IFRSs show examples of how specific IFRS rules must or can be applied, and the guidances are integrated parts of the Standards.

manual de aplicación

= guía de aplicación

▲ *consult the application guidance* consultar el manual de aplicación

appoint

To appoint means to choose or select a person for a specific job.

nombrar

▲ *power to appoint the majority of the members of the board of directors* el poder para nombrar a la mayoría de los miembros del consejo de administración

appointed

When a group of persons has been established to solve one or more specific tasks, the group is said to have been appointed.

nombrado

▲ *an appointed liaison committee* un comité de enlace nombrado ▲ *an appointed working team* un equipo de trabajo nombrado

appointment

An appointment is the selection of a person to a specific job.

nombramiento

▲ *during the appointment of the director* durante el nombramiento del director ▲ *the appointment of the board of directors or equivalent governing body* el nombramiento del consejo de administración o equivalente

appraisal

= measurement, valuation

Appraisal is the professional opinion of the market value of a property.

valoración

= evaluación

▲ *appraisal normally undertaken by professionally qualified valuers* valoración normalmente llevada a cabo por profesionales cualificados ▲ *determined by appraisal* determinado por valoración ▲ *plant and equipment at market value, normally determined by appraisal* instalaciones y equipos a valor de mercado, normalmente determinados por valoración

appraisal cost

Appraisal costs are costs incurred that are related to assessment of the quality level or the inspection for and detection of defects and deficiencies related to products and services such as employee training, product testing or repair and maintenance of plant and equipment.

coste de evaluación

▲ *an estimate of appraisal costs* una estimación de los costes de evaluación ▲ *recognise appraisal costs* reconocer los costes de evaluación ▲ *the appraisal costs incurred* los costes de evaluación incurridos

⇛ external failure cost, internal failure cost, prevention cost

appropriate

Appropriate means correct, suitable or right for a particular time, purpose, situation or occasion.

apropiado

▲ *amounts or appropriate proportions of outstanding items* cantidades o proporciones apropiadas de partidas pendientes ▲ *an appropriate distribution* una distribución apropiada ▲ *an appropriate method* un método apropiado ▲ *an appropriate mix of members of the supervisory board* una combinación apropiada de los miembros del consejo de supervisión ▲ *an appropriate solution* una solución apropiada ▲ *apply the appropriate discount rate to future cash flows* aplicar el tipo de descuento apropiado a los flujos de efectivo futuros ▲ *appropriate accounting policies* políticas contables apropiadas ▲ *appropriate adjustments* ajustes apropiados ▲ *appropriate application* aplicación apropiada ▲ *appropriate information* información apropiada ▲ *if appropriate* si es apropiado ▲ *lay down appropriate strategies* formular las estrategias apropiadas ▲ *make appropriate economic decisions* tomar las decisiones económicas apropiadas ▲ *the appropriate accounting treatment* el tratamiento contable apropiado

appropriateness

Appropriateness is the suitability of something for a particular time, purpose or situation.

adecuación

▲ *assess the appropriateness of something* evaluar la adecuación de algo ▲ *their different appropriateness* sus diferentes adecuaciones

appropriation of net income US

= distribution of net income

Appropriation of net income refers to a statement in the annual or interim report of an enterprise specifying how net income for an accounting period is allocated. Part of the income may typically be distributed to shareholders in the form of dividends, leaving the remainder to be transferred to retained earnings.

aplicación del beneficio neto

▲ *allocation transferred from appropriation of net income* asignación transferida desde la aplicación del beneficio neto del ejercicio ▲ *comments on the appropriation of net income* comentarios sobre la aplicación del beneficio neto del ejercicio ▲ *proposal for the appropriation of net income* propuesta para la aplicación del beneficio neto del ejercicio

approval

An approval is an acceptance of something, e.g work done or the use of a specific method.

aprobación

▲ *issue the financial statements to a supervisory board for approval* remitir los estados financieros a un consejo de supervisión para su aprobación ▲ *legal or regulatory approvals* aprobaciones legales o estatutarias ▲ *obtain approval for payment from a regulatory authority* obtener la aprobación de una autoridad reguladora para efectuar el pago ▲ *obtain the approval of the owners of the minority interest* obtener la aprobación de los accionistas minoritarios ▲ *subject to board approval* sujeto a la aprobación del consejo ▲ *submit for approval* remitir para la aprobación ▲ *the approval and announcement of a plan for discontinuance of an operation* la aprobación y el anuncio de un plan para interrumpir la operación

Arabic numeral UK

Arabic numerals are applied to number and divide the items ranging below the principal items preceded by Roman numerals in the balance sheet as well as the main items in the profit and loss account in the accounts formats required by the UK Companies Act and the Danish Financial Statements Act.

número arábigo

▲ *items preceded by Arabic numerals* partidas precedidas por números arábigos

Arabic numeral level

The Arabic numeral level is the lowest level for items in the layout of the balance sheet, ranging below the Roman numeral and the principal item levels. For instance, in the profit and loss account, Arabic numerals precede the main items. This applies to the accounts formats required in the UK Companies Act and the Danish Financial Statements Act.

nivel numérico arábigo

▲ *at Arabic numeral level* al nivel numérico arábigo

ARC IAS/IFRS

= Accounting Regulatory Committee IAS/IFRS

ARC is the abbreviation for the Accounting Regulatory Committee (ARC) set up by the European Commission under the IAS Regulation. The Committee has a regulatory function and gives opinions on proposals made by the EU Commission for the adoption of international financial reporting standards (IFRS). The ARC is chaired by the European Commission, and ARC members are representatives from EU Member States.

ARC

= Comité de Regulación Contable

NOTE The Spanish equivalent body is 'Instituto de Contabilidad y Auditoría de Cuentas' (ICAC).

▲ *at the 30 November ARC meeting* en la reunión del ARC de 30 de noviembre

⇛ IAS Regulation, International Accounting Standard, International Financial Reporting Standard

ARM

= adjustable-rate mortgage

ARM is the abbreviation for adjustable-rate mortgage, which is a loan secured on real property, and the interet rate payable is reset at fixed intervals during the term of the loan. The interest rates fixed for the intervals vary according to changes in the market rates of interest, and the interest rate is therefore adjusted regularly.

hipoteca de interés variable

= hipoteca a interés variable, préstamo hipotecario a interés variable, préstamo hipotecario de interés variable

▲ *calculate the price of the ARM* calcular el precio de la hipoteca de interés variable ▲ *convert an ARM to a fixed-rate mortgage* convertir una hipoteca de interés variables en una de interés fijo

arm's length

If transactions are made at arm's length, the transactions are conducted on terms and at prices that would have applied if the transactions had been made between knowledgeable, willing, independent parties.

en condiciones de igualdad

= a precio de mercado

▲ *an arm's length exchange motivated by normal business considerations* un cambio a precio de mercado motivado por razones de negocio habituales ▲ *recent arm's length market transactions* transacciones bursátiles recientes en condiciones de igualdad ▲ *recent market transactions on arm's length terms* transacciones bursátiles recientes en condiciones de igualdad

⇛ arm's length principle

arm's length adjustment

An arm's length adjustment is an adjustment of an enterprise's taxable income as a consequence of an increase in the taxable income of another enterprise that is a related party, involving the recalculation of certain intercompany transactions to other (higher) values that would have been achieved in transactions between independent enterprises under similar circumstances.

ajuste en condiciones de igualdad

▲ *make an arm's length adjustment* hacer un ajuste en condiciones de igualdad

arm's length basis

Transactions made on an arm's length basis are transactions made between knowledgeable, willing, independent parties.

a precio de mercado

= en condiciiones de igualdad, en condiciones de plena competencia

NOTE The Spanish equivalent is not a noun but a phrase.

▲ *make on an arm's length basis* realizar a precio de mercado ▲ *regularly occurring market transactions on an arm's length basis* transacciones bursátiles habituales en condiciones de plena competencia

arm's length price

An arm's length price is the price obtained in a transaction between two knowledgeable, willing, independent parties that are not related financially, commercially or in any other way. Therefore, an arm's length price reflects the fair market value of the asset or services traded.

precio en condiciones de plena competencia

= precio de mercado

▲ *details of arm's length prices* detalles de los precios en condiciones de plena competencia ▲ *pay an arm's length price* pagar un precio en condiciones de plena competencia

arm's length principle

The arm's length principle involves that transactions are made at arm's length, i.e. conducted on terms and at prices identical to the terms applied and prices obtained by independent parties that are not related financially, commercially or in any other way in the open market.

principio del precio de mercado

= principio del valor razonable

▲ *consistent with the arm's length principle* consistente con el principio del precio de mercado ▲ *the statutory arm's length principle* el principio reglamentario del precio de mercado ▲ *use the general arm's length principle* usar el principio general del precio de mercado

arm's length transaction

≠ related party transaction

An arm's length transaction is a transaction between independent parties who are not related in any way and act in their own best interest. The price resulting from such a transaction is deemed to reflect the fair market value.

transacción a precio de mercado

= transacción realilzada en condiciones de independencia mutua, transacción realizada en condiciones de plena competencia

NOTE Spanish accountants prefer 'transacción a precio de mercado' to the IAS/IFRS term 'transacción realizada en condiciones de independencia mutua'.

▲ *a price agreed in an arm's length transaction* un precio acordado en una transacción a precio de mercado ▲ *an arm's length transaction between knowledgeable and willing parties* una transacción a precio de mercado entre partes con conocimiento y voluntad

⇛ fair value

arm's length value

Arm's length value is the value of a given transaction as if that transaction had been made between knowledgeable, willing, independent parties under similar circumstances.

valoración a precio de mercado

= valoración en condiciones de plena competencia

▲ *establish an arm's length value* establecer una valoración a precio de mercado ▲ *exceed the arm's length value of the services* exceder la valoración a precio de mercado de los servicios ▲ *reflect the arm's length value of the goods supplied* reflejar la valoración a precio de mercado de los bienes suministrados

ARR

= accounting rate of return

ARR is the abbreviation for the accounting rate of return that is applied to forecast return on an investment as it measures the profitability of an enterprise expressed as a ratio between the profit including or excluding interest and tax and the capital employed at the end of an accounting period. Discounted-cash-flow models are often preferred instead of the accounting rate of return.

tasa de rendimiento contable

= tasa de beneficio contable

▲ *calculate the ARR* calcular la tasa de rendimiento contable ▲ *changes in ARR* cambios en la tasa de rendimiento contable ▲ *the ARR of the investment* la tasa de rendimiento contable de la inversión

⇛ capital employed, return on invested capital

arrange

To arrange is to plan or organize something, e.g. a meeting.

organizar

▲ *arrange a general meeting* organizar una junta general ▲ *arrange borrowings* organizar el endeudamiento ▲ *arrange for something* organizar algo

articles of association UK

The articles of association is a document that contains the regulations governing the internal affairs of a company, i.e. the relationship between the company and its members.

estatutos

▲ *a management body provided by the articles of association* un órgano de gestión previsto en los estatutos ▲ *a right of redemption provided by the articles of association* un derecho de cancelación previsto en los estatutos ▲ *absence of a quorum for alterations to the articles of association approved by an annual general meeting* ausencia de quorum para modificar los estatutos aprobados en la junta general anual ▲ *according to the articles of association* de acuerdo con los estatutos ▲ *according to the company's articles of association* de acuerdo con los estatutos de la compañía ▲ *alteration to the articles of association* modificación de los estatutos ▲ *amend the articles of association* enmendar los estatutos ▲ *reserves provided for by the articles of association* reservas previstas por los estatutos

articles of incorporation US

The articles of incorporation is the document that creates a corporation under the laws of the state of incorporation and must be filed with the relevant authorities. The articles must include informatiion about the corporation's name, authorised capital, registered office and incorporators.

estatutos

▲ *file the articles of incorporation* presentar los estatutos ▲ *prepare articles of incorporation* preparar los estatutos ▲ *provided in the articles of incorporation* previsto en los estatutos

⇛ certificate of incorporation

articles of organization US

→ articles of incorporation

artificial costs

= complete reciprocated costs

Artificial costs, i.e. complete reciprocated costs, constitute all own costs incurred by a service department plus the costs allocated to it for services provided by other service departments.

costes artificiales

= costes contractuales, costes recíprocos completos

▲ *calculate artificial costs* calcular los costes artificiales ▲ *recognise artificial costs* reconocer los costes artificiales ▲ *reduce artificial costs* reducir los costes artificiales

ASB UK

= Accounting Standards Board UK

ASB is the abbreviation for Accounting Standards Board that develops, issues and withdraws accounting standards in the UK.

ASB

▲ *accounting standards issued by the ASB* normas de contabilidad emitidas por la ASB

ascertain

To ascertain means to discover or learn something with certainty.

verificar

= constatar

▲ *ascertain a loss* verificar una pérdida ▲ *ascertain a value* verificar un valor ▲ *ascertain any obvious violations of statutory provisions* verificar cualesquiera violaciones obvias de las estipulaciones estatutarias ▲ *ascertain the amount outstanding at the balance sheet date* verificar la cantidad pendiente a fecha de balance ▲ *ascertain the selling price* verificar el precio de venta

ascertainable

When something can be confirmed, learned or discovered with certainty, it is called ascertainable.

verificable

▲ *ascertainable errors* errores verificables ▲ *ascertainable errors and omissions* errores y omisiones verificables ▲ *readily ascertainable* fácilmente verificable

ascertainment

Ascertainment is the discovery of something with certainty or the confirmation of something.

verificación

▲ *ascertainment of the value of goodwill* verificación del valor del fondo de comercio

assertions

Assertions are implied or expressed representations by management embodied in the financial statements.

afirmaciones

▲ *adjust assertions* ajustar las afirmaciones

assess

= evaluate

To assess means to make a judgement about something, taking into consideration all relevant facts.

valorar

= evaluar

▲ *assess a risk* valorar un riesgo ▲ *assess the future cash flows of the enterprise* valorar los flujos de efectivo futuros de la empresa ▲ *assess the future possibilities of the enterprise* valorar las posibilidades futuras de la empresa ▲ *assess the probability of expected future economic benefits* valorar la probabilidad de beneficios económicos futuros esperados ▲ *assess the specific risks associated with the asset's estimated cash flows* valorar los riesgos específicos asociados a los flujos de efectivo estimados del activo ▲ *assess whether the information of the intellectual capital report is relevant and reliable* valorar si la información del informe sobre el capital intelectual es relevante y fiable ▲ *in assessing whether* al valorar si

assessment

= evaluation

An assessment is a judgement of something, taking into consideration all relevant facts.

valoración

= evaluación

▲ *a contract-by-contract assessment* una valoración contrato a contrato ▲ *a market assessment of* una valoración de mercado de ▲ *an assessment of whether* una valoración de si ▲ *an indefinite useful life assessment* una valoración de la vida útil indefinida ▲ *an independent professional assessment* una valoración profesional independiente ▲ *assessment of equity for the purpose of analysis* valoración del patrimonio a efectos de análisis ▲ *claims assessment costs* costes de valoración de las reclamaciones ▲ *make an assessment* hacer una valoración ▲ *recoverability assessments* valoraciones de la recuperabilidad ▲ *review of useful life assessment* revisión de la valoración de la vida útil ▲ *the accuracy of past assessments of future cash flows* la precisión de las valoraciones pasadas de flujos de efectivo futuros

asset

≠ liability

An asset is an economic resource that belongs to an individual or an enterprise due to past financial transactions or events and is expected to provide future economic benefits. Assets are generally expressed in money terms and may be fixed or current assets.

NOTE The term asset is also used metaphorically to describe things that cannot actually be owned, e.g. the skills, loyalty and commitment of employees.

activo

▲ *a depreciable asset* un activo amortizable ▲ *a non-depreciable asset* un activo no amortizable ▲ *assets adjusted upward* activos ajustados al alza ▲ *assets held by a long-term employee benefit fund* activos mantenidos por un plan de pensiones a largo plazo ▲ *assets held for sale* activos mantenidos para la venta ▲ *assets leased under finance leases* activos en arrendamiento financiero ▲ *assets that are continuously adjusted to fair value* activos que se ajustan continuamente a valor razonable ▲ *assets, total* activos, total ▲ *charged assets* activos cargados ▲ *combined assets* activos combinados ▲ *generate assets* generar activos ▲ *identifiable assets* activos identificables ▲ *prepare the asset for its intended use* preparar el activo para su utilización prevista ▲ *recognised assets* activos reconocidos ▲ *retirement of assets* retirada de activos ▲ *ring-fenced assets* activos de protección ▲ *self-constructed assets* activos autogenerados ▲ *separable asset* activos separables ▲ *the ability to operate an asset* la habilidad para gestionar un activo ▲ *the asset transferred* los activos transferidos ▲ *the assets acquired* los activos adquiridos ▲ *the assets disposed of* los activos eliminados ▲ *the date of the assets' entry into service* la fecha de la entrada en servicio de los activos ▲ *the leased asset* los activos arrendados ▲ *the lost assets* los activos deteriorados ▲ *the right to operate the asset* el derecho a gestionar el activo ▲ *the scrapped assets* los activos desmantelados

⇛ current asset, fixed asset, non-current asset

asset allocation US

= distribution of assets UK

Asset allocation is the way in which the total assets are mixed in the investment portfolio of an enterprise or a person. The assets may be allocated on domestic and foreign investments in different types of shares, bonds, properties and other investments, depending on investment criteria such as return and risk.

asignación de activos

= distribución de activos

▲ *asset allocation by geography* asignación de activos por criterio geográfico

asset deal

≠ share deal UK, stock deal US

An asset deal is a specific structure applied in connection with acquiring or taking over an enterprise. In an asset deal, an enterprise is acquired through the acquisition of that enterprise's individual tangible fixed assets. The buyer may choose to assume only certain liabilities of the target, leaving others behind, which is why such a deal is generally less advantageous to the vendor than a share deal, where the seller does not retain any liabilities.

venta de activos

▲ *conclude an asset deal* concluir una venta de activos ▲ *enter into an asset deal* acordar una venta de activos

asset held under a capital lease US

When an asset is held under a capital lease, the lessor has conveyed to the lessee the right to use the asset for an agreed period of time, and where –except for the legal title– all the risks and rewards associated with the ownership of the asset is transferred. Title of the asset is transferred to the lessee at the end of the lease term.

activo en régimen de arrendamiento financiero

▲ *capitalization of assets held under a capital lease* capitalización de activos en régimen de arrendamiento financiero ▲ *recognize assets held under a capital lease in the balance sheet* reconocer activos en régimen de arrendamiento financiero

asset held under a finance lease IAS/IFRS

When an asset is held under a finance lease, the lessor has conveyed to the lessee the right to use the asset for an agreed period of time, and where - except for the legal title - all the risks and rewards associated with the ownership of the asset is transferred. Title of the asset may or may not be transferred to the lessee at the end of the lease term.

activo en régimen de arrendamiento financiero

▲ *an intangible asset held under a finance lease* un activo intangible en régimen de arrendamiento financiero ▲ *capitalisation of assets held under a finance lease* capitalización de activos en régimen de arrendamiento financiero ▲ *lessee's biological assets held under finance leases* activos biológicos del arrendatario en régimen de arrendamiento financiero ▲ *recognise assets held under a finance lease in the balance sheet* reconocer activos en régimen de arrendamiento financiero en el balance

asset item

An asset item is a group of similar assets that are shown on the asset side of the balance sheet.

partida de activo

▲ *interest amount for each asset item* suma de intereses por cada partida de activo

asset management

= portfolio management

Asset management involves planning and deciding how funds are invested and property administered to generate the highest possible profit to an individual or an enterprise.

gestión del activo

▲ *a contractual asset management agreement* un acuerdo por contrato de gestión del activo ▲ *asset management expenses* gastos por gestión del activo ▲ *proper asset management* gestión del activo apropiada ▲ *the asset management policy of the entity* la política de gestión del activo de la entidad

asset manager

= portfolio manager

An asset manager is a physical or legal person that administers funds and property on behalf of somebody else to generate the highest possible profit. Examples of asset managers are pension funds and investment banks.

gestor de activos

▲ *the asset manager of the year* el gestor de activos del año

asset retirement obligation US

= cost of restoring

Asset retirement obligations refer to costs incurred when reconstructing or repairing something that has been destroyed or damaged.

coste de reparación

▲ *measure the asset retirement obligation* medir el coste de reparación ▲ *pay the majority of the asset retirement obligation* pagar la mayor parte del coste de reparación

asset side

The asset side constitutes one half of the balance sheet as

presented in the horizontal format, and states the enterprise's total assets and how the enterprise has used the invested capital.

columna del activo

= activo

▲ *recognise an item in the asset side* reconocer una partida en la columna del activo ▲ *recognise assets in the asset side* reconocer activos en la columna del activo ▲ *recognise capital in the asset side* reconocer capital en la columna del activo ▲ *recognise expenses in the asset side* reconocer gastos en la columna del activo

asset write-offs US

= amounts written off investments UK, impairment of financial assets IAS/IFRS

Asset write-offs constitute the part of write-downs for impairment of non-current assets for the accounting period that are expensed in the income statement. Impairment may be caused by decreases in market value, damage or, for loans, by non-performance. Asset write-offs typically concern financial assets.

eliminaciones de activos no corrientes

▲ *account for asset write-offs* contabilizar eliminaciones de activos no corrientes ▲ *significant asset write-offs* eliminaciones significativas de activos no corrientes

⇛ financial asset, impairment

assets

= property

The totality of what a person or enterprise owns is called his or its assets.

activos

▲ *all assets* todos los activos ▲ *total assets* total activos ▲ *transfer the assets* transferir los activos ▲ *use of the company's assets* uso de los activos de la empresa

assignment of shares

The transaction whereby a shareholder sells or otherwise transfers his shares to someone else is called an assignment of assets.

traspaso de acciones

▲ *gain on assignment of shares* ganancia por traspaso de acciones ▲ *loss on assignment of shares* pérdida por traspaso de acciones ▲ *plans for the assignment of shares* planes para el traspaso de acciones ▲ *restrictions on assignment of shares* restricciones en el traspaso de acciones

assistance

Assistance is the help given or received in order to perform a task.

asistencia

= ayuda

▲ *accounting assistance* asistencia contable ▲ *external assistance* asistencia externa ▲ *financial assistance* asistencia financiera ▲ *government assistance* asistencia gubernamental ▲ *legal assistance* asistencia legal ▲ *periodic assistance* asistencia periódica ▲ *receive assistance* recibir asistencia ▲ *render assistance* prestar asistencia ▲ *technical assistance* asistencia técnica

assistant audit manager

An assistant audit manager reports to the audit manager in an enterprise and has a professional background as a qualified accountant. The assistant audit manager works in the audit department with the internal audit and the internal control procedures as well as other accountancy tasks.

auditor auxiliar

▲ *an internal assistant audit manager* un auditor auxiliar interno ▲ *appoint a new assistant audit manager* nombrar un nuevo auditor auxiliar

associate US, IAS/IFRS

= associated enterprise, associated undertaking

An associate is an enterprise which is not a subsidiary, but in which another enterprise and its subsidiaries hold equity investments, and over which these enterprises exercise significant influence in making operating and financial decisions.

empresa asociada

= asociada

▲ *amounts owed by associates* cantidades debidas por empresas asociadas ▲ *an investor in an associate* un inversor en una empresa asociada ▲ *disposal of associates* enajenación de empresas asociadas ▲ *dividends received from an associate* dividendos recibidos de una empresa asociada ▲ *income from investments in associates* ingresos procedentes de inversiones en empresas asociadas ▲ *investments in associates* inversiones en empresas asociadas ▲ *payables to associates* cantidades a pagar a empresas asociadas ▲ *proportionally consolidated associates* empresas asociadas consolidadas proporcionalmente ▲ *sales of assets from an associate to an investor* ventas de activos de una empresa asociada a un inversor ▲ *share of profits and losses of associates* porcentaje de resultados de empresas asociadas ▲ *share of results before tax of associates* porcentaje de resultados antes de impuestos de empresas asociadas ▲ *substantially all of the associate's operations* sustancialmente todas las operaciones de las empresas asociadas ▲ *the associate's financial statements* los estados financieros de las empresas asociadas ▲ *the capital commitments of an associate* los compromisos de capital de una empresa asociada ▲ *the carrying amount of associates* el valor contable de las empresas asociadas ▲ *the contingent liabilities of an associate* los pasivos contingentes de una empresa asociada ▲ *the performance of the associate* el resultado de la empresa asociada ▲ *the principal associates* las principales empresas asociadas ▲ *undistributed profits of associates* beneficios no distribuidos de empresas asociadas ▲ *winding up of associates* disolución de empresas asociadas

⇛ associated company, associated undertaking

associated

Associated means related to. In the context of a group, associated is used about enterprises in which a parent company has a significant influence, typically by holding between 20 and 50 per cent of the voting shares.

asociado

▲ *any associated future economic benefits* cualesquiera beneficios económicos futuros asociados ▲ *directly associated liabilities* directamente pasivos asociados ▲ *goodwill associated with the transaction* fondo de comercio asociado a la transacción ▲ *revenue associated with a transaction involving the rendering of services* ingresos asociados a una transacción que implica la prestación de servicios ▲ *the excess of the associated current or deferred tax* el excedente del impuesto diferido o corriente asociado

⇛ associate

associated company UK

An associated company is a company which is not a subsidiary, in which the investor has a participating interest and over whose operating and financial policies it exercises a significant influence.

empresa asociada

= asociada

▲ *pledge all the shares in all the associated companies* pignorar todas las acciones de todas las empresas asociadas ▲ *the executive or managing director of the associated company* el director ejecutivo o consejero delegado de la empresa asociada ▲ *the rate of tax on payments of interest or royalties made to an associated company* el tipo impositivo por pagos de intereses o royalties hechos a una empresa asociada

⇛ associate, associated undertaking

associated undertaking UK

= associate IAS/IFRS, associated enterprise DK

An associated undertaking is an enterprise over which another enterprise has significant influence, typically by holding a participating interest of between 20 and 50 per cent.

empresa asociada

= asociada

▲ *an amount corresponding to the proportion of the associated undertaking's capital and reserves represented by the participating interest* una cantidad correspondiente a la proporción del capital y reservas de la empresa asociada representado por las participaciones ▲ *provide access services to end-users either directly or through an associated undertaking* proveer servicios de acceso a los clientes, bien directamente o bien a través de una empresa asociada ▲ *the capital of the associated undertaking* el capital de la empresa asociada ▲ *the conclusion*

of contracts with an associated undertaking la finalización de los contratos con una empresa asociada
⇛ associated company, subsidiary

association
An association is a group of persons or enterprises that have a common aim or perform the same kind of activities.
asociación
▲ *association of stock exchanges* asociación de bolsas de valores ▲ *economic association* asociación económica

Association of Chartered Certified Accountants UK
= ACCA UK
The Association of Chartered Certified Accountants replaced the Chartered Association of Certified Accountants in 1996 as the organisation for certified accountants. It is the largest international professional accountancy body with students and members in 160 countries and an entensive worldwide network. The ACCA is on the six chartered bodies of accountants in the UK.
Asociación de Auditores del Reino Unido
▲ *become a member of Association of Chartered Certified Accountants* ser un miembro de la Asociación de Auditores del Reino Unido ▲ *four core qualifications offered by Association of Chartered Certified Accountants* cuatro opiniones centrales ofrecidas por la Asociación de Auditores del Reino Unido
⇛ certified accountant, chartered accountant

assume
1 To assume means to take something for granted, correct or possible.
asumir
▲ *assume that the figures are correct* asumir que las cifras son correctas ▲ *assume that the information can be verified* asumir que la información puede verificarse ▲ *assume the residual value to be zero* asumir que el valor residual es cero
2 To assume is to accept or take on something such as responsibility, control, a liability, a task or an assignment.
NOTE Liabilities which are assumed are liabilities accepted by another party, e.g. a company when acquiring another company.
asumir
▲ *assume an obligation* asumir una obligación ▲ *assume liability* asumir deuda

assuming company
= assuming insurer, reinsurer
≠ cedant, ceding company
An assuming company is an insurance company that agrees to assume the risk or part of the risk of another insurance company, the cedant or ceding company, against part of the premium on a given policy.
reaseguradora
▲ *deposits received from assuming companies* depósitos recibidos de reaseguradoras ▲ *receive compensation for losses from the assuming company* recibir compensación por pérdidas de la reaseguradora

assumption
Assumptions are hypotheses, statements or estimates concerning future events that are accepted without evidence to form the basis for decisions, analyses or calculations.
suposición
= hipótesis, supuesto
▲ *assumptions affecting the possible future resolution of the uncertainties* suposiciones que afectan a la posible resolución futura de las incertidumbres ▲ *be based on an assumption* basarse en una suposición ▲ *changes made to past assumptions concerning the liabilities* cambios hechos en las hipótesis pasadas concernientes a los pasivos ▲ *disclose information about the key assumptions concerning the future* publicar información sobre las suposiciones claves concernientes al futuro ▲ *inaccurate assumptions* suposiciones imprecisas ▲ *incorrect assumptions* suposiciones incorrectas ▲ *major assumptions concerning future events* hipótesis importantes concernientes a sucesos futuros ▲ *make an assumption* hacer una suposición ▲ *reasonable and supportable assumptions* suposiciones razona-

bles y fiables ▲ *significant assumptions applied in estimating fair values of financial liabilities* suposiciones significativas aplicadas al estimar los valores razonables de los pasivos financieros ▲ *under appropriate assumptions* bajo suposiciones apropiadas

assurance

1 Assurance is an auditor's examination method for assessing an enterprise's financial reporting systems and processes and checking management's assertion as to appropriateness. Assurance may also include other investigation and attestation services than audit.

NOTE The level of assurance obtained by the auditor may be expressed positively in the audit report as "reasonable assurance that the annual report is free of material misstatement".

opinión

▲ *limited assurance* opinión limitada ▲ *reasonable assurance* opinión razonable

2 Assurance is insurance against an event that is certain to occur (e.g. death), but where the time is uncertain.

NOTE In British English "assurance" or "life assurance" is used for "life insurance", however, the application of "life insurance" is gaining ground.

aseguramiento

NOTE In Spanish "life assurance" is translated by "seguro de vida".

▲ *assurance services* servicios de aseguramiento ▲ *life assurance* seguro de vida

⇛ insurance, life assurance, life insurance

at the beginning of

= beginning-of-year

For accounting purposes, 'at the beginning of' refers to the start of the accounting period.

al inicio de

▲ *at the beginning of the financial year* al inicio del año económico ▲ *cash and cash equivalents at the beginning of the year* efectivo y equivalentes de efectivo al inicio del año ▲ *deferred tax at the beginning of the year* impuesto diferido al inicio del año ▲ *equity at the beginning of the year* patrimonio al inicio del año ▲ *minority interests at the beginning of the year* intereses de los accionistas minoritarios al inicio del año ▲ *other provisions at the beginning of the year* otras provisiones al inicio del año ▲ *payable at the beginning of the year* a pagar al inicio del año ▲ *recognition in the equity at the beginning of the year* reconocimiento en el patrimonio al inicio del año ▲ *revaluation adjustment at the beginning of the year* ajuste por revalorización al inicio del año ▲ *the quoted price of the share at the beginning of 2005* la cotización de la acción al inicio de 2005

at the end of

= year-end

For accounting purposes, 'at the end of' refers to the end of the accounting period.

al final de

= a final de

▲ *a reconciliation of the number of shares outstanding at the beginning and at the end of the period* una conciliación del número de acciones pendientes al principio y al final del periodo ▲ *at the end of the financial year* al final del año económico ▲ *equity at the end of period* patrimonio al final del año ▲ *the exchange rates quoted at the end of the year* los tipos de cambio vigentes al final del año

attention directing US

Attention directing is the reporting and interpreting data helping management to focus on operating problems, inefficiencies, opportunities, etc.

sistema de alerta

▲ *the use of attention directing* el uso del sistema de alerta

attributable to

When something is related to a specific amount, asset, liability or section, belongs to a certain person or enterprise, or results from a particular event, it is attributable to it.

atribuible a

▲ *assets attributable to a discontinuing operation* activos atribuibles a una operación interrumpida ▲ *cash flows of the hedged item that are attributable to a hedged risk* flujos de efectivo de las partidas protegidas que son atribuibles a los fondos de riesgo ▲ *costs directly attributable to something* costes directamente atribuibles a algo ▲ *costs directly attributable to the acquisition of finished goods* costes directamente atribuibles a la adquisición de productos terminados ▲ *costs that are attributable to contract activity in general* costes que son atribuibles a la actividad contractual en general ▲ *decreases attributable to biological assets classified as held for sale* decrementos atribuibles a activos biológicos clasificados como dispuestos para la venta ▲ *disposing of assets or settling liabilities attributable to a discontinued operation* eliminar activos o colocar pasivos atribuibles a una operación interrumpida ▲ *goodwill that is directly attributable to a segment* fondo de comercio directamente atribuible a un segmento ▲ *increases in benefits attributable to a salary increase* incrementos en beneficios atribuibles a un aumento salarial ▲ *issued capital and reserves attributable to equity holders of the parent* capital emitido y reservas atribuibles a los accionistas de la matriz ▲ *net asset value attributable to unitholders* valor del activo neto atribuible a los partícipes ▲ *net profit attributable to ordinary shareholders* beneficio neto atribuible a accionistas ordinarios ▲ *profit or loss attributable to minority interests* resultado atribuible a los intereses de los accionistas minoritarios ▲ *profit or loss from continuing operations attributable to the parent entity* resultado de operaciones interrumpidas atribuibles a la matriz ▲ *settlement of liabilities attributable to discontinuing operations* pago de pasivos atribuibles a operaciones interrumpidas ▲ *the net cash flows attributable to the operating, investing and financing activities of discontinued operations* los flujos de efectivo netos atribuibles a actividades de explotación, inversión y financiación de operaciones interrumpidas

attribute[1] *noun* <an, the, -s>

An attribute is any detail or characteristic serving to qualify, identify, classify or quantify an entity. For example, historical cost and current cost are attributes of an asset.

atributo

▲ *measurement attributes* medición de atributos ▲ *qualitative attributes* atributos cualitativos
⇛ measurement attribute

attribute[2] *verb* <-s, -d, has -d, attributing> *passive* <is -d, was -d>

1 To attribute means to decide that something belongs to a particular class, scheme or event.

asignar
= atribuir

▲ *attribute benefit on a straight-line basis* atribuir beneficios según el método lineal ▲ *attribute benefit to periods of service* atribuir beneficios a años de servicio ▲ *attribute benefit to the current period* atribuir beneficios al periodo actual ▲ *attribute expenditure directly to a particular intangible asset* atribuir gastos directamente a un activo intangible particular ▲ *attribute the interest-bearing liability to the segment* atribuir la deuda con interés al segmento

2 To attribute means to accredit an object or a person with specific properties or characteristics.

conferir

▲ *attribute a value to the equity instruments* conferir un valor a los instrumentos patrimoniales ▲ *attribute importance to something* conferir importancia a algo

audit[1] *noun*

1 = auditing

An audit is an examination of the financial report and statements of an enterprise by an independent auditor after which the audit gives an opinion which is expressed in an audit report.

auditoría

▲ *an objective and impartial audit* una auditoría imparcial y objetiva ▲ *audit and non-audit services* servicios de auditoría y no auditoría ▲ *audit matters of governance interest* la auditoría analiza el interés de la dirección ▲ *audit of the annual report* auditoría del informe anual ▲ *audit of the supplementary reports* auditoría de los informes adicionales ▲ *audit qualifications* opiniones de la auditoría ▲ *au-*

dit quality assurance review revisión de aseguramiento de la calidad de la auditoría ▲ *audit working papers* documentos de trabajo de la auditoría ▲ *basis of audit opinion* bases de la opinión de auditoría ▲ *be subject to statutory audit* estar sujeto a auditoría reglamentaria ▲ *conduct an audit* llevar a cabo una auditoría ▲ *good audit quality* buena calidad de la auditoría ▲ *perform an audit* realizar una auditoría ▲ *plan an audit* planificar una auditoría ▲ *the audit also includes* la auditoría también incluye ▲ *the scope of the statutory audit* el alcance de la auditoría reglamentaria ▲ *the statutory audit* la auditoría reglamentaria ▲ *voluntary audit* auditoría voluntaria

⇛ audit report, statutory audit

2 = examination

An audit is an official, methodical examination or review by an expert.

auditoría

▲ *annual audits* auditorías anu ales ▲ *audit and quality assurance* auditoría y aseguramiento de la calidad

audit[2] *verb*

1 To audit is to independently examine and subsequently express an opinion on the financial statements of an organisation.

auditar

▲ *audit the accounts independently* auditar las cuentas de forma independiente ▲ *have the annual report audited* tener el informe anual auditado

2 To audit is to check something officially.

auditar

▲ *audit the accounts* auditar las cuentas

audit client

An audit client is a customer who requires and pays for audit services.

cliente de la auditoría

= cliente de auditoría

▲ *a direct financial interest in the audit client* un interés económico directo en el cliente de la auditoría ▲ *a direct or indirect shareholding in the audit client* una participación accionarial directa o indirecta en el cliente de auditoría ▲ *an affiliate of the audit client* una filial del cliente de la auditoría ▲ *an audit client of public interest* un cliente de auditoría de interés público ▲ *an indirect financial interest in the audit client* un interés financiero indirecto en el cliente de la auditoría ▲ *loan staff assignments to an audit client* acuerdos de cesión de empleados a un cliente de la auditoría ▲ *offer non-audited services to an audit client* ofrecer servicios no auditados a un cliente de la auditoría ▲ *the audited financial statements of the audit client* los estados financieros auditados del cliente de la auditoría ▲ *the governance body of the audit client* el órgano de gobierno del cliente de la auditoría ▲ *the governance infrastructure of the audit client* la infraestructura de gobierno del cliente de la auditoría ▲ *the legal and organisational structure of the audit client* la estructura legal y organizativa del cliente de auditoría ▲ *the provision of legal services to an audit client* la provisión de servicios legales a un cliente de auditoría ▲ *the services provided to the audit client* los servicios prestados al cliente de la auditoría ▲ *the total amount of fees charged to the audit client* la cantidad total de honorarios cargados al cliente de la auditoría

audit committee

An audit committee is a committee set up by a company's board of directors with responsibility for oversight of the company's financial reporting and evaluation of the external and internal audit procedures to ensure transparency and confidence of its stakeholders. Listed companies are required to form audit committees composed of outside directors.

NOTE For companies whose shares trade in the US, audit committees are mandatory under the Sarbanes-Oxley Act.

comité de auditoría

▲ *a recommendation made by the audit committee* una recomendación hecha por el comité de auditoría ▲ *an audit committee composed of non-executive members of the administrative body or members of the supervisory body* un comité de auditoría compuesto por miembros no ejecutivos del órgano administrativo o por miembros del comité de supervisión ▲ *an independent audit committee* un comité de auditoría independiente ▲ *FSR's Audit Committee* Comité de Auditoría de FSR ▲ *report to the audit committee on key matters arising from the statutory audit* informar al comité de auditoría sobre aspectos esenciales procedentes de la auditoría reglamentaria ▲ *set up an audit committee* nombrar un comité de auditoría ▲ *the audit committee of the audited entity* el comité de auditoría de la entidad auditada ▲ *the duties of the audit committee* las obligaciones del comité de auditoría ▲ *the function of the audit committee* la función del comité de auditoría ▲ *the malfunctioning of audit committees* el mal funcionamiento de los comités de auditoría

⇛ Sarbanes-Oxley Act

audit cost

Audit costs are the costs associated with an independent examination of and the subsequent expression of opinion by an auditor on the financial statements of an organisation.

coste de auditoría

▲ *incur audit costs* incurrir en costes de auditoría

audit evidence

Audit evidence is the information gathered by auditors in order to reach the conclusions underlying the audit opinion.

prueba de auditoría

▲ *collect audit evidence* reunir prueba de auditoría ▲ *obtain audit evidence* obtener prueba de auditoría

audit fee

An audit fee is the remuneration payable to an accountant or accountancy firm for performing the audit of an enterprise.

honorario de auditoría

= tarifa de auditoría

▲ *audit fee payable* honorario de auditoría a pagar ▲ *require disclosure of the audit fee* requerir la publicación del honorario de auditoría ▲ *the audit fees charged* los honorarios de auditoría cargados ▲ *the basis for calculating the audit fee* la base de cálculo del honorario de auditoría ▲ *the consolidated audit fee* el honorario de auditoría consolidado

audit firm

An audit firm is a firm or an enterprise which provides audit services.

empresa auditora

= firma auditora

▲ *a non-audit owner of the audit firm* un propietario no auditor de la empresa auditora ▲ *an affiliate of an audit firm* una filial de una empresa auditora ▲ *an integral function of the audit firm's quality review structure* una función integral de la estructura de revisión de la calidad de la firma auditora ▲ *be associated with an audit firm* estar asociado con una empresa auditora ▲ *employed by or associated as partner or otherwise with the audit firm* empleado por o asociado como socio o de otra forma con la firma auditora ▲ *registration of audit firms* inscripción de firmas auditoras ▲ *the audit firm's independence policies* las políticas de independencia de la firma auditora ▲ *the audit firm's internal safeguarding system* el sistema de salvaguarda interno de la empresa auditora ▲ *the audit firms of public interest entities* las empresas auditoras de las entidades públicas ▲ *the conditions for approval of audit firms* las condiciones para la autorización de las empresas auditoras ▲ *the majority of voting rights in the audit firm* la mayoría de los derechos de voto en la empresa auditora ▲ *the majority ownership of an audit firm* la propiedad mayoritaria de una empresa auditora ▲ *the members of the administrative or management body of the audit firm* los miembros del cuerpo administrativo o de gestión de la firma auditora ▲ *the members of the management of the audit firm* los miembros de la dirección de la empresa auditora ▲ *the natural persons who carry out statutory audits on behalf of the audit firm* las personas físicas que realizan auditorías reglamentarias en nombre de la firma auditora ▲ *the owners or shareholders of an audit firm* los propietarios o accionistas de una firma auditora ▲ *wi-*

thdraw the approval of audit firms retirar la autorización de firmas auditoras

⇛ audit

audit opinion

= opinion

The audit opinion is the auditor's conclusion after having audited the financial statements of an enterprise as expressed in the audit report. The wording is that the financial statements "give a true and fair view" in British English, or "present fairly, in all material respects" in US English if the opinion is unqualified.

NOTE The expression "audit opinion" may also refer to the whole audit report.

opinión de auditoría

▲ *basis of audit opinion* base de la opinión de auditoría ▲ *express an audit opinion* expresar una opinión de auditoría

⇛ audit report

audit program US

= audit programme UK, IAS/IFRS

An audit program is a set of instructions defining the nature, timing and extent of the audit procedures necessary to carry out the overall audit plan.

programa de auditoría

▲ *an internal audit program* un programa de auditoría interna

audit programme UK, IAS/IFRS

= audit program US

An audit programme is a set of instructions defining the nature, timing and extent of the audit procedures necessary to carry out the overall audit plan.

programa de auditoría

▲ *an internal audit programme* un programa de auditoría interna

audit provision

= audit regulation

Audit provisions are rules contained in statutes and administrative regulations governing the audit of the financial statements of enterprises.

norma de auditoría

= regla de auditoría

▲ *Danish audit provisions* normas de auditoría danesas ▲ *foreign audit provisions* normas de auditoría extranjeras

audit report

= auditors' report

An audit report is a written statement signed by one or two independent accountants and included in the annual report or the financial statements. The report states whether an enterprise's financial statements give a true and fair view of the financial position, operating results and cash flows of the enterprise and may offer recommendations along with findings and conclusions.

informe de auditoría

▲ *a common standard for audit reports* una norma común para los informes de auditoría ▲ *audit report issued by auditors that are independent of the company* informe de auditoría emitido por auditores independientes de la empresa ▲ *qualified audit report* informe de auditoría con reservas ▲ *unqualified audit report* informe de auditoría sin reservas

⇛ disclaimer, modified audit report, qualified audit report, unqualified audit report

audit risk

Audit risk is the probability that the auditor gives an inappropriate audit opinion because of failure to discover material misstatement, deficiency, abuse or other unacceptable matter in the financial statements.

riesgo de auditoría

▲ *potential audit risks* riesgos de auditoría potenciales ▲ *the acceptable level of audit risk* el nivel aceptable de riesgo de auditoría

⇛ control risk, detection risk, inherent risk

audit sampling

Audit sampling is the application of audit procedures to less than 100% of a population of financial data to obtain audit evidence.

muestreo de auditoría

▲ *carry out an audit sampling* realizar un muestreo de auditoría ▲ *evaluate on the basis of audit sampling* evaluar empleando el muestreo de auditoría

⇛ population

audit trail

An audit trail is a step-by-step record of transactions, typically a computer system, that allows financial data to be tra-

ced through all the stages in an accounting system.
rastro de auditoría
▲ *a break in the audit trail* una discontinuidad en el rastro de auditoría ▲ *a sufficient audit trail* un rastro de auditoría suficiente ▲ *check the audit trail* comprobar el rastro de auditoría ▲ *follow an audit trail* seguir un rastro de auditoría ▲ *in the absence of an adequate audit trail* en ausencia de un rastro de auditoría adecuado

audit work
Audit work comprises the activities performed by an auditor in connection with the audit of the financial statements and the annual report of an enterprise, including audit procedures such as investigation and verifying the accounting records, audit sampling, computation as well as the issuing of an audit report on completion of the audit.
trabajo de auditoría
▲ *carry out audit work in accordance with generally accepted auditing standards* llevar a cabo el trabajo de auditoría de acuerdo con normas de auditoría generalmente aceptadas ▲ *decisions that directly relate to the audit work* decisiones que se relacionan directamente con el trabajo de auditoría ▲ *external audit work* trabajo de auditoría externa ▲ *internal audit work* trabajo de auditoría interna ▲ *statutory audit work* trabajo de auditoría reglamentaria ▲ *unexpected factors in the audit work* factores inesperados en el trabajo de auditoría

auditable
When financial statements are auditable, sufficient evidence exists to support the information and assertions made in the statements. Insufficient evidence for accounting items may result in the auditor not being able to carry out an audit.
auditable
▲ *the auditable part of* la parte auditable de

Auditing Practices Board UK
= APB
The Auditing Practices Board (APB) was established in 2002 as a substitute for the previous APB set up in 1991 and is committed to leading the development of auditing practice in the United Kingdom and the Republic of Ireland. The APB is supervised by the Financial Reporting Council.
Auditing Practices Board
= Comité de Prácticas de Auditoría
NOTE The Spanish body for performing similar functions is called 'Instituto de Contabilidad y Auditoría de Cuentas' (ICAC).
▲ *in accordance with auditing standards issued by the Auditing Practices Board* de acuerdo con las normas de auditoría emitidas por el Auditing Practices Board
⇛ APB

auditing standard
Auditing standards lay down the basic principles for the scope and procedures that auditors must follow when performing audits of financial reports and statements. International auditing rules are laid down in the International Standards on Auditing (ISA).
norma de auditoría
▲ *a revised auditing standard* una norma de auditoría revisada ▲ *apply a national auditing standard* aplicar una norma de auditoría nacional ▲ *conduct the audit in accordance with applicable auditing standards* llevar a cabo la auditoría de acuerdo con las normas de auditoría aplicables ▲ *in accordance with auditing standards issued by the Auditing Practices Board* de acuerdo con las normas de auditoría emitidas por el Auditing Practices Board

auditing standards
= auditing practices
An audit of financial statements that has been performed according to generally accepted auditing standards complies with the broad rules and guidelines for auditing procedures that auditors are obliged to observe when carrying out audit work for their clients.
normas de auditoría
▲ *carry out audit work in accordance with generally accepted auditing standards* llevar a cabo un trabajo de auditoría de acuerdo con normas de audito-

ría generalmente aceptadas ▲ *generally accepted auditing standards* normas de auditoría generalmente aceptadas

auditor

An auditor is a person or accountancy firm appointed to perform and have final responsibility for an independent audit of an enterprise. To audit a listed enterprise, the auditor must be a qualified, authorised accountant.

auditor

▲ *a supplementary report with an opinion expressed by the auditor* un informe auxiliar con una opinión expresada por el auditor ▲ *an aptitude test for the approval of auditors from other countries* un test de aptitud para aceptar auditores de otros países ▲ *an independent auditor* un auditor independiente ▲ *auditor rotation* rotación del auditor ▲ *auditors elected by the annual general meeting* auditores elegidos por la junta general anual ▲ *auditors' remuneration* remuneración de los auditores ▲ *compromise the auditor's independece* poner a prueba la independencia del auditor ▲ *dismissal of the auditor* despido del auditor ▲ *group auditor* auditor del grupo ▲ *reduce the auditor's independence risk to an acceptable level* reducir el riesgo de independencia del auditor a un nivel aceptable ▲ *resignation of the auditor* dimisión del auditor ▲ *the auditor's ability to act objectively* la capacidad del auditor para actuar de forma objetiva ▲ *the auditor's duties, independence and ethics* las obligaciones del auditor, independencia y comportamiento ético ▲ *the confidentiality and professional secrecy rules relating to auditors* las normas de secreto profesional y confidencialidad relacionadas con los auditores ▲ *the duration of the auditor's appointment* la duración del nombramiento del auditor ▲ *the enterprise's auditor* el auditor de la empresa ▲ *the ethical requirements that apply to auditors* los requisitos éticos que se aplican a los auditores ▲ *the parent's auditor* el auditor de la matriz

⇛ accountant

auditor's report

= audit opinion US, audit report UK, independent auditor's report

The auditor's report is a written statement signed by an independent accountant and included in the annual report or the financial statements. The report states whether an enterprise's financial statements give a true and fair view of the financial position, operating results and cash flows of the enterprise and may offer recommendations along with findings and conclusions.

informe de auditor

▲ *a qualified auditor's report* un informe de auditor con reparos ▲ *an unqualified auditor's report* un informe de auditor sin reparos ▲ *be responsible for the auditor's report* ser responsable del informe de auditor ▲ *issue an auditor's report* emitir un informe de auditor

auditors' records

= audit minutes

The auditors' records contain the long-form audit reports by the auditor(s) for various accounting periods on the scope and procedures of the audit performed as well as the audit opinions expressed for each accounting period. Such records are required by Danish legislation and must be addressed internally to the board of directors or other top management of an enterprise.

registros de los informes de auditores

= actas de auditores, registro de los informes de los auditores

▲ *comment on something in the auditors' records* comentar algo en los registros de los informes de auditores ▲ *express an opinion in the auditors' records* expresar una opinión en los registros de los informes de los auditores ▲ *the auditors' records concerning the financial statements* los registros de los informes de auditores relativos a los estados financieros

⇛ long-form audit report

auditors' remuneration

= audit fee, auditors' fee

The auditors' remuneration is the payment made to the auditors for performing the audit of the financial statements of the enterprise.

remuneración de los auditores

▲ *disclosure of auditors' remuneration* publicación de la remuneración de los auditores

auditors' report
= audit opinion US, audit report UK, auditor's report UK, independent auditors' report
The auditors' report is a written statement signed by two independent accountants and included in the annual report or the financial statements. The report states whether an enterprise's financial statements give a true and fair view of the financial position, operating results and cash flows of the enterprise and may offer recommendations along with findings and conclusions.
informe de auditores
= informe de los auditores
▲ *a qualified auditors' report* un informe de auditores con reparos ▲ *an unqualified auditors' report* un informe de auditores sin reparos ▲ *be responsible for the auditors' report* ser responsable del informe de auditores ▲ *issue an auditors' report* emitir un informe de auditores
⇛ management report, statement of directors' responsibilities

Australian Society of Certified Practising Accountants
→ CPA Australia

authorise
To authorise is to delegate power to a person or body to act in a particular way on behalf of someone else.
autorizar
▲ *authorise the supervisory board to increase capital* autorizar al consejo de supervisión la ampliación de capital ▲ *authorise the supervisory board to issue warrants* autorizar al consejo de supervisión la emisión de warrants ▲ *the financial statements are authorised for issue* se autoriza la publicación de los estados financieros ▲ *the number of shares authorised* el número de acciones autorizadas
⇛ authority

authorised capital UK
= authorised share capital, authorized capital stock US, nominal capital, registered capital
A company's authorised capital is the maximum nominal value of the shares that the company is authorised by its memorandum of association to issue in order to raise capital.
capital autorizado
= capital delegado
▲ *decide to double the amount of authorised capital* decidir doblar la cantidad de capital autorizado ▲ *payment of the subscribed, non-paid-in portion of authorised capital* pago del capital suscrito, no pagado en proporción al capital autorizado

authorised market place
= AMP, authorized market place US
An authorised market place is an official, regulated market for regular trade in transferable securities admitted for trading, but not listed on a stock exchange, such as money-market instruments, derivative financial instruments, depository receipts and investment association units. Authorised market places have been set up in EU member states under the EU Investment Services and must be recognised by the national competent authorities.
mercado autorizado
▲ *activities as an authorised market place* actividades como en un mercado autorizado ▲ *admitted for trading at an authorised market place* admitido a negociación en un mercado autorizado ▲ *operate as an authorised market place* operar como un mercado autorizado ▲ *trade at an authorised market place* negociar en un mercado autorizado

authorised marketplace
→ authorised market place

authorised share capital
→ authorised capital

authority[1] *noun* <no indefinite article, the, no plural>
Authority is the power delegated to a person or body, usually called the agent, to act in a particular way on behalf of someone else, called the principal, thereby creating rights and obligations binding on the principal.
autorización
= delegación
▲ *act within the scope of the authority* actuar dentro del límite de la autorización ▲ *actual authority* autorización actual ▲ *apparent authority* autorización aparente ▲ *apply for the authority to increase the share capital* solicitar autorización para ampliar el capital social ▲ *by*

authority por delegación ▲ *general authority* autorización general ▲ *implied authority* autorización implícita ▲ *incidental authority* autorización incidental ▲ *ostensible authority* autorización manifiesta ▲ *revoke the authority* revocar la autorización ▲ *special authority* autorización especial ▲ *the duration of the period for which the authority is given* la duración del periodo para el que se otorga la autorización ▲ *those persons having authority and responsibility for planning, directing and controlling the activities of the reporting enterprise* esas personas que tienen autorización y responsabilidad para planificar, dirigir y controlar las actividades de la empresa informante

authority[2] *noun* <an, the, authorities>
An authority is an official organisation with the power or right to direct, control or judge the actions of other people.
autoridad
▲ *local authorities* autoridades locales ▲ *obtain approval for payment from a regulatory authority* obtener aprobación de una autoridad reguladora para el pago ▲ *public authorities* autoridades públicas ▲ *regulatory authorities* autoridades reguladoras ▲ *supervisory authority* autoridad supervisora ▲ *taxation authorities* autoridades fiscales ▲ *the competent authority* la autoridad competente

authorize US
= authorise UK
To authorize is to delegate power to a person or body to act in a particular way on behalf of someone else.
autorizar
= delegar
▲ *authorize the board of directors to increase capital* autorizar al consejo de administración la ampliación de capital ▲ *authorize the board of directors to issue warrants* autorizar al consejo de administración la emisión de warrants ▲ *the financial statements are authorized for issue* se autoriza la publicación de los estados financieros ▲ *the number of shares authorized* el número de acciones autorizadas

authorized capital stock US
= authorised capital UK, authorised share capital UK, nominal share capital, registered capital UK
The authorized capital stock of a corporation is the maximum amount of common stock that can be issued of that corporation under its Articles of Incorporation. The issued common stock is usually less than the authorized capital stock.
capital social autorizado
= capital delegado
▲ *a reduction of the authorized capital stock* una reducción del capital social autorizado ▲ *an increase of the authorized capital stock* un aumento del capital social autorizado

authorized market place US
= AMP, authorised market place
An authorized market place is an official, regulated market for regular trade in transferable securities admitted for trading, but not listed on a stock exchange, such as money-market instruments, derivative financial instruments, depository receipts and investment association units. Authorized market places have been set up in EU member states under the EU Investment Services and must be recognised by the national competent authorities.
mercado autorizado
▲ *activities as an authorized market place* actividades como un mercado autorizado ▲ *admitted for trading at an authorized market place* admitido a negociación en un mercado autorizado ▲ *operate as an authorized market place* operar como un mercado autorizado ▲ *trade at an authorized market place* negociar en un mercado autorizado

authorized marketplace US
→ authorized market place

available
To be available is to be accessible, obtainable or at disposal.
disponible
▲ *based on the latest information available* basado en la última información disponible ▲ *based on the most reliable evidence available* basado en la evidencia disponible más fiable ▲ *consolidated financial statements available*

for public use estados financieros consolidados disponibles para el uso público ▲ *make available* poner a disposición ▲ *on the basis of the evidence available* de acuerdo con la evidencia disponible ▲ *substantial documentation must be available* la documentación sustancial debe estar disponible ▲ *take into account all available information* tomar en cuenta toda la información disponible

available-for-sale financial asset IAS/IFRS

= available-for-sale investment IAS/IFRS

Available-for-sale financial assets are financial assets that are ready to be sold, i.e. financial assets other than loans and receivables originated by an enterprise, held-to-maturity investments or financial assets held for trading.

activo financiero disponible para la venta

▲ *accounted for as available-for-sale financial assets* contabilizado como activos financieros disponibles para la venta ▲ *available-for-sale financial assets that are not monetary items* activos financieros disponibles para la venta que no son partidas monetarias ▲ *gains or losses on remeasuring available-for-sale financial assets* resultados al volver a reclasificar los activos financieros disponibles para la venta ▲ *recognise a decline in the fair value of an available-for-sale financial asset* reconocer un descenso en el valor razonable de un activo financiero disponible para la venta ▲ *transaction costs on the initial and subsequent measurement of an available-for-sale financial asset* costes de transacción en la valoración inicial y subsiguiente de un activo financiero disponible para la venta

⇛ held-for-trading financial asset

available-for-sale instrument IAS/IFRS, US

Available-for-sale instruments are financial assets other than derivative financial instruments classified as held with the purpose of sale rather than being held until maturity. Usually 20 per cent or less of this investment type is held in another company. The instruments are equity or debt instruments recognised at fair value in the balance sheet and do not include loans and receivables originated by the enterprise or financial assets held for trading, referred to by IFRS as financial assets at fair value through profit or loss.

instrumento financiero disponible para la venta

▲ *changes in the value of an available-for-sale instrument* cambios en el valor de un instrumento financiero disponible para la venta ▲ *convert into an available-for-sale instrument* convertir en un instrumento financiero disponible para la venta

available-for-sale investment IAS/IFRS

= available-for-sale financial asset IAS/IFRS

Available-for-sale investments are equity or debt instruments classified as financial assets held with the purpose of sale rather than being held until maturity. The investments are recognised at fair value in the balance sheet and do not include loans and receivables originated by the enterprise or financial assets held for trading, referred to by IFRS as financial assets at fair value through profit or loss.

inversión disponible para la venta

▲ *sale of long term available-for-sale investments* venta de inversiones a largo plazo disponibles para la venta

available-for-sale security IAS/IFRS, US

Available-for-sale securities are equity or debt instruments classified as financial assets held with the purpose of sale rather than being held until maturity. The securities are recognised at fair value in the balance sheet and do not include loans and receivables originated by the enterprise or financial assets held for trading, referred to by IFRS as financial assets at fair value through profit or loss.

título disponible para la venta

▲ *impairment of available-for-sale securities* deterioro de los títulos disponibles para la venta ▲ *the fair value of available-for-sale securities* el valor razonable de los títulos disponibles para la venta

average cost

= AVCO

Average cost is the average unit cost of an inventory, within cost accounting calculated by dividing total production costs by the number of total output units or, within stock valuation, by dividing total stock value during a period by the number of units in stock.

coste medio

▲ *average cost calculation* cálculo del coste medio ▲ *calculate average cost* calcular el coste medio

average cost formula

→ weighted average cost formula

average cost method

→ weighted average cost formula

average exchange rate

→ average rate of exchange

average price

The average price is the price paid on average for a unit calculated as total costs divided by the total number of units.

precio medio

▲ *a representative average price* un precio medio representativo ▲ *acquired at an average price of 6.2 times EBITA* adquirido a un precio medio de 6,2 veces el EBITA ▲ *annual average price* precio medio anual ▲ *determination of an average price* determinación de un precio medio

average rate method US

The average rate method is a currency translation method under which all income statement items are translated at weighted average exchange rates, because it is impractical to apply the different current exchange rates at the various dates when the many revenue and expense items are recognised.

método del tipo de cambio medio

▲ *use the average rate method* utilizar el método del tipo de cambio medio

SOURCE SFAS 52

⇛ current rate method

average rate of exchange

= average exchange rate

The average rate of exchange is an average that is calculated over a specific period for one or more exchange rates.

tipo de cambio medio

▲ *calculate the average rate of exchange* calcular el tipo de cambio medio ▲ *determine the average rate of exchange* determinar el tipo de cambio medio ▲ *the average rate of exchange during the year* el tipo de cambio medio durante el año ▲ *the weighted average rate of exchange for the year* el tipo de cambio medio ponderado durante el año ▲ *use a weighted average rate of exchange* utilizar un tipo de cambio medio ponderado

avoidable cost

Avoidable costs are costs that are not incurred if the activity to which they relate is scaled down or discontinued.

coste de subactividad

▲ *identify the avoidable costs* identificar los costes de subactividad ▲ *the avoidable costs of the project* los costes de subactividad del proyecto

B

B

B

B+

B+ is the credit rating B modified by a plus used by the credit rating agency Standard & Poor's. The rating B states that adverse business, financial, or economic conditions will likely impair the capacity or willingness of the enterprise to meet its financial commitments, and that the obligation is more vulnerable to nonpayment than obligations rated BB. The ratings from below BBB –are speculative– grade ratings. Ratings from AA to CCC may be modified by the addition of a plus or a minus sign to show relative standing within the major rating categories.

B+

▲ *assign a B+ rating* calificar con un rating de B+ ▲ *receive a B+ rating* recibir un rating de **B**

1 The rating B used by the credit rating agencies Moody's and Standard & Poor's states that adverse business, financial, or economic conditions will likely impair the capacity or willingness of the enterprise to meet its financial commitments, and that the obligation is more vulnerable to nonpayment than obligations rated Ba or BB. The ratings from below Baa3 (Moody's) or BBB- (Standard & Poor's) are speculative-grade ratings. S&P ratings from AA to CCC may be modified by the addition of a plus or a minus sign to show relative standing within the major rating categories, while Moody's applies the figures 1, 2 or 3 for Aa to B ratings.

B

▲ *assign a B rating* calificar con un rating B ▲ *rating B* rating B ▲ *receive a B rating* recibir un rating B

2 The letter 'B' is applied for differentiation between shares in share classes.

B

▲ *redeem B shares at par* rescatar acciones de clase B a la par ▲ *share class B* acción de clase B

B share

= class B share

A B share is an ordinary share carrying other rights than A shares. Usually, B shares have less voting rights, e.g. 10 times less votes per share than A shares.

acción de clase B

▲ *redeem B shares* rescatar acciones de clase B ▲ *redemption of B shares* rescate de acciones de clase B ▲ *subscribe for B shares* suscribir acciones de clase B ▲ *subscribe for new B shares at a discount to the market price* suscribir acciones nuevas de clase B con descuento sobre el valor de mercado

⇛ A share, preference share, preferred stock, share class

B1

B1 is a notch on the credit rating agency Moody's rating scale for long-term debt ratings. B1 is a speculative-grade rating and signifies that the debt lacks characteristics of a desirable investment.

B1

▲ *assign a B1 rating* calificar con un rating B1 ▲ *receive a B1 rating* recibir un rating B1

B2

B2 is a notch on the credit rating agency Moody's rating scale for long-term debt ratings. B2 is a speculative-grade rating and signifies that the debt lacks characteristics of a desirable investment.

B2

▲ *assign a B2 rating* calificar con un rating B2 ▲ *receive a B2 rating* recibir un rating B2

B3

B3 is a notch on the credit rating agency Moody's rating scale for long-term debt ratings. B3 is a speculative-grade rating and signifies that the debt lacks characteristics of a desirable investment.

B3

▲ *assign a B3 rating* calificar con un rating B3 ▲ *receive a B3 rating* recibir un rating B3

Ba

Ba signifies speculative-grade rating and is used by the credit rating agency Moody's for long-term debt ratings.

Ba

▲ *assign a Ba rating* calificar con un rating de Ba ▲ *receive a Ba rating* recibir un rating de Ba

Ba1

Ba1 is a notch on the credit rating agency Moody's rating scale for long-term debt ratings, classified as the highest speculative grade meaning that this debt has speculative elements.

Ba1

▲ *a credit rating of Ba1 with a Stable Outlook* un rating crediticio de Ba1 con Stable Outlook ▲ *achieve a Ba1 credit rating* obtener un rating crediticio de Ba1

Ba2

Ba2 is a notch on the credit rating agency Moody's rating scale for long-term debt ratings classifying this debt as having speculative elements.

Ba2

▲ *assign a Ba2 rating* calificar con un rating Ba2 ▲ *receive a Ba2 rating* recibir un rating Ba2

Ba3

Ba3 is a notch on the credit rating agency Moody's rating scale for long-term debt ratings classifying this debt as having speculative elements.

Ba3

▲ *assign a Ba3 rating* calificar con un rating Ba3 ▲ *receive a Ba3 rating* recibir un rating Ba3

Baa

Baa signifies investment-grade rating and is used by the credit rating agency Moody's for long-term debt ratings. The lowest investment-grade rating is Baa3, and the highest speculative-grade rating is Ba1.

Baa

▲ *assign a Baa rating* calificar con un rating de Baa ▲ *receive a Baa rating* recibir un rating de Baa

Baa1

Baa1 is a notch on the credit rating agency Moody's rating scale for long-term debt ratings classified as medium-grade. The lowest investment-grade rating is Baa3, and the highest speculative-grade rating is Ba1.

Baa1

▲ *assign a Baa1 rating* calificar con un rating Baa1 ▲ *receive a Baa1 rating* recibir un rating Baa1

Baa2

Baa2 is a notch on the credit rating agency Moody's rating scale for long-term debt ratings classified as medium-grade. The lowest investment-grade rating is Baa3, and the highest speculative-grade rating is Ba1.

Baa2

▲ *assign a Baa2 rating* calificar con un rating Baa2 ▲ *receive a Baa2 rating* recibir un rating Baa2

Baa3

Baa3 is a notch on the credit rating agency Moody's rating scale for long-term debt ratings classified as medium-grade. The lowest investment-grade rating is Baa3, and the highest speculative-grade rating is Ba1.

Baa3

▲ *assign a Baa3 rating* calificar con un rating Baa3 ▲ *receive a Baa3 rating* recibir un rating Baa3

back charge

A back charge is the invoicing back to another party costs incurred or expenses for work performed by the party receiving the invoice. For instance, general contractors will back charge subcontractors for expenses relating to repair or damage.

recargo

▲ *make a back charge* facturar un recargo

back pay

Back pay is money an employer owes to workers for work already done, e.g. to cover a wage increase in the past.

atrasos

NOTE Always plural in Spanish accounting texts

▲ *the accounting treatment of back pay* el tratamiento contable de los atrasos ▲ *the total back pay* los atrasos totales

backflush costing

Backflush costing is a costing system under which the recording of costs-rather than being made sequentially through the stages of direct materials purchase, production, completion and sale - is deferred and delayed until the products have reached the stage of sale as finished goods at which time the budgeted or standard costs are allocated backwards through the recording system, in this way "flushing out" the manufacturing costs of the products.

NOTE Backflush costing is typically used in just-in-time production systems where inventories are at a low level.

sistema de coste retroactivo

sistema de coste de efecto retardado

▲ *apply backflush costing* aplicar un sistema de coste retroactivo ▲ *use a backflush costing approach* usar un sistema de coste retroactivo

⇛ just-in-time production system

background information

Background information is information or data about a specific issue, and it is provided in order to enlighten and for further understanding. Background information may concern one or more persons, an enterprise or an event.

antecedente

= información previa

▲ *background information on* antecedentes de ▲ *gather background information* obtener información previa ▲ *use something as background information* usar algo como antecedente

bad debt

A sum of money that is legally owed to an enterprise but has become impossible to collect from the debtor is called a bad debt. The bad debt is treated as a loss.

fallido

= impagado

▲ *a change in the estimate of the amount of bad debts* un cambio en la cantidad estimada de fallidos ▲ *bad debt allowance* provisionar fallidos ▲ *the real level of bad debts* el nivel actual de fallidos

badwill

→ negative goodwill

balance[1] *noun*

1 = account balance

A balance is the net amount or amount remaining after part has been taken away, i.e. the difference between debits and credits in an account.

saldo

▲ *a balance not written down* un saldo no amortizado ▲ *a negative balance* un saldo negativo ▲ *a positive balance* un saldo positivo ▲ *balance at 1 January 2005* saldo a 1 de enero de 2005 ▲ *balance brought forward* saldo previsto ▲ *closing balance* saldo de cierre ▲ *equity balances* saldos de capital ▲ *equity balances recognised in the consolidated financial statements* saldos de capital reflejados en los estados financieros consolidados ▲ *opening balance* saldo de apertura ▲ *the balance of accumulated profit or loss at the beginning of the period* el saldo de la cuenta de pérdidas y ganancias a principios del periodo ▲ *the balance of retained earnings at the beginning of the period* el saldo de los resultados no distribuidos al inicio del periodo

2 = account

A balance is an amount owed, i.e. an outstanding debt payable.

deuda

▲ *a comprehensive analysis of related party balances* un análisis global de las deudas de las partes implicadas ▲ *balances in foreign currencies* deudas en divisas extranjeras ▲ *balances with associated enterprises* deudas con empresas asociadas ▲ *balances with other banks* deudas con otros bancos ▲ *balances with the central bank* deudas con el banco central ▲ *elimination of intra-group balances* eliminación de las deudas intragrupo ▲ *identification of outstanding balances* identificación de las deudas pendientes de pago ▲ *intercompany balances* deudas entre empresas ▲ *intra-group balances* deudas intragrupo

▲ *outstanding balances between an entity and its related parties* deudas pendientes de pago entre una entidad y las partes implicadas

balance[2] *verb*

To balance means to reconcile the debit and the credit side of an account to determine the balance.

saldar

▲ *balance off* saldar ▲ *balance the books* saldar las cuentas

balance on the operating equipment account

The balance on the operating equipment account shows the difference between the debit entries and the credit entries on the account.

saldo de la cuenta de explotación

▲ *additions relating to the balance on the operating equipment account* sumas del saldo de la cuenta de explotación ▲ *balance on the operating equipment account at the beginning of the year* saldo de la cuenta de explotación al inicio del ejercicio ▲ *balance on the operating equipment account at the end of the year* saldo de la cuenta de explotación al final del año ▲ *be included in the balance on the operating equipment account* se incluye en el saldo de la cuenta de explotación ▲ *disposals relating to the balance on the operating equipment account* disposición del saldo de la cuenta de explotación

balance scorecard

→ balanced scorecard

balance sheet

= statement of financial position US

The balance sheet is a statement of the enterprise's assets, equity and liabilities at the balance sheet date. The statement is a status report estimating the enterprise's assets, equity and liabilities as a snapshot at a certain date.

balance

▲ *a comparative balance sheet as of the end of the immediately preceding financial year* un balance comparativo al final del año económico inmediatamente anterior ▲ *a condensed balance sheet* un balance consolidado ▲ *abridged balance sheet* balance abreviado ▲ *account form balance sheet* balance con forma de cuenta ▲ *account-format balance sheet* balance con formato de cuenta ▲ *balance sheet amounts* saldos del balance ▲ *balance sheet as at 31 December 2005* balance a 31 de diciembre de 2005 ▲ *balance sheet as of the end of the current interim period* balance al final del periodo interino actual ▲ *balance sheet at year-end* balance a final de año ▲ *balance sheet in report form* balance formalizado ▲ *balance sheet lay-out* formato del balance ▲ *consolidated balance sheet* balance consolidado ▲ *derecognise in the balance sheet* eliminar del balance ▲ *disclose on the face of the balance sheet* dar a conocer a la vista del balance ▲ *eliminate from the balance sheet* eliminar del balance ▲ *extensive balance sheet disclosures* divulgación extensa del balance ▲ *group balance sheet* balance del grupo ▲ *horizontal balance sheet* balance horizontal ▲ *horizontal balance sheet format* formato de balance horizontal ▲ *incorporate an item in the balance sheet* incorporar una partida al balance ▲ *net liability recognised in balance sheet* pasivo exigible reconocido en el balance ▲ *notes to the balance sheet* anotaciones al balance ▲ *off balance sheet items* partidas fuera de balance ▲ *offset in the balance sheet* compensar en el balance ▲ *present in the balance sheet* figurar en el balance ▲ *recognise as assets and liabilities in the balance sheet* reconocer como activos y pasivos en el balance ▲ *recognise in the balance sheet* reconocer en el balance ▲ *recognise initially as a separate item in the balance sheet* reconocer inicialmente como una partida separada en el balance ▲ *report form balance sheet* balance formalizado ▲ *statement-format balance sheet* balance normalizado ▲ *the changes in the amounts recognised in the balance sheet* los cambios en las cantidades reconocidas en el balance ▲ *the date of the balance sheet* la fecha del balance ▲ *vertical balance sheet* balance vertical ▲ *vertical balance sheet format* formato de balance vertical

⇛ statement of financial position

balance sheet account

= revenue and expenditure account

A balance sheet account records the entries concerning the enterprise's assets and liabilities with resulting balances and forms the basis of the balance sheet.

cuenta de balance

≠ cuenta de explotación, cuenta de ingresos y gastos

▲ *entries to balance sheet accounts* anotaciones en las cuentas de balance

balance sheet at year-end

= closing balance sheet, year-end balance sheet

The balance sheet at year-end is the balance sheet with all items at the last day in the financial year.

balance final

= balance al cierre

▲ *account for in the balance sheet at year end* reflejar en el balance final ▲ *consolidated balance sheet at year-end* balance consolidado al cierre ▲ *record in the balance sheet at year-end* registrar en el balance final

balance sheet date

The balance sheet date is the closing date of the financial year and the statement of assets, equity and liabilities.

fecha de cierre del balance

= fecha de cierre, fecha de final de ejercicio

▲ *adjusting events after the balance sheet date* ajustes por hechos posteriores a la fecha de cierre ▲ *after the balance sheet date* después de la fecha de cierre del balance ▲ *as of the balance sheet date* como si fuera la fecha de cierre ▲ *at each balance sheet date* en cada una de las fechas de cierre del balance ▲ *at the balance sheet date* a fecha de cierre del balance ▲ *at the last balance sheet date* en la última fecha de cierre del balance ▲ *change the balance sheet date* cambiar la fecha de cierre del balance ▲ *changes in an enterprise's equity between two balance sheet dates* cambios en el patrimonio de la empresa entre dos fechas de cierre ▲ *events after the balance sheet date* hechos posteriores a la fecha de cierre del balance ▲ *exist at the balance sheet date* existir a fecha de cierre del balance ▲ *immediately prior to a balance sheet date* inmediatamente anterior a la fecha de cierre del balance ▲ *non-adjusting events after the balance sheet date* hechos no ajustables después de la fecha de cierre del balance ▲ *non-current receivables due within 5 years from the balance sheet date* derechos de cobro no corrientes con vencimiento dentro de los cinco años siguientes a la fecha de cierre del balance ▲ *potential ordinary shares outstanding at the balance sheet date* acciones ordinarias no emitidas a fecha de cierre del balance ▲ *the balance sheet date for the joint financial statements* la fecha de cierre para el total de estados financieros ▲ *the balance sheet date or the period covered by the financial statements* la fecha de cierre del balance o el periodo comprendido por los estados financieros ▲ *the last annual balance sheet date* la última fecha de cierre del balance ▲ *the value at the balance sheet date* el valor a fecha de cierre del balance ▲ *up to the balance sheet date* hasta la fecha de cierre del balance ▲ *updating of disclosures about conditions at the balance sheet date* actualización de las divulgaciones de las condiciones a fecha de cierre del balance ▲ *within a reasonable period after the balance sheet date* en un periodo razonable posterior a la fecha de cierre del balance ▲ *within twelve months of the balance sheet date* en los doce meses siguientes a la fecha de cierre de balance

balance sheet entry

A balance sheet entry is made in connection with the recording of a transaction in one of the balance sheet items.

entrada en el balance

▲ *make a balance sheet entry* crear una entrada en el balance

balance sheet format

A balance sheet format is a presentation form and layout of a statement of assets, liabilities and equity prescribed by legislation or accounting standards, e.g. the UK Companies Act, the Danish Financial Statements Act, IFRS and FASB.

formato de balance
▲ *a uniform balance sheet format* un formato de balance uniforme
⇛ balance sheet, format, horizontal format

balance sheet item
The balance sheet is sub-divided into balance sheet items under assets, equity and liabilities. The balance sheet is divided into principal items and into items preceded by Roman numerals.
partida del balance
▲ *balance sheet items adjusted in accordance with US GAAP* partidas del balance ajustadas según los criterios contables generalmente aceptados en Estados Unidos ▲ *currency translation adjustment of balance sheet items* ajustes por conversión monetaria de las partidas del balance ▲ *hedging of balance sheet items* cobertura de las partidas del balance ▲ *measurement of balance sheet items* valoración de las partidas del balance ▲ *monetary balance sheet items* partidas monetarias del balance ▲ *non-monetary balance sheet items* partidas no monetarias del balance ▲ *notes to balance sheet items* anotaciones a las partidas del balance ▲ *translate balance sheet items at the closing rate* conversión de las partidas del balance al tipo de cierre ▲ *translation of balance sheet items* conversión de las partidas del balance

balance sheet liability method
→ balance-sheet liability method

balance sheet sum
The balance sheet sum is the total assets and liabilities of an enterprise at a specific balance sheet date.
suma del balance
= total del balance
▲ *the balance sheet sum at year-end* la suma del balance a final de año ▲ *the decrease of the balance sheet sum* el descenso de la suma del balance ▲ *the total growth of the balance sheet sum* el crecimiento total de la suma del balance
⇛ sum

balance sheet total
The total balance sheet amount at year-end, which is the sum of all assets and the sum of all liabilities and equity present in the enterprise at the balance sheet date, is referred to as the balance sheet total. The balance sheet total for assets will always be equivalent to the balance sheet total of equity and liabilities.
total del balance
= suma del balance
▲ *aggregate balance sheet total* calcular el total del balance ▲ *increase the balance sheet total* aumentar el total del balance

balance sheet value
The balance sheet value is the value at which an asset is recognised in the balance sheet.
valor en el balance
▲ *balance sheet value at 31 December 2005* valor en el balance a 31 de diciembre de 2005 ▲ *calculation of balance sheet values* cálculo de los valores en el balance

balance-sheet liability method
≠ income-statement liability method IAS/IFRS
The balance-sheet liability method implies that the tax liabilities and the tax expenses are calculated on the basis of the differences between the carrying amount of an asset or liability in the balance sheet and its tax base (temporary differences).
método de la deuda basado en el balance
= método del pasivo basado en el balance
≠ método de la deuda basado en resultados
▲ *account for using the balance-sheet liability method* justificar el uso del método de la deuda basado en el balance ▲ *measure under the balance-sheet liability method* medir según el método de la deuda basado en el balance ▲ *use the balance-sheet liability method* usar el método de la deuda basado en el balance
⇛ temporary difference

balanced scorecard
A balanced scorecard is a management system that measures the performance of a business. It provides a method of balancing financial and operating measures as well as linking performance to rewards while recognising the diversity of strategic goals.
cuadro de mando integral
▲ *use a balanced scorecard* usar un cuadro de mando integral

bank

A bank is a financial institution that accepts deposits, makes loans and acts as an intermediary by channelling money into lending activities or investments and by providing financial services for its customers.

banco

= entidad financiera, institución financiera

▲ *advances given by the bank* anticipos concedidos por el banco ▲ *appoint a bank agent* nombrar un agente bancario ▲ *assess the liquidity of the bank* valorar la liquidez del banco ▲ *assess the performance of the separate activities of a bank* valorar la rentabilidad de las actividades separadas de un banco ▲ *bank borrowings* créditos bancarios ▲ *bank debt* deuda bancaria ▲ *bank deposit* depósito bancario ▲ *bank overdrafts* descubiertos ▲ *bank reconciliation* conciliación bancaria ▲ *cash and balances with the central bank* el disponible en el banco central ▲ *cash at bank* dinero en efectivo en el banco ▲ *cash at bank and in hand* dinero en efectivo en el banco y en mano ▲ *deposits from other banks* depósitos de otros bancos ▲ *disclosures in the financial statements of banks and similar financial institutions* publicaciones en los informes financieros de los bancos e instituciones financieras similares ▲ *in the ordinary course of the bank's business* en el transcurso ordinario de la actividad bancaria ▲ *placements with, and loans and advances to, other banks* depósitos, préstamos y anticipos a otros bancos ▲ *receivables from a bank* cuentas bancarias ▲ *the acceptance and repayment of demand deposits of a bank* la aceptación y reembolso de los depósitos bancarios a la vista ▲ *the adequacy of the bank's capital* el coeficiente de solvencia del banco ▲ *the bank's own trading position* la posición comercial propia del banco ▲ *the financial position and performance of the bank* la situación financiera y la rentabilidad del banco ▲ *the funds available to the bank* los fondos disponibles en el banco ▲ *the level of risk to which the bank is exposed* el nivel de riesgo al que se expone el banco ▲ *the nature and amount of off balance sheet transactions undertaken by a bank* la naturaleza y cantidad de las transacciones fuera del balance ▲ *the principal types of expenses arising from the operations of a bank* los principales tipos de gastos resultantes de las operaciones bancarias ▲ *the principal types of income arising from the operations of a bank* los principales tipos de ingresos resultantes de las operaciones bancarias ▲ *the risks associated with the operations of the bank* los riesgos asociados con las operaciones bancarias ▲ *the special characteristics of the operations of a bank* las características especiales de las operaciones bancarias

Bank Accounts Directive

The Bank Accounts Directive is a directive adopted by the European Council on the annual and consolidated accounts of certain types of companies, banks and other financial institutions and insurance undertakings.

Directiva de Cuentas Bancarias

▲ *Article 39.3 of the Bank Accounts Directive* El artículo 39.3 de la Directiva de Cuentas Bancarias ▲ *comply with the national transposition of the EU Bank Accounts Directive (BAD) (86/635/EEC)* cumplir con la trasposición nacional de la Directiva de Cuentas Bancarias del Banco Europeo (86/635/CEE) ▲ *reference to Article 23 of the Bank Accounts Directive (86/635/EEC)* referencia al artículo 23 de la Directiva de Cuentas Bancarias (86/635/CEE)

bank accounts directive

The bank accounts directive is a directive adopted by the European Council on the annual and consolidated accounts of certain types of companies, banks and other financial institutions and insurance undertakings.

directiva de cuentas bancarias

▲ *comply with the national transposition of the EU Bank Accounts Directive (BAD)*

(86/635/EEC) cumplir con la trasposición de la Directiva de Cuentas Bancarias del Banco Europeo (86/635/CEE) al ordenamiento nacional ▲ *reference to Article 23 of the Bank Accounts Directive (86/635/EEC)* referencia al artículo 23 de la Directiva de Cuentas Bancarias (86/635/CEE)

bank balance
A bank balance is an amount available on a deposit or checking account with a bank.
saldo bancario
▲ *cash and bank balances* dinero en efectivo y saldos bancarios ▲ *interest on bank balances etc.* interés de los saldos bancarios, etc.

bank borrowings US
Bank borrowings refer to amounts that have been raised with a bank usually in the form of interest-bearing loans.
préstamos bancarios
▲ *bank borrowings payable in foreign currencies* préstamos bancarios a pagar en divisas ▲ *changes in bank borrowings* modificaciones en los préstamos bancarios ▲ *current bank borrowings* préstamos bancarios corrientes ▲ *fixed-rate bank borrowings* préstamos bancarios con interés fijo ▲ *floating-rate bank borrowings* préstamos bancarios con interés variable ▲ *non-current bank borrowings* préstamos bancarios no corrientes ▲ *reduction of bank borrowings* disminución de los préstamos bancarios ▲ *security provided for bank borrowings* garantía ofrecida por los préstamos bamcarias ▲ *US dollar denominated bank borrowings* préstamos bancarios nominados en dólares

bank deposit
A bank deposit is money paid into a bank account and is part of an enterprise's cash.
depósito bancario
= depósito
▲ *a large bank deposit* un depósito bancario cuantioso ▲ *make a bank deposit* efectuar un depósito bancario ▲ *short-term bank deposit* depósito bancario a corto plazo

bank loan
= bank borrowings
A loan that has been raised with a bank is called a bank loan.
préstamo bancario
currencies préstamos bancarios a pagar en divisas ▲ *fixed-rate bank loan* préstamo bancario a un tipo fijo ▲ *floating-rate bank loan* préstamo bancario a un tipo variable ▲ *guarantee a bank loan* avalar un préstamo bancario ▲ *ordinary bank loans* préstamos bancarios ordinarios ▲ *other bank loans* otros préstamos bancarios ▲ *provide guarantee for a bank loan* aportar avales para un préstamo bancario ▲ *raising of bank loan* obtención de un préstamo bancario ▲ *repayment of bank loan* devolución de un préstamo bancario ▲ *secured bank loans* préstamos bancarios garantizados

bank loans and overdrafts UK
Bank loans and overdrafts is an item under creditors: amounts falling due within one year or under creditors: amounts falling due after more than one year –depending on whether short-or long-term– in the balance sheet according to the Companies Act 1985 required report format.
préstamos y descubiertos
NOTE In Spain bank loans and overdrafts are not usually regulated together.
▲ *long-term bank loans and overdrafts* préstamos y descubiertos a largo plazo ▲ *lower the effective interest rate on bank loans and overdrafts* reducir el tipo de interés aplicado a los préstamos y descubiertos ▲ *secured bank loans and overdrafts* préstamos y descubiertos garantizados ▲ *short-term bank loans and overdrafts* préstamos y descubiertos a corto plazo ▲ *unsecured bank loans and overdrafts* préstamos y descubiertos sin garantizar

bank overdraft
A bank overdraft is a loan facility provided by a bank to a customer allowing a custormer to overdraw a cheque account by an agreed amount for a fixed period against an interest charge on the debit balance.
descubierto
= descubierto bancario
▲ *bank overdraft withdrawals* retiradas de dinero en descubierto ▲ *bank overdrafts which*

are repayable on demand descubiertos reintegrables a petición ▲ *include bank overdrafts as a component of cash and cash equivalents* incluir los descubiertos como un componente del efectivo y otros activos líquidos equivalentes ▲ *interest on bank overdrafts* interés de los descubiertos ▲ *payment into a bank overdraft account* pago en una cuenta en descubierto ▲ *security for a bank overdraft* aval para un descubierto bancario

banker

A banker is a person or business performing banking activities that the entreprise uses when doing bank transactions or raising capital.

banca

NOTE Spanish accountants do not mention the person who performs banking activities. They typically refer to the institutions.

▲ *banker's acceptance* aceptación de la banca ▲ *banker's credit* crédito de la banca ▲ *banker's draft* giro bancario ▲ *banker's opinion* opinión bancaria ▲ *banker's reference* referencia bancaria ▲ *our bankers* nuestra banca

banking

Banking is the principal business activities of a bank.

banca

NOTE If used as adjective, the Spanish equivalent must be 'bancario' or 'de la banca'

▲ *banking arrangements* acuerdos de la banca ▲ *banking business* negocio bancario ▲ *banking operations* operaciones de la banca ▲ *banking secrecy* secreto bancario ▲ *general banking risks* riesgos bancarios generales ▲ *local banking practices* prácticas bancarias locales

banking activity

The banking activity of a bank comprises that part of its revenue that is attributable to business transactions with private and corporate customers.

actividad bancaria

▲ *cost/income ratio for banking activities* ratio coste/beneficio de las actividades bancarias ▲ *foreign banking activities* actividades bancarias en el extranjero ▲ *net interest income from banking activities, etc.* ingresos netos por intereses provenientes de las actividades bancarias

bankruptcy US

Bankruptcy is the process whereby an insolvent individual or company is made bankrupt and the estate is administered for the benefit of the creditors.

NOTE In the UK the term 'bankruptcy' only applies to individuals, sole proprietors and partnerships, but not to companies.

quiebra

= bancarrota

NOTE The Spanish term 'concursal' is a synonym of 'quiebra' and 'bancarrota' in Spanish legal discourse.

▲ *adjudication of bankruptcy* declaración judicial de quiebra ▲ *bankruptcy court* juzgado concursal ▲ *bankruptcy estate* masa de la quiebra ▲ *bankruptcy filing* solicitud de quiebra ▲ *bankruptcy fraud* quiebra fraudulenta ▲ *bankruptcy order* auto judicial declarativo de quiebra ▲ *bankruptcy petition* solicitud de declaración de quiebra ▲ *bankruptcy proceedings* procedimientos de la ley concursal ▲ *bankruptcy remote corporation* sociedad instrumental en la titulización ▲ *bankruptcy trustee* administrador concursal de la quiebra ▲ *in bankruptcy* en quiebra ▲ *the bankruptcy of a customer* la bancarrota de un cliente ▲ *the US Bankruptcy Code* la Ley Concursal Española

bankruptcy filing US

A bankruptcy filing is a petition to a court to declare a person, company or other business enterprise bankrupt.

solicitud de declaración de quiebra

= solicitud de procedimiento concursal

▲ *as of the bankruptcy filing* desde la solicitud de declaración de quiebra

⇛ bankruptcy petition

bankruptcy petition

A bankruptcy petition is a request to a court to declare a person, company or other business enterprise bankrupt.

NOTE In the UK the term 'bankruptcy petition' only applies to individuals, sole proprietors and partnerships, but not to companies.

petición de declaración de quiebra

= solicitud de procedimiento concursal

▲ *present a bankruptcy petition* presentar una petición de declaración de quiebra

⇛ bankruptcy filing

bargain price

A bargain price is the list price or suggested retail price for a product or service less a discount, price reduction or rebate.

precio rebajado

▲ *at a bargain price* a un precio rebajado ▲ *at the bargain price of €6000* al precio rebajado de 6.000 euros. ▲ *purchase the property at a bargain price* comprar la propiedad a un precio rebajado

barrier

= obstacle

A barrier is an obstacle impeding free movement, blocking access or restricting progress.

barrera

= obstáculo

▲ *barriers to entry* barreras a la entrada ▲ *barriers to trade* barreras al comercio ▲ *economic barriers* barreras económicas ▲ *external barriers* barreras externas ▲ *internal barriers* barreras internas ▲ *operational barriers* barreras operacionales ▲ *overcome a barrier* superar una barreras ▲ *remove barriers to the admission of securities to regulated markets* eliminar las barreras a la admisión de valores en los mercados regulados ▲ *structural barriers* barreras estructurales ▲ *trade barriers* barreras comerciales

base

To base on is to use as a basis or background for something.

basar

▲ *base the consolidated financial statements on estimated figures* basar los estados financieros consolidados en cifras estimadas ▲ *based on an assessment of* basado en la valoración de ▲ *being based on the International Financial Reporting Standards* se están basando en las Normas Internacionales de Información Financiera

base stock

The base stock is the minimum inventory level necessary to maintain effective and continuous operations.

stock base

= inventario base, stock mínimo

▲ *the base stock method* el método de stock base ▲ *use base stock for income tax purposes* usar el método de stock base a efectos fiscales

base stock method

= normal stock method

The base stock method is an inventory valuation method in which the base amount of goods is valued at acquisition cost; this method is also referred to as the normal stock method.

método de stock base

= método del inventario mínimo, método del stock mínimo

▲ *use the base stock method* usar el método de stock base

basic earnings per share

= basic EPS, BEPS

≠ diluted earnings per share

Basic earnings per share is a financial ratio defined as the profit for the accounting period attributable to ordinary shareholders divided by the average number of ordinary shares outstanding for the same period. This ratio is applied for valuation of the share and the enterprise's ability to generate profit to the owners and is calculated on a non-diluted basis as it disregards any dilutive convertible bonds or share options.

ganancias básicas por acción

= beneficios básicos por acción, ganancias por acción básicas, PER básico

▲ *calculation of basic earnings per share* cálculo de las ganancias básicas por acción ▲ *consolidated basic earnings per share* ganancias básicas por acción consolidadas ▲ *determination of basic earnings per share* determinación de las ganancias básicas por acción ▲ *disclose basic earnings per share* publicar las ganancias básicas por acción ▲ *have a dilutive effect on the basic earnings per share* tener un efecto de dilución sobre las ganancias básicas por acción ▲ *included in the computation of basic earnings per share* incluido en el cómputo de las ganancias básicas por acción ▲ *maximise the dilution of basic earnings per share* maximizar la dilución de las ganancias básicas por acción ▲ *presentation of basic earnings per share* presentación de las ganancias básicas por acción ▲ *the objective of basic earnings per share information* el objetivo de la información sobre ganancias básicas por acción

basic EPS

= basic earnings per share

Basic EPS is the abbreviation for basic earnings per share, which is a financial ratio defined as the profit for the accounting period attributable to ordinary shareholders divided by the average number of ordinary shares outstanding for the same period. This ratio is applied for valuation of the share and the enterprise's ability to generate profit to the owners and is calculated on a non-diluted basis as it disregards any dilutive convertible bonds or share options.

ganancia básica por acción

= beneficios básicos por acción, ganancias por acción básicas, PER básico

▲ *basic EPS calculations* cálculo de la ganancia básica por acción ▲ *calculate basic EPS* calcular la ganancia básica por acción ▲ *restatement of previous years' basic EPS* actualización de la ganancia básica por acción de los años anteriores

basic values

= standards of value

The basic values of an enterprise are the values that must be present in the work performed and services rendered by that enterprise. Basic values are often presented in a mission statement and include such values as timeliness, care, quality, environmental policy as well as cost and product optimisation.

valores fundamentales

▲ *common basic values* valores fundamentales comunes ▲ *live up to the agreed basic values* estar a la altura de los valores fundamentales acordados ▲ *the basic values of the enterprise* los valores fundamentales de la empresa

⇛ corporate mission

basis

A basis is a foundation, background or starting point for something.

base

▲ *a fundamental change in the basis of financial reporting* un cambio radical en la base del informe financiero ▲ *a suitable basis* una base adecuada ▲ *calculate cost on the basis of weighted average prices* calcular el coste en base a los precios medios ponderados ▲ *calculated on a periodic basis* calculado sobre una base periódica ▲ *cost recovery basis* base de recuperación de costes ▲ *fail to report on a timely basis* no publicarse en una base adecuada ▲ *financial basis* base financiera ▲ *form a basis* establecer una base ▲ *measurement basis* base de cálculo ▲ *on a long-term basis* a largo plazo ▲ *on a rational and consistent basis* sobre una base racional y consistente ▲ *on a systematic basis* sobre una base sistemática ▲ *on a timely basis* sobre una base adecuada ▲ *on the basis of* sobre la base de ▲ *primary basis of accounting* base primaria de la contabilidad ▲ *recognise lease payments as an expense on a straight-line basis* reconocer los pagos por alquiler como un gasto según el método lineal ▲ *reported on a net basis* publicado en una base neta ▲ *the basis for allocation of costs between segments* la base para el reparto de costes entre sectores ▲ *the basis on which the financial statements are prepared* la base conforme a la cual se preparan los estados financieros ▲ *the basis used to revalue the assets* la base usada para revalorizar los activos ▲ *write down to net realisable value on an item by item basis* anotar a valor realizable neto partida por partida

basis for decisions

The basis for decisions is typically a collection of data, calculations, statements etc., that ensure that the decision to be made will be correct and advantageous.

base para la toma de decisiones

▲ *constitute a qualified basis for decisions* establecer una base cualificada para la toma de decisiones

basis of accounting

= accounting basis

The basis of accounting is a method of recognising revenues and expenses.

principio de contabilidad

= base contable, base de la contabilidad

▲ *a fundamental change in the basis of accounting* un cambio radical en la base de la contabilidad ▲ *disclosure of bases of accounting* divulgación de los principios de contabilidad ▲ *primary basis of accounting* base de la contabilidad primaria ▲ *the accrual basis of accounting* el principio del devengo ▲ *the going concern basis of accounting* el principio de empresa en funcionamiento ▲ *the historical cost basis of accounting* el principio de coste histórico ▲ *the original basis of accounting* el principio original de la contabilidad ▲ *the primary basis of accounting* el principio primario de la contabilidad

basis of advance depreciation

The basis of advance depreciation is the aggregate calculated acquisition cost exceeding a determined basic amount. If the acquisition cost is lower than the basic amount of a particular asset, advance depreciation is not allowed of that asset.

principio de depreciación acelerada

▲ *provide for advance depreciation of 10% of the basis of advance depreciation* establecer un 10% del precio de adquisición como principio de depreciación acelerada

⇛ advance depreciation

basis of amortisation UK

1 = amortisation basis UK, amortization base US

The basis of amortisation or amortisable amount means the historical cost of an amortisable intangible asset or other revalued amount substituted for historical cost, less the residual value and any write-downs.

base de amortización

▲ *basis of amortisation for tax purposes* base de amortización a efectos fiscales ▲ *determination of the basis of amortisation* determinación de la base de amortización ▲ *measurement of the basis of amortisation* cálculo de la base de amortización ▲ *the basis of amortisation of the asset* la base de amortización del activo ▲ *the buyer's basis of amortisation* la base de amortización del adquirente ▲ *the enterprise's basis of amortisation* la base de amortización de la empresa ▲ *the future basis of amortisation* la base de amortización futura ▲ *the reduced basis of amortisation* la base de amortización reducida

⇛ straight-line method

2 = amortisation method UK, basis of amortization US, method of amortisation UK

The basis of amortisation is the method of amortisation chosen to reflect the depletion of an intangible asset over its estimated economic life in the financial statements. Normally, the straight-line method is the most appropriate for intangible assets.

base de amortización

▲ *declining-balance basis of amortisation* base de amortización degresiva ▲ *diminishing-balance basis of amortisation* base de amortización decreciente ▲ *reducing-balance basis of amortisation* base de amortización degresiva ▲ *straight-line basis of amortisation* base de amortización constante

3 = basis of amortization US

A basis of amortisation is a method for reducing debt by paying instalments of interest and principal according to a predetermined schedule over the maturity period.

base de amortización

▲ *the basis of amortisation of mortgage credit loans* la base de amortización de los préstamos hipotecarios

basis of amortization US

1 = amortisation basis UK, amortization base US

The basis of amortization or amortizable amount means the historical cost of an amortizable intangible asset or other revalued amount substituted for historical cost, less the residual value and any write-downs.

base de amortización

▲ *basis of amortization for tax purposes* base de amortización a efectos fiscales ▲ *determination of the basis of amortization* determinación de la base de amortización ▲ *measurement of the basis of amortization* cálculo de la base de amortización ▲ *the basis of amortization of the asset* la base de amortización del activo ▲ *the buyer's basis of amortization* la base de amortización del adquirente ▲ *the enterprise's basis of amortization* la base de amortización de la empresa ▲ *the future basis of amortization* la base de amortización futura ▲ *the reduced basis of amortization* la base reducida de amortización

2 = basis of amortisation UK, method of amortisation UK

The basis of amortization is the method of amortization chosen to reflect the depletion of an intangible asset over its estimated economic life in the financial statements. Normally, the straight-line method is the most appropriate for intangible assets.

base de amortización

▲ *change the basis of amortization* cambiar la base de amortización ▲ *disclosure of the basis of amortization for R&D* divulgación de la base de amortización para I+D ▲ *the straight line basis of amortization* la base de amortización continua

3 = basis of amortisation UK

A basis of amortization is a method for reducing debt by paying instalments of interest and principal according to a predetermined schedule over the maturity period.

base de amortización

▲ *change the basis of amortization* cambiar la base de amortización

basis of calculation

The data that form the basis of a calculation are called the basis of calculation.

base de cálculo

▲ *be part of the basis of calculation* integrar en la base de cálculo ▲ *specification of the basis of calculation* especificación de la base de cálculo

basis of comparison

The basis of comparison is the data or facts that make it possible to compare someone or something with someone or something else.

base de comparación

= criterio de comparación

▲ *establish a basis of comparison* establecer una base de comparación ▲ *form the basis of comparison* formar la base de comparación

basis of depreciation UK

= depreciable amount IAS/IFRS, depreciation base US, depreciation basis

The basis of depreciation or depreciable amount is the cost of a tangible fixed asset, or other amount substituted for cost in the financial statements, less its scrap value. In the case of depreciated assets, the depreciation charge is deducted, and in the case of assets written-up, the revaluation surplus is added.

base de amortización

= base de depreciación

▲ *basis of depreciation for tax purposes* base de amortización a efectos fiscales ▲ *determination of the basis of depreciation* determinación de la base de amortización ▲ *measurement of the basis of depreciation* cálculo de la base de amortización ▲ *the basis of depreciation of the asset* la base de amortización del activo ▲ *the buyer's basis of depreciation* la base de amortización del adquirente ▲ *the enterprise's basis of depreciation* la base de amortización de la empresa ▲ *the future basis of depreciation* la base de amortización futura

basis of measurement

A basis of measurement is a base for determining the value of an asset or a liability for recognition in the financial statements. Bases of measurement include cost, fair value, amortised cost, replacement cost and net realisable value.

criterio de valoración

▲ *a clear description of the basis of measurement* una descripción clara del criterio de valoración ▲ *a clearly described basis of measurement* un criterio de valoración bien determinado ▲ *regardless of the basis of measurement* con independencia del criterio de valoración

basis of valuation

The basis of valuation is the basis, data or value concept

used for determining the value of something, e.g. assets or property.

método de valoración

▲ *the basis of valuation of assets* el método de valoración de los activos ▲ *the basis of valuation of recognised deferred tax assets* el método de valoración de activos por impuestos diferidos reconocidos

⇛ measurement basis

basis point

One basis point is one hundredth of one percent.

punto básico

▲ *100 basis points* 100 puntos básicos

⇛ percentage point

batch

A batch is a quantity of goods regarded as an entity in that the goods in a batch have been produced under the same conditions and in the same manner and thus have identical characteristics.

lote estable

= serie

▲ *batch production* producción en serie

batch costing

Batch costing is a method or system for calculation of the total costs attributable to a particular job or batch.

sistema de coste por lote

▲ *use of batch costing* empleo del sistema de coste por lote

batch-level cost

Batch-level costs are costs incurred when a batch of a product is being produced. Such costs will depend on the number of times a batch is processed rather than on the number of units produced. Batch-level costs are e.g. costs incurred in connection with the adjustment of a machine for batch production.

coste por lote

▲ *batch-level cost per unit* coste por lote unitario ▲ *calculate batch-level costs* calcular los costes por lote

BB

BB is a credit rating used by the credit rating agency Standard & Poor's stating the obligation is less vulnerable to nonpayment than other speculative issues, but faces major ongoing uncertainties or exposure to adverse business. The ratings below BBB- are speculative-grade ratings. Ratings from AA to CCC may be modified by the addition of a plus or a minus sign to show relative standing within the major rating categories.

BB

▲ *assign a BB credit rating* calificar con un rating de solvencia crediticia BB

BBB

BBB is a credit rating used by the credit rating agency Standard & Poor's stating that adverse economic conditions or changing circumstances are more likely to lead to a weakened capacity of the enterprise to meet its financial commitments. The ratings from AAA to BBB- are investment-grade ratings. Ratings from AA to CCC may be modified by the addition of a plus or a minus sign to show relative standing within the major rating categories.

BBB

▲ *assign a BBB credit rating* calificar con un rating de solvencia crediticia BBB

bear

To bear is to carry, to have or to produce something.

cargar

= soportar

▲ *bear a loss* soportar una pérdida ▲ *bear a risk* soportar un riesgo ▲ *bear interest* cargar intereses ▲ *bear interest at the rate of 5%* cargar intereses al 5% ▲ *bear some similarity to biological transformation* se asemejan en parte a la transformación biológica ▲ *bear the cost of meeting the obligations* cargar con los costes del cumplimiento de las obligaciones ▲ *bear the costs of* cargar con los costes de ▲ *the proportion that contract costs incurred for work performed to date bear to the estimated total contract costs* la proporción que los costes contractuales incurridos por trabajo realizado hasta la fecha carga a los gastos contractuales totales estimados

bearer

A bearer is a person who is in possession of a document such as a share, bond or bill of exchange.

portador
▲ *bearer bill* cuenta del portador ▲ *bearer bond* bono al portador ▲ *bearer paper* efecto al portador ▲ *bearer security* título al portador ▲ *bearer share* acción al portador ▲ *issue to bearer* extender al portador ▲ *make out to bearer* extender al portador ▲ *payable to bearer* a pagar al portador

bearer bond
A bearer bond is a bond that is regarded as being owned by the person who has the bond in his possession.
bono al portador
▲ *issue a bearer bond* emitir un bono al portador ▲ *the owner of a bearer bond* el propietario del bono al portador

bearer share
= bearer stock US
≠ registered share
A bearer share is a share for which no register of ownership is kept. Consequently, ownership of the share belongs to the person in possession of the share certificate.
acción al portador
≠ acción nominativa
▲ *disclosure of registered or bearer shares* divulgación de acciones al portador o acciones nominativas

bearer stock US
= bearer share UK
Bearer stock is stock for which no register of ownership is kept. Consequently, ownership of the stock belongs to the person in possession of the stock certificate.
acción al portador
≠ acción nominativa
▲ *disclosure of registered or bearer stock* divulgación de acciones nominativas o acciones al portador

beginning
The start or the first phase of a period or sequence of events is referred to as the beginning.
inicio
▲ *a reconciliation of the number of shares outstanding at the beginning and at the end of the year* una conciliación del número de acciones en circulación al inicio y al final del ejercicio ▲ *at the beginning of the current period* al inicio del ejercicio actual ▲ *at the beginning of the financial year* al inicio del ejercicio ▲ *at the beginning of the period* al inicio del periodo ▲ *at the beginning of the year* al inicio del año ▲ *periods beginning on or after 1 January 2005* periodos que se inician el 1 de enero de 2005 o posteriormente ▲ *the beginning of the first IFRS reporting period* el inicio del periodo de publicación de la primera NIIF

beginning inventory
→ opening inventory

benchmark[1] *noun* <a, the, -s>
A benchmark is a standard or measurement by which an enterprise measures its organisational performance and practices against others in the same or different industries, or something used as a basis of comparison or standard of reference, such as a particular bond or interest rate.
benchmark
= índice de referencia
▲ *a stable benchmark basic interest rate* un tipo de interés básico correspondiente a un benchmark estable ▲ *external benchmarks* benchmarks externos ▲ *identification benchmarks* identificación de los benchmarks ▲ *the amount that is not attributable to changes in a benchmark interest rate* la cantidad que no se atribuye a las modificaciones en un benchmark ▲ *the benchmark cost formula* la fórmula de coste benchmark
⇛ benchmark treatment

benchmark[2] *verb* <-s, -ed, has -ed, -ing> *passive* <is -ed, was -ed>
To benchmark means to use as a reference standard for comparison, e.g. the organisational performance and practices of an enterprise with others in the same or different industries, or the performance of a bond or an interest rate.
fijar criterios comparativos
= fijar un benchmark, llevar a cabo un benchmark
▲ *benchmark the company against peers* fijar los criterios comparativos de la empresa frente a otras similares ▲ *to benchmark financial reporting* fijar criterios comparativos para realizar informes financieros

benchmark accounting policy IAS/IFRS

= benchmark treatment IAS/IFRS

≠ allowed alternative treatment IAS/IFRS

The benchmark accounting policy or benchmark treatment is one of two possible accounting treatments allowed in some limited cases in the International Financial Reporting Standards. The other policy is referred to as an allowed alternative treatment. However, no preference is suggested between the two treatments, and financial statements will meet the IFRS presentation requirements irrespective of which treatment is chosen.

método de comparación

▲ *apply the benchmark accounting policy* aplicar el método de comparación

benchmark comparison

A benchmark comparison is an evaluation of something against a reference standard, such as the financial ratios of an enterprise, based on the general rules of thumb or best practices ratios.

benchmark

▲ *make a benchmark comparison* llevar a cabo un benchmark

benchmark treatment IAS/IFRS

= benchmark accounting policy IAS/IFRS

≠ allowed alternative treatment IAS/IFRS

The benchmark treatment is one of two possible accounting treatments allowed in some limited cases in the International Financial Reporting Standards. The other policy is referred to as an allowed alternative treatment. However, no preference is suggested between the two treatments, and financial statements will meet the IFRS presentation requirements irrespective of which treatment is chosen.

método de comparación

= método benchmark

▲ *designate as the benchmark treatment* designar como método de comparación ▲ *in accordance with the benchmark treatment under IFRS* de acuerdo con el método de comparación según NIIF ▲ *the benchmark treatment for joint ventures* el método de comparación para joint ventures ▲ *under the benchmark treatment* según el método de comparación

⇛ benchmark

benchmarking

Benchmarking is a method applied by enterprises to evaluate their organisational performance by means of comparison with the general rules of thumb or best practices ratios.

benchmarking

= evaluación comparativa

▲ *benchmarking against the industry* benchmarking frente al sector ▲ *benchmarking of capital requirements* benchmarking de necesidades de capital ▲ *benchmarking of financial results against competitors* benchmarking de resultados financieros frente a competidores ▲ *external benchmarking* benchmarking externo ▲ *functional benchmarking* benchmarking funcional ▲ *internal benchmarking* benchmarking interno ▲ *strategic benchmarking* benchmarking estratégico

beneficial owner

The beneficial owner of payments of interest or royalties is an enterprise or a permanent establishment that holds those payments for its own benefit and not as an agent, trustee or nominee for some other person.

beneficiario

▲ *make payments of interest or royalties to the beneficial owner* pagar intereses o royalties al beneficiario ▲ *the beneficial owner of payments of interest or royalties* el beneficiario de intereses o royalties ▲ *the beneficial owner of the dividends* el beneficiario de dividendos ▲ *the royalties that have been agreed by the payer and the beneficial owner* los royalties acordados entre el pagador y el beneficiario

benefit

1 A benefit is an advantage, preference or privilege provided by a product or service. Examples include increased cash inflow and low running costs.

beneficio

▲ *allow the benefit of the loss to be realised* permite compensar el beneficio con una pérdida que se va a materializar ▲ *be commensurated with the benefits* estar en proporción con los beneficios ▲ *defer recognition of the benefit of tax losses until the period of realisation* aplazar el reconocimiento del beneficio fiscal hasta el periodo de liquidación ▲ *recognise the benefit as an asset* reconocer el beneficio como un activo

2 Benefits are payments from an insurance policy or pension scheme to which a participant or beneficiary may be entitled under specified circumstances.

prestación

ditional benefits un derecho contractual a recibir prestaciones complementarias ▲ *a significant portion of the total contractual benefits* una parte importante de las prestaciones contractuales totales ▲ *employee benefits* prestaciones a los trabajadores ▲ *guarenteed benefits* prestaciones garantizadas ▲ *past service cost that arose from benefit changes* coste de servicio anterior procedente de cambios en las prestaciones ▲ *pay significant additional benefits* pagar prestaciones complementarias significativas ▲ *promise death benefits* prometer prestaciones por fallecimiento

⇛ compensation

benefit/years of service method

= accrued benefit method prorated on service, projected unit credit method

Within the context of pension plans, the benefit/years of service method is a method for calculating the final benefit obligation of a pension plan by measuring benefit entitlements through the allocation of these entitlements to separate units related to individual periods of service.

método de prestaciones por año cotizado

▲ *use the benefit/years of service method to determine the present value of defined benefit obligations* utilizar el método de prestaciones por año cotizado para fijar el valor actual de las obligaciones de las prestaciones definidas ▲ *use the benefit/years of service method to measure obligations and costs* usar el método de prestaciones por año cotizado para valorar obligaciones y costes

BEPS

= basic earnings per share

BEPS is the abbreviation for basic earnings per share, which is a financial ratio defined as the profit for the accounting period attributable to ordinary shareholders divided by the average number of ordinary shares outstanding for the same period. This ratio is applied for valuation of the share and the enterprise's ability to generate profit to the owners and is calculated on a non-diluted basis as it disregards any dilutive convertible bonds or share options.

rentabilidad por acción

= beneficio básico por acción, ganancia básica por acción, PER básico

▲ *calculate BEPS* calcular la rentabilidad por acción ▲ *restatement of previous years' BEPS* actualización de la rentabilidad básica por acción de los años anteriores ▲ *the share price required for the BEPS calculation* se necesita conocer el precio de la acción para calcular la rentabilidad básica por acción ▲ *time-weighted shares for use in BEPS calculation* acciones ponderadas temporalmente para calcular la rentabilidad básica por acción

beta

= beta coefficient

Beta or the beta coefficient is a measure of the sensitivity of the price of a share to market changes and shows how risky the share is. If the beta is less than 1, the share price fluctuates less than the market average or index, when higher than 1, the price will be more volatile than the market average, and if equal to 1, the volatility of the share corresponds to that of the market average.

beta

▲ *high beta* beta alto ▲ *low beta* beta bajo ▲ *negative beta* beta negativo ▲ *positive beta* beta positivo

bi-annual

→ biannual

biannual

= half-yearly, semiannual

Biannual means half-yearly, i.e. every six months.

bianual

= semestral

▲ *biannual allocation* asignación bianual

bid

= bid price

≠ offer

A bid or bid price is a buying price and may be the price at which a market maker will buy shares, the price offered by a company wanting to buy the share capital of another company, or any price a buyer is ready to pay.

licitación

▲ *fix a bid* amañar una licitación

bid price

= bid, buying price

≠ ask price, offer price

The bid price is the quoted bid or the highest price a buyer is willing to pay at a particular time for a certain security.

precio de licitación

= precio de la licitación

▲ *the current bid price* el precio de licitación actual ▲ *the most recently quoted bid price* el precio de la licitación más reciente ▲ *the official bid price* el precio de la licitación actual ▲ *the stock exchange quoted bid price* el precio de licitación cotizado en bolsa

bifurcation

Bifurcation means the splitting apart, dividing or forking of something into two branches or separate parts.

split

NOTE Spanish accountants use the English term, usually in the collocation 'hacer un split'.

▲ *necessitate bifurcation* tener que hacer un split ▲ *require bifurcation* precisar hacer un split ▲ *the bifurcation of financial instruments* el split de los instrumentos financieros

bilateral

If something is bilateral, it involves two parties.

bilateral

▲ *a bilateral agreement* un contrato bilateral ▲ *bilateral loan agreements* contrato bilateral de préstamos ▲ *bilateral negotiations* negociaciones bilaterales

bilateral netting

Bilateral netting refers to the offsetting of amounts receivable and amounts payable subject to agreement between two parties, typically on an intragroup basis between multinationals, leaving a net balance payable or receivable.

compensación bilateral

= liquidación bilateral

▲ *a legally enforceable bilateral netting arrangement* una compensación bilateral de obligado cumplimiento ▲ *a legally valid bilateral netting agreement* una compensación bilateral legalmente válida

⇛ multilateral netting, netting agreement

bill[1] US *noun* <a, the, -s>

= invoice UK

A bill is a document drafted by a supplier requesting payment for goods or services already supplied or about to be supplied.

factura

= cuenta

▲ *a bill for $1000* una factura de 1000 dólares ▲ *according to the bill* según la factura ▲ *prepare a bill* preparar una factura

bill[2] US *verb* <-s, -ed, has -ed, -ing> *passive* <is -ed, was -ed>

= invoice UK

To bill means to request payment for supplied goods or services by way of an invoice.

facturar

▲ *bill a product* facturar un producto ▲ *bill in EUR* facturar en euros ▲ *bill in foreign currency* facturar en divisa extranjera ▲ *bill periodically* facturar periódicamente ▲ *bill sales* facturar ventas ▲ *bill the customer* facturar al cliente

bill of exchange

= B/E, bill

A bill of exchange is a written order drawn by the seller/lender and signed by the purchaser/borrower who thereby accepts the terms of payment included in the agreement.

letra de cambio

▲ *bills of exchange payable* letras de cambio a pagar ▲ *bills of exchange receivable* letras de cambio a cobrar

billability ratio

The billability ratio is a financial ratio calculated as the number of hours billed to clients divided by the billability, i.e. the total number of hours available that can be directly billed to clients. This ratio is typically used in the consultancy industry to show the revenue production either per assignment or per consultant.

facturación por horas

▲ *increase the billability ratio* aumentar la facturación por horas

billed US

= invoiced UK

When something has been billed, a bill has been prepared for it, describing the date, customer's and vendor's names, quantity, price, freight, and credit terms of the transaction.

facturado

▲ *a billed amount* una cantidad facturada ▲ *a billed price* un precio facturado ▲ *billed directly to the borrower* facturado directamente al acreedor ▲ *billed expenses* gastos facturados ▲ *billed income* ingresos facturados ▲ *billed sales for the year* ventas facturadas al año

billing US

Billing means requesting payment for supplied goods or services by way of an invoice.

facturación

▲ *advance billing* facturación anticipada ▲ *billing and collection activities* facturación ▲ *billing date* fecha de facturación ▲ *billing department* departamento de facturación ▲ *billing manager* director de facturación ▲ *billing of orders* facturación de pedidos ▲ *billing on account* facturación a cuenta ▲ *billing system* sistema de facturación ▲ *continuous billing* facturación continua ▲ *progress billing* facturación parcial

bills of exchange payable UK

= notes payable US, IAS/IFRS

Bills of exchange payable is an item under creditors: amounts falling due within one year or under creditors: amounts falling due after more than one year –depending on whether short-or long-term– in the balance sheet according to the Companies Act 1985 required report format.

letra de cambio a pagar

▲ *foreign bills of exchange payable* letras de cambio a pagar en divisas ▲ *long-term bills of exchange payable* letras de cambio a pagar a largo plazo ▲ *non-interest bearing bills of exchange payable* letras de cambio a pagar sin interés

bills payable UK

= notes payable US, IAS/IFRS

Bills payable is an item under current liabilities in the balance sheet recognising the bills of exchange written by an enterprise that have to be paid on maturity.

cuentas a pagar

= cuentas acreedoras

▲ *a decrease in bills payable* una disminución en las cuentas a pagar ▲ *an increase in bills payable* un aumento en las cuentas a pagar ▲ *foreign bills payable* cuentas a pagar nominadas en moneda extranjera

⇛ note payable

bills receivable UK

= notes receivable IAS/IFRS, US

Bills receivable is an item under current assets in the balance sheet recognising the bills of exchange to be received by the enterprise at a future date.

cuentas a cobrar

= cuentas deudoras

▲ *a decrease in bills receivable* una disminución en las cuentas a cobrar ▲ *an increase in bills receivable* un aumento en las cuentas a cobrar ▲ *discount bills receivable* cuentas a cobrar con descuento ▲ *foreign exchange bills receivable* cuentas a cobrar en divisa extranjera

⇛ note receivable

bind

= commit

To bind oneself means being committed, obliged or compelled to do something, i.e. by a contract or a promise that has been made.

obligar

= vincular

▲ *be bound by an agreement* estar obligado por acuerdo ▲ *bind the promissor* obligar al pagador

⇛ subscribe

binding

Binding means committed, obliged or compelled to do something.

vinculante

= obligado cumplimiento

▲ *a binding agreement* un acuerdo vinculante ▲ *a binding contract* un contrato vinculante ▲ *a binding obligation* una obligación vinculante ▲ *a binding sale agreement* un contrato de venta vinculante ▲ *a legally binding arrangement* un acuerdo de obligado cumplimiento legal ▲ *an overall binding sale agreement* un contrato de venta vinculante total ▲ *have a binding obligation to, and be able to, make good the losses* tener una obligación vinculante y ser capaz de compensar las pérdidas

biological asset

Biological assets are living animals or plants.

activo biológico

▲ *a group of biological assets* un grupo de activos biológicos ▲ *an active market for biological assets* un mercado dinámico de activos biológicos ▲ *biological assets related to agricultural activity* actividades biológicas relacionadas con la actividad agrícola ▲ *cessation of a biological asset's life processes* cese de los procesos vitales de un activo biológico ▲ *consumable biological assets* activos biológicos consumibles ▲ *contract for the sale of biological assets* contrato de venta de activos biológicos ▲ *estimated point-of-sale costs of a biological asset* costes estimados de venta de un activo biológico ▲ *fair value reserve for biological assets* reserva de valor razonable para activos biológicos ▲ *immature biological assets* activos biológicos no vencidos ▲ *mature biological assets* activos biológicos vencidos ▲ *qualitative changes in a biological asset* cambios cualitativos en un activo biológico ▲ *quantitative changes in a biological asset* cambios cuantitativos en un activo biológico

biological transformation

Biological transformation is the effect of growth, degeneration, production and procreation on the quantity or quality of a biological asset.

transformación biológica

▲ *bear some similarity to biological transformation* asemejarse a la transformación biológica ▲ *brought about by biological transformation* producido por la transformación biológica ▲ *enhance the future biological transformation* incentivar la transformación biológica futura ▲ *facilitate biological transformation* facilitar la transformación biológica ▲ *increases in value from additional biological transformation* aumentos en el valor de la transformación biológica adicional ▲ *the biological transformation of living animals* la transformación biológica de los animales vivos ▲ *the impact of the biological transformation on price* el impacto de la transformación biológica sobre el precio

Black & Scholes formula

= Black-Scholes option pricing model

The Black & Scholes formula is an option pricing model. The pricing of options is based on the price of the underlying asset, price fluctuations, remaining maturity and the risk-free interest rate.

fórmula de Black & Scholes

▲ *based on the Black & Scholes formula* en base a la fórmula de Black & Scholes

Black-Scholes option pricing model

→ Black & Scholes formula

board

1 → board of directors

2 → executive board

board of directors US, UK, IAS/IFRS

The board of directors is the management of a company, and its members are appointed for a specified term by the shareholders at a general meeting. A member of the board of directors is called a director.

consejo de administración

▲ *appoint the majority of the members of the board of directors* nombrar a la mayoría de los miembros del consejo de administración ▲ *at meetings of the board of directors* en las reuniones del consejo de administración ▲ *chairman of the board of directors* presidente del consejo de administración ▲ *decisions made by the board of directors* decisiones tomadas por el consejo de administración ▲ *internal reporting to the board of directors* informe interno para el consejo de administración ▲ *join the board of directors* integrarse en el consejo de administración ▲ *remove the majority of the members of the board of directors* cesar a la mayoría de los miembros del consejo de administración ▲ *report to the board of directors* informar al consejo de administración ▲ *representation on the board of directors* representación en el consejo de administración

▲ *the appointment of the board of directors* el nombramiento del consejo de administración ▲ *the board of directors and/or other governing body of an enterprise* el consejo de administración y/u otros órganos de dirección de una empresa
⇛ supervisory board

bond
= debt security
A bond is an interest-bearing debt security issued by a borrower promising to pay the bondholder interest for a fixed period of time and to repay the principal of the loan at maturity. Bonds are usually long-term securities carrying fixed or variable interest and are issued by central and local governments, mortgage banks as well as enterprises.
bono
▲ *a callable bond* un bono amortizable ▲ *a called bond* un bono amortizado ▲ *a convertible bond* un bono convertible ▲ *a corporate bond* un bono de empresa ▲ *a government bond* un bono público ▲ *a non-convertible bond* un bono no convertible ▲ *a short bond* un bono a corto plazo ▲ *accounting for bonds* contabilidad de bonos ▲ *an uncallable bond* un bono no amortizable ▲ *covered bonds* bonos cubiertos ▲ *early retirement of bonds* amortización anticipada de bonos ▲ *fixed-rate bond* bono a interés fijo ▲ *high-coupon bond* bono de rendimiento alto ▲ *high-quality bonds* bonos de alta solvencia ▲ *high-yield bond* bono de alta rentabilidad ▲ *index-linked bonds* bonos indexados ▲ *issue bonds* emitir bonos ▲ *issue of bonds* emisión de bonos ▲ *long-term bond* bono a largo plazo ▲ *low-coupon bond* bono de rendimiento bajo ▲ *municipal bond* bono municipal ▲ *number of ordinary shares resulting from conversion of the bond* número de acciones ordinarias que resultan de la conversión de los bonos ▲ *on maturity of the bonds* al vencimiento de los bonos ▲ *redeem a bond* amortizar un bono ▲ *secured bonds* bonos garantizados ▲ *short-term bond* bono a corto plazo ▲ *the interest expense on the bond* el coste del interés del bono ▲ *the liability component of the convertible bond* el componente pasivo del bono convertible ▲ *the term of the bond* el vencimiento del bono ▲ *Treaury bond* bono del Tesoro ▲ *unsecured bonds* bonos no garantizados ▲ *zero-coupon bond* bono de cupón cero

bond issue
= bond issuance
The act of issuing bonds, i.e. making bonds available for purchase by the public, is called a bond issue. Bonds are issued by companies or governments in order to raise money.
emisión de bonos
▲ *bond issue costs* costes de la emisión de bonos ▲ *fixed-rate bond issue* emisión de bonos a interés fijo ▲ *rating of bond issues* rating de la emisión de bonos

bond issuer
Bond issuers include governments, enterprises or mortgage banks issuing bonds for sale, i.e. government bonds, corporate bonds or mortgage bonds, respectively, typically on a stock exchange with a view to raising a long-term loan.
emisor de bonos
▲ *dealings by the management in the bond issuer's bonds* acuerdos administrativos sobre los bonos del emisor de bonos

bond loan
A loan raised by issuing bonds is called a bond loan.
empréstito
▲ *a bond loan with a maturity of 13 years* un empréstito con un vencimiento a 13 años ▲ *bond and debenture loans* empréstitos y préstamos con obligaciones ▲ *issue a bond loan* emitir un empréstito ▲ *raise a bond loan* suscribir un empréstito

bond portfolio
= bond holding
The total money value of bonds held by an enterprise is called a bond portfolio.
cartera de renta fija
▲ *a risk profile of the bond portfolio* un perfil de riesgo de la cartera de renta fija ▲ *adjustment for change in the market value of the bond portfolio* ajuste por modificación en el valor de mercado de la cartera de renta fija ▲ *adjustment for changes in the market value of bond portfolio* ajuste por modificaciones en el valor de mercado de la

cartera de renta fija ▲ *duration of bond portfolio* plazo de vigencia de la cartera de renta fija ▲ *losses on the bond portfolio* pérdidas en la cartera de renta fija ▲ *profit or loss on bond portfolio* resultados de la cartera de renta fija ▲ *realised capital gain on bond portfolio* ganancia de capital devengada de la cartera de renta fija ▲ *the market value of the bond portfolio* el valor de mercado de la cartera de renta fija ▲ *yield to maturity on bond portfolio* rentabilidad al vencimiento de la cartera de renta fija

bond yield

= bond interest rate

The bond yield is the real rate of return paid on a bond expressed as the coupon rate as a percentage of the current market price rather than the par value of the bond. Bond yields fluctuate depending on supply and demand in the stock market.

rentabilidad del bono

= rendimiento del bono

▲ *average bond yield* rentabilidad media del bono

⇛ nominal interest rate, yield

bondholder

A person or enterprise that owns a bond is called a bondholder.

obligacionista

▲ *the holding of meetings of bondholders* la celebración de juntas de obligacionistas ▲ *the representative of the bondholders* el representante de los obligacionistas ▲ *the rights of the bondholder* los derechos del obligacionista

bonus

1 = performance-related bonus

Bonus refers to extra remuneration, such as a cash bonus, which is awarded to employees on the basis of their performance or to employees who meet specified criteria. The purpose of bonuses is to motivate and induce employees to participate in meeting the goals of the enterprise.

bonificación

▲ *a cash bonus* una bonificación en efectivo ▲ *a contingent bonus* una bonificación contingente ▲ *the bonus granted* la bonificación concedida

⇛ performance-related pay

2 Generally, bonus refers to a monetary amount paid in addition to the amount which is expected or agreed on. E.g. a holder of a life insurance policy may receive regular bonuses, usually once a year, and/or a terminal bonus on maturity.

paga extra

= bonus

▲ *a cash bonus* una paga extra en efectivo ▲ *bonus awards* concesiones de paga extra ▲ *bonuses and deferred compensation* pagas extras y prestaciones diferidas ▲ *bonuses payable within 12 months* pagas extras a satisfacer en los próximos 12 meses ▲ *have a legal obligation to pay a bonus* tener obligación legal de abonar pagas extras ▲ *provisions for bonuses and rebates* provisiones para pagas extras y desgravaciones fiscales ▲ *without receiving a bonus* sin recibir una paga extra

bonus issue

= capitalisation issue, scrip issue

A bonus issue is the act of increasing a company's issued capital by issuing additional share certificates for free to its existing shareholders in proportion to their shareholdings, in this way converting accumulated reserves into issued share capital. However, no additional capital is contributed and total equity remains the same; the effect is a reduction of the share price that increases the liquidity of the company's shares in the stock market.

emisión gratuita

= emisión liberada

▲ *a two-for-one bonus issue* una emisión gratuita de dos por uno

⇛ rights issue

bonus plan

= bonus scheme

A bonus plan is an arrangement under which extra remuneration, such as a cash bonus, is awarded to employees on the basis of their performance or to employees who meet specified criteria. The purpose of a bonus plan is to motivate and induce employees to participate in meeting the goals of the enterprise.

plan de incentivos

▲ *an obligation under a bonus plan* una obligación según un plan de incentivos ▲ *bonus plan for managers and specialists* plan de incentivos para ejecutivos y expertos ▲ *end a bonus plan* terminar un plan de incentivos ▲ *extraordinary bonus plans* planes extraordinarios de incentivos ▲ *introduce a bonus plan* introducir un plan de incentivos ▲ *legal or constructive obligations under a bonus plan* obligaciones legales o tácitas según un plan de incentivos ▲ *participate in a bonus plan* participar en un plan de incentivos ▲ *recognise the cost of bonus plans as an expense* reconocer el coste de los planes de incentivos como un gasto ▲ *share-option-based bonus plans* planes de incentivos basados en opciones sobre acciones

bonus program US

A bonus program is an arrangement under which extra remuneration, such as a cash bonus, is awarded to employees on the basis of their performance or to employees who meet specified criteria. The purpose of a bonus plan is to motivate and induce employees to participate in meeting the goals of the enterprise.

programa de incentivos

▲ *be covered by a 1-year bonus program* comprendido en un programa de incentivos a un año ▲ *introduce a bonus program* introducir un programa de incentivos

bonus programme UK

A bonus programme is an arrangement under which extra remuneration, such as a cash bonus, is awarded to employees on the basis of their performance or to employees who meet specified criteria. The purpose of a bonus plan is to motivate and induce employees to participate in meeting the goals of the enterprise.

programa de incentivos

▲ *be covered by a 1-year bonus programme* comprendido en un programa de incentivos a un año ▲ *introduce a bonus programme* introducir un programa de incentivos

bonus share

Bonus shares are shares issued for free to shareholders in proportion to their existing shareholdings. Consequently no additional capital is contributed, and the share value is reduced, which may have been the purpose in order to boost share marketability and turn accumulated retained earnings into shares. In a one-for-one bonus share issue, the amount of shares is doubled and the share price generally halved.

acción gratuita

= acción liberada

▲ *bonus share issue* emisión de acciones gratuitas ▲ *issue bonus shares* emitir acciones gratuitas

⇛ scrip issue

book

= recognise

≠ derecognise

To book is to recognise or record an entry in the accounts.

anotar

= contabilizar, registrar

▲ *book an item* anotar una partida ▲ *book as income* anotar como ingreso

⇛ recognise

book depreciation

= accounting depreciation

≠ tax depreciation

Book depreciation is the systematic allocation of the cost of a tangible asset over its useful life in the financial statements.

cuota de amortización

▲ *determine book depreciation* fijar la cuota de amortización ▲ *straight-line book depreciation* cuota de amortización constante ▲ *the accumulated book depreciation* la cuota de amortización acumulada ▲ *the calculation of book depreciation* el cálculo de la cuota de amortización

book value UK

= carrying amount IAS/IFRS, UK, carrying value US

The book value or net book value (NBV) is the value at which an asset appears in the books of an enterprise (usually at the date of the last balance sheet) less any depreciation (amortisation) or writedowns applied since its purchase or its last revaluation.

valor contable

= valorado en libros

▲ *book value at year-end* valor contable a final de año ▲ *book value of charged assets* valor contable de los activos cargados ▲ *book value of leased assets* valor contable de los activos arrendados ▲ *book value per share* valor contable por acción ▲ *difference between the book value and the tax base* diferencia entre el valor contable y el fiscal ▲ *include in the book value* incluir en el valor contable ▲ *less the book value* menos el valor contable ▲ *realisation of goodwill at book value* reconocimiento del fondo de comercio a valor contable ▲ *recovery of the book value* recuperación del valor contable ▲ *reduce the book value to nil* reducir el valor contable a cero ▲ *sale at book value* venta a valor contable ▲ *take over the assets at book value* adquirir los activos a valor contable ▲ *the book value at the date of discontinuation* el valor contable a la fecha de baja en el inventario ▲ *the book value of goodwill* el valor contable del fondo de comercio ▲ *the book value of net assets* el valor contable de los activos netos ▲ *the book value of the share* el valor contable de la acción ▲ *the total book value of the assets mortgaged* el valor contable total de los activos hipotecados

⇛ net asset value

book value per share

= BVPS

The book value per share is a financial ratio calculated as the value of an enterprise's equity (i.e. share capital and reserves) as recognised in the financial statements at the balance sheet date divided by the number of shares outstanding.

valor contable por acción

▲ *calculate the book value per share* calcular el valor contable por acción ▲ *diluted book value per share* valor contable diluido por acción ▲ *year-end book value per share* valor contable a final de año por acción

book-entry security

= dematerialised security, uncertificated security

A book-entry security is a security that does not exist in a certificated form, but exist as an electronic entry in a register and is issued and tranferred as an uncertificated financial instrument.

título intangible

= valor anotado en cuenta, valor sin soporte material

▲ *a party to a book-entry securities transaction* una parte de la transacción de los títulos intangibles ▲ *attachment or enforcement proceedings with respect to book-entry securities* diligencias de embargo o incautación con respecto a los títulos intangibles ▲ *collateralisation of book-entry securities* garantía de los títulos intangibles ▲ *issue and registration of book-entry securities* emisión y registro de títulos intangibles ▲ *multi-tiered holdings of book-entry securities* valores anotados en cuenta depositados en intermediarios ▲ *the proprietary aspects of book-entry securities* los aspectos patrimoniales de los títulos intangibles ▲ *transfer of book-entry securities* transferencia de títulos intangibles

book-keeping

→ bookkeeping

bookkeeper

= accountant

A bookkeeper is a person who keeps the financial records of an enterprise.

tenedor de libros

= contable

▲ *the firm's bookkeeper* el tenedor de libros de la empresa ▲ *work as a bookkeeper* trabaja como tenedor de libros

⇛ accountant

bookkeeping

Bookkeeping is the systematic recording of financial transactions in the records and accounts of an enterprise, usually according to the double-entry bookkeeping system.

teneduría de libros

▲ *the internal bookkeeping of the enterprise* la teneduría de libros interna de la empresa

⇛ bookkeeping records, double-entry bookkeeping

bookkeeping records

The bookkeeping records constitute the accounting data that have been compiled and recorded on a daily basis to keep track of all transactions in an enterprise, kept on computer files and divided up into various ledgers.

registros contables
▲ *accurate bookkeeping records* registros contables exactos
⇛ double-entry bookkeeping

borrow against
To raise a loan by providing security in a particular asset is to borrow against that asset.
hipotecar
NOTE Spanish accountants use the term 'pignorar' when an enterprise borrows against equities.
▲ *borrow against the equity in the house* pignorar títulos propios ▲ *borrow against the property* hipotecar el edificio
⇛ charge, security

borrower
A borrower is a person or enterprise that raises a loan and thereby contracts a debt.
prestatario
▲ *a future act of default by the borrower* un posible riesgo de insolvencia del prestatario ▲ *adverse changes in the payment status of borrowers* cambios adversos en el nivel de solvencia de los prestatarios ▲ *an exchange between an existing borrower and lender of debt instruments* un intercambio de instrumentos de deuda entre el prestamista y el prestatario ▲ *credit card borrowers who have reached their credit limit* los titulares de las tarjetas de crédito que han llegado al límite de crédito ▲ *economic or legal reasons relating to the borrower's financial difficulty* razones económicas o legales relativas a las dificultades financieras del prestatario ▲ *subprime borrowers* prestatarios de sub-prime ▲ *the borrower's financial position* la posición financiera del prestatario ▲ *the borrower's investment securities* los valores mobiliarios que respaldan al prestatario ▲ *the level of creditworthiness of groups of borrowers* el nivel de solvencia de los grupos de prestatarios ▲ *undertakings by the borrower* garantías del prestatario

borrowing
Borrowing means the raising of a loan.
crédito
▲ *amortisation of ancillary costs incurred in connection with the arrangement of borrowings* amortización de costes adicionales incurridos en conexión con la contratación de créditos ▲ *amortisation of discounts or premiums relating to borrowings* amortización de los descuentos o bonificaciones relacionados con los créditos ▲ *bank overdrafts and other short-term borrowings* descubiertos bancarios y otros créditos a corto plazo ▲ *borrowing agreements* acuerdos de crédito ▲ *borrowing limit* límite de crédito ▲ *borrowing of funds* línea crediticia ▲ *borrowing requirements* requisitos crediticios ▲ *borrowings and similar liabilities* créditos y obligaciones similares ▲ *borrowings of the enterprise* créditos de la empresa ▲ *current borrowings* créditos corrientes ▲ *discounts related to borrowings* descuentos relacionados con los créditos ▲ *exchange differences arising from foreign currency borrowings* diferencias de cambio derivadas de créditos en divisa ▲ *financed by borrowing* financiado con crédito ▲ *long-term borrowings* créditos a largo plazo ▲ *noncurrent borrowings* créditos no-corrientes ▲ *report as borrowings* informar sobre créditos ▲ *short-term borrowings* créditos a corto plazo ▲ *the amounts of borrowing and lending* las cantidades de créditos y préstamos ▲ *the period of the borrowings* el plazo de los créditos ▲ *total borrowings* total créditos ▲ *undrawn borrowing facilities* líneas de crédito no dispuestas

borrowing charges
Borrowing charges are fees, commission or other charges to be paid on the raising of a loan, however not interest which is the cost of the loan.
cargas crediticias
▲ *borrowing charges in the amount of €3.5 million* cargas crediticias por un total de 3.5 millones de euros ▲ *increased borrowing charges* cargas crediticias aumentadas ▲ *reduce borrowing charges* reducir las cargas crediticias ▲ *the borrowing charges incurred* las cargas crediticias incurridas

borrowing cost
= cost of borrowing
Borrowing costs are the costs an enterprise incurs when bor-

rowing funds, such as interest and fees.

coste por intereses

= coste financiero

▲ *a weighted average of the borrowing costs* una media ponderada de los costes por intereses ▲ *accounting policy for borrowing costs* política contable para los costes finacieros ▲ *associated borrowing costs* costes financieros asociados ▲ *borrowing costs eligible for capitalisation* costes financieros elegibles para capitalización ▲ *borrowing costs previously capitalised* costes financieros previamente capitalizados ▲ *capitalisation of borrowing costs* capitalización de los costes financieros ▲ *capitalise borrowing costs* capitalizar los costes financieros ▲ *cessation of the capitalisation of borrowing costs* suspensión de la capitalización de los costes financieros ▲ *classify all borrowing costs* clasificar todos los costes financieros ▲ *general borrowing costs* costes por intereses generales ▲ *incur borrowing costs* incurrir en costes financieros ▲ *recognise borrowing costs as an expense* reconocer los costes financieros como un gasto ▲ *reduce the borrowing costs of the enterprise* reducir los costes financieros de la empresa ▲ *specific borrowing costs* costes por intereses específicos ▲ *suspension of the capitalisation of borrowing costs* suspensión de la capitalización de los costes financieros ▲ *the actual borrowing costs incurred* los costes financieros reales incurridos ▲ *the amount of borrowing costs capitalised during the financial year* la cantidad de costes por intereses capitalizados durante el ejercicio ▲ *the weighted average of the borrowing costs* la media ponderada de los costes financieros ▲ *total borrowing costs* total costes por intereses

borrowing facility

= credit facility, credit line, loan facility

A borrowing facility is an arrangement with a bank or financial institution that gives the right to borrow money in case this is necessary.

línea de crédito

▲ *committed borrowing facilities* línea de crédito concedida ▲ *revolving borrowing facilities* líneas de crédito autorrenovable ▲ *undrawn borrowing facilities* líneas de crédito disponible

borrowing rate

The borrowing rate is price of money or liquidity, i.e. the interest rate charged by a lender for providing a loan expressed as a certain percentage of the loan amount. The borrowing rate varies depending on the general interest rate level, the availability of credit, the term of the loan and the borrower's credit situation.

tipo de interés del crédito

▲ *fluctuations in the borrowing rate* fluctuaciones en el tipo de interés del crédito ▲ *include the amount of the borrowing rate in the cost* incluir la cantidad del tipo de interés del crédito en el coste ▲ *incremental borrowing rate* el tipo de interés de crédito incremental ▲ *other market borrowing rates* otros tipos de interés del crédito en el mercado ▲ *the lessee's incremental borrowing rate* tipo de interés incremental del crédito del arrendatario ▲ *the marginal borrowing rate* el tipo de interés marginal del crédito

bottleneck

A bottleneck is a resource in the production process which is scarce or at capacity and which therefore puts a limit to the target achievement of an enterprise, e.g. a machine or an employee group.

estrangulamiento

= cuello de botella, embotellamiento

▲ *physical bottlenecks* estrangulamientos físicos ▲ *technical bottlenecks* estrangulamientos técnicos ▲ *the removal of bottlenecks* la dilución de los estrangulamientos

bottom line

= net income US, profit for the period

≠ top line

The bottom line refers to the last line in the profit and loss account that shows the performance of an enterprise for the accounting period, i.e. the profit for the period after tax. Some enterprises operate with several bottom lines, each showing the performance of the enterprise with regard to e.g. environmental, knowledge and social reporting.

resultado neto

▲ *a clearly integrated bottom line* un resultado neto claramente integrado ▲ *a partially integrated bottom line* un resultado neto integrado parcialmente ▲ *below the bottom line* por debajo del resultado neto ▲ *bottom line result* resultado neto ▲ *the three bottom lines* los tres resultados netos

⇛ environmental bottom line, financial bottom line, social bottom line

branch

A branch is a department, shop, plant or office that is part of a large enterprise. The branch is not a separate legal entity and may be located in another city or country.

sucursal

▲ *a branch of a foreign enterprise* una sucursal de una empresa extranjera ▲ *a branch of the reporting enterprise* una sucursal de la empresa declarante ▲ *branch network* red de sucursales ▲ *establish a branch* establecer una sucursal ▲ *have a branch in another country* tener una sucursal en otro país ▲ *investments in branches* inversiones en sucursales ▲ *open a branch* abrir una sucursal ▲ *register a branch with the Danish Commerce and Companies Agency* registrar una sucursal en el Registro Mercantil danés ▲ *the branch managers of a branch* los directores de una sucursal ▲ *the cancellation of the branch from the register* la baja de la sucursal en el registro ▲ *the deregistration of the branch from the register* la baja de la sucursal en el registro ▲ *the financial statements of the branch* los estados financieros de la sucursal ▲ *the organisational structure of the branch* la estructura organizativa de la sucursal ▲ *undistributed profits of subsidiaries, branches, associates and joint ventures* beneficios no distribuidos de las filiales, sucursales, asociadas y joint ventures ▲ *with a branch in Denmark* con una sucursal en Dinamarca

branch accounts UK

Branch accounts are separate financial statements of a branch that is part of a large enterprise.

cuentas de la sucursal

▲ *produce separate branch accounts for consolidation* elaborar cuentas separadas de la sucursal para la consolidación

branch financial statements US

Branch financial statements are separate financial statements of a branch that is part of a large enterprise.

estados financieros de la sucursal

▲ *prepare monthly branch financial statements* elaborar estados financieros mensuales de la sucursal ▲ *submit separate branch financial statements* emitir estados financieros separados de la sucursal ▲ *the preparation of branch financial statements* la elaboración de los estados financieros de la sucursal

branch supervisory board

A branch supervisory board is the top executive board of a branch. If a branch has more than one branch manager, the senior management is the branch supervisory board which corresponds to the executive board in a public limited company. No board of directors is required as is the case for a public limited company.

junta de supervisión de la sucursal

▲ *the members of the branch supervisory board* los miembros de la junta de supervisión de la sucursal

brand[1] *noun* <a, the, -s>

1 = trademark

A brand is a name, design, symbol or any other feature given to a product or group of products in order to distinguish them from those of other sellers.

marca

▲ *a dominating brand* una marca dominante ▲ *brand awareness* reconocimiento de la marca ▲ *brand image* imagen de marca ▲ *internally generated brands* marcas generadas internamente ▲ *subsequent expenditure on brands* gastos posteriores en marcas

2 = branded product

A brand is a product or a group of products from a known company or organisation. The brand value is an expression of the competitiveness of the product or group of products in a particular market.

marca

▲ *a dominating brand* una marca dominante ▲ *acquire the status as a brand* adquirir el status de marca ▲ *brand extension* extensión de la marca ▲ *brand loyalty* fidelidad a una marca ▲ *brand names* nombres de marca

brand[2] *verb* <-s, -ed, has -ed, -ing> *passive* <is -ed, was -ed>
To brand means to give a product or group of products a name, design, symbol or any other feature in order to distinguish them from those of other sellers.

etiquetar

▲ *to brand a product* etiquetar un producto

brand equity
= brand value
Brand equity represents the added value endowed to a product as a result of past investments in the marketing and communication mix elements for the brand.

valor de marca

▲ *a quantitative measurement of brand equity* una medición cuantitativa del valor de marca

brand portfolio
A brand portfolio is an enterprise's total collection of owned brands.

cartera de marcas

▲ *strengthen the brand portfolio* fortalecer la cartera de marcas

break-even analysis
→ breakeven analysis

break-even point
→ breakeven point

break-even sales
= break-even turnover
Break-even sales means sales with no profit or loss, also called break-even point. It is the sales volume, in units or in dollars, where total sales revenue equals total costs. In this way, zero profit results.

umbral de rentabilidad

▲ *future break-even sales* umbral de rentabilidad futuro ▲ *reduce break-even sales* reducir el umbral de rentabilidad

breakdown
= specification
A breakdown is a statement showing information or amounts separated into components, parts or elements for higher detail.

desglose

▲ *breakdown by categories of activity* desglose por categorías de actividad ▲ *breakdown of provisions and changes during the year* desglose de las provisiones y cambios durante el año

breakeven analysis
A breakeven analysis is an analysis that makes it possible to calculate the breakeven point and constitutes the first step in a cost-volume-profit analysis.

análisis del punto muerto
= análisis del umbral de rentabilidad

▲ *an expanded breakeven analysis* un análisis del punto muerto ampliado ▲ *do a breakeven analysis* llevar a cabo un análisis del punto muerto
⇛ breakeven chart, breakeven point, cost-volume-profit analysis

breakeven chart UK
A breakeven chart is a chart showing the approximate profit or loss at various levels of sales volume within a limited range. Types of chart include conventional breakeven charts based on different cost structures, as well as the contribution and profit-volume charts.

gráfico del punto muerto

▲ *complete a breakeven chart* completar un gráfico del punto muerto ▲ *use a breakeven chart* utilizar un gráfico del punto muerto
⇛ breakeven analysis, breakeven point

breakeven point
The breakeven point is the level of activity at which revenue equals costs and net profit is zero. The breakeven point is ascertained through a breakeven chart or analysis.

punto muerto
= umbral de rentabilidad

▲ *calculate the breakeven point* calcular el punto muerto ▲ *compute the breakeven point* computar el punto muerto ▲ *determine the breakeven point* determinar el punto muerto ▲ *shift the breakeven point* cambiar el umbral de rentabilidad

⇛ breakeven analysis, breakeven chart

bring forward *verb* <brings forward, brought forward, has brought forward, bringing forward> *passive* <is brought forward, was brought forward>
To bring forward means to transfer an item from a previous accounting period to the current period.
transferir
▲ *bring deductions forward* transferir las deducciones ▲ *brought forward from previous years* transferido de ejercicios anteriores ▲ *loss brought forward* pérdida transferida ▲ *profit brought forward* beneficio transferido ▲ *profit or loss brought forward* resultados transferidos
⇛ carry forward

budget
A budget is a quantitative statement or plan of action covering a defined period of time including planned revenues, expenses, assets, liabilities and cash flows. A budget also helps coordinate and implement plans.
presupuesto
▲ *a reliable budget* un presupuesto fiable ▲ *a revised budget* un presupuesto modificado ▲ *activity-based budgets* presupuestos basados en la actividad ▲ *an annual budget* un presupuesto anual ▲ *an approved budget* un presupuesto aprobado ▲ *budget period* periodo presupuestario ▲ *budget variance* desviación presupuestaria ▲ *cash flow projections based on financial budgets* proyecciones de flujos de caja basados en los presupuestos financieros ▲ *consolidated report on implementation of the budget* informe consolidado sobre la implementación del presupuesto ▲ *detailed, explicit and reliable financial budgets/forecasts of future cash flows for periods longer than five years* presupuestos financieros detallados, explícitos y fiables/proyecciones de flujos de caja futuros para periodos superiores a los cinco años ▲ *prepare a budget* preparar un presupuesto ▲ *publish a budget* publicar un presupuesto ▲ *reductions in the budget* reducciones en el presupuesto ▲ *the budgets approved by the management* los presupuestos aprobados por la dirección ▲ *the most recent financial budgets* los presupuestos financieros más recientes

budget slack
= budgetary slack
Budget slack involves the underestimation of revenues or overestimation of costs by managers, often intentionally, when preparing budgets.
presupuesto conservador
▲ *create budget slack* formular un presupuesto conservador

budgetary slack
Budgetary slack involves the underestimation of revenues or overestimation of costs by managers, often intentionally, when preparing budgets.
conservadurismo presupuestario
▲ *create budgetary slack* emplear conservadurismo presupuestario

budgeted
Amounts budgeted for have been anticipated as income or expenses in a budget.
presupuestado
▲ *a significant decline in budgeted net cash flows* una disminución importante en la pérdida presupuestaria ▲ *a significant increase in budgeted loss* un aumento importante en la pérdida presupuestaria ▲ *budgeted balance sheet* balance presupuestado ▲ *budgeted figures for the future* cifras presupuestadas para el futuro ▲ *budgeted income statement* cuenta de resultados presupuestada ▲ *budgeted market share* cuota de mercado presupuestada ▲ *cash flows that are significantly higher than those originally budgeted* flujos de caja que son significativamente más altos que los originalmente presupuestados

budgeted cost
≠ actual cost
The budgeted costs are the planned and expected costs of an enterprise according to the budget for a particular accounting period.
coste presupuestado
▲ *compare actual and budgeted costs* comparar los costes reales y los presupuestados ▲ *determi-*

ne the budgeted costs determinar los costes presupuestados ▲ *total budgeted costs* total costes presupuestados

budgeted costing

Budgeted costing is a costing method according to which both direct and indirect costs are assigned to a cost object at budgeted rates.

sistema de coste presupuestado

▲ *approved budgeted costing for the project* sistema de coste presupuestado aprobado para el proyecto

budgeted factory-overhead rate

The budgeted factory-overhead rate is a budgeted rate at which indirect production costs are allocated to the individual activity cost pools in a period. The rate is calculated by dividing the budgeted fixed indirect production costs for each cost pool by a selected cost-allocation base, e.g. the number of machine hours.

ratio de coste indirecto de fabricación presupuestado

▲ *compute the budgeted factory-overhead rate* calcular el ratio de coste indirecto de fabricación presupuestado

budgeted financial statements

Budgeted financial statements are financial statements that are planned for a future accounting period.

presupuestos

▲ *an analysis of the budgeted financial statements* un análisis de los presupuestos ▲ *significant changes to the budgeted financial statements* cambios significativos en los presupuestos

budgeted indirect-cost rate

The budgeted indirect-cost rate is the calculated as the total indirect costs in a cost pool divided by the relevant cost allocation base, e.g. the budgeted production capacity such as the number of machine-hours.

ratio de coste indirecto presupuestado

▲ *compute the budgeted indirect-cost rate* calcular el ratio de coste indirecto presupuestado ▲ *use a budgeted indirect-cost rate* utilizar el ratio de coste indirecto presupuestado

⇛ cost pool

building society UK

Building societies in the UK are financial institutions whose objectives include accepting deposits for saving, granting mortgage loans as well as unsecured loans to the depositors for the purchase, construction or improvement of owner-occupied dwellings as well as offering various financial services.

sociedad de crédito hipotecario

NOTE In Spain, mortgage-related activities are carried out by banks and savings banks.

▲ *major building societies* principales sociedades de crédito hipotecario ▲ *raise a loan with a building society* conseguir un préstamo en una sociedad de crédito hipotecario

⇛ mortgage bank

bullet loan

A bullet loan is a loan where the borrower only pays interest during the term of the loan. When the term of the loan expires, the borrower must pay the principal sum, i.e. the original amount of the loan, in a single payment, referred to as the bullet.

préstamo de reembolso único

▲ *a bullet loan with a maximum term of 12 years* un préstamo de reembolso único con una carencia máxima de 12 años ▲ *fixed-rate bullet loans* préstamos de reembolso único a tipos de interés fijos ▲ *grant a bullet loan* conceder un préstamo de reembolso único

bundled product

A bundled product consists of two or more products and/or services which are sold both as a package and separately. The aggregate price for a bundled product is lower than the sum of the prices quoted on a separate basis. A typical example of a bundled product is a vacation package which can include airfare, hotel accommodation as well as car hire.

producto conjunto

▲ *efficient pricing of a bundled product* fijación de precios eficiente de un producto conjunto ▲ *market a bundled product* sacar al mercado un producto conjunto ▲ *produce a bundled product* fabricar un producto conjunto

burden

A burden is a load, typically in the form of a liability, an obligation, or a responsibility.

carga

▲ *burden of proof* carga de la prueba ▲ *tax burden* carga tributaria

business[1] *noun* <no indefinite article, the, no plural>

Business is the production, buying, and selling of goods or services for profit.

negocio

NOTE As an adjective, Spanish accountants prefer 'mercantil' to 'negocio' .

▲ *a fixed place of business* un lugar fijo de negocio ▲ *in the normal course of business* en el curso normal del negocio ▲ *in the ordinary course of business* en el curso ordinario del negocio ▲ *in the same line of business* en la misma línea del negocio ▲ *principal place of business* sitio principal del negocio ▲ *public sector business enterprises* empresas mercantiles del sector público ▲ *sale or termination of a line of business* liquidación o terminación de una línea de negocio ▲ *the business ordinarily carried on by the enterprise* el negocio tradicionalmente realizado por la empresa

business[2] *adjective*

= commercial, corporate

Business means related to or belonging to an enterprise or commercial purposes.

comercial

▲ *a business context* un contexto comercial ▲ *business approach* enfoque comercial ▲ *business area* área comercial ▲ *business investment* inversión comercial ▲ *business law* ley de comercio ▲ *business tenancy* arrendamiento comercial

business[3] *noun* <a, the, -es>

= enterprise, firm, organisation UK, organization US, undertaking UK

A business is a general expression for a firm or a commercial enterprise run for the purpose of earning a profit. Businesses may be small, medium-size or large enterprises, organisations or companies that produce and sell goods or provide services.

negocio

▲ *a business combination involving businesses under common control* una combinación de negocios implica negocios bajo un mismo control ▲ *acquire a group of assets that does not constitute a business* adquirir un grupo de activos que no constituyen un negocio ▲ *small businesses* negocios pequeños ▲ *the purchase of some of the net assets of another entity that together form one or more businesses* la compra de algunos activos netos de otra entidad que juntos forman uno o más negocios

business activity

A business activity is an activity undertaken or engaged in by a commercial enterprise with the purpose of making a profit, i.e. it is the production and/or sales of goods or the provision of services.

actividad comercial

▲ *business activities in certain industry sectors* actividades comerciales en ciertos sectores industriales ▲ *slow business activities* actividades comerciales ralentizadas ▲ *the different business activities of subsidiaries* las actividades comerciales diferentes de las filiales ▲ *the relocation of business activities from one country to another* el traslado de las actividades comerciales de un país a otro ▲ *the significance of different business activities within the group* la importancia de las diferentes actividades comerciales dentro del grupo ▲ *the uncertainties inherent in business activities* las incertidumbres inherentes a las actividades comerciales

business angel

A business angel is an investor, typically an individual, who provides equity investments and experience to enterprises in their early stage of business.

inversor ángel

▲ *a business angel with the right skills* un inversor ángel con las destrezas adecuadas ▲ *business angel network* cadena de inversores ángel

business combination IAS/IFRS

A business combination is defined as the combining of separate enterprises to form one economic entity as a result of one enterprise uniting with or obtaining control over the net assets and operations of another enterprise.

combinación de negocios

▲ *a business combination achieved in stages* una combinación de negocios realizada en etapas ▲ *a business combination agreement* un acuerdo de combinación de negocios ▲ *a business combination that is an acquisition* una combinación de negocios que es una adquisición ▲ *a major business combination* una combinación de negocios importante ▲ *accounting for business combinations* contabilidad para las combinaciones de negocios ▲ *acquisitions through business combinations* adquisiciones mediante combinaciones de negocios ▲ *an intercompany business combination* una combinación de negocios interempresarial ▲ *at the date of the business combination* a la fecha de la combinación de negocios ▲ *deferred tax arising from a business combination* impuesto diferido procedente de una combinación de negocios ▲ *deferred tax assets and liabilities acquired in a business combination* activos y pasivos por impuestos diferidos adquiridos en una combinación de negocios ▲ *effect a business combination* efectuar una combinación de negocios ▲ *fair value adjustments made on a business combination* ajustes a valor razonable realizados en una combinación de negocios ▲ *goodwill arising on a business combination* el fondo de comercio surgido de una combinación de negocios ▲ *operations resulting from the business combination* operaciones resultantes de la combinación de negocios ▲ *prior to the business combination* anterior a la combinación de negocios ▲ *restate all business combinations that occurred between 30 June 2002 and the date of transition to IFRSs* reformular todas las combinaciones de negocios que ocurrieron entre el 30 de junio de 2002 y el periodo de transición a las NIIF ▲ *subsequent to the business combination* posterior a la combinación de negocios ▲ *temporary differences that may arise in a business combination* diferencias temporarias que pueden surgir en una combinación de negocios ▲ *the cost of a business combination* el coste de una combinación de negocios ▲ *the residual cost of the business combination* el coste residual de la combinación de negocios ▲ *undertake a business combination* asumir una combinación de negocios

SOURCE IFRS 3, Appendix 3

business combination involving entities or businesses under common control

A business combination involving entities or businesses under common control is the bringing together of entities and businesses that were controlled by the same party or parties prior to the combination and continue to be so afterwards; furthermore the control must not be temporary.

combinación de negocios entre entidades o negocios bajo control común

= combinación de negocios entre empresas controladas conjuntamente

▲ *accounting for a business combination involving entities or businesses under common control* contabilizar una combinación de negocios entre entidades o negocios bajo control común

SOURCE IFRS 3, Appendix A

business day

A business day is a day on which financial markets are open for trading, i.e. Monday to Friday excluding holidays.

día laborable

= día hábil

▲ *at the business day* en día laborable ▲ *the last business day of the year* el último día laborable del año ▲ *the sixth business day after the publication of the earnings release* el sexto día laborable después de la publicación de los beneficios

Business Excellence Model

The Business Excellence Model is a framework to support the management of enterprises by making quality decisive for the achievement of global competitive advantage, i.e. excellence. The Business Excellence Model was introduced by the European Foundation for Quality Management (EFQM) in 1992 for assessing organisations for a

European Quality Award. The model can be used by enterprises *for* self-assessment to identify strengths and weaknesses and states key criteria for achieving excellent results: leadership, strategy and policy as well as people, partnerships, resources and processes.

Modelo de Excelencia Empresarial

▲ *the European Business Excellence Model* El Modelo de Excelencia Empresarial Europeo ⇛ comprehensive report, holistic report

business foundation

The business foundation of an enterprise shows its role, goals, strategies, and objectives in the business community, e.g. business area, segments, functions and competitive platform, also appearing from the enterprise's corporate mission.

proyecto empresarial

▲ *a stable business foundation* un proyecto empresarial estable

business function costs

Business function costs comprise the total costs, i.e. variable as well as fixed costs, which are incurred by a department in an enterprise such as e.g. the marketing function.

costes de funcionamiento de la sección

▲ *the business function costs incurred* los costes de funcionamiento de la sección incurridos ⇛ function

business process re-engineering

UK, US <no inflections>

→ business process reengineering

business process reengineering

UK, US

= process reengineering, reengineering

Business process reengineering is the rethinking and radical redesign of business processes with a view to improving performance in areas such as cost, quality, speed and service and creating and delivering better customer value.

reestructuración empresarial

▲ *conduct a business process reengineering study* dirigir un proyecto de reestructuración empresarial ▲ *use business process reengineering to identify opportunities for improving* utilizar la reestructuración empresarial para identificar oportunidades de mejora

business risk

Business risk is the risk that the cash flow of an enterprise will be impaired because of adverse economic conditions, making it difficult for the enterprise to meet its operating expenses, and the risk that is associated with the unique circumstances of a particular company.

riesgo empresarial

▲ *general business risks* riesgos empresariales generales ▲ *normal business risks* riesgos empresariales normales

business sector

= business, corporate sector

The business sector is made up of all the enterprises in a country or area that do business with a view to profit.

sector empresarial

▲ *strengthen the competitiveness of the business sector* fortalecer la competitividad del sector empresarial ▲ *strong ties with the business sector* lazos fuertes con el sector empresarial ▲ *the European business sector* el sector empresarial europeo

business segment

A business segment is a component of an enterprise that can be distinguished from the rest of the enterprise in that it provides products or services that are subject to risk and returns different from those of other business segments.

segmento empresarial

▲ *combine as a single business segment* reunir en un segmento empresarial único ▲ *each individual business segment* cada segmento empresarial individual ▲ *externally reportable business segments* segmentos empresariales que rinden cuentas externamente ▲ *have a business segment* tener un segmento empresarial ▲ *have several business segments* tener varios segmentos empresariales ▲ *identify a business segment* identificar un segmento empresarial ▲ *internally reported business segments* segmentos empresariales internamente informados ▲ *provide information about business segments* ofrecer información sobre los segmentos empresariales ▲ *sell a business segment* vender un segmento empresarial ▲ *separate business segments* segmentos empresariales separados ▲ *transfers between business segments* transferencias entre segmentos empresariales ▲ *vertically integrated business segments* segmentos empresariales integrados verticalmente SOURCE IAS 14, paragraph 9

business taxation

Business taxation is the taxation of enterprises that do business with a view to profit.

tributación empresarial

= impuesto empresarial

▲ *business taxation of small and medium-sized enterprises* la tributación empresarial de las pequeñas y medianas empresas

business trend

= business cycle

Business trends are the periodic developments in the business cycles, typically over periods of five years during which the development moves in various phases from a trough over stages of pick-up with increasing demand and recovery to a peak or a boom, followed by a slowdown with negative growth and a recession which will again move into an upturn etc.

tendencia empresarial

▲ *positive business trends* tendencias empresariales positivas ▲ *upward business trends* tendencias empresariales ascendentes

business unit

= business entity

A business unit refers to an enterprise within an organisation or group or part of an enterprise engaging in a specific activity, e.g. a sales department. A business unit may be a separate legal entity of its own or part of a legal entity.

unidad de negocio

▲ *a divested business unit* una unidad de negocio abandonada ▲ *a strategic business unit* una unidad de negocio estratégica ▲ *acquisition of business units* adquisición de unidades de negocio ▲ *an international business unit* una unidad de negocio internacional ▲ *balance sheets for the business units* balances de las unidades de negocio ▲ *disposal of business units* enajenación de unidades de negocio ▲ *form a business unit* constituir una unidad de negocio ▲ *include something in the business unit* incluir algo en la unidad de negocio ▲ *the expectations of business units* las expectativas de las unidades de negocio ▲ *the income statements for the business units* las cuentas de resultados para las unidades de negocio ▲ *the objectives of the business units* los objetivos de las unidades de negocio ▲ *transactions between business units* transacciones entre unidades de negocio

buyer

= purchaser

A buyer is a party to a contract who acquires the ownership of property from a seller, usually for a money consideration.

comprador

= adquiriente

▲ *a buyer unrelated to the seller* un comprador independiente del vendedor ▲ *a knowledgeable, willing buyer* un comprador interesado, con conocimiento ▲ *a potential buyer* un comprador potencial ▲ *a prospective buyer* un posible comprador ▲ *a willing buyer* un comprador interesado ▲ *actively seeking a buyer* buscando activamente un comprador ▲ *buyer's market* el mercado del comprador ▲ *buyer's option* opción del comprador ▲ *contracts negotiated between individual buyers and sellers* los contratos negociados entre compradores y vendedores particulares ▲ *provide interest free credit to the buyer* ofrecer crédito sin interés al comprador ▲ *the buyer or user of the asset* el comprador o usuario del activo ▲ *the passing of the risk to the buyer* el traslado del riesgo al comprador ▲ *transfer the significant risks and rewards of ownership to the buyer* transferir la propiedad por cuenta y riesgo al comprador ▲ *transfer to the buyer* transferir al comprador

buying rate

= bid rate

The buying rate is the bid rate, i.e. the rate at which money or

foreign exchange is bought in the market.
tipo de cambio para la compra
▲ *the most recently quoted buying rate* el tipo de cambio para la compra más recientemente cotizado ▲ *the official buying rate* el tipo de cambio oficial para la compra

BVPS
= book value per share
BVPS is the abbreviation for book value per share, which is a financial ratio calculated as the value of an enterprise's equity (i.e. share capital and reserves) as recognised in the financial statements at the balance sheet date divided by the number of shares outstanding.
valor contable por acción
▲ *calculate BVPS* calcular el valor contable por acción

by-product
= byproduct
A by-product is an incidental or secondary product generated in the process of manufacturing another product. By-products typically constitute the output from joint production in the form of joint products with positive, but limited, i.e. relatively insignificant sales values. By-products can only be identified as separate products after the split-off point.
subproducto
▲ *a main product and a by-product* un producto principal y un subproducto ▲ *accounting for by-products* contabilizando los subproductos ▲ *elimination of by-products* eliminación de los subproductos ▲ *vegetable residues and by-products* residuos vegetales y subproductos
⇛ joint production, joint products, main product, split-off point

bye-laws US
→ bylaws

bylaws US
Bylaws are the rules governing the internal affairs of a corporation or other business entity. They specify the rights and duties of the officers and members of the enterprise.
estatutos
▲ *absence of a quorum for alterations to the bylaws approved by an annual general meeting* falta de quorun para la modificación de los estatutos aprobados en la junta general anual ▲ *according to the bylaws* de acuerdo con los estatutos ▲ *according to the company's bylaws* de acuerdo con los estatutos de la empresa ▲ *alteration to the bylaws* modificación de los estatutos ▲ *amend the company's bylaws* modificar los estatutos de la empresa ▲ *any further accounting and reporting requirements provided by bylaws or by agreement* cualesquiera requisitos contables y de publicidad recogidos en los estatutos o en el acuerdo ▲ *make a proposal for altering the company's bylaws* hacer una propuesta para modificar los estatutos de la empresa

byproduct
→ by-product

C

C

C

1 The letter 'C' is used as a rating symbol by the credit rating agencies Moody's and Standard & Poor's. The 'C' rating is the lowest speculative-grade rating of both agencies and may be used to cover a situation where a bankruptcy petition has been filed or similar action has been taken but payment on this obligation are being continued. 'C' is also used for preferred stock in arrears.

C

▲ *assign a C rating* calificar con un rating C ▲ *receive a C rating* recibir un rating C

Ca

Ca is a notch on the credit rating agency Moody's rating scale for long-term debt ratings. Ca is a speculative-grade rating and signifies that the debt is highly speculative.

Ca

▲ *assign a Ca rating* calificar con un rating Ca ▲ *receive a Ca rating* recibir un rating Ca

CA UK

= chartered accountant UK, CPA US

CA is the abbreviation for chartered accountant. A CA is a person who has qualifications as an accountant and belongs to one of the three institutes of accountants in the UK and Ireland: the Institute of Chartered Accountants in England and Wales, the Institute of Chartered Accountants in Scotland and the Institute of Chartered Accountants in Ireland.

contable colegiado

▲ *employ a CA in the firm* emplear un contable colegiado en la empresa ▲ *use the designation CA* usar el título de contable colegiado

Caa

Caa is a notch on the credit rating agency Moody's rating scale for long-term debt ratings. Caa is a speculative-grade rating and signifies that the debt is of poor standing.

Caa

▲ *assign a Caa rating* calificar con un rating Caa ▲ *receive a Caa rating* recibir un rating Caa

Caa1

Caa1 is a notch on the credit rating agency Moody's rating scale for long-term debt ratings. Caa1 is a speculative-grade rating and signifies that the debt is of poor standing.

Caa1

▲ *assign a Caa1 rating* calificar con un rating Caa1 ▲ *receive a Caa1 rating* recibir un rating Caa1

Caa2

Caa2 is a notch on the credit rating agency Moody's rating scale for long-term debt ratings. Caa2 is a speculative-grade rating and signifies that the debt is of poor standing.

Caa2

▲ *assign a Caa2 rating* calificar con un rating Caa2 ▲ *receive a Caa2 rating* recibir un rating Caa2

Caa3

Caa3 is a notch on the credit rating agency Moody's rating scale for long-term debt ratings. Caa3 is a speculative-grade rating and signifies that the debt is of poor standing.

Caa3

▲ *assign a Caa3 rating* calificar con un rating Caa3 ▲ *receive a Caa3 rating* recibir un rating de

CAGR

= compound annual growth rate

CAGR is the abbreviation for annual compound growth rate which is a geometric average of the year-to-year growth rate over a number of years.

tasa de crecimiento anual

▲ *a CAGR of 11%* una tasa de crecimiento anual del 11%

calculate

To calculate means to determine a number, value, sum etc. using a mathematical process.

calcular

▲ *calculate earnings per share* calcular los beneficios por acción ▲ *calculate expenses at USD 5000* calcular gastos por importe de 5.000 dólares USA ▲ *calculate financial ratios* calcular ratios financieros ▲ *calculate objectively* calcular objetivamente ▲ *calculate on a periodic basis* calcular periódicamente ▲ *calculate the actuarial present value of promised retirement benefits* calcular el valor actuarial presente de las prestaciones comprometidas del plan de pensiones ▲ *calculate the necessary adjustments* calcular los ajustes necesarios ▲ *calculate the net profit or loss for the period attributable to ordinary shareholders* calcular el resultado neto durante el periodo computable a los accionistas ordinarios ▲ *calculate the present value of the expected payments by a retirement benefit plan* calcular el valor actual de los pagos previstos de un plan de pensiones ▲ *calculated in accordance with* calculado de acuerdo con ▲ *calculated on the basis of the average price of the ordinary shares during the financial year* calculado en base al precio medio de las acciones ordinarias durante el ejercicio ▲ *calculated using current salary levels or projected salary levels* calculado utilizando los niveles de salario actuales o los proyectados para el futuro ▲ *calculated using the weighted average number of ordinary shares* calculado usando el número medio ponderado de acciones ordinarias

calculated

When something is calculated it has been determined by using a mathematical process.

calculado

▲ *a calculated amount* una cantidad calculada ▲ *a calculated carrying amount* un valor contable calculado ▲ *a calculated cost* un coste calculado ▲ *a calculated minimum payment* un pago mínimo calculado ▲ *a calculated present value* un valor actual calculado ▲ *a calculated profit* un beneficio calculado ▲ *a calculated selling price* un precio de venta calculado ▲ *calculated costs* costes calculados ▲ *calculated resources* recursos calculados ▲ *calculated risk* riesgo calculado

calculation

A calculation is a mathematical procedure using numbers to determine or estimate the amount or value of something.

cálculo

▲ *a detailed calculation* un cálculo detallado ▲ *an annual calculation of the recoverable amount of goodwill* un cálculo anual de la cantidad de fondo de comercio recuperable ▲ *calculation of comparatives* cálculo de valores comparativos ▲ *calculation of deferred tax* cálculo del impuesto diferido ▲ *calculation of the depreciable amount* cálculo de la cantidad depreciada ▲ *determine something on the basis of calculations* determinar algo en base a los cálculos ▲ *pension calculations* cálculos de pensiones ▲ *revise the calculations* revisar los cálculos ▲ *the effect of a future restructuring on a value in use calculation* el efecto de una reestructuración futura en el cálculo del valor en uso ▲ *up-dated calculations* cálculos actualizados

calculation error

A calculation error occurs when a calculation is incorrect.

error de cálculo

▲ *correct a calculation error* corregir un error de cálculo

calculation method

= method of calculation

A method used for calculating an item prior to its recognition in the balance sheet or income statement is called a calculation method.

método de cálculo

▲ *approximate calculation method* método de cálculo aproximado ▲ *the calculation method adopted* el método de cálculo adoptado ▲ *the calculation method concerning amortisation and depreciation* el método de cálculo concerniente con la amortización y la depreciación ▲ *the calculation method used for determining bad debts* el método de cálculo usado para determinar los fallidos ▲ *the calculation method used for determining the useful life of an asset* el método de cálculo usado para determinar la vida útil de un activo

calculation of financial ratios

The calculation of financial ratios involves comparing two financial statement figures to offer a tool for analysing an enterprise's performance and financial position over several accounting periods at a glance. Some ratios are percentages,

such as "operating margin" and "return on invested capital", where others are multiples, such as "price earnings" and "price/book value".
cálculo de ratios financieros
▲ *adjusted calculations of financial ratios* cálculos de ratios financieros ajustados

calculation of the present value
A calculation of the present value is a multiplication of projected net cash flows expected from an asset by a discount factor to evaluate the net present value, i.e. the current value of future amounts.
cálculo del valor actual
= cálculo del valor presente
▲ *calculation of the present value of expected net cash flows* cálculo del valor actual de los flujos de caja netos previstos ▲ *the objective of a calculation of the present value* el objetivo de cálculo del valor actual

calendar year
A calendar year is the period from 1 January to 31 December.
año natural
▲ *during the past calendar year* durante el pasado año natural ▲ *end of the calendar year* a finales del año natural ▲ *per calendar year* por año natural ▲ *subsequent calendar years* los años naturales posteriores ▲ *within a calendar year* a lo largo del año natural

calendar year financial statements
US, IAS/IFRS
Calendar financial statements are financial statements for a calendar year, i.e. the period from 1 January to 31 December.
estados financieros del año natural
▲ *change to calendar year financial statements* cambiar a los estados financieros del año natural ▲ *prepare calendar year financial statements* preparar los estados financieros del año natural

call in
1 To call in means to ask somebody to assist in a situation requiring e.g. specific knowledge or extra resources.
pedir ayuda
= solicitar
▲ *call in assistance* solicitar asesoramiento
2 To call in means to require payment of a loan.
pedir
▲ *call in share certificates for cancellation* pedir los certificados de acciones para su cancelación

call option
A call option gives the buyer the right, but not the obligation, to buy an underlying asset at a specified price at a specified future date.
opción de compra
▲ *a call option embedded in an equity instrument* una opción de compra implícita en un título de patrimonio ▲ *a call option right retained by the entity* un derecho de opción de compra mantenido por la entidad ▲ *a call option that is deeply out of the money* una opción de compra que pierde gran cantidad de dinero ▲ *a covered call option write* una venta de la opción de compra con seguro de cobertura ▲ *a deep in-the-money call option* una opción de compra con mucho dinero ▲ *American call option* opción de compra americana ▲ *an attractive call option* una opción de compra atractiva ▲ *call options sold* opciones de compra vendidas ▲ *European call option* opción de compra europea ▲ *hold share call options that are convertible into ordinary shares* tener opciones de compra sobre acciones convertibles en acciones ordinarias ▲ *purchased call options* opciones de compra adquiridas ▲ *share call options* opciones de compra sobre acciones ▲ *the intrinsic value of a call option* el valor intrínseco de una opción de compra ▲ *the obligation under a call option written* la obligación según la opción de compra vendida ▲ *the right under a call option held* el derecho según la opción de compra adquirida ▲ *the time value of the call option* el valor en el tiempo de una opción de compra ▲ *the writer of the call option* el vendedor de la opción de compra ▲ *write a call option on the debt instrument to a third party* vender una opción de compra de la deuda a un tercero ▲ *written call options* opciones de compra vendidas
⇛ warrant

callable
≠ prepayable

A bond or loan that may be redeemed by the issuer before maturity under pre-determined conditions is termed callable.
rescatable
▲ *a callable loan* un préstamo rescatable ▲ *a written call option used to hedge a callable liability* una opción de compra vendida para cubrir un pasivo rescatable ▲ *callable bond series* series de bonos rescatables ▲ *callable convertible debt instrument* obligación convertible rescatable ▲ *callable mortgage-credit bonds* bonos hipotecarios rescatables

callable bond
A callable bond is a bond that may be redeemed at par by the issuer during the life of the bond before the maturity date.
bono rescatable
▲ *options in callable bonds* opciones en bonos rescatables ▲ *the duration of the callable bond* la vigencia del bono rescatable ▲ *the price of the callable bond* el precio del bono rescatable

called up share capital UK
The called up share capital of a company is that part of the issued capital that the company has required the shareholders to pay, in whole or in part. Called up share capital is also an item under capital and reserves in the balance sheet showing the total amount due from all shareholders to the company - whether paid or not-at the balance sheet date. Under the Companies Act 1985, issued shares may be paid in instalments when called up for payment.
capital no desembolsado exigido
= dividendo pasivo exigido
▲ *called up share capital shown as an asset* capital no desembolsado exigido reflejado como activo ▲ *called up share capital shown under liabilities* capital no desembolsado exigido reflejado en el pasivo
⇛ called up share capital not paid, issued capital, share capital, shareholders' funds

called up share capital not paid UK
Called up share capital not paid is an item in the balance sheet according to the Companies Act 1985 required report format. The item contains the amount of authorised share capital that remains to be fully paid in by shareholders.
capital no desembolsado exigido
= dividendo pasivo exigido
▲ *balance of called up share capital not paid at beginning of period* saldo de capital no desembolsado exigido al inicio del periodo ▲ *called up share capital not paid due from parent undertaking* capital no desembolsado exigido vencido procedente de la matriz
⇛ called up share capital, capital and reserves

called-up capital
→ called up share capital

called-up share capital UK
→ called up share capital

Canadian Institute of Chartered Accountants
= CICA
The Canadian Institute of Chartered Accountants (CICA) is a professional accountancy body whose members may audit the financial statements of companies. CICA acts as a coordinating organisation for the Canadian autonomous provincial institutes of accountants and issues the CICA Handbook according to whose standards Canadian financial statements must be prepared and audited.
Canadian Institute of Chartered Accountants
= Instituto Canadiense de Auditores
NOTE The Spanish equivalent body is called ICAC ('Instituto de Contabilidad y Auditoría de Cuentas').
▲ *become a member of the Canadian Institute of Chartered Accountants* inscribirse en el Canadian Institute of Chartered Accountants ▲ *the mission of the Canadian Institute of Chartered Accountants* el cometido del Canadian Institute of Chartered Accountants
⇛ chartered accountant, financial statements

cancel
To cancel means to bring an arrangement, e.g. a contract, to an end as from a particular date.
cancelar
▲ *cancel a contract or an agreement* cancelar un contrato o un acuerdo ▲ *cancel a contract without paying compensation to the other par-*

ty cancelar un contrato sin indemnización a la otra parte ▲ *cancel a lease* cancelar un alquiler ▲ *cancel a retirement benefit plan* cancelar un plan de pensiones ▲ *cancel a sale* cancelar una venta ▲ *cancel a transaction without significant penalty* cancelar una transacción sin penalización significativa ▲ *cancel potential ordinary shares* cancelar acciones ordinarias potenciales ▲ *cancel treasury shares* cancelar acciones propias

cancellation

Cancellation is the act of bringing an arrangement, e.g. a contract, to an end as from a particular date.

cancelación

▲ *cancellation of a branch* cancelación de una rama ▲ *cancellation of shares* cancelación de acciones ▲ *cancellation of the lease* cancelación del alquiler ▲ *cancellation of treasury shares* cancelación de acciones propias ▲ *exercise of cancellation rights* ejercicio de los derechos de cancelación ▲ *the lessor's losses associated with the cancellation* las pérdidas del arrendador asociadas a la cancelación

capacity

Capacity is the ability to contain something within a certain space or to achieve, fulfill or produce something.

capacidad

= rendimiento

▲ *adjust capacity* ajustar la capacidad ▲ *an equivalent productive capacity* una capacidad productiva equivalente ▲ *capacity ratio* ratio de capacidad ▲ *capacity to pay* capacidad de pago ▲ *capacity utilisation* utilización de la capacidad ▲ *earnings-generating capacity* capacidad para generar beneficios ▲ *estimated capacity* capacidad estimada ▲ *excess capacity* exceder la capacidad ▲ *existing capacity* capacidad existente ▲ *idle capacity* capacidad ociosa ▲ *increase capacity* aumentar la capacidad ▲ *increases in operating capacity* aumentos de capacidad operativa ▲ *invest in new capacity* invertir en capacidades productivas nuevas ▲ *loss of capacity resulting from planned maintenance* pérdida de capacidad resultante del mantenimiento previsto ▲ *production capacity* capacidad productiva ▲ *reduce capacity* reducir la capacidad ▲ *the asset's capacity* la capacidad del activo ▲ *the asset's expected capacity* la capacidad prevista del activo ▲ *the enterprise's capacity to generate earnings and cash flows* la capacidad de la empresa para generar beneficios y flujos de caja ▲ *the normal capacity of the production facilities* el rendimiento normal de las instalaciones ▲ *unutilised capacity* capacidad no utilizada ▲ *utilise the full capacity* usar a pleno rendimiento

capacity cost

Capacity costs are an alternate form for fixed costs that measure the cost of providing the capability to operate at a particular capacity for such activities as manufacturing, sales, administration and research.

coste de capacidad

= coste a pleno rendimiento

▲ *capacity cost variances* discrepancias en los costes a pleno rendimiento ▲ *capacity costs excluding depreciation, amortisation and write-downs on fixed assets* costes de capacidad excluyendo la depreciación, amortización y devaluación de los activos fijos ▲ *incur capacity costs* incurrir en costes de capacidad

⇛ fixed cost

capex

= capital cost, investment expenditure

Capex is the abbreviation of capital expenditure which is expenditure or expenses relating to investments in or improvements of fixed assets. Capital expenditure is capitalised in the balance sheet.

capex

= gasto de capital

▲ *a reduction in capex* una reducción en capex ▲ *capex, excluding share acquisitions* capex, excluyendo las adquisiciones de acciones ▲ *EBITDA less capex* EBITDA menos capex

⇛ capital expenditure

capital

Capital is the funds provided for the long-term financing of an enterprise and refers to the resources of an enterprise. Capital may take the form of either equity or loan capital.

capital

= financiación básica

▲ *affect the capital and asset structure of an enterprise* afectar el capital y la estructura de activos de una empresa ▲ *allocated capital* capital asignado ▲ *average invested capital* capital invertido medio ▲ *average working capital* capital circulante medio ▲ *capital appreciation* revalorización de capital ▲ *capital employed* capital empleado ▲ *contribute additional capital* aportar capital adicional ▲ *financial capital* capital financiero ▲ *holdings of a particular class of capital* carteras de una clase concreta de capital ▲ *idle capital* capital ocioso ▲ *inflow of capital* entrada de capital ▲ *invest capital in an enterprise* invertir capital en una empresa ▲ *maintain capital* mantener capital ▲ *nominal money capital* capital monetario autorizado ▲ *outflow of capital* salida de capital ▲ *physical capital* capital físico ▲ *preferred capital* capital preferente ▲ *provide a return on the allocated capital* rentabilizar el capital asignado ▲ *providers of capital to the enterprise* aportantes de capital a la empresa ▲ *repayment of capital* amortización de capital ▲ *return on invested capital* rentabilidad sobre el capital invertido ▲ *risk capital* capital riesgo ▲ *the increase in the capital during the financial year* el aumento de capital durante el ejercicio ▲ *total capital* total capital ▲ *weighted average cost of capital* coste medio ponderado de capital

capital account

A capital account is an account recording the capital contributed and ownership interest held in an enterprise. In a partnership the account lists the capital and retained earnings attributable to each partner, as it does to the single proprietor in the case of a one-man firm. In a limited liability company, the capital account shows the amounts contributed for each class of share capital.

cuenta de patrimonio

▲ *credit an amount to the capital account* abonar una cantidad a la cuenta de patrimonio ▲ *data related to the capital account* información relativa a la cuenta de patrimonio ▲ *separate capital account from drawing accounts* cuenta de patrimonio independiente de las cuentas corrientes

capital adequacy

Capital adequacy refers to the amount of capital funds (liabilities) a bank or other financial institution must maintain in proportion to funds lent (assets) as sufficient protection against losses. On an international basis, minimum capital requirements have been set by the Bank for International Settlements in the Basle Agreement. In 2004, this agreement was supplemented with a new accord, Basle II, which has introduced a new framework.

ratio de solvencia

▲ *capital adequacy requirements* requisitos del ratio de solvencia ▲ *capital adequacy statement* informe del ratio de solvencia ▲ *Council Directive 93/6/EEC on the capital adequacy of investment firms and credit institutions* Directiva del Consejo Europeo 93/6/CEE en relación con el ratio de solvencia de las instituciones financieras y crediticias

⇛ capital adequacy ratio

capital adequacy ratio

= solvency ratio

The capital adequacy ratio is a key performance indicator for banks and other credit institutions, defined as base capital as a ratio of risk-weighted assets (credit exposures) and off-balance sheet items.

ratio de adecuación del capital

▲ *a high capital adequacy ratio* un ratio de adecuación del capital alto ▲ *a low capital adequacy ratio* un ratio de adecuación del capital bajo

⇛ core capital ratio

capital adequacy rule

Capital adequacy rules are the rules for the amount of capital funds an enterprise must maintain to protect against credit and other risks. Such rules are typically relevant for banks and other financial institutions, and on an international basis, minimum capital requirements have been laid down by the Bank for International Settlements in the

Basle Agreement, succeeded by the Basle II Accord in 2004.
norma de solvencia crediticia
▲ *lay down capital adequacy rules* fijar las normas de solvencia crediticia ▲ *proposal for new capital adequacy rules* proposición de nuevas normas de solvencia crediticia
⇛ capital adequacy ratio

capital and reserves UK, IAS/IFRS, UK
= equity attributable to equity holders of the parent IAS/IFRS, shareholders' funds, stockholders' equity US
Capital and reserves is an item in the balance sheet according to the Companies Act 1985 required report format, representing the share capital contributed by owners plus retained earnings. In a group, capital and reserves is the equity share attributable to the parent company and exclude minority interests.
capital y reservas
= fondos propios
▲ *capital and reserves at the beginning of the financial year* capital y reservas al inicio del ejercicio ▲ *changes in capital and reserves* cambios en el capital y reservas ▲ *show as part of capital and reserves* reflejar como parte del capital y reservas ▲ *the aggregate amount of capital and reserves* la cantidad agregada de capital y reservas
⇛ equity, owners' equity

capital asset
= fixed asset
Capital assets are fixed assets, i.e. assets that are intended for permanent ownership or use by the enterprise. A capital asset may be an intangible asset, a tangible asset or an investment.
inmovilizado
= activo fijo
▲ *major capital assets* inmovilizado principal ▲ *tangible capital assets* inmovilizado tangible
⇛ asset

capital base
1 = capital resources
The capital base is the capital foundation or capital structure of an enterprise, i.e. equity plus loan capital.
financiación básica
▲ *analysis of the capital base* análisis de la financiación básica
2 The capital base is the capital resources of a bank and must comply with the statutory capital adequacy requirements. The capital base consists of core capital (tier 1 capital) and supplementary capital (tier 2 capital). The requirements are laid down in the Basel Capital Accord by the Basel Committee on Banking Supervision.
financiación básica
▲ *the size of the bank's capital base* el volumen de la financiación básica del banco

capital budget
A capital budget is a long-term plan for investment projects and capital expenditure, i.e. investments in and acquisition of fixed assets such as machinery, equipment and facilities.
presupuesto de inversión
= plan de inversión
▲ *a capital budget prepared by management* un presupuesto de inversión preparado por la dirección ▲ *a long-term capital budget* un presupuesto de inversión a largo plazo ▲ *a short-term capital budget* un presupuesto de inversión a corto ▲ *adjustments of certain items in the capital budget* ajustes de determinadas partidas en el presupuesto de inversión ▲ *the preparation of the capital budget* la preparación del presupuesto de inversión

capital charge
The capital charge is calculated as invested capital multiplied by the weighted average cost of capital (WACC) in per cent.
coste de capital
▲ *calculate the capital charge* calcular el coste de capital
⇛ WACC

capital commitment UK
Capital commitments refer to the future obligations of an enterprise to undertake capital expenditure, i.e. to invest in fixed assets. E.g. an enterprise may have agreed to buy new machinery at a future date. Capital commitments are accounted for in the notes to the financial statements.
compromiso de capital
▲ *any capital commitments in relation to interests in joint ventures* cualesquiera compromisos de capital en relación con las joint ven-

tures ▲ *settle capital commitments* establecer los compromisos de capital ▲ *the share of the contingent liabilities and capital commitments of an associate* la proporción de los pasivos contingentes y los compromisos de capital de una asociada

capital contribution

= supply of capital

Capital contribution is the contribution of capital by equity investment, e.g. share capital, or by capital similar to equity e.g. subordinate debt or subordinate loan capital.

aportación de capital

▲ *a cash capital contribution* una aportación de capital en efectivo ▲ *capital contributions by the venturers* aportaciones de capital por los participantes en una empresa de capital riesgo ▲ *capital contributions in kind* aportaciones de capital en especie ▲ *securities with indefinite maturity and other capital contributions* títulos con vencimiento indefinido y otras aportaciones de capital

capital cost

1 → cost of capital

2 Capital cost is an enterprise's expenditure on investments in or improvements of fixed assets. Capital costs are not charged to the profit and loss account, but capitalised in the balance sheet.

coste de capital

▲ *accounting for capital costs* contabilidad de costes de capital ▲ *high capital costs* costes de capital elevados ▲ *long-term capital costs* costes de capital a largo plazo

⇛ capital expenditure

capital employed

= invested capital

Capital employed is the total amount of capital used to generate profits, expressed as the sum of shareholders' equity and long-term interest-bearing debt of a company, or total non-current assets plus working capital. Capital employed is an important element of financial ratio analysis, although not legally defined.

capital utilizado

▲ *comparable returns in similar industries on turnover or capital employed* los rendimientos comparables en sectores similares sobre facturación o capital utilizado ▲ *return on average capital employed* rendimiento del capital utilizado medio ▲ *return on capital employed* rendimiento del capital utilizado

⇛ working capital

capital equipment

= fixed asset

Capital equipment is fixed assets used by an enterprise when producing goods or providing services. The concept includes plant, buildings and machinery but not land.

bienes de capital

NOTE Always plural in Spanish

▲ *costs of installation of capital equipment* costes de instalación de bienes de capital ▲ *costs of moving capital equipment to the site* costes de traslado de los bienes de capital al lugar ▲ *costs of removal of capital equipment* costes de eliminación de bienes de capital ▲ *costs of removing capital equipment* costes de eliminación de bienes de capital ▲ *costs of transport of capital equipment* costes de transporte de bienes de capital ▲ *depreciation of capital equipment* depreciación de los bienes de capital ▲ *development and production of capital equipment* desarrollo y producción de bienes de capital ▲ *lease of capital equipment* alquiler de bienes de capital ▲ *maintenance of capital equipment* mantenimiento de los bienes de capital ▲ *rationalisation and increase in the efficiency of the capital equipment* racionalización y aumento de la eficiencia de los bienes de capital ▲ *self-constructed capital equipment* bienes de capital de fabricación propia

capital expenditure

= capex, capital investment

An investment in or an improvement of a fixed asset is referred to as capital expenditure. Capital expenditure is capitalised in the balance sheet.

inversión en capital

= inversión en bienes de capital

▲ *capital additions or capital expenditure* sumas de capital o inversión en capital ▲ *capital expenditure excluding share acquisitions* inversión en capital excluyendo la adquisición de acciones ▲ *capital expenditure financed by borrowing* inversión en capital financiada con endeudamiento ▲ *financial capital expenditure* inversión en capital financiero ▲ *fixed capital expenditure* inversión en bienes de capital fijo ▲ *future capital expenditure necessary to maintain or sustain an asset at its originally assessed standard of performance* la inversión futura en capital necesaria para mantener o sostener un activo según el estándar de eficiencia inicialmente fijado ▲ *future capital expenditure that will improve or enhance the asset in excess of its originally assessed standard of performance* inversión en capital futura que mejorará o aumentará el activo excedente sobre el estándar de eficiencia inicialmente fijado ▲ *hedging of capital expenditure* cobertura de la inversión en capital ▲ *incur capital expenditure* incurrir en gastos en bienes de capital ▲ *intangible capital expenditure* inversión en capital intangible ▲ *tangible capital expenditure* inversión en capital tangible

capital gain

1 A capital gain refers to the profit made when an asset is sold or an increase in the value of an asset that is not sold, i.e. a capital gain may be either realised or unrealised. Usually, the person or enterprise holding or selling the asset is liable to pay tax.

plusvalía

▲ *a long-term capital gain* plusvalía a largo ▲ *a short-term capital gain* plusvalía a corto ▲ *any capital gains on disposal* cualesquiera plusvalías en la venta ▲ *capital gain on resale* plusvalía en la reventa ▲ *defer tax on capital gains* impuesto diferido de las plusvalías ▲ *realised capital gains* plusvalías liquidadas ▲ *tax on capital gains* impuesto sobre plusvalías ▲ *taxation of capital gains* tributación de la plusvalía ▲ *the capital gain of the investors* la plusvalía de los inversores

2 = capital gain on shares

A capital gain occurs when the original purchase price of securities is lower than the current selling price. A capital gain may be either unrealised or realised. Usually, the person or enterprise holding or selling the securities is liable to pay tax.

plusvalía

▲ *a realised capital gain* una plusvalía liquidada ▲ *calculate a capital gain* calcular una plusvalía ▲ *capital gain on shares* plusvalía por acciones

capital gains tax

= capital gains tax on shares, CGT

Capital gains tax is a tax that is levied on the increase in the value of assets. The capital gains tax is usually only collected when the assets are sold.

impuesto sobre plusvalías

▲ *be subject to capital gains tax* estar sujeto al impuesto sobre plusvalías ▲ *capital gains tax calculation* cálculo del impuesto sobre plusvalías ▲ *charge capital gains tax* cobrar el impuesto sobre plusvalías ▲ *deferral of capital gains tax* diferimiento del impuesto sobre plusvalías ▲ *give rise to capital gains tax* dar lugar al impuesto sobre plusvalías ▲ *introduce capital gains tax* introducir el impuesto sobre plusvalías ▲ *levy capital gains tax on the share options* gravar las opciones sobre acciones con el impuesto sobre plusvalías ▲ *pay capital gains tax* pagar el impuesto sobre plusvalías

capital in excess of par value US

= additional paid-in capital, paid-in surplus, premium on capital stock

Capital in excess of par value represents the amounts paid to the company for shares in excess of their nominal value. Capital in excess of par value is recognised as an item under equity in the balance sheet of an enterprise, representing the undistributable reserve of such share premiums.

prima de emisión

▲ *capital in excess of par value as at January 1* prima de emisión a 1 de enero ▲ *capital in excess of par value during the year* prima de emisión a lo largo del año

capital increase

A capital increase is the increase of the contributed capital either through cash or non-cash contribution or by conversion of debt.

ampliación de capital

▲ *a planned capital increase* una ampliación de capital planificada ▲ *costs of the capital increase* costes de la ampliación de capital ▲ *notice of capital increase* notificación de la ampliación de capital ▲ *proposal for a capital increase* propuesta de ampliación de capital ▲ *the estimated costs of the capital increase* los costes previstos de la ampliación de capital ▲ *the right to subscribe for new shares issued in connection with a capital increase* el derecho a suscribir nuevas acciones emitidas en una ampliación de capital

capital increase by way of non-cash contributions

A capital increase by way of non-cash contributions is an increase of the share capital made through the contribution of other assets than cash.

ampliación de capital con aportaciones no dinerarias

= ampliación de capital con aportaciones en especie

▲ *complete a capital increase by way of non-cash contributions* realizar una ampliación de capital con aportaciones no dinerarias ▲ *propose a capital increase by way of non-cash contributions* proponer una ampliación de capital con aportaciones no dinerarias

capital injection

= capital infusion, raising of additional capital

A capital injection is the supply of additional cash and cash equivalents to an enterprise that may be effected through the increase of the loan capital or the contributed capital.

inyección de capital

▲ *at the date of any subsequent capital injection* en la fecha de cualquier inyección de capital posterior ▲ *capital injection by minority interests* inyección de capital por intereses de los minoritarios

capital investment

= capital expenditure

≠ short-term investment

A capital investment refers to the expenditure by an enterprise to purchase or improve a fixed asset. Capital investments are not expensed in the profit and loss account when made, but instead the carrying amount of the fixed assets resulting from the investments is capitalised in the balance sheet and depreciated over their estimated useful lives.

inversión de capital

= inversión en bienes de capital

▲ *detailed capital investment plans* planes de inversión de capital detallados ▲ *major capital investments* inversiones de capital sustanciales ▲ *make capital investments* llevar a cabo inversiones de capital

⇛ financial investment, trading investment

capital lease US

= finance lease, finance lease agreement IAS/IFRS, UK

A capital lease is a lease that under Financial Accounting Standard 13 must be reflected on a company's balance sheet as an asset and corresponding liability. Generally, this applies to leases where the lessee acquires essentially all the economic benefits and risks related to the ownership of the leased asset - except for the legal title. The title of the asset is transferred to the lessee at the end of the lease term.

arrendamiento financiero

= leasing

▲ *accounting treatment of capital leases* tratamiento contable de los arrendamientos financieros ▲ *acquisition using capital leases* adquisición utilizando arrendamientos financieros ▲ *enter into capital leases* contratar arrendamientos financieros ▲ *investment property held under a capital lease* inversión en bienes raíces realizada mediante un arrendamiento financiero ▲ *lease out assets under a capital lease* alquilar activos mediante un arrendamiento financiero ▲ *leased property under capital leases* bienes raíces arrendados mediante arrendamientos financieros ▲ *net investment in a capital lease* inversión neta en un arrendamiento financiero ▲ *pre-existing capital leases* arrendamientos financieros preexistentes ▲ *the capitalized remaining lease obligation on capital leases* la obligación por alquiler vigente capitalizada en el arrendamiento financiero ▲ *the inception of a capital lease* el comienzo de un arrendamiento financiero ▲ *the interest rate implicit in a capital lease* el tipo de interés implícito en un arrendamiento financiero

capital loss

= investment loss

A capital loss is the loss that occurs when the price paid for a security is higher than its actual or estimated sales price.
minusvalía
▲ *capital losses on securities* minusvalías en los títulos ▲ *capital losses on shares* minusvalías en las acciones ▲ *deductible capital loss* minusvalía deducible ▲ *make deductions for capital losses* deducciones por minusvalías ▲ *realised capital losses* minusvalías realizadas ▲ *significant capital losses* minusvalías importantes ▲ *unrealised capital losses* minusvalías no realizadas

capital loss on shares
= capital loss on equities
A capital loss on shares is a loss due to fluctuations in the price of particular shares.
minusvalía en acciones
▲ *the capital losses on shares already realised* las minusvalías en acciones ya realizadas

capital maintenance
The concept of capital maintenance implies that an enterprise has as much capital at the end of the financial year as it had at the beginning of the financial year. Any amount over and above that required to maintain the capital at the beginning of the year is profit.
mantenimiento del capital
▲ *financial capital maintenance* mantenimiento del capital financiero ▲ *measure financial capital maintenance in nominal monetary units* medición del mantenimiento del capital financiero en unidades monetarias nominales ▲ *measure financial capital maintenance in units of constant purchasing power* medición del mantenimiento del capital financiero en unidades de poder adquisitivo costantes ▲ *physical capital maintenance* mantenimiento del capital físico

capital maintenance adjustment
The revaluation or restatement of assets and liabilities held over the financial year and which gives rise to increase or decrease in equity are accounted for as capital maintenance adjustments.
ajuste en el mantenimiento del capital
▲ *include in equity as capital maintenance adjustments* incluir en el patrimonio como ajustes en el mantenimiento del capital ▲ *reserves representing capital maintenance adjustments* reservas que representan los ajustes en el mantenimiento del capital

capital management
Capital management is the planning and administration of an enterprise's cash and cash equivalents to ensure that optimum liquidity resources are available to hedge against business and financial risk.
gestión de capital
▲ *risk and capital management* gestión de riesgo y capital

capital market
A capital market is a physical or virtual market place such as a stock exchange where long-term finance in the form of equity or loan capital is channelled from suppliers of capital (investors) to those demanding capital (enterprises).
mercado de capital
▲ *a competitive capital market* un mercado de capital competitivo ▲ *a strong capital market* un mercado de capital fuerte ▲ *access to a capital market* acceso al mercado de capital ▲ *an active capital market* un mercado de capital dinámico ▲ *an efficient capital market* un mercado de capital eficiente ▲ *developments in the capital markets* desarrollos en los mercados de capitales ▲ *increase the efficiency in a capital market* aumentar la eficiencia en un mercado de capital ▲ *the capital market in the EU* el mercado de capital en la UE ▲ *the Danish capital market* el mercado de capital danés ▲ *the global capital markets* los mercados de capitales globales ▲ *the interrelationship of capital markets* la interrelación de los mercados de capital ▲ *turnover in a capital market* facturación en un mercado de capital
⇛ money market

capital market day
A capital market day is a road show or meeting arranged and conducted by a particular company in various cities around the world with a view to providing capital markets, e.g. potential and existing investors,

with information about the company.

reunión promocional con analistas

= capital market day

▲ *hold a capital market day* tener una reunión promocional con analistas

capital receivable

→ uncalled capital

capital redemption reserve UK

= reserve for own shares UK, treasury stock US

A capital redemption reserve is a non-distributable reserve that is created when a company buys or redeems its own shares.

reserva para acciones propias

▲ *transfer to a capital redemption reserve* constituir una reserva para acciones propias

⇛ capital reserve, non-distributable reserve

capital reduction

= reduction of capital

A capital reduction is a write-down of the contributed capital, e.g. when a company buys back its own shares and cancels them.

reducción de capital

▲ *adopt a capital reduction* aprobar una reducción de capital ▲ *capital reduction by way of redemption* reducción de capital por medio de amortización ▲ *capital reduction with payment to shareholders* reducción de capital con pago a los accionistas ▲ *formalities concerning capital reduction* trámites concernientes a la reducción de capital ▲ *implement a capital reduction* implementar una reducción de capital ▲ *notification of capital reduction* notificación de reducción de capital ▲ *recommend the adoption of a capital reduction* recomendar la adopción de una reducción de capital ▲ *resolution for a capital reduction* resolución para una reducción de capital

capital requirement

Capital requirement is the amount of capital required by an enterprise to operate formulated by the Bank for International Settlements (BIS). For credit institutions, special capital requirements were laid down in the 1988 Basel Accord, which has been followed up by the Basel II Capital Accord to be implemented from 2006. The regulatory framework of Basel II rests on three interacting pillars: (1) minimum capital requirements which maintain an unchanged 8% minimum capital ratio, but include stricter calculation of risk weights, (2) a supervisory review process of banks' internal risk measurement procedures, and (3) market discipline which is to be encouraged through increased disclosures from banks.

requisito de capital mínimo

▲ *capital requirements for credit to small enterprises* requisitos de capital mínimo para conceder créditos a las pequeñas empresas ▲ *capital requirements for intra-group interbank lending* requisitos de capital mínimo para préstamo interbancario dentro del grupo ▲ *capital requirements to cover credit risk* requisitos de capital mínimo para cubrir el riesgo crediticio ▲ *compliance with regulatory capital requirements* cumplimiento de los requisitos de capital mínimo regulado ▲ *maintain a capital requirement* exigir un requisito de capital mínimo ▲ *measurement of capital requirements* medición de los requisitos de capital mínimo ▲ *options to waive capital requirements at various levels within a group* opciones para soslayar los requisitos del capital mínimo a varios niveles dentro del grupo ▲ *revise EU capital requirements* revisar los requisitos de capital mínimo de la UE ▲ *satisfy a capital requirement* cumplir con un requisito de capital mínimo ▲ *the risk-adjusted capital requirement* el requisito de capital mínimo ajustado al riesgo ▲ *to exempt investment firms from capital requirements for operational risk* eximir a las empresas de inversión de los requisitos de capital mínimo por riesgo operativo

capital reserve UK

= non-distributable reserve, restricted surplus US, undistributable reserve

≠ distributable reserve, revenue reserve UK, unrestricted earnings US

A capital reserve is a reserve in a company's balance sheet that is not available for distribution to shareholders.

reserva indisponible

▲ *an estimated balance on the capital reserve* un equilibrio estimado en la reserva indisponible ▲ *the value of the capital reserve* la cuantía de la reserva indisponible

capital reserve

= capital strength, capital strengthening, strengthening

A capital reserve reinforces the financial position of an enterprise. It can be obtained through a new issue of shares, which increases the share capital and consequently the equity, by repayment of debt or by the conversion of debt to share capital.

reserva patrimonial

▲ *the capital reserve of the enterprise* la reserva patrimonial de la empresa

capital resources

The capital resources of an enterprise consist of the financial funds available to the enterprise for its operations.

fondos propios

= recursos financieros, recursos propios

▲ *liquidity and capital resources* liquidez y fondos propios ▲ *safeguarding of the company's capital resources* salvaguardando los recursos financieros de la empresa ▲ *secure the capital resources* asegurar los recursos financieros ▲ *strengthen the capital resources* fortalecer los recursos financieros ▲ *the propriety of the company's capital resources* la propiedad de los recursos financieros de la empresa

capital stock US

Capital stock is the share capital or total amount of equity shares in a corporation. Basically, capital stock consists of two types of stock: common stock and preferred stock.

capital social

▲ *a minimum of 5% of the voting rights of the capital stock* un mínimo del 5% de los derechos de voto del capital social ▲ *amount to a minimum of 5% of the capital stock* representar un mínimo del 5% del capital social ▲ *fully paid-in capital stock* capital social completamente desembolsado ▲ *increase the capital stock* aumentar el capital social ▲ *increase the company's capital stock* aumentar el capital social de la empresa ▲ *issue of capital stock* emisión de capital social ▲ *paid-in capital stock* capital social desembolsado ▲ *reduce the capital stock by USD 10m* reducir el capital social en 10 millones de dólares USA ▲ *return on capital stock* rendimiento del capital social ▲ *the capital stock acquired* el capital social suscrito ▲ *the capital stock issued* el capital social emitido ▲ *the total nominal capital stock* el capital social nominal total

⇛ common stock, preferred stock, share capital

capital strength

= capital reserve, capital strengthening, strengthening

Capital strength is the reinforcement of the financial position of an enterprise. It can be obtained through a new issue of shares, which increases the share capital and consequently the equity, by repayment of debt or by the conversion of debt to share capital.

reforzamiento del capital

▲ *improve the capital strength of the enterprise* mejorar el reforzamiento del capital de la empresa

capital strengthening

= capital reserve, capital strength, strengthening

Capital strengthening is a way of reinforcing the financial position of an enterprise. It can be obtained through a new issue of shares, which increases the share capital and consequently the equity, by repayment of debt or by the conversion of debt to share capital.

reforzamiento del capital

▲ *capital strengthening of the position of the enterprise* reforzamiento del capital de posicionamiento de la empresa

capital structure

The capital structure of an enterprise is the composition of, on the one part, shareholders' funds and reserves and, on the other part, loan capital.

estructura de capital

▲ *affect the capital structure of the enterprise* afectar a la estructura de capital de la empresa ▲ *capital structure leverage* apalancamiento de la estructura de capital ▲ *changes in capital structure* cambios en la estructura de capital ▲ *evaluate the group capital structure* evaluar la estructura de capital del grupo ▲ *independent of the enterprise's capital structure* independiente de la estructura de capital de la empresa ▲ *optimisation of the capital structure* optimización de la estructura de capital ▲ *represent a significant element in the enterprise's capital structure* representar un elemento importante en la estructura de capital de la empresa ▲ *the development of the group capital structure* el desarrollo de la estructura de capital del grupo

capital surplus US
= paid-in surplus US, share premium IAS/IFRS, UK
Capital surplus is a type of reserves under equity representing a paid-in surplus in the form of a premium on issued shares, i.e. amounts contributed in excess of the nominal or stated value to a company.
prima de emisión
▲ *capital surplus as at January 1* prima de emisión a fecha de 1 de enero ▲ *capital surplus during the year* prima de emisión durante el año

capital transaction
A capital transaction is a transaction that changes the asset or debt position. Capital transactions may be investments in assets or repayment of debt.
transacción de capital
▲ *capital transactions with owners and distributions to owners* transacciones de capital con los propietarios y distribuciones a los propietarios ▲ *changes in equity other than those arising from capital transactions with owners* cambios en el patrimonio diferente al que surge de las transacciones de capital con los propietarios ▲ *reporting of capital transactions* registro de las transacciones de capital

capitalisation IAS/IFRS, UK
1 = capitalization US
Capitalisation means recognising a cost in the balance sheet as part of an asset's cost instead of charging it as an expense in the profit and loss account. Examples of capitalised items are costs, goodwill and other intangibles.
capitalización
= activación
▲ *borrowing costs eligible for capitalisation* costes por intereses susceptibles de capitalización ▲ *capitalisation of assets under finance leases* activación de activos en régimen de arrendamientos financieros ▲ *capitalisation of borrowing costs and other expenditure* capitalización de los costes financieros y otros gastos ▲ *capitalisation of concessions* activación de concesiones ▲ *capitalisation of development projects* activación de los proyectos de desarrollo ▲ *capitalisation of intangible assets* activación de activos intangibles ▲ *capitalisation of licences* activación de licencias ▲ *capitalisation of losses resulting from severe currency devaluations* capitalización de pérdidas resultantes de devaluaciones severas de divisas ▲ *capitalisation of negative deferred tax* capitalización del impuesto diferido negativo ▲ *capitalisation of the rights acquired* activación de los derechos adquiridos ▲ *capitalisation rate* tipo de capitalización ▲ *cessation of capitalisation* suspensión de capitalización ▲ *commencement of capitalisation* inicio de capitalización ▲ *meet the criteria for capitalisation* cumplir los criterios para la activación ▲ *suspension of capitalisation* suspensión de capitalización ▲ *writeback and capitalisation of an asset previously written off* reversión y capitalización de un activo previamente eliminado
2 = capitalization US
Capitalisation involves the computation of future payments into present value by means of an interest rate.
capitalización
▲ *capitalisation of borrowing costs* capitalización de costes financieros

capitalisation issue UK
= capitalization issue US, issue of bonus shares, scrip issue
A capitalisation issue is the act of increasing a company's issued capital by issuing additional share certificates for free to the company's existing shareholders in proportion to their shareholdings, this way converting accumulated reserves into issued share capital.

However, no additional capital is contributed and total equity remains the same; the effect is a reduction of the share price that increases the liquidity of the company's shares in the stock market.

ampliación de capital liberada
= emisión liberada
▲ *approve the capitalisation issue* aprobar la ampliación de capital liberada ▲ *recommend a capitalisation issue* recomendar una ampliación de capital liberada
⇛ rights issue

capitalise UK, IAS/IFRS
1 = capitalize US
To capitalise is to recognise an amount as an asset in the financial statements.
capitalizar
= activar
≠ actualizar
▲ *capitalise concessions* activar concesiones ▲ *capitalise costs* activar costes ▲ *capitalise development projects* activar proyectos de desarrollo ▲ *capitalise goodwill* capitalizar el fondo de comercio ▲ *capitalise intangible assets* activar activos intangibles ▲ *capitalise interest* capitalizar intereses ▲ *capitalise licences* activar licencias ▲ *capitalise negative deferred tax* capitalizar el impuesto diferido negativo ▲ *capitalise patents* activar patentes ▲ *capitalise the tax value of losses* capitalizar el valor fiscal de las pérdidas ▲ *capitalise trademarks* activar marcas ▲ *write back and capitalise an asset previously written off* reversión y capitalización de un activo previamente eliminado
2 = capitalize US
To capitalise is to compute future payments into present value using an interest rate.
capitalizar
▲ *capitalise a residual lease obligation* capitalizar una obligación de arrendamiento residual

capitalization US
1 = capitalisation UK
Capitalization means recognizing a cost in the balance sheet as part of an asset's cost instead of charging it as an expense in the income statement. Examples of capitalized items are costs, goodwill and other intangibles.
capitalización
▲ *borrowing costs eligible for capitalization* costes financieros susceptibles de capitalización ▲ *capitalization of assets under finance leases* activación de activos en régimen de arrendamientos financieros ▲ *capitalization of borrowing costs and other expenditure* capitalización de costes financieros y otros gastos ▲ *capitalization of concessions* activación de concesiones ▲ *capitalization of development projects* activación de proyectos de desarrollo ▲ *capitalization of intangible assets* activación de activos intangibles ▲ *capitalization of licences* activación de licencias ▲ *capitalization of losses resulting from severe currency devaluations* capitalización de pérdidas resultantes de devaluaciones de divisas severas ▲ *capitalization of negative deferred tax* capitalización del impuesto diferido negativo ▲ *capitalization of the rights acquired* activación de los derechos adquiridos ▲ *capitalization rate* tipo de capitalización ▲ *cessation of capitalization* suspensión de capitalización ▲ *commencement of capitalization* inicio de capitalización ▲ *meet the criteria for capitalization* cumplir los criterios para la capitalización ▲ *suspension of capitalization* suspensión de la capitalización ▲ *writeback and capitalization of an asset previously written off* reversión y capitalización de un activo previamente eliminado
2 = capitalisation UK
Capitalization involves the computation of future payments into present value by mean of an interest rate.
capitalización
≠ actualización
▲ *capitalization of borrowing costs* capitalización de costes financieros

capitalization issue US
= capitalisation issue, issue of bonus shares, scrip issue
A capitalization issue is the act of increasing a company's issued capital by issuing additional share certificates for free to the company's existing shareholders in proportion to their shareholdings, this way converting accumulated reserves

into issued share capital. However, no additional capital is contributed and total equity remains the same; the effect is a reduction of the share price that increases the liquidity of the company's shares in the stock market.

ampliación de capital liberada

▲ *approve the capitalization issue* aprobar la ampliación de capital liberada ▲ *recommend a capitalization issue* recomendar una ampliación de capital liberada

⇛ rights issue

capitalize US

1 = capitalise UK

To capitalize is to recognise an amount as an asset in the financial statements.

capitalizar

▲ *capitalize concessions* activar concesiones ▲ *capitalize costs* capitalizar costes ▲ *capitalize development projects* activar proyectos de desarrollo ▲ *capitalize goodwill* activar fondo de comercio ▲ *capitalize intangible assets* activar activos intangibles ▲ *capitalize interest* capitalizar intereses ▲ *capitalize licences* activar licencias ▲ *capitalize negative deferred tax* capitalizar el impuesto diferido negativo ▲ *capitalize patents* activar patentes ▲ *capitalize the tax value of losses* capitalizar el valor fiscal de las pérdidas ▲ *capitalize trademarks* activar marcas ▲ *write back and capitalize an asset previously written off* reversión y capitalización de un activo previamente eliminado

2 = capitalise UK

To capitalize is to compute future payments into present value using an interest rate.

capitalizar

≠ actualizar

▲ *capitalize a residual lease obligation* capitalizar una obligación de alquiler residual

carry

= book

For accounting purposes, to carry means to recognise or book an item or an amount in the financial statements.

contabilizar

= anotar, registrar

▲ *assets carried at fair value* activos contabilizados a valor razonable ▲ *carried as inventory* anotado en el inventario ▲ *carried at a revalued amount* registrado a una cantidad revalorizada ▲ *carried at cost* contabilizado al coste ▲ *carried at net realisable value* contabilizado al valor realizable neto ▲ *carried in terms of historical cost* contabilizado en términos de coste histórico ▲ *carried under the benchmark treatment* registrado según el tratamiento benchmark ▲ *intangible assets carried under the allowed alternative treatment* activos intangibles contabilizados según el tratamiento alternativo permitido ▲ *non-monetary items carried at amounts current at the balance sheet date* partidas no monetarias contabilizadas por el valor actual al cierre del balance

carry back

≠ carry forward

To carry back is to take back an accounting item to a previous accounting period.

trasladar a cuenta anterior

= trasladar a la cuenta anterior

▲ *carry back allowable losses* trasladar las pérdidas permitidas a la cuenta anterior

carry forward

≠ carry back

To carry forward is to transfer an accounting item to a future accounting period.

trasladar a cuenta nueva

▲ *carried forward for one calendar year* trasladar a cuenta nueva durante un año natural ▲ *carried forward until the related revenues are recognised* trasladar a cuenta nueva hasta que se reconozcan los ingresos relacionados ▲ *carry forward against future income* trasladar a cuenta nueva contra ingresos futuros ▲ *to be carried forward* ser trasladado a cuenta nueva

⇛ bring forward

carry interest

= provide return

To carry interest is to provide return, accumulate profit or get yield on an investment or a loan provided.

devengar interés

▲ *the loan carries interest at 8%* el préstamo devenga un interés del 8%

carry out

To carry out means to do something or put it into practice.

ejecutar

▲ *carry out a detailed valuation of the obligation before the balance sheet date* ejecutar una valoración detallada de la obligación antes de la fecha de cierre del balance ▲ *carry out a liability adequacy test* ejecutar una evaluación de suficiencia de pasivo ▲ *carry out disproportionate and costly changes to the entity's asset/liability management* ejecutar cambios desproporcionados y costosos para la gestión de activo/pasivo de la entidad ▲ *carry out expenditure to operate in a particular way in the future* ejecutar un gasto para operar en el futuro de una forma concreta ▲ *carry out repairs* ejecutar reparaciones ▲ *carry out the restructuring* ejecutar la reestructuración

carryback IAS/IFRS, UK

≠ carryforward

A carryback is a process by which the deductions or credits of one taxable year that cannot be used to reduce tax liability in that year are applied against a tax liability in an earlier year or years.

imputación a un ejercicio anterior

≠ imputación a un ejercicio siguiente

▲ *loss carryback* imputación de pérdidas a un ejercicio anterior

carryforward

= amount carried forward, carryover

≠ carryback

A carryforward is an amount which is carried forward from one accounting period to a future period, e.g. a tax loss carryforward.

imputación a un ejercicio siguiente

≠ imputación a un ejercicio anterior

▲ *carryforward of unused tax credits* imputación a un ejercicio siguiente de los créditos fiscales no utilizados ▲ *carryforward of unused tax losses* imputación a un ejercicio siguiente de las pérdidas fiscales no utilizadas ▲ *possibility of loss carryforward* posibilidad de imputación de la pérdida a un ejercicio siguiente ▲ *the benefit of income tax loss carryforwards* el beneficio de las imputaciones al ejercicio siguiente de la pérdida de ingresos fiscales ▲ *the tax loss or tax credit carryforward* la imputación al ejercicio siguiente de pérdida o crédito fiscal

⇛ tax credit carryforward, tax loss carryforward

carrying amount IAS/IFRS, UK

The carrying amount is the amount at which an asset or a liability is recognised in the balance sheet. For a fixed asset the carrying amount is the asset value recognised after adding to cost any revaluation and deducting any accumulated depreciation (amortisation) as well as any impairment losses thereon.

NOTE Depreciation is used about tangible fixed assets, and amortisation applies to intangible fixed assets.

valor contable

= importe en libros, valor en libros

▲ *a change in carrying amount arising from revaluation* un cambio en el valor contable que surge de la revalorización ▲ *add expenditure to the carrying amount of the asset* añadir gastos al valor contable del activo ▲ *adjust the carrying amount* ajustar el valor contable ▲ *amortise any remaining carrying amount of the goodwill over its remaining useful life* amortizar cualquier valor contable restante del fondo de comercio sobre su vida útil restante ▲ *average carrying amount* valor contable medio ▲ *carrying amount at year-end* el valor contable al final del año ▲ *determine by reference to the carrying amount* determinar por referencia al valor contable ▲ *excess of the carrying amount of the qualifying asset over recoverable amount* exceso del valor contable del activo garantizado sobre el valor recuperable ▲ *increase the carrying amount* aumentar el valor contable ▲ *initial carrying amount* valor contable inicial ▲ *realisation of goodwill at carrying amount* reconocimiento del fondo de comercio a valor contable ▲ *reconciliation of the carrying amount* conciliación del valor contable ▲ *recover the carrying amount* recuperar el valor contable ▲ *recover the carrying amount of certain assets or liabilities* recuperar el valor contable de ciertos activos o pasivos ▲ *recoverability of the carrying amount* recuperación del valor contable ▲ *reductions in the carrying amount* reducciones en el valor contable ▲ *revalued carrying amount* valor contable revalorizado ▲ *review the carrying amount* revisar el valor contable ▲ *revised carrying amount* valor contable revisado ▲ *sale at carrying amount* venta a valor contable ▲ *settle the carrying amount* determinar el valor contable ▲ *the aggregate carrying amount of the assets mortgaged* el valor contable agregado de los activos hipotecados ▲ *the carrying amount of net assets* el valor contable de los activos netos ▲ *the carrying amount of the share* el valor contable de la acción ▲ *the entire carrying amount of the asset* el valor contable íntegro del activo ▲ *the gross carrying amount of the goodwill* el valor contable bruto del fondo de comercio ▲ *the net carrying amount of the goodwill* el valor contable neto del fondo de comercio ▲ *the pre-acquisition carrying amounts of the identifiable liabilities* los valores contables anteriores a la adquisición de los pasivos identificables ▲ *the total carrying amount of inventories* el valor contable total de inventarios ▲ *write-down of the carrying amount* amortización del valor contable

carrying cost
= inventory cost
Carrying costs are costs incurred by holding stock of materials or products for a particular period, typically from time of receipt to time of use in production or sale. Such costs include e.g. storage, insurance and spoilage.
coste de almacenamiento
= coste de inventario
▲ *a decrease in carrying costs* una disminución en los costes de almacenamiento ▲ *an increase in carrying costs* un aumento en los costes de almacenamiento ▲ *reduce carrying costs* reducir los costes de almacenamiento
⇛ storage cost

carrying value US
= book value
Carrying value is the amount shown on an entity's books for assets, liabilities, or owners' equity, net of reductions of offsets such as for accumulated depreciation, allowance for bad debts, and bond discount.
valor contable
= valor en libro
▲ *carrying value at year-end* el valor contable al final del año ▲ *carrying value of net assets* el valor contable de los activos netos ▲ *difference between the carrying value and the tax base* diferencia entre el valor contable y el fiscal ▲ *realization of goodwill at carrying value* reconocimiento del fondo de comercio a valor contable ▲ *sale at carrying value* venta a valor contable ▲ *the carrying value of the share* el valor contable de la acción ▲ *the total carrying value of the assets mortgaged* el valor contable agregado de los activos hipotecados

carryover US
Carryover is a process by which the deductions and credits of one taxable year that cannot be used to reduce tax liability in that year are applied against tax liability in subsequent years.
crédito por pérdidas a compensar
▲ *automatic carryovers from 2004 to 2005* créditos por pérdidas a compensar automáticos del año 2004 a 2005 ▲ *non-automatic carryovers* créditos por pérdidas a compensar no automáticos ▲ *possibility of loss carryover* posibilidad de crédito por pérdidas a compensar

cash[1] *noun*
1 Cash includes cash on hand and deposits on current accounts with banks.
tesorería
= efectivo
NOTE Spanish accountants prefer 'tesorería' to the IAS/IFRS term 'efectivo'.
▲ *cash acquired* tesorería adquirida ▲ *cash disposed of* tesorería dispuesta ▲ *convert securities into cash* convertir títulos en tesorería
2 Cash is an item in the cash flow statement referring to cash in hand and bank deposits with up to 24 hours' notice.
tesorería
= efectivo
▲ *cash or a cash equivalent asset not restricted in use* tesorería u otros activos líquidos equivalentes sin restricción de uso ▲ *instruments that are readily convertible into cash* instrumentos que se convierten fácilmente en efectivo

⇛ cash and cash equivalents, cash at bank and in hand

3 Cash is money in the form of notes and coins instead of e.g. cheques, debit or credit cards.
efectivo
▲ *additional consideration in the form of cash* contraprestación adicional en forma de efectivo ▲ *as cash or its equivalent is received or paid* se recibe o paga en efectivo o equivalente ▲ *cash and bank balances* efectivo y saldos bancarios ▲ *cash and/or another form of consideration* en efectivo y/u otra forma de contraprestación ▲ *cash on hand and demand deposits* efectivo y depósitos a la vista ▲ *collect cash* cobrar en efectivo ▲ *consideration in cash* contraprestación en efectivo ▲ *movements of cash* movimientos de efectivo

4 = in cash
Cash payment means payment immediately with money, by cheque or debit card instead of buying on credit.
efectivo
= en efectivo, en metálico
▲ *a cash amount* una cantidad en efectivo ▲ *cash bid* oferta en efectivo ▲ *cash budget* presupuesto en efectivo ▲ *cash dividends* dividendos en metálico ▲ *cash funds* fondos efectivos ▲ *cash issue* emisión de efectivo ▲ *cash profit* beneficio en efectivo

cash[2] *verb*
To cash a checque or similar instrument means to exchange it for cash.
cobrar
▲ *cash a cheque* cobrar un cheque

cash accounting
= cash basis, cash basis accounting US, cash-flow accounting
≠ accrual accounting
Cash accounting means recording cash receipts and cash payments rather than revenues when earned and expenses as incurred.
contabilidad de caja
▲ *the use of cash accounting* el uso de la contabilidad de caja ▲ *under cash accounting* según la contabilidad de caja
⇛ cash basis of accounting

cash and cash equivalents IAS/IFRS, US
Cash and cash equivalents are defined as cash, i.e. cash in hand and at bank as demand deposits, as well as cash equivalents, i.e. highly liquid investments which may be immediately converted into known cash amounts at short notice, typically within three months or less, and which will not risk any significant change in value. The item "cash and cash equivalents" is the bottom line in the cash flow statement.
tesorería
= efectivo y otros medios líquidos equivalentes
NOTE Spanish accountants prefer 'tesorería' to the IAS/IFRS term 'efectivo'.
▲ *accumulate cash and cash equivalents and other monetary items* acumular tesorería y otras partidas monetarias ▲ *cash and cash equivalents as previously reported* tesorería como registrada previamente ▲ *cash and cash equivalents as restated* tesorería reestructurada ▲ *cash and cash equivalents at 1 January 2006* tesorería a uno de enero de 2006 ▲ *cash and cash equivalents at beginning of period* tesorería al inicio del periodo ▲ *cash and cash equivalents at beginning of year* tesorería a principio de año ▲ *cash and cash equivalents at end of period* tesorería al final del periodo ▲ *cash and cash equivalents at end of year* tesorería a final de año ▲ *changes in cash and cash equivalents* cambios en la tesorería ▲ *changes in cash and cash equivalents for the financial year* cambios en la tesorería para el ejercicio ▲ *contractual obligation to deliver cash and cash equivalents* obligación contractual para traspasar tesorería ▲ *contractual right to receive cash and cash equivalents* derecho contractual para recibir tesorería ▲ *define as cash and cash equivalents* calificar como tesorería ▲ *easy access to cash and cash equivalents* fácil acceso a la tesorería ▲ *generate cash and cash equivalents* generar tesorería ▲ *group cash and cash equivalents at end of year* grupo de tesorería a final del año ▲ *include as a component of cash and cash equivalents* incluir como componente de tesorería ▲ *net change in cash and cash equivalents* cambio neto en tesorería ▲ *net increase in cash and cash equivalents* incremento neto en tesorería ▲ *net of cash and cash equivalents acquired* neto de teso-

tesorería ▲ *net of cash and cash equivalents disposed of* neto de tesorería dispuesto ▲ *receive cash and cash equivalents* recebir tesorería ▲ *the ability of the enterprise to generate cash and cash equivalents* la capacidad de la empresa para generar tesorería ▲ *the historical changes in cash and cash equivalents* los cambios históricos en tesorería

cash at bank and in hand UK
= cash
Cash at bank and in hand is the balance sheet item comprising the total amount of money held at the bank by a company and the amount of cash on hand.
tesorería
▲ *cash at bank and in hand acquired* tesorería adquirida ▲ *cash at bank and in hand disposed of* tesorería dispuesta ▲ *convert securities into cash at bank and in hand* convertir los títulos en tesorería
⇛ cash and cash equivalents

cash balance
The cash balance is the money in the form of notes and coins held by the enterprise.
saldo de efectivo
▲ *a low cash balance* un saldo de efectivo bajo ▲ *a substantial cash balance* un saldo de efectivo importante ▲ *an increased cash balance* un saldo de efectivo incrementado

cash basis[1] *noun* <a, the, cash bases>
= cash
≠ credit
A settlement made on a cash basis is made against payment in cash. Prices quoted on a cash basis typically reflect a cash discount that the customer foregoes if buying on credit.
al contado
≠ a crédito
▲ *computed on a cash basis* contabilizado al contado ▲ *effect on a cash basis* efectuar al contado ▲ *modified cash basis* al contado modificado ▲ *on a cash and debt free basis* al contado y libre de cargas

cash basis[2] *noun* <a, the, no plural>
≠ accrual basis of accounting
The cash basis is a method of accounting in which revenue and expenses are recorded only when payments are actually received or made.
criterio de caja
≠ principio del devengo
▲ *modified cash basis* criterio de caja modificado

cash basis accounting
= cash basis of accounting, cash flow accounting
Cash basis accounting implies that revenues and expenses are recognised when cash is received or paid rather than when earned or incurred.
contabilidad por el criterio de caja
≠ contabilidad por el principio del devengo
▲ *financial reporting under cash basis accounting* información financiera según la contabilidad por el criterio de caja

cash basis of accounting
= cash basis accounting, cash flow accounting
≠ accrual basis of accounting
The cash basis of accounting implies that revenues and expenses are recognised when cash is received or paid rather than when earned or incurred.
contabilidad por el criterio de caja
≠ contabilidad por el principio del devengo
▲ *financial reporting under the cash basis of accounting* información financiera según la contabilidad por el criterio de caja

cash book
A cash book is a record in chronological order of cash receipts and cash payments including transactions made via bank accounts.
libro de caja
▲ *keep a cash book* mantener un libro de caja ▲ *record in the cash book* anotar en el libro de caja

cash budget
A cash budget is a financial document showing planned cash income and expenditure for a particular period of time.
presupuesto de caja
▲ *prepare a cash budget* preparar un presupuesto de caja
⇛ cash flow projection, financial budget

cash capacity cost
Cash capacity costs are indirect costs paid during the year and necessary for production and sa-

les. Examples are taxes, interest on loans, office and management expenses, and insurance as opposed to e.g. depreciation which is a non-cash expense.

coste de producción con variación de cash-flow

≠ coste de producción sin variación del cash flow

▲ *cash capacity costs payable* costes de producción con variación de cash-flow debidos ▲ *fixed-term cash capacity costs* costes de producción con variación de cash-flow fijos ▲ *incur cash capacity costs* incurrir en costes de producción con variación de cash-flow ▲ *prepaid cash capacity costs* costes de producción con variación de cash-flow ya pagados

cash disbursement

A cash disbursement is payment made in money by somebody on behalf of another person.

pago en efectivo

▲ *cash disbursement reconciliations* conciliaciones de pago en efectivo

cash discount

= sales discount US

A cash discount is a percentage reduction in an invoice amount given in return for cash or quick payment.

descuento por pronto pago

▲ *allow a cash discount* permitir un descuento por pronto pago ▲ *cash discounts allowed* descuento por pronto pago permitido ▲ *cash discounts received* descuento por pronto pago recibido ▲ *receive a cash discount* recibir un descuento por pronto pago

cash earnings

= CE

Cash earnings is a financial ratio measuring an enterprise's performance and profitability defined as profit before non-cash charges such as depreciation, amortisation and write-downs and share-based payments, less share in associates and minorities' share of non-cash charges.

dividendo

▲ *cash earnings after tax* dividendo después de impuestos ▲ *cash earnings per share* dividendo por acción

cash earnings per share

= CEPS

Cash earnings per share is an investment ratio defined as cash earnings divided by the average number of shares diluted.

dividendo por acción

= beneficio por acción

▲ *fully diluted adjusted cash earnings per share* los dividendos por acción totalmente diluidos

⇛ cash earnings

cash equivalent

Cash equivalents are short-term investments of such high liquidity and safety that they may be easily and quickly converted into cash without any significantly changed value.

equivalente de efectivo

= equivalente al efectivo

NOTE Spanish accountants prefer 'equivalente de efectivo' to the IAS/IFRS term 'equivalente al efectivo'. The IAS/IFRS term is nonsensical in Spanish.

▲ *consider to be cash equivalents* considerarse equivalentes de efectivo ▲ *hold cash equivalents* tener equivalentes de efectivo ▲ *investments not included in cash equivalents* inversiones no incluidas en los equivalentes de efectivo ▲ *the investment of excess cash in cash equivalents* la inversión del exceso de liquidez en equivalentes de efectivo

cash flow

Cash flow is the movement of cash and cash equivalents flowing in and out of an enterprise.

flujo de efectivo

= cash flow, flujo de caja

▲ *adjust for daily-weighted cash flows* ajustar los flujos de efectivo ponderados diariamente ▲ *cash flow description* descripción de flujos de efectivo ▲ *cash flow for the year* flujos de efectivo para el año ▲ *cash flow forecast* previsión de flujos de efectivo ▲ *cash flow information* información de flujos de efectivo ▲ *cash flows from financing activities* flujos de efectivo de actividades de financiación ▲ *cash flows from investing activities* flujos de efectivo de actividades de inversión ▲ *cash flows from operating activities* flujos de efectivo de actividades de explotación ▲ *cause ma-*

jor movements in the cash flow of an enterprise originar movimientos mayores en el flujo de efectivo de una empresa ▲ *discount future cash flows* descontar flujos de efectivo futuros ▲ *discounted cash flow projections* proyecciones de flujos de efectivo descontadas ▲ *estimated future net cash flows* flujos de efectivo neto futuros estimados ▲ *future cash flows* flujos de efectivo futuros ▲ *generate cash flows* generar flujos de efectivo ▲ *operating cash flow* flujos de efectivo de explotación ▲ *present cash flows* flujos de efectivo actuales ▲ *reliable estimates of future cash flows* estimaciones fiables de los flujos de efectivo futuros ▲ *report cash flows on a net basis* registrar flujos de efectivo por valor neto ▲ *segment cash flows* fraccionar flujos de efectivo ▲ *the amount of cash flows arising from operating activities* la cantidad de flujos de efectivo procedentes de operaciones de explotación ▲ *the amounts and timing of cash flows* las cantidades y periodificación de los flujos de efectivo ▲ *the enterprise having the cash flow difficulties* la empresa que tiene dificultades de efectivo ▲ *the expected cash flow approach* el enfoque del flujo de efectivo esperado ▲ *the financial position, performance and cash flows of an enterprise* la posición financiera, actividad y los flujos de efectivo de una empresa ▲ *the present value of the future cash flows* el valor actual de los flujos de efectivo futuros ▲ *utilise cash flows* utilizar flujos de efectivo

cash flow accounting

= cash basis accounting, cash basis of accounting

Cash flow accounting implies that revenues and expenses are recognised when cash is received or paid rather than when earned or incurred.

contabilidad de caja

= contabilidad de efectivo

▲ *financial reporting under cash flow accounting* registro financiero según la contabilidad de caja

cash flow analysis

By means of the cash flow analysis the future cash flows of the enterprise are assessed on the basis of changes in cash and cash equivalents in the financial year in question.

análisis de flujo de efectivo

= análisis del cash flow, análisis del flujo de caja, análisis del flujo de efectivo

▲ *discounted cash flow analysis* análisis de flujo de efectivo descontado ▲ *prepare a cash flow analysis* preparar un análisis de flujo de efectivo

cash flow from financing activities

UK

Cash flow from financing activities is an item in the cash flow statement that shows the net cash flow attributable to long-term financing such as the issuance of equity or the raising and servicing of loan capital.

flujo de efectivo de las actividades de financiación

= cash flow de las actividades de financiación, flujo de caja de las actividades de financiación

▲ *changes in cash flow from financing activities* cambios en el flujo de efectivo de las actividades de financiación ▲ *determine the cash flow from financing activities* determinar el flujo de efectivo de las actividades de financiación

⇛ cash flow statement, financing activity

cash flow from investing activities

UK

Cash flow from investing activities is an item in the cash flow statement that shows the net cash flow in connection with investments, i.e. cash receipts from fixed asset disposals or investments, such as dividend and interest, less cash payments attributable to the fixed asset acquisitions.

flujo de efectivo de las actividades de inversión

= cash flow de las actividades de inversión, flujo de caja de las actividades de inversión

▲ *beginning-of-period cash flow from investing activities* flujo de efectivo de las actividades de inversión al inicio del periodo ▲ *other cash flow from investing activities* otro flujo de efectivo de las actividades de inversión

⇛ cash flow statement

cash flow from operating activities UK

Cash flow from operating activities is an item in the cash flow statement that shows the net cash flow (actual cash receipts less cash payments) generated from an enterprise's operations during the accounting period as calculated by applying either the direct or the indirect method.

flujo de efectivo de las actividades de explotación

= cash flow de las actividades de explotación, flujo de caja de las actividades de explotación

▲ *calculate cash flow from operating activities* calcular el flujo de caja de las actividades de explotación

⇛ cash flow from operations, cash flow statement

cash flow from operations

= CFFO

Cash flow from operations is a financial profitability and efficiency ratio defined as cash flow before capital expenditure, dividend payment, share buybacks and proceeds from issues, also expressed as free cash flow to equity plus capex.

flujo de efectivo operativo

= cash flow operativo, flujo de efecto operativo

▲ *calculate cash flow from operations* calcular el flujo de efectivo operativo

⇛ capital expenditure, cash flow from operating activities, free cash flow to equity

cash flow hedge

A cash flow hedge is a transaction intending to offset or minimize risk exposure to changes in future cash flows of a particular asset or liability (the hedged item) that are e.g. due to fluctuations in interest rates or foreign currencies. The hedging transaction involves use of derivative financial instruments as hedging instruments such as swaps.

cobertura de flujo de efectivo

= cobertura del cash flow, cobertura del flujo de caja, cobertura del flujo de efectivo

▲ *derivative financial instruments designated for cash flow hedges* instrumentos financieros derivados diseñados para coberturas de flujo de efectivo ▲ *fair value gains on cash flow hedges* ganancias del valor razonable de las coberturas de flujo de efectivo ▲ *fair value losses on cash flow hedges* pérdidas del valor razonable de las coberturas de flujo de efectivo ▲ *qualify as cash flow hedges* habilitar como coberturas de flujo de efectivo ▲ *qualify as hedging instruments in a cash flow hedge* habilitar como instrumentos de cobertura en una cobertura de flujo de efectivo ▲ *use interest rate swaps as cash flow hedges of future interest payments* utilizar swaps de tipo de interés como coberturas de flujo de efectivo de los pagos de intereses futuros

cash flow hedging

Cash flow hedging refers to an enterprise's use of derivative financial instruments to hedge against changes in future cash flows of a particular asset or liability (the hedged item) that are e.g. due to fluctuations in interest rates or foreign currencies. The hedging transaction involves use of derivative financial instruments as hedging instruments such as swaps.

operaciones de cobertura de flujo de efectivo

NOTE Always plural in Spanish accounting texts.

▲ *cash flow hedging of variable interest payments* operaciones de cobertura de flujo de efectivo para pagos de intereses variables ▲ *designate as cash flow hedging instruments* designar como instrumentos de operaciones de cobertura de flujo de efectivo ▲ *ongoing cash flow hedging* operaciones de cobertura de flujo de efectivo en marcha ▲ *use cash flow hedging* utilizar operaciones de cobertura de flujo de efectivo

⇛ cash flow hedge, derivative financial instrument, hedged item, hedging instrument

cash flow per share

= CFPS

Cash flow per share is an investment ratio defined as cash flow from operations divided by the average number of shares diluted.

cash flow por acción

= flujo de caja por acción, flujo de efectivo por acción

▲ *free cash flow per share* cash flow por acción gratis ▲ *net cash flow per share* cash flow por acción neto

⇛ cash flow from operations

cash flow projection
= cash budget
A cash flow projection is a forecast or budget for future in- and outflows of cash of an enterprise during a period, often a month. The projection may also include plans for managing any cash surpluses or cash deficits from operations.
previsión de flujo de efectivo
= previsión de cash flow, previsión del flujo de caja
▲ *cash flow projections based on reasonable and supportable assumptions* previsiones de flujo de efectivo basadas en supuestos documentados y razonables ▲ *cash flow projections until the end of an asset's useful life* previsiones de flujo de efectivo hasta el fin de la vida útil de un activo ▲ *current cash flow projections* previsiones de flujo de efectivo actual ▲ *extrapolate cash flow projections beyond the period covered by the most recent budgets and forecasts* extrapolar las previsiones de flujo de efectivo más allá del periodo cubierto por los presupuestos más actuales y los proyectados ▲ *the difference between past cash flow projections and actual cash flows* la diferencia entre las previsiones de flujo de efectivo futuras y los flujos de efectivo actuales ▲ *the discount rates applied to the cash flow projections* los tipos de descuento aplicados a las previsiones de flujo de efectivo

cash flow risk
A cash flow risk is the risk that future cash flows associated with a monetary financial instrument will fluctuate in amount.
riesgo de flujo de efectivo
= riesgo de cash flow, riesgo de flujo de caja
▲ *exposed to cash flow risk from changes in market interest rates* expuesto al riesgo de flujo de efectivo procedente de cambios en los tipos de interés del mercado

cash flow statement IAS/IFRS
The cash flow statement must, as a minimum, show the cash flows for the period classified by operating, investing and financing activities. Furthermore, the cash flow statement must show changes in cash and cash equivalents for the accounting period and the cash and cash equivalents as at the beginning and end of the period.
estado de flujo de efectivo
= estado de cash flow, estado de flujo de caja, estado de tesorería
▲ *cash flow statement per quarter* estado de flujo de efectivo por trimestre ▲ *cash flow statement per segment* estado de flujos de efectivo por segmento ▲ *condensed cash flow statement* estado de flujo de efectivo abreviado ▲ *disclose as separate items in the cash flow statement* publicar como partidas separadas en el estado de flujo de efectivo ▲ *exclude from a cash flow statement* excluir de un estado de flujo de efectivo ▲ *include a cash flow statement in the financial statements* incluir un estado de flujos de efectivo en los estados financieros ▲ *main items in the consolidated cash flow statement* partidas principales en el estado de flujos de efectivo consolidado ▲ *notes to the cash flow statement* notas al estado de flujos de efectivo ▲ *prepare a cash flow statement* preparar un estado de flujos de efectivo ▲ *prepare a separate cash flow statement for the parent* preparar un estado de flujos de efectivo separado para la matriz ▲ *present a cash flow statement* presentar un estado de flujos de efectivo ▲ *present a consolidated cash flow statement* presentar un estado de flujos de efectivo consolidado ▲ *present a reconciliation of the amounts in the cash flow statement* presentar una conciliación de las cantidades en el estado de flujo de efectivo ▲ *present on the face of the cash flow statement* presentar a la vista del estado de flujo de efectivo ▲ *present the cash flow statement in accordance with the direct method* presentar el estado de flujos de efectivo de acuerdo con el método directo ▲ *present the cash flow statement in accordance with the indirect method* presentar el estado de flujo de efectivo consolidado de acuerdo con el método indirecto ▲ *presentation of the cash flow*

statement presentación del estado de flujos de efectivo ▲ *report in the cash flow statement* informar en el estado de flujos de efectivo
⇛ direct method, indirect method, statement of cash flows

cash generated from operations
Cash generated from operations is an item in the cash flow statement classifying the cash flowing into an enterprise for an accounting period as an effect of transactions and other events relating to the ordinary activities, also appearing from the operating profit in the profit and loss account. The two other main cash flow categories are cash flow from investing activities and cash flow from financing activities.
efectivo generado por las actividades de explotación
▲ *actual cash generated from operations* efectivo generado por las actividades de explotación actual ▲ *measure the cash generated from operations* medir el efectivo generado por las actividades de explotación

cash generating unit
→ cash-generating unit

cash inflow
≠ cash outflow
Cash inflow is an ingoing movement of cash to an enterprise.
entrada de efectivo
≠ salida de efectivo
▲ *cash inflows from an asset or group of assets* entradas de efectivo procedentes de un activo o un grupo de activos ▲ *future cash inflows* entradas de efectivo futuras ▲ *generate cash inflows* generar entradas de efectivo ▲ *generate independent cash inflows from continuing use* generar entradas de efectivo independientes del uso continuado ▲ *generate separate cash inflows* generar entradas de efectivo separadas ▲ *independent of the cash inflows from other assets* independiente de las entradas de efectivo de otros activos ▲ *the lowest level of identifiable cash inflows* el nivel más bajo de entradas de efectivo identificables ▲ *the present value of future cash inflows* el valor actual de las entradas de efectivo futuras
⇛ cash flow, net cash inflow

cash loan
A cash loan is a loan where the borrower receives the entire loan amount in cash from the lender.
préstamo
▲ *amortisation account for cash loans* cuenta de amortización de los préstamos ▲ *raise a cash loan* obtener un préstamo

cash management
= liquidity management
Cash management is the administration and control of the enterprise's cash, so that it is able to meet its payment obligations and have a clear picture of its cash flows.
gestión de efectivo
▲ *an integrated part of the enterprise's cash management* una parte integrada de la gestión de efectivo de la empresa ▲ *coordinate cash management* cordinar la gestión de efectivo ▲ *form an integral part of an enterprise's cash management* formar una parte integral de la gestión de efectivo de una empresa ▲ *include securities in the continuous cash management* incluir títulos en la gestión de efectivo permanente ▲ *the continuous cash management of the enterprise* la gestión de efectivo permanente de la empresa ▲ *the variety of cash management practices* la variedad de prácticas de gestión de efectivo

cash outflow
≠ cash inflow
Cash outflow is an outgoing movement of cash from an enterprise.
salida de efectivo
≠ entrada de efectivo
▲ *cash outflows that are necessary to generate the cash inflows* salidas de efectivo que son necesarias para generar entradas de efectivo ▲ *estimates of future cash inflows and cash outflows* cálculos de entradas y salidas de efectivo futuras ▲ *estimates of future cash outflows for the restructuring* cálculos de salidas de efectivo futuras para la reestructuración ▲ *future cash outflows* salidas de efectivo futuras ▲ *net cash outflows for the asset* salidas de efectivo netas para el activo ▲ *projections of cash outflows* proyecciones de salidas de efectivo ▲ *provisions relating to cash outflows that arise soon after the balance sheet*

date provisiones relacionadas con las salidas de efectivo que surgen poco después de la fecha de cierre del balance
⇛ cash flow

cash payment
≠ cash receipt
Cash payment is payment or settlement in money rather than in kind.
pago en efectivo
≠ cobro en efectivo
▲ *cash payments to and on behalf of employees* pagos en efectivo en nombre de los trabajadores ▲ *cash payments to owners to acquire or redeem the enterprise's shares* pagos en efectivo a los propietarios para adquirir o amortizar las acciones de la empresa ▲ *cash payments to suppliers for goods and services* pagos en efectivo a proveedores de bienes y servicios ▲ *major classes of gross cash payments* clases mayores de pagos en efectivo brutos

cash proceeds
Cash proceeds constitute the amount of money received from asset sales or the issuance of securities such as shares and bonds.
efectivo generado
▲ *cash proceeds from issuing debentures, notes, mortgages and other short or long-term borrowings* efectivo generado por emisión de empréstitos, pagarés, hipotecas, y otros préstamos a corto o largo plazo ▲ *cash proceeds from issuing shares or other equity instruments* efectivo generado por emisión de acciones u otros instrumentos de patrimonio

cash receipt
≠ cash payment
A cash receipt is money received as payment in the form of notes, coins, cheques, debit card payments and similar payments from customers such as trade debtors.
cobro en efectivo
= cobro procedente
≠ pago en efectivo
NOTE The IAS/IFRS term 'cobro procedente' is very ambiguous in Spanish. Spanish accountants prefer the traditional Spanish term 'cobro en efectivo'.
▲ *cash receipts and payments from contracts held for dealing or trading purposes* cobros y pagos en efectivo por contratos suscritos por razones comerciales y otras actividades empresariales ▲ *cash receipts from royalties, fees, commissions and other revenue* cobros en efectivo por royalties, tarifas, comisiones y otros ingresos ▲ *cash receipts from the sale of goods and the rendering of services* cobros en efectivo por la venta de bienes y por la prestación de servicios ▲ *deferrals or accruals of past or future operating cash receipts or payments* anticipos o devengos de operaciones pasadas o futuras por cobros en efectivo ▲ *major classes of gross cash receipts* clases mayores de cobros en efectivo brutos

cash resources
= cash and credit available, cash reserves, financial resources
Cash resources are the cash funds of an enterprise, typically consisting of cash in hand and demand deposits at banks, which are available at short term to finance operations and settlement of debts.
tesorería
= caja y bancos
▲ *group cash resources at 31 December 2005* la tesorería del grupo a 31 de diciembre de 2005 ▲ *group cash resources including undrawn credit facilities* la tesorería del grupo que incluye créditos disponibles ▲ *improve cash resources* mejorar tesorería ▲ *set goals for cash resources* establecer objetivos de tesorería

cash value
The cash value is the fair market value of property or the monetary amount receivable, e.g. on a loan or on the surrender of a life insurance policy.
valor en efectivo
= valor al contado
▲ *cash value of land and buildings* valor en efectivo de terrenos y construcciones ▲ *conversion into cash value* transformación en valor en efectivo ▲ *convert into cash value* convertir en valor en efectivo ▲ *the cash value of the loan* el valor en efectivo del préstamo ▲ *the underlying cash value of the loan at the date of borrowing* el valor en

efectivo subyacente del préstamo a fecha de formalización

cash-basis accounting US

→ cash accounting

cash-flow accounting

→ cash accounting

cash-generating unit IAS/IFRS

= CGU

A cash-generating unit is the smallest group of assets that can be identified to generate cash inflows on a separate basis compared with other assets or groups of assets.

unidad generadora de efectivo

= UGE

▲ *determine the recoverable amount of a cash-generating unit* determinar la cantidad recuperable de una unidad generadora de efectivo ▲ *determine the value in use of a cash-generating unit* determinar el valor en uso de una unidad generadora de efectivo ▲ *disclosures of cash-generating units* desgloses de las unidades generadoras de efectivo ▲ *identification of an asset's cash-generating unit* identificación de la unidad generadora de efectivo de un activo ▲ *identify as a separate cash-generating unit* identificar como una unidad generadora de efectivo independiente ▲ *impairment losses for a cash-generating unit* pérdidas por deterioro del valor en una unidad generadora de efectivo ▲ *make write-downs in a cash-generating unit* hacer amortizaciones en una unidad generadora de efectivo ▲ *net selling price of a cash-generating unit* precio de venta neto de una unidad generadora de efectivo ▲ *test a cash-generating unit for impairment* hacer una prueba a una unidad generadora de efectivo por deterioro patrimonial ▲ *the assets of cash-generating units* los activos de las unidades generadoras de efectivo ▲ *the carrying amount of cash-generating units* el valor contable de las unidades generadoras de efectivo ▲ *the cash-generating unit's output* la producción de una unidad generadora de efectivo ▲ *the estimated future cash flows of the cash-generating unit* los flujos de efectivo futuros estimados de la unidad generadora de efectivo

SOURCE IFRS 5, Appendix A

cash-settled share-based payment transaction IAS/IFRS, UK

Cash-settled share-based payment transactions are transactions with suppliers of goods and services where the liability incurred in return by the enterprise is the transfer of an amount in cash or other assets based on the fair value or price of the enterprise's equity instruments.

transacción liquidada en efectivo con pagos basados en acciones

▲ *account for the transaction, as a cash-settled share-based payment transaction* contabilizar la transacción como una transacción liquidada en efectivo con pagos basados en acciones ▲ *goods or services acquired in a cash-settled share-based payment transaction* bienes o servicios adquiridos en una transacción liquidada en efectivo con pagos basados een acciones ▲ *in accordance with the requirements applying to cash-settled share-based payment transactions* de acuerdo con los requisitos que requieren las transacciones liquidadas en efectivo con pagos basados en acciones

SOURCE IFRS 2, Appendix A

cause[1] *noun*

= reason

A cause is a reason for an event.

causa

= motivo

▲ *a potential cause* una causa potencial ▲ *cause and effect* causa y efecto ▲ *cause for complaint* motivo de la protesta ▲ *cause of damage* causa del daño ▲ *root cause* causa raíz

cause[2] *verb*

To cause something is to result in something or make something happen.

causar

▲ *cause a significant loss* causar una pérdida significativa ▲ *factors that cause changes in fair value* factores que causan cambios en el valor razonable

CC

The letters 'CC' are used as a rating symbol by the credit rating agency Standard & Poor's. The 'CC' rating is a speculative-grade rating and rates an obligation as currently highly vulnerable to nonpayment.

CC

▲ *assign a CC rating* calificar con un rating CC ▲ *receive a CC rating* recibir un rating CC

CCA

= current cost accounting

CCA is the abbreviation for current cost accounting, which is a method of accounting in which the costs and revenues of an enterprise are recorded after taking into account the assets' current replacement cost as well as the effect of inflation on asset values and liabilities.

contabilidad a coste constante

▲ *CCA depreciation* depreciación de contabilidad a coste constante ▲ *use CCA* utilizar contabilidad a coste constante

CCC

The letters 'CCC' are used as a rating symbol by the credit rating agency Standard & Poor's to signify a speculative-grade rating. An obligation rated 'CCC' is currently vulnerable to nonpayment, and is dependent upon favorable business, financial, and economic conditions for the obligor to meet its financial commitment on the obligation. Speculative-grade ratings are ratings below BB.

CCC

▲ *assign a CCC rating* calificar con un rating CCC ▲ *receive a CCC rating* recibir un rating CCC

cedant

= ceding company

≠ assuming company, reinsurer

A cedant is an insurer who passes on (cedes) the risk to a reinsurer.

cedente

= compañía cedente

≠ reaseguradora

▲ *a cedant's net contractual rights under a reinsurance contract* los derechos contractuales netos de un cedente de acuerdo con un contrato de reaseguro ▲ *losses on one or more contracts issued by the cedant* pérdidas en uno o más contratos emitidos por el cedente ▲ *the cedant's accounting policies* las prácticas contables del cedente

SOURCE IFRS 4, Appendix A

⇛ reinsurance

ceding company

= cedant, ceding insurer, primary company

≠ assuming company, reinsurer

A ceding company or ceding insurer is an insurance company that passes on (cedes) the risk to a reinsurer.

compañía cedente

= cedente

≠ reaseguradora

▲ *a ceding company's net contractual rights under a reinsurance contract* los derechos contractuales netos de la compañía cedente de acuerdo con un contrato de reaseguro ▲ *losses on one or more contracts issued by the ceding company* pérdidas en uno o más contratos emitidos por una compañía cedente ▲ *the ceding company's accounting policies* las prácticas contables de la compañía cedente

central bank

A central bank is a country's supreme bank and it is responsible for and controls the money supply and monetary and exchange rate policies in the country or a monetary union.

NOTE The name of the central bank in the UK is the Bank of England, in Denmark it is Danmarks Nationalbank; in the US, however, central banking is the responsibility of the Federal Reserve System consisting of 12 Federal Reserve Banks governed by the Federal Reserve Board in Washington, D.C.

banco central

▲ *balances with the central bank* saldos con el banco central ▲ *cash and balances with the central bank* efectivo y saldos con el banco central ▲ *exchange control restrictions imposed by a government or a central bank* restricciones en el control del tipo de cambio impuestos por un gobierno o un banco central ▲ *the European Central Bank, ECB* el Banco Central Europeo, BCE ▲ *treasury bills and other bills eligible for rediscounting with the central bank* fondos propios y otros fondos elegibles para redescontar con el banco central

CEO

= chief executive officer

CEO is an abbreviation for chief executive officer, the highest ranking and most senior officer of an enterprise, positioned at the top and responsible for the decision-making and running of that enterprise.

NOTE In some jurisdictions where the management is a one-tier system, the chief executive officer sits on the board of directors. In listed companies, it is usually not possible for the chief executive officer to be chairman of the board of directors.

consejero delegado

▲ *appoint a new CEO* nombrar un nuevo consejero delegado ▲ *the company's CEO* el consejero delegado de la empresa ▲ *the former CEO* el anterior consejero delegado ▲ *the incoming CEO* el consejero delegado entrante ▲ *the retiring CEO* el consejero delegado saliente

CEPS

= Cash Earnings Per Share

CEPS is the abbreviation for cash earnings per share and an investment ratio defined as cash earnings divided by the average number of shares diluted.

dividendo por acción

= beneficio por acción

▲ *a decerase in CEPS* un descenso en el dividendo por acción ▲ *an increase in CEPS* un aumento en el dividendo por acción ▲ *calculate CEPS* calcular el dividendo por acción

⇛ cash earnings

certainty

Certainty means that there is no doubt about the state or existence of something.

certeza

▲ *a high degree of certainty* un alto grado de certeza ▲ *assess the degree of certainty attached to the flow of future economic benefits* valorar el grado de certeza vinculado con el flujo de beneficios económicos futuros ▲ *reasonable certainty* certeza razonable ▲ *sufficient certainty* certeza suficiente

certificate

A certificate is an official, written and signed document that provides evidence of particular rights or facts.

certificado

▲ *admit certificates for listing* admitir certificados para cotización en bolsa ▲ *certificates representing shares* certificados que representan acciones ▲ *draw up a certificate* extender un certificado ▲ *exchange of certificates for original securities* cambio de certificados por títulos originales ▲ *green certificates* certificados verdes ▲ *issue a certificate* emitir un certificado ▲ *prepare a certificate* preparar un certificado ▲ *the shares forming the basis of the certificate* las acciones que forman la base del certificado

certificate holder

A certificate holder is a person or an enterprise in possession of a certificate.

titular del certificado

▲ *the total number of certificate holders* el número total de titulares de certificados

⇛ certificate

certificate of incorporation US, UK

A certificate of incorporation is a legal document issued by the appropriate authority certifying that a company has started to have a legal existence. In the UK, the Registrar of Companies will issue the certificate. In the US, a company is given a charter as a private corporation by the state in which it is to carry on business according to the corporation laws of that state.

certificado de inscripción

▲ *amend the certificate of incorporation* enmendar el certificado de inscripción ▲ *amended and restated certificate of incorporation* certificado de inscripción enmendado y actualizado ▲ *the original certificate of incorporation* el certificado de inscripción original

⇛ articles of incorporation, memorandum of association

certified accountant UK

A certified accountant works within private practice, industry, commerce and the public sector, providing accountancy and other services within the fields of taxation, insolvency, corporate finance. Services may also include the auditing of financial records.

NOTE To become a chartered certified accountant and member of the Association of Chartered Certified Accountants (ACCA) you must –besides three to four years of training– have passed ACCA's examinations which is one of the examinations qualifying for the performance of statutory audits.

auditor

= censor de cuentas

NOTE The Spanish 'auditor' is a member of the 'Registro Oficial de Auditores de Cuentas' (ROAC).

▲ *become a certified accountant* convertirse en un auditor

⇛ Association of Chartered Certified Accountants

certified management accountant US

= CMA

A certified management accountant is a professional accountant within management accounting and as such a counterpart to the certified public accountant within financial accounting.

auditor

= censor de cuentas

▲ *become a certified management accountant* llegar a ser un auditor

certified public accountant US

= chartered accountant UK, CPA US, state authorized public accountant DK

A certified public accountant is an independent accountant in the United States who is licensed to practice and give an audit opinion on the fairness of a company's published financial statements. A CPA meets stringent professional qualifications and must satisfy the experience requirements of a particular state in the US.

auditor

= censor de cuentas

▲ *become a certified public accountant* llegar a ser un auditor

certifying body

A certifying body is a person, enterprise or authority that has been empowered to prepare official certificates and gives them legal effect.

supervisor

= órgano de supervisión

▲ *the certifying body's internal report* el informe interno del supervisor

CFC

1 = controlled foreign company

UK definition: A CFC is a controlled foreign company in which a UK company has a 10% stake or more.

empresa extranjera controlada

▲ *a CFC engaged in 'exempt activities'* una empresa extranjera controlada ocupada en 'actividades exentas' ▲ *CFC legislation* legislación relacionada con la empresa extranjera controlada ▲ *regard a company as a CFC* considerar una empresa como una empresa extranjera controlada

2 = controlled foreign corporation

US definition: A CFC is a controlled foreign corporation whose voting stock is more than 50% owned by US stockholders, each of whom owns at least 10% of the voting power.

empresa extranjera controlada

▲ *regard a corporation as a CFC* considerar una empresa como una empresa extranjera controlada

CFC rule

A CFC rule is a rule that governs cross-border joint taxation of enterprises. CFC rules are designed to ensure certainty about the tax effects of establishing subsidiaries in other countries.

normativa sobre empresa extranjera controlada

= disposición sobre empresa extranjera controlada

▲ *escape CFC rules* escapar a las disposiciones sobre empresa extranjera controlada ▲ *the new CFC rule* la nueva normativa sobre empresa extranjera controlada ▲ *under the CFC rules* según las disposiciones sobre empresa extranjera controlada

CFFO

= Cash Flow From Operations

CFFO is the abbreviation for cash flow from operations, which is a financial profitability and efficiency ratio defined as cash flow before capital expenditure, dividend payment, share buybacks and proceeds from issues, also expressed as free cash flow to equity plus capex.

flujo de efectivo operativo

▲ *a model for CFFO calculation* un modelo para el cálculo del flujo de efectivo operativo ▲ *calculate CFFO* calcular el flujo de efectivo operativo

⇛ capital expenditure, free cash flow to equity

CFO US
= chief financial officer US
The CFO (chief financial officer) is the top finance director of an enterprise dealing with the financial issues, decisions and activities in the enterprise.
director financiero
▲ *be appointed CFO* ser nombrado director financiero ▲ *the incoming CFO* el director financiero entrante ▲ *the retiring CFO* el director financiero saliente

CFPS
= cash flow per share
CFPS is the abbreviation of cash flow per share, which is an investment ratio defined as cash flow from operations divided by the average number of shares diluted.
efectivo por acción
▲ *calculate CFPS* calcular el efectivo por acción ▲ *make a CFPS calculation* hacer un cálculo del efectivo por acción

CGT UK
CGT is the abbreviation of capital gains tax, i.e. a tax that is levied on the increase in the value of assets. The capital gains tax is usually only collected when the assets are sold.
impuesto por ganancias de capital
▲ *charge CGT* cargar el impuesto por ganancias de capital ▲ *levy CGT on the share options* exigir el impuesto por ganancias de capital en las opciones sobre acciones ▲ *pay CGT* pagar el impuesto por ganacias de capital
⇛ capital gains tax

CGU
= cash-generating unit
CGU is the abbreviation for cash-generating unit, i.e. the smallest set of assets possible to identify that generates cash flows on a separate basis.
UGE
= unidad generadora de efectivo
▲ *grouping in a CGU* agrupar en una UGE

chairman
A chairman is a person presiding over a governing body such as a board of directors or a committee, or a person directing a meeting.
presidente
▲ *appoint a chairman* nombrar un presidente ▲ *chairman and CEO* presidente y consejero delegado ▲ *chairman emeritus* presidente emérito ▲ *chairman of* presidente de ▲ *chairman of the audit commitee* presidente del comité de auditoría ▲ *chairman of the remuneration committee* presidente del comité de retribuciones ▲ *chairman of the supervisory board* presidente del órgano supervisor ▲ *deputy chairman* vicepresidente ▲ *former chairman* anterior presidente ▲ *honorary chairman* presidente honorario ▲ *stand for chairman* presentarse como candidato a presidente ▲ *the chairman of the supervisory board* el presidente del órgano supervisor
⇛ chairman of the board of directors

chairman of the board of directors UK, US, IAS/IFRS
The chairman of the board of directors is the person presiding over the board of directors –i.e. the management– of a company with responsibility for company decision-making. Under corporate governance rules, the offices of chief executive officer and chairman should not be held by the same person. Usually, the chairman is a non-executive or outside director.
presidente del consejo de administración
▲ *act as chairman of the board of directors* actuar como presidente del consejo de administración ▲ *appoint a chairman of the board of directors* nombrar un presidente del consejo de administración ▲ *the former chairman of the board of directors* el anterior presidente del consejo de administración

chairman's report UK
= chairman's statement UK
The chairman's report is a non-mandatory statement by the chairman of the board of directors in the annual report of most large companies in the UK. The statement is a review of the past financial year together with an outlook for the future period and supplements the mandatory directors' report.
informe del presidente
▲ *as stated in the chairman's report* como se recoge en el informe del presidente ▲ *the con-*

tents of the chairman's report los contenidos del informe del presidente

chairman's statement UK
= chairman's report
The chairman's statement is a non-mandatory statement by the chairman of the board of directors in the annual report of most large companies in the UK. The statement is a review of the past financial year together with an outlook for the future period and supplements the mandatory directors' report.
informe del presidente
▲ *the contents of the chairman's statement* los contenidos del informe del presidente

change[1] *noun* <a, the, -s>
A change occurs when something develops from one stage to another, is transformed or altered.
cambio
▲ *a statement of changes in equity* un estado de cambios en el patrimonio ▲ *a strategic change* un cambio estratégico ▲ *change in accounting policies* cambio en las políticas contables ▲ *change in activities* cambio en las actividades ▲ *change in deferred tax* cambio en el impuesto diferido ▲ *change in depreciation method* cambio en el método de depreciación ▲ *change in the accounting estimate* cambio en la contabilidad estimada ▲ *change in the accounting policies adopted* cambio en las políticas contables adoptadas ▲ *change in the methods of recognition and measurement bases* cambio en los métodos de reconocimiento y en las bases de cálculo ▲ *change in working capital* cambio en el capital circulante

change[2] *verb* <-s, -d, has -d, changing> *passive* <is -d, was -d>
To change is to alter or modify something so that it becomes different.
cambiar
▲ *change accounting policies* cambiar las políticas contables ▲ *change accounting systems* cambiar los sistemas contables ▲ *change the measurement basis* cambiar la base de cálculo

change in accounting policies
A change in accounting policies occurs when an enterprise alters all or some of the accounting bases or methods of recognition and measurement applied to prepare its financial statements.
cambio en las prácticas contables
= cambio en las políticas contables
▲ *adjustment due to change in accounting policies* ajuste debido a un cambio en las prácticas contables

change in equity
A change in equity is the debiting or crediting of an amount relating to an equity item.
variación patrimonial
= cambio patrimonial
▲ *a statement showing changes in equity* un estado que muestra los cambios patrimoniales ▲ *an analysis of changes in equity* un análisis de los cambios patrimoniales ▲ *changes in equity* variaciones patrimoniales ▲ *current and deferred tax related to changes in equity* impuesto actual y diferido relacionado con variaciones patrimoniales ▲ *other changes in equity for the year ended 31 December 2005* otras variaciones patrimoniales correspondientes al año que finaliza el 31 de diciembre de 2005 ▲ *recognise directly as changes in equity* reconocer directamente como variaciones patrimoniales

change in foreign exchange rates
A change in foreign exchange rates is a change of the exchange rate of a given currency resulting in a gain or loss for an enterprise having payables or receivables in that currency.
variación en los tipos de cambio
▲ *a change in foreign exchange rates after the balance sheet date* una variación en los tipos de cambio después de la fecha de cierre del balance ▲ *a change in foreign exchange rates after the transaction date* una variación en los tipos de cambio después de la fecha de la transacción ▲ *a change in foreign exchange rates on borrowings* una variación en los tipos de cambio de los préstamos ▲ *a change in foreign exchange rates on financial instruments* una variación en los tipos de cambio de los instrumentos financieros ▲ *a negative change in foreign exchange rates* una variación en los tipos de cambio negativa ▲ *a positive change in foreign exchange rates* una variación en los

tipos de cambio positiva ▲ *unrealised gains and losses arising from changes in foreign currency exchange rates* resultados no realizados como consecuencia de variaciones en los tipos de cambio

change in inventory

A change in inventory is a change in the size of an enterprise's inventory, i.e. changes in finished goods and goods for resale held on stock, representing either a decrease or an increase. Included as a separate item in the profit and loss account as presented in the vertical format classified by nature.

variación en el inventario

▲ *the amount of the net change in inventories for the financial year* la cantidad de variación neta en los inventarios correspondientes al año financiero

change in liquidity

= change in cash

A change in liquidity is the effect of transactions that increases or decreases liquidity. The change is seen as the net liquidity or net cash and cash equivalents at the end of an accounting period.

variación de efectivo

= variación de liquidez

▲ *change in liquidity for the period* variación de efectivo para el periodo

change in stocks of finished goods and in work in progress UK

= changes in inventories of finished goods and work in progress IAS/IFRS

Change in stocks of finished goods and in work in progress is an item in the profit and loss account as presented in the report format classified by nature. The item shows the increase or decrease of stocks of finished goods and work in progress.

variación de existencias

▲ *included in change in stocks of finished goods and in work in progress* incluido en la variación de existencia

change in value

A change in value occurs when the value is increased or decreased.

cambio de valor

▲ *a realised change in value* un cambio de valor realizado ▲ *changes in value of identifiable assets and liabilities* cambios de valor en los activos y pasivos identificables ▲ *changes in value of investments* cambios de valor de las inversiones ▲ *insignificant risk of changes in value* riesgo insignificante de cambios de valor

changes in inventories of finished goods and work in progress IAS/IFRS

= change in stocks of finished goods and in work in progress UK

Changes in inventories of finished goods and work in progress is an item in the income statement that shows the increase or decrease of stocks of finished goods and work in progress, as presented in the vertical format as classified by the nature of expense method.

variación de existencias de productos terminados y en curso de fabricación

▲ *the total value of changes in inventories of finished goods and work-in-progress* el valor total de la variación de existencias de productos terminados y en curso de fabricación

SOURCE IAS 1, paragraph 91

charge[1] *noun*

1 A charge is a legal right over assets (land or other property) belonging to another person. A charge provides guarantee for compensation e.g. in case of non-repayment of a loan.

carga

= hipoteca

▲ *a prior charge* una carga anterior ▲ *charges and securities* hipotecas y valores mobiliarios ▲ *company charge* carga empresarial ▲ *create a charge* crear una carga ▲ *free from all charges and encumbrances* libre de todas las cargas y gravámenes ▲ *grant a second charge* conceder una segunda hipoteca ▲ *land charges* hipotecas sobre la tierra

⇛ mortgage

2 Charge is an amount of money to be paid for goods or services or the act of requesting that amount.

tasa

▲ *a charge for exceeding the 1-month time limit* una tasa por sobrepasar el límite de tiempo de un mes ▲ *free of charge* gratis ▲ *impose a charge* imponer una tasa ▲ *levy charges* recaudar tasas

3 A charge is an expense or cost.
gasto
▲ *a charge based on the expected use or output of the asset* un gasto basado en el uso esperado o salida del activo ▲ *a constant charge over the useful life of the asset* un gasto constante sobre la vida útil del activo ▲ *a decreasing charge over the useful life of the asset* un gasto decreciente sobre la vida útil del activo ▲ *incur an explicit interest charge* incurrir en un gasto por interés explícito ▲ *interest expense and similar charges* gastos financieros y gastos similares ▲ *the related finance charges* los gastos financieros relacionados

4 A charge is a debit to an account.
cargo
= adeudo, débito
▲ *make a charge to an account* hacer un cargo en una cuenta

charge[2] UK *verb*

1 = debit
≠ credit
To charge is to recognise an amount in the profit and loss account as an expense or to debit the cost of something to an account.
cargar
= adeudar
≠ abonar, acreditar
▲ *charge an amount to an account* cargar una cantidad en una cuenta ▲ *charge to the financial statements* cargar en los estados financieros ▲ *charge to the income statement* cargar la cuenta de resultados ▲ *charge to the profit and loss account* cargar la cuenta de resultados ▲ *items credited or charged directly to equity* partidas abonadas o cargadas directamente en el patrimonio neto
⇛ expense

2 To charge is to ask for payment for goods and services.
cobrar
▲ *charge a price* cobrar un precio ▲ *prices charged by service providers* precios cobrados por proveedores de servicios ▲ *the current fees charged by other market participants for similar services* las tarifas actuales cobradas por otros participantes en el mercado por servicios similares

3 To charge is to mortgage or pledge an asset as security for a loan.
hipotecar
▲ *charge debts on a property* hipotecar un edificio

charge exemption
= tax exemption
To be granted a charge exemption means to be allowed to avoid paying any charges, i.e. amounts of money payable as a special fee in connection with e.g. overdue payment or late delivery.
exento de carga
▲ *be entitled to a charge exemption* tener derecho a estar exento de carga

charge production
Charge production is a production process which is characterised by high production volume and high product standardisation. Fixed quantities of e.g. steel and food are produced, and the quantities are determined and limited by the production capacity.
producción en continuo
▲ *charge production costs* costes de producción en continuo

charge to the income statement
IAS/IFRS
= recognise as an expense
To charge to the income statement is to expense an amount.
cargar en la cuenta de resultados
= imputar como gasto en la cuenta de resultados
▲ *charge intangible assets to the income statement* imputar como gasto los activos intangibles en la cuenta de resultados ▲ *charge to the income statement on a straight-line basis over the period of the lease* cargar en la cuenta de resultados por el método directo durante el periodo de arrendamiento ▲ *the depreciation charged to the income statement* la depreciación cargada en la cuenta de resultados

charge to the profit and loss account UK
To charge to the profit and loss account is to expense an amount.
cargar en la cuenta de resultados
= imputar como gasto en la cuenta de resultados
▲ *charge expenses to the profit and loss account* cargar gastos en la cuenta de resultados

chart of accounts
A list of all the accounts contained in the double entry sys-

tem used by an enterprise is called a chart of accounts.

cuadro de cuentas

▲ *a harmonised chart of accounts* un cuadro de cuentas armonizado ▲ *adopt a new chart of accounts* adoptar un cuadro de cuentas nuevo ▲ *finalise the chart of accounts* finalizar el cuadro de cuentas

charter US

= articles of incorporation, corporate charter

The charter is the document that creates a corporation under the laws of the state of incorporation and must be filed with the relevant authorities. The charter must include information about the corporation's name, authorised capital, registered office and incorporators.

escritura de constitución

▲ *amendment of the charter* modificación de la escritura de constitución ▲ *copy of the charter* copia de la escritura de constitución ▲ *the charter and bylaws of an organization* la escritura de constitución y los estatutos de una organización ▲ *the date of signature of the charter* la fecha de la firma de la escritura de constitución ▲ *the signing of the charter* el acto de la firma de la escritura de constitución

chartered accountant UK

= CA UK, certified public accountant US, state authorised public accountant DK

A chartered accountant is a person who is a qualified accountant and a member of one of the three institutes of accountants in the UK and Ireland: the Institute of Chartered Accountants in England and Wales, the Institute of Chartered Accountants in Scotland and the Institute of Chartered Accountants in Ireland.

auditor

▲ *become a chartered accountant* llegar a ser un auditor ▲ *independent chartered accountants* auditores independientes

⇛ accountant, Institute of Chartered Accountants in England and Wales, Institute of Chartered Accountants in Ireland, Institute of Chartered Accountants of Scotland

check list

A check list is a record of jobs that must be performed, often in a strict order, in connection with a particular activity. The check list ensures that the performance of all jobs may be controlled.

hoja de control

▲ *prepare a check list* preparar una hoja de control

chief executive

= CEO, chief executive officer

The chief executive is the most senior officer of an enterprise, positioned at the top and responsible for the decision-making and running of that enterprise. In some jurisdictions where the management is a one-tier system, the chief executive sits on the board of directors. In listed companies, it is usually not possible for the chief executive to be chairman of the board of directors.

consejero delegado

▲ *chairman and chief executive* presidente y consejero delegado

chief executive officer

= CEO, chief executive

The chief executive officer (CEO) is the highest ranking and most senior officer of an enterprise, positioned at the top and responsible for the decision-making and running of that enterprise. In some jurisdictions where the management is a one-tier system, the chief executive officer sits on the board of directors. In listed companies, it is usually not possible for the chief executive officer to be chairman of the board of directors.

consejero delegado

▲ *appoint a new chief executive officer* nombrar un nuevo consejero delegado ▲ *the company's chief executive officer* el consejero delegado de la empresa ▲ *the former chief executive officer* el anterior consejero delegado ▲ *the incoming chief executive officer* el consejero delegado entrante ▲ *the position of chief administrative officer* el puesto de consejero delegado ▲ *the retiring chief executive officer* el consejero delegado saliente

chief financial officer US
= CFO US, corporate treasurer US, finance director UK
The chief financial officer is the top finance director of an enterprise dealing with the financial issues, decisions and activities in the enterprise.
director financiero
▲ *be appointed chief financial officer* ser nombrado director financiero
▲ *the incoming chief financial officer* el director financiero entrante
▲ *the retiring chief financial officer* el director financiero saliente

chief information officer US
= CIO
The chief information officer (CIO) is responsible for the supervision, monitoring and coordination of the information technology systems, including acquisition, maintenance, programmes and planning as well as the personnel. The CIO reports to the CEO or the CFO.
director de información
▲ *appoint a new chief information officer* nombrar un nuevo director de información ▲ *the company's chief information officer* el director de información de la empresa
▲ *the former chief information officer* el anterior director de información ▲ *the incoming chief information officer* el director de información entrante ▲ *the retiring chief information officer* el director de información saliente

chief operating decision maker IAS/IFRS
The chief operating decision maker is a function that assesses the performance of operating segments and allocates ressources to those segments. The chief executive officer often performs the function of chief operating decision maker of the enterprise.
dirección de operaciones
= máxima instancia de toma de decisiones operativas
NOTE The IAS/IFRS term 'máxima instancia de toma de decisiones operativas' is conceptually vague.
▲ *segment assets reviewed by the chief operating decision maker* segmentos de activos revisados por la dirección de operaciones
▲ *the entity's chief operating decision maker* la dirección de operaciones de la organización
SOURCE IFRS 8, paragraph 7

chief operating officer US
= COO
The chief operating officer (COO) is among the highest-ranking officers in an enterprise and responsible for the day-to-day management of the enterprise's operations. The COO reports directly to the CEO.
director de operaciones
▲ *appoint a new chief operating officer* nombrar un nuevo director de operaciones ▲ *the former chief operating officer* el anterior director de operaciones
▲ *the incoming chief operating officer* el director de operaciones entrante ▲ *the retiring chief operating officer* el director de operaciones saliente

choice criterion
A choice criterion is a standard based on a set of characteristics, qualities or other attributes by which an assessment or judgment can be made resulting in a decision.
criterio de selección
▲ *apply a choice criterion* aplicar un criterio de selección

CIO US
= chief information officer
CIO is an abbreviation for chief information officer. The CIO is responsible for the supervision, monitoring and coordination of the information technology systems, including acquisition, maintenance, programmes and planning as well as the personnel. The CIO reports to the CEO or the CFO.
director de información
▲ *appoint a new CIO* nombrar un nuevo director de información ▲ *the company's CIO* el director de información de la empresa ▲ *the former CIO* el anterior director de información ▲ *the incoming CIO* el director de información entrante
▲ *the retiring CIO* el director de información saliente

claim
A claim is the making of a demand and asserting a right for money due, for property, from damages or for enforcement of a right. If a claim fails to be honoured, this may result in a lawsuit.
demanda
= reclamación

▲ *actual claims compared with previous estimates* demandas reales comparadas con estimaciones anteriores ▲ *claims assessment costs* costes de evaluación de demandas ▲ *claims brought against the enterprise by customers* demandas contra la empresa interpuestas por los clientes ▲ *claims handling costs* costes de tramitación de demandas ▲ *convert a claim into equity investments* convertir una demanda en inversiones de patrimonio ▲ *convert a claim into shares* convertir una demanda en acciones ▲ *legal claims* demandas legales ▲ *other claims payable* otras demandas a pagar ▲ *provisions for possible future claims* provisiones para posibles reclamaciones futuras ▲ *redemption of a claim* cancelación de una demanda ▲ *related claims for or payments of compensation from third parties* demandas relacionadas o pagos de compensación de terceras partes ▲ *set off a claim* compensar una demanda ▲ *the outcome of legal claims* el resultado de las demandas legales ▲ *the supplier's claim against the customer* la demanda del proveedor contra el cliente ▲ *the value of the claim* el valor de la demanda ▲ *warranty claims* demandas de garantía

claims outstanding provision

= provision for claims outstanding

The claims outstanding provision is a provision under equity for the payment of future compensation or damages relating to claims against the enterprise.

provisión para responsabilidades pendientes

▲ *changes in claims outstanding provisions* cambios en las provisiones para responsabilidades pendientes

clarity

Clarity is one of the fundamental accounting assumptions underlying the preparation of financial statements and implies that financial data must be presented in a clear and understandable manner and not include any misrepresentation.

transparencia

▲ *ensure clarity* garantizar la transparencia

⇛ transparency, understandability

clarity concept

The clarity concept is a fundamental accounting assumption which provides that financial statements must be prepared in a clear and understandable manner.

concepto de transparencia

▲ *according to the clarity concept* de acuerdo con el concepto de transparencia ▲ *comply with the clarity concept* cumplir con el concepto de transparencia ▲ *the application of the clarity concept* la aplicación del concepto de transparencia ▲ *use the clarity concept* utilizar el concepto de transparencia

⇛ transparency, understandability

class A share

→ A share

class B share

→ B share

class of assets

A class of assets is a classification of assets that have common significant characteristics which distinguish them from other classes of assets. For instance, assets are typically classified as either tangibles or intangibles.

categoría de activos

= clase de activos

▲ *complete the revaluation of the class of assets* completar la revalorización de la clase de activos ▲ *revalue a class of assets on a rolling basis* revalorizar una clase de activos mediante el método de rotación constante ▲ *the amount of the impairment loss recognised by class of assets* la cantidad de deterioro reconocida por clase de activos ▲ *the main classes of assets affected by impairment losses* las principales clases de activos afectadas por deterioro ▲ *the return obtained on particular classes of assets* el rendimiento obtenido por clases concretas de activos ▲ *the use of different measurement bases for different classes of assets* el uso de diferentes bases de medida para las diferentes clases de activos

class of shares UK

→ share class

class of stock US

= share class UK

Common stock may be divided into classes of stock with different characteristics as determined by the bylaws of the corporation in question. One class of stock has certain advantages, such as more voting rights, compared with another class of stock.

NOTE In the US and Denmark, class A stock typically has more voting rights than class B stock, however, in the UK the opposite may be the case.

clase de acciones

▲ *contributed capital consisting of several classes of stock* capital contribuido consistente en varias clases de acciones ▲ *different classes of stock* diferentes clases de acciones ▲ *issue special classes of stock* emitir clases de acciones especiales ▲ *issue two classes of stock* emitir dos clases de acciones ▲ *the stockholders of the same class of stock* los accionistas de la misma clase de acciones

classification

A classification is the organisation of something into different existing or new classes, i.e. categories.

clasificación

▲ *a change in the classification of financial instruments* un cambio en la clasificación de los instrumentos financieros ▲ *a revised classification* una clasificación revisada ▲ *allocate operating expenses between functional classifications* distribuir los gastos operativos entre las clasificaciones funcionales ▲ *appropriate classification* clasificación apropiada ▲ *classification by activity* clasificación por actividad ▲ *classification of foreign operations* clasificación de operaciones en moneda extranjera ▲ *classification of items* clasificación de partidas ▲ *classification of leases* clasificación de arrendamientos ▲ *common classifications of inventories* clasificaciones comunes de inventarios ▲ *determine the appropriate classification* determinar la clasificación adecuada ▲ *different classifications of inventories* clasificaciones diferentes de inventarios ▲ *each major classification of assets, liabilities, income and expenses* cada clasificación mayor de activos, pasivos, ingresos y gastos ▲ *give rise to a new classification for accounting purposes* dar lugar a una nueva clasificación por motivos contables ▲ *job classification* clasificación laboral ▲ *separate classification* clasificación separada ▲ *the carrying amount in classifications appropriate to the enterprise* el valor contable en las clasificaciones apropiadas a la empresa ▲ *the most useful approach to the classification of liabilities* el enfoque más útil para proceder a la clasificación de pasivos ▲ *the nature of the change in classification* la naturaleza del cambio en la clasificación

classification by function

Classification by function refers to the presentation method that analyses items of expense in the profit and loss account by function. When classifying items of expense by function, costs and expenses are referred to their origin and not by type. By classifying items by function, the costs and expenses from ordinary activities are distributed on production, administration, sales and distribution.

clasificación por función

= clasificación funcional

▲ *according to the classification by function* de acuerdo a la clasificación por función ▲ *an alternative classification by function* una clasificación por función alternativa

classification by nature

Classification by nature refers to the presentation method that analyses items of expense in the profit and loss account by nature, such as amortisation and depreciation, costs of raw materials, transportation costs, wages and salaries, advertising costs.

clasificación por naturaleza

▲ *classification by nature of assets* clasificación por naturaleza de activos ▲ *use a classification by nature* utilizar una clasificación por naturaleza

classified

When something has been classified, it has been organised into different existing or new classes, i.e. categories.

clasificado

▲ *classified according to the nature of the assets* clasificado de acuerdo a la naturaleza de los activos ▲ *classified as a current asset* clasificado como un activo corriente ▲ *classified as non-current assets* clasificado como activos no corrientes ▲ *classified by operating, investing and financing activities* clasificado por actividades de explotación, inversión y financiación ▲ *classified in a manner appropriate to the enterprise's operations* clasificado de una manera apropiada a las operaciones de la empresa ▲ *classified primary financial instruments* instrumentos financieros primarios clasificados ▲ *the presentation of condensed and classified data* la presentación de datos condensados y clasificados

classified by function

= by-function format, classification by function, functional

≠ classified by nature

Classified by function refers to the presentation method that analyses items of expense in the profit and loss account by business functions. When classifying items of expense by function, costs and expenses are referred to their origin and not by nature or type. Costs and expenses from ordinary activities are e.g. distributed on production, administration, sales and distribution.

clasificado por función

▲ *income statement classified by function* cuenta de resultados clasificada por función

classified by nature IAS/IFRS, US

= by-nature format

≠ classified by function

Classified by nature refers to the presentation method that discloses items of expense in the profit and loss account by nature, such as amortisation and depreciation, costs of raw materials, transportation costs, wages and salaries, advertising costs.

clasificado por tipo de gasto

= clasificado por naturaleza

NOTE Spanish accountants prefer 'clasificado por tipo de gasto' to the IAS/IFRS term 'clasificado por naturaleza'.

▲ *income statement classified by nature* cuenta de resultados clasificada por tipo de gasto ▲ *presentation of costs classified by nature* presentación de costes clasificados por tipo de gasto

classified by type of expenditure UK

= classified by items of expense UK

≠ classified by function IAS/IFRS, classified by type of operation and function UK

Classified by type of expenditure refers to the presentation method that analyses items of expense in the profit and loss account by nature, such as amortisation and depreciation, costs of raw materials, transportation costs, wages and salaries, advertising costs.

clasificado por tipo de gasto

▲ *presentation of costs classified by type of expenditure* presentación de costes clasificados por tipo de gasto ▲ *profit and loss account classified by type of expenditure* cuenta de resultados clasificada por tipo de gasto

classified by type of operation and function UK

= classified by function IAS/IFRS

≠ classified by nature IAS/IFRS

Classified by type of operation and function refers to the presentation method that analyses items of expense in the profit and loss account by business functions. When classifying items of expense by functions, costs and expenses are referred to their origin. Costs and expenses from ordinary activities are e.g. distributed on production, administration, sales and distribution.

clasificado por tipo de operación y función

≠ clasificado por naturaleza

▲ *profit and loss account classified by type of operation and function* cuenta de resultados clasificada por tipo de operación y función

classify

To classify is to organise something into different existing or new classes, i.e. categories.

clasificar

▲ *classify as extraordinary expenses* clasificar como gastos extraordinarios ▲ *classify as extraordinary income* clasificar como ingreso extraordinario ▲ *classify as receivables* clasificar como cuentas a cobrar ▲ *classify expenses by function* clasificar gastos por función ▲ *classify expenses by nature* clasificar gastos por naturaleza ▲ *classify the items in accordance with the nature of the enterprise and the extent of its activities* clasificar las partidas de acuerdo con la naturaleza de la empresa y alcance de sus actividades

clean-up cost

Clean-up costs are costs associated with the cleaning or removal of contaminated soil.

coste de descontaminación

▲ *clean-up cost insurance* seguro para coste de descontaminación ▲ *clean-up costs for unlawful environmental damage* costes de descontaminación por daño medioambiental ilegal ▲ *total clean-up costs* total costes de descontaminación

clear

To clear is to settle payments and debts or securities transactions. In the context of payment by cheque, to clear is to make sure that there is coverage for the amount specified on the cheque after which the amount is credited to the payee's account.

compensar

▲ *clear a liability* compensar una obligación ▲ *clear a security* compensar un título ▲ *clear a transaction* compensar una transacción ▲ *clear money transactions* compensar las transacciones monetarias ▲ *the obligation to clear* la obligación de compensar

clearing

Clearing is the settlement of payments and debts or securities transactions. In the context of payment by cheque, clearing is the affirmation that there is coverage for the amount specified on the cheque and the subsequent crediting of that amount to the payee's account.

compensación

▲ *accept for clearing* aceptar la compensación ▲ *clearing of money* compensación de dinero ▲ *clearing of payments* compensación de pagos ▲ *clearing of securities* compensación de títulos ▲ *clearing of transactions concluded on the regulated market* compensación de transacciones finalizadas en el mercado regulado ▲ *electronic clearing* compensación electrónica ▲ *lay down rules governing clearing* establecer reglas que gobiernen la compensación

clearing center US

= clearing centre UK, clearing house UK

A clearing center is an organisation that carries out settlements of payments and claims or securities transactions between members, e.g. financial institutions.

centro de compensación

▲ *a participant in a clearing center* un participante en un centro de compensación ▲ *agreement with a clearing center* acuerdo con un centro de compensación ▲ *conclude an agreement with a clearing center* llegar a un acuerdo con un centro de compensación ▲ *efficient and stable clearing centers* centros de compensación eficientes y estables ▲ *settle through a clearing center* pagar a través de un centro de compensación

⇛ securities clearing house

clearing centre UK

= clearing center US, clearing house UK

A clearing centre is an organisation that carries out settlements of payments and claims or securities transactions between members, e.g. financial institutions.

centro de compensación

▲ *a participant in a clearing centre* un participante en un centro de compensación ▲ *agreement with a clearing centre* acuerdo con un centro de compensación ▲ *conclude an agreement with a clearing centre* concluir un acuerdo con un centro de compensación ▲ *effi-*

cient and stable clearing centres centros de compensación eficientes y estables ▲ *settle through a clearing centre* pagar a través de un centro de compensación
⇛ securities clearing house

clearing house
= clearing center US, clearing centre UK
A clearing house is an organisation that carries out computerised settlements of payments and claims or securities transactions between members, e.g. financial institutions.
centro de compensación
▲ *enter into appropriate arrangements with a clearing house* entrar en acuerdos apropiados con un centro de compensación ▲ *recognised clearing houses* centros de compensación reconocidos ▲ *the clearing house which has a direct contractual relationship with the central counterparty* el centro de compensación que tiene una relación contractual directa con la parte contratante central ▲ *the margin required by the clearing house* el margen requerido por el centro de compensación

clearing member
A clearing member is an enterprise affiliated to a clearing house or centre. Clearing members participate in the settlement and clearing of payments, debts and securities transactions.
miembro de un centro de compensación
▲ *the services of a general clearing member* los servicios de un miembro de un centro de compensación general
⇛ clearing house

clock card UK
= time card
≠ job card UK, labor time ticket US
A clock card records the exact time that an employee arrives at and leaves the job by means of a mechanical time clock.
tarjeta de reloj
= tarjeta de reloj de control de asistencia, tarjeta de tiempo
▲ *electronic clock cards* tarjetas de reloj electrónicas ▲ *suppliers of clock cards* proveedores de tarjetas de reloj

close
= end
To close means to end, to finish or to finalise.
cerrar
= finalizar
▲ *close a deal* cerrar un trato ▲ *close a transaction* cerrar una transacción ▲ *close down* cerrar ▲ *close facilities* cerrar las instalaciones ▲ *close negotiations* cerrar las negociaciones ▲ *close the accounts* cerrar las cuentas ▲ *close the meeting* finalizar la reunión

close company US, UK
= close corporation US
A close company is a private limited company in the UK or a privately-held corporation in the US whose voting shares are held by one or few shareholders.
sociedad cerrada
▲ *own shares in close companies* tener acciones en sociedades cerradas ▲ *voting rights in a close company* derechos de voto en una sociedad cerrada
⇛ private limited company, privately-held company

close corporation US
= close company US, closed corporation US, closely-held corporation US, private corporation US
A close corporation is a privately-held corporation whose voting shares are held by one or few shareholders.
sociedad cerrada
▲ *form a close corporation* formar una sociedad cerrada ▲ *shareholders of close corporations* accionistas de sociedades cerradas

close-out netting
A settlement of all agreed, not due liabilities to and claims against a counterparty by a single liability or a single claim is called close-out netting. This type of close-out netting is mainly used in connection with financial collateral arrangements.
liquidación por compensación exigible anticipadamente
= liquidación bilateral por compensación
▲ *close-out netting provisions* cláusulas de liquidación por compensación exigible anticipadamente

closed corporation US
→ close corporation

closely-held corporation US
→ close corporation

closing balance
≠ opening balance
The closing balance is the total amount of assets or liabilities in the balance sheet at the end of an accounting period.
saldo final
≠ saldo inicial
▲ *reconcile the opening and closing balances of each element within equity* conciliar el saldo inicial y final de cada elemento en el patrimonio

closing balance sheet
= balance sheet at year-end, year-end balance sheet
The closing balance sheet is the balance sheet with all items at the last day in the financial year.
balance de cierre
= saldo al cierre
▲ *be equivalent to the closing balance sheet for the previous financial year* ser equivalente al balance de cierre del ejercicio anterior ▲ *closing balance sheet as at the merger date for accounting purposes* balance de cierre en la fecha de la fusión a efectos contables ▲ *consolidated closing balance sheet* balance de cierre consolidado ▲ *the closing balance sheet for the previous year* el balance de cierre del ejercicio anterior

closing date
The closing date is the date by which you must terminate a project, a task or an assignment, or provide something.
fecha de cierre
▲ *actual closing date* la fecha de cierre real ▲ *the closing date of the financial year* la fecha de cierre del ejercicio

closing entry
Closing entries are entries recorded in financial records and statements at the end of an accounting period to close the accounts and transfer balances to e.g. the profit and loss account.
asiento de cierre
▲ *make closing entries* hacer los asientos de cierre

closing inventory US, IAS/IFRS
= closing stock UK
≠ opening inventory US, IAS/IFRS, opening stock UK
Closing inventory is the inventory remaining within an enterprise at the end of an accounting period as raw materials, work in progress, or finished goods.
inventario final
▲ *closing inventories* inventarios finales ▲ *intercompany profit included in closing inventory* beneficio entre empresas incluido en el inventario final

closing of the accounts
Closing of the accounts is the process of completing and closing all the accounts.
cierre de las cuentas
▲ *after the closing of the accounts* después del cierre de las cuentas ▲ *at the closing of the accounts* al cierre de las cuentas ▲ *at the time of the closing of the accounts* en el momento del cierre de las cuentas ▲ *before the annual closing of the accounts* antes del cierre anual de las cuentas ▲ *events after the closing of the accounts* hechos posteriores al cierre de las cuentas ▲ *on the day of closing of the accounts* en la fecha del cierre de las cuentas

closing of the annual accounts UK
= closing of the financial statements US
The closing of the annual accounts is a process involving the closing of all accounts at the end of the accounting period by transfer of the balances to the profit and loss account or the balance sheet.
cierre de las cuentas anuales
▲ *at the time of closing of the annual accounts* en el momento del cierre de las cuentas anuales ▲ *significant events subsequent to the closing of the annual accounts* hechos significativos posteriores al cierre de las cuentas anuales ▲ *within six months after the closing of the annual accounts* en los seis meses posteriores al cierre de las cuentas anuales

closing of the financial statements US, IAS/IFRS
= closing of the annual accounts UK
The closing of the financial statements is a process involving the closing of all accounts at the end of the accounting period by transfer of the balances to the profit and loss account or the balance sheet.
cierre de los estados financieros
▲ *at the closing of the financial statements at December 31, 2005*

al cierre de los estados financieros a 31 de diciembre de 2005 ▲ *at the date of closing of the financial statements* a fecha de cierre de los estados financieros ▲ *subsequent to the closing of the financial statements* después del cierre de los estados financieros

closing price

= end-of-period price, year-end price

Closing prices are the last bid or offer prices quoted in an organised financial market or stock exchange at the end of the trading day.

precio de cierre

= cotización al cierre, cotización de cierre

▲ *adjustment at closing price* ajuste a precio de cierre ▲ *highest closing price* el precio de cierre más alto ▲ *lowest closing price* el precio de cierre más bajo ▲ *the quoted closing price of a share* el precio de cierre cotizado de una acción

closing rate

The closing rate is the spot exchange rate between two currencies quoted at the close of business on the balance sheet date.

tipo de cambio de cierre

= tipo de cambio al cierre

▲ *adjustment at closing rate* ajuste al tipo de cambio de cierre ▲ *highest closing rate* tipo de cambio de cierre más alto ▲ *measure at closing rates* medir a los tipos de cambio de cierre ▲ *report foreign currency monetary items using the closing rate* informar de las partidas en divisas usando el tipo de cambio de cierre ▲ *the closing rate existing at the date of the most recent balance sheet presented* el tipo de cambio al cierre a fecha del último balance presentado ▲ *translate at the closing rate* ajustar al tipo de cambio de cierre ▲ *translate into the reporting currency at the closing rate* trasladar la divisa utilizada al tipo de cambio de cierre

⇛ transaction rate

closing rate method

The closing rate method is a method applied for translating financial statements of foreign subsidiaries from their local currencies into the presentation currency of the parent on consolidation. Assets and liabilities are translated at balance-sheet-date exchange rates, whereas profit-and-loss-account items are translated at recognition-date rates, average rates or balance-sheet-date rates.

método del tipo de cambio de cierre

= método de tipo de cambio al cierre

▲ *application of the closing rate method* aplicación del método del tipo de cambio de cierre ▲ *apply the closing rate method* aplicar el método del tipo de cambio de cierre ▲ *use the closing rate method* usar el método de tipo de cambio de cierre

⇛ current rate method, temporal method

closing stock UK

= closing inventory IAS/IFRS, US

≠ opening inventory IAS/IFR, US, opening stock UK

Closing stock is the stock remaining within an enterprise at the end of an accounting period as raw materials, work in progress, or finished goods.

inventario final

= existencias finales

▲ *closing stock of goods* inventario final de existencias ▲ *closing stock of manufactures* inventario final de productos terminados ▲ *closing stock of raw materials* inventario final de materias primas ▲ *closing stocks* inventarios finales

closing stocks UK

Closing stocks are the stocks remaining within an enterprise at the end of an accounting period as raw materials, work in progress, or finished goods.

inventarios finales

= existencias finales

▲ *intercompany profit included in closing stocks* el beneficio entre compañías del grupo incluido en los inventarios finales

CMA US

= certified management accountant US

CMA is the abbreviation for certified management accountant. A CMA is a professional accountant within management accounting and as such a counterpart to the certified

public accountant within financial accounting.
experto contable en contabilidad de gestión
▲ *acquire the designation of CMA* conseguir el nombramiento de experto contable en contabilidad de gestión ▲ *the designation of CMA* la designación del experto contable en contabilidad de gestión

CMS US
= cost management system US
CMS is the abbreviation for cost management system. A cost management system is a system of techniques to identify how management decisions influence costs. The purpose of a cost management system is to provide cost information for strategic decisions and operational control as well as measures of inventory value and cost of goods manufactured for external stakeholders.
sistema de contabilidad de costes
▲ *an integrated CMS* un sistema de contabilidad de costes integrado ▲ *implement a new CMS* implementar un nuevo sistema de contabilidad de costes
⇛ cost accounting system

co-operation
→ cooperation

co-operation agreement
→ cooperation agreement

co-operative partner
→ cooperative partner

co-operative savings bank
→ cooperative savings bank

co-operative society
→ cooperative society

co-partner
A co-partner is a co-owner of a partnership.
socio comanditario
▲ *be jointly and severally liable for a co-partner's tortious act* ser responsable conjunta y forzosamente por un acto ilícito del socio comanditario ▲ *liability for a co-partner's debts* responsabilidad por las deudas de un socio comanditario ▲ *the express approval of the co-partners* la aprobación expresa de los socios comanditarios ▲ *without the consent of the co-partners* sin el consentimiento de los socios comanditarios

co-payment
Co-payment applies in health insurance and means the partial payment of medical expenses by the insured party.
copago
▲ *a 20% co-payment* un 20% de copago ▲ *introduce co-payment* introducir el copago ▲ *reduce the co-payment* reducir el copago

code of conduct UK, US
A code of conduct is a statement or document setting the ethical standards within a certain area or organisation.
código de conducta
= código ético
▲ *amend or change the code of conduct* reformar o modificar el código de conducta ▲ *comply with the code of conduct* cumplir con el código de conducta ▲ *draft code of conduct* código de conducta provisional

coefficient of determination
A coefficient of determination is a measurement of the proportional changes (variance) in a given variable (the dependent variable) which result from changes in another variable (the independent variable), e.g. the degree to which changes in costs which can be explained by cost driver changes.
coeficiente de determinación
= índice de determinación
▲ *calculate the coefficient of determination* calcular el coeficiente de determinación ▲ *interpret the adjusted coefficient of determination* interpretar el coeficiente de determinación ajustado

COGS
COGS is the abbreviation of cost of goods sold, i.e. the cost during a period of the merchandise or products an enterprise acquires or produces and then sells.
coste de mercancías vendidas
= coste de artículos vendidos
▲ *calculate COGS* calcular el coste de mercancías vendidas
⇛ cost of goods sold

collateral
Collateral is additional security provided in the form of assets pledged, such as personal or real property, which a lender can seize in the event of default by a borrower.
garantía secundaria
= colateral

▲ *adequate collateral* garantía secundaria adecuada ▲ *book entry securities collateral* registro de garantías secundarias de títulos ▲ *collateral agreements* acuerdos de colateral ▲ *collateral held in the case of a financial asset* garantía secundaria aportada en el caso de un activo financiero ▲ *collateral pledged in the case of a financial liability* garantía secundaria pignorada en el caso de un pasivo financiero ▲ *collateral sold or repledged* garantía secundaria liquidada o vuelta a pignorar ▲ *date-sensitive collateral* garantía secundaria adaptada a la fecha ▲ *deliver financial collateral* aportar garantías secundarias financieras ▲ *equivalent collateral* garantía secundaria equivalente ▲ *fashion-sensitive collateral* garantía secundaria adaptada al uso ▲ *financial assets pledged as collateral for liabilities* activos financieros pignorados como garantía secundaria para deudas ▲ *financial collateral arrangements* acuerdos de garantías secundarias financieras ▲ *guarantees and collaterals* garantías primarias y secundarias ▲ *material terms and conditions relating to assets pledged as collateral* condiciones materiales relativas a los activos pignorados como garantía secundaria ▲ *pledge as collateral* prenda como garantía secundaria ▲ *potential recoveries from realisation of collateral* cobro potencial de la liquidación de la garantía secundaria ▲ *shares in listed companies held as collateral for loans* acciones en empresas cotizadas guardadas como garantía secundaria para los préstamos ▲ *the collateral provider* el aportante de la garantía secundaria ▲ *the collateral taker* el tomador de la garantía secundaria ▲ *the effective realisation of financial collateral* la liquidación efectiva de las garantías secundarias financieras ▲ *the fair value of any collateral* el valor razonable de cualquier garantía secundaria ▲ *the value of the collateral* el valor de la garantía secundaria ▲ *top-up collateral* colateral complementario ▲ *transfer collateral* traspasar la garantía secundaria
⇛ security

Collegio dei Ragionieri e Periti Commerciali

The Collegio dei Ragionieri e Periti Commerciali is a leading Italian professional accountancy body set up on a local basis. The Collegio is one of the two leading Italian professional accountancy bodies, the other being the Consiglio Nazionale dei Dottori Commercialisti that operates on a national basis.

Collegio dei Ragionieri e Periti Commerciali

▲ *become a member of the Collegio dei Ragionieri e Periti Commerciali* inscribirse en el Collegio dei Ragionieri e Periti Commerciali
⇛ Consiglio Nazionale dei Dottori Commercialisti

collusive pricing

Collusive pricing constitutes the secret price-fixing by one or more producers in a particular line of business. Collusive pricing agreements are prohibited in most countries.

fijación colusoria de precios

▲ *be engaged in collusive pricing* verse implicado en la fijación colusoria de precios ▲ *the impact of cyclical fluctuations on collusive pricing* el impacto de las fluctuaciones cíclicas en la fijación colusoria de precios
⇛ collusive pricing agreement

collusive pricing agreement

A collusive pricing agreement is an agreement where one or more producers in a particular line of business collude, i.e. work secretly and illegally together, to fix the prices of certain products. Collusive pricing agreements are prohibited in most countries.

pacto de fijación colusoria de precios

▲ *a court investigation into collusive pricing agreements* una investigación judicial sobre pactos de fijación colusoria de precios ▲ *create collusive pricing agreements* acordar pactos de fijación colusoria de precios ▲ *enter into a collusive pricing agreement* participar en un pacto de fijación colusoria de precios
⇛ collusive pricing

combination

A combination is the organisation of individual elements so as to form one unit.

combinación

▲ *a combination of* una combinación de ▲ *combination of a class of intangible assets* combinación de una clase de bienes intangibles ▲ *combination of the 'bottom-up' and the 'top-down' test* combinación de pruebas 'bottom-up' y 'top-down' ▲ *in combination with* en combinación con ▲ *individually or in combination* individualmente o en combinación

combine

To combine means to organise individual elements so as to form one unit.

combinar

▲ *combine activities in a particular line of business* combinar actividades en una línea concreta de negocio ▲ *combine amounts* combinar cantidades ▲ *combine as a single business segment* combinar como un segmento empresarial único ▲ *combine controlled items with jointly controlled items* combinar partidas controladas con partidas controlados conjuntamente ▲ *combine on a line-by-line basis* combinar sobre una base línea por línea ▲ *combine with a similar significant segment* combinar con un segmento significativo similar

combined financial instrument

A combined financial instrument is a financial instrument that, from the issuer's perspective, contains both a liability and an equity element.

instrumento financiero compuesto

▲ *the cash flows of the combined financial instrument* los flujos de efectivo del instrumento financiero compuesto ▲ *the liability component of the combined financial instrument* el componente de pasivo del instrumento financiero compuesto ▲ *treat the combined financial instrument as held for trading* tratar el instrumento financiero compuesto como dispuesto para la venta

combined financial statement

A combined financial statement covers two or more affiliated enterprises and presents the assets, liabilities, equity and operating figures of these enterprises to provide a financial overview of all the enterprises as a whole. Intercompany transactions may or may not be eliminated in a combined statement. However, combined financial statements are not consolidated financial statements as they do not relate to a group.

estado financiero combinado

▲ *disclose in the combined financial statement* divulgar en el estado financiero combinado ▲ *prepare a combined financial statement* preparar un estado financiero combinado ▲ *present in a combined financial statement* presentar en un estado financiero combinado

comfort letter

= letter of support

A comfort letter is a declaration made by a parent in which it declares its intention to support a subsidiary if the subsidiary should become unable to fulfil its obligations under a contract with the recipient of the comfort letter, e.g. a lender providing a loan to the subsidiary.

carta de garantía

▲ *issue a comfort letter* emitir una carta de garantía

commercial activities

= business activities, operations

The commercial activities of an enterprise is its business activities in the form of the production of products and services for profit.

actividad comercial

▲ *carry on commercial activities* llevar a cabo actividades comerciales ▲ *meet the definition of commercial activities* cumplir con la definición de actividades comerciales ▲ *promote something through commercial activities* promover algo mediante actividades comerciales

commercial enterprise

A commercial enterprise is an enterprise that provides goods, rights, funds, services etc. for a money consideration with a view to profit.

empresa comercial

▲ *a medium-sized commercial enterprise* una empresa comercial de tamaño medio

commercial paper US
= CP US
Commercial paper is a short-term, unsecured, negotiable loan issued by enterprises to obtain funding, usually on a discount basis with a maturity of 2 to 270 days.
efectos comerciales
NOTE Always plural in Spanish accounting texts.
▲ *commercial paper borrowing* deuda en forma de efectos comerciales ▲ *commercial paper issued by other companies* efectos comerciales emitidos por otras empresas ▲ *commercial paper programme* programa de efectos comerciales ▲ *issue commercial paper* emitir efectos comerciales

commission
Commission is the amount paid to a person or enterprise that has assisted in completing a sale. The commission is usually calculated as a percentage of the sales price.
comisión
▲ *cash receipts from fees and commissions* cobros en efectivo procedentes de comisiones y honorarios ▲ *commission relating to payments transfer* comisión relativa a transferencia de pagos ▲ *commissions paid* comisiones liquidadas ▲ *directly attributable fees and commissions* comisiones y honorarios directamente atribuibles ▲ *fee and commission income* ingreso por comisión y honorario ▲ *fee and commission income, net* ingreso por comisión y honorario, neto ▲ *interest and commission payable* cuenta acreedora por interés y comisión ▲ *interest and commission receipts* cobros por interés y comisión ▲ *interest and commission receivable* cuenta deudora por interés y comisión ▲ *other commissions* otras comisiones ▲ *payment of commissions* pago de comisiones

commission expense
= commissions paid
Commission expenses are payments made by an enterprise to persons or other enterprises for work done on the basis of commission.
gastos por comisiones
NOTE Always plural in Spanish accounting texts.
▲ *fee and commission expense* gastos por comisiones y honorarios

commission income
Commission income refers to income generated by performing work on commission. Typically, commission income is based on a percentage of the sales price of goods or services sold on commission.
ingresos por comisiones
NOTE Always plural in Spanish accounting texts.
▲ *fee and commission income* ingresos por comisiones y honorarios ▲ *fee and commission income from share market related transactions* ingresos por comisiones y honorarios procedente de transacciones relacionadas con el mercado de valores
⇛ fee income

commit
To commit oneself is to bind oneself and be obliged or compelled to do something i.e. give your time, money or loyalty to a particular purpose or person.
comprometerse
= comprometer
▲ *a future restructuring to which an enterprise is not yet committed* una reestructuración futura a la que una empresa no se compromete todavía ▲ *commit oneself* comprometerse ▲ *demonstrably committed to* demostrablemente comprometido con

commitment
A commitment is an obligation or an agreement to do something.
compromiso
▲ *distressed commitments* compromisos embargados ▲ *enter into commitments* comprometerse ▲ *long-term commitments* compromisos a largo ▲ *professional commitments* compromisos profesionales ▲ *reduce a commitment* reducir un compromiso ▲ *risky commitments* compromisos arriesgados ▲ *settlement of a commitment* establecimiento de un compromiso ▲ *short-term commitments* compromisos a corto ▲ *the total of large commitments* la suma de grandes compromisos

committed
Committed means guaranteed, binding or unavoidable.
comprometido
▲ *an undrawn committed credit line* una línea de crédito com-

prometida sin utilizar ▲ *committed costs* costes comprometidos ▲ *committed credit facility* línea de crédito comprometida ▲ *committed facility* línea comprometida ▲ *committed syndicated credit lines* líneas de crédito comprometidas sindicadas

committed cost UK, US

= committed fixed cost

≠ discretionary cost

Committed costs are costs, typically fixed costs, which relate to long-term expenditures and prior management decisions such as production equipment, IT infrastructure and the fundamental capacity of an enterprise, and therefore constitute costs which cannot be reduced or avoided if the enterprise is to continue operations in future.

NOTE Committed costs are often capacity costs such as depreciation and other costs stemming from the ownership of plant, facilities and equipment.

coste comprometido

= coste discrecional

▲ *control of committed costs* control de los costes comprometidos

⇛ capacity cost, committed fixed cost, fixed cost

committed fixed cost UK,US

Committed fixed costs are costs incurred relating to long-term expenditures and prior management decisions such as production equipment, IT infrastructure and the fundamental capacity of an enterprise, and therefore constitute costs which cannot be reduced or avoided if the enterprise is to continue operations in future.

coste fijo comprometido

▲ *less committed fixed costs* menos los costes fijos comprometidos

⇛ committed cost

committee of directors US, UK, IAS/IFRS

= board committee

A committee established within the board of directors is called a committee of directors. Such committees are usually established to allow non-executive directors to play an effective role in key areas.

comité de dirección

= junta directiva

▲ *appoint a committee of directors* nombrar un comité de dirección ▲ *set up a committee of directors* constituir un comité de dirección ▲ *the primary purpose of the committee of directors* el objetivo principal del comité de dirección ▲ *the terms of reference of the committee of directors* los términos de referencia del comité de dirección

committee on auditing

→ audit committee

commodity

A commodity is a physical thing such as a raw material that can be measured and traded on an exchange, and which can be the subject-matter of a contract, e.g. as an asset underlying a futures contract.

mercancía

▲ *a cash settlement of the obligation to receive or deliver the commodity* una liquidación en efectivo de la obligación de recibir o enviar la mercancía ▲ *a contract to buy or sell a commodity at a fixed price at a future date* un contrato para comprar o vender una mercancía a un precio fijo en una fecha futura ▲ *settlement through the physical receipt or delivery of a commodity* liquidación mediante la recepción física o envío de una mercancía ▲ *the underlying commodity* la mercancía subyacente

commodity contract

Commodity contract refers to an agreement between a buyer and a seller for the purchase or sale of commodities mainly for investment purposes, whether or not actual delivery is intended. Commodity contracts include forward and futures contracts.

contrato de producto

= contrato de materia prima, contrato de mercancía

▲ *the ability to buy or sell a commodity contract for cash* la posibilidad de comprar o vender un contrato de producto en efectivo

commodity future

A commodity future is a futures contract involving the future purchase or sale of a fixed

amount of commodities at a fixed price at a fixed date.
futuro de mercancías
▲ *a commodity futures market* un mercado de futuros de mercancías ▲ *commodity futures trading* negociación de futuros de mercancías ▲ *identical commodity futures* futuros de mercancías idénticos

commodity instrument
A commodity instrument is a financial instrument based on an underlying asset, the commodity, used to hedge a fixed contract, e.g. for a future sale of a specific commodity. Commodity instruments are derivative financial instruments, typically options or futures, and the underlying assets may be various types of commodities such as wheat, cotton, crude oil, natural gas or silver.
instrumento de materia prima
▲ *use commodity instruments* usar instrumentos de materia prima

common cost
Common costs are costs shared by several products, services, departments or segments.
coste conjunto
▲ *profit before common costs* beneficio antes de los costes conjuntos ▲ *the accounting treatment of common costs* el tratamiento contable de los costes conjuntos

common equity US
→ common stockholders' equity

common share US
= equity share, share of common stock
Common shares are the ordinary shares or stock of a company and entitles the owner to proportionate dividends if the company makes a profit. Common shares carry voting rights, but no priorities over other classes of shares.
acción ordinaria
▲ *a substantially equal exchange of voting common shares between the combining enterprises* un intercambio sustancialmente igualitario de acciones ordinarias con derecho a voto entre empresas participantes en una combinación de negocios ▲ *an exchange of voting common shares for cash* un intercambio de acciones ordinarias con derecho a voto por efectivo ▲ *the percentage of voting common shares exchanged* el porcentaje de acciones ordinarias con derecho a voto intercambiadas ▲ *the substantial majority of the voting common shares* la mayoría sustancial de acciones ordinarias con derecho a voto
⇛ common stock, ordinary share

common shareholders' equity US
= common stockholders' equity, shareholders' funds UK
The common shareholders' equity is the ownership interest - shareholdings and retained earnings - held by holders of common stock in a corporation.
fondos propios
= recursos propios
▲ *a return on common shareholders' equity of 15%* una rentabilidad de los fondos propios del 15% ▲ *reconciliation of common shareholders' equity* conciliación de fondos propios

common stock[1] US *noun* <a, the, no plural>
Common stock is semantically plural, grammatically uncountable singular. To state a given number of shares of common stock, the terms common share(s) or X shares of common stock are applied.
= common shares US, equity share, ordinary shares UK, stock of common shares US
≠ preferred stock US
Common stock represents the shares issued to owners in a corporation. Shares of common stock carry voting and dividend rights, but rank subordinately to preferred stockholders and creditors for payment in the event of corporate bankruptcy.
acción ordinaria
▲ *proceeds from the issue of common stock* beneficios de la emisión de acciones ordinarias ▲ *total number of common stock* total número de acciones ordinarias ▲ *weighted average number of shares of common stock* número medio ponderado de acciones ordinarias
⇛ common share

common stock[2] US *noun* <a, the, -s>
When referring to an investor's equity investment portfolios or

aggregate stockholdings in several companies, the plural form "common stocks" applies. However, to state a given number of shares of common stock in an individual company, the terms common share(s) or X shares of common stock applies.
Common stock refers to the legal capital of a corporation and refers to a portfolio of shares of common stock held in one or more corporations, i.e. an investor's aggregate amount of shares of common stock.
acción ordinaria
⇛ common share

common stockholders' equity US
= capital and reserves UK, common shareholders' equity, shareholders' funds UK
The common stockholders' equity is the ownership interest –stockholdings and retained earnings– held by holders of common stock in a corporation.
fondos propios
= recursos propios
▲ *average common stockholders' equity* fondos propios medios ▲ *beginning common stockholders' equity* inicio de fondos propios ▲ *ending common stockholders' equity* fin de fondos propios ▲ *return on common stockholders' equity* rentabilidad sobre fondos propios

common-size analysis
A common-size analysis is a method clarifying the performance of an enterprise by an analysis of the level and development of individual items or elements compared with totals in the financial statements. Costs items may e.g. be compared with sales (revenue), and individual operating activities seen in proportion to invested capital. As the analysis will show the development in the proportion in between various accounting items in e.g. the profit or loss account or the balance sheet, it is possible to assess the performance of an enterprise by comparing the percentages achieved with those of another enterprise.
análisis proporcional
= análisis equiparable
▲ *carry out a common-size analysis* llevar a cabo un análisis proporcional ▲ *prepare a common-size analysis* preparar un análisis proporcional

Compagnie Nationale des Commissaires aux Comptes
= CNCC
The Compagnie Nationale des Commissaires aux Comptes (CNCC) is the French government-controlled professional accountancy body that supervises statutory audits and of which accountants that audit companies must be members. The private-sector accountancy body is the Ordre des Experts Comptable.
Compagnie Nationale des Commissaires aux Comptes
▲ *become a member of Compagnie Nationale des Commissaires aux Comptes* inscribirse en la Compagnie Nationales des Commissaires aux Comptes
⇛ Ordre des Experts Comptable

Companies Act UK
= CA
The Companies Act contains the rules that allow one or more persons to form an incorporated company with or without limited liability by registration. It contains special rules about issues such as the required documents, share capital, the management and administration of companies, directors and other officers, meetings, financial reporting and audit.
Ley de Sociedades Mercantiles
▲ *comply with the Companies Act 1989* cumplir con la Ley de Sociedades Mercantiles de 1989 ▲ *in accordance with section 235 of the Companies Act 1989* según la sección 235 de la Ley de Sociedades Mercantiles de 1989 ▲ *Schedule 1 of the Companies Act 1989* Anexo 1 de la Ley de Sociedades Mercantiles de 1989

company
A company is an association of people that has been formed to conduct business or other activities in the name of the company. In most jurisdictions a company is a separate legal entity, and may be formed by only one person.
empresa
= compañía, sociedad

▲ *a company acquired in a business combination* una empresa adquirida en una combinación de negocios ▲ *a dominant company* una sociedad dominante ▲ *a related company* una sociedad relacionada ▲ *an associated company* una compañía asociada ▲ *brass-plate company* empresa de alto nivel ▲ *carry on business as a general commercial company* llevar a cabo negocios como una empresa comercial general ▲ *dissolve a company* disolver una empresa ▲ *dormant company* empresa inactiva ▲ *form a company* formar una empresa ▲ *medium-sized companies* medianas empresas ▲ *ready-made company* empresa ya constituida ▲ *registered company* empresa registrada ▲ *small companies* pequeñas empresas ▲ *the investing company* la empresa inversora ▲ *the reporting company* la sociedad informante ▲ *transactions between a company and its principal shareholder* transacciones entre una sociedad y su principal accionista ▲ *unlimited company* sociedad colectiva ▲ *wind up a company* liquidar una empresa

company information

Company information is any information about a particular company, including its name, address, incorporation date, names of board members and auditors, dates of general meetings etc.

información de la empresa

▲ *access to company information* acceder a la información de la empresa ▲ *submit company information* remitir la información de la empresa

company law

The term 'company law' refers to all the legal rules in a country or area governing companies. The rules may be found in statutes, regulations or case law.

derecho de sociedades

▲ *comply with company law* cumplir con el derecho de sociedades ▲ *in accordance with company law* de acuerdo con el derecho de sociedades ▲ *pursuant to company law* conforme al derecho de sociedades

Company Law Directive

The Company Law Directive is a legal act concerning the activities of companies adopted by the EU, and it is implemented in the individual member states by national statutes or administrative regulations.

Directiva de Sociedades

▲ *EU's Seventh Company Law Directive (consolidated accounts)* la Séptima Directiva de Sociedades de la UE (cuentas consolidadas) ▲ *the provisions of the EC Fourth and Seventh Company Law Directives* las disposiciones de la Cuarta y la Séptima Directivas de Sociedad de la CEE

company law directive

A company law directive is a legal act concerning the activities of companies adopted by the EU, and it is implemented in the individual member states by national statutes or administrative regulations.

directiva de sociedades

▲ *EU's seventh company law directive (consolidated accounts)* la séptima directiva de sociedades de la UE (cuentas consolidadas) ▲ *the provisions of the EC Fourth and Seventh Company Law Directives* las disposiciones de la cuarta y la séptima directivas de sociedad de la CEE

company taxation UK

When tax is imposed on the income of a company for a specific year, this is referred to as company taxation.

tributación del impuesto de sociedades

▲ *Danish company taxation* tributación del impuesto de sociedades danés ▲ *international company taxation* tributación del impuesto de sociedades internacional ▲ *reduce company taxation* reducir la tributación del impuesto de sociedades

company transfer

A company transfer is a transfer of a company by way of sale, gift or merger.

traspaso empresarial

▲ *an intercompany transfer of company ownership* un traspaso empresarial de la propiedad empresarial entre empresas ▲ *part in a company transfer* participar en un traspaso empresarial

comparability

Comparability means having the ability to be compared. For

accounting purposes, comparability may refer to the possibility of making valid comparisons between financial reporting items or financial statements presented by different enterprises.

comparabilidad

▲ *achieve a reasonable degree of comparability* conseguir un grado razonable de comparabilidad ▲ *comparability of accounting figures* comparabilidad de cifras contables ▲ *enhance comparability* incentivar la comparabilidad ▲ *ensure comparability* asegurar la comparabilidad ▲ *ensure the comparability of annual reports of different financial years* asegurar la comparabilidad de los informes anuales de diferentes ejercicios ▲ *maintain comparability in financial reporting among enterprises* mantener la comparabilidad de la información financiera entre empresas ▲ *non-comparability* no comparabilidad ▲ *the comparability of financial statements* la comparabilidad de los estados financieros ▲ *the comparability of information* la comparabilidad de la información ▲ *the comparability of the per share amounts disclosed* la comparabilidad de las cantidades por acción divulgadas

⇛ consistency

comparable

Comparable means having the ability to be compared.

comparable

▲ *a comparable price* un precio comparable ▲ *a comparable quality* un atributo comparable ▲ *an interim financial report for the comparable interim period of the immediately preceding financial year* un informe financiero provisional para el ejercicio intermedio comparable al del ejercicio inmediatamente anterior ▲ *be comparable to* ser comparable a ▲ *broadly comparable to* comparable en gran medida a ▲ *comparable financial reporting* información financiera comparable ▲ *comparable goods sold to a buyer unrelated to the seller* bienes comparables vendidos al comprador no relacionado con el vendedor ▲ *comparable information* información comparable ▲ *comparable market transactions* transacciones de mercado comparables ▲ *comparable over all periods presented* comparable para los periodos presentados ▲ *comparable returns* rendimientos comparables ▲ *comparable with* comparable con ▲ *expected growth rates of comparable securities* tasa de crecimiento previsto de valores comparables ▲ *lack of comparable market data* pérdida de información de mercado comparable ▲ *the end of the comparable period* el final del periodo comparable

comparative figure

= comparative amount, comparatives

Comparative figures are figures presented with a view to making comparisons between corresponding amounts reported in financial statements for different accounting periods or between corresponding amounts presented by different enterprises.

cifra comparativa

▲ *comparative figures for 2005* cifras comparativas para 2005 ▲ *restate comparative figures* actualizar las cifras comparativas

⇛ comparative information

comparative information

Comparative information constitutes data that can be compared. For accounting purposes, such data include reporting figures included in the financial reports for comparison with previous accounting periods.

información comparativa

▲ *comparative information for the previous financial year* información comparativa para el ejercicio anterior ▲ *disclose comparative information* divulgar la información comparativa ▲ *present full comparative information* presentar la información comparativa completa ▲ *reclassify comparative information* reclasificar la información comparativa ▲ *restate comparative information* actualizar la información comparativa

⇛ comparative figure

comparator company

= peer company

A comparator company is an enterprise that is comparable with another enterprise because it operates within the same industry and has more or less the same size, therefore constituting a useful benchmark for analyses of performance and other criteria.

empresa homóloga

▲ *a comparator company that is listed* una empresa homóloga que cotiza en bolsa ▲ *choice of comparator company* elección de empresa homóloga ▲ *outperform the comparator company* superar a la empresa homóloga

⇛ peer group

compare

To compare means to examine or analyse two or more things in order to find similarities and differences.

comparar

▲ *compare prices* comparar precios ▲ *compare the financial statements of an enterprise over a period of time* comparar los estados financieros de una empresa durante un periodo de tiempo ▲ *compare the present value of the future cash flows* comparar el valor actual de los flujos de efectivo futuros ▲ *compare the profit or loss for the year with expected developments for the year* comparar el resultado del ejercicio con los rendimientos previstos para el mismo ▲ *compare the recoverable amount of the cash-generating unit to its carrying amount* comparar el valor recuperable de la unidad generadora de efectivo con su valor contable ▲ *compare with* comparar con

comparison

A comparison is an examination or analysis of two or more things made in order to find similarities and differences.

comparación

▲ *a direct comparison* una comparación directa ▲ *a step-by-step comparison* una comparación paso a paso ▲ *a systematic comparison* una comparación sistemática ▲ *a year-on-year comparison of the enterprise* comparación de la empresa año a año ▲ *basis of comparison* base de comparación ▲ *comparison of an enterprise's financial statements with those of prior periods* comparación de los estados financieros de una empresa con los de ejercicios anteriores ▲ *comparison of consolidated financial statements* comparación de estados financieros consolidados ▲ *comparison of cost with net realisable value* comparación del coste con el valor realizable neto ▲ *comparison of data* comparación de datos ▲ *comparison of performance* comparación de rendimientos ▲ *comparison with other expenses* comparación con otros gastos ▲ *for the purpose of comparison* a efectos de comparación ▲ *in comparison with* en comparación con ▲ *make a comparison* realizar una comparación ▲ *perform a meaningful comparison* llevar a cabo una comparación significativa

compensate

To compensate is to pay somebody for a service or a job done or to provide damages for a loss incurred or injury suffered.

compensar

= remunerar, retribuir

▲ *accumulating compensated absences* acumulando bajas remuneradas ▲ *adjust revenues to compensate for any increase in market rates* ajustar los ingresos para compensar por cualquier incremento en los tipos de mercado ▲ *compensate a loss by future lease payments at below market price* compensar una pérdida por pagos futuros de arrendamiento a un precio inferior al del mercado ▲ *compensate an employee on retirement* compensar a un empleado por jubilación ▲ *compensate employees for absence* remunerar a los empleados por baja ▲ *entitlement to future compensated absences* derecho a futuras bajas remuneradas ▲ *matched with the associated costs which the grant is intended to compensate* igualado con los costes asociados que se pretende que la subvención compense ▲ *non-accumulating compensated absences* bajas remuneradas no acumuladas ▲ *prices that compensate for the expected loss of purchasing power during the credit period* precios que compensan las pérdidas del poder adquisitivo previstas durante el periodo del crédito ▲ *short-term compensated absences* bajas remuneradas a corto

compensation

Compensation is a payment made because something bad has occurred such as damage or loss of office or earnings.

indemnización

▲ *a compensation for expenses or losses already incurred* indemnización por gastos o pérdidas ya devengados ▲ *bonuses and deferred compensation* primas e indemnización diferida ▲ *cancel a contract without paying compensation to the other party* cancelar un contrato sin indemnizar a la otra parte ▲ *compensation for employees* indemnización para los empleados ▲ *compensation for the impairment or loss of items* indemnización por el deterioro o pérdida de partidas ▲ *compensation in cash or in kind* indemnización en efectivo o en especie ▲ *compensation received* indemnización percibida ▲ *compensation related to the involuntary conversion of items of property, plant and equipment* indemnización relativa a conversión involuntaria de partidas de edificios, instalaciones y equipos ▲ *deferred compensation arrangement* acuerdo de indemnización diferida ▲ *employee compensation plans* planes de indemnizaciones para empleados ▲ *equity compensation benefits* indemnizaciones según beneficios patrimoniales ▲ *monetary compensation* indemnización monetaria ▲ *non-monetary compensation* indemnización no monetaria ▲ *payment of compensation* pago por indemnización ▲ *provide compensation for the uncertain future event* percibir indemnización por un acontecimiento futuro imprevisto ▲ *receive compensation* percibir indemnización ▲ *receive compensation for losses from a reinsurer* percibir indemnización por pérdidas de una reaseguradora ▲ *repay compensation* volver a indemnizar

⇛ benefit

compensation alternative

A compensation alternative is a way to pay employees other than paying money.

forma alternativa de indemnización

▲ *offer a favourable compensation alternative* ofrecer una forma alternativa de indemnización favorable

compensation plan

A compensation plan is an agreement between an employer and its employees specifying the ways in which the employees are or may be remunerated.

plan de compensación

= plan de compensaciones

▲ *employee compensation plan* plan de compensación al empleado ▲ *equity compensation plan* plan de compensación patrimonial ▲ *incentive compensation plan* incentivar el plan de compensación ▲ *performance-related compensation plan* plan de compensación según beneficios ▲ *share-based compensation plan* plan de compensación basado en acciones ▲ *stock-based compansation plan* plan de compensación basado en acciones

compensation programme

A compensation programme is an agreement between an employer and an employee specifying the ways in which the employee is or may be remunerated.

programa de compensación

= programa de compensaciones, programa de remuneración

▲ *introduction of a compensation programme* introducción de un programa de compensación ▲ *prepare a compensation programme* preparar un programa de compensación ▲ *share-based compensation programme* programa de compensación basado en acciones

compensatory amount

A compensatory amount is payment made to offset a claim or fully settle a loss or an injury. In connection with an exchange of shares, a shareholder may e.g. receive shares in another company plus a monetary compensatory amount in full settlement of the purchase price agreed.

cantidad compensatoria

▲ *calculate the compensatory amount* calcular la cantidad compensatoria ▲ *pay a compensatory amount* pagar una cantidad compensatoria ▲ *the size of the compensatory amount* el importe de la cantidad compensatoria

competence report

A competence report is a review that gives an overview of the competencies held by individuals, e.g. employees, enterprises or the society as a whole. The competencies may be social, intellectual, managerial or communicative.

informe de competencias

▲ *the National Competence Report* el Informe Nacional de Competencias

competitive

Something is competitive when it has reached a level at which it is just as good or better than other enterprises or offers.

competitivo

▲ *a competitive advantage* una ventaja competitiva ▲ *a competitive disadvantage* una desventaja competitiva ▲ *a competitive edge* un margen competitivo ▲ *a competitive market* un mercado competitivo ▲ *competitive bidding* oferta competitiva ▲ *competitive factors* factores competitivos ▲ *competitive power* poder competitivo ▲ *competitive prices* precios competitivos ▲ *competitive pricing* fijación de precios competitiva ▲ *competitive tendering* licitación competitiva ▲ *gain a competitive edge* obtener un margen competitivo

competitive parameter

Competitive parameters refer to aspects and factors that influence customers' willingness to buy a specific product or the product of a specific enterprise, e.g. price, design, packaging or efficiency.

parámetro competitivo

▲ *a central competitive parameter* un parámetro competitivo central ▲ *a crucial competitive parameter* un parámetro competitivo crucial

competitiveness

= competitive power, competitive strength

Competitiveness is the ability of an enterprise to gain a competitive edge in relation to other enterprises by possessing specific cost and product differentiation advantages.

competitividad

▲ *affect competitiveness* afectar a la competitividad ▲ *improve competitiveness* mejorar la competitividad ▲ *strengthen competitiveness* fortalecer la competitividad ▲ *the company's competitiveness on international markets* la competitividad de la empresa en los mercados internacionales ▲ *the competitiveness of companies* la competitividad de las empresas ▲ *weaken competitiveness* debilitar la competitividad

complaint

A complaint is a claim that a product is defective or does not otherwise conform to the contract.

queja

= reclamación

▲ *complaints received* quejas recibidas ▲ *dealing with complaints* ocupándose de las quejas ▲ *number of orders with complaints* número de pedidos con reclamaciones

complaints cost

Complaints costs are those costs that an enterprise incurs as a result of complaints about its products received from customers.

coste de reclamaciones

= coste por reclamaciones

▲ *realised complaints costs* costes de reclamaciones liquidados

complete reciprocated costs

= artificial costs

Complete reciprocated costs constitute all own costs incurred by a service department plus the costs allocated to it for services provided by other service departments.

costes recíprocos completos

= costes artificiales, costes contractuales

▲ *calculate the complete reciprocated costs* calcular los costes recíprocos completos ▲ *recognise the complete reciprocated costs* reconocer los costes recíprocos completos ▲ *reduce complete reciprocated costs* reducir los costes recíprocos completos

completed contract method

→ completed-contract method

completed-contract method

= sales method

The completed-contract method is an accounting method whereby recognition of profits and related costs from long-term contracts is subject to completion on the contract and delivery of the product or service in question.

método del contrato cumplido

= método de reconocimiento de beneficios al terminarse la obra

▲ *change from the completed-contract method to the percentage of completion method* cambio desde el método del contrato cumplido al método del porcentaje de obra ejecutada ▲ *recognise revenue and expenses using the completed-contract method* identificar los ingresos y gastos usando el método del contrato cumplido ▲ *use the completed-contract method* usar el método del contrato cumplido

⇛ percentage of completion method

completeness

Completeness is one of the basic assumptions for the preparation of annual reports. To be reliable, the information in financial statements must be complete within the bounds of materiality and cost. An omission can cause information to be false or misleading and thus unreliable and deficient in terms of its relevance.

integridad

▲ *clarity, completeness and transparency* claridad, integridad y transparencia ▲ *the underlying assumption of completeness* el supuesto subyacente de integridad

compliance

Compliance means the obeyance of rules, regulations, standards, contracts or other requirements, often within a particular subject area.

cumplimiento

▲ *an explicit and unreserved statement of compliance with IFRSs* un estado explícito y no reservado de cumplimiento de las NIIFs ▲ *compliance in all material respects* cumplimiento de todas las consideraciones materiales ▲ *compliance risk* riesgo de cumplimiento ▲ *compliance with a requirement* cumplimiento de un requisito ▲ *disclosure of compliance with IFRS* publicación del cumplimiento con las NIIFs ▲ *fair presentation and compliance with international accounting standards* justa presentación y cumplimiento de las normas de contabilidad internacional ▲ *in compliance with* en cumplimiento de ▲ *past or future compliance with certain conditions* cumplimiento pasado o futuro de ciertas condiciones

compliance audit

A compliance audit is typically performed by internal auditors to review and ascertain whether an enterprise complies with appropriate rules and regulations in carrying out its activities and whether the enterprise has the necessary competencies, including adequate system controls, to perform its activities.

auditoria de cumplimiento

▲ *carry out a compliance audit* llevar a cabo una auditoría de cumplimiento ▲ *planning of the compliance audit* planificación de la auditoría de cumplimiento ▲ *the results of the compliance audit* los resultados de la auditoría de cumplimiento

comply with

When you obey rules, regulations, standards, contracts or other requirements, you comply with them.

cumplir con

▲ *comply with conditions* cumplir con las condiciones ▲ *comply with each IFRS effective at the reporting date for its first IFRS financial statements* cumplir con cada NIIF en vigor a la fecha de publicación de los estados financieros elaborados según la primera NIIF ▲ *comply with provisions* cumplir con las disposiciones ▲ *comply with requirements* cumplir con los requisitos ▲ *comply with the disclosure requirements, where appropriate* cumplir con los requisitos de información, si son apropiados ▲ *comply with the recognition and measurement requirements of IFRSs* cumplir con el reconocimiento y los requisitos de valoración de las NIIFs

component of an entity IAS/IFRS

A component of an entity is a distinct part of an entity that is separate and independent regarding operations, cash flows and financial reporting.

NOTE In the context of the International Financial Reporting Standards (IFRS), components of entities typically refer to non-current assets held for sale or discontinued operations.

componente de una entidad

▲ *a component of an entity that has been disposed of* un componente de una entidad que se ha liquidado ▲ *a component of an entity that is classified as held for sale* un componente de una en-

tidad que está clasificado como preparado para la venta
SOURCE IFRS 5, Appendix A

composite financial statements
Composite financial statements are financial statements that have been prepared by combining the individual financial statements of two or more enterprises, e.g. consolidated financial statements.
estados financieros consolidados
▲ *prepare composite financial statements* preparar los estados financieros consolidados ▲ *publish composite financial statements* publicar los estados financieros consolidados

composite unit
A composite unit is a theoretical unit calculated on the basis of a weighting of the individual products in the total sales mix.
unidad de cuenta
▲ *budgeted contribution margin per composite unit* margen de contribución presupuestado por unidad de cuenta ▲ *budgeted sales price per composite unit* precio de ventas presupuestado por unidad de cuenta
⇛ sales mix

composition
A composition is the organisation and relationship between several independent elements.
composición
▲ *a balanced composition* una composición equilibrada ▲ *the composition of holders of class B shares* la composición de accionistas de acciones de clase B ▲ *the composition of the balance sheet* la composición del balance ▲ *the composition of the credit portfolio* la composición de la cartera de crédito ▲ *the composition of the enterprise's knowledge resources* la composición de los recursos de conocimiento de la empresa ▲ *the composition of the equity and borrowings of the enterprise* la composición del patrimonio y deudas de la empresa ▲ *the composition of the executive board* la composición del consejo ejecutivo ▲ *the composition of the management* la composición de la dirección ▲ *the composition of the share capital* la composición del capital social ▲ *the composition of the supervisory board* la composición del consejo de supervisión ▲ *the composition of the total receivables* la composición de las cuentas deudoras totales

compound annual growth rate
= CAGR, compounded annual growth rate
The annual compound growth rate (CAGR) is a geometric average of the year-to-year growth rate over a number of years.
tasa de crecimiento anual compuesta
= tasa de crecimiento interanual
▲ *achieve a compound annual growth rate of 10%* lograr una tasa de crecimiento anual compuesta del 10%

compound financial instrument IAS/IFRS
= compound instrument IAS/IFRS, debt and equity security
Compound financial instruments are securities with partly equity and partly liability or debt components, such as a convertible bond.
instrumento financiero híbrido
= instrumento financiero compuesto
NOTE Spanish accountants prefer 'instrumento financiero híbrido' to the IAS/IFRS term 'instrumento financiero compuesto'.
▲ *issue a compound financial instrument* emitir un instrumento financiero híbrido ▲ *split a compound financial instrument into separate liability and equity components* dividir un instrumento financiero híbrido en los componentes de pasivo y de patrimonio ▲ *the equity component of a compound financial instrument* el componente de patrimonio de un instrumento financiero híbrido ▲ *the issuer of a compound financial instrument* el emisor de un instrumento financiero híbrido
SOURCE IAS 32, paragraph 28
⇛ equity component, liability component

compound instrument IAS/IFRS
→ compound financial instrument

compounded annual growth rate
→ compound annual growth rate

comprehensive income
Comprehensive income is the change in equity for an accounting period arising from

transactions and other events excluding investments by owners and distribution of dividends. As an all-inclusive income concept, comprehensive income includes e.g. gains and losses not included in income, such as those arising from changes in market value of investments.

variaciones en el patrimonio neto

= resultado global

NOTE Spanish accountants prefer 'variaciones en patrimonio neto' to the IAS/IFRS term 'resultado global'. The Spanish term is always plural.

▲ *amounts reclassified from other comprehensive income to profit or loss* cuentas reclasificadas desde otras variaciones en el patrimonio neto a la cuenta de resultados ▲ *comprehensive income and its components* variaciones en el patrimonio neto y sus componentes ▲ *display comprehensive income* mostrar variaciones en el patrimonio neto ▲ *income tax relating to components of other comprehensive income* el impuesto sobre la renta relativo a los componentes de otras variaciones en el patrimonio neto ▲ *items included in other comprehensive income* partidas incluidas en otras variaciones en el patrimonio neto ▲ *other comprehensive income* otras variaciones en el patrimonio neto ▲ *total comprehensive income* resultado global total

⇛ statement of total recognised gains and losses

comprehensive income model

Under the comprehensive income model all value adjustments in the balance sheet resulting in an increase or a decrease of equity must be recognised in the profit and loss account. The value adjustments include gains and losses, but exclude owner transactions.

modelo de variaciones en el patrimonio neto

▲ *apply the comprehensive income model* aplicar el modelo de variaciones en el patrimonio neto

⇛ statement of total recognised gains and losses

comptroller UK

= controller

The controller is the top accounting officer of an enterprise and typically responsible for financial reporting, taxation, and internal auditing.

director financiero

= controller

▲ *appoint a new comptroller* nombrar a un nuevo director financiero ▲ *the incoming comptroller* el director financiero entrante ▲ *the outgoing comptroller* el director financiero saliente

⇛ treasurer

compulsory

When something is compulsory it must be done and cannot be derogated from.

obligatorio

= forzoso

▲ *a compulsory offer* una oferta obligatoria ▲ *a compulsory requirement* un requisito obligatorio ▲ *be subject to compulsory accounting provisions* estar sometido a provisiones contables obligatorias ▲ *compulsory benefits* beneficios obligatorios ▲ *compulsory formats* formatos obligatorios ▲ *compulsory licence* licencia obligatoria ▲ *compulsory redundancy* despido forzoso ▲ *compulsory retirement* jubilación forzosa ▲ *make something compulsory under current law* hacer algo obligatorio según la ley vigente ▲ *the compulsory elements of the annual report* los elementos obligatorios del informe anual

compulsory dissolution

A compulsory dissolution of a business enterprise is the involuntary closing down of that enterprise and occurs as a consequence of the enterprise's insolvency or violation of legal requirements relating to management, audit or financial reporting.

disolución obligatoria

= disolución forzosa

▲ *the compulsory dissolution of the company* la disolución obligatoria de la empresa

compulsory redemption

= mandatory redemption

Compulsory redemption means the unavoidable and enforced exchange for cash of typically shares or bonds by the issuer. Shares that are at a regulatory, legal, taxation or other disadvantage to the issuer or its shareholders may be subject to compulsory redemption.

amortización obligatoria

▲ *apply section 20B of the Danish Public Limited Companies Act on compulsory redemption* aplicar la sección 20B de la Ley danesa de Sociedades Anónimas sobre amortización obligatoria ▲ *deregistration without compulsory redemption* anulación de una inscripción en un registro público sin amortización obligatoria ▲ *introduce a redemption right to replace a compulsory redemption* introducir un derecho de amortización para sustituir una amortización obligatoria ▲ *make a compulsory redemption* realizar una amortización obligatoria ▲ *replace a mandatory offer by a compulsory redemption* sustituir una oferta preceptiva por una amortización obligatoria

⇛ redemption obligation

concept

A concept is an idea or understanding of something.

concepto

▲ *a common concept* un concepto común ▲ *apply the concept of cash-generating units* aplicar el concepto de unidades generadoras de efectivo ▲ *central concepts* conceptos centrales ▲ *concepts of capital and capital maintenance* conceptos de capital y de mantenimiento de capital ▲ *the application of the control concept* la aplicación del concepto de control ▲ *the concept of fair value* el concepto del valor razonable ▲ *the concept of materiality* el concepto de materialidad

conceptual framework

= statement of principles

A conceptual framework consists of the basic theoretical study and foundations for the rules and principles underlying financial reporting and accounting. Such a framework was initiated by the Financial Accounting Standards Board in the US (the Statements of Financial Accounting Concepts); later similar frameworks have been adopted by Accounting Standards Board in the UK (the Statement of Principles) and the International Accounting Standards Board (the Framework for the Preparation and Presentation of Financial Statements).

marco conceptual

▲ *develop a conceptual framework* desarrollar un marco conceptual ▲ *outside the scope of the conceptual framework* fuera del alcance del marco conceptual ▲ *prepare a conceptual framework* preparar un marco conceptual ▲ *within the scope of the conceptual framework* dentro del alcance del marco conceptual

⇛ regulatory framework, Statement of Principles

concern

= entity

A concern is a business or firm.

empresa

= entidad

▲ *a large concern* una gran empresa ▲ *establish a new concern* montar una nueva empresa

⇛ going concern, going-concern concept

concession

A concession is a right granted by a public authority to an enterprise, usually against payment, to carry out certain business activities.

concesión

▲ *at the beginning of the concession period* al principio del periodo de la concesión ▲ *at the end of the concession period* al final del periodo de concesión ▲ *capitalisation of concessions* capitalización de concesiones ▲ *concessions acquired* concesiones adquiridas ▲ *during the concession period* durante el periodo de concesión ▲ *service concession arrangements* acuerdos de concesión de servicios ▲ *the concession operator* el beneficiario de la concesión ▲ *the concession provider* el proveedor de la concesión ▲ *the period of the concession* el periodo de la concesión

concluded

= closed, finished, settled, terminated

When something is concluded, it has been brought to an end or finished.

concluido

= acabado, finalizado, terminado

▲ *concluded negotiations* negociaciones concluidas ▲ *concluded transactions* transacciones concluidas

conclusion

= finalización

Conclusion is the act of entering into an agreement.

conclusión

▲ *conclusion of contracts* conclusión de contratos

condensed IAS/IFRS

≠ complete

Financial statements are condensed when, as a minimum, they contain the separate headings and subtotals which were recognised in the financial statements most recently published by an enterprise, also including selected notes. Other line items and notes must also be recognised if failure to disclose them would result in misleading condensed statements.

abreviado

= condensado

NOTE Spanish accountants use 'abreviado' instead of the IAS/IFRS term 'condensado'.

▲ *a condensed balance sheet* un balance abreviado ▲ *a condensed cash flow statement* un estado de flujo de efectivo abreviado ▲ *a condensed income statement* un estado de resultados abreviado ▲ *a condensed set of financial statements* una serie abreviada de estados financieros ▲ *condensed interim financial statements* estados financieros a cuenta abreviados ▲ *condensed items* partidas abreviadas ▲ *condensed statement of changes in equity* estado abreviado de cambios en el patrimonio neto ▲ *presentation of condensed and classified data* presentación de datos clasificados y abreviados ▲ *the condensed set of half-yearly financial statements* el conjunto abreviado de estados financieros semestrales

condition

1 A condition is a term of an agreement, contract or other formal arrangement that must be agreed to and complied with for the contract or agreement to remain in force and valid. Consequently, a condition is something that is a prerequisite for something else.

condición

▲ *a condition precedent* una condición precedente ▲ *a condition subsequent* una condición posterior ▲ *conditions of sale* condiciones de venta

2 A condition is a particular situation or state of something or somebody.

condición

▲ *conditions existing at the end of the financial year* condiciones existentes al final del ejercicio ▲ *conditions have improved* las condiciones han mejorado ▲ *conditions requiring disclosure* condiciones que requieren divulgación ▲ *conditions that existed at the balance sheet date* condiciones que existían a la fecha de balance ▲ *economic conditions* condiciones económicas ▲ *in the light of current conditions* a la luz de las condiciones actuales ▲ *market conditions* condiciones de mercado ▲ *under normal conditions* bajo condiciones normales

conditional

Conditional means subject to restrictions or depending on something.

condicionado

▲ *a conditional bonus* una prima condicionada ▲ *a conditional government grant* una subvención pública condicionada ▲ *a conditional statement* un estado condicionado ▲ *conditional benefits* beneficios condicionados ▲ *conditional on future employment* condicionado a empleo futuro ▲ *conditional sale* venta condicionada ▲ *conditional upon* condicionado a ▲ *whether or not the benefits are conditional on further service* tanto si los beneficios están condicionados a un mejor servicio como si no lo están

conditional sale

A conditional sale is a contract where a buyer has bought goods or real property and agreed to pay the price by instalments over a specified period on the condition that he will not become the owner of the goods or real property until he has paid the entire price or fulfilled some other condition.

venta condicionada

▲ *conditional sale agreements* contratos de venta condicionada ▲ *the subject-matter of a conditional sale* el contenido de una venta condicionada

conditional-sale debtor

A conditional-sale debtor is a person or enterprise that has bought goods or real property under a conditional sale agreement and still owes the seller money under the contract.

deudor en la venta condicionada

▲ *the obligations of the conditional-sale debtor* las obligaciones del deudor en la venta condicionada

⇛ conditional sale

conference method

The conference method is an interdepartmental cooperation approach for estimating costs where experts from the various functions of an enterprise contribute with analyses and information concerning future costs. Examples of departments involved are purchasing, manufacturing and employee relations departments.

método de conferencia

= método de la conferencia

▲ *an alternative to the conference method* una alternativa al método de conferencia

⇛ account analysis method, high-low method

conglomerate

A conglomerate is an enterprise or group that conducts business activities in a number of industries that have little or nothing in common.

conglomerado de empresas

▲ *the Financial Conglomerates Committee* el Comité de los Conglomerados de Empresas Financieras ▲ *the supplementary supervision of credit institutions, insurance undertakings and investment firms in a financial conglomerate* la supervisión adicional de instituciones crediticias, aseguradoras y empresas de inversión en un conglomerado de empresas financiero

Conglomerates Directive

The Conglomerates Directive is a legislative act adopted by the European Parliament and the Council on the supplementary supervision of credit institutions, insurance undertakings and investment firms in a financial conglomerate, i.e. a financial group which provides services and products in different sectors of the financial markets.

Directiva sobre Conglomerado de empresas

▲ *in compliance with the provisions of the Conglomerates Directive* en cumplimiento de las provisiones de la Directiva sobre Conglomerados de empresas

connection

= relation

A connection is some sort of relation between two or more points, persons or entities that are linked together.

conexión

▲ *in connection with* en conexión con ▲ *Internet connections* conexiones a Internet

⇛ affiliation

consequence

A consequence is the result or effect that naturally or logically follows from previous events or acts.

consecuencia

▲ *a direct consequence* una consecuencia directa ▲ *additional consequences* consecuencias adicionales ▲ *an immediate consequence* una consecuencia inmediata ▲ *an inevitable consequence* una consecuencia inevitable ▲ *an operational consequence* una consecuencia operativa ▲ *as a consequence of* como consecuencia de ▲ *elimination of the consequences* eliminación de las consecuencias ▲ *have consequences for* tener consecuencias para ▲ *in consequence* en consecuencia ▲ *income tax consequences of dividends* consecuencias fiscales de los dividendos ▲ *tax consequences* consecuencias fiscales

conservatism US

= conservatism convention US, principle of conservatism US, prudence UK, IAS/IFRS

Conservatism is an accounting concept implying being prudent in measuring assets and ensuring that uncertainty and risks are adequately disclosed. In the financial statements, revenues are only included when realised, and liabilities are provided for whether certain or uncertain.

prudencia

= conservadurismo

▲ *appropriate conservatism* prudencia apropiada ▲ *the concept of conservatism* el concepto de prudencia ▲ *various degrees of conservatism* varios grados de prudencia

conservatism convention US
= principle of conservatism, prudence concept IAS/IFRS, UK
The conservatism convention is an accounting concept implying being prudent in measuring assets and ensuring that uncertainty and risks are adequately disclosed. In the financial statements, revenues are only included when realised, and liabilities are provided for whether certain or uncertain.
norma de prudencia
▲ *apply the conservatism convention* aplicar la norma de prudencia ▲ *in accordance with the conservatism convention* de acuerdo con la norma de prudencia

consideration[1] *noun* <a, the, -s>
Consideration means payment for something in money or money's worth.
remuneración
= contraprestación
▲ *consideration for treasury shares* remuneración por valores del tesoro ▲ *consideration received from the equity compensation plans* remuneración percibida de los planes de compensación en acciones ▲ *contingent consideration payable* remuneración contingente a pagar ▲ *contingent consideration receivable* remuneración contingente a percibir ▲ *identifiable non-cash consideration* contraprestación identificable no dineraria ▲ *issue securities as consideration for contributions other than cash* emitir valores como remuneración por contribuciones que no sean en efectivo ▲ *nominal consideration* remuneración nominal ▲ *sale consideration* remuneración por venta ▲ *the cash consideration* la remuneración en efectivo ▲ *the consideration receivable* la remuneración a percibir ▲ *the consideration to be exchanged* la remuneración a modificar ▲ *the fair value of consideration received or receivable* el valor razonable de la remuneración percibida o a percibir ▲ *the net consideration agreed* la remuneración neta acordada ▲ *the nominal amount of the consideration* la cantidad nominal de la remuneración ▲ *total purchase or disposal consideration* total compra o remuneración disponible

consideration[2] *noun* <no indefinite article, the, no plural>
= regard
Consideration is the thorough and careful deliberation of an issue, typically in a decision-making process before making a judgment or giving an opinion.
consideración
▲ *give due consideration to* dar debida consideración a ▲ *pay consideration to* otorgar consideración a ▲ *take something into consideration* tomar algo en consideración

considerations of prudence
Considerations of prudence are required for the preparation of financial statements. These considerations are based on the prudence concept and ensure that assets are cautiously valued and liabilities provided for so that accounting disclosures are reliable and realistic.
consideraciones de prudencia
▲ *be guided by considerations of prudence* guiarse por consideraciones de prudencia ▲ *disregard of all considerations of prudence* desestimación de todas las consideraciones de prudencia ▲ *ordinary considerations of prudence* consideraciones de prudencia ordinarias

Consiglio Nazionale dei Dottori Commercialisti
= CNDC
The Consiglio Nazionale dei Dottori Commercialisti (CNDC) is the national Italian professional accountancy body representing at national level over 50,000 accountants in public practice, providing services in the field of business law, assurance accounting and taxation, both to private and public entities. The Institute is supervised by the Ministry of Justice and is responsible for the coordination of the 153 local branches and acts as technical adviser in all the relevant parliamentary committees.
Consiglio Nazionale dei Dottori Commercialisti
▲ *become a member of the Consiglio Nazionale dei Dottori Commercialisti* ser un miembro del

Consiglio Nazionale dei Dottori Commercialisti
⇛ Collegio dei Ragionieri e Periti Commerciali

consignment inventory US
= consignment stock UK
Consignment inventory is merchandise or goods given to and held by an enterprise (the dealer or consignee) that can act for the legal owner (the consignor). The dealer can either sell the goods to a third party on the owner's behalf against a commission or return them to the owner. The goods are physically held by the dealer, however, they remain part of the owner's inventory.
inventario en consignación
= mercancía consignada, mercancía en consignación, stock en depósito
▲ *a vendor-financed consignment inventory* unos inventarios en consignación financiados por el vendedor ▲ *consignment inventory arrangements* acuerdos de inventario en consignación

consignment stock UK
= consignment inventory US
Consignment stock is stock or goods given to and held by an enterprise (the dealer or consignee) that can act for the legal owner (the consignor). The dealer can either sell the goods to a third party on the owner's behalf against a commission or return them to the owner. The goods are physically held by the dealer, however, they remain part of the owner's stocks.
mercancía en consignación
= inventario en consignación, mercancía consignada, stock en depósito
▲ *consignment stock arrangements* acuerdos sobre mercancías en consignación ▲ *vendor-financed consignment stocks* mercancía en consignación financiadas por el vendedor

consistency
Consistency is one of the fundamental accounting concepts underlying the presentation of financial statements. The consistency concept implies that conformity must exist in accounting treatment from one accounting period to the next and that recognition methods and measurement bases must be applied uniformly to the same category of items.
uniformidad
▲ *consistency in valuation* uniformidad en la valoración ▲ *consistency of presentation* uniformidad de presentación ▲ *consistency requirements* requisitos de uniformidad ▲ *the consistency principle dictates that* el principio de uniformidad dicta que ▲ *the underlying assumption of consistency* el supuesto de uniformidad subyacente

consistency concept
The consistency concept is one of the fundamental accounting concepts and implies that conformity must exist in accounting treatment from one accounting period to the next and that recognition methods and measurement bases must be applied uniformly to the same category of items.
concepto de uniformidad
= concepto de consistencia
▲ *satisfy the consistency concept* satisfacer el concepto de uniformidad

consistency principle
The consistency principle is one of the fundamental accounting concepts and implies that conformity must exist in accounting treatment from one accounting period to the next and that recognition methods and measurement bases must be applied uniformly to the same category of items.
principio de uniformidad
= principio de consistencia
▲ *comply with the consistency principle* cumplir con el principio de uniformidad ▲ *departure from the consistency principle* desviación del principio de uniformidad ▲ *exemptions to the consistency principle* exenciones al principio de uniformidad

consistent
When something is consistent, it takes place or develops in a similar way as or is in agreement with something else.
consistente
▲ *allocate on a reasonable and consistent basis* asignar sobre una base consistente y razonable ▲ *be consistent with* ser con-

sistente con ▲ *consistent application* aplicación consistente ▲ *consistent assumptions* supuestos consistentes ▲ *consistent measurement* valoración consistente ▲ *consistent recognition* reconocimiento consistente ▲ *consistent use* uso consistente ▲ *in a consistent manner* de una manera consistente ▲ *on a rational and consistent basis* sobre una base consistente y racional

consistently

When something is done consistently, it is done in the same way in accordance with the same rules or principles each time, e.g. an enterprise may use specific accounting policies each year when preparing its financial statements.

consistentemente

= de forma consistente

▲ *a consistently determined denominator* un denominador fijado consistentemente ▲ *apply consistently from period to period* aplicar consistentemente de un periodo a otro ▲ *follow the enterprise's accounting policies consistently* seguir las normativas contables de una empresa consistentemente ▲ *measure something consistently* medir algo de forma consistente ▲ *recognise something consistently* reconocer algo consistentemente ▲ *use something consistently* usar algo consistentemente

consolidate

To consolidate means to combine and refers to the adding together of the financial statements of a parent with those of its consolidated subsidiaries to present the financial statements of the group enterprises as if they were one single entity.

consolidar

▲ *consolidate all subsidiaries, foreign and domestic* consolidar todas las filiales, extranjeras y nacionales ▲ *consolidate an SPE* consolidar una Entidad de Fines Especiales ▲ *consolidate on a pro rata basis* consolidar sobre una base proporcional

consolidated

Consolidated means combined and refers to the adding together of the financial statements of a parent with those of its consolidated subsidiaries to present the financial statements of the group enterprises as if they were one single entity.

consolidado

▲ *a consolidated balance sheet* un balance consolidado ▲ *a consolidated company* una empresa consolidada ▲ *a consolidated enterprise* una empresa consolidada ▲ *a consolidated income statement* una cuenta de resultados consolidada ▲ *a consolidated report* un informe consolidado ▲ *a consolidated subsidiary* una filial consolidada ▲ *consolidated annuities* bonos anuales consolidados ▲ *consolidated financial statements* estados financieros consolidados

⇛ consolidated accounts, consolidated financial statements

consolidated accounts UK

= consolidated financial statements US, IAS/IFRS, group accounts UK

≠ parent company accounts UK, parent-company financial statements US

Consolidated accounts combine the accounts of a parent and its subsidiaries and present the results, cash flows and financial position after elimination of intercompany balances as if the enterprises were a single entity.

cuentas consolidadas

= cuentas del grupo

▲ *prepare consolidated accounts* preparar las cuentas consolidadas ▲ *publish the consolidated accounts* publicar las cuentas consolidadas

consolidated accounts directive UK

The consolidated accounts directive is an EU directive concerning the presentation of consolidated accounts.

directiva sobre cuentas consolidadas

▲ *comply with the consolidated accounts directive* cumplir con la directiva sobre cuentas consolidadas ▲ *in accordance with the consolidated accounts directive* de acuerdo con la directiva sobre cuentas consolidadas

consolidated act

→ consolidation act

consolidated annual accounts UK

= consolidated accounts, consolidated financial statements US, IAS/IFRS, group accounts UK

Consolidated annual accounts combine the accounts of a parent and its subsidiaries and present the results, cash flows and financial position after elimination of intercompany balances as if the enterprises were a single entity.

cuentas anuales consolidadas

= estados financieros consolidados

▲ *be included in the enterprise's consolidated annual accounts by consolidation* estar incluido en los estados financieros consolidados de la empresa por consolidación ▲ *exemption from preparing consolidated annual accounts* exención de preparar estados financieros consolidados ▲ *general requirements for consolidated annual accounts* requisitos generales de los estados financieros consolidados ▲ *include in the consolidated annual accounts* incluir en las cuentas anuales consolidadas ▲ *obligation to prepare consolidated annual accounts* obligación de preparar cuentas anuales consolidadas ▲ *obligation to present consolidated annual accounts* obligación de presentar cuentas anuales consolidadas ▲ *omit to present consolidated annual accounts* eximir la presentación de estados financieros consolidados ▲ *prepare consolidated annual accounts* preparar estados financieros consolidados ▲ *present consolidated annual accounts* presentar estados financieros consolidados ▲ *publish the consolidated annual accounts* publicar los estados financieros consolidados ▲ *receive a demand for the presentation of consolidated annual accounts* recibir una petición de presentación de los estados financieros consolidados ▲ *submit the consolidated annual accounts* presentar los estados financieros consolidados ▲ *the balance sheet of the consolidated annual accounts* el balance de los estados financieros consolidados ▲ *the cash flow statement of the consolidated annual accounts* el estado de flujo de efectivo de los estados financieros consolidados ▲ *the consolidated annual accounts of the foreign parent* las cuentas anuales consolidadas de la matriz extranjera ▲ *the contents of the consolidated annual accounts* los contenidos de los estados financieros consolidados ▲ *the information about the group disclosed in the consolidated annual accounts* la información sobre el grupo divulgada en las cuentas anuales consolidadas ▲ *the profit and loss account of the consolidated annual accounts* la cuenta de resultados de los estados financieros consolidados

consolidated annual report

= group annual report

The consolidated annual report is a document including the financial statements, the management's review, the statement by the executive and supervisory boards on the annual report, the auditors' report and any supplementary statements of a group.

informe anual consolidado

▲ *prepare a consolidated annual report* preparar un informe anual consolidado ▲ *present a consolidated annual report* presentar un informe anual consolidado ▲ *publish a consolidated annual report* publicar un informe anual consolidado

consolidated balance sheet

= group balance sheet

The consolidated balance sheet combines the balance sheets of a parent and its subsidiaries and presents them, after elimination of intercompany balances, as if the enterprises were a single entity.

balance consolidado

▲ *foreign currency in the consolidated balance sheet* moneda extranjera en el balance consolidado ▲ *included in the consolidated balance sheet* incluir en el balance consolidado ▲ *prepare a consolidated balance sheet* preparar un balance consolidado ▲ *present a consolidated balance sheet* presentar un balance consolidado ▲ *recognise assets and liabilities in the consolidated balance sheet* reconocer activos y pasivos en el balance consolidado ▲ *the completed consolidated balance sheet* el balance consolidado normal

consolidated cash flow

The consolidated cash flow is the combined cash flow of a group of enterprises under common control as presented in the consolidated cash flow statement.

flujo de efectivo consolidado

= cash flow consolidado, flujo de caja consolidado

▲ *a summary of the consolidated cash flows* un resumen de los flujos de efectivo consolidados ▲ *disclosure of consolidated cash flows* divulgación de flujos de efectivo consolidados

consolidated cash flow statement

IAS/IFRS, UK

= consolidated statement of cash flows US

The consolidated cash flow statement combines the cash flow statements of a parent and its subsidiaries and presents the cash flows after elimination of intercompany balances as if the enterprises were a single entity.

estado de flujo de efectivo consolidado

= estado de cash flow consolidado, estado de flujo de caja consolidado

▲ *prepare a consolidated cash flow statement* preparar un estado de flujo de caja consolidado ▲ *presented in the consolidated cash flow statement* presentado en el estado de flujo de caja consolidado

consolidated company

A consolidated company is a parent and its subsidiaries.

empresa consolidada

▲ *a German consolidated company* una empresa consolidada alemana

⇛ group enterprise

consolidated enterprise

= consolidated undertaking

A consolidated enterprise is a parent and its subsidiaries.

empresa consolidada

▲ *a Danish consolidated enterprise* una empresa consolidada danesa ▲ *as if the consolidated enterprises together were one single enterprise* como si las empresas consolidadas fueran una sola empresa ▲ *debt owed to another consolidated enterprise* importe adeudado a otra empresa consolidada ▲ *exclusion of a consolidated enterprise* exclusión de una empresa consolidada ▲ *interest income from another consolidated enterprise* ingresos financieros de otra empresa consolidada ▲ *sell goods to another consolidated enterprise* vender mercancías a otra empresa consolidada ▲ *the consolidated enterprises' share of the subsidiary's contributed capital and voting rights* la proporción de empresas consolidadas en el capital y derechos de voto aportados por la filial ▲ *the share of the equity which is held by the consolidated enterprises overall* el patrimonio común que tienen el total de las empresas consolidadas ▲ *the sum of all the consolidated enterprises' balance sheet totals* la suma de los totales de todos los balances de las empresas consolidadas ▲ *transactions between consolidated enterprises* transacciones entre empresas consolidadas

⇛ group enterprise

consolidated equity

= group equity

The consolidated equity is the total equity of a group presented in the group balance sheet combining the equity of the parent company and ownership interests in subsidiaries.

patrimonio consolidado

▲ *determination of consolidated equity* determinación del patrimonio consolidado ▲ *minority interests' share of the consolidated equity* la proporción de patrimonio consolidado de las participaciones minoritarias ▲ *specification of the consolidated equity* especificación del patrimonio consolidado

consolidated financial statements

US, IAS/IFRS

= consolidated annual accounts, consolidated statements US

Consolidated financial statements combine the financial statements of a parent and its subsidiaries and present the results, cash flows and financial position after elimination of intercompany balances as if the enterprises were a single entity.

estados financieros consolidados

= cuentas anuales consolidadas

▲ *be included in the enterprise's consolidated financial statements by consolidation* estar incluido en los estados financieros consolidados de la empresa por consolidación ▲ *exemption from preparing consolidated financial statements* exención de preparar estados financieros consolidados ▲ *general requirements for consolidated financial statements* requisitos generales de los estados financieros consolidados ▲ *include in the consolidated financial statements* incluir en las cuentas anuales consolidadas ▲ *omit to present consolidated financial statements* eximir la presentación de estados financieros consolidados ▲ *prepare consolidated financial statements* preparar estados financieros consolidados ▲ *present consolidated financial statements* presentar estados financieros consolidados ▲ *publish the consolidated financial statements* publicar los estados financieros consolidados ▲ *receive a demand for the presentation of consolidated financial statements* recibir una petición de presentación de los estados financieros consolidados ▲ *submit the consolidated financial statements* presentar los estados financieros consolidados ▲ *the balance sheet of the consolidated financial statements* el balance de los estados financieros consolidados ▲ *the cash flow statement of the consolidated financial statements* el estado de flujo de efectivo de los estados financieros consolidados ▲ *the contents of the consolidated financial statements* los contenidos de los estados financieros consolidados ▲ *the income statement of the consolidated financial statements* la cuenta de resultados de los estados financieros consolidados

⇛ parent-company financial statements

consolidated financial statements audit US, IAS/IFRS

A consolidated financial statements audit is the audit of consolidated financial statements, i.e. the financial statements of a group.

auditoría de los estados financieros consolidados

▲ *perform the annual consolidated financial statements audit* realizar la auditoría de los estados financieros consolidados anuales ▲ *results of our annual consolidated financial statements audit* resultados de la auditoría de nuestros estados financieros consolidados anuales

consolidated goodwill

= goodwill on consolidation, group goodwill

Consolidated goodwill arises where the price paid by an acquiring enterprise, e.g. the parent, for an acquisition of another enterprise, e.g. a subsidiary, exceeds the fair value of the subsidiary's identifiable net assets.

fondo de comercio consolidado

▲ *amortisation of consolidated goodwill* amortización del fondo de comercio consolidado ▲ *capitalise consolidated goodwill* capitalizar el fondo de comercio consolidado ▲ *determination of consolidated goodwill* determinación del fondo de comercio consolidado ▲ *offset consolidated goodwill and negative goodwill* compensar el fondo de comercio consolidado y el fondo de comercio negativo ▲ *realisation of consolidated goodwill at carrying amount* cálculo del fondo de comercio consolidado al valor contable ▲ *tax related to consolidated goodwill* impuesto relativo al fondo de comercio consolidado ▲ *write off consolidated goodwill directly against equity* amortizar el fondo de comercio consolidado imputándolo directamente en el patrimonio

consolidated income statement US, IAS/IFRS

= consolidated profit and loss account UK, consolidated statement of income US

A consolidated income statement combines the income statements of a parent and its subsidiaries and presents them, after elimination of intercompany balances, as if the enterprises were a single entity.

cuenta de resultados consolidada

= cuenta de pérdidas y ganancias consolidada

▲ *be included in the consolidated income statement* estar incluido en la cuenta de pérdidas y ganancias consolidada ▲ *explanatory notes to the consolidated income statement* notas aclaratorias a la cuenta de pérdidas y ganancias consolidada ▲ *present a consolidated income statement* presentar una cuenta de pérdidas y ganancias consolidada ▲ *recognise in the consoli-*

dated income statement reconocer en la cuenta de resultados consolidada ▲ *show separately in the consolidated income statement* mostrar por separado en la cuenta de pérdidas y ganancias consolidada

consolidated loss

= consolidated net loss US

A consolidated loss is the combined net loss of a group of enterprises under common control as presented in the consolidated profit and loss account after elimination of intra-group balances.

pérdida consolidada

▲ *consolidated loss before taxes* pérdida consolidada antes de impuestos ▲ *the consolidated loss in Q1 2006* la pérdida consolidada en el primer trimestre de 2006

consolidated negative goodwill

= negative goodwill on consolidation

Consolidated negative goodwill arises where the price paid by an acquiring enterprise, e.g. the parent, for an acquisition of another enterprise, e.g. a subsidiary, is less than the fair value of the subsidiary's identifiable net assets.

fondo de comercio negativo consolidado

▲ *adjustment of consolidated negative goodwill* ajuste del fondo de comercio negativo consolidado ▲ *recognised consolidated negative goodwill* el fondo de comercio negativo consolidado reconocido

consolidated net income US

The consolidated net income is the bottom line of the income statement of a group showing the total results of the parent and the subsidiaries consolidated in the group after elimination of intra-group balances.

ingreso neto consolidado

▲ *consolidated net income before tax* ingreso neto consolidado antes de impuestos ▲ *consolidated net income under UK GAAP* ingreso neto consolidado según los principios contables generalmente aceptados en el Reino Unido ▲ *transactions that will affect consolidated net income* transacciones que afectarán al ingreso neto consolidado

consolidated net loss US

= consolidated loss

A consolidated net loss is the combined net loss of a group of enterprises under common control as presented in the consolidated profit and loss account after elimination of intra-group balances.

pérdida neta consolidada

▲ *consolidated net loss before taxes* pérdida neta consolidada antes de impuestos ▲ *the consolidated net loss in Q1 2006* la pérdida neta consolidada en el primer trimestre de 2006

consolidated profit UK

A consolidated profit is the combined profit for an accounting period of a group of enterprises under common control as presented in the consolidated profit and loss account after elimination of intra-group balances.

beneficio consolidado

▲ *consolidated profit after taxes* beneficio consolidado después de impuestos ▲ *consolidated profit before tax* beneficio consolidado antes de impuesto ▲ *the consolidated profit for the financial year* el beneficio consolidado del ejercicio

consolidated profit and loss account UK

= consolidated income statement US, IAS/IFRS

The consolidated profit and loss account combines the profit and loss accounts of a parent and its subsidiaries and presents them, after elimination of intercompany balances, as if the enterprises were a single entity.

cuenta de pérdidas y ganancias consolidada

= cuenta de resultados consolidada

▲ *be included in the consolidated profit and loss account* estar incluido en la cuenta de pérdidas y ganancias consolidada ▲ *explanatory notes to the consolidated profit and loss account* notas aclaratorias a la cuenta de pérdidas y ganancias consolidada ▲ *present a consolidated profit and loss account* presentar una cuenta de pérdidas y ganancias consolidada ▲ *show separately in the consolidated profit and loss account* mostrar por separado en la cuenta de pérdidas y ganancias consolidada

consolidated results

= group earnings

The consolidated results constitute the total profit or loss of a group presented in the group profit and loss account as a combination of the profits and losses of the individual companies in the group after elimination of intra-group balances.

resultados consolidados

▲ *have a substantial effect on the consolidated results* tener un efecto considerable en los resultados consolidados ▲ *reflected in the consolidated results* reflejado en los resultados consolidados ▲ *the quarterly consolidated results* los resultados consolidados trimestralmente

consolidated revenue IAS/IFRS, US

= consolidated sales US, consolidated turnover UK

Consolidated revenue is the total revenue of a parent and its subsidiaries in a group after eliminating intra-group balances.

facturación consolidada

= ingresos consolidados, ventas consolidadas

▲ *analysis of consolidated revenue by product category* análisis de la facturación consolidada por tipos de productos

consolidated sales US

= consolidated revenue, consolidated turnover UK, group sales

Consolidated sales constitute the total sales of a parent and its subsidiaries in a group after eliminating intra-group balances.

facturación consolidada

= ingresos consolidados, ventas consolidadas, ventas del grupo

▲ *analysis of consolidated sales by product category* análisis de la facturación consolidada por tipos de productos

consolidated statement of cash flows US

= consolidated cash flow statement UK, IAS/IFRS

The consolidated statement of cash flows combines the cash flow statements of a parent and its subsidiaries and presents the cash flows after elimination of intercompany balances as if the enterprises were a single entity.

estado de flujo de efectivo consolidado

= estado de cash flow consolidado, estado de flujo de caja consolidado

▲ *condensed consolidated statement of cash flows* estado de flujo de efectivo consolidado abreviado ▲ *unaudited consolidated statement of cash flows* estado de flujo de efectivo consolidado no auditado

consolidated statement of income

→ consolidated income statement

consolidated statements US

→ consolidated financial statements

consolidated subsidiary

≠ non-consolidated subsidiary

A consolidated subsidiary is an enterprise that is under control of a parent and combined with other enterprises to make up a consolidated group as if they were a single entity.

filial consolidada

≠ filial no consolidada

▲ *an investment in a consolidated subsidiary* una inversión en una filial consolidada ▲ *losses applicable to the minority in a consolidated subsidiary* pérdidas aplicables a los minoritarios en una filial consolidada ▲ *minority interests in the net assets of consolidated subsidiaries* participación minoritaria en los activos netos de filiales consolidadas ▲ *minority interests in the profit or loss of consolidated subsidiaries* participación minoritaria en los resultados de filiales consolidadas

consolidated turnover UK

= group revenue, group turnover

Consolidated turnover constitutes the total turnover of a parent and its subsidiaries in a group after eliminating intra-group balances.

facturación consolidada

= facturación del grupo, ingresos consolidados, ventas consolidadas, ventas del grupo

▲ *3% growth in consolidated turnover* 3% de crecimiento de la facturación consolidada ▲ *analysis of consolidated turnover by product category* análisis de la facturación consolidada por tipos de productos ▲ *pre-*

tax consolidated turnover facturación consolidada antes de impuestos

consolidation

1 Consolidation is the presentation of a parent company and its subsidiaries as one entity. The financial statements of the group enterprises are combined in consolidated financial statements where intra-group balances are eliminated.

consolidación

▲ *basis of consolidation* base de consolidación ▲ *be included in the consolidated financial statements by full consolidation* estar incluido en los estados financieros consolidados por consolidación completa ▲ *be included in the consolidation* estar incluido en la consolidación ▲ *consolidation of shares* consolidación de acciones ▲ *consolidation principles* principios de consolidación ▲ *eliminated as part of the consolidation process* eliminado como parte del proceso de consolidación ▲ *exclusion from consolidation* exclusión de la consolidación ▲ *fall within the scope of consolidation* incluir dentro del ámbito de la consolidación ▲ *for consolidation purposes* a efectos de consolidación ▲ *full consolidation* consolidación completa ▲ *negative goodwill arisen on consolidation* fondo de comercio negativo surgido cuando la consolidación ▲ *procedures for the consolidation of investments in subsidiaries* procedimientos para la consolidación de las inversiones en las filiales ▲ *proportionate consolidation* consolidación proporcionada

2 = debt consolidation

Consolidation of debt is a strategy to improve debt management which implies the restructuring and refinancing of a loan portfolio consisting of several small loans by repayment of the loans with the proceeds from a new large loan provided by one lender. This may involve lower amounts for debt servicing and a longer repayment period.

consolidación

▲ *consolidation of debt* consolidación de deuda

consolidation accounting

Consolidation accounting is the preparation of financial statements for a group as one entity, combining the statements of the parent company and its subsidiaries after elimination of intercompany balances and transactions.

contabilidad de consolidación

▲ *change the consolidation accounting rules* cambiar las normas de contabilidad de consolidación ▲ *consolidation accounting in a multinational company* contabilidad de consolidación en una multinacional ▲ *tax consolidation accounting* contabilidad fiscal de consolidación

consolidation act

= consolidated act, consolidating act

A consolidation act is a statute that repeals and re-enacts the provisions of existing statutes governing a particular subjet in order to show their combined effect and make the presentation of the law simpler.

norma de consolidación

= texto refundido

▲ *cf. Consolidation Act no. 725 of 25 July 2000* cf. la Norma de Consolidación número 725 de 25 de julio de 2000

constant currency

Constant currency is a currency that has the same value as one or more indexed currencies and therefore is seen as a unit of general purchasing power. For reporting financial performance relating to foreign operations, enterprises may show figures in a constant currency to exclude foreign exchange translation adjustments.

moneda constante

▲ *apply a constant currency in the calculation* aplicar una moneda constante en el cálculo ▲ *approximately 3% at constant currency* aproximadamente 3% a moneda constante ▲ *flat at constant currency* fijo a moneda constante

constitute

To constitute means to amount to or to be equal to.

equivaler

= equivaler a

▲ *constitute a change in accounting policy* equivaler a un cambio en la política contable ▲ *constitute a financing transac-*

tion equivaler a una transacción financiera ▲ *constitute a partial disposal* equivaler a una enajenación parcial ▲ *constitute a return of the investment* equivaler a un beneficio de la inversión ▲ *constitute a separate item of property, plant and equipment* equivaler a una partida independiente de edificios, instalaciones y equipos ▲ *constitute less than 75% of the total consolidated or enterprise revenue* equivaler a menos del 75% del total consolidado o de los ingresos empresariales ▲ *exclude movements between items that constitute cash or cash equivalents* excluir movimientos entre partidas que equivalen a efectivo o equivalentes

constraint

A constraint is a limitation or restriction, often imposed by regulation.

condicionante

= limitación, restricción

▲ *an existing legal constraint* un condicionante legal existente ▲ *be subject to a cost-benefit constraint* estar supeditado a un condicionante coste-beneficio

construction[1] *noun* <no indefinite article, the, no plural>

Construction refers to the act of setting up or building tangible fixed assets, such as plants or office buildings.

construcción

▲ *a building under construction* un edificio en construcción ▲ *assets in the course of construction* activos en el transcurso de la construcción ▲ *at the time of construction* al tiempo de la construcción ▲ *borrowing costs that are directly attributable to the construction of a qualifying asset* costes del empréstito que son directamente atribuibles a la construcción de un activo calificado ▲ *commence a construction project* comenzar un proyecto de construcción ▲ *construction in progress* obra en curso ▲ *construction of an asset* construcción de un activo ▲ *construction of immovable property* construcción de bienes inmuebles ▲ *construction work* trabajo de construcción ▲ *the design, construction and operation of a pilot plant* el diseño, construcción y operación de una planta piloto ▲ *the physical construction of the asset* la construcción física del activo ▲ *when the construction of a qualifying asset is completed in parts* cuando la construcción de un activo en curso se ha completado parcialmente ▲ *while construction continues* mientras la construcción continúe

construction[2] *noun* <a, the, -s>

A construction is a building, bridge, factory, plant or other structure.

construcción

= obra

▲ *a tall construction* una construcción elevada

construction contract

A construction contract is a legal document in which the particulars regarding the construction, repair, renovation or restoration of an asset is specified.

contrato de construcción

= contrato por obra

▲ *advances received on construction contracts* anticipos recibidos de los contratos de construcción ▲ *amounts due for construction contracts* cantidades debidas por contratos de construcción ▲ *an expected loss on the construction contract* una pérdida estimada en el contrato de construcción ▲ *assets arising from construction contracts* activos procedentes de contratos de construcción ▲ *award of a construction contract* concesión de un contrato de construcción ▲ *combine and segment construction contracts* combinar y segmentar los contratos de construcción ▲ *construction contract work in progress* contrato por obra en curso ▲ *directly related to construction contracts* directamente relacionado con contratos de construcción ▲ *long-term construction contracts* contratos de construcción a largo plazo ▲ *the costs of a construction contract* los costes de un contrato de cosntrucción ▲ *treat as a separate construction contract* tratar como un contrato de construcción independiente ▲ *treat as a single construction contract* tratar como un contrato de construcción único ▲ *when the outcome of a construction contract can be estimated reliably* cuando el resultado de un contrato de construcción puede estimarse de forma fidedigna ▲ *work in progress arising under construction contracts* obra en curso procedente de los contratos de construcción

constructive obligation

A constructive obligation is an obligation that arises as a result of an enterprise creating a valid expectation on the part of other parties that it will fulfil certain responsibilities as indicated by e.g. the enterprise's pattern of best practice and published policies.

compromiso tácito

= obligación tácita

▲ *a present constructive obligation* un compromiso tácito actual ▲ *assume a constructive obligation* asumir una obligación tácita ▲ *create a constructive obligation* crear un compromiso tácito ▲ *give rise to a constructive obligation* dar lugar a un compromiso tácito ▲ *have a constructive obligation* tener un compromiso tácito ▲ *measurement of constructive obligations* valoración de obligaciones tácitas ▲ *settle a constructive obligation* pagar un compromiso tácito ▲ *the amount of the constructive obligations* la cantidad de las obligaciones tácitas

consultancy fee

= consulting fee

A consultancy fee is the payment a consultant, such as an auditor, receives for his services.

honorario por asesoría

= honorario por consultoría

▲ *charge a consultancy fee* abonar un honorario por asesoría

consumable

1 = consumable material

≠ direct material

Consumables are goods that are bought by companies and used in the production process but not directly associated with the end-product. Examples of consumables are lubricating oil and packaging.

insumo

= material consumible, material fungible

▲ *changes in inventories of finished goods and consumables* cambios en inventarios de productos terminados e insumos ▲ *cost of consumables* coste de insumos ▲ *raw materials and consumables* materias primas e insumos ▲ *raw materials and consumables used* materias primas e insumos usados ▲ *the cost of consumables* el coste de insumos

2 Consumables are goods which are bought by companies and used up in administrative work rather than in production.

insumo

= consumible, fungible

▲ *buy consumables* comprar insumos ▲ *the cost of consumables* el coste de los insumos

Consumer Price Index US

= CPI US, Retail Price Index UK, RPI UK

The Consumer Price Index, CPI, is an index showing the rise and fall in prices of consumer goods and services sold in the retail market over a period of time.

Índice de Precios al Consumo

= IPC

▲ *a change in the Consumer Price Index* un cambio en el Índice de Precios al Consumo

consumption of resources

Consumption of resources refers to an enterprise's use of items, such as labour, raw materials and facilities, which are necessary to produce its goods or provide its services.

consumo de recursos

▲ *data on the consumption of resources* datos sobre el consumo de recursos ▲ *estimated consumption of resources* consumo de recursos estimado

contingency

A contingency is an item constituting a contingent asset, liability, gain or loss. Contingencies refer to events that may or may not occur in future and are, because of their uncertainty, off-balance sheet items disclosed in the notes.

contingencia

▲ *a loss recognised on the outcome of a contingency* una pérdida reconocida en el supuesto de una contingencia ▲ *reserve for contingencies* reserva para contingencias

contingent

Contingent means dependent on something.

contingente

= condicionado, eventual, supeditado

▲ *be contingent on* estar supeditado a ▲ *contingent adjustment* ajuste eventual ▲ *contingent amounts* cantidades contingentes ▲ *contingent assets* activos contingentes ▲ *contingent consideration* contrapartida supeditada ▲ *contingent gain* ganancia contingente ▲ *contingent liabilities* pasivos contingentes ▲ *contingent loss* pérdida contingente ▲ *contingent on one or more future events* supeditado a uno o más acontecimientos futuros ▲ *contingent rent payments* pagos de alquiler contingentes ▲ *contingent rents* alquileres contingentes ▲ *contingent reserve* reserva contingente ▲ *contingent settlement provision* provisión por pago contingente ▲ *contingent share agreement* acuerdo condicionado de emisión de acciones ▲ *contingent stock agreement* acuerdo condicionado de emisión de acciones ▲ *contingent workers* trabajadores eventuales

contingent asset

A contingent asset is a possible asset that exists at the balance sheet date as a result of past events and that may result in future economic benefits, but where the existence of the assets can only be confirmed by one or more uncertain future events not entirely within the control of the enterprise.

activo contingente

▲ *a group of contingent assets* un grupo de activos contingentes ▲ *assess contingent assets continually* valorar activos contingentes continuamente ▲ *changes in contingent assets since the last balance sheet date* cambios en los activos contingentes desde la última fecha de balance ▲ *disclose contingent assets* divulgar activos contingentes ▲ *measure contingent assets continuously* medir activos contingentes continuamente ▲ *recognition of a contingent asset* reconocimiento de un activo contingente ▲ *tax-related contingent assets* activos contingentes relativos a impuestos ▲ *the nature of contingent assets* la naturaleza de activos contingentes ▲ *the value of the enterprise's contingent assets* el valor de los activos contingentes de la empresa

contingent consideration

Contingent consideration is a payment that is held in escrow during a contingency period and/or depends on the occurrence of certain future events or factors such as the performance of a company acquired under a contingent contract.

contrapartida eventual

▲ *contingent consideration payable* contrapartida eventual a pagar ▲ *contingent consideration receivable* contrapartida eventual a percibir ▲ *contracts for contingent consideration* contratos para contrapartida eventual

contingent item

A contingent item is an item that is dependent on a potential future event that may or may not occur. Contingent items are not recognised in the financial statements, but disclosed in the notes.

partida contingente

▲ *as recognised in contingent items* como se reconoce en las partidas contingentes ▲ *relevant contingent items* partidas contingentes relevantes

⇛ contingent asset, contingent liability

contingent liability

A contingent liability is 1) a possible obligation that exists at the balance sheet date as a result of past events and that may result in the outflow of future economic benefits, but where the existence of the obligation can only be confirmed by one or more uncertain future events not entirely within the control of the enterprise or 2) a possible obligation that exists at the balance sheet date as a result of past events, but where it is not probable that an outflow of resources embodying economic benefits will be required to settle the obligation, or 3) an obligation, the amount of which cannot be measured with sufficient reliability.

pasivo contingente

▲ *a contingent liability that existed at the balance sheet date* un pasivo contingente existente a fecha del balance ▲ *changes in contingent liabilities since the last balance sheet date* cambios en los pasivos contingentes desde la fecha del último balance ▲ *disclose contingent liabilities* divulgar los pasivos contingentes ▲ *enter into significant contingent liabilities* incurrir en pasivos contingentes significativos ▲ *measure a contingent liability* cuantificar un pasivo contingente ▲ *recognise a contingent liability* reconocer un pasivo contingente ▲ *short-term self-liquidating trade-related contingent liabilities* pasivos contingentes comerciables con capacidad de autoliquidación a corto plazo ▲ *tax-related contingent liabilities* pasivos contingentes relativos a impuestos ▲ *the amount of contingent liabilities arising from off balance sheet items* la cantidad de pasivos contingentes resultante de las partidas fuera de balance ▲ *the nature of the contingent liability* la naturaleza del pasivo contingente ▲ *the relationship between provisions and contingent liabilities* la relación entre las provisiones y los pasivos contingentes ▲ *transaction-related contingent liabilities* pasivos contingentes relativos a transacciones

contingent obligation US

→ contingent liability

contingent rent

Contingent rent is that part of the lease payment that is not fixed in amount but is based on a factor other than just the passage of time (e.g. percentage of sales, amount of usage, price indices, market rates of interest).

cuota contingente por arrendamiento

▲ *contingent rent based on related sales* cuota contingente por arrendamiento basada en ventas relacionadas ▲ *contingent rent payments* pagos de cuota contingente por arrendamiento ▲ *contingent rents based on variable interest rates* cuotas contingentes por arrendamiento basadas en tipos de interés variable ▲ *contingent rents recognised in income by lessors* cuotas contingentes por arrendamiento especificadas en la cuenta de resultados por prestamistas ▲ *contingent rents recognised in the income statement* cuotas contingentes por arrendamiento especificadas en la cuenta de resultados ▲ *disclosure of contingent rents* divulgación de cuotas contingentes por arrendamiento ▲ *the basis on which contingent rent payments are determined* la base sobre la que se determinan los pagos de la cuota contingente por arrendamiento ▲ *total contingent rents* total cuotas contingentes por arrendamiento

contingent rental

→ contingent rent

continual budgeting

= continuous budgeting, perpetual budgeting,

Continual budgeting is a budgeting process which is followed-up on a current basis, so that the budget is updated every month or quarter by adding another monthly or quarterly period to the end of the budget ensuring that the budget will always be updated for a minimum of 12 months.

presupuestación continua

▲ *the purpose of continual budgeting* la finalidad de la presupuestación continua

⇛ rolling budget

continued

Continued is used about something which is done or takes place at a regular basis or for a long period of time.

continuado

= contínuo

▲ *a continued commitment* un compromiso continuado ▲ *allow the continued use of the asset* permitir el uso continuado del activo ▲ *conditional on continued employment* condicionado a empleo continuado ▲ *redevelop for continued future use as investment property* volver a desarrollar para uso futuro continuado como propiedad de inversión

continuing

= ongoing

Continuing means having existed or been in progress for some time and continuing to do so.

continuo

= continuado

▲ *adjustment on a continuing basis* ajuste de forma continua ▲ *be of continuing significance* ser de relevancia continua ▲ *charge to income on a conti-*

nuing basis cargar en ingresos de forma continua ▲ *continuing activities* actividades continuas ▲ *continuing improvements* mejoras continuas ▲ *continuing improvements of efficiency* mejoras continuas de eficiencia ▲ *continuing investments* inversiones continuas ▲ *continuing involvement* implicación continua ▲ *continuing losses of an investee* pérdidas continuas de una compañía en la que se invierte ▲ *continuing managerial involvement* implicación gerencial continua ▲ *continuing ordinary operations* operaciones ordinarias continuas ▲ *continuing use* uso continuo ▲ *continuing value adjustment* ajuste de valor continuo ▲ *on a continuing basis* de forma continua ▲ *part of a continuing business* parte de una empresa continua ▲ *recognition of income on a continuing basis* identificación de ingresos de forma continua ▲ *recognition on a continuing basis* identificación de forma continua ▲ *retraining or relocating continuing staff* volver a formar o recolocar al personal fijo ▲ *segregate continuing and discontinuing assets* segregar activos continuos e interrumpidos ▲ *the continuing enterprise* la empresa en marcha

continuing auditor

A continuing auditor is the independent, external auditor who performed the audit of the financial statements for the previous year(s) and carries on performing auditing services in the following period(s).

auditor continuo

▲ *assure continuing auditor independence* asegurar la independencia del auditor continuo

⇛ auditor

continuing operation

≠ discontinued operation, discontinuing operation

Continuing operations are operations of an enterprise that are not expected terminated, disposed of or sold in the foreseeable future contrary to discontinued operations.

operación continua

▲ *earnings per share for continuing operations* ganancias por acción por operaciones continuas ▲ *gains or losses relating to continuing operations* resultados relativos a operaciones continuas ▲ *include in profit or loss from continuing operations* incluir en los resultados procedentes de operaciones continuas ▲ *loss per share from continuing operations* pérdida por acción procedente de operaciones continuas ▲ *net income from continuing operations* ingresos netos procedentes de operaciones continuas ▲ *segment result from continuing operations* segmentar los resultados procedentes de operaciones continuas

continuity

= going concern

Continuity is the accounting assumption that an enterprise will continue in operational existence for the foreseeable future. This means that the enterprise is not anticipated to be subject to any voluntary or compulsory winding-up.

continuidad

▲ *prepare financial statements on a continuity basis* preparar estados financieros sobre una base de continuidad

continuity convention US

= going concern convention UK

The continuity convention is one of the fundamental accounting concepts and the assumption that an enterprise will continue in operational existence, i.e. as a going concern, for the foreseeable future. This means that the enterprise is not anticipated to be subject to any voluntary or compulsory winding-up.

principio de empresa en funcionamiento

= principio de continuidad

▲ *under the continuity convention* según el principio de empresa en funcionamiento

⇛ going concern

continuous

Continuous is used about something that continues without interruptions.

continuo

▲ *a continuous improvement* una mejora continua ▲ *a continuous process* un proceso continuo ▲ *continuous billing* facturación continua ▲ *continuous budget* presupuesto continuo ▲ *continuous compounding* acumulación continua ▲ *continuous de-*

velopment of staff competence mejora continua de la competencia de la plantilla ▲ *continuous invoicing* facturación continua ▲ *continuous operation* operación continua ▲ *continuous personal consulting* asesoría personal continua ▲ *continuous production* producción continua ▲ *continuous updating of knowledge* continua actualización del conocimiento ▲ *in a continuous sequence* en una secuencia continua

continuous budget

= rolling budget

A continuous budget is a budget that is continuously updated, typically on a monthly or quarterly basis, i.e. compared with the bookkeeping records for the previous month or quarter for adjustment if and as required, e.g. because of changed competition, technology development, changes in raw material prices or foreign exchange rates etc. Another monthly or quarterly budget period is added on expiry of the previous period ensuring that an enterprise will always have an updated budget for a minimum of 12 months.

presupuesto continuo

▲ *prepare a continuous budget* preparar un presupuesto continuo ▲ *present a continuous budget* presentar un presupuesto continuo

⇛ master budget

continuous budgeting

= continual budgeting, perpetual budgeting

Continuous budgeting is a budgeting process which is followed-up on a current basis, so that the budget is updated every month or quarter by adding another monthly or quarterly period to the end of the budget ensuring that the budget will always be updated for a minimum of 12 months.

presupuestación continua

▲ *the purpose of continuous budgeting* la finalidad de presupuestación continua

contra account

A contra account is an account where entries representing amounts owed and owing between two enterprises are offset completely or partially.

cuenta de contrapartida

= cuenta compensatoria

▲ *the balance of the contra account* el saldo de la cuenta de contrapartida ▲ *transfer to the contra account* transferir a la cuenta de contrapartida

contra entry

= set-off

A contra entry is an offsetting entry in a ledger or an account whereby a previous entry is reversed and cancelled. Contra entries may also be debit entries offsetting credit entries in the double-entry bookkeeping system.

asiento de contrapartida

= asiento compensatorio, contraasiento

▲ *delete a contra entry* borrar un asiento de contrapartida ▲ *make a contra entry* anotar un asiento de contrapartida

contract

1 A contract is a legally enforceable agreement made orally or in writing between two or more parties.

contrato

▲ *a derivative contract* un contrato derivado ▲ *a group of contracts* una serie de contratos ▲ *an executory contract* un contrato para ser cumplido ▲ *beneficial contracts* contratos ventajosos ▲ *binding contract* contrato vinculante ▲ *breach of contract* incumplimiento de contrato ▲ *contract income* ingresos contractuales (o por contrato) ▲ *contract loss* pérdida contractual (o por contrato) ▲ *contracts for the rendering of services* contratos por prestación de servicios ▲ *contracts held for dealing or trading purposes* contratos a efectos de contratación o negociación ▲ *enter into a contract* firmar un contrato ▲ *financial contract* contrato financiero ▲ *fraudulent contract* contrato fraudulento ▲ *meet the obligations under the contract* cumplir las obligaciones según el contrato ▲ *offsetting contract* contrato de compensación ▲ *perform a contract* cumplir un contrato ▲ *renew a contract* renovar un contrato ▲ *terminate a contract* finalizar un contrato ▲ *termination of an existing contract* finalización de un contrato existente

2 → construction contract

contract amount

The total amount payable for goods or servives bought under a contract is called the contract amount.

importe del contrato

= importe contractual

▲ *contract amount determined at market price at 31 December 2005* importe del contrato fijado a precio de mercado a 31 de diciembre ▲ *the contract amount of futures contracts* el importe contractual de los contratos de futuros

contract cost

The costs that are attributable to a particular construction contract are called the contract costs.

coste de contrata

▲ *by reference to the contract costs incurred to date* por referencia a los costes de contrata generados hasta la fecha ▲ *contract costs associated with the construction contract* costes de contrata asociados con el contrato de construcción ▲ *contract costs incurred for work performed to date* costes de contrata generados por trabajo realizado hasta la fecha ▲ *contract costs incurred in the period* costes de contrata incurridos en el periodo ▲ *contract costs that relate to future activity on the contract* costes de contrata relativos a la actividad futura reflejada en el contrato ▲ *determination of contract costs* fijación de costes de contrata ▲ *identify the contract costs attributable to the contract* identificar los costes de contrata atribuibles al contrato ▲ *included as part of the contract costs* incluido como parte de los costes de contrata ▲ *recognise contract costs* reconocer costes de contrata ▲ *recover the contract costs incurred* recuperar los costes de contrata incurridos ▲ *recoverability of contract costs incurred* recuperabilidad de los costes de contrata incurridos ▲ *the actual contract costs incurred* los costes de contrata presentes generados ▲ *the contract costs to complete the contract* los costes de contrata para ejecutar el contrato ▲ *the estimated total contract costs* los costes de contrata totales estimados ▲ *total estimated contract costs* total costes de contrata estimados

contract period

= period of the contract

Contract period refers to the period of time during which the terms of a contract are in effect, e.g. an enterprise may have the right to use an asset during a specified period of time in pursuance of a contractual agreement.

periodo contractual

▲ *amortise or depreciate something over the contract period* amortizar o depreciar algo en el periodo contractual ▲ *the commencement of the contract period* el inicio del periodo contractual ▲ *the expiry of the contract period* el vencimiento del periodo contractual

contract revenue

Contract revenue is the total income generated from a construction or project contract for a particular accounting period.

ingreso contractual

= ingreso del contrato, ingreso por contrato

▲ *accumulated contract revenue* ingreso contractual acumulado ▲ *an adjustment of the amount of contract revenue* un ajuste de la cantidad de ingreso contractual ▲ *contract revenue associated with the construction contract* ingreso contractual asociado con el contrato de construcción ▲ *current estimates of contract revenue* estimaciones actuales de ingreso contractual ▲ *determine the contract revenue recognised* fijar el ingreso contractual reconocido ▲ *incentive payments included in contract revenue* pagos incentivados incluidos en ingreso contractual ▲ *recognition of contract revenue* reconocimiento de ingreso contractual ▲ *revise the estimates of contract revenue* revisar las estimaciones de ingreso contractual ▲ *total contract revenue* total ingreso contractual

contract term

= term of contract, term of the contract

The contract term is the period during which a contract is valid and legally binding.

periodo contractual

= duración del contrato, periodo del contrato

▲ *during the contract term* durante el periodo contractual ▲ *the beginning of the contract term* el inicio del periodo contractual ▲ *the end of the contract term* el fin del periodo contractual ▲ *the remaining contract term* el periodo contractual restante

contract work in process US

Contract work in process is an inventory item under current assets in the balance sheet representing work that has been started on a job or combination of interrelated jobs, but not completed, under a project or construction contract. Examples of such work are constructions of bridges, buildings and ships. The revenue and expenses by reference to the stage of completion of the contract at the balance sheet date must be disclosed.

contrato por obra en curso

= contrato por construcción

▲ *amounts due for contract work in process* cantidades adeudadas por contrato por obra en curso ▲ *determine the stage of completion of contract work in process* fijar la etapa de finalización de contrato por obra en curso ▲ *loss on contract work in process* pérdida en contrato por obra en curso ▲ *measurement of contract work in process* valoración de contrato por obra en curso ▲ *recognition of contract work in process* reconocimiento de contrato por obra en curso ▲ *value of contract work in process* valor de contrato por obra en curso

contract work in progress IAS/IFRS

Contract work in progress is an item under stocks and current assets in the balance sheet representing work that has been started on a job or combination of interrelated jobs, but not completed, under a project or construction contract. Examples of such work are constructions of bridges, buildings and ships. The revenue and expenses by reference to the stage of completion of the contract at the balance sheet date must be disclosed.

trabajo en curso de contrato de construcción

▲ *amounts due for contract work in progress* cantidades adeudadas por trabajo en curso de contrato de construcción ▲ *classified as contract work in progress* clasificado como trabajo en curso de contrato de construcción ▲ *construction contract work in progress* ejecución de trabajo en curso de contrato de construcción

contracting company

A contracting company or firm of contractors operates within the building and construction industry.

empresa de contratación

▲ *domestic contracting companies* empresas de contratación nacionales ▲ *quotations from different contracting companies* licitaciones procedentes de diferentes empresas de contratación

contractor

A contractor is a person or enterprise undertaking to carry out a specified task, usually a construction project, under the terms of a contract.

contratista

▲ *the annual reports of contractors* los informes anuales de los contratistas

contractual

Something that complies with the requirements, terms etc. specified in a contract are referred to as contractual.

contractual

▲ *a contractual agreement* un acuerdo contractual ▲ *a contractual rent increase* un incremento de alquiler contractual ▲ *a contractual right* un derecho contractual ▲ *contractual basis* base contractual ▲ *contractual commitment* acuerdo contractual ▲ *contractual dates of repayment* fechas de amortización contractuales ▲ *contractual maturity dates* fechas de vencimiento contractual ▲ *contractual obligations* obligaciones contractuales ▲ *contractual revaluation dates* fechas de revalorización contractual ▲ *contractual terms and conditions* términos y condiciones contractuales ▲ *under a contractual arrangement* según un acuerdo contractual

contractual amount

A contractual amount is an amount specified in a contract

that is receivable or payable under the terms of the contract.

cantidad contractual

▲ *the contractual amount of dividends that must be paid* la cantidad contractual de dividendos que se deben pagar

contribute

= invest

To contribute is to provide funds for and to invest in an enterprise etc.

aportar

= contribuir, invertir

▲ *contribute assets into a jointly controlled entity* aportar activos a una entidad controlada conjuntamente ▲ *contribute capital to a company* aportar capital a una empresa ▲ *contribute to* aportar a ▲ *contribute to multi-employer plans* aportar a planes multi-empresa ▲ *contribute to the medical costs covered by the plan* contribuir a los costes médicos cubiertos por el plan

contributed

A contributed amount is an amount that is invested in something, e.g. in a company in return for an ownership interest.

contribuido

= aportado, invertido

▲ *contributed assets* activos contribuidos ▲ *contributed capital* capital contribuido ▲ *contributed equity* patrimonio invertido ▲ *contributed liabilities* pasivos contribuidos ▲ *the fair values of non-monetary assets contributed* los valores razonables de los activos no monetarios contribuidos ▲ *the significant risks and rewards of ownership of the contributed non-monetary assets* los riesgos y recompensas importantes de la propiedad de los activos no monetarios contribuidos

contributed capital

= paid-in capital

Contributed capital is capital that the owners have contributed to the enterprise, and which is part of the enterprise's equity. In public limited companies and private limited companies, the contributed capital is the share capital.

capital contribuido

▲ *a reduction of the contributed capital* una reducción del capital contribuido ▲ *contributed capital in excess of par* capital contribuido por encima del valor nominal ▲ *the value of the contributed capital* el valor del capital contribuido

⇛ share capital

contributed equity IAS/IFRS

= equity capital UK, IAS/IFRS

Contributed equity is the capital paid in by investors in return for an ownership interest in an enterprise with the purpose of contributing to the activities of the enterprise through the exercise of control or significant influence, or with a view to gaining a long-term return on investment.

patrimonio aportado

= patrimonio contribuido

▲ *the carrying amount of contributed equity* el valor contable del patrimonio aportado

⇛ equity interest, investment, participating interest

contribution

1 A contribution is something provided such as money, assistance or time. Contributions may e.g. be amounts paid to insurance companies or given to charity.

aportación

= contribución

▲ *a reduction in future contributions* una reducción en las aportaciones futuras ▲ *consolidated contributions* aportaciones consolidadas

2 = investment

A contribution is an amount of money paid or an asset assigned to an enterprise against a future share of profit.

aportación

▲ *a cash contribution* una aportación en efectivo ▲ *a contribution transaction lacking commercial substance* una aportación que no es de naturaleza comercial ▲ *equity contributions in cash or in kind* aportaciones de patrimonio en efectivo o en especie

3 = contribution margin US, UK, contribution per unit UK, marginal income US, marginal revenue UK, US, total contribution UK, unit contribution margin US

Contribution is calculated by deducting variable costs from the sales value, arriving at the amount that contributes to cover fixed costs and generate profits.

The expression is used to mean either total contribution or unit contribution margin.
ingreso marginal
▲ *expected contribution* ingreso marginal previsto ▲ *reduce the contribution* reducir el ingreso marginal
⇛ contribution ratio

contribution approach
The contribution approach is a method of income statements that separates variable costs from fixed costs in order to emphasise the importance of cost behavior patterns for purposes of planning and control.
método contributivo
▲ *statement using a contribution approach* estado que utiliza un método contributivo

contribution income statement
= contribution-margin income statement US
A contribution income statement is an income statement dividing costs into variable and fixed costs. First, variable costs are deducted from sales resulting in contribution margin from which total fixed costs are then deducted. This way of presenting costs relating to sales is typically applied as part of management accounting and will rarely appear from the external income statement for competitive reasons.
estado de resultados del ingreso marginal
▲ *prepare a contribution income statement* preparar un estado de resultados del ingreso marginal
⇛ contribution, contribution margin

contribution margin UK, US
= contribution UK, US, contribution per unit UK, marginal income US, marginal revenue UK, total contribution UK, unit contribution margin US
The contribution margin is the excess amount resulting when variable costs are deducted from the sales value, e.g. the amount that contributes to cover fixed costs and generate profits. The expression is used to mean either total contribution or unit contribution margin.
ingreso marginal
▲ *adjust the contribution margin downwards* ajustar a la baja el ingreso marginal ▲ *contribution margin per unit* ingreso marginal por unidad ▲ *expected contribution margin* ingreso marginal previsto ▲ *increase the contribution margin* aumentar el ingreso marginal ▲ *reduce the contribution margin* reducir el ingreso marginal
⇛ contribution ratio

contribution margin ratio UK
→ contribution ratio

contribution per unit
→ unit contribution margin

contribution ratio
= contribution margin ratio, contribution-margin percentage
The contribution ratio is the contribution margin calculated as a ratio: the contribution margin as a percentage of sales, often calculated by unit or product.
ratio de contribución
= ratio de aportación
▲ *a falling contribution ratio* un ratio de contribución descendente ▲ *a rising contribution ratio* un ratio de contribución ascendente ▲ *lower the contribution ratio* bajar el ratio de contribución ▲ *raise the contribution ratio* aumentar el ratio de contribución
⇛ contribution margin, total contribution, unit contribution margin

contribution-margin percentage US
= contribution margin ratio, contribution ratio
The contribution-margin percentage is calculated as the total contribution margin (i.e. total sales less variable cost of sales) multiplied by 100 divided by total sales.
porcentaje del ingreso marginal
▲ *determine the contribution-margin percentage* fijar el porcentaje del ingreso marginal ▲ *the budgeted contribution margin percentage of sales* el porcentaje del ingreso marginal de ventas presupuestado
⇛ total contribution, unit contribution margin, variable cost percentage

contribution-margin ratio US
→ contribution ratio

control[1] *noun*
1 = dominant influence
≠ significant influence

To have control of an enterprise means to have dominant influence over it. The controlling enterprise consequently has the power to determine the financial and operating policies of the controlled enterprise so as to gain benefits from its activities.
NOTE Control may e.g. result when an enterprise holds more than 50 per cent of the voting shares of another enterprise; this enterprise is then referred to as a subsidiary.

control

▲ *because of the absence of control* debido a la falta de control ▲ *before control effectively passes to the acquirer* antes de que el control se transfiera efectivamente al adquirente ▲ *enterprises that are not under common control* empresas que no están bajo control común ▲ *establish joint control* establecer control conjunto ▲ *have control over the combining enterprises* tener control sobre las combinaciones de empresas ▲ *have joint control over a jointly controlled entity* tener control conjunto sobre una empresa controlada conjuntamente ▲ *interests which involve joint control* intereses que implican control conjunto ▲ *joint control* control conjunto ▲ *subject to control by the reporting enterprise* supeditado al control de la empresa informante ▲ *the date of obtaining control* la fecha de obtención del control ▲ *the date on which control of the acquiree is effectively transferred to the acquirer* la fecha en la que el control de lo adquirido se transfiere efectivamente al adquirente ▲ *the date on which the parent ceases to have control of the subsidiary* la fecha en la que la matriz deja de tener control sobre la filial ▲ *the period of control over the acquired business* el periodo de control sobre la empresa adquirida ▲ *transactions among enterprises under common control* transacciones entre empresas bajo control común ▲ *transitory control* control transitorio ▲ *where control exists* donde hay control

⇛ direct control, indirect control

2 Control (of an asset) means that the enterprise has the power to gain the future economic benefits that flow from the asset.

control

▲ *beyond the control of the enterprise* fuera del control de la empresa ▲ *control over a resource* control sobre un recurso ▲ *exercise control* ejercer el control ▲ *insufficient control* control insuficiente ▲ *joint control* control conjunto ▲ *obtain control* conseguir el control ▲ *obtain control over the net assets and operations of another enterprise* conseguir el control sobre los activos netos y las operaciones de otra empresa ▲ *the period of control over the asset* el periodo de control sobre el activo ▲ *wholly within the control of the enterprise* completamente bajo el control de la empresa

control[2] *verb*

To control means to have decisive power over somebody or something.

controlar

▲ *control the timing of the reversal of the temporary difference* controlar la programación de la reversión de la diferencia temporal ▲ *have the ability to control a party* tener la capacidad para controlar una parte ▲ *the enterprise whose shareholders now control the combined enterprise* la empresa cuyos accionistas controlan ahora la combinación de empresas

control procedure

Control procedures are activities and practices to check actions, products, services, accounting systems etc. with a view to detecting, correcting, minimising or preventing errors and irregularities, thereby securing reliability, accuracy and quality.

procedimiento de control

▲ *internal control procedures* procedimientos de control interno

control risk

Control risk is the type of audit risk that involves misstatements that have not been detected and corrected in the accounting and internal control systems.

riesgo de control

▲ *evaluation of control risk* evaluación del riesgo de control

▲ *the assessment of control risk* la valoración del riesgo de control
⇛ audit risk, detection risk, inherent risk

control system

A control system is a system of units functioning as a whole, usually constituted by people or electronic devices acting or performing in specified ways to secure that something meets demands or expectations when realised.

sistema de control

▲ *an internal control system* un sistema de control interno ▲ *effective internal control systems* sistemas de control interno efectivos ▲ *material weaknesses in the internal control system* debilidades materiales en el sistema de control interno ▲ *operation, review and disclosure of internal control systems* operación, revisión y divulgación de los sistemas de control interno ▲ *supervision by internal control systems* supervisión mediante sistemas de control interno

controllability

Controllability is the ability to influence something by means of actions, decisions or statements, i.e. it refers to the extent to which a person or enterprise can influence the outcome of something.

controlabilidad

▲ *the controllability principle* el principio de controlabilidad

controllable cost

≠ uncontrollable cost

Controllable costs refer to costs of which the level can be influenced by the actions and decisions of managers or other persons having responsibilities in the enterprise.

coste controlable

▲ *actual controllable costs* costes controlables reales ▲ *reduce controllable costs by 20%* reducir los costes controlables un 20% ▲ *total controllable costs* total costes controlables
⇛ cost, expense

controller

= chief accounting executive, comptroller UK

The controller is the top accounting officer of an enterprise and typically responsible for financial reporting, taxation, and internal auditing.

controller

▲ *controller letter* carta del controller ▲ *corporate controller* controller empresarial ▲ *group controller* controller del grupo ▲ *group financial controller* controller financiero del grupo
⇛ treasurer

controlling director

A controlling director is a member of an enterprise's board of directors that holds a 20% share ownership or more in the enterprise. For a director, such a holding constitutes a controlling interest.

director por participación de control

= director por participación dominante

▲ *the relatives of the controlling director* los familiares del director por participación de control
⇛ controlling interest

controlling financial interest US

= controlling interest

A controlling financial interest in a company is an interest that gives e.g. a shareholder control over the operating and financial policies of an enterprise. To have a controlling financial interest a shareholder will need to own or control more than half the voting shares (the majority). If the shareholder is a member of the board of directors, 20% ownership is a controlling financial interest.

participación de control

= participación dominante, participación mayoritaria

▲ *acquire the controlling financial interest in a company* adquirir la participación de control de una empresa ▲ *acquisition of a controlling financial interest* adquisición de una participación de control ▲ *be secured the controlling financial interest in a company* asegurarse la participación de control de una empresa ▲ *hold a controlling financial interest* tener una participación de control ▲ *secure the controlling financial interest in a company* asegurar la participación de control en una empresa ▲ *sell one's controlling financial interest* vender su participación de control
⇛ controlling director, majority interest

controlling interest
= controlling financial interest US, majority of shares, share majority
A controlling interest in a company is an interest that gives e.g. a shareholder control over the operating and financial policies of an enterprise. To have a controlling interest a shareholder will need to own or control more than half the voting shares (the majority). If the shareholder is a member of the board of directors, 20% ownership is a controlling interest.
participación mayoritaria
= participación de control, participación dominante
▲ *acquire the controlling interest in a company* adquirir la participación mayoritaria en una empresa ▲ *acquisition of a controlling interest* adquisición de una participación mayoritaria ▲ *be secured the controlling interest in a company* asegurarse la participación mayoritaria en una empresa ▲ *hold a controlling interest* tener una participación mayoritaria ▲ *secure the controlling interest in a company* asegurar la participación mayoritaria en una empresa ▲ *sell one's controlling interest* vender su participación mayoritaria
⇛ controlling director, majority interest

convergence
Convergence is the act of achieving some sort of common result, characteristics or quality.
convergencia
▲ *convergence criteria* criterios de convergencia ▲ *convergence requirements* requisitos de convergencia ▲ *increase convergence of accounting standards around the world* aumentar la convergencia de las normas contables en todo el mundo ▲ *sustained convergence* convergencia sostenida

conversion
1 = refinancing
Conversion is the exchange of an existing security, such as a bond, or debt into another security or into new debt with extended maturity or increased amount of debt.
conversión
= canje
▲ *conversion into equity interests* conversión a capital social ▲ *conversion of potential ordinary shares* conversión de acciones ordinarias potenciales ▲ *conversion of the dilutive potential ordinary shares* conversión de las acciones ordinarias potenciales reajustadas a la baja ▲ *conversion ratio* ratio de conversión ▲ *conversion rights* derechos de conversión ▲ *conversion risk* riesgo de conversión ▲ *date of conversion* fecha de conversión ▲ *equity conversion component* componente de canje de patrimonio ▲ *extinguishment on conversion* pérdida de valor por canje ▲ *the conversion of a debt instrument to ordinary shares* la conversión de un instrumento de deuda en acciones ordinarias ▲ *the conversion of debt to equity* la conversión de deuda en patrimonio ▲ *the exercise of conversion rights* el ejercicio de los derechos de conversión
2 = rebuilding
Conversion is the act or process of changing something that is already in existence.
conversión
= reconstrucción
▲ *conversion of a production site* conversión de un lugar de producción
⇛ refurbishment

conversion cost
→ cost of conversion

conversion date
= date of conversion
The conversion date is the date on which convertible bonds or other instruments are converted into shares.
fecha de conversión
= fecha de canje
▲ *the market price of the claim at the conversion date* el precio de mercado de la reclamación a la fecha de conversión

conversion of financial statements
A conversion of financial statements means a change of the preparation and presentation of the financial statements, e.g. to meet international or other generally accepted accounting principles than those applied so far, or a change of the accounting period to e.g. follow the calendar year. Conversions

may result from a changed group structure or a takeover.

conversión de los estados financieros

▲ *conversion of financial statements to IFRS accounting norms* conversión de los estados financieros a normas contables NIIF ▲ *gains from conversion of financial statements* beneficios procedentes de la conversión de los estados financieros

⇛ translation

conversion option

If a bond or convertible preference share contains a conversion option, the holder has the right to convert the bond or preference share into a specified number of ordinary shares at a specified conversion price within a specified period.

opción de conversión

▲ *exercise a conversion option* ejercer una opción de conversión ▲ *extinguishment of a conversion option* extinción de una opción de conversión

conversion premium

A conversion premium is an extra amount that has to be paid when buying ordinary shares via a convertible bond or convertible preference share instead of buying ordinary shares directly.

prima de conversión

▲ *pay a conversion premium* pagar una prima de conversión

conversion price

The conversion price is the nominal bond price used when converting a bond into a share.

precio de conversión

= precio de canje

▲ *initial conversion price* precio de conversión inicial ▲ *original conversion price* precio de conversión original ▲ *reduce the conversion price* reducir el precio de conversión ▲ *the agreed conversion price* el precio de conversión acordado ▲ *the conversion price of convertible bonds* el precio de conversión de los bonos convertibles

convert

To convert something means to change it into a different form or state.

convertir

▲ *convert a claim into share capital* convertir una deuda en capital social ▲ *convert convertible bonds into shares* convertir bonos convertibles en acciones ▲ *convert into cash and cash equivalents* convertir en efectivo y equivalentes de efectivo ▲ *convert one financial instrument into another* convertir un instrumento financiero en otro ▲ *convert one's claim into equity interests in the enterprise* convertir su deuda en capital social de la empresa ▲ *convert one's claim into shares* convertir su deuda en acciones ▲ *converted into the enterprise's ordinary shares at the holder's option* convertidas en acciones ordinarias de la empresa a petición del accionista ▲ *the right to convert into equity* el derecho a convertir en patrimonio

convertible asset

A convertible asset is an asset, such as a bond or a share, that can be changed into another type of security, i.e. into another legal form, on certain conditions. Convertible bonds may e.g. be changed into shares.

activo financiero convertible

▲ *easily convertible assets* activos financieros convertibles fácilmente ▲ *freely convertible assets* activos financieros convertibles libremente ▲ *readily convertible asset* activo financiero convertible de forma rápida

convertible bond

A convertible bond gives the owner the right to convert the bond into shares at one or more future points in time and at an agreed price.

bono convertible

▲ *5% convertible bond* bono convertible al 5% ▲ *face value of convertible bond* el valor nominal del bono convertible ▲ *issue convertible bonds* emitir bonos convertibles ▲ *proceeds from issue of convertible bonds* ingresos procedentes de la emisión de bonos convertibles ▲ *the consideration received for the convertible bond* la prestación recibida por el bono convertible ▲ *the embedded option in a convertible bond* la opción integrada en un bono convertible ▲ *the equity component of the convertible bond* el componente de patrimonio del bono convertible ▲ *the liability compo-*

nent of the convertible bond el componente de pasivo del bono convertible

convertible debenture UK

A convertible debenture is a bond that can be exchanged at the lender's option at some date in the future for another security, typically an ordinary share.

obligación convertible

▲ *an offering of convertible debentures* una oferta de obligaciones convertibles ▲ *issuance of convertible debentures* emisión de obligaciones convertibles ▲ *redeem the convertible debentures* amortizar las obligaciones convertibles ▲ *secured convertible debentures* obligaciones convertibles garantizadas ▲ *unsecured convertible debentures* obligaciones convertibles no garantizadas

⇛ debenture

convertible debt

Convertible debt is a debt owed by an enterprise that, at the request of the creditor, can be converted into shares in the enterprise within a specified period of time.

deuda convertible

▲ *conversion of convertible debt* conversión de deuda convertible ▲ *convert the convertible debt into ordinary shares* transformar la deuda convertible en acciones ordinarias ▲ *convertible debt instruments issued* instrumentos de deuda convertible emitidos ▲ *interest expense on convertible debt, net of tax* gasto por interés de deuda convertible, neto de impuesto ▲ *issue convertible debt instruments* emitir instrumentos de deuda convertible

convertible debt instrument

= convertible instrument of debt

Convertible debt instruments are bonds and debentures issued by a company and which the owner may convert into shares in the company within a specified period of time or at a specified date.

instrumento de deuda convertible

▲ *convertible and profit-sharing debt instruments* instrumentos de deuda convertible y con reparto de beneficios ▲ *shares resulting from the conversion of convertible debt instruments* acciones resultantes del canje de deuda convertible ▲ *the issuer of a convertible debt instrument* el emisor de un instrumento de deuda convertible

convertible loan

A convertible loan is a loan that can be exchanged at the lender's option at some date in the future for other securities, typically equity.

empréstito convertible

▲ *issue a convertible loan* emitir un empréstito convertible ▲ *raise a convertible loan* contraer un empréstito convertible

convertible loan note

A convertible loan note is a medium-term debt instrument issued by an enterprise that may be changed into a share at a future date on certain conditions.

obligación convertible

▲ *the issue of secured convertible loan notes* la emisión de obligaciones convertibles garantizadas ▲ *the nominal value of convertible loan notes* el valor nominal de las obligaciones convertibles ▲ *unsecured convertible loan notes* obligaciones convertibles no garantizadas

convertible loan stock UK

Convertible loan stock consists of bonds or debentures that can be converted into equity share capital at the option of the holder in the future at a definite price. For convertible government bonds the option is to convert into new stock rather than obtaining repayment.

obligación convertible

▲ *holders of convertible loan stock* titulares de obligaciones convertibles ▲ *issue secured convertible loan stock* emitir obligaciones convertibles garantizadas ▲ *the issue of unsecured convertible loan stock* la emisión de obligaciones convertibles no garantizadas

convey

To convey means to give, transfer or move something to another person or another place.

ceder

▲ *convey something to someone* ceder algo a alguien ▲ *convey the right to use the asset* ceder el derecho a usar el activo

COO US

= chief operating officer

COO is an abbreviation for chief operating officer who is among the highest-ranking officers in an enterprise and responsible for the day-to-day management of the enterprise's operations. The COO reports directly to the CEO.

Director General

▲ *appoint a new COO* nombrar un nuevo Director General ▲ *the former COO* el Director General anterior ▲ *the incoming COO* el Director General entrante ▲ *the retiring COO* el Director General saliente

cooperation

= co-operation, collaboration

Cooperation is the act of persons or groups working together towards a common goal or for a common purpose.

cooperación

= colaboración

▲ *cooperation in* cooperación en ▲ *cross-border cooperation* cooperación transfronteriza ▲ *in close cooperation with* en estrecha cooperación con ▲ *in cooperation with* en cooperación con ▲ *international cooperation* cooperación internacional

cooperative agreement

= co-operative agreement, cooperation agreement

A cooperative agreement is a contractual agreement between one or more parties to jointly undertake specified activities, e.g. commercial activities, or to cooperate in order to meet specified objectives.

acuerdo de cooperación

= acuerdo colaborativo, acuerdo de colaboración

▲ *a local cooperative agreement* un acuerdo de cooperación local ▲ *enter into a cooperative agreement* adherirse a un acuerdo de cooperación

cooperative partner

= cooperator

A cooperative partner is a person or enterprise with whom or which a cooperation agreement has been entered for the joint implementation, performance or development of a specific project, job or other assignment.

socio cooperativo

▲ *a foreign cooperative partner* un socio cooperativo extranjero ▲ *carry out a credit rating of cooperative partners* calificar con un índice de solvencia crediticia a los socios cooperativos

cooperative savings bank

= co-operative savings bank

A cooperative savings bank is a bank organised as a cooperative and owned by the members of the cooperative.

caja laboral

= caja de ahorros laboral

▲ *own a chain of 35 co-operative savings banks* poseer una cadena de 35 cajas de ahorro laborales

cooperative society

= co-operative society

A cooperative society is an enterprise or organisation operated in the common interest of and for the benefit of its members.

sociedad cooperativa

▲ *cooperative societies with limited liability* sociedades cooperativas con responsabilidad limitada

copyright

A copyright is the exclusive right to reproduce or authorise others to reproduce an intellectual creation, i.e. a musical, artistic, literary or dramatic work, and software.

derecho de autor

= copyright

▲ *amortise fully the costs of a copyright* amortizar por completo los costes de un derecho de autor ▲ *charges for the use of long-term assets of the enterprise, for example, patents, trademarks, copyrights and computer software* gastos por el uso de activos a largo plazo de la empresa, por ejemplo patentes, marcas registradas, derechos de autor y software ▲ *claim copyright* reclamar el derecho de autor ▲ *copyright infringement* violación de copyright ▲ *copyright notice* aviso de derecho de autor ▲ *copyrights, patents and other industrial property rights, service and operating rights* derechos de autor, patentes y otros derechos de propiedad intelectual, servicios y derechos de explotación ▲ *expenditure incurred in securing copyrights* gasto incurrido en el registro de los derechos de autor ▲ *holder of copyright* titular del copyright ▲ *no copyright subsisted in the drawings* no subsistía derecho de autor en los dibujos ▲ *protected by copyright* protegido por copyright ▲ *protected by legal rights such as copyrights* protegido por derechos legales, tales como los derechos de autor ▲ *the first owner of a copyright* el primer propietario de un derecho de autor ▲ *the subject-matter of the copyright* la materia del derecho de autor

core activity

A core activity is the principal activity of an enterprise, justifying the existence, goal and purpose of that enterprise.

actividad principal

▲ *a review of core activities* una revisión de las actividades principales ▲ *expand core activities* ampliar las actividades principales

core business

= core business area, principal activity

Core business refers to the activities of an enterprise that generate most of the sales or revenue, i.e. the enterprise's main products or services.

corazón del negocio

= actividad empresarial central, actividad empresarial principal

▲ *strengthen our core business* reforzar nuestro corazón del negocio

core business area

= core business, principal activity

A core business area refers to the main activity of an enterprise that generates most of the sales or revenue, i.e. the most central product or service.

corazón del negocio

= actividad empresarial central, actividad empresarial principal

▲ *develop new core business areas* desarrollar nuevas actividades comerciales centrales ▲ *future core business areas* corazón del negocio futuro

core capital

= tier 1 capital

Core capital or tier 1 capital is the capital of a bank corresponding to the equity of other enterprises, i.e. share capital, premium on share issues and reserves.

capital básico

= capital más reservas preferentes, core capital

▲ *a core capital injection of EUR 1 billion* una inyección de capital básico de mil millones de euros ▲ *core capital after statutory deductions* capital básico después de deducciones legales ▲ *decrease in the core capital* disminución en el capital básico ▲ *minimum core capital requirements* requisitos de capital básico mínimos ▲ *the hybrid core capital* el capital básico híbrido ▲ *the impact on the bank's consolidated core capital* el impacto sobre el capital básico consolidado del banco

core capital ratio

= tier 1 capital ratio

The core capital ratio is defined as core capital after statutory deductions as a percentage of total risk-weighted assets. The core capital after statutory deductions includes paid-up share or guarantee capital, as well as the premium on share issue and reserves, less the portfolio of treasury shares, intangible assets and the current loss for the year. Total risk-weighted assets are credit-risk-weighted assets and off balance sheet items as well as market risk.

ratio de capital básico

= ratio de core capital

▲ *a reduction of the core capital ratio* una reducción del ratio de capital básico ▲ *core capital ratio excluding profit/loss for the period* ratio de capital básico excluyendo beneficios/pérdidas durante el ejercicio ▲ *the average core capital ratio of the group* el ratio medio de capital básico del grupo ▲ *the group core capital ratio* el ratio de capital básico del grupo

⇛ capital adequacy ratio

core competence

Core competences are those competences that give an enterprise a competitive edge over its competitors.

ventaja competitiva esencial

▲ *development of core competences* desarrollo de ventajas competitivas esenciales

core earnings

= core income

Core earnings appear as a separate item in the highlights of the annual report or the notes to the financial statements of a financial institution and comprise earnings generated by the main operations, i.e. the customer-related activities such as net interest income, fee and commission income as well as trading income.

beneficios obtenidos en operaciones centales

= beneficios en operaciones centrales

▲ *core earnings as a percentage of average equity* beneficios obtenidos en operaciones centrales como un porcentaje del patrimonio medio

⇛ investment portfolio earnings

core income

Core income appears as a separate item in the highlights of the annual report or the notes to the financial statements of a financial institution and comprises income generated by the main operations, i.e. the customer-related activities such as net interest income, fee and commission income as well as trading income.

ingresos básicos

NOTE Always plural in Spanish accounting texts.

▲ *cost/core income ratio as a percentage* ratio coste/ingresos básicos como un porcentaje ▲ *other core income* otros ingresos básicos ▲ *total core income* total ingresos básicos

core value

Core values are a set of factors or attitudes that together form the image and position of an enterprise in the minds of consumers.

valor corporativo

▲ *determination of core values* determinación de valores corporativos

corporate

= business

Corporate means related to or belonging to a company.

corporativo

▲ *corporate activities* actividades corporativas ▲ *corporate advertising* publicidad corporativa ▲ *corporate body* organismo corporativo ▲ *corporate brand* marca corporativa ▲ *corporate by-laws* estatutos corporativos ▲ *corporate charter* escritura de constitución corporativa ▲ *corporate citizen* ciudadano corporativo ▲ *corporate citizenship* ciudadanía corporativa ▲ *corporate communication* comunicación corporativa ▲ *corporate customer* cliente corporativo ▲ *corporate development* desarrollo corporativo ▲ *corporate executive* ejecutivo corporativo ▲ *corporate finance* finanza corporativa ▲ *corporate identity* identidad corporativa ▲ *corporate image* imagen corporativa ▲ *corporate malpractice* malas prácticas profesionales corporativas ▲ *corporate objective* objetivo corporativo ▲ *corporate performance* rentabilidad corporativa ▲ *corporate planning* planificación corporativa ▲ *corporate responsibility* responsabilidad corporativa ▲ *corporate social responsibility* responsabilidad social corporativa ▲ *corporate strategy* estrategia corporativa ▲ *good corporate behaviour* buen comportamiento corporativo ▲ *the corporate sector* el sector corporativo

corporate asset

Corporate assets are assets contributing to generating future cash flows of enterprises. The enterprise may be both the cash-generating unit under review and other cash-generating units. Goodwill is not considered to be a corporate asset.

activo corporativo

= activo común de la compañía, activo de la sociedad

▲ *allocate a corporate asset to a cash-generating unit* asignar un activo corporativo de una unidad de producción de efectivo ▲ *corporate assets such as head office assets* activos corporativos tales como activos de la matriz ▲ *corporate assets that relate to the cash-generating unit* los activos corporativos que se refieren a la unidad de producción de efectivo ▲ *key characteristics of corporate assets* características básicas de los activos corporativos ▲ *meet the definition of corporate assets* cumplir la definición de activos corporativos ▲ *the carrying amount of the corporate asset* el valor contable del activo corporativo ▲ *the cash-generating unit to which the corporate asset belongs* la unidad de producción de efectivo a la que pertenece el activo corporativo

▲ *the recoverable amount of an individual corporate asset* la cantidad a cobrar de un activo corporativo individual

corporate bond

A corporate bond is a debt instrument issued by a private enterprise, as distinct from one e.g. issued by a government.

bono corporativo

▲ *corporate bond issuance* emisión de bonos corporativos ▲ *high quality corporate bonds* bonos corporativos de alta calidad ▲ *market yields at the balance sheet date on high quality corporate bonds* rendimientos comerciales a fecha de balance de los bonos corporativos de alta calidad ▲ *the currency and term of the corporate bonds* la divisa y las condiciones de los bonos corporativos

⇛ debenture

corporate charter US

→ charter

corporate culture

= company culture, enterprise culture

Corporate culture is a constellation of the corporate image, the values, norms, policies and attitudes as well as the basic beliefs and assumptions of an enterprise. A consensus about the corporate culture must be reached and shared by all employees.

cultura corporativa

▲ *be protective of one's corporate culture* proteger su cultura corporativa ▲ *common corporate culture* cultura corporativa común

corporate financial statements

= corporate accounts

The financial statements of an incorporated enterprise are called corporate financial statements.

estados financieros corporativos

▲ *audit corporate financial statements* auditar los estados financieros corporativos ▲ *the quality of corporate financial statements* la calidad de los estados financieros corporativos

corporate form

Corporate form means the way an enterprise has been established and from which appears the legal structure, i.e. how it has been organised and how its liability is for payments of debts etc. Corporate forms include private or public limited companies, partnerships and sole proprietorships.

estructura corporativa

▲ *choose a corporate form* elegir una estructura corporativa ▲ *the most appropriate corporate form* la estructura corporativa más adecuada

corporate governance

Corporate governance is a code of conduct focusing on the management, accountability and control of corporate entities, particularly listed companies, and the interaction between management, owners and other stakeholders in the achievement of defined goals. Since the introduction of the Cadbury Report in 1992 in the UK, corporate governance has become increasingly important, and compliance with corporate governance rules by listed companies are required by most stock exchanges and the US Sarbanes-Oxley Act.

gobierno corporativo

= gobernanza corporativa

▲ *be incompatible with corporate governance* ser compatible con la gobernanza corporativa ▲ *comply with the corporate governance rules of NYSE* cumplir con las reglas de gobernanza corporativa del NYSE ▲ *corporate governance codes* códigos de gobierno corporativo ▲ *introduce corporate governance requirements applicable to both US issuers and non-US issuers* introducir requisitos de gobierno corporativo aplicables a los emisores norteamericanos y no norteamericanos ▲ *the corporate governance task* la labor de gobierno corporativo ▲ *uphold high corporate governance standards* mantener normas de gobierno corporativo elevadas

⇛ Sarbanes-Oxley Act

corporate governance report

= corporate governance statement

A corporate governance report is a report included in the annual report of an enterprise disclosing particulars about its governance structure, accountability, management goals, risk management, internal controls and other major principles, typically on a "comply or explain" basis against the relevant national code. Listed companies are required by most stock exchanges and the US Sarbanes-Oxley Act to comply with corporate governance rules; in the UK, the Combined Code on Corporate Governance lays down such rules.

informe de gobierno corporativo

= informe de gobernanza corporativa

▲ *disclose in a separate corporate governance report* divulgar en un informe de gobierno corporativo independiente ▲ *prepare a corporate governance report* preparar un informe de gobierno corporativo

⇛ corporate governance

corporate governance statement

= corporate governance report

A corporate governance statement is a statement included in the annual report of an enterprise disclosing particulars about its governance structure, accountability, management goals, risk management, internal controls and other major principles, typically on a "comply or explain" basis against the relevant national code. Listed companies are required by most stock exchanges and the US Sarbanes-Oxley Act to comply with corporate governance rules; in the UK, the Combined Code on Corporate Governance lays down such rules.

informe de gobierno corporativo

= informe de gobernanza corporativa

▲ *disclose in the corporate governance statement* divulgar en un informe de gobierno corporativo ▲ *prepare a corporate governance statement* preparar un informe de gobierno corporativo

⇛ corporate governance

corporate income tax US

= corporation tax UK, income tax IAS/IFRS

Corporate income tax is the tax imposed on the profits earned by a corporation.

impuesto sobre sociedades

= impuesto de sociedades

▲ *corporate income tax paid* impuesto sobre sociedades pagado ▲ *corporate income tax payable* impuesto de sociedades a pagar ▲ *Danish corporate income tax* impuesto sobre sociedades danés ▲ *domestic corporate income tax* impuesto sobre sociedades nacional ▲ *foreign corporate income tax* impuesto sobre sociedades extranjero ▲ *maximum corporate income tax of 18%* impuesto sobre sociedades máximo del 18% ▲ *payment of corporate income tax* pago del impuesto de sociedades ▲ *proportionate allocation of corporate income tax* asignación proporcional del impuesto sobre sociedades

corporate income taxation US

Corporate income taxation is the imposition of tax on the profit earned by a corporation.

tributación del impuesto de sociedades

= tributación del impuesto sobre sociedades

▲ *City of Copenhagen Corporate Income Taxation Office* El Organismo de Tributación del Impuesto de Sociedades de la ciudad de Copenhague ▲ *Danish corporate income taxation* tributación del impuesto de sociedades danés ▲ *international corporate income taxation* tributación del impuesto de sociedades internacional ▲ *reduce corporate income taxation* reducir la tributación del impuesto de sociedades

corporate mission

= business foundation

The corporate mission identifies the scope of an enterprise's operations in product and market terms and states its broad-ranging goals and purposes. The corporate mission is often defined in a mission statement that also reflects the values and priorities of the enterprise.

misión corporativa

▲ *be included in the corporate mission* estar incluido en la misión corporativa

⇛ basic values

corporate social responsibility

= CSR, social responsibility

Corporate social responsibility is the obligation and awareness of enterprises to employees, stakeholders and the society at large to act in decision-making and business operations in a way that meets the ethical, business, pu-

blic and legal expectations of society to a business organisation. The focus is on obtaining sustainable development not only economically, but also for social and environmental purposes.
responsabilidad social corporativa
▲ *adopt a corporate social responsibility policy* adoptar una política de responsabilidad social corporativa ▲ *develop a best practice on corporate social responsibility* desarrollar una mejor práctica en responsabilidad social corporativa ▲ *enhance the development and transparency of corporate social responsibility* fomentar el desarrollo y transparencia de la responsabilidad social corporativa

corporate treasurer US
= chief financial officer US, finance director UK
The corporate treasurer in an enterprise is the top financial officer responsible for dealing with the financial issues, decisions and activities within the enterprise.
director financiero corporativo
▲ *appoint a new corporate treasurer* nombrar un nuevo director financiero corporativo ▲ *the former corporate treasurer* el anterior director financiero corporativo ▲ *the retiring corporate treasurer* el director financiero corporativo saliente
⇛ controller

corporation US
A corporation is an association of shareholders created under the rules of law and recognised in law as a separate legal entity that is entirely separate from its owners.
sociedad
= compañía
▲ *a dominant corporation* una sociedad dominante ▲ *a related corporation* una sociedad relacionada ▲ *an associated corporation* una compañía asociada ▲ *close corporation* compañía cercana ▲ *corporation law* derecho de sociedades ▲ *dual listed corporations* sociedades con doble cotización ▲ *the reporting corporation* la sociedad informante ▲ *transactions between a corporation and its principal stockholder* transacciones entre una sociedad y su principal accionista

corporation tax UK
= corporate income tax US, CT, income tax IAS/IFRS
Corporation tax is the tax payable by UK incorporated and unincorporated companies (excluding partnerships and local authorities) on earned profits, i.e. the value added gained. In the balance sheet, the item “Corporation tax” refers to the tax payable by a company for the year under review.
impuesto sobre sociedades
= impuesto de sociedades
▲ *corporation tax paid* impuesto sobre sociedades pagado ▲ *corporation tax payable* impuesto de sociedades a pagar ▲ *Danish corporation tax* impuesto sobre sociedades danés ▲ *domestic corporation tax* impuesto sobre sociedades nacional ▲ *exempt from corporation tax* eximir del impuesto de sociedades ▲ *foreign corporation tax* impuesto sobre sociedades extranjero ▲ *payment of corporation tax* pago del impuesto de sociedades ▲ *proportionate allocation of corporation tax* asignación proporcional del impuesto sobre sociedades
⇛ corporation tax rate

corporation tax rate UK
Corporation tax rate is the percentage of the separate tax charged on taxable profits by incorporated and unincorporated companies in the UK, excluding partnerships and local authorities, for each accounting period. The corporation tax rates are fixed for the financial year ending each 31 March.
NOTE Depending on the profit level of the company, there are different rate thresholds: a main rate and a small companies rate, supplemented by marginal rates.
tipo del impuesto de sociedades
▲ *change the corporation tax rate* modificar el tipo del impuesto de sociedades ▲ *lower the corporation tax rate* bajar el tipo del impuesto de sociedades ▲ *the reduction in the corporation tax rate* la reducción del tipo del impuesto de sociedades

⇛ corporate income tax, corporation tax

correct[1] *verb*

To correct means to change something so as to remove errors and inconsistencies.

corregir

▲ *correct an error* corregir un error ▲ *correct material prior period errors retrospectively* corregir restrospectivamente errores materiales del ejercicio anterior ▲ *correct the error prospectively from the earliest date practicable* corregir el error con posterioridad a la fecha anterior posible

correct[2] *adjective*

If something is correct it is true and free from errors and inconsistencies.

correcto

▲ *publish the correct information* publicar la información correcta ▲ *the correct data* los datos correctos

corrected

If something is corrected it has been checked and is free from errors and inconsistencies.

corregido

▲ *a corrected value* un valor corregido ▲ *corrected figures* cifras corregidas

correction

= adjustment

A correction is an alteration to correct an error or a modification or adjustment to a calculation.

corrección

▲ *changes in accounting estimates and correction of errors* modificaciones en estimaciones contables y corrección de errores ▲ *correction for tax* corrección fiscal ▲ *correction of fundamental errors* corrección de errores fundamentales ▲ *correction of misstated amounts* corrección de cantidades incorrectas ▲ *correction of the recorded result* corrección del resultado registrado ▲ *including the effects of the correction of fundamental errors* incluyendo los efectos de la corrección de errores fundamentales ▲ *make a correction* llevar a cabo una corrección ▲ *the amount of the correction of an error* la cantidad de la corrección de un error

correction amount

= amount of correction

The correction amount is the amount constituting the difference between an amount before and after the correction. The amount of the correction e.g. of a fundamental error that relates to prior periods should be reported by adjusting the opening balance of retained earnings and comparative information should be restated.

corrección

▲ *disclosure of correction amounts* divulgación de las correcciones ▲ *include a correction amount* incluir una corrección

corresponding

Corresponding means equivalent or comparable.

correspondiente

▲ *corresponding amounts for each prior period presented* cantidades correspondientes a cada periodo anterior presentado ▲ *corresponding figures for the previous period* cifras correspondientes al periodo anterior ▲ *corresponding gains and losses* resultados correspondientes ▲ *eliminate against a corresponding amount* eliminar contra una cuenta correspondiente ▲ *recognise a corresponding expense* reconocer un gasto correspondiente ▲ *with a corresponding adjustment to the amount of goodwill* con un ajuste correspondiente a la cantidad de fondo de comercio ▲ *without a corresponding change in resources* sin la correspondiente modificación en recursos

corresponding figure

→ comparative figure

corridor

A corridor is a range of 10% around an enterprise's best estimate of its post-employment benefit obligations, set as the larger of the present value of the obligation and the fair value of the plan assets. Any actuarial gains or losses outside the corridor must be recognised as income or expense and cannot be offset.

banda de fluctuación

= corredor pasillo

▲ *a corridor around the best estimate* una banda de fluctuación en torno a la mejor estimación ▲ *apply a corridor* aplicar una banda de fluctuación ▲ *both within and outside the corridor* tanto dentro como fuera de la banda de fluctuación ▲ *fall outside the 10% corridor* caer fuera de la banda de fluctuación del 10% ▲ *set the limits of the corridor* fijar los límites de la banda de fluctuación ▲ *the portion of the actuarial losses that fall outside a corridor of plus or minus 10%* la parte de pérdidas actuariales que no se incluye en una banda de fluctuación de más o menos el 10%

corridor approach

The corridor approach is a method applied in accounting for defined benefit plans, which requires, as a minimum, the recognition of accumulated actuarial gains and losses that exceed a corridor or range of plus/minus 10% of the projected post-employment benefit obligation. Gains and losses falling within the corridor may or may not be recognised.

enfoque corredor

= enfoque corridor

▲ *retrospective application of the corridor approach* aplicación restrospectiva del enfoque corredor ▲ *use the corridor approach* usar el enfoque corredor ▲ *use the corridor approach for later actuarial gains and losses* usar el enfoque corredor para resultados actuariales posteriores

SOURCE IAS 19, paragraph 95

COSA

= cost of sales adjustment

COSA is the abbreviation for cost of sales adjustment, a downward adjustment of operating profit in the context of current cost accounting made because of a higher value of the quantity of stocks at the end of an accounting period than at the beginning of the period. The increased value results from rising prices and therefore constitutes a holding gain rather than a profit from operations. The profit resulting from the higher stock value is tied up in stocks and remains unrealised until the goods are sold.

NOTE Cost of sales adjustment (incl. current-cost accounting) has been largely abandoned since the late 1980s/early 1990s because of the lower inflation rates.

ajuste al coste de ventas

▲ *items utilised in computing COSA* partidas utilizadas al calcular el ajuste al coste de ventas

cost[1] *noun* <a, the, -s>

Costs represent the sacrifice or decrease in economic benefits in an accounting period measured by asset outflows or the using up of assets or incurrence of liabilities, resulting in a reduction of equity, excluding expenses in the form of distribution to owners.

coste

= costo

NOTE 'Costo' is used in American Spanish.

▲ *achieve a cost saving* conseguir un ahorro de costes ▲ *claims handling costs* costes de gestión de reclamaciones ▲ *costs associated with insured events* costes asociados con acontecimientos asegurados ▲ *costs directly attributable to the business combination* costes directamente atribuibles a la combinación de negocio ▲ *costs expected to be incurred as a result of a combination* costes en los que se prevé incurrir como resultado de una combinación ▲ *costs incurred during the period* costes incurridos durante el ejercicio ▲ *costs of conducting business in a new location* coste por gestionar actividades empresariales en una nueva localización ▲ *costs of employee benefits* costes por prestaciones al trabajador ▲ *costs of introducing a new product or service* costes de introducción de un nuevo producto o servicio ▲ *costs of testing whether the asset is functioning properly* costes de comprobación sobre el funcionamiento adecuado del activo ▲ *direct incremental costs to dispose of the asset* costes incrementales directos para la venta del activo ▲ *possible future costs arising in respect of the acquiree* posibles costes futuros surgidos en relación a la adquisición ▲ *recognise costs in the carrying amount of an intangible asset* reconocer costes en el valor contable de un activo intangible ▲ *the cost of generating an intangible asset internally* el coste de generación interna de un activo intangible ▲ *the costs of arranging and issuing financial liabilities* los costes de planificación y emisión de pasivos financieros ▲ *the costs of maintaining an acquisitions department* los costes de mantener un departamento de adquisiciones

cost[2] *noun* <a, the, no plural>
The cost of an asset is the amount of consideration given to acquire that asset whether it was acquired from an external party or internally generated, while the cost of a liability is the amount received as consideration for that liability.
coste
= gasto
NOTE 'Costo' is used in American Spanish.
▲ *accumulated cost* coste acumulado ▲ *be included in the cost* estar incluido en el coste ▲ *calculate the cost based on the FIFO method* calcular el gasto basado en el método FIFO ▲ *calculate the cost based on weighted average costs* calcular el gasto basado en los costes medios ponderados ▲ *cost at beginning of year* coste al inicio de ejercicio ▲ *cost at end of year* coste al final del ejercicio ▲ *cost at the end of the previous financial year* coste al final del ejercicio anterior ▲ *deemed cost* coste considerado ▲ *determination of cost* determinación del coste ▲ *estimate at cost* estimar al coste ▲ *include in the cost* incluir en el coste ▲ *indexed cost* coste indexado ▲ *inflation-adjusted cost* coste ajustado a la inflación ▲ *measure an asset at cost* valorar un activo al coste ▲ *measure at cost* medir al coste ▲ *original cost* coste inicial ▲ *recognise an asset at cost* reconocer un activo al coste ▲ *recognise interest expenses as part of the cost* reconocer los gastos financieros como parte del coste ▲ *the cost of inventories* el coste de inventarios ▲ *total cost at the balance sheet date* total gasto a la fecha de balance

cost[3] *verb* <-s, cost, cost, -ing>
If a product or a service costs something it means that a certain price has to be paid or consideration given to acquire that product or service.
costar
▲ *cost a fortune* costar una fortuna

cost[4] *verb* <-s, -ed, has -ed, -ing> *passive* <is -ed, was -ed>
To cost is to calculate or decide the cost of an activity.
valorar
▲ *cost the goods* valorar los bienes

cost accounting
Cost accounting is that part of the cost management system that measures costs for the purpose of management decisions and financial reporting. Cost accounting involves budgeting, breaking down of costs and revenues by product and location as well as analysing variances, profitability and use of funds.
contabilidad de costes
▲ *managerial cost accounting concepts* conceptos de contabilidad de costes de gestión ▲ *the application of cost accounting principles* la aplicación de principios de contabilidad de costes
⇛ cost accounting system, cost management system

cost accounting system
= management control system, management information system
ost accounting systems support all other cost management systems and include techniques to analyse and measure the cost of a product, service, customer or other cost object. A cost accounting system must measure costs to meet the cost management system purposes.
sistema de contabilidad de costes
▲ *a centralised cost accounting system* un sistema de contabilidad de costes centralizado ▲ *deficiencies in the cost accounting system* deficiencias en el sistema de contabilidad de costes ▲ *implement a cost accounting system* implementar un sistema de contabilidad de costes
⇛ cost accounting, cost management system

cost accumulation US
Cost accumulation is the organised recording and collection of costs by natural classification such as materials, labor or activities performed.
acumulación de costes
NOTE By referring to 'costes' (plural), Spanish accountants assume that the concept always refers to various types of costs.

▲ *the measurement of cost accumulation* la medición de la acumulación de costes

cost advantage

An enterprise has a cost advantage when it is able to produce specific goods or deliver specific services at a considerably lower cost in comparison with the costs of competing enterprises.

ventaja de coste

= ventaja comparativa

▲ *a relative cost advantage* una ventaja de coste relativa ▲ *a significant cost advantage* una ventaja de coste significativa ▲ *an absolute cost advantage* una ventaja de coste absoluta

cost allocation

Cost allocation is the act of assigning overhead expenses to cost centres using reliable cost drivers.

asignación de costes

NOTE By referring to 'costes' (plural), Spanish accountants assume that the concept always refers to various types of costs.

▲ *actuarial cost allocation* asignación de costes actuariales ▲ *cost allocation base* base de asignación de costes ▲ *the incremental common cost allocation method* el método de asignación de costes común incremental

cost assignment US

Cost assignment means allocating or tracing costs to one or more cost objectives such as activities, departments, customers or products.

asignación de costes

NOTE By referring to 'costes' (plural), Spanish accountants assume that the concept always refers to various types of costs.

▲ *an effective tool for cost assignment* un instrumento efectivo de asignación de costes ▲ *the improvement in cost assignment* una mejora en la asignación de costes

cost behavior US

= cost behaviour

Cost behavior is the way an entity's activities affect its costs.

comportamiento de costes

= comportamiento de los costes

NOTE By referring to 'costes' (plural), Spanish accountants assume that the concept always refers to various types of costs.

▲ *guidelines for managing cost behavior* directrices para gestionar el comportamiento de costes

cost behaviour

= cost behavior US

Cost behaviour is the way an entity's activities affect its costs.

comportamiento de costes

NOTE By referring to 'costes' (plural), Spanish accountants assume that the concept always refers to various types of costs.

▲ *guidelines for managing cost behaviour* directrices para gestionar el comportamiento de costes

cost center US

= cost centre UK

Cost centers are responsibility centers, i.e. a particular unit or function for which costs are accumulated. Usually, only one manager is in charge of a particular cost center and the planning, budgeting and control of costs related to that center. Cost centers can be divided into two main types: production cost centers or service cost centers.

centro de coste

▲ *an independent cost center* un centro de coste independiente ▲ *costs attributable to a cost center* costes atribuibles a un centro de coste

⇛ responsibility center

cost centre UK

= cost center US

Cost centres are responsibility centres, i.e. a particular unit or function for which costs are accumulated. Usually, only one manager is in charge of a particular cost centre and the planning, budgeting and control of costs related to that centre. Cost centres can be divided into two main types: production cost centres or service cost centres.

centro de coste

▲ *an independent cost centre* un centro de coste independiente ▲ *costs attributable to a cost centre* costes atribuibles a un centro de coste

⇛ responsibility centre

cost control

Cost control refers to an enterprise's preparation and

implementation of procedures and systems to keep costs at a reasonable level.

control de costes

NOTE By referring to 'costes' (plural), Spanish accountants assume that the concept always refers to various types of costs.

▲ *strict cost control* control de costes estricto ▲ *tight cost control* control de costes riguroso ▲ *to strengthen cost control* reforzar el control de costes

cost convention

The cost convention is a basic accounting concept assuming that the cost of an asset is the value at which the asset should be recognised in the financial statements. Typically, the historical cost convention is applied; other cost measures are current cost and replacement cost.

convención del coste

▲ *the historical cost convention* la convención del coste histórico

⇛ current cost, historical cost convention, replacement cost

cost development

Cost development refers to the upward or downward trend in an enterprise's total costs or in one or more specific parts of the enterprise's costs.

desarrollo de costes

NOTE By referring to 'costes' (plural), Spanish accountants assume that the concept always refers to various types of costs.

▲ *a satisfactory cost development* un desarrollo de costes satisfactorio ▲ *a stable cost development* un desarrollo de costes estable ▲ *to focus on the cost development* centrarse en el desarrollo de costes

cost driver

A cost driver is any factor or output measure causing a change in the cost of an activity or the use of costly resources. An activity may have multiple cost drivers, examples are number of labour hours, number of parts per product, number of advertisements etc.

generador de coste

▲ *expenditure that can be attributed to a single cost driver* gastos atribuibles a un generador de coste único ▲ *identify a cost driver* identificar un generador de coste

⇛ cost function, cost measurement

cost effective

→ cost-effective

cost estimation

Cost estimation is a process applied in cost accounting for determining the approximate future costs of defined products or services by analysing historical cost behaviour.

estimación de costes

NOTE By referring to 'costes' (plural), Spanish accountants assume that the concept always refers to various types of costs.

▲ *commonly agreed cost estimation methods* métodos de estimación de costes comúnmente acordados

cost formula

= cost function

A cost formula is a method for calculating the total costs, typically both fixed and variable, at a certain activity or output level and shows the relationship, expressed as an equation, between costs and one or more cost drivers.

fórmula de coste

= función de coste, método de coste

▲ *different cost formulas for inventories* diferentes fórmulas de coste para inventarios ▲ *the cost formula used* la fórmula de coste empleada ▲ *the cost formulas that are used to assign costs to inventories* las fórmulas de coste que se usan para asignar costes a inventarios ▲ *the weighted average cost formula* la fórmula de coste medio ponderado

⇛ cost driver

cost function UK/US

= cost formula

The cost function is a formula or an equation applied by managers to describe the relationship between a cost and its cost drivers.

función de coste

▲ *a nonlinear cost function* una función de coste no lineal ▲ *compute a cost function* computar una función de coste

⇛ cost driver

cost hierarchy

A cost hierarchy is an arrangement of costs in separated cost pools based on different cost driver categories at different levels, typically divided into four levels: output unit-level costs, batch-level costs, product-sustaining costs and facility-sustaining costs.

jerarquía de costes

NOTE By referring to 'costes' (plural), Spanish accountants assume that the concept always refers to various types of costs.

▲ *use the cost hierarchy* usar la jerarquía de costes

⇛ batch-level cost, cost pool, facility-sustaining cost, output unit-level cost, product-sustaining cost

cost incurrence

Cost incurrence is the consumption of resources or sacrifice of benefits, e.g. in a production process, to achieve a specific target.

incurrencia de costes

= incurrencia en costes

NOTE By referring to 'costes' (plural), Spanish accountants assume that the concept always refers to various types of costs.

▲ *a defined location of cost incurrence* una localización definida de la incurrencia de costes ▲ *an accurate determination of cost incurrence* una determinación exacta de la incurrencia de costes ▲ *the pattern of cost incurrence* el modelo de incurrencia de costes

cost leadership

Cost leadership is a strategy where an enterprise sets out to become the lowest-cost producer in a specific industry by focusing on low costs, low prices and high volumes.

liderazgo de costes

= liderazgo en costes

NOTE By referring to 'costes' (plural), Spanish accountants assume that the concept always refers to various types of costs.

▲ *sustainable cost leadership* liderazgo de costes sostenible

cost management

Cost management is management and control of activities to help set enterprise strategies and to determine an accurate product and service cost, improve business procedures, eliminate waste, identify cost drivers, and plan operations.

gestión de costes

NOTE By referring to 'costes' (plural), Spanish accountants assume that the concept always refers to various types of costs.

▲ *comprehensive streamlining of cost management* aerodinamización exhaustiva de la gestión de costes ▲ *efficient cost management* gestión de costes eficiente ▲ *focus on cost management* centrarse en la gestión de costes ▲ *implement strict cost management* implementar la gestión de costes estricta

cost management system US

= CMS US

A cost management system is a system of techniques to identify how management decisions influence costs. The purpose of a cost management system is to provide cost information for strategic decisions and operational control as well as measures of inventory value and cost of goods manufactured for external stakeholders.

sistema de gestión de costes

NOTE By referring to 'costes' (plural), Spanish accountants assume that the concept always refers to various types of costs.

▲ *a strategic cost management system* un sistema de gestión de costes estratégico ▲ *an integrated cost management system* un sistema de gestión de costes integrado ▲ *develop a cost management system* desarrollar un sistema de gestión de costes

⇛ cost accounting system

cost measurement

Cost measurement means estimating cost behaviour as a function of appropriate cost drivers.

medición de costes

NOTE By referring to 'costes' (plural), Spanish accountants assume that the concept always refers to various types of costs.

▲ *guidelines for cost measurement* directrices para la medición de costes ▲ *improve cost measurement* mejorar la medición de costes ▲ *methods for cost measurement* métodos para la medición de costes

⇛ cost driver

cost method

= cost formula

A cost method is a valuation method according to which assets are measured and recognised at cost in the balance sheet.

método de coste

= fórmula de coste

NOTE Spanish accountants prefer 'método de coste' to the IAS/IFRS term 'fórmula de coste'.

▲ *account for by use of the cost method* contabilizar usando el método de coste ▲ *prepared under the historical cost method* preparado según el método de coste histórico ▲ *the historical cost method* el método de coste histórico ▲ *the standard cost method* el método de coste estándar ▲ *under a cost method* según un método de coste ▲ *use the cost method* utilizar el método de coste

cost object
= cost objective
A cost object is an activity (such as a particular product, service, division or department) to which costs are attributed and for which cost data are required with a view to separate measurement, e.g. for cost management purposes.
objeto de coste
= objetivo de coste
▲ *a new cost object* un nuevo objeto de coste ▲ *total cost for a cost object* total coste por un objeto de coste
⇛ cost unit

cost objective
1 = cost target
A cost objective is the cost target or limit determined for a particular activity or product, typically in a budget.
coste límite
▲ *establish a cost objective* estable cer un coste límite ▲ *meet the cost objective* cumplir el coste límite
2 = cost object
A cost objective is an activity (such as a particular product, service, division or department) to which costs are attributed and for which cost data are required with a view to separate measurement, e.g. for cost management purposes.
objetivo de coste
= objeto de coste
▲ *costs incurred in meeting the cost objective* costes incurridos al cumplir el objetivo de coste ▲ *establish a cost objective* establecer un objetivo de coste
⇛ cost unit

cost of borrowing
→ borrowing cost

cost of capital
The cost of capital is the price or return paid by an enterprise for raising capital. For equity, the return constitutes dividends or value added reflected in share prices, whereas for loan capital the return is interest paid on the borrowed funds.
coste de capital
▲ *average cost of capital* coste de capital medio ▲ *disclosure of cost of capital* divulgación del coste de capital ▲ *weighted average cost of capital* coste de capital medio ponderado ▲ *weighted cost of capital* coste de capital ponderado

cost of completion
= coste de realización
Costs of completion are those costs that are incurred in completing a project or product so that it is ready for sale or delivery to the customer.
coste de finalización
= coste de realización
▲ *estimated costs of completion* costes de finalización estimados ▲ *the total cost of completion of the project* el coste total de finalización del proyecto

cost of conversion
Costs of conversion of inventories comprise the costs incurred and directly related to the production process where raw materials are converted into finished products. Such costs include fixed and variable manufacturing overheads and direct labour related to the conversion.
coste de transformación
= coste de conversión
▲ *allocate fixed production overheads to the costs of conversion* asignar costes indirectos de producción fijos a los costes de transformación ▲ *direct costs of conversion* costes de transformación directos ▲ *the costs of conversion of inventories* los costes de transformación de inventarios
SOURCE IAS 2, paragraph 12

cost of dismantling
Costs of dismantling refer to costs related to the taking down or removal of assets, such as machinery or other types of equipment, when they are no longer used or at the end of their useful lives.
coste de desmantelamiento
▲ *estimated selling price less costs of dismantling* precio de venta estimado menos costes de desmantelamiento ▲ *the estimated*

costs of dismantling los costes de desmantelamiento estimados

cost of disposal

= disposal cost

Costs of disposal are the costs directly incurred when selling or otherwise disposing of an asset, not including finance costs and tax expenses.

coste de enajenación

= coste de disposición

▲ *after deducting the expected costs of disposal* despues de deducir los costes de enajenación esperados ▲ *less the costs of disposal* menos los costes de enajenación ▲ *the asset's market price less the costs of disposal* el precio de mercado del activo menos los costes de enajenación

cost of goods manufactured

The cost of goods manufactured refers to the total production costs for a specific accounting period.

coste de producción

= coste de fabricación

▲ *calculate the cost of goods manufactured for the month of May* calcular el coste de fabricación del mes de mayo ▲ *determine the costs of goods manufactured* determinar los costes de fabricación

cost of goods sold

= COGS, cost of sales

Cost of goods sold is an item in the profit and loss account or income statement showing the cost during a period of the merchandise or products an enterprise acquires or produces and then sells.

coste de ventas

▲ *calculate cost of goods sold* calcular coste de ventas ▲ *determine the cost of goods sold* determinar el coste de ventas

cost of labour

Cost of labour includes wages, social security and pension contributions to employees for an accounting period. The expression can refer both to employees at all levels in an enterprise or to direct labour only.

coste de personal

▲ *direct cost of labour* coste de personal directo ▲ *pay costs of labour in local currency* pagar costes de personal en moneda nacional ▲ *settle costs of labour in local currency* pagar costes de personal en moneda nacional

cost of materials

The cost of materials is the price paid for those materials that are used in manufacturing products or providing serivces.

coste de materiales

= coste de materias primas

▲ *costs of materials used in construction* costes de materiales utilizados en la construcción ▲ *direct costs of materials incurred* costes de materiales incurridos directos

cost of premises

= costs relating to premises, occupancy costs

The costs of premises are those costs that are attributable to premises and offices including rent, repair and maintenance, power, heating, insurance, cleaning etc.

coste de funcionamiento de instalaciones

▲ *other costs of premises* otros costes de funcionamiento de instalaciones

cost of restoring

Costs of restoring refer to costs incurred when reconstructing or repairing something that has been destroyed or damaged.

coste de rehabilitación

▲ *incur costs of restoring* incurrir en costes de rehabilitación ▲ *measure the cost of restoring* medir el coste de rehabilitación ▲ *pay the majority of the costs of restoring* pagar la mayoría de los costes de rehabilitación

cost of sales

= cost of goods sold

Cost of sales is an item in the profit and loss account or income statement showing the cost during a period of the merchandise or products an enterprise acquires or produces and then sells.

coste de ventas

▲ *an increase in the cost of sales* un aumento en el coste de ventas ▲ *calculate the cost of sales* calcular el coste de ventas ▲ *classify expenses according to their function as part of cost of sales* clasificar gastos de acuerdo a su función como parte del coste de ventas ▲ *cost of sales figures* cifras de coste de ventas ▲ *cost of sales method* método de coste de ventas ▲ *the adjusted amount of cost of sales* la cantidad ajustada de coste de ventas ▲ *the amount of the adjustment to cost of sales* la cantidad del ajuste a coste de ventas

cost of sales adjustment

= COSA

In the context of current cost accounting, a cost of sales adjustment is a downward adjustment in operating profit made because of a higher value of the quantity of stocks at the end of an accounting period than at the beginning of the period. The increased value results from rising prices and therefore constitutes a holding gain rather than a profit from operations. The profit resulting from the higher stock value is tied up in stocks and remains unrealised until the goods are sold.

NOTE Cost of sales adjustment (incl. current-cost accounting) has been largely abandoned since the late 1980s/early 1990s because of the lower inflation rates.

coste de ventas ajustado

▲ *items utilised in computing cost of sales adjustment* partidas utilizadas en el cálculo del coste de ventas ajustado

⇛ current cost accounting, historical cost convention

cost of sales method

→ classification by function

cost plus contract

≠ fixed price contract

A cost plus contract is a construction contract that determines the contract price as the agreed and defined costs of construction, such as labour and materials costs, plus an added percentage markup or a fixed fee.

contrato a coste más beneficio

= contrato de margen sobre el coste

≠ contrato a precio fijo

NOTE Spanish accountants use 'contrato a coste más beneficio' considering that the IAS/IFRS term 'contrato de margen sobre el coste' can be easily misunderstood.

▲ *a cost plus contract with an agreed maximum price* un contrato a coste más beneficio con un precio máximo acordado ▲ *classify as cost plus contracts* clasificar como contratos a coste más beneficio ▲ *revenue from cost plus contracts* ingreso de contratos a coste más beneficio ▲ *the outcome of a cost plus contract* el resultado de un contrato a coste más beneficio

SOURCE IAS 11, paragraph 3

cost plus method

The cost plus method is a pricing model which seeks to add an appropriate mark-up to the supplier's cost.

método coste más beneficio

▲ *use the cost plus method* usar el método coste más beneficio

cost pool

A cost pool is an aggregation of costs that are based on the same cost driver in an activity-based costing system.

agrupación de costes

NOTE By referring to 'costes' (plural), Spanish accountants assume that the concept always refers to various types of costs.

▲ *a cost pool for each activity* una agrupación de costes para cada actividad ▲ *allocate to a cost pool* asignar a una agrupación de costes ▲ *charge to the wrong cost pool* cargar la agrupación de costes equivocada

cost prediction

Cost prediction is an estimation and calculation of future costs.

predicción de costes

NOTE By referring to 'costes' (plural), Spanish accountants assume that the concept always refers to various types of costs.

▲ *a valid cost prediction* una predicción de costes válida

cost price

The cost price is the price of something that is sold for what it cost to produce, without any profit for the producer.

precio de coste

= precio al coste

▲ *calculate the cost price* calcular el precio de coste

cost ratio

The cost ratio is the relation of total costs to another amount, typically revenue i.e. income, expressed as a percentage and applied as a performance indicator. For banks, the cost ratio is defined as costs excluding losses and provisions in relation to revenue, whereas for insurance companies it is the relationship between operating costs and earned premiums expressed on a net or gross basis, i.e. before and after reinsurance cover.

ratio de coste

▲ *an improved cost ratio* un ratio de coste mejorado ▲ *calculation of the cost ratio* cálculo del ratio de coste ▲ *reach one's cost ratio target* alcanzar su objetivo de ratio de coste ▲ *reduce the cost ratio* reducir el ratio de coste ▲ *set up a cost ratio target* establecer un objetivo de ratio de coste

⇛ cost/income ratio

cost recovery

Cost recovery is the carrying forward of assets such as stocks, equipment or amounts paid in advance, because the costs are expected to be recovered via cash inflows in future periods.

recuperación del coste

= recuperación de coste

▲ *achieve cost recovery* conseguir la recuperación del coste ▲ *the ultimate aim of achieving cost recovery* el objetivo final de lograr la recuperación del coste

cost reduction

= cost cutting

A cost reduction is a lowering or a relative lowering of an enterprise's total costs, categories of costs or the costs related to a specific product or service.

reducción de coste

= reducción del coste

▲ *achieve cost reductions* lograr reducciones de coste ▲ *annual cost reductions* reducciones de coste anuales ▲ *constant cost reductions* reducciones de coste constantes ▲ *make cost reductions* hacer reducciones de coste ▲ *realisation of cost reductions* materialización de reducciones de coste ▲ *timing difference in cost reduction on capacity adjustment* diferencia temporal en la reducción de coste en el ajuste de capacidad

cost saving

= savings on costs

A cost saving is a reduction in costs compared to the expected or planned level of costs.

ahorro de coste

▲ *achieve cost savings* lograr ahorros de coste ▲ *an annual cost saving* un ahorro de coste anual ▲ *closing of a facility to achieve productivity improvements or other cost savings* cierre de una instalación para conseguir mejoras de productividad u otros ahorros de coste ▲ *cost savings or other benefits resulting from the use of the asset* ahorros de coste u otros beneficios resultantes del uso del activo ▲ *plan cost savings* planificar ahorros de coste ▲ *realisation of cost savings* materialización de ahorros de coste ▲ *realise cost savings* llevar a cabo ahorros de coste ▲ *related cost savings* ahorros de coste relacionados

cost smoothing

= peanut-butter costing US

Cost smoothing is a costing method according to which resource costs are allocated evenly on all cost objects on the basis of broad averages even though the individual products, services or customers are not equally resource demanding.

reparto uniforme del coste

▲ *use cost smoothing* utilizar el reparto uniforme del coste

cost structure

= structure of costs

Cost structure refers to the relative proportion of a specific type of costs, classified as fixed, variable or mixed costs, incurred by an enterprise when producing goods or providing services.

estructura de coste

▲ *the general cost structure of the industry* la estructura de coste general de la industria

cost to sell

Costs to sell are differential costs related to the disposal of assets held for sale or disposal groups. Such costs do not include finance costs and income tax.

coste de venta

▲ *an increase in the present value of the costs to sell* un aumento en el valor actual de los costes de venta ▲ *higher of value in use and fair value less costs to sell* el mayor del valor en uso y el valor razonable menos costes de venta ▲ *less costs to sell* menos costes de venta ▲ *measure the costs to sell at their present value* valorar los costes de venta a su valor actual

SOURCE IFRS 5, Appendix A

cost tracing

= cost tracking

Cost tracing is the process of attributing direct costs to the appropriate cost objects.

guía de coste

▲ *improve the accuracy of the cost tracing* mejorar la precisión de la guía de coste ▲ *show cost tracing for three activities* mostrar la guía de coste de tres actividades ▲ *the conditions for cost tracing* las condiciones para la guía de coste

cost tracking

= cost tracing

Cost tracking is the process of attributing direct costs to the appropriate cost objects.

guía de coste

▲ *do simple cost tracking* hacer una guía de coste simple

cost unit

The cost unit is the smallest unit of product or service for which the cost is being calculated.

unidad de coste

▲ *a suitable cost unit* una unidad de coste adecuada

⇛ cost object

cost variance

Cost variance is the difference between actual costs and budgeted costs. This difference may be positive or negative compared with the budgeted costs.

desviación en coste

▲ *favorable cost variance* desviación en coste favorable ▲ *unfavorable cost variance* desviación en coste desfavorable

cost-accumulation US

→ cost accumulation

cost-allocation base

The cost-allocation base is a method for cause-and-effect allocation or assigning of indirect costs to various cost objects using cost drivers to identify the relation between the costs and the cause of the costs.

NOTE Cost-allocation base is also referred to as cost-application base when the cost object is a product, a job or a customer rather than e.g. a department, a division or an organisational unit.

método de asignación de coste

▲ *identify the cost-allocation base for each indirect-cost pool* identificar el método de asignación de coste para cada agregación de coste indirecto

⇛ cost driver, cost-application base

cost-application base

A cost-application base is a method for the allocation of costs to relevant cost centres, activities etc., based on e.g. the number of machine hours paid or the number of hectolitres consumed, when the cost object is a job, a product or a customer.

NOTE Cost-application base can also be referred to as cost-allocation base, but only when the cost object is a product, a job or a customer and not in cases where the cost object is e.g. a department, a division or an organisational unit.

método de aplicación de coste

▲ *an appropriate cost-application base* un método de aplicación de coste adecuado ▲ *determine an indirect cost-application base* determinar un método de aplicación de coste indirecto

⇛ cost-allocation base

cost-benefit analysis

= cost-benefit evaluation, cost-effectiveness assessment

A cost-benefit analysis is an economic analysis that assesses and compares expected costs and benefits of different solutions and actions, the purpose being to choose the most profitable solution and action.

análisis coste-beneficio

▲ *environmental cost-benefit analysis* análisis coste-beneficio medioambiental ▲ *the use of cost-benefit analysis* el uso de análisis coste-beneficio ▲ *use a cost-benefit analysis* utilizar un análisis coste-beneficio

cost-benefit balance

The cost-benefit balance or the weighing of estimated costs against probable benefits is a decisive factor in the choice between various projects, products or services, such as an accounting system or a bridge.

saldo coste-beneficio

▲ *a negative cost-benefit balance* un saldo coste-beneficio negativo ▲ *a positive cost-benefit balance* un saldo coste-beneficio positivo ▲ *attain the optimum cost-benefit balance* conse-

guir el saldo coste-beneficio óptimo
⇛ cost-benefit criterion

cost-benefit criterion
A cost-benefit criterion is an approach where estimated costs are weighed against probable benefits in the choice between various projects, products or services, such as an accounting system or a bridge.
criterio coste-beneficio
▲ *apply a cost-benefit criterion* utilizar un criterio coste-beneficio ▲ *be at odds with the cost-benefit criterion* ser contrario al criterio coste-beneficio ▲ *financial reporting based on the cost-benefit criterion* información financiera basada en el criterio coste-beneficio ▲ *make decisions according to the cost-benefit criterion* tomar decisiones de acuerdo con el criterio coste-beneficio
⇛ cost-benefit balance

cost-benefit evaluation
= cost-benefit analysis, cost-effectiveness assessment
A cost-benefit evaluation is an economic evaluation that assesses and compares expected costs and benefits of different solutions and actions, the purpose being to choose the most profitable solution and action.
evaluación coste-beneficio
▲ *conduct a cost-benefit evaluation* llevar a cabo una evaluación coste-beneficio ▲ *form the basis of a cost-benefit evaluation* formar la base de una evaluación coste-beneficio

cost-effective
Cost-effective refers to actions or transactions that result in a reduction or a relative reduction of costs; new production processes may e.g. be cost effective.
coste-eficiente
= coste eficiente
▲ *a cost-effective production* una producción coste-eficiente ▲ *cost-effective access to relevant information* acceso coste-eficiente a información relevante ▲ *cost-effective funding* financiación coste-eficiente ▲ *cost-effective implementation* implementación coste-eficiente

cost-plus contract
→ cost plus contract

cost-plus pricing
= cost plus method, full cost pricing
Cost-plus pricing is a pricing model which seeks to add an appropriate mark-up to the supplier's cost.
contrato a coste más beneficio
▲ *use cost-plus pricing* utilizar un contrato a coste más beneficio

cost-volume-profit analysis UK/US
= CVP UK/US, CVP analysis UK/US
A cost-volume-profit analysis is the study of the effects of future output volume on sales or revenue, costs and net profit.
análisis coste-volumen-beneficio
▲ *cost-volume-profit analysis under uncertainty* análisis coste-volumen-beneficio en condiciones de incertidumbre ▲ *data collection for cost-volume-profit analysis* colección de datos para análisis coste-volumen-beneficio
⇛ breakeven analysis

cost/benefit analysis
→ cost-benefit analysis

cost/benefit balance
→ cost-benefit balance

cost/benefit evaluation
→ cost-benefit evaluation

cost/income ratio
= CIR
The cost/income ratio is a profitability ratio relevant for comparing the operating efficiency of banks. This ratio is defined as operating expenses divided by either total operating income or by total operating income and investment income.
ratio coste-beneficio
= ratio coste-ingreso
▲ *an increase in the cost/income ratio* un aumento en el ratio coste-beneficio ▲ *measure efficiency by the cost/income ratio* medir la eficiencia por el ratio coste-beneficio
⇛ cost ratio

counsel
Counsel is a term used for a legally qualified person who gives legal advice and assistance to someone.
consejero
▲ *counsel's opinion* opinión del consejero ▲ *general counsel* consejero general ▲ *in-house counsel* consejero interno ▲ *retain counsel* mantener al consejero

counter purchase transaction
= counter purchase deal
A counter purchase transaction is the exchange of goods or services between a buyer and a seller not involving consideration in the form of money. This practice is referred to as countertrading.
permuta
= trueque
▲ *the value of counter purchase transactions* el valor de las permutas

counterclaim
A counterclaim is a claim by a debtor against his creditor that can be offset against the amount the debtor owes the creditor, thereby reducing or eliminating the debt.
reclamación
▲ *anti-trust counterclaims* reclamaciones anti-trust ▲ *make a counterclaim* efectuar una reclamación ▲ *set up a counterclaim* fijar una reclamación

counterparty
A counterparty is the other party to a sale, contract, legal proceedings, negotiations etc.
parte contratante
▲ *a financial counterparty* una parte contratante financiera ▲ *an uncertain future event that adversely affects the counterparty* un acontecimiento futuro incierto que afecta negativamente a la parte contratante ▲ *contracts entered into simultaneously with a single counterparty* contratos firmados simultáneamente con una única parte contratante ▲ *counterparty credit risk* riesgo de crédito de parte contratante ▲ *counterparty failure* fallo de parte contratante ▲ *incur a loss in the event of a default by the counterparty* incurrir en una pérdida en caso de impago por la parte contratante ▲ *the same counterparty as in the barter transaction* la misma parte contratante como en el trueque ▲ *transactions executed with eligible counterparties* transacciones ejecutadas con partes contratables elegibles

counterparty risk
= counterparty exposure
Counterparty risk is the risk that an enterprise may suffer a loss due to the act or default of a counterparty to a contract, sale etc.
riesgo de parte contratante
▲ *calculate the counterparty risk* calcular el riesgo de parte contratante ▲ *counterparty risk management* gestión del riesgo de parte contratante ▲ *exposure to counterparty risk* exposición al riesgo de parte contratante ▲ *minimise the counterparty risk* minimizar el riesgo de parte contratante

countervalue
= equivalent value
The countervalue is the currency value of a transaction done by a person who buys another currency against that currency.
contracambio
= valor equivalente
▲ *the accounting countervalue of a share* el contracambio contable de una acción ▲ *the countervalue to be paid* el contracambio a pagar

country of domicile
The country in which an enterprise has its head office is called the country of domicile.
país del domicilio social
= domicilio social, nación de domicilio socia, país de la sede central
▲ *a subsidiary operating in a country other than the country of domicile of the parent* una filial que opera en un país de domicilio social distinto del de su matriz ▲ *a subsidiary operating in the country of domicile of its parent* una filial que opera en el país de domicilio social de su matriz ▲ *Denmark as the country of domicile* Dinamarca como país de domicilio social

country risk
= sovereign risk
Country risks are risks associated with operating in, trading with or holding assets in foreign countries, such as risks related to political, legal, economic, financial and social conditions.
riesgo país
= riesgo-país
≠ riesgo soberano
▲ *country risk rating* rating de riesgo país ▲ *provisions for country risk* provisiones por riesgo país ▲ *provisions for losses excluding country risk* provisiones por pérdidas excluyendo riesgo país ▲ *the applicable*

country risk classification la clasificación de riesgo país aplicable

coupon

1 The coupon or coupon rate is the nominal interest rate on a fixed-interest bond, i.e. the stated rate that determines the interest payable on the bond, expressed as a percentage of the face value of the bond.

cupón

▲ *a bond with a 7% coupon* un bono con un cupón del 7% ▲ *a high coupon* un cupón alto ▲ *a low coupon* un cupón bajo

2 A coupon is one of several detachable tags attached to a bearer security certificate, typically a bond certificate, which the holder must submit to the issuer to obtain payment of interest.

cupón

▲ *a sheet of coupons* una hoja de cupones ▲ *the clipped coupons* los cupones recortados

course cost

Course costs are costs attributable to having employees attend courses that can improve their competences related to the activities of the business.

coste de formación

▲ *invoiced course costs* costes de formación facturados ▲ *the course costs incurred* el coste de formación incurrido

course expense

Course expenses are expenses attributable to having employees attend courses that can improve their competences related to the activities of the business.

gasto de formación

= gasto en formación

▲ *invoiced course expenses excluding own payroll costs* gastos de formación facturados excluyendo los costes de sus nóminas

course of business

The course of business is the way in which an enterprise conducts, carries on and develops its business activities.

curso del negocio

▲ *an ordinary course of business* un curso ordinario del negocio ▲ *assets for sale in the normal course of business* activos para la venta en el curso normal del negocio ▲ *other matters arising in the ordinary course of business* otros asuntos surgidos en el curso ordinario del negocio ▲ *sale in the ordinary course of business* venta en el curso ordinario del negocio ▲ *the estimated selling price in the ordinary course of business* el precio estimado de venta en el curso ordinario del negocio

cover of losses

An enterprise's cover of losses constitutes the reduction of certain reserves under equity by an amount equivalent to the loss for the accounting period. Typically, capital reserves (non-distributable reserves) cannot be used to cover losses.

cobertura de pérdidas

▲ *information about the cover of losses* información sobre la cobertura de pérdidas

covered bond

Covered bonds are debt instruments secured by a cover pool of mortgage loans issued by credit institutions subject to special financial market regulation such as the EU Directive on Undertakings for Collective Investments in Transferable Securties (UCITS) and the EU Capital Requirements Directive.

bono garantizado

= bono cubierto

▲ *assign a risk weight to the covered bonds* asignar una tasa de riesgo a los bonos garantizados ▲ *claims in the form of covered bonds* reclamaciones en la forma de bonos garantizados ▲ *exposures in the form of covered bonds* riesgos en la forma de bonos garantizados ▲ *holders of covered bonds* titulares de bonos garantizados ▲ *issue covered bonds* emitir bonos garantizados ▲ *real estate collateralising covered bonds* bienes raíces como aval de fondos garantizados ▲ *the nominal amount of outstanding covered bonds* la cantidad nominal de bonos garantizados pendientes ▲ *the nominal amount outstanding on the covered bonds* el nominal pendiente de los bonos garantizados ▲ *the obligor's own issues of covered bonds* las emisiones propias de bonos garantizados por el obligacionista ▲ *the value of the total assets pledged as collaterel for the covered bonds* el valor de los activos totales pignorados como garantía de los bonos garantizados

⇛ credit institution, mortgage bond

CP

= commercial paper

CP is an abbreviation for commercial paper, which is a short-term, unsecured, negotiable loan issued by enterprises to obtain funding, usually on a discount basis with a maturity of 2 to 270 days.

papel comercial

= efecto comercial

▲ *a CP programme* un programa de papel comercial ▲ *CP issued by other companies* papel comercial emitido por otras compañías ▲ *issuance of CP* emisión de papel comercial

CPA Australia

= CPAA

CPA Australia (CPAA) is the successor to the former Australian Society of Certified Practising Accountants, one of the two major Australian professional accountancy bodies whose members may audit the financial statements of companies. The roles of the CPAA overlap with those of its sister organisation, the Institute of Chartered Accountants in Australia (ICAA), but a significant number of CPAA members are employees in the public sector, whereas most ICAA members perform audits.

CPA Australia

= Instituto Australiano de Auditores de Cuentas

▲ *become a member of CPA Australia* llegar a ser un miembro del CPA Australia

⇛ Institute of Chartered Accountants in Australia

CPI US

= Consumer Price Index US, Retail Price Index UK, RPI UK

CPI stands for Consumer Price Index and is an index showing the rise and fall in prices of consumer goods and services sold in the retail market over a period of time.

IPC

= Índice de precios al consumo

▲ *calculate the CPI* calcular el IPC ▲ *goods and services represented in the CPI* bienes y servicios representados en el IPC ▲ *measure price changes in the CPI* medir variaciones de precios en el IPC

creative accounting UK

= window dressing US

Creative accounting refers to forms of accounting that are intended to present misleadingly optimistic financial statements (window-dressing). This is not illegal as generally accepted accounting principles may be interpreted in different ways, and therefore the establishment of rules in accounting standards and for corporate governance have been established to counteract this practice.

contabilidad creativa

▲ *detect creative accounting* detectar la contabilidad creativa

⇛ accounting standard, generally accepted accounting principle

credit[1] *noun* <no indefinite article, the, no plural>

1 The term credit refers to a period of time allowed to a purchaser of goods or services before the purchaser is required to pay for them.

crédito

▲ *a credit assessment* una valoración crediticia ▲ *allow credit* permitir crédito ▲ *credit balance* saldo acreedor ▲ *credit controller* controller crediticio ▲ *credit information* información crediticia ▲ *credit sale* venta a crédito ▲ *defer payment beyond normal credit terms* diferir el pago más allá de los términos crediticios normales ▲ *extend credit* extender el crédito ▲ *open credit* crédito abierto ▲ *provide interest free credit* ofrecer crédito sin interés ▲ *purchase on credit* comprar a crédito ▲ *receive security for sale on credit* recibir garantías para la venta a crédito ▲ *recognise as interest expense over the period of credit* reconocer como gasto de interés a lo largo de la vida del crédito ▲ *sale on credit* venta a crédito ▲ *the extension of free credit on a debt* la extensión de crédito libre en una deuda

2 ≠ debit

The term credit refers to the right-hand side of an account and represents either the liabilities and equity or income of the enterprise.

haber
≠ debe
▲ *credit entry* anotación al haber ▲ *credit memorandum* memorandum de haber ▲ *credit note* abono ▲ *debit and credit balances representing deferred taxes* saldo del debe y del haber mostrando impuestos diferidos ▲ *the account shows a credit balance* la cuenta muestra un saldo en el haber

credit[2] *noun* <a, the, -s>
→ credit item

credit[3] *verb*
≠ debit
To credit is to recognise an item as a credit entry, i.e. in the right hand side of an account.

abonar
≠ cargar
▲ *credit an account with an amount* abonar una cuenta con una cantidad ▲ *credit an amount to an account* abonar una cantidad en una cuenta ▲ *credit goods returned* abonar artículos devueltos ▲ *credit to the income statement on a straight-line basis over the expected lives of the related assets* abonar al estado de ingreso en una base uniforme sobre las vidas útiles previstas de los activos relacionados ▲ *items credited or charged directly to equity* partidas abonadas o cargadas directamente a patrimonio neto ▲ *items previously charged or credited to equity* partidas previamente cargadas o abonadas a patrimonio neto ▲ *tax charged to equity* impuestos cargados a patrimonio neto

credit agreement
A credit agreement is a contract that provides for deferred payment of a debt, so that capital is available to the borrower.

póliza de crédito
▲ *a credit agreement for GBP 1.3m* una póliza de crédito por valor de 1,3 millones de libras esterlinas ▲ *a long-term credit agreement* una póliza de crédito a largo plazo ▲ *a short-term credit agreement* una póliza de crédito a corto plazo ▲ *completion of credit agreements* finalización de pólizas de crédito ▲ *sign a credit agreement* firmar una póliza de crédito

credit commitment
A credit commitment is a contract granting credit and entered into by two or more parties.

compromiso de crédito
= póliza de crédito
▲ *accept a credit commitment* aceptar un compromiso de crédito ▲ *issue letters of intent and letters of comfort for credit commitments* emitir cartas de intenciones y seguridad de compromisos de crédito ▲ *monitoring of credit commitments* control de compromisos de crédito ▲ *the company's total credit commitments* los compromisos de crédito totales de la empresa

credit derivative
A credit derivative is an over-the-counter financial instrument that can hedge against credit risk, default and credit rating downgrades. Examples are credit default swaps, credit default options and credit linked notes.

derivado de crédito
▲ *extensive use of credit derivatives* uso extensivo de derivados de crédito ▲ *the market for credit derivatives* el mercado de derivados de crédito ▲ *trading of credit derivatives* negociación de derivados de crédito

credit exposure
Credit exposure is the risk run by an enterprise that an amount receivable from a counterparty may be lost, in whole or in part, because of the default of the counterparty.

riesgo crediticio
= exposición crediticia
▲ *a cash outflow from other credit exposures* una salida de flujo de efectivo de otros riesgos crediticios ▲ *disclose information about credit exposures* divulgar información sobre riesgos crediticios

credit facility
= credit line
A credit facility is a service provided by a bank or similar type of financial institution in the form of a credit allowance within a particular limit, the credit line, which the customer may use as required subject to defined terms and conditions.

línea de crédito
▲ *a credit facility at an interest rate which is substantially below*

market rates un línea de crédito a un tipo de interés que está sustancialmente por debajo de los tipos de mercado ▲ *agreed credit facilities* líneas de crédito acordadas ▲ *an undrawn credit facility* una línea de crédito no dispuesta

credit item

A credit item is a record on the right side of an account. According to the double-entry bookkeeping system, credit items show decreases in assets and expenses or increases in liabilities, revenue and equity.

abono

▲ *a negative credit item* un abono negativo ▲ *other credit items* otros abonos ▲ *the corresponding credit item* el abono correspondiente

credit line

= line of credit

A credit line is a specified maximum amount of credit extended to a person or an enterprise by a bank or other lending institution usually based on creditworthiness. A credit line enables the person or enterprise to borrow the entire maximum amount in one borrowing or in several borrowings without having to reapply each time as long as the maximum amount is not exceeded.

línea de crédito

▲ *a counterparty credit line* una línea de crédito de la contraparte ▲ *committed credit lines* líneas de crédito comprometidas ▲ *long-term credit lines* líneas de crédito a largo plazo ▲ *short-term credit lines* líneas de crédito a corto plazo ▲ *undrawn credit lines* líneas de crédito no utilizadas ▲ *use a credit line* usar una línea de crédito

credit method

The credit method is a method for eliminating double taxation and appears from the OECD Model Tax Convention. Under the credit method, two countries that have contracted a double tax treaty agree that a resident of one contracting country that generates income or owns capital that is taxed in the other contracting country will be allowed a deduction equal to the amount of income tax paid to that other country.

método para evitar la doble imposición

▲ *grant relief under the credit method* conceder una exención aplicando el método para evitar la doble imposición

⇛ exemption method

credit period

= period of credit

The credit period is the period for which credit has been granted to a customer.

periodo de crédito

▲ *compensate for the expected loss of purchasing power during the credit period* compensar por la pérdida esperada de poder adquisitivo durante el periodo de crédito

credit rating

= credit standing

A credit rating is an assessment of the creditworthiness of a person or an enterprise to establish whether and to which extent that person or enterprise can safely be granted credit. Credit ratings are expressed by letter grades in various forms such as A, AA, Aa, BB, CCC, often combined with plus, minus or figures, and provided by credit rating agencies such as Moody's, Standard & Poor's or Dun & Bradstreet.

rating crediticio

= calificación crediticia

▲ *a high credit rating* un rating crediticio alto ▲ *a long-term credit rating* un rating crediticio a largo plazo ▲ *a satisfactory credit rating* un rating crediticio satisfactorio ▲ *a short-term credit rating* un rating crediticio a corto plazo ▲ *an attractive credit rating* un rating crediticio atractivo ▲ *an issuer with a similar credit rating* un emisor con un rating crediticio similar ▲ *make a credit rating* hacer un rating crediticio

⇛ credit rating agency

credit rating agency

A credit rating agency is a commercial enterprise engaged in assessing the creditworthiness of enterprises and debt securities and grading these according to risk and quality.

agencia de rating

= agencia de calificación

▲ *an international credit rating agency* una agencia de rating internacional ▲ *IOSCO's Code of Conduct Fundamentals for*

credit rating agencies Código de Conducta del IOSCO para las agencias de rating
⇛ credit rating

credit relief

Credit relief is a tax relief granted and corresponds to the difference between the foreign corporation tax and the higher domestic corporation tax.

dedución por doble imposición

▲ *grant credit relief* conceder deducción por doble imposición ▲ *grant credit relief* conceder deducción por doble imposición ▲ *maximum credit relief* deducción por doble imposición máxima

credit risk

A credit risk is the risk involved in granting credit. It is the risk that the borrower will fail to discharge the obligations related to the loan, including the payment of interest and instalments, in this way causing the lender to incur a financial loss.

riesgo crediticio

= riesgo de crédito, riesgo de insolvencia

▲ *assume a credit risk* asumir un riesgo crediticio ▲ *assume the credit risk* asumir el riesgo crediticio ▲ *assumption of credit risk* asunción de riesgo crediticio ▲ *be exposed to credit risks* estar expuestos a riesgos crediticios ▲ *credit risk management* gestión del riesgo crediticio ▲ *derivative instruments for the transfer of credit risk* instrumentos derivados para el traspaso del riesgo crediticio ▲ *enterprise-specific credit risk* riesgo crediticio específico de empresa ▲ *exposed to credit risk* expuesto a riesgo crediticio ▲ *financial assets exposed to credit risk* activos financieros expuestos a riesgo crediticio ▲ *fully eliminated credit risk* riesgo crediticio eliminado completamente ▲ *hedge a credit risk* cubrir un riesgo crediticio ▲ *hedging of credit risk* cobertura de riesgo crediticio ▲ *increase the credit risk* aumentar el riesgo crediticio ▲ *limit the credit risk* limitar el riesgo crediticio ▲ *manage the credit risk* gestionar el riesgo crediticio ▲ *mediation of credit risk* mediación de riesgo crediticio ▲ *monitor the credit risk* controlar el riesgo crediticio ▲ *quantify the credit risk* cuantificar el riesgo crediticio ▲ *reduce the credit risk* reducir el riesgo crediticio ▲ *reduce the credit risk significantly* reducir el riesgo crediticio significativamente ▲ *significant concentrations of credit risk* concentraciones significativas de riesgo crediticio ▲ *spread the credit risk* extender el riesgo crediticio ▲ *subject to credit risk* supeditado a riesgo crediticio ▲ *substantially different credit risks* riesgos crediticios sustancialmente diferentes ▲ *the amount exposed to credit risk* la cantidad expuesta a riesgo crediticio ▲ *transfer the credit risk* traspasar el riesgo crediticio

creditor

A creditor is an individual or business to whom money, goods or services are owed by the enterprise.

acreedor

▲ *creditor suit* demanda al acreedor ▲ *creditor turnover* facturación al acreedor ▲ *eliminate all or a portion of an amount due to a creditor* eliminar toda o parte de una cantidad adeudada a un acreedor ▲ *other creditors including taxation and social security* otros acreedores incluyendo tributación y seguridad social ▲ *preferential creditor* acreedor preferente ▲ *present and prospective creditors* acreedores actuales y potenciales ▲ *secured creditor* acreedor asegurado ▲ *subordinate a claim to rank after all the enterprise's other creditors* condicionar una reclamación a situar después de todos los demás acreedores de la empresa ▲ *the debtor's primary obligation to the creditor* la obligación primaria del deudor al acreedor ▲ *the enterprise's creditors* los acreedores de la empresa ▲ *the reporting enterprise's own creditors* los acreedores propios de la empresa informante ▲ *unsecured creditor* acreedor no asegurado
⇛ debtor

creditor, amount falling due after more than one year UK

= creditor due after more than one year GB, long-term creditor, long-term debt US, IAS/IFRS
≠ creditor, amount falling due within one year UK

Creditors, amounts falling due after more than one year is an item in the balance sheet constituting long-term liabilities other than provisions, such as bank loans and overdrafts as well as other long-term creditors.

cuenta acreedora con vencimiento superior a un año

= cuenta acreedora a largo plazo

▲ *include under creditors, amounts falling due after more than one year* incluir en cuentas acreedoras con vencimiento superior a un año

⇛ long-term borrowing, non-current liability

creditor, amount falling due within one year UK

= account payable IAS/IFRS, creditor due within one year UK, payable IAS/IFRS/US, short-term creditor, short-term debt IAS/IFRS, US

≠ long-term debt UK

Creditors falling due within one year are recognised as current liabilities other than provisions in the balance sheet and constitute businesses or individuals to whom an organisation owes money on a short term.

cuenta acreedora con vencimiento inferior a un año

= cuenta acreedora a corto plazo

▲ *current assets less amounts falling due within one year* activos actuales menos cuentas acreedoras con vencimiento inferior a un año

⇛ account payable, short-term borrowing

creditor days ratio

= days' payable outstanding, DPO

Creditor days ratio is a financial ratio measuring how long it takes an enterprise on average to pay its trade payables, i.e. trade creditors.

rotación de acreedores

≠ rotación de deudores

▲ *a decrease in the creditor days ratio* una disminución en la rotación de acreedores ▲ *an increase in the creditor days ratio* un incremento en la rotación de acreedores

creditor due after more than one year

→ creditor, amount falling due after more than one year

creditor due within one year

→ creditor, amount falling due within one year

creditors

Creditors is an item in the balance sheet under liabilities, expressing short-term debt, i.e. debt falling due within one year, or long-term debt: debt falling due after more than one year.

acreedores

▲ *long-term creditors* acreedores a largo plazo ▲ *short-term creditors* acreedores a corto plazo

⇛ creditor, creditors, amount falling due after more than one year, creditors, amount falling due within one year

creditors' ledger UK

= bought ledger, purchases ledger US

≠ debtors' ledger UK, sales ledger US

A creditors' or purchases ledger is a book or group of accounts containing the individual creditors' accounts, i.e. amounts owed to suppliers. The creditors' ledger records purchases, payments made and discounts received. Today, creditors' ledgers are usually stored on computer files that have replaced the old-time binders.

libro mayor de acreedores

= registro de acreedores

≠ registro de deudores

▲ *balances from creditors' ledger* saldos del libro mayor de acreedores

⇛ nominal ledger

creditworthy

If a person or enterprise is creditworthy, it means that the financial position of the person or enterprise justifies the granting of credit to that person or enterprise.

solvente

▲ *a creditworthy third party* una tercera parte solvente ▲ *confirmation that the guarantor is creditworthy in relation to the size of the guaranteed debt* confirmación de que el avalista es solvente en relación con la cantidad de la deuda garantizada

cross currency

Cross-currencies are two currencies that are compared, typically non-standard currencies in the country where they are quoted. The exchange rate between the two currencies is the cross rate, appearing as e.g. the DKK/JPY cross. The exchange rate between the two currencies may also be based on a third currency, typically the US dollar.

divisa cruzada

▲ *cross currency trading* negociación en divisa cruzada

cross-sectional comparison

A cross-sectional comparison is an assessment of an individual, enterprise, industry or country based on the comparison of a number of selected variables with variables from peer groups or industry averages for the same period.

comparación intersectorial

▲ *a cross-sectional comparison of compensation and wage costs* una comparación intersectorial de costes por salarios semanales e indemnización ▲ *conduct a cross-sectional comparison* realizar una comparación intersectorial

CSR

= corporate social responsibility, social responsibility

CSR is the abbreviation for corporate social responsibility, which is the obligation and awareness of enterprises to employees, stakeholders and the society at large to act in decision-making and business operations in a way that meets the ethical, business, public and legal expectations of society to a business organisation. The focus is on obtaining sustainable development not only economically, but also for social and environmental purposes.

responsabilidad social corporativa

▲ *adopt a CSR policy* adoptar una política de responsabilidad social corporativa ▲ *develop a best practice on CSR* desarrollar mejores prácticas de responsabilidad social corporativa ▲ *enhance the development and transparency of CSR* fomentar el desarrollo y transparencia de la responsabilidad social corporativa

CT UK

CT is the abbreviation of corporation tax, i.e. the tax payable by UK incorporated and unincorporated companies (excluding partnerships and local authorities) on earned profits, i.e. the value added gained.

impuesto de sociedades

▲ *CT paid* impuesto de sociedades pagado ▲ *exempt from CT* exención del impuesto de sociedades

⇛ corporation tax

cum

= with

"Cum" is a Latin preposition meaning "with"or "including".

con

= cum

▲ *cum coupon* con cupón ▲ *cum div.* con dividendo incluido

cum dividend

→ cum-dividend

cum-dividend

≠ ex-dividend

Cum-dividend means "with dividend" and refers to securities sold with the benefit of the next dividend payable.

con dividendo

= cum dividendo

≠ ex dividendo

▲ *a purchaser of securities cum-dividend* un comprador de títulos con dividendo ▲ *the purchase of a share cum-dividend* la compra de una acción con dividendo

cumdividend

→ cum-dividend

cumulative average-time learning model

The cumulative average-time learning model is a learning-curve model which shows that the accumulated average time per unit produced decreases by a constant percentage each time the accumulated quantity of units produced is doubled.

NOTE Learning curves are functions used in management and cost accounting to predict how labour costs will decline as more units are produced, i.e. as workers become more efficient from learning.

modelo de aprendizaje acumulativo temporal

▲ *under a cumulative average-time learning model* según un modelo de aprendizaje acumulativo temporal

⇛ incremental unit-time learning model

cumulative preference share

With a cumulative preference share any preference dividend not paid in one year will be carried forward so that, in a future year, any arrears will be paid before any other shareholders will get a dividend.

acción preferente por dividendo acumulado

▲ *cumulative preference shares that are classified as equity* acciones preferentes por dividendo acumulado que se clasifican como patrimonio neto ▲ *cumulative preference shares that are held by minority interests* acciones preferentes por dividendo acumulado que mantienen los accionistas minoritarios ▲ *outstanding cumulative preference shares* acciones preferentes por dividendo acumulado pendiente de pago ▲ *the after-tax amount of the preference dividends for cumulative preference shares required for the period* la cantidad después de impuestos de los dividendos preferentes por acciones preferentes por dividendo acumulado requerida en el ejercicio

⇛ cumulative preferred stock

cumulative preferred stock US

Cumulative preference stock is a type of stock whose dividends not paid in one year accumulate to be carried forward so that, in a future year, any arrears will be paid before any other stockholders will get a dividend.

acción preferente por dividendo acumulado

▲ *tier 1 capital plus cumulative preferred stock* capital tier 1 más acción preferente por dividendo acumulado

⇛ cumulative preference share

currency

Currency refers to the monetary unit applied by and in circulation in a particular state or country.

divisa

= moneda extranjera

▲ *a foreign currency* una divisa extranjera ▲ *a severe devaluation or depreciation of a currency* una devaluación o apreciación significativa de una divisa ▲ *capitalisation of losses resulting from severe currency devaluations* capitalización de pérdidas resultantes de devaluaciones significativas de divisas ▲ *convertible currency* divisa convertible ▲ *currency adjustment* ajuste de divisa ▲ *currency invoicing* facturación en divisa ▲ *domestic currency* divisa nacional ▲ *index-linked bonds of the same currency and term* bonos indexados de la misma divisa y término ▲ *local currency* divisa local ▲ *report in the currency of a hyperinflationary economy* informe en la divisa de una economía hiperinflacionista ▲ *risks arising from currency fluctuations* riesgos surgidos de las fluctuaciones de la divisa ▲ *specify the currency in which the enterprise presents its financial statements* especificar la divisa en la que la empresa presenta sus estados financieros ▲ *the currency in which the benefits are to be paid* la divisa en la que se tienen que pagar los beneficios ▲ *the currency of the corporate bonds* la divisa de los bonos corporativos ▲ *the currency of the country in which the enterprise is domiciled* la divisa del país en el que la empresa está domiciliada ▲ *translated into Danish currency* convertido a divisa danesa

⇛ foreign currency

currency contract

= foreign currency contract

A currency contract is a contract for the purchase or sale of a given currency. Currency contracts are often applied as hedges against foreign exchange risk, e.g. foreign exchange fluctuations affecting debt, payables or receivables. Examples are currency futures and forward contracts.

contrato de divisa

= contrato en divisa

▲ *loss on currency contracts* pérdida en los contratos de divisa ▲ *use currency contracts to hedge foreign exchange risks at market value* usar contratos de divisa para cubrir los riesgos del tipo de cambio al valor de mercado

⇛ forward contract, futures contract

currency cost

Currency costs are costs incurred in local or foreign currencies, e.g. in connection with loan financing.

coste de conversión de moneda

▲ *total currency costs* total costes de conversión de moneda

currency exposure

= currency translation exposure, foreign currency exposure

Currency exposure is the risk that the actual value of assets, liabilities and earnings may change because of exchange rate fluctuations.

exposición en divisa

= operación en divisa

▲ *currency exposure related to net assets in foreign companies* exposición en divisa relacionada con activos netos en empresas extranjeras ▲ *hedge of currency exposure* cobertura de la exposición en divisa ▲ *reduce the currency exposure* reducir la exposición en divisa ▲ *special currency exposure* exposición en divisa especial

currency hedging

= currency hedge, foreign currency hedging

Currency hedging is the use of financial transactions to offset currency exposures arising from foreign exchange fluctuations. These transactions typically involve hedging instruments, i.e. derivative financial instruments such as options and forward contracts.

cobertura en divisa

▲ *currency hedging of a future goods purchase* cobertura en divisa de una compra futura de bienes

⇛ derivative financial instrument, forward contract

currency mix

The currency mix shows the distribution of currencies, often as percentages, related to the international operations of an enterprise, used e.g. to illustrate the foreign currency exposure and the net currency position.

combinación de divisas

▲ *currency mix changes* fluctuaciones en la combinación de divisas ▲ *the currency mix of borrowings* la combinación de divisas de los créditos

currency option

= foreign currency option

A currency option is the right to buy or sell a particular currency within a specified period at an agreed fixed exchange rate.

opción en divisa

▲ *currency options signed* opciones en divisa firmadas ▲ *exercise a currency option* ejercer una opción en divisa ▲ *sign a currency option* firmar una opción en divisa ▲ *using currency options* usando opciones en divisa

currency position

= foreign currency position

A currency position is a placement in one or more specified currencies that entails foreign exchange risk. The currency position reflects the unhedged cash flows that are exposed to exchange rate changes.

posición en divisa

▲ *a long currency position* una posición en divisa a largo ▲ *a short currency position* una posición en divisa a corto ▲ *an open currency position* una posición en divisa abierta ▲ *the underlying currency position* la posición en divisa subyacente

currency risk

= foreign currency risk, foreign exchange risk

Currency risk is the exposure to losses as a consequence of developments in foreign exchange rates being different from what was expected at the time of decision-making.

riesgo de divisa

= riesgo de cambio

▲ *an expected currency risk* un riesgo de divisa previsto ▲ *changes in currency risk* fluctuaciones en riesgo de divisa ▲ *commercial currency risks* riesgos de divisa comerciales ▲ *currency risk of Danish subsidiaries with foreign business* riesgo de divisa de las filiales danesas con negocios en el extranjero ▲ *hedge a currency risk* cubrir un riesgo de divisa ▲ *hedging of a currency risk* cobertura de un riesgo de divisa ▲ *measures against future currency risks* medidas contra riesgos de divisa futuros ▲ *reduce the currency risk* reducir el riesgo de divisa ▲ *the underlying currency risks* los riesgos de divisa subyacentes

⇛ currency translation exposure, translation

currency swap

= currency swap agreement

A currency swap is a financial contract involving the exchange of a particular amount of both interest and the principal in one currency for another currency on agreed terms. A currency swap transaction can also involve the simultaneous purchase or sale of an amount in one currency in the spot market against a corresponding sale or purchase of the same amount in the same currency in the forward market.

swap de divisa

= permuta financiera de divisa

▲ *hedge via currency swaps* cubrir mediante swaps de divisa ▲ *use currency swaps to minimise currency risks* usar swaps de divisa para minimizar los riesgos en divisa

currency translation

Currency translation is the translation of one currency, typically the foreign currency of a subsidiary, into the presentation currency of the parent company of the subsidiary's assets, liabilities, operating results and other items for recognition in the consolidated financial statements.

conversión de divisa

▲ *currency translation differences* diferencias por conversión de divisa ▲ *currency translation gains and losses* pérdidas y ganancias por conversión de divisa ▲ *currency translation of goodwill* conversión de divisa del fondo de comercio ▲ *exposed to currency translation risk* expuesto al riesgo de conversión de divisa

currency translation difference

Currency translation differences are the differences arising when restating amounts in foreign currencies to the presentation currency. Depending on the changes in exchange rates between the transaction and translation dates, gains or losses will arise.

diferencia de cambio

= diferencia en la conversión de divisa

▲ *accounting classification of currency translation differences* clasificación contable de las diferencias de cambio ▲ *accumulated currency translation difference* diferencia de cambio acumulada ▲ *currency translation differences arising in the year* diferencias de cambio resultantes en el ejercicio ▲ *currency translation differences arising on non-monetary items* diferencias de cambio resultantes de partidas no monetarias ▲ *currency translation differences classified in equity* diferencias de cambio imputadas a patrimonio neto

currency translation reserve

→ foreign currency translation reserve

currency unit

A currency unit refers to the type of money or currency of a particular country such as kroner, euro, yen or dollar.

unidad de divisa

▲ *pay two million currency units* pagar dos millones en unidades de divisa ▲ *the insignificant risk of losing one currency unit* el riesgo insignificante de perder una unidad de divisa

current

1 ≠ long-term UK, non-current IAS/IFRS, US

Within the context of accounting, current refers to something that takes place or falls due within a year.

corriente

▲ *current and non-current liabilities* pasivo corriente y no corriente ▲ *current borrowings* empréstitos corrientes ▲ *current debt* deuda corriente ▲ *current liabilities* pasivos corrientes ▲ *current maturities of long-term debt* vencimientos corrientes de la deuda a largo plazo ▲ *current portion of interest-bearing borrowings* parte corriente de empréstitos que generan intereses ▲ *current portion of long-term liabilities* parte corriente del pasivo a largo plazo ▲ *current receivable* cuenta deudora corriente ▲ *total assets less current liabilities* total activos menos pasivos corrientes

2 = continuing, ongoing

Current means occuring or in force at present or belonging to the present time.

actual

= presente

▲ *a current liability* un pasivo actual ▲ *current actuarial assumptions* supuestos actuariales actuales ▲ *current and deferred tax assets and liabilities* activos y pasivos por impuesto corriente y diferido ▲ *current and prior periods* periodos actual y anterior ▲ *current commitments* compromisos actuales ▲ *current employees* empleados actuales ▲ *current estimates of contract revenue and contract costs* estimaciones actuales de ingresos y costes contractuales ▲ *current expenditure* gasto actual ▲ *current expenses* gastos actuales ▲ *current IASB practice* práctica IASB actual ▲ *current income* ingreso actual ▲ *current market interest rates* tipos de interés de mercado actual ▲ *current payments* pagos actuales ▲ *current portion of interest-bearing borrowings* parte actual de empréstitos que generan intereses ▲ *current receipts* recibos actuales ▲ *current replacement costs* costes de sustitución actuales ▲ *current salary levels* niveles salariales actuales ▲ *current sales* ventas actuales ▲ *current service cost* costes de servicios actuales ▲ *have a direct impact on current cash flows* tener un impacto directo en los flujos de efectivo actuales ▲ *in the light of current conditions* a la luz de las condiciones presentes ▲ *net profit or loss for the current period* resultado neto del periodo actual ▲ *the current and future tax consequences* las consecuencias presentes y futuras de los impuestos ▲ *the current cash sales price of the goods or services* el precio actual en efectivo de venta de los bienes o servicios ▲ *the current financial year* el ejercicio presente ▲ *the current interim period* el periodo intermedio actual ▲ *the current period* el periodo actual ▲ *the net current selling price of the asset* el precio actual neto de venta del activo

current amount payable US
= current payable
A current amount payable is money owed on a short term, i.e. payable within one year. In the balance sheet, current amounts payable are recognised under current liabilities.
deuda a corto plazo
= deuda con vencimiento en el año
▲ *current assets less current amounts payable* activos corrientes menos deudas a corto plazo ▲ *payables to suppliers and other current amounts payable* deudas a proveedores y otras deudas a corto plazo

current asset
An asset must be classified as a current asset if that asset is expected to be realised in, or is held for sale or consumption in, the normal course of the enterprise's operating cycle, is held primarily for trading purposes and not for permanent ownership or use, and is expected to be realised within the foreseeable future or is cash or cash equivalents that are not restricted in use.
activo corriente
= activo circulante
≠ activo no corriente
NOTE Spanish traditional accounting texts used 'activo circulante' before the introduction of 'activo corriente' through the translations of IAS/IFRS texts.
▲ *a manufactured current asset* un activo corriente manufacturado ▲ *changes in the value of current assets* cambios en el valor de activos corrientes ▲ *classified as a current asset* clasificado como un activo corriente ▲ *current and non-current assets and liabilities* activos y pasivos corrientes y no corrientes ▲ *current asset investments* inversiones en activos corrientes ▲ *current assets: inventory* activos corrientes: inventario ▲ *current assets: receivables* activos corrientes: cuentas a cobrar ▲ *current assets that are used in the operating activities of the segment* activos corrientes que se utilizan en las actividades de explotación del segmento ▲ *investments held as current assets* inversiones mantenidas como activos corrientes ▲ *part of the current assets of the consolidated group* parte de los activos corrientes del grupo consolidado ▲ *presentation of current assets and current liabilities* presentación de activos y pasivos corrientes ▲ *the net realisable value of current assets* el valor neto realizable de activos corrientes

current cost
Current cost is the amount of cash or cash equivalents required to buy an asset (or an equivalent asset) now, regardless of the amount paid for the asset in the past.
valor actual
= coste corriente
NOTE The IAS/IFRS term 'coste corriente' is an anglicism that is not used in Spanish accounting texts.
▲ *current cost financial statements* estados financieros a va-

lor actual ▲ *current cost income statement* estado de ingresos a valor actual ▲ *determine current costs* determinar valores actuales ▲ *disclose the current cost of property, plant and equipment* publicar el valor actual de edificios, instalaciones y equipos ▲ *in terms of current costs* en términos de valores actuales ▲ *items stated at current cost* partidas reflejadas a valor actual ▲ *shows current cost in place of historical cost* muestra valor actual en lugar de coste histórico ▲ *the current cost approach* el criterio de valor actual ▲ *the lower of current cost at the balance sheet date and net realisable value* el valor actual más bajo a la fecha del balance y valor neto realizable

⇛ fair value, historical cost

current cost accounting

= CCA

Current cost accounting is a method of accounting in which the costs and revenues of an enterprise are recorded after taking into account the assets' current replacement cost as well as the effect of inflation on asset values and liabilities.

contabilidad a valor actual

= contabilidad a coste corriente

▲ *current cost accounting report* informe de contabilidad a valor actual ▲ *evaluation of current cost accounting methods* evaluación de los métodos de contabilidad a valor actual

⇛ cost of sales adjustment, historical cost convention

current cost accounts

Current cost accounts are presented under the current cost approach and use replacement cost as the primary measurement basis.

cuentas a valor actual

= cuentas a coste corriente

▲ *prepare current cost accounts* preparar las cuentas a coste corriente ▲ *published current cost accounts* cuentas a valor actual publicadas

current cost approach IAS/IFRS

The current cost approach is an alternative to the historical cost approach. Under this method of accounting, balance sheet items are typically measured at replacement cost, i.e. the amount of cash required to buy an asset now, rather than the amount paid for the asset in the past, in this way reflecting the changes in the value of assets, however, not including any inflation adjustments. The current cost income statement reports the costs that were current when transactions were made, cost of sales when consumption occurred, and sales when made, and therefore restatement of all income statement amounts into the measuring unit at the balance sheet date must be made on the basis of a general price index.

NOTE IAS 15 Information Reflecting the Effects of Changing Prices was withdrawn with effect from January 1, 2005. In an IFRS context, current cost financial statements are dealt with in IAS 29 Financial Reporting in Hyperinflationary Economies.

método del coste corriente

= criterio del coste actual, criterio del valor actual

▲ *financial statements based on a current cost approach* estados financieros basados en un método del coste corriente

SOURCE IAS 15

⇛ cost of sales adjustment, historical cost convention, replacement cost

current currency unit

1 The current currency unit is the currency applicable in a country at present.

unidad de moneda corriente

= unidad de cuenta corriente

▲ *apply the current currency unit* aplicar la unidad de moneda corriente ▲ *calculated in current currency units* calculado en las unidades de moneda corriente

2 Current currency units are currency amounts restated and adjusted for any inflation occurring between the transaction date and the balance sheet date.

unidad de cuenta corriente

▲ *restatement of accounting figures in terms of current currency units* actualización de cifras contables en términos de unidad de cuenta corriente

current exchange rate

The current exchange rate is the spot rate quoted for delivery now rather than in future.

tipo de cambio en el mercado al contado
≠ tipo de cambio en el mercado de futuros
▲ *at the current exchange rate* al tipo de cambio en el mercado al contado ▲ *use the current exchange rate for translation* usar el tipo de cambio en el mercado al contado para conversión

current exit value
= CEV
The current exit value is the amount that an insurer expects it will have to pay on the balance sheet date for immediately transferring its remaining contractual obligations and rights to another enterprise.
valor de realización actual
▲ *measure at current exit value* medir al valor de realización actual ▲ *the current exit value of reinsurance assets* el valor de realización actual de los activos de reaseguro

current interest rate
= current rate, current rate of interest
The current interest rate is the rate that is prevailing or quoted today.
tipo de interés actual
▲ *determine at appropriate current interest rates* determinar a tipos de interés actuales apropiados ▲ *the current interest rate levels* los niveles del tipo de interés actual

current liability IAS/IFRS, US
≠ long-term liability US, non-current liability IAS/IFRS
Current liabilities are liabilities representing amounts expected settled in the normal course of an enterprise's operations or due for settlement within one year from the balance sheet date. As a balance sheet item under liabilities, current liabilities include e.g. payables, short-term debt and provisions.
pasivo corriente
≠ pasivo no corriente
▲ *any liability that has been excluded from current liabilities* cualquier pasivo que ha sido excluido de pasivos corrientes ▲ *classified as a current liability* clasificado como un pasivo corriente ▲ *current liabilities: payables* pasivos corrientes: cuentas a pagar ▲ *make provisions for dividends as a current liability* incluir provisiones para dividendos como un pasivo corriente ▲ *presentation of current assets and current liabilities* presentación de activos y pasivos corrientes

current liability other than provision IAS/IFRS
= short-term liabilities other than provisions
Current liabilities other than provisions are liabilities representing amounts expected to be settled in the normal course of an enterprise's operations or due for settlement within one year from the balance sheet date excluding provisions, i.e. amounts set aside for anticipated liabilities.
pasivo corriente diferente de provisión
▲ *current assets less current liabilities other than provisions* activos corrientes menos pasivos corrientes diferentes de provisiones

current maturities of long-term debt US
= current portion of long-term borrowings IAS/IFRS, current portion of long-term debt UK, portion of long-term debt due within one year US
The current maturities of long-term debt is an item under current liabilities in the balance sheet recognising the amount of the debt falling due and payable within the next financial year.
vencimientos corrientes de la deuda a largo plazo
▲ *repayment of current maturities of long-term debt* refinanciación de los vencimientos corrientes de la deuda a largo plazo ▲ *report current maturities of long-term debt as current liabilities* informar de vencimientos corrientes de la deuda a largo plazo ▲ *total current maturities of long-term debt* total vencimientos corriente de la deuda a largo plazo

current portion of long-term borrowings IAS/IFRS
= current maturities of long-term debt US, current portion of long-term debt UK
The current portion of long-term borrowings is an item under current liabilities in the

balance sheet recognising the amount of the debt falling due and payable within the next financial year.

parte actual de los empréstitos a largo plazo

▲ *decrease in current portion of long-term borrowings* disminución de la parte actual de los empréstitos a largo plazo ▲ *less current portion of long term borrowings* menos la parte actual de los empréstitos a largo plazo ▲ *short-term borrowings and current portion of long term borrowings* empréstitos a corto plazo y la parte actual de los empréstitos a largo plazo

current portion of long-term debt

UK

= current maturities of long-term

debt US, current portion of long-term borrowings IAS/IFRS

The current portion of long-term debt is an item under current liabilities in the balance sheet recognising the amount of the debt falling due and payable within the next financial year.

parte actual de los empréstitos a largo plazo

▲ *a drop in the current portion of long-term debt* una caída en la parte actual de los empréstitos a largo plazo ▲ *less current portion of long-term debt from continuing operations* menos la parte actual de los empréstitos a largo plazo de las operaciones continuas ▲ *short-term borrowings and current portion of long-term debt* empréstitos a corto plazo y la parte actual de los empréstitos a largo plazo

current price

1 The current price is the latest price quoted on the stock exchange for a security.

precio actual

▲ *current prices for similar financial instruments* el precio actual de los instrumentos financieros similares ▲ *the current price of the underlying securities* el precio actual de los títulos subyacentes ▲ *the current price of the underlying shares* el precio actual de las acciones subyacentes

SOURCE IAS 39, paragraph AG 72, IFRS 2, paragraph B6(c)

⇛ market price

2 = spot price

≠ forward price

The current price is today's price in an active market for an asset, e.g. properties, commodities or other products or services.

precio actual

▲ *current prices on an active market* precios actuales en un mercado activo

SOURCE IAS 40, paragraphs 45 and 46

current rate

1 = current exchange rate, current rate of exchange, spot rate

≠ forward rate

The current rate is the spot rate, i.e. the rate of exchange quoted for delivery now rather than in future.

tipo de cambio vigente

= tipo de cambio actual, tipo de cambio al contado

≠ tipo de cambio futuro

▲ *the current rate of the underlying shares* el tipo de cambio vigente de las acciones subyacentes

⇛ foreign exchange

2 = current interest rate, current rate of interest

The current rate is the interest rate that is prevailing or quoted today.

tipo de interés corriente

= tipo de interés actual

▲ *at the current rate* al tipo de interés actual

current rate method

The current rate method is a foreign currency translation method applied for translating financial statements of foreign subsidiaries from their local currencies into the presentation currency of the parent on consolidation. By this method all balance sheet and income statement elements are translated at the current exchange rates, i.e. at the rates at the balance sheet date for assets and liabilities and at the dates of recognition for revenues, expenses, gains and losses.

método de tipo de cambio corriente

= método al tipo de cambio actual, método al tipo de cambio vigente

▲ *translate the income statement using the current rate method* convertir el estado de resultados usando el método de tipo de cambio corriente ▲ *under the current rate method* según el método de tipo de cambio corriente ▲ *use the current rate method* usar el método de tipo de cambio corriente
⇛ average rate method, closing rate method, temporal method

current rate of exchange
The current rate of exchange is the spot rate quoted for delivery now rather than in future.
tipo de cambio al contado
= tipo de cambio actual, tipo de cambio corriente
≠ tipo de cambio futuro
▲ *at the current rate of exchange* al tipo de cambio al contado ▲ *use the current rate of exchange on translation* usar el tipo de cambio al contado en la conversión

current rate of interest
= current interest rate, current rate
The current rate of interest is the rate that is prevailing or quoted today.
tipo de interés corriente
= tipo de interés actual, tipo de interés vigente
▲ *at the current rate of interest* al tipo de interés corriente

current ratio
= working capital ratio UK
The current ratio is a financial ratio defined as total current assets divided by total current liabilities at balance sheet date. The ratio measures the liquidity of an enterprise, and the higher the ratio is, the more it is probable that the enterprise is able to pay its creditors; however, a ratio that is too high may indicate poor liquidity management.
ratio de liquidez
▲ *compute the current ratio* calcular el ratio de liquidez
⇛ acid test ratio, liquidity ratio, liquidity test, quick ratio

current service cost IAS/IFRS
≠ past service cost
Current service cost is the increase in the value of pension obligations as a result of services rendered by employees in the current accounting period.
coste de los servicios del ejercicio corriente
= coste de los servicios del periodo corriente
▲ *determine the current service costs* determinar los costes de los servicios del ejercicio corriente ▲ *measurement of current service costs* medición de costes de los servicios del ejercicio corriente ▲ *recognition of current service costs* reconocimiento de costes de los servicios del periodo corriente
SOURCE IAS 19

current tax
Current tax is the amount of income taxes payable to, or recoverable from, the tax authorities based on the taxable profit, or tax loss, for the financial year.
impuesto corriente
▲ *any adjustments recognised in the period for current tax of prior periods* cualesquiera ajustes reconocidos en el ejercicio por impuesto corriente de ejercicios anteriores ▲ *current tax expense* gasto por impuesto corriente ▲ *current tax for current and prior financial years* impuesto corriente para el ejercicio presente y el anterior ▲ *current tax income* ingreso por impuesto corriente ▲ *current tax on the profit for the year* impuesto corriente sobre el beneficio del ejercicio ▲ *current tax receivable* impuesto corriente a cobrar ▲ *recover current tax* recuperar impuesto corriente
⇛ current tax asset, current tax liability

current tax expense
Current tax expense refers to the amount of tax payable or estimated to be payable by an enterprise in respect of its taxable profit or loss for the current accounting period. The payment of tax is recognised in the profit and loss account.
gasto por impuesto corriente
▲ *gross-up current tax expense* calcular el bruto del gasto por impuesto corriente ▲ *reduce current tax expense* reducir el gasto por impuesto corriente

current tax for the year
The current tax for the year is the tax on the taxable income for the year plus any ad-

justments of current tax for previous years.
impuesto corriente del ejercicio
▲ *current tax for the year concerning changes in equity* impuesto corriente del ejercicio relativo a variaciones en patrimonio neto ▲ *current tax for the year including enterprises participating in the joint taxation* impuesto corriente del ejercicio incluyendo las empresas que participan en la tributación conjunta

current tax liability
A current tax liability is current tax for the current and previous financial years that is still unpaid.
pasivo por impuesto corriente
▲ *have an immediate effect on the enterprise's current tax liabilities or assets* tener un efecto inmediato en el activo o pasivo por impuesto corriente de la empresa ▲ *offset current tax assets and current tax liabilities* compensar activos por impuesto corriente y pasivos por impuesto corriente ▲ *recognition of current tax liabilities* reconocimiento de pasivos por impuesto corriente ▲ *set off a current tax asset against a current tax liability* compensar un activo por impuesto corriente con un pasivo por impuesto corriente ▲ *settle current tax liabilities on a net basis* pagar pasivos por impuesto corriente en base a un método neto
⇛ deferred tax

current tax payable IAS/IFRS
= corporation tax UK, income taxes payable US
"Current tax payable" is an item recognised under current liabilities in the balance sheet and relates to the tax expense for the current and previous financial years that remains to be paid.
hacienda pública acreedora por impuesto sobre sociedades
= impuesto corriente a pagar
NOTE Spanish accountants use 'hacienda pública acreedora por impuesto sobre sociedades' instead of the IAS/IFRS term 'impuesto corriente a pagar'.
▲ *current tax payable for the financial year* hacienda pública acreedora por impuesto sobre sociedades del ejercicio ▲ *total current tax payable* total hacienda pública acreedora por impuesto sobre sociedades
⇛ deferred tax

currently attainable standard
= normal standard
A currently attainable standard is an average standard or level of performance that is normally reached under usual efficient operating conditions allowing for normal breakdowns etc.
nivel de funcionamiento estándar
▲ *approach the currently attainable standard* acercarse al nivel de funcionamiento estándar

curtailment
A curtailment is a reduction of the headcount or activities of an enterprise or a partial closing-down of production plant or the like, typically in connection with related restructuring activities. In the context of pension plans, besides relating to the an enterprise's reduction in the number of employees covered by a defined benefit plan, curtailment also refers to the enterprise's amendments to the terms of the plan to the effect that existing employees will not qualify for benefits in respect of some future service or only for reduced benefits.
recorte
= reducción
▲ *a curtailment arising from an isolated event* un recorte originado por un acontecimiento puntual ▲ *a curtailment of retirement benefits* un recorte de las prestaciones por jubilación ▲ *make curtailments* hacer recortes ▲ *qualify as a curtailment* calificar como un recorte ▲ *recognise gains or losses on the curtailment of a defined benefit plan* reconocer los resultados por el recorte en un plan de prestación definida ▲ *the effect of any curtailments* el efecto de cualesquiera recortes ▲ *when the curtailment occurs* cuando se lleva a cabo el recorte
SOURCE IAS 19, paragraph 111
⇛ curtailment gain, curtailment loss, defined benefit plan

curtailment gain
A curtailment gain is a gain resulting from any changes in the present value of defined

benefit obligations or in the fair value of pension plan assets arising in connection with a reduction of the headcount or total or partial closing down of activities or plan, typically in connection with a restructuring. Such a reduction will lead to a reduction in the pension plan obligation and lower pension plan expenses to be recognised in the financial statements after restating the pension obligations and the plan assets involved on the basis of current actuarial assumptions.

ganancia por reducción
= beneficio por recorte
▲ *recognition of a curtailment gain* reconocimiento de una ganancia por reducción

curtailment loss
= loss on curtailment
A curtailment loss is a loss resulting from any change in the present value of defined benefit obligations or in the fair value of pension plan assets arising in connection with a reduction of the headcount or total or partial closing down of activities or plan, typically in connection with a restructuring. Such a reduction will lead to higher pension plan expenses to be recognised in the financial statements after restating the pension obligations and the plan assets involved on the basis of current actuarial assumptions.

pérdida por reducción
= pérdida por recorte
▲ *recognition of a curtailment loss* reconocimiento de una pérdida por reducción

custodian
= account-holding
A custodian or custodian bank is a bank or other financial institution that has the legal responsibility for a customer's securities. This implies registration of share certificates and other investment securities with a securities centre on behalf of legal and natural persons.

custodio
▲ *the custodian bank* el banco custodio
⇛ depositary bank

custodian bank
A custodian bank is a bank, usually a commercial bank, that holds securities under a written agreement for a corporate client and buys or sells securities when instructed. Custodian services include securities safekeeping, and collection of dividends and interest. The bank acts only as transfer agent and makes no buy-sell recommendations.

banco custodio
▲ *a domestic custodian bank* un banco custodio nacional ▲ *a local custodian bank* un banco custodio local ▲ *as custodian bank* como banco custodio

custody account
A custody account is an account with a bank and the place where an investor keeps his financial instruments such as shares and bonds.

cuenta de custodia
▲ *keep a custody account* mantener una cuenta de custodia ▲ *keep securities in the same custody account* mantener los títulos en la misma cuenta de custodia

custody commission
Custody commission is money earned by a bank for keeping shares, bonds, mortgages and other financial instruments for their customers.

comisión de custodia
▲ *securities and custody commission* títulos y comisión de custodia

customer
A customer is a buyer of a product, i.e. goods or services.

cliente
▲ *a credit balance with a customer* un saldo a favor de un cliente ▲ *a customer with a high credit risk* un cliente con un alto riesgo crediticio ▲ *amounts receivable from trade customers* cuentas a cobrar de clientes ▲ *at the option of the customer* a gusto del cliente ▲ *cash advances and loans made to customers* anticipos y préstamos en efectivo realizados a los clientes ▲ *cash receipts and payments on behalf of customers* pagos y cobros en efectivo en nombre de los clientes ▲ *costs that are specifically chargeable to the customer under the terms of the contract* costes que son específica-

mente imputables al cliente según los términos del contrato ▲ *customer caused delays* el cliente causó retrasos ▲ *customer lists* listas de clientes ▲ *customer loyalty* lealtad del cliente ▲ *from supplier to customer* del proveedor al cliente ▲ *funds held for customers by an investment enterprise* fondos custodiados para clientes por una empresa de inversión ▲ *large customers* grandes clientes ▲ *progress payments and advances received from customers* tramitar pagos y anticipos recibidos de los clientes ▲ *regular customer* cliente habitual ▲ *revenue derived from customers outside the enterprise* ingresos originados por clientes externos a la empresa ▲ *the activities of the customer* las actividades del cliente ▲ *the costs of designing products for specific customers* los costes de diseño del producto para clientes concretos ▲ *the gross amount due from customers for contract work* el importe bruto debido por los clientes por contrato de obra ▲ *the gross amount due to customers for contract work* el importe bruto exigible a clientes por ejecución de obra ▲ *total revenue from sales to external customers* total ingresos por ventas a clientes externos ▲ *with a single customer or with several customers* con uno o varios clientes

customer capital

Customer capital is that part of an enterprise's intellectual capital that is attributable to its customers. The other parts constitute individual capital and structural capital.

clientela

▲ *protect the customer capital* proteger la clientela ▲ *the concept of customer capital* el concepto de clientela ▲ *the diversity of customer capital* la diversidad de la clientela

⇛ individual capital, intellectual capital, structural capital

customer cost hierarchy

A customer cost hierarchy is a categorisation of costs related to customers into different cost pools based on different cost-drivers, cost-allocation bases and determination difficulties in connection with cause-and-effect or benefits-received relationships.

NOTE A typical customer cost hierarchy includes the following five categorisations: customer-sustaining costs, customer output unit-level costs, customer batch-level costs, distribution-channel costs and business-sustaining costs.

jerarquización de costes de cliente

▲ *according to the customer cost hierarchy* de acuerdo con la jerarquización de costes de cliente ▲ *the categories in a customer cost hierarchy* las categorías en una jerarquización de costes de cliente ▲ *use a customer cost hierarchy* utilizar una jerarquización de costes de cliente

customer relationship

Customer relationships are any direct or indirect links between an enterprise and its customers.

relación con el cliente

▲ *a close customer relationship* una estrecha relación con el cliente ▲ *customer relationship management* gestión de la relación con el cliente ▲ *customer relationship marketing* marketing de relaciones con el cliente ▲ *development of customer relationships* desarrollo de relaciones con el cliente ▲ *expand customer relationships* ampliar las relaciones con el cliente ▲ *good customer relationships* buenas relaciones con el cliente ▲ *profitable customer relationships* relaciones con el cliente rentables ▲ *the duration of customer relationships* la duración de relaciones con el cliente

customer-profitability analysis

A customer-profitability analysis evaluates an enterprise's portfolio of customers by an investigation of the profitability attributable to an individual customer or a group of customers. The analysis also shows how many customers are unprofitable and why as well as the amount of resources they use.

análisis de la rentabilidad por cliente

= análisis rentabilidad-cliente

▲ *the most accurate customer-profitability analysis* el análisis rentabilidad-cliente más preciso ▲ *use of a customer-profitability analysis* empleo de un análisis de la rentabilidad por cliente

customs duty

Customs duty is a tax levied on imports to provide government financing and protection of domestic production from foreign competition.

arancel

▲ *exempt from customs duty* eximir de aranceles ▲ *impose a customs duty on the goods* imponer un arancel a los bienes ▲ *reduce the customs duty* reducir los aranceles

cut-off date

The cut-off date is the last day in an accounting period, i.e. the balance sheet date. To ensure a true and fair view of the results and financial position of an enterprise, transactions and events occurring after this date are not relevant and not recognised in the financial statements for the period.

fecha de cierre

▲ *an appropriate cut-off date* una fecha de cierre apropiada ▲ *set a cut-off date* fijar una fecha de cierre

cut-off procedure

Cut-off procedures involve determining whether there are revenues and expenses which relate to the accounting period under review, irrespective of the time of payment. The cut-off procedures are decisive for delivering true annual results and also determine the tax assessment for the period.

procedimiento de cierre

⇛ cut-off date

CVP analysis UK, US

= cost-volume-profit analysis UK, US

A CVP (cost-volume-profit) analysis is the study of the effects of future output volume on sales or revenue, costs and net profit.

análisis coste-volumen-beneficio

▲ *the CVP analysis* el análisis coste-volumen-beneficio ▲ *use CVP analysis* usar el análisis coste-volumen-beneficio

⇛ breakeven analysis

cycle

A cycle is a period of time during which a series of events recur regularly in the same order.

ciclo

▲ *a clearly identifiable operating cycle* un ciclo operativo claramente identificable ▲ *the typical product life cycle for the asset* el ciclo de vida útil del producto típico del activo

cycle time

= throughput time

For manufactured goods, cycle time is the time span in a production process from purchase of raw materials over production to finished product, or, for finished goods or services, the time span from an order is placed to delivery.

ciclo de fabricación

= tiempo de fabricación

▲ *a long cycle time* un ciclo de fabricación largo ▲ *a very short cycle time* un ciclo de fabricación muy corto ▲ *average cycle time* un ciclo de fabricación medio ▲ *reduce cycle time* reducir el ciclo de fabricación

D

damages
= compensation
Damages constitute the pecuniary compensation payable, often by a court order, to the claimant. Damages may be awarded for various losses such as loss of earnings or chattels and impairment loss. Payment is made by the tortfeasor or person causing the loss or from the claimant's or the tortfeasor's insurance.
indemnización por daños y perjuicios
= responsabilidad por daños y perjuicios
▲ *an action for damages* una demanda de indemnización por daños y perjuicios ▲ *assessment of damages* valoración de la indemnización por daños y perjuicios ▲ *claim for damages* reclamación de la indemnización por daños y perjuicios ▲ *damages for breach of contract* indemnización por daños y perjuicios por incumplimiento de contrato ▲ *damages for pain and suffering* indemnización por daños y perjuicios causados por dolor físico y sufrimiento ▲ *liability in damages* responsabilidad por daños y perjuicios ▲ *measure of damages* cuantificación de la indemnización por daños y perjuicios ▲ *pay damages* pagar por indemnización de daños y perjuicios ▲ *recover damages* cobrar la indemnización por daños y perjuicios

data
Information that can be stored and processed on a computer is referred to as data.
datos
▲ *based on central data* basado en datos centrales ▲ *based on consolidated data* basado en datos consolidados ▲ *based on real time data* basado en datos en tiempo real ▲ *condensed and classified data* datos clasificados y condensados ▲ *have access to extensive data* tener acceso a una gran cantidad de datos ▲ *historical summaries of financial data* resúmenes históricos de datos financieros ▲ *interim period data* datos del periodo intercalario ▲ *lack of comparable market data* carencia de datos de mercado comparables

data collection
Data collection is the retrieval of information with the object of establishing a basis for analyses and decision-making.
recogida de datos
= recopilación de datos
▲ *systematisation of data collection* sistematización de la recogida de datos
⇛ data retrieval

data retrieval
Data retrieval means finding and fetching data stored on a computer.
recuperación de datos
▲ *requirements for data retrieval* requisitos para la recuperación de datos
⇛ data collection

date of acquisition
= acquisition date, time of acquisition
The date of acquisition in a business combination is the date when one enterprise (the acquirer) obtains control over the acquired enterprise (the acquiree).
fecha de adquisición
▲ *at, or before, the date of acquisition* a, o antes de, la fecha de adquisición ▲ *fixing of the date of acquisition* determinación de la fecha de adquisición ▲ *market price at the date of acquisition* precio de mercado a la fecha de adquisición ▲ *market price at the date of acquisition* precio de mercado a la fecha de adquisición ▲ *recognition and determination of goodwill at the date of acquisition* reconocimiento y determinación del fondo de comercio a la fecha de adquisición ▲ *the actual date of acquisition* la fecha real de adquisición ▲ *the carrying amount on the date of acquisition* el valor contable en la fecha de adquisición ▲ *three months after the date of acquisition* tres meses después de la fecha de adquisición ▲ *with effect from the date of*

acquisition con efecto desde la fecha de adquisición
⇛ acquisition date

date of adjustment
The date on which an adjustment is made is called the date of adjustment.
fecha de ajuste
▲ *value at the date of adjustment* valor a la fecha de ajuste

date of borrowing
The date of borrowing is the date on which the loan contract is made, i.e. the date of raising the loan.
fecha de formalización del crédito
▲ *the effective interest rate at the date of borrowing* el tipo de interés efectivo a la fecha de formalización del crédito

date of conclusion
The date on which a contract or similar arrangement is made is called the date of conclusion.
fecha de vencimiento
▲ *at the date of conclusion* a la fecha de vencimiento ▲ *prior to the date of conclusion* anterior a la fecha de vencimiento

date of deduction
The date of deduction is the time when expenses may be deducted in the tax return. Depending on type, some expenses are deductible for tax purposes in the income tax year, and others, e.g. depreciation charges, are allocated over several years.
fecha de la deducción
▲ *dates of deduction for tax purposes* fechas de deducción por motivos fiscales

date of demerger
→ demerger date

date of disposal
= disposal date US
The date of disposal is the time of sale, transfer or abandonment of an asset.
fecha de baja del inventario
▲ *at the date of disposal* a la fecha de baja del inventario ▲ *determine the date of disposal for investment property* determinación de la fecha de baja del inventario de la inversión inmobiliaria ▲ *included in the consolidated income statement until the date of disposal* incluido en la cuenta de resultados consolidados hasta la fecha de baja del inventario ▲ *the expected date of disposal* la fecha prevista de baja del inventario ▲ *up to the date of disposal* hasta la fecha de baja del inventario

date of entry into service
Date of entry into service refers to the date on which an enterprise begins to use an asset in its course of business.
fecha de entrada en funcionamiento
= fecha de entrada en servicio
▲ *on the date of entry into service* en la fecha de entrada en funcionamiento ▲ *prior to the date of entry into service* anterior a la fecha de entrada en funcionamiento

date of exchange
1 = date of conversion
The date of exchange is the time when a given exchange takes place. In an exchange of shares, this date is decisive for the amount payable to shareholders exchanging their shares, as the share price quoted on this date determines the amount.
fecha de intercambio
= fecha de canje
▲ *recognised at the market price on the date of exchange* reconocido al precio de mercado en la fecha de intercambio
2 ≠ acquisition date IAS/IFRS
The date of exchange in a business combination involving the acquisition of more than one entity is the date when each acquisition is recognised in the financial statements of the acquiring enterprise (the acquirer). The date of exchange in a business combination involving one acquisition only is the acquisition date.
fecha de intercambio
▲ *the fair value at the date of exchange* el valor razonable a la fecha de intercambio ▲ *the present value at the date of exchange* el valor actual a la fecha de intercambio ▲ *the published price at the date of exchange of a quoted equity instrument* el valor de cotización a la fecha de inercambio de un instrumento de patrimonio cotizado
SOURCE IFRS 3, Appendix A
⇛ acquisition date, business combination

date of formation
The date of formation is the date on which the memoran-

dum of association is signed by the promoters of a company.
fecha de constitución
▲ *at the date of formation* a la fecha de constitución ▲ *listed by date of formation* incluido en bolsa por fecha de constitución

date of grant
→ grant date

date of purchase
= time of acquisition
The date on which something has been bought is called the date of purchase.
fecha de compra
= fecha de adquisición
▲ *the equity value of the investment at the date of purchase* el valor patrimonial de la inversión en la fecha de compra ▲ *the rate at the date of purchase* el tipo en la fecha de compra ▲ *translation at the rate at the date of purchase* conversión al tipo en la fecha de compra ▲ *use of the exchange rate prevailing at the date of purchase of the asset* uso del tipo de cambio existente en la fecha de compra del activo

date of realisation UK
= date of realization US
The date of realisation is the time when an asset is sold and the sales proceeds recognised.
fecha de enajenación
= fecha de venta
▲ *the planned date of realisation* la fecha de enajenación prevista

date of realization US
= date of realisation UK
The date of realization is the time when an asset is sold and the sales proceeds recognized.
fecha de enajenación
= fecha de venta
▲ *the planned date of realization* la fecha de enajenación prevista

date of reassessment
The date of reassessment is the time when a restatement of something takes place, e.g. an asset, a liability or a contract.
fecha de valoración posterior
▲ *contractual date of reassessment* fecha de valoración posterior contraactual ▲ *disclosure of the dates of reassessment* publicación de las fechas de valoración posterior

date of recognition
The date of recognition is the time when assets or liabilities are included in the balance sheet or when income or expenses are recorded in the profit and loss account.
fecha de registro
= fecha de reconocimiento
▲ *assessment of the date of recognition* valoración de la fecha de registro ▲ *at the date of recognition* a la fecha de registro

date of the revaluation
= time of revaluation
The date on which something has been revalued is called the date of revaluation.
fecha de la valoración posterior
▲ *the effective date of the revaluation* la fecha de la valoración posterior efectiva ▲ *the exchange rate prevailing at the date of the revaluation* el tipo de cambio existente a la fecha de la valoración posterior ▲ *the fair value at the date of the revaluation* el valor razonable a la fecha de la valoración posterior ▲ *translate revalued items using the exchange rate prevailing at the date of the revaluation* reevaluar las partidas utilizando el tipo de cambio existente a la fecha de la valoración posterior

date of transaction
= transaction date
The date of transaction is the day when a transaction, e.g. a purchase or a sale, has been registered to have taken place and control of the asset traded passes from the seller to the buyer, or, for a contract, the date when a transaction has been agreed.
fecha de transacción
▲ *at the date of transaction* a la fe cha de transacción ▲ *before the date of transaction* antes de la fecha de transacción ▲ *from the date of transaction to the balance sheet date* desde la fecha de transacción a la fecha del balance ▲ *the exchange rate ruling at the date of transaction* el tipo de cambio oficial a la fecha de transacción

date of transition to IFRSs IAS/IFRS
The first date in the accounting period for which an enterprise prepares and presents its financial statements in accordance with the International

Financial Reporting Standards is referred to as the date of transition to IFRSs.
fecha de transición a las NIIFs
▲ *a business combination that occurred before the date of transition to IFRSs* una combinación de negocio que tuvo lugar antes de la fecha de transición a las NIIFs ▲ *an entity's estimates under IFRSs at the date of transition to IFRSs* estimaciones de una entidad según las NIIFs a la fecha de transición a las NIIFs ▲ *based on the parent's date of transition to IFRSs* basado en la fecha de transición a las NIIFs de la matriz ▲ *based on the subsidiary's date of transition to IFRSs* basado en la fecha de transición a las NIIFs de la filial ▲ *events and transactions before the date of transition to IFRSs* hechos y operaciones antes de la fecha de transición a las NIIFs ▲ *prepare an opening IFRS balance sheet at the date of transition to IFRSs* preparar un balance de apertura NIIF a la fecha de transición a las NIIFs ▲ *the conditions that existed at the date of transition to IFRSs* las condiciones existentes a la fecha de transición a las NIIFs
SOURCE IFRS 1, Appendix A

day-to-day management
Day-to-day management refers to the direction, running and control of the operations of an enterprise on a current and continuing basis.
gestión del día a día
▲ *responsible for day-to-day management* responsable de la gestión del día a día ▲ *the day-to-day management of the company* la gestión del día a día de la empresa

days payable outstanding
→ days' payable outstanding

days' payable outstanding
= creditor days ratio, Days' Payable Outstanding, DPO
≠ days' sales outstanding, DSO
Days' payable outstanding (DPO) is a financial ratio measuring how long it takes an enterprise on average to pay its trade payables, i.e. trade creditors.
rotación de proveedores
= plazo promedio de proveedores, rotación de pagos comerciales
≠ rotación de clientes, rotación de cobros comerciales
▲ *a decrease in days' payable outstanding* un descenso en la rotación de proveedores ▲ *an increase in days' payable outstanding* un aumento en la rotación de proveeedores ▲ *reduce days' payable outstanding by 10%* reducir la rotación de proveedores en un 10%

Days' Payable Outstanding
= creditor days ratio, days' payable outstanding, DPO
≠ Days' Sales Outstanding, DSO
Days' Payable Outstanding (DPO) is a financial ratio measuring how long it takes an enterprise on average to pay its trade payables, i.e. trade creditors.
rotación de proveedores
= plazo promedio de proveedores, rotación de pagos comerciales
≠ rotación de clientes, rotación de cobros comerciales
▲ *a decrease in Days' Payable Outstanding* un descenso en la rotación de proveedores ▲ *an increase in Days' Payable Outstanding* un aumento en la rotación de proveedores ▲ *reduce Days' Payable Outstanding by 10%* reducir la rotación de proveedores en un 10%

days sales in inventory
→ days' sales in inventory

days' sales in inventory
= Days' Sales in Inventory, days' sales of inventory, Days' Sales of Inventory, DSI
Days' sales in inventory (DSI) is a financial ratio measuring an enterprise's performance by showing the average time spent for turning the enterprise's inventory (preferably including work in progress) into sales. A low DSI implies a short amount of days and is therefore preferable, however, the ratio varies with type of industry.
rotación de inventario
= plazo promedio de inventario, rotación de existencias
▲ *a 10% reduction in days' sales in inventory* una reducción del 10% en la rotación de inventario ▲ *a drop in days' sales in inventory* una caída en la rotación de inventario ▲ *calculate the number of days' sales in inventory* calcular el número de días en la rotación de inventario

Days' Sales in Inventory
= days' sales in inventory, days sales in inventory, days' sales of

inventory, Days' Sales of Inventory, days sales of inventory, DSI
Days' Sales in Inventory (DSI) is a financial ratio measuring an enterprise's performance by showing the average time spent for turning the enterprise's inventory (preferably including work in progress) into sales. A low DSI implies a short amount of days and is therefore preferable, however, the ratio varies with type of industry.
rotación de inventario
= plazo promedio de inventario, rotación de existencias
▲ *a 10% reduction in Days' Sales in Inventory* una reducción del 10% en la rotación de inventario ▲ *a drop in Days' Sales in Inventory* una caída en la rotación de inventario ▲ *calculate the number of Days' Sales in Inventory* calcular la rotación de inventario

days' sales in receivables
= days' sales outstanding, debtor collection period, DSO
≠ days' payable outstanding, DPO
Days' sales in receivables is a financial ratio measuring how long it takes an enterprise on average to collect amounts receivable (revenue) after making a sale. A low days' sales in receivables ratio implies a small amount of days and is therefore positive, whereas a high amount indicates a long debtor collection period and that the enterprise is selling on credit.
rotación de clientes
= plazo promedio de clientes, rotación de cobros comerciales
≠ rotación de pagos comerciales, rotación de proveedores
▲ *a decrease in days' sales in receivables* un descenso en la rotación de clientes ▲ *an increase in days' sales in receivables* un aumento en la rotación de clientes ▲ *compare the days' sales in receivables with the company's credit terms* comparar la rotación de clientes con las condiciones crediticias de la empresa ▲ *determine the number of days' sales in receivables* determinar la rotación de clientes ▲ *reduce days' sales in receivables* reducir la rotación de clientes

days sales of inventory
→ days' sales of inventory

days' sales of inventory
= days' sales in inventory, Days' Sales in Inventory, Days' Sales of Inventory, DSI
Days' sales of inventory (DSI) is a financial ratio measuring an enterprise's performance by showing the average time spent for turning the enterprise's inventory (preferably including work in progress) into sales. A low DSI implies a short amount of days and is therefore preferable, however, the ratio varies with type of industry.
rotación de inventario
= plazo promedio de inventario
▲ *a 10% reduction in days' sales of inventory* una reducción del 10% en la rotación de inventario ▲ *a drop in days' sales of inventory* una caída en la rotación de inventario ▲ *calculate the number of days' sales of inventory* calcular la rotación de inventario

Days' Sales of Inventory
= days' sales in inventory, Days' Sales in Inventory, days' sales of inventory, DSI
Days' Sales of Inventory (DSI) is a financial ratio measuring an enterprise's performance by showing the average time spent for turning the enterprise's inventory (preferably including work in progress) into sales. A low DSI implies a short amount of days and is therefore preferable, however, the ratio varies with type of industry.
rotación de inventario
= plazo promedio de inventario
▲ *a 10% reduction in Days' Sales of Inventory* una reducción del 10% en la rotación de inventario ▲ *a drop in Days' Sales of Inventory* una caída en la rotación de inventario ▲ *calculate the number of Days' Sales of Inventory* calcular la rotación de inventario

days sales outstanding
→ days' sales outstanding

days' sales outstanding
= days' sales in receivables, debtor collection period, DSO
≠ days' payable outstanding
Days' sales outstanding (DSO) is a financial ratio measuring

how long it takes an enterprise on average to collect amounts receivable (revenue) after making a sale. A low DSO implies a small amount of days and is therefore positive, whereas a high amount indicates a long debtor collection period and that the enterprise is selling on credit.

rotación de clientes

= plazo medio de clientes, rotación de cobros comerciales

≠ rotación de pagos comerciales, rotación de proveedores

▲ *a decrease in days' sales outstanding* un descenso en la rotación de clientes ▲ *an increase in days' sales outstanding* un aumento en la rotación de clientes ▲ *compare the days' sales outstanding with the company's credit terms* comparar la rotación de clientes con las condiciones crediticias de la empresa ▲ *determine the number of days' sales outstanding* determinar la rotación de clientes ▲ *reduce days' sales outstanding* reducir la rotación de clientes

Days' Sales Outstanding

= days' sales outstanding, debtor collection period, DSO

≠ Days' Payable Outstanding, DPO

Days' Sales Outstanding (DSO) is a financial ratio measuring how long it takes an enterprise on average to collect amounts receivable (revenue) after making a sale. A low DSO implies a small amount of days and is therefore positive, whereas a high amount indicates a long debtor collection period and that the enterprise is selling on credit.

rotación de clientes

= plazo promedio de clientes, rotación de cobros comerciales

≠ rotación de pagos comerciales, rotación de proveedores

▲ *a decrease in Days' Sales Outstanding* un descenso en la rotación de clientes ▲ *an increase in Days' Sales Outstanding* un aumento en la rotación de clientes ▲ *compare the Days' Sales Outstanding with the company's credit terms* comparar la rotación de clientes con las condiciones crediticias de la empresa ▲ *determine the number of Days' Sales Outstanding* determinar la rotación de clientes ▲ *reduce Days' Sales Outstanding* reducir la rotación de clientes

DB method

→ declining-balance method

DB plan

= DB scheme, defined benefit plan, defined benefit scheme

A DB plan (defined benefit plan) is a pension plan from which the benefits payable to pensioners are based on salary at or near retirement and years of service and not on the contributions paid into the plan and the returns on the plan's investments. DB plans do not include personal pension plans, but are typically occupational pension plans under which it is the enterprise's obligation to provide the agreed benefits to current and former employees whether or not the amount of such benefits exceed the contributions.

plan de prestaciones definidas

▲ *accounting for DB plans* contabilizando planes de prestaciones definidas ▲ *an overfunded DB plan* un plan de prestaciones definidas sobredotado ▲ *curtailment of a DB plan* reducción de un plan de prestaciones definidas ▲ *funded DB plans* planes de prestaciones definidas dotados ▲ *multi-employer DB plans* planes de prestación definida multiempresa ▲ *settlement of a DB plan* pago de un plan de prestaciones definidas ▲ *the formal terms of a DB plan* los términos formales de un plan de prestaciones definidas ▲ *the present value of the DB plan* el valor actual del plan de prestaciones definidas ▲ *transitional liability for a DB plan* pasivo de transición para un plan de prestación definida ▲ *unfunded DB plans* planes de prestaciones definidas insuficientemente dotados ▲ *wholly or partly funded DB plan* plan de prestaciones definidas total o parcialmente dotado

DB scheme

= DB plan, defined benefit plan, defined benefit scheme

A DB scheme (defined benefit scheme) is a pension scheme from which the benefits payable to pensioners are based on salary at or near retirement and years of service and not on the contributions paid into the scheme and the returns on the scheme's investments. DB schemes do not include personal pension schemes, but are typically occupational pension schemes under which it is the enterprise's obligation to provide the agreed benefits to current and former employees whether or not the amount of such benefits exceed the contributions.

plan de prestaciones definidas

▲ *accounting for DB schemes* contabilizando planes de prestaciones definidas ▲ *curtailment of a DB scheme* reducción de un plan de prestaciones definidas ▲ *settlement of a DB scheme* pago de un plan de prestaciones definidas ▲ *the present value of the DB scheme* el valor actual del plan de prestaciones definidas ▲ *wholly or partly funded DB schemes* planes de prestaciones definidas total o parcialmente dotados

DC plan

= DC scheme, defined contribution plan, defined contribution scheme

A DC plan (defined contribution plan) is a pension plan from which the benefits payable to pensioners are based entirely on the contributions paid into the plan by the member, or on behalf of the member, and on the returns on the plan's investments. All personal pension plans are of the DC type, however, occupational pension plans may also be of this type.

plan de aportaciones definidas

▲ *accounting for DC plans* contabilizando planes de aportaciones definidas ▲ *classify a multi-employer plan as a DC plan* clasificar un plan multiempresa como un plan de aportaciones definidas ▲ *contributions to a DC plan* contribuciones a un plan de aportaciones definidas ▲ *recognised as an expense for DC plans* reconocido como un gasto en los planes de aportaciones definidas ▲ *the contribution payable to a DC plan* la contribución a pagar al plan de aportaciones definidas

DC scheme

= DC plan, defined contribution plan defined contribution scheme

A DC scheme (defined contribution scheme) is a pension scheme from which the benefits payable to pensioners are based entirely on the contributions paid into the scheme by the member, or on behalf of the member, and on the returns on the scheme's investments. All personal pension schemes are of the DC type, however, occupational pension schemes may also be of this type.

plan de aportaciones definidas

▲ *accounting for DC schemes* contabilizando planes de aportaciones definidas ▲ *contributions to a DC scheme* contribuciones a un plan de aportaciones definidas ▲ *recognised as an expense for DC schemes* reconocido como un gasto en los planes de aportaciones definidas ▲ *the contribution payable to a DC scheme* la contribución a pagar a un plan de aportaciones definidas

DCF

1 = discounted cash flow

DCF is the abbreviation for discounted cash flow, i.e. the future cash flow shown at its present value following a discounted cash flow calculation where the projected annual cash flow figure is multiplied by a discount factor. Discounting projected cash flows is important to capital investment appraisal.

flujo de efectivo actualizado

▲ *calculate DCF* calcular el flujo de efectivo actualizado ▲ *the calculation of DCF* el cálculo del flujo de efectivo actualizado

⇛ discounted-cash-flow model, free cash flow to firm

2 = discounted-cash-flow model

A DCF model is a method for budgeting the capital needed for a given project. Future cash inflows and outflows related to the project are discounted to a specified point of time using a given

discount factor allowing for comparison with other projects.
modelo de flujo de efectivo actualizado
▲ *use a DCF model* utilizar un modelo de flujo de efectivo actualizado

3 = discounted-cash-flow model
A DCF model is a method for valuation of an enterprise. The free cash flow from the budget period and the terminal period are discounted at a discount rate corresponding to the weighted average capital costs. The value of the enterprise is found after deduction of the market value of the interest-bearing debt of the enterprise.
modelo de flujo de efectivo actualizado
▲ *use a DCF model* utilizar un modelo de flujo de efectivo actualizado

DDM
= dividend discount model
DDM is the abbreviation for the dividend discount model which is a direct valuation method to estimate the present value of expected future dividend payments, thereby estimating the value of a share or a company to a shareholder.
modelo de dividendo actualizado
▲ *estimates based on the DDM* estimaciones basadas en el modelo de dividendo actualizado ▲ *under the DDM* según el modelo de dividendo actualizado ▲ *use the DDM* utilizar el modelo de dividendo actualizado

debenture UK
A debenture is a fixed-interest debt instrument representing a long-term loan to an enterprise. Debentures are usually secured on specific assets of the issuing enterprise (fixed charge) or by a floating charge on the assets.
obligación
▲ *convert debentures into shares* convertir las obligaciones en acciones ▲ *convertible debentures* obligaciones convertibles ▲ *issue a debenture* emitir una obligación ▲ *perpetual debentures* obligaciones perpetuas ▲ *secured debentures* obligaciones garantizadas ▲ *unsecured debentures* obligaciones no garantizadas
⇛ fixed charge, floating charge

debit[1] *noun* <a, the, -s>
≠ credit
The term debit refers to the left-hand side of an account and represents either the assets or expenses of the enterprise.
debe
= deudor
≠ acreedor, haber
▲ *place an amount to the debit of an account* colocar una cantidad en el debe de una cuenta ▲ *the account shows a debit balance* la cuenta muestra un saldo deudor
⇛ double-entry bookkeeping

debit[2] *noun* <a, the, -s>
→ debit item

debit[3] *verb*
≠ credit
To debit is to recognise an item as a debit entry in an account, i.e. in the left hand side.
cargar
= adeudar, debitar
≠ abonar, acreditar
▲ *debit an amount against a customer* cargar una cantidad a un cliente

debit item
A debit item is a record on the left side of an account. According to the double-entry bookkeeping system, debit items show increases in assets and expenses or decreases in liabilities, revenue and equity.
cargo
≠ abono
▲ *other debit items* otros cargos ▲ *show as a debit item* mostrar un cargo ▲ *the aggregate of all the debit items* el total de todos los cargos

debt
= payable US, IAS/IFRS
≠ receivable
Debt is money or services owed to an outside party and a legal obligation of the business arising from written or oral agreement, through the granting of credit or through raising of loan capital. Debt may be either short-term or long-term.
deuda
= obligación, pago
≠ cobro, crédito
▲ *a long-term debt* una deuda a largo plazo ▲ *a short-term debt* una deuda a corto plazo ▲ *an interest-bearing long-term debt*

una deuda con interés a largo plazo ▲ *be discharged of a debt* estar eximido de una deuda ▲ *doubtful debts* deudas de dudoso cobro ▲ *doubtful debts allowances on receivables* provisiones para insolvencia sobre deudores ▲ *mortgage debt* deudas a instituciones de crédito hipotecario ▲ *other debts* otras deudas ▲ *recognise proposed dividends as a debt* reconocer los dividendos devengados como una deuda ▲ *the date when the debt was incurred* la fecha en la que la deuda fue contraída ▲ *total debts* total deudas

debt and equity instrument
= debt and equity security
Debt and equity instruments are compound financial instruments, i.e. securities with partly equity and partly liability or debt components, such as a convertible bond.
instrumento híbrido
▲ *issuing of debt and equity instruments* emisión de instrumentos híbridos

debt and equity security IAS/IFRS
= compound instrument IAS/IFRS, debt and equity instrument, hybrid, hybrid security
Debt and equity securities are compound financial instruments, i.e. securities with partly equity and partly liability or debt components, such as a convertible bond.
instrumento híbrido
▲ *issuing of debt and equity securities* emisión de instrumentos híbridos

debt capital
= loan capital
≠ equity
Debt capital refers to the non-current liabilities or long-term borrowings of an enterprise.
pasivo no corriente
= pasivo ajeno a largo plazo
≠ patrimonio
▲ *changes in debt capital* cambios en el pasivo no corriente ▲ *source debt capital in US dollars* origen de pasivo no corriente en dólares norteamericanos ▲ *subordinate debt capital* pasivo no corriente subordinado ▲ *the debt capital market* el mercado de pasivo no corriente

debt consolidation
= consolidation of debt
Debt consolidation is a strategy to improve debt management which implies the restructuring and refinancing of a loan portfolio consisting of several small loans by repayment of the loans with the proceeds from a new large loan provided by one lender. This may involve lower amounts for debt servicing and a longer repayment period.
reunificación de deuda

debt conversion
Debt conversion is the conversion of debt to equity capital, e.g. the conversion of debentures to shares.
conversión de deuda
▲ *a proposed debt conversion* una conversión de deuda propuesta

debt extinguishment
→ extinguishment of debt

debt factoring
= factoring of debt
Debt factoring is the sale of trade receivables, i.e. trade debt, to a factor, typically a finance company, which assumes the debt collection and the right to receive payment from the debtors against immediate payment at a discount of a cash amount to the seller. The debt may be sold with or without recourse to the seller.
factoring
▲ *the accounting treatment of debt factoring* el tratamiento contable del factoring
⇛ factor, factoring, factoring liability

debt guarantee
≠ closing rate method
A debt guarantee is a promise made by a guarantor to repay a loan and accept liability on behalf of a borrower in the event of the latter failing to meet the repayment obligations. A guarantee typically involves providing security in the form of particular assets to the lender.
aval
▲ *debt guarantee commitments* compromisos por aval ▲ *expiration of the debt guarantee* finalización del aval ▲ *provide debt guarantee for major shareholders* ofrecer el aval a los accionistas mayoritarios
⇛ guarantee, guarantee debtor

debt instrument
= document of indebtedness, instrument of debt

A debt instrument is a written promise to repay a debt, typically a short-term loan, and constitutes a formal loan document stipulating the terms and conditions of the loan. Examples are bills, notes, bonds, banker's acceptances, certificates of deposit or commercial paper.

instrumento de deuda

▲ *a convertible debt instrument with an embedded call or put option feature* un instrumento de deuda convertible con opciones de futuro para vender o comprar incluidas ▲ *a range of debt instruments* un abanico de instrumentos de deuda ▲ *acquire equity or debt instruments of other enterprises* adquirir instrumentos de patrimonio o de deuda de otras empresas ▲ *cash receipts from sales of debt instruments of other enterprises* recibos de efectivo procedentes de las ventas de los instrumentos de deuda de otras empresas ▲ *conversion of convertible debt instruments* conversión de los instrumentos de deuda convertibles ▲ *refinance debt instruments in central banks* refinanciar los instrumentos de deuda en los bancos centrales ▲ *the amortised cost of the host debt instrument* el coste amortizado del instrumento de deuda anfitrión ▲ *the conversion of a debt instrument to ordinary shares* la conversión de un instrumento de deuda en acciones ordinarias ▲ *under the original or modified terms of a debt instrument* según los términos iniciales o modificados de un instrumento de deuda

debt obligation

A debt obligation is a requirement, often legally enforceable, to pay an amount owed to another party.

obligación de deuda

▲ *assume a debt obligation* asumir una obligación de deuda ▲ *derecognise the debt obligation* anular la obligación de deuda ▲ *recognise a new debt obligation* reconocer una nueva obligación de deuda ▲ *service existing and normally expected debt obligations* pagar las obligaciones de deuda existentes y las normalmente esperadas

debt payable on demand

A debt payable on demand is a debt the lender can require paid without a period of notice to the borrower.

deuda a pagar a la presentación

▲ *long-term debt payable on demand at the balance sheet date* deuda a pagar a la presentación a largo plazo a la fecha de balance ▲ *repayment of a debt payable on demand* amortización de una deuda a pagar a la presentación

debt ratio

The debt ratio is defined as total debt divided by total assets.

ratio de garantía

▲ *calculate the debt ratio* calcular el ratio de garantía ▲ *long-term debt ratio* ratio de garantía a largo plazo

debt repayment obligation

A debt repayment obligation is a borrower's duty to repay a loan.

obligación de amortización de deuda

▲ *fulfill a debt repayment obligation* cumplir una obligación de amortización de deuda ▲ *release from the debt repayment obligation* eludir la obligación de amortización de deuda

debt security

A debt security is a financial instrument giving a written promise to repay debt, typically with interest, e.g. a bill, a note or a bond.

título de deuda

▲ *debt securities admitted to trading on a regulated market* títulos de deuda admitidos a cotización en bolsa ▲ *debt securities and other fixed-income securities* títulos de deuda y otros títulos de renta fija ▲ *debt securities ranking pari passu* títulos de deuda con categoría pari passu ▲ *issue debt securities in public securities markets* sacar a bolsa títulos de deuda ▲ *publicly traded debt securities* títulos de deuda cotizados ▲ *the initial carrying amount of a debt security* el valor contable inicial de un título de deuda

⇛ instrument of debt

debt structure

Debt structure refers to an enterprise's combination of different types of debt as well as

to the debt's maturity dates and the timing of instalment and interest payment.
estructura de la deuda
▲ *assess the debt structure* examinar la estructura de la deuda ▲ *the company's debt structure* la estructura de la deuda de la empresa

debt-equity ratio
= financial gearing
The debt-equity ratio is a ratio used to define the financial structure or gearing of an enterprise and equals total net interest-bearing debt divided by total equity. A high ratio indicates that the enterprise has a high amount of debt or loan capital in proportion to its equity.
ratio de endeudamiento
▲ *an increase in the debt-equity ratio* un incremento en el ratio de endeudamiento
⇛ equity ratio

debt-financed
= funded by loans
An investment is debt-financed when the investor has raised a separate loan for the specific purpose of financing that particular investment.
financiado con préstamo
▲ *a debt-financed acquisition* una adquisición financiada con préstamo

debt/equity ratio
→ debt-equity ratio

debtor
= amount outstanding, receivable
≠ creditor
A debtor is a person or entity with a debit balance, i.e. an outstanding amount or service due to another person or entity. In the balance sheet, debtors are recognised as current assets.
deudor
≠ acreedor
▲ *a foreign currency debtor* un deudor en moneda extranjera ▲ *a group of debtors* un grupo de deudores ▲ *a right of set-off is a debtor's legal right to settle* un derecho de compensación es un derecho legal de un deudor a pagar ▲ *debtors arising out of reinsurance operations* deudores procedentes de operaciones de reaseguro
⇛ trade debtors

debtor collection period
= days' sales in receivables, days' sales outstanding, DSO
≠ days' payable outstanding, DPO
Debtor collection period is a financial ratio measuring how long it takes an enterprise on average to collect amounts receivable (revenue) after making a sale. A low debtor collection period ratio implies a small amount of days and is therefore positive, whereas a high amount indicates a long debtor collection period and that the enterprise is selling on credit.
rotación de clientes
= plazo promedio de clientes, rotación de cobros comerciales
≠ rotación de pagos comerciales, rotación de proveedores
▲ *a decrease in the debtor collection period* una disminución en la rotación de clientes ▲ *an increase in the debtor collection period* un incremento en la rotación de clientes ▲ *reduce the debtor collection period* reducir la rotación de clientes

debtor company
A debtor company is an enterprise set up as a limited liability company that owes money or other services to another enterprise.
sociedad deudora
≠ sociedad acreedora
▲ *share capital of the debtor company* el capital social de la sociedad deudora ▲ *the debtor company's parent* la matriz de la sociedad deudora

debtor days ratio
≠ creditor days ratio
The debtor days ratio is defined as average trade debtors divided by sales multiplied by 365 days. This ratio shows the average number of days that credit is granted to customers by measuring the time it takes them to pay.
rotación de deudores
= plazo promedio de deudores
≠ rotación de acreedores
▲ *a small improvement in the debtor days ratio* una pequeña mejora en la rotación de deudores ▲ *annualised debtor days ratio* rotación de deudores anualizada

debtor due after one year
→ debtor falling due after more than one year

debtor due within one year
→ debtor falling due within one year

debtor falling due after more than one year UK
Debtors falling due after more than one year are outstanding balances that do not fall due until after more than one year.
deudores a largo plazo
NOTE Always plural in Spanish balance sheets.
▲ *a decrease in debtors falling due after more than one year* un descenso en deudores a largo plazo ▲ *recognise within debtors falling due after more than one year* reconocer dentro de deudores a largo plazo ▲ *total debtors falling due after more than one year* total deudores a largo plazo

debtor falling due within one year UK
"Debtors falling due within one year" is recognised under current assets in the balance sheet meaning outstanding balances that fall due within one year, typically amounts of money owed by customers.
deudores a corto plazo
NOTE Always plural in Spanish balance sheets.
▲ *increase in debtors falling due within one year* aumento en deudores a corto plazo ▲ *total debtors falling due within one year* total deudores a corto plazo

debtor insurance
Debtor insurance is an arrangement whereby an enterprise takes out insurance covering any losses that may result if one or more debtors do not pay what they owe the enterprise.
seguro de impago
= seguro contra impago
▲ *optional debtor insurance* seguro de impago opcional

debtor risk
The risk that the debtors of an enterprise cannot meet their obligations towards the enterprise is called debtor risk.
riesgo de impago
= riesgo de insolvencia
▲ *manage the debtor risk* gestionar el riesgo de impago ▲ *the relative debtor risk* el riesgo de impago relativo

debtors' ledger UK
= sales ledger US
≠ creditors' ledger UK, purchases ledger US
A debtors' or sales ledger is a book or group of accounts containing the individual debtors' accounts, i.e. amounts owed by customers. The debtors' ledger records sales made on credit, amounts received and discounts given. Today, debtors' ledgers are usually stored on computer files that have replaced the old-time binders.
libro de deudores
= libro de ventas
≠ libro de acreedores, libro de compras
▲ *balance as per debtors' ledger* saldo según el libro de deudores
⇛ nominal ledger

decide
To decide means to make a decision based on careful consideration of the data and options available.
decidir
▲ *decide to change accounting policy for borrowing costs* decidir cambiar la política contable de los costes de préstamo ▲ *decide to change the balance sheet date* decidir cambiar la fecha de balance ▲ *operations that the entity has decided to dispose of as a result of the business combination* operaciones que una entidad ha decidido eliminar como resultado de la combinación de negocios

decision
A decision is a choice made, or an opinion or judgment arrived at, after careful consideration.
decisión
▲ *a decision to do something* una decisión para hacer algo ▲ *a management decision to restructure taken before the balance sheet date* una decisión para reestructurar tomada por la dirección antes de la fecha del balance ▲ *assist users in making economic decisions* asistir a los usuarios en la toma de decisiones económicas ▲ *influence the economic decisions of users* influir en las decisiones económicas de los usuarios ▲ *make economic decisions* tomar decisiones económicas ▲ *the financial and operating policy decisions of an entity* las decisiones de política financiera y operativa de una entidad

decision model
A decision model is a method for choosing between alternatives, often involving quantita-

tive and/or qualitative analyses.

modelo de decisión

▲ *a microeconomic decision model* un modelo de decisión microeconómico ▲ *a rational decision model* un modelo de decisión racional ▲ *an economic decision model* un modelo de decisión económico

decision table

A decision table is a matrix showing various conditions for decisions and any values or contingencies of decision results. A decision table is used in a decision-making process.

cuadro de decisión

▲ *make a decision table* hacer un cuadro de decisión ▲ *use a decision table* utilizar un cuadro de decisión

decision-making process

A decision-making process is the sequence of stages through which a decision debate passes.

proceso de toma de decisiones

▲ *an efficient decision-making process* un proceso de toma de decisiones eficiente ▲ *participate in the decision-making process* participar en el proceso de toma de decisiones ▲ *take part in the decision-making process* participar en el proceso de toma de decisiones

declaration

A declaration is a formal written or oral statement about a specific matter.

anotación

▲ *a declaration on the annual report* una anotación en el informe anual ▲ *make a declaration* hacer una anotación

declare

To declare means to make a formal written or oral statement about a specific matter.

declarar

▲ *declare oneself satisfied* declararse satisfecho

declare for tax purposes

To declare an amount for tax purposes is to state the amount on which taxes, e.g. VAT or excise duties, are payable.

declarar por motivos fiscales

▲ *fail to declare for tax purposes* no declarar por motivos fiscales ▲ *failure to declare for tax purposes* inclumiento al declarar por motivos fiscales

⇛ excise duty, VAT

declared for tax purposes

Amounts declared for tax purposes are amounts disclosed to the tax authorities on which e.g. VAT or excise duties are payable.

declarado por motivos fiscales

▲ *purchases declared for tax purposes* compras declaradas por motivos fiscales ▲ *revenue declared for tax purposes* ingresos declarados por motivos fiscales

decline

≠ increase

A decline is a fall or a setback compared with an earlier level or situation.

disminución

≠ incremento

▲ *a decline in market value of investments* una disminución en el valor de mercado de las inversiones ▲ *a decline in revenue* una disminución en los ingresos ▲ *a decline in the price of materials* una disminución en el precio de los materiales ▲ *a decline of 3%* una disminución del 3% ▲ *a seasonal decline* una disminución estacionaria ▲ *a significant decline in budgeted net cash flows or operating profit* una disminución significativa en los flujos de efectivo netos presupuestados o en el beneficio de explotación ▲ *decline in activities* disminución en actividades ▲ *decline in the activities of the company* disminución en las actividades de la empresa ▲ *rapid decline* disminución rápida ▲ *slow decline* disminución lenta

declining balance amortization US

→ declining-balance amortization

declining balance depreciation US

→ declining-balance depreciation

declining balance method US

→ declining-balance method

declining-balance amortization US

= diminishing-balance amortisation IAS/IFRS, reducing-balance amortisation UK

≠ straight-line amortisation UK, straight-line amortization US

Declining-balance amortization is a method of allocating the cost of an intangible asset over its useful life by charging against income for each accounting period a percentage of each year's amortisable amount, which means that the amortisation charge is reduced each year.

amortización decreciente
= amortización degresiva
≠ amortización lineas y constante
▲ *the calculation of declining balance amortization* el cálculo de la amortización decreciente ▲ *use the declining balance amortization method* utilizar el método de amortización decreciente

declining-balance depreciation US
= diminishing-balance depreciation, reducing-balance depreciation
Declining-balance depreciation is a method of allocating the cost of a tangible asset over its useful life, in which the depreciation charge for each accounting period in the profit and loss account is based on a percentage of each year's depreciable amount which means that each year's charge is reduced.

depreciación decreciente
= depreciación degresiva
▲ *declining-balance depreciation for tax purposes* depreciación decreciente por motivos fiscales ▲ *total declining-balance depreciation* total depreciación decreciente

declining-balance method US
= declining balance method US, diminishing-balance method IAS/IFRS, UK, reducing-balance method UK
≠ straight-line method
The declining-balance method is a method of allocating the cost of a tangible or an intangible asset over its useful life, in which the depreciation or amortisation charge for each accounting period is based on a percentage of the asset's depreciable or amortisable amount at the beginning of the period, which means that the depreciation or amortisation charge is reduced each year.

método de amortización decreciente
= método de amortización degresiva
▲ *the declining-balance method for tax purposes* el método de amortización decreciente por motivos fiscales

decrease
= reduction
A decrease is a reduction in amount or a limitation of scope.

disminución
= decrecimiento
▲ *a decrease in the present value of the economic benefits* una disminución en el valor actual de los beneficios económicos ▲ *a decrease in value of asset items* una disminución en el valor de las partidas del activo ▲ *a decrease of a liability* una disminución del pasivo ▲ *a material decrease in recoverable amount* una disminución material en la cantidad recuperable ▲ *a permanent decrease in value* una disminución permanente de valor ▲ *a revaluation increase or decrease* un aumento o disminución de la revalorización ▲ *a temporary decrease in value* una disminución temporal de valor ▲ *the decrease in the purchasing power of the shareholders' interests* la disminución en el poder adquisitivo de los minoritarios ▲ *the increase or decrease in carrying amount* el incremento o disminución en el valor contable

deduct
To deduct is to subtract an amount from another amount, i.e. reduce an amount by another amount resulting in a lowering of the original amount.

deducir
= sustraer
▲ *deduct a loss from the taxable income* deducir una pérdida de los ingresos imponibles ▲ *deduct a value* deducir un valor ▲ *deduct an amount* sustraer una cantidad ▲ *deduct consolidated goodwill* deducir el fondo de comercio consolidado ▲ *deduct costs* deducir costes ▲ *deduct expenses* deducir gastos ▲ *deduct for tax purposes on a cash basis* deducir a efectos fiscales aplicando el criterio de caja ▲ *deduct prepayments from customers* deducir los anticipos de los clientes ▲ *deduct tax losses* deducir pérdidas fiscales ▲ *right to deduct* derecho a deducir

deductibility US
Deductibility is the right to deduct an amount that is deductible for tax purposes.

derecho a deducir
= deducibilidad
▲ *allow deductibility* permitir un derecho a deducir ▲ *deductibility in full* derecho a deducir la totalidad ▲ *deductibility of an amount* derecho a deducir una cantidad ▲ *deductibility of an expense* derecho a deducir un gasto ▲ *deductibility of insurance premiums* derecho a deducir primas de seguro ▲ *deductibility of interest* derecho a deducir intereses ▲ *deductibility of losses* derecho a deducir pérdidas ▲ *deductibility of royalties* derecho a deducir royalties

deductible

An expense that is deductible is an expense that may be deducted from the taxable income thereby reducing the amount payable for tax purposes by the tax payer. Both natural persons and legal persons or entities are entitled to deductions or allowances if the deduction or allowance comply with the tax requirements.

deducible
▲ *a deductible expense* un gasto deducible ▲ *a deductible loss* una pérdida deducible ▲ *a deductible maintenance cost* un coste de mantenimiento deducible ▲ *a deductible operating cost* un coste de explotación deducible ▲ *deductible for tax purposes* deducible fiscalmente ▲ *deductible temporary differences* diferencias temporarias deducibles ▲ *deductible VAT* IVA deducible ▲ *expenses not deductible for tax purposes* gastos no deducibles fiscalmente

deductible temporary difference
IAS/IFRS
≠ taxable temporary difference
IAS/IFRS

Deductible temporary differences are temporary differences giving rise to amounts that will be deductible in determining taxable profit (loss) of future accounting periods. Deductible temporary differences usually result in deferred tax assets.

diferencia temporaria deducible
= diferencia temporal deducible
≠ diferencia temporaria imponible
▲ *a deductible temporary difference arises* una diferencia temporaria deducible surge ▲ *amounts arising from deductible temporary differences* cantidades que surgen de las diferencias temporarias deducibles ▲ *deductible temporary differences associated with investments* diferencias temporarias deducibles asociadas con inversiones ▲ *expiry date of deductible temporary differences* fecha de vencimiento de las diferencias temporarias deducibles ▲ *recover the benefit of deductible temporary differences* reconocer el beneficio de las diferencias temporarias deducibles ▲ *reversal of deductible temporary differences* reversión de las diferencias temporarias deducibles ▲ *utilise the deductible temporary difference* aplicar la diferencia temporaria deducible
SOURCE IAS 12
⇛ deferred tax asset, temporary difference

deduction
= subtraction
≠ addition

A deduction is the subtraction of an amount from another amount resulting in a reduction of the original amount.

deducción
▲ *after deduction of VAT and rebates* después de la deducción del IVA y bonificaciones ▲ *net actuarial gains of the current period after the deduction of past service cost of the current period* ganancias actuariales netas del periodo actual después de la deducción de los costes por servicio prestado del periodo actual ▲ *recognise goodwill as a deduction from equity* reconocer el fondo de comercio como una deducción del patrimonio ▲ *the amount of the tax deduction* la cantidad de la deducción fiscal
⇛ tax deduction

deem to be zero IAS/IFRS

To deem to be zero is to consider to be of no value and recognise an item at the figure 0. In the context of IFRS, a first-time IFRS adopter e.g. may not recognise existing cumulative translation differences on foreign activities according to a special exemption rule, but may deem such differences to be zero.

saldo cero

▲ *deemed to be zero at the date of transition to IFRSs* saldo cero a la fecha de transición a las NIIFs

SOURCE IFRS 1

deemed cost

Deemed cost is an amount used instead of cost or depreciated cost at a specific date. Any following amortisation or depreciation is made on the assumption that the enterprise initially recognised the asset or liability at a cost equal to the deemed cost.

coste atribuido

= coste asignado

▲ *fair value or revaluation as deemed cost* valor razonable o revalorización como coste atribuido ▲ *have a deemed cost of zero in the opening IFRS balance sheet* tener cero como coste atribuido en el balance de apertura basado en la NIIF ▲ *the deemed cost of goodwill* el coste atribuido del fondo de comercio ▲ *use an event-driven fair value measurement as deemed cost* utilizar una medición del valor razonable de un acontecimiento inevitable como coste atribuido

SOURCE IFRS 1, Appendix A

defer

To defer is to postpone e.g. a process, a time limit or deadline.

diferir

▲ *defer expenses for subsequent recognition* diferir gastos para su reconocimiento posterior ▲ *defer payment without incurring an explicit interest charge* diferir el pago sin incurrir en gasto por interés explícito ▲ *defer recognition of the benefit of tax losses until the period of realisation* diferir el reconocimiento del beneficio por pérdidas fiscales hasta el periodo de realización ▲ *defer settlement of the liability for at least twelve months after the balance sheet date* diferir el pago de la obligación hasta al menos doce meses después de la fecha del balance

⇛ deferred income, deferred tax

deferral

A deferral is a postponement or extension of e.g. a process, a time limit, payment or deadline or of the recognition of an item in the financial statements.

diferimiento

▲ *deferral of capital gains taxation* diferimiento del impuesto de sociedades ▲ *deferral of gains and losses on hedging transactions* diferimiento de las ganancias y pérdidas en las transacciones con cobertura ▲ *deferral of recognition* diferimiento del reconocimiento ▲ *deferral of tax loss* diferimiento de las pérdidas fiscales ▲ *deferral of the recognition of hedging transactions in the income statement* diferimiento del reconocimiento de las transacciones con cobertura en el balance

deferral method

The deferral method is a method for computing deferred tax. Under this method, tax payments are deferred to subsequent periods and calculated at the tax rates applicable at the balance sheet date of the period when the deferred tax asset or liability originated. Another more commonly used method is the liability method which, by contrast, applies tax rates currently in force.

método del diferimiento

▲ *follow the deferral method* seguir el método del diferimiento ▲ *under the deferral method* según el método del diferimiento ▲ *use the deferral method of accounting for income taxes* utilizar el método del diferimiento para contabilizar el impuesto sobre beneficios

⇛ deferred tax, deferred tax asset, deferred tax liability

deferred asset

Deferred assets are assets representing cash or other assets receivable after more than one year from the balance sheet date.

cobro diferido

▲ *give rise to deferred assets* dar lugar a cobros diferidos

deferred income

Under the accruals concept, deferred income is an item recognised under liabilities in the balance sheet concerning a payment received in advance of the period to which it relates.

ingreso diferido
▲ *classify as deferred income* clasificar como ingreso diferido ▲ *negative goodwill that is treated as deferred income* fondo de comercio negativo que se trata como ingreso diferido ▲ *reduce the deferred income balance by the amount repayable* reducir el ingreso diferido del balance por la cantidad reembolsable
⇛ accruals and deferred income

deferred income tax US
Deferred income tax is tax expected paid in future that is attributable to timing or temporary differences between the carrying amount and the tax value of assets and liabilities of an enterprise at the balance sheet date. Deferred tax comprises both deferred tax liabilities and deferred tax assets.
impuesto diferido
▲ *a significant increase in deferred income tax* un aumento significativo en el impuesto diferido ▲ *the aggregate amount of current and deferred income tax credited or charged to equity* la cantidad agregada de impuesto corriente y diferido
⇛ deferred tax asset, deferred tax liability

deferred liability
A deferred liability is a liability that has not yet been recognised in the financial statements, but is postponed to a future accounting period, because the recognition requirements have not been met. Deferred tax is an example of a deferred liability.
pago diferido
▲ *give rise to deferred liabilities* dar lugar a pagos diferidos

deferred maintenance
Deferred maintenance is maintenance that should have been carried out as part of the regular maintenance, but which has not yet been effected. Provisions cannot be made for such maintenance.
mantenimiento extraordinario
= reparación extraordinaria
▲ *deferred maintenance of property, plant and equipment* mantenimiento extraordinario de propiedad, planta y equipo ▲ *provision for deferred maintenance* provisión por mantenimiento extraordinario

deferred payment
= additional payment
Deferred payment is payment delayed until a later time or date.
pago diferido
= pago aplazado
▲ *make a deferred payment* hacer un pago aplazado

deferred revenue
Deferred revenue refers to cash payments from customers prior to the enterprise's provision of the goods or services to which the payments relate, i.e. the revenue is not earned yet, but payment has been received.
ingreso diferido
▲ *deferred revenue and most warranty obligations* ingreso diferido y obligaciones garantizadas

deferred tax
= deferred taxation
Deferred tax is tax expected paid in future that is attributable to timing or temporary differences between the carrying amount and the tax value of assets and liabilities of an enterprise at the balance sheet date. Deferred tax comprises both deferred tax liabilities and deferred tax assets.
impuesto diferido
▲ *a significant increase in deferred tax* un aumento significativo en el impuesto diferido ▲ *adjustment of deferred tax* ajuste del impuesto diferido ▲ *change in deferred tax* cambio en el impuesto diferido ▲ *change in deferred tax* cambio en el impuesto diferido ▲ *deferred tax for the year* el impuesto diferido del ejercicio ▲ *determination of deferred tax* determinación del impuesto diferido ▲ *estimated deferred tax* impuesto diferido estimado ▲ *make full provision for deferred tax* hacer una provisión completa por impuesto diferido ▲ *make partial provision for deferred tax* hacer una provisión parcial por impuesto diferido ▲ *negative deferred tax* impuesto diferido negativo ▲ *provision for deferred tax* provisión por impuesto diferido ▲ *release deferred tax as current tax* calificar el impuesto diferido como corriente

⇛ deferred tax asset, deferred tax liability, temporary difference, timing difference

deferred tax adjustment

Deferred tax adjustments are changes in and reversals of deferred tax previously recognised in the financial statements, e.g. because of differences between deferred tax provided and actual tax incurred on assets sold during the financial year, any impairment losses, or any restatements to new accounting policies involving changes in the recognition of items, such as depreciation or amortisation changes.

ajuste por impuesto diferido

▲ *an immaterial deferred tax adjustment* un ajuste por impuesto diferido intangible ▲ *give rise to a deferred tax adjustment* dar lugar a un ajuste por impuesto diferido ▲ *total before deferred tax adjustment* total antes del ajuste por impuesto diferido

deferred tax asset

Deferred tax assets are income tax amounts that an enterprise can recover in future accounting periods concerning carryforwards of unutilised tax losses or tax credits and deductible temporary differences.

activo por impuesto diferido

▲ *discounting of deferred tax assets acquired* descuento de los activos por impuesto diferido adquiridos ▲ *give rise to a deferred tax asset* dar lugar a un activo por impuesto diferido ▲ *measurement of deferred tax assets* medición de los activos por impuesto diferido ▲ *realisation of a deferred tax asset* realización de un activo por impuesto diferido ▲ *recognised deferred tax assets* activos por impuesto diferido reconocidos ▲ *recover a deferred tax asset* recuperar un activo por impuesto diferido ▲ *set off a deferred tax asset against a deferred tax liability* compensar un activo por impuesto diferido con un pasivo por impuesto diferido ▲ *the carrying amount of a deferred tax asset* el valor contable de un activo por impuesto diferido

SOURCE IAS 12

⇛ deferred tax

deferred tax expense

Deferred tax expense adds to deferred tax liability and arises from any changes during the accounting year of an enterprise's deferred tax liabilities and assets because of e.g. changes in tax rates, write-downs or reversals or any temporary differences that arise or are reversed.

gasto por impuesto diferido

▲ *classify as deferred tax expense* clasificar como gasto por impuesto diferido ▲ *deferred tax expense arising from the write-down of a deferred tax asset* gasto por impuesto diferido resultante de la amortización de un cobro por impuesto diferido ▲ *recognise the resulting deferred tax expense in the income statement* reconocer el gasto por impuesto diferido resultante en el balance ▲ *the amount of deferred tax expense relating to changes in tax rates* la cantidad de gasto por impuesto diferido relacionado con cambios en los tipos impositivos ▲ *the amount of deferred tax expense relating to the origination and reversal of temporary differences* la cantidad de gasto por impuesto diferido relacionada con el origen y la reversión de las diferencias temporales

deferred tax for the year

Deferred tax for the year represents the change in deferred tax from the beginning to the end of the accounting period excluding changes resulting from the acquisition or disposal of enterprises.

impuesto diferido del ejercicio

▲ *recognition of deferred tax for the year* reconocimiento del impuesto diferido del ejercicio ▲ *specification of the tax for the year as current tax and deferred tax for the year* desglose del impuesto del ejercicio como impuesto corriente e impuesto diferido

⇛ deferred tax

deferred tax liability

A deferred tax liability is the income tax amount payable in future accounting periods related to a taxable temporary difference.

pasivo por impuesto diferido

▲ *give rise to a deferred tax liability* dar lugar a un pasivo por

impuesto diferido ▲ *recognise a deferred tax liability* reconocer un pasivo por impuesto diferido ▲ *set off a deferred tax asset against a deferred tax liability* compensar un activo por pasivo diferido con un pasivo por pasivo diferido ▲ *subsequent changes in the unrecognised deferred tax liability* cambios posteriores en el pasivo por impuesto diferido no reconocido ▲ *the measurement of deferred tax liabilities* la medición de los pasivos por impuesto diferido
SOURCE IAS 12
⇛ deferred tax

deferred tax recognition
Deferred tax recognition is the recording of deferred tax as an item in the financial statements.
reconocimiento del impuesto diferido
= contabilización del impuesto diferido
▲ *changes in deferred tax recognition* cambios en el reconocimiento del impuesto diferido

deferred taxation
= deferred tax
Deferred taxation is tax expected paid in future that is attributable to timing or temporary differences between the carrying amount and the tax value of assets and liabilities of an enterprise at the balance sheet date. Deferred tax comprises both deferred tax liabilities and deferred tax assets.
tributación diferida
▲ *changes in deferred taxation* cambios en tributación diferida ▲ *make provision for deferred taxation* hacer una provisión por tributación diferida ▲ *transfer to deferred taxation* transferir a tributación diferida
⇛ deferred tax asset, deferred tax liability, temporary difference, timing difference

deficit
≠ surplus
A deficit arises when a negative amount is higher than a positive amount, e.g. when expenditure exceeds income or imports exceed exports, or when there is a shortfall of something required or expected.
NOTE In a non-profit organisation, a negative bottom line is referred to as a deficit.
déficit
≠ superávit
▲ *a budget deficit* un déficit presupuestario ▲ *a large deficit* un gran déficit ▲ *alter the revaluation surplus or deficit previously recognised on the asset* alterar el superávit o déficit previamente reconocido en el activo ▲ *revaluation surpluses and deficits* superávits y déficits ▲ *reverse a revaluation deficit* revertir un déficit
⇛ loss

defined benefit
= DB
≠ DC, defined contribution
Defined benefit is a term used in connection with a type of pension plan, defined benefit plans, from which the benefits payable to pensioners are based on salary at or near retirement and years of service and not on the contributions paid into the plan and the returns on the plan's investments. Defined benefit plans do not include personal pension plans, but are typically occupational pension plans under which it is the enterprise's obligation to provide the agreed benefits to current and former employees whether or not the amount of such benefits exceed the contributions.
prestación definida
≠ aportación definida
▲ *a defined benefit asset* un activo por prestación definida ▲ *a defined benefit liability* un pasivo por prestación definida ▲ *a defined benefit obligation* una obligación por prestación definida ▲ *a defined benefit plan* un plan de prestación definida ▲ *defined benefit multiemployer plan* plan de prestación definida multiempresa ▲ *defined benefit retirement plan* plan de pensiones de prestación definida
⇛ defined benefit plan

defined benefit liability
A defined benefit liability is the net total amount of the defined benefit obligation's present value less the fair value of any plan assets out of which the obligations are to be settled. This amount may be increased by unrecognised net

actuarial gains and decreased by unrecognised past service cost.

obligación por prestación definida

▲ *recognise as a defined benefit liability* reconocer como una obligación por prestación definida

defined benefit obligation

Defined benefit obligation refers to an enterprise's obligation to pay pension benefits to current and former employees who are members of the enterprise's defined benefit plan. The value of this obligation is calculated as the present value of expected benefits payable to members in the future without deducting the value of the plan assets.

obligación por prestación definida

▲ *determine the present value of the defined benefit obligation* determinar el valor actual de la obligación por prestación definida ▲ *measure the defined benefit obligation* cuantificar la obligación por prestación definida ▲ *settle a defined benefit obligation* pagar una obligación por prestación definida ▲ *the actuarial gains and losses on the defined benefit obligation* los resultados actuariales de la obligación por prestación definida

defined benefit pension plan

→ defined benefit plan

defined benefit plan IAS/IFRS, US

= DB plan, defined benefit scheme UK, final salary scheme UK, salary-related scheme UK

≠ DC plan, defined contribution plan US, IAS/IFRS, defined contribution scheme UK, money-purchase scheme UK

A defined benefit plan is a pension plan from which the benefits payable to pensioners are based on salary at or near retirement and years of service and not on the contributions paid into the plan and the returns on the plan's investments. Defined benefit plans do not include personal pension plans, but are typically occupational pension plans under which it is the enterprise's obligation to provide the agreed benefits to current and former employees whether or not the amount of such benefits exceed the contributions.

plan de prestación definida

▲ *accounting for defined benefit plans* contabilizando planes de prestación definida ▲ *an overfunded defined benefit plan* un plan de prestación definida sobredotado ▲ *curtailment of a defined benefit plan* reducción de un plan de prestación definida ▲ *funded defined benefit plans* planes de prestación definida suficientemente dotados ▲ *multi-employer defined benefit plans* planes de prestación definida multiempresas ▲ *settlement of a defined benefit plan* pago de un plan de prestación definida ▲ *the formal terms of a defined benefit plan* las condiciones formales de un plan de prestación definida ▲ *the present value of the defined benefit plan* el valor actual del plan de prestación definida ▲ *transitional liability for a defined benefit plan* obligación transitoria para un plan de prestación definida ▲ *unfunded defined benefit plans* planes de prestación definida insuficientemente dotados ▲ *wholly or partly funded defined benefit plan* plan de prestación definida total o parcialmente dotado

SOURCE IAS 19

defined benefit scheme UK

= DB plan, defined benefit plan IAS/IFRS, US, final salary scheme UK, salary-related scheme UK

≠ DC plan, defined contribution plan IAS/IFRS, US, defined contribution scheme UK, money-purchase plan UK

A defined benefit scheme is a pension scheme from which the benefits payable to pensioners are based on salary at or near retirement and years of service and not on the contributions paid into the scheme and the returns on the scheme's investments. Defined benefit schemes do not include personal pension schemes, but are typically occupational pension schemes under which it is the enterprise's obligation to provide the agreed benefits to current and former employees whether or not the amount of such benefits exceed the contributions.

plan de prestación definida

▲ *accounting for defined benefit schemes* contabilizando los pla-

nes de prestación definida ▲ *curtailment of a defined benefit scheme* reducción de un plan de prestación definida ▲ *settlement of a defined benefit scheme* pago de un plan de prestación definida ▲ *the present value of the defined benefit scheme* el valor actual de un plan de prestación definida ▲ *wholly or partly funded defined benefit schemes* planes de prestación definida total o parcialmente dotados
SOURCE FRS 17

defined contribution
= DC
≠ DB, defined benefit
Defined contribution is a term used in connection with a type of pension plan, defined contribution plans, from which the benefits payable to pensioners are based entirely on the contributions paid into the plan by the member, or on behalf of the member, and on the returns on the plan's investments. All personal pension plans are of the defined contribution type, however, occupational pension plans may also be of this type.
aportación definida
≠ prestación definida
▲ *defined contribution plan* plan de aportación definida
⇛ defined contribution plan

defined contribution pension plan
→ defined contribution plan

defined contribution plan US, IAS/IFRS
= DC plan, defined contribution scheme UK, money-purchase scheme UK
≠ DB plan, defined benefit plan IAS/IFRS, US, defined benefit scheme UK, final salary scheme UK, salary-related scheme
A defined contribution plan is a pension plan from which the benefits payable to pensioners are based entirely on the contributions paid into the plan by the member, or on behalf of the member, and on the returns on the plan's investments. All personal pension plans are of the defined contribution type, however, occupational pension plans may also be of this type.
plan de aportación definida
≠ plan de prestación definida
▲ *accounting for defined contribution plans* contabilizando los planes de aportación definida ▲ *classify a multi-employer plan as a defined contribution plan* clasificar un plan multiempresa como un plan de aportación definida ▲ *contributions to a defined contribution plan* aportaciones a un plan de aportación definida ▲ *recognised as an expense for defined contribution plans* reconocido como un gasto por planes de aportación definida ▲ *the contribution payable to a defined contribution plan* la aportación a ingresar en un plan de aportación definida

defined contribution scheme UK
= DC plan, defined contribution plan IAS/IFRS, US, money-purchase scheme UK
≠ DB plan, defined benefit plan IAS/IFRS, US, defined benefit scheme UK, final salary scheme UK, salary-related scheme UK
A defined contribution scheme is a pension scheme from which the benefits payable to pensioners are based entirely on the contributions paid into the scheme by the member, or on behalf of the member, and on the returns on the scheme's investments. All personal pension schemes are of the defined contribution type, however, occupational pension schemes may also be of this type.
plan de aportación definida
≠ plan de prestación definida
▲ *accounting for defined contribution schemes* contabilizando los planes de aportación definida ▲ *contributions to a defined contribution scheme* aportaciones a un plan de aportación definida ▲ *recognised as an expense for defined contribution schemes* reconocido como un gasto por planes de aportación definida ▲ *the contribution payable to a defined contribution scheme* la aportación a ingresar en un plan de aportación definida
SOURCE FRS 17

degressive
Degressive means going down gradually in percentage terms.
degresivo
≠ progresivo
▲ *degressive cost* coste degresivo
▲ *degressive tax* impuesto degresivo

delist
To delist means to remove the shares of a company from the

official list of quotations on a stock exchange.
retirar de bolsa
= sacar de bolsa
▲ *apply for the delisting of a company* solicitar la retirada de bolsa de una empresa ▲ *delist shares* retirar de bolsa las acciones ▲ *have a company delisted* retirar una empresa de bolsa

delisting
Delisting is the act of removing the shares of a company from the official list of quotations on a stock exchange.
salida de bolsa
= retirada de bolsa
▲ *apply for delisting* solicitar la salida de bolsa ▲ *delisting of the company* la salida de bolsa de la empresa ▲ *the company's delisting on the Stock Exchange* la salida de la empresa de la Bolsa

delivery cost
Delivery costs are the expenses incurred in bringing inventories to their existing location and condition from the supplier, such as freight, dispatch expenses and handling charges.
coste de envío
= gasto de envío
NOTE Spanish accountants prefer 'gasto de envío' to the IAS 'coste de envío'.
▲ *plus delivery costs* más costes de envío

demand[1] *noun*
A demand is a requirement for something or a firm request that something be done.
demanda
▲ *become payable on demand* pagadero a la presentación ▲ *comply with a demand* cumplir con una demanda ▲ *make a demand* demandar ▲ *meet a demand* satisfacer una demanda ▲ *place heavy demands on* colocar demandas graves sobre ▲ *repayable on demand* reembolsable a la presentación ▲ *withdraw deposits on demand* retirar depósitos a la vista

demand[2] *noun*
≠ supply
Demand is the quantity of goods and services that enterprises and consumers want to buy in a particular period of time.
demanda
≠ oferta
▲ *changes in the market demand for the products* cambios en la demanda de los productos ▲ *declining demand* demanda descendente ▲ *growing demand* demanda creciente ▲ *initial operating losses incurred while demand for the asset's output builds up* pérdidas de explotación iniciales incurridas durante el tiempo en el que aumenta la demanda de activos ▲ *meet the demand* satisfacer la demanda ▲ *poor demand* demanda débil

demand[3] *verb*
To demand is to require something or firmly request that something be done.
demandar
= exigir
▲ *demand immediate repayment* demandar el reembolso inmediato ▲ *demand information* demandar información ▲ *demand payment* exigir el pago

demand deposit
Demand deposits are receivables that may be withdrawn on demand without notice of intended withdrawal.
depósito a la vista
▲ *a non-interest-bearing demand deposit* un depósito a la vista no remunerado ▲ *cash demand deposit* depósito a la vista en efectivo ▲ *demand deposit with Danmarks Nationalbank* depósito a la vista en el Banco Nacional danés ▲ *demand deposit with no interest and instalment payable* depósitos a la vista sin intereses y pago a plazos ▲ *demand deposits with central banks* depósitos a la vista en los bancos centrales ▲ *demand deposits with credit institutions* depósitos a la vista en instituciones crediticias ▲ *the repayment of demand deposits of a bank* el reembolso de los depósitos a la vista de un banco

dematerialised security
= book-entry security UK, uncertificated security
A dematerialised security is a book-entry security that does not exist in a certificated form, but exists as an electronic entry in a register and is issued and transferred as an uncertificated financial instrument.
título intangible
= anotación en cuenta
▲ *issue and registration of dematerialised securities* emisión y registro de títulos intangibles

demerge

To demerge a company is to transfer all its assets and liabilities to one or more existing or newly formed enterprises against the payment of compensation to the owners of the demerged company.

escindir

▲ *demerge the company* escindir la empresa

demerged

= split

A demerged enterprise is an enterprise that has been sold off or divested from a group or is the result of a company split. A demerged enterprise continues in operation as an independent entity.

escindida

NOTE Always feminine in Spanish accounting texts as this adjective is part of a Spanish collocation with the feminine noun 'empresa'.

▲ *a demerged company* una empresa escindida ▲ *a demerged enterprise* una empresa escindida

⇛ demerger, merger

demerged subsidiary

A demerged subsidiary is a subsidiary that has been divested and disposed of by the parent company, either by a sell-off or by a transfer to another independent company following a split-up of a group.

filial escindida

▲ *repayment of debt from demerged subsidiaries* reembolso de la deuda de las filiales escindidas

⇛ demerger, merger

demerger

A demerger is a strategic transaction whereby a large enterprise or group of companies splits up into two or more legally independent entities which carry on the activities.

escisión

▲ *by demerger* por escisión ▲ *complete a demerger* completar una escisión ▲ *Danish Act on Merger, Demerger and Addition of Assets etc.* La Ley danesa sobre Fusión, Escisión y Canje de Activos, etc. ▲ *demerger by acquisition* escisión por adquisición ▲ *demerger by the formation of new companies* escisión mediante la formación de nuevas empresas ▲ *disposal on demerger and divestment* enajenación por escisión y desinversión ▲ *enterprises' acquisition of assets and liabilities in connection with a demerger* la adquisición de activos y pasivos de las empresas en conexión con una escisión ▲ *merger and demerger accounting* contabilidad de la fusión y escisión ▲ *notification of an adopted demerger* notificación de una escisión adoptada ▲ *tax-exempt demerger* escisión exenta de impuestos ▲ *the companies involved in the demerger* las empresas implicadas en la escisión

demerger accounts UK

≠ joint and opening balance sheets, joint balance sheet for the merger

Demerger accounts are financial statements prepared in connection with the splitting of a part or parts of an enterprise into separate entities. On the demerger, all or part of the enterprise's assets and liabilities are transferred to one or more existing or newly established enterprises.

balance de la escisión

▲ *merger and demerger accounts* balances de la fusión y escisión ▲ *prepare demerger accounts* preparar el balance de la escisión

demerger cost

Demerger costs are the expenses involved in a demerger, i.e. the split up of a large company or group into independent entities.

coste de escisión

▲ *other demerger costs* otros costes de escisión ▲ *the demerger costs incurred* los costes de escisión incurridos

demerger date

= date of demerger

The demerger date is the date when a large company or group is split up into independent entities.

fecha de escisión

▲ *at the demerger date* a la fecha de escisión

⇛ demerger

demerger financial statements

US, IAS/IFRS

= financial statements in respect of demerger

Financial statements in respect of demerger are prepared on

the split of an enterprise into two or more entities.
estados financieros de la escisión
▲ *prepare demerger financial statements* preparar los estados financieros de la escisión

denominate
To denominate is to state the value in a particular currency unit. Debt denominated in US dollar must be paid in US dollar.
denominar
▲ *a transaction which is denominated in a foreign currency* una transacción que se denomina en una moneda extranjera ▲ *cash flows denominated in a foreign currency* flujos de efectivo denominados en una moneda extranjera ▲ *denominate in several currencies* denominar en varias monedas ▲ *denominate in USD* denominar en dólares norteamericanos ▲ *denominated in euro* denominado en euros ▲ *payments denominated in units of an internal or external investment fund* pagos denominados en unidades de un fondo de inversión interno o externo

denominator level
= production-denominator level
A denominator level is a chosen production level based on e.g. the budgeted sales or the production capacity. The denominator level serves as a calculation basis for the rate of fixed indirect production costs used for allocation of these costs on various cost objects.
tasa predeterminada de distribución de costes indirectos
▲ *find a common denominator level* encontrar una tasa predeterminada de distribución de costes indirectos ▲ *fix the denominator level* fijar la tasa predeterminada de distribución de costes indirectos

denominator-level variance
= output level overhead variance, output-level variance, production-volume variance
Denominator-level variance is the difference between the budgeted fixed indirect production costs (overheads) and the fixed indirect production costs (overheads) that have been allocated to the produced units.
variación de la tasa predeterminada de distribución de costes indirectos
▲ *a favourable denominator-level variance* una variación de la tasa predeterminada de distribución de costes indirectos favorable ▲ *the denominator-level variance of a period* la variación de la tasa predeterminada de distribución de costes indirectos de un periodo

department
A department is a section or division of an organisation or enterprise with special responsibilities in which particular activities are carried out, e.g. the sales department.
departamento
▲ *an autonomous department* un departamento autónomo ▲ *set up a department* crear un departamento ▲ *the group's department of* el departamento del grupo de

department manager
A department manager is a manager heading a department in an enterprise and the employees within. Typically, a department manager guides the employees and is in control of the department's day-to-day operations.
director de departamento
▲ *be appointed department manager* ser nombrado director de departamento ▲ *the department manager of* el director del departamento de ▲ *under the control of the department manager* bajo el control del director de departamento

dependant variable
"Dependant" is a misspelling of "dependent".
→ dependent variable

dependent variable
≠ independent variable
A variable that is dependent is a variable whose value depends on the value or effect of an independent variable and which cannot be controlled. An example of a dependent variable is the number of defective units produced. The higher the amount of produced units is, the higher the amount of defective units will be. It is difficult for an enterprise to control the number of defects that oc-

cur as this number will depend on the number of produced units.

variable dependiente

≠ variable independiente

▲ *calculate a value of a dependent variable* calcular un valor de una variable dependiente ▲ *mean of dependent variable* mediana de la variable dependiente ▲ *standard deviation of dependent variable* desviación estándar de la variable dependiente

depletion

Depletion applies to wasting assets such as oil or mineral ores and refers to the physical using up and reducing of the supply of such assets.

agotamiento

▲ *a depletion of assets* un agotamiento de activos

deployment cost

Deployment costs are costs related to the use and maintenance of a product and include both fixed and variable costs, e.g. costs related to labour, installation, infrastructure and equipment. Deployment costs typically relate to telecommunications, IT and data networks.

coste de despliegue

▲ *a reduction in deployment costs* una reducción en los costes de despliegue ▲ *an increase in deployment costs* un aumento en los costes de despliegue ▲ *recognise deployment costs* reconocer los costes de despliegue ▲ *the deployment costs incurred* los costes de despliegue incurridos

deposit[1] *noun*

1 A deposit is an amount of money that is paid in advance as a down payment for goods or services to be rendered or lodged as security for renting something.

anticipo

= entrada

▲ *pay a deposit* pagar un anticipo ▲ *pay a deposit of USD 10,000* pagar un anticipo de 10.000 dólares norteamericanos ▲ *put down a deposit* dar una entrada

2 ≠ advance, withdrawal

A deposit constitutes funds or amounts of money placed with a bank or other financial institution in an account to be withdrawn on demand or at notice, depending on the type of account.

depósito

▲ *a deposit of cash with a bank* un depósito de efectivo en un banco ▲ *custody account deposits* depósitos en cuenta custodia ▲ *deposits held in banks* depósitos guardados en bancos ▲ *deposits with ceding undertakings* depósitos en empresas cedentes ▲ *make a deposit in a current account* abrir un depósito en una cuenta corriente

3 = depositing

Deposit is the act of leaving funds or valuables somewhere for safekeeping, e.g. at a bank or other financial institution.

depósito

▲ *deposit of mortgages* depósito de hipótecas ▲ *deposit of securities* depósito de valores ▲ *deposit of shares* depósito de acciones

deposit[2] *verb*

1 ≠ withdraw

To deposit is to leave something somewhere for safekeeping, e.g. money or other valuables at a bank or other financial institution.

depositar

≠ retirar

▲ *deposit money as security for a debt* depositar dinero como garantía de una deuda ▲ *deposit mortgages* depositar hipotecas ▲ *deposit securities* depositar valores ▲ *deposit shares* depositar acciones

2 ≠ withdraw

To deposit is to pay money into a bank account.

depositar

= ingresar

≠ retirar

▲ *deposit money with a bank* depositar dinero en un banco

deposit component

Besides an insurance component, insurance contracts, typically certain reinsurance contracts, may contain a deposit component consisting of premiums that are paid by policyholders before the period of risk. In the context of IFRS, a deposit component is a component that, according to IAS 39, is not recognised as a separate derivative financial instrument, but can be unbundled, i.e. separated, if it is possible to measure it separately from the insurance component.

componente de depósito

▲ *measure the deposit component separately* medir el componente de depósito por separado ▲ *obligations and rights arising from the deposit component* obligaciones y derechos procedentes del componente de depósito ▲ *unbundle an insurance contract into a deposit component and an insurance component* separar un contrato de seguros en un componente de depósito y un componente de seguro ▲ *unbundling of deposit components* separación de los componentes de depósito

SOURCE IFRS 4, Appendix A

depositary bank

= depository bank

A depositary bank is a bank holding funds or marketable securities, usually under a specific agreement. In connection with the listing of an alien company on a US stock exchange, a depositary bank will hold the alien (e.g. Danish) shares and issue American Depositary Receipts or American Depositary Shares representing such shares for trading purposes.

banco depositario

▲ *equity instruments issued by a depositary bank* instrumentos de patrimonio emitidos por un banco depositario ▲ *pay directly into the depositary bank* pagar directamente al banco depositario

⇛ American Depositary Receipt, American Depositary Share

depository bank

→ depositary bank

depreciable

When an asset is depreciable, the enterprise may depreciate and allocate that asset's value over time instead of recognising it as an expense on acquisition.

NOTE The term depreciable applies to tangible assets.

amortizable

▲ *a depreciable amount* una cantidad amortizable ▲ *the depreciation policy for depreciable leased assets* la política de amortización aplicada a los activos arrendados amortizables

⇛ amortisable

depreciable amount

The depreciable amount is the cost of a tangible fixed asset, or other revalued amount substituted for cost, less the residual value and any write-downs.

cantidad amortizable

= importe depreciable

▲ *systematic allocation of the depreciable amount of an asset over its useful life* distribución sistemática de la cantidad amortizable de un activo ▲ *the adjusted depreciable amount of the asset* la cantidad amortizable ajustada del activo ▲ *the calculation of the depreciable amount* el cálculo de la cantidad amortizable ▲ *the depreciable amount of an asset with a finite useful life* la cantidad amortizable de un activo con una vida útil limitada ▲ *the depreciable amount of an intangible asset* la cantidad amortizable de un activo intangible ▲ *the depreciable amount of an item of property, plant and equipment* la cantidad amortizable de una partida de edificios, instalaciones y equipos

⇛ amortisable amount

depreciable asset

When an asset is depreciable or amortisable, the enterprise may depreciate or amortise and allocate that asset's value over time instead of recognising it as an expense on acquisition.

NOTE The term depreciable applies to intangible assets and amortisable applies to tangible assets.

activo amortizable

▲ *depreciation of the depreciable assets based on their fair values* amortización de los activos amortizables basada en sus valores razonables ▲ *give rise to a depreciation expense for depreciable assets* originar un gasto de amortización para activos amortizables ▲ *grants related to depreciable assets* subvenciones relacionadas con activos amortizables ▲ *the expected pattern of consumption of economic benefits of a depreciable asset* el patrón esperado de agotamiento de beneficios económicos de un activo amortizable ▲ *treated as separate depreciable assets* trata-

do como activos amortizables independientes
⇛ amortisable asset

depreciate

To depreciate is to allocate the depreciable amount systematically over the useful life of a tangible asset.

amortizar

▲ *depreciate assets under finance leases* amortizar activos en régimen de arrendamiento financiero ▲ *depreciate fully* amortizar completamente ▲ *depreciate over a time period not exceeding the useful life of the asset* amortizar durante un periodo que no exceda la vida útil del activo ▲ *depreciate prospectively over the remaining useful life* amortizar prospectivamente durante la vida útil restante ▲ *depreciate the asset on a straight-line basis over its estimated useful life* amortizar el activo usando un método lineal durante el periodo estimado de vida útil

depreciated cost model

The depreciated cost model is a method for recognising investment properties where, subsequent to initial measurement, an enterprise is to measure investment properties at depreciated cost, i.e. cost less accumulated depreciation and impairment losses.

modelo de coste amortizado

▲ *under the depreciated cost model* según el modelo de coste amortizado ▲ *use the depreciated cost model under IAS 16* utilizar el modelo de coste amortizado según la NIC 16
SOURCE IAS 16, paragraph 30, IAS 40, IN 12
⇛ fair value model

depreciation

1 Depreciation is the systematic allocation of the cost of an asset over its useful life. Several depreciation methods exist. Depreciation for accounting purposes is differentiated from depreciation for tax purposes, as different rules apply. The term 'amortisation' is generally used when referring to intangible assets, whereas the term 'depreciation' applies to tangible assets.

amortización

▲ *a particular item of depreciation* una partida concreta de amortización ▲ *accelerated depreciation* amortización acelerada ▲ *accelerated depreciation allowances* bonificaciones por amortización acelerada ▲ *accounting depreciation* amortización contable ▲ *cumulative additional depreciation* amortización acumulada ▲ *cumulative depreciation for tax purposes* amortización acumulada por motivos fiscales ▲ *depreciation addback* amortización inversa ▲ *depreciation of plant and equipment used on the contract* amortización de instalaciones y equipos usados en el contrato ▲ *depreciation of the depreciable assets based on their fair values* amortización de los activos amortizables basada en sus valores razonables ▲ *depreciation/amortisation of tangible and intangible assets* depreciación/amortización de activos tangibles e intangibles ▲ *net of depreciation* neto de amortización ▲ *tax depreciation* amortización fiscal ▲ *the depreciation policy for depreciable leased assets* la política de amortización de los activos arrendados amortizables ▲ *the depreciation used in determining taxable profit* la amortización utilizada al determinar el beneficio imponible
⇛ amortisation, reducing-balance depreciation, straight-line depreciation

2 Depreciation means a reduction in value, e.g. a currency's fall in value.

depreciación

⇛ impairment

depreciation account

A depreciation account is an account in the accounting system recording the periodic depreciation charges on an enterprise's tangible assets.

cuenta de amortización

▲ *the depreciation account shows depreciation on plant and machinery for the year* la cuenta de amortización muestra la depreciación de instalaciones y maquinaria del año
⇛ amortisation account

depreciation accounting

Depreciation accounting is the financial reporting for and measuring of the cost of consumption, including the wearing out and using up, of a tangible fixed asset over its useful life. Depreciation is carried out by systematically allocating over time the cost of the asset under a chosen depreciation method, such as the straight-line or reducing-balance methods.

amortización contable

▲ *prescribe a method of depreciation accounting* prescribir un método de amortización contable

⇛ depreciation

depreciation adjustment

Depreciation adjustment is the adjustment made either to reflect the actual wear and tear on a particular fixed asset, or, in current cost accounting, to eliminate the difference arising between depreciation based on the current cost of assets and depreciation based on the historical cost of assets.

ajuste por depreciación

▲ *compute the depreciation adjustment* computar el ajuste por depreciación ▲ *depreciation adjustment of property, plant and equipment* ajuste por depreciación de edificios, instalaciones y equipos ▲ *make a depreciation adjustment* hacer un ajuste por depreciación

depreciation amount

= amount of depreciation US

The depreciation amount or charge is the amount calculated on the basis of the systematic allocation of the depreciable amount over the useful life of the asset that is written off each accounting period.

NOTE The term depreciation amount applies to tangible assets.

cuota de amortización

▲ *a fictitious depreciation amount* una cuota de amortización ficticia ▲ *a fixed depreciation amount* una cuota de amortización fija ▲ *an annual depreciation amount of EUR 250,000* una cuota de amortización anual por valor de 250.000 euros ▲ *the accumulated depreciation amount* la cuota de amortización acumulada ▲ *the total depreciation amount* la cuota de amortización total

⇛ amortisation amount

depreciation and amortisation expense IAS/IFRS

Depreciation and amortisation expense is an item in the income statement recognising the part of the cost of non-current assets charged against profit for the period under review in connection with an enterprise's allocation of the cost of a tangible asset over its useful life.

gasto por depreciación y amortización

▲ *total depreciation and amortisation expense* total gasto por depreciación y amortización

⇛ depreciation and other amounts written off tangible and intangible fixed assets

depreciation and other amounts written off tangible and intangible fixed assets UK

Depreciation and other amounts written off tangible and intangible fixed assets is an item in the profit and loss account as presented in the report format classified by nature.

depreciación y otras cantidades eliminadas de activos fijos tangibles e intangibles

⇛ depreciation and amortisation expense, impairment of property, plant and equipment

depreciation balance

The depreciation balance shows the net book value, i.e. carrying amount of a tangible asset less depreciation for the period.

NOTE The term depreciation balance applies to tangible assets.

saldo de depreciación

▲ *a negative depreciation balance* un saldo de depreciación negativo ▲ *increase in the depreciation balance* aumento en el saldo de depreciación

⇛ amortisation balance

depreciation base

= basis of depreciation UK, depreciable amount IAS/IFRS

The depreciation base is the cost of a tangible fixed asset, or other amount substituted for cost in the financial statements, less its scrap value. In the case of depreciated assets, the depreciation charge is deducted, and in the case of assets written-up, the revaluation surplus is added.

NOTE The term "depreciation base" applies to tangible assets.

base de depreciación

= cuota de depreciación

▲ *depreciation base for tax purposes* base de depreciación por motivos fiscales
⇛ amortisation base

depreciation basis for tax purposes
The depreciation basis for tax purposes is the amount of a tangible fixed asset subject to depreciation allowed under tax rules. This amount constitutes the cost of that asset plus any revaluations and less the residual value and any write-downs.
base de depreciación por motivos fiscales
▲ *depreciation basis for tax purposes according to assessed cash value* base de amortización por motivos fiscales de acuerdo al valor en efectivo estimado ▲ *difference between nominal purchase sum and depreciation basis for tax purposes* diferencia entre el valor de compra nominal y la base de amortización por motivos fiscales ▲ *the depreciation basis for tax purposes of an asset* la base de amortización por motivos fiscales de un activo
⇛ amortisation basis for tax purposes

depreciation charge UK
= depreciation cost UK, depreciation expense US, IAS/IFRS
A depreciation charge is the amount recognised as an expense in the profit and loss account relating to the depreciation provided for a particular accounting period in connection with an enterprise's allocation of the cost of a tangible asset over its useful life.
gasto por depreciación
▲ *a reduced depreciation charge* un gasto por depreciación reducido ▲ *adjust the depreciation charge for the current period* ajustar el gasto por depreciación para el periodo actual ▲ *determination of the depreciation charges to be recognised* determinación de los gastos por depreciación a reflejar ▲ *make a depreciation charge* hacer un gasto por depreciación ▲ *the depreciation charge for each period* el gasto por depreciación para cada periodo
⇛ depreciation

depreciation cost UK
= depreciation charge UK, depreciation expense US, IAS/IFRS
Depreciation costs refer to the costs related to an enterprise's allocation of the cost of a tangible asset over its useful life by means of depreciation. In each accounting period, part of the cost is recognised in the profit and loss account in the form of depreciation costs.
coste por depreciación
= coste de depreciación
▲ *a reduction in depreciation costs* una reducción en los costes por depreciación ▲ *less depreciation costs* menos costes por depreciación
⇛ depreciation

depreciation expense US, IAS/IFRS
= depreciation charge UK, depreciation cost UK
Depreciation expenses refer to the expenses related to an enterprise's allocation of the cost of a tangible asset over its useful life by means of depreciation. In each accounting period, part of the cost is recognised in the profit and loss account in the form of depreciation expenses.
gasto por depreciación
▲ *depreciation expense included after the acquisition date in the acquirer's income statement* gasto por depreciación incluido posteriormente a la fecha de adquisición en la cuenta de resultados del adquirente ▲ *give rise to a depreciation expense for depreciable assets* originar un gasto por depreciación de activos amortizables ▲ *the sum of the depreciation expense for the asset and the finance expense for the period* la suma del gasto por amortización del activo y del gasto financiero del periodo

depreciation for tax purposes
= tax depreciation
≠ accounting depreciation, depreciation for accounting purposes
Depreciation for tax purposes is the depreciation of a tangible asset allowed under tax legislation.
amortización fiscal
NOTE The presence of 'cumulative' in the collocation indicates that we are dealing with 'amortización' instead of 'depreciación', as Spanish accoun-

tants never use 'cumulative' with 'depreciación'.

▲ *cumulative depreciation for tax purposes* amortización fiscal acumulada

⇛ amortisation for tax purposes

depreciation method

The depreciation method is the policy applied by an enterprise for gradually writing down a tangible asset and allocating the cost over its useful life.

método de amortización

▲ *the choice of depreciation method* la elección del método de amortización ▲ *the depreciation method used* el método de amortización utilizado ▲ *the selected depreciation method* el método de amortización seleccionado

⇛ amortisation method

depreciation period

The depreciation period is the expected useful life of the asset, i.e. the period over which that asset is expected to be used by the enterprise, and the period over which the cost of the asset is allocated.

NOTE The term depreciation period applies to tangible assets.

periodo de amortización

= vida útil

▲ *a long depreciation period* un periodo de amortización largo ▲ *a short depreciation period* un periodo de amortización corto ▲ *reassess the depreciation period* volver a estimar el periodo de amortización ▲ *the remaining depreciation period* el periodo de amortización restante

⇛ amortisation period

depreciation policy

The depreciation policy is the method applied by an enterprise for allocating the costs of tangible assets over their useful lives.

NOTE The term depreciation policy applies to tangible assets.

política de amortización

▲ *depreciate in accordance with the group's depreciation policy* amortizar de acuerdo con el método de amortización del grupo ▲ *normal depreciation policy* política de amortización corriente ▲ *the depreciation policy for depreciable leased assets* la política de amortización para activos arrendados amortizables

⇛ amortisation policy, reducing-balance depreciation, straight-line depreciation

depreciation profile

The depreciation profile shows the allocation of the depreciation charges on an asset over the useful life.

NOTE The term depreciation profile applies to tangible assets.

perfil de la amortización

= perfil de amortización

▲ *expectations to the depreciation profile of an investment* previsiones con respecto al perfil de amortización de una inversión ▲ *the buyer's depreciation profile* el perfil de amortización del comprador ▲ *the discounted value of a depreciation profile* la bonificación por consumo de un perfil de amortización

⇛ amortisation profile

depreciation rate

The depreciation rate is the percentage rate at which tangible fixed assets are depreciated under a chosen depreciation method to determine the depreciation charge written off for an accounting period.

tasa de amortización

= porcentaje de amortización

▲ *a wrong depreciation rate* una tasa de amortización errónea ▲ *adjust the depreciation rate for the current period* ajustar la tasa de amortización para el periodo actual ▲ *depreciation rate change* cambio en la tasa de amortización ▲ *reduction of the depreciation rate* reducción de la tasa de amortización ▲ *straight-line depreciation rates* tasas de amortización linéales ▲ *the general depreciation rate* la tasa de amortización general ▲ *the use of different depreciation rates* el uso de porcentajes de amortización diferentes

⇛ amortisation rate, reducing-balance depreciation, straight-line depreciation

depreciation rule

Depreciation rules are official instructions for depreciation for financial reporting purposes and for tax purposes as provided by accounting standards and tax legislation respectively.

NOTE The term depreciation rule applies to tangible assets.

norma de amortización

▲ *a generous depreciation rule* una norma de amortización amplia

⇛ amortisation rule

depreciation schedule

A depreciation schedule shows the allocation of the depreciation amounts on a tangible asset over its useful life.

plan de amortización

▲ *amend the depreciation schedule* modificar el plan de amortización ▲ *changes in the depreciation schedule* cambios en el plan de amortización

⇛ amortisation schedule

deprival value

= DV

The deprival value of an asset is the loss that a business would suffer if it were to be deprived of the use of the asset.

valor de sustitución

▲ *carry at deprival value* llevar a valor de sustitución ▲ *measure the deprival value* medir el valor de sustitucion ▲ *revalue the assets to their deprival value* revalorizar los activos a sus valores de sustitución

deputy chairman

= vice chairman, vice-chairman

A deputy chairman is the vice chairman e.g. the person next in rank to the chairman.

vicepresidente

▲ *be appointed deputy chairman* ser nombrado vicepresidente

deputy chief executive

The deputive chief executive normally acts on behalf of the chief executive when he or she is absent.

viceconsejero delegado

▲ *be appointed deputy chief executive* ser nombrado viceconsejero delegado

deputy managing director

A deputy managing director is second-in-command to the managing director and acts as a substitute in his absence. The deputy managing director is authorised to act and make decisions on behalf of the managing director.

subdirector gerente

▲ *the former deputy managing director* el anterior subdirector gerente ▲ *the new deputy managing director* el nuevo subdirector gerente ▲ *the retiring deputy managing director* el subdirector gerente saliente

derecognise

To derecognise an item is to remove that item from the financial statements.

dar de baja

= eliminar

▲ *derecognise financial assets or financial liabilities* dar de baja los activos y pasivos financieros ▲ *derecognise negative goodwill* dar de baja el fondo de comercio negativo ▲ *financial assets derecognised under previous GAAP* activos financieros eliminados según los principios contables generalmente aceptados anteriores ▲ *immediately derecognise the asset given up* inmediatamente dar de baja el activo abandonado ▲ *the date that the asset is derecognised* la fecha en la que el activo se da de baja

derecognition

Derecognition takes place when (a part of) a previously recognised asset or liability is eliminated from the balance sheet of an enterprise.

baja en cuenta

= eliminación en cuenta

NOTE Spanish accountants prefer 'baja en cuenta' to the IAS/IFRS term 'eliminación en cuentas'.

▲ *apply the derecognition requirements in IAS 39* aplicar los requisitos de baja en cuenta previstos en la NIC 39 ▲ *at the date of derecognition* a la fecha de baja en cuenta ▲ *derecognition of financial assets* baja en cuenta de activos financieros ▲ *derecognition of financial liabilities* baja en cuenta de pasivos financieros ▲ *derecognition of items of property, plant and equipment retired or disposed of* baja en cuenta de partidas de edificios, instalaciones y equipos ▲ *derecognition provisions* disposiciones para baja en cuenta ▲ *qualify for derecognition* acceder a baja en cuenta ▲ *requirements relating to derecognition* requisitos relacionados con la eliminación en cuenta ▲ *retained after the derecognition transaction* mantenido después de la operación de eliminación en cuenta

derecognize US
= derecognise UK
To derecognize an item is to remove that item from the financial statements.
dar de baja
= eliminar
▲ *derecognize financial assets or financial liabilities* dar de baja los activos o pasivos financieros ▲ *derecognize negative goodwill* dar de baja el fondo de comercio negativo ▲ *financial assets derecognized under previous GAAP* activos financieros eliminados según los principios contables generalmente aceptados anteriores ▲ *immediately derecognize the asset given up* inmediatamente dar de baja el activo abandonado ▲ *the date that the asset is derecognized* la fecha en la que el activo se da de baja

deregistration
Deregistration is the cancellation of a previously made registration so that it is no longer effective.
eliminación
▲ *deregistration of a branch* eliminación de una sucursal

derivative
= derivative financial instrument
A derivative is a transaction or contract whose value depends on or is derived from an underlying asset and is short for derivative financial instrument. The value of a derivative depends on the performance of the underlying and related asset. The most common derivatives are options and futures.
derivado
▲ *a compound financial instrument with multiple embedded derivatives* un instrumento financiero compuesto con múltiples instrumentos derivados implícitos ▲ *a credit derivative default product* un producto contra impago de un derivado de crédito ▲ *a derivative based on climatic, geological, or other physical variables* un derivado basado en variables climáticas, geológicas, u otras variables físicas ▲ *a derivative that is embedded in an insurance contract* un derivado que está implícito en un contrato de seguros ▲ *acquisition of derivatives* adquisición de derivados ▲ *an embedded foreign currency derivative* un derivado en moneda extranjera implícito ▲ *eliminate all deferred losses and gains arising on derivatives* eliminar todos los resultados diferidos procedentes de derivados ▲ *embedded derivatives* derivados implícitos ▲ *exchange-traded derivatives* derivados en moneda extranjera ▲ *measure all derivatives at fair value* valorar todos los derivados a valor razonable ▲ *sale of derivatives* venta de derivados ▲ *separate an embedded derivative from its host contract* separar un derivado implícito de su principal ▲ *the term of the derivative* el plazo del derivado ▲ *trade in derivatives* negociar derivados ▲ *use a derivative to hedge an underlying non-financial variable* usar un derivado como protección de las variaciones del tipo de interés subyacente

derivative contract
= derivative
A derivative contract is a contract whose value depends on or derives from an underlying asset and refers to a derivative financial instrument. The value of a derivative contract depends on the performance of the underlying and related asset. The most common derivative contracts are options and futures.
contrato de derivado
▲ *credit derivative contract* contrato de derivado de crédito ▲ *enter into a derivative contract* suscribir un contrato de derivado

derivative financial instrument
A derivative financial instrument is a financial instrument whose value depends on changes in value of the underlying financial asset from which it is derived. These changes arise from fluctuations in interest rates, foreign exchange rates, commodity prices, security prices, credit ratings or credit indices, or similar variables. Derivative financial instruments include options, swaps, futures and forward contracts.
NOTE The short form “derivative” is also applied.
instrumento financiero derivado
▲ *a contractual obligation arising from a derivative financial*

instrument una obligación contractual procedente de un instrumento financiero derivado ▲ *account for something as a derivative financial instrument* contabilizar algo como un instrumento financiero derivado ▲ *enter into a hedging contract with a derivative financial instrument* suscribir un contrato de cobertura con un instrumento financiero derivado ▲ *liabilities resulting from derivative financial instruments* pasivos resultantes de instrumentos financieros derivados ▲ *regard a derivative financial instrument as a hedge instrument* considerar un instrumento financiero derivado como un instrumento de cobertura
⇛ futures contract

derivative instrument
→ derivative financial instrument

derivative market
The derivative market is a market where individuals and enterprises may hedge interest-rate and currency risks by investing in futures, swaps, options etc.
mercado de derivados
▲ *a liquid derivative market* un mercado de derivados con liquidez ▲ *a well-functioning derivative market* un mercado de derivados eficiente ▲ *an active derivative market* un mercado de derivados activo ▲ *an illiquid derivative market* un mercado de derivados sin liquidez ▲ *the size of the total derivative market* el tamaño del mercado de derivados total

derivative transaction
A derivative transaction refers to a transaction involving the purchase of derivative instruments via an intermediary, such as a bank or stock exchange, in order to reduce e.g. operational, currency or interest rate risk.
transacción de derivados
▲ *collateral in connection with derivative transactions* colateral en conexión con transacciones de derivados ▲ *enter into a derivative transaction* realizar una transacción de derivados

describe
To describe something is to give an oral or written account of the principal or special features of it, so that you have a clear and comprehensive understanding or idea of it.
describir
▲ *describe something in detail* describir algo con detalle ▲ *describe the core activities of the enterprise* describir las actividades principales de la empresa ▲ *describe the development in the enterprise's cash flow* describir la evolución en el flujo de efectivo de la empresa ▲ *describe the main features of the enterprise's financial performance* describir los principales rasgos de la actuación financiera de la empresa ▲ *describe the value of the product to the users* describir el valor del producto a los usuarios ▲ *describe the value of the service to the users* describir el valor del servicio a los usuarios ▲ *except as described in paragraphs 3-5* excepto como se describe en los párrafos 3 a 5

description
A description is an oral or written account of the principal or special features of something, so that you have a clear and comprehensive understanding or idea of it.
descripción
▲ *description of environmental factors* descripción de factores medioambientales ▲ *description of knowledge resources* descripción de recursos de conocimiento ▲ *description of principal activities* descripción de actividades básicas ▲ *description of related party transactions* descripción de transacciones entre partes vinculadas ▲ *description of special risks* descripción de riesgos especiales

designate
To designate is to classify or describe something for a specific purpose.
designar
▲ *a designated derivative* un derivado designado ▲ *designate a previously recognised financial asset as a financial asset at fair value through profit or loss* designar un activo financiero previamente reconocido como un activo financiero a valor razonable mediante beneficio o pérdida ▲ *designate as investments at fair value through pro-*

fit or loss calificar como inversiones a valor razonable mediante beneficio o pérdida ▲ *designate assets as available for sale* designar activos como mantenidos para la venta ▲ *remeasure designated insurance liabilities* volver a medir los pasivos del seguro designado ▲ *to designate irrevocably* designar irrevocablemente

designation

Designation means classification or description for a specific purpose.

designación

▲ *designation of an investment as held to maturity* designación de una inversión como mantenida hasta el vencimiento ▲ *designation of financial assets or financial liabilities* designación de activos o pasivos financieros ▲ *designation of financial items as hedged items* designación de partidas financieras como partidas protegidas ▲ *designation of groups of items as hedged items* designación de grupos de partidas como partidas protegidas ▲ *designation of hedging instruments* designación de instrumentos de cobertura ▲ *designation of non-financial items as hedged items* designación de partidas no financieras como partidas protegidas ▲ *designation of previously recognised financial instruments* designación de instrumentos financieros previamente reconocidos ▲ *formal designation of the hedging relationship* designación formal de la relación de cobertura ▲ *revoke the designation* revocar la designación

designed-in cost

= locked-in cost

Designed-in costs are costs related to goods and services not yet incurred by an enterprise that will invariably be incurred at a later time as a consequence of previous decisions made, typically at the design stage.

coste inevitable

▲ *determine the designed-in costs* determinar los costes inevitables ▲ *reduce designed-in costs* reducir los costes inevitables

detection risk

Detection risk is the type of audit risk that involves the failure of an auditor's substantive procedures to detect an error or misstatement in the financial records.

riesgo de detección

▲ *an acceptable detection risk* un riesgo de detección aceptable ▲ *limit detection risk* limitar el riesgo de detección

⇛ audit risk, control risk, inherent risk

determination

1 Determination refers to the statement, measurement or calculation of accounting results, values, amounts or assumptions as well as to the fixing or calculation of interest rates or prices.

determinación

▲ *determination of a value* determinación de un valor ▲ *determination of an amount* determinación de una cantidad

2 Determination means making up, assessing or setting, for accounting purposes, the measurement basis, accounting policy or treatment, or the value or amount of a transaction, element or item such as the fair value, cost, assets, liabilities, revenue, income or expense as well as the profit or loss of an enterprise for a particular period.

determinación

▲ *a current recoverable amount determination* una determinación de la cantidad recuperable actual ▲ *affect the determination of the useful life of the building* afectar a la determinación de la vida útil de el edificio ▲ *determination of accounting profit* determinación de beneficio contable ▲ *determination of net profit or loss for the period* determinación del resultado neto del periodo ▲ *the determination of an enterprise's financial position* la determinación de la posición financiera de la empresa ▲ *the determination of cost and its subsequent recognition as an expense* la determinación del coste y su reconocimiento subsiguiente como un gasto ▲ *the determination of fair value for agricultural produce* la determinación del valor razonable para la producción agrícola ▲ *the reliable determination of deferred tax assets on a discounted basis* la determinación fiable de los activos por impuesto diferido según un método interrumpido

determine

To determine is to fix after a calculation, investigation, study, inquiry or other effort.

fijar

= determinar

▲ *determine a difference* determinar una diferencia ▲ *determine a requirement* fijar un requisito ▲ *determine provisionally* fijar provisionalmente ▲ *determine reasonably* fijar razonablemente ▲ *determine the fair values of identifiable assets acquired in a business combination* fijar los valores razonables de los activos identificables adquiridos en una combinación de negocios ▲ *determine the stage of completion of contracts in progress* fijar la etapa de finalización de los contratos en curso ▲ *determined by reference to the carrying amount of a liability* fijado por referencia al valor contable de un pasivo ▲ *properly determined* fijado adecuadamente ▲ *the methods used to determine the contract revenue recognised* los métodos utilizados para fijar los ingresos contractuales reconocidos

development[1] *noun* <no indefinite article, the, no plural>

Development refers to the employment of research findings or other knowledge in order to produce new or improved products, render new or improved services or to improve or enhance the efficiency of processes prior to carrying out the changes in practice for commercial use.

desarrollo

▲ *development of concessions* desarrollo de concesiones ▲ *development of intangible assets* desarrollo de activos intangibles ▲ *development of new products* desarrollo de productos nuevos ▲ *development of patents* desarrollo de patentes ▲ *in-process research and development* investigación y desarrollo en curso ▲ *research and development* investigación y desarrollo ▲ *research and development costs* costes de investigación y desarrollo ▲ *research and development grants* subvenciones por investigación y desarrollo ▲ *the amount of commitments for the development of biological assets* la cantidad de compromisos para el desarrollo de activos biológicos ▲ *the development of alternative products and processes* el desarrollo de productos y procesos alternativos ▲ *the development of an entity's own web site* el desarrollo de la propia página web de una entidad ▲ *the web site's stage of development* la etapa de desarrollo de la página web ▲ *transfer of research and development* transferencia de investigación y desarrollo

⇛ R&D

development[2] *noun* <a, the, -s>

Development refers to the change of or in something, i.e. when something increases, decreases, improves or deteriorates, it undergoes a development.

modificación

▲ *a negative development* una modificación negativa ▲ *a positive development* una modificación positiva ▲ *investment in skills development* inversión en la modificación de habilidades ▲ *keep track of developments* seguir la pista a las modificaciones

development activity

Development activities are activities of which the purpose is to create or improve new or existing products, services or processes.

actividades de desarrollo

NOTE Always plural in Spanish accounting texts.

▲ *expenditure on development activities* gasto en actividades de desarrollo ▲ *expenditure that is directly attributable to development activities* gasto directamente atribuible a actividades de desarrollo ▲ *funding of development activities* financiación de actividades de desarrollo ▲ *property, plant and equipment used for development activities* edificios, instalaciones y equipos utilizados para las actividades de desarrollo

development cost

Development costs are the expenses incurred by an enterprise by producing improved products or more advanced process, typically through research work and technical investigation.

coste de desarrollo

▲ *capitalisation of development costs* capitalización de los costes de desarrollo ▲ *capitalised development costs* costes de desarrollo capitalizados ▲ *development costs incurred* costes de desarrollo incurridos ▲ *incur development costs* incurrir en costes de desarrollo ▲ *operating and development costs* costes de explotación y desarrollo ▲ *recognition of development costs* reconocimiento de costes de desarrollo ▲ *research and development costs* costes de investigación y desarrollo

⇛ development expenditure, R&D

development effort

Development efforts refer to the activities and actions that have been carried out by an enterprise in order to create or improve new or existing products, services or processes.

esfuerzo de desarrollo

▲ *major new development efforts* mayores esfuerzos de desarrollo nuevos

development expenditure

Development expenditure includes the costs incurred by an enterprise in the development and improvement of products or processes, typically through research work and technical investigation.

gasto en desarrollo

= desembolso por desarrollo

NOTE Spanish accountants prefer 'gasto en desarrollo' to the IAS/IFRS term 'desembolso por desarrollo'.

▲ *goodwill and assets arising from development expenditure* fondo de comercio y activos procedentes del gasto en desarrollo ▲ *research and development expenditure* gasto en investigación y desarrollo ▲ *the aggregate amount of development expenditure recognised as an expense during the financial year* la cantidad agregada del gasto en desarrollo reconocida como gasto durante el ejercicio

⇛ development cost, R&D

development opportunity

Development opportunity refers to an enterprise's opportunity to develop new products, services or processes or to develop further existing products, services or processes in order to improve them or enhance their efficiency.

oportunidad de desarrollo

▲ *an overview of new development opportunities* una panorámica de nuevas oportunidades de desarrollo ▲ *professional development opportunities for employees* oportunidades de desarrollo profesionales para empleados

development project

A development project is a targeted project, usually within a framework in terms of time and finances, which is undertaken by an enterprise for the purpose of producing new or improved products, rendering new or improved services or improving or enhancing the efficiency of processes prior to carrying out the changes in practice for commercial use.

proyecto de desarrollo

▲ *a development project that is not yet completed* un proyecto de desarrollo que no está todavía finalizado ▲ *an ambitious development project* un proyecto de desarrollo ambicioso ▲ *an in-process development project* un proyecto de desarrollo en curso ▲ *capitalisation of development projects* capitalización de proyectos de desarrollo ▲ *clearly defined and identifiable development projects* proyectos de desarrollo claramente definidos e identificables ▲ *completed development projects* proyectos de desarrollo finalizados ▲ *completed development projects, including concessions, patents, trademarks and similar rights that originate from development projects* proyectos de desarrollo finalizados, incluyendo concesiones, patentes, marcas y derechos similares procedentes de proyectos de desarrollo ▲ *depreciation of recognised development projects* depreciación de proyectos de desarrollo reconocidos ▲ *development projects in progress* proyectos de desarrollo en curso ▲ *expenditure relating to development projects* gasto relacionado con proyectos de desarrollo ▲ internal development projects proyectos de desarrollo internos ▲ recognised development *projects* proyectos de desarrollo reconocidos ▲ *set up a development project* poner en funcionamiento un proceso de desarrollo

development stage enterprise

A development stage enterprise is an enterprise that is in the process of establishment. This means that it has not yet started its principal operations or it has not generated any significant revenue even though principal operations are in process.

empresa en constitución

▲ *financial reporting for development stage enterprises* informe financiero para empresas en constitución ▲ *investments in development stage enterprises* inversiones en empresas en constitución

differ

When something differs, it is not like what is usual or expected.

diferir

= ser diferente, ser distinto

▲ *assets and liabilities that differ in nature or function* activos y pasivos que difieren por naturaleza o función ▲ *differ from* diferir de ▲ *differ from past experience* diferir de la experiencia pasada ▲ *differ in terms of stability* ser diferente en términos de estabilidad ▲ *differ materially from* diferir materialmente de ▲ *the risk that future experience may differ from actuarial assumptions* el riego de que la experiencia futura pueda diferir de las suposiciones actuariales ▲ *the risk that the future cash flows will differ in amount or timing from estimates* el riesgo de que los flujos de efectivo futuros puedan ser diferentes en cantidad o momento a los esperados

difference

1 = balance

The difference is the number that remains after a subtraction.

diferencia

= saldo

▲ *recognise the entire difference in profit or loss* reconocer la diferencia completa en el resultado

2 A difference refers to a situation where something is not like what is usual or expected.

diferencia

▲ *a difference in geographical location of inventories* una diferencia en la localización geográfica de los inventarios ▲ *any difference between the carrying amount of goodwill and its tax base of nil* una diferencia entre el valor contable del fondo de comercio y la base imponible es cero ▲ *difference from cost* diferencia de coste ▲ *difference in accounting policies* diferencia en las políticas contables ▲ *recognise the entire difference in profit or loss* reconocer la diferencia completa en el resultado ▲ *the difference between the nominal and discounted amounts* la diferencia entre las cantidades nominales y descontadas ▲ *the economic differences between assets* las diferencias económicas entre activos

differential

Differential refers to a measurable difference between two quantities, values or rates.

diferencial

▲ *a severe differential* un diferencial importante ▲ *reduce the differential* reducir el diferencial

differential cost

= incremental cost

Differential cost is the incremental cost resulting from a decision, i.e. the difference in total cost between two alternatives, where the alternative includes the total cost plus additional costs.

coste diferencial

▲ *recognise the differential costs* reconocer los costes diferenciales ▲ *take account of the differential costs of providing services* total cantidad de los costes diferenciales por servicios prestados

⇛ differential revenue

differential revenue

Differential revenue is the increase (decrease) in revenue per unit on a rise (fall) in sales by a given number of units above one unit.

ingreso diferencial

▲ *a differential revenue requirement* un requisito de ingreso diferencial

⇛ differential cost

diluted

When earnings per share are diluted, this means that earnings may be subject to a reduction in value because of an increase in the number of ordinary shares issued resulting from e.g. convertible bonds, warranties or share options being turned into ordinary shares.

diluido

▲ *disclose the diluted amount per share for the discontinuing operation* divulgar la cantidad diluida por acción por la operación interrumpida

⇛ earnings per share

diluted earnings per share

= diluted EPS, EPS diluted

≠ basic earnings per share, basic EPS

Diluted earnings per share is an investment ratio defined as profit for the accounting period attributable to shareholders divided by the average number of shares diluted, i.e. adjusted for dilutive effects from any options, convertible bonds etc.

beneficios por acción diluidos

= ganancias por acción diluidas, ganancia por acción diluida

NOTE Spanish accountants prefer 'beneficios' to the IAS term 'ganancias'.

▲ *calculation of diluted earnings per share* cálculo de los beneficios por acción diluidos ▲ *consolidated diluted earnings per share* beneficios por acción diluidos consolidados ▲ *fully diluted earnings per share* beneficios por acción diluidos totalmente ▲ *restate diluted earnings per share* replantear los beneficios por acción diluidos ▲ *the amounts used as the numerators in calculating diluted earnings per share* las cantidades usadas como numeradores al calcular los beneficios por acción diluidos ▲ *the diluted earnings per share computation* cómputo de los beneficios por acción diluidos ▲ *the effects of share options on diluted earnings per share* los efectos de las opciones sobre acciones sobre los beneficios por acción diluidos ▲ *the number of ordinary shares used to compute diluted earnings per share* el número de acciones ordinarias utilizadas para calcular los beneficios por acción diluidos

SOURCE IAS 33, paragraph 31

diluted EPS

→ EPS diluted

dilution

Dilution is the reduction of or weakening effect on the ownership share and consequently in earnings per share of a shareholder resulting from an increase in shares. An increase in the number of shares may result from the exercise of e.g. convertible securities, options or warrants.

dilución

▲ *dilution of equity* dilución de patrimonio ▲ *dilution of the value of a share* dilución del valor de una acción ▲ *earnings dilution* dilución de beneficios ▲ *maximise the dilution of basic earnings per share* maximizar la dilución de los beneficios básicos por acción ▲ *maximum dilution from options* dilución máxima de opciones ▲ *maximum dilution from warrants* dilución máxima de warrants ▲ *theoretical dilution from options* dilución teórica de opciones ▲ *theoretical dilution from warrants* dilución teórica de warrants

dilution adjustment factor

= adjustment factor

The dilution adjustment factor compensates for the dilution of the per-share values of earnings, cash flow etc. that results when additional shares are issued by a company at prices lower than market prices with the effect that the proceeds of the company will be comparatively lower than the value of the new shares. The dilution adjustment factor is applied to adjust financial ratios prior to the share issue, making year-on-year comparisons possible.

factor de ajuste de la dilución

▲ *calculate a dilution adjustment factor* calcular un factor de ajuste de la dilución ▲ *computation of dilution adjustment factor* cómputo del factor de ajuste de la dilución ▲ *dilution adjustment factor by increases in share capital* el factor de ajuste de la dilución por ampliaciones del capital social

dilutive potential ordinary shares

Dilutive potential ordinary shares are shares whose conversion to ordinary shares would decrease net profit per share from continuing ordinary operations or increase loss per share from continuing ordinary operations.

acciones ordinarias con potencial de dilución

▲ *adjust for the effects of dilutive potential ordinary shares* ajustar los efectos de las acciones ordinarias con potencial de dilución ▲ *changes in income or expense resulting from the conversion of the dilutive potential ordinary shares* cambios en el resultado procedente de la conversión de las acciones ordinarias con potencial de dilución ▲ *conversion of all dilutive potential ordinary shares* conversión de todas las acciones ordinarias con potencial de dilución ▲ *dilutive potential ordinary shares with the lowest 'earnings per incremental share'* acciones ordinarias con potencial de dilución con los beneficios más bajos por ampliación de capital ▲ *dividends on dilutive potential ordinary shares* dividendos en acciones ordinarias con potencial de dilución ▲ *interest recognised for the dilutive potential ordinary shares* interés reconocido en las acciones ordinarias con potencial de dilución

dilutive security

Dilutive securities are financial instruments that may result in a reduction of earnings per share when turned into ordinary shares, as they contribute to increasing the total number of shares. Examples of dilutive securities are convertible bonds, warranties and share options.

título con potencial de dilución

▲ *adjustment for dilutive securities on net income* ajuste por títulos con potencial de dilución en el ingreso neto ▲ *conversion of dilutive securities* conversión de los títulos con potencial de dilución ▲ *effect of dilutive securities* efecto de los títulos con potencial de dilución

diminishing balance amortisation

→ diminishing-balance amortisation

diminishing balance depreciation

→ diminishing-balance depreciation

diminishing balance method UK, IAS/ IFRS

→ diminishing-balance method

diminishing-balance amortisation IAS/IFRS, UK

= reducing-balance amortisation UK

≠ straight-line amortisation UK

Diminishing-balance amortisation is a method of allocating the cost of an intangible asset over its useful life, in which the amortisation charge for each accounting period in the profit and loss account is based on a percentage of each year's amortisable amount which means that each year's charge is reduced.

amortización decreciente

= amortización degresiva, amortización regresiva

▲ *diminishing-balance amortisation for tax purposes* amortización degresiva a efectos fiscales ▲ *total diminishing-balance amortisation* total amortización decreciente

⇛ diminishing-balance depreciation

diminishing-balance depreciation UK, IAS/IFRS

= reducing-balance depreciation

Diminishing-balance depreciation is a method of allocating the cost of a tangible asset over its useful life, in which the depreciation charge for each accounting period in the profit and loss account is based on a percentage of each year's depreciable amount which means that each year's charge is reduced.

depreciación decreciente

▲ *diminishing-balance depreciation for tax purposes* depreciación decreciente por motivos fiscales ▲ *total diminishing-balance depreciation* total depreciación decreciente

diminishing-balance method IAS/IFRS, UK

= declining-balance method US, diminishing balance method IAS/IFRS, UK, reducing-balance method UK

≠ straight-line method

The diminishing-balance method is a method of allocating the cost of a tangible or an intangible asset over its useful life, in which the depreciation or amortisation charge for each accounting period is based on a percentage of the asset's depreciable or amortisable amount at the beginning of the period, which means that the depreciation or amortisation charge is reduced each year.

método de amortización decreciente

= método de saldo decreciente

≠ método de amortización lineal

▲ *the diminishing-balance method for tax purposes* el método de amortización decreciente por motivos fiscales

direct allocation method

≠ step-down method

The direct allocation method is a method for allocating the costs of service or support departments directly to operating or production departments, disregarding the services provided in between the service or support departments.

método de asignación directa

= método de proporción directa

▲ *use the direct allocation method* utilizar el método de asignación directa

direct control UK

≠ indirect control UK

That an entity (the controlling entity) has direct control of an asset (the controlled entity) means that it can utilise the economic resources of that asset and obtain the resulting future economic benefits as well as restrict the access of other parties to these benefits.

control directo

≠ control indirecto

▲ *obtain direct control of an entity* obtener el control directo de una entidad

⇛ control

direct cost

= direct expense

≠ indirect cost

A direct cost is a cost which can be identified with and measured in respect of a relevant costing object such as a product or a department.

coste directo

≠ coste indirecto

▲ *direct costs for administration* costes directos de administración ▲ *direct costs incurred* costes directos incurridos ▲ *incur direct costs relating to the acquisition* incurrir en costes directos relacionados con la adquisición ▲ *the accounting treatment of initial direct costs incurred by a lessee* el tratamiento contable de los costes directos iniciales incurridos por un arrendatario ▲ *the direct costs incurred* los costes directos incurridos ▲ *the related direct costs* los costes directos relacionados

direct cost of a cost object

The direct costs of a cost object are costs that can be economically traced to, identified with and separately measured for a specified cost object. The full costs of the cost object constitute the direct costs and the indirect costs allocated to the cost object.

coste directo de un objeto de coste

▲ *calculate the direct cost of a cost object* calcular el coste directo de un objeto de coste ▲ *determine the direct cost of a cost object* determinar el coste directo de un objeto de coste

direct costing

= variable costing

Direct costing is a method for fixing the value of the inventory of an enterprise, which is based on recognition of all direct production costs and variable indirect production costs. The fixed indirect production costs are not included as part of the inventory value, but are considered as period costs.

sistema de coste directo

= direct costing

▲ *consequences of using direct costing* consecuencias de la utilización del sistema de coste directo

⇛ marginal costing, period cost

direct expense US

= direct cost

A direct expense is an expense which can be identified with and measured in respect of a relevant costing object such as a product or a department.

coste directo

▲ *an increase in direct expenses* un aumento en los costes directos ▲ *net of direct expenses* neto de costes directos ▲ *total direct expenses* total costes directos

direct insurance contract

A direct insurance contract is an insurance contract that has been directly entered between an underwriter (the insurer) and another party (the insured), contrary to a reinsurance contract which is entered between two insurance companies where one company (the cedant) transfers part of or all its risk to the other company (the reinsurer).

contrato de seguro directo

▲ *direct insurance contracts in which the entity is the policyholder* los contratos de seguro directo en el que la entidad es el tomador del seguro ▲ *direct insurance contracts that the entity holds* los contratos de seguro directo que la entidad tiene

SOURCE IFRS 4, Appendix A

⇛ cedant

direct labor cost US

= direct labour cost UK

Direct labor costs are wage costs that can be attributed directly or traced logically to a specific cost unit, product type, service or division.

coste de personal directo

▲ *average direct labor cost* coste de personal directo medio ▲ *direct labor cost per hour* coste de personal directo por hora ▲ *direct labor cost per unit of output* coste de personal directo por unidad de producto

direct labour cost UK

Direct labour costs are wage costs that can be attributed directly or traced logically to a specific cost unit, product type, service or division.

coste de personal directo

▲ *average direct labour cost* coste de personal directo medio ▲ *direct labour cost per hour* coste de personal directo por hora ▲ *direct labour cost per unit of output* coste de personal directo por unidad de producto

direct manufacturing expense

= direct manufacturing cost, direct production cost, direct production expense, prime cost

A direct manufacturing expense is the total of all expenses that directly relate to manufacturing including direct materials costs, direct labour costs as well as other direct costs.

coste de fabricación directo

= coste de producción directo

▲ *5% of direct manufacturing expenses* 5% de los costes de fabricación directos ▲ *accounting for direct manufacturing expenses* contabilidad de costes de fabricación directos ▲ *reduce direct manufacturing expenses by 10%* reducir los costes de fabricación directos en un 10%

direct manufacturing labor cost US

Direct manufacturing labor costs are wage costs that can be attributed directly or traced logically to the production of a specific cost unit or product type.

coste de personal de fabricación directo

▲ *additional direct manufacturing labor cost* coste de personal de fabricación directo adicional ▲ *budgeted direct manufacturing labor cost per hour* coste de personal de fabricación directo presupuestado ▲ *total direct manufacturing labor cost* total coste de personal de fabricación directo

⇛ direct labor cost

direct materials cost

Direct materials costs refer to the costs of raw materials and components directly used in the production processes.

coste de materias primas directo

= coste de materiales directo

▲ *a significant reduction in direct materials cost* una reducción significativa en coste de materias primas directo ▲ *total direct materials cost* total coste de materias primas directo

direct materials inventory US

= raw materials inventory US

The direct materials inventory is a type of inventory under current assets in the balance sheet representing raw materials and components held on stock for use in the production processes.

inventario de materiales directos

▲ *beginning direct materials inventory* iniciando el inventario de materiales directos ▲ *ending direct materials inventory* finalizando el inventario de materiales directos

direct method

≠ indirect method

The direct method is one of two methods of preparing the cash flow statement. The direct method of reporting cash flows shows operating cash in- and outflows listed separately by main class to arrive at the aggregated cash flow from operations as the difference between the cash in- and outflows, i.e. receipts and payments.

método directo

▲ *present the cash flow statement using the direct method* presentar el estado de flujo de efectivo usando el método directo

⇛ cash flow from operating activities, cash flow statement

direct production expense

= direct manufacturing cost, direct manufacturing expense, direct production cost, prime cost

A direct production expense is the total of all expenses that directly relate to production including direct materials costs, direct labour costs as well as other direct costs.

coste de producción directo

▲ *5% of direct production expenses* 5% de los costes de producción directos ▲ *accounting for direct production expenses* contabilidad de costes de producción directos ▲ *reduce direct production expenses by 10%* reducir los costes de producción directos en un 10%

direct-material cost

Direct-material costs are costs of materials directly attributable to a cost pool based on registration.

coste de materias primas directo

= coste de materiales directo

▲ *an overall direct-material cost reduction of 5% per unit* una reducción del 5% por unidad en el coste de materias primas directo general ▲ *reduce direct-material costs by 5%* reducir los costes de materias primas directos en un 5%

directive

A directive is a legal act adopted by the EU addressed to one or more member states requiring them to achieve specified results, often within a specified framework, by passing national legislation or issuing national administrative rules.

directiva

▲ *address a directive to somebody* aplicar una directiva a alguien ▲ *adopt a directive* adoptar una directiva ▲ *apply a directive to somebody* aplicar una directiva a alguien ▲ *Council Directive 83/349/EEC* Directiva del Consejo 83/349/CEE ▲ *directive on annual accounts* directiva sobre cuentas anuales ▲ *directive on consolidated accounts* directiva de cuentas consolidadas ▲ *in accordance with the seventh directive* de acuerdo con la séptima directiva ▲ *provisions in a directive* provisiones en una directiva

director

1 A director is a member of the board of directors of an enterprise.

director

▲ *a new director* un nuevo director ▲ *alternate director* director alternativo ▲ *directors and officers' liability insurance* seguro de responsabilidad de directores y funcionarios ▲ *managerial posts held by the directors of the enterprise* puestos de dirección en manos de los directores de la empresa

⇛ member of the supervisory board

2 A director is a person who is responsible for controlling and managing (part of) the operations of an enterprise.

director

▲ *director of market development* director de desarrollo de mercados ▲ *managing director* director gerente

directors' civil liability

→ directors' liability

directors' liability US, UK, IAS/IFRS

Directors' liability is the liability that a person may incur when acting as a director of a company.

responsabilidad del director

▲ *the overall directors' liability* responsabilidad del director general

directors' meeting US, UK, IAS/IFRS

A directors' meeting is a meeting held between the members of a company's board of directors.

reunión del consejo

= junta de directores, junta del consejo

▲ *call a directors' meeting* convocar una reunión del consejo ▲ *discuss a matter at the directors' meeting* discutir un tema en la reunión del consejo

▲ *hold a directors' meeting* mantener una reunión del consejo ▲ *present a matter for transaction at the directors' meeting* presentar un tema para su aprobación en la reunión del consejo
⇛ board of directors

directors' remuneration US, UK, IAS/IFRS
= emolument
Directors' remuneration is the payment received by and given to the directors of a company for their work and services.
remuneración del consejo
= emolumentos de los consejeros, remuneración de los consejeros
▲ *enter into an agreement regulating the directors' remuneration* llegar a un acuerdo de regulación de la remuneración de los consejeros ▲ *half directors' remuneration* la remuneración de la mitad del consejo ▲ *ordinary directors' remuneration* remuneración ordinaria del consejo

directors' remuneration report UK
The directors' remuneration report is a report issued by the remuneration committee of a UK listed company, in which the committee reports on the remuneration policy applied in the company with a view to determining and accounting for rewards to executive directors in line with the Greenbury Report's recommendations and the principles of good corporate governance as defined in the 1998 Combined Code and the Directors' Remuneration Report Regulations 2002. At the annual general meeting, shareholders may vote on the remuneration report.
informe sobre la remuneración del consejo
▲ *approve the directors' remuneration report* aprobar el informe sobre la remuneración del consejo
⇛ remuneration committee, remuneration policy

directors' report UK
= management's review, operating and financial review UK
The directors' report is the operating and financial review in the annual report in a company and appears as a separate, stand-alone, narrative statement containing the directors' analysis of the company's performance and financial position in the period under review together with an assessment of future developments.
informe de dirección
= informe de la dirección
▲ *approval and signing of the directors' report* aprobación y rúbrica del informe de dirección ▲ *duty to prepare directors' report* el deber de preparar el informe de dirección ▲ *the preparation of a directors' report* la preparación de un informe de la dirección

directorship US, UK, IAS/IFRS
A directorship is the position held by a person as director of a company.
dirección
▲ *hold a directorship* mantener una dirección ▲ *non-executive directorship* dirección no ejecutiva

disallowed for tax purposes
If an expense is disallowed for tax purposes that expense is not deductible for tax purposes which means that it will not reduce the taxable income.
desestimado por motivos fiscales
= no deducible
▲ *book amortisation of goodwill disallowed for tax purposes* amortización en libro del fondo de comercio desestimada por motivos fiscales ▲ *capital expenditure disallowed for tax purposes* gasto de capital no deducible ▲ *expenses disallowed for tax purposes* gastos desestimados por motivos fiscales ▲ *expenses disallowed for tax purposes* gastos no deducibles ▲ *part of the entertainment expenses disallowed for tax purposes* parte no deducible de los gastos de representación

disclaimer IAS/IFRS
A disclaimer of opinion is a modified audit report that is expressed because of the auditor's inability to give any opinion on whether the financial statements give a true and fair view due to large uncertainties or lack of appropriate audit evidence (e.g. insufficient accounting records).
claúsula de exención de responsabilidad
▲ *an issuance of a disclaimer* una emisión de una claúsula de exención de responsabilidad

⇛ audit report, modified audit report

disclose

Within the context of accounting, to disclose is to provide information about the financial and non-financial activities of an enterprise, typically in interim and annual reports, financial statements and the notes to the financial statements. Accounting legislation and standards contain certain disclosure requirements.

divulgar

= informar, revelar

▲ *disclose a reconciliation of the carrying amount of goodwill at the end of the financial year* divulgar una conciliación del valor contable del fondo de comercio al final del periodo ▲ *disclose in the notes information about the key assumptions concerning the future* divulgar en las notas información sobre las suposiciones básicas futuras ▲ *disclose information on impaired intangible assets* divulgar la información sobre activos intangibles deteriorados ▲ *disclose publicly the fair value of the equity instruments* divulgar públicamente el valor razonable de los instrumentos de patrimonio ▲ *disclose segment result for each reportable segment* divulgar el resultado del segmento para cada segmento del que se informa ▲ *disclose the weighted average share price during the financial year* divulgar el precio medio ponderado de la acción durante el periodo ▲ *the basic earnings per share disclosed for each comparative period* los beneficios básicos por acción divulgados para cada periodo comparativo

⇛ disclosure requirement

disclosure

Disclosures constitute information provided, typically referring to the financial and non-financial information in the financial reports and statements which is required announced by companies to the public.

divulgación

= información

▲ *additional disclosures* divulgaciones adicionales ▲ *appropriate disclosure* divulgaciones adecuadas ▲ *be exempted from certain disclosure requirements* estar exento de ciertos requisitos de divulgación ▲ *improve disclosure about corporate governance practices* mejorar la divulgación sobre las prácticas de gobierno corporativo ▲ *related party disclosures* divulgaciones de la parte vinculada

⇛ disclosure requirement

disclosure requirement

Disclosure requirements are the requirements in accounting legislation or accounting standards for the minimum provision of financial and non-financial information in the financial statements.

requisito de información

= requisito de divulgación

▲ *comply with disclosure requirements* cumplir con los requisitos de información ▲ *exemptions from the presentation and disclosure requirements* exenciones relacionadas con los requisitos de presentación e información ▲ *identify the disclosure requirements to be applied to each reportable segment* identificar los requisitos de información para ser aplicados a cada segmento del que se informa ▲ *set out certain disclosure requirements for reporting impairment losses by segment* establecer ciertos requisitos de información para recoger las pérdidas por deterioro por segmento ▲ *significant disclosure requirements* requisitos de información significativos ▲ *specific disclosure requirements* requisitos de información específicos

⇛ disclose, disclosure

discontinue

To discontinue is to bring something to a stop or an end, e.g. activities or operations.

interrumpir

▲ *a plan to discontinue an operation* un plan para interrumpir una operación ▲ *discontinue a business segment* interrumpir un segmento de negocio ▲ *discontinue the use of proportionate consolidation* interrumpir la utilización de la consolidación proporcional ▲ *discontinue the use of the equity method* interrumpir el uso del método de participación

⇛ continuing operation, discontinued operation, discontinuing operation

discontinued business

→ discontinued operation

discontinued operation

≠ continuing operation

A discontinued operation is a major, separate business segment or other operating activity of an entity that is discontinued because of planned sale, sale or other disposal.

operación interrumpida

= operación discontinua

▲ *abandon a discontinued operation* abandonar una operación interrumpida ▲ *assets and liabilities relating to a discontinued operation* activos y pasivos relacionados con una operación interrumpida ▲ *disclosures about discontinued operations* informaciones sobre operaciones interrumpidas ▲ *dispose of a discontinued operation in its entirety or piecemeal* eliminación de una operación interrumpida en su totalidad o pieza a pieza ▲ *included in the annual report as a discontinued operation* incluido en el informe anual como una operación interrumpida ▲ *presentation of discontinued operations* presentación de operaciones interrumpidas ▲ *sale of discontinued operations* venta de operaciones interrumpidas ▲ *separate disclosure for each discontinued operation* publicación por separado de cada operación interrumpida ▲ *the assets attributable to the discontinued operation* los activos atribuibles a la operación interrumpida ▲ *the carrying amount of the discontinued operation* el valor contable de la operación interrumpida

SOURCE IFRS 5, Appendix A

⇛ abandoned activity, discontinuing operation

discontinuing

When something is discontinuing, such as an activity, it is in the process of being brought to an end.

liquidativo

= en liquidación

▲ *discontinuing activities* actividades liquidativas ▲ *discontinuing activities after tax* actividades liquidativas después de impuestos ▲ *discontinuing cash flows* flujos de efectivo liquidativos ▲ *discontinuing company* empresa en liquidación ▲ *discontinuing operations* operaciones liquidativas

discontinuing operation

≠ continuing operation

A discontinuing operation is a component of an enterprise that the enterprise, pursuant to a single plan, is disposing of substantially in its entirety or piecemeal or terminate through abandonment, and that represents a separate major line of business or geographical area of operations, and that can be distinguished operationally and for financial reporting purposes.

operación de liquidación

= operación en liquidación

▲ *abandon a discontinuing operation* abandonar una operación de liquidación ▲ *assets and liabilities relating to a discontinuing operation* activos y pasivos relacionados con una operación en liquidación ▲ *disclosures about discontinuing operations* publicaciones sobre operaciones de liquidación ▲ *dispose of a discontinuing operation in its entirety or piecemeal* cancelación de una operación de liquidación en su totalidad o parte a parte ▲ *included in the annual report as a discontinuing operation* incluido en el informe anual como una operación de liquidación ▲ *sale of discontinuing operations* venta de operaciones en liquidación ▲ *separate disclosure for each discontinuing operation* publicación separada de cada operación de liquidación ▲ *the assets attributable to the discontinuing operation* los activos atribuibles a la operación de liquidación ▲ *the carrying amount of the discontinuing operation* el valor contable de la operación de liquidación

⇛ discontinued operation

discount[1] *noun*

1 A discount is a reduction in the full scheduled price of goods or services.

descuento

= deducción

▲ *deferred rebates and discounts* bonificaciones y deducciones diferidas ▲ *discount allowed* descuento permitido ▲ *discount received* descuento recibido ▲ *grant a discount* ofrecer un descuento ▲ *less rebates and discounts* menos bonificaciones y deducciones ▲ *the amount of any trade discounts and volume rebates allowed by the enterprise* la cantidad de cualesquiera descuentos comerciales y bonificaciones por volumen permitidas por la empresa

2 A security that is traded at a discount is traded at a price below its nominal value or at a price below its quoted market price.

descuento

▲ *an increase in the discount on the initial issue* un aumento en el descuento en la emisión inicial ▲ *any original issue discount on increasing rate preference shares* cualquier descuento en la emisión sobre el tipo ascendente de las acciones preferentes ▲ *at a discount* con un descuento ▲ *sell the preference shares at a discount* vender las acciones preferentes con un descuento ▲ *the discount arising on initial recognition of the liability component* el descuento que surge en el reconocimiento inicial del pasivo

discount[2] *verb*

1 To discount is to purchase a bill of exchange prior to its maturity date at a lower price than the face value, so that the purchaser makes a profit when the bill is paid in full at maturity. Usually, bills are discounted by banks.

descontar

2 To discount is to apply a discount factor to a future cash flow with a view to calculating the net present value of that cash flow allowing for the time value of money.

actualizar

≠ capitalizar

▲ *discount a liability* actualizar un pasivo ▲ *discount deferred tax assets and liabilities* actualizar activos y pasivos por impuesto diferido ▲ *discount provisions by the average bond yield* actualizar las provisiones al rendimiento medio del bono ▲ *discount the stream of future cash receipt expected over the life of the asset* actualizar la corriente de efectivo futuro esperado durante la vida del activo

⇛ discount factor

3 = factor in, price in

To discount is to allow for the factual or possible effects of events or announcements in a decision-making process, in a price fixing (typically of shares, bonds etc.), in acquisitions, disposals, investments or other transactions, or in expectations for future developments.

tener en cuenta

▲ *discount greater uncertainty* tener en cuenta una mayor incertidumbre ▲ *discount interest rate hikes* tener en cuenta las subidas del tipo de interés ▲ *discount shareholders' expectations for the company's future performance* tener en cuenta las expectativas de los accionistas sobre el futuro de la actividad de la compañía

discount factor

A discount factor is an interest rate used for discounting a future cash flow to net present value, i.e. adjusting the future cash flow downwards to allow for the time value of money.

factor de descuento

▲ *a decrease in the discount factor* un descenso en el factor de descuento ▲ *the discount factor used for the net present value calculations* el factor de descuento utilizado en los cálculos del valor actual neto ▲ *the risk-free discount factor* el factor de descuento sin riesgo ▲ *use the interest rate implicit in the lease as the discount factor* utilizar el tipo de interés implícito en el arrendamiento como el factor de descuento

⇛ discount, net present value, time value of money

discount rate

1 = discount factor

The discount rate used for capitalisation is the interest rate applied for the computation of the present value.

tipo de descuento

= tasa de actualización, tasa de descuento

▲ *a current market discount rate* un tipo de descuento de mercado actual ▲ *a discount rate equal to the sum of the benchmark interest rate* un tipo de descuento igual a la suma del tipo de interés de referencia ▲ *a discount rate without direct reference to market conditions* un tipo de descuento sin referencia directa a las condiciones de mercado ▲ *a pre-tax discount rate* un tipo de descuento antes de impuestos ▲ *adjustments to the discount rate* ajustes al tipo de descuento ▲ *an asset-based discount rate* un tipo de descuento basado en activos ▲ *apply a single weighted average discount rate* aplicar un tipo de descuento medio ponderado único ▲ *apply the appropriate discount rate to the future cash flows* aplicar el tipo de descuento adecuado a los flujos de efectivo futuros ▲ *determination of the discount rate* determinación del tipo de descuento ▲ *determine the discount rate* determinar el tipo de descuento ▲ *embedded in the discount rate* implícito en el tipo de descuento ▲ *post-tax discount rate* tipo de descuento después de impuestos ▲ *the current discount rate* el tipo de descuento actual ▲ *the discount rate used in calculating the asset's value in use* el tipo de descuento utilizado para calcular el valor en uso del activo ▲ *the effect of changes in the discount rate* el efecto de los cambios en el tipo de descuento ▲ *use a discount rate that reflects the estimated return on the insurer's assets* utilizar un tipo de descuento que refleja el rendimiento estimado sobre los activos de la aseguradora ▲ *use a single discount rate for the estimate of an asset's value in use* utilizar un tipo de descuento único para la estimación del valor en uso de un activo

2 = official discount rate

The discount rate is the official interest rate set by a central bank, either as a signal or benchmark rate or as an actual rate charged for short-term loans to banks as a monetary policy tool. The discount rate typically functions as a reference rate for money-market interest rates.

tipo de descuento

▲ *lower the discount rate* bajar el tipo de descuento ▲ *raise the discount rate* elevar el tipo de descuento ▲ *the official discount rate* el tipo de descuento oficial

discount to net present value

To discount to net present value is to adjust a future cash flow downwards by applying a discount factor and allowing for the time value of money.

descontar al valor actual neto

⇛ net present value

discounted

When a future cash flow has been discounted, it has been restated to net present value after a downward adjustment allowing for the time value of money.

descontado

▲ *discounted amount* cantidad descontada ▲ *discounted bills of exchange* letras de cambio descontadas ▲ *discounted cash flow projections based on reliable estimates of future cash flows* proyecciones de flujos de efectivo descontados basadas en estimaciones fiables de flujos de efectivo futuros ▲ *discounted cash flows* flujos de efectivo descontados ▲ *discounted letters of credit* pólizas de crédito descontadas ▲ *measure on a discounted basis* medir a un valor actual ▲ *present discounted value* valor actual descontado ▲ *the future net receipts appropriately discounted* los efectos a cobrar futuros netos adecuadamente descontados

⇛ discount factor, net present value

discounted cash flow

= DCF

The discounted cash flow is the future cash flow shown at its present value following a discounted cash flow calculation where the projected annual cash flow figure is multiplied by a discount factor. Discounting projected cash flows is important to capital investment appraisal.

flujo de efectivo descontado

= flujo de efectivo actual

▲ *discounted cash flow projections based on reliable estimates of future cash flows* proyecciones de flujo de efectivo descontados basadas en estimaciones fiables de flujos de efectivo futuros

⇛ discounted-cash-flow model, free cash flow to firm, net present value, weighted average cost of capital

discounted dividend model
→ dividend discount model

discounted value
= present value
The discounted value is the result arrived at in a discounted cash flow calculation by multiplying a projected annual cash flow figure by a discount factor. The discounted value shows the economic present value of a future amount.
valor descontado
= valor actual
▲ *estimated discounted value* valor descontado estimado ▲ *the discounted value of future net cash inflows* el valor descontado de entradas de efectivo netas futuras ▲ *the discounted value of future net cash outflows* el valor descontado de salidas de efectivo netas futuras
⇛ present value

discounted-cash-flow model
1 = DCF model
The discounted-cash-flow model is a method for budgeting the capital needed for a given project. Future cash inflows and outflows related to the project are discounted to a specified point of time using a given discount factor allowing for comparison with other projects.
modelo del flujo de efectivo descontado
▲ *use a discounted cash flow model* utilizar un modelo del flujo de efectivo descontado
⇛ discount factor, discounted cash flow, net present value
2 = DCF model
The discounted-cash-flow model is a method for valuation of an enterprise. The free cash flow from the budget period and the terminal period are discounted at a discount rate corresponding to the weighted average capital costs. The value of the enterprise is found after deduction of the market value of the interest-bearing debt of the enterprise.
modelo del flujo de efectivo descontado
▲ *use a discounted-cash-flow model* utilizar un modelo del flujo de efectivo descontado
⇛ free cash flow, terminal value, weighted average cost of capital

discounting
Discounting is the application of a discount factor to a future cash flow with a view to calculating the net present value of that cash flow allowing for the time value of money.
descuento
▲ *determined by the use of discounting* determinado por el uso del descuento ▲ *discounting of deferred tax* descuento del impuesto diferido ▲ *prohibit the discounting of deferred tax assets and liabilities* prohibir el descuento de activos y pasivos fiscales diferidos ▲ *the effect of discounting* el efecto del descuento
⇛ discount factor, discounted-cash-flow model, net present value

discounting basis
The discounting basis constitutes the cash inflows or outflows that are discounted to net present value using a discount factor and which are relevant to the assessment of investment projects.
base de descuento
▲ *determination of the discounting basis* determinación de la base de descuento

discretionary cost UK, US
= discretionary fixed cost UK, US, managed cost UK, management cost US, policy cost UK, programmed cost US
≠ committed cost UK, US
Discretionary costs are fixed costs that are determined by managerial decisions without any obvious relationship with capacity or production activity. Examples are marketing, training, research and development costs.
coste discrecional
≠ coste inevitable
▲ *a reduction in discretionary costs* una reducción en los costes discrecionales ▲ *control discretionary costs* controlar los costes discrecionales ▲ *current discretionary costs* costes discrecionales actuales ▲ *incur discretionary costs* incurrir en costes discrecionales
⇛ engineered cost, fixed cost

discretionary fixed cost UK, US
= discretionary cost UK, US, managed cost UK, management cost US, policy cost UK, programmed cost US

≠ committed cost UK, US

Discretionary fixed costs are costs that are determined by and subject to change because of managerial decisions without any obvious relationship with capacity or production activity. Examples are marketing, training, research and development costs.

coste fijo discrecional

▲ *adjust discretionary fixed costs periodically* ajustar los costes fijos discrecionales de forma periódica

⇛ fixed cost, management cost

discretionary participation feature

In the context of an insurance contract, a discretionary participation feature is a right under the contract to receive supplementary benefits in addition to the guaranteed benefits. Such benefits are benefits that constitute a significant portion of the total benefits where, under the contract, the issuer can decide the amount or timing of the benefits, and benefits that contractually depend on the performance of a defined amount of contracts or type of contract, on whether or not the return on a defined investment held by the issuer has been realised, or on the performance of the issuing company, fund or enterprise.

componente de participación discrecional

▲ *contain a discretionary participation feature* contiene un componente de participación discrecional ▲ *discretionary participation features in financial instruments* componente de participación discrecional en instrumentos financieros ▲ *financial instruments with a discretionary participation feature* instrumentos financieros con un componente de participación discrecional ▲ *the portion of the discretionary participation feature classified as a liability* la parte del componente de participación discrecional clasificada como un pasivo

SOURCE IFRS 4, Appendix A

discriminatory pricing

Discriminatotory pricing is the practice of charging different prices for the same product in different markets or when offered to different buyers in the same market.

fijación de precios discriminatorios

▲ *engage in discriminatory pricing* implicarse en la fijación de precios discriminatorios ▲ *unreasonable and unjustifiable discriminatory pricing activities* actividades de fijación de precios discriminatorios injustificables y no razonables

dismantling

To dismantle an asset is to remove it because the enterprise no longer needs it or its useful life has expired.

desmantelamiento

▲ *dismantling of assets* desmantelamiento de activos ▲ *the estimated costs of dismantling items of property, plant and equipment* los costes estimados de desmantelamiento de las partidas de edificios, instalaciones y equipos ▲ *the initial estimate of the costs of dismantling and removing the item* la estimación inicial de los costes de desmantelamiento y retirada de la partida

dismiss

To dismiss means to terminate a person's employment with an employer, i.e. the person is removed from his job.

despedir

▲ *dismiss an employee* despedir a un empleado ▲ *dismiss the statutory auditor* despedir al auditor estatutario

dismissal

= termination of employment

A dismissal is the employer's act of removing an employee from the job.

despido

▲ *dismissal of employees* despido de empleados ▲ *dismissal of the auditor during the term of appointment* despido del auditor durante el periodo de nombramiento ▲ *payment of post-employment benefits on dismissal* pago de prestaciones por despido

dismissal payment US

= severance benefit

Dismissal payment refers to a monetary benefit payable to an employee upon involuntary termination before normal retirement.

indemnización por despido

▲ *dismissal payments falling due more than 1 year after the balan-*

ce sheet date indemnizaciones por despido que vencen en el largo plazo ▲ *dismissal payments for key management personnel* indemnizaciones por despido para el personal de alta dirección ▲ *make dismissal payments* pagar las indemnizaciones por el despido ▲ *measurement of dismissal payments* valoración de las indemnizaciones por despido ▲ *provide dismissal payments* ofrecer indemnizaciones por despido ▲ *provisions for dismissal payments* provisiones para indemnizaciones por despido ▲ *recognize dismissal payments* reconocer las indemnizaciones por despido
⇛ termination benefit

disposal
≠ acquisition, addition
A disposal is a sale, transfer or abandonment of an asset.
enajenación
▲ *asset and business disposals* enajenaciones de activo y negocio ▲ *disposal of a property* enajenación de una propiedad ▲ *disposal of activities* enajenación de actividades ▲ *disposal of enterprises* enajenación de empresas ▲ *disposal of investments* enajenación de inversiones ▲ *disposal of operations* enajenación de operaciones ▲ *disposal of property, plant and equipment* enajenación de edificios, instalaciones y equipos ▲ *disposal of treasury shares* enajenación de acciones propias ▲ *disposal on a piecemeal basis* enajenación parcial ▲ *disposals during the year* enajenaciones durante el año ▲ *gains or losses arising from disposal of property, plant and equipment* resultados que proceden de la enajenación de edificios, instalaciones y equipos ▲ *partial disposal* enajenación parcial

disposal consideration UK
The disposal consideration is the sales amount received on the sale of an asset.
importe de la enajenación
= suma de la enajenación
▲ *purchase and disposal consideration* compra e importe de la enajenación ▲ *reasonable disposal consideration* importe de la enajenación razonable ▲ *the portion of the disposal consideration discharged by means of cash and cash equivalents* la porción del importe de la enajenación saldada mediante efectivo o equivalentes de efectivo ▲ *the total purchase or disposal consideration* la compra total o importe de la enajenación

disposal group
A disposal group is a group of fixed assets subject to be sold or otherwise disposed of in a single transaction.
grupo enajenable de elementos
▲ *a disposal group available for immediate sale in its present condition* un grupo enajenable de elementos disponible para la venta inmediata en su condición actual ▲ *a disposal group that is to be abandoned* un grupo enajenable de elementos que se va a abandonar ▲ *a disposal group that was part of a cash-generating unit* un grupo enajenable de elementos que era parte de una unidad generadora de efectivo ▲ *an impairment loss for any initial or subsequent write-down of the disposal group* una pérdida por deterioro por cualquier amortización inicial o subsiguiente del grupo enajenable de elementos ▲ *disposal groups classified as held for sale* grupos enajenables de elementos clasificados como mantenidos para la venta ▲ *goodwill included in a disposal group* fondo de comercio incluido en un grupo enajenable de elementos ▲ *the individual assets and liabilities within the disposal group* los activos y pasivos individuales dentro del grupo enajenable de elementos
SOURCE IFRS 5, Appendix A

disposal sum
= disposal amount, sum of disposal
The disposal sum is the amount received on the sale or disposal of an asset.
suma de la enajenación
= importe de la enajenación
▲ *a disposal sum in excess of £5000* una suma de la enajenación superior a 5.000 libras esterlinas ▲ *disposal sum of £10000* la suma de la enajenación de 10.000 libras esterlinas

dispose of
= sell off
≠ acquire

To dispose of is to get rid of or sell something e.g. an asset that is no longer needed or wanted.

enajenar

▲ *dispose of a business segment* enajenar un segmento de negocios ▲ *dispose of an activity* enajenar una actividad ▲ *dispose of the assets received* enajenar los activos recibidos

⇛ divest

disposed subsidiary

A disposed subsidiary is a subsidiary that has been divested by the parent company.

filial enajenada

▲ *finance leases of the disposed subsidiary* arrendamientos financieros de la filial enajenada ▲ *the carrying value of the disposed subsidiary* el valor contable de la filial enajenada ▲ *the net assets of the disposed subsidiary* los activos netos de la filial enajenada

dissolve

To dissolve means to officially bring something, e.g. a company, to an end.

disolver

▲ *dissolve a company* disolver una empresa ▲ *dissolve a partnership* disolver una sociedad comanditaria

distributable reserves

= revenue reserves

Distributable reserves refer to undistributed profits of previous accounting periods that may legally be distributed to shareholders in the form of dividends.

reservas distribuibles

▲ *increase distributable reserves* aumento de las reservas distribuibles ▲ *transfer to distributable reserves* transferir a reservas distribuibles

distribute

1 To distribute means to divide the enterprise's profit for a period, or part of the profit, and pay it to the owners.

distribuir

= asignar

▲ *distribute a 10% dividend* distribuir un dividendo del 10% ▲ *distribute the entire profits to the parent or investor* distribuir los beneficios totales a la matriz o al inversor ▲ *distribute the specific future economic benefits attributable to the asset* distribuir los beneficios económicos futuros específicos atribuibles al activo ▲ *the enterprise's own equity financial instruments distributed by equity compensation plans to employees* los instrumentos financieros de patrimonio propios de la empresa distribuidos a los empleados como compensación mediante acciones

2 = allocate

To distribute means to make things, e.g. goods or services, available to persons or enterprises.

distribuir

▲ *decide to distribute dividends* decidir distribuir dividendos ▲ *distribute money* distribuir dinero ▲ *the methods used to distribute the product or provide the service* los métodos utilizados para distribuir el producto u ofrecer el servicio

3 To distribute means to spread something over a gradually increasing area.

asignar

▲ *distribute tasks among the employees* asignar tareas entre los empleados

distribution

1 Distribution refers to the division and payment of an enterprise's profit, or of part of the profit, to the owners of the enterprise, e.g. to the shareholders of a company in the form of dividends.

distribución

▲ *capital reduction with distribution to shareholders* reducción de capital con distribución a los accionistas ▲ *distribution of dividend* distribución de dividendos ▲ *distribution of dividends from subsidiaries* distribución de dividendos procedentes de filiales ▲ *distribution to owners* distribución a propietarios ▲ *distribution to shareholders* distribución a los acionistas ▲ *distributions from accumulated profits* distribuciones de beneficios acumulados ▲ *distributions of profits to holders of equity investments in proportion to their holdings of a particular class of capital* distribuciones de beneficios a los poseedores de inversiones de patrimonio en proporción a sus posesiones de una clase concreta de capital ▲ *distributions received* distribuciones recibidas ▲ *distribu-*

tions to owners distribuciones a propietarios ▲ *proposal for distribution of dividend* propuesta para la distribución del dividendo

2 Distribution refers to the act of allocating something between several units or people.
reparto
▲ *distribution of market values* reparto de valores de mercado ▲ *distribution of responsibility* reparto de responsabilidades ▲ *risk-neutral distribution* reparto de riesgo neutral

3 When something is spread over a volume of something or over an area, there is a distribution.
asignación
▲ *distribution of responsibility* asignación de responsabilidad ▲ *distribution of risk* asignación de riesgo

4 Distribution refers to the sale and delivery of goods or services from manufacturers to consumers.
distribución
▲ *distribution channel* canal de distribución ▲ *distribution vehicle* vehículo de distribución ▲ *exclusive distribution* distribución exclusiva ▲ *physical distribution* distribución física ▲ *selective distribution* distribución selectiva

distribution cost
Distribution costs are costs attributable to delivering products to customers, e.g. transportation costs, storing costs, loading and unloading costs as well as fuel costs. "Distribution costs" is a separate item in some profit and loss account formats.
coste de distribución
▲ *a fall in distribution costs* una caída en costes de distribución ▲ *an increase in distribution costs* un aumento en costes de distribución ▲ *distribution costs as a percentage of total costs* costes de distribución como un porcentaje de costes totales
⇛ selling cost

distribution expense
Distribution expenses are expenses attributable to delivering products to customers, e.g. transportation expenses, storing expenses, loading and unloading expenses as well as fuel expenses. "Distribution expenses" is a separate item in some profit and loss account formats.
gasto de distribución
▲ *a decrease in distribution expense* un descenso en el gasto de distribución ▲ *recognise distribution expenses* reconocer los gastos de distribución ▲ *total distribution expense* total gasto de distribución

distribution method
The distribution method is a cost accounting method under which fixed costs are allocated to specific products or departments.
método de distribución
▲ *apply the distribution method* aplicar el método de distribución

distribution of assets UK
= asset allocation US
The distribution of assets is a way in which the total assets are mixed in the investment portfolio of an enterprise or a person. The assets may be allocated on domestic and foreign investments in different types of shares, bonds, properties and other investments, depending on investment criteria such as return and risk.
diversificación de activos
▲ *distribution of assets by geography* diversificación de activos por criterio geográfico

distribution of dividend
= dividend distribution, dividend payment, payment of dividend
Distribution of dividend is the actual payment to shareholders of the dividends recommended by the board of directors and approved at the annual general meeting.
distribución de dividendos
▲ *affect the distribution of dividend* afectar a la distribución de dividendos ▲ *distribution of dividend and reserve funds* distribución de dividendos y fondos de reserva

distribution of net income US
Distribution of net income refers to a statement in the annual or interim report of an enterprise specifying how net income for an accounting period is allocated. Part of the income may typically be distributed to shareholders in the

form of dividends, leaving the remainder to be transferred to retained earnings.
distribución del beneficio
▲ *announcement of distribution of net income* anuncio de la distribución del beneficio

distribution of net profit IAS/IFRS
= distribution to owners, distribution to shareholders
The distribution of net profit shows how the enterprise has appropriated the profit for the financial year for distribution of dividends or to retained earnings.
aplicación del beneficio neto
= distribución de la ganancia neta
▲ *allocation transferred from distribution of net profit* asignación transferida desde la aplicación del beneficio neto del ejercicio ▲ *comments on the distribution of net profit* comentarios sobre la aplicación del beneficio neto del ejercicio ▲ *proposal for the distribution of net profit* propuesta para la aplicación del beneficio neto del ejercicio

distribution of profit UK, IAS/IFRS
= allocation of profits, appropriation of profit, distribution of net profit
The distribution of profit shows how the enterprise has appropriated the profit for the financial year for distribution of dividends or to retained earnings.
aplicación del beneficio
= distribución de la ganancia
NOTE Spanish accountants prefer 'aplicación del beneficio' to the IAS term 'distribución de la ganancia'.
▲ *announcement of distribution of profit* anuncio de la aplicación del beneficio

distribution of the profit for the year UK
The distribution of the profit for the year depends on the allocation attributed by the enterprise of the net profits, for example to dividends or to reserves.
aplicación del beneficio del ejercicio
= distribución de la ganancia del año
▲ *allocation transferred from distribution of the profit for the year* asignación transferida desde la aplicación del beneficio neto del ejercicio ▲ *comments on the distribution of the profit for the year* comentarios sobre la aplicación del beneficio neto del ejercicio ▲ *proposal for distribution of the profit for the year* propuesta para la aplicación del beneficio neto del ejercicio

divert
To divert means to take the attention away from something.
desviar
▲ *divert attention from* desviar la atención de ▲ *divert someone's attention* desviar la atención de alguien

divest
= dispose of, sell off
≠ invest
To divest is to realise an asset or an activity by selling it off or closing it down.
desinvertir
= abandonar
≠ invertir
▲ *divest interests* desinvertir
▲ *the divested business* el negocio abandonado
⇛ divestment

divested subsidiary
= disposed subsidiary
A divested subsidiary is a subsidiary that has been disposed by the parent company.
filial enajenada
= filial abandonada
▲ *finance leases of the divested subsidiary* arrendamientos financieros de la filial enajenada
▲ *the carrying value of the divested subsidiary* el valor contable de la filial enajenada ▲ *the net assets of the divested subsidiary* los activos netos de la filial enajenada

divestiture US
= divestment UK
Divestiture means the selling off or realisation of an asset or several assets, or the selling off or closing down of activities.
desinversión
▲ *a total divestiture* una desinversión total ▲ *disposals relating to the divestiture of enterprises* enajenaciones relacionadas con la desinversión de empresas
▲ *divestiture of enterprises* desinversión de empresas ▲ *loss on divestiture* pérdida por desinversión ▲ *profit on divest-*

iture beneficio por desinversión

⇛ disposal

divestment

≠ investment

Divestment means the selling off or realisation of an asset, or the selling off or closing down of activities.

desinversión

= enajenación

≠ inversión

▲ *a total divestment* una desinversión total ▲ *disposals relating to the divestment of enterprises* enajenaciones relacionadas con la desinversión de empresas ▲ *divestment of enterprises* desinversión de empresas ▲ *loss on divestment* pérdida por desinversión ▲ *profit on divestment* beneficio por desinversión

⇛ divest

dividend

Dividend is the periodic distribution of the enterprise's profits to holders of equity investments. The amount of dividend is determined at the annual general meeting of the enterprise. Dividend represents the return on investment, except for capital gains, that a shareholder receives on his or her investment.

dividendo

▲ *an item disposable for dividend* una partida disponible para dividendo ▲ *be entitled to participate in dividends* tener derecho a participar en la distribución de dividendos ▲ *cumulative dividend* dividendo acumulado ▲ *distribution of dividend* distribución del dividendo ▲ *distribution of dividends to shareholders* distribución de dividendos a los accionistas ▲ *dividend for the year* dividendo para el año ▲ *dividend not subject to tax* dividendo no sujeto a impuestos ▲ *dividend of EUR 80 per share* dividendo de 80 euros por acción ▲ *dividend paying shares* acciones que generan dividendos ▲ *dividend per share for the year* dividendo por acción para el año ▲ *dividends computation* cómputo de dividendos ▲ *dividends declared* dividendos declarados ▲ *dividends declared for 2005* dividendos declarados para el 2005 ▲ *dividends distributed* dividendos distribuidos ▲ *dividends distributed to minority interests* dividendos distribuidos a los minoritarios ▲ *dividends distributed to parent shareholders* dividendos distribuidos a los accionistas de la matriz ▲ *dividends on treasury shares* dividendos en acciones propias ▲ *dividends payable* dividendos a pagar ▲ *dividends receivable* dividendos a cobrar ▲ *dividends received* dividendos recibidos ▲ *dividends to holders of equity instruments* dividendos a propietarios de instrumentos de patrimonio ▲ *dividends to owners* dividendos a propietarios ▲ *final dividend* dividendo final ▲ *interim dividend* dividendo provisional ▲ *net of dividends paid out* neto de dividendos pagados ▲ *ordinary dividend* dividendo ordinario ▲ *preference dividend* dividendo preferente ▲ *proposed dividend for the year* dividendo propuesto para el año ▲ *tax on dividends received* impuesto sobre dividendos recibidos ▲ *the amount of dividends* la cuantía de los dividendos ▲ *the management's recommendation for dividends* la recomendación de la dirección para la aplicación de dividendos ▲ *unclaimed dividend* dividendo no reclamado ▲ *undistributed dividends* dividendos no distribuidos

dividend cover UK

≠ payout ratio

The dividend cover shows the number of times a company's dividends to equity shareholders can be paid out of its net profits after tax in the same period and is calculated as earnings per share divided by dividend per share.

cobertura de dividendo

= ratio de dividendo neto por dividendo distribuido

▲ *recommend a dividend cover of 25-30% of the net profit for the year* recomendar una cobertura de dividendo del 25-30% del beneficio neto para el año ▲ *set targets for the dividend cover* fijar objetivos para la cobertura de dividendo

⇛ dividend per share, dividend yield, earnings per share

dividend discount model

= DDM, discounted dividend model

The dividend discount model is a direct valuation method to estimate the present value of expected future dividend payments, thereby estimating the value of a share or a company to a shareholder.

modelo de descuento del dividendo

▲ *a variant of the classic dividend discount model* una variante del modelo de descuento del dividendo clásico ▲ *use a dynamic dividend discount model* utilizar un modelo de descuento del dividendo dinámico

dividend distribution

= distribution of dividend, dividend payment, payment of dividend

Dividend distribution is the actual payment to shareholders of the dividends approved at the general meeting.

distribución del dividendo

= distribución de dividendos

▲ *dividend distribution per preferred share* distribución del dividendo por acciones preferentes ▲ *shares eligible for dividend distribution* acciones elegibles para distribución del dividendo ▲ *the right to participate in dividend distributions* el derecho a participar en las distribuciones del dividendo

dividend equalisation fund

= dividend equalisation reserve

A dividend equalisation fund is a distributable reserve under equity in the balance sheet established in profitable financial years as a buffer reserve to provide for funds to be distributed as dividends or bonus shares in future non-profitable financial years.

fondo para la distribución de dividendos

▲ *allocated to the dividend equalisation fund* asignado al fondo para la distribución de dividendos ▲ *establish a dividend equalisation fund* establecer un fondo para la distribución de dividendos

⇛ distributable reserves

dividend in kind

→ dividend-in-kind

dividend income

Dividend income is that part of a person's or enterprise's total income that is attributable to dividends received from (other) companies.

ingreso por dividendos

▲ *interest and dividend income, after tax payable by the fund* ingreso por intereses y dividendos, después del impuesto a pagar por el fondo ▲ *interest and dividend income net of tax payable* ingreso neto sujeto a impuesto por intereses y dividendos ▲ *taxation of dividend income* imposición del ingreso por dividendos

dividend per share

= DPS

Dividend per share is a financial ratio defined as the amount of dividend distributed for the period divided by the number of outstanding ordinary shares.

dividendo por acción

▲ *imputed dividend per share* dividendo por acción imputado ▲ *increase dividend per share* aumentar el dividendo por acción

dividend policy

Dividend policy refers to an enterprise's policy as to how large a proportion of its profit should be distributed to its shareholders in the form of dividends and how large a proportion should be retained in the enterprise, i.e. transferred to retained earnings.

política de dividendos

▲ *adopt a dividend policy* adoptar una política de dividendos ▲ *control the dividend policy of subsidiaries* controlar la política de dividendos de las filiales ▲ *future dividend policy* política de dividendos futura

dividend ratio

Dividend ratios are financial ratios relating to dividend distribution to shareholders such as earnings per share, dividend yield, and payout ratio.

ratio de dividendo

▲ *share and dividend ratios* ratios de acción y dividendo

dividend tax

= coupon tax, withholding tax

Dividend tax is tax on dividends that is deducted at source by the payer who is responsible for paying the tax to the tax authorities on behalf of the recipient.

impuesto por dividendo

▲ *Danish dividend tax* impuesto por dividendo danés ▲ *dividend tax on ordinary dividend* impuesto por dividendo sobre el dividendo ordinario ▲ *dividend tax receivable* impuesto por dividendo a cobrar ▲ *dividend tax refund* cobro del impuesto por dividendo ▲ *omit to withhold dividend tax* omitir para retener el impuesto por dividendo ▲ *pay dividend tax* pagar el impuesto por dividendo ▲ *payment of dividend tax* pago del impuesto por dividendo ▲ *re-introduction of dividend tax* reintroducción del impuesto por dividendo ▲ *withhold dividend tax on dividends declared* retener el impuesto por dividendo en los dividendos declarados ▲ *withholding of dividend tax* retención del impuesto por dividendo

dividend yield

= gross yield dividend

Dividend yield expresses the direct yield on a share, i.e. the return on market value offered by the share and is calculated as dividend per share divided by the market price per share.

rentabilidad del dividendo

= rendimiento del dividendo

▲ *annual dividend yield* rentabilidad del dividendo anual ▲ *debt whose rate of interest depends on the dividend yield* deuda cuyo tipo de interés depende de la rentabilidad del dividendo ▲ *take dividend yields into consideration* tener en consideración los rendimientos del dividendo ▲ *the parent's dividend yield* la rentabilidad del dividendo de la matriz

⇛ dividend cover, payout ratio

dividend-in-kind

= dividend in kind

Dividend-in-kind is non-monetary dividend distributed to shareholders, i.e. in the form of assets such as property or shares in addition to or instead of cash dividends.

dividendo en especie

▲ *cash dividend or dividend-in-kind* dividendo monetario o en especie ▲ *disbursement of dividend-in-kind* desembolso del dividendo en especie ▲ *distribute by way of a dividend-in-kind* distribuir mediante un dividendo en especie ▲ *pro rata dividend-in-kind* prorratear el dividendo en especie ▲ *receive dividend-in-kind* recibir el dividendo en especie

⇛ stock dividend

DKK thousand

= DKK '000

DKK thousand applied about an amount signifies that the amount is stated in thousands and in Danish kroner, i.e. the Danish currency, e.g. DKK 478 thousand.

NOTE For the heading of a column of figures, DKK '000 typically applies.

miles de coronas danesas

= en miles de coronas danesas

▲ *DKK 67,890 thousand* 67.890 miles de coronas danesas ▲ *operating income per employee (DKK thousand)* ingreso de explotación por empleado (en miles de coronas danesas)

document

A document is a paper or set of papers with written or printed information, esp. of an official type.

documento

▲ *a cross-reference to another published document* una referencia cruzada a otro documento publicado ▲ *a legal document* un documento legal ▲ *document granting agency authority* documento de concesión de autoridad ▲ *IFRS 1 First-time Adoption of International Financial Reporting Standards and its accompanying documents* Primera Adopción de la NIIF 1 y sus documentos adjuntos ▲ *information presented in an annual report or other document* información presentada en un informe anual u otro documento

document of indebtedness

= debt instrument

A document of indebtedness is a written, unilateral and unconditional acknowledgment of debt from the debtor.

documento de deuda

= instrumento de deuda

▲ *issue a document of indebtedness* emitir un documento de deuda

documentation

Documentation is material that can be produced as evidence or proof for the correctness or truth of something.

documentación

▲ *comply with the other documentation requirements* cumplir con los otros requisitos de documentación ▲ *documentation of something* documentación de algo ▲ *documentation of the hedging relationship* documentación de la relación de cobertura ▲ *legal documentation* documentación legal ▲ *the entity's documentation of its hedging strategy* la documentación de la entidad de su estrategia de cobertura

documentation requirement

Documentation requirements refer to the criteria that must be satisfied to prove the value or existence of something.

requisito de documentación

▲ *comply with the documentation requirements* cumplir con los requisitos de documentación ▲ *meet the documentation requirements* satisfacer los requisitos de documentación

documentation system

A documentation system is a knowledge base and information reference system, often computerised, from which data may be retrieved, identified, validated or substantiated for a specific purpose.

sistema de documentación

▲ *store data in a documentation system* almacenar datos en un sistema de documentación ▲ *the transition from printed to electronic documentation systems* la transacción de la documentación escrita a la electrónica

domicile

A domicile is the country in which a person or enterprise has it permanent address.

domicilio

▲ *a subsidiary operating in the country of domicile of its parent* una filial que opera en el país de domicilio de su matriz ▲ *fiscal domicile* domicilio fiscal ▲ *the Danish domicile* el domicilio danés ▲ *the domicile and legal form of the enterprise* el domicilio y la forma legal de la empresa

domicile address

A domicile address is the address where an enterprise has its permanent address, i.e. its head office.

sede central

▲ *the domicile address of the company* la sede central de la empresa

dominant influence

= control

≠ significant influence

To have dominant influence of an enterprise means to have control of it. The controlling enterprise consequently has the power to determine the financial and operating policies of the controlled enterprise so as to gain benefits from its activities.

NOTE Dominant influence may e.g. result when an enterprise holds more than 50 per cent of the voting shares of another enterprise; this enterprise is then referred to as a subsidiary.

influencia dominante

= control

▲ *before dominant influence effectively passes to the acquirer* antes de que la influencia dominante pase de forma efectiva al adquirente ▲ *subject to dominant influence by the reporting enterprise* sujeto a influencia dominante por la empresa informante ▲ *transitory dominant influence* influencia dominante transitoria

double entry bookkeeping

→ double-entry bookkeeping

double taxation

Double taxation occurs when a person or enterprise has to pay tax on the same income to the tax authorities of two countries.

doble imposición

▲ *double taxation convention* convenio de doble imposición ▲ *double taxation relief* desgravación por doble imposición ▲ *double taxation treaty* tratado de doble imposición ▲ *less double taxation relief* menos desgravación por doble imposición ▲ *prevent double taxation* prevenir la doble imposición ▲ *relief from double taxation* desgravación por doble imposición ▲ *risk of double taxation* riesgo de doble imposición

double taxation agreement

→ double taxation convention

double taxation convention

A double taxation convention is an agreement between two countries in which they agree how to avoid double taxation of the same income and specify which country has the right to tax different types of income if a taxpayer has connections to both countries.

convenio de doble imposición

▲ *draft double taxation convention* borrador del convenio de doble imposición ▲ *sign a double taxation convention* firmar un convenio de doble imposición ▲ *the general scope of the double taxation convention* el alcance general del convenio de doble imposición ▲ *the provisions of the double taxation convention* las disposiciones del convenio de doble imposición ▲ *the US/UK Double Taxation Convention* el convenio de doble imposición de EEUU/ Reino Unido

⇛ thin capitalisation

double taxation treaty

→ double taxation convention

double-entry bookkeeping

Double-entry bookkeeping is a system of bookkeeping that requires simultaneous recording of a transaction in two accounts, in this way reflected both as an entry of debit and as an entry of credit.

contabilidad por partida doble

= contabilidad de doble entrada

▲ *the invention of double entry bookkeeping* la invención de la contabilidad por partida doble

⇛ credit, debit, dual aspect convention

double-entry system

The double-entry system is a system of bookkeeping that requires simultaneous recording of a transaction in two accounts, in this way reflected both as an entry of debit and as an entry of credit.

sistema de partida doble

= sistema de doble entrada

▲ *form part of the double-entry system* formar parte del sistema de partida doble

⇛ dual aspect convention

doubtful accounts US

→ doubtful receivables

doubtful debts UK

Doubtful debts refer to amounts owed to an enterprise or individual that it does not expect to receive due to the debtor's inability to pay. Usually, provisions are made for such debts.

deudores de dudoso cobro

= deudores morosos

▲ *impairment charge for bad and doubtful debts* cargo por deterioro de cuentas a cobrar dudosas o deudores de dudoso cobro ▲ *material doubtful debts* cuentas a cobrar materiales procedentes de deudores de dudoso cobro ▲ *net of doubtful debts allowances on receivables* cuentas a cobrar netas de bonificaciones por deudores de dudoso cobro ▲ *provisions for doubtful debts related to the amount of outstanding balances* provisiones por deudores de dudoso cobro relativas a la cuantía de los saldos pendientes ▲ *the expense in respect of bad or doubtful debts due from related parties* los gastos en relación con las cuentas a cobrar dudosas o deudores de dudoso cobro vencidas procedentes de partes vinculadas

doubtful receivables

Doubtful receivables refer to amounts owed to an enterprise or individual that it does not expect to receive due to the debtor's inability to pay. Usually, provisions are made for such receivables.

cuentas a cobrar de dudoso cobro

▲ *less an estimate made for doubtful receivables* menos una estimación hecha por cuentas a cobrar de dudoso cobro ▲ *material doubtful receivables* cuentas a cobrar materiales procedentes de deudores de dudoso cobro

downsizing

Downsizing is the reduction of an enterprise's workforce and/ or operating units in order to cut costs.

reestructuración

▲ *corporate downsizing* reestructuración empresarial ▲ *start downsizing* empezar la reestructuración

downward adjustment

When something is reduced compared to previously, a downward adjustment is made.

ajuste a la baja

▲ *downward adjustment of expectations* ajuste a la baja de las expectativas

DPO

= days' payable outstanding, Days' Payable Outstanding, days payable outstanding

≠ days' sales outstanding, DSO

DPO is the abbreviation for days' payable outstanding, which is a financial ratio measuring how long it takes an enterprise on average to pay its trade payables, i.e. trade creditors.

rotación de proveedores
= plazo promedio de proveedores, rotación de pagos comerciales
≠ rotación de clientes, rotación de cobros comerciales
▲ *a decrease in DPO* un descenso de la rotación de proveedores ▲ *an increase in DPO* un aumento de la rotación de proveedores ▲ *reduce DPO by 10%* reducir la rotación de proveedores en un 10%

DPS
= dividend per share
DPS is the abbreviation for dividend per share, a financial ratio defined as the amount of dividend distributed for the period divided by the number of outstanding ordinary shares.
dividendo por acción
▲ *adjusted DPS* dividendo por acción ajustado ▲ *calculate DPS* calcular el dividendo por acción ▲ *DPS calculations* cálculos del dividendo por acción

drawdown
= drawing
A drawdown is the withdrawal of money from a bank account with available funds such as a line of credit or a savings account. A flexible drawdown allows the money to be withdrawn in stages.
disposición
▲ *requirements for drawdown of funds* requisitos para la disposición de fondos ▲ *violate the drawdown rules* violar las normas de la disposición

drawing
= withdrawal
≠ deposit
Drawings are amounts withdrawn from e.g. bank accounts, reserves etc.
disposición
= retirada
▲ *drawing account* cuenta corriente ▲ *drawing facility* servicio de giro ▲ *drawing right* derecho de disposición ▲ *drawings account* cuenta de disposiciones

drop in share prices UK, IAS/IFRS
= decline in share prices
A drop in share prices signals a depreciation of the share value.
caída en los precios de la acción
▲ *withstand a drop in share prices* resistir una caída en el precio de la acción

DSI
= days' sales in inventory, Days' Sales in Inventory, days' sales of inventory, Days' Sales of Inventory
DSI is an abbreviation of days' sales in inventory, which is a financial ratio measuring an enterprise's performance by showing the average time spent for turning the enterprise's inventory (preferably including work in progress) into sales. A low DSI implies a short amount of days and is therefore preferable, however, the ratio varies with type of industry.
rotación de inventario
= plazo promedio de inventario
▲ *a 10% reduction in DSI* una reducción del 10% en la rotación de inventario ▲ *a drop in DSI* una caída en la rotación de inventario ▲ *calculate DSI* calcular la rotación de inventario

DSO
= days' sales outstanding, Days' Sales Outstanding, debtor collection period
≠ days' payable outstanding, DPO
DSO is the abbreviation for days' sales outstanding, which is a financial ratio measuring how long it takes an enterprise on average to collect amounts receivable (revenue) after making a sale. A low DSO implies a small amount of days and is therefore positive, whereas a high amount indicates a long debtor collection period and that the enterprise is selling on credit.
rotación de clientes
= plazo promedio de clientes, rotación de cobros comerciales
≠ rotación de pagos comerciales, rotación de proveedores
▲ *a decrease in DSO* un descenso en la rotación de clientes ▲ *an increase in DSO* un aumento en la rotación de clientes

dual aspect convention
The dual aspect convention is an accounting convention according to which transactions are treated as having two aspects, i.e. an increase in assets and a decrease in cash, which both must be recognised in the financial statements. This leads to double-entry bookkeeping according to which tran-

sactions are recognised simultaneously as debit and credit items.

principio de partida doble

= principio de doble entrada

▲ *correspond to the dual aspect convention* corresponde al principio de partida doble

⇛ double-entry bookkeeping

dual pricing

Dual pricing is a transfer pricing method where affiliated, intra-group enterprises, divisions or units use two different transfer-pricing methods in their price setting of internal transfers and interdivisional transactions, where e.g. full-cost transfer prices are received by selling divisions, whereas market-based transfer prices are paid by buying divisions.

método de desdoblamiento de precios

▲ *counter argument used to defend dual pricing* contraargumento utilizado para defender el método de desdoblamiento de precios ▲ *use dual pricing* utilizar el método de desdoblamiento de precios

⇛ transfer pricing

due

To be due means to be payable or deliverable at a particular time.

vencido

▲ *an amount due* una cantidad vencida ▲ *due date* fecha vencida ▲ *fall due more than 12 months after the balance sheet date* vencido a largo plazo ▲ *liabilities that are due for settlement* pasivos vencidos para la liquidación ▲ *obligations that are due to be repaid within the next operating cycle* obligaciones vencidas para ser liquidadas en el próximo ciclo de explotación ▲ *the gross amount due from customers for contract work* la cantidad bruta vencida procedente de clientes por contrato de obra ▲ *the gross amount due to customers for contract work* la cantidad bruta vencida a clientes por contrato por construcción

due diligence

A due diligence is a detailed analysis and investigation of the financial position of a company with a view to a potential flotation on a stock exchange or a large capital investment e.g. by a venture capitalist, typically performed by an independent accountant. Due diligences are also performed by banks or other lenders to evaluate the debt of a company with a view to assessing the risk involved.

NOTE The expression "due diligence" refers to the prudence involved. Therefore, due diligences are typically performed by a third party.

diligencia debida

= due diligence, prudencia debida

▲ *allow due diligence to take place* permitir que la diligencia debida tenga lugar ▲ *commercial and financial due diligence* diligencia debida financiera y comercial ▲ *due diligence documents* documentos de la diligencia debida ▲ *environmental due diligence* diligencia debida medioambiental ▲ *legal due diligence* diligencia debida legal ▲ *limitation of access to due diligence* limitación del acceso a la diligencia debida ▲ *perform due diligence* llevar a cabo una diligencia debida ▲ *performance of satisfactory due diligence* llevar a cabo una diligencia debida satisfactoria ▲ *prepare a due diligence report* preparar un informe de diligencia debida ▲ *the due diligence methods used* los métodos de diligencia debida utilizados ▲ *the nature of the agreed due diligence* la naturaleza de la diligencia debida acordada ▲ *the scope of due diligence* el alcance de la diligencia debida ▲ *undertake due diligence* hacer una diligencia debida

dumping

Dumping is the selling of products below market prices in international trade typically with a view to gaining market shares or securing a monopoly, consequently involving unfair competition.

dumping

▲ *illegal dumping* dumping ilegal ▲ *standards dumping* dumping de normas

duration

Duration expresses the term-to-maturity of a debt, typically a bond, or a portfolio of debts on the basis of interest rates and/or the amounts and the

time aspect of the individual payments. The longer the term-to-maturity, the higher the price sensitivity.
vencimiento
▲ *achieve the intended duration* conseguir el vencimiento pretendido ▲ *actual duration* vencimiento actual ▲ *average duration* vencimiento medio ▲ *changes in the duration of the contract* cambios en el vencimiento del contrato ▲ *modified duration* vencimiento modificado ▲ *the activity, duration and reporting obligations of the joint venture* la actividad, vencimiento y las obligaciones de informar de la joint venture ▲ *the duration of debt stock* el vencimiento del título de deuda ▲ *the duration of the bond portfolio* el vencimiento de la cartera de bonos

duty

1 = tax
Duty is any tax levied by a public authority, particularly that imposed on imports, exports and manufactured goods.
tributo
= impuesto
▲ *charge duty* cargar el tributo ▲ *customs duty* impuesto arancelario ▲ *duty exemption* libre de impuesto ▲ *excise duty* impuesto especial ▲ *stamp duty* impuesto del timbre

2 A duty is a moral or legal obligation.
obligación
= deber
▲ *duty of care* deber de amparo ▲ *duty of disclosure* deber de publicación

DV

= deprival value
DV is the abbreviation for deprival value, i.e. the loss that a business would suffer if it were to be deprived of the use of the asset.
valor de abandono
▲ *assets valued at DV* activos valorados al valor de abandono ▲ *calculate DV* calcular el valor de abandono

E

earn
= accumulate
To earn is to generate income or profit.
ganar
= acumular
▲ *earn a profit* acumular un beneficio ▲ *earn a taxable amount* ganar una cantidad imponible ▲ *earn rentals* ganar por alquileres ▲ *recognise income as earned* reconocer ingresos como acumulados

earning capacity
→ earnings capacity

earning of income
→ income earning

earnings
For accounting purposes, earnings are the net income from operations; earnings may arise from ordinary or extraordinary operations.
beneficios
= ganancias
NOTE Spanish accountant prefer 'beneficios' to the IAS/IFRS term 'ganancias'.
▲ *a specified level of earnings* un nivel especificado de beneficios ▲ *accrued earnings* beneficios devengados ▲ *an adjustment to the opening balance of retained earnings* un ajuste de beneficios no distribuidos en el balance de apertura ▲ *earnings dilution* dilución de beneficios ▲ *earnings sustainability* sostenibilidad de beneficios ▲ *investment earnings* beneficios de inversión ▲ *retained earnings* beneficios no distribuidos

earnings before interest and tax
= EBIT
Earnings before interest and tax refers to the profit of an enterprise prior to the deduction of tax and interest expenses, and it is used both as a key figure and an item in the income statement.
beneficios antes de interes e impuestos
= EBIT, ganancias antes de intereses e impuestos, resultado neto de explotación
NOTE Spanish accountants prefer 'beneficios' to the IAS/IFRS term 'ganancias'.
▲ *a decrease in earnings before interest and tax* un descenso en beneficios antes de intereses e impuestos ▲ *an increase in earnings before interest and tax* un aumento en beneficios antes de intereses e impuestos ▲ *earnings before interest and tax excluding one-time items* beneficios antes de impuestos excluyendo partidas extraordinarias ▲ *earnings before interest and tax including one-time items* beneficios antes de intereses e impuestos incluyendo partidas extraordinarias

earnings capacity
= cash generating ability, earning capacity
Earnings capacity is the ability of the enterprise per time unit to generate net cash from operating acitivites.
capacidad de beneficios
= capacidad de ganancias
▲ *a high earnings capacity* una alta capacidad de beneficios ▲ *future earnings capacity* capacidad de beneficios futura ▲ *sustain an earnings capacity* sustentar una capacidad de beneficios

earnings decrease US
A decrease in earnings means that results of the enterprise are poorer as compared with prior fiscal years.
disminución de beneficios
= disminución de ganancias
▲ *a pretax earnings decrease of $23.4 million* una disminución de beneficios de 23,4 millones de dólares antes de impuestos ▲ *earnings decrease before tax* disminución de beneficios antes de impuestos ▲ *year-on-year earnings decrease* disminución de beneficios interanual

earnings development
= earnings performance
The development in earnings means the historical or future performance of results.
desarrollo de beneficios
= curva de beneficios
▲ *achieve above-average earnings development* conseguir una curva de beneficios por

encima de la media ▲ *have a negative influence on earnings development* tener una influencia negativa en el desarrollo de beneficios ▲ *have a positive impact on earnings development* tener un impacto positivo en el desarrollo de beneficios

earnings element

Earnings elements are the various aspects of the financial results of an enterprise from which the user will get a more detailed picture of the earnings capacity of the enterprise. The earnings elements appearing in the annual report include: EBITDA or operating profit/loss, profit or loss on ordinary activities and profit or loss for the accounting period.

componente de beneficios

▲ *extraordinary earnings elements* componentes de beneficios extraordinarios ▲ *ordinary earnings elements* componentes de beneficios ordinarios

earnings expectations

The expectations to the development in earnings for the year compared with prior periods or up to the end of the financial year are referred to as earnings expectations.

expectativas de beneficios

▲ *adjust earnings expectations for the year downwards* ajustar las expectativas de beneficios del ejercicio a la baja ▲ *adjust earnings expectations for the year upwards* ajustar las expectativas de beneficios al alza ▲ *changed earnings expectations for the financial year* expectativas de beneficios modificadas para el ejercicio

earnings from investment portfolios

= investment portfolio income

Earnings that are attributable to a portfolio of securities are called earnings from investment portfolios.

beneficios de las carteras de inversión

= ingresos de las carteras de inversión

▲ *net interest income excluding earnings from investment portfolios* ingresos financieros netos excluyendo los beneficios de las carteras de inversión ▲ *total earnings from investment portfolios* total beneficios de las carteras de inversión

earnings growth

Earnings growth is an increase in net profits.

aumento de beneficios

= aumento de ganancias

▲ *earnings growth forecasts* previsiones de aumento de beneficios ▲ *pre-tax earnings growth* aumento de beneficios antes de impuestos ▲ *private sector earnings growth* aumento de beneficios del sector privado ▲ *short-term earnings growth* aumento de beneficios a corto plazo ▲ *strong earnings growth* fuerte aumento de beneficios

earnings impact

An event that makes earnings rise or fall has an earnings impact. Events impacting earnings include profitable sales, depreciation and amortisation, decrease in expenses attributable to unchanged earnings etc. Events not impacting earnings include transactions recognised direct in equity such as share issues, revaluation of fixed assets, capital decreases etc.

impacto en los beneficios

= impacto de beneficios, impacto de ganancias, impacto en beneficios, impacto en las ganancias

▲ *estimated earnings impact* impacto en los beneficios previstos ▲ *total pre-tax earnings impact of consolidated adjustments* total impacto en beneficios de los ajustes consolidados antes de impuestos

earnings improvement

An earnings improvement occurs where the results for the period are better than the results for the previous period.

mejora de beneficios

= mejora de ganancias, mejora de las ganancias, mejora de los beneficios

▲ *a good earnings improvement* una buena mejora de beneficios

earnings management

Earnings management involves the preparation of financial statements that ensures that earnings are managed to be at the same level over a number of years without any wide fluctuations.

gestión de beneficios

= gestión de ganancias, gestión de las ganancias, gestión de los beneficios

▲ *abusive earnings management* gestión abusiva de los beneficios ▲ *traditional earnings management techniques* técnicas de gestión de beneficios tradicionales

earnings multiple
= P/E ratio, price/earnings ratio
The earnings multiple or price/earnings ratio is defined as the market price per share divided by earnings per share (EPS). This investment ratio compares the market price of an ordinary share with the EPS and is used to analyse the performance potential of a company. A high earnings multiple indicates future earnings growth and signals that investors have high confidence in the company.
ratio precio/beneficios
▲ *an earnings multiple of approximately 20* un ratio precio/beneficios de aproximadamente 20 ▲ *calculate the earnings multiple* calcular el ratio precio/beneficios

earnings per share
= EPS
Earnings per share is a financial ratio stating the amount of net profit for the period that is attributable to ordinary shareholders divided by the weighted average number of ordinary shares outstanding during the period. This ratio is applied for valuation of the share and the enterprise's ability to generate profit to the owners.
beneficios por acción
= ganancias por acción
NOTE Spanish accountants prefer 'beneficios por acción' to the IAS/IFRS term 'ganancias por acción'.
▲ *a reduction in earnings per share* una reducción de los beneficios por acción ▲ *adjusted earnings per share* beneficios por acción ajustados ▲ *basic earnings per share* beneficios por acción básicos ▲ *calculate earnings per share* calcular los beneficios por acción ▲ *changes in the assumptions used in earnings per share calculations* modificaciones en los supuestos usados en los cálculos de los beneficios por acción ▲ *computation of earnings per share* cómputo de los beneficios por acción ▲ *consolidated basic earnings per share* beneficios por acción básicos consolidados ▲ *decrease earnings per share* disminuir los beneficios por acción ▲ *diluted earnings per share* beneficios por acción diluidos ▲ *disclose earnings per share* divulgar los beneficios por acción ▲ *earnings per share amounts* cantidades de beneficios por acción ▲ *have an antidilutive effect on earnings per share* tener un efecto antidilutivo en los beneficios por acción ▲ *increase earnings per share* aumentar los beneficios por acción ▲ *previously reported earnings per share* beneficios por acción sobre los que previamente se ha informado ▲ *principles for the determination of earnings per share* principios para la determinación de los beneficios por acción ▲ *principles for the presentation of earnings per share* principios para la presentación de los beneficios por acción ▲ *the denominator of the earnings per share calculation* el denominador para el cálculo de los beneficios por acción

earnings performance
= earnings development
The earnings performance shows the historical or future development of results.
curva de beneficios
= desarrollo de beneficios
▲ *a negative earnings performance* una curva de beneficios negativa ▲ *a positive earnings performance* una curva de beneficios positiva ▲ *a satisfactory earnings performance* una curva de beneficios satisfactoria ▲ *a stable earnings performance* una curva de beneficios estable ▲ *affect the earnings performance of the group* afectar a la curva de beneficios del grupo ▲ *contribute negatively to the earnings performance* contribuir negativamente a la curva de beneficios ▲ *contribute positively to the earnings performance* contribuir positivamente a la curva de beneficios ▲ *quarterly earnings performance* curva de beneficios trimestral ▲ *revenue and earnings performance* curva de bene-

ficios e ingresos fiscales ▲ *semi-annual earnings performance* curva de beneficios semestral

earnings release US

An earnings release is a financial reporting announcement presented to the public and the stock markets by an enterprise on a quarterly or annual basis containing information about earnings and results of operations. Earnings releases usually contain the enterprise's financial highlights, management's interpretation of the period under review together with outlook and expectations as well as summary financial statements.

publicación de resultados

= informe de resultados

▲ *after the publication of the earnings release* después de la publicación del informe de resultados ▲ *as specified in the group earnings release No. 01/02 of March 6, 2005* tal y como están especificados en la publicación de resultados del grupo nº 01/02 de 6 de marzo de 2005 ▲ *earnings release for the year* publicación de resultados del ejercicio ▲ *earnings release of April 16, 2005* publicación de resultados del 16 de abril de 2005 ▲ *in a separate earnings release* en una publicación de resultados separada ▲ *publication through an earnings release* publicación mediante un informe de resultados ▲ *publish earnings releases* publicar informes de resultados

⇛ stock exchange announcement

earnings statement US

→ income statement

earnings warning US

An earnings warning is an announcement by an enterprise that its results for a specific period will be lower than expected.

aviso de menores beneficios

= profit warning

▲ *issue an earnings warning* emitir un profits warning ▲ *release an earnings warning* divulgar un aviso de menores beneficios

earnings yield

= E/P

Earnings yield is an investment ratio defined as earnings per share divided by market price. The reciprocal value is the price/earnings ratio.

ratio precio por beneficios

▲ *an earnings yield of 10%* un ratio precio por beneficios de 10%

⇛ price/earnings ratio

EBIT

EBIT is the abbreviation for earnings before interest and tax, which refers to the profit of an enterprise prior to the deduction of tax and interest expenses, and it is used both as a key figure and an item in the income statement.

BAII

= beneficio antes de intereses e impuestos, EBIT, resultado neto de explotación

▲ *a decrease in EBIT* una disminución del BAII ▲ *an increase in EBIT* un aumento del BAII ▲ *EBIT excluding one-time items* BAII excluyendo partidas excepcionales ▲ *EBIT including one-time items* BAII incluyendo partidas excepcionales

EBIT margin

= operating margin

EBIT margin or operating margin is a measure of operating profitability, calculated as earnings before interest and tax or operating profit divided by sales.

margen de BAII

= margen BAII, margen operativo

▲ *achieve an EBIT margin of 10%* conseguir un margen de BAII del 10% ▲ *an increasing EBIT margin* un margen de BAII en aumento ▲ *maintain an EBIT margin of 10%* mantener un margen de BAII del 10%

EBITA

EBITA is the abbreviation for earnings before interest, tax and amortisation, i.e. the profit of a company as shown in the profit and loss account before deducting interest, tax and amortisation expenses on intangible assets.

EBITA

= beneficio antes de intereses, impuestos y amortización

▲ *a decrease in EBITA* una disminución del EBITA ▲ *an increase in EBITA* un aumento del EBITA

EBITA margin

EBITA margin is a measure of operating profitability, calculated as earnings before interest, tax and goodwill amortisation divided by sales.

margen de EBITA

= margen de beneficios antes de intereses, impuestos y amortización

▲ *achieve an EBITA margin of 10%* conseguir un margen de EBITA del 10% ▲ *adjust the EBITA margin downwards* ajustar el margen de EBITA a la baja ▲ *an increasing EBITA margin* un margen de EBITA al alza ▲ *increase the EBITA margin* aumentar el margen de EBITA ▲ *maintain an EBITA margin of 10%* mantener un margen de EBITA del 10%

EBITDA

= operating income US, operating profit UK

EBITDA is the abbreviation for earnings before interest, taxes, depreciation and amortisation. For accounting purposes, this concept is applied both as a key figure and as an item in the income statement.

EBITDA

= beneficio bruto de explotación, resultado bruto de explotación

▲ *EBITDA from international ac*

tivities el EBITDA de las actividades internacionales ▲ *EBITDA growth of 5% in the second half of 2005* aumento del EBITDA del 5% en el segundo semestre de 2005 ▲ *EBITDA less capex and plus working capital changes* EBITDA menos gastos en bienes de capital más modificaciones del capital operativo ▲ *improved EBITDA* EBITDA mejorado

EBITDA margin

= operating margin

EBITDA margin is a measure of operating profitability, calculated as earnings before interest, tax, depreciation, amortisation and write-downs divided by sales.

margen de EBITDA

▲ *achieve an EBITDA margin of 10%* conseguir un margen de EBITDA del 10% ▲ *adjust the EBITDA margin downwards* ajustar el margen de EBITDA a la baja ▲ *EBITDA margin (%)* margen de EBITDA (%) ▲ *increase the EBITDA margin* aumentar el margen de EBITDA ▲ *maintain an EBITDA margin of 10%* mantener un margen de EBITDA del 10%

economic

Economic means concerned with or relating to economics, money, finance, trade and industry within a region, country or sector.

económico

▲ *a difficult economic situation* una situación económica difícil ▲ *a future economic benefit* un futuro beneficio económico ▲ *an economic decline* un declive económico ▲ *an economic slowdown* una ralentización económica ▲ *an economic unit* una unidad económica ▲ *an economic upswing* alza económica ▲ *economic benefit* beneficio económico ▲ *economic capital* capital económico ▲ *economic development* desarrollo económico ▲ *economic environments* ámbitos económicos ▲ *economic growth* crecimiento económico ▲ *economic life* vida económica ▲ *economic value added* valor económico añadido ▲ *from an economic perspective* desde una perspectiva económica ▲ *in making economic decisions* a la hora de tomar decisiones económicas

economic benefit

Economic benefits are potential gains resulting in net cash inflows to an enterprise because of its ability to generate such cash inflows through transactions and events. In a broader sense, economic benefits refer to financial gains attributable to infrastructure and facility improvements provided by central and local authorities.

beneficio económico

▲ *a diminution of economic benefits* una disminución de beneficios económicos ▲ *an outflow of resources embodying economic benefits* una salida de recursos incorporados a los beneficios económicos ▲ *future economic benefits arising from assets that are not capable of being individually identified* beneficios económicos futuros resultantes de los activos que no se pueden identificar individualmente ▲ *future economic benefits associated with the item* beneficios económicos futuros asociados con la partida ▲ *the economic benefits that may be obtained from the asset* los beneficios económicos que se pueden obtener del activo ▲ *the expected pattern of consumption of the future economic benefits* el modelo previsto de consumo de los beneficios económicos futuros ▲ *the future economic benefits embodied in depreciable assets* los beneficios económicos futuros incorporados en los activos depreciables

economic life

Economic life is the period over which an asset is expected to provide economic benefits and be economically usable by one or more users.

vida útil

= vida económica

NOTE Spanish accountants use 'vida útil' instead of the IAS/IFRS term 'vida económica' considering that the IAS/IFRS term is not a specific accounting term, but a general economic one.

▲ *an indefinite economic life* una vida útil indefinida ▲ *an unlimited economic life* una vida útil ilimitada ▲ *economic life of goodwill* vida útil del fondo de comercio ▲ *economic life of property, plant and equipment* vida útil de edificios, instalaciones y equipos ▲ *estimated economic life of consolidated goodwill* vida útil prevista del fondo de comercio consolidado ▲ *the economic life of the entire leased asset* la vida útil de todo el activo alquilado ▲ *the end of the economic life of the assets* el final de la vida útil de los activos

⇛ useful life

economic mismatch IAS/IFRS

≠ accounting mismatch IAS/IFRS

Economic mismatch occurs particularly in insurance accounting where the values of assets (in which premiums have been invested) are not subject to the same economic influences as the liabilities (to policyholders). This gives rise to a mismatch that should be reflected in the financial statements as economic reality.

desequilibrio económico

▲ *manage the economic mismatch* gestionar el desequilibrio económico ▲ *report all the economic mismatch that exists* anotar todo el desequilibrio económico existente

SOURCE IFRS 4

economic order quantity

= EOQ

The economic order quantity is a mathematical method for calculating the most economically advantageous order size for the purchase of products to be held on stock which contributes to optimising stock holdings and reducing costs of holding goods on stock.

gestión económica de inventarios

▲ *calculate the economic order quantity* calcular la gestión económica de inventarios ▲ *economic order quantity spreadsheet* hoja de cálculo de la gestión económica de inventarios

economic profit

= EP

Economic profit is a performance measure defined as the difference between operating profit after tax and a cost of capital charge on invested capital. Economic profit measures the real profit rather than the accounting profit, and shows the value added to an enterprise by its operations in a given period.

beneficio económico

▲ *base control on economic profit* basar el control en el beneficio económico ▲ *measurement of economic profit* medición del beneficio económico ▲ *pay compensation on the basis of economic profit* pagar la indemnización en base al beneficio económico

economic trend

= economic conditions

Economic trends are the periodic developments in the business cycles, typically over periods of five years during which the development moves in various phases from a trough over stages of pick-up with increasing demand and recovery to a peak or a boom, followed by a slowdown with negative growth and a recession which will again move into an upturn etc.

tendencia económica

▲ *a weak economic trend* una débil tendencia económica

▲ *the underlying economic trend* una tendencia económica subyacente ▲ *uncertain economic trends* tendencias económicas inciertas

economic value

→ value in use

economic value added

= economic profit, EP, EVA

Economic value added (EVA) is a performance measure defined as the difference between operating profit after tax and a cost of capital charge on invested capital and measures economic profit rather than accounting profit. EVA was introduced in the 1990s and focuses the attention on the drivers that contribute to creating shareholder wealth.

valor económico añadido

= valor añadido económico, valor económico agregado, EVA

▲ *an effective measure of economic value added* una medición efectiva de valor económico añadido ▲ *the main principle of economic value added* el principio básico de valor económico añadido

economy[1] *noun* <an, the, economies>

An economy refers to a particular country's or group of countries' system of business activities and way of organising production and wealth.

economía

▲ *a hyperinflationary economy* una economía hiperinflacionaria ▲ *a sound economy* una economía sólida ▲ *the American economy* la economía estadounidense ▲ *the Danish economy* la economía danesa ▲ *the European economy* la economía europea ▲ *the global economy* la economía global ▲ *the new economy* la nueva economía ▲ *the old economy* la vieja economía

economy[2] *noun* <no indefinite article, the, no plural>

Economy refers to the spending of money, time or efforts while carefully considering the amount spent, i.e. with a view to spending less or wishing to avoid waste.

economía

= ahorro

▲ *for reasons of economy* por razones de economía ▲ *practice economy* ahorrar ▲ *strict economy* ahorro riguroso

ED IAS/IFRS, UK

= exposure draft

ED is the abbreviation for exposure draft, which is a discussion document issued before the final document. Typically, exposure drafts are the drafts of new International Financial Reporting Standards (IFRSs), or amendments to existing International Accounting Standards (IASs), issued for public comments in connection with the consultative procedures of the International Accounting Standards Board (IASB).

ED

= documento de discusión

▲ *as stated in ED 10* como se especifica en el ED 10 ▲ *publish ED 10* publicar el ED 10

education and training expenditure

Education and training expenditure is the expenditure incurred by the enterprise that is attributable to education and training of staff, including retraining.

gasto en educación y formación

▲ *recognise education and training expenditure* reconocer el gasto en educación y formación ▲ *the economic benefits from the education and training expenditure incurred* los beneficios económicos del gasto efectuado en educación y formación

educational level

= level of education

Educational level refers to the educational qualifications of a person or group of persons. An enterprise may require that employees have a certain educational level, e.g. a bachelor's or a master's degree.

nivel educativo

▲ *number of employees by educational level* número de empleados por nivel educativo

effect

An effect is the way an act, event etc. changes or affects something.

efecto

▲ *a direct effect* un efecto directo ▲ *a modest effect* un efecto modesto ▲ *a monetary effect* un efecto monetario ▲ *a negative effect* un efecto negativo ▲ *a prospective effect* un efecto futuro ▲ *a significant effect* un efecto significativo ▲ *accumulated effect of changes in accounting policies* efecto acumulado de las variaciones en las políticas contables ▲ *an indirect effect* un efecto indirecto ▲ *effect of changes in accounting estimates* efecto de las variaciones en las estimaciones contables ▲ *effect of changes in exchange rates* efecto de las variaciones en los tipos de cambio ▲ *effect of correction of fundamental errors* efecto de la corrección de errores fundamentales ▲ *effect of expected future restructurings* efecto de las reestructuraciones futuras esperadas ▲ *effect on cash flows* efecto en los flujos de efectivo ▲ *effect on equity* efecto sobre el patrimonio neto ▲ *the effect of changes in exchange rates on the reporting enterprise* el efecto de las variaciones en los tipos de cambio de la empresa informante

effect on cash flow

= cash flow effect

When an action has an effect on cash flow, this results in an outflow of cash from or an inflow of cash to an enterprise. Some actions, such as depreciation, amortisation and credit selling, do not have an immediate effect on cash flow.

efecto en el flujo de efectivo

= efecto en el cash flow, efecto en el flujo de caja

▲ *a negative effect on cash flow* un efecto negativo en el flujo de efectivo ▲ *a negligible effect on cash flow* un efecto poco significativo en el flujo de efectivo ▲ *a positive effect on cash flow* un efecto positivo en el flujo de efectivo ▲ *a substantial effect on cash flow* un efecto considerable en el flujo de efectivo

effective

1 To be effective means to function and produce the intended result.

efectivo

▲ *an effective measurement tool* un instrumento de medida efectivo ▲ *the effective interest method* el metódo del tipo de interés efectivo ▲ *the effective interest rate of the financial instrument* el tipo de interés efectivo del instrumento financiero ▲ *the effective yield* el rendimiento efectivo

2 To become effective means to enter into force.

efectivo

= en funcionamiento

▲ *be effective* ser efectivo ▲ *become effective for financial periods beginning on or after 1 April 2007* entrar en funcionamiento en los ejercicios que empiezan el 1 de abril de 2007 o con posterioridad ▲ *effective date* fecha efectiva

effective date

The effective date is the date when a rule, standard, agreement, contract etc. become applicable and enters into force.

fecha de vigencia

= fecha efectiva

▲ *after the effective date of the IFRS* después de la fecha de vigencia de la NIIF ▲ *costs incurred after the effective date of the Standard* costes incurridos después de la fecha de vigencia de la Norma ▲ *the effective date of application of this interpretation* la fecha efectiva de aplicación de esta interpretación ▲ *the effective date of the revaluation* la fecha efectiva de la revalorización ▲ *the effective date paragraph* el párrafo de la fecha de vigencia ▲ *transitional provisions and effective date* disposiciones transitorias y fecha de vigencia

effective interest method

The effective interest method is a method of calculating amortisation using the effective interest rate of a financial asset or financial liability.

método del interés efectivo

= método de interés efectivo

▲ *accounted for in accordance with the effective interest method* contabilizado según el método del interés efectivo ▲ *calculated using the effective interest method* calculado empleando el método del interés efectivo ▲ *measure at amortised cost using the effective interest method* medir al coste amortizado usando el método del interés efectivo ▲ *use the effective interest method* usar el método del interés efectivo

effective interest rate

The effective interest rate refers to the total actual costs related to a loan, such as nominal interest, compounded interest, fees, etc., and constitutes the price for the loan.

tipo de interés efectivo

▲ *a constant effective interest rate* un tipo de interés efectivo constante ▲ *a weighted average effective interest rate* un tipo de interés efectivo medio ponderado ▲ *average effective interest rate* tipo de interés efectivo medio ▲ *change in the effective interest rate of the financial instrument* variación en el tipo de interés efectivo del instrumento financiero ▲ *financial instruments having substantially different effective interest rates* instrumentos financieros que tienen tipos de interés efectivo considerablemente diferentes ▲ *the current effective interest rate* el tipo de interés efectivo corriente ▲ *the original effective interest rate* el tipo de interés efectivo original

⇛ effective yield

effective interest rate method

→ effective interest method

effective tax rate

The effective tax rate is the average percentage resulting when total tax expenses for the period are divided by taxable income.

tipo impositivo efectivo

▲ *a decrease in the effective tax rate* un descenso del tipo impositivo efectivo ▲ *a higher effective tax rate* un tipo impositivo efectivo más alto ▲ *a lower effective tax rate* un tipo impositivo efectivo más bajo ▲ *an effective tax rate of 30%* un tipo impositivo efectivo del 30% ▲ *an increase in the effective tax rate* un aumento del tipo impositivo efectivo ▲ *reconciliation of effective tax rate* reconciliación del tipo impositivo efectivo ▲ *the effective tax rate for the whole group* el tipo impositivo efectivo para todo el grupo

effective yield

= yield to maturity

The effective yield is the internal rate of return on a debt instrument, such as a bond, purchased at a specified price and held until maturity. The effective yield is calculated on the basis of the market price, the coupon rate, the time between interest payments and the maturity period.

rentabilidad efectiva

= rendimiento efectivo

▲ *the effective yield on the consideration* la rentabilidad efectiva al considerar

⇛ effective interest rate

effectiveness

Effectiveness is a measure of the capability of reaching a desired objective, for instance how well a piece of equipment performs an intended task.

efectividad

▲ *assess the effectiveness* valorar la efectividad ▲ *hedge effectiveness* cubrir la efectividad ▲ *measure the effectiveness* medir la efectividad ▲ *test effectiveness periodically* comprobar la efectividad periódicamente ▲ *the effectiveness of the hedges* la efectividad de las coberturas ▲ *the effectiveness of the hedging relationship* la efectividad de la relación de cobertura

efficiency

Efficiency is a measure of the ability to reach an intended objective using the time, money and means at one's disposal with the least possible waste of effort or energy. Often used about persons who are competent and practical.

eficiencia

▲ *efficiency control* control de la eficiencia ▲ *enhanced efficiency* eficiencia reforzada ▲ *measures to improve efficiency* medidas para mejorar la eficiencia

efficiency variance

= quantity variance, usage variance

Efficiency variance is the difference between the actual quantity used and the budgeted quantity which was expected to be used.

variación en la eficiencia

= varianza de la eficiencia

▲ *an adverse efficiency variance* una variación en la eficiencia adversa ▲ *the efficiency variance for direct labour* la variación en la eficiencia por trabajo directo

efficient

To be efficient means to produce quick and satisfactory results.

eficiente

▲ *an efficient use of resources* un uso eficiente de los recursos

efficient capital market

An efficient capital market refers to a situation on a capital

market where the prices of securities traded reflect all the information and news that are publicly available.
mercado de capital eficiente
▲ *a transparent and efficient capital market* un mercado de capital eficiente y transparente ▲ *build an efficient capital market* construir un mercado de capital eficiente ▲ *develop an efficient capital market* desarrollar un mercado de capital eficiente

effort
An effort is an attempt to perform a specific action or to meet an objective which requires mental or physical energy.
esfuerzo
▲ *make a great effort to do something* llevar a cabo un gran esfuerzo para hacer algo ▲ *make every reasonable effort* hacer todo esfuerzo razonable

EFRAG IAS/IFRS
= European Financial Reporting Advisory Group IAS/IFRS
EFRAG is the abbreviation for the European Financial Reporting Advisory Group. EFRAG is responsible for giving a pro-active contribution to the standard setting work of IASB (International Accounting Standards Board), and for providing advice and technical expertise to the European Commission concerning the IFRSs and the interpretations for their European application. EFRAG was established in June 2001 by financial reporting stakeholders, i.e. national standard setters, accountants, reporting enterprises and users.
EFRAG
= Grupo Asesor Financiero para la Información Financiera
▲ *a special subcommittee of EFRAG* un subcomité especial del EFRAG ▲ *an EFRAG endorsement* una autorización EFRAG ▲ *the Technical Expert Group of EFRAG* el Grupo de Expertos Técnicos del EFRAG
⇛ International Accounting Standard, International Financial Reporting Standard

EGM
= extraordinary general meeting
EGM is the abbreviation for extraordinary general meeting which is any meeting of the shareholders of a company and its directors that is not an annual general meeting, and its purpose is to discuss and vote on issues that cannot wait to be resolved at the next annual general meeting.
junta general extraordinaria
▲ *at the EGM* en la junta general extraordinaria ▲ *call an EGM* convocar una junta general extraordinaria ▲ *close the EGM* finalizar la junta general extraordinaria ▲ *hold an EGM* llevar a cabo una junta general extraordinaria ▲ *resolve at the EGM* resolver en la junta general extraordinaria
⇛ AGM

EITF US
= Emerging Issues Task Force US
EITF is the abbreviation for Emerging Issues Task Force. The EITF is a task force assisting the FASB on emerging accounting issues.
EITF
= Emerging Issues Task Force, Grupo Especial de Asuntos Emergentes
▲ *as required by the new EITF rules* como requieren las nuevas reglas del EITF
⇛ FASB

element of uncertainty
An element of uncertainty is a factor that is connected with not having precise knowledge as to a particular size, amount, effect, development, outcome, etc.
factor de incertidumbre
▲ *a substantial element of uncertainty* un factor de incertidumbre considerable

eliminate
1 To eliminate is to completely get rid of something.
eliminar
= amortizar
▲ *eliminate a difference* eliminar una diferencia ▲ *eliminate a profit* eliminar un beneficio ▲ *eliminate a reserve* eliminar una reserva ▲ *eliminate a risk* eliminar un riesgo ▲ *eliminate an effect* eliminar un efecto ▲ *eliminate an item* eliminar una partida ▲ *eliminate counterparty risk* eliminar el riesgo de la contraparte ▲ *eliminate*

intercompany profit eliminar el beneficio entre empresas ▲ *eliminate intercompany receivables and payables* eliminar las cuentas a cobrar y pagar entre empresas ▲ *eliminate uncertainties* eliminar incertidumbres

2 To eliminate is to settle an obligation, e.g. to pay a debt in full.

eliminar

▲ *eliminate investments in subsidiaries* eliminar inversiones en las filiales

elimination

1 Elimination is the offsetting consolidation adjustment made for intra-group balances and transactions in connection with the preparation of consolidated financial statements for a group. As the consolidated financial statements are presented as if the parent company and its subsidiaries were a single entity, the combining of the individual financial statements of the parent and the subsidiaries must ignore items relating to intra-group activities.

eliminación

▲ *elimination of accumulated depreciation* eliminación de la depreciación acumulada ▲ *elimination of accumulated depreciation on revaluation* eliminación de la depreciación acumulada por revalorización ▲ *elimination of unrealised profits and losses on transactions with associates* eliminación de los resultados no realizados en transacciones con asociadas ▲ *the elimination of unrealised profits and losses resulting from intra-group transactions* la eliminación de los resultados no realizados resultantes de las transacciones intragrupo

2 Elimination is the removal, offsetting, netting, settlement or neutralisation of something, e.g. an obligation.

eliminación

▲ *capital elimination* eliminación de capital

embedded derivative

In a combined, hybrid instrument, an embedded derivative is one of the components, the other being the host contract. When embedded in another financial instrument, a derivative is not contractually transferable independently of that instrument and must have the same counterparty as the instrument.

derivado implicito

= derivado incrustado

▲ *an embedded derivative linked to an interest rate index* un derivado implícito ligado a un índice de tipo de interés ▲ *embedded derivatives that are regarded as closely related to a host contract* derivados implícitos que se consideran como muy relacionados con un contrato anfitrión ▲ *fixed rate debt with an embedded derivative* deuda a tipo fijo con un derivado implícito ▲ *measure an embedded derivative separately* medir un derivado implícito por separado ▲ *measure the embedded derivatives at fair value* medir los derivados implícitos a valor razonable ▲ *separate an embedded derivative from the host contract* separar un derivado implícito del contrato anfitrión ▲ *the economic characteristics and risks of an embedded derivative* las características y riesgos económicos de un derivado implícito SOURCE IAS 39, paragraph 10

⇛ combined financial instrument, compound financial instrument, financial instrument, host contract

Emerging Issues Task Force US

= EITF US

The Emerging Issues Task Force (EITF) is a task force assisting the FASB on emerging accounting issues.

Emerging Issues Task Force

= Grupo Especial de Asuntos Emergentes

▲ *an implementation guidance promulgated by the Emerging Issues Task Force* una guía de implementación promulgada por la Emerging Issues Task Force ▲ *the make-up of the Emerging Issues Task Force* la estructura de la Emerging Issues Task Force ▲ *the mission of the Emerging Issues Task Force* la misión de la Emerging Issues Task Force

⇛ Financial Accounting Standards Board

employ

To employ means to engage a person to do some work or

provide services in return for payment.

emplear

▲ *employ 1000 persons* emplear a 1.000 personas

employee

An employee is a person who is engaged by an enterprise to perform work or provide services against payment.

empleado

▲ *12 months after the end of the period in which the employees render the related service* 12 meses después del fin del periodo en el que los empleados dan cuentas del servicio relacionado ▲ *a number of new employees* un número de nuevos empleados ▲ *cash payments to and on behalf of employees* pagos en efectivo a y en nombre de empleados ▲ *employee turnover* rotación de empleados ▲ *the number of employees at the end of the period* el número de empleados al final del periodo

employee benefit

Employee benefits constitute consideration offered by an employer to employees including normal wages and salaries as well as insurance, pension contributions, income protection, etc.

retribución a los empleados

= beneficio a los empleados, prestación a los empleados

NOTE The IAS/IFRS term 'beneficio a los empleados' is rarely used in Spanish accounting texts.

▲ *accrual of employee benefits* devengo de retribuciones a los empleados ▲ *assets arising from employee benefits* activos resultantes de las retribuciones a los empleados ▲ *assets held by a fund for long-term employee benefits* activos mantenidos en un fondo para prestaciones a los empleados a largo plazo ▲ *costs of employee benefits arising directly from bringing the asset to its working condition* costes de las prestaciones a los empleados resultantes directamente de hacer que el activo sea operativo ▲ *employee benefits costs* costes de las retribuciones a los empleados ▲ *employee benefits expense* gasto por retribuciones a los empleados ▲ *employee benefits for key management personnel* retribuciones a los empleados para el personal de alta dirección ▲ *employers' assets and liabilities under employee benefit plans* activos y pasivos de los empleadores según los planes de prestaciones a los empleados ▲ *long-term employee benefits* prestaciones a los empleados a largo plazo ▲ *net employee benefit assets or liabilities for defined benefit plans* activos y pasivos por retribuciones a los empleados netas por planes de prestación definida ▲ *non-vested employee benefits* retribuciones a los empleados revocables ▲ *pay employee benefits when they fall due* pagar prestaciones a los empleados cuando vencen ▲ *pensions and other employee benefits to be paid in cash* pensiones y otras prestaciones a los empleados a pagar en efectivo ▲ *settlement of employee benefit obligations* liquidación de obligaciones por retribuciones a los empleados ▲ *short-term employee benefits* prestaciones a los empleados a costo plazo ▲ *the enterprise's obligation for employee benefits* la obligación de la empresa por retribuciones a los empleados ▲ *vested employee benefits* prestaciones a los empleados irrevocables

employee benefit plan

= pension benefit plan, pension plan US, pension scheme UK, post-employment benefit plan, retirement benefit plan

An employee benefit plan is an arrangement under which an enterprise provides monetary benefits such as lump sums or periodic payments for its employees on or after retirement.

plan de pensiones

▲ *employers' assets and liabilities under employee benefit plans* activos y pasivos de los empleadores por planes de pensiones ▲ *the settlement of employee benefit plan obligations* la liquidación de las obligaciones del plan de pensiones

employee benefits expense IAS/IFRS

Employee benefits expense is an item in the income statement as presented according to the nature of expense method. This item aggregates both short-term and long-term benefits provided by an enterprise to its employees for services rendered, e.g. wages and salaries, pension and termination benefits etc.

gasto por beneficios a los empleados

▲ *disclosure of employee benefits expense* divulgación del gasto por beneficios a los empleados

employee board member US

= employee director, employee representative, worker director UK

An employee board member is a person employed in a company elected and appointed by the employees to serve on the board of directors of the company. Employee board members have the same rights, duties and responsibilities as other board members.

representante de los empleados en el consejo

▲ *a newly elected employee board member* un representante de los empleados en el consejo recién nombrado ▲ *alternate employee board member* alternar al representante de los empleados en el consejo ▲ *elect a new employee board member* elegir a un nuevo representante de los empleados en el consejo ▲ *election of employee board members* nombramiento del representante de los empleados en el consejo

employee cost

= employee expense US, staff cost, staff expense

Employee costs constitute the costs of an enterprise relating to salaries, wages, pension costs, uniforms, training etc.

coste de personal

▲ *breakdown of employee costs* distribución de costes de personal ▲ *comparatives for employee costs* comparativas para costes de personal ▲ *disclose employee costs* publicar costes de personal ▲ *employee costs in proportion to total costs* costes de personal en proporción a costes totales ▲ *employee costs payable* costes de personal a pagar ▲ *other employee costs* otros costes de personal ▲ *reductions in employee costs* reducciones en costes de personal

employee director US/UK

= employee board member, employee representative, worker director

An employee director is a person employed in a company elected and appointed by the employees to serve on the board of directors of the company. Employee directors have the same rights, duties and responsibilities as other board members.

representante de los empleados en el consejo

▲ *a newly appointed employee director* un representante de los empleados en el consejo recién nombrado ▲ *alternate employee director* alternar al representante de los empleados en el consejo ▲ *appoint a new employee directors* elegir a un nuevo representante de los empleados en el consejo ▲ *appointment of employee director* nombramiento del representante de los empleados en el consejo

employee expense US

= employee cost, staff cost, staff expense

Employee expenses constitute the costs of an enterprise relating to salaries, wages, pension costs, uniforms, training etc.

gasto de personal

▲ *breakdown of employee expenses* desglose de los gastos de personal ▲ *comparatives for employee expenses* comparativas por gastos de personal ▲ *disclose employee expenses* divulgar los gastos de personal ▲ *employee expenses in proportion to total costs* gastos de personal en proporción a costes totales ▲ *employee expenses payable* gastos de personal a pagar ▲ *other employee expenses* otros gastos de personal ▲ *reductions in employee expenses* reducciones en gastos de personal

employee satisfaction

Employee satisfaction is the satisfaction perceived by an employee involving commitment, motivation, inspiration, job meaningfulness and involvement as well as physical needs. An enterprise's approach to employee satisfaction is a key consideration in strategic planning and of importance to the retention of its employees.

grado de satisfacción de los empleados

= grado de satisfacción laboral

▲ *declining employee satisfaction* grado de satisfacción de los empleados decreciente ▲ *employee satisfaction measurement* medida del grado de satisfacción de los empleados ▲ *increase employee satisfaction* aumentar el grado de satisfacción de los empleados ▲ *increasing employee satisfaction* grado de satisfacción de los empleados creciente

employee share IAS/IFRS, UK

= employee stock US

An employee share is a share in a company provided and offered by the company to its employees, either for free or at a favourable price, typically under an employee share ownership plan.

acción de los empleados

▲ *buy-back of employee shares* recompra de acciones de los empleados ▲ *employee shares held in custody accounts* acciones de los empleados en cuentas custodiadas ▲ *issue of employee shares at a favourable price* emisión de acciones de los empleados a un precio favorable ▲ *subscription of employee shares* suscripción de acciones de los empleados ▲ *tax adjustment relating to employee shares* ajuste fiscal relativo a las acciones de los empleados ▲ *the total number of employee shares sold* el número total de acciones de los empleados vendidas

⇛ employee share ownership plan

employee share ownership plan IAS/IFRS, UK

= employee stock ownership plan US, ESOP

An employee share ownership plan is an incentive programme set up by an enterprise with the purpose of offering shares to employees. Typically, the shares are offered at a discount to the market price.

plan de opciones sobre acciones para empleados

= plan de propiedad de acciones para empleados, plan de titularidad de acciones de los empleados

NOTE Spanish accountants prefer 'plan de opciones sobre acciones para empleados' to the IAS/IFRS term 'plan de titularidad de acciones de los empleados'.

▲ *allocation to an employee share ownership plan* asignación a un plan de opciones sobre acciones para empleados ▲ *an employee share ownership plan for senior employees with more than three years' service* un plan de opciones sobre acciones para empleados para los empleados senior con más de tres años de servicio

⇛ share incentive plan

employee stock US

= employee share UK, IAS/IFRS

Employee stock refers to shares of stock in a company provided and offered by the company to its employees, either for free or at a favourable price, typically under an employee stock ownership plan.

acción de los empleados

▲ *buy-back of employee stock* recompra de acciones de los empleados ▲ *employee stock held in custody accounts* acciones de los empleados en cuentas custodiadas ▲ *issue of employee stock at a favorable price* emisión de acciones de los empleados a un precio favorable ▲ *subscription of employee stock* suscripción de acciones de los empleados ▲ *tax adjustment relating to employee stock* ajuste fiscal relativo a las acciones de los empleados ▲ *the total number of employee stock sold* el número total de acciones de los empleados vendidas

⇛ employee stock ownership plan

employee stock ownership plan US

= employee share ownership plan UK, ESOP

An employee stock ownership plan is an incentive programme set up by an enterprise with the purpose of offering stock to employees. Typically, the shares of stock are offered at a discount to the market price.

plan de opciones sobre acciones para empleados

= plan de titularidad de acciones de los empleados

▲ *allocation to an employee stock ownership plan* asignación a un plan de opciones sobre acciones para empleados ▲ *an employee stock ownership plan for senior employees with more than three years' service* un plan de opciones sobre acciones para empleados para los empleados senior con más de tres años de servicio

employee turnover US
= staff turnover UK
Employee turnover is a financial ratio measuring the rate of employee replacement in per cent and shows whether employees are replaced frequently or whether the headcount is rather stable during a particular accounting period.
rotación de personal
= plazo promedio de personal
▲ *a decrease in employee turnover* un descenso en la rotación de personal ▲ *an increase in employee turnover* un aumento en la rotación de personal ▲ *employee turnover rate* tasa de rotación de personal ▲ *high employee turnover* rotación de personal alta

employee-related cost
Employee-related costs are wages and salaries, social security contributions, pension and termination benefits, bonuses, car allowances, payroll taxes etc.
coste de personal
▲ *an analysis of the trend in employee-related costs* un análisis de la tendencia en costes de personal ▲ *an increase in employee-related costs* un aumento en costes de personal ▲ *severance and other employee-related costs* indemnización por rescisión de contrato y otros costes de personal ▲ *total employee-related costs* total costes de personal

employees and others providing similar services
Defined for share-based payment purposes, employees and others providing similar services are persons providing services to an enterprise and that are employees for legal and tax purposes or of a similar standing, such as management employees as well as non-executive directors.
empleados y terceros que prestan servicios similares
▲ *transactions with employees and others providing similar services* transacciones con empleados y terceros que prestan servicios similares
SOURCE IFRS 2, Appendix A

employment
Employment is a macroeconomic figure showing how many persons in a particular area, such as a country, who are employed. Typically, employment is specified as a number of persons or as a percentage of persons of a specific group, e.g. persons aged 18-60.
empleo
NOTE The collocation 'employment security' is transalted by 'seguridad laboral' in Spanish as the term 'employment' in attributive position is 'laboral' in Spanish.
▲ *employment contract* contrato de empleo ▲ *employment numbers* cifras de empleo ▲ *employment security* seguridad laboral

employment policy
Employment policies refer to an enterprise's policies in relation to employment and recruitment of employees, including policies related to pay, benefits, rewards, facilities, conduct, dismissal procedures as well as recruitment and selection procedures.
política de empleo
▲ *adopt a new employment policy* adoptar una nueva política de empleo ▲ *change the existing employment policy* modificar la política de empleo existente

enclosure
An enclosure is a document that is put inside an envelope together with a letter.
documento adjunto
▲ *see the enclosure* ver el documento adjunto

encumbent
→ incumbent

encumbrance
1 An encumbrance is a right or interest in the land held by someone other than the owner of the land, for example easements, mortgages and leases.
gravamen
= gravamen
▲ *easements and other encumbrances* facilidades y otros gravámenes ▲ *free of all encumbrances* libre de todo gravamen ▲ *otherwise free from encumbrances* por lo demás libre de gravámenes ▲ *subject to the encumbrances and other entries*

appearing in the register sujeto a gravámenes y otras entradas que aparecen en el registro

2 In US government accounting encumbrances are commitments arising out of unperformed contracts relating to the purchase or sale of goods and services.

compromiso de gasto

▲ *accounting for encumbrances* contabilizando los compromisos de gasto ▲ *recognize encumbrances* reconocer los compromisos de gasto

end[1] *noun*

End refers to the last part of something or to the last element in a row.

final

= finalización

▲ *at the beginning or end of the accounting period* al principio o final del periodo contable ▲ *at the end of the period* al final del periodo ▲ *at the end of the previous reporting period* al final del periodo de información anterior ▲ *disposal of plant and equipment at the end of the contract* eliminación de instalaciones y equipos al final del contrato ▲ *dispose of an asset at the end of its useful life* eliminación de un activo al final de su vida útil ▲ *financial year end* final del ejercicio ▲ *the end of a specified notice period* el final del periodo de notificación especificado ▲ *the end of the comparable interim period* el final del periodo intermedio comparable ▲ *the number of employees at the end of the period* el número de empleados al final del periodo

end[2] *verb*

When something is ended, it is finished or terminated.

finalizar

▲ *end the financial year on specific days of the week* finalizar el ejercicio en días específicos de la semana

end-of-life salvage value

→ salvage value

end-of-period entry

End-of-period entries are entries recorded in financial records and statements at the end of an accounting period to close the accounts and transfer balances to e.g. the profit and loss account.

entrada al final del ejercicio

end-of-year inventory

→ closing inventory

endeavour

To endeavour to do something means to try very hard to do it or avoid doing it.

esforzarse

▲ *endeavour to avoid conflicts of interest* esforzarse por evitar conflictos de intereses ▲ *endeavour to perform as budgeted for this year* esforzarse por obtener los beneficios presupuestados para este ejercicio

ending balance US

→ closing balance

ending inventory

→ closing inventory

endorse

To endorse means to add a signature often together with a statement to a document to verify the validity or fair presentation of the document. As an example, annual reports must be endorsed by a management statement and an audit report to verify that the annual report gives a true and fair view of the assets, liabilities and financial position as well as the operations and cash flow of a specific enterprise.

ratificar

▲ *endorse the financial statements* ratificar los estados financieros

endorsement

= endorsement of approval

In the context of financial reporting, an endorsement is a written statement from the auditor declaring that the auditing is completed. The endorsement also states whether the accounts, according to the assessment of the auditor, give a true and fair view of the company's performance and financial position.

opinión del auditor

▲ *a separate endorsement* una opinión del auditor separada

endorsement of approval

→ endorsement

engage

To engage means to hire a person or enterprise to do work or provide services against payment.

contratar

▲ *engage new employees* contratar nuevos empleados

engage in

To be engaged in something means to do a particular job or

to be actively interested in soemthing.

implicarse en

= participar en

▲ *engage in certain activities* implicarse en ciertas actividades ▲ *engage in financial consultancy* implicarse en asesoría financiera ▲ *engage in research and development* participar en investigación y desarrollo

engagement

Engagement means the act of employing personnel.

contratación

▲ *the engagement of an auditor* la contratación de un auditor ▲ *the engagement of new staff* la contratación de nuevo personal

engineered cost

Engineered costs are costs with a direct connection to the output of an enterprise, such as e.g. direct materials costs.

coste diseñado

▲ *engineered costs per unit of measure* costes diseñados por unidad de medida ▲ *generate engineered costs* generar costes diseñados ▲ *use engineered costs data* utilizar datos de costes diseñados

⇛ discretionary cost

engineering analysis US

The engineering analysis measures the cost behaviour ex ante, i.e. beforehand, based on a systematic review of what the costs should be, not by what the costs have been. The costs reviewed are typically cost of materials, supplies, labour, support services and facilities needed for services and products. Based on actual experience and experiments, cost analysts gain information to determine what future costs should be.

analisis de desviación de costes

= análisis de la desviación de costes

▲ *detailed engineering analysis* análisis detallado de desviación de costes ▲ *in-depth engineering analysis* análisis de desviación de costes en profundidad

⇛ account analysis

engineering approach

The engineering approach measures the cost behaviour ex ante, i.e. beforehand, based on a systematic review of what the costs should be, not by what the costs have been. The costs reviewed are typically cost of materials, supplies, labour, support services and facilities needed for services and products. Based on actual experience and experiments, cost analysts gain information to determine what future costs should be.

análisis de desviación de costes

= análisis de la desviación de costes

▲ *the traditional engineering approach* el análisis de desviación de costes tradicional ▲ *use the engineering approach* utilizar el análisis de desviación de costes

enter

= post US, recognise UK, IAS/IFRS, recognize US, state

To enter an item in the balance sheet or the income statement means to show it separately.

anotar

= entrar, reconocer, registrar

▲ *enter an item in the balance sheet* anotar una partida en el balance de situación ▲ *enter an item in the income statement* anotar una partida en la cuenta de resultados

enter into

To enter into an agreement or contract means to make a binding arrangement.

suscribir

▲ *enter into a separate agreement to repurchase the goods* suscribir un acuerdo independiente para recomprar los bienes ▲ *enter into contracts to sell biological assets at a future date* suscribir contratos para vender activos biológicos a una fecha futura ▲ *enter into transactions in foreign currencies* suscribir transacciones en divisas ▲ *enter into transactions that are presently not recognised in the balance sheet* suscribir transacciones que no están actualmente reconocidas en el balance de situación

enter into service

When an enterprise begins to use an asset in its course of business, the asset enters into service.

entrar en servicio

▲ *enter into service early in May 2005* entrar en servicio a principios de mayo de 2005

enterprise
= undertaking UK
An enterprise is a business organisation, whether set up as a body corporate, partnership or unincorporated association, defined as a separate legal entity that carries on business, with or without a view to profit.
empresa
▲ *a consolidated enterprise* una empresa consolidada ▲ *acquire or redeem the enterprise's shares* adquirir o rescatar las acciones de la empresa ▲ *cash receipts and cash payments of an insurance enterprise* recibos en efectivo y pagos en efectivos de una empresa de seguros ▲ *determine the ability of an enterprise to pay dividends out of operating cash flows* determinar la capacidad de una empresa para pagar dividendos aparte de los flujos de efectivo de explotación ▲ *enterprise committee* comité de empresa ▲ *enterprise culture* cultura empresarial ▲ *enterprise visit* visita empresarial ▲ *equity financial instruments issued by the enterprise* instrumentos financieros de patrimonio emitidos por la empresa ▲ *funds held for customers by an investment enterprise* fondos que los clientes tienen en una empresa de inversión ▲ *revenue arising from the use by others of enterprise assets yielding interest, royalties and dividends* ingresos resultantes del uso por terceros de los activos de la empresa que generan interés, royalties y dividendos

enterprise resource planning UK, US
= ERP US, UK
Enterprise resource planning is an integrated information software system that is designed to support and automate the functional areas of an enterprise.
planificación de los recursos de una empresa
▲ *an effective system for enterprise resource planning* un sistema efectivo de planificación de los recursos de una empresa
⇛ enterprise resource planning system

enterprise resource planning system UK, US
= ERP system UK, US
An enterprise resource planning system is an accounting oriented information software system designed to support and automate the business processes and all functional areas of an enterprise such as the managing of finance, inventories, customer orders, fixed assets and real estate.
sistema de planificación de los recursos de una empresa
▲ *an effective enterprise resource planning system* un sistema efectivo de planificación de los recursos de una empresa
⇛ enterprise resource planning

enterprise value
= EV, firm value
Enterprise value is an investment ratio defined as an enterprise's market capitalisation plus its net interest-bearing debt. The definition also includes the value of minority interests minus the value of the share of any associates minus the value of other non-operating assets. This key figure shows the market value of the underlying invested capital and illustrates how the enterprise's operations are valued on the stock market irrespective of capital structure.
valor de la empresa en el mercado
▲ *an enterprise value over $14 billion* un valor de la empresa en el mercado superior a 14 millardos de dólares ▲ *an increase in enterprise value* un aumento en el valor de la empresa en el mercado ▲ *calculate the enterprise value* calcular el valor de la empresa en el mercado ▲ *debt to enterprise value* deuda a valor de la empresa en el mercado

enterprise with limited liability
An enterprise with limited liability is an enterprise in which none of the participants is liable personally or severally, or has unlimited liability. Therefore, satisfaction or payment in full can only be claimed in the contributed capital.
empresa con responsabilidad limitada
liability constituir una empresa con responsabilidad limitada

entertainment expense
Entertainment expenses are expenses incurred in connection with meals, hotel ac-

commodation and other hospitality provided in connection with trade and business activities. A percentage tax deduction is allowed subject to documentation requirements and approval by the tax authorities.

gastos de representación

NOTE Always plural in Spanish accounting texts.

▲ *deductible entertainment expenses* gastos de representación deducibles ▲ *deductible part of the entertainment expenses* parte deducible de los gastos de representación ▲ *incur entertainment expenses* incurrir en gastos de representación ▲ *non-deductible part of the entertainment expenses* parte no deducible de los gastos de representación

entity

= concern

An entity is a separate, independent, economic unit such as an enterprise involved in carrying on business on its own with or without profit-making as an objective.

entidad

▲ *a component of an entity* una sección de una entidad ▲ *a jointly controlled entity* una entidad controlada conjuntamente ▲ *a listed entity* una entidad cotizada ▲ *a mutual cooperative entity* una entidad cooperativa mutual ▲ *a mutual entity* una entidad mutual ▲ *an entity's first IFRS financial statements* los primeros estados financieros NIIF de una entidad ▲ *an investor-owned entity* una entidad propiedad del inversor ▲ *an unincorporated entity* una entidad no inscrita en el registro oficial ▲ *assets used for general entity or head office purposes* activos usados para llevar a cabo propósitos de la entidad general o de la oficina central ▲ *circumstances beyond the entity's control* circunstancias que escapan al control de la entidad ▲ *owner-managed entities* entidades gestionadas por el propietario ▲ *private entity* entidad privada ▲ *public entity* entidad pública ▲ *reconcile segment revenue to entity revenue from external customers* reconciliar ingresos del segmento con ingresos de la entidad debidos a clientes externos ▲ *the audited entity* la entidad auditada ▲ *the combined entity* la entidad combinada ▲ *the combining entity* la entidad dirigente ▲ *the entity giving up cash* la entidad que presta efectivo en nombre de otra ▲ *the entity's reported financial position, financial performance and cash flows* la posición financiera de la que informa la empresa, los resultados financieros y los flujos de efectivo ▲ *the issuing entity* la entidad emisora ▲ *the issuing public entity* la entidad pública emisora

⇛ accounting entity, reporting entity

entity concept

= entity theory

≠ proprietary view

The entity concept is a view which focuses on the entity as an enterprise existing as a legal entity separate from its owners. This concept is a fundamental accounting concept, as it views the enterprise's financial statements as separate from its owners. The focus is on assets as the basis for carrying out operating activities rather than as an investment made by owners.

concepto de entidad

= teoría de la entidad

▲ *a violation of the entity concept* una violación de la teoría de la entidad ▲ *use the entity concept* usar el concepto de entidad

⇛ entity

entity theory US

= entity concept

≠ proprietary view

The entity theory is a concept or view which focuses on the entity as an enterprise existing as a legal entity separate from its owners. The theory is a fundamental accounting concept, as it views the enterprise's financial statements as separate from its owners. The focus is on assets as the basis for carrying out operating activities rather than as an investment made by owners.

teoría de la entidad

= concepto de entidad

▲ *a violation of the entity theory* una violación de la teoría de la entidad

⇛ entity, entity concept

entity-specific cash flow

Entity-specific cash flows are cash flows that are specific to a particular insurer and which do not arise for other market participants even though they have identical obligations.

flujo de efectivo específico de la entidad

= flujo de caja específico de la entidad

entity-specific value

→ value in use

entrepreneur

An entrepreneur is an innovative person who develops profit-making ideas or projects or who sets up an enterprise and assumes the financial risk, typically for the purpose of selling new products or providing new services.

emprendedor

▲ *encourage potential entrepreneurs* estimular a los posibles emprendedores ▲ *establish a network for entrepreneurs* establecer una red de emprendedores ▲ *the visions and commitment of the entrepreneurs* las posturas y compromisos de los emprendedores

entrepreneurial business

An entrepreneurial business is a business or enterprise set up by an entrepreneur or business innovator.

empresa emprendedora

▲ *form an entrepreneurial business* constituir una empresa emprendedora

entry

= posting US

An entry is the recognition of income or expense in the financial statements or bookkeeping records of an enterprise.

entrada

= anotación, apunte

▲ *a setoff to an entry* una compensación a una entrada ▲ *accounting entries* entradas contables ▲ *correct an entry* corregir una entrada ▲ *duplicated entry* entrada duplicada ▲ *make an entry* hacer una entrada

entry into service

When an enterprise begins to use an asset in its course of business, this is the asset's entry into service.

entrada en servicio

▲ *ready for entry into service* listo para la entrada en servicio ▲ *the date of the asset's entry into service* la fecha de entrada en servicio del activo

entry on shareholders' equity UK

An entry on shareholders' equity is an amount recognised in, and changing the balance of, an item under shareholders' equity. Entries include amounts recognised that concern asset revaluation, capital increases, retained earnings etc.

anotación en recursos propios

= entrada en recursos propios

▲ *tax on entries on shareholders' equity for the period* impuesto en las anotaciones en recursos propios del periodo

entry on shareowners' equity US

An entry on shareowners' equity is an amount recognised in, and changing the balance of, an item under shareowners' equity. Entries include amounts recognised concerning asset revaluation, capital increases, retained earnings etc.

anotación en recursos propios

= entrada en recursos propios

▲ *income tax on entries on shareowners' equity for the period* ingreso fiscal en las anotaciones en recursos propios del periodo

environment

The environment is all the circumstances, events, people, nature etc. that are found around the enterprise and which influence and are influenced by its activities and decisions.

entorno

▲ *a healthy environment* un entorno saludable ▲ *changes in the environment in which the enterprise operates* cambios en el entorno en el que opera la empresa ▲ *expenditure on the environment* gastos en el entorno ▲ *harmful to the environment* perjudicial para el entorno ▲ *measures to prevent damage to the environment* medidas para prevenir daños en el entorno ▲ *remedying damage to the environment* reparando los daños ocasionados al entorno ▲ *restoration of the environment* restauración del entorno ▲ *the economic environment in which the transaction takes place* el entorno económico en el que la transacción tiene lugar ▲ *the enterprise's impact on the external environment* el impacto de la empresa sobre el entorno externo ▲ *the state of the environment* el estado del entorno

environmental accounting policy

Environmental accounting policy is the practice developed and characterised as generally accepted accounting practice for the preparation of environmental reports. This practice is being continuously developed in step with the widening scope of the reporting on environmental issues by business enterprises.

sistema de contabilidad medioambiental

▲ *applied environmental accounting policies* sistemas aplicados de contabilidad medioambiental

environmental accounts

= environmental report

Environmental accounts are an enterprise's accounts on environmental issues such as the consumption of energy, water and raw materials, contaminants used in production and subsequently emitted, as well as the treatment of waste.

cuentas medioambientales

▲ *prepare environmental accounts* preparar las cuentas medioambientales ▲ *publish social and environmental accounts* publicar las cuentas medioambientales y sociales ▲ *standalone environmental accounts* individualizar las cuentas medioambientales

environmental approval

An environmental approval is an approval obtained by an enterprise from the regulatory authorities following an assessment of whether the enterprise's products, waste, emissions, noise, odour etc. comply with environmental regulations.

certificación medioambiental

= aprobación medioambiental

▲ *apply for the renewal of one's environmental approval* solicitar la renovación de su certificación medioambiental ▲ *comply with an environmental approval* ajustarse a una certificación medioambiental ▲ *obtain a new environmental approval* obtener una nueva certificación medioambiental

environmental audit

= environmental auditing, green audit

An environmental audit is an internal audit examining the environmental report with the objective of confirming that the environmental issues referred to in the report have been properly dealt with and comply with the environmental policies of the enterprise.

auditoría medioambiental

▲ *carry out an environmental audit* llevar a cabo una auditoría medioambiental

⇛ environmental report, green accounts

environmental audit scheme

An environmental audit scheme is part of the Eco-Management and Audit Scheme (EMAS), a voluntary management tool offered by the EU to public and private enterprises in the EU and the European Economic Area for the evaluation, reporting and improvement of their environmental performance. The objective of the audit is to consider the relevance and adequacy of the environmental policy pursued by the EMAS-registered enterprise as well as its compliance with the requirements of the EMAS Regulation for environmental performance.

programa de auditoría medioambiental

▲ *a comprehensive environmental audit scheme* un programa completo de auditoría medioambiental

⇛ environmental management scheme

environmental auditing scheme

→ environmental audit scheme

environmental bottom line

The environmental bottom line contains information about the enterprise's impact on the environment through its decisions and activities.

última línea de la cuenta de resultados dedicada al medio ambiente

▲ *improve the environmental bottom line* mejorar la última línea de la cuenta de resultados dedicada al medio ambiente

⇛ financial bottom line, social bottom line

environmental cost

Environmental costs are costs incurred by an enterprise in relation to actions or efforts to protect the environment or to deal with existing environmental damage caused by the enterprise when carrying out its activities.

coste medioambiental

▲ *less than half the external environmental costs* menos de la mitad de los costes medioambientales extrernos ▲ *provisions for environmental costs* provisiones por costes medioambientales ▲ *reduce environmental costs* reducir los costes medioambientales ▲ *significant environmental costs* costes medioambientales significativos ▲ *the requirement of notes on significant environmental costs* el requerimiento de notas en los costes medioambientales significativos ▲ *total environmental costs* total costes medioambientales

environmental data

Environmental data are data about the environment and the enterprise's impact on the environment through its decisions and activities.

información medioambiental

▲ *supplementary environmental data* información medioambiental complementaria

environmental expenditure

= environmental expense

Environmental expenditure refers to the costs of an enterprise, which are related to its activities and measures taken in order to prevent environmental harm and pollution.

gasto medioambiental

▲ *capitalisation of environmental expenditure* capitalización del gasto medioambiental ▲ *incur environmental expenditure* incurrir en gasto medioambiental

environmental issues

Environmental issues refer to matters, especially damage, relating to the environment such as a particular enterprise's consumption of energy, water and raw materials or contaminants used in production and subsequently emitted, as well as recycling and the treatment of waste.

aspectos medioambientales

▲ *description of environmental issues* descripción de los aspectos medioambientales ▲ *increased publicity concerning environmental issues* mayor divulgación de los aspectos medioambientales ▲ *reference to environmental issues* referencia a los aspectos medioambientales

environmental management

Environmental management refers to an enterprise's planning and implementation of activities, measures and standards to protect the environment or to reduce the environmental impacts of its operations. Environmental management is a continuing process implying e.g. the formulation and assessment of environmental policies and objectives as well as the preparation and performance of action plans in order to meet the objectives.

gestión medioambiental

▲ *implementation of environmental management* implementación de la gestión medioambiental ▲ *improved environmental management* gestión medioambiental mejorada

environmental management scheme

An environmental management scheme is part of the Eco-Management and Audit Scheme (EMAS), a voluntary management tool offered by the EU to public and private enterprises in the EU and the European Economic Area for the evaluation, reporting and improvement of their environmental performance. The scheme requires the implementation of an environmental management system (EMS), which is a system for managing, identifying and evaluating the environmental data of the EMAS-registered enterprise.

programa de gestión medioambiental

= gestión medioambiental

▲ *conform in all respects to an environmental management scheme suitable for the progressive reduction of the environmental impact of the activities* conforme con todos los aspectos de una gestión medioambiental adecuada para la reducción progresiva del impacto medioambiental de las actividades ▲ *voluntary participation in an environmental management scheme* participación voluntaria en un programa de gestión medioambiental

⇛ environmental audit scheme, environmental management

environmental policy

Environmental policy refers to an enterprise's formulated statement of its intentions and principles in relation to protection of the environment or to reducing environmental impacts. The environmental policy forms part of the enterprise's environmental management and provides the framework for action plans and formulation of actual objectives.

política medioambiental

▲ *the group's environmental policy* la política medioambiental del grupo

environmental report

= environmental accounts, environmental statement, green accounts

An environmental report is an enterprise's report on environmental issues such as the consumption of energy, water and raw materials, contaminants used in production and subsequently emitted, as well as the treatment of waste.

informe medioambiental

▲ *prepare an environmental report* preparar un informe medioambiental ▲ *publish a social and environmental report* publicar un informe medioambiental y social ▲ *stand-alone environmental report* informe medioambiental independiente

environmental risk

An enterprise's environmental risk is the probability of unforseen environmental damage and its consequences.

riesgo medioambiental

▲ *economic impact of environmental risks* impacto económico de los riesgos medioambientales ▲ *significant possible environmental risks* posibles riesgos medioambientales significativos

environmental statement

= environmental report, green accounts

An environmental statement is an enterprise's report on environmental issues such as the consumption of energy, water and raw materials, contaminants used in production and subsequently emitted, as well as the treatment of waste.

informe medioambiental

▲ *a voluntary environmental statement* un informe medioambiental voluntario ▲ *reliable information in the environmental statement* información fiable en el informe medioambiental ▲ *the annual environmental statement* el informe medioambiental anual

EP

= economic profit, economic value added, EVA

EP is the abbreviation for economic profit, a performance measure defined as the difference between operating profit after tax and a cost of capital charge on invested capital. EP measures the economic profit, i.e. the real profit rather than the accounting profit, and shows the value added to an enterprise by its operations in a given period.

beneficio económico

= valor económico agregado, valor económico añadido, EVA

▲ *base control on EP* basar el control en el beneficio económico ▲ *EP-based compensation* compensación basada en el beneficio económico ▲ *future expectations to EP* previsiones futuras a beneficio económico ▲ *measurement of EP* medición del beneficio económico ▲ *pay compensation on the basis of EP* pagar compensación en base al beneficio económico

EPS

EPS is the abbreviation for earnings per share, a financial ratio stating the amount of net profit for the period that is attributable to ordinary shareholders divided by the weighted average number of ordinary shares outstanding during the period. This ratio is applied for valuation of the share and the enterprise's ability to generate profit to the owners.

beneficios por acción

= ganancias por acción

NOTE Spanish accountants prefer 'beneficios por acción' to the IAS/IFRS term 'ganancias por acción'.

▲ *basic EPS* beneficios por acción básicos ▲ *computation of EPS* cómputo de beneficios por acción ▲ *diluted EPS* beneficios por acción diluidos

▲ *EPS as originally reported* beneficios por acción tal y como se informó originalmente ▲ *EPS including effects of rights issue* beneficios por acción incluyendo los efectos de los derechos preferentes de suscripción ▲ *EPS restated for rights issue* beneficios por acción actualizados por derechos preferentes de suscripción ▲ *profit from operating activities and EPS* beneficio de actividades de explotación y beneficios por acción

EPS basic

= basic earnings per share, basic EPS

EPS basic is the abbreviation for earnings per share basic, which is a financial ratio defined as the profit for the accounting period attributable to ordinary shareholders divided by the average number of ordinary shares outstanding for the same period. This ratio is applied for valuation of the share and the enterprise's ability to generate profit to the owners and is calculated on a non-diluted basis as it disregards any dilutive convertible bonds or share options.

beneficio por acción básico

= ganancia por acción básica

NOTE Spanish accountants prefer 'beneficio por acción básico' to the IAS/IFRS term 'ganancia por acción básica'.

▲ *calculate EPS basic* calcular el beneficio por acción básico ▲ *EPS basic calculations* cálculos del beneficio por acción básico ▲ *restatement of previous years' EPS basic* actualización del beneficio por acción básico de los ejercicios anteriores

EPS diluted

= diluted earnings per share

EPS diluted is an abbreviation for diluted earnings per share, i.e. an investment ratio defined as profit for the accounting period attributable to shareholders divided by the average number of shares diluted, i.e. adjusted for dilutive effects from any options, convertible bonds etc.

beneficio por acción diluido

= ganancia por acción diluida

NOTE Spanish accountants prefer 'beneficio por acción diluido' to the IAS/IFRS term 'ganancia por acción diluida'. The Spanish term can be accompanied by a singular or plural verb form.

▲ *calculation of EPS diluted* cálculo del beneficio por acción diluido ▲ *restate EPS diluted* actualizar el beneficio por acción diluido ▲ *the amounts used as the numerators in calculating EPS diluted* las cantidades empleadas como numeradores en el cálculo del beneficio por acción diluido ▲ *the number of ordinary shares used to compute EPS diluted* el número de acciones ordinarias empleadas para computar el beneficio por acción diluido

equal[1] *verb*

In US English, it is also correct not to double the final consonant in "equal" when the past-tense, past- and present-participle endings are added. To equal something means that it is the same, e.g. two sums that are identical in value.

ser igual a

= equivaler

▲ *equal 4%* ser igual al 4%

equal[2] *adjective*

Equal means to be identical to in terms of measure, quantity or value.

equivalente

= igual

▲ *an amount equal to the asset's carrying amount* una cantidad equivalente al valor contable del activo ▲ *at an amount equal to the net investment in the lease* a una cantidad equivalente a la inversión neta en el arrendamiento ▲ *be equal to a value of EUR 1 million* ser equivalente a un millón de euros ▲ *equal to the carrying amount of the asset disposed of* equivalente al valor contable del activo eliminado de

equalisation UK

= equalization US

Equalisation means adjustment or offsetting to make equal in size, rank, amount or value.

nivelación

▲ *an equalisation of differences* una nivelación de las diferencias

equalization US

= equalisation UK

Equalization means adjustment or offsetting to make equal in size, rank, amount or value.

nivelación

▲ *an equalization of differences* una nivelación de las diferencias

equate with

= align with, compare with

To equate one thing with another means to give the two things the same status.

igualar con

▲ *equate non-residents with residents* igualar los no residentes con los residentes

equipment

Equipment consists of machinery, furniture, vehicles, and tools used in the operation of a business.

equipos

= equipo

NOTE Spanish accountants prefer the plural 'equipos' to the IAS/IRFS singular 'equipo'.

▲ *a damaged item of equipment* una partida de equipos defectuosa ▲ *administrative equipment* equipos administrativos ▲ *delivery of equipment* envío de equipos ▲ *disposal of equipment* eliminación de equipos ▲ *maintenance of equipment* mantenimiento de equipos ▲ *production of equipment* fabricación de equipos ▲ *provide for advance depreciation of equipment* prever la amortización anticipada de equipos ▲ *servicing equipment* poner a punto los equipos ▲ *stand-by equipment* equipos de reserva ▲ *the written-down tax value of the equipment* el valor impositivo devaluado de los equipos ▲ *write-off an item of equipment* devaluar una partida de equipos

⇛ property, plant and equipment

equities

= ordinary shares

Equities refer to the ordinary shares issued to the owners of an enterprise. Equities carry voting and dividend rights, but rank subordinately to preferred shareholders and creditors for payment in the event of bankruptcy of the enterprise.

acciones ordinarias

▲ *available-for-sale equities in a foreign currency* acciones ordinarias disponibles para la venta en una moneda extranjera ▲ *equities portfolio* cartera de acciones ordinarias ▲ *investments in equities and bonds* inversiones en acciones ordinarias y bonos

⇛ equity, equity market

equity

1 Equity is defined as total assets less total liabilities. Equity consists of the capital contributed by owners (e.g. the share capital in a company) plus retained earnings (reserves). In a group, equity is distributed on equity attributable to equity holders in the parent company and equity attributable to minority interests.

patrimonio neto

▲ *a change in equity* una modificación en patrimonio neto ▲ *a net increase in equity* un aumento neto en patrimonio neto ▲ *a net reduction in equity* una reducción neta en patrimonio neto ▲ *a statement of changes in equity* un estado de cambios en patrimonio neto ▲ *accumulated equity capital* patrimonio neto acumulado ▲ *adjust against equity* ajustar contra patrimonio neto ▲ *adjusted equity at 1 January 2005* patrimonio neto ajustado a 1 de enero de 2005 ▲ *changes in equity* modificaciones en patrimonio neto ▲ *changes in group equity* modificaciones en el patrimonio neto del grupo ▲ *classify as equity* clasificar como patrimonio neto ▲ *equity at the beginning of the financial year* patrimonio neto al inicio del ejercicio ▲ *equity per share* patrimonio neto por acción ▲ *fully diluted equity* patrimonio neto completamente diluido ▲ *interest on equity contributions* interés en las contribuciones de patrimonio neto ▲ *negative equity capital* patrimonio neto negativo ▲ *paid-up equity capital* patrimonio neto desembolsado ▲ *recognise directly in equity* reconocer directamente en patrimonio neto ▲ *show as part of equity* mostrar como parte del patrimonio neto ▲ *the aggregate amount of equity* la cantidad agregada de patrimonio neto ▲ *the consolidated equity* patrimonio neto consolidado

SOURCE IFRS Framework, F 49(c)

2 Equity is the residual value of a property that an owner has after and above all loans, liens and outstanding mortgages in that property.
valor neto
▲ *borrow from the equity in the house* pedir prestado sobre el valor neto del inmueble ▲ *equity release* redención del valor neto ▲ *homeowner's equity* el valor neto del propietario del inmueble

equity accounting
= one-line consolidation
Equity accounting is the accounting for investments in subsidiaries and associates using the equity method of accounting (equity method).
método de puesta en equivalencia
= método de la participación, método de participación
NOTE Spanish accountants prefer 'método de puesta en equivalencia' to the IAS/IFRS terms 'método de la participación', and 'método de participación'.
▲ *equity accounting method* método de puesta en equivalencia ▲ *use the equity accounting method* utilizar el método de puesta en equivalencia

equity and liabilities IAS/IFRS
= liabilities and equity US, liabilities and stockholders' equity US, shareholders' equity and liabilities UK
Equity and liabilities constitute the balance sheet total in the credit side of the balance sheet when presented in the horizontal format and represent the sources of funds for the assets presented in the debit side.
patrimonio neto y pasivo
= patrimonio neto y pasivos
NOTE Spanish accountant prefer 'patrimonio neto y pasivo' to the IAS 'patrimonio neto y pasivos'.
▲ *significant changes in equity and liabilities* cambios importantes en patrimonio neto y pasivo ▲ *total equity and liabilities* total patrimonio neto y pasivo
⇛ equity, liability

equity and liabilities side
The equity and liabilities side constitutes one half of the balance sheet as presented in the horizontal format, and states how the enterprise has been financed.
columna de patrimonio neto y pasivo

▲ *record an amount on the equity and liabilities side* apuntar una cantidad en la columna del patrimonio neto y pasivo ▲ *record an item on the equity and liabilities side* apuntar una partida en la columna del patrimonio neto y pasivo

equity at the beginning of the year
Equity at the beginning of the year is the opening equity balance, i.e. the amount of equity recognised in the financial statements of an enterprise at the start of the financial year.
patrimonio neto al inicio del año
= patrimonio neto al inicio del ejercicio
▲ *recognise directly to equity at the beginning of the year* reconocer directamente en patrimonio neto al inicio del año ▲ *translation of the equity at the beginning of the year at the closing rate* conversión del patrimonio neto al inicio del año al tipo de cierre

equity attributable to equity holders of the parent IAS/IFRS
Equity attributable to equity holders of the parent is the amount of capital and reserves held in subsidiaries that are not wholly owned, excluding the amount held by minority interests. Under IFRS, the amounts must be presented separately in the consolidated balance sheet and the statement of changes in equity.
patrimonio neto atribuible a los tenedores de instrumentos de patrimonio neto de la dominante
▲ *total equity attributable to equity holders of the parent* total patrimonio neto atribuible a los tenedores de instrumentos de patrimonio neto de la dominante
SOURCE IAS 1, paragraphs 68 and 96
⇛ minority interest

equity capital
1 = contributed equity IAS/IFRS, equity share capital UK

Equity capital refers to the total amount of capital invested in an enterprise by its shareholders in exchange for ordinary shares (equities) issued.

capital social

▲ *disaggregate equity capital and reserves into various classes* desagregar capital social y reservas en varias clases

2 = equity

Equity capital is defined as total assets less total liabilities. Equity capital consists of the capital contributed by owners (the common stock in a corporation) plus retained earnings (reserves).

patrimonio neto

▲ *an entity that has no equity capital* una entidad que no tiene patrimonio neto ▲ *disaggregate equity capital and reserves into various classes* desagregar patrimonio neto en varias clases ▲ *equity capital and reserves* patrimonio y reservas

equity compensation benefit IAS/IFRS

Equity compensation benefits constitute employee benefits of two types: employee benefits in the form of equity financial instruments issued by the enterprise or, if in a group, the parent of an enterprise, and employee benefits where the amount of the benefit obligation to the employee is subject to the future price of equity financial instruments issued by the enterprise or its parent.

prestación basada en instrumentos de patrimonio

▲ *assess the effect of equity compensation benefits on an enterprise's financial position, performance and cash flows* valorar el efecto de las prestaciones basadas en instrumentos de patrimonio sobre la posición financiera de una empresa, sus resultados y sus flujos de efectivo ▲ *provide equity compensation benefits for one or more employees* conceder prestaciones basadas en instrumentos de patrimonio a uno o más empleados ▲ *provide equity compensation benefits in the form of instruments issued by the enterprise's parent* conceder prestaciones basadas en instrumentos de patrimonio en forma de instrumentos emitidos por la matriz de una empresa ▲ *provide equity compensation benefits to key management personnel* conceder prestaciones basadas en instrumentos de patrimonio al personal de alta dirección ▲ *recognition and measurement requirements for equity compensation benefits* reconocimiento y valoración de los requisitos para acceder a prestaciones basadas en instrumentos de patrimonio

equity compensation plan

Equity compensation plans are schemes arranged formally or informally by an enterprise for its employees with a view to providing equity compensation benefits to them.

plan de prestaciones basado en instrumentos de patrimonio

▲ *enter into related party transactions with equity compensation plans* llevar a cabo transacciones entre las partes implicadas en los planes de prestaciones basados en instrumentos de patrimonio ▲ *expenses incidental to equity compensation plans* gastos puntuales relativos a planes de prestaciones basados en instrumentos de patrimonio ▲ *introduction of equity compensation plans* introducción de los planes de prestaciones basados en instrumentos de patrimonio ▲ *recognition and measurement requirements for equity compensation plans* requisitos de reconocimiento y valoración para los planes de prestaciones basados en instrumentos de patrimonio ▲ *the accounting policy for equity compensation plans* la política contable para los planes de prestaciones basados en instrumentos de patrimonio ▲ *the amounts recognised in the financial statements for equity compensation plans* las cantidades reconocidas en los estados financieros en concepto de planes de prestaciones basados en instrumentos de patrimonio ▲ *the enterprise's own equity financial instruments which are held by equity compensation plans* los propios instrumentos financieros de patrimonio de la empresa que mantienen los planes de prestaciones basados

en instrumentos de patrimonio ▲ *the nature and terms of equity compensation plans* la naturaleza y los términos de los planes de prestaciones basados en instrumentos de patrimonio
SOURCE IAS 19, paragraph 7 (1993)

equity component IAS/IFRS
≠ liability component
A compound financial instrument is a security which is split into two elements or components: an equity component and a liability component. The liability component consists of the amount the issuer is obliged to repay to the holder (i.e. the principal), whereas the equity component represents the residual that results after deduction of the fair value of the liability component from the value of the compound instrument at the issue date. In the financial statements the components are recognised separately in the balance sheet: the liability component as a financial liability and the equity component as an equity instrument under equity. Examples of compound financial instruments are convertible bonds and warrants.
componente de patrimonio
= componente de pasivo
▲ *an equity component previously recognised* un componente de patrimonio previamente reconocido ▲ *an instrument that contains both a liability and an equity component* un instrumento que incluye tanto un componente de patrimonio como un componente de pasivo ▲ *measure the equity component of a compound financial instrument* medir el componente de patrimonio de un instrumento financiero compuesto ▲ *on initial recognition of the equity component* al reconocer inicialmente el componente de patrimonio ▲ *the carrying amount of the equity component* el valor contable del componente de patrimonio ▲ *the fair value of the equity component* el valor razonable del componente de patrimonio ▲ *the original equity component* el componente de patrimonio original
⇛ compound financial instrument

equity financial statements
Equity financial statements are financial statements of the parent company in a group, where entries are adjusted to the equity method.
estados financieros consolidados según el método de participación
▲ *analysis of the equity financial statements* análisis de los estados financieros consolidados según el método de participación ▲ *prepare equity financial statements* preparar los estados financieros consolidados según el método de participación ▲ *publish equity financial statements* publicar los estados financieros consolidados según el método de participación ▲ *the equity financial statements of the parent* los estados financieros consolidados según el método de participación de la matriz

equity financing
= equity funding
≠ debt financing
Equity financing is the part of the total financing or funding of an enterprise that is provided by the owners contrary to debt financing. In the public limited company, equity financing is provided via the sale of shares.
financiación propia
= financiación con fondos propios, financiación por fondos propios
≠ financiación ajena
▲ *raise capital through debt and equity financing* recaudar capital por medio de emisión de deuda y financiación propia ▲ *the actual costs of equity financing* los costes reales de la financiación propia

equity holder IAS/IFRS
An equity holder is an individual or an enterprise holding equity interests or shares in another enterprise that represent title of ownership and the legal right to participate in the enterprise's profit as well as any other rights attached to the equity interests or shares such as voting rights.
socio
▲ *equity attributable to equity holders of the parent* patrimonio neto atribuible a los socios de

la matriz ▲ *profit for the period attributable to equity holders of the parent* beneficio para el periodo atribuible a los socios de la matriz

equity holding

An equity holding is the holding by an individual or an enterprise of equity interests or shares in another enterprise, representing title of ownership and the legal right to participate in the enterprise's profit as well as any other rights attached to the equity interests or shares such as voting rights.

participación en patrimonio
= participación en el patrimonio, participación en patrimonio neto

▲ *secure a 90% equity holding in another enterprise* asegurar un 90% de participación en el patrimonio de otra empresa

equity income

Equity income is the share of earnings in a subsidiary or associate that a parent company is entitled to receive in proportion to the ownership share in that subsidiary or associate.

dividendo de la filial

▲ *determination of equity income* determinación del dividendo de la filial ▲ *equity income from investments* dividendo de la filial procedente de inversiones

equity instrument

An equity instrument is a contract that provides evidence of a residual ownership interest in the assets of an enterprise after deduction of all its liabilities. Equity instruments are shares or other evidence of ownership interest.

instrumento de patrimonio

▲ *acquisition of equity instruments* adquisición de instrumentos de patrimonio ▲ *an equity instrument of another enterprise* un instrumento de patrimonio de otra empresa ▲ *an exchange of voting ordinary equity instruments for cash* un cambio de instrumentos de patrimonio ordinarios por efectivo ▲ *attribute a value to the equity instruments* atribuir un valor a los instrumentos de patrimonio ▲ *cancel own equity instruments* cancelar instrumentos de patrimonio propios ▲ *cash proceeds from issuing equity instruments* el efectivo procede de la emisión de instrumentos de patrimonio ▲ *dividends on an available-for-sale equity instrument* dividendos de un instrumento de patrimonio disponible para la venta ▲ *dividends to holders of equity instruments* dividendos a los propietarios de los instrumentos de patrimonio ▲ *equity instruments that are convertible into ordinary shares* instrumentos de patrimonio convertibles en acciones ordinarias ▲ *host equity instrument* instrumento de patrimonio receptor ▲ *investments in equity instruments that do not have a quoted market price in an active market* inversiones en instrumentos de patrimonio que no tienen precio de mercado cotizado en un mercado activo ▲ *issue of equity instruments* emisión de instrumentos de patrimonio ▲ *participating equity instruments* participando en instrumentos de patrimonio ▲ *pledged equity instruments* instrumentos de patrimonio pignorados ▲ *prices of traded equity instruments* precios de los instrumentos de patrimonio cambiados ▲ *quoted equity instruments* instrumentos de patrimonio cotizados ▲ *reacquire own equity instruments* volver a adquirir instrumentos de patrimonio propios ▲ *the costs of issuing equity instruments* los costes de la emisión de los instrumentos de patrimonio ▲ *the equity instruments of the legal subsidiary* los instrumentos de patrimonio de la filial legal ▲ *the fair value of equity instruments granted* el valor razonable de los instrumentos de patrimonio concedidos ▲ *the number and type of equity instruments issued* el número y tipo de instrumentos de patrimonio emitidos ▲ *the number of equity instruments issued or issuable* el número de instrumentos de patrimonio emitidos o a emitir ▲ *the percentage of voting equity instruments acquired* el porcentaje de instrumentos de patrimonio con derecho a voto adquiridos ▲ *the published price of the equity instruments* el precio publicado de los instrumentos de

patrimonio ▲ *unquoted equity instruments* instrumentos de patrimonio no cotizados
SOURCE IAS 32, paragraph 11, IFRS 2, Appendix A

equity instrument granted
An equity instrument granted is the conditional or unconditional right to such an instrument that has been transferred from an enterprise to another party according to a share-based payment arrangement.
instrumento de patrimonio concedido
▲ *a cancellation of some equity instruments granted* una cancelación de algunos instrumentos de patrimonio concedidos ▲ *estimating the fair value of equity instruments granted* estimando el valor razonable de los instrumentos de patrimonio concedidos ▲ *modify the terms or conditions of the equity instruments granted* modificar los términos o condiciones de los instrumentos de patrimonio concedidos ▲ *the additional equity instruments granted* los instrumentos de patrimonio concedidos adicionales ▲ *the date at which the fair value of the equity instruments granted is measured* la fecha en la que se calcula el valor razonable de los instrumentos de patrimonio concedidos ▲ *the measurement of the amount recognised for services received as consideration for the equity instruments granted* el cálculo de la cantidad reconocida por servicios recibidos como consideración por los instrumentos de patrimonio concedidos
SOURCE IFRS 2, Appendix A

equity interest
An equity interest represents contributed capital to and equity ownership in an enterprise, e.g. represented by a shareholding in that enterprise.
inversión en patrimonio
▲ *a gain or loss attributable to the equity interests of the other venturers* un resultado atribuible a las inversiones en patrimonio de los otros inversores en sociedades de capital riesgo ▲ *a reduction in the equity interest* una reducción de la inversión en patrimonio ▲ *accounted for on the basis of the direct equity interest* contabilizado en base a la inversión en patrimonio directa ▲ *an equity interest of 30%* una inversión en patrimonio del 30% ▲ *an increase in the equity interest* un aumento de la inversión en patrimonio ▲ *the entity that issues the equity interests* la entidad que emite las inversiones en patrimonio

equity investment UK, IAS/IFRS
= investment IAS/IFRS, US, participating interest UK
Equity investments are investments in public limited companies (shares), in private limited companies (shares) and in the equity of other enterprises.
inversión en patrimonio
▲ *a qualified equity investment* una inversión en patrimonio cualificada ▲ *distributions of profits to holders of equity investments in proportion to their holdings of a particular class of capital* distribución de beneficios a los titulares de inversiones en patrimonio en proporción a sus inversiones en un tipo concreto de capital ▲ *increase in equity investments* aumento de inversiones en patrimonio ▲ *private equity investment in a number of diverse portfolio companies* inversión en patrimonio privada en un número variado de sociedades de cartera ▲ *proceeds from equity investments* ingresos procedentes de inversiones en patrimonio

equity issue
= share issue
An equity issue refers either to the authorisation and provision of equity for sale to new or existing shareholders for the purpose of creating share capital or to the distribution of equity to existing shareholders in relation to their shareholdings.
emisión de acciones
= ampliación de capital
▲ *adjust ratios for equity issues* ajustar los ratios para las emisiones de acciones ▲ *carry out an equity issue* llevar a cabo una emisión de acciones ▲ *cross-border equity issues* emisiones de acciones internacionales ▲ *equity issue costs* costes de la emisión de acciones ▲ *new shares via equity issue* nuevas acciones vía ampliación de capital ▲ *proceeds from equity issue* in-

gresos procedentes de de la emisión de acciones

equity item

An equity item is any of the items under equity in the balance sheet, e.g. share capital, share premium account, revaluation reserve, other reserves and retained earnings.

partida de patrimonio neto

▲ *adjust the carrying amount of the equity item in the period of the change* ajustar el valor contable de la partida de patrimonio neto en el periodo del cambio ▲ *equity items, income and expenses, including comparatives* partidas de patrimonio neto, ingresos y gastos, incluyendo comparativos

equity market

= share market UK, stock market US

An equity market is a market place where trading takes place in equities, i.e. shares providing ownership of a company.

mercado de valores

= bolsa

▲ *equity market turbulence* turbulencia en el mercado de valores ▲ *falling equity markets* mercados de valores a la baja ▲ *the Danish equity market* el mercado de valores danés ▲ *the global equity markets* los mercados de valores globales ▲ *the implicit volatility of the equity market* la volatibilidad implícita del mercado de valores ▲ *the international equity markets* los mercados de valores internacionales ▲ *the trends on the equity market* las tendencias en el mercado de valores ▲ *unsettled equity markets* mercados de valores inestables

⇛ equities, stock exchange

equity method

= equity method of accounting

The equity method is a method of accounting whereby equity investments in subsidiaries and associated enterprises are recorded in the financial statements. Under the equity method, the value of the investments are measured by adjusting their value at the proportionate share of net profit in the company in question, dividends and other adjustments, e.g. capital reductions or revaluations.

método de participación

= método de la participación, método de patrimonio, método de patrimonio neto

▲ *account for under the equity method* contabilizar según el método de participación ▲ *equity method investment* inversión según el método de participación ▲ *investments accounted for using the equity method* inversiones contabilizadas usando el método de participación ▲ *measured under the equity method* calculado según el método de participación ▲ *net revaluation reserve according to the equity method* reserva de revalorización neta según el método de participación ▲ *omit to apply the equity method* omitir para aplicar el método de participación ▲ *recognise under the equity method* reconocer según el método de participación ▲ *use the equity method* usar el método de participación

equity ownership

= equity interest IAS/IFRS, US, interest, investment, share, stake

Equity ownership is the investment in the form of an equity interest in an enterprise held by an individual or another enterprise on a long-term basis, typically in the form of a shareholding, representing title of ownership and the legal right to participate in the enterprise's profit as well as any other rights attached to the equity ownership.

participación en el patrimonio

▲ *a 19% equity ownership in the enterprise* un 19% de participación en el patrimonio de la empresa ▲ *director compensation and equity ownership* indemnización al director y participación en el patrimonio ▲ *the company's equity ownership in unconsolidated subsidiaries* la participación en el patrimonio de la empresa en filiales no consolidadas

equity ratio

= solvency ratio

The equity ratio is a solvency ratio defined as shareholders' equity at year-end divided by total assets that shows the capital adequacy of an enterprise. The solvency of an enterprise is improved if shareholders' equity increases because of generated profits or repaid debt.

ratio de solvencia
▲ *calculate the equity ratio* calcular el ratio de solvencia ▲ *compare equity ratios* comparar ratios de solvencia ▲ *equity ratio calculations* cálculos del ratio de solvencia
⇛ debt-equity ratio

equity security
An equity security is a financial instrument, such as a share, that represents title of ownership of the assets of an enterprise after deduction of all its liabilities as well as the legal right to participate in the enterprise's profits as well as other rights attached to the equity security such as voting rights.
título de patrimonio
▲ *a demerger of the assets via spin-off of a separate equity security to the enterprise's shareholders* una escisión de los activos vía spin-off de un título de patrimonio separado realizada a los propietarios de la empresa ▲ *a recovery of part of the cost of the equity securities* una recuperación de parte del coste de los títulos de patrimonio ▲ *dividends on equity securities* dividendos de los títulos de patrimonio ▲ *enterprises whose debt or equity securities are publicly traded* empresas cuya deuda o títulos de patrimonio cotizan en bolsa ▲ *issuances, repurchases, and repayments of debt and equity securities* emisiones, recompras y reembolsos de deuda y títulos de patrimonio ▲ *the costs of registering and issuing equity securities* los costes de registro y emisión de títulos de patrimonio

equity share
= common share US, ordinary share UK
≠ non-equity share UK
An equity share is an ordinary share in a company that carries rights to participate in the distribution of dividends and a surplus in a winding up not limited to a specified amount.
acción ordinaria
▲ *acquire equity shares* adquirir acciones ordinarias ▲ *dividends on equity shares* dividendos de acciones ordinarias ▲ *illiquid equity shares* acciones ordinarias no convertibles en efectivo ▲ *issue equity shares* emitir acciones ordinarias ▲ *NASDAQ-listed equity shares* acciones ordinarias indexadas en el NASDAQ ▲ *repurchase of equity shares* recompra de acciones ordinarias ▲ *security investments other than equity shares* inversiones en títulos distintos de acciones ordinarias ▲ *subscribe for equity shares* suscribir acciones ordinarias
⇛ ordinary share

equity share capital UK
= equity capital UK, IAS/IFRS
Equity share capital is the part of the share capital of a company consisting of equities, i.e. ordinary shares.
capital social en acciones
▲ *called-up equity share capital* capital social en acciones exigido ▲ *issue of equity share capital* emisión de capital social en acciones ▲ *issued equity share capital* capital social en acciones emitido ▲ *paid-up equity share capital* capital social en acciones contribuido ▲ *subscribed equity share capital* capital social en acciones suscrito
⇛ non-equity share

equity structure
Equity structure refers to the distribution of the equity components, i.e. between the contributed capital (the share capital in a company) and the different types of reserves such as distributable and undistributable reserves or share premium, revaluation reserve, retained earnings etc. Also, for a company, the equity structure may refer to the equity components represented by different classes of shares with different rights attached.
estructura patrimonial
▲ *the equity structure appearing in the consolidated financial statements* la estructura patrimonial que aparece en los estados financieros consolidados ▲ *the equity structure of the legal parent* la estructura patrimonial de la matriz legal
⇛ contributed capital, reserve, share capital

equity trading
= share trading
Equity trading constitutes the purchase or sale of one or more equities.
contratación de accciones
= negociación de acciones

▲ *increase equity trading* aumentar la contratación de acciones ▲ *reduce equity trading* reducir la contratación de acciones

equity transaction

An equity transaction is a transaction which results in an increase or decrease of equity or a transfer between equity accounts.

transacción de acciones

▲ *incremental costs directly attributable to the equity transaction* costes marginales directamente atribuibles a la transacción de acciones ▲ *the costs of an equity transaction that is abandoned* los costes de una transacción de acciones abortada ▲ *the transaction costs of an equity transaction* los costes de la transacción de una transacción de acciones

equity value

= net asset value

Equity value is the ownership interest in or net asset value of a company, i.e. total assets less total liabilities.

valor del patrimonio neto

▲ *determination of the equity value* determinación del valor del patrimonio neto ▲ *equity value per share* valor del patrimonio neto por acción

⇛ book value

equity-settled share-based payment transaction

An equity-settled share-based payment transaction is a transaction where, instead of payment in money terms, an enterprise will receive consideration in the form of goods or services in return for the enterprise's equity instruments, e.g. equities or share options.

transacción con pagos basados en acciones liquidada mediante instrumentos de patrimonio

▲ *account for the transaction as an equity-settled share-based payment transaction* contabilizar la transacción como una transacción con pagos basados en acciones liquidada mediante instrumentos de patrimonio ▲ *goods or services received in an equity-settled share-based payment transaction* bienes o servicios recibidos en una transacción con pagos basados en acciones liquidada mediante instrumentos de patrimonio

SOURCE IFRS 2, Appendix A

⇛ compensation

equivalent

If something is equivalent to something, it corresponds to it or is comparable to it.

equivalente

▲ *a reconciliation of the amounts in the cash flow statement with the equivalent items reported in the balance sheet* una conciliación de las cantidades en el estado de flujos de efectivo con las partidas equivalentes recogidas en el balance ▲ *enter into a new lease for the same or an equivalent asset* realizar un nuevo alquiler sobre el mismo activo u otro equivalente ▲ *equivalent to 6.75% annually* equivalente al 6,75% anual ▲ *pay the equivalent in euro* pagar el equivalente en euros ▲ *profit or loss equivalent to the profit or loss resulting from an outright sale of the asset* resultado equivalente al resultado originado por una venta en firme del activo ▲ *revalue assets without an equivalent adjustment being made for tax purposes* revalorizar activos sin realizar un ajuste equivalente a efectos fiscales ▲ *the board of directors or equivalent governing body* el consejo de administración u organismo directivo equivalente

equivalent unit

An equivalent unit refers to the number of completed units and goods in progress that can be produced on the basis of the applied inputs.

unidad equivalente

▲ *calculate costs per equivalent unit* calcular los costes por unidad equivalente ▲ *replacement cost per equivalent unit* coste de sustitución por unidad equivalente

ERP UK, US

= enterprise resource planning US, UK

ERP is the abbreviation for enterprise resource planning, an integrated information software system that is designed to support and automate the functional areas of an enterprise.

planificación de recursos empresariales

▲ *ERP software* software de planificación de recursos empresariales

⇛ ERP system

ERP system US, UK
= enterprise resource planning system US, UK
An ERP system is an accounting oriented information software system designed to support and automate the business processes and all functional areas of an enterprise such as the managing of finance, inventories, customer orders, fixed assets and real estate.
sistema de planificación de recursos empresariales
▲ *develop a new ERP system* desarrollar un sistema nuevo de planificación de recursos empresariales ▲ *implement a new ERP system* implementar un sistema nuevo de planificación de recursos empresariales ▲ *select an ERP system* seccionar un sistema de planificación de recursos empresariales
⇛ enterprise resource planning system, ERP

error
An error is something that is unintentionally misleading.
error
▲ *a prior period error* un error del periodo anterior ▲ *account for an error correction retrospectively* calcular una corrección de errores retrospectivamente ▲ *accounting errors* errores de contabilidad ▲ *anomalous error* error anómalo ▲ *as a result of errors* como un resultado de errores ▲ *correct an error* corregir un error ▲ *correct the error prospectively from the earliest date practicable* corregir el error prospectivo desde la fecha más antigua ▲ *correction of fundamental errors* correcciones de errores fundamentales ▲ *determine the amount of an error* determinar la cantidad de un error ▲ *errors in measuring the fair value* errores en el cálculo del valor razonable ▲ *errors in the preparation of the annual report* errores en la preparación del informe anual ▲ *free from material errors* libre de errores materiales ▲ *fundamental errors* errores fundamentales ▲ *reversal of fundamental errors* revocación de errores fundamentales ▲ *the period-specific effects or the cumulative effect of the error* los efectos específicos del periodo o el efecto acumulativo del error

ESOP
1 ESOP is the abbreviation for employee share ownership plan, an incentive programme set up by an enterprise with the purpose of offering shares to employees. Typically, the shares are offered at a discount to the market price.
plan de retribuciones a empleados mediante acciones
▲ *guaranteed ESOP obligation* obligación de llevar a cabo un plan garantizado de retribuciones a empleados mediante acciones ▲ *liabilities of the ESOP* obligaciones del plan de retribuciones a empleados mediante acciones
2 ESOP is the abbreviation for employee stock ownership plan, an incentive program set up by an enterprise with the purpose of offering shares of stock to employees. Typically, the shares are offered at a discount to the market price.
plan de retribuciones a empleados mediante acciones
▲ *guaranteed ESOP obligation* obligación de llevar a cabo un plan garantizado de retribuciones a empleados mediante acciones
▲ *liabilities of the ESOP* obligaciones del plan de retribuciones a empleados mediante acciones

establish
To establish means to create or introduce something.
establecer
▲ *establish a contractual obligation to deliver cash or another financial asset* establecer una obligación contractual para entregar efectivo u otro activo financiero ▲ *establish joint control* establecer el control conjunto

establishment[1] *noun* <an, the, -s>
An establishment is the physical location of an organisation's operations. Examples include product and service sales offices, factories and warehouses.
establecimiento
▲ *constitute a permanent establishment of an enterprise* constituir un establecimiento permanente de una empresa ▲ *permanent establishment* establecimiento permanente

establishment[2] *noun* <an, the, -s>
An establishment is the creation or introduction of something.

establecimiento

▲ *establishment account* cuenta de establecimiento ▲ *establishment fee* tasa de establecimiento ▲ *freedom of establishment* libertad de establecimiento ▲ *right of establishment* derecho de establecimiento

estimate[1] *noun* <an, the, no plural>

An estimate is the result of an approximate calculation.

estimación

▲ *a changed estimate* una estimación modificada ▲ *a reasonable estimate* una estimación razonable ▲ *a reliable estimate* una estimación fiable ▲ *estimate of future cash flows* estimación de flujos de efectivo futuros ▲ *explicit and unbiased estimates* estimaciones explícitas y no sesgadas ▲ *highly subjective estimates* estimaciones altamente subjetivas ▲ *make a formal estimate of the recoverable amount* realizar una estimación formal de la cantidad a cobrar

estimate[2] *verb*

To estimate means to fix the value, number or size of something based on an approximate calculation.

estimar

▲ *estimate an amortisation period* estimar un periodo de amortización ▲ *estimate something reliably* estimar algo con fiabilidad ▲ *estimate the recoverable amount of the asset* estimar la cantidad a cobrar del activo ▲ *estimate the result* estimar el resultado ▲ *estimate the useful life of goodwill* estimar la vida útil del fondo de comercio ▲ *estimate using statistical models* estimar usando modelos estadísticos

estimated

If the value of something has been estimated, the value has been fixed on the basis of an approximate calculation.

estimado

▲ *a single set of estimated cash flows* un único conjunto de flujos de efectivo estimados ▲ *an estimated measurement* una valoración estimada ▲ *estimated amounts* cantidades estimadas ▲ *estimated point-of-sale costs* costes estimados en el punto de venta ▲ *the estimated amount of output* la cantidad estimada de producto ▲ *the estimated costs of completion* los costes estimados de finalización ▲ *the estimated selling price in the ordinary course of business* el precio de venta estimado en el curso ordinario del negocio ▲ *the present value of estimated future cash flows expected to arise from the continuing use of an asset* el valor actual de las estimaciones de los flujos de efectivo futuros previstos que se deriven de la utilización continua de un activo

estimated residual value UK, IAS/IFRS

= estimated salvage value US

The estimated residual value is the calculated recoverable value of a fixed asset on disposal after depreciation or amortisation at the end of its useful economic life.

valor residual estimado

▲ *depreciate to estimated residual value on a straight line basis* depreciar a valor residual estimado según el método lineal ▲ *less the estimated residual value of the relevant assets* menos el valor residual estimado de los activos relevantes

⇛ amortisation, depreciation, economic life

estimated salvage value US

= estimated residual value UK, IAS/IFRS

The estimated salvage value is the calculated recoverable value of a non-current asset on disposal after depreciation or amortisation at the end of its useful economic life.

valor residual estimado

▲ *a nominal estimated salvage value* un valor residual estimado nominal ▲ *less estimated salvage value of the asset* menos el valor residual estimado del activo ▲ *net of estimated salvage value* neto del valor residual estimado

estimation

An estimation is an attempt of predicting or calculating factors on which other calculations or judgments are to be based. Estimations are made for sales growth, demand, price changes, economic lives of fixed assets, etc.

estimación

▲ *estimation of* estimación de ▲ *key sources of estimation uncer-*

tainty fuentes claves de estimación de la incertidumbre ▲ *previous estimation* estimación previa ▲ *the discount factor in the current estimation* el factor de descuento en la estimación corriente ▲ *the estimation of the useful life of an item of property, plant and equipment* la estimación de la vida útil de una partida de edificios, instalaciones y equipos ▲ *the estimation of the value of the identifiable assets at the date of acquisition* la estimación del valor de los activos identificables a la fecha de adquisición ▲ *the nature of the assumption or other estimation uncertainty* la naturaleza de la suposición u otra estimación de la incertidumbre

ethical report

= ethical statement

An ethical report is an enterprise's report on ethical issues, such as working and environmental conditions, animal protection, human resource management and community development. The report aims at giving a true and fair view of the enterprise's ethical performance compared with its values and objectives. The ethical report may be part of the annual report or issued as a separate statement.

informe ético

▲ *prepare an ethical report* preparar un informe ético ▲ *publish an ethical report* publicar un informe ético

EURIBOR

= Euro Interbank Offered Rate

EURIBOR is an abbreviation of Euro Interbank Offered Rate, which is the benchmark rate for euro money market transactions and the euro interbank lending interest rate.

Euribor

= EURIBOR

▲ *3-month EURIBOR* Euribor a tres meses ▲ *EURIBOR + 0.10* Euribor + 0,10

⇛ LIBOR

Euro Interbank Offered Rate

= EURIBOR

The Euro Interbank Offered Rate (EURIBOR) is the benchmark rate for euro money market transactions and the euro interbank lending interest rate.

Euribor

= EURIBOR

▲ *charge interest on the basis of Euro Interbank Offered Rate* cargar el interés según el Euribor

⇛ LIBOR

eurobond

Eurobonds are long-term bearer bonds that are issued in a European currency other than that of the country of origin. As they are issued in bearer form and the interest payments are free of withholding taxes, eurobonds are particularly attractive to investors wishing to remain anonymous e.g. for the purpose of avoiding tax.

eurobono

▲ *issue eurobonds* emitir eurobonos

European Financial Reporting Advisory Group IAS/IFRS

= EFRAG IAS/IFRS

The European Financial Reporting Advisory Group (EFRAG) is responsible for giving a pro-active contribution to the standard setting work of IASB (International Accounting Standards Board), and for providing advice and technical expertise to the European Commission concerning the IFRSs and the interpretations for their European application. EFRAG was established in June 2001 by financial reporting stakeholders in Europe, i.e. national standard setters, accountants, reporting enterprises and users.

European Financial Reporting Advisory Group

= Grupo Asesor Financiero de Información Financiera, EFRAG

▲ *chairman of European Financial Reporting Advisory Group* presidente del European Financial Reporting Advisory Group ▲ *endorsements by European Financial Reporting Advisory Group* visados por el European Financial Reporting Advisory Group

⇛ International Accounting Standard, International Financial Reporting Standard

EV

= Enterprise Value

EV is the abbreviation for enterprise value, an investment ratio defined as an enterprise's market capitalisation plus its net interest-bearing debt. The definition also includes the value of minority interests minus the value of the share of any associates minus the value of other non-operating assets. This key figure shows the market value of the underlying invested capital and illustrates how the enterprise's operations are valued on the stock market irrespective of capital structure.

valor de la empresa en el mercado

▲ *EV calculations* cálculos del valor de la empresa en el mercado ▲ *increase EV in the long run* incrementar el valor de la empresa en el mercado a largo plazo

EVA

= economic value added, EP

EVA is the abbreviation for economic value added, which is a performance measure defined as the difference between operating profit after tax and a cost of capital charge on invested capital and measures economic profit rather than accounting profit. EVA was introduced in the 1990s and focuses the attention on the drivers that contribute to creating shareholder wealth.

EVA

= valor económico agregado, valor económico añadido

▲ *EVA growth* crecimiento del EVA ▲ *to calculate EVA* calcular el EVA ▲ *to measure EVA* medir el EVA

event

An event is an occurrence or a transaction of importance to an enterprise that influences the financial reporting of the enterprise.

acontecimiento

= suceso

▲ *a non-adjusting event* un acontecimiento no modificable ▲ *a past event* un acontecimiento pasado ▲ *a single event* un acontecimiento único ▲ *an adjusting event* un acontecimiento modificable ▲ *as a result of past events* como un resultado de acontecimientos pasados ▲ *contingent on future events* dependiendo de acontecimientos futuros ▲ *differ from previously occurring events* diferir de los acontecimientos previamente ocurridos ▲ *evaluate past, present or future events* evaluar acontecimientos pasados, presentes o futuros ▲ *events materially affecting the financial position of the enterprise* acontecimientos que afectan materialmente a la posición financiera de la empresa ▲ *events occurring after the end of the financial year* acontecimientos que ocurren después del cierre del ejercicio ▲ *events that are distinct from the ordinary activities* acontecimientos distintos de las actividades ordinarias ▲ *external event* acontecimiento externo ▲ *favourable events* acontecimientos favorables ▲ *revise as events occur* revisar a medida que ocurran los acontecimientos ▲ *separate economic events* acontecimientos económicos aislados ▲ *significant events occurring in the financial year* acontecimientos significativos que ocurren en el ejercicio ▲ *the obligating event* el acontecimiento obligatorio ▲ *unfavourable events* acontecimientos desfavorables

event after the balance sheet date

IAS/IFRS, UK

= post balance sheet event UK, subsequent event IAS/IFRS/US

An event occurring after the balance sheet date is an event - positive or negative - that occurs in the period between the balance sheet date and the time of adoption of the annual report.

NOTE Events after the balance sheet date may be adjusting or non-adjusting events, i.e. events evidencing conditions at the balance sheet or events arising after the balance sheet date, respectively.

hecho posterior a la fecha del balance

= hecho ocurrido después de la fecha de balance

NOTE Although both Spanish terms are IAS translations, the term 'hecho posterior a la fecha del balance' is typically used in Spanish accounting texts.

▲ *accounting for events after the balance sheet date* contabilizando los hechos posteriores a la fecha del balance ▲ *adjust the annual report for events after the balance sheet date* ajustar el informe anual por hechos posteriores a la fecha del balance ▲ *adjusting events after the balance sheet date* ajustando los hechos posteriores a la fecha del balance ▲ *disclosure of*

events after the balance sheet date publicación de los hechos posteriores a la fecha del balance ▲ *non-adjusting events after the balance sheet date* no ajustando los hechos posteriores a la fecha del balance
⇛ adjusting event, non-adjusting event

ex

1 Ex is a Latin preposition meaning "from" or "out of".
franco
= ex
≠ con
▲ *ex warehouse* franco almacén
▲ *ex works* franco fábrica

2 ≠ cum
Ex is a Latin preposition meaning "without".
sin
= ex
▲ *ex coupon* sin cupón ▲ *ex div.* sin dividendo
⇛ ex-coupon, ex-dividend, ex-rights

ex coupon
→ ex-coupon

ex dividend
→ ex-dividend

ex rights
→ ex-rights

ex-coupon
= ex-interest
Ex-coupon means "without interest" and refers to securities sold without the benefit of the next interest instalment payable.
sin cupón
= ex cupón
▲ *ex-coupon Treasury bonds* bonos del Tesoro sin cupón
⇛ coupon, ex-dividend

ex-dividend
Ex-dividend means "without dividend" and refers to securities sold without the benefit of the next dividend payable.
sin dividendo
= ex dividendo
▲ *on the ex-dividend date* en la fecha sin dividendo
⇛ ex-coupon

ex-rights
Ex-rights means "without rights" and refers to shares sold without the right for the purchaser to participate in a rights issue.
sin derechos de suscripción
▲ *theoretical ex-rights fair value per share* valor razonable teórico sin derecho de suscripción por acción

examination
= analysis, review
An examination is a careful investigation, a review of documents, procedures or personnel or an audit of financial records.
análisis
= revisión
▲ *a detailed examination* un análisis detallado ▲ *an examination on a test basis* un análisis basado en pruebas ▲ *make an examination* hacer un análisis ▲ *require further examination* requerir una nueva revisión

examine
= analyse, review
To examine is to inspect or investigate something, e.g. to find errors and omissions.
examinar
= analizar, revisar
▲ *examine all facts and circumstances that affect potential voting rights* examinar todos los hechos y circunstancias que afectan a los derechos de voto potenciales ▲ *examine an annual report* examinar un informe anual ▲ *examine something in detail* examinar algo detalladamente ▲ *examine the accounts* revisar las cuentas

exceptional
Exceptional means unusual. In the context of accounting, exceptional is used about items that refer to events or transactions that relate to the ordinary activities of an enterprise, but are unusual in size or occurrence.
excepcional
= extraordinario
▲ *an exceptional event* un acontecimiento excepcional ▲ *an exceptional item* una partida extraordinaria ▲ *an exceptional ordinary item* una partida ordinaria excepcional ▲ *an exceptional transaction* una transacción excepcional ▲ *exceptional circumstances* circunstancias excepcionales ▲ *exceptional costs* costes extraordinarios ▲ *exceptional income* ingreso extraordinario ▲ *exceptional transfers of capital to the shareholders* transferencias excepcionales de capital a los accionistas ▲ *in exceptional cases* en casos excepcionales
⇛ extraordinary item, unusual item

exceptional item UK
≠ extraordinary item

An exceptional item is a material, unusual item recognised in the profit and loss account within the ordinary and normal activities of the enterprise. The item is exceptional because of its size or incidence.

partida excepcional

▲ *excluding exceptional items* excluyendo partidas excepcionales ▲ *operating profit before exceptional items* beneficio de explotación antes de partidas excepcionales

⇛ extraordinary item, unusual item

exceptionals UK

→ exceptional item

excess

Excess means surplus or additional.

excedente

▲ *excess capacity* capacidad excedente ▲ *excess demand* demanda excedente ▲ *excess reserves* reservas excedentes

excess capacity

= unused capacity

Excess capacity constitutes the difference between the capacity available and the capacity required to carry out the production necessary for the period in question.

capacidad excedente

▲ *a build-up of excess capacity* una acumulación de la capacidad excedente ▲ *a decrease in excess capacity* un descenso en la capacidad excedente ▲ *an increase in excess capacity* un aumento de la capacidad excedente ▲ *reduce excess capacity by 10%* reducir la capacidad excedente en un 10% ▲ *substantial excess capacity* capacidad excedente sustancial

excess liquidity

= surplus liquidity

An enterprise with excess liquidity has more cash resources than needed to e.g. pay debts as they fall due. Enterprises usually carry out liquidity management to ensure that sufficient liquidity is available and to avoid having idle funds.

liquidez excedente

= exceso de liquidez

▲ *investment of excess liquidity* inversión de la liquidez excedente ▲ *place excess liquidity in foreign currency* colocar la liquidez excedente en divisas

exchange[1] *noun*

1 An exchange is an open market or authorised marketplace for buying and selling goods, commodities, securities, currencies etc.

mercado

▲ *a domestic or foreign exchange* un mercado nacional o internacional ▲ *traded on the exchange* contratado en el mercado

⇛ stock exchange

2 Exchange is the act of giving something, e.g. goods or money, and receiving something else in return of a similar value.

intercambio

▲ *acquire an item of property, plant and equipment in exchange for a non-monetary asset* adquirir una partida de edificios, instalaciones y equipos por intercambio de un activo no monetario ▲ *an exchange of one non-monetary asset for another* un intercambio de un activo no monetario por otro ▲ *an exchange that has commercial substance* un intercambio que tiene una naturaleza comercial ▲ *an item of property, plant and equipment acquired in an exchange of assets transaction* una partida de edificios, instalaciones y equipos adquirida en un intercambio de transacción de activos ▲ *ordinary shares issued in exchange for cash* acciones ordinarias emitidas por intercambio de efectivo

exchange[2] *noun* <an, the, no plural>

Exchange is the act where you change one currency for another.

▲ *an exchange of currencies* un cambio de monedas

exchange[3] *verb*

To exchange is to change for something else of a similar value or type.

intercambiar

▲ *exchange one financial instrument with another* intercambiar un instrumento financiero por otro ▲ *the fair value of the assets exchanged* el valor razonable de los activos intercambiados

exchange adjustment

→ foreign exchange adjustment

exchange difference

An exchange difference is the difference resulting from reporting the same number of units of a foreign currency in the reporting currency at different exchange rates.

diferencia de cambio

▲ *accumulated exchange differences* diferencias de cambio acumuladas ▲ *changes that result from exchange differences* cambios que resultan de las diferencias de cambio ▲ *exchange differences arising on a foreign currency liability* diferencias de cambio procedentes de un pasivo en moneda extranjera ▲ *exchange differences arising on the settlement of monetary items* diferencias de cambio procedentes de la liquidación de partidas monetarias ▲ *exchange differences arising on the translation of the financial statements of a foreign operation* diferencias de cambio procedentes de la conversión de los estados financieros de una operación extranjera ▲ *exchange differences that result from a severe devaluation or depreciation of a currency* diferencias de cambio como resultado de una devaluación o depreciación severa de una divisa ▲ *exchange differences which have been deferred* diferencias de cambio que han sido diferidas ▲ *recognition of exchange differences* reconocimiento de las diferencias de cambio ▲ *tax effects of exchange differences* efectos fiscales de las diferencias de cambio ▲ *the amount of exchange differences* el importe de las diferencias de cambio

exchange gain

= currency gain, foreign exchange gain

≠ exchange loss

An exchange gain appears from exchange rate differences or fluctuations resulting from the translation or conversion of foreign currency amounts into the domestic currency.

ganancia de cambio

= diferencia de cambio positiva, ganancia en el cambio

≠ pérdida de cambio

▲ *a realised exchange gain* una ganancia de cambio realizada ▲ *an unrealised exchange gain* una ganancia de cambio no realizada ▲ *exchange gains and losses related to hedges of the currency risk of a forecast transaction* ganancias y pérdidas de cambio relacionadas con coberturas de riesgo de moneda extranjera de una transacción prevista ▲ *foreign exchange gain* ganancia de cambio

exchange loss

= foreign currency loss, foreign exchange loss

≠ exchange gain

An exchange loss appears from exchange rate differences or fluctuations resulting from the translation or conversion of foreign currency amounts into the domestic currency.

pérdida de cambio

= diferencia de cambio negativa, pérdida en el cambio

≠ ganancia de cambio

▲ *a capitalised exchange loss* una pérdida de cambio capitalizada ▲ *capitalise an exchange loss* capitalizar una pérdida de cambio ▲ *exchange losses on hedging contracts* pédidas de cambio en contratos de cobertura ▲ *exchange losses on liabilities* pérdidas de cambio en pasivos ▲ *exchange losses relating to hedged transactions* pérdidas de cambio relativas a operaciones de cobertura ▲ *exchange losses resulting from a severe devaluation* pérdidas de cambio resultantes de una depreciación severa ▲ *make deductions for exchange losses* efectuar deducciones por pérdidas de cambio ▲ *realised exchange losses* pérdidas en el cambio realizadas ▲ *significant exchange losses* pérdidas en el cambio significativas ▲ *the carrying amount of a capitalised exchange loss* el valor contable de una pérdida de cambio capitalizada ▲ *unrealised exchange losses* pérdidas de cambio no realizadas

exchange of shares

= share exchange

In an exchange of shares one company, the acquirer, acquires an ownership share of another company, the acquiree, by acquiring shares in that company in exchange for shares in the acquirer and/or consideration in cash. On the transaction, the acquirer obtains control of the acquiree which becomes a subsidiary with the acquirer as its parent company.

intercambio de acciones

= canje de acciones

▲ *a public offer for the exchange of shares* una oferta pública por el intercambio de acciones

▲ *an exchange of shares that is determined by factors other than the current market valuation of the share* un intercambio de acciones que se determina por factores distintos a la valoración de mercado actual de la acción ▲ *German based exchange of shares* intercambio de acciones basado en el método alemán
⇛ acquiree, acquirer, parent company, subsidiary

exchange rate
= foreign exchange rate, rate of exchange
The exchange rate is the price of a currency in terms of another, expressed as a number of units of one (domestic) currency in terms of a unit of another (foreign) currency. In some countries, e.g. the UK, the exchange rate is expressed as the amount of foreign currency one unit of domestic currency will buy.
tipo de cambio
▲ *a flexible exchange rate* un tipo de cambio flexible ▲ *an approximate exchange rate* un tipo de cambio aproximado ▲ *at different exchange rates* a tipos de cambio diferentes ▲ *subsequent changes in exchange rates* cambios posteriores en los tipos de cambio ▲ *the exchange rate at the date of the transaction* el tipo de cambio a la fecha de la transacción ▲ *the exchange rate for immediate delivery* el tipo de cambio para entrega inmediata ▲ *the exchange rate of the functional currency and the foreign currency* el tipo de cambio de la moneda funcional y la moneda extranjera ▲ *the exchange rates at the date when the fair value was determined* los tipos de cambio en la fecha en la que se determinaba el valor razonable

exchange rate adjustment UK
= currency translation adjustment, foreign currency adjustment
An exchange rate adjustment is a change of the recognised amount of an asset or a liability because of a change in the reporting exchange rate.
ajuste por tipo de cambio
▲ *exchange rate adjustment of a hedging transaction* ajuste por tipo de cambio de una transacción con cobertura ▲ *exchange rate adjustment of goodwill* ajuste por tipo de cambio del fondo de comercio ▲ *exchange rate adjustment of investments in foreign operations* ajuste por tipo de cambio de una inversión en operaciones extranjeras ▲ *exchange rate adjustment of loans and advances* ajuste por tipo de cambio por préstamos y anticipos ▲ *exchange rate adjustment of the equity of subsidiaries* ajuste por tipo de cambio del patrimonio neto de las filiales ▲ *exchange rate adjustment relating to foreign subsidiaries* ajuste por tipo de cambio relacionado con filiales extranjeras

exchange rate fluctuation
An exchange rate fluctuation is a change in the exchange rate of a given currency.
fluctuación del tipo de cambio
= fluctuación de tipo de cambio, fluctuación en el tipo de cambio
▲ *changes in cash flows caused by exchange rate fluctuations* cambios en flujos de efectivo causados por fluctuaciones del tipo de cambio ▲ *effect of exchange rate fluctuations* efecto de las fluctuaciones del tipo de cambio ▲ *hedges against exchange rate fluctuations* coberturas contra fluctuaciones del tipo de cambio ▲ *significant exchange rate fluctuations* fluctuaciones significativas de tipo de cambio

exchange value
1 The exchange value of a product or a service is a measure of how much the product or service, if traded, is worth in terms of other products or services.
valor de intercambio
▲ *the exchange value of the goods* el valor de intercambio de los bienes
2 The exchange value is the value of one currency in terms of another, e.g. the value of US dollars in euro. A country may decide to peg its currency to a key currency such as the US dollar or a basket of currencies.
valor de cambio
= valor del intercambio

▲ *expected exchange value* valor de cambio previsto ▲ *measure at exchange value* medir a valor de cambio

excise duty

Excise duty is an indirect tax levied on certain goods within a country. Examples of such goods are liquor and tobacco.

impuesto especial

▲ *charge an excise duty* cargar un impuesto especial ▲ *goods subject to excise duty* bienes sujetos al impuesto especial ▲ *impose an excise duty* imponer un impuesto especial ▲ *the lowering of the rates of excise duty* la bajada de los tipos del impuesto especial ▲ *the minimum rate of excise duty on cigarettes* el tipo mínimo del impuesto especial sobre los cigarrillos

exclude

= leave out

To exclude means to disregard or ignore.

excluir

▲ *exclude a consolidated enterprise from consolidation* excluir a una empresa consolidada de la consolidación ▲ *exclude in-process research and development acquired in the business combination* excluir la investigación y el desarrollo en marcha adquiridos en la combinación de negocios ▲ *exclude the subsidiary from the consolidation* excluir a la filial de la consolidación

excluding

Excluding means without, i.e. not including.

excluyendo

= sin contar

≠ incluyendo

▲ *balance sheet excluding pooled schemes* balance excluyendo planes agrupados ▲ *capital expenditure excluding share acquisitions* gasto de capital excluyendo adquisiciones de acciones ▲ *equity excluding minority interests* patrimonio excluyendo intereses minoritarios ▲ *excluding restoration costs* excluyendo costes de reparación ▲ *net income excluding one-time items* ingreso neto excluyendo partidas excepcionales

exclusion

Exclusion is the deliberate leaving out or ignoring something.

exclusión

▲ *exclusion from consolidation* exclusión de la consolidación ▲ *exclusion of an enterprise from consolidation* exclusión de una empresa de la consolidación ▲ *exclusion of information to the Stock Exchange* exclusión de la información a la Bolsa de Valores ▲ *exclusion of non-cash transactions from the cash flow statement* exclusión de operaciones no monetarias del estado de flujos de efectivo ▲ *exclusion of subsidiaries due to insignificance* exclusión de las filiales debido a su insignificancia ▲ *the reason for exclusion* la razón para la exclusión

exclusive right

An exclusive right is the right to e.g. distribute, sell, copy or produce a particular product in a specified market as the sole person or organisation that holds or has been given the right, typically under a contract.

derecho exclusivo

▲ *acquire an exclusive right* adquirir un derecho exclusivo ▲ *recognise exclusive rights* reconocer derechos exclusivos

excoupon

→ ex-coupon

exdividend

→ ex-dividend

executive[1] *noun*

= executive officer

An executive is an employee who manages and is responsible for a specific department, activity or function of an enterprise.

ejecutivo

▲ *the executives of the company* los ejecutivos de la compañía ▲ *top-level executives* ejecutivos de alto nivel

executive[2] *adjective*

Executive is used about a person or group of persons, typically within an enterprise or government, who has the power to manage, control or organise something or who has the power to carry out decisions or day-to-day operations in practice.

ejecutivo

▲ *an executive position* una posición ejecutiva ▲ *any director, whether executive or otherwise, of the entity* cualquier director de la entidad, sea o no sea ejecutivo ▲ *executive candidate* candidato ejecutivo ▲ *executive chairman* presidente ejecutivo

executive board

= executive committee US, management board

The executive board is the governing body in charge of the day-to-day affairs of the enterprise within the general policy and planning laid down by the supervisory board (i.e. the board of directors). The executive board exercises its powers and duties under the authority granted by the supervisory board and the articles of association.

órgano ejecutivo

= comité ejecutivo, órgano de gestión

▲ *a change of the executive board* un cambio en el órgano ejecutivo ▲ *member of the executive board* miembro del comité ejecutivo ▲ *remuneration for the parent's executive board* remuneración para el comité ejecutivo de la matriz ▲ *retire from the executive board* retirarse del órgano ejecutivo ▲ *the composition of the executive board* la composición del órgano ejecutivo ▲ *the Danish members of the executive board* los miembros daneses del órgano ejecutivo ▲ *the powers of the executive board* las competencias del comité ejecutivo

⇛ board of directors, management, supervisory board

executive board makeup

Executive board makeup refers to the way in which the executive board is organised and indicates the allocation of responsibility among its members.

funcionamiento del comité ejecutivo

▲ *group executive board makeup* funcionamiento del comité ejecutivo del grupo

executive committee US

= executive board

The executive committee is the governing body in charge of the day-to-day affairs of the enterprise within the general policy and planning laid down by the supervisory board (i.e. the board of directors). The executive committee exercises its powers and duties under the authority granted by the supervisory board and the articles of association.

comité ejecutivo

= órgano de gestión, órgano ejecutivo

▲ *a change of the executive committee* un cambio en el comité ejecutivo ▲ *member of the executive committee* miembro del comité ejecutivo ▲ *remuneration for the parent's executive committee* remuneración para el comité ejecutivo de la matriz ▲ *retire from the executive committee* retirarse del órgano ejecutivo ▲ *the composition of the executive committee* la composición del órgano ejecutivo ▲ *the Danish members of the executive committee* los miembros daneses del órgano ejecutivo ▲ *the powers of the executive committee* las competencias del comité ejecutivo

⇛ board of directors, management

executive committee makeup US

Executive committee makeup refers to the way in which the executive committee is organised and indicates the allocation of responsibility among its members.

funcionamiento del comité ejecutivo

▲ *group executive committee makeup* funcionamiento del comité ejecutivo del grupo

executive director

≠ non-executive director

An executive director is a member of a company' s board of directors who also holds a position as a manager in the company.

director ejecutivo

⇛ director

executive officer US

= management employee

An executive officer is an employee who manages and is responsible for a specific department, activity or function of an enterprise.

ejecutivo

▲ *appoint a new executive officer* nombrar a un nuevo ejecutivo ▲ *compensation of named executive officers* remuneración de los ejecutivos nombrados ▲ *highly-compensated executive officers* ejecutivos altamente remunerados ▲ *performance goals for executive officers* objetivos a conseguir por los ejecutivos

▲ *the executive officers of the company* los ejecutivos de la compañía

executive order

An executive order is a legally binding edict issued by a member of the executive branch of a government, usually the head of that branch.

orden ejecutiva

▲ *Danish Executive Order on Green Accounts* Orden Ejecutiva danesa sobre Cuentas Verdes ▲ *Danish Executive Order on the Conditions for the Admission of Securities to Stock Exchange Listing* Orden Ejecutiva danesa sobre las condiciones para la admisión de valores mobiliarios a cotización ▲ *Executive Order no. XX* Orden Ejecutiva nº XX ▲ *issue an executive order* emitir una orden ejecutiva

executive vice president

An executive vice president is a senior officer in a group who refers directly to the CEO and takes part in the day-to-day management of the group.

vicepresidente ejecutivo

▲ *appoint a new executive vice president* nombrar a un nuevo vicepresidente ejecutivo ▲ *name an interim executive vice president* nombrar un vicepresidente ejecutivo interino ▲ *the former executive vice president* el anterior vicepresidente ejecutivo ▲ *the incoming executive vice president* el vicepresidente ejecutivo entrante ▲ *the retiring executive vice president* el vicepresidente ejecutivo saliente

executory contract

An executory contract is a contract where neither party has performed its obligations or where both parties have performed part of their obligations to an equal extent.

contrato pendiente de ejecución

▲ *onerous executory contracts* contratos pendientes de ejecución onerosos ▲ *provisions, contingent liabilities and contingent assets that result from executory contracts* provisiones, pasivos y activos contingentes como resultado de contratos pendientes de ejecución

executory cost US

Executory costs are costs related to the maintenance and operation of assets under finance leases that are not included in the lease payments. Executory costs are paid by the lessor and reimbursed by the lessee.

coste del arrendatario en un arrendamiento de capital

▲ *gross rent less any executory costs* renta bruta menos cualesquiera costes del arrendatario en un arrendamiento de capital ▲ *less executory costs* menos costes del arrendatario en un arrendamiento de capital ▲ *one-time executory costs* costes del arrendatario en un arrendamiento de capital de una sola vez

exemption method

The exemption method is a method for eliminating double taxation and appears from the OECD Model Tax Convention. Under the exemption method, two countries that have contracted a double tax treaty agree that a resident of one contracting country that generates income or owns capital that is taxed in the other contracting country will be exempt from tax on such income or capital.

método de exención

▲ *grant double taxation relief under the exemption method* deducción por doble imposición según el método de exención ▲ *grant relief under the exemption method* deducción según el método de exención

⇛ credit method

exemption relief

Exemption relief is a tax relief regulation for enterprises for whom double taxation is a possibility. Where the exemption relief rule applies, the income earned abroad is added to the domestic income, but the added income from abroad is not subject to domestic taxation if tax has already been deducted abroad.

devolución de impuestos

▲ *eligible for exemption relief* elegible para devolución de impuestos ▲ *grant exemption relief* conceder devolución de impuestos ▲ *partial exemption relief* devolución de impuestos parcial

exercisable

Exercisable means available for carrying out or implementing and may be used about e.g. voting rights or options.

ejercitable

▲ *at the date the option becomes exercisable* en la fecha la opción se convierte en ejercitable ▲ *exercisable during the period between vesting date and the end of the option's life* ejercitable durante el periodo comprendido entre la fecha de adquisición y el final de la vida de la opción ▲ *options exercisable at the end of the period* opciones ejercitables al final del periodo ▲ *the existence and effect of potential voting rights that are currently exercisable or convertible* la existencia y el efecto de los derechos de voto potenciales que actualmente son ejercitables o convertibles

exercise[1] *noun*

Exercise refers to the use of rights, power or capabilities, e.g. the holder of an option may exercise his right to buy the underlying securities.

ejercicio

▲ *assume the exercise of dilutive options and warrants* asumir el ejercicio de opciones y warrants dilutivos ▲ *the expected date of exercise of the purchase option* la fecha prevista del ejercicio de la opción de compra ▲ *the possible exercise of potential voting rights* el posible ejercicio de los derechos de voto potenciales ▲ *the terms of exercise of the potential voting rights* los términos del ejercicio de los derechos de voto potenciales

exercise[2] *verb*

To exercise means to make use of rights, power or capabilities, e.g. the holder of an option may exercise his right to buy the underlying securities.

ejercer

▲ *a put option that can be exercised if a stock market index reaches a specified level* una opción de venta que puede ejercerse si un índice bursátil alcanza un nivel especificado ▲ *exercise the right to use the leased asset* ejercer el derecho de uso del activo arrendado ▲ *options exercised on 30 June 2006* opciones ejercidas el 30 de junio de 2006 ▲ *the ability to exercise a contractual right* la capacidad para ejercer un derecho contractual ▲ *the holder's ability to exercise a put option* la capacidad del titular para ejercer una opción de venta

exercise date

= vesting date

The exercise date is the date at which you exercise the rights on your option, buying the underlying security.

fecha de ejercicio

▲ *share price at the exercise date* precio de la acción a la fecha de ejercicio ▲ *the debt instrument's amortised cost on each exercise date* el coste amortizado del instrumento de deuda en cada fecha de ejercicio ▲ *the difference between the exercise price and the market price at the exercise date* la diferencia entre el precio de ejercicio y el precio de mercado en la fecha de ejercicio ▲ *the option exercise date* la fecha de ejercicio de la opción ▲ *the value of the option at the exercise date* el valor de la opción a la fecha de ejercicio

exercise period

The exercise period is the time frame or the stipulated validity span of time during which options or share acquisition rights may be exercised at a pre-determined exercise price.

periodo de ejercicio

= periodo del ejercicio

▲ *expected exercise period* periodo de ejercicio esperado

exercise price

= strike price

Exercise price is the agreed specified price at which a holder of an option or a warrant may exercise his right to buy the underlying shares.

precio de ejercicio

= periodo de compra

▲ *an effective exercise price* un precio de ejercicio efectivo ▲ *an exercise price below the current market price* un precio de ejercicio por debajo del precio de mercado actual ▲ *average exercise price* precio de ejercicio medio ▲ *tender debt or other instruments of the entity in payment of all or a portion of the exercise price* deuda ofertada u otros instrumentos de la entidad como pago de todo o parte del precio de ejercicio ▲ *the call exercise price* el precio de ejercicio de compra ▲ *the exercise price of the option* el precio de ejercicio de la opción ▲ *the most advantageous exercise price* el precio de ejercicio más ventajoso ▲ *the option exercise price less the time value of the option if the option is in or at the money* el precio de ejercicio de la opción menos el valor temporal de la opción si la opción está dentro de dinero o en dinero ▲ *the present value of the exercise price* el valor actual del precio de ejercicio

exhibition cost

Exhibition costs are expenses incurred in connection with an exhibition of products for the purpose of selling. Exhibition costs are included in an enterprise's distribution costs along with other sales and marketing costs.

coste de exhibición

▲ *the exhibition costs incurred* los costes de exhibición incurridos

exist

= be available

To exist means to be available and accessible.

existir

▲ *all other hedging relationships that existed at the date of transition to IFRSs* todas las demás relaciones de cobertura que existían en la fecha de adaptación a las NIIFs ▲ *conditions that existed at the balance sheet date* condiciones que existían en la fecha del balance ▲ *control exists* el control existe ▲ *to the extent that the events confirm conditions existing at the end of the period* en la medida en que los hechos confirmen las condiciones existentes al cierre del periodo

expand

To expand is to extend, make larger or widen.

ampliar

▲ *expand on* ampliar ▲ *expand the market share* ampliar la cuota de mercado ▲ *retain and expand the customer base* mantener y ampliar la base de clientes ▲ *use an expanded presentation that splits the fair value of acquired insurance contracts into two components* usar una presentación ampliada que divide el valor razonable de los contratos de seguro adquiridos en dos componentes

expect

To expect is to anticipate the coming or occurrence of a future event or to regard something as probable.

esperar

▲ *be expected to be realised within 1 year of the balance sheet date* esperarse que se realicen dentro de un año de la fecha del balance ▲ *be expected to generate future economic benefits* esperarse que generen beneficios económicos futuros ▲ *be expected to result in* esperarse que resulte en ▲ *dividends expected to be distributed for the year* dividendos esperados para ser distribuidos durante el año ▲ *events expected to occur in the future* sucesos esperados que ocurran en el futuro ▲ *expect to receive economic benefits* esperar a recibir los beneficios económicos ▲ *expect to utilise the provision fully* esperar la utilización completa de la disposición ▲ *sales that are no longer expected to occur* ventas que se esperan que no ocurran más ▲ *the tax rates that are expected to apply at the balance sheet date* los tipos impositivos que se esperan aplicar a fecha de balance

expectation

The anticipation of how events will develop in future is referred to as expectations.

expectativa

▲ *changes in prepayment expectations* cambios en las expectativas de los pagos anticipados ▲ *expectations about future defaults from loans with particular characteristics* expectativas sobre impagos futuros procedentes de los préstamos con características particulares ▲ *expectations about possible variations in the amount or timing of future cash flows* expectativas sobre posibles variaciones en la cantidad o programación de los flujos de efectivo futuros ▲ *raise a valid expectation* suscitar una expectativa válida ▲ *reflect market expectations* reflejar expectativas de mercado

expected cost UK

= expected expense US

Expected costs are costs that are anticipated and highly probable to be incurred.

coste previsto
= coste esperado
▲ *measure the expected cost of accumulating compensated absences* medir el coste previsto acumulando bajas compensadas ▲ *recognise the expected cost of short-term employee benefits* reconocer el coste previsto de prestaciones a corto plazo ▲ *the expected cost of profit-sharing* el coste previsto de distribución de beneficios ▲ *the expected costs of disposal* los costes previstos de publicación

expected expense US
= expected cost UK
Expected expenses are expenses that are anticipated and highly probable to be incurred.
gasto previsto
= gastos esperados
▲ *cover expected expenses* cubrir los gastos previstos ▲ *expected expenses for the year* gastos previstos para el ejercicio ▲ *the total expected expenses* los gastos previstos totales

expected spoilage
= normal spoilage
Expected spoilage refers to spoilage that is inherent in a specific production process and which may therefore occur even under optimum operating conditions.
residuo previsto
▲ *calculate expected spoilage* calcular el residuo previsto ▲ *take into account expected spoilage* tener en cuenta el residuo previsto ▲ *write off expected spoilage* eliminar el residuo previsto

expected value
The expected value is the aggregate value of a random variable such as an asset or a liability which is statistically calculated by adding up potential outcomes and multiplying them by the probabilities of their occurrence. The expected monetary value, or EMV, results when the outcomes are measured in monetary terms. The expected value is typically used in decision making.
valor previsto
▲ *calculate the expected value* calcular el valor previsto ▲ *determination of the expected value* determinación del valor previsto
⇛ monetary value

expenditure
Expenditure is an outlay of a monetary amount or a commitment to pay a monetary amount by an enterprise, which leads to a reduction of its financial resources.
gasto
▲ *attribute subsequent expenditure directly to a particular intangible asset* atribuir directamente el gasto subyacente a un activo intangible concreto ▲ *expenditure incurred after the initial recognition of an acquired intangible asset* gasto incurrido después del reconocimiento inicial de un activo intangible adquirido ▲ *expenditure on advertising, training, start-up, research and development activities* gasto en publicidad, formación, puesta en funcionamiento y actividades de investigación y desarrollo ▲ *expenditure on an intangible item that was initially recognised as an expense in previous financial statements* gasto en una partida intangible que inicialmente se reconoció como gasto en las cuentas anuales anteriores ▲ *expenditure on developing a website* gasto en desarrollo de una página web ▲ *expenditure on purchasing or creating content specifically for a web site* gasto en la adquisición o en la creación de contenidos específicos para una página web ▲ *expenditure on relocating or reorganising part or all of an entity* gasto parcial o total de recolocación o reorganización de una entidad ▲ *expenditure on the exploration for minerals, oil, natural gas and similar non-regenerative resources* gasto en exploración de minerales, petróleo, gas natural y fuentes de energía no renovables similares ▲ *internal expenditure on the development and operation of an entity's own website* gasto interno en el desarrollo y funcionamiento de la propia página web de una entidad ▲ *reinstatement of expenditure previously recognised as an expense in the balance sheet* confirmación del gasto previamente reconocido como un gasto en el balance ▲ *research and development expenditure* gasto en investigación y desarrollo ▲ *selling, administrative and other general overhead ex-*

penditure coste indirecto en venta, costes administrativos y otros gastos generales ▲ *subsequent expenditure on an acquired in-process research and development projects* gasto subsiguiente en una investigación en curso adquirida y en proyectos de desarrollo ▲ *the expenditure incurred* el gasto incurrido
⇛ expense

expense[1] *noun*
= cost, expenditure
Expenses represent the sacrifice or decrease in economic benefits in an accounting period measured by asset outflows or the using up of assets or incurrence of liabilities, resulting in a reduction of equity, excluding expenses in the form of distribution to owners.
gasto
▲ *a deductible expense* un gasto deducible ▲ *accounting policies for insurance contracts and related assets, liabilities, income and expense* politicas contables para contratos de seguros y activos relacionados, pasivos, ingresos y gastos ▲ *actual expenses* gastos reales ▲ *an unexpected increase in expenses* un aumento imprevisto en los gastos ▲ *executive and general administrative expenses* gastos ejecutivos y administrativos generales ▲ *expense risks* riesgo de gasto ▲ *income or expense from reinsurance contracts* ingreso o gasto procedente de contratos de reaseguros ▲ *past expenses not to be recognised as an asset* gastos anteriores que no se reconocen como un activo ▲ *recognise expenditure as an expense when it is incurred* reconocer los gastos una vez devengados ▲ *recognition of an expense* reconocimiento de un gasto ▲ *the revenue, expenses and pre-tax profit or loss of discontinued operations* los ingresos, gastos y el beneficio o pérdida antes de impuestos de operaciones interrumpidas

expense[2] US *verb*
= recognise as an expense
To expense is to recognise an amount as expense in the income statement.
reconocer como gasto
▲ *expense in the income statement* reconocer como gasto en la cuenta de resultados ▲ *expense intangible assets in the income statement* reconocer como gasto activos intangibles en la cuenta de resultados ▲ *expense on a straight-line basis over the period of the lease* reconocer como gasto usando el método lineal durante la duración del alquiler ▲ *expense the development costs in the income statement as incurred* reconocer como gasto devengado los costes de desarrollo en la cuenta de resultados ▲ *recognize expenses in the income statement* reconocer gastos en la cuenta de resultados

expense account
1 ≠ revenue account
An expense account records entries and balances concerning the ordinary operations of an enterprise. Expense accounts form the bases of the profit and loss account.
cuenta de gasto
≠ cuenta de ingreso
▲ *charge off through the expense account* cancelar a través de la cuenta de gasto
2 An expense account is an account for an employee to be used for job-related expenses such as travelling, hotel and entertainment expenses.
cuenta de gastos de representación
▲ *abuse the expense account* abusar de la cuenta de gastos de representación

expense as incurred
To expense costs as incurred is to charge the costs to the profit and loss account in the accounting period to which they relate rather than deferring them until a later date.
gasto incurrido
= gasto devengado
▲ *expense repairs and maintenance expenditures as incurred* cargar gastos incurridos por reparaciones y mantenimiento

expense item
= item of expense
An expense item is an item in the income statement that records the amount of a particular expense or cost incurred during the accounting period.
partida de gasto
▲ *a main category of expense items* una categoría principal de partidas de gasto ▲ *all expense*

items recognised todas las partidas de gasto reconocidas

experience adjustment

In the accounting for post-employment defined benefit plans, experience adjustments are the actuarial gains and losses that arise because of differences between the actuarial assumptions made at the beginning of an accounting period and the actual experience during the period.

ajuste por experiencia

▲ *experience adjustment of actuarial assumptions* ajuste por experiencia de los supuestos actuariales ▲ *the effect of experience adjustments* el efecto de los ajustes por experiencia

SOURCE IAS 19, paragraph 7

experience curve

The experience curve is a curve showing the interrelation between decreasing costs and increasing volume of production of a product or service explained by the higher efficiency of workers that become more skilful.

curva de experiencia

▲ *calculations based on the experience curve* cálculos basados en la curva de experiencia

expert[1] *noun*

An expert is a person with special skills, knowledge and experience in a particular area or subject.

experto

▲ *engage an expert* implicar a un experto

expert[2] *adjective*

= professional, specialist

Expert as an adjective means being professional or specialist in connection with job, special knowledge, education or expertise.

experto

= profesional

▲ *expert assessment* valoración experta ▲ *expert evaluation* evaluación experta ▲ *expert knowledge* conocimiento experto ▲ *expert opinion* opinión experta

expiration date US

= expiry date UK

The expiration date is the date when a contract is terminated and ceases to be effective, e.g. the last date when an option can be exercised and a lease will end.

fecha de vencimiento

= fecha del vencimiento

▲ *the amortised cost of the transferred asset at the expiration date of the option* el coste amortizado del activo transferido a la fecha de vencimiento de la opción

expire

To expire means to cease being valid or exercisable.

vencer

▲ *an option that will expire after 5 years* una opción que vence a los 5 años ▲ *the contract has expired* el contrato ha vencido

⇛ lapse

expiry date UK

= expiration date US

The expiry date is the date when a contract is terminated and ceases to be effective, e.g. the last date when an option can be exercised and a lease will end.

fecha de vencimiento

▲ *the amortised cost of the transferred asset at the expiry date of the option* el coste amortizado del activo transferido a la fecha de vencimiento de la opción

explicit transactions

Explicit transactions are transactions which have been completed and can be documented by means of basic vouchers or other vouchers, e.g. sale on credit, purchase on credit, salary payments or purchase of investment goods.

transacciones explícitas

▲ *make explicit transactions* llevar a cabo transacciones explícitas ▲ *recognise explicit transactions* reconocer las transacciones explícitas

exposure

An exposure is the extent of risk involved in a particular position, such as the loss that may occur in connection with e.g. a loan provided or an amount invested.

exposición

= exposición al riesgo

▲ *information about exposures to interest rate risk under embedded derivatives contained in a host insurance contract* información sobre exposiciones al riesgo por variación en el tipo de interés en los derivados implícitos incluidos en un contrato de seguros principal ▲ *mitigate an underlying risk exposure* mitigar una exposición al riesgo subyacente ▲ *reduce the profit or loss exposure of a hedged item* reducir la exposición al riesgo de pérdida o beneficio de una partida cubierta ▲ *significant exposure* exposición significativa

exposure draft IAS/IFRS, UK

= ED

An exposure draft is a discussion document issued before the final document. Typically, exposure drafts are the drafts of new International Financial Reporting Standards (IFRSs), or amendments to existing International Accounting Standards (IASs), issued for public comments in connection with the consultative procedures of the International Accounting Standards Board (IASB).

documento de discusión

= borrador de discusión, borrador para discusión

▲ *issue an exposure draft* emitir un borrador de discusión ▲ *publish an exposure draft* publicar un documento de discusión

exrights

→ ex-rights

extend

To extend is to expand, make larger or widen.

ampliar

= extender

▲ *an automatic provision to extend the remaining term to maturity of a debt instrument* una provisión automática para ampliar el plazo restante hasta el vencimiento de un instrumento de deuda ▲ *an average of market prices over a period of time that extends beyond the end of the reporting period* una media de precios de mercado que se amplia más allá del final del periodo de información ▲ *extend the period required to complete the sale* ampliar el periodo exigido para cerrar la venta ▲ *extend the period to complete the sale beyond one year* ampliar el periodo para cerrar la venta después de un año

eXtensible Business Reporting Language

= XBRL

eXtensible Business Reporting Language is an XML-based accounting language that facilitates the electronic communication of financial information including the comparison across enterprises.

eXtensible Business Reporting Language

= EBRL, lenguaje extensible de informes de negocios

▲ *a national eXtensible Business Reporting Language taxonomy* una taxonomía nacional del eXtensible Business Reporting Language

extension

An extension is an extra addition to something such as extra facilities, buildings, time or influence.

ampliación

▲ *an extension of the disclosure requirement* una ampliación del requisito de divulgación ▲ *an extension of the entity's investment in the associate* una ampliación de la inversión de la entidad en la asociada ▲ *an extension of the period required to complete a sale* una ampliación del periodo requerido para cerrar una venta ▲ *an ongoing extension* una ampliación en curso ▲ *build an extension to a factory* realizar una ampliación de una fábrica ▲ *complete an extension* finalizar una ampliación ▲ *extension expenses* gastos de ampliación

extensive

= large-scale, substantial

Extensive means comprehensive, i.e. containing, implying or covering rather much.

sustancial

= a gran escala

▲ *an extensive updating* una actualización a gran escala ▲ *extensive measures* medidas sustanciales ▲ *have access to extensive data* tener acceso a datos sustanciales

external audit

≠ internal audit

An external audit is a type of audit conducted by a qualified accountant, who is independent of the enterprise he or she audits. An external audit includes the periodic examination of the accounting records and the auditing of the published financial statements.

auditoría externa

≠ auditoría interna

▲ *an independent external audit* una auditoría externa independiente ▲ *carry out an external audit* llevar a cabo una auditoría externa ▲ *external audit policies* políticas de auditoría externa ▲ *the obligation to undertake an external audit* la obligación de realizar una auditoría externa

external auditor

An external auditor is a person, often a qualified accountant, who is independent of the enterprise he or she audits and responsible for the periodic examination of the accounting records and the auditing of the published financial statements.

auditor externo

▲ *the appointment of the external auditor* el nombramiento del auditor externo ▲ *the external auditor engaged by the company* el auditor externo contratado por la empresa ▲ *the external auditor's independence, objectivity and effectiveness* la independencia, objetividad y efectividad del auditor externo ▲ *the external auditor's work programme* el programa de trabajo del auditor externo ▲ *the former external auditor of the company* el anterior auditor externo de la empresa ▲ *the present external auditor of the company* el actual auditor externo de la empresa ▲ *the reappointment of the external auditor* la confirmación del auditor externo ▲ *the recommendations made in the external auditor's management letter* las recomendaciones hechas en la carta a la dirección por el auditor externo ▲ *the removal of the external auditor* el cambio de auditor externo ▲ *the resignation of the external auditor* la renuncia del auditor externo ▲ *the selection of the external auditor* la selección del auditor externo

external cost

External costs are costs caused by a person or an enterprise to the economy or another party, e.g. by pollution, which are not borne by that person or enterprise, or costs incurred by an enterprise which are related to external factors, e.g. costs for raw materials and supplies.

coste externo

≠ coste interno

▲ *external costs directly attributable to the issue of new shares* costes externos directamente atribuibles a la emisión de nuevas acciones

external debt

External debt owed by an enterprise typically consists of loans raised abroad in foreign currencies which may give rise to currency risk. For a country as a whole, foreign debt is the total debt owed to creditors abroad by the country's government as well as private sector households or institutions. Such creditors typically include other governments, foreign banks, the International Monetary Fund or the World Bank.

deuda externa

▲ *gross external debt* deuda externa bruta ▲ *long-term external debt* deuda externa a largo plazo ▲ *medium-term external debt* deuda externa a medio plazo ▲ *short-term external debt* deuda externa a corto plazo ▲ *the company's total external debt* la deuda externa total de la compañía ▲ *total external debt* total deuda externa

external expense

External expenses are expenses caused by a person or an enterprise to the economy or another party, e.g. by pollution, which are not borne by that person or enterprise, or costs incurred by an enterprise which are related to external factors, e.g. costs for raw materials and supplies.

gasto externo

▲ *external expenses incurred* gastos externos incurridos ▲ *external expenses on goods and services* gastos externos en bienes y servicios ▲ *other external expenses* otros gastos externos

external failure cost

External failure costs are costs incurred because of defects and deficiencies related to manufactured products such as warranty claims or repair costs that are detected after delivery to customers.

coste por fallos externos

≠ coste por fallos interno

▲ *estimate external failure costs* estimar los costes por fallos externos ▲ *huge external failure costs* costes por fallos externos enormes ▲ *reduce external fa-*

ilure costs reducir los costes por fallos externos
⇛ appraisal cost, internal failure cost, prevention cost

external funding
External funding is the raising of capital by an enterprise by means of sources from outside the enterprise, such as banks and other enterprises.
financiación externa
▲ *obtain external funding for research* obtener financiación externa para investigación ▲ *sources for external funding* fuentes de financiación externa ▲ *substantial external funding* financiación externa sustancial ▲ *the potential for future external funding* el potencial para financiación externa futura

external growth
= inorganic growth
≠ internal growth, organic growth
External growth is the inorganic growth achieved by an enterprise by acquisition of or merger with other enterprises with a view to e.g. increasing their market share or competitiveness.
crecimiento externo

extinguishment of debt US
= repayment UK, retirement US, UK
Extinguishment of debt means the repayment or retirement of debt which may take place before or after maturity by repayment, refunding or conversion.
extinción de deuda
▲ *account for as an extinguishment of debt* contabilizar como una extinción de deuda ▲ *accounting for extinguishment of debt* contabilizando la extinción de deuda ▲ *early extinguishment of debt* extinción anticipada de la deuda ▲ *gains and losses from extinguishment of debt* pérdidas y ganancias por extinción de deuda

extraordinary expense
Expenses originating from events that do not fall within the ordinary activities and are therefore not expected to be recurring must be classified as extraordinary expenses.
gasto extraordinario
▲ *extraordinary expenses and income* ingresos y gastos extraordinarios ▲ *the extraordinary expenses incurred* los gastos extraordinarios incurridos

extraordinary general meeting
= EGM
An extraordinary general meeting is any meeting of the shareholders of a company and its directors that is not an annual general meeting, and its purpose is to discuss and vote on issues that cannot wait to be resolved at the next annual general meeting.
junta general extraordinaria
▲ *call an extraordinary general meeting* convocar una junta general extraordinaria ▲ *hold an extraordinary general meeting* llevar a cabo una junta general extraordinaria ▲ *notice of an extraordinary general meeting* notificación de una junta general extraordinaria ▲ *resolve at an extraordinary general meeting* resolver en una junta general extraordinaria
⇛ annual general meeting

extraordinary income
≠ extraordinary loss
Income originating from events that do not fall within the ordinary activities and is therefore not expected to be recurring must be classified as extraordinary income.
ingresos extraordinarios
NOTE Always plural in Spanish accounting texts.
▲ *extraordinary income and expenses* gastos e ingresos extraordinarios ▲ *record income in the item extraordinary income* registrar los ingresos en la partida de ingresos extraordinarios

extraordinary income or loss US
The extraordinary income or loss of the enterprise is the income or loss from ordinary activities of the enterprise including extraordinary income and excluding extraordinary expenses.
resultado extraordinario
▲ *extraordinary income or loss after tax* resultado extraordinario después de impuestos ▲ *extraordinary income or loss before tax* resultado extraordinario antes de impuestos ▲ *tax on extraordinary income or loss* impuesto sobre el resultado extraordinario

extraordinary item

Extraordinary items include income and expenses that arise from events or transactions that are clearly distinct from the ordinary activities of the enterprise and therefore are not expected to recur frequently or regularly.

partida extraordinaria

▲ *cash flows associated with extraordinary items* flujos en efectivo asociados a partidas extraordinarias ▲ *extraordinary items after tax* partidas extraordinarias después de impuestos ▲ *net loss after tax on extraordinary items* pérdida neta después de impuestos en partidas extraordinarias ▲ *present items of income and expense as extraordinary items* presentar partidas de gastos e ingresos como partidas extraordinarias ▲ *remove references to extraordinary items* eliminar referencias a partidas extraordinarias ▲ *results before tax and extraordinary items* resultados antes de impuestos y partidas extraordinarias ▲ *results from extraordinary items* resultados de partidas extraordinarias ▲ *tax on extraordinary items* impuesto sobre partidas extraordinarias ▲ *the nature and the amounts of extraordinary items* el tipo y las cantidades de las partidas extraordinarias ▲ *the tax effects of extraordinary items* los efectos impositivos de las partidas extraordinarias

⇛ non-recurring item, unusual item

extraordinary loss

pérdida extraordinaria

1 ≠ extraordinary income US, extraordinary profit UK, IAS/IFRS

The extraordinary loss of the enterprise is the loss from ordinary activities of the enterprise including extraordinary income and excluding extraordinary expenses.

gasto extraordinario

▲ *an extraordinary loss for financial reporting purposes* un gasto extraordinario a efectos de información financiera ▲ *pre-tax extraordinary loss* gasto extraordinario antes de impuestos

2 ≠ extraordinary gain

An extraordinary loss is a nonrecurrent, material loss outside the ordinary activities of an enterprise.

pérdida extraordinaria

▲ *income before extraordinary loss* ingreso antes de pérdida extraordinaria

extraordinary profit or loss

The extraordinary profit or loss of the enterprise is the profit or loss from ordinary activities of the enterprise including extraordinary income and excluding extraordinary expenses.

resultado extraordinario

= pérdidas y ganancias extraordinarias

▲ *extraordinary profit or loss after tax* resultado extraordinario después de impuestos ▲ *extraordinary profit or loss before tax* resultado extraordinario antes de impuestos ▲ *tax on extraordinary profit or loss* impuesto sobre el resultado extraordinario

F

face value

= face amount US, nominal value, par value, principal
≠ market value
The face value is the value appearing on a financial instrument, a cheque, a banknote or a coin and represents the stated and nominal value when it is issued.

valor nominal

= valor a la par
▲ *a liability with no face value* un pasivo sin valor nominal ▲ *accrete to face value* incrementar a valor nominal ▲ *carry at face value* trasladar a valor nominal ▲ *provide deferred tax on the difference between book and face value of bond debt* ofrecer impuesto diferido sobre la diferencia entre el valor en libro y el valor nominal del bono ▲ *record at face value* apuntar a valor nominal ▲ *represent 5.5% of the face value of EUR 2.24m* representar el 5% del valor nominal de 2,24 millones de euros

facility-sustaining cost

Facility-sustaining costs are costs incurred that relate to activities that support an enterprise in general and are therefore not attributable to any concrete individual products. Examples of such costs are administrative expenses as well as management and accounting costs.

coste de mantenimiento de la instalación

▲ *less facility-sustaining costs* menos los costes de mantenimiento de la instalación

factor

1 A factor is a thing or cause that contributes to an accomplishment, a decision, an event, an outcome, a process, or a situation.

factor

▲ *a critical factor* un factor crítico ▲ *a decisive factor* un factor decisivo ▲ *a favourable resolution of the delaying factors* una resolución favorable de los factores que retrasan ▲ *a significant factor* un factor significativo ▲ *a time-weighting factor* un factor ponderado con el tiempo ▲ *an important factor* un factor importante ▲ *based on an analysis of all of the relevant factors* basado en un análisis de todos los factores relevantes ▲ *economic and legal factors influencing the useful life of an intangible asset* factores económicos y legales que influyen en la vida útil de un activo intangible ▲ *non-quantifiable factors* factores no cuantificables ▲ *operational factors* factores operacionales ▲ *quantifiable factors* factores cuantificables ▲ *the risk-return factors inherent in the financial instrument* los factores riesgo-rendimiento inherentes al instrumento financiero

2 A factor is an enterprise such as a finance company or a bank, to which an enterprise can outsource the collection of its debts via the transfer, i.e. sale, of its portfolio of debtors for later collection of the amounts owed against payment of a fee, typically a percentage of the amount owed. Often, the factor will also assume the credit risk involved and be responsible for carrying the debtor accounts.

empresa de factoring

▲ *operate as a factor* operar como una empresa de factoring ▲ *perform invoice discounting activities as factor within the group* llevar a cabo actividades de descuento de facturas como una empresa de factoring dentro del grupo
⇛ debt factoring, factoring

factor in

= discount, price in
To factor in is to allow for the factual or possible effects of events or announcements in a decision-making process, in a price fixing (typically of shares, bonds etc.), in acquisitions, disposals, investments or other transactions, or in expectations for future developments.

contar con

▲ *factor in greater uncertainty* contar con una incertidumbre mayor ▲ *factor in interest rate hikes* contar con subidas en los tipos de interés ▲ *factor in shareholders' expectations for the company's future performance* contar con las expectativas de los accionistas sobre la actividad futura de la empresa

factoring

Factoring is the sale of trade receivables by an enterprise to a factor, i.e. a firm that accepts the credit risk and collects the debt against a fee or a discount, in this way providing cash funds to the enterprise.

factoring

▲ *disclosed factoring* factoring publicado ▲ *factoring agreement* acuerdo de factoring ▲ *factoring company* empresa de factoring ▲ *undisclosed factoring* factoring no publicado

⇛ 2 factor

factoring liability

A factoring liability is the enterprise's liability as a consequence of having transferred its debtors to a factor that has a right of recourse if the debtor fails to pay. Factoring liabilities are contingent liabilities.

pasivo por factoring

= deudas por factoring

▲ *the factoring liability in the balance sheet* el pasivo por factoring en el balance

factory

= plant

A factory is a production facility consisting of buildings and machinery in which one or more production operations of an enterprise take place, e.g. manufacturing, packaging or labelling.

planta

= fábrica

▲ *ex factory* fuera de fábrica ▲ *fit smoke filters in the factory* colocar filtros de humo en la planta ▲ *the cost of factory management* el coste de gestión de la planta

factory burden US

= factory overhead US, factory overhead cost, indirect manufacturing cost, indirect manufacturing expense US, indirect production cost, indirect production expense US, manufacturing overhead US, production overhead IAS/IFRS

Factory burdens are costs that are not directly related to the production of goods, i.e. costs for which single products or activities cannot be identified. Examples of factory burdens are indirect labor and materials, rent and insurance of manufacturing units.

coste de fabricación indirecto

= coste de producción indirecto

▲ *direct labor and related factory burden* mano de obra directa y coste de fabricación indirecto relacionado ▲ *include all factory burden* incluir todos los costes de fabricación indirectos

factory manager

= plant manager

A factory manager is responsible for the day-to-day operations and financial performance of a factory.

gerente de fábrica

▲ *appoint a new factory manager* nombrar un nuevo gerente de fábrica

factory overhead US

= factory burden US, factory overhead cost, indirect manufacturing cost, indirect production cost, manufacturing overhead US, production overhead IAS/IFRS

Factory overheads are costs that are not directly related to the production of goods, i.e. costs for which single products or activities cannot be identified. Examples of factory overheads are indirect labour and materials, rent and insurance of manufacturing units.

coste de fabricación indirecto

= coste de producción indirecto

▲ *calculate and interpret factory overhead* calcular e interpretar el coste de fabricación indirecto ▲ *direct labor and factory overhead* mano de obra directa y coste de fabricación indirecto

factory overhead cost

→ factory overhead

failing

A failing enterprise is one that has financial difficulties to the extent that it is unable to meet its obligations.

insolvente

▲ *a failing company* una empresa insolvente

fair

In order for financial reporting information to be fair it must be relevant, reliable and reflect the actual circumstances surrounding the enterprise.

razonable

▲ *a fair market value* un valor de mercado razonable ▲ *a fair presentation* una presentación razonable ▲ *achieve a fair presentation* lograr una presentación razonable ▲ *fair accounting information* información contable razonable ▲ *give a fair presentation in all material respects* dar una presentación razonable en todos los aspectos materiales

fair presentation IAS/IFRS, US

= true and fair view UK

Fair presentation refers to the overriding requirement that the financial statements must give a true and fair view of, or present fairly, in all material respects, the results and financial position of an enterprise. Fair presentation means that generally accepted accounting principles and conventions have been consistently applied when preparing the financial statements. In the EU, the requirement is statutory.

imagen fiel

= presentación razonable

NOTE Spanish accountants prefer 'imagen fiel' to the IAS/IFRS term 'presentación razonable'.

▲ *achieve a fair presentation* conseguir una imagen fiel ▲ *give a fair presentation* dar una imagen fiel ▲ *give a qualified opinion as to the fair presentation in the annual report* dar una opinión con salvedades en cuanto a la imagen fiel en el informe anual ▲ *information of importance to the fair presentation* la información de importancia para la imagen fiel ▲ *information that is necessary for a fair presentation* información que es necesaria para una imagen fiel ▲ *meet the fair presentation requirement* cumplir el requisito de imagen fiel ▲ *the fair presentation of the enterprise's financial position* la imagen fiel de la posición financiera de la empresa ▲ *the general requirement of a fair presentation* el requisito general de una imagen fiel

fair value

Fair value is the amount at which it is assumed that an asset or a liability could be exchanged in an arm's length transaction between knowledgeable, willing parties. The market price in an active market is considered to be fair value.

NOTE Fair value may refer to the value in an active market, i.e. the market price, net realisable value, replacement value or value in use.

valor razonable

= justiprecio

▲ *adjust to fair value* ajustar a valor razonable ▲ *an amount approximating to the fair value of the asset* una cantidad que se aproxima al valor razonable del activo ▲ *calculate the fair value* calcular el valor razonable ▲ *changes in the fair value* cambios en el valor razonable ▲ *determine the fair value* determinar el valor razonable ▲ *fair value adjustment* ajuste a valor razonable ▲ *fair value at beginning of year* valor razonable al inicio del año ▲ *fair value at end of year* valor razonable a final de año ▲ *fair value at the date of acquisition* valor razonable a la fecha de adquisición ▲ *fair value hedge* cobertura a valor razonable ▲ *measure at fair value* medir a valor razonable ▲ *negative fair values* valores razonables negativos ▲ *positive fair values* valores razonables positivos ▲ *recognise at fair value* reconocer a valor razonable ▲ *remeasure to fair value* volver a medir a valor razonable ▲ *revalue to fair value* revalorizar a valor razonable ▲ *the fair value of the hedged asset* el valor razonable del activo cubierto ▲ *theoretical fair value* valor razonable teórico

SOURCE IAS 2, paragraph 6

⇛ current cost

fair value adjustment

Fair value adjustments imply the write up or write down of assets and liabilities recognised in the financial statements to reflect their actual fair values for the financial year in accordance with the fair value method.

ajuste a valor razonable

= ajuste de valor razonable

▲ *any fair value adjustments to the carrying amounts of assets and liabilities* cualesquiera ajustes a valor razonable a los valores contables de activos y pasivos ▲ *fair value adjustments made on a business combination* ajustes a valor razonable realizados en una combinación de negocios ▲ *fair value adjustments recognised in equity* ajustes a valor razonable reconocidos en patrimonio neto ▲ *net gains or losses from fair value adjustments* pérdidas o ganancias netas por ajustes a valor razonable ▲ *tax related to fair value adjustments* impuestos relacionados con ajustes a valor razonable

fair value directive

The fair value directive is a term used about Directive 2001/65/EC of the European Parliament and of the Council of 27 September 2001 amending Directives 78/660/EEC, 83/349/EEC and 86/635/EEC as regards the valuation rules for the annual and consolidated accounts of certain types of companies as well as of banks and other financial institutions. Under the directive Member States shall permit or require in respect of all companies or any classes of companies valuation at fair value of financial instruments, including derivatives.

directiva sobre el valor razonable

▲ *implement the fair value directive* implementar la directiva sobre el valor razonable ▲ *the provisions of the fair value directive* las disposiciones de la directiva sobre el valor razonable

fair value gain

≠ fair value loss

A fair value gain is a gain arising from the measurement of an asset, e.g. a financial instrument, at fair value that results in an upward revaluation of the asset. Fair value gains are typically unrealised and recognised in equity, e.g. in a special fair value adjustment reserve.

ganancia a valor razonable

= ganancia de valor razonable

▲ *fair value gains on cash flow hedges* ganancias a valor razonable en los instrumentos de cobertura del flujo de efectivo ▲ *fair value gains on financial instruments* ganancias a valor razonable en instrumentos financieros ▲ *fair value gains on property, plant and equipment* ganancias a valor razonable en edificios, instalaciones y equipos ▲ *fair value gains on sale* ganancias a valor razonable en ventas

⇛ fair value, fair value reserve

fair value hedge IAS/IFRS

A fair value hedge is a transaction intending to offset or minimize risk exposure to changes in the fair value of a particular asset or liability (the hedged item). The hedging transaction involves use of derivative financial instruments as hedging instruments such as futures.

cobertura de valor razonable

= cobertura a valor razonable

▲ *a fair value hedge of the change in the value of the investment* una cobertura de valor razonable del cambio en la valoración de la inversión ▲ *a fair value hedge of the interest rate exposure* una cobertura de valor razonable de la exposición al tipo de interés ▲ *acquire an asset that is a hedged item in a fair value hedge* adquirir un activo que es una partida cubierta en una cobertura a valor razonable ▲ *designated fair value hedges* coberturas de valor razonable designadas ▲ *recognition and measurement on fair value hedge accounting* reconocimiento y cálculo de la contabilidad de cobertura de valor razonable ▲ *redesignate the hedge as a fair value hedge* rediseñar la cobertura como una cobertura de valor razonable

fair value hedging

Fair value hedging refers to an enterprise's use of derivative financial instruments to hedge against any changes in the fair value of a recognised asset or liability impacting an enterprise's profit or loss for an accounting period.

sistema de cobertura a valor razonable

▲ *available-for-sale assets available for fair value hedging* activos disponibles para la venta listos para sistema de cobertura a valor razonable ▲ *the ability to apply fair value hedging* la capacidad para aplicar el sistema de cobertura a valor razonable ▲ *use of fair value hedging* usar un sistema de cobertura a valor razonable

fair value hierarchy

The fair value hierarchy is made up of three levels of input based on the relative relia-

bility of the input in the method used to estimate fair value. Officially quoted prises on an active market for identical assets or liabilities are the most reliable input and belong to level 1. Non-observable market input based on reporting assumptions is the least reliable input and belong to level 3.
jerarquía para el cálculo del valor razonable

fair value less costs to sell IAS/IFRS
= net realisable value IAS/IFRS, UK
The fair value less costs to sell of an asset is the sum of the future cash flows which the asset is expected to generate at the balance sheet date in the ordinary course of business less the selling costs, i.e. the net realisable value. The fair value less costs to sell of a liability is the sum of the future cash flows from the enterprise during the life of the liability.
valor razonable menos costes de venta
▲ *clear evidence of an increase in fair value less costs to sell* prueba clara de un aumento en valor razonable menos costes de venta ▲ *estimates of fair value less costs to sell* estimaciones de valor razonable menos costes de venta ▲ *evidence of a reduction in the fair value less costs to sell of current assets* prueba de una reducción en el valor razonable menos los costes de venta de los activos corrientes ▲ *make a new assessment of fair value less costs to sell* hacer una nueva valoración de valor razonable menos costes de venta ▲ *measure liabilities at fair value less costs to sell* medir pasivos a valor razonable menos costes de venta ▲ *revalue to fair value less costs to sell* revalorizar a valor razonable menos costes de venta ▲ *the fair value less costs to sell at the balance sheet date* el valor razonable menos costes de venta a la fecha del balance ▲ *the revised fair value less costs to sell* el valor razonable menos costes de venta revisado ▲ *write down to fair value less costs to sell* amortizar a valor razonable menos costes de venta ▲ *write-downs of inventories to fair value less costs to sell* eliminaciones de inventarios a valor razonable menos costes de venta
SOURCE IAS 36, paragraph 6

fair value loss
≠ fair value gain
A fair value loss is a loss arising from the measurement of an asset, e.g. a financial instrument, at fair value that results in a downward revaluation of the asset. Fair value losses are typically unrealised and recognised in equity, e.g. in a special fair value adjustment reserve.
pérdida a valor razonable
= pérdida de valor razonable
▲ *fair value losses on land and buildings* pérdidas a valor razonable en bienes raíces y edificios
⇛ fair value, fair value reserve

fair value measurement
Fair value measurement is the determining of the amount of an asset or a liability at fair value, i.e. the amount at which the asset could be exchanged, or the liability settled, in an arm's length transaction.
valoración a valor razonable
= medición a valor razonable
NOTE Spanish accountants prefer 'valoración a valor razonable' to the IAS/IFRS term 'medición a valor razonable'.
▲ *fair value measurement considerations* consideraciones de valoración a valor razonable ▲ *fair value measurement of assets and liabilities* valoración a valor razonable de activos y pasivos ▲ *on a fair value measurement basis* en base a una valoración a valor razonable ▲ *the fair value measurement of financial assets* la valoración a valor razonable de activos financieros ▲ *the fair value measurement of the intangible asset* la valoración a valor razonable del activo intangible
⇛ arm's length basis

fair value method
Fair value method is a method of accounting according to which assets and liabilities are measured at fair value in the financial statements, i.e. at the amount for which an asset or liability could be exchanged between knowledgeable and willing parties in an arm's length transaction.
método del valor razonable
= método de valor razonable
▲ *apply the fair value method* aplicar el método del valor ra-

zonable ▲ *use the fair value method* utilizar el método del valor razonable

fair value model

The fair value model is a recognition method according to which, following initial recognition, an enterprise must measure all its assets at fair value. Any gains or losses arising because of the restatement to fair value must be recognised in the profit for the period in which the gain or loss arises.

modelo del valor razonable

= modelo de valor razonable

▲ *apply the fair value model* aplicar el modelo del valor razonable

⇛ depreciated cost model

fair value principle

= fair value adjustment

The fair value principle implies the write up or write down of assets and liabilities recognised in the financial statements to reflect their actual fair values for the financial year in accordance with the fair value method.

principio de valor razonable

▲ *net gains or losses from the fair value principle* resultados netos procedentes de aplicar el principio de valor razonable ▲ *tax related to the fair value principle* impuestos relacionados con el principio de valor razonable

fair value reserve

= fair value adjustment reserve

Fair value reserves are reserves for changes in the fair value of financial instruments, e.g. gains and losses arising from translation adjustments because of exchange differences. Examples of such financial instruments are hedging instruments and available for sale financial assets.

reserva de valor razonable

= reserva del valor razonable

▲ *a separate fair value reserve* una reserva de valor razonable separada ▲ *a table showing movements in the fair value reserve during the financial year* una tabla que muestra los movimientos en la reserva de valor razonable durante el ejercicio ▲ *adjust the fair value reserve* ajustar la reserva de valor razonable ▲ *include a change directly in equity in a fair value reserve* incluir un cambio directamente en el patrimonio neto en una reserva de valor razonable ▲ *lay down rules governing the use of the fair value reserve* establecer normas que regulan el uso de la reserva de valor razonable ▲ *remove from the fair value reserve* quitar de la reserva de valor razonable ▲ *transfer to the fair value reserve* transferir a reserva de valor razonable

⇛ hedging reserve

fair value-based

When e.g. a method or a measurement is fair-value based, the underlying assumption of that method or measurement is the fair value. The fair-value based accounting method typically applies to the accounting for employee share options where the fair value of the compensation cost is measured at the grant date and recognised over the service period, i.e. the vesting period of the options.

basado en el valor razonable

▲ *fair value-based reporting* el sistema de registro basado en el valor razonable ▲ *the fair value-based method of accounting* el método de contabilidad basado en el valor razonable

⇛ fair value, historical cost, intrinsic value

fall due

= mature

To fall due means to become payable or deliverable at a particular time.

vencer

▲ *fall due after 5 years* vencer después de 5 años

FAR SRS

FAR SRS is the professional institute for the Swedish accountants: authorised public accountants (auktoriserade revisorer), approved public accountants (godkända revisorer) and other highly qualified professionals in the accountancy sector in Sweden.

NOTE FAR SRS was established in 2006, combining the former two associations Föreningen Auktoriserade Revisorer (FAR) and Svenska Revisorsamfundet (SRS).

FAR SRS

= Asociación de Auditores Suecos

▲ *become a member of FAR SRS* llegar a ser miembro del FAR SRS

FAS US

= Financial Accounting Standard US

FAS stands for Financial Accounting Standard. Financial Accounting Standards are accounting standards issued by the US Financial Accounting Standards Board to set disclosure requirements and to establish generally accepted accounting principles for companies registered with the Securities and Exchange Commission when preparing their financial statements.

Norma de Contabilidad Financiera

= FAS

▲ *comply with the provisions of the relevant FAS* cumplir con las disposiciones de la Norma de Contabilidad Financiera relevante ▲ *in accordance with the relevant FAS* de acuerdo con la Norma de Contabilidad Financiera relevante

⇛ accounting standard, SFAS

FASB US

FASB is an abbreviation for the Financial Accounting Standards Board, which is the American independent body that issues generally accepted accounting principles in the form of FASB statements.

FASB

▲ *a FASB Exposure Document* un Documento de Exposición FASB ▲ *FASB's weekly newsletter* una circular semanal del FASB

⇛ SFAS

FASB Interpretation US

= FIN US

FASB Interpretations are issued by the Financial Accounting Standards Board to clarify, explain and elaborate on existing Statements of Financial Accounting Standards to promote application and provide extra guidance for the benefit of users. The Interpretations are part of US Generally Accepted Accounting Principles.

Interpretación FASB

▲ *according to the FASB interpretation* de acuerdo con la interpretación FASB ▲ *rescission of FASB Interpretation No. 34* rescisión de la interpretación FASB nº 34 ▲ *the effective date of the FASB Interpretation* la fecha efectiva de la interpretación FASB

⇛ generally accepted accounting principles

favorable price US

= favourable price UK

A favorable price is a price below a given market price that makes it advantageous to the person who may subscribe for shares of stock at such a price. A company may e.g. issue stock to its stockholders or employees at a favorable price enabling them to sell such shares of stock, typically after a vesting period, with a profit.

precio favorable

= precio ventajoso

▲ *at a favorable price* a un precio favorable

favorable variance US

= favourable variance UK

≠ unfavorable variance US, unfavourable variance UK

A favorable variance is a variance between the budgeted amount of e.g. costs or sales and the actual level to the benefit of the enterprise.

desviación favorable

≠ desviación desfavorable

▲ *a favorable variance of $1.7m* una desviación favorable de 1,7 millones de dólares ▲ *a year-end favorable variance* una desviación favorable a fin de año

favourable price UK

= favorable price US

A favourable price is a price below a given market price that makes it advantageous to the person who may subscribe for shares at such a price. A company may e.g. issue shares to its shareholders or employees at a favourable price enabling them to sell such shares, typically after a vesting period, with a profit.

precio favorable

= precio ventajoso

▲ *at a favourable price* a un precio favorable

favourable variance UK

= favorable variance US

≠ unfavorable variance US, unfavourable variance UK

A favourable variance is a variance between the budgeted amount of e.g. costs or sales and the actual level to the benefit of the enterprise.

desviación favorable

≠ desviación desfavorable

▲ *a favourable variance of £1.7m* una desviación favorable de 1,7 millones de dólares ▲ *a year-end favourable variance* una desviación favorable a fin de año

FCF

= free cash flow

FCF is the abbreviation for free cash flow, which is the amount of cash that remains after deducting the funds a company must commit to continue operating at its planned level; net cash flows from operating activities, minus dividends, minus net capital expenditures. The measure is used for the valuation and risk assessment of enterprises.

flujo de efectivo de libre disposición

= FEL, flujo de efectivo libre

▲ *calculate FCF* calcular el flujo de efectivo de libre disposición ▲ *determine FCF* determinar el flujo de efectivo de libre disposición

FCFE

= free cash flow to equity

FCFE is the abbreviation for free cash flow to equity which is a key figure defined as cash flow before dividend payment and share buybacks, but including e.g. financial income and expenses in contrast to free cash flow to firm.

flujo de efectivo disponible para el accionista

▲ *calculate FCFE* calcular el flujo de efectivo disponible para el accionista ▲ *FCFE calculations* cálculos del flujo de efectivo disponible para el accionista ▲ *generate FCFE of £1200 a year* generar un flujo de efectivo disponible para el accionista de 1.200 libras por año

⇛ free cash flow, free cash flow to firm

FCFF

= free cash flow to firm

FCFF is the abbreviation for free cash flow to firm, a key figure used in discounted cash flow models as a measure of the cash flow left to service the return requirements of the debt and equity of the enterprise. FCFF is defined as cash flow before dividend payment, share buybacks and net financials, but after tax.

flujo de efectivo disponible para la empresa

▲ *calculate FCFF* calcular el flujo de efectivo disponible para la empresa ▲ *determine FCFF* determinar el flujo de efectivo disponible para la empresa ▲ *FCFF calculations* cálculos del flujo de efectivo disponible para la empresa

⇛ FCFE

federal regulator US

A federal regulator is a supervisory body and governmental agency in the United States overseeing compliance with federal laws and regulations within a particular area, such as the Securities and Exchange Commission.

regulador federal

▲ *work with federal regulators* trabajar con los reguladores federales

fee

= remuneration

A fee is a fixed charge for professional services.

honorario

= remuneración, tarifa

▲ *a comparison with current fees charged by other market participants for similar services* una comparación con los honorarios actuales cargados por otros partícipes en el mercado por servicios similares ▲ *a fixed fee* un honorario fijo ▲ *a split fee* un honorario fraccionado ▲ *auditors' fee* honorario de los auditores ▲ *early repayment fee* honorario reembolsado anticipadamente ▲ *fee for the auditors performing the statutory audit* honorario de los auditores que llevan a cabo la auditoría estatutaria ▲ *fees for employees stationed in Denmark* honorarios para empleados ubicados en Dinamarca ▲ *future investment management fees* honorarios por gestión de inversiones futuras ▲ *professional fees* honorarios profesionales ▲ *professional fees arising directly from bringing the asset to its working condition* honorarios profesionales que proceden directamente de poner el activo en condiciones de funcionamiento ▲ *professional fees paid to accountants* honorarios profesionales pagados a los contables ▲ *the overall fee for the financial year for the firm of auditors performing the statutory audit* el honorario completo para el ejercicio para la firma de auditores ▲ *the total amount of fees charged to the audit client* la cantidad total de honorarios cargados al cliente de la auditoría

fee earnings US

Fee earnings are earnings or income resulting from charging fees.

ingresos por honorarios

▲ *net interest and fee earnings* intereses netos e ingresos por honorarios

fee expense

Money paid as fees to external persons or enterprises are referred to as fee expense.

gasto por honorarios

▲ *incur fee expenses* incurrir en gastos por honorarios

fee income

1 Fee income refers to income in the form of amounts charged by a person or enterprise for providing a professional service such as accounting and legal services.

ingreso por honorarios

▲ *fee income in the professions* ingreso por honorarios por actividades profesionales ▲ *finance charge collections and other fee income received in respect of the securitised exposures net of costs and expenses* cobros de cargas financieras y otros ingresos por los honorarios recibidos en relación con los riesgos titulizados netos de costes y gastos

2 Fee income refers to income in the form of amounts charged by financial institutions for providing financial services.

ingreso por comisiones

▲ *net interest and fee income* intereses e ingreso por comisiones netos

⇛ commission income

fellow subsidiary

= sister subsidiary

Fellow subsidiraies are two or more enterprises that are all subsidiaries under the same parent.

filial hermana

▲ *acquisition by the parent of a fellow subsidiary* adquisición por la matriz de una filial hermana ▲ *amounts payable to and receivable from fellow subsidiaries* cantidades a pagar a y a recibir de las filiales hermanas

fictitious

Something that is fictitious does not exist in reality but has been accepted as a convention in specific circumstances.

ficticio

▲ *a fictitious interest rate* un tipo de interés ficticio ▲ *fictitious assets* activos ficticios ▲ *fictitious interest income* ingresos por interés ficticios

FIFO

= first-in, first-out

FIFO is the abbreviation for first-in, first-out, which is a stock valuation method where the cost of stock is calculated on the assumption that stock items purchased first will always be sold first. Therefore, the FIFO method implies that the oldest stock prices are used for measuring cost of sales in the profit and loss account, and the most recent prices are used for measuring the stock value in the balance sheet.

FIFO

= primera entrada-primera salida, primera entrada, primera salida

NOTE Spanish accountants prefer 'FIFO' to the IAS/IFRS term 'primera entrada - primera salida'.

▲ *the FIFO formula* la fórmula FIFO

⇛ LIFO

FIFO formula

→ FIFO method

FIFO method

The FIFO method is a stock valuation method where the cost of stock is calculated on the assumption that stock items purchased first will always be sold first. Therefore, the FIFO method implies that the oldest stock prices are used for measuring cost of sales in the profit and loss account, and the most recent prices are used for measuring the stock value in the balance sheet.

método FIFO

▲ *calculate using the FIFO method* calcular usando el método FIFO ▲ *determine cost by using the FIFO method* determinar el

coste usando el método FIFO ▲ *measure by using the FIFO method* medir utilizando el método FIFO ▲ *use the FIFO method* usar el método FIFO
⇛ LIFO method

figure

A figure symbols a number or an amount stated in monetary terms.

cifra

= resultado

▲ *aggregate current period figures with budgeted figures for the future* cifras del periodo corriente agregadas con las cifras presupuestadas para el futuro ▲ *consolidated figures* cifras consolidadas ▲ *corresponding figures* correspondiente a cifras ▲ *enterprise-wide figures* cifras de toda la empresa ▲ *interim figures* resultados intermedios ▲ *presentation of figures* presentación de resultados ▲ *the balance sheet figures* las cifras del balance ▲ *the difference between the two net assets figures* la diferencia entre las dos cifras de activos netos ▲ *the figures for the year* las cifras del año ▲ *the figures of the intellectual capital report* las cifras del informe de capital intelectual ▲ *the income statement figures* las cifras de la cuenta de resultados ▲ *the level of precision used in the presentation of figures in the financial statements* el nivel de precisión utilizado en la presentación de resultados en los estados financieros

FIN US

= Financial Accounting Standards Board Interpretation No.

FIN is the abbreviation for Financial Accounting Standards Board Interpretation No. and refers to the number added to the interpretations issued by the Financial Accounting Standards Board to clarify, explain and elaborate on existing Statements of Financial Accounting Standards. By 2005, 47 interpretations have been issued.

NOTE The abbreviation FIN followed by the relevant number of the interpretation is used for reference purposes.

Interpretación FASB

▲ *as required by FIN 46* como requiere la Interpretación FASB 46 ▲ *the adoption of FIN 46* la adopción de la Interpretación FASB 46 ▲ *under FIN 44* según la Interpretación FASB 46

final dividend

Final dividend is remaining dividend payable at the end of the financial year. The final dividend constitutes the difference between any interim dividend paid during the year and the total dividend declared at a company's annual general meeting.

dividendo final

▲ *declare final dividend of 10%* declarar un dividendo final del 10% ▲ *entitled to the 2006 final dividend* tenía derecho al dividendo final del 2006 ▲ *proposed final dividend* dividendo final propuesto ▲ *recommend a final dividend of 9.5%* recomendar un dividendo final del 9,5%
⇛ interim dividend

final salary plan

→ defined benefit plan

finance

= fund

To finance is to provide funds, capital or money or to make funds, capital or money available for a particular purpose.

financiar

▲ *continue to finance the investment until maturity* continuar para financiar la inversión hasta su vencimiento ▲ *finance a production* financiar una producción ▲ *finance a purchase* financiar una compra ▲ *finance an acquisition* financiar una adquisición ▲ *finance by raising a mortgage loan* financiar por medio de una hipoteca ▲ *the way the entity financed the purchase of the asset* la forma en la que la entidad financió la compra del activo

finance charge

= finance cost, financial expense
≠ financial income

Finance charges are expenses recognised in the profit and loss account relating to borrowings and investments. The item is mainly constituted by interest payments, but foreign exchange adjustments and capital losses may also be included.

carga financiera

= coste financiero, gasto financiero
≠ ingreso financiero

▲ *allocate the finance charge to periods during the lease term* distribuir la carga financiera en periodos durante el arrendamiento ▲ *an imputed finance charge* una carga financiera imputada ▲ *finance charges in respect of finance leases* cargas financieras por arrendamientos financieros ▲ *net of finance charges* neto de cargas financieras ▲ *the related finance charge* la carga financiera relacionada

finance cost IAS/IFRS
= finance charge, financial expense UK, US
≠ finance income IAS/IFRS

Finance costs are expenses recognised in the income statement relating to borrowings and investments. The item is mainly constituted by interest payments, but foreign currency adjustments and capital losses may also be included.

coste financiero
= gasto financiero
▲ *excluding finance costs* excluyendo costes financieros ▲ *inclusion of finance costs in the purchase price* inclusión de costes financieros en el precio de compra ▲ *measurement of finance costs* medición de costes financieros ▲ *net finance costs* costes financieros netos ▲ *recognise in the income statement as finance costs* reconocer en el estado de ingresos como costes financieros ▲ *recognised finance costs* costes financieros reconocidos ▲ *the interest element of the finance cost* el interés del coste financiero

finance director

The finance director in an enterprise is the top financial officer responsible for dealing with the financial issues, decisions and activities within the enterprise.

director financiero
= director de finanzas
▲ *be appointed finance director* ser nombrado director financiero ▲ *Group Finance Director* Director Financiero del Grupo ▲ *the incoming finance director* el director financiero entrante ▲ *the retiring finance director* el director financiero saliente
⇛ director

finance director's review
= financial review

The finance director's review is a statement in the annual report of an enterprise containing the management's discussion of the capital structure of the company and its treasury policy. The review comments on the actual financial statements and may be presented as part of the management's review or as a separate statement.

informe del director financiero
= informe financiero
▲ *prepare a finance director's review* preparar un informe del director financiero

finance income

1 In accounting for finance leases, finance income is income received by the lessor in the form of lease payments made by the lessee and recognised to reflect the periodic rate of return on the net investment outstanding concerning the finance lease. For operating leases, finance income constitutes the contingent rent paid by the lessee to the lessor and is recognised as incurred.

ingreso por arrendamiento financiero
= ingreso por el arrendamiento financiero
▲ *allocate finance income over the lease term on a systematic and rational basis* distribuir el ingreso por arrendamiento financiero durante el periodo del arrendamiento de forma sistemática y racional ▲ *allocation of finance income by a lessor* distribución por el arrendador del ingreso por arrendamiento financiero ▲ *finance income over the lease term* ingreso por arrendamiento financiero durante el periodo de arrendamiento ▲ *less unearned finance income* menos el ingreso por el arrendamiento financiero no realizado ▲ *produce finance income* producir ingresos por arrendamiento financiero ▲ *recognition of finance income* reconocimiento del ingreso por arrendamiento financiero ▲ *unearned finance income* ingreso por arrendamiento financiero no realizado

2 → financial income

finance lease IAS/IFRS, UK
= capital lease US, finance lease agreement UK, IAS/IFRS
≠ operating lease

A finance lease is a lease under which essentially all risks and rewards related to the ownership of the asset being leased - except for the legal title - are transferred to the lessee. For accounting purposes, the leased asset is treated as if owned by the lessee. The title of the asset may or may not be transferred to the lessee at the end of the lease term.

arrendamiento financiero

= leasing

▲ *a lessee's residual value guarantee embedded in a finance lease* una garantía del valor residual del arrendatario implícita en un arrendamiento financiero ▲ *accounting treatment of finance leases* tratamiento contable de los arrendamientos financieros ▲ *an intangible asset held under a finance lease* un activo intangible mantenido bajo un arrendamiento financiero ▲ *enter into finance leases* contratar arrendamientos financieros ▲ *finance lease payables recognised by a lessee* arrendamiento financiero a pagar reconocido por un arrendatario ▲ *investment property held under a finance lease* inversión en bienes raíces realizada mediante un arrendamiento financiero ▲ *lease out assets under a finance lease* alquilar activos mediante un arrendamiento financiero ▲ *net investment in a finance lease* inversión neta en un arrendamiento financiero ▲ *pre-existing finance leases* arrendamientos financieros preexistentes ▲ *the capitalised remaining lease obligation on the finance lease* la obligación por alquiler vigente capitalizada en el arrendamiento financiero ▲ *the inception of a finance lease* el comienzo de un arrendamiento financiero ▲ *the interest rate implicit in a finance lease* el tipo de interés implícito en un arrendamiento financiero

finance lease agreement IAS/IFRS, UK

= capital lease US, finance lease IAS/IFRS, UK

A finance lease agreement is a lease agreement under which all risks and rewards related to the ownership of the asset being leased are transferred to the lessee. For accounting purposes, the leased asset is treated as if owned by the lessee.

acuerdo de arrendamiento financiero

▲ *at the inception of the financial lease agreement* en el comienzo del acuerdo de arrendamiento financiero ▲ *enter into a financial lease agreement* firmar un acuerdo de arrendamiento financiero

finance lease liability

A finance lease liability is not a financial liability, but an enterprise's obligation to pay future lease payments, i.e. rent. The lease liability must be disclosed in the balance sheet.

obligación por arrendamiento financiero

= pasivo por arrendamiento financiero

▲ *present value of finance lease liabilities* valor actual de las obligaciones por arrendamiento financiero

financial

If something is financial it relates to or involves money or capital.

financiero

▲ *a difficult financial situation* una situación financiera difícil ▲ *designation of financial items as hedged items* designación de las partidas financieras como partidas cubiertas ▲ *financial and operating policies* políticas financieras y operativas ▲ *financial assets* activos financieros ▲ *financial guarantee contracts* contratos de garantía financiera ▲ *financial performance* actuación financiera ▲ *financial solutions* soluciones financieras ▲ *the financial system* el sistema financiero

financial accounting

≠ management accounting

Financial accounting is concerned with the provision of accounting information to owners, investors and other external users who are not involved in the day-to-day running of the business. The accounting information provided for these users is disclosed in the annual report and the financial statements.

contabilidad financiera

▲ *high-quality financial accounting* contabilidad financiera de alta calidad ▲ *the fundamentals of financial accounting* los fun-

damentos de la contabilidad financiera
⇛ accounting

Financial Accounting Standard US
→ Statement of Financial Accounting Standards

financial accounting standard
Financial accounting standards are official accounting rules for financial reporting that must be followed for financial statements to achieve a true and fair view. The standards are issued to set disclosure requirements and establish accepted accounting principles by authoritative accountancy bodies such as the UK Accounting Standards Board, the US Financial Accounting Standards Board and the International Accounting Standards Board.
norma de contabilidad financiera
▲ *according to a financial accounting standard* de acuerdo con una norma de contabilidad financiera ▲ *comply with a financial accounting standard* cumplir con una norma de contabilidad financiera
⇛ Financial Accounting Standard, Financial Reporting Standard, International Accounting Standard

Financial Accounting Standards Board US
= FASB US
The Financial Accounting Standards Board is the American independent body that sets and issues generally accepted accounting principles in the form of FASB statements.
Financial Accounting Standards Board
= FASB

Financial Accounting Standards Board Interpretation US
= FASB Interpretation US
Financial Accounting Standards Board Interpretations are the interpretations issued by the Financial Accounting Standards Board to clarify, explain and elaborate on existing Statements of Financial Accounting Standards. The Interpretations are part of US Generally Accepted Accounting Principles, and by 2005, 47 interpretations have been issued.
Interpretación FASB
▲ *adoption of Financial Accounting Standards Board Interpretation No. 46* adopción de la Interpretación FASB nº 46 ▲ *in accordance with Financial Accounting Standards Board Interpretation No. 32* de acuerdo con la Interpretación FASB nº 32 ▲ *pursuant to Financial Accounting Standards Board Interpretation No. 25* en aplicación de la Interpretación FASB nº 25 ▲ *the provisions of Financial Accounting Standards Board Interpretation No. 39* las disposiciones de la Interpretación FASB nº 39

Financial Accounting Standards Board Interpretation No. US
= FIN
Financial Accounting Standards Board Interpretation No. refers to the number added to the interpretations issued by the Financial Accounting Standards Board to clarify, explain and elaborate on existing Statements of Financial Accounting Standards. By 2005, 47 interpretations have been issued.
NOTE The abbreviation FIN followed by the relevant number of the interpretation is used for reference purposes.
Interpretación FASB No.
▲ *as required by Financial Accounting Standards Board Interpretation No. 46* como exige la Interpretación FASB No. 46 ▲ *the adoption of Financial Accounting Standards Board Interpretation No. 46* la adopción de la Interpretación FASB No. 46 ▲ *under Financial Accounting Standards Board Interpretation No. 44* según la Interpretación FASB No. 44

financial analysis
A financial analysis is the processing of financial data with a view to obtaining a better and more detailed view of the financial position of an enterprise than that directly provided by the financial statements.
análisis financiero
▲ *a good financial analysis of an annual report* un buen análisis financiero de un informe anual ▲ *financial analysis and business evaluation* análisis financiero y evaluación empresarial ▲ *make a financial analysis* realizar un análisis financiero ▲ *strategic*

financial analysis análisis financiero estratégico

financial analyst

A financial analyst is a specialist who studies and assesses the financial performance and value of an enterprise or company using certain prerequisites as e.g. calculated financial ratios. On the basis of this assessment, the financial analyst is able to give investment advice to potential investors.

analista financiero

▲ *general recommendations issued by financial analysts* recomendaciones generales emitidas por los analistas financieros

financial and operating data

= financial highlights

Financial and operating data are key figures presented in annual reports by enterprises showing important highlights such as sales or revenue, operating profit (EBITDA), profit for the period, balance sheet total and equity, often on a comparative basis for the last five years.

resultados financieros y de gestión

▲ *comparable financial and opera ting data* comparar los resultados financieros y de gestión ▲ *restate financial and operating data for previous years in accordance with the changed accounting policies* replantear los datos financieros y de gestión para los años anteriores de acuerdo con los principios contables modificados ▲ *selected financial and operating data* resultados financieros y de gestión seleccionados

financial asset

≠ financial liability

Financial assets include cash and equity instruments in other enterprises as well as rights under a contract to payment of cash, receipt of financial assets and exchange on favourable conditions of financial instruments.

activo financiero

▲ *a financial asset held for trading* un activo financiero mantenido para operar ▲ *a group of financial assets* un grupo de activos financieros ▲ *adjust financial assets on an ongoing basis* ajustar los activos financieros según el principio de empresa en funcionamiento ▲ *available-for-sale financial assets* activos financieros disponibles para la venta ▲ *deliver a financial asset to a third party* traspasar un activo financiero a un tercero ▲ *derecognition of financial assets and liabilities* baja en cuenta de los activos y pasivos financieros ▲ *financial asset at fair value through profit or loss* cambios en la cuenta de resultados por valoración de activos financieros por su valor razonable ▲ *held-to-maturity financial assets* activos financieros mantenidos hasta vencimiento ▲ *impairment of financial assets* deterioro de los activos financieros ▲ *interest rates of financial assets* tipos de interés de los activos financieros ▲ *maturity profile of financial assets* perfil de vencimiento de los activos financieros ▲ *measure a financial asset* valorar un activo financiero ▲ *non-derivative financial assets* activos financieros no derivados ▲ *purchase of financial assets* compra de activos financieros ▲ *receive a financial asset from a third party* recibir un activo financiero de un tercero ▲ *regular way purchases of financial assets* compras regulares de activos financieros ▲ *remove a previously recognised financial asset from the enterprise's balance sheet* quitar un activo financiero previamente reconocido del balance de la empresa ▲ *retain the risks and rewards of ownership of the financial asset* mantener los riesgos y recompensas de la propiedad del activo financiero ▲ *sale of financial assets* venta de activos financieros ▲ *the amortised cost of financial assets* el coste depreciado de los activos financieros ▲ *the carrying amount of a financial asset* el valor contable de un activo financiero ▲ *the fair value of a financial asset* el valor razonable de un activo financiero ▲ *transfer a financial asset* transferir un activo financiero ▲ *transfer of financial assets* transferencia de activos financieros ▲ *transfer the contractual rights to receive the cash flows of the financial asset* transferir los derechos contractuales para re-

cibir los flujos de efectivos de los activos financieros
SOURCE IAS 32, paragraph 11

financial asset at fair value through profit or loss
Financial assets at fair value through profit or loss are financial assets held for trading that are initially recognised at fair value in the income statement, excepting equity investments for which no quoted market value exists or no fair value can be reliably measured.
cambios en la cuenta de resultados por valoración de activos financieros por su valor razonable
= activo financiero a valor razonable con cambios en resultados
▲ *designate an asset as a financial asset at fair value through profit or loss* designar cambios en la cuenta de resultados por valoración de activos financieros por su valor razonable ▲ *measure a financial asset at fair value through profit or loss* medir cambios en la cuenta de resultados por valoración de activos financieros por su valor razonable ▲ *recognise as a financial asset at fair value through profit or loss* reconocer cambios en la cuenta de resultados por valoración de activos financieros por su valor razonable
SOURCE IAS 39, paragraph 9
⇛ financial asset, financial liability at fair value through profit or loss, held-for-trading financial asset

financial assumption
Financial assumptions are estimates of financial variables used to evaluate future benefits, typically used for the valuation of pension plans. Such variables typically include the inflation rate, the rate of increase in salaries, and the expected rate of return on assets. Also, financial assumptions underlie financial planning and funding strategies where appropriate factors are market conditions, bond yields, expected return on equities and other financial data as well as analyses of financial statements.
supuesto financiero
▲ *determine financial assumptions in nominal terms* fijar supuestos financieros en términos nominales ▲ *financial assumptions based on market expectations* supuestos financieros basados en expectativas de mercado
⇛ actuarial assumption, assumption

financial audit
A financial audit constitutes the audit procedures that form the basis of the auditor's independent assessment of the financial annual report. The auditor will assess i.a. whether the annual report is without material misstatement and errors by evaluating the business procedures and internal controls relevant to the financial reporting.
auditoría financiera
▲ *carry out a financial audit* llevar a cabo una auditoría financiera ▲ *planning of the financial audit* planificación de la auditoría financiera ▲ *the positive outcome of the financial audit* el resultado positivo de la auditoría financiera

financial bottom line
The financial bottom line refers to the last line of the profit and loss account and shows the performance of an enterprise for the accounting period, i.e. the profit or loss for the period. Some enterprises also show bottom lines with regard to e.g. environmental, knowledge and social reporting.
última línea para resultados financieros
= última línea para los resultados financieros
▲ *a positive financial bottom line* una última línea para resultados financieros positivos ▲ *the impact on the financial bottom line* el impacto en la última línea para resultados financieros
⇛ environmental bottom line, social bottom line

financial budget
A financial budget refers to the part of the total budget system of an enterprise that includes the capital budget, the cash budget and the budgeted balance sheet.
presupuesto financiero
▲ *financial budget planning* planificación del presupuesto fi-

nanciero ▲ *prepare a financial budget* preparar un presupuesto financiero ▲ *the proposed financial budget for 2007* el presupuesto financiero propuesto para 2007
⇛ capital budget, cash budget, master budget, operating budget

financial commitment
A financial commitment is a contractual obligation to surrender cash or cash equivalents, or other assets, to another enterprise or to exchange financial assets or liabilities with another enterprise on potentially unfavourable terms.
compromiso financiero
▲ *a legally enforceable financial commitment* un compromiso financiero legalmente exigible ▲ *the ability of the enterprise to meet its financial commitments* la capacidad de la empresa para cumplir sus compromisos financieros ▲ *the availability of sufficient funds to meet financial commitments as they fall due* la disponibilidad de fondos suficientes para cumplir los compromisos financieros cuando venzan

financial condition
Financial condition refers to the value and proportions of an enterprise's assets and liabilities and its amount of equity at a specific point of time.
NOTE Statement of financial condition is another term for balance sheet.
situación financiera
▲ *assess the financial condition of the defined benefit plan* examinar la situación financiera del plan de prestación definida ▲ *understand an enterprise's financial condition and liquidity* entender una situación financiera y de liquidez de una empresa

financial contract
Financial contracts are financial market agreements under which payment or delivery must be effected at a defined time or within a defined time period in future. The underlying assets of such contracts may be physical, such as commodities, currencies, securities etc., or synthetic, such as share indices or interest rates. Types of financial contracts include swaps, options and futures, forward rate agreements and forward exchange contracts.
contrato financiero
▲ *a capital loss on a financial contract* una pérdida de capital en un contrato financiero ▲ *a counterparty to financial contracts* una contraparte en los contratos financieros ▲ *a financial contract based on shares* un contrato financiero basado en acciones ▲ *conclude a financial contract* concluir un contrato financiero ▲ *financial contracts concluded* contratos financieros concluidos

financial control
= corporate financial management, financial management
Financial control is the actions of the management of an organisation taken to ensure that the costs incurred and revenue generated are at acceptable levels.
control financiero
▲ *separate financial control from internal auditing* separar el control financiero de la auditoría interna

financial expense
= finance charge, finance cost
≠ financial income
Financial expenses are expenses recognised in the profit and loss account relating to borrowings and investments. The item is mainly constituted by interest payments, but foreign exchange adjustments and capital losses may also be included.
gasto financiero
= carga financiera, coste financiero
≠ ingreso financiero
▲ *excluding financial expenses and tax* excluyendo gastos financieros e impuestos ▲ *financial expenses arising from group enterprises* gastos financieros procedentes de las empresas del grupo ▲ *other financial expenses* otros gastos financieros

financial gearing
= debt-equity ratio
Financial gearing shows the relationship between an enterprise's net interest-bearing debt, i.e. loan capital, and equity. If an enterprise is highly geared, its loan capital is larger than its equity.
ratio de endeudamiento
▲ *high financial gearing* ratio de endeudamiento alto ▲ *low fi-*

nancial gearing ratio de endeudamiento bajo

financial highlight

= key figure

Financial highlights are financial statement figures of particular interest and importance typically appearing as part of management's review in financial reports.

resumen financiero

▲ *semiannual financial highlight* resumen financiero semestral

⇛ financial ratio

financial income

Financial income refers to income in the form of dividends, interest accrued on funds invested and interest paid by borrowers as well as other income earned in relation to loans and guarantees, e.g. in the form of fees. Financial income is recognised in the profit and loss account as a separate item or as part of the item net financials.

ingreso financiero

▲ *financial income and expenses* ingresos y gastos financieros ▲ *financial income from group enterprises* ingreso financiero de las empresas del grupo ▲ *other financial income* otro ingreso financiero

financial income or expense item

Financial income or expense items are expense and income attributable to the entreprise's funding of its operations, e.g. interest expenses and interest income.

partida de resultado financiero

▲ *record an amount as a finance income or expense item* anotar una cantidad como una partida de resultado financiero

financial information

= financial disclosure

Financial information contains news, analyses, charts, key figures and ratios, or data concerning company financial statements and company performance.

información financiera

▲ *announce profit and selected other financial information* anunciar beneficio y otra información financiera seleccionada ▲ *condensed interim financial information* información financiera intermedia resumida ▲ *disclose financial information by segment voluntarily* publicación voluntaria de la información financiera por segmento ▲ *give someone access to current financial information* darle a alguien acceso a la información financiera actual ▲ *reporting financial information by segment* anotación de la información financiera por segmento ▲ *the assessment of trends in financial information for predictive purposes* la evaluación de las tendencias en la información financiera para predecir el futuro ▲ *translation of financial information into a foreign currency* conversión de la información financiera a una divisa

financial institution

A financial institution is an organisation whose primary activity is to channel funds in the financial markets and provide financial transactions and services, typically as an intermediary, such as taking deposits, lending money, investing and giving financial advice. Financial institutions may be deposit-taking or non-deposit-taking; examples are commercial banks, mortgage banks, pension funds and insurance companies.

institución financiera

▲ *banks and similar financial institutions* bancos e instituciones financieras similares ▲ *cash advances and loans made by financial institutions* anticipos y préstamos hechos por instituciones financieras ▲ *interest and similar income and interest expense and similar charges for a financial institution* interés e ingreso similar y gasto por interés y cargas similares para una institución financiera ▲ *operating cash flows for financial institutions* flujo de efectivo de explotación de instituciones financieras ▲ *the placement of deposits with and withdrawal of deposits from financial institutions* el lugar de los depósitos en y la retirada de depósitos de una institución financiera

financial instrument

A financial instrument is a marketable, legally enforceable contract involving a financial obligation and transferring monetary value; it therefore creates a financial asset in one entity as well as a financial liability in another entity. A typical example is a share or a bond.

instrumento financiero

▲ *a derivative that is attached to a financial instrument* un derivado que se une a un instrumento financiero ▲ *a fixed rate financial instrument* un instrumento financiero de interés fijo ▲ *a portfolio of identified financial instruments that are managed together* una cartera de instrumentos financieros identificados que se gestiona conjuntamente ▲ *accepted economic methodologies for pricing financial instruments* metodologías económicas aceptadas para calcular los precios de los instrumentos financieros ▲ *an agreement concerning a financial instrument* un acuerdo concerniente a un instrumento financiero ▲ *compound financial instruments* instrumentos financieros compuestos ▲ *convert a financial instrument* convertir un instrumento financiero ▲ *deliver a financial instrument* enviar un instrumento financiero ▲ *estimated future cash payments or receipts through the expected life of the financial instrument* pagos en efectivo futuros estimados o recibos durante la vida esperada de los instrumentos financieros ▲ *exchange a financial instrument* cambiar un instrumento financiero ▲ *exchange financial instruments* intercambiar instrumentos financieros ▲ *financial instrument prices* precios de los instrumentos financieros ▲ *financial instruments issued to members of cooperatives* instrumentos financieros emitidos para los miembros de las cooperativas ▲ *financial instruments that give the holder the right to purchase ordinary shares* instrumentos financieros que otorgan al poseedor el derecho a comprar acciones ordinarias ▲ *fixed interest financial instruments* instrumentos financieros con interés fijo ▲ *future cash flows relating to financial instruments* flujos de efectivo futuros relacionados con instrumentos financieros ▲ *future changes in price of the financial instrument* cargas futuras en el precio del instrumento financiero ▲ *maturities of financial instruments* vencimientos de los instrumentos financieros ▲ *non-insurance financial instruments* instrumentos financieros no asegurados ▲ *primary financial instruments* instrumentos financieros primarios ▲ *receive a financial instrument* recibir un instrumento financiero ▲ *similar financial instruments* instrumentos financieros similares ▲ *synthetic financial instruments* instrumentos financieros sintéticos ▲ *the contractual terms of the financial instrument* los términos contractuales del instrumento financiero ▲ *the financial instrument's original effective interest rate* el tipo de interés efectivo original del instrumento financiero ▲ *the foreign currency component of the financial instruments* el componente en divisas de los instrumentos financieros ▲ *the holder of a financial instrument* el tenedor de un instrumento financiero ▲ *the risk-return factors inherent in the financial instrument* los factores de riesgo-rentabilidad inherentes a los instrumentos financieros ▲ *the total interest rate exposure of a hedged financial instrument* la exposición al tipo de interés total de un instrumento financiero cubierto ▲ *the value of a financial instrument* el valor de un instrumento financiero ▲ *trade a financial instrument* intercambiar un instrumento financiero

SOURCE IAS 32, paragraph 11

⇛ security

financial investment

Financial investments constitute acquisition of financial assets such as bonds, equities and other securities with a view to getting a return in the form of income on a current basis, i.e. dividend or interest, or a capital gain on disposal.

inversión financiera

▲ *make a financial investment* hacer una inversión financiera

⇛ capital investment

financial lease

→ finance lease

financial leverage US

Financial leverage shows the relationship between an enterprise's net interest-bearing debt, i.e. loan capital, and equity. If an enterprise is highly leveraged, its loan capital is larger than its equity.

apalancamiento financiero

= leverage financiero

▲ *high financial leverage* apalancamiento financiero alto ▲ *low financial leverage* apalancamiento financiero bajo ▲ *reduce financial leverage* reducir el apalancamiento financiero ▲ *substantial financial leverage* apalancamiento financiero importante ▲ *the impact of financial leverage* el impacto del apalancamiento financiero

financial liability IAS/IFRS

≠ financial asset

Financial liabilities are contractual obligations to deliver cash or other financial assets to another enterprise, or to exchange financial assets or liabilities with another enterprise under potentially adverse terms.

pasivo financiero

▲ *a financial liability held for trading* un pasivo financiero mantenido para operar ▲ *a gain or loss on a financial asset or financial liability* una ganancia o pérdida en un activo o pasivo financiero ▲ *a legally enforceable financial liability* un pasivo financiero exigible legalmente ▲ *a non-derivative financial liability* un pasivo financiero no derivado ▲ *assume a new financial liability* asumir un pasivo financiero nuevo ▲ *derecognition of financial assets and financial liabilities* eliminación de los activos y pasivos financieros ▲ *designate as financial liabilities at fair value through profit or loss* designar como pasivos financieros a valor razonable en la cuenta de resultados ▲ *expected surrender patterns for financial liabilities* modelos de rendición esperados para los pasivos financieros ▲ *financial liabilities issued by insurers* pasivos financieros emitidos por las aseguradoras ▲ *financial liabilities that are designated as hedged items* pasivos financieros que se designan como partidas cubiertas ▲ *financial liabilities that provide financing on a long-term basis* pasivos financieros que ofrecen financiación a largo plazo ▲ *floating rate financial liabilities* pasivos financieros a interés variable ▲ *initial measurement of financial liabilities* mediciones iniciales de los pasivos financieros ▲ *recognise any expense incurred on the financial liability* reconocer cualquier gasto incurrido en el pasivo financiero ▲ *servicing costs for a financial liability* costes de servicio por un pasivo financiero ▲ *the costs of arranging and issuing financial liabilities* los costes de formalización y emisión de los instrumentos financieros ▲ *the fair value of a financial liability with a demand feature* el valor razonable de un pasivo financiero con un rasgo de demanda ▲ *the incurrence of a financial liability* la incurrencia de un pasivo financiero ▲ *the maturity dates of financial liabilities* las fechas de vencimiento de los pasivos financieros

financial liability at fair value through profit or loss

Financial liabilities at fair value through profit or loss are financial liabilities held for trading that are initially recognised at fair value in the income statement, excepting equity investments for which no quoted market value exists or no fair value can be reliably measured.

cambios en la cuenta de resultados por valoración de pasivos financieros por su valor razonable

= pasivo financiero a valor razonable con cambios en resultados

▲ *measure a financial liability at fair value through profit or loss* medir cambios en la cuenta de resultados por valoración de pasivos financieros por su valor razonable

SOURCE IAS 39, paragraph 9

⇛ financial asset at fair value through profit or loss

financial management

= corporate financial management, financial control

Financial management is the management of acquisitions and the use of long- and short-term capital by a business.

gestión financiera

▲ *risk and financial management* gestión financiera y del riesgo

financial manager

1 A financial manager is a key executive who oversees the day-to-

day finances and financial operations of an enterprise. Depending on the size of enterprise, a financial manager has various responsibilities which typically include strategic financial planning, preparation of financial information including financial statements, monitoring of budgetary control and cash flows as well as supervision of staff in one or more divisions.

director financiero

▲ *be appointed financial manager* ser designado director financiero ▲ *the incoming financial manager* el director financiero entrante ▲ *the retiring financial manager* el director financiero saliente

⇛ chief financial officer, financial director

2 A financial manager is a financial expert, typically with professional background in corporate finance or accountancy, who is responsible for giving financial advice to the enterprise or clients he works for. Some financial managers are financial analysts.

director financiero

▲ *appoint a new financial manager* nombrar un nuevo director financiero ▲ *the incoming financial manager* el director financiero entrante ▲ *the retiring financial manager* el director financiero saliente

⇛ financial analyst

financial performance UK, US

The financial performance of an enterprise shows the capacity of an enterprise to generate cash flows and a return on the resources it controls, i.e. the profitability of the enterprise. Performance measures profit or income for the accounting period, EBITDA, operating margin (EBIT margin) and EPS.

rendimiento financiero

▲ *the combined entity's financial performance* el rendimiento financiero de la entidad combinada ▲ *the financial position and financial performance of an entity* la posición y rendimiento financieros de una entidad ▲ *the main features of the entity's financial performance* los rasgos principales del rendimiento financiero de la entidad

⇛ EBITDA, net income, net profit, operating margin

financial position

The financial position of an enterprise shows its economic resources through the assets, liabilities and equity as reported in the balance sheet, thereby encompassing the financial structure, liquidity and solvency as well as the enterprise's capacity to manage risk and changes in its operating environment.

posición financiera

▲ *changes in the financial position of an enterprise* cambios en la posición financiera de una empresa ▲ *deterioration in operating results and financial position after the balance sheet date* deterioro en los resultados de explotación y en la posición financiera después de la fecha del balance ▲ *effect on the financial position of the enterprise* efecto en la posición financiera de la empresa ▲ *events that materially affect the financial position of the enterprise* sucesos que afectan materialmente la posición financiera de la empresa ▲ *measurement of the financial position* valoración de la posición financiera ▲ *represent faithfully the financial position and financial performance of the entity* representar fielmente la posición financiera y la actuación financiera de la entidad

SOURCE IFRS Framework, F 47, Statement of Principles for Financial Reporting, 1.15

financial profit

Financial profit describes a situation in which an enterprise has purposely planned that a sum of money is in excess after all the expenses have been covered. This is in contrast to profit of a more intangible nature or to the surplus of nonprofit organisations.

beneficio financiero

= ganancia financiera

▲ *generate sufficient financial profit* generar suficiente beneficio financiero

financial ratio

Financial ratios express a proportional relationship between two figures, usually from an enterprise's financial statements and provide an indication of the financial performance and position of an enterprise. Ratios may be expressed as percentages or as multiples. Ratios can be grouped as profitability, liquidity, activity, leverage, and market value ratios.

ratio financiero

▲ *calculate financial ratios* calcular los ratios financieros ▲ *distort financial ratios* falsear los ratios financieros ▲ *evolution of selected key financial ratios* evolución de los ratios financieros claves seleccionados

financial report

A financial report is the financial statement of an enterprise disclosing financial information such for a defined period, i.e. an annual report, a half year report or a quarterly report.

informe financiero

▲ *a single financial report* un informe financiero único ▲ *a special purpose financial report* un informe financiero con un fin específico ▲ *an annual financial report* un informe financiero anual ▲ *an interim financial report* un informe financiero provisional ▲ *prepare a financial report* preparar un informe financiero

⇛ interim financial report, interim report

financial reporting

= presentation of financial statements

≠ management accounting

Financial reporting is the preparation of financial reports and financial statements under accounting rules and regulations in force with a view to present financial disclosures about an enterprise to its external stakeholders.

presentación de los estados financieros

= presentación de estados financieros

▲ *a principles-based approach to financial reporting* un enfoque a la presentación de los estados financieros basado en principios ▲ *a rules-based approach to financial reporting* un enfoque a la presentación de los estados financieros basado en reglas ▲ *annual financial reporting* presentación anual de los estados financieros ▲ *assessment for the purpose of financial reporting* valorar el objetivo de la presentación de los estados financieros ▲ *at a subsequent financial reporting date* en una fecha posterior a la presentación de los estados financieros ▲ *be subject to the financial reporting requirements of IFRSs* estar sujetos a los requisitos de presentación de los estados financieros según NIIFs ▲ *ensure proper financial reporting* asegurar la presentación de los estados financieros adecuados ▲ *for financial reporting purposes* para la presentación de los estados financieros ▲ *high-quality financial reporting* la presentación de los estados financieros de alta calidad ▲ *interim financial reporting* presentación provisional de los estados financieros

Financial Reporting Council UK

= FRC UK

The Financial Reporting Council (FRC) was set up by the UK Government in 1990 as the supervisory body for the setting of accounting standards. The FRC appoints the members of and provides guidance to the Accounting Standards Board that is concerned with the accounting standards setting in the UK.

Consejo de Información Financiera

▲ *the Board of the Financial Reporting Council* la Dirección del Consejo de Información Financiera

⇛ Accounting Standards Board, Financial Reporting Standard

Financial Reporting Exposure Draft UK

= FRED

Financial Reporting Exposure Drafts (FREDs) are discussion documents preceding the issue of Financial Reporting Standards (FRSs) developed and issued by the Accounting Standards Board in the UK. The intention of issuing an exposure draft is to attract comments from accountants, investment analysts, financial institutions and other experts.

Borrador para la Discusión sobre Información Financiera

▲ *issue a Financial Reporting Exposure Draft* emitir un Borrador para la Discusión sobre Información Financiera ▲ *issue a new Financial Reporting Exposure Draft (FRED) for comment* emitir un nuevo Borrador para la Discusión sobre Información Financiera para su discusión

⇛ Accounting Standards Board, Financial Reporting Standard

financial reporting period

The financial reporting period is the period covered by a financial report. The period may be longer or shorter than 12 months.

periodo cubierto por los estados financieros

▲ *a financial reporting period shorter than a full financial year* un periodo cubierto por los estados financieros inferior a un año completo ▲ *acquisitions occurring after the beginning of the financial reporting period* adquisiciones que ocurren después del periodo cubierto por los estados financieros ▲ *during the current financial reporting period* durante el periodo actual cubierto por los estados financieros ▲ *publicly announced after the end of the enterprise's financial reporting period* anunciado públicamente después del final del periodo cubierto por los estados financieros ▲ *throughout the financial reporting period* a lo largo de todo el periodo cubierto por los estados financieros

Financial Reporting Review Panel UK

= FRRP UK

The Financial Reporting Review Panel (FRRP) is a body referring to the Financial Reporting Council and set up in the UK in 1991. The FRRP investigates the annual accounts of large companies if they fail to comply with the requirements of the Companies Act, e.g. if they do not give a true and fair view. The FRRP can refer issues to court.

Panel de Análisis de Información Financiera

▲ *the Financial Reporting Review Panel's current objectives* los objetivos actuales del Panel de Análisis de Información Financiera

⇛ Companies Act, Financial Reporting Council, true and fair view

financial reporting standard

A financial reporting standard is an accounting standard containing provisions specifying how a particular transaction or event must or should be treated, disclosed and presented in the financial statements of an enterprise.

norma de información financiera

▲ *comply with a financial reporting standard* cumplir con una norma de información financiera

⇛ accounting standard, financial accounting standard, International Financial Reporting Standard

Financial Reporting Standard UK

= FRS UK

Financial Reporting Standards (FRSs) are accounting standards issued by the UK Accounting Standards Board to set disclosure requirements and to establish generally accepted accounting principles for enterprises in the preparation of their financial reporting to ensure that their financial statements give a true and fair view. The FRSs have been issued since 1990 to supplement or replace the Statements of Standard Accounting Practice (SSAPs).

Norma de Información Financiera

▲ *comply with the provisions of a Financial Reporting Standard* cumplir con las estipulaciones de una Norma de Información Financiera ▲ *issue a Financial Reporting Standard* emitir una Norma de Información Financiera ▲ *the requirements contained in the Financial Reporting Standard concerned* los requisitos contenidos en la Norma de Información Financiera

⇛ Statement of Standard Accounting Practice

financial resources IAS/IFRS

Financial resources are those financial funds that are available to an enterprise for carrying out its operations.

recursos financieros

▲ *safeguarding of the company's financial resources* salvaguardando los recursos financieros de la empresa ▲ *secure the financial resources* asegurar los recursos financieros ▲ *strengthen the financial resources* fortalecer los recursos financieros ▲ *the propriety of the company's financial resources* la propiedad de los recursos financieros de la empresa

financial results

= net results, reported earnings

Financial results constitute the revenue, profits, gains, expenses and losses recognised by a reporting enterprise during an accounting period.

resultados financieros

▲ *benchmarking of the financial results against those of the competitors* evaluación comparativa de los resultados financieros con los de los competidores

financial review UK

= finance director's review UK

The financial review is a statement in the annual report of an enterprise containing the management's discussion of the capital structure of the company and its treasury policy. The review comments on the actual financial statements and may be presented as part of the management's review or as a separate statement.

revisión financiera

= debate y análisis de la gestión financiera

▲ *a financial review by management* una revisión financiera realizada por la dirección ▲ *a separate financial review* un debate y análisis de la gestión financiera separada ▲ *provide information in the financial review* ofrecer información en el debate y análisis de la gestión financiera

⇛ financial and operating review, operating review

financial risk

Financial risk is 1) the risk involved in the use of financial instruments and comprises foreign exchange risk, interest rate risk and credit risk, and 2) the risk involved in the way the enterprise has been financed, i.e. how the capital structure may impact earnings or financial expenses.

riesgo financiero

▲ *a contract that exposes the issuer to financial risk* un contrato que expone al emisor al riesgo financiero ▲ *create financial risk* crear riesgo financiero ▲ *derivatives that expose one party to financial risk* derivados que exponen a una parte al riesgo financiero ▲ *evaluate financial risks* evaluar los riesgos financieros ▲ *financial risks assumed* riesgos financieros asumidos ▲ *hedge financial risks* cubrir los riesgos financieros ▲ *identify financial risks* identificar los riesgos financieros ▲ *minimise exposures to financial risks* minimizar las exposiciones a los riesgos financieros ▲ *the entity's financial risk management objectives and policies* los objetivos y políticas de gestión del riesgo financiero de la entidad ▲ *the financial risks associated with a financial instrument* los riesgos financieros asociados con un instrumento financiero ▲ *transfer of financial risks* transferencia de riesgos financieros

SOURCE IFRS 4, Appendix A

financial service

Generally, financial services refer to all types of banking, investment and insurance services provided by financial institutions such as banks, insurance companies, investment companies, etc.

servicio financiero

▲ *a single financial services market* un mercado único de servicios financieros ▲ *an e-commerce policy for financial services* una política de e-comercio para los servicios financieros ▲ *financial services policies* políticas de los servicios financieros ▲ *income from financial service* ingresos del servicio financiero ▲ *provide financial services* ofrecer servicios financieros ▲ *retail financial services* servicios financieros minoristas ▲ *transaction costs of financial services* costes de transacción de los servicios financieros

Financial Services Act UK

= FSA UK

The Financial Services Act is a UK Act of Parliament enacted 1986 that came into force in 1988 to regulate investment business in the UK and set up the Securities and Investment Board. The SIB was reorganised and renamed the Financial

Services Authority following the adoption in 2000 of the Financial Services and Markets Act that superseded the Financial Services Act.

Financial Services Act

= Ley de Servicios Financieros

▲ *according to the Financial Services Act* de acuerdo con la Financial Services Act ▲ *the provisions of the Financial services Act* las disposiciones de la Financial Services Act

⇛ Financial Services and Markets Act

Financial Services and Markets Act UK

= FSMA

The Financial Services and Markets Act was adopted in 2000 and came into force in 2001 as the sucessor to the Financial Services Act. The new act substituted the Securities and Investment Board with a new regulatory body for the entire UK financial sector, the Financial Services Authority, and introduced a new Code of Market Conduct for the financial markets.

Financial Services and Markets Act

= Ley de Servicios Financieros y de Mercados

▲ *according to the Financial Services and Markets Act* de acuerdo con la Financial Services and Markets Act ▲ *section 23 of the Financial Services and Markets Act* la sección 23 de la Financial Services and Markets Act ▲ *the provisions of the Financial Services and Markets Act* las disposiciones de la Financial Services and Markets Act

⇛ Financial Services Act, Financial Services Authority

Financial Services Authority UK

= FSA UK

The Financial Services Authority (FSA) was introduced by the Financial Services and Markets Act in 2000 as a new regulatory body for the entire UK financial sector to substitute the former Securities and Investment Board and some of the self-regulatory organisations regulating investment activities. The supervision and authority by the Bank of England and the Treasury over the banking and insurance sectors were surrendered to the FSA, as was the listing authority of the London Stock Exchange.

Financial Services Authority

NOTE The Spanish regulatory body is the Banco de España.

▲ *authorised by the Financial Services Authority* autorizados por la Financial Services Authority ▲ *the chairman of the Financial Services Authority's board* el presidente del consejo de la Financial Services Authority ▲ *the objectives of the Financial Services Authority* los objetivos de la Financial Services Authority

financial statement

A financial statement is a report containing financial data about an enterprise such as a profit and loss account, a balance sheet, a statement of changes in equity or a cash flow statement.

estado financiero

▲ *a detailed financial statement* un estado financiero detallado

▲ *prepare a financial statement* preparar un estado financiero

⇛ financial statements

financial statement assertion

The financial statement assertions are explicit or other assertive statements by management embodied in the financial statements.

opinión sobre el estado financiero

▲ *all relevant financial statement assertions* todas las opiniones relevantes sobre el estado financiero ▲ *detect a material error in financial statement assertions* detectar un error material en las opiniones sobre el estado financiero ▲ *specific financial statement assertions* opiniones específicas sobre el estado financiero

financial statement user

= user of financial statements

A financial statement user is a person or an enterprise that uses financial statements prepared by enterprises.

usuario de los estados financieros

▲ *enhance financial statement users' understanding of the significance of financial instruments to an entity's financial position, performance and cash flows* mejorar el entendimiento de los usuarios de los estados financieros relativo al significado de los instrumentos financieros para la posición financiera de la empresa, su resultado y sus flujos de efectivo ▲ *useful to financial statement users* útil para los usuarios de los estados financieros

financial statements

1 = accounts UK

A complete set of financial statements includes the balance sheet, the income statement, a statement showing changes in equity, a cash flow statement, the accounting policies and explanatory notes.

cuentas anuales

▲ *prepare financial statements* preparar las cuentas anuales

2 = annual accounts UK

The financial statements constitute an enterprise's financial information for the financial year and include the balance sheet, the income statement, a statement showing changes in equity, a cash flow statement, the accounting policies and explanatory notes.

cuentas anuales

= conjunto completo de estados financieros, estados financieros

▲ *a complete set of financial statements* un conjunto completo de estados financieros ▲ *approval of the financial statements* aprobación de las cuentas anuales ▲ *audit the financial statements* auditar las cuentas anuales ▲ *consolidated financial statements* cuentas anuales consolidadas ▲ *consolidated financial statements of a group controlled by the enterprise* cuentas anuales consolidadas de un grupo controlado por la empresa ▲ *financial statements for previous periods* cuentas anuales de los periodos anteriores ▲ *financial statements under IFRSs* cuentas anuales según NIIFs ▲ *include a cash flow statement in the financial statements* incluir un estado de efectivo en las cuentas anuales ▲ *net profit or loss according to the last financial statements* resultado neto de acuerdo con las últimas cuentas anuales ▲ *preparation of financial statements* preparación de las cuentas anuales ▲ *prepare financial statements in accordance with the Danish Financial Statements Act* preparar las cuentas anuales de acuerdo con la Ley danesa de Estados Financieros ▲ *prepare financial statements in accordance with the International Financial Reporting Standards* preparar las cuentas anuales conforme a las Normas Internacionales de Información Financiera ▲ *prepare financial statements in conformity with the International Accounting Standards* preparar las cuentas anuales conforme a las Normas Internacionales de Información Financiera ▲ *presentation of financial statements* presentación de las cuentas anuales ▲ *publication of the financial statements* publicación de las cuentas anuales ▲ *reading of the financial statements* lectura de las cuentas anuales ▲ *result in more relevant information for the users of the financial statements* dar como resultado información más relevante para los usuarios de las cuentas anuales ▲ *submission of the financial statements* rendición de las cuentas anuales ▲ *the component parts of the financial statements* los componentes de las cuentas anuales ▲ *the financial statements presented by the management* las cuentas anuales presentadas por la dirección ▲ *the first IFRS financial statements* las primeras cuentas anuales NIIFs ▲ *the latest financial statements* las últimas cuentas anuales ▲ *the most recent previous financial statements* las cuentas anuales anteriores más recientes ▲ *the next financial statements* las próximas cuentas anuales

⇛ financial statement

financial statements audit US, IAS/IFRS

A financial statements audit is the audit of financial statements carried out by the auditor.

auditoría de las cuentas anuales

= auditoría de los estados financieros, auditoría del conjunto completo de los estados financieros

NOTE Spanish accountants prefer 'auditoría de las cuentas

anuales' to the IAS/IFRS terms 'auditoría del conjunto completo de los estados financieros' and 'auditoría de los estados financieros'.

▲ *conduct a financial statements audit* dirigir una auditoría de las cuentas anuales ▲ *plan and perform the financial statements audit* planificar y llevar a cabo la auditoría de las cuentas anuales

financial statements based on activity-based costing

Financial statements based on activity-based costing use a costing system that identifies the various activities performed in the enterprise and uses multiple cost drivers to assign overhead costs or indirect costs to products.

cuentas anuales basadas en el sistema de coste basado en la actividad

▲ *prepare financial statements based on activity-based costing* preparar las cuentas anuales basadas en el sistema de coste basado en la actividad

financial statements in respect of dissolution

Financial statements in respect of dissolution are the final statements prepared in connection with a solvent liquidation of an enterprise.

cuentas anuales de la disolución

▲ *prepare financial statements in respect of dissolution* preparar las cuentas anuales de la disolución

financial year IAS/IFRS, UK

= accounting year UK, fiscal year US

A financial year is the accounting period for twelve consecutive months, i.e. the reporting period for which an enterprise prepares its financial statements. Typically, a financial year follows the calendar year, but may also run in an alternative twelve-month period, e.g. from April 1 to March 31.

ejercicio

= año, año financiero, ejercicio económico

▲ *after the end of the financial year* después del cierre del ejercicio ▲ *at the end of the financial year* a final del ejercicio ▲ *beyond the current financial year* más allá del ejercicio actual ▲ *change the financial year* cambiar el ejercicio ▲ *during the financial year* durante el ejercicio ▲ *in the course of the financial year* en el curso del ejercicio ▲ *in two consecutive financial years* en dos ejercicios consecutivos ▲ *income concerning the financial year* ingresos concernientes al ejercicio ▲ *the financial year in question* el ejercicio en cuestión ▲ *the previous financial year* el ejercicio anterior

⇛ accounting period

financials, net

= net financials

Financials, net are interest and other financial income/expenses, net.

financieros, neto

▲ *total financials, net* total financieros, neto

⇛ other interest receivable and similar income

financing

1 = funding

Financing is providing funds, capital or money for capital expenditure or operating expenses in the form of loans, subsidies, equity financing, retained profits or funds generated from operations in the company.

financiación

▲ *any liabilities incurred in financing the share of the assets* cualesquiera pasivos incurridos en la financiación de la participación de los activos ▲ *expenses related to financing the venturer's interest in the assets* gastos relacionados con la financiación de intereses en los activos de la sociedad de capital riesgo

2 = financial base

Financing is the money provided for an investment and the arrangements for providing it.

financiación

▲ *poor financing* financiación pobre ▲ *strong financing* financiación fuerte

financing activity

Financing activities are transactions that include the distribution, acquisition, movement and management of cash, affecting the amount and composition of equity and debt in an enterprise.

actividad de financiación

▲ *cash flow from financing activities* flujo de efectivo procedente de las actividades de financiación ▲ *cash inflows or*

outflows from financing activities entradas o salidas de efectivo procedentes de las actividades de financiación ▲ *the currency in which funds from financing activities are generated* la moneda en la que se generan los fondos de las actividades de financiación ▲ *the net cash flows attributable to the financing activities of discontinued operations* los flujos de efectivo netos atribuibles a las actividades de financiación de las operaciones interrumpidas
SOURCE IAS 7, paragraph 6
⇛ cash flow from financing activities

financing company

A financing company is a company whose sole business activity is the provision of financial funds to customers.

compañía financiera

▲ *mitigate the risks normally associated with a financing company* mitigar los riesgos normalmente asociados a una compañía financiera

financing cost

= finance cost IAS/IFRS, financial expense UK, US

Financing costs are expenses recognised in the profit and loss account which are attributable to the investments and borrowings of an enterprise for operating and financing activities. Finance costs typically constitute interest paid, but foreign exchange adjustments and capital losses may also be included.

coste financiero

▲ *financing costs attributed to a discontinued operation* costes financieros atribuidos a una operación interrumpida ▲ *present in profit or loss as a financing cost* presentar en la cuenta de resultados como un coste financiero

financing interest

Financing interest is the amount of interest paid in connection with loans and borrowings of funds for a project or an enterprise.

interés financiero

▲ *capitalised financing interest* interés financiero capitalizado ▲ *interest expenses including capitalised financing interest* gasto por intereses incluyendo interés financiero capitalizado

financing interest rate

The financing interest rate is the rate of interest that determines the interest payable in connection with loans and borrowings of funds for a project or an enterprise.

tipo de interés financiero

▲ *a high financing interest rate* un tipo de interés financiero alto ▲ *calculate the financing interest rate* calcular el tipo de interés financiero

finished goods

= finished product, manufactured goods, manufactured product

Finished goods refer to products that have completed an enterprise's manufacturing processes and that are in a saleable form. Products that are considered as finished goods by one enterprise may be considered as raw products or components by another enterprise.

productos terminados

▲ *an increase in finished goods during the period* un aumento de los productos terminados durante el periodo ▲ *changes in inventories of finished goods and work in progress* cambios en los inventarios de los productos terminados y en curso ▲ *costs directly attributable to the acquisition of finished goods* costes directamente atribuibles a la adquisición de productos terminados ▲ *finished goods at cost* productos terminados al coste ▲ *finished goods at net realisable value* productos terminados a valor realizable neto ▲ *finished goods produced by the enterprise* productos terminados producidos por la empresa ▲ *fixed and variable production overheads that are incurred in converting materials into finished goods* costes indirectos de producción fijos y variables que se incurren al convertir las materias primas en productos terminados ▲ *inventories of finished goods and merchandise* inventarios de productos terminados y mercaderías ▲ *the cost of finished goods and work in progress* el coste de los productos terminados y en curso ▲ *the selling prices of finished goods* los precios de venta de los productos terminados

finished goods and goods for resale UK

Finished goods and goods for resale is an item under current assets in the balance sheet according to the Companies Act 2006 required report format. This item contains stocks of products which have completed the manufacturing process and products which have been purchased to be sold on.

productos terminados y otros activos mantenidos para la venta

▲ *stocks of finished goods and goods for resale* stocks de productos terminados y otros activos mantenidos para la venta

⇛ finished goods, goods for resale, merchandise inventories

finished-goods inventory

The finished-goods inventory is a type of inventory under current assets in the balance sheet representing manufactured goods held on stock ready for sale. Other types include work-in-process inventory and merchandise inventory.

inventario de productos terminados

▲ *finished goods inventory beginning of the period* inventario de productos terminados iniciados en el ejercicio ▲ *finished goods inventory end of the period* inventario de productos terminados al cierre del periodo ▲ *overstate finished goods inventory* sobreestimar el inventario de productos terminados

⇛ inventory

finite life

≠ indefinite life

A finite life is a life with a limited period in time. The useful lives of intangible assets are either finite or indefinite, depending on whether the periods in which the assets are expected to contribute to the cash flows of an enterprise have or do not have foreseeable limits. Intangibles with finite lives are amortised over their useful lives, whereas intangibles with indefinite lives are no longer amortised, but regularly tested for impairment.

NOTE In the context of accounting, indefinite does not mean infinite, but not limited by any legal, contractual or other factors.

vida determinada

= vida finita

≠ vida infinita

▲ *finite life intangible assets* activos intangibles de vida determinada ▲ *intangible assets with a finite life* activos intangibles con una vida determinada

SOURCE FAS 142, IAS 36, BC 119, IAS 38

Finnish Institute of Authorised Public Accountants

The Finnish Institute of Authorised Public Accountants (KHT-yhdistys) is the professional accountancy body of Finland. The Institute is the representative organisation of authorised public accountants and has a key role in developing generally accepted auditing standards and ethical codes in Finland.

Instituto Finlandés de Expertos Contables Autorizados

NOTE The Spanish equivalent body is called Instituto de Contabilidad y Auditoría de Cuentas (ICAC).

▲ *become a member of the Finnish Institute of Authorised Public Accountants* llegar a ser un miembro del Instituto Finlandés de Expertos Contables Autorizados

firm commitment

1 A firm commitment is a committed agreement for the exchange of a particular asset at a defined price and date.

compromiso en firme

▲ *a firm commitment to acquire an enterprise* un compromiso en firme para adquirir una empresa ▲ *a firm commitment to make a purchase* un compromiso en firme para llevar a cabo una compra ▲ *a firm commitment to make a sale* un compromiso en firme para llevar a cabo una venta ▲ *a hedge of a firm commitment* una cobertura de un compromiso en firme ▲ *a previously unrecognised firm commitment* un compromiso en firme no reconocido previamente ▲ *an unrecognised firm commitment* un compromiso en firme no reconocido ▲ *as a result of a firm commitment* como resultado de un compromiso en firme ▲ *assets to be acquired as a result of a firm commitment to purchase goods or services* activos

para ser adquiridos como un resultado de un compromiso en firme para comprar bienes o servicios ▲ *the hedged firm commitment* el compromiso en firme cubierto
SOURCE IAS 39, paragraph 9

2 A firm commitment is a committed undertaking, e.g. by a bank to lend to a particular customer a specified amount of money over a particular period at a particular rate.
crédito
▲ *make a firm commitment* formalizar un crédito

firm purchase commitment
= firm purchase contract IAS/IFRS
A firm purchase commitment is a binding agreement with an unrelated party in which all material terms and conditions, such as price and time limits, have been specified, and where an included disincentive for non-performance is large enough to make performance highly probable.
compromiso de compra en firme
▲ *after a firm purchase commitment is obtained* después de que se obtenga un compromiso de compra en firme ▲ *obtain a firm purchase commitment* obtener un compromiso de compra en firme
SOURCE IFRS 5, Appendix A

firm value
= enterprise value, EV
Firm value is an investment ratio defined as an enterprise's market capitalisation plus its net interest-bearing debt. The definition also includes the value of minority interests minus the value of the share of any associates minus the value of other non-operating assets. This key figure shows the market value of the underlying invested capital and illustrates how the enterprise's operations are valued on the stock market irrespective of capital structure.
valor de la empresa
= VE
▲ *a firm value over $14 billion* un valor de la empresa alrededor de 14 mil millones de dólares ▲ *an increase in firm value* un aumento en el valor de la empresa ▲ *calculate the firm value* calcular el valor de la empresa ▲ *debt to firm value* deuda a valor de la empresa

first IFRS financial statements
The first IFRS financial statements constitute the annual financial statements prepared for the first time under the International Financial Reporting Standards (IFRSs) by an enterprise that has explicitly, and with no reservations, stated to adopt and comply with the International Financial Reporting Standards (IFRSs).
primeras cuentas anuales según NIIF
= primeros estados financieros según NIIF
NOTE Spanish accountants prefer 'primeras cuentas anuales según NIIF' to the IAS/IFRS term 'primeros estados financieros según NIIF'.
▲ *at the reporting date for the first IFRS financial statements* en la fecha de información para las primeras cuentas anuales según NIIF ▲ *part of the period covered by the first IFRS financial statements* parte del periodo cubierto por las primeras cuentas anuales según NIIF ▲ *the period covered by the first IFRS financial statements* el periodo cubierto por las primeras cuentas anuales según NIIF
SOURCE IFRS 1, Appendix A

first in, first out
→ FIFO

first-in, first-out
= FIFO
First-in, first-out (FIFO) is a stock valuation method where the cost of stock is calculated on the assumption that stock items purchased first will always be sold first. Therefore, the FIFO method implies that the oldest stock prices are used for measuring cost of sales in the profit and loss account, and the most recent prices are used for measuring the stock value in the balance sheet.
primera entrada, primera salida
= FIFO
▲ *use the first-in, first-out method* utilizar el método FIFO
⇛ last-in, first-out

first-quarter
= Q1

First-quarter is used about financial reports, items or statements that relate to the first three months of the accounting year.

primer trimestre

▲ *first quarter earnings* beneficios del primer trimestre ▲ *first-quarter highlights* hechos relevantes del primer trimestre ▲ *first-quarter results* resultados del primer trimestre

first-time adopter

An enterprise that prepares its first financial statements under the International Financial Reporting Standards (IFRS) is referred to as a first-time adopter.

adoptante por primera vez

▲ *become a first-time adopter later than one's parent* llegar a ser adoptante por primera vez con posterioridad a su matriz ▲ *the basis of accounting that a first-time adopter used immediately before adopting IFRSs* la base de la contabilidad que utilizó un adoptante por primera vez

SOURCE IFRS 1, Appendix A

fiscal authority

→ tax authority

fiscal period US

The fiscal period is the period for which an enterprise prepares its financial statements, e.g. a quarter of a year, half a year or a whole year.

periodo contable

▲ *a subsequent fiscal period* un periodo contable subsiguiente ▲ *increases in the economic benefits during the fiscal period* incrementos en los beneficios económicos durante el periodo contable ▲ *starting from the earliest fiscal period forming part of the financial statements* comenzando con el periodo contable más antiguo que forma parte de las cuentas anuales ▲ *the beginning of the fiscal period* el inicio del periodo contable ▲ *the current fiscal period* el periodo contable actual ▲ *the end of the fiscal period* el final del periodo contable ▲ *the fiscal period under review* el periodo contable en revisión ▲ *the previous fiscal period* el periodo contable anterior ▲ *within the same fiscal period* dentro del mismo periodo contable

fiscal year

1 = tax year US

A fiscal year is the tax year, i.e. the twelve-month period for which taxpayers must file a tax return, and for which the government estimates the annual budget.

NOTE In the US, the fiscal year runs from October 1 to September 30, whereas the tax year dates in the UK are April 6 to April 5, respectively.

año fiscal

▲ *after the end of the fiscal year* después del cierre del año fiscal ▲ *in the 2004/05 fiscal year* en el año fiscal 2004/2005

2 = accounting year UK, financial year IAS/IFRS, UK

A fiscal year is the accounting period for twelve consecutive months, i.e. the reporting period for which an enterprise prepares its financial statements. Typically, a fiscal year follows the calendar year, but may also run in an alternative twelve-month period, e.g. from April 1 to March 31.

año contable

= ejercicio contable

▲ *after the end of the fiscal year* después del cierre del año contable ▲ *during the current fiscal year* durante el año contable actual ▲ *over the past fiscal year* sobre el año contable anterior

⇛ accounting period

fix

= determine

To fix is to determine precisely and to make firm or permanent.

fijar

▲ *fix a price* fijar un precio ▲ *fix a time-limit* fijar un límite de tiempo ▲ *fix an amount* fijar una cantidad ▲ *fix the time for a meeting* fijar la hora para una reunión

fixed asset UK

= capital asset, long-lived asset, non-current asset

Fixed assets are assets that are intended for permanent ownership or use by the enterprise. A fixed asset may be an intangible asset, a tangible asset or an investment.

activo fijo

= activo no corriente

▲ *a constructed fixed asset* un activo fijo construido ▲ *any fixed assets that are no longer required for their original use* cualesquiera activos fijos que ya no se usan para su destino original ▲ *gains or losses on disposals of fixed assets* pérdidas o ganancias por enajenaciones de activos fijos ▲ *inventory and fixed assets* inventario y activos fijos ▲ *investments held as fixed assets* inversiones mantenidas como activos fijos ▲ *total fixed assets* total activos fijos

fixed asset investment

Fixed asset investments include equity investments in group enterprises and associates, receivables from group enterprises and associates, other investments and receivables as well as receivables from owners and management that have the common characteristic of being non-current assets. Fixed asset investments are line items under assets in the balance sheet.

inversión en activos fijos

▲ *cost of a fixed asset investment* coste de una inversión en activos fijos ▲ *disposal of fixed asset investments* enajenación de inversiones en activos fijos ▲ *other fixed asset investments* otras inversiones en activos fijos ▲ *profit on sale of fixed asset investments* beneficio por venta de inversiones en activos fijos ▲ *purchase of fixed asset investments* compra de inversiones en activos fijos ▲ *the fair value of fixed asset investments* el valor razonable de las inversiones en activos fijos ▲ *unlisted fixed asset investments* inversiones en activos fijos no catalogadas

⇛ long-term investment

fixed asset turnover

Fixed asset turnover is a financial ratio defined as sales divided by average fixed assets for the accounting period. This ratio measures the activity of an enterprise and the management's effectiveness in using fixed assets over the accounting period.

rotación del activo fijo

= plazo promedio del activo fijo

▲ *a sharp decline in fixed asset turnover* un descenso pronunciado en la rotación del activo fijo ▲ *an increase in fixed asset turnover* un incremento en la rotación del activo fijo ▲ *compute the fixed asset turnover for 2006* calcular la rotación del activo fijo para el 2006

fixed capital

Fixed capital refers to the amount of capital invested in fixed assets that are used by an enterprise when producing goods or providing services.

inversión en activo fijo

▲ *an increase in fixed capital* un aumento en inversión en activo fijo

fixed charge UK

≠ floating charge UK

A fixed charge is a legal right to an asset agreed on in a company, such as a building or equipment, provided as security by that company for money owed.

gravamen fijo

≠ gravamen variable

▲ *create a fixed charge* crear un gravamen fijo ▲ *land and buildings subject to a fixed charge* bienes raíces y edificios sujetos a un gravamen fijo ▲ *secured by a fixed charge over property* asegurado por un gravamen fijo sobre la propiedad

⇛ charge

fixed cost

≠ variable cost

Fixed costs are expenses which remain constant regardless of changes in the level of activity (production or sales) and the cost-driver level.

coste fijo

= coste variable

▲ *a decrease in fixed costs of 2.5%* un descenso del 2,5% en costes fijos ▲ *incur fixed costs* incurrir en costes fijos ▲ *rising fixed costs* costes fijos en aumento ▲ *tight control of fixed costs* control restrictivo de costes fijos

⇛ variable cost

fixed interest rate

≠ floating rate, variable interest rate

A fixed interest rate is an interest rate that is unchanged throughout the loan period or life of the financial instrument.

tipo de interés fijo

≠ tipo de interés variable

▲ *a commitment to lend funds at a fixed interest rate* un compromiso para prestar fondos a un tipo de interés fijo ▲ *financial assets with a fixed interest rate* activos financieros con un tipo de interés fijo ▲ *financial liabilities with a fixed interest rate* pasivos financieros con un tipo de interés fijo ▲ *operate in a fixed interest rate environment* operar en un entorno de tipo de interés fijo ▲ *the fixed interest rate on a hedged item* el tipo de interés fijo en una partida cubierta

fixed overhead

Fixed overheads are indirect costs that remain relatively constant regardless of the volume of production or changes in activity, i.e. costs that are indirectly associated with the units of productions or production processes. Examples are management and administration costs, depreciation, rent and insurance.

coste indirecto fijo

▲ *the amount of fixed overhead* la cantidad de coste indirecto fijo ▲ *the amount of fixed overhead allocated to each unit of production* la cantidad de coste indirecto fijo asignado a cada unidad de producción ▲ *the fixed overhead incurred* el coste indirecto fijo incurrido

fixed overhead cost variance

The difference between the actual fixed overhead amount and the budgeted fixed overhead amount for actual output is the fixed overhead cost variance. This variance may arise if the amount of fixed costs actually spent exceeds the amount of budgeted fixed costs, or if the forecast volume used as basis for the overhead application rate differs from the actual production.

desviación en costes indirectos fijos

= desviación en los costes indirectos fijos

▲ *calculate the fixed overhead cost variance* calcular la desviación en los costes indirectos fijos ▲ *total fixed overhead cost variance* total desviación en costes indirectos fijos

fixed overhead flexible-budget variance

= fixed overhead spending variance

The difference between the actual fixed overhead costs and the budgeted fixed overhead costs in the flexible budget is referred to as fixed overhead flexible-budget variance.

variación en un presupuesto flexible por coste indirecto fijo

▲ *calculate the fixed overhead flexible-budget variance* calcular la variación en un presupuesto flexible por coste indirecto fijo

⇛ flexible budget, overhead cost

fixed overhead spending variance

= fixed overhead flexible-budget variance

The difference between the actual fixed overhead costs and the budgeted fixed overhead costs in the flexible budget is referred to as fixed overhead spending variance.

variación en el gasto por coste indirecto fijo

▲ *calculate the fixed overhead spending variance* calcular la variación en el gasto por coste indirecto fijo

⇛ flexible budget, overhead cost

fixed price contract IAS/IFRS

= fixed-price contract

≠ cost-plus contract IAS/IFRS

A fixed price contract is a construction contract under which a fixed contract price, or a fixed rate per output unit, typically subject to cost escalation clauses, has been agreed by a contractor.

contrato a precio fijo

= contrato de precio fijo

▲ *a fixed price contract involving a fixed price per unit of output* un contrato a precio fijo que incluye un precio fijo por unidad de producto ▲ *revenue from a fixed price contract* ingresos de un contrato a precio fijo ▲ *revenue from fixed price contracts* ingresos de contratos a precio fijo ▲ *the amount of revenue agreed in a fixed price contract* la cantidad de ingresos acordados en un contrato a precio fijo ▲ *the outcome of a fixed price contract* el resultado de un contrato de precio fijo

SOURCE IAS 11, paragraph 3

fixed production overhead

Fixed production overheads are the indirect production costs that are associated with, but not directly part of, the units or processes of production, and that are fairly constant regardless of changes in the volume of activity. Examples are administrative expenses, depreciation or costs of factory and equipment maintenance.

coste indirecto de producción fijo

▲ *the allocation of fixed production overheads to the costs of conversion* la asignación de los costes indirectos de producción fijos a los costes por conversión ⇛ variable production overhead

fixed rate of interest

→ fixed interest rate

fixed-asset movement schedule

UK

A fixed-asset movement schedule is a specification in the notes to the financial statement of the fixed assets recognised in the balance sheet. This note states the costs, revaluation, depreciation or amortisation and write-downs for impairment of the fixed assets.

llamada por cambio en activos fijos

▲ *fixed-asset movement schedule, goodwill and negative goodwill* llamada por cambio en activos fijos, fondo de comercio y fondo de comercio negativo ▲ *fixed-asset movement schedule, investment properties* llamada por cambio en activos fijos, inversiones propiedades ▲ *fixed-asset movement schedule, investments* llamada por cambio en activos fijos, inversiones ▲ *requirement of fixed-asset movement schedule* obligación de llamada por cambio en activos fijos

fixed-income corporate bond

A fixed-income corporate bond is a debt instrument issued by a business enterprise that pays a fixed rate of return, i.e. interest, at periodic intervals until maturity.

bono corporativo de ingreso fijo

▲ *high-quality fixed-income corporate bonds* bonos corporativos de ingreso fijo de calidad alta ▲ *issue fixed-income corporate bonds* emitir bonos corporativos de ingreso fijo ▲ *long-term fixed income corporate bond* bono corporativo de ingreso fijo a largo plazo ▲ *short-term fixed-income corporate bond* bono corporativo de ingreso fijo a corto plazo

fixed-overhead rate

A fixed-overhead rate is an addition calculated per production unit, which is meant to cover the fixed production costs because these costs are not directly attributable to the individual production units.

proporción de coste indirecto fijo

▲ *a fixed-overhead rate of 12%* una proporción de coste indirecto fijo del 12% ▲ *the budgeted fixed-overhead rate* la proporción de coste indirecto fijo presupuestada ▲ *the predetermined fixed-overhead rate* la proporción de coste indirecto fijo predeterminda

fixed-price contract

→ fixed price contract

fixed-rate

A fixed-rate investment or loan yields a rate of return or interest that does not vary.

fijo

▲ *a fixed-rate asset* un activo fijo ▲ *a fixed-rate claim* una reclamación fija ▲ *a fixed-rate debt* una deuda fija ▲ *a fixed-rate loan* un préstamo fijo ▲ *a fixed-rate obligation* una obligación fija ▲ *fixed-rate financial instruments* instrumentos financieros fijos

fixing

= determination

Fixing means determining and setting a level for amounts, prices, interest rates, values etc.

fijación

= determinación

▲ *advance fixing* avanzar la fijación ▲ *fixing of prices* fijación de precios ▲ *the criteria for fixing the amount* los criterios para la fijación de la cantidad

fixtures and equipment US

Fixtures and equipment is a category of tangible assets comprising immovables and movables, such as office furniture and computers. As an item in the balance sheet, fixtures and equipment appears under tangible fixed assets.

utillaje y equipo

▲ *lease of fixtures and equipment* alquiler de utillaje y equipo ▲ *machinery, fixtures and equipment* maquinaria, utillaje y equipo ▲ *provide for depreciation on fixtures and equipment* provisión por depreciación de utillaje y equipo ▲ *purchase of fixtures and equipment* compra de utillaje y equipo

fixtures and fittings IAS/IFRS

Fixtures and fittings is a category of tangible assets comprising immovables and movables, such as office furniture and computers. As an item in the balance sheet, fixtures and fittings appears under tangible fixed assets.

mobiliario y enseres

= mobilliario y utillaje

▲ *expenditure on furniture, fixtures and fittings* gasto en muebles de oficina, mobiliario y enseres ▲ *fixtures and fittings including improvements to leasehold buildings* mobiliario y enseres incluyendo mejoras en edificios arrendados ▲ *other fixtures and fittings, tools and equipment* otro mobiliario y enseres, herramientas y equipos

fixtures, fittings, tools and equipment UK

Fixtures, fittings, tools and equipment is an item under fixed assets in the balance sheet according to the Companies Act 2006 required report format. This item contains tangible assets typically not directly used in the production processes such as cars, office furniture and computers.

utillaje, accesorios, herramientas y equipo

▲ *other fixtures, fittings, tools and equipment* otro utillaje, accesorios, herramientas y equipo ▲ *the cost of fixtures, fittings, tools and equipment* el coste de utillaje, accesorios, herramientas y equipo

flexible budget

= variable budget

A flexible budget is a budget that allows for continuous adjustments depending on the actual cost-driver activities of an enterprise such as the volume of sales or production.

presupuesto flexible

= presupuesto variable

▲ *activity-based flexible budgets* presupuestos flexibles basados en la actividad ▲ *prepare a flexible budget* preparar un presupuesto flexible ▲ *the purpose of a flexible budget* el propósito de un presupuesto flexible ▲ *use a flexible budget* utilizar un presupuesto flexible

flexible-budget variance

A flexible-budget variance is the variance between the actual results for a period and the flexible budget for the period, based on the production for that period.

variación en un presupuesto flexible

▲ *determine the flexible-budget variance* calcular la variación en un presupuesto flexible

floatation

→ flotation

floating charge UK

A floating charge is a legal right to any asset in a company, such as a building or equipment, provided as security by that company for money owed.

garantía flotante

▲ *create a floating charge* crear una garantía flotante ▲ *land and buildings subject to a floating charge* bienes raíces y edificios sujetos a una garantía flotante ▲ *secured by a floating charge over the property* asegurado por una garantía flotante sobre la propiedad

⇛ charge

floating interest rate

= floating rate, floating rate of interest

A floating interest rate is a rate of interest that varies or may be changed over time according to the market rate of interest.

tipo de interés variable

= tipo de interés flotante

▲ *financial assets with a floating interest rate* activos financieros con un tipo de interés variable ▲ *financial liabilities with a floating interest rate* pasivos financieros con un tipo de interés variable ▲ *reset the floating interest rate to market rates* reconvertir el tipo de interés variable a tipos de mercado

floating rate

= floating interest rate, floating rate of interest

A floating rate is a rate of interest that varies or may be changed over time according to the market rate of interest.

tipo de interés variable

= tipo de interés flotante

▲ *a premium resulting from a change in the credit spread over the floating rate specified in the instrument* una prima procedente de un cambio en el margen del crédito sobre el tipo de interés variable especificado en el instrumento ▲ *groups of floating rate financial assets maturing within various future time periods* grupos de activos financieros con tipo de interés variable que vencen en diferentes periodos futuros de tiempo

floating rate debt

A floating rate debt is a debt on which the debtor pays a rate of interest that varies according to the market interest rate over the agreed period.

deuda a tipo de interés variable

▲ *change floating rate debt to fixed rate debt* cambio de la deuda a tipo de interés variable a tipo de interés fijo

floating rate instrument

A floating rate instrument is a financial instrument on which the interest rate payable varies according to the market rate over the life of the instrument.

instrumento a tipo de interés variable

▲ *a premium or discount on a floating rate instrument* una prima o descuento en un instrumento a tipo de interés variable

floating rate loan

A floating rate loan is a loan on which the borrower pays a rate of interest that varies according to market interst rates over the loan period.

préstamo a tipo de interés variable

▲ *convert a floating rate loan into a fixed rate loan* convertir un préstamo a tipo de interés variable en un préstamo a tipo de interés fijo ▲ *the interest rate for the floating-rate loan* el tipo de interés para un préstamo a tipo de interés variable ▲ *unsecured floating rate loan* préstamo a tipo de interés variable no asegurado

floating rate note

= FRN

A floating rate note is a eurocurrency bond with a coupon that is not fixed, but variable and fluctuates according to market interest rates.

pagaré a tipo de interés fijo

▲ *a floating rate note listed on the London Stock Exchange* un pagaré a tipo de interés fijo que cotiza en la Bolsa de Londres ▲ *a floating rate note whose interest rate is reset once a year* un pagaré a tipo de interés fijo cuyo tipo de interés se recalcula una vez al año ▲ *purchase of floating rate note* compra de pagarés a tipo de interés fijo ▲ *unsecured floating rate note* pagaré a tipo de interés fijo no asegurado

floating rate of interest

→ floating interest rate

floating-rate

A floating-rate loan is a loan carrying a variable interest rate that floats, i.e. varies periodically instead of being fixed at the time of issue. Changes in floating rates typically depend on e.g. the general interest level, certain indices or other factors.

a interés variable

▲ *a floating-rate coupon linked to an interest rate reference* cupón a interés variable unido a un tipo de interés de referencia ▲ *a floating-rate loan* un préstamo a interés variable ▲ *a floating-rate note* un pagaré a interés variable ▲ *floating-rate financial assets* activos financieros a interés variable ▲ *floating-rate financial liabilities* pasivos financieros a interés variable

flotation UK

= admission for listing on the stock exchange UK, initial public offering US, IPO US

Flotation is a privately held company's first offering of shares to the public. Usually an investment bank will assist the company with the flotation and may underwrite the share offering. After the flotation, the shares will be publicly traded on a stock exchange, giving the issuing company the advantage of access to a market for additional capital and providing the shares with a fair market value.

NOTE A flotation is also referred to as "going public".

flotación

= salida a bolsa

▲ *carry through a flotation* llevar a cabo una salida a bolsa ▲ *flotation costs* costes de flotación

flow from

≠ flow to

When something, e.g. economic benefits, cash or other resources, flows from an enterprise it means that it has been separated from or left the enterprise.

separar de

= separarse de

≠ unir a

▲ *economic benefits that flow from the asset* beneficios económicos que se separan del activo ▲ *flow from the enterprise* separar de la empresa ▲ *future economic benefits that will flow from the enterprise* beneficios económicos futuros que se separaran de la empresa ▲ *the economic benefits that are expected to flow from the property* los beneficios económicos que se espera separar de la propiedad

flow to

≠ flow from

When something, e.g. cash, income or economic benefits, flows to an enterprise it means that it accrues to the enterprise.

unir a

= unirse a

≠ separar de

▲ *a resource from which future economic benefits are expected to flow to the entity* un recurso del que los beneficios económicos futuros se esperan unir a la entidad ▲ *flow to the acquirer* unir al adquirente ▲ *let something flow to the enterprise* menos algo que se une a la empresa

fluctuation

Fluctuation refers to changes, either upward or downward, in relation to a given starting point. In the context of finance and managerial economics, fluctuations refer to e.g. movements in interest rates, exchange rates and share, bond or product prices. In macroeconomics, fluctuations often refer to market conditions: when business activity is high and the business cycle is peaking, it is boom time, and when business activity is at its lowest, the economy is experiencing a depression.

fluctuación

▲ *exchange rate fluctuations* fluctuaciones en el tipo de cambio ▲ *fluctuation in prices* fluctuaciones en los precios ▲ *fluctuations in the enterprise's operating income* fluctuaciones en los ingresos de explotación de la empresa ▲ *fluctuations in values* fluctuaciones en los valores ▲ *interest rate fluctuations* fluctuaciones de los tipos de interés ▲ *long-term fluctuations* fluctuaciones a largo plazo ▲ *seasonal fluctuations* fluctuaciones estacionales ▲ *share price fluctuations* fluctuaciones en el precio de la acción ▲ *short-term fluctuations* fluctuaciones a corto plazo ▲ *show fluctuations* mostrar fluctuaciones ▲ *temporary fluctuations* fluctuaciones temporales

forecast transaction IAS/IFRS

= forecasted transaction UK, US

A forecast transaction is a transaction which an enterprise expects to carry out, but which it is not obligated to carry out under a firm commitment.

transacción prevista

▲ *a forecast transaction for a non-financial liability* una transacción prevista para un instrumento no financiero ▲ *a forecast transaction that is no longer highly probable* una transacción prevista que no es muy probable ▲ *a highly probable forecast transaction* una transacción prevista altamente probable ▲ *the forecast transaction that is the subject of the hedge* la transacción prevista que está sujeta a la cobertura ▲ *the hedged forecast transaction* la transacción prevista cubierta

SOURCE IAS 39, paragraph 9

forecasted transaction UK, US

= forecast transaction IAS/IFRS

A forecasted transaction is a transaction which an enterprise expects to carry out, but which it is not obligated to carry out under a firm commitment.

transacción prevista

▲ *a highly probable forecasted transaction* una transacción prevista altamente probable ▲ *foreign-currency-denominated forecasted transaction* transacción prevista denominada en moneda extranjera ▲ *hedge of a foreign currency forecasted transaction* cobertura de una transacción prevista en moneda extranjera ▲ *recognise a forecasted transaction* reconocer una transacción prevista ▲ *the documentation of the forecasted transaction* la documentación de la transacción prevista

⇛ forecast transaction

foreign currency

= local currency

A foreign currency is a currency other than the reporting currency of an enterprise.

moneda extranjera

▲ *an embedded foreign currency derivative* un derivado en moneda extranjera incluido ▲ *buy shares in foreign currency* comprar acciones en moneda extranjera ▲ *denominated in foreign currency* denominado en moneda extranjera ▲ *foreign currency balances* saldos en moneda extranjera ▲ *foreign currency future cash flows* flujos de efectivo futuros en moneda extranjera ▲ *foreign currency liabilities* pasivos en moneda extranjera ▲ *foreign currency receivables* cantidades a cobrar en moneda extranjera ▲ *foreign currency transactions* transacciones en moneda extranjera ▲ *foreign currency translation* conversión de moneda extranjera ▲ *lack of access to foreign currency* falta de acceso a moneda extranjera ▲ *prepare financial statements in foreign currency* preparar las cuentas anuales en moneda extranjera ▲ *translation from foreign currency to the monetary unit chosen* conversión de la moneda extranjera a la unidad monetaria elegida

foreign currency adjustment

= foreign currency translation adjustment, foreign exchange adjustment UK

A foreign currency adjustment is a restatement of the recognised amounts of assets and liabilities e.g. in the reporting currency of a parent company as a result of changes in the presentation currency of a foreign subsidiary.

ajuste en moneda extranjera

= ajuste de monera extranjera, ajuste por moneda extranjera

▲ *calculate the foreign currency adjustment* calcular el ajuste en moneda extranjera ▲ *net foreign currency adjustments* ajustes netos en moneda extranjera

foreign currency debt

Foreign currency debt is debt denominated in the currency of another country than that of the presentation currency.

deuda en moneda extranjera

▲ *long-term foreign currency debt* deuda en moneda extranjera a largo palzo ▲ *service the foreign currency debt* pagar la deuda en moneda xtranjera ▲ *short-term foreign currency debt* deuda en moneda extranjera a corto plazo

foreign currency exposure

A foreign currency exposure is the currency risk of an enterprise to one or several foreign currencies that arises because of payment inflows or outflows in other currencies than the presentation currency of the enterprise or changes in the value of financial instruments denominated in foreign currencies resulting from exchange rate fluctuations. The enterprise may hedge against currency exposure through derivative financial instruments.

exposición al riesgo en moneda extranjera

= exposición a monera extranjera

NOTE The IAS/IFRS term 'exposición a moneda extranjera' is nonsensical in Spanish.

▲ *a hedge of the foreign currency exposure* una cobertura de la exposición al riesgo en moneda extranjera ▲ *hedge the foreign currency exposure of the contract commitments* cubrir la exposición al riesgo en moneda extranjera por obligaciones contractuales

foreign currency hedging

= foreign currency hedge

Foreign currency hedging refers to an enterprise's use of derivative financial instruments to hedge against risks of losses in relation to foreign exchange rate movements.

cobertura por riesgo de cambio

= moneda extranjera cubierta de riesgo

NOTE Spanish accountants prefer 'cobertura por riesgo de cambio' to the IAS/IFRS term 'moneda extranjera cubierta de riesgo'. This IAS expression is nonsensical in Spanish.

▲ *unrealised net losses on derivatives used for foreign currency hedging* pérdidas netas no realizadas en los derivados utilizados para cobertura por riesgo de cambio

foreign currency loan

A foreign currency loan is a loan raised and denominated in the currency of another country than that of the borrower.

préstamo en moneda extranjera

▲ *exchange differences on foreign currency loans* diferencias en el tipo de cambio en los préstamos en moneda extranjera ▲ *raise a foreign currency loan* conseguir un préstamo en moneda extranjera

foreign currency loss

= exchange loss

A foreign currency loss appears from exchange rate differences or fluctuations resulting from the translation or conversion of foreign currency amounts into the domestic currency.

pérdida en moneda extranjera

= pérdida de moneda extranjera, pérdida en divisas, pérdida por diferencia de cambio

▲ *a capitalised foreign currency loss* una pérdida en moneda extranjera capitalizada ▲ *capitalise a foreign currency loss* capitalizar una pérdida en moneda extranjera ▲ *foreign currency losses on hedging contracts* pérdidas en moneda extranjera en los contratos de cobertura ▲ *foreign currency losses on liabilities* pérdidas en moneda extranjera en pasivos ▲ *foreign currency losses relating to hedged transactions* pérdidas en moneda extranjera relacionadas con transacciones cubiertas ▲ *foreign currency losses resulting from a severe devaluation* pérdidas en moneda extranjera resultantes de una devaluación severa ▲ *make deductions for foreign currency losses* llevar a cabo deducciones por pérdidas en moneda extranjera ▲ *realised foreign currency losses* pérdidas en moneda extranjera realizadas ▲ *significant foreign currency losses* pérdidas en moneda extranjera significativas ▲ *the carrying amount of a capitalised foreign currency loss* el valor contable de una pérdida en moneda extranjera capitalizada ▲ *unrealised foreign currency losses* pérdidas no realizadas en moneda extranjera

foreign currency receivable

A foreign currency receivable is a receivable in another currency than the enterprise's presentation currency.

cuenta a cobrar en moneda extranjera

= moneda extranjera liquidable

NOTE Spanish accountants prefer 'cuenta a cobrar en moneda extranjera' to the IAS/IFRS term 'moneda extranjera liquidable'.

▲ *hedge an existing foreign currency receivable* cubrir una cuenta a cobrar en moneda extranjera existente

foreign currency risk US, IAS/IFRS

= currency risk, foreign exchange risk

Foreign currency risk is the exposure to losses stemming from exchange-rate changes affecting receivables, investments, financial instruments etc. denominated in foreign currencies.

riesgo por diferencia de cambio

= riesgo de moneda extranjera, riesgo en moneda extranjera, riesgo por diferencias de cambio

NOTE Spanish accountants prefer 'riesgo por diferencia de cambio' to the IAS/IFRS terms 'riesgo en moneda extranjera', and 'riesgo de moneda extranjera'.

▲ *eliminate a foreign currency risk* eliminar un riesgo por diferencia de cambio ▲ *enter into financial contracts to hedge a foreign currency risk* firmar contratos para cubrir el riesgo por diferencia de cambio ▲ *foreign currency risk of investments in foreign subsidiaries* riesgo por diferencia de cambio de las inversiones en filiales extranjeras ▲ *foreign currency risk on incoming orders* riesgo por diferencias de cambio en los pedidos entrantes ▲ *foreign currency risk on orders received* riesgo por diferencia de cambio en los pedidos recibidos ▲ *hedge a foreign currency risk* cubrir un riesgo por diferencia de cambio ▲ *hedge the exposure to foreign currency risk* cubrir la exposición al riesgo por diferencias de cambio ▲ *reduce a foreign currency risk* reducir un riesgo por diferencia de cambio ▲ *the fo-*

reign currency risk of an intragroup monetary item el riesgo por diferencia de cambio en una partida monetaria intragrupo
⇛ translation

foreign currency translation
Foreign currency translation means the translation of items denominated or measured in one currency into another currency, usually the presentation currency.
conversión en moneda extranjera
= conversión a moneda extranjera, traspaso a moneda extranjera
▲ *exchange adjustment on foreign currency translation* ajuste por tipo de cambio en conversión en moneda extranjera ▲ *foreign currency translation method* método de conversión en moneda extranjera ▲ *foreign currency translation of foreign entities* conversión en moneda extranjera de entidades extranjeras ▲ *general foreign currency translation principles* principios de conversión en moneda extranjera generales ▲ *the enterprise's foreign currency translation policies* políticas de conversión en moneda extranjera de la empresa

foreign currency translation adjustment US, IAS/IFRS
A foreign currency translation adjustment is a restatement of the recognised amounts of assets and liabilities e.g. in the reporting currency of a parent company as a result of changes in the presentation currency of a foreign subsidiary.
ajuste por conversión en moneda extranjera
= ajuste por tipo de cambio, ajuste por traspaso a moneda extranjera
▲ *foreign currency translation adjustment relating to foreign subsidiaries* ajuste por conversión en moneda extranjera en relación con subsidiarias en el extranjero

foreign currency translation reserve
= currency translation reserve, translation reserve
Foreign currency translation reserves represent foreign exchange differences (gains or losses) arising on the translation of financial statements prepared by foreign entities and operations, such as subsidiaries, on consolidation in the group financial statements. Foreign currency translation reserves appear under equity in the balance sheet and may constitute a credit or a debit balance.
reserva por conversión de moneda extranjera
= reserva por traspaso a moneda extranjera
NOTE Spanish accountants prefer 'reserva por conversión de moneda extranjera' to the IAS/IFRS term 'reserva por traspaso a moneda extranjera'.
▲ *reset the foreign currency translation reserve to zero* llevar a cero la reserva por conversión de moneda extranjera
⇛ foreign currency, foreign currency translation adjustment, foreign exchange, foreign exchange gain, foreign exchange loss

foreign enterprise
A foreign enterprise is a company or business domiciled or based in another country than the country of the reporting enterprise.
empresa extranjera
▲ *a branch of a foreign enterprise* una rama de una empresa extranjera ▲ *annual report of a foreign enterprise* informe anual de una empresa extranjera ▲ *exemption statement for a foreign enterprise* declaración de exención por una empresa extranjera ▲ *translation of the financial statements of a foreign enterprise* conversión de los estados financieros de una empresa extranjera

foreign entity
A foreign entity is an operation that is domiciled in another country than that of the reporting entity and whose activities are not an integral part of those of the reporting enterprise.
entidad extranjera
▲ *acquire a foreign entity* adquirir una entidad extranjera ▲ *balances with a foreign entity* saldos con una entidad extranjera ▲ *changes to equity in the foreign entity* cambios a patrimonio neto en la entidad extranjera ▲ *dispose of a foreign entity*

eliminación de una entidad extranjera ▲ *dispose of an investment in a foreign entity* eliminación de una inversión en una entidad extranjera ▲ *hedge of a net investment in a foreign entity* cobertura de una inversión neta en una entidad extranjera ▲ *net investment in a foreign entity* inversión neta en una entidad extranjera ▲ *the carrying amount of a foreign entity* el valor contable de una entidad extranjera ▲ *translation of goodwill arising on the acquisition of a foreign entity* conversión del fondo de comercio surgido de la adquisición de una entidad extranjera ▲ *translation of the financial statements of a foreign entity* conversión de los estados financieros de una entidad extranjera

foreign exchange

1 Foreign exchange refers to the currencies of other countries.

divisa

▲ *a related foreign exchange component* un componente de divisa relacionado ▲ *foreign exchange translation differences* diferencias por conversión de divisa

⇛ foreign exchange market

2 Foreign exchange refers to the trading of currencies of different countries.

operación en moneda extranjera

= operación en divisas

▲ *make a large profit on foreign exchange* conseguir un beneficio sustancial en la operación en moneda extranjera

⇛ foreign exchange market

foreign exchange adjustment

= foreign currency translation adjustment

Foreign exchange adjustments result from the process of translating financial statements from foreign currencies into the reporting currency of the enterprise.

ajuste por tipo de cambio

▲ *calculate the foreign exchange adjustment* calcular el ajuste por tipo de cambio ▲ *net foreign exchange adjustments* ajustes netos por tipo de cambio

⇛ translation

foreign exchange contract

A foreign exchange contract is a contract for the purchase or sale of a specific currency. Foreign exchange contracts are often used as hedging against exchange rate fluctuations on debt or receivables in which case they are referred to as forward exchange contracts.

contrato de compra venta de divisas

▲ *external foreign exchange contracts* contratos de compra venta de divisas externos ▲ *the fair value of forward foreign exchange contracts* el valor razonable de los contratos de compraventa de divisas futuros

⇛ forward exchange contract

foreign exchange exposure

A foreign exchange exposure is the risk of incurring losses because of exchange rate fluctuations affecting an enterprise's transactions, assets or liabilities in foreign currencies.

exposición al riesgo por tipo de cambio

= riesgo por tipo de cambio

▲ *changes in foreign exchange exposures* cambios en la exposición al riesgo por tipo de cambio

⇛ currency risk, translation

foreign exchange gain

= exchange gain

≠ foreign exchange loss

A foreign exchange gain appears from exchange rate differences or fluctuations resulting from the translation of foreign currency amounts into the domestic currency. Examples are increases in amounts receivable in foreign currencies or the value of foriegn investments.

beneficio por tipo de cambio

= ganancia por tipo de cambio

≠ pérdida por tipo de cambio

▲ *accounting policies for the recognition of foreign exchange gains* políticas contables para el reconocimiento de los beneficios por tipo de cambio ▲ *all foreign exchange gains arising on the translation of a borrowing* todos los beneficios por tipo de cambio en la conversión de un préstamo ▲ *deferred foreign exchange gain* beneficio por tipo de cambio diferido ▲ *foreign exchange gain whose recognition in the income statement has been deferred* beneficio por tipo de cambio cuyo reconocimiento en la cuenta de resultados se ha diferido ▲ *foreign exchange gains on monetary assets and monetary liabilities* beneficios por tipo de cambio en los activos y pasivos monetarios ▲ *unrealised foreign exchange gains* beneficios por tipo de cambio no realizados

foreign exchange loss
= exchange loss
≠ foreign exchange gain
A foreign exchange loss appears from exchange rate differences or fluctuations resulting from the translation or conversion of foreign currency amounts into the domestic currency.
pérdida por tipo de cambio
≠ beneficio por tipo de cambio
▲ *a realised foreign exchange loss* una pérdida por tipo de cambio realizada ▲ *an unrealised foreign exchange loss* una pérdida por tipo de cambio no realizada ▲ *foreign exchange losses on hedging transactions* pérdidas por tipo de cambio al cubrir las transacciones ▲ *foreign exchange losses on liabilities* pérdidas por tipo de cambio en pasivos ▲ *operating profit adjusted for foreign exchange losses* beneficio de explotación ajustado por pérdidas por tipo de cambio ▲ *risk of foreign exchange loss* riego de pérdida por tipo de cambio ▲ *significant foreign exchange losses* pérdidas por tipo de cambio significativas

foreign exchange market
The foreign exchange market is the market for buying and selling currencies. This is an international, computerised money market where supply and demand determine the exchange rates for currencies traded such as the dollar, the pound, the euro and other leading currencies. In the spot market currencies are traded with delivery within two business days, whereas in the forward exchange market, delivery will takes place at a future date specified in the relevant forward contract.
mercado de divisas
▲ *a currency traded in a foreign exchange market* una moneda que cotiza en el mercado de divisas ▲ *intervene in the foreign exchange market* intervenir en el mercado de divisas ▲ *liberalisation of the foreign exchange market* liberalización del mercado de divisas ▲ *purchase US Dollars in the foreign exchange market* comprar dólares norteamericanos en el mercado de divisas ▲ *strengthen the development of the foreign exchange market* fortalecer el desarrollo del mercado de divisas

foreign exchange rate
= exchange rate
The foreign exchange rate is the price of a currency in terms of another, expressed as a number of units of one (domestic) currency in terms of a unit of another (foreign) currency. In some countries, e.g. the UK, the foreign exchange rate is expressed as the amount of foreign currency one unit of domestic currency will buy.
tipo de cambio de moneda extranjera
= tasa de cambio de moneda extranjera, tasa de cambio externa, tipo de cambio externo
NOTE Spanish accountants prefer 'tipo de cambio de moneda extranjera' to the IAS/IFRS terms 'tasa de cambio de moneda extranjera', 'tasa de cambio externa', and 'tipo de cambio externo'.
▲ *abnormally large changes after the balance sheet date in foreign exchange rates* variaciones anormalmente significativas después de la fecha del balance en los tipos de cambio de moneda extranjera ▲ *exposure to foreign exchange rate gains or losses* exposición a beneficios o pérdidas por tipo de cambio de moneda extranjera ▲ *the effects of changes in foreign exchange rates* los efectos de las variaciones en los tipos de cambio de moneda extranjera

foreign exchange reserve
The foreign exchange reserve constitutes the amount of foreign currency held by an enterprise, typically a bank.
efectivo en moneda extranjera
▲ *a separate foreign exchange reserve* un efectivo en moneda extranjera separado ▲ *movement on foreign exchange reserve* movimiento en el efectivo en moneda extranjera
⇛ foreign currency translation reserve

foreign exchange risk UK
= currency risk, foreign currency risk
Foreign exchange risk is the exposure to losses because of exchange rate fluctuations affecting an enterprise's transactions, assets or liabilities in foreign currencies.
riesgo por diferencia de cambio
= riesgos por diferencias de cambio
▲ *eliminate a foreign exchange risk* eliminar un riesgo por diferencia de cambio ▲ *enter into financial contracts to hedge a foreign exchange risk* firmar contratos para cubrir el riesgo por diferencia de cambio ▲ *foreign exchange risk on foreign investments* riesgo por diferencia de cambio en inversiones extranjeras ▲ *foreign exchange risk on incoming orders* riesgo por diferencias de cambio en los pedidos entrantes ▲ *foreign exchange risk on orders received* riesgo por diferencia de cambio en los pedidos recibidos ▲ *foreign exchange risks of investments in foreign subsidiaries* riesgo por diferencia de cambio de las inversiones en filiales extranjeras ▲ *hedge a foreign exchange risk* cubrir un riesgo por diferencia de cambio ▲ *reduce a foreign exchange risk* reducir un riesgo por diferencia de cambio
⇛ translation

foreign operation
From the point of view of the reporting enterprise, a foreign operation is a subsidiary, associate, joint venture, branch or other entity whose activities are located or carried on in another country and whose assets, liabilities and results are reported in a foreign currency.
negocio en el extranjero
= operación extranjera
▲ *a foreign operation that is integral to the operations of the reporting entity* un negocio en el extranjero que está integrado en los negocios de la principal ▲ *a significant foreign operation* un negocio en el extranjero significativo ▲ *an enterprise that has significant foreign operations* una empresa que tiene negocios en el extranjero significativos ▲ *classification of foreign operations* clasificación de los negocios en el extranjero ▲ *disposal of a foreign operation* eliminación de un negocio en el extranjero ▲ *gains and losses arising from translating the financial statements of foreign operations* beneficios y pérdidas procedentes de conversión de los estados financieros de los negocios en el extranjero ▲ *hedge of a net investment in a foreign operation* cobertura de una inversión neta en un negocio en el extranjero ▲ *investment in a foreign operation* inversión en un negocio en el extranjero ▲ *measurement of investments in a foreign operation* medición de las inversiones en un negocio en el extranjero ▲ *net investment in a foreign operation* inversión neta en un negocio en el extranjero ▲ *reclassification of a foreign operation* reclasificación de un negocio en el extranjero ▲ *significant foreign operations in foreign currencies* negocios en el extranjero significativos en divisas ▲ *the foreign operation's taxable profit or tax loss* resultado sujeto a impuestos del negocio en el extranjero ▲ *the translation of a foreign operation into the presentation currency of the entity* la conversión de un negocio en el extranjero a la moneda de presentación de la entidad ▲ *translation of cash flows in a foreign operation* conversión de flujos de efectivo en un negocio en el extranjero
SOURCE IAS 21, paragraph 8

foreign-exchange adjustment
→ foreign exchange adjustment

foreign-exchange contract
→ foreign exchange contract

foreign-exchange exposure
→ foreign exchange exposure

foreign-exchange gain
→ foreign exchange gain

foreign-exchange loss
→ foreign exchange loss

foreign-exchange market
→ foreign exchange market

foreign-exchange rate
→ foreign exchange rate

foreign-exchange reserve
→ foreign exchange reserve

foreign-exchange risk
→ foreign exchange risk

Föreningen Auktoriserade Revisorer
→ FAR SRS

foreseeable
An event or outcome which can reasonably be predicted or anticipated before it occurs is referred to as foreseeable. When used about the future, foreseeable refers to a time period for which it is immediately possible to predict events or results.
previsible
▲ *a foreseeable limit* un límite previsible ▲ *in the foreseeable future* en el futuro previsible

forgivable loan
A forgivable loan is a loan where the lender, often a public or non-profit organisation, has no repayment obligation or has waived repayment subject to certain circumstances or requirements.
préstamo no reintegrable
= préstamo condonable
NOTE Spanish accountants prefer 'préstamo no reintegrable' yo the IAS/IFRS term 'préstamo condonable'.
▲ *a forgivable loan from government* un préstamo no reintegrable del gobierno
SOURCE IAS 20, paragraph 3

form of business enterprise
A form of business enterprise is a type of business organisation from which appears how it has been organised and how its liability is for payments of debts etc. Types include private or public limited companies, partnerships and sole proprietorships.
tipo de empresa
= tipo de organización empresarial
▲ *forms of business enterprises with limited liability* tipos de empresa con responsabilidad limitada
⇛ limited liability, partnership, private limited company, public limited company

form of financial statement US
= format, layout
The form of a financial statement is the presentation format or layout of a balance sheet or an income statement. The balance sheet generally follows one of two formats: the account (horizontal) form or the report (vertical) form. The profit and loss account is typically presented in the account form classified either by type of expenditure or by type of operation and function.
formato de presentación de cuentas anuales
▲ *a completed form of financial statement* un formato completo de presentación de las cuentas anuales ▲ *an improved form of financial statement* un formato de presentación de cuentas anuales mejorado ▲ *use of another form of financial statement* utilización de otro formato de presentación de cuentas anuales
⇛ classified by operation and function, classified by type of expenditure, horizontal format, vertical format

formalities
= formal requirements
Formalities are conditions regarding order, method, arrangement, use of technical expressions, performance of specific acts, etc., which are required by the law in the making of contracts or conveyances, or in the taking of legal proceedings, to insure their validity and regularity. Formalities generally refer to 'procedure' in contrast to 'substance'.
formalidades
= formalismos
▲ *a number of formalities* un número de formalidades ▲ *comply with formalities* cumplir con las formalidades ▲ *legal formalities* formalidades legales ▲ *satisfy the formalities* satisfacer los formalismos

format UK
= form, layout, presentation form, reporting format
A format (of accounts) is the layout in which or method according to which the financial statements are arranged and presented, e.g. the horizontal and the vertical formats.
formato
▲ *a common format* un formato común ▲ *adopt a different format for the income statement* adoptar un formato diferente para el estado de resultados ▲ *balance sheet formats* formatos del balance ▲ *the entity's primary or the entity's secondary reporting format* el formato de presentación de información de la empresa principal o secundaria ▲ *the format of the balance sheet* el formato del balance

formation

Formation means the setting up or establishment of something new such as a business organisation, a committee or an association.

constitución

▲ *companies in the course of formation* empresa en constitución ▲ *deem the enterprise's activities to have commenced on the date of formation* considerar que las actividades de la empresa han comenzado en la fecha de constitución ▲ *formation having tax implications* constitución con implicaciones fiscales ▲ *formation of a public limited company* constitución de una sociedad anónima cotizada ▲ *retroactive formation* constitución sucesiva ▲ *the actual expenses in connection with the formation of a public limited company* los gastos actuales en relación con la constitución de una sociedad anónima cotizada ▲ *the formation of a new company* la constitución de una nueva empresa ▲ *the formation of public limited companies* la constitución de sociedades anónimas cotizadas

formation expense

= set-up cost, start-up cost

Formation expenses are the costs incurred by establishing a business enterprise.

gasto de constitución

= gasto de establecimiento

▲ *formation expenses receivable* gastos de constitución a cobrar ▲ *incur formation expenses* incurrir en gastos de constitución ▲ *value adjustments in respect of formation expenses* valorar los ajustes en relación con los gastos de constitución

forward contract

A forward contract is a legally binding agreement between two parties on a future purchase/sale of an asset at a predetermined price at a specified date. The contract specifies the terms of the forward transaction. Unlike futures contracts, forward contracts are not standardised. Usually, a forward contract is an agreement to exchange a specified amount of one currency for another in order to hedge against foreign currency exchange rate changes.

contrato de futuros

▲ *a forward contract to be settled in five months' time* un contrato de futuros para materializarse a los cinco meses ▲ *a forward contract to purchase a fixed rate debt instrument* un contrato de futuros para comprar un instrumento de deuda de tipo fijo ▲ *a sale assured under a forward contract* una venta asegurada según un contrato de futuros ▲ *an entity's obligation under a forward contract to purchase its own equity instruments for cash* una obligación de una entidad según un contrato de futuros para intercambiar sus propios instrumentos de patrimonio por efectivo ▲ *become a party to a forward contract* ser un partícipe en un contrato de futuros ▲ *conclusion of forward contracts* conclusión de los contratos de futuros ▲ *forward contracts purchased* contratos de futuros comprados ▲ *gains and losses on forward contracts* pérdidas y ganancias en los contratos de futuros ▲ *separate the interest element and the spot price of a forward contract* separar el interés y el precio al contado de un contrato de futuros ▲ *the discount or premium on the forward contract* el descuento o prima en el contrato de futuros ▲ *the fair value of the forward contract at inception* el valor razonable del contrato de futuros al inicio ▲ *value adjustments of forward contracts* valorar los ajustes de los contratos de futuros

⇛ derivative financial instrument, forward transaction

forward exchange contract

A forward exchange contract is a legally binding agreement between two parties on a future purchase or sale of foreign currency at a specified exchange rate at a specified date. Forward exchange contracts are typically made with a view to hedging against foreign exchange risk.

contrato de compraventa de divisas a plazo

▲ *adjustment of forward exchange contracts to fair value* ajuste de los contratos de compraventa de divisas a plazo a valor razonable ▲ *an open forward exchange contract* un contrato de compraventa de divisas a plazo abierto ▲ *become a party to an unperformed forward exchange contract* ser un partícipe en un contrato de compraventa de divisas a plazo no materializado ▲ *convert a forward exchange contract* convertir un contrato de compraventa de divisas a plazo ▲ *deferred gain on forward exchange contracts* beneficio diferido por contratos de compraventa de divisas a plazo ▲ *deferred loss on forward exchange contracts* pérdida diferida por contratos de compraventa de divisas a plazo ▲ *enter into a forward exchange contract* firmar un contrato de compraventa de divisas a plazo ▲ *hedge a foreign currency receivable using a forward exchange contract* cubrir una divisa a cobrar utilizando un contrato de compraventa de divisas a plazo ▲ *hedge by using forward exchange contracts* cubrir utilizando contratos de compraventa de divisas a plazo ▲ *the notional value of a forward exchange contract* el valor teórico de un contrato de compraventa de divisas a plazo

⇛ forward exchange transaction

forward exchange market

The forward exchange market is a subcategory of the foreign exchange market. In the forward exchange market, traded currencies are delivered at a future date specified in the relevant forward contract as opposed to the spot market, where currencies are traded with delivery within two business days.

mercado de divisas a plazo

▲ *intervene in the forward exchange market* intervenir en el mercado de divisas a plazo ▲ *the liquidity in the forward exchange market* la liquidez en el mercado de divisas a plazo ▲ *turnover on the forward exchange market* facturación en el mercado de divisas a plazo

⇛ foreign exchange market, spot market

forward exchange rate

= forward rate

The forward exchange rate is the fixed exchange rate at which a given amount of a currency is to be delivered on a specified date in the future. The forward exchange rate consists of the spot rate of the underlying currency plus a premium or less a discount depending on the interest rate differential between the two currencies involved in the transaction.

tipo de cambio a plazo

= tipo de cambio a futuro

NOTE Spanish accountants prefer 'tipo de cambio a plazo' to the IAS/IFRS term 'tipo de cambio a futuro'.

▲ *at the forward exchange rate* al tipo de cambio a plazo ▲ *the average forward exchange rate* el tipo de cambio a plazo medio ▲ *the contracted forward exchange rate* el tipo de cambio a plazo contratado ▲ *the forward exchange rate agreed to* el tipo de cambio a plazo acordado

forward exchange transaction

= forward exchange contract

A forward exchange transaction is a transaction made on the basis of a previously agreed forward exchange contract involving the purchase or sale of a specified amount of foreign currency at a specified exchange rate agreed on the inception of the contract with delivery and settlement at a specified future date. Such transactions are typically made with a view to hedging against foreign exchange risk.

transacción en divisas a plazo

▲ *accrued premiums on forward exchange transactions* primas devengadas en transacciones en divisas a plazo

⇛ forward exchange contract

forward premium

≠ forward discount

A forward premium is the (positive) difference between the spot and the forward prices (or rates where currency is the underlying asset), typically expressed as a percentage of the underlying price or spot exchange rate. A negative difference is referred to as a forward discount.

prima a plazo

≠ descuento a plazo

▲ *accrual of forward premiums and discounts* devengo de primas y descuentos a plazo

forward price

The forward price is the fixed price at which a given amount of a commodity, currency, or a financial instrument is to be delivered on a fixed date in the future. The forward price consists of the spot price of the underlying asset plus a premium or less a discount depending on the interest rate differential involved.

precio a plazo

= precio pactado

▲ *based on the forward price for the commodity* basado en el precio a plazo de la materia prima ▲ *the forward price at the balance sheet date* el precio a plazo a la fecha de balance ▲ *the forward price at year-end* el precio a plazo a final de año

⇛ forward contract

forward rate

= forward exchange rate

The forward rate is the fixed exchange rate at which a given amount of a currency is to be delivered on a specified date in the future. The forward rate consists of the spot rate of the underlying currency plus a premium or less a discount depending on the interest rate differential between the two currencies involved in the transaction.

tipo de cambio a plazo

▲ *forward rate agreements* acuerdos de tipo de cambio a plazo

forward transaction

= forward deal

A forward transaction is a transaction made on the basis of a previously agreed forward contract involving the purchase or sale of a specified amount of foreign currency, commodity or other at a specified exchange rate or price agreed on the inception of the contract with delivery and settlement at a specified future date.

transacción a plazo

▲ *long-term forward transactions* transacciones a plazo a largo ▲ *revaluation of forward transaction* revalorización de la transacción a plazo ▲ *settlement of a forward transaction* pago de una transacción a plazo ▲ *short-term forward transactions* transacciones a plazo a corto

⇛ forward contract

forward-looking statement

= safe harbor statement US

A forward-looking statement is a cautionary statement made by a reporting company under the Private Securities Litigation Reform Act 1995 providing current expectations or forecasts of events such as new product introductions, product approvals and financial performance. The statement is included in earnings releases and annual reports and represents a warning to users that the forward-looking statement is subject to risks and uncertainties, in this way protecting the company and providing 'a safe harbor' from legal action because of false or misleading information.

informe de previsión

= declaración de puesto seguro, informe previsional

▲ *identify forward-looking statements* identificar informes de previsión ▲ *projections and other forward-looking statements* proyecciones y otros informes de previsión ▲ *rely on forward-looking statements* confiar en los informes de previsión

⇛ safe harbor statement

foundation

A foundation is an institution or organisation which is established and supported by an endowment. The objective of a foundation may be to support causes such as educational, business or charitable activities by granting money. Foundations are usually non-profit and tax-exempt organisations.

fundación

▲ *a commercial foundation* una fundación comercial ▲ *a newly established foundation* una fundación nuevamente establecida ▲ *an existing foundation* una fundación existente ▲ *Danish Act on Commercial Foundations* Ley danesa sobre Fundaciones Comerciales ▲ *the continuing foundation* la fundación continua

⇛ commercial foundation

founder

A founder is a natural or artificial person who sets up an organisation or an enterprise. An organisation or enterprise may be established by several founders, and an organisation can be the founder of another organisation. For companies, the founders' names will appear from the memorandum of association.

fundador

▲ *founder member* miembro fundador ▲ *founder's share* participación del fundador ▲ *requirements as to the domicile and address of the founder* requisitos en cuanto al domicilio y dirección postal del fundador

fragmented

Fragmented means incomplete or separated into several fragments, i.e. pieces or parts.

fragmentado

▲ *the fragmented global market* el mercado global fragmentado

framework

A framework is a system containing theoretical rules, concepts and principles on which the development of more detailed rules, e.g. accounting standards, is based.

marco

▲ *IASB Framework for the Preparation and Presentation of Financial Statements* el Marco IASB para la Preparación y Presentación de Estados Financieros ▲ *meet the Framework definitions of income or expense* cumplir con las definiciones de ingreso o gastos del Marco ▲ *the definitions and recognition criteria for assets, liabilities, income and expenses set out in the Framework* las definiciones y criterios de registro de activos, pasivos, ingresos y gastos fijados en el Marco

⇛ conceptual framework, regulatory framework

franchise right

A franchise right is a right given to an enterprise allowing it to manufacture or sell a specific product or service under a name owned by someone else.

derecho de franquicia

▲ *acquire a franchise right* adquirir un derecho de franquicia ▲ *grant a franchise right* conceder un derecho de franquicia

franchisee

A franchisee is a person or enterprise that has acquired a franchise right. This franchise right allows the franchisee to manufacture or sell a specific product or service under a name owned by someone else, called a franchisor, usually against payment.

franquiciado

▲ *provide financial support to the franchisee* ofrecer apoyo financiero al franquiciado ▲ *the area in which the franchisee is permitted to operate* el área en la que se permite operar al franquiciado ▲ *transactions between the franchisor and the franchisee* transacciones entre el franquiciador y el franquiciado

⇛ franchisor

franchisor

A franchisor is a person or enterprise that has granted a franchisee a franchise right that allows the franchisee to manufacture or sell a specific product or service under a name owned by the franchisor, usually against payment to the franchisor.

franquiciador

▲ *the decision-making authority of the franchisor* el poder de toma de decisiones del franquiciador ▲ *transactions between the franchisor and the franchisee* transacciones entre el franquiciador y el franquiciado

⇛ franchisee

fraudulent

If something has been done or said in order to intentionally deceive someone in order to gain some advantage, it is fraudulent.

fraudulento

▲ *fraudulent conversion* conversión fraudulenta ▲ *fraudulent financial reporting* informe financiero fraudulento ▲ *fraudulent practices* prácticas fraudulentas ▲ *fraudulent preference* preferencia fraudulenta ▲ *fraudulent procurement of a patent* licitación fraudulenta de una patente ▲ *fraudulent trading* cotización fraudulenta ▲ *material amounts of work in progress and receivables in respect of fraudulent contracts which cannot be enforced* cantidades materiales de trabajo en curso y a cobrar con respecto a contratos fraudulentos sin obligación de cumplimiento

FRC UK

= Financial Reporting Council UK

FRC is the abbreviation for the Financial Reporting Council, a body set up by the UK Government in 1990 to supervise the setting of accouting standards.

FRC

= Consejo de Información Financiera

▲ *The Board of the FRC* El Consejo de la FRC

⇛ Accounting Standards Board

FRED UK

FRED is the abbreviation for Financial Reporting Exposure Draft. FREDs are discussion documents preceding the issue of Financial Reporting Standards (FRSs) developed and issued by the Accounting Standards Board in the UK. The intention of issuing an exposure draft is to attract comments from accountants, investment analysts, financial institutions and other experts.

Borrador para la Discusión sobre Información Financiera

▲ *publish FRED 19* publicar el Borrador para la Discusión sobre Información Financiera 19 ▲ *release a new FRED* dar a conocer un nuevo Borrador para la Discusión sobre Información Financiera

free cash flow

= FCF

Free cash flow is the net cash that remains after deducting operating expenses, i.e. net cash flows from operating activities, minus dividends, minus net capital expenditures. The measure is used for the valuation and risk assessment of enterprises.

flujo de efectivo disponible

= cash flow disponible, flujo de caja disponible

▲ *calculate free cash flow* calcular el flujo de efectivo disponible ▲ *expected free cash flow* flujo de efectivo disponible esperado ▲ *free cash flow of USD 10 million* flujo de efectivo disponible de 10 millones de dólares norteamericos ▲ *negative free cash flow* flujo de efectivo disponible negativo ▲ *positive free cash flow* flujo de efectivo disponible positivo

free cash flow to equity

= FCFE

Free cash flow to equity (FCFE) is a key figure defined as cash flow before dividend payment and share buybacks, but including e.g. financial income and expenses in contrast to free cash flow to firm.

flujo de efectivo disponible para los accionistas

= FCFE, flujo de caja disponible para ccionistas, flujo de efectivo disponible para accionistas, free cash flow to equity

▲ *discounted free cash flow to equity* flujo de efectivo disponible para los accionistas descontado ▲ *measure free cash flow to equity* medir el flujo de efectivo disponible para los accionistas ▲ *spreadsheet for free cash flow to equity* hoja de cálculo para flujo de efectivo disponible para los accionistas ▲ *the entity's ability to generate and sustain free cash flow to equity* la capacidad de la entidad para generar y sostener el flujo de efectivo disponible para los accionistas

⇛ equity, free cash flow, free cash flow to firm

free cash flow to firm

= FCFF

Free cash flow to firm (FCFF) is defined as cash flow before dividend payment, share buybacks and net financials, but after tax. FCFF is a key figure used in discounted cash flow models as a measure of the cash flow left to service the return requirements of the debt and equity of the enterprise.

flujo de efectivo disponible para la empresa

= FCFF, free cash flow to firm

▲ *compute free cash flow to the firm* computar el flujo de efectivo disponible para la empresa ▲ *use a free cash flow to firm valuation model* utilizar un flujo de efectivo disponible para la empresa como modelo de valoración

⇛ free cash flow to equity

free cash flow to firm yield

The free cash flow to firm yield is a financial ratio defined as free cash flow to firm divided by enterprise value. This ratio expresses a company's capacity for debt servicing, dividend payments and share buy-backs.

ratio de flujo de efectivo disponible para la empresa por el valor de la empresa

▲ *calculate free cash flow to firm yield* calcular el ratio de flujo

de efectivo disponible para la empresa por el valor de la empresa
⇛ free cash flow to firm

free cash flow yield
The free cash flow yield is a financial ratio defined as free cash flow to equity, i.e. cash flow before dividend payment and share buybacks, divided by market capitalisation and the value of minority interests. This ratio expresses a company's capacity for dividends and share buybacks.
ratio de flujo de efectivo disponible por valor bursátil
▲ *a free cash flow yield of somewhere around 10%* un ratio de flujo de efectivo disponible por valor bursátil de más o menos el 10% ▲ *an above sector average free cash flow yield* un sector por encima de la media del ratio de flujo de efectivo disponible por valor bursátil ▲ *generate a free cash flow yield of about 8%* generar un ratio de flujo de efectivo disponible por valor bursátil de cerca del 8%
⇛ free cash flow to equity

freehold[1] UK *noun* <a, the, no plural>
Freehold is the most complete form of ownership of real property, and the right is of uncertain duration, i.e. may last for ever.
pleno dominio
= dominio absoluto, dominio pleno
▲ *acquire the freehold to land* adquirir el pleno dominio sobre bienes raíces ▲ *freehold estate* propiedades de dominio pleno ▲ *freehold ownership* propiedad de pleno dominio
⇛ freehold property

freehold[2] *noun* <a, the, -s>
→ freehold property

freehold property UK
Freehold property is property owned completely with no limit in time.
propiedad de dominio pleno
▲ *buy freehold property* comprar propiedad de dominio pleno
⇛ freehold

front-end fee
A front-end fee is a one-time fee payable by a borrower when obtaining a loan. A front-end fee may be a fixed amount or a percentage of the loan amount.
cuota de suscripción
▲ *pay a front-end fee* pagar una cuota de suscripción

FRRP UK
= Financial Reporting Review Panel UK
FRRP is the abbreviation for the Financial Reporting Review Panel, a body referring to the Financial Reporting Council and set up in the UK in 1991. The FRRP investigates the annual accounts of large companies if they fail to comply with the requirements of the Companies Act, e.g. if they do not give a true and fair view. The FRRP can refer issues to court.
Panel de Revisión de la Información Financiera
= FRRP
▲ *a formal enquiry conducted by the FRRP* una investigación formal dirigida por el Panel de Revisión de la Información Financiera ▲ *a press note issued by the FRRP* una nota de prensa emitida por el Panel de Revisión de la Información Financiera ▲ *the chairman of FRRP* el presidente del Panel de Revisión de la Información Financiera

FRS UK
= Financial Reporting Standard UK
FRS is the abbreviation for Financial Reporting Standard. FRSs are accounting standards issued by the UK Accounting Standards Board to set disclosure requirements and to establish generally accepted accounting principles for enterprises in the preparation of their financial reporting to ensure that their financial statements give a true and fair view. The FRSs have been issued since 1990 to supplement or replace the Statements of Standard Accounting Practice (SSAPs).
Norma de Información Financiera
= NIF
▲ *compliance with an FRS* cumplimiento de una Norma de Información Financiera ▲ *follow an FRS* seguir una Norma de Información Financiera ▲ *issue an FRS* emitir una Norma de Información Financiera ▲ *the requirements of an*

FRS los requisitos de una Norma de Información Financiera
⇛ accounting standard, IFRS, SFAS

FSA

1 = Financial Services Authority UK
FSA is an abbreviation for the Financial Services Authority (FSA) that was introduced by the Financial Services and Markets Act in 2000 as a new regulatory body for the entire UK financial sector to substitute the former Securities and Investment Board and some of the self-regulatory organisations regulating investment activities. The supervision and authority by the Bank of England and the Treasury over the banking and insurances sectors were surrendered to the FSA, as was the listing authority of the London Stock Exchange.

FSA
= Autoridad de Servicios Financieros
▲ *authorised by the FSA* autorizado por la FSA ▲ *comply with the FSA rules* cumplir con las normas de la FSA ▲ *on behalf of the FSA* en nombre de la FSA

2 = Financial Services Act UK
FSA is an abbreviation for the Financial Services Act, a UK Act of Parliament enacted 1986 that came into force in 1988 to regulate investment business in the UK and set up the Securities and Investment Board. The SIB was reorganised and renamed the Financial Services Authority following the adoption in 2000 of the Financial Services and Markets Act that superseded the Financial Services Act.

FSA
= Ley de Servicios Financieros
▲ *comply with the FSA* cumplir con la FSA ▲ *the provisions of the FSA* las disposiciones de la FSA ▲ *the scope of FSA* el alcance de la FSA

FSMA UK

= Financial Services and Markets Act UK
FSMA is the abbreviation for the Financial Services and Markets Act that was adopted in 2000 and came into force in 2001 as the sucessor to the Financial Services Act. The new act substituted the Securities and Investment Board with a new regulatory body for the entire UK financial sector, the Financial Services Authority, and introduced a new Code of Market Conduct for the financial markets.

FSMA
= Ley de Servicios Financieros y Mercados
▲ *according to the FSMA* de acuerdo con la FSMA ▲ *comply with the provisions of FSMA* cumplir con lo dispuesto en la FSMA ▲ *governed by FSMA* regulado por la FSMA ▲ *the scope of FSMA* el alcance de la FSMA

full absorption

= absorption approach, absorption costing, allocation costing
Full absorption is a costing method which seeks to estimate the value of an inventory by assigning all variable manufacturing costs and all fixed manufacturing costs to each production unit. The fixed costs are typically allocated to output units based on direct labour hours, machine hours or material costs.

sistema de coste integral
= sistema de coste completo
▲ *full absorption of projected spending* sistema de coste integral del gasto proyectado ▲ *full absorption of the costs* sistema de coste integral de los costes
⇛ overhead absorption rate

full consolidation

= global consolidation, line-by-line consolidation
≠ proportionate consolidation
Full consolidation is a consolidation method where 100% of the assets, liabilities, revenues and expenses of a subsidiary are recognised in the financial statements of the parent company. This is the normal method of consolidation, and it is also used even if the subsidiary is not wholly owned by the parent company.

consolidación global
= consolidación total
▲ *be included in the consolidated financial statements by full consolidation* estar incluido en los estados financieros consolida-

dos por consolidación global ▲ *financial statements by full consolidation* estados financieros por consolidación global

full cost pricing

= cost plus method, cost-plus pricing

Full cost pricing is a pricing model which seeks to add an appropriate mark-up to the supplier's cost.

contrato a coste más beneficio

= sistema de coste total

▲ *use full cost pricing* usar el contrato a coste más beneficio

full costing

Full costing is a costing method where all costs related to the production of a product or providing a service are calculated by including both direct and indirect costs (overheads) in the cost unit using overhead absorption rates.

criterio de coste completo

= método de coste completo, sistema de coste completo

▲ *recommend full costing* recomendar el criterio de coste completo ▲ *use full costing* utilizar el criterio de coste completo

⇛ overhead absorption rate

full costing method

= absorption approach

The full costing method is a method where all costs related to the production of a product or providing a service are calculated by including both direct and indirect costs (overheads) in the cost unit, using overhead absorption rates.

criterio de coste completo

= método de coste completo, sistema de coste completo

▲ *calculated by the full costing method* calculado por el criterio de coste completo ▲ *under the full costing method* según el criterio de coste completo ▲ *use the full costing method* utilizar el criterio de coste completo

full costs

= fully allocated costs

Full costs constitute the total costs, i.e. the sum of all production, marketing, distribution and development costs as well as administrative expenses attributable to a product or a service.

costes totales

▲ *estimate the full costs* estimar los costes totales ▲ *the full costs of every project* los costes totales de cada proyecto

⇛ full costs of the product

full costs of the product

The full costs of the product refer to the total costs that relate to a specific product, e.g. the costs of research & development, production, marketing, distribution and customer service.

costes totales del producto

▲ *calculate the full costs of the product* calcular los costes totales del producto ▲ *pay the full costs of the product* pagar los costes totales del producto ▲ *reflect the full costs of the product* reflejar los costes totales del producto

⇛ full costs

full-time

Full-time work involves working for the complete time that is the standard for a particular job, often defined by a specific number of hours per day or week.

tiempo completo

= full time

▲ *a full-time employee* un empleado a tiempo completo ▲ *conversion to full-time positions* conversión a posiciones a tiempo completo ▲ *provide services to an enterprise on a full-time, part-time, permanent, casual or temporary basis* ofrecer servicios a una empresa a tiempo completo, a tiempo parcial, de forma permanente, casual o estacional

full-time employed[1] *noun*

A full-time employed person works for the complete time that is the standard for a particular job, often defined by a specific number of hours per day or week.

personal a tiempo completo

▲ *the total number of full-time employed* el número total de personal a tiempo completo

full-time employed[2] *adjective*

A person who is full-time employed is a person working full time in an enterprise. The scope of full time will depend on the definition of full time in the collective agreement under which the person is employed.

empleado a tiempo completo

▲ *full-time employed staff* personal empleado a tiempo completo

full-time employee
A full-time employee is a person employed on full time in an enterprise, where the scope of full time will depend on the definition of full time in the collective agreement under which the person is employed. A full-time employee pays social security contributions in full.
trabajador a tiempo completo
▲ *an average number of full-time employees* un número medio de trabajadores a tiempo completo ▲ *full-time employee equivalents* equivalentes a trabajadores a tiempo completo

full-year figure
Full-year figures are the results for a financial reporting period covering a full financial year.
cifra anual
▲ *be in excess of the full year figure for 2005* estar por encima de la cifra anual de 2005 ▲ *divide the full-year figure by four* dividir la cifra anual por cuatro ▲ *the corresponding full-year figure for 2005* la cifra anual correspondiente para el 2005 ▲ *the restated full-year figure for 2005* la cifra anual recalculada para el 2005

full-year financial statements
The full-year financial statements are financial statements that cover a financial year that must comprise a whole accounting period of 12 months.
estados financieros anuales
▲ *prepare full-year financial statements* preparar los estados financieros anuales ▲ *quarterly and full-year financial statements* estados financieros trimestrales y anuales

fully allocated costs
= full costs
Fully allocated costs constitute the total costs, i.e. the sum of all production, marketing, distribution and development costs as well as administrative expenses attributable to a product or a service.
costes totales
▲ *the development of fully allocated costs* el desarrollo de los costes totales

function
In a business context, a function is a unit or division of an enterprise which is responsible for particular, relatively uniform, separate activities such as production, logistics, finance, accounting or marketing. A particular function may refer both to such a division and to the activity it performs, e.g. the accounting function.
función
= tarea
▲ *the audit function* la función de auditoría ▲ *the functions assigned to the audit committee* las funciones asignadas al comité de auditoría ▲ *the public-interest function of statutory auditors* la función de interés público de los auditores estatutarios ▲ *the risk management function* la función de gestión del riesgo

functional budget
A functional budget is a budget of costs and, if possible, income prepared for a particular function, sector or division of an enterprise, e.g. sales, production or administration.
presupuesto funcional
▲ *adjust the functional budget* ajustar el presupuesto funcional ▲ *prepare a functional budget* preparar un presupuesto funcional ▲ *the proposed functional budget* el presupuesto funcional propuesto

functional budgeting
Functional budgeting is a budget procedure focusing on preparing a budget of the costs and possible income for a particular function, sector or division of an enterprise, e.g. sales, production or administration.
procedimiento de elaboración del presupuesto funcional
▲ *introduce functional budgeting* introducir el procedimiento de elaboración del presupuesto funcional
⇛ functional budget

functional currency
The functional currency is the currency applied in the primary economic environment of an enterprise's operations and as such the currency in which the enterprise has determined to measure the individual items in the financial statements.
NOTE Under IFRS (IAS 21), the former "reporting currency" has been split up in two concepts: "presentation currency" and "functional currency".
moneda funcional
▲ *an item denominated in the functional currency of the fo-*

reign operation una partida denominada en la moneda funcional de la operación en divisas ▲ *change in functional currency* cambio en la moneda funcional ▲ *changes in the general purchasing power of the functional currency* cambios en el poder de compra general de la moneda funcional ▲ *determining the functional currency of a foreign operation* determinar la moneda funcional de una operación extranjera ▲ *reporting foreign currency transactions in the functional currency* informar en la moneda funcional de las transacciones realizadas en moneda extranjera ▲ *the functional currency of any substantial party to the contract* la moneda funcional de cualquier contraparte importante del contrato ▲ *the functional currency used* la moneda funcional utilizada ▲ *translate foreign currency items into the functional currency* traducir las partidas en moneda extranjera a la moneda funcional ▲ *translation from functional currency to reporting currency* conversión de la moneda funcional a la moneda del informe ▲ *use of a presentation currency other than the functional currency* uso de una moneda de presentación diferente a la moneda funcional
⇛ local currency, presentation currency

fund[1] *noun*
A fund is a pool of cash or other resources designated for a particular purpose.
fondo
▲ *allocation to a special fund* asignación a un fondo especial ▲ *assets held by a long-term employee benefit fund* activos cubiertos por un fondo de pensiones a largo plazo ▲ *contributions paid to a fund* contribuciones pagadas al fondo ▲ *interest and dividend income, after tax payable by the fund* ingresos por intereses y dividendos, después de impuestos pagables por el fondo ▲ *operate an internal property fund that issues notional units* operar con un fondo de propiedad interna que emite unidades nocionales ▲ *the property held by the fund* la propiedad cubierta por el fondo
⇛ pension fund

fund[2] *verb*
= finance
To fund means to raise or otherwise provide capital or money for something, e.g. an activity, organisation or event.
financiar
▲ *fund a pension plan* financiar un plan de pensiones ▲ *fund employee benefits under a defined benefit plan* financiar las prestaciones a empleados según un plan de prestación definida ▲ *pay insurance premiums to fund a post-employment benefit plan* pagar primas de seguro para financiar un plan de jubilación

fund by loans
To fund by loans means to finance an investment or other activity by raising loans rather than e.g. financing it out of internally generated profits.
financiar con préstamos
▲ *buildings funded by loans* edificios financiados con préstamos

fundamental accounting principle
Fundamental accounting principles are the basic assumptions that underlie the preparation of financial statements such as the accruals, consistency, going concern, separate valuation and prudence concepts.
principio contable fundamental
▲ *the fundamental accounting principles relating to derivatives* los principios contables fundamentales relacionados con derivados

fundamental error
Fundamental errors are errors discovered in the current period that are of such significance that the financial statements of one or more prior periods can no longer be considered to have been reliable at the date of their issue.
error fundamental
▲ *change as a result of fundamental errors* cambio como un resultado de errores fundamentales ▲ *correction of a fundamental error* corrección de un error fundamental ▲ *discover a fundamental error* descubrir un error fundamental ▲ *reversal*

due to fundamental errors modificación debido a errores fundamentales ▲ *the effects of fundamental errors* los efectos de los errores fundamentales ▲ *the nature of the fundamental error* la naturaleza del error fundamental

fundamental principle

A fundamental principle is the basic principle underlying something.

principio fundamental

▲ *based on a fundamental principle* basado en un principio fundamental ▲ *the fundamental principle of securities law* el principio fundamental de la ley de valores

funded IAS/IFRS

≠ unfunded

When something has been funded, it has been secured by a fund of assets. Pension plans are typically funded by a legally separate fund of assets, e.g. pension contribution, investments or other resources, to secure the payment of benefits.

asegurado

▲ *funded plans* planes asegurados ▲ *the payment of funded benefits* el pago de prestaciones aseguradas ▲ *wholly or partly funded defined benefit plans* planes de pensiones de prestación definida asegurados total o parcialmente

funded obligation

A funded obligation is an obligation to pay employee benefits, which has been secured by a legally separate fund of assets.

obligación garantizada

= obligación asegurara

▲ *present value of funded obligations* valor actual de las obligaciones garantizadas

⇛ funded

funded pension scheme UK

= funded scheme UK

A funded pension scheme is a pension scheme that has been secured by a separate fund of assets, which ensures that future payments of benefits are covered.

plan de pensiones garantizado

= plan de pensiones asegurado

▲ *a mandatory funded pension scheme* un plan de pensiones garantizado obligatorio ▲ *introduce a funded pension scheme* introducir un plan de pensiones garantizado

SOURCE FRS 17

⇛ funded

funded status

Within the context of pension plans, the funded status is the difference between the plan assets of a pension fund and the projected benefit obligation (PBO), i.e. the future liability to pay employee benefits. When the fair value of the plan assets exceed the PBO the plan is overfunded, and when the PBO exceeds the fair value of the plan assets the plan is underfunded.

situación financiera del plan

▲ *development of funded status for pensions* desarrollo de la situación financiera del plan de pensiones ▲ *reconciliation of funded status* conciliación de la situación financiera del plan ▲ *the current funded status of the plan* la situación financiera del plan actual

⇛ plan asset, projected benefit obligation

funding

1 = financing, raising of funds

Funding is the providing of capital by an enterprise to finance its business and investment activities. Funding may be obtained by various methods, e.g. by issuing shares or by raising loan capital via bank borrowings or corporate bond issues.

financiación

▲ *as part of funding* como parte de la financiación ▲ *available funding* financiación disponible ▲ *committed funding* financiación comprometida ▲ *cross-border funding* financiación transnacional ▲ *funding assets* financiando activos ▲ *funding liabilities* financiando pasivos ▲ *funding vehicle* vehículo de financiación ▲ *the entity's sources of funding* las fuentes de financiación de la entidad

2 Funding is the covering of employee benefits by contributions paid by employers, and in some cases employees, into a legally separate fund of assets.

aportación

▲ *full funding* aportación completa ▲ *partial funding* aportación parcial ▲ *pension schemes changing from non-funding to full funding* planes de pensiones que cambian de no aportación a aportación completa

funding policy

A funding policy refers to an enterprise's procedures for transferring assets to a legally separate fund to secure future payments of benefits under various funded post-employment benefit plans or pension schemes.

política de aportaciones

▲ *a description of the funding policy* una descripción de la política de aportaciones ▲ *information about the funding policy based on salary projections* información sobre la política de aportaciones basada en proyecciones salariales

funding source

Funding sources refer to entities or parties providing financial resources to an enterprise to finance its activities, e.g. a bank may provide loans and credit facilities.

fuente de financiación

▲ *serve as a funding source* servir como una fuente de financiación ▲ *the entity's funding sources* las fuentes de financiación de la entidad

funds flow statement UK

= source and application of funds statement UK, statement of changes in financial position US, statement of source and application of funds UK

A funds flow statement shows the source and application of funds and the changes in an enterprise's working capital for an accounting period. In modern financial reporting, this statement has been replaced by a cash flow statement, as movements in working capital may not give a true and fair view of the liquidity and solvency of an enterprise.

estado del flujo de fondos

= estados de cambios en la posición financiera

▲ *prepare a funds flow statement* preparar un estado de cambios en la posición financiera

SOURCE FRS 1, Appendix III

funds generated from operations

Funds generated from operations are cash flows that constitute earnings resulting from an enterprise's own activities rather than from loan financing.

fondos generados por actividades de explotación

▲ *funds generated from operations for first quarter 2006* fondos generados por actividades de explotación durante el primer trimestre del 2006

funds tied up

Funds tied up represent the liquidity directly or indirectly invested in activities and assets and therefore not available for alternative use.

fondos cautivos

= fondos condicionados

▲ *an increase in funds tied up* un aumento en los fondos cautivos ▲ *funds tied up according to geographical segment* fondos cautivos de acuerdo al segmento geográfico ▲ *funds tied up in net operating assets* fondos cautivos en activos de explotación netos ▲ *funds tied up in operations* fondos cautivos en actividades de explotación ▲ *funds tied up in products and services* fondos cautivos en productos y servicios ▲ *funds tied up in receivables* fondos cautivos en cuentas a cobrar ▲ *funds tied up in trade receivables* fondos cautivos en clientes y cuentas a cobrar ▲ *funds tied up in working capital* fondos cautivos en el capital circulante ▲ *increased funds tied up in assets* fondos cautivos aumentados en activos ▲ *increasing funds tied up in assets* incrementando los fondos cautivos en activos ▲ *reduced funds tied up in assets* fondos cautivos reducidos en activos

funds tied-up

→ funds tied up

future

→ futures contract

future benefit

Future benefits are projected benefits or potential gains resulting in net cash inflows to an enterprise because of its ability to generate such cash inflows through transactions and events.

beneficio proyectado

▲ *the expected future benefits and obligations associated with assets and liabilities* los beneficios proyectados esperados y

las obligaciones asociadas con activos y pasivos ▲ *the related future benefits from the future costs* los beneficios proyectados relacionados con los costes proyectados
⇛ future economic benefit

future contract
→ futures contract

future economic benefit
Future economic benefits are projected benefits or potential gains resulting in net cash inflows to an enterprise because of its ability to generate such cash inflows through transactions and events.
beneficio económico futuro
= beneficio económico proyectado
▲ *generate sufficient future economic benefits to recover the carrying amount* generar beneficios económicos proyectados suficientes para recuperar el valor contable ▲ *in anticipation of future economic benefits* anticipando los beneficios económicos futuros ▲ *obtain future economic benefits* obtener beneficios económicos futuros ▲ *the expected future economic benefits from the asset* los beneficios económicos futuros esperados procedentes del activo ▲ *the expected pattern of consumption of the future economic benefits embodied in depreciable assets* el modelo de consumo esperado de los beneficios económicos proyectados incluidos en activos amortizables ▲ *the future economic benefits embodied in an asset* los beneficios económicos futuros incluidos en un activo
SOURCE IAS Framework, F 53

futures contract
A futures contract is a standardised mutual binding agreement involving the future purchase or sale of a fixed amount of an underlying asset at a fixed price at a fixed date. The underlying asset may be a share, a share index or a basket of bonds. Unlike options, futures contracts involve a definite purchase or sale and are typically used for hedging purposes.
NOTE The short form "futures" or "a future" is sometimes applied.
contrato de futuros
▲ *financial futures contracts* contratos de futuros financieros ▲ *futures contracts exchange* intercambio de contratos de futuros ▲ *futures contracts trading* operaciones de contratos de futuros
⇛ derivative financial instrument

FX
1 = foreign exchange
FX is an abbreviation for foreign exchange which refers to the currencies of other countries.
divisa
▲ *FX products* productos en divisas
2 = foreign exchange
FX is an abbreviation for foreign exchange which refers to the trading of currencies of different countries.
divisa
▲ *FX trading* operaciones en divisas

G

GAAP

GAAP is the abbreviation for generally accepted accounting principles, i.e. the conventions, rules and procedures that define and dictate accepted accounting practice. The concept includes not only broad guidelines but also detailed rules. When an enterprise complies with generally accepted accounting principles, the financial statements give a true and fair view

principios contables generalmente aceptados

= PCGA

▲ *approximate amounts as adjusted to conform with US GAAP* cantidades aproximadas ajustadas según los principios contables generalmente aceptados estadounidenses ▲ *balance sheet items as adjusted in accordance with US GAAP* partidas del balance ajustadas según los principios contables generalmente aceptados estadounidenses ▲ *differ significantly from US GAAP* diferir significativamente de los principios contables generalmente aceptados estadounidenses ▲ *in accordance with US GAAP* de acuerdo con los principios contables generalmente aceptados estadounidenses ▲ *net income for the year in accordance with US GAAP* ingresos netos del ejercicio según los principios contables generalmente aceptados estadounidenses ▲ *reclassify items recognised under previous GAAP* reclasificar partidas reconocidas según los principios contables generalmente aceptados anteriores ▲ *restatement to US GAAP* actualización de los principios contables generalmente aceptados estadounidenses ▲ *UK GAAP* los principios contables generalmente aceptados del Reino Unido ▲ *US GAAP* los principios contables generalmente aceptados estadounidenses

gain[1] *noun*

= profit

Seen in relation to the balance sheet, gains are profits from activities outside the normal operations of an enterprise resulting in increases in equity, i.e. economic benefits, and as such similar in nature to revenue. Gains may arise as differences between the proceeds of disposing of an asset and the cost of acquiring that asset.

beneficio

= ganancia

▲ *a deferred gain* un beneficio diferido ▲ *a foreign currency gain* un beneficio en divisa ▲ *a post-tax gain* un beneficio después de impuestos ▲ *any cumulative gains* cualesquiera beneficios acumulativos ▲ *consolidated statement of total gains and losses* estado consolidado de pérdidas y beneficios y totales ▲ *deferral of gains and losses on hedging transactions* diferimiento de pérdidas y beneficios en transacciones de cobertura ▲ *expected gain* beneficio previsto ▲ *fair value gains* ganancias en el valor razonable ▲ *gain and loss* pérdida y beneficio ▲ *gain on disposal of assets* beneficio por venta de activos ▲ *gain on sale of group enterprises* beneficio por venta de las empresas del grupo ▲ *gain on sale of property, plant and equipment* beneficio por venta de edificios, instalaciones y equipos ▲ *gain to redemption* beneficio para amortización ▲ *gains on extinguishment of debt* beneficios en extinción de deuda ▲ *gains or losses relating to continuing operations* resultados relativos a las operaciones en curso ▲ *gains reclassified from equity* beneficios reclasificados de patrimonio neto ▲ *realised gains* beneficios realizados ▲ *recognise a gain* reconocer un beneficio ▲ *the gain arising from the derecognition of an intangible asset* el beneficio resultante del no reconocimiento de un activo intangible ▲ *unrealised gains* beneficios no realizados

SOURCE IAS Framework, F 75

gain[2] *verb*

To gain something means to get an advantage or benefit from it.

ganar

▲ *gain experience* ganar experiencia ▲ *gain recognition* ganar reconocimiento ▲ *gain synergies* ganar sinergias

gain on curtailment

→ curtailment gain

gain on disposal

≠ loss on disposal

A gain on disposal refers to the amount by which the proceeds obtained by an enterprise on the sale of an asset exceed the carrying amount of the asset, i.e. the value of the asset less depreciation charges.

beneficio por enajenación

= ganancia por enajenación

▲ *determine the gain on disposal* determinar el beneficio por enajenación ▲ *recognise the gain on disposal* reconocer el beneficio por enajenación

gain on realisation UK

= gain on realization US

A gain on realisation is the profit achieved from a disposal or sale of an asset arising as the difference between the amount received as compensation and the carrying amount of the asset.

beneficio de liquidación

= ganancia de liquidación

▲ *taxation of gains on realisation* tributación de los beneficios de liquidación

⇛ realise

gain on realization US

= gain on realisation UK

A gain on realization is the profit achieved from a disposal or sale of an asset arising as the difference between the amount received as compensation and the carrying value of the asset.

beneficio de liquidación

= ganancia de liquidación

▲ *taxation of gains on realization* tributación de los beneficios de liquidación

⇛ realize

gearing

Gearing refers to either financial or operating gearing. Financial gearing refers to the relationship between an enterprise's net interest-bearing debt, i.e. loan capital, and equity. Operating gearing refers to how high the percentage of an enterprise's fixed costs is in relation to total costs.

apalancamiento

= endeudamiento

▲ *high gearing* apalancamiento alto ▲ *low gearing* apalancamiento bajo ▲ *the enterprise's policy on gearing* la política de la empresa sobre el apalancamiento

⇛ contribution margin, financial gearing, operating gearing

gearing ratio

Gearing ratios deal with an enterprise's financial gearing, i.e. the relationship between loan capital and equity, typically seen as net interest-bearing debt divided by total equity or, in a more operations-oriented version, as invested capital divided by total equity.

ratio de apalancamiento

= ratio de endeudamiento a largo plazo

▲ *supplementary gearing ratios* ratios de apalancamiento adicionales

⇛ financial gearing

general

When something is general, it is common and prevailing, and thus it applies to the majority of members of a category or group.

general

▲ *a general obligation* una obligación general ▲ *changes in a general or specific price index* cambios en un índice de precios general o específico ▲ *general audit* auditoría general ▲ *general balance sheet* balance general ▲ *general principles* principios generales ▲ *general risks* riesgos generales ▲ *general terms* condiciones generales ▲ *the general objective* el objetivo general

general clause

= catch-all provision, general provision, overriding principle

A general clause is a general provision and an overriding principle in an act. For accounting purposes, the general clause has specific importance as the overall objective of financial reporting.

cláusula general

▲ *comply with the general clause* cumplir con la cláusula general ▲ *extension of the general clause* extensión de la cláusula general ▲ *revision of the general clau-*

se revisión de la cláusula general ▲ *supplement the general clause* suplementar la cláusula general ▲ *the extent of the general clause* el alcance de la cláusula general ▲ *the general clause of the Danish Financial Statements Act* la cláusula general de la Ley danesa de Estados Financieros

general ledger

→ nominal ledger

general meeting

= annual general meeting

A general meeting is a meeting of members of a company where they can discuss issues and vote in order to make decisions.

junta general

= asamblea general

▲ *attend a general meeting* asistir a una junta general de accionistas ▲ *call a general meeting* convocar una junta general de accionistas ▲ *hold a general meeting* celebrar una junta general de accionistas ▲ *notice of general meeting* notificación de junta general de accionistas ▲ *proposed resolution for the general meeting* resolución propuesta para la junta general de accionistas ▲ *recommend the annual report for approval by the general meeting* recomendar el informe anual para su aprobación por la junta general de accionistas ▲ *the approval of the annual report by the general meeting* la aprobación del informe anual de la junta general de accionistas ▲ *time and place of the general meeting* hora y lugar de la junta general de accionistas

general partner

A general partner is a partner in a partnership who is fully liable for the partnership's debts.

socio con responsabilidad ilimitada

= socio colectivo

▲ *a retiring general partner* un socio con responsabilidad ilimitada saliente ▲ *an incoming general partner* un socio con responsabilidad ilimitada entrante

general partnership

→ partnership

general price index

A general price index is an index measuring the changes in the price level of a representative selection of products and services, e.g. consumer prices, over a period of time.

índice general de precios

= IPC, índice de precios general

▲ *a general price index that reflects changes in general purchasing power* un índice general de precios que refleje los cambios en el poder adquisitivo general ▲ *restate corresponding figures applying a general price index* reafirmar las cifras correspondientes aplicando un índice general de precios ▲ *selection and use of the general price index* selección y uso del índice general de precios ▲ *the change in a general price index from the date of acquisition to the balance sheet date* el cambio en un índice general de precios desde la fecha de adquisición hasta la fecha del balance

⇛ Consumer Price Index, specific price index

general purchasing power approach IAS/IFRS

The general purchasing power approach is an accounting method under which financial statements presented according to the historical cost convention are adjusted to allow for inflationary effects, typically by restating the items on the basis of a current general price index.

NOTE IAS 15 Information Reflecting the Effects of Changing Prices was withdrawn with effect from January 1, 2005. In an IFRS context, current cost financial statements are dealt with in IAS 29 Financial Reporting in Hyperinflationary Economies.

método general del poder adquisitivo

▲ *according to the general purchasing power approach* de acuerdo con el método general del poder adquisitivo ▲ *use the general purchasing power approach* utilizar el método general del poder adquisitivo

SOURCE IAS 15, paragraph 11

general purpose financial report UK

≠ special purpose financial report UK

A general purpose financial report is financial information

such as an annual report and the statements and reports included or another general purpose financial report such as letters to shareholders, press releases and other announcements.

informe financiero de uso general

≠ informe financiero de uso especial

⇛ annual report, general purpose financial statements

general purpose financial statements UK, IAS/IFRS

General purpose financial statements are usually referred to as "financial statements", meaning the financial statements or accounts contained in annual and interim reports, preliminary releases as well as summary financial statements.

estados financieros de uso general

▲ *the basis for presentation of general purpose financial statements* la base para la presentación de los estados financieros de uso general ▲ *the objective of general purpose financial statements* el objetivo de los estados financieros de uso general

⇛ general purpose financial report, special purpose financial report

general risk

General risks are commercial and financial risks that are normal in the ordinary course of business.

riesgo general

▲ *disclosure of the enterprise's general risks* publicación de los riesgos generales de la empresa ▲ *management of general risks* gestión de los riesgos generales

generally accepted accounting principles

= GAAP

Generally accepted accounting principles are the conventions, rules and procedures that define and dictate accepted accounting practice. The concept includes not only broad guidelines but also detailed rules. When an enterprise complies with generally accepted accounting principles, the financial statements give a true and fair view.

principios contables generalmente aceptados

= PCGA

▲ *requirement of generally accepted accounting principles* requisito de los principios contables generalmente aceptados

generally accepted auditing standards

An audit of financial statements that has been performed according to generally accepted auditing standards complies with the broad rules and guidelines for auditing procedures that auditors are obliged to observe when carrying out audit work for their clients.

normas de auditoría generalmente aceptadas

▲ *in accordance with generally accepted auditing standards* de acuerdo con las normas de auditoría generalmente aceptadas

generate

To generate is to create or produce something. For example, enterprises generate earnings.

generar

▲ *a transaction which generates revenue* una transacción que genera ingresos ▲ *assess the ability of the entity to generate cash and cash equivalents* evaluar la capacidad de la entidad para generar efectivo y equivalentes de efectivo ▲ *generate an intangible asset* generar un activo intangible ▲ *generate cash flows* generar flujos de efectivo ▲ *generate future economic benefits* generar beneficios económicos futuros ▲ *generate income* generar ingreso ▲ *internally generated goodwill* fondo de comercio generado internamente ▲ *the period over which the asset is expected to generate net cash inflows for the enterprise* el periodo durante el cual el activo se espera que genere flujos de efectivo neto para la empresa ▲ *the total gains and losses generated by the enterprises activities* los beneficios y pérdidas totales generados por las empresas

generated

Something that has been generated has been created or produced. For example, earnings are generated by enterprises.

generado

▲ *cost of an internally generated intangible asset* coste de un activo intangible generado internamente ▲ *internally generated computer software* sofware generado internamente ▲ *internally generated goodwill* fondo de comercio generado internamente ▲ *internally generated intangible assets* activos intangibles generados internamente ▲ *internally generated intellectual property rights* derechos de propiedad intelectual generados internamente

geographic segment

= geographical segment

A geographic segment is a component of an enterprise, i.e. reportable segment, operating in, supplying products or services to, and generating revenue in a particular geographic area, and which is subject to risks and returns that differ from those of the segments operating in other economic environments.

segmento geográfico

▲ *an enterprise that operates in a single geographic segment* una empresa que opera en un único segmento geográfico ▲ *asset-based geographic segment* segmento geográfico basado en activos ▲ *combine as a single geographic segment* combinar como un único segmento geográfico ▲ *customer-based geographic segment* segmento geográfico basado en el cliente ▲ *identification of geographic segments* identificación de los segmentos geográficos ▲ *information about geographic segments* información sobre segmentos geográficos ▲ *internally reported geographic segments* segmentos geográficos informados internamente ▲ *similar geographic segments* segmentos geográficos similares ▲ *the basis of the enterprise's geographic segments* la base de los segmentos geográficos de la empresa ▲ *the determination of the composition of a geographic segment* la determinación de la composición de un segmento geográfico ▲ *the total assets of all geographic segments* los activos totales de todos los segmentos geográficos ▲ *transfers between geographic segments* transferencias entre segmentos geográficos

geographical segment

= geographic segment US

A geographical segment is a component of an enterprise, i.e. reportable segment, operating in, supplying products or services to, and generating revenue in a particular geographical area, and that is subject to risks and returns that differ from those of the segments operating in other economic environments.

segmento geográfico

▲ *an enterprise that operates in a single geographical segment* una empresa que opera en un segmento geográfico único ▲ *asset-based geographical segment* segmento geográfico basado en activos ▲ *combine as a single geographical segment* combinar como un único segmento geográfico ▲ *customer-based geographical segment* segmento geográfico basado en el cliente ▲ *identification of geographical segments* identificación de los segmentos geográficos ▲ *information about geographical segments* información sobre segmentos geográficos ▲ *internally reported geographical segments* segmentos geográficos informados internamente ▲ *similar geographical segments* segmentos geográficos similares ▲ *the basis of the enterprise's geographical segments* la base de los segmentos geográficos de la empresa ▲ *the determination of the composition of a geographical segment* la determinación de la composición de un segmento geográfico ▲ *the total assets of all geographical segments* los activos totales de todos los segmentos geográficos ▲ *transfers between geographical segments* transferencias entre segmentos geográficos

SOURCE IAS 14, paragraph 9

gilt UK

= gilt-edged security UK, government bond UK, treasury bond US

Gilts refer to British government bonds, i.e. interest-bearing securities issued by the British government for the purpose of borrowing money. Investment in gilts is regarded as safe.

título de renta fija pública

= deuda pública, renta fija pública

NOTE The synonym 'renta fija pública' is always singular in Spanish accounting texts.

▲ *gilts and equities* renta fija pública y renta variable ▲ *index-linked gilts* títulos de renta fija pública indexada ▲ *invest in gilts* invertir en títulos de renta fija pública ▲ *short gilts* renta fija pública a corto ▲ *the gilts market* el mercado de renta fija pública

⇛ bond

gilt-edged security UK

= gilt UK, government bond UK, treasury bond US

Gilt-edged securities refer to British government bonds, i.e. interest-bearing securities issued by the British government for the purpose of borrowing money. Investment in gilt-edged securities is regarded as safe.

título de renta fija pública

= deuda pública, renta fija pública

NOTE The synonym 'renta fija pública' is always singular in Spanish accounting texts.

▲ *invest in gilt-edged securities* invertir en títulos de renta fija pública ▲ *provide returns above equivalent gilt-edged securities* proporcionar rentabilidades por encima de los títulos de renta fija pública equivalentes ▲ *yields on gilt-edged securities* rendimientos de los títulos de renta fija pública

giro credit balance

The amount constituting the balance on a giro account is the giro credit balance.

saldo de la cuenta de giro

▲ *bank and other giro credit balances* saldos en el banco y en otra cuenta de giro

give an account

To give an account of something means to explain or clarify it.

dar cuenta

▲ *give an account of the enterprise's objective* dar cuenta del objetivo de la empresa

global consolidation

→ full consolidation

goal

= objective, target

A goal is the final target, result or purpose of a plan which persons or businesses strive to reach.

objetivo

▲ *a financial goal* un objetivo financiero ▲ *achieve a goal* conseguir un objetivo ▲ *areas essential to the goals of the joint venture* áreas esenciales para los objetivos de la joint venture ▲ *reach a goal* alcanzar un objetivo ▲ *the overriding goal* el objetivo primordial

goal congruence

Goal congruence is the situation where managers and employees cooperate in their own interest to promote the overall goals and objectives of their enterprise.

congruencia de objetivos

▲ *achieve goal congruence* conseguir una congruencia de objetivos ▲ *result in goal congruence* dar lugar a una congruencia de objetivos

going concern

= continuity US

Going concern is the accounting assumption that an enterprise will continue in operational existence for the foreseeable future. This means that the enterprise is not anticipated to be subject to any voluntary or compulsory winding-up.

empresa en funcionamiento

= negocio en marcha

NOTE Spanish accountants prefer 'empresa en funcionamiento' to the IAS/IFRS term 'negocio en marcha'.

▲ *an assessment of an enterprise's ability to continue as a going concern* una valoración de la capacidad de una empresa para continuar como una empresa en funcionamiento ▲ *prepare financial statements on a going concern basis* preparar estados financieros aplicando el principio de empresa en funcionamiento ▲ *significant doubt about the enterprise's ability to continue as a going concern* dudas significativas sobre la capacidad de la empresa para continuar como una empresa en funcionamiento ▲ *the assumption that the enterprise is a going concern* el supuesto de que la empresa sea una empresa en funcionamiento ▲ *the going concern assumption* el supuesto de empresa en funcionamiento ▲ *the going concern basis of accounting* el principio contable de empresa en funcionamiento

⇛ concern, going-concern concept

going concern concept

→ going-concern concept

going concern convention

= continuity convention US, going-concern concept

The going concern convention is one of the fundamental accounting concepts and the assumption that an enterprise will continue in operational existence for the foreseeable future. This means that the enterprise is not anticipated to be subject to any voluntary or compulsory winding-up.

principio de empresa en funcionamiento

= principio de negocio en marcha

▲ *prepare the financial statements under the going concern convention* preparar los estados financieros según el principio de empresa en funcionamiento ▲ *use the going concern convention* usar el principio de empresa en funcionamiento

⇛ concern

going forward

Going forward means continuing and progressing from this point in time into the future.

en adelante

▲ *results for 2005, and going forward* resultados para el 2005, y en adelante

going-concern concept

= continuity concept US, going concern convention UK

The going-concern concept is one of the fundamental accounting concepts and the assumption that an enterprise will continue in operational existence for the foreseeable future. This means that the enterprise is not anticipated to be subject to any voluntary or compulsory winding-up.

principio de empresa en funcionamiento

= principio de empresa en marcha, principio de negocio en marcha

▲ *prepare the annual report under the going-concern concept* preparar el informe anual según el principio de empresa en funcionamiento ▲ *use the going-concern concept* usar el principio de empresa en funcionamiento

⇛ concern

goods for resale UK

Goods for resale are finished goods purchased for resale.

bienes para la reventa

▲ *costs for goods for resale* costes para bienes para la reventa ▲ *disposal of goods for resale* liquidación de bienes para la reventa ▲ *gross margin on goods for resale* margen bruto en bienes para la reventa ▲ *the cost of goods for resale* el coste de bienes para la reventa

goodwill

≠ negative goodwill

Goodwill is any excess of the cost of the acquisition over the acquirer's interest in the fair value of the identifiable assets and liabilities acquired as at the date of the exchange transaction. Goodwill is an intangible asset.

fondo de comercio

= plusvalía, diferencia positiva en la adquisición

NOTE Although some IAS/IFRS texts use 'plusvalia' as translation equivalent of 'goodwill', Spanish accountants consider this translation erroneous. It can lead to misinterprations. In Spanish accounting texts, 'goodwill' is always 'fondo de comercio'.

▲ *a decrease in the service potential of goodwill* una disminución del potencial de servicio del fondo de comercio ▲ *amortisation of goodwill disallowed for tax purposes* amortización del fondo de comercio no deducible a efectos fiscales ▲ *amortise goodwill over 20 years* amortizar el fondo de comercio durante unos 20 años ▲ *calculate goodwill* calcular el fondo de comercio ▲ *capitalise goodwill* capitalizar el fondo de comercio ▲ *expense goodwill in the year of acquisition* fondo de comercio depreciado en el año de la adquisición ▲ *goodwill arising on acquisition* fondo de comercio resultante de una adquisición ▲ *goodwill transferred to the income statement* fondo de comercio transferido a la cuenta de resultados ▲ *goodwill with a tax base of nil* fondo de comercio con una base fiscal de cero ▲ *internally generated goodwill* fondo de comercio generado internamente ▲ *notional goodwill* fondo de comercio nocional ▲ *purchased goodwill* fondo de comercio adquirido ▲ *recognition of goodwill* reconocimiento del fondo de comercio ▲ *the book value of goodwill* el valor contable del fondo de comercio ▲ *the carrying amount of goodwill* el valor contable del fondo de comercio ▲ *the cost of goodwill* el coste del fondo de comercio ▲ *the future economic benefits arising from the goodwill* los futuros beneficios económicos resultantes del fondo de comercio ▲ *unamortised goodwill* fondo de comercio no amortizado ▲ *with addition of residual goodwill value* con la suma del valor residual del fondo de comercio ▲ *write off goodwill to equity* pasar el fondo de comercio a patrimonio neto ▲ *write-down of goodwill* devaluación del fondo de comercio ▲ *write-off of goodwill* anulación en libros del fondo de comercio

goodwill amortisation UK

= goodwill amortization US

Goodwill amortisation is the systematic allocation of the amortisable amount of goodwill over its economic life.

amortización del fondo de comercio

▲ *accounting for goodwill amortisation* contabilizando la amortización del fondo de comercio ▲ *results before goodwill amortisation* resultados antes de la amortización del fondo de comercio

goodwill amortization US

= goodwill amortisation UK, IAS/IFRS

Goodwill amortization is the systematic allocation of the amortizable amount of goodwill over its economic life.

amortización del fondo de comercio

▲ *accounting for goodwill amortization* contabilizando la amortización del fondo de comercio ▲ *results before goodwill amortization* resultados antes de la amortización del fondo de comercio

goodwill on acquisition IAS/IFRS

= acquired goodwill IAS/IFRS, purchased goodwill UK

Goodwill on acquisition is the goodwill arising from the acquisition of an enterprise or activity, representing the excess price paid over the net assets' fair value. Goodwill on acquisition is initially recognised at cost less impairment losses and must be tested for impairment regularly, where formerly it used to be capitalised and amortised over the expected economic life, usually a maximum of 20 years.

plusvalía por adquisición

= diferencia positiva en la adquisición, fondo de comercio por adquisición

▲ *calculation of goodwill on acquisition* cálculo de la plusvalía por adquisición ▲ *estimated goodwill on acquisition* fondo de comercio por adquisición estimado ▲ *measurement of goodwill on acquisition* cálculo de la plusvalía por adquisición ▲ *negative goodwill on acquisition* fondo de comercio negativo por adquisición

goodwill value

Goodwill value is the carrying value at which acquired goodwill has been recognised in the balance sheet.

valor del fondo de comercio

▲ *determine the goodwill value* determinar el valor del fondo de comercio ▲ *pay the full goodwill value* pagar el valor total del fondo de comercio ▲ *the estimated goodwill value* el valor previsto del fondo de comercio

governing body

A governing body is a general term for a single person or a group of persons that supervises the operations of an enterprise on a certain level in specific situations. For instance, in a public limited company, the governing body is the board of directors.

organismo regulador

▲ *power to cast the majority of votes at meetings of the board of directors or equivalent governing body* capacidad para emitir la mayoría de los votos en reuniones del consejo de administración u organismo regulador equivalente ▲ *remove the majority of the members of the board of directors or equivalent governing body* destituir a la mayoría de los miembros del consejo de administración u organismo regulador equivalente ▲ *representation on the governing body of the investee* representación en el organismo regulador de la empresa en la que se ha invertidido

government

1 The government refers to the community system of legislation and rules, typically the central government that has the authority for enacting legislation and administering public services and programmes on a national basis.

administraciones públicas

= gobierno

NOTE Spanish accountants use 'administraciones públicas' (plural) instead of the IAS/IFRS term 'gobierno'. This term indicates the existence of different regional governments in Spain.

▲ *a forgivable loan from government* un préstamo no reintegrable proveniente de las administraciones públicas ▲ *an incentive provided by government without related costs* un incentivo facilitado por las administraciones públicas sin gastos asociados ▲ *conclude business contracts with government and government agencies* cerrar contratos de negocios con agencias gubernamentales y administraciones públicas ▲ *government participation in the ownership of an enterprise* participación de las administraciones públicas en el capital de una empresa ▲ *in close interaction with government and government agencies* en estrecha colaboración con las agencias gubernamentales o administraciones públicas ▲ *late payments from government and government agencies* pagos aplazados de las agencias gubernamentales y de las administraciones públicas ▲ *liabilities to the government* obligaciones para las administraciones públicas ▲ *supervision by government or a government agency* supervisión por parte de una agencia gubernamental o por las administraciones públicas ▲ *the expropriation of major assets by government* la expropiación de los principales activos de las administraciones públicas

⇛ government bond, government grant

2 A government is a group of officials whose responsibility is to run, control and direct a country or state.

gobierno

▲ *government intervention* intervención gubernamental ▲ *heads of government* jefes de gobierno ▲ *the national government* el gobierno nacional

government assistance

Government assistance constitutes grants, funds or other support provided as assistance by government and resulting in economic benefits to qualifying enterprises.

ayuda pública

= ayuda gubernamental, ayudas públicas, subvención oficial

NOTE Spanish accountants use 'ayuda pública' instead of the IAS/IFRS term 'ayuda gubernamental'. This term may be misleading in Spain where there are 17 regional governements and 1 central government.

▲ *contingencies attaching to government assistance* contingencias que atañen a las ayudas públicas ▲ *government assistance from which the enterprise has directly benefited* ayudas públicas de las que la empresa se ha beneficiado directamente ▲ *government assistance which cannot reasonably have a value placed upon them* ayudas públicas que no pueden valorarse de forma razonable ▲ *intangible assets acquired with government assistance* activos intangibles adquiridos con ayudas públicas ▲ *provide government assistance* ofrecer ayuda pública ▲ *segregate the trading activities from government assistance* segregar las actividades comerciales de la ayuda pública ▲ *the receipt of government assistance* el comprobante de la ayuda pública ▲ *unfulfilled conditions attaching to government assistance* condiciones incumplidas que atañen a la ayuda pública

SOURCE IAS 20, paragraph 3

government bond UK

= gilt UK, gilt-edged security UK, treasury bond US

Government bonds are interest-bearing securities issued by a government for the purpose of borrowing money. Investment in government bonds is regarded as safe.

bono del estado

= renta fija pública, título de renta fija pública

▲ *a contractual obligation to deliver government bonds* una obligación contractual para emitir bonos del estado ▲ *a note payable in government bonds* un pagaré en bonos del estado ▲ *Danish government bonds* bonos del estado daneses ▲ *derive basic interest rates from observable government bond prices* derivar tipos de interés básicos de los precios de los bonos del estado a la vista ▲ *fixed rate government bonds* tipo fijo de los bonos del estado ▲ *foreign government bonds* bonos del estado extranjero ▲ *invest free funds in government bonds* invertir los fondos disponibles en bonos del estado ▲ *long-term government bonds* bonos del estado a largo plazo ▲ *rating for government bonds* rating de los bonos del estado ▲ *the market yields of high-quality or government bonds* los rendimientos del mercado de los bonos del estado o de alta calificación ▲ *the yield of a government bond* el rendimiento de un bono del estado

⇛ bond

government grant

Government grants refer to government assistance for defined purposes in the form of transfers of assets (usually money) to an enterprise in return for past or future fulfilment of certain specified conditions relating to the enterprise's operating activities.

subvención oficial

= ayuda pública, subvención del gobierno

NOTE Spanish accountants prefer 'subvención oficial' to the IAS/IFRS term 'subvención del gobierno'. The IAS term may be easily misinterpreted in Spain where there are 17 regional governments and 1 central government.

▲ *accounting treatment of government grants* tratamiento contable de las subvenciones oficiales ▲ *award a government grant* conceder una subvención oficial ▲ *government grants related to assets* subvenciones oficiales relacionadas con activos ▲ *government grants related to income* subvenciones oficiales relacionadas con ingresos ▲ *gratuitous government grants* subvenciones oficiales a fondo perdido ▲ *non-monetary government grants* subvenciones oficiales no monetarias ▲ *non-taxable government grants* subvenciones oficiales exentas de tributación ▲ *receive government grants* recibir subvenciones oficiales ▲ *recognise a government grant* reconocer una subvención oficial ▲ *repayment of government grants* reembolso de las subvenciones oficiales ▲ *the accounting policy adopted for government grants* la política contable adoptada para subvenciones oficiales ▲ *the nature and extent of government grants recognised in the financial statements* la naturaleza y la extensión de las subvenciones oficiales reconocidas en los estados financieros

government security

Government securities are bonds issued by a government for the purpose of borrowing money.

deuda pública

▲ *determine a fair value for government securities* determinar el valor razonable de la deuda pública ▲ *invest in government securities* invertir en deuda pública ▲ *short-term government securities* deuda pública a corto plazo ▲ *the issuance of government securities* la emisión de deuda pública ▲ *the market yields on government securities* el mercado da rendimientos en deuda pública

grant[1] *noun*

A grant is an endowment, often in the form of financial aid and usually awarded by a government, which is meant to serve a particular purpose and which does not have to be repaid.

subvención

▲ *a government grant* una subvención oficial ▲ *a grant related to assets* una subvención relacionada con activos ▲ *a grant related to income* una subvención de explotación ▲ *credit a grant directly to equity* abonar una subvención directamente a patrimonio neto ▲ *deduct the grant from the asset's carrying amount* deducir la subvención del valor contable del activo ▲ *grants and refunds* subvenciones y bonificación ▲ *grants for research and development* subvenciones para investigación y desarrollo ▲ *grants for the acquisition of property, plant and equipment* subvenciones para la adquisición de edificios, instalaciones y equipos ▲ *grants for the purchase of assets and development activities* subvenciones para la adquisición de activos y actividades de desarrollo ▲ *grants related to depreciable assets* subvenciones relativas a activos depreciables ▲ *grants related to non-depreciable assets* subvenciones relativas a los activos no depreciables ▲ *investment grants* subvenciones para inversión ▲ *non-monetary grants* subvenciones no monetarias ▲ *non-taxable government grants related to assets* subvenciones oficiales no tributables relativas a activos ▲ *receive a grant* recibir una subvención ▲ *repay a grant* reintegrar una subvención ▲ *set up the grant as deferred income* anotar una subvención como ingreso diferido ▲ *take a grant to income* reflejar una subvención como ingreso ▲ *the conditions attaching to the grant* las condiciones anexas a la subvención

grant[2] *verb*

To grant means to provide someone with financial aid, a right or a privilege, usually without compensation.

subvencionar

▲ *grant an option to the holder of the instrument to convert it into an equity instrument of the entity* subvencionar una opción al titular del instrumento para convertirlo en un instrumento de patrimonio de la entidad ▲ *grant options at a discount on the market price* subvencionar opciones con descuento sobre el precio de mercado ▲ *grant share options to employees with more than four years of service* subvencionar opciones sobre acciones a los trabajadores con más de cuatro años de servicio

grant date

= date of grant, time of granting

The grant date is the date when an option, e.g. an employee share option, or other share-based payment arrangement is granted, agreed between an enterprise and an employee or approved, and when the rights under that option or arrangement to cash, assets or equity instruments are conferred to the employee subject to any particular vesting conditions.

fecha de concesión

= fecha de la concesión

▲ *at grant date* a fecha de concesión ▲ *estimate the grant date fair value of the shares granted* estimar el valor razonable a fecha de concesión de las acciones otorgadas ▲ *estimate the length of the expected vesting period at grant date* estimar la longitud del periodo de carencia esperado a fecha de concesión ▲ *information available at the grant date* información disponible en la fecha de concesión ▲ *measure at the grant date fair value of the equity instruments* medir en la fecha de concesión el valor razonable de los instrumentos de patrimonio ▲ *on grant date* a fecha de concesión ▲ *satisfy a vesting condition that was specified at grant date* satisfacer la carencia especificada a fecha de concesión ▲ *shares outstanding on the grant date* acciones pendientes en la fecha de concesión ▲ *the grant date valuation of the rights to shares* la valoración a fecha de concesión de los derechos sobre acciones ▲ *the period of time from grant date to the date on which the option is expected to be exercised* el periodo de tiempo desde la fecha de concesión a la fecha en la que se espera ejercer la opción

⇛ share option, share-based payment, vesting condition

grant related to assets IAS/IFRS, UK

Grants related to assets are government grants paid to an enterprise that are capital-based, i.e. conditioned on and made as a contribution towards the construction and purchase or other acquisition of non-current assets. Such grants are typically recognised as income in the profit and loss account over the useful economic lives of the related assets.

subvenciones relacionadas con activos

= subvenciones relacionadas con los activos

▲ *non-taxable government grants related to assets* subvenciones públicas relacionadas con activos exentas de impuestos ▲ *presentation of grants related to assets* presentación de las subvenciones relacionadas con activos ▲ *the appropriate portions of grants related to assets* las partes apropiadas de subvenciones relacionadas con los activos

SOURCE IAS 20, paragraph 3, SSAP 4

⇛ grant related to income

grant related to income

Grants related to income are government grants paid to an enterprise that are not related to assets, but revenue-based, i.e. related to a particular category of revenue expenditure. Such grants should be recognised in the profit and loss account in the same period as the related revenue expenditure.

subvención de explotación

= subvención relacionada con ingresos, subvención relacionada con los ingresos

NOTE Spanish accountants prefer 'subvención de explotación' to the IAS/IFRS term 'subvención relacionada con ingresos'.

▲ *presentation of grants related to income* presentación de las subvenciones de explotación

SOURCE IAS 20, paragraph 3, SSAP 4

⇛ grant related to asset

granting

When someone, a person or a group of persons, has been chosen to receive a grant, a granting has taken place.

concesión

▲ *the date of granting* la fecha de concesión ▲ *the granting of share options* la concesión de opciones sobre acciones

⇛ grant

green accounts

= environmental report, environmental statement

Green accounts constitute an enterprise's environment report on environmental issues such as the consumption of energy, water and raw materials, contaminants used in production and subsequently emitted, as well as the treatment of waste. Green accounts may be separate reports or an integral part of the annual report.

cuentas medioambientales

▲ *be liable to prepare green accounts* ser responsable de la preparación de las cuentas medioambientales ▲ *be under an obligation to prepare green accounts* estar obligado a preparar las cuentas medioambientales ▲ *prepare green accounts* preparar las cuentas medioambientales ▲ *publish green accounts* publicar las cuentas medioambientales ▲ *submit green accounts* enviar las cuentas medioambientales

gross

Gross is used about a total amount of something, e.g. income, profit or weight, before deducting another amount, e.g. tax, expenses or packing. Gross dividend e.g. is the total amount of dividend before deduction of tax.

bruto

▲ *depreciation transfer, gross* transferencia por depreciación, bruta ▲ *eliminate against the gross carrying amount of the asset* eliminar contra el valor contable bruto del activo ▲ *gross profit* beneficio bruto ▲ *gross purchase sum* importe de adquisición bruto ▲ *gross selling price* precio de venta bruto ▲ *non-current assets, gross* activos no corrientes, brutos ▲ *other administrative expenses, gross* otros gastos administrativos, brutos ▲ *recognise an item on a gross basis* reconocer una partida sobre una base bruta ▲ *revaluation, gross* revalorización, bruta ▲ *settle an amount gross* liquidar una cantidad bruta ▲ *the gross amount of loans and advances* la cantidad bruta de préstamos y anticipos ▲ *the gross investment in the lease discounted at the interest rate implicit in the lease* la inversión bruta en el alquiler descontada al tipo de interés implícito del alquiler

gross amount

A gross amount is the total amount before any costs or taxes have been taken away.

cantidad bruta
= importe bruto
▲ *gross amount of gains and losses* importe bruto de pérdidas y ganancias ▲ *the gross amount and accumulated impairment losses at the beginning of the financial year* la cantidad bruta y pérdidas por deterioro acumuladas al inicio del año ▲ *the gross amount due from customers for contract work* la cantidad bruta adeuda por los clientes por trabajos contratados ▲ *the gross amount of loans and advances* la cantidad bruta de préstamos y adelantos

gross book value
The gross book value constitutes the cost including installation costs of an asset on a gross basis, i.e. before deduction of accumulated depreciation.
valor contable bruto
= valor en libros bruto
▲ *estimated gross book value* valor contable bruto previsto ▲ *gross book value less depreciation* valor contable bruto menos depreciación ▲ *measure the assets at their gross book value* medir los activos a su valor contable bruto ▲ *the gross book value of property, plant and equipment* el valor contable bruto de edificios, instalaciones y equipos

gross cash flow
Gross cash flow is the total cash flow of an enterprise before offsetting cash outflow against cash inflow. Consequently, gross cash flow is also seen to be operating profit less taxes, i.e. the after-tax cash flow generated by an enterprise's operations.
flujo de efectivo bruto
= cash flow bruto, flujo de caja bruto
▲ *show cash flows as gross cash flows* reflejar los flujos de efectivo como flujos de efectivo brutos

gross income
= gross receipts
≠ net income, net receipts
Gross income is income before deduction of expenses and/or tax.
ingreso bruto
▲ *total gross income* total ingreso bruto

gross investment
Under a finance lease, the gross investment in a lease is the total of the minimum lease payments receivable by the lessor and any not-guaranteed, residual value of the leased asset accruing to the lessor.
inversión bruta
▲ *computation of the lessor's gross investment in a lease* cómputo de la inversión bruta del arrendador en un arrendamiento ▲ *gross investment in a finance lease* inversión bruta en un arrendamiento financiero ▲ *the gross investment in assets* la inversión bruta en activos ▲ *total gross investment* total inversión bruta
SOURCE IAS 17, paragraph 4

gross loss
= trading loss
A gross loss arises when production costs exceed net sales or revenue.
pérdida bruta
▲ *compared with a gross loss of $125000 in the first quarter of 2005* comparado con una pérdida bruta de 125.000 dólares en el primer trimestre de 2005 ▲ *make a gross loss* hacer una pérdida bruta ▲ *suffer a gross loss* sufrir una pérdida bruta

gross margin
1 = gross profit
Gross margin results after deducting direct and indirect production costs from revenue.
beneficio bruto
▲ *a realised gross margin* un beneficio bruto realizado
⇛ cost of goods sold
2 = gross margin ratio, gross profit margin, gross profit percentage
Gross margin is a profitability and efficiency ratio calculated as gross profit divided by sales.
margen bruto
▲ *calculate the gross margin* calcular el margen bruto ▲ *the estimated gross margin* el margen bruto estimado ▲ *the expected gross margin* el margen bruto previsto ▲ *the gross margin per unit* el margen bruto por unidad
3 = gross profit UK, IAS/IFRS, US
Gross margin is the excess of sales over cost of goods sold.
beneficio bruto
▲ *a gross margin of 21.0% in Q1 2007* un beneficio bruto de

21,0% en el primer trimestre de 2007

gross margin percentage

The gross margin percentage is the gross profit expressed as a percentage of sales and is calculated as sales less cost of sales multiplied by 100 divided by sales for the period.

porcentaje de margen bruto

▲ *a decrease in gross margin percentage* un descenso en el porcentaje de margen bruto ▲ *adjusted gross margin percentage* porcentaje de margen bruto ajustado ▲ *an increase in gross margin percentage* un aumento en el porcentaje de margen bruto

gross margin ratio

= gross profit margin, gross profit percentage

The gross margin ratio is a ratio of financial performance calculated as gross profit divided by sales.

ratio de utilidad bruta sobre ventas

= ratio de beneficio bruto sobre ventas

▲ *a decline in the gross margin ratio* una disminución en el ratio de utilidad bruta sobre ventas ▲ *an increase in the gross margin ratio* un aumento en el ratio de utilidad bruta sobre ventas

gross proceeds

The gross proceeds constitute the total amount resulting from a share issue before deducting the costs of issuance.

ingresos por emisión de títulos

▲ *earn the enterprise gross proceeds of GBP 750m* ganar la empresa ingresos por emisión de títulos de 750 millones de libras esterlinas ▲ *subscribe for shares with gross proceeds of GBP 750m* suscribir acciones con ingresos por emisión de títulos de 750 millones de libras esterlinas ▲ *total gross proceeds* total ingresos por emisión de títulos

gross profit

= gross margin US

Gross profit is the excess of sales over cost of sales.

beneficio bruto

= ganancia bruta

▲ *a realised gross profit* un beneficio bruto realizado ▲ *gross profit or loss* ganancia o pérdida bruta

⇛ cost of sales

gross profit margin

= gross margin ratio, gross profit percentage

The gross profit margin is a profitability and efficiency ratio showing the difference between the sales revenue of a business and the cost of goods sold.

margen de beneficio bruto

= margen de ganancia bruta

▲ *a strong improvement in gross profit margin* una mejora sustancial en el margen de beneficio bruto ▲ *calculate the gross profit margin* calcular el margen de beneficio bruto ▲ *the gross profit margin decrease* el descenso en el margen de beneficio bruto ▲ *the increase in gross profit margin* el aumento en el margen de beneficio bruto

gross profit margin ratio

= gross margin ratio

The gross profit margin ratio is a profitability and efficiency ratio calculated as gross profit divided by sales.

ratio del beneficio bruto sobre ventas

= ratio de ganancia bruta sobre ventas, ratio de la utilidad bruta sobre ventas

▲ *a gross profit margin ratio of 10%* un ratio del beneficio bruto sobre ventas del 10% ▲ *an improved gross profit margin ratio* un ratio del beneficio bruto sobre ventas mejorado ▲ *calculate the gross profit margin ratio* calcular el ratio del beneficio bruto sobre ventas

gross profit percentage

= gross margin ratio, gross profit margin

The gross profit percentage is a profitability and efficiency ratio calculated as gross profit divided by sales.

porcentaje de beneficio bruto

= porcentaje de ganancia bruta

▲ *average gross profit percentage* porcentaje de beneficio bruto medio

gross profit rate

→ gross profit margin

gross receipts

= gross income

≠ net income, net receipts

Gross receipts are receipts before deduction of expenses.

ingresos brutos
▲ *gross receipts for financial reporting purposes* ingresos brutos a efectos de información financiera ▲ *total annual gross receipts of $200,000* total ingresos brutos anuales de 200.000 dólares estadounidenses

gross redemption yield
= effective yield
The gross redemption yield is the internal rate of return on a debt instrument, such as a bond, purchased at a specified price and held until maturity. The gross redemption yield is calculated on the basis of the market price, the coupon rate, the time between interest payments and the maturity period.
rentabilidad bruta de un efecto en la fecha de rescate
▲ *the gross redemption yield on the consideration* la rentabilidad bruta de un efecto en la fecha de rescate en la consideración

gross revenue
The gross revenue of an enterprise is its total revenue before any deduction of costs is made.
ingreso bruto
▲ *agreed gross revenue* ingreso bruto acordado ▲ *gross revenue and expense amounts* cuentas de ingresos y gastos brutos ▲ *total gross revenue* total ingreso bruto

gross tax
Gross tax is tax deducted before payment of wages which means that this tax is levied on gross pay without any deductions and without differentiation for the wage earners' individual taxable capacity.
impuesto bruto
▲ *gross tax payable* impuesto bruto a pagar

gross value
The gross value of e.g. an asset is the total value of that asset before any deductions, e.g. of costs such as depreciation or tax.
valor bruto
▲ *the gross value of all debts* el valor bruto del total de deudas

group
A group consists of a parent company and its subsidiaries, i.e. one or more legal entities under common control.
grupo
▲ *a group comprising a parent and all of its subsidiaries* un grupo compuesto por una matriz y todas sus filiales ▲ *a group containing individual entities with different functional currencies* un grupo que contiene entidades individuales con diferentes monedas funcionales ▲ *a group's share in an associate* una participación de un grupo en una asociada ▲ *financial statements of a group presented as those of a single economic entity* los estados financieros de un grupo presentados como los de una entidad económica única ▲ *formation of the group* formación del grupo ▲ *group accounting policies* políticas contables del grupo ▲ *members of the consolidated group* miembros del grupo consolidado ▲ *minority interests in the profit or loss of the group* intereses minoritarios en los resultados del grupo ▲ *outstanding balances with other entities in a group* saldos pendientes de pago con otras entidades de un grupo ▲ *overview of group companies* visión general de las empresas del grupo ▲ *terms and conditions agreed between members of the group* términos y condiciones acordados por los miembros del grupo ▲ *the group as a whole* el grupo como un todo ▲ *the measurement currencies of the enterprises in the group* las divisas empleadas en la medición de las empresas del grupo ▲ *the name of the parent and the ultimate parent of the group* el nombre de la matriz y la anterior matriz del grupo ▲ *the preparation of consolidated financial statements of the group* la preparación de los estados financieros consolidados del grupo

group accounts UK
= consolidated accounts, consolidated financial statements
The group accounts combine the accounts of a parent and its subsidiaries and present the results, cash flows and financial position after elimination of intercompany balances as if the enterprises were a single entity.
cuentas del grupo
= cuentas consolidadas
▲ *audit the group accounts* auditar las cuentas del grupo ▲ *prepare group accounts* preparar las

cuentas del grupo ▲ *publish group accounts* publicar las cuentas del grupo

group annual review

= group management's review

The group annual review is a statement in the parent's financial statements containing information about the group as a whole, i.e. a management's review of the entire group.

informe anual del grupo

▲ *prepare the group annual review* preparar el informe anual del grupo

group auditor

A group auditor is the auditor or audit firm that carries out the audit of consolidated financial statements.

auditor del grupo

▲ *audited by the group auditor* auditado por el auditor del grupo ▲ *based on the group auditor's professional judgment* basado en la opinión profesional del auditor del grupo

group chart

= overview of group companies

A group chart is a specification containing the names of the parent and the subsidiaries that together make up the group.

organigrama del grupo

▲ *appear from the group chart* aparecer procedente del organigrama del grupo ▲ *prepare a group chart* preparar un organigrama del grupo ▲ *present the group chart in the financial statements* mostrar el organigrama del grupo en los estados financieros

group chief executive

A group chief executive is the highest ranking and most senior officer of the group, responsible for the decision-making and running of the group and a member of the group executive management.

consejero delegado del grupo

▲ *be appointed group chief executive* ser nombrado consejero delegado del grupo ▲ *take up the position as group chief executive* asumir el cargo de consejero delegado del grupo ▲ *the former group chief executive* el anterior consejero delegado del grupo ▲ *the incoming group chief executive* el consejero delegado del grupo entrante ▲ *the retiring group chief executive* el consejero delegado del grupo saliente

group executive management

= group executive board, group management board

The executive board or committee that is responsible for the day-to-day management of the group is collectively called the group executive management.

comité ejecutivo del grupo

▲ *become a member of the group executive management* convertirse en miembro del comité ejecutivo del grupo

group finance director UK

A group finance director is the top financial officer of a group, responsible for dealing with the financial issues, decisions and activities of the entire group.

director financiero del grupo

▲ *appoint a new group finance director* nombrar un director financiero del grupo nuevo ▲ *retire as group finance director* jubilarse como director financiero del grupo ▲ *the former group finance director* el anterior director financiero del grupo ▲ *the retiring group finance director* el director financiero del grupo saliente

⇛ chief financial officer, corporate treasurer, director

group of shareholders

A group of shareholders is a number or class of shareholders with the same characteristics who share specific interests in relation to the company.

grupo de accionistas

▲ *a large group of shareholders* un grupo de accionistas amplio ▲ *companies controlled by the same group of shareholders* empresas controladas por el mismo grupo de acionistas

group profit or loss UK

= group earnings

The group profit or loss refers to the bottom line of the consolidated income statement that shows the total results for the accounting period as a combination of the net profits or losses from the parent company and its subsidiaries on consolidation after elimination of any intra-group profits or losses.

pérdida o ganancia del grupo
= resultado del grupo
▲ *determination of the group profit or loss* determinación de la pérdida o ganancia del grupo ▲ *group profit or loss before minority interest* pérdida o ganancia del grupo antes de intereses de los minoritarios ▲ *group profit or loss before tax* pérdida o ganancia del grupo antes de impuestos

grow
= increase
To grow means to become larger in real or relative terms compared with a specific base.
crecer
▲ *grow by 10%* crecer un 10%

growth
The growth of something is the increase in and development of its importance, size, structure, wealth etc.
crecimiento
▲ *a high growth rate* una tasa de crecimiento alta ▲ *an indicator of growth* un indicador del crecimiento ▲ *further growth in earnings* mayor crecimiento de beneficios ▲ *future growth in revenues and earnings* crecimiento futuro de ingresos y beneficios ▲ *restrict growth* restringir el crecimiento

growth component
A growth component is a measure of the amount of change in profit before interest and tax (EBIT) which is attributable to changes in the volume of sales.
componente de crecimiento
▲ *the growth component of investments* el componente de crecimiento de las inversiones
⇛ EBIT

growth market
A growth market is a specific market in which the growth rate is or is expected to be higher than in other markets.
mercado en expansión
▲ *selected growth markets* mercados en expansión seleccionados

growth potential
Growth potential constitutes the sales possibilities of a product or service on a given market.
potencial de crecimiento
▲ *a contract with growth potential* un contrato con potencial de crecimiento ▲ *future growth potential* potencial de crecimiento futuro ▲ *possess growth potential* tener potencial de crecimiento

growth rate
A growth rate is the percentage by which something increases.
tasa de crecimiento
▲ *a falling growth rate* una tasa de crecimiento a la baja ▲ *a high growth rate* una tasa de crecimiento alta ▲ *a steady or declining growth rate* una tasa de crecimiento estable o a la baja ▲ *exceed the long-term average growth rate for the products* superar la tasa de crecimiento media a largo plazo para los productos ▲ *the average historical growth rate over the long term* la tasa de crecimiento media histórica a largo plazo ▲ *the growth rate used to extrapolate cash flow projections beyond the period covered by the most recent forecasts* la tasa de crecimiento usada para extrapolar las proyecciones de flujo de efectivo más allá del periodo que cubren las previsiones más recientes

growth strategy
A growth strategy is a plan specifying or outlining how the enterprise intends to meet one or more growth targets.
estrategia de crecimiento
▲ *a natural growth strategy* una estrategia de crecimiento natural ▲ *accountability for the growth strategy* dar cuentas de de la estrategia de crecimiento ▲ *an organic growth strategy* una estrategia de crecimiento orgánico

growth target
A growth target is a particular result that you intend to achieve.
objetivo de crecimiento
▲ *achieve a growth target* conseguir un objetivo de crecimiento ▲ *high annual growth target of 10%* alto objetivo de crecimiento anual del 10% ▲ *meet a growth target* cumplir un objetivo de crecimiento

guarantee[1] *noun*
1 A guarantee is a promise made by a guarantor to repay a loan and accept liability on behalf of a borrower in the event of the latter failing to meet the

repayment obligations. A guarantee typically involves providing security in the form of particular assets to the lender.

garantía

= aval

▲ *a financial guarantee contract* un contrato de garantía financiera ▲ *a guarantee provided by the entity for default losses on the transferred asset* una garantía aportada por la entidad por pérdidas por morosidad en los activos transferidos ▲ *a legally binding guarantee* una garantía legalmente vinculante ▲ *a lessee's residual value guarantee embedded in a finance lease* una garantía del valor residual de un arrendatario incrustada en un arrendamiento financiero ▲ *cash flows resulting from embedded options and guarantees* flujos de efectivo resultantes de las garantías y opciones incrustadas ▲ *obtain payments under the guarantee* obtener pagos según la garantía ▲ *the fair value of the guarantee* el valor razonable de la garantía ▲ *the guarantee amount* la cantidad de la garantía ▲ *the intrinsic value of embedded options and guarantees* el valor intrínseco de las garantías y opciones incrustadas ▲ *the time value of embedded options and guarantees* el valor temporal de las garantías y opciones incrustadas

⇛ debt guarantee

2 A guarantee is a contract whereby a person or an enterprise, the guarantor, agrees to become liable for the debt of another, the principal debtor, in case the principal debtor defaults on the obligations he owes to the creditor.

aval

▲ *discharge a guarantee* cancelar un aval ▲ *guarantee for a bank loan* aval de un préstamo bancario ▲ *guarantee for a subsidiary* aval para una filial ▲ *guarantees provided* avales aportados ▲ *loan against guarantee* préstamo con aval ▲ *provide a guarantee* aportar un aval ▲ *provide guarantee* aportar el aval

3 = guaranty US, warranty

A guarantee is a promise made by a supplier, manufacturer or seller to give compensation for, or to repair or replace any defective or malfunctioning goods or services delivered subject to defined conditions concerning extent and guarantee period.

garantía

▲ *give a guarantee* dar una garantía ▲ *issue a guarantee* emitir una garantía

⇛ guarantee claim

guarantee[2] *verb*

1 To guarantee means to accept liability for a debt on behalf of another party, the debtor, and repay the debt to the creditor in the event of the debtor failing to meet the repayment requirements.

avalar

▲ *guarantee a loan* avalar un préstamo ▲ *guarantee for a subsidiary* avalar a una filial

⇛ debt guarantee

2 = warrant

To guarantee means to promise something orally or in writing and give certainty it will happen.

garantizar

= avalar

▲ *guarantee a payment* garantizar un pago ▲ *guarantee debt securities* garantizar títulos de deuda ▲ *guarantee loan exposures* garantizar los riesgos crediticios ▲ *guarantee obligations* garantizar obligaciones ▲ *guarantee the market price of shares or bonds* garantizar el precio de mercado de las acciones o bonos ▲ *guarantee the payment of retirement benefits* garantizar el pago de las prestaciones por jubilación

guarantee claim UK

= guaranty claim US, warranty claim

A guarantee claim is a claim submitted by a customer against a seller for damages, compensation or repair because a product is defective or malfunctioning. A guarantee claim must be asserted while the product is still under guarantee, i.e. within a defined guarantee period running from the date of purchase.

reclamación de garantía

= reclamación de la garantía

▲ *enforcement of a guarantee claim* ejecución de una reclamación de garantía ▲ *make a guarantee claim* llevar a cabo una reclamación de garantía

▲ *the risk of guarantee claims* el riesgo de las reclamaciones de garantía
⇛ guarantee

guarantee debtor
= guarantor
A guarantee debtor is a debtor, e.g. a bank or an enterprise, that has provided a guarantee or security for a debt to a third party.
avalista
▲ *loans, advances and guarantee debtors* avalistas de préstamos, anticipos y garantías
⇛ debt guarantee

guarantee liability
Guarantee liability is the liability a person or an enterprise, the guarantor, assumes by agreeing to be liable for the debt of another, the principal debtor, in case the principal debtor defaults on the obligations he owes to the creditor.
responsabilidad de garantía
▲ *the carrying amount of the guarantee liability* el valor contable de la responsabilidad de garantía

guarantee work
Guarantee work is repair work done to a defective product under the terms of a product guarantee issued when the product was sold.
trabajo en garantía
▲ *estimated costs of rectification and guarantee work* costes previstos de arreglo y trabajo en garantía ▲ *provide guarantee work* ofrecer trabajo en garantía

guaranteed
When something has been guaranteed, something has been provided as security for it, or somebody has promised to ensure that it will happen. If e.g. debt has been guaranteed by a guarantor, the guarantor will pay the debt if the debtor defaults on the payment.
garantizado
▲ *a guaranteed amount* una cantidad garantizada ▲ *a guaranteed benefit* un beneficio garantizado ▲ *a guaranteed contract* un contrato garantizado ▲ *a guaranteed minimum price* un precio mínimo garantizado ▲ *a guaranteed return* un rendimiento garantizado ▲ *guaranteed debt securities* títulos de deuda garantizados ▲ *guaranteed investment contract* contrato de inversión garantizado ▲ *loans guaranteed* préstamos garantizados ▲ *the holder of the guaranteed debt* el titular de la deuda garantizada

guaranteed benefit
In the context of an insurance contract, guaranteed benefit refers to payments or other benefits to which a specific policyholder or investor is unconditionally entitled and which are not subject to contractual influence from the issuer of the insurance contract.
prestación garantizada
▲ *a supplement to guaranteed benefits* un suplemento a las prestaciones garantizadas ▲ *an obligation to pay guaranteed benefits* una obligación a pagar prestaciones garantizadas
SOURCE IFRS 4, Appendix A

guaranteed element
In an insurance contract with a discretionary participation feature, a guaranteed element is an obligation to pay the benefits guaranteed in the contract.
elemento garantizado
▲ *changes in the guaranteed element* cambios en el elemento garantizado ▲ *classify the guaranteed element as a liability* clasificar el elemento garantizado como una obligación ▲ *contain a guaranteed element* incluir un elemento garantizado ▲ *recognise the guaranteed element separately from the discretionary participation feature* reconocer el elemento garantizado independientemente del rasgo de participación discrecional
SOURCE IFRS 4, Appendix A

guaranteed residual value UK, IAS/IFRS
For the lessee, the guaranteed residual value is the predetermined, maximum amount payable of the residual value that has been guaranteed by either the lessee or a third party associated with the lessee. For the lessor, the guaranteed residual value is the maximum amount of the residual value that has been guaranteed by either the lessee or a third party, who is not associated with the lessor, and who has the financial means to settle the obligations under the guarantee.

valor residual garantizado

▲ *including any guaranteed residual value* incluyendo cualquier valor residual garantizado

guarantor

1 = guarantee debtor

A guarantor is a person or enterprise who has contractually agreed to become liable for the debt of another, the principal debtor, in case the principal debtor defaults on the obligations he owes to the creditor.

avalista

▲ *be a guarantor for somebody* ser avalista de alguien

2 A guarantor is a person or enterprise that has guaranteed, i.e. promised, something, e.g. to repay a loan on behalf of a borrower.

avalista

▲ *a primary guarantor* un avalista principal ▲ *a secondary guarantor* un avalista subsidiario ▲ *complete rating histories on recognised guarantors* completar el historial de clasificación crediticia de los avalistas reconocidos ▲ *the financial condition of the guarantor* la condición financiera del avalista ▲ *third-party guarantors* avalistas de terceras partes

guaranty US

= guarantee UK, warranty

A guaranty is a promise made by a supplier, manufacturer or seller to give compensation for, or to repair or replace any defective or malfunctioning goods or services delivered subject to defined conditions concerning extent and guaranty period.

garantía

▲ *meet a guaranty* cumplir una garantía

⇛ guaranty claim

guaranty claim US

= guarantee claim UK, warranty claim

A guaranty claim is a claim submitted by a customer against a seller for damages, compensation or repair because a product is defective or malfunctioning. A guaranty claim must be asserted while the product is still under guaranty, i.e. within a defined guaranty period running from the date of purchase.

reclamación de garantía

= reclamación de la garantía

▲ *enforcement of a guaranty claim* ejecución de una reclamación de garantía ▲ *make a guaranty claim* llevar a cabo una reclamación de garantía ▲ *the risk of guaranty claims* el riesgo de las reclamaciones de garantía

⇛ guaranty, warranty

guideline

A guideline is a recommended or customary method of working or a document that recommends methods used to accomplish an objective; it is not enforced but is generally followed, or a statement providing guidance for interpretation and application of a policy.

directriz

▲ *generally accepted guidelines* directrices generalmente aceptadas ▲ *in the absence of explicit guidelines* en ausencia de directrices explícitas ▲ *the guidelines recommended by the Danish Society of Financial Analysts* las directrices recomendadas por la Sociedad danesa de Analistas Financieros

H1 or H2 earnings release US
An H1 or H2 earnings release is a financial reporting announcement for the first or second half of a financial year presented to the public and the stock markets by an enterprise on a quarterly or annual basis containing information about earnings and results of operations. Earnings releases usually contain the enterprise's financial highlights, management's interpretation of the period under review together with outlook and expectations as well as summary financial statements.
anuncio de ganancias del primer o segundo semestre
= anuncio de beneficios del primer o segundo trimestre
▲ *publication of an H1 or H2 earnings release* publicación de un anuncio de ganancias del primer o segundo semestre

half year
= six months
Half a year is six months.
NOTE The abbreviation H is often used in preliminary announcements of financial statements, e.g. H1 and H2.
semestre
▲ *during the first half year of 2005* durante el primer semestre del 2005 ▲ *half year highlights 1* noticias más importantes del primer semestre

half year report
= half-year interim report
The half year (interim) report is prepared after half a year of the full financial year.
informe semestral
▲ *half year report for the period 1 January - 30 June 2005* informe semestral para el periodo del 1 de enero al 30 de junio del 2005 ▲ *information included in a half year report* información incluida en un informe semestral ▲ *preparation of a half year report* preparación de un informe semestral ▲ *prepare a half year report* preparar un informe semestral ▲ *present a half year report* presentar un informe semestral ▲ *publication of the half year report* publicación del informe semestral ▲ *submission of the half year report* remisión del informe semestral ▲ *the balance sheet date of the half year report* la fecha del balance del informe semestral

half-yearly settlement
A half-yearly settlement is the payment of amounts or money owed at the end of a six-month period.
pago semestral
▲ *half-yearly settlement of interest* pago semestral de intereses

half-yearly statement
= statement for the six months ended
A half-yearly statement is a survey or settlement for six months of the year.
estado semestral
▲ *prepare a half-yearly statement* preparar un estado semestral

handle
To handle a problem or situation means to deal with it with the intent to achieve a useful or successful outcome.
ocuparse de
▲ *handle the collection of debts* ocuparse de la recaudación de las deudas

handling
In a business context, handling is the management and organisation in an enterprise of a particular function, e.g. logistics, marketing, bookkeeping and finance. Handling may be outsourced against payment to another enterprise.
manipulación
▲ *claims handling* manipulación de las reclamaciones

handling cost
Handling costs are costs incurred that relate to the physical transportation of materials and products from one place to another as well as storage and packaging in the different stages of production.
coste de manipulación
= coste de la manipulación
▲ *handling costs directly attributable to the acquisition of finished goods, materials and services* costes de manipulación directamente atribuibles a la adqui-

sición de productos terminados, materias primas y servicios ▲ *initial delivery and handling costs* costes de manipulación y envío iniciales

harvest IAS/IFRS

Harvest is the intentional gathering of plants, animals or other renewable natural resources by humans.

cosecha

= recoleción

▲ *agricultural produce at the point of harvest* producción agrícola hasta la cosecha ▲ *assets that are able to sustain regular harvests* activos que son capaces de ofrecer cosechas regulares ▲ *decrease due to harvest* disminución debido a la cosecha ▲ *processing of agricultural produce after harvest* procesamiento de los productos agrícolas después de la cosecha ▲ *products that are the result of processing after harvest* productos que son el resultado del proceso de transformación después de la cosecha ▲ *re-establishment of biological assets after harvest* restablecimiento de los activos biológicos después de la cosecha ▲ *recognition of biological assets up to the point of harvest* reconocimiento de los activos biológicos hasta la cosecha ▲ *throughout the period between planting and harvest* durante todo el periodo entre la siembra y la cosecha

HC

= historical cost

HC is the abbreviation for historical cost, i.e. the original cost.

coste histórico

▲ *HC reporting* informe del coste histórico

head office

Head office refers to the premises of an enterprise where the principal management, administration and perhaps also production take place. Usually, the head office is the registered office.

oficina central

= sede

▲ *assets used for general entity or head office purposes* activos utilizados para fines de la oficina central o de la entidad general ▲ *debt issued at the head office level* deuda emitida por la oficina central ▲ *head office assets* activos de la oficina central ▲ *head office expenses* gastos de la oficina central

headcount

Headcount refers to the aggregate number of employees in an enterprise.

número de personal

= número de empleados, número de trabajadores

▲ *increase the headcount* aumentar el número de personal ▲ *reduce the headcount* reducir el numero de personal

headline earnings UK

Headline earnings is a measure of an enterprise's earnings excluding non-recurring or non-operating items such as profits and losses from the sale of fixed assets or discontinued operations. The measure has been implemented by the Institute of Investment Management and Research in the UK.

beneficios ordinarios

= beneficios corrientes

▲ *a 10% increase in headline earnings* un incremento del 10% en los beneficios ordinarios ▲ *calculate headline earnings* calcular los beneficios ordinarios ▲ *headline earnings per share* beneficios ordinarios por acción

⇛ headline earnings per share

headline earnings per share UK

= headline EPS UK

Headline earnings per share is an investment ratio defined as the headline earnings for the latest accounting period of a company divided by the average number of ordinary shares.

beneficios ordinarios por acción

▲ *adjusted headline earnings per share* beneficios ordinarios por acción ajustados ▲ *an increase in headline earnings per share* un aumento en los beneficios ordinarios por acción

⇛ headline earnings

headline EPS UK

Headline EPS is an abbreviation for headline earnings per share which is an investment ratio defined as the headline earnings for the latest accounting period of a company divided by the average number of ordinary shares.

beneficios ordinarios por acción

▲ *a marginal increase in headline EPS* un aumento marginal

en los beneficios ordinarios por acción ▲ *disclose the headline EPS* publicar los beneficios ordinarios por acción
⇛ headline earnings

health care cost

Health care costs refer to the costs incurred by an enterprise in connection with the preventive, diagnostic and treatment services offered to employees, such as chiropractic and physiotherapy services, hospital stays, medications etc.

coste de prevención y enfermedad

▲ *estimate the annual health care costs* estimar los costes anuales de prevención y enfermedad ▲ *health care cost insurance* seguro contra el coste de prevención y enfermedad ▲ *rising health care costs* costes crecientes de prevención y enfermedad

hedge[1] *noun*

1 A hedge is a financial arrangement made to offset gains or losses because of changes in the fair value or cash flows of a hedged item. Such transactions are typically investments in derivative financial instruments.

contrato de cobertura

= cobertura

▲ *cash flow hedge* contrato de cobertura del flujo de efectivo ▲ *fair value hedge* contrato de cobertura a valor razonable ▲ *foreign currency hedge* contrato de cobertura de divisas ▲ *hedge accounting* contabilidad de cobertura ▲ *hedge of a net investment* contrato de cobertura de una inversión neta ▲ *hedge of expected future transactions* cobertura de las transacciones de futuros esperadas ▲ *hedge of expected sales in foreign currency* contrato de cobertura de las ventas esperadas en moneda extranjera ▲ *hedge of foreign currency receivables* contrato de cobertura de las divisas a cobrar ▲ *hedge of future cash flows* contrato de cobertura de los flujos de efectivo futuros ▲ *hedge of the value of assets and liabilities* contrato de cobertura del valor de los activos y pasivos ▲ *hedge reserve* reserva por contrato de cobertura

2 = hedge transaction

A hedge is a transaction made with the aim of eliminating risk and protecting against exposures relating to changes in foreign currency exchange rates, interest rates, fair value or cash flows.

operación de cobertura

= operación de la cobertura

▲ *at the inception of the hedge* al inicio de la operación de cobertura

hedge[2] *verb*

To hedge is to offset risk exposures arising from changes in prices, exchange rates or interest rates by using hedging instruments, typically derivative financial instruments.

cubrir

= proteger

▲ *hedge a currency position against subsequent exchange rate movements* cubrir una posición en divisas contra movimientos posteriores del tipo de cambio ▲ *hedge a liability* cubrir un pasivo ▲ *hedge a portion of the interest rate risk* cubrir una parte del riesgo por tipo de interés ▲ *hedge foreign currency investments* cubrir las inversiones en divisas ▲ *hedge investments in foreign currencies by currency borrowings* cubrir las inversiones en divisas con préstamos en divisas ▲ *use a derivative to hedge an underlying non-financial variable* utilizar un derivado para cubrir una variable financiera subyacente ▲ *use contract currency swaps to hedge net assets in subsidiaries* utilizar swaps de divisas para proteger activos netos en filiales

hedge accounting

Hedge accounting means offsetting gains or losses because of changes in the fair value or cash flows of a hedged item by using hedging instruments, typically derivative financial instruments.

contabilidad de cobertura

▲ *discontinue hedge accounting* interrumpir la contabilidad de cobertura ▲ *each main type of forecast transaction for which hedge accounting is used* cada tipo principal de transacción previsto para el que se usa la contabilidad de cobertura ▲ *for hedge accounting purposes* por razones de contabilidad de cobertura ▲ *hedge ac-*

counting for foreign currency items contabilidad de cobertura para las partidas en moneda extranjera ▲ *hedge accounting of foreign currency* contabilidad de la cobertura de moneda extranjera ▲ *hedge accounting rules* normas de contabilidad de cobertura ▲ *meet the criteria for hedge accounting* cumplir los criterios para la contabilidad de cobertura ▲ *qualify for hedge accounting* cumplir los requisitos de la contabilidad de cobertura ▲ *recognition and measurement on fair value hedge accounting* reconocimiento y medición de la contabilidad de cobertura a valor razonable ▲ *the application of hedge accounting* la aplicación de la contabilidad de cobertura

hedge effectiveness

Hedge effectiveness is the degree to which offsetting changes in fair value or cash flows attributable to a hedged risk are achieved by the hedging instrument.

efectividad de la cobertura

▲ *assess hedge effectiveness* examinar la efectividad de la cobertura ▲ *compliance with hedge effectiveness* cumplir con la efectividad de la cobertura ▲ *measure hedge effectiveness* medir la efectividad de la cobertura ▲ *meet hedge effectiveness criteria* cumplir los criterios de efectividad de la cobertura ▲ *specify a single method for assessing hedge effectiveness* especificar un único método para valorar la efectividad de la cobertura ▲ *test hedge effectiveness prospectively* examinar la efectividad de la cobertura prospectivamente ▲ *test hedge effectiveness retrospectively* examinar la efectividad de la cobertura retrospectivamente

hedge fund

A hedge fund is a diversified, managed investment fund that is open to a limited number of private investors that are accredited (i.e. very wealthy). Hedge funds are administered by professional investment managers and focus on financial asset investments of many types. They hold long and short positions attempting to generate a high return by using a wide array of investment strategies that may involve hedging and leverage. By combining investments assumed to be safe with high-risk investments they aim at reducing (hedging) the risk of loss. Hedge fund managers are paid a performance fee.

NOTE In 1949, the first hedge fund was set up in the US by Alfred Jones who designed it with a view to extracting returns from the market with less risk than inherently required.

fondo de cobertura

= fondo alternativo, hedge fund

hedge transaction

= hedge

A hedge transaction is a transaction made with the aim of eliminating risk and protecting against exposures relating to changes in foreign currency exchange rates, interest rates, fair value or cash flows.

operación de cobertura

= operación de la cobertura

▲ *accounting for hedge transactions* contabilizando las operaciones de cobertura ▲ *gains or losses on hedge transactions* resultados en las operaciones de cobertura

hedgeable risk

≠ non-hedgeable risk

Hedgeable risks are risks that can be effectively neutralised by the purchase or sale of financial instruments.

riesgo a cubrir

= riesgo progegible

▲ *hedgeable risks arising from insurance obligations* riesgos a cubrir procedentes de obligaciones de seguro

hedged exchange rate

Hedged exchange rate are exchange rates exposed to risk of exchange rate fluctuations which have been offset by a hedging transaction, typically a forward contract.

tipo de cambio cubierto

▲ *receivables translated at the hedged exchange rate* cuentas a cobrar convertidas al tipo de cambio cubierto

hedged item

Hedged items are assets, liabilities, fixed commitments, net foreign investments or expected future transactions that constitute a risk exposure to changes in fair value or future cash flows and that are classified as being items that are hedged.

partida cubierta

▲ *changes in the fair value or cash flows of a designated hedged item* cambios en el valor razonable o flujos de efectivo de una partida cubierta designada ▲ *financial assets that are designated as hedged items* activos financieros que se designan como partidas cubiertas ▲ *foreign currency hedged items* partidas cubiertas de divisas ▲ *gain on a hedged item* ganancia en una partida cubierta ▲ *loss on a hedged item* pérdida en una partida cubierta ▲ *qualify as a hedged item in the consolidated financial statements* calificar como una partida cubierta en los estados financieros consolidados ▲ *the carrying amount of the hedged item* el valor contable de la partida cubierta ▲ *the fair value of the hedged item* el valor razonable de la partida cubierta ▲ *the fixed interest rate on a hedged item* el tipo de interés fijado en una partida cubierta ▲ *the gain or loss on the hedged item attributable to the hedged risk* el resultado en la partida cubierta que se atribuye al riesgo cubierto ▲ *the payment date of the hedged item* la fecha de pago de la partida cubierta ▲ *the repricing time periods for which the hedged item is a liability* los periodos de tiempo de actualización de precios para los que la partida cubierta es un pasivo ▲ *the separate component of equity associated with the hedged item* el componente individual de patrimonio neto asociado con la partida cubierta

hedging

Hedging means taking measures to cover risk and involves using hedging instruments, i.e. derivative financial instruments such as futures and options, to offset changes in the fair value or cash flow of the item to be hedged. Examples of hedged items are assets, liabilities, firm commitments, probable anticipated transactions or foreign investments.

cobertura

= operación de cobertura

▲ *a designated hedging relationship* una relación de cobertura designada ▲ *a dynamic hedging strategy* una estrategia de cobertura dinámica ▲ *central hedging* cobertura central ▲ *for hedging purposes* por motivos de cobertura ▲ *hedging activities* actividades de cobertura ▲ *policies for hedging of risk exposures* políticas para la cobertura de la exposición al riesgo ▲ *the hedging of a net investment in a foreign operation* la cobertura de una inversión neta en una operación de divisas

⇛ cash flow hedging, currency hedging, derivative financial instrument, fair value hedging, hedged item

hedging activity

Hedging activities are activities performed by enterprises to minimise or eliminate risk exposures by using hedging instruments to offset changes in fair value or cash flows.

actividad de cobertura

= operación de cobertura

▲ *comply with the disclosure requirements for hedging activities* cumplir con los requisitos de publicidad de las actividades de cobertura ▲ *risk management policies and hedging activities* políticas de gestión del riesgo y actividades de cobertura ▲ *structure the ongoing hedging activities* estructura de las actividades de cobertura en marcha

hedging instrument

For accounting hedging, hedging instruments are designated derivative financial instruments or (in limited circumstances) other financial assets or liabilities used to offset fair value or cash flow changes of designated hedged items.

instrumento de cobertura

= instrumento de la cobertura

▲ *a specification of the hedging instruments* una especificación de los instrumentos de cobertura ▲ *acquire a hedging instrument* adquirir un instrumento de cobertura ▲ *an expired hedging instrument* un instrumento de cobertura vencido ▲ *changes in the value of the hedging instrument* cambios en el valor del instrumento de cobertura ▲ *derivative liabilities that are not accounted for as hedging instruments* obligaciones

por derivados que no están contabilizadas como instrumentos de cobertura ▲ *gain on a hedging instrument* ganancia en un instrumento de cobertura ▲ *hedging instruments used to hedge expected future transactions* instrumentos de cobertura utilizados para cubrir transacciones futuras esperadas ▲ *loss on a hedging instrument* pérdida en un instrumento de cobertura ▲ *qualify as a hedging instrument* calificar como un instrumento de cobertura ▲ *reversal of value adjustment of hedging instruments* reversión del ajuste de valor de los instrumentos de cobertura ▲ *the cumulative gain on the hedging instrument from inception of the hedge* la ganancia acumulada en el instrumento de cobertura desde el inicio de la cobertura ▲ *the fair value of a hedging instrument* el valor razonable de un instrumento de cobertura ▲ *the ineffective portion of the gain or loss on the hedging instrument* la parte no efectiva del resultado en el instrumento de cobertura ▲ *the principal terms of the hedging instrument* los términos principales del instrumento de cobertura ▲ *the replacement or rollover of a hedging instrument into another hedging instrument* el reemplazo o rotación de un instrumento de cobertura a otro instrumento de cobertura ▲ *the time period during which the hedging instrument remains outstanding* el periodo de tiempo durante el cual el instrumento de cobertura sigue vigente ▲ *translation adjustments on hedging instruments* ajustes por conversión en los instrumentos de la cobertura ▲ *value adjustment of hedging instruments* ajuste del valor de los instrumentos de cobertura
SOURCE IAS 32, paragraph 11

hedging policy

An enterprise's hedging policy is a dynamic statement based on strategic decisions to manage and remove risk as well as maximising profit, e.g. by minimising the effect of exchange rate fluctuations on transactions, cash flows and earnings. The hedging policy is typically set out in the financial review of the annual report and identifies derivative financial instruments used and methods to determine hedge effectiveness.

política de cobertura

▲ *a dynamic hedging policy* una política de cobertura dinámica ▲ *adopt a new hedging policy* adoptar una nueva política de cobertura ▲ *an appropriate hedging policy* una política de cobertura apropiada ▲ *revise the hedging policy* revisar la política de cobertura

⇛ derivative financial instrument, hedging

hedging reserve

Hedging reserves are reserves for changes in the fair value of derivative financial instruments designated and qualifying as effective cash flow hedges. The gains and losses arising from the changes are deferred to the hedging reserves.

reserva de cobertura

= reserva por cobertura

▲ *fair value gains and losses transferred from the hedging reserve in shareholders' equity* pérdidas y ganancias a valor razonable transferidos de la reserva de cobertura en el patrimonio neto de los accionistas ▲ *movements on the hedging reserve in shareholders' equity* movimientos en la reserva de cobertura en el patrimonio neto de los accionistas

⇛ cash flow hedge, fair value reserve, hedging

hedging transaction

= hedge

A hedging transaction is a transaction which is made with the intention to hedge or eliminate the risk of an asset or a liability exposed to risk, referred to as the hedged item.

operación de cobertura

= cobertura

▲ *a specification of a hedging transaction* una especificación de una operación de cobertura ▲ *an effective hedging transaction* una operación de cobertura efectiva ▲ *conclude a hedging transaction* finalizar una operación de cobertura ▲ *enter into hedging transactions with other entities within the group* firmar una operación de cobertura con otras entidades dentro del grupo ▲ *record a financial instru-*

ment as a hedging transaction anotar un instrumento financiero como una operación de cobertura ▲ *the value of a hedging transaction* el valor de una operación de cobertura ▲ *translation adjustment of a hedging transaction* ajuste por conversión de una operación de cobertura

held-for-trading financial asset
Held-for-trading financial assets are financial assets at fair value through profit or loss that are acquired with the intention of early sale or repurchase and profit-taking.
activo financiero mantenido para negociar
▲ *classify as held-for-trading financial assets* clasificar como activos financieros mantenidos para negociar ▲ *recognise a held-for-trading financial asset* reconocer un activo financiero mantenido para negociar
⇛ available-for-sale financial asset, financial asset at fair value through profit or loss

held-to-maturity
Held-to-maturity is used of financial instruments and refers to financial assets with fixed or determinable payments and fixed maturity that are non-derivative instruments and are intended held to maturity by the investor enterprise. Examples of such assets are mortgage, government and corporate bonds.
mantenido hasta el vencimiento
▲ *classified as held-to-maturity* clasificado como mantenido hasta el vencimiento ▲ *the held-to-maturity classification* la clasificación mantenida hasta el vencimiento

held-to-maturity instrument
= held-to-maturity security
Held-to-maturity instruments are financial assets with fixed or determinable payments and fixed maturity that are non-derivative instruments and intended held to maturity by the investor enterprise. Exceptions are financial assets at fair value through profit or loss, available-for-sale financial assets as well as loans and receivables.
instrumento mantenido hasta el vencimiento
▲ *impaired held-to-maturity instruments* instrumentos deteriorados mantenidos hasta el vencimiento

held-to-maturity investment
Held-to-maturity investments are financial assets with fixed or determinable payments and fixed maturity that are non-derivative instruments and intended held to maturity by the investor enterprise. Exceptions are financial assets at fair value through profit or loss, available-for-sale financial assets as well as loans and receivables.
inversión mantenida hasta el vencimiento
▲ *a significant increase in the risk weights of held-to-maturity investments* un aumento significativo en las ponderaciones de riesgo de las inversiones mantenidas hasta el vencimiento ▲ *amortise to profit or loss over the remaining life of the held-to-maturity investment* amortizar a resultados durante la vigencia de la inversión mantenida hasta el vencimiento ▲ *dispose of a held-to-maturity investment* eliminación de una inversión mantenida hasta el vencimiento ▲ *held-to-maturity investments carried at amortised cost* inversiones mantenidas hasta el vencimiento llevadas a coste amortizado ▲ *interest risk in a held-to-maturity investment* riesgo de interés en una inversión mantenida hasta el vencimiento ▲ *measurement of financial assets previously classified as held-to-maturity investments* medición de activos financieros previamente clasificados como inversiones mantenidas hasta el vencimiento ▲ *reclassify any remaining held-to-maturity investments* reclasificar cualesquiera inversiones mantenidas hasta el vencimiento vigentes ▲ *satisfy the criteria for a held-to-maturity investment* satisfacer los criterios por una inversión mantenida hasta el vencimiento ▲ *the sale or transfer of held-to-maturity investments* la venta o transferencia de las inversiones mantenidas hasta el vencimiento
SOURCE IAS 39, paragraph 9

held-to-maturity security
= held-to maturity instrument
Held-to-maturity securities are financial assets with fixed or

determinable payments and fixed maturity that are non-derivative instruments and intended held to maturity by the investor enterprise. Exceptions are financial assets at fair value through profit or loss, available-for-sale financial assets as well as loans and receivables.

título mantenido hasta el vencimiento

▲ *carry held-to-maturity securities at amortised cost* llevar los títulos mantenidos hasta el vencimiento a coste amortizado ▲ *losses on held-to-maturity securities sold prior to maturity* pérdidas en los títulos mantenidos hasta el vencimiento vendidos con anterioridad ▲ *sale of held-to-maturity securities* venta de los títulos mantenidos hasta el vencimiento

hidden reserve

= secret reserve

Hidden reserves are secret reserves that will not appear from the balance sheet, i.e. resources that an enterprise accumulates e.g. by recognising assets at understated values. The fair value method of accounting assets seeks to avoid this by measuring assets at current market value.

reserva oculta

= reserva secreta

▲ *constitute a hidden reserve* constituir una reserva oculta ▲ *create hidden reserves* crear reservas ocultas

high-low method US, UK

The high-low method is a method of predicting cost behaviour through a comparison of the total costs associated with two extreme levels of output: the highest activity and the lowest activity points. The resulting difference is presumed to be caused by an increase in variable costs, which allows a calculation of unit variable cost. Fixed costs can now be derived, as total cost is known. In this way, mixed cost or semi-variable cost may be separated into the fixed and variable components.

método alto-bajo

= método alto/bajo

▲ *use the high-low method* utilizar el método alto-bajo

⇛ conference method, least-square regression method, visual-fit method

highlight

Highlights refer to the most essential, significant or memorable parts of something. In financial reports, highlights include financial statement figures of particular interest and importance.

aspectos destacados

NOTE Always plural in Spanish accounting texts.

▲ *financial highlights for the year* aspectos destacados financieros para el año ▲ *present the highlights* presentar los aspectos destacados ▲ *the financial highlight* los aspectos destacados financieros

highly liquid

Highly liquid assets are assets that may be turned into cash at very short notice with insignificant risk of material loss. Such assets include marketable securities, e.g. bonds with short maturities or financial instruments that can be sold before maturity.

muy líquido

▲ *highly liquid investments with an original maturity of three months or less* inversiones muy líquidas con un vencimiento original de tres meses o menos ▲ *highly liquid securities* títulos muy líquidos ▲ *short-term highly liquid investments* inversiones muy líquidas a corto plazo

⇛ cash and cash equivalents

highly probable

Highly probable means that something is very likely to happen or to be true or real.

altamente probable

▲ *a firm purchase commitment that is highly probable within one year* un compromiso de compra de una empresa que es altamente probable dentro de un año ▲ *a hedge of a highly probable forecast purchase of a commodity with a forward contract* una cobertura de una compra altamente probable de una mercancía con un contrato de futuros ▲ *a hedged highly probable forecast transaction* una operación cubierta altamente probable ▲ *make performance highly probable* actuación altamente probable

SOURCE IFRS 5, Appendix A

hire purchase contract

= hire-purchase contract

A hire purchase contract is an agreement whereby a person or an enterprise hires goods in return for periodical payments for a specified period and has an option to buy the goods when the period expires. No ownership passes unless the option to buy is exercised.

contrato de alquiler con opción de compra

= arrendamiento financiero, leasing

▲ *assets held under a hire purchase contract* activos mantenidos según un contrato de alquiler con opción de compra ▲ *enter into a hire purchase contract* firmar un contrato de alquiler con opción de compra ▲ *payments of capital under hire purchase contract* pagos de principal según el contrato de alquiler con opción de compra

hire-purchase contract

→ hire purchase contract

historic cost convention

→ historical cost convention

historical

Within the context of accounting, historical means original, as in e.g. historical cost, which refers to the original cost or purchase price at the date of acquisition.

histórico

▲ *estimate on the basis of historical market data* estimar en base a datos de mercado históricos ▲ *exceed the average historical growth rate over the long term* exceder la tasa de crecimiento histórica media a largo plazo ▲ *historical cash flow information* información de flujo de efectivo histórico ▲ *historical changes in cash and cash equivalents* cambios históricos en efectivo y equivalentes ▲ *historical loss experience* experiencia de pérdida histórica ▲ *historical summaries of financial data* resúmenes históricos de los datos financieros ▲ *historical volatility* volatilidad histórica ▲ *information about historical loss rates* información sobre las tasas de pérdida históricas ▲ *information about the specific components of historical operating cash flows* información sobre los componentes específicos de los flujos de efectivo de explotación históricos ▲ *the historical pattern of increases in dividends* el modelo histórico de los aumentos de dividendos ▲ *unadjusted historical experience* experiencia histórica no ajustada ▲ *valuation of inventories in the context of the historical cost system* valoración de inventarios en el contexto del sistema de coste histórico

historical conversion rate

Historical conversion rate is the foreign exchange rate at the transaction date of an asset.

tipo de cambio histórico

▲ *translate at the historical conversion rate* convertir al tipo de cambio histórico ▲ *use the historical conversion rate* utilizar el tipo de cambio histórico

historical cost

= HC

The historical cost of an asset is the original cost of the asset, i.e. the cash (or amount of cash equivalents) paid, or the fair value of any consideration given, in return for the acquisition of the asset. For a liability, the historical cost amounts to the proceeds received in satisfaction of the liability.

coste histórico

▲ *an item measured in terms of historical cost* una partida valorada en términos de coste histórico ▲ *based on a historical cost approach* basado en un criterio de coste histórico ▲ *historical cost financial statements* estados financieros a coste histórico ▲ *measured at historical cost* valorado a coste histórico ▲ *prepare financial statements on the historical cost basis of accounting* preparar los estados financieros según el criterio contable del coste histórico ▲ *recoverable historical costs* costes históricos recuperables ▲ *state assets at historical cost* registrar activos a coste histórico ▲ *the depreciated historical cost* el coste histórico amortizado ▲ *the historical cost carrying amount* el valor contable a coste histórico ▲ *use historical cost as measurement basis* utilizar el coste histórico como método de medida

historical cost convention

The historical cost convention is an accounting convention of valuing items in the balance sheet requiring all items to be

recognised at historical cost, i.e. at original cost.
criterio de coste histórico
= criterio del coste histórico
▲ *based on the historical cost convention* basado en el criterio de coste histórico ▲ *prepare the finansial statements under the historical cost convention* preparar los estados financieros según el criterio de coste histórico

historical price
The historical price is the price on the transaction date at initial recognition of a non-monetary asset.
precio histórico
▲ *report using historical price* informar utilizando el precio histórico

HM Revenue and Customs
→ HM Revenue & Customs

HM Revenue & Customs UK
HM Revenue & Customs (HMRC) is the name of the tax authorities in the UK, which was formed in 2005 when the former Inland Revenue and HM Customs and Excise departments merged. The HMRC is responsible for collecting tax revenues in the UK by collecting and administering direct and indirect taxes such as income tax, corporation tax, capital gains tax, VAT and excise duties.
Agencia Tributaria del Reino Unido
= HM Revenue & Customs
▲ *statistics from HM Revenue & Customs* estadística de la Agencia Tributaria del Reino Unido

hold
1 = own
To hold is to be in possession of, to own or have rightfully.
tener
= poseer
▲ *hold for trading* poseer para operar ▲ *hold investments* poseer inversiones ▲ *hold more than 5% of the share capital* tener más del 5% del capital social ▲ *hold more than 50% of the voting rights* tener más del 50% de los derechos de voto ▲ *hold the majority of the voting rights in the company* poseer la mayoría de los derechos de voto en la empresa
2 = arrange
To hold is to arrange, to be responsible for, to organise or to plan a meeting, a conference etc.
celebrar
▲ *hold an annual general meeting* celebrar una junta general de accionistas ▲ *hold information meetings* celebrar reuniones informativas
3 To hold is to keep something in one's possession instead of disposing of it.
mantener
▲ *hold receivables to maturity* mantener cuentas a cobrar hasta el vencimiento

holding
1 = possession
The holding of something means the amount of a particular type of investment owned, e.g. real property or shares.
agrupación
▲ *holding costs* costes de la agrupación ▲ *holding of voting rights* agrupación de derechos de voto ▲ *major holdings of financial instruments* agrupación principal de instrumentos financieros ▲ *the holdings of the group's other associates or joint ventures* las agrupaciones de las otras asociadas del grupo o joint ventures ▲ *the reporting entity's holding of instruments of the subsidiary or associate* la agrupación de instrumentos de la filial o asociada de la empresa que informa
2 Holding is the arrangement, organisation or planning of a meeting, a conference etc.
celebración
▲ *holding of a general meeting* celebración de una junta general
3 A holding is a portfolio of assets i.e. shares, bonds or properties owned by an enterprise.
cartera
▲ *a holding of shares* una cartera de acciones

holding company
A holding cormpany is a company that owns a majority of voting rights in one or more other companies, called subsidiaries, thereby obtaining control of the other companies. Many holding companies do not carry out any business activities themselves.
holding de empresas
▲ *a financial holding company* un holding de empresas financieras ▲ *form a holding company* forma un holding de empresas
⇛ parent company

holding group

A holding group is a group of companies in which the parent is a holding company without significant activities of its own.

holding

▲ *creating a new holding group organisation* creando una nueva organización del holding ▲ *the holding group management bodies* los organismos de gestión del holding

holiday pay

Holiday pay is a, usually predetermined, sum of money that the employer has to pay to his employee when the employee is on holiday.

paga de vacaciones

▲ *adjustment of holiday pay payable* ajuste de la paga de vacaciones a pagar ▲ *calculated holiday pay* paga de vacaciones calculada ▲ *payable holiday pay* paga de vacaciones a pagar ▲ *the employer's obligation to pay holiday pay* la obligación del empleador de pagar la paga de vacaciones

holiday pay obligation

Holiday pay obligation refers to an employer's obligation to pay compensation in excess of base wages and salaries to employees in respect of holidays.

obligación por paga de vacaciones

▲ *assess the holiday pay obligation* evaluar la obligación por paga de vacaciones ▲ *provision for holiday pay obligations* provisión para obligaciones por paga de vacaciones

horisontal format UK

→ horizontal format

horisontal group UK

→ horizontal group

horizontal format

= account form

≠ narrative form US, report form, vertical format

The horizontal format is a presentation form of a financial statement in which debit items are listed in one column in the left hand side and credit items in one column in the right hand side.

formato horizontal

▲ *present a balance sheet in horizontal format* presentar un balance en formato horizontal ▲ *the horizontal format balance sheet* el formato de balance horizontal

⇛ vertical format

horizontal group

A group consisting of enterprises involved in the same stage of the production or distribution process of a particular product is designated a horizontal group.

grupo horizontal

▲ *establish a horizontal group* establecer un grupo horizontal ▲ *the activities of a horizontal group* las actividades de un grupo horizontal ▲ *within the horizontal group* dentro del grupo horizontal

host bond

A host bond is the debt instrument underlying a warrant, and to which the warrant is attached.

bono anfitrión

= host bond

▲ *convert the host bond to a variable rate instrument* convertir el bono anfitrión en un instrumento de interés variable ▲ *the fair value of the host bond* el valor razonable del bono anfitrión

host contract

A host contract is the underlying contract of a derivative financial instrument.

contrato anfitrión

▲ *a host contract with an embedded foreign currency derivative* un contrato anfitrión con un derivado de divisas incluido ▲ *a non-derivative host contract* un contrato anfitrión no derivado ▲ *be closely related to the host contract* estar muy relacionado con el contrato anfitrión ▲ *pay on the host contract* pagar en base al contrato anfitrión ▲ *separate an embedded derivative from the host contract* separar un derivado incrustado del contrato anfitrión ▲ *the economic characteristics and risks of the host contract* las características y riesgos económicos del contrato anfitrión ▲ *the fair value of the host contract* el valor razonable del contrato anfitrión ▲ *the holder's initial rate of return on the host contract* la tasa de rentabilidad inicial del propietario en el contrato anfitrión ▲ *the host contract itself* el mismo contrato anfitrión

human capital

Within the context of intellectual capital reports, human capital is the part of the intellectual capital that relates to skills, competencies, etc. of the employees as well as the company values and culture.

capital humano

▲ *a strong pool of human capital* un fondo poderoso de capital humano ▲ *continuous improvement in human capital* mejora continua en capital humano ▲ *improve investments in human capital* mejorar las inversiones en capital humano

⇛ intellectual capital report

hurdle rate

= required rate of return

A hurdle rate is the rate of return that is considered sufficiently profitable to encourage enterprises and other investors to engage in an investment.

tasa crítica de rentabilidad

▲ *calculation of the hurdle rate* cálculo de la tasa crítica de rentabilidad ▲ *the hurdle rate of the investor* la tasa crítica de rentabilidad del inversor ▲ *the hurdle rate of the owners* la tasa crítica de rentabilidad de los propietarios ▲ *the hurdle rate on the investment* la tasa crítica de rentabilidad de la inversión ▲ *the weighted average hurdle rate* la tasa crítica de rentabilidad media ponderada

⇛ opportunity cost of capital

hybrid costing system

A hybrid costing system a costing system where costs are allocated to products, typically when manufactured in batches, where the products share some common characteristics, but also have some individual characteristics. This system applies techniques from both job-order costing and the process-costing system.

sistema híbrido de cálculo de costes

▲ *use a hybrid costing system* utilizar un sistema híbrido de cálculo de costes

⇛ job-order costing, process-costing system

hybrid-costing system

→ hybrid costing system

hyperinflation

Hyperinflation occurs when very rapid price increases cause the inflation rate to increase 50% to 100% or more over a short period of time, consequently reducing the purchasing value of money dramatically. In the context of accounting, hyperinflation therefore makes comparative figures misleading.

hiperinflación

▲ *identify the existence of hyperinflation in the country in whose currency the enterprise reports* identificar la existencia de hiperinflación en el país en cuya moneda la empresa informa

SOURCE IAS 29, paragraph 3

hyperinflationary economy

A hyperinflationary economy is an economy characterised by an inflation rate ranging from 50% to 100% or more over a short period of time causing its currency to lose purchasing power very rapidly.

economía hiperinflacionaria

▲ *financial reporting in hyperinflationary economies* información financiera de economías hiperinflacionarias ▲ *report in the currency of a hyperinflationary economy* informar en la moneda de una economía hiperinflacionaria

SOURCE IAS 29, paragraph 3

⇛ hyperinflation

I

IAS IAS/IFRS

IAS is an abbreviation of International Accounting Standard. IASs were issued by the IASC which was replaced in 2001 by IASB as the new global standards issuer. A number of IASs will remain in force until changed or withdrawn; new standards issued by the IASB are called IFRSs.

NIC

▲ *change to IAS* cambiar a las NIC ▲ *financial reporting in accordance with IAS* información financiera de acuerdo con las NIC ▲ *first time adoption of IAS* la primera adopción de las NIC ▲ *in accordance with IAS* de acuerdo con la NIC ▲ *in accordance with IAS 29* de acuerdo con la NIC 29 ▲ *present financial statements in accordance with IAS* presentar los estados financieros de acuerdo con la NIC ▲ *restate in accordance with IAS 29* reformular de acuerdo con la NIC 29 ▲ *the compatibility of the IAS with the accounting directives* la comparabilidad de las NIC con las directivas contales ▲ *the effect of IAS 29* el efecto de la NIC 29

⇛ accounting standard, International Financial Reporting Standard

IAS disclosure requirement

= IFRS disclosure requirement

IAS/IFRS

IAS disclosure requirements refer to the requirements for information to be entered in the financial statements if these are prepared in accordance with IAS.

requerimiento de publicación NIC

▲ *compliance with IAS disclosure requirements* cumplimiento de los requerimientos de publicación NIC ▲ *comply with the IAS disclosure requirements* cumplir con los requerimientos de publicación NIC

⇛ IFRS disclosure requirement

IAS financial statements IAS/IFRS

IAS financial statements are financial statements that are prepared and presented according to IAS.

estados financieros NIC

▲ *full set of IAS financial statements* conjunto completo de estados financieros NIC ▲ *presentation of IAS financial statements* presentación de los estados financieros NIC ▲ *publication of IAS financial statements* publicación de estados financieros NIC

⇛ first IFRS financial statements, IFRS financial statements

IAS Regulation IAS/IFRS

The IAS Regulation (EC) 1606/2002 concerns the application and adoption of the International Accounting Standards (IAS) on 19 July 2002 by the European Parliament and the Council. According to the Regulation, to achieve a better functioning of the internal market and to ensure that Community enterprises participating in financial markets are accepted internationally, publicly traded enterprises are required to apply a single set of global standards such as the International Accounting Standards for the preparation of their consolidated financial statements.

Normativa NIC

▲ *implement the IAS Regulation* implementar la Normativa NIC ▲ *the effect of the IAS Regulation* el efecto de la Normativa NIC ▲ *under the IAS Regulation* según la Normativa NIC

SOURCE IAS Regulation

⇛ International Accounting Standard, International Financial Reporting Standard

IAS requirement

An IAS requirement is a requirement that is specified in IAS. An IAS requirement must be complied with if the enterprise reports under IAS.

requerimiento NIC

▲ *compliance with IAS requirements* cumplimiento de los requerimientos NIC ▲ *comply with IAS requirements* cumplir con los requerimientos NIC

IASB IAS/IFRS

IASB is the abbreviation for International Accounting Standards Board. In 2001, IASB replaced IASC as international standard-issuing organ. In 2003, IASB started issuing international accounting standards, now referred to as IFRSs. The standards issued by the former IASC are named IASs.

Comité Internacional de Normas de Contabilidad

= IASB, IASC

▲ *adopted by the IASB* adoptado por el Comité Internacional de Normas de Contabilidad ▲ *comply with the financial reporting standards from IASB* cumplir con las normas de información financiera del Comité Internacional de Normas de Contabilidad ▲ *documents and papers issued by IASB* documentos y artículos emitidos por el Comité Internacional de Normas de Contabilidad ▲ *exposure drafts issued by IASB* documentos de discusión emitidos por el Comité Internacional de Normas de Contabilidad ▲ *Implementation Guidance for Standards issued by the IASB* Manual de Implementación de las Normas emitido por el Comité Internacional de Normas de Contabilidad ▲ *unfinished discussions between the IASB, the European Central Bank, prudential supervisors and the banking industry* discusiones no finalizadas entre el Comité Internacional de Normas de Contabilidad, el Banco Central Europeo, los organismos supervisores y el sector bancario

⇛ IAS, IFRS

IASB standard

An IASB standard, referred to as IFRS plus the relevant number, is one of the international accounting standards developed and issued from 2003 by the International Accounting Standards Board that in 2001 replaced the International Accounting Standards Committee (IASC) as the new global accounting standards issuer. Standards issued by IASC are referred to as IASs.

Norma NIIF

▲ *comply with every IASB standard in force* cumplir con cada Norma NIIF en vigor ▲ *the proposed IASB standard* la Norma NIIF propuesta

IASC

IASC is the abbreviation of International Accounting Standards Committee. IASC has now been replaced by IASB.

IASC

= Comité Internacional de Normas de Contabilidad, IASB

▲ *approved by the IASC Board* aprobado por el Consejo del IASC ▲ *IASC framework for the preparation and presentation of financial statements* marco IASC para la preparación y presentación de estados financieros

⇛ IASB

IASC standard

An IASC standard, referred to as IAS plus the relevant number, is one of the 34 international accounting standards developed and issued by the International Accounting Standards Committee that was replaced in 2001 by the International Accounting Standards Board (IASB) as the new global accounting standards issuer. Standards issued by IASB are referred to as IFRSs.

Norma NIC

▲ *an alternative provided in an IASC standard* una alternativa provista en una norma NIC ▲ *as provided for by the IASC standard* como provisto por la norma NIC ▲ *comply with the provisions of the IASC standard* cumplir con la provisiones de la norma NIC ▲ *meet the IASC standard's definition* cumplir la definición de la norma NIC ▲ *pass an IASC standard* pasar una norma NIC ▲ *revalue assets under the IASC standard* revalorizar activos según la norma NIC

IASCF

= International Accounting Standards Committee Foundation

IASCF is the abbreviation for the International Accounting Standards Committee Foundation, the top, not-for-profit corporation overseeing and appointing the members of the International Accounting Standards Board to whom it has delegated the sole responsibility for setting the international accounting standards. The IASCF consists of 19 trustees with diverse geographical and functional background, appointed for a period of three years with the possibility of being renewed once.

Fundación del IASC

= Fundación del Comité Internacional de Normas de Contabilidad

▲ *the objectives of the IASCF* los objetivos de la Fundación del IASC ▲ *the Trustees of IASCF* los Patronos de la Fundación del IASC

ICAEW

= Institute of Chartered Accountants in England and Wales

= Instituto de Auditores de Inglaterra y Gales

ICAEW is an abbreviation of the Institute of Chartered Accountants in England and Wales which is the largest UK professional accountancy body. The objectives of the ICAEW are primarily focussed on the education and training of chartered accountants and the maintenance of high standards for members' professional conduct. As well as providing various services to members, the ICAEW plays an important role, both internationally and in the UK, with regard to advancing accounting theory and practice as well as developing corporate reporting, corporate governance and auditing.

Institute of Chartered Accountants in England and Wales

= Instituto de Auditores de Inglaterra y Gales

▲ *become a member of the ICAEW* llegar a ser un miembro del Institute of Chartered Accountants in England and Wales

ID code

= ISIN code

ID code is the abbreviation for a stock exchange identification code and is a code attached to a financial instrument, used to identify that instrument, e.g. a share, issued by a particular listed company in a particular country. The ID code is unique to each instrument and consists of an alpha country code and a number consisting of a standardised amount of digits. CSE1158 is e.g. the ID code for shares of the Danish company Novo Nordisk listed on the OMX Nordic Exchange (Copenhagen Stock Exchange). On an international basis, ID codes comprise the International Securities Identification Number (ISIN) which is ISO-standardized. Other ID codes are SEDOL (the Stock Exchange Official List) for all securities issued in the UK and Eire and CUSIP, the system used by US and Canadian companies, a system developed by the Committee on Uniform Security Identification Procedures under the American Bankers' Association.

código ISIN

▲ *a previously used ID code* un código ISIN previamente utilizado ▲ *change to a previously deleted ID code* cambiar a un código ISIN previamente eliminado ▲ *registered under the ID code* registrado según el código ISIN

ideal standard

= perfection standard

Ideal standards set as their goal peak performance under perfect operating conditions based on existing specifications and equipment and do not allow for defective materials, waste or machine breakdowns. Being extremely difficult to live up to, ideal standards are not favoured by employees who find them demotivating as they set unrealistic benchmarks.

norma estándar ideal

= norma estándar perfecta

▲ *comply with an ideal standard* cumplir con una norma estándar ideal ▲ *live up to an ideal standard* vivir conforme a una norma estándar ideal ▲ *the old ideal standard* la norma estándar ideal antigua

⇛ currently attainable standard, flexible budget, normal standard

identifiability

Identifiability means that something is capable of being

identified meaning that it can be recognised and distinguished clearly from something else.

identificabilidad

▲ *a necessary condition for identifiability* una condición necesaria para la identificabilidad ▲ *meet the identifiability criterion in the definition of an intangible asset* cumplir el criterio de identificabilidad en la definición de un activo intangible

identifiable

≠ unidentifiable

When something is identifiable, e.g. an asset, it means that it is possible to define its identity and distinguish it from something else.

identificable

▲ *an identifiable and separately measurable portion of the interest rate exposure of an interest-bearing asset* una parte identificable y claramente medible de la exposición al riesgo de tipo de interés de un activo sujeto a interés ▲ *an identifiable asset* un activo identificable ▲ *an identifiable liability* un pasivo identificable ▲ *an identifiable non-monetary asset without physical substance* un activo no monetario identificable sin sustancia física ▲ *identifiable goods and services* bienes y servicios identificables ▲ *identifiable non-cash consideration* contraprestación identificable no dineria ▲ *measure identifiable net assets acquired at an amount that is not fair value* medir activos netos identificables adquiridos a una cantidad que no es su valor razonable ▲ *supply goods or services within a clearly identifiable operating cycle* suministrar bienes o servicios sin un ciclo operativo claramente identificable ▲ *the identifiable consideration received* la contraprestación identificable recibida ▲ *the identifiable segment assets and segment liabilities* los activos y pasivos del segmento identificables ▲ *the parent's interest and the minority interest in the identifiable net assets of the unit* el interés de la matriz y de los accionistas minoritarios en los activos netos identificables de la unidad

identification

Identification means to recognise something so that it can be clearly distinguished from something else.

identificación

▲ *electronic identification* identificación electrónica ▲ *identification of assets* identificación de activos ▲ *identification of hedging transactions* identificación de transacciones con cobertura ▲ *identification of liabilities* identificación de pasivos ▲ *identification of segments* identificación de segmentos ▲ *identification of the cash-generating units* identificación de las unidades generadoras de efectivo ▲ *reassess the identification and measurement of the acquiree's identifiable assets* reexaminar la identificación y medición de los activos identificables del adquirente ▲ *specific identification of cost* identificación específica del coste

identify

To identify means to recognise something so that it can be clearly distinguished from something else.

identificar

▲ *an explicitly identified asset* un activo identificado explícitamente ▲ *an implicitly identified asset* un activo identificado implícitamente ▲ *identify a liability* identificar un pasivo ▲ *identify risks* identificar riesgos ▲ *identify the facts* identificar los hechos

idle time

Idle time is the period of time measured in labour or machine hours when a production facility or workstation is able to operate, but not used because of lack of operators or materials. Idle time is a cost of direct labour and part of production overheads.

tiempo muerto

= tiempo vacío

▲ *budgeted idle time* el tiempo muerto presupuestado ▲ *eliminate idle time* eliminar el tiempo muerto ▲ *minimise idle time* minimizar el tiempo muerto

IFRIC IAS/IFRS

= International Financial Reporting Interpretations Committee IAS/IFRS

IFRIC is an abbreviation for International Financial Reporting Interpretations Committee, which in 2002 replaced the former Standing Interpretations Committee (SIC) set up in 1997. The role of the IFRIC is to prepare interpretations of International Financial Reporting Standards for approval by the IASB and, in the context of the Framework and as appropriate, to clarify and explain issues of financial reporting which are not covered by existing IASs or IFRSs.

IFRIC

= CINIIF, Comité de Interpretación de Normas Internacionales de Información Financiera, SIC

▲ *be within the scope of IFRIC 1* estar dentro del alcance de la IFRIC 1.

IFRIC interpretation IAS/IFRS

IFRIC is an abbreviation for International Financial Reporting Interpretations Committee which in 2002 replaced the former Standing Interpretations Committee (SIC) set up in 1997. IFRIC interpretations of International Financial Reporting Standards are issued by the IFRIC for approval by the IASB.

interpretación IFRIC

= interpretación NIIF

▲ *IFRIC Interpretation 1 Changes in existing decommissioning, restoration and similar liabilities* la interpretación IFRIC 1 cambia lo existente sobre decomisos, reparaciones y pasivos similares ▲ *release an IFRIC interpretation* publicar una interpretación IFRIC

IFRS IAS/IFRS

IFRS is an abbreviation of International Financial Reporting Standard. Starting in 2003, IFRSs are issued by the IASB that in 2001 replaced IASC as the new global standards issuer. A number of IASs, or International Accounting Standards, issued by IASC, remain in force until changed or withdrawn.

NIIF

▲ *an integral part of IFRS 3* una parte integral de la NIIF 3 ▲ *an unreserved statement of compliance with IFRS* un estado no reservado de cumplimiento con la NIIF ▲ *apply IFRS* aplicar la NIIF ▲ *apply the latest version of IFRSs* aplicar la versión última de las NIIFs ▲ *explanation of transition to IFRSs* explicación de la transición a las NIIFs ▲ *financial statements under IFRSs* estados financieros según las NIIFs ▲ *first-time adoption of IFRS* adopción por vez primera de la NIIF ▲ *IFRS for small and medium-sized entities* NIIF para pequeñas y medianas empresas ▲ *in conformity with IFRSs in all respects* de acuerdo con las NIIFs en todos los aspectos ▲ *make an explicit and unreserved statement in the annual report of compliance with IFRSs* llevar a cabo un estado explícito y sin reserva en el informe anual de acuerdo con las NIIFs ▲ *opening balance sheet at the date of transition to IFRS* balance de apertura a la fecha de transición a la NIIF ▲ *opening IFRS balance sheet* balance de apertura NIIF ▲ *prepare a reporting package under IFRSs* preparar un paquete de información según las NIIFs ▲ *presentation of the annual report under IFRS* presentación del informe anual según la NIIF ▲ *provide a suitable starting point for accounting under IFRSs* ofrecer un punto de partida adecuado para contabilizar según las NIIFs ▲ *the first IFRS financial statements* los primeros estados financieros NIIF ▲ *transition to IFRS* transición a la NIIF ▲ *use full IFRSs* utilizar las NIIFs completas

⇛ accounting standard, FRS, IAS, SFAS

IFRS disclosure requirement

IFRS disclosure requirements refer to the requirements for information to be entered in the financial statements if these are prepared in accordance with IFRS.

requisito de información según NIIF

= necesidad de divulgación según NIIF

▲ *compliance with IFRS disclosure requirements* cumplimiento de los requisitos de información según NIIF ▲ *comply with the IFRS disclosure requirements* cumplir con los requisitos de información según NIIF

⇛ IAS disclosure requirement

IFRS financial statements

IFRS financial statements are financial statements that are prepared and presented according to IFRS.

estados financieros presentados con arreglo a las NIIF

▲ *full set of IFRS financial statements* juego completo de estados financieros presentados con arreglo a las NIIF ▲ *prepare IFRS financial statements* preparar los estados financieros presentados con arreglo a las NIIF ▲ *presentation of IFRS financial statements* presentación de los estados financieros con arreglo a las NIIF ▲ *publication of IFRS financial statements* publicación de los estados financieros presentados con arreglo a las NIIF

⇛ IAS financial statements

IGU UK

= income generating unit UK

IGU is the abbreviation for income generating unit, i.e. the smallest group of assets, liabilities or associated goodwill identified to generate income independently of the other income streams of the reporting entity. The separation of total income into income generating units is made to perform impairment reviews as accurately as possible.

unidad generadora de ingresos

▲ *esstablish an IGU* establecer una unidad generadora de ingresos

illiquid

1 An enterprise which is illiquid has insufficient cash, or assets that can be readily converted into cash, to continue operations and pay its debts as they fall due.

sin liquidez

▲ *illiquid person* persona sin liquidez ▲ *illiquid share* acción sin liquidez ▲ *unlisted and illiquid equities* títulos no cotizados y sin liquidez

2 An illiquid asset is an asset that is not easily convertible into cash and which is not readily negotiable. An illiquid share is a rarely traded share.

no líquido

▲ *illiquid assets* activos no líquidos ▲ *illiquid shares* acciones no líquidas

IMA US

= Institute of Management Accountants US

IMA is the abbreviation for the Institute of Management Accountants, a US professional organisation of accountants within management accounting. The Institute oversees the Certified Management Accountant (CMA) program and continued professional development of management accountants.

IMA

= Instituto de Contabilidad de Gestión

▲ *a study published by IMA* un estudio publicado por el IMA ▲ *become a member of IMA* llegar a ser un miembro del IMA

⇛ Institute of Management Accountants

immediate income recognition

Immediate income recognition is the act of recognising revenues in the profit and loss account as they are earned.

reconocimiento inmediato de ingresos

▲ *immediate income recognition in part* reconocimiento inmediato de ingresos en parte

immediate recognition

Immediate recognition is the act of recognising revenues as earned or expenses as incurred in the profit and loss account.

reconocimiento inmediato

▲ *immediate recognition of actuarial gains and losses* reconocimiento inmediato de pérdidas y ganancias actuariales

impairment

= write-down for impairment

Impairment is the fall in the balance sheet value of an asset because of damage or reduced market value seen by a reduction in the recoverable amount of an asset below its carrying amount.

deterioro

= depreciación

▲ *an impairment in value* una depreciación en el valor ▲ *an indication of an impairment* una indicación de una depreciación ▲ *annual impairment test of goodwill* evaluación del deterioro del fondo de comercio ▲ *at the time of impairment testing* a la hora de la comprobación del deterioro ▲ *compensation for impairment* compensación por deterioro ▲ *evidence of impairment* evidencia de deterioro ▲ *for the purpose of impairment testing* por motivo de la comprobación del deterioro ▲ *impairment of a financial asset carried at amortised cost* deterioro de un activo financiero llevado a coste amortizado ▲ *interest income after impairment recognition* ingreso por interés después del reconocimiento del deterioro ▲ *objective evidence of impairment* evidencia objetiva de deterioro ▲ *recognise a credit impairment on the recognised assets* reconocer una depreciación en un crédito en los activos reconocidos ▲ *recognition of a loss from the impairment of property, plant and equipment* reconocimiento de una pérdida por depreciación de edificios, instalaciones y equipos ▲ *review an asset for impairment* revisar la depreciación de un activo ▲ *test a cash-generating unit for impairment* evaluar una unidad generadora de efectivo por depreciación ▲ *the collective assessment of impairment* el examen colectivo de la depreciación ▲ *the process for estimating impairment* el proceso de estimación de la depreciación

impairment cost

An impairment cost is the write-down recognised in the financial statements when an impairment review shows that the carrying amount of a fixed asset exceeds the recoverable amount.

pérdida por deterioro

= coste de deterioro, coste del deterioro, pérdida por el deterioro

NOTE Spanish accountants prefer 'pérdida por deterioro' to the IAS/IFRS term 'coste de deterioro'.

▲ *accumulated impairment cost* pérdida por deterioro acumulada ▲ *reversal of an impairment cost* reversión de una pérdida por deterioro

⇛ impairment loss

impairment loss UK

An impairment loss arises when the value of a fixed asset is impaired because the carrying amount exceeds the estimated recoverable amount.

NOTE In the US, an impairment loss arises when the value of a fixed asset is impaired because the carrying amount exceeds the fair value.

pérdida por deterioro

= pérdida por el deterioro

▲ *a goodwill impairment loss* una pérdida por deterioro del fondo de comercio ▲ *a reversal of an impairment loss* una reversión de una pérdida por deterioro ▲ *accumulated impairment losses* pérdidas por deterioro acumuladas ▲ *an arbitrary allocation of an impairment loss between the assets* una asignación arbitraria de una pérdida por deterioro entre los activos ▲ *determine the amount of an impairment loss* determinar la cantidad de una pérdida por deterioro ▲ *disclosure requirements for reporting impairment losses by segment* publicar requisitos para informar sobre pérdidas por deterioro por segmento ▲ *impairment loss for a cash-generating unit* pérdida por deterioro para una unidad generadora de efectivo ▲ *indications that an impairment loss may have occurred* indicaciones de que una pérdida por deterioro puede haber ocurrido ▲ *recognise impairment losses* reconocer pérdidas por deterioro ▲ *recognise the impairment loss in profit or loss* reconocer la pérdida por deterioro en la cuenta de resultados ▲ *recognising and measuring an impairment loss* reconocimiento y medición de una pérdida por deterioro ▲ *result in a material impairment loss* resultar en una pérdida por deterioro material ▲ *reverse impairment losses* revertir pérdidas por deterioro ▲ *reversing an impairment loss for an individual asset* reversión de una pérdida por deterioro de un activo individual ▲ *test an intangible asset for impairment loss* examinar un activo intangible por pérdida por deterioro ▲ *the aggregate reversals of impairment losses recognised during the period* las reversiones agregadas de pérdidas por deterioro reconocidas ▲ *the amount estimated for an impairment loss* la cantidad estimada de una pérdida por deterioro ▲ *the main classes of assets affected by impairment losses* las clases principales de activos afectados por pérdidas por deterioro

⇛ impairment cost

impairment of financial assets IAS/IFRS

= amounts written off investments UK, asset write-offs US

Impairment of financial assets is a reduction in the recoverable amount of a financial asset below its carrying amount. As an item in the financial statements, "Impairment of financial assets" recognises the impairment loss by writing down the carrying amount of impaired financial assets to the present value of estimated future cash flows discounted at the financial assets' original effective interest rate.

deterioro del activo financiero

= deterioro de los activos financieros

▲ *recognition of a loss from the impairment of financial assets* reconocimiento de una pérdida por el deterioro de los activos financieros

impairment of property, plant and equipment IAS/IFRS

Impairment of property, plant and equipment is a line item in the income statement when presented classifying expenses by nature. This item recognises the expense for the period under review representing impairment losses.

depreciación de edificios, instalaciones y equipos

= deterioro de propiedad, planta y equipo

NOTE Spanish accountants prefer 'depreciación de edificios, instalaciones y equipos' to the IAS/IFRS term 'deterioro de propiedades, planta y equipo'.

▲ *recognition of a loss from the impairment of property, plant and equipment* reconocimiento de una depreciación de edificios, instalaciones y equipos

impairment review UK

= impairment test IAS/IFRS, US

An impairment review is a process aimed at identifying any impairment loss on a fixed asset by comparing the carrying amount of the fixed asset with its recoverable amount. If the recoverable amount of the asset is lower than its carrying amount, a write-down must be recognised in the financial statements.

NOTE In the US, the carrying amount of the fixed asset is compared with the fair value.

evaluación del deterioro

= examen del deterioro

▲ *the annual impairment review* la evaluación anual del deterioro ▲ *undertake an annual impairment review* llevar a cabo una evaluación anual del deterioro

impairment test US, IAS/IFRS

= impairment review UK

An impairment test is a review of an asset for any reduction in value to ascertain whether a write-down must be made of that asset. If the recoverable amount of the asset is lower than its carrying amount, a write-down must be recognised in the financial statements.

NOTE In the US, the carrying amount of the fixed asset is compared with the fair value.

evaluación del deterioro

= comprobación del deterioro

▲ *annual impairment test* evaluación del deterioro anual ▲ *perform an impairment test* llevar a cabo una evaluación del deterioro ▲ *the annual impairment test for a cash-generating unit to which goodwill has been allocated* la evaluación del deterioro anual para una unidad generadora de efectivo a la que se le ha asignado el fondo de comercio ▲ *timing of impairment tests* fecha escogida para las evaluaciones del deterioro

imperfect competition

≠ perfect competition

Imperfect condition is a market situation where an individual enterprise is aware that its behaviour will influence the price prevailing on the market and therefore adapts and plans accordingly.

competencia imperfecta

≠ competencia perfecta

▲ *markets with imperfect competition* mercados con competencia imperfecta ▲ *the interplay of imperfect competition and incomplete information* la interrelación de la competencia imperfecta y la información incompleta

implement

To implement means to do or carry out something so that it has practical effect.

implementar

▲ *implement a directive* implementar una directiva ▲ *start to implement the restructuring plan* empezar a implementar el plan de reestructuración

implementation

Implementation is the act or process of doing or carrying out something so that it has practical effect.

implementación

▲ *announcing or commencing the implementation of a major restructuring* anunciando o comentando la implementación de una reestructuración importante ▲ *design and implementation of new processes or systems* diseño e implementación de nuevos procesos o sistemas ▲ *implementation guidance* manual de implementación ▲ *the implementation of IAS 39* la implementación de la NIC 39

implicit interest rate IAS/IFRS

Within the context of leases, the implicit interest rate is the discount rate which, applied at the inception, i.e. the beginning, of a lease term to the minimum lease payments and the unguaranteed residual value of the lease, would cause the resulting total present value to be equal to the fair value of a leased asset, e.g. equipment or property.

tipo de interés implicito

▲ *an implicit interest rate of 8%* un tipo de interés implícito del 8%

SOURCE IAS 17, paragraph 4

⇛ interest rate implicit in the lease

important

= material

If something is significant, necessary or highly valued, it is important.

importante

▲ *certain important provisions in IAS 39* ciertas provisiones importantes en la NIC 39 ▲ *disclose the important features of the income tax system* publicar los rasgos importantes del sistema del impuesto sobre la renta ▲ *important elements of the operating capacity of the enterprise* elementos importantes de la capacidad operativa de la empresa ▲ *obscure important information as a result of too much aggregation* ocultar información importante como un resultado de demasiada agregación ▲ *regard as an important user group* considerar como un grupo importante de usuarios

improvement

An improvement is an increase in value or a change in condition for the better. An improvement in the performance of an enterprise means higher earnings.

mejora

▲ *an improvement in the debtor's credit rating* una mejora en el rating crediticio del deudor ▲ *an improvement of the result for the year* una mejora del resultado del año ▲ *an improvement project* un proyecto de mejora ▲ *limited improvements to accounting by insurers for insurance contracts* mejoras limitadas a la contabilidad de los contratos de seguros por los aseguradores ▲ *technical or commercial obsolescence arising from changes or improvements in production* obsolescencia técnica o comercial procedente de cambios o mejoras en la producción

improvement expense

Improvement expenses refer to expenses incurred to improve the condition of an asset. These expenses are capitalised in the balance sheet together with the underlying asset rather than being expensed in the profit and loss account.

gasto de mejora

= gasto por mejora

▲ *improvement expenses written off* eliminación de gastos de mejora ▲ *plus improvement expenses* más gastos de mejora ▲ *reconstruction and improvement expenses* reconstrucción y gastos de mejora ▲ *write off improvement expenses* eliminar gastos de mejora

impute

To impute means to calculate the value or size of something by reference to similar things because it is difficult to measure it in the normal way.

imputar

▲ *impute the amount of interest* imputar el importe del interés ▲ *imputed cost of equity* coste de patrimonio neto imputado ▲ *imputed rate of interest* tipo de interés imputado

imputed cost

Imputed costs are calculated costs with no cash flow effect such as depreciation charges.

coste de producción sin variación de efectivo

= coste imputado

≠ coste de producción con variación de cash flow

NOTE Spanish accountants use 'coste de producción sin variación de efectivo' instead of the IAS/IFRS term 'coste imputado'. This term is not precise and can easily lead to misunderstandings.

▲ *estimates of imputed costs* estimaciones de costes de producción sin variación de efectivo ▲ *excluding imputed costs* excluyendo costes de producción sin variación de efectivo ▲ *recognition of imputed costs* reconocimiento de costes de producción sin variación de efectivo

in arrears

When a liability, e.g. payment, is in arrears, it is overdue for settlement.

en mora

▲ *be in arrears with respect to the payment of interest or principal* estar en mora con respecto al pago de intereses o capital ▲ *be in arrears with the repayments* estar en mora con los pagos ▲ *interest, royalty or dividend revenue received in arrears* ingresos por intereses, royalties y dividendos devengados en mora

in process US

= in progress UK

Something in process is ongoing and not yet completed.

en curso

= en marcha, en proceso

▲ *a sale in process at the balance sheet date* una venta en marcha a la fecha del balance ▲ *production in process* producción en curso ▲ *research and development in process* investigación y desarrollo en curso ▲ *work in process* trabajo en curso

⇛ contract work in process

in progress UK

= in process US

Something in progress is ongoing and not yet completed.

en curso

= en marcha, en proceso

▲ *a delevopment project in progress* un proyecto de desarrollo en curso ▲ *a sale in progress* una venta en marcha ▲ *an in progress development project* un proyecto de desarrollo en curso ▲ *changes in inventories of finished goods and work in progress* cambios en inventarios de productos terminados y trabajo en curso ▲ *construction contract work in progress* trabajo en curso por contrato de obra ▲ *provisions subject to the future outcome of litigation in progress* provisiones sujetas al resultado futuro del litigio en curso ▲ *work in progress arising under construction contracts* trabajo en curso procedente de contratos por obra

⇛ contract work in progress

in terms of time

When something is referred to, measured or calculated in terms of time it means that time is used as a measurement basis.

en términos de tiempo

▲ *demand considerable resources both in terms of time and money* demandar recursos considerables tanto en términos de tiempo como de dinero ▲ *savings in terms of time* ahorros en términos de tiempo

in the longer term

In the longer term means sometime in future.

en el largo plazo

= a largo plazo

▲ *a slight improvement in the longer term* una mejora ligera en el largo plazo ▲ *improve production in the longer term* mejorar la producción a largo plazo ▲ *reduce financial exposure in the longer term* reducir la exposición al riesgo financiero en el largo plazo

in total

The expression "in total" refers to an aggregate sum or amount, typically appearing as the bottom line of an account or financial statement.

en total

= de forma conjunta, en conjunto

▲ *disclose key management personnel compensation in total* publicar la compensación del personal de alta dirección de forma conjunta ▲ *disclosures made in total* revelaciones hechas en conjunto ▲ *result in the loss of 250 jobs in total* resultar en la pérdida de 250 empleos en total

⇛ total

in-process

In-process activities are ongoing and in progress.

en curso

= en marcha, en proceso

▲ *in-process research and development* investigación y desarrollo en curso ▲ *related to an in-process development project acquired in a business combination* relacionado con un proyecto de desarrollo en curso adquirido en una combinación de negocios ▲ *subsequent expenditure on an acquired in-process development project* gasto subsiguiente en un proyecto de desarrollo en curso adquirido ▲ *the carrying amount of the acquired in-process research project* el valor contable de la investigación en curso adquirida

Inc. US

= incorporated US

Inc. is the abbreviation for "incorporated" and is used about an incorporated business organisation. Inc. appears after and as part of the firm name.

SA

= sociedad anónima

▲ *choose to do business as an Inc.* elegir hacer un negocio como una SA ▲ *form an Inc.* formar una SA

⇛ corporation, incorporate

incentive

An incentive is an encouragement inducing a person to act in a certain way, e.g. performing in the best interests of the enterprise.

incentivo

▲ *a financial incentive* un incentivo financiero ▲ *a personal incentive* un incentivo personal ▲ *an incentive to the employees to remain in the entity's employ* un incentivo a los empleados para permanecer en la empresa ▲ *an incentive to undertake specific expenditures* un incentivo para llevar a cabo gastos específicos ▲ *incentive payments* pagos de incentivos ▲ *incentives for the agreement of a new or renewed lease* incentivos para el acuerdo de un arrendamiento nuevo o renovado ▲ *irrespective of the incentive's nature or form* independiente de la naturaleza o forma del incentivo ▲ *provide incentives for the lessee to enter into the contract* ofrecer incentivos al arrendatario para firmar el contrato ▲ *recognise incentives* reconocer incentivos ▲ *share-based incentives* incentivos basados en acciones ▲ *the aggregate benefit of incentives* el beneficio agregado de los incentivos ▲ *the aggregate cost of incentives* el coste agregado de los incentivos

incentive compensation US

Incentive compensation constitutes a reward offered subject to a manager or other employee of an enterprise achieving certain performance goals. One of the objectives of incentive compensation is to motivate employee performance. Incentive compensation may consist in bonus pay or stock options.

remuneración por incentivo

= remuneración por incentivos

▲ *incentive compensation for the members of the board of directors* remuneración por incentivos para los miembros del consejo de administración ▲ *incentive compensation for the members of the executive committee* remuneración por incentivos para los miembros del comité ejecutivo ▲ *performance-based incentive compensation* remuneración por incentivos basada en resultados ▲ *share-based incentive compensation* remuneración por incentivos basada en acciones

⇛ employee share ownership plan, incentive pay

incentive pay

Incentive pay refers to a system of remuneration under which employees or managers are remunerated on the basis of their individual results or performance or on the basis of the enterprise's results or performance.

remuneración por incentivo

= remuneración por incentivos

▲ *incentive pay for the members of the executive board* remuneración por incentivos para los miembros del comité ejecutivo ▲ *incentive pay for the members of the supervisory board* remuneración por incentivos para los miembros del consejo de administración ▲ *performance-based incentive pay* remuneración por incentivos basada en resultados ▲ *share-based incentive pay* remuneración por incentivos basada en acciones

⇛ incentive compensation

incentive program US

= incentive scheme UK

An incentive program is a scheme adopted for the purpose of encouraging someone to do something. An enterprise may e.g. offer incentive programs to urge its employees and managers to meet defined performance targets or work harder. Incentive programs may include rewards in the form of cash bonuses, shares or share options.

programa de incentivos

▲ *a bonus-based incentive program* un programa de incentivos basado en primas ▲ *a share-based incentive program* un programa de incentivos basado en acciones ▲ *a special incentive program* un programa de incentivos especial ▲ *be subject to an incentive program* estar sujeto a un programa de incentivos ▲ *introduce an incentive program* introducir un programa de incentivos ▲ *introduce incentive programs for the company's board of directors and management* introducir programas de incentivos para el consejo y la dirección de la empresa ▲ *introduce special incentive programs* introducir programas de incentivos especiales

⇛ share option

incentive programme

= incentive program US

An incentive programme is a scheme adopted for the purpose of encouraging someone to do something. An enterprise may e.g. offer incentive programs to urge its employees and managers to meet defined performance targets or work harder. Incentive programs may include rewards in the form of cash bonuses, shares or share options.

programa de incentivos

▲ *a bonus-based incentive programme* un programa de incentivos basado en primas ▲ *a share-based incentive programme* un programa de incentivos basado en acciones ▲ *a special incentive programme* un programa de incentivos especial ▲ *introduce an incentive programme* introducir un programa de incentivos ▲ *introduce incentive programmes for the company's board of directors and management* introducir programas de incentivos para el consejo y la dirección de la empresa

incentive scheme

An incentive scheme is an arrangement under which extra remuneration such as cash bonuses is awarded to employees who meet specified criteria. The purpose of an incentive scheme is to motivate and induce employees to participate in meeting the goals of the enterprise.

plan de incentivos

▲ *a long-term incentive scheme* un plan de incentivos a largo plazo ▲ *amounts awarded under an incentive scheme* cantidades otorgadas según un plan de incentivos ▲ *introduce an incentive scheme* introducir un plan de incentivos

inception

The inception is the date at which the parties under a particular contract are committed to complying with the provisions of that contract, i.e. the date when the contractual terms and conditions become effective. In the context of leases, the inception of a lease is the date of the signing of the lease, if earlier than the date of commitment, which is the date when the parties are committed to meeting the principal provisions of the lease, e.g. when the lessor acquires the leased asset. Other examples of contracts are insurance contracts, derivative financial instruments and hedges.

inicio

▲ *at the inception of an insurance contract* al inicio de un contrato de seguros ▲ *at the inception of the hedge* al inicio de la cobertura ▲ *inception of a lease* inicio del arrendamiento ▲ *on inception of the contract* en el inicio del contrato ▲ *the cumulative gain on the hedging instrument from inception of the hedge* la ganancia acumulada en el instrumento de cobertura desde el inicio de la cobertura ▲ *the fair value at inception of the contractual rights* el valor razonable al inicio de los derechos contracturales ▲ *the measurement of the liability at inception* la medición del pasivo al inicio ▲ *the terms of the exchange determined on inception of the derivative instrument* los términos del intercambio determinados en el inicio del instrumento derivado

include

1 To include is to integrate as part of a whole or to embed into something.

incluir

▲ *included in income from continuing operations* incluido en ingreso procedente de operaciones continuas

2 = recognise UK, IAS/IFRS, recognize US

To include an item or an amount is to recognise that item or amount in the financial statements, as an asset or liability item in the balance sheet, or as a revenue or expense item in the income statement.

reconocer

▲ *include depreciation, amortisation and impairment of assets* reconocer depreciación, amortización y deterioro de activos ▲ *include interest expenses in the cost* reconocer gastos por intereses en el coste

inclusion

1 Inclusion is the integration or embeddedment of something into something else.

inclusión

▲ *exemption from the inclusion of information* exento de la inclusión de información ▲ *inclusion of interest expenses in the cost of fixed assets* inclusión de gastos por intereses en el coste de los activos fijos

2 Inclusion is the recognition of asset or liability items in the balance sheet or of revenue or expense items in the income statement.

reconocimiento

▲ *inclusion of interest expenses in the cost of fixed assets* reconocimiento de los gastos por interés en el coste de los activos fijos

income

1 Income is inflows or improvements of assets as well as increases in equity arising from decreases of liabilities that result in increases in economic benefits during an accounting period of an enterprise.

ingreso

▲ *a calculated income* un ingreso calculado ▲ *an income of EUR 100m* un ingreso de 100 millones de euros ▲ *an item of income* una partida de ingresos ▲ *consolidated negative goodwill taken to income* fondo de comercio negativo llevado a ingresos ▲ *contingent rents recognised as income in the period* rentas contingentes reconocidas como ingreso en el periodo ▲ *extraordinary income* ingreso extraordinario ▲ *future income* ingreso futuro ▲ *income from investments* ingreso procedente de inversiones ▲ *income from investments in associates* ingreso procedente de inversiones en asociadas ▲ *income from investments in group enterprises* ingreso procedente de inversiones en empresas del grupo ▲ *income from other investments and receivables that are fixed assets* ingreso procedente de otras inversiones y partidas a cobrar que son activos fijos ▲ *recognise income as earned* reconocer el ingreso cuando se realiza ▲ *recognition of income* reconocimiento de ingresos ▲ *total income* total ingresos

2 Income refers to a monetary amount earned by a person or enterprise during a specified period for providing services, delivering goods or from investments. Usually, income is taxable.

renta

▲ *determination of taxable income* determinación de la renta imponible

3 = net income, profit UK, IAS/IFRS ≠ loss UK, US, IAS/IFRS

For an accounting period, income constitutes the earnings of an enterprise, i.e. the amount by which revenue exceeds expenses, resulting in increased total assets. NOTE UK English uses "income" instead of "profit" in non-profit organisations.

beneficio

▲ *appropriation of net income* apropiación del beneficio neto ▲ *income turnaround* cambiar positivamente el beneficio ⇛ income and expenditure account

income after income tax US

= post-tax profit IAS/IFRS, UK, profit after tax UK

≠ income before income tax US, pre-tax profit IAS/IFRS, UK, profit before tax UK, IAS/IFRS

Income after income tax is the net income of an enterprise for an accounting period after deduction of tax expense.

ingreso después de impuestos

= beneficios después de impuestos

▲ *an improvement of income after tax* una mejora del ingreso después de impuestos ▲ *an increase in income after tax* un aumento en el ingreso después de impuestos

income and expenditure account

= income and expenditure statement, income statement US, IAS/IFRS, profit and loss account UK, revenue account

≠ balance sheet

An income and expenditure account is the statement in a non-profit organisation that corresponds to the profit and loss account or income statement in an enterprise trading for a profit. The income and expenditure account covers a fixed period of time and its balance shows the excess of income over expenditure (or vice versa) instead of a profit or loss.

cuenta de ingresos y gastos

= cuenta de pérdidas y ganancias, cuenta de resultados

▲ *consolidated income and expenditure account* cuenta de ingresos y gastos consolidada ▲ *prepare an income and expenditure account* preparar una cuenta de ingresos y gastos

⇛ revenue and expenditure account

income and expenditure statement

→ income and expenditure account

income base

The income base is the total amount of income earned by a taxpayer for a defined period on which tax is assessed.

base imponible

▲ *maintenance of the company's income base* mantenimiento de la base imponible de la empresa ▲ *the income base for calculating earnings per share* la base imponible para el cálculo de los beneficios por acción

income before income tax US

= pre-tax profit IAS/IFRS, UK, profit before tax UK, IAS/IFRS

≠ income after income tax US, post-tax profit IAS/IFRS, profit after tax UK

Income before income tax is the income of an enterprise for an accounting period before deduction of tax expense.

beneficio antes de impuetos

▲ *an improvement of income before tax* una mejora en el beneficio antes de impuestos ▲ *an increase in income before tax* un aumento en el beneficio antes de impuestos

income earning

Income earning takes place when a person or enterprise carries out tasks, actions or efforts, receiving in return some form of remuneration or compensation.

percepción de renta

▲ *a company with high income earning* una compañía con percepción de renta alta

⇛ income-earning

income from interests in associated undertakings UK

Income from interests in associated undertakings is an item in the profit and loss account relating to income from long-term investments in undertakings in which the parent holds a significant interest i.e. 20 per cent or more. The item does not include interests in group undertakings.

ingresos por intereses en asociadas

= ingreso por inversiones en asociadas

▲ *a decrease in income from interests in associated undertakings* un descenso en ingresos por intereses en asociadas ▲ *an increase in income from interests in associated undertakings* un aumento en ingresos por inversiones en asociadas ▲ *total income from interests in associated undertakings* total ingresos por intereses en asociadas

⇛ income from shares in group undertakings

income from ordinary activities

Income from ordinary activities is the income or loss from the recurring business operations and activities incidental to or arising from these operations, such as investing and financing, contributing to an increase or decrease in net assets.

NOTE In the income statement, income from ordinary activities is recognised below operating income or loss, depreciation, amortisation and net financial income and expenses, usually both before and after tax and before any extraordinary items.

ingresos por actividades ordinarias

▲ *other income from ordinary activities* otro ingreso por actividades ordinarias ▲ *total income from ordinary activities* total ingreso por actividades ordinarias

income from other fixed asset investments UK

Income from other fixed asset investments is an item in the profit and loss account relating to income from long-term holdings of securities other than equity investments in group enterprises and associates.

ingresos por inversiones en otros activos fijos

▲ *a decrease in income from other fixed asset investments* un descenso en los ingresos por inversiones en otros activos fijos ▲ *an increase in income from other fixed asset investments* un aumento en los ingresos por inversiones en otros activos fijos

⇛ income from interests in associated undertakings, income from other participating interests, income from shares in group undertakings

income from other participating interests UK

Income from other participating interests is an item in the profit and loss account relating to income from long-term interests other than interests in group or associated undertakings.

ingresos por intereses en otras participaciones

NOTE Always plural in Spanish accounting texts.

▲ *a decrease in income from other participating interests* un descenso en ingresos por intereses en otras participaciones ▲ *an increase in income from other participating interests* un aumento en ingresos por intereses en otras participaciones

⇛ income from interests in associated undertakings, participating interest

income from shares in group undertakings UK

Income from shares in group undertakings is an item in the profit and loss account relating to income from an interest or investment on a long-term basis in a subsidiary or parent undertaking within the same group.

ingresos por participaciones en empresas del grupo

NOTE Always plural in Spanish accounting texts.

▲ *profit before income from shares in group undertakings* beneficio antes de ingresos por participaciones en empresas del grupo

income generating unit UK

= IGU

An income generating unit is the smallest group of assets, liabilities or associated goodwill identified to generate income independently of the other income streams of the reporting entity. The separation of total income into income generating units is made to perform impairment reviews as accurately as possible.

unidad generadora de ingresos

= unidad generadora de los ingresos

▲ *the carrying amount of each income generating unit* el valor contable de cada unidad generadora de ingresos

SOURCE FRS 11

income item

= item of income, revenue item

An income item is an item in the income statement that records an amount of income generated or earned during the accounting period.

partida de ingresos

▲ *a main category of income items* una categoría principal de partidas de ingresos ▲ *all income items recognised* todas las partidas de ingresos reconocidas

income or loss from ordinary activities IAS/IFRS

= income or loss from ordinary operations US, profit or loss on ordinary activities

Income or loss from ordinary activities is the income or loss from the recurring business operations and activities incidental to or arising from these operations, such as investing and financing, contributing to an increase or decrease in net assets.

NOTE In the income statement, income or loss from ordinary activities is recognised below operating income or loss, depreciation, amortisation and net financial income and expenses, usually both before and after tax and before any extraordinary items.

resultado de actividades ordinarias

= ingreso o pérdida por actividades ordinarias, resultado de operaciones ordinarias, resultado por actividades ordinarias, resultado por operaciones ordinarias

▲ *income or loss from ordinary activities after tax* resultado de actividades ordinarias después de impuestos

income or loss from ordinary operating operations US

= profit or loss from ordinary operating activities UK

Income or loss from ordinary operating operations is a subtotal derived from the income statement appearing as income or loss before tax and extraordinary items adjusted for other operating income and expenses as well as interest income and expenses.

ingresos o pérdidas por operaciones de explotación ordinarias

= ingreso o pérdida por actividades de explotación, ingreso o pérdida por operaciones de explotación

income or loss from ordinary operations US

= income or loss from ordinary activities IAS/IFRS

Income or loss from ordinary operations is the income or loss from the recurring business operations and activities incidental to or arising from these operations, such as investing and financing, contributing to an increase or decrease in net assets.

NOTE In the income statement, income or loss from ordinary operations is recognised below operating income or loss, depreciation, amortisation and net financial income and expenses, usually both before and after tax and before any extraordinary items.

resultado de operaciones ordinarias

= ingreso o pérdida por operaciones ordinarias, resultado de actividades ordinarias, resultado por actividades ordinarias, resultado por operaciones ordinarias

▲ *estimated income or loss from ordinary operations* resultado estimado de operaciones ordinarias ▲ *income or loss from ordinary operations after income tax* resultado de operaciones ordinarias después de impuestos

income smoothing

1 = profit smoothing UK
Income smoothing is the levelling of an enterprise's income for the year as a result of the application of different applicable accounting principles.

nivelación de resultados

▲ *single-period income smoothing* nivelación de resultados en un periodo único ▲ *the relationship between income smoothing and return and risk* la relación entre la nivelación de resultados y la rentabilidad y el riesgo

2 Income smoothing is the levelling of personal income in an economy, e.g. by taxation, to counteract an unequal income distribution.

nivelación de ingresos

income statement IAS/IFRS, US

= profit and loss account UK, profit and loss statement US

The income statement shows revenues and expenses and, where appropriate, results from continuing and discontinued operations recognised during an accounting period arriving at the earnings or income for the accounting period.

cuenta de pérdidas y ganancias

= cuenta de resultados, estado de resultados

▲ *aggregate expenses in the income statement* gastos agregados en la cuenta de pérdidas y ganancias ▲ *an item in the income statement* una partida en la cuenta de pérdidas y ganancias ▲ *comparative figures for the income statement* figuras comparativas para la cuenta de pérdidas y ganancias ▲ *format for the income statement* formato para la cuenta de pérdidas y ganancias ▲ *include in the income statement* incluir en la cuenta de pérdidas y ganancias ▲ *income statement classified by function* cuenta de pérdidas y ganancias clasificada por función ▲ *income statement classified by nature* cuenta de pérdidas y ganancias clasificada por tipo de gasto ▲ *income statement in report form* cuenta de pérdidas y ganancias en formato vertical ▲ *information to be presented on the face of the income statement* información para ser presentada en el anverso de la cuenta de pérdidas y ganancias ▲ *notes to the income statement* notas a la cuenta de pérdidas y ganancias ▲ *offsetting in the income statement* compensando en la cuenta de pérdidas y ganancias ▲ *present an income statement* presentar una cuenta de pérdidas y ganancias ▲ *present in the income statement* presentar en la cuenta de pérdidas y ganancias ▲ *recognise immediately in the income statement* reconocer inmediatamente en la cuenta de pérdidas y ganancias ▲ *recognition in the income statement* reconocer en la cuenta de pérdidas y ganancias ▲ *the effect on the income statement* el efecto en la cuenta de pérdidas y ganancias ▲ *the line item in the income statement in which the excess is recognised* la linea en la cuenta de pérdidas y ganancias en la que se reconoce el excedente ▲ *the predictive value of the income statement* el valor predictivo de la cuenta de pérdidas y ganancias

income statement format US, IAS/IFRS

= profit and loss account format UK

An income statement format is a presentation form and layout of a statement of income or loss prescribed by legislation or accounting standards, e.g. the Danish Financial Statements Act, IFRS and FASB.

formato de la cuenta de pérdidas y ganancias

= formato de la cuenta de resultados, formato del estado de resultados

▲ *income statement format for groups* formato de la cuenta de pérdidas y ganancias por grupos ▲ *items in the income statement format* partidas en el formato de la cuenta de pérdidas y ganancias

⇛ account form, report form

income statement item US, IAS/IFRS

Income statement items are elements in the income statement such as revenue or sales, cost of sales etc.

partida de la cuenta de pérdidas y ganancias

= partida del estado de resultados

▲ *other income statement items, such as interest income and expense* otras partidas de la cuenta de pérdidas y ganancias, tales como ingresos y gastos por intereses ▲ *ranging from a few income statement items to extensive income statement disclosures* que van desde algunas partidas de la cuenta de pérdidas y ganancias a la publicación de la cuenta de pérdidas y ganancias extensiva ▲ *the restatement of non-monetary assets, owners' equity and income statement items* la regularización de activos no monetarios, patrimonio neto y partidas de la cuenta de pérdidas y ganancias

income statement liability method

→ income-statement liability method

income tax

Income tax is the tax payable by individuals to the tax authorities on their computed taxable income.

impuesto sobre la renta

▲ *an entity subject to income taxes* una entidad sujeta al impuesto sobre la renta ▲ *calculation of income tax* cálculo del impuesto sobre la renta ▲ *cash flows arising from income taxes* flujos de efectivo procedentes de los impuestos sobre la renta ▲ *cash payment of income tax* pagos en efectivo del impuesto sobre la renta ▲ *current income tax* impuesto sobre la renta corriente ▲ *Danish Act on Income Tax and Property Tax pertaining to Individuals etc.* Ley danesa sobre el impuesto sobre la renta y el patrimonio de particulares. etc. ▲ *deferred income tax* impuesto sobre la renta diferido ▲ *disclose accounting policies for income taxes* publicar las políticas contables para el impuesto sobre la renta ▲ *foreign income tax* impuesto sobre la renta extranjero ▲ *income tax receipts or payments* recibos o pagos del impuesto sobre la renta ▲ *income taxes paid* impuestos sobre la renta pagados ▲ *income taxes payable* impuestos sobre la renta a pagar ▲ *income taxes that are created as a result of statutory requirements imposed by governments* impuestos sobre la renta que se crean como un resultado de los requisitos normativos impuestos por el gobierno ▲ *levy income tax* recaudar el impuesto sobre la renta ▲ *net cash from operating activities before income tax* efectivo neto procedente de actividades de explotación antes del impuesto sobre la renta ▲ *pay income tax* pagar el impuesto sobre la renta ▲ *payable income taxes* impuesto sobre la renta a pagar ▲ *payments relating to income tax* pagos relacionados con el impuesto sobre la renta ▲ *recognition of income tax* reconocimiento del impuesto sobre la renta ▲ *recoverable income taxes* impuestos sobre la renta a recuperar ▲ *refund of income tax* reembolso del impuesto sobre la renta ▲ *the aggregate amount of current and deferred income tax credited or charged to equity* la cantidad agregada del impuesto sobre la renta corriente y diferido ▲ *the potential benefit of the acquiree's income tax loss carry-forwards* el beneficio potencial del adquirente por pérdidas a compensar en el impuesto sobre la renta ▲ *the related amount of income taxes recognised directly in equity* la cantidad del impuesto sobre la renta relacionada reconocida directamente en el patrimonio

income tax benefit US/IAS/IFRS

An income tax benefit is a reduction in or exemption from payment of income tax granted as financial support or business incentives in particular circumstances, in the form of tax allowances, loss carryforwards, exemption from tax on dividends or other types of tax and other tax relief.

deducción en el impuesto sobre beneficios

= beneficio en el impuesto a las ganancias

NOTE The IAS/IFRS term 'beneficio por impuesto a las ganancias' is not used in Spanish accounting texts.

▲ *net of any related income tax benefit* neto de cualquier deducción en el impuesto sobre beneficios relacionada

income tax convention US

→ double taxation convention

income tax credit US

= tax credit

An income tax credit is a direct, monetary reduction of the tax liability, i.e. amount of tax payable as opposed to tax relief, tax allowances or tax deductions that are offset against the taxable income. An example of an income tax credit is the offsetting of taxes paid abroad against national taxes payable.

crédito por impuesto sobre beneficios

= crédito fiscal

▲ *grant an income tax credit* garantizar un crédito por impuesto sobre los beneficios ▲ *total income tax credit* total crédito por impuestos sobre beneficios

⇛ allowance, tax deduction, tax relief

income tax expense

Income tax expense represents the aggregate amount of current and deferred income tax expenses, also represented as an item in the income statement for the accounting period under review.

gasto por impuesto sobre beneficios

▲ *excluding finance costs and income tax expense* excluyendo los costes financieros y el gasto por impuesto sobre los beneficios ▲ *income tax expense for an interim period* gasto por impuesto sobre beneficios para un periodo intermedio ▲ *income tax expense relating to the gain or loss* gasto por impuesto sobre beneficios relacionado con pérdidas o ganancias ▲ *related income tax expense* gasto por impuesto sobre beneficios relacionado

income tax law US

Income tax law is the legislation and set of rules and regulations according to which taxes must be paid. In the US, all federal tax laws are embodied in the Internal Revenue Code, whereas state taxes are paid under the rules of each individual state where state tax is payable.

NOTE In the UK, tax charged on the profits of companies is referred to as corporation tax.

normativa sobre impuestos

= normativa fiscal

▲ *under the income tax laws applicable* según la normativa sobre impuestos aplicable

⇛ corporation tax, Internal Revenue Service

income tax rate

Income tax rate refers to the percentage at which tax is levied on taxable income. The income tax rate is applied to the computed taxable income to determine the amount of income tax payable.

tipo impositivo

▲ *an estimated average annual effective income tax rate* un tipo impositivo efectivo anual medio estimado ▲ *reduced income tax rates* tipos impositivos reducidos ▲ *the weighted average annual income tax rate expected for the full financial year* el tipo impositivo anual medio ponderado esperado para el año completo

income tax receivable US

= tax receivable UK

An income tax receivable is an asset for an enterprise and arises because the enterprise has paid too much tax.

impuesto a devolver

▲ *an increase in income tax receivable* un aumento en el impuesto a devolver ▲ *recognition of an income tax receivable* reconocimiento de un impuesto a devolver ▲ *recognize as an income tax receivable* reconocer como un impuesto a devolver

income tax return UK

= statement of income, tax return IAS/IFRS, US

An income tax return is a taxpayer's annual statement of income submitted to the tax authorities showing details of taxable amounts of income, gains and profits and tax-deductible expenses.

declaración de la renta

▲ *complete the income tax return* completar la declaración de la renta ▲ *submit the income tax return* remitir la declaración de la renta

income taxes payable US

= corporation tax UK, current tax payable IAS/IFRS

"Income taxes payable" is an item in the balance sheet under current liabilities representing current tax payable after adjustments and deduction of taxes paid during the accounting period.

impuestos a pagar

▲ *a decrease in income taxes payable* un descenso en impuestos a pagar ▲ *an increase in income taxes payable* un aumento en impuestos a pagar ▲ *deferred income taxes payable* impuestos a pagar diferidos

⇛ current tax, deferred tax, income tax expense

income taxes related to net income US

The income taxes related to net income is the share of income taxes for the year not attributable to the items recognised directly in equity.

impuestos relacionados con ingresos imputados al patrimonio neto

▲ *current income taxes related to net income* impuestos corrientes sobre resultados del ejercicio

income-earning

An income-earning activity is an activity that generates income.

generador de ingresos

= generador de los ingresos

▲ *income-earning activities* actividades generadoras de ingresos

⇛ income earning

income-generating unit UK

→ income generating unit

income-statement liability method

≠ balance-sheet liability method IAS/IFRS

The income-statement liability method implies that the tax liabilities and the tax expenses are calculated on the basis of the differences between the taxable profit and the accounting profit that arise in one accounting period and are reversed in the following period(s) (timing differences).

método de pasivo basado en resultados

= método del pasivo basado en los resultados

≠ método de pasivo basado en el balance, método del pasivo basado en el balance

▲ *use of the income statement liability method* utilizar el método de pasivo basado en resultados

⇛ timing difference

incoming auditor

= successor auditor

≠ predecessor auditor

An incoming auditor is a newly appointed, independent, external auditor who did not perform the audit of the financial statements for the previous accounting period.

auditor entrante

▲ *audits performed by the incoming auditor* auditorías realizadas por el auditor entrante ▲ *pass to the incoming auditor* trasladar al auditor entrante

⇛ auditor, continuing auditor

incomplete

Something that lacks some of its necessary parts or details or is not yet finished is incomplete.

incompleto

▲ *an incomplete earnings process* un proceso de rendimientos incompleto ▲ *an incomplete operating cycle* un ciclo de explotación incompleto ▲ *incomplete documentation* documentación incompleta

incorporate

1 To incorporate is to create a legal entity (corporation) under the authority of the laws of the relevant jurisdiction by filing the corporation's articles of incorporation or certificate of incorporation with the appropriate state or other governmental agency.

fundar

= constituir

▲ *incorporate a company* fundar una empresa

⇛ articles of incorporation, certificate of incorporation, corporation, Inc., incorporated

2 To incorporate is to include in, combine with, or add to something, e.g. a plan, system, document, or group.

incorporar

▲ *be incorporated in* estar incorporado en ▲ *personal property incorporated in real property* propiedad personal incorporada en la propiedad real

incorporated US

= Inc. US

Incorporated or Inc. used as part of a firm name signifies that the firm is created as a corporate, legal entity with certain attributes, e.g. limited liability, which will appear from the articles of incorporation.

sociedad anónima

= SA

▲ *an incorporated enterprise* una sociedad anónima

⇛ articles of incorporation, corporation, incorporate

increase[1] *noun*

1 = rise

≠ decrease

An increase is a rise in amount, number or degree.

aumento

= incremento

▲ *a considerable increase* un aumento considerable ▲ *a price increase* un aumento de precio ▲ *a revaluation increase* un aumento por revalorización ▲ *a significant increase in budgeted loss flowing from the asset* un aumento significativo en la pérdida presupuestada procedente del activo ▲ *an increase in expenses* un aumento en los gastos ▲ *an increase in inventories* un incremento en los inventarios ▲ *an increase in net realisable value* un aumento en el valor realizable neto ▲ *an increase in nominal money capital* un aumento en el capital monetario nominal ▲ *an increase in provisions* un aumento en provisiones ▲ *an increase in the financial resources of the enterprise* un aumento en los recursos financieros de la empresa ▲ *an increase in the value in use of a fixed asset* un aumento en el valor en uso de un activo fijo ▲ *any increase in the present value of the costs to sell that arises from the passage of time* cualquier aumento en el valor actual de los costes por ventas que surgen con el paso del tiempo ▲ *consistent assumptions about price increases attributable to general inflation* suposiciones consistentes sobre aumentos de precio atribuibles a la inflación general ▲ *increases in short-term interest rates* aumentos en los tipos de interés a corto plazo ▲ *the risk of unexpected increases in the administrative costs* el riesgo de aumentos inesperados en los costes administrativos

2 = expansion
An increase is an expansion or extension of something.
incremento
= aumento
▲ *an increase by USD 10m in bonus shares* un incremento de 10 millones de dólares norteamericanos en bonos

increase[2] *verb*
= raise
≠ decrease
To increase means to make something larger in amount, degree, level or number.
aumentar
= incrementar
≠ disminuir
▲ *increase a value* incrementar un valor ▲ *increase convergence of accounting standards around the world* incrementar la convergencia de las normas contables en todo el mundo ▲ *increase earnings per share from continuing operations* aumentar los beneficios por acción procedentes de operaciones continuas ▲ *increase loss per share from continuing operations* aumentar las pérdidas por acción procedentes de operaciones continuas ▲ *increase the carrying amount of goodwill* incrementar el valor contable del fondo de comercio ▲ *increase to an amount equal to or greater than the asset's carrying amount* incrementar a una cantidad igual o mayor que el valor contable del activo

increase in activities
An increase in activities occurs when the volume of activities, i.e. the production level, for one period rises compared with another period.
aumento de actividades
▲ *an appreciable increase in activities* un aumento de actividades apreciable

increase in exchange rate
An increase in exchange rate represents a rise in the price of a currency in terms of another seen in relation to the previous exchange rate level.
incremento en el tipo de cambio
= aumento en el tipo de cambio
▲ *a significant increase in the exchange rate* un incremento significativo en el tipo de cambio ▲ *subsequent increases in exchange rates* aumentos en los tipos de cambio subsiguientes

increase in price
An increase in price represents a rise in the price of a security compared with the previous price level.
incremento en precio
= incremento en el precio
▲ *increases in the price of a listed asset* incrementos en el precio de un activo cotizado

increase in turnover UK
An increase in turnover is a rise in the total turnover of an enterprise, i.e. sales or revenue for products and services, during an accounting period compared with the previous period.
incremento en facturación
= incremento en la facturación
▲ *realise a substantial increase in turnover* constatar un incremento sustancial de facturación

increase in value
= appreciation in value
An increase in value means growth in the value of or value added to something.
aumento de valor
▲ *a future increase in value* un aumento de valor futuro ▲ *a permanent increase in value* un aumento de valor permanente ▲ *increases in value from additional biological transformation and future activities of the enterprise* aumentos de valor procedentes de la transformación biológica adicional y de las actividades futuras de la empresa

increase of share capital
An increase of share capital means a higher amount of share capital as a result of further capital contributed via the issue of additional shares.
incremento de capital social
= ampliación de capital social, aumento del capital social, incremento del capital social

▲ *adjustment factor in increases of share capital* factor de ajuste en los incrementos de capital social

incremental

Incremental is used about something that increases step by step.

marginal

= incremental

NOTE Spanish accountants prefer 'marginal' to the IAS/IFRS term 'incremental'.

▲ *dilutive potential ordinary shares with the lowest earnings per incremental share* acciones ordinarias con potencial dilutivo con los beneficios más bajos por acción marginal ▲ *incremental staff skills leading to future economic benefits* destrezas del personal marginal que conducen a beneficios económicos futuros ▲ *the direct incremental costs to dispose of the asset* los costes marginales directos para eliminar el activo ▲ *the entity's incremental borrowing rate* el tipo de interés marginal de la entidad ▲ *the incremental costs directly attributable to the disposal of an asset* los costes marginales directamente atribuibles a la eliminación de un activo ▲ *the incremental fair value granted* el valor razonable marginal acordado ▲ *the incremental ordinary shares* las acciones ordinarias marginales ▲ *the lessee's incremental borrowing rate of interest* el tipo de interés del empréstito marginal del arrendatario

incremental cost

= differential cost

Incremental cost is the differential cost resulting from a decision, i.e. the difference in total cost between two alternatives, where the alternative includes the total cost plus additional costs.

coste marginal

= coste incremental

NOTE Although traditional Spanish accounting texts used 'coste marginal' the Nuevo Plan General Contable has adopted the IAS/IFRS term 'coste incremental'.

▲ *an estimate of the incremental costs* una estimación de los costes marginales ▲ *incremental costs directly attributable to the disposal of an asset* costes marginales directamente atribuibles a la eliminación de un activo ▲ *incremental costs of production* costes marginales de producción ▲ *the future incremental costs* los costes marginales futuros

incremental cost-allocation method

The incremental cost-allocation method ranks users of a cost object in a prioritised order and allocate costs to users based on this ranking. Stand-alone costs are allocated to the first-ranked user seen as a stand-alone user (the primary party) and the additional costs arising from an increased number of users to the following users (the incremental parties).

método de asignación del coste marginal

▲ *develop the incremental cost-allocation method* desarrollar el método de asignación del coste marginal ▲ *under the incremental cost-allocation method* según el método de asignación del coste marginal ▲ *use the incremental cost-allocation method* utilizar el método de asignación del coste marginal

⇛ incremental cost

incremental effect US, UK

The incremental effect means the change in total results (costs and revenues) caused by an activity change or a new condition compared with another given or known condition.

efecto marginal

= efecto incremental

▲ *examine the incremental effect* examinar el efecto marginal ▲ *incremental effect of the acquisition upon the earnings* efecto incremental de la adquisición sobre los beneficios ▲ *measure the incremental effect* medir el efecto marginal

incremental revenue

Incremental revenue constitutes the increase added to existing revenue.

ingreso marginal

= ingreso incremental

▲ *a 10% increase in incremental revenue* un 10% de aumento en el ingreso marginal ▲ *boost incremental revenue* aumentar el ingreso marginal ▲ *generate incremental revenue* generar ingreso incremental

incremental revenue allocation method
→ incremental revenue-allocation method

incremental revenue-allocation method
The incremental revenue-allocation method is a method which ranks revenue to bundled products by ranking the individual products according to certain management-determined criteria, e.g. the highest sales. The primary product in the bundle is the product ranked first; ranking second is the first incremental product, and ranking third is the second incremental product etc.
método de asignación del ingreso marginal
▲ *under the incremental revenue-allocation method* de acuerdo con el método de asignación del ingreso marginal ▲ *use the incremental revenue-allocation method* utilizar el método de asignación del ingreso marginal

incremental unit-time learning model
The incremental unit-time learning model is a learning-curve model which shows that the incremental unit time, i.e. the time needed to produce the last unit, decreases by a constant percentage each time the accumulated quantity of units produced is doubled.
NOTE Learning curves are functions used in management and cost accounting to predict how labour costs will decline as more units are produced, i.e. as workers become more efficient from learning.
modelo de aprendizaje del tiempo unitario incremental
▲ *use an incremental unit-time learning model* utilizar un modelo de aprendizaje del tiempo unitario incremental
⇛ cumulative average-time learning model

incumbent
1 When an expense, a debt or a duty is incumbent on an enterprise, this means that the enterprise has an obligation to pay the expense or debt or perform the duty.
incumbencia
▲ *a task incumbent on the Board* una tarea de la incumbencia del Consejo
2 Incumbent means in office now and is used about a person who is in a certain official position at present.
incumbente
▲ *the incumbent auditor* el auditor incumbente ▲ *the incumbent members of the board* los miembros incumbentes del consejo
3 In a business context, an incumbent supplier, e.g. a mobile operator, is a supplier holding a dominant position in a market, typically as a consequence of previously having had a monopoly and now having a large market share in a free market for its products.
dominante
▲ *the incumbent mobile operator* el operador móvil dominante

incumbrance
→ encumbrance

incur
= pay
If an enterprise incurs a cost, expense or debt it has a liability to pay money.
incurrir
= materializar
▲ *costs are recognised when incurred* los costes se reconocen cuando se incurren ▲ *incur costs* incurrir en costes ▲ *incur legal or constructive obligations* incurrir en obligaciones legales o constructivas ▲ *incur liabilities* incurrir en pasivos ▲ *net of transaction costs incurred* neto de costes incurridos por transacción ▲ *other expenditure incurred* otros gastos incurridos ▲ *pay expenses as incurred* pagar gastos cuando se incurren ▲ *recognise expenditure in profit or loss as incurred* reconocer gastos en resultados cuando se materializan

incurred cost
Incurred costs are costs which have arisen in connection with an activity and which are payable.
coste incurrido
▲ *calculate the incurred costs* calcular los costes incurridos ▲ *recognise incurred costs* reconocer costes incurridos ▲ *total incurred costs* total costes incurridos

incurrence
= payment

Incurrence of a cost, expense or debt means that the enterprise has a liability to pay money for that cost, expense or debt.

materialización

▲ *concurrently with the incurrence of related costs* concurrentemente con la materialización de los costes relacionados ▲ *incurrence of a financial liability* materialización de un pasivo financiero ▲ *initial cost incurrence* materialización de costes iniciales

indefinite economic life

An indefinite economic life means a life not limited by a specified time period or by any legal, regulatory, contractual, competitive, economic or other factors. Examples of assets with indefinite economic lives may be land, brands, goodwill and trademarks. Assets with indefinite economic lives are not depreciated or amortised, but subject to impairment review on an annual basis.

vida útil indefinida

= vida económica indefinida

▲ *goodwill with indefinite economic life* fondo de comercio con una vida útil indefinida ▲ *land with an indefinite economic life* bien raíz con una vida útil indefinida

⇛ economic life

indefinite life IAS/IFRS

≠ definite life IAS/IFRS

An indefinite life means a life not limited by a specified time period or by any legal, regulatory, contractual, competitive, economic or other factors. Examples of assets with indefinite lives may be land, brands, goodwill and trademarks. Assets with indefinite lives are not depreciated or amortised, but subject to impairment review.

NOTE In the context of accounting, indefinite does not mean infinite, but not limited by any legal, contractual or other factors.

vida indefinida

≠ vida determinada

▲ *held-to-maturity investments with an indefinite life* inversiones mantenidas hasta vencimiento con una vida indefinida ▲ *indefinite life intangibles* intangibles de vida indefinida

⇛ indefinite economic life, indefinite useful life

indefinite useful life IAS/IFRS

An indefinite useful life means a life not limited by a specified time period or by any legal, regulatory, contractual, competitive, economic or other factors. Examples of assets with indefinite useful lives may be land, brands, goodwill and trademarks. Assets with indefinite useful lives are not depreciated or amortised, but subject to impairment review.

vida útil indefinida

▲ *an indefinite useful life assessment of an asset* una valoración de la vida útil indefinida de un activo ▲ *an intangible asset assessed as having an indefinite useful life* un activo intangible examinado suponiéndole una vida útil indefinida ▲ *an intangible asset with an indefinite useful life* un activo intangible con una vida útil indefinida ▲ *test an intangible asset with an indefinite useful life for impairment* examinar por deterioro un activo intangible con una vida útil indefinida

⇛ useful life

indemnification asset

A contractual promise from the seller in a business combination to the buyer in which the seller undertakes to indemnify a loss on one or more specified uncertain liabilities is called an indemnification asset. The buyer, i.e. the acquirer, must account for the promise as an asset.

compensación por reducción en el valor de los activos entregados

▲ *measure an indemnification asset* medir una compensación por reducción en el valor de los activos entregados ▲ *recognise an indemnification asset* reconocer una compensación por reducción en el valor de los activos entregados

independant variable

"Independant" is a misspelling of "independent".

→ independent variable

independence

Independence refers to the state of being free from any influence or control by other parties and considerations to other parties which e.g. exist because of a related party relationship. It is a statutory and regulatory professional requirement that external auditors must be independent of an enterprise and its management when appointed to audit the annual report or financial statements of that enterprise, as independence is a prerequisite for making an objective and unbiased evaluation.

independencia

▲ *compromise the auditor's independence* comprometer la independencia del auditor ▲ *create a significant threat to the auditor's independence* crear un riesgo significativo a la independencia del auditor ▲ *independence from audit client's decision-making* independencia del auditor en la toma de decisiones del cliente ▲ *independence from providers of loan capital* independencia de los proveedores de financiación ▲ *reduce the auditor's independence risk to an acceptable level* reducir el riesgo de independencia del auditor a un nivel aceptable ▲ *the independence of the supervisory board* la independencia del consejo supervisor ▲ *the potential self-interest threat to the auditor's independence* el riesgo potencial para la independencia del auditor por intereses particulares

independent

An independent person or enterprise is free from any influence or control by other parties and considerations to other parties and able to make unbiased and objective decisions and judgments. It is a statutory and regulatory professional requirement that external auditors must be independent of an enterprise and its management when appointed to audit the annual report or financial statements of that enterprise.

independiente

▲ *an external and independent person* una persona independiente y externa ▲ *an independent professional assessment of the value of the items* una valoración profesional independiente del valor de las partidas ▲ *an independent valuer who holds recognised professional qualification* un valor independiente que mantiene una cualificación profesional independiente ▲ *independent qualified actuaries* actuarios cualificados independientes ▲ *resell the assets to an independent party* revender los activos a un partícipe independiente ▲ *stand alone as an independent reporting period* reflejar como un periodo independiente de presentación de informes ▲ *the lowest aggregation of assets that generate largely independent cash inflows* la suma más pequeña de activos que generan fundamentalmente entradas independientes de efectivo

independent auditor

An independent auditor is an external auditor who is not employed by, or in any way connected or committed to, the enterprise or the products of the enterprise whose financial statemens he or she examines.

auditor independiente

▲ *approve the fees to be paid to the independent auditor* aprobar las tarifas que se van a pagar al auditor independiente ▲ *engage an independent auditor* contratar un auditor independiente ▲ *selection of independent auditor* selección del auditor independiente ▲ *the role of the independent auditor* el papel del auditor independiente

⇛ external auditor, internal auditor

independent auditors' report

The independent auditors' report is a written statement signed by two independent accountants or auditing firms and included in the annual report or the financial statements. The report states whether an enterprise's financial statements give a true and fair view of the financial position, operating results and cash flows of the enterprise and may offer recommendations along with findings and conclusions.

informe de los auditores independientes

= informe de auditores independientes

▲ *as mentioned in the independent auditors' report* como se menciona en el informe de los auditores independientes

independent variable

≠ dependent variable

If a variable can be controlled, it is referred to as an independent variable. An independent variable can e.g. be the number of produced units which the enterprise itself may determine.

variable independiente

≠ variable dependiente

▲ *a change in the independent variable* un cambio en la variable independiente ▲ *more than one independent variable* más de una variable independiente

index-linked bond

= indexed bond

An index-linked bond is a bond whose interest and repayments are adjusted to the price development in an economy's retail price index. In case of an increasing inflation rate, the repayments payable by the borrower, and receivable by the lender, will increase at the same rate.

bono indexado

▲ *a deep market in index-linked bonds of the same currency and term* un mercado profundo en los bonos indexados de la misma moneda y término ▲ *issue index-linked bonds* emitir bonos indexados ▲ *redeem an index-linked bond* redimir un bono indexado ▲ *state index-linked bonds on the basis of the December 31 index* reflejar los bonos indexados de acuerdo con el índice a 31 de diciembre

indication of impairment IAS/IFRS

Indications of impairment of assets are signs of reduction in the value of an enterprise's assets during the accounting period, observed from e.g. obsolescence or damage of the assets, substantial reduction in their market value, considerable changes in the operating environment of the enterprise or from a lower market capitalisation of the enterprise than the carrying amount of its net assets.

indicio de deterioro del valor

▲ *an indication of an impairment of an asset* un indicio de deterioro del valor de un activo ▲ *an indication of impairment of a CGU* un indicio de deterioro del valor de una unidad generadora de efectivo

SOURCE IAS 36, paragraph 12

⇛ impairment test

indirect control UK

≠ direct control

If an entity indirectly controls an asset, it has control of another entity that has direct control of the asset. A parent company has indirect control of its subsidiaries' activities and resources.

control indirecto

≠ control directo

▲ *acquire indirect control of over an entity* adquirir el control indirecto de una entidad ▲ *exercise indirect control* ejercer un control indirecto ▲ *retain indirect control of the entity* retener el control indirecto de la entidad

⇛ control

indirect cost

≠ direct cost

Costs that are not directly attributable to a specific cost object, e.g. a product or a division, are called indirect costs.

coste indirecto

≠ coste directo

▲ *attributable indirect costs* costes indirectos atribuibles ▲ *pay remuneration over indirect costs* pagar remuneración sobre costes indirectos

indirect cost of a cost object

The indirect costs of a cost object constitute the share of indirect costs (overheads) allocated to a specific cost object, i.e. the costs that cannot be specifically and economically traced to or identified with the cost object. Examples of indirect costs are costs of labour and services.

coste indirecto de un objeto de coste

▲ *calculate the indirect costs of a cost object* calcular los costes indirectos de un objeto de coste ▲ *identify the indirect costs of a cost object* identificar los costes indirectos de un objeto de coste

indirect manufacturing cost

= factory burden US, factory overhead US, factory overhead cost, indirect manufacturing expense US, indirect production cost, indirect production expense US, manufacturing overhead US, production overhead IAS/IFRS

≠ direct manufacturing cost

Indirect manufacturing costs are costs that are not directly related to the production of goods, i.e. costs for which single products or activities cannot be identified. Examples of indirect manufacturing costs are indirect labour and materials, rent and insurance of manufacturing units.

coste de producción indirecto
= overheads
≠ coste de producción directo
▲ *annual indirect manufacturing cost budget* presupuesto anual de coste de producción indirecto ▲ *materials, labour and indirect manufacturing costs* materias primas, salarios y costes de producción indirectos

indirect manufacturing expense
= indirect production cost, indirect production expense
An indirect manufacturing expense is an expense that is not directly related to the manufacturing of goods, i.e. expenses for which single products or activities cannot be identified. Examples of indirect manufacturing expenses are indirect labour and materials, rent and insurance of manufacturing units.

gasto indirecto de fabricación
= gasto indirecto de producción
≠ gasto directo de fabricación
▲ *capitalise indirect manufacturing expenses* capitalizar los gastos indirectos de fabricación ▲ *compulsory recognition of indirect manufacturing expenses* reconocimiento obligatorio de los gastos indirectos de fabricación ▲ *fixed indirect manufacturing expenses* gastos indirectos de fabricación fijos ▲ *measurement basis for indirect manufacturing expenses* base para la medición de los gastos indirectos de fabricación ▲ *recognise indirect manufacturing expenses* reconocer los gastos indirectos de fabricación ▲ *recognition methods for indirect manufacturing expenses* métodos de reconocimiento de los gastos indirectos de fabricación ▲ *related indirect manufacturing expenses* gastos indirectos de fabricación relacionados ▲ *systematic allocation of indirect manufacturing expenses* asignación sistemática de los gastos indirectos de fabricación ▲ *the amount of indirect manufacturing expenses* la cuantía de los gastos indirectos de fabricación ▲ *unallocated indirect manufacturing expenses* gastos indirectos de fabricación no asignados ▲ *variable indirect manufacturing expenses* gastos indirectos de fabricación variables

indirect method
= reconciliation method US
≠ direct method
The indirect or reconciliation method is one of two applied methods of preparing the cash flow statement. Under the indirect method, the net cash flow from operating activities is reported indirectly by stating as a starting point operating income or profit for the accounting period and next adjusting this amount for, i.e. reconciling it with, the items included in income or profit that have not had any influence on cash in- or outflows, i.e. all accrual or non-cash components.

método indirecto
▲ *under the indirect method* según el método indirecto ▲ *use the indirect method* usar el método indirecto
⇛ cash flow from operating activities, cash flow statement

indirect production cost
= factory burden US, factory overhead US, factory overhead cost, indirect manufacturing cost, indirect manufacturing expense US, indirect production expense US, manufacturing overhead US, production overhead IAS/IFRS
Indirect production costs are costs that are not directly related to the production of goods, i.e. costs for which single products or activities cannot be identified. Examples of indirect production costs are indirect labour and materials, rent and insurance of manufacturing units.

coste de producción indirecto
= overheads
≠ coste de producción directo
▲ *capitalise indirect production costs* capitalizar los costes de producción indirectos ▲ *compulsory recognition of indirect production costs* reconocimiento obligatorio de los costes de producción indirectos ▲ *fixed indirect production costs* costes

de producción indirectos fijos ▲ *include indirect production costs* incluir los costes de producción indirectos ▲ *measurement basis for indirect production costs* criterio de medición para los costes de producción indirectos ▲ *recognise indirect production costs* reconocer los costes de producción indirectos ▲ *recognition methods for indirect production costs* métodos de reconocimiento para los costes de producción indirectos ▲ *recognition of indirect production costs* reconocimiento de los costes de producción indirectos ▲ *related indirect production costs* costes de producción indirectos relacionados ▲ *systematic allocation of indirect production costs* asignación sistemática de los costes de producción indirectos ▲ *the amount of indirect production costs* la cuantía de los costes de producción indirectos ▲ *unallocated indirect production costs* costes de producción indirectos no asignados ▲ *variable indirect production costs* costes de producción indirectos variables

indirect production expense

= indirect manufacturing expense, indirect production cost

An indirect production expense is an expense that is not directly related to the production of goods, i.e. expenses for which single products or activities cannot be identified. Examples of indirect production expenses are indirect labour and materials, rent and insurance of manufacturing units.

gasto indirecto de producción

= gasto indirecto de fabricación

≠ gasto directo de producción

▲ *capitalise indirect production expenses* capitalizar los gastos indirectos de producción ▲ *compulsory recognition of indirect production expenses* reconocimiento obligatorio de los gastos indirectos de producción ▲ *fixed indirect production expenses* gastos indirectos de producción fijos ▲ *measurement basis for indirect production expenses* base de medición de los gastos indirectos de producción ▲ *recognise indirect production expenses* reconocer los gastos indirectos de producción ▲ *recognition methods for indirect recognition expenses* métodos de reconocimiento de los gastos indirectos de producción ▲ *related indirect production expenses* gastos indirectos de producción relacionados ▲ *systematic allocation of indirect production expenses* asignación sistemática de los gastos indirectos de producción ▲ *the amount of indirect production expenses* la cuantía de los gastos indirectos de producción ▲ *unallocated indirect production expenses* gastos indirectos de producción no asignados ▲ *variable indirect production expenses* gastos indirectos de producción variables

indirect-cost rate

The indirect-cost rate is calculated as the total indirect costs in a cost pool divided by the relevant cost allocation base, e.g. the production capacity such as the number of machine-hours.

ratio coste indirecto

≠ ratio coste directo

▲ *a new three-year indirect cost rate* un nuevo ratio de coste indirecto a tres años ▲ *indirect cost rate proposal* propuesta de ratio de coste indirecto ▲ *the unadjusted indirect cost rate* el ratio de coste indirecto no ajustado

individual asset

An individual asset is an asset that can be recognised and measured separately from other assets.

activo individual

▲ *acquisition of individual assets* adquisición de activos individuales ▲ *reversal of an individual asset* reversión de un activo individual ▲ *sale of individual assets* venta de activos individuales ▲ *the cost of individual assets* el coste de los activos individuales ▲ *the recoverable amount of the individual assets* la cantidad a recuperar de los activos individuales ▲ *treat as an individual asset* tratar como un activo individual ▲ *write-down of an individual asset* amortización de un activo individual

individual capital

Individual capital is the part of the intellectual capital related to the skills, competencies, etc. of the employees. The concept includes all indicators that concern employees. The values of individual capital are part of the invisible balance sheet as they will not appear from the financial balance sheet. The other part of the invisible balance sheet constitutes the structural capital and often also customer capital.

NOTE In connection with human resource accounting, individual capital is referred to as human capital, but within the context of the intellectual capital report, human capital will typically also include company values and culture.

capital individual intelectual

⇛ customer capital, intellectual capital, intellectual capital report, structural capital

individual component part

The term 'individual component part' is used about one of several component parts that together form a larger whole.

componente individual

▲ *individual component parts in a consolidation* el componente individual en una consolidación ▲ *the individual component parts of a fixed asset* los componentes individuales de un activo fijo

Individual Savings Account UK

= ISA UK

An Individual Savings Account (ISA) is a tax efficient savings account introduced by the UK Government that offers savers tax relief through holding savings invested in cash deposits, shares or life insurance products or a combination of all three types of asset.

Cuenta con Desgravación Fiscal

▲ *a new tax-free Individual Savings Account* una nueva Cuenta con Desgravación Fiscal libre de impuestos ▲ *open an Individual Savings Account* abrir una Cuenta con Desgravación Fiscal

individual transaction

An independent transaction is a transaction that can be recognised and measured separately from other transactions.

transacción individual

▲ *gains and losses from individual transactions* pérdidas y ganancias de transacciones individuales ▲ *recurring individual transactions* transacciones individuales recurrentes

industry area

An industry area defines the scope of the enterprise's operations either by business segment or by geographical segment.

área de influencia de la empresa

▲ *a significant part of the enterprise's industry area* una parte significativa del área de influencia de la empresa

industry segment

An industry segment refers to a distinguishable part of the total activities of an enterprise, e.g. a specific department or product category.

segmento industrial

▲ *disclose cash flow information for each industry segment* publicar información de flujos de efectivo para cada segmento industrial ▲ *identification of industry segments* identificación de los segmentos industriales ▲ *operate an industry segment* gestionar un segmento industrial

inflation

Inflation is the situation where general increases in prices persistently occur in an economy together with a decline in the purchasing power of money. Inflation can be measured by the retail price index.

inflación

▲ *future price increases due to general inflation* aumentos futuros de precios debidos a la inflación general ▲ *high inflation economies* economías con inflaciones elevadas ▲ *price increases attributable to general inflation* aumentos de precios atribuibles a la inflación general ▲ *the effect of general inflation* el efecto de la inflación general

inflation adjustment

= adjustment for inflation

Inflation adjustment refers to the restatement of the value of financial statement items in order to eliminate the effects of inflation, i.e. adjusting the items for price movements.

ajuste a la inflación

▲ *applied method of inflation adjustment* método aplicado de ajuste a la inflación ▲ *expected cash flows before inflation adjustment* flujos de efectivo esperados antes del ajuste a la inflación

inflation rate

= rate of inflation

The inflation rate is the percentage change in the prices of goods and services over a specified period of time, usually a year. It is an important economic indicator denoting the purchasing power of money, and it is usually calculated on the basis of consumer price indices.

tasa de inflación

▲ *a high inflation rate* una tasa de inflación alta ▲ *a low inflation rate* una tasa de inflación baja ▲ *annual inflation rate* tasa de inflación anual ▲ *current estimates of future inflation rates* estimaciones actuales de las tasas de inflación futuras ▲ *the cumulative inflation rate* la tasa de inflación acumulada

inflow

≠ outflow

Inflow is an ingoing movement of cash, funds or other assets from an enterprise.

flujo de entrada

≠ flujo de salida

▲ *estimated future cash inflows* flujos de entrada futuros estimados ▲ *generate an inflow of cash or another financial asset* generar un flujo de entrada u otro activo financiero ▲ *inflow of cash* flujo de entrada de efectivo ▲ *inflows of cash and cash equivalents received from parties external to the enterprise* flujos de entrada de efectivo y equivalentes de efectivo recibidos de partícipes externos a la empresa

information systems audit

= information technology audit, IT audit

An information systems audit is typically an internal audit involving the application of various audit procedures to examine the extent to which the information systems of an enterprise supports its management and financial reporting as well as the information security and IT capacity of the enterprise.

auditoría de los sistemas de información

▲ *carry out an information systems audit* llevar a cabo una auditoría de los sistemas de información ▲ *planning of the information systems audit* planificación de la auditoría de los sistemas de información ▲ *the results of the information systems audit audit* los resultados de la auditoría de los sistemas de información

information technology audit

= information systems audit, IT audit

An information technology audit is typically an internal audit involving the application of various audit procedures to examine the extent to which the information systems of an enterprise supports its management and financial reporting as well as the information security and IT capacity of the enterprise.

auditoría de la tecnología de información

▲ *carry out an information technology audit* llevar a cabo una auditoría de la tecnología de información ▲ *planning of the information technology audit* planificación de la auditoría de la tecnología de información ▲ *the results of the information technology audit audit* los resultados de la auditoría de la tecnología de información

inherent goodwill

→ internally generated goodwill

inherent risk

Inherent risk is the type of audit risk that involves susceptibility to material risks resulting from the particular type of business segment of an enterprise.

riesgo inherente

▲ *bear the inherent risks* soportar los riesgos inherentes ▲ *involve inherent risks and uncertainties* incluir riesgos e incertidumbres inherentes ▲ *manage the inherent risk* gestionar el riesgo inherente

⇛ audit risk, control risk, detection risk

initial expense

Initial expenses are those expenses that are directly associated with the raising of a loan or the formation of a company.

gasto inicial

▲ *deduction of initial expenses on borrowing* deducción de los gastos iniciales en el empréstito ▲ *incur initial expenses* incurrir en gastos iniciales ▲ *initial expenses on borrowing* gastos iniciales en el empréstito

initial public offering US

= admission for listing on the stock exchange UK, flotation UK, IPO US

An initial public offering (IPO) is a privately held company's first offering of shares to the public. Usually an investment bank will assist the company with the IPO and may underwrite the share offering. After the IPO, the shares will be publicly traded on a stock exchange, giving the issuing company the advantage of access to a market for additional capital and providing the shares with a fair market value.

NOTE An IPO is also referred to as "going public" or "floating on the market".

oferta pública inicial

= OPI

▲ *carry through an initial public offering* llevar a cabo una oferta pública inicial

initial recognition

Initial recognition is the first time an asset, liability or transaction is recognised for accounting purposes.

reconocimiento inicial

▲ *at the time of initial recognition* al tiempo del reconocimiento inicial ▲ *deferred tax liabilities arising from the initial recognition of goodwill* pasivos fiscales diferidos procedentes del reconocimiento inicial del fondo de comercio ▲ *expenditure incurred after the initial recognition of a purchased intangible asset* gasto incurrido después del reconocimiento inicial de la compra de un activo intangible ▲ *for initial recognition purposes* por motivos de reconocimiento inicial ▲ *initial recognition of an asset or liability* reconocimiento inicial de un activo o pasivo ▲ *on initial recognition* al reconocimiento inicial ▲ *on the basis of the evidence available at the time of initial recognition* en base a la evidencia disponible en el momento del reconocimiento inicial ▲ *subsequent to initial recognition* siguiente al reconocimiento inicial ▲ *the basis for initial recognition* la base para el reconocimiento inicial ▲ *the initial recognition and measurement of internally generated intangible assets* el reconocimiento inicial y valoración de los activos intangibles generados internamente

initial revaluation

Initial revaluation is the act whereby the value of an asset is revalued upwards for the first time for accounting purposes.

revalorización inicial

▲ *prospective treatment of initial revaluation* tratamiento prospectivo de la revalorización inicial

Inland Revenue UK

The Inland Revenue is the name of the former UK tax authorities, since 2005 referred to as the HM Revenue Customs.

Agencia Tributaria del Reino Unido

▲ *approved by the Inland Revenue* aprobado por la Agencia Tributaria del Reino Unido ▲ *enter into an Inland Revenue approved savings contract* firmar un contrato de ahorro autorizado por la Agencia Tributaria del Reino Unido

⇛ HM Revenue Customs

inorganic growth

= external growth

≠ internal growth, organic growth

Inorganic growth is the external growth achieved by an enterprise by acquisition of or merger with other enterprises with a view to e.g. increasing their market share or competitiveness.

crecimiento inorgánico

= crecimiento externo

≠ crecimiento interno, crecimiento orgánica

input tax UK

= input VAT UK

≠ output tax UK, output VAT UK

Input tax is a value added tax (VAT) that is included in the price paid for goods purchased by buyers. When accounting for VAT to the tax authorities, a VAT-registered enterprise offsets input taxes paid against output taxes charged.

impuesto soportado

▲ *input tax credit* crédito por impuesto soportado ▲ *input tax on purchases* impuesto soportado por compras ▲ *input tax refunds for previous years* devoluciones del impuesto soportado de años anteriores

input VAT

= input tax

Input VAT is value added tax that is included in the price paid for goods purchased by buyers. When accounting for VAT to the tax authorities, a VAT-registered enterprise offsets input VAT paid against output VAT charged.

IVA soportado

▲ *an account for input VAT* una cuenta para el IVA soportado ▲ *deduct input VAT* deducir el IVA soportado ▲ *entitlement to deduct input VAT* derecho a deducir el IVA soportado ▲ *the right of deduction of input VAT* el derecho de deducción del IVA soportado

⇛ value added tax

input-price variance

= price variance, rate variance

An input-price variance is the difference between the budgeted price per unit and the actual purchase or input price per unit of raw materials, semi-manufactures, secondary materials and labour, multiplied by the purchased quantity.

desviación de precio

▲ *direct-labour input-price variance* desviación de precio de costes de personal directos ▲ *direct-material input-price variance* desviación de precio de costes de materiales directos

insider dealing

= insider trading

Insider dealing is the exploitation of insider information on the purchase or sale of securities, in this way making profits or avoiding losses because of possessing knowledge that has not yet been communicated to the stock exchange and that will affect the price development of such securities. Insider dealing is illegal.

información privilegiada

▲ *ban on insider dealing* prohibir la información privilegiada ▲ *constitute insider dealing* constituir información privilegiada ▲ *prevent insider dealing* evitar la información privilegiada

⇛ insider information

insider information

= inside information

Insider information is information about a company that has not yet been made public, e.g. on matters that may affect the price development of the company's shares or bonds when released. Buying or selling securities with a view to making a profit or avoiding a loss on insider information is illegal.

información confidencial

▲ *abuse of insider information* abusar de la información confidencial ▲ *exploitation of insider information* explotación de la información confidencial ▲ *have access to insider information of another company* tener acceso a la información confidencial de otra empresa

⇛ insider dealing

insourcing

≠ outsourcing

Insourcing means carrying out activities that were previously delegated to external suppliers internally in the enterprise.

internalización

≠ externalización

▲ *insourcing of activities* internalización de las actividades ▲ *insourcing of jobs* internalización de los empleos ▲ *insourcing of services* internalización de los servicios

installment US

= instalment UK

An installment is a pre-determined part of an amount that is paid regularly over a period of time in order to reduce a debt.

plazo

= cuotas

≠ contado

▲ *by installments* a plazos ▲ *delivery by installments* entrega a plazos ▲ *installment credit* crédito a plazos ▲ *installment lending* prestar a plazos ▲ *installment loans* préstamos a plazos ▲ *installment mortgage* hipoteca a plazos ▲ *installment repayments* cuotas a plazo ▲ *pay out the loan in installments* devolver el préstamo a plazos ▲ *payable by monthly installments* a pagar mediante plazos mensuales ▲ *payment by installments* pago a plazos

instalment UK, IAS/IFRS
= installment US
An instalment is a pre-determined part of an amount that is paid regularly over a period of time in order to reduce a debt.
plazo
NOTE Spanish accountants tend to use the terms 'plazo' and 'contado' preceded by a preposition, typically 'a' or 'en'.
▲ *by instalments* a plazos ▲ *delivery by instalments* entrega a plazos ▲ *instalment credit* crédito a plazo ▲ *instalment lending* prestar a plazo ▲ *instalment loans* préstamos a plazo ▲ *instalment mortgage* hipoteca a plazo ▲ *instalment repayments* devoluciones a plazos ▲ *pay out the loan in instalments* pagar el préstamo a plazos ▲ *payable by monthly instalments* pagadero en plazos mensuales ▲ *payment by instalments* pago a plazos

Institut der Wirtschaftsprüfer
= German Institute of Auditors, IdW
As the German Institute of Auditors, Institut der Wirtschaftsprüfer is the German private-sector professional accountancy body. To audit companies, members must also join the state-auditing government-controlled Wirtschaftsprüferkammer.
Institut der Wirtschaftsprüfer
= Colegio de Auditores de Alemania
▲ *become a member of the Institut der Wirtschaftsprüfer* llegar a ser un miembro del Institut der Wirtschaftsprüfer
⇛ Wirtschaftsprüferkammer

Institute of Certified Public Accountants of Singapore
= ICPAS
The Institute of Certified Public Accountants of Singapore (ICPAS) is the national organisation of the accountancy profession in Singapore.
Institute of Certified Public Accountants of Singapore
= Colegio de Auditores de Singapur
▲ *become a member of the Institute of Certified Public Accountants of Singapore* llegar a ser un miembro del Institute of Certified Public Accountants of Singapore

Institute of Chartered Accountants in Australia
= ICAA
The Institute of Chartered Accountants in Australia (ICAA) is a professional accountancy body whose members may audit the financial statements of companies. The ICAA's roles overlap with those of its sister organisation CPA Australia (CPAA), but most ICAA members are in public practice and perform audits, where CPAA members are mostly employees in the public sector.
Institute of Chartered Accountants in Australia
= Colegio de Auditores de Australia
▲ *become a member of the Institute of Chartered Accountants in Australia* llegar a ser un miembro del Institute of Chartered Accountants in Australia
⇛ chartered accountant, CPA Australia

Institute of Chartered Accountants in England and Wales
= ICAEW
The Institute of Chartered Accountants in England and Wales (ICAEW) is the largest UK professional accountancy body. The objectives of the ICAEW are primarily focussed on the education and training of chartered accountants and the maintenance of high standards for members' professional conduct. As well as providing various services to members, the ICAEW plays an important role, both internationally and in the UK, with regard to advancing accounting theory and practice as well as developing corporate reporting, corporate governance and auditing.
Institute of Chartered Accountants in England and Wales
= Colegio de Auditores de Inglaterra y Gales
▲ *become a member of the Institute of Chartered Accountants in England and Wales* llegar a ser un miembro del Institute of Chartered Accountants in England and Wales
⇛ chartered accountant

Institute of Chartered Accountants in Ireland
= ICAI

The Institute of Chartered Accountants in Ireland (ICAI) is an accountancy body and association of chartered accountants in Ireland.

Institute of Chartered Accountants in Ireland

= Colegio de Auditores de Irlanda

▲ *become a member of the Institute of Chartered Accountants in Ireland* llegar a ser un miembro del Institute of Chartered Accountants in Ireland

⇛ chartered accountant

Institute of Chartered Accountants of New Zealand

= ICANZ

The Institute of Chartered Accountants of New Zealand (ICANZ) is New Zealand's only professional accountancy body and only members of ICANZ may use the title of 'chartered accountant'. ICANZ succeeded the former New Zealand Society of Accountants in 1996 and develops financial reporting standards - the New Zealand equivalents to the International Financial Reporting Standards (NZ IFRS) - that are enforced by the New Zealand Accounting Standards Review Board.

Institute of Chartered Accountants of New Zealand

= Colegio de Auditores de Nueva Zelanda

▲ *become a member of the Institute of Chartered Accountants of New Zealand* llegar a ser un miembro del Institute of Chartered Accountants of New Zealand

Institute of Chartered Accountants of Scotland

= ICAS

The Institute of Chartered Accountants in Scotland (ICAS) is an association of chartered accountants in Scotland and the world's oldest accountancy body.

Institute of Chartered Accountants of Scotland

= Colegio de Auditores de Escocia

▲ *become a member of the Institute of Chartered Accountants of Scotland* llegar a ser un miembro del Institute of Chartered Accountants of Scotland

⇛ chartered accountant

Institute of Management Accountants US

= IMA US

The Institute of Management Accountants is a US professional organisation of accountants within management accounting. The Institute oversees the Certified Management Accountant (CMA) program and continued professional development of management accountants.

Institute of Management Accountants

= Colegio de Auditores de Gestión

▲ *become a member of the Institute of Management Accountants* llegar a ser un miembro del Institute of Management Accountants

institutional investor

Institutional investors refer to financial institutions such as banks, insurance companies, pension funds and investment companies investing in large quantities of securities. Institutional investors are important players on the stock market.

inversor institucional

▲ *a market dominated by institutional investors* un mercado dominado por los inversores institucionales ▲ *attract institutional investors* atraer a inversores institucionales ▲ *private placement with institutional investors* colocación privada con inversores institucionales ▲ *supervision of institutional investors* supervisión de los inversores institucionales

instrument

→ financial instrument

instrument of debt

= debt instrument

An instrument of debt is a written promise to repay a debt, typically a short-term loan, and constitutes a formal loan document stipulating the terms and conditions of the loan. Examples are bills, notes, bonds, banker's acceptances, certificates of deposit or commercial paper.

instrumento de deuda

▲ *convertible instruments of debt* instrumentos de deuda convertibles ▲ *issue instruments of debt* emitir instrumentos de deuda ▲ *negotiable instruments of debt* instrumentos de deuda negociables

insurance[1] *noun* <no indefinite article, the, no plural>

Insurance is the assumption of a risk against payment of a premium.

seguro
▲ *a mutual insurance company* una mutua de seguros ▲ *consequential loss insurance* seguro de daños emergentes ▲ *creditors arising out of direct insurance operations* acreedores procedentes de operaciones de seguro directas ▲ *Danish Insurance Association* Asociación danesa del Seguro ▲ *insurance against damage in transit* seguro de daños en tránsito ▲ *insurance against personal injury to passengers* seguro de daños personales a los pasajeros ▲ *insurance against theft* seguro de robo ▲ *insurance benefit* póliza de seguro ▲ *insurance claim* reclamación por siniestro ▲ *insurance for goods in transit* seguro de bienes en tránsito ▲ *insurance fraud* fraude en el seguro ▲ *insurance of machinery and equipment* seguro de maquinaria y equipo ▲ *mutual insurance* seguro recíproco ▲ *pay an insurance benefit* pagar una prima de seguro ▲ *prepaid insurance* seguro con pago adelantado ▲ *take out insurance* tomar un seguro

insurance[2] *noun* <an, the, -s>
An insurance is a written contract covering a specific type of risk.
seguro
▲ *an insurance against theft* un seguro contra hurto ▲ *take out an insurance* hacerse un seguro

Insurance Accounts Directive
The Insurance Accounts Directive is a term for Council Directive 91/674/EEC of 19 December 1991 on the annual accounts and consolidated accounts of insurance undertakings.
Directiva sobre Cuentas de Empresas Aseguradoras
▲ *comply with the provisions of the Insurance Accounts Directive* cumplir con las disposiciones de la Directiva sobre Cuentas de Empresas Aseguradoras

insurance asset
When an insurer, i.e. an insurance company, enters into an insurance contract, the insurer acquires certain rights under the contract. Such rights net of obligations are referred to as insurance assets and are recognised as assets in the financial statements of the insurer.
activo de seguro
= activo derivado de contrato de seguro
NOTE Spanish accountants prefer 'activo de seguro' to the IAS/IFRS term 'activo derivado de contrato de seguro'.
▲ *changes in assumptions used to measure insurance assets* cambios en los supuestos utilizados para medir activos de seguro ▲ *insurance assets acquired in a business combination* activos derivados de contratos de seguro adquiridos en una combinación de negocios
SOURCE IFRS 4, Appendix A

insurance broker
An insurance broker is an agent acting on behalf of the insured who negotiates with insurance companies for favourable insurance offers as well as terms and cover in insurance policies. An insurance broker is independent of insurance companies.
corredor de seguros
▲ *an international insurance broker* un corredor de seguros internacional

insurance business[1] *noun* <an, the, -es>
An insurance business is an enterprise, usually a company, which carries on business activities within insurance.
compañía de seguros
= aseguradora
▲ *start up an insurance business* crear una compañía de seguros

insurance business[2] *noun* <singular, no plural>
Insurance business is the providing of compensation for a financial loss resulting from an occurrence that will happen (life insurance), or an eventuality that may or may not happen (general insurance). Compensations are paid out of funds created by payment of a premium by the insured.
negocio de seguros
▲ *insurance business earnings* ganancias en el negocio de seguros ▲ *insurance business revenue expenditure* ingresos y gastos del negocio de seguros ▲ *minimum capital requirements related to insurance business* requisitos de capital mínimo re-

lacionados con el negocio de seguros

insurance contract

= insurance agreement

An insurance contract is a contract between an insurer (an insurance company) and an insured under which the insurer agrees to compensate the insured should a specified event occur in the future. By entering into this agreement, the insurer accepts a transfer of risk from the insured in return for the regular payment of specified premiums by the insured.

contrato de seguro

= contrato de seguros, póliza de seguro, póliza de seguros

▲ *a credit insurance contract* un contrato de seguro de crédito ▲ *accounting for insurance contracts* la contabilización de los contratos de seguro ▲ *acquire a portfolio of insurance contracts* adquirir una cartera de contratos de seguro ▲ *an insurance contract unbundled into a deposit component and an insurance component* un contrato de seguro que diferencia entre un componente de depósito y un componente de seguro ▲ *at the inception of an insurance contract* al suscribir un contrato de seguro ▲ *benefits insured by an insurance contract* riesgos cubiertos por un contrato de seguro ▲ *embedded derivatives contained in a host insurance contract* derivativos implícitos contenidos en un contrato de seguro anfitrión ▲ *enter into an insurance contract* firmar un contrato de seguro ▲ *financial instruments that are embedded in insurance contracts* instrumentos financieros que se incluyen en los contratos de seguro ▲ *insurance contracts acquired in a business combination or portfolio transfer* contratos de seguro adquiridos en una combinación de negocios o en una transferencia de cartera de inversiones ▲ *insurance contracts of insurance companies* contratos de seguro de las compañías de seguro ▲ *issue an insurance contract* emitir un contrato de seguro ▲ *net contractual rights under an insurance contract* derechos contractuales netos de acuerdo con un contrato de seguro ▲ *post-employment benefit plans involving insurance contracts* contratos de seguro que incluyen un plan de jubilación de prestaciones definidas ▲ *rights and obligations under insurance contracts* derechos y obligaciones según los contratos de seguro ▲ *split the fair value of acquired insurance contracts into two components* dividir en dos componentes el valor razonable de los contratos de seguro ▲ *the amount, timing and uncertainty of future cash flows from insurance contracts* la cuantía, periodificación e incertidumbre de los flujos de efectivo futuros de los contratos de seguro ▲ *the essence of an insurance contract* la esencia de un contrato de seguros ▲ *the insurer's accounting policies for insurance contracts* las políticas contables de la aseguradora para el tratamiento de los contratos de seguro ▲ *the recognised assets, liabilities, income and expense arising from insurance contracts* los activos, pasivos, ingresos y gastos reconocidos procedentes de los contratos de seguro

SOURCE IFRS 4, Appendix A

insurance cover

Insurance cover refers to a third party taking over a risk from the original insurer, i.e. an insurance company, against a premium. Insurance cover can also be the insurer's own hedging with financial instruments.

cobertura de seguro

= cobertura del seguro

▲ *insufficent insurance cover* cobertura de seguro insuficiente ▲ *provide insurance cover* ofrecer la cobertura de seguro ▲ *sufficient insurance cover* cobertura de seguro suficiente

insurance coverage

Insurance coverage refers to the risks covered within specified monetary limits by an insurer under an insurance contract.

cobertura de seguro

= cobertura del seguro

▲ *appropriate insurance coverage* cobertura de seguro adecuada ▲ *increase the insurance coverage* aumentar la cobertura del seguro ▲ *sufficient insurance co-*

verage cobertura de seguro suficiente
⇛ insurance cover

insurance expense

Insurance expenses refer to expenses in the form of periodic premiums paid to an insurance company for assuming specified risks.

gasto del seguro
= gasto de seguro, prima de seguro, prima del seguro
▲ *incur insurance expenses* incurrir en gastos del seguro ▲ *recognise insurance expenses* reconocer los gastos del seguro

insurance liability

Insurance liability refers to the obligation of an insurance company towards an insured in pursuance of an insurance contract, i.e. an insurance company may be liable to pay out a specified amount to the insured should a specific event occur.

responsabilidad de la aseguradora
= obligación de la aseguradora, pasivo derivado del contrato de seguro
▲ *accounting policies for insurance liabilities* políticas contables para los pasivos derivados del contrato de seguro ▲ *measure insurance liabilities on an undiscounted basis* medir las responsabilidades de la aseguradora en una base no descontada ▲ *offset reinsurance assets against the related insurance liabilities* compensar activos de reaseguro contra las responsabilidades de la aseguradora relacionados ▲ *reconciliation of changes in insurance liabilities* conciliación de cambios en las responsabilidades de la aseguradora ▲ *remove an insurance liability from the balance sheet* eliminar una responsabilidad de la aseguradora del balance ▲ *the carrying amount of the host insurance liability* el valor contable de la responsabilidad de la aseguradora anfitrión ▲ *the insurance liabilities assumed in a business combination* las responsabilidades de la aseguradora asumidas en una combinación de negocios ▲ *the related adjustment to the insurance liability* el ajuste relacionado a la responsabilidad de la aseguradora ▲ *the relevant insurance liabilities* las responsabilidades relevantes de la aseguradora
SOURCE IFRS 4, Appendix A

insurance policy

An insurance policy is an insurance contract that covers a specific risk. The policy also contains the specific terms and conditions for the insurance cover.

póliza de seguro
= póliza del seguro
▲ *a qualifying insurance policy* una póliza de seguro cualificada ▲ *take out an insurance policy* hacerse una póliza de seguro
⇛ insurance contract

insurance premium

= premium
The price that the insurer charges for assuming a risk is called the insurance premium. The premium is usually paid by regular instalments over a period of time.

prima de seguro
= prima del seguro
▲ *insurance premium deduction* deducción de la prima de seguro ▲ *insurance premium expenses* gastos de la prima de seguro ▲ *pay insurance premiums* pagar las primas del seguro ▲ *prepaid insurance premiums* primas de seguro anticipadas ▲ *right to deduct insurance premiums* derecho a la deducción de las primas del seguro ▲ *taxes on insurance premiums* impuestos sobre las primas del seguro ▲ *the Group's total general insurance premiums* las primas de seguro generales totales del Grupo

insurance provision

Insurance provisions are amounts allocated by an insurance company for the settlement of the company's liabilities in connection with its issued insurance policies, typically referred to as technical provisions.

provisión de seguro
= provisión del seguro
▲ *disclose movements in insurance provisions* publicar los movimientos en las provisiones de seguro ▲ *insurance provisions for life-assurance policies where the investment risk is borne by the policyholders* provisiones de seguro para pólizas de seguro de vida en las que los riesgos

de inversión recaen en los tenedores de las pólizas ▲ *the discounting of annuities included in insurance provisions* el descuento de las anualidades incluidas en las provisiones de seguro ▲ *the insurance provisions for claims outstanding at the end of the last financial year* las provisiones de seguro por reclamaciones pendientes al final del último año financiero ▲ *the total increase in percentage terms in insurance provisions* el incremento total en términos de porcentaje en las provisiones de seguro ▲ *the value of insurance provisions* el valor de las provisiones de seguro ▲ *undiscounted insurance provisions* provisiones de seguro no descontadas

insurance risk

An insurance risk is the risk that an insurer (an insurance company) accepts when entering into an insurance contract.

riesgo de seguro

▲ *accept significant insurance risks* aceptar riesgos de seguro significativos ▲ *an increase in the insurance risk* un aumento en el riesgo de seguro ▲ *assessment of insurance risks* valoración de los riesgos de seguro ▲ *changes in the level of insurance risk* cambios en el nivel del riesgo de seguro ▲ *concentrations of insurance risk* concentraciones de riesgo de seguro ▲ *expose the insurer to significant insurance risk* exponer a la aseguradora a riesgo de seguro significativo ▲ *including insurance risk* incluyendo el riesgo de seguro ▲ *insurance risks accepted* riesgos de seguro aceptados ▲ *pass all significant insurance risk back to the policyholder* pasar todo riesgo de seguro significativo al tenedor de la poliza ▲ *transfer of insurance risk* transferencia del riesgo de seguro

SOURCE IFRS 4, Appendix A

insured event

Insured event refers to an uncertain event, act or omission which is covered under an insurance contract. Should the event, act or omission occur, the insured is entitled to make an insurance claim against the insurer.

evento asegurado

= suceso asegurado, evento abierto

▲ *costs associated with insured events* costes asociados con los eventos asegurados ▲ *the occurrence of the insured event* el hecho del evento asegurado ▲ *the payment that is contingent on the insured event* el pago que es contingente en el evento asegurado

SOURCE IFRS 4, Appendix A

insurer

The insurer is the party in an insurance arrangement who is obligated to compensate a policyholder for losses should an insured event occur.

aseguradora

= compañía de seguros

▲ *a mutual insurer* una aseguradora mutual ▲ *a pre-existing risk transferred from the policyholder to the insurer* un riesgo anterior transferido desde el tenedor de la póliza a la aseguradora ▲ *an insurer's contractual rights under insurance contracts* derechos contractuales de una aseguradora según los contratos de seguro ▲ *expose the insurer to significant insurance risk* exponer a la aseguradora a un riesgo de seguro significativo ▲ *financial assets held by insurers* activos fiscales mantenidos por las aseguradoras ▲ *financial liabilities issued by insurers* pasivos fiscales emitidos por las aseguradoras ▲ *the current annuity rates charged by the insurer* las anualidades corrientes cargadas por la aseguradora ▲ *the direct insurer* la aseguradora directa

SOURCE IFRS 4, Appendix A

intangible[1] US *noun*

≠ tangible asset

Intangibles are intangible assets, i.e. non-monetary, fixed assets that have no physical presence, such as goodwill, patents, copyrights and trademarks.

activo intangible

▲ *acquired intangibles* activos intangibles adquiridos ▲ *amortization of intangibles* amortización de los activos intangibles ▲ *impairment of intangibles* deterioro de los activos intangibles ▲ *internally developed intangibles* activos intangibles desarrollados internamente ▲ *investment in intangibles* inversión en activos intangibles

▲ *prepayments for intangibles* pagos anticipados por activos intangibles ▲ *purchase of intangibles* compra de activos intangibles ▲ *recognise intangibles separately from goodwill* reconocer activos intangibles por separado del fondo de comercio ▲ *recognition of intangibles* reconocimiento de los activos intangibles ▲ *revaluation of intangibles* revalorización de los activos intangibles ▲ *sale of intangibles* venta de activos intangibles ▲ *the cost of intangibles* el coste de los activos intangibles ▲ *the fair value of intangibles* el valor razonable de los activos intangibles ▲ *the recoverable amount of intangibles* la cantidad recuperable de los activos intangibles ▲ *write down intangibles to the recoverable amount* amortizar los activos intangibles al importe recuperable

intangible[2] *adjective*

≠ tangible

When something is intangible, it has no physical presence. Intangible assets comprise fixed assets such as goodwill, patents, copyrights and trademarks.

intangible

▲ *an intangible asset* un activo intangible ▲ *capitalise internally generated intangible assets* capitalizar los activos intangibles generados internamente ▲ *expenditure on an intangible item* gasto en una partida intangible ▲ *incur liabilities on the acquisition and maintenance of intangible resources* incurrir en pasivos en la adquisición y mantenimiento de los recursos intangibles

intangible asset

≠ tangible asset

Intangible assets refer to nonmonetary, fixed assets that have no physical presence, such as goodwill, patents, copyrights and trademarks.

activo intangible

▲ *a market for the output of the intangible asset* un mercado para la salida del activo intangible ▲ *acquired intangible assets* activos intangibles adquiridos ▲ *amortisation of intangible assets* amortización de los activos intangibles ▲ *an intangible asset held under a finance lease* un activo intangible mantenido mediante un arrendamiento financiero ▲ *an intangible asset with an indefinite useful life* un activo intangible con una vida útil indefinida ▲ *costs incurred in using or redeploying an intangible asset* costes incurridos usando o reorganizando un activo intangible ▲ *costs of materials and services used in generating the intangible asset* costes de materiales y servicios utilizados generando el activo intangible ▲ *disposal of an intangible asset* eliminación de un activo intangible ▲ *impairment of intangible assets* deterioro de los activos intangibles ▲ *indefinite-lived intangible assets* activos intangibles de vida indefinida ▲ *intangible assets under development* activos intangibles en desarrollo ▲ *intangible assets with finite useful lives* activos intangibles con vidas útiles limitadas ▲ *internally developed intangible assets* activos intangibles desarrollados internamente ▲ *internally generated intangible assets* activos intangibles generados internamente ▲ *investment in intangible assets* inversión en activos intangibles ▲ *measure the recoverable amount of an intangible asset* medir la cuantía a recuperar de un activo intangible ▲ *non-current intangible assets classified as held for sale* activos intangibles no corrientes clasificados como disponibles para la venta ▲ *prepayments for intangible assets* pagos anticipados por activos intangibles ▲ *purchase of intangible assets* compra de activos intangibles ▲ *recognition of intangible assets* reconocimiento de los activos intangibles ▲ *revaluation of intangible assets* revalorización de los activos intangibles ▲ *sale of intangible assets* venta de activos intangibles ▲ *test an intangible asset with an indefinite useful life for impairment* examinar el deterioro de un activo intangible con una vida útil indefinida ▲ *the cost of intangible assets* el coste de los activos intangibles ▲ *the fair value of intangible assets* el valor razonable de los activos intangibles ▲ *the purchase and sale of unique in-*

tangible assets la compra y venta de activos intangibles únicos ▲ *the recoverable amount of intangible assets* la cantidad recuperable de los activos intangibles ▲ *the technical feasibility of completing the intangible asset* la viabilidad técnica de completar el activo intangible ▲ *write down intangible assets to the recoverable amount* amortizar los activos intangibles al importe recuperable

integrated foreign entity

An integrated foreign entity is a foreign enterprise whose activities and cash flows are interrelated with those of the reporting enterprise.

empresa extranjera integrada

▲ *translation of integrated foreign entities* conversión de las empresas extranjeras integradas

intellectual

Intellectual characterises certain kinds of assets that are not tangible in nature. The term is used in connection with knowledge-based assets, i.e. intellectual capital, and assets over which an enterprise has legal rights in the form of e.g. patents, trademarks and copyrights, i.e. intellectual property.

intelectual

▲ *an intellectual property right* un derecho de propiedad intelectual ▲ *internally generated intellectual property rights* derechos de propiedad intelectual generados internamente ▲ *protection of an intellectual property right* protección de un derecho de propiedad intelectual ▲ *the use of intellectual property in a production process* el uso de la propiedad intelectual en un proceso de producción

intellectual capital

Intellectual capital refers to the market value of an enterprise, i.e. the aggregate value of assets or, for a listed company, the market capitalisation, minus the carrying value. Within the context of intellectual capital reports, intellectual capital typically constitutes the sum of customer capital, organisational capital and individual capital.

capital intelectual

▲ *resources to build intellectual capital* recursos para construir el capital intelectual ▲ *the enhancement of intellectual capital* la mejora del capital intelectual ▲ *the maintenance of intellectual capital* el mantenimiento del capital intelectual

⇛ customer capital, individual capital, intellectual capital report, organisational capital, structural capital

intend

Intend means to have as a plan or purpose.

tener intención de

= tener la intención de

▲ *assets intended to be held to maturity* activos con la intención de ser mantenidos hasta el vencimiento ▲ *intend to hold the financial asset for an undefined period* tener la intención de mantener el activo financiero durante un periodo indefinido ▲ *intend to hold to maturity* tener intención de mantener hasta el vencimiento ▲ *intend to liquidate the entity or to cease trading* tener intención de liquidar la entidad o de cesar la actividad comercial ▲ *intend to settle on a net basis or to realise the asset* tener intención de pagar en neto o de realizar el activo ▲ *not intend to hold to maturity* no tener la intención de mantener hasta el vencimiento

intercompany

= intra-group

Intercompany refers to transactions involving or occurring between two or more companies of the same group.

intragrupo

▲ *adjustment for intercompany trade* ajuste por actividad comercial intragrupo ▲ *elimination of an intercompany receivable* eliminación de una cuenta a cobrar intragrupo ▲ *elimination of intercompany dividend payable* eliminación del dividendo intragrupo a pagar ▲ *intercompany balances* saldos intragrupo ▲ *intercompany debt* deuda intragrupo ▲ *intercompany dividends* dividendos intragrupo ▲ *intercompany expenses* gastos intragrupo ▲ *intercompany gains and losses* pérdidas y ganancias intragrupo ▲ *intercompany income* ingresos intragrupo ▲ *intercompany payables* cuentas a pagar intragrupo ▲ *intercompany profits* beneficios intragrupo ▲ *intercompany purchased goods* bienes comprados intragrupo ▲ *intercompany receivables* cuentas a cobrar intragrupo ▲ *intercompany sales and purchases* ventas y compras intragrupo ▲ *intercompany shareholdings* participaciones accionariales intragrupo ▲ *intercompany transactions* transacciones intragrupo ▲ *intercompany transfer of enterprise ownership* trasferencia intragrupo de la propiedad de la empresa

intercompany account
= intra-group account
An intercompany account is an account recognising the transactions between enterprises that are members of the same group. Such transactions include intercompany purchases and sales as well as receivables and payables. When presenting the consolidated financial statements, such intercompany balances have to be eliminated.
cuenta entre empresas
▲ *charge an amount to the intercompany account* cargar una cantidad a la cuenta entre empresas ▲ *to credit the intercompany account with an amount* abonar la cuenta entre empresas con una cantidad ▲ *to debit the intercompany account with an amount* cargar la cuenta entre empresas con una cantidad

intercompany balance
= intercompany account, intra-group balance
Intercompany balances represent all forms of internal transactions between the members of a group such as intercompany profits, purchases, sales, receivables and payables. When preparing the consolidated financial statements, intercompany balances must be eliminated.
saldo intragrupo
▲ *long-term intercompany balances* saldos intragrupo a largo plazo ▲ *the elimination of intercompany balances* la eliminación de saldos intragrupo ▲ *translation of intercompany balances* conversión de saldos intragrupo

intercompany debt
= intra-group debt
Intercompany debt refers to amounts due to one company in a group by another in the form of loans, fees or other obligations payable.
deuda intragrupo
▲ *elimination of intercompany debt* eliminación de la deuda intragrupo

intercompany loan
= intra-group loan
An intercompany loan is a loan or other credit extension made by one or more companies in a group to one or more other companies in the same group.
préstamo intragrupo
▲ *fund activities by intercompany loans* financiar actividades por préstamos intragrupo ▲ *proceeds from intercompany loan* ingresos de préstamo intragrupo

intercompany loss
= intra-group loss
An intercompany loss is a loss incurred by a company in a group by selling goods or services to one or more other companies in the same group.
pérdida intragrupo
▲ *changes in intercompany losses* cambios en pérdidas intragrupo

intercompany position
= intra-group position
An intercompany position is a position recognised on the basis of interrelated or group enterprises, e.g. of a group, and discloses business transactions between such enterprises. An example of an intercompany position is intercompany accounts payable or intercompany profits, i.e. profits generated from intra-group sales. In group financial statements, intercompany positions must be eliminated.
posición intragrupo
▲ *monitor the intercompany position* controlar la posición intragrupo

intercompany profit
= intra-group profit
Intercompany profit refers to the profit generated by one company in a group, e.g. by selling goods or services to one or more other companies in the group. When preparing the consolidated financial statements, such profits must be

eliminated or adjusted so that they do not appear in the consolidated financial statements.
beneficio intragrupo
▲ *eliminate intercompany profit* eliminar beneficio intragrupo ▲ *less unrealised intercompany profits* menos beneficios intragrupo no realizados ▲ *unrealised intercompany profit* beneficio intragrupo no realizado
⇛ transfer pricing

intercompany receivable
= intra-group receivable
An intercompany receivable is an amount owed by one company to another in the same group, one company having the amount due from the other.
cuenta a cobrar intragrupo
▲ *accounting for intercompany receivables* contabilizar las cuentas a cobrar intragrupo ▲ *interest-bearing intercompany receivables* cuentas a cobrar intragrupo que devengan intereses ▲ *total short-term intercompany receivables* total cuentas a cobrar intragrupo a corto plazo

intercompany sales
= intra-group sales
Intercompany sales refer to the turnover generated by one enterprise in a group by selling goods or services to one or more other enterprises in the group. When preparing the consolidated financial statements, intercompany sales must be eliminated or adjusted so that they do not appear in the consolidated financial statements.
ventas intragrupo
▲ *elimination of intercompany sales* eliminación de ventas intragrupo
⇛ transfer pricing

intercompany settlement
= intra-group settlement
Intercompany settlement refers to the payment of amounts due to one or more companies in a group by one or more other companies in the same group, e.g. as a result of exchanges of goods or services.
liquidación intragrupo
▲ *management of intercompany settlement* gestión de la liquidación intragrupo
⇛ transfer pricing

intercompany shareholding
= intra-group shareholding
An intercompany shareholding is a share ownership held by one group company, i.e. parent company or subsidiary, in another company within the same group of companies.
participación accionarial intragrupo
▲ *elimination of intercompany shareholdings* eliminación de la participación accionarial intragrupo

intercompany trade
= intra-group trade
Intercompany trade is trade that takes place between companies in a group, e.g. when one company in a group sells goods or services to another company in the same group. When preparing the consolidated financial statements, intercompany trade must be eliminated or adjusted so that it does not appear in the consolidated financial statements.
actividad comercial intragrupo
▲ *elimination of intercompany trade* eliminación de la actividad comercial intragrupo ▲ *intercompany trade in fixed assets* actividad comercial intragrupo en activos fijos ▲ *intercompany trade in raw materials, consumables and goods for resale* actividad comercial intragrupo en materias primas, insumos y bienes para la reventa
⇛ transfer pricing

intercompany transaction
= intra-group transaction
An intercompany transaction is a transaction that takes place between companies in a group, e.g. when one company in a group sells goods or services to another company in the same group. When preparing the consolidated financial statements, intercompany transactions must be eliminated or adjusted so that they do not appear in the consolidated financial statements.
transacción intragrupo
▲ *disclosures of significant intercompany transactions and investments in and balances with group and associated companies and with directors* publicaciones de las transacciones intragrupo

significativas e inversiones en y saldos con el grupo y asociadas y directivos ▲ *material intercompany transactions* transacciones intragrupo materiales
⇛ transfer pricing

interest[1] *noun* <no indefinite article, the, no plural>
Interest is the amount paid for borrowing money or the amount received as return on an investment. Interest is usually measured as a percentage on an annual basis.
interés
NOTE Usually plural in Spanish accounting texts.
▲ *accrue interest on the recognised asset using the effective interest method* devengar intereses sobre el activo reconocido utilizando el método del tipo de interés efectivo ▲ *catastrophe bonds that provide for reduced payments of principal and interest* bonos de catástrofe que ofrecen pagos reducidos de principal e intereses ▲ *change the amount of interest* cambiar la cantidad de intereses ▲ *commodity-indexed interest or principal payments* intereses indexados a materia prima o pagos del principal ▲ *equity-indexed interest or principal payments* intereses indexados a patrimonio o pagos del principal ▲ *interest and principal payments* pagos por intereses y principal ▲ *interest at the basic or risk-free rate* interés a tipo fijo básico ▲ *reduce the tax-exempt status of interest on the held-to-maturity investment* reducir el estado impositivo del interés en la inversión mantenida hasta el vencimiento ▲ *the time value of money represented by the current market risk-free rate of interest* el valor temporal del dinero representado por el tipo de interés fijo en el mercado actual
⇛ interest rate

interest[2] *noun* <an, the, -s>
= equity interest US, IAS/IFRS, investment US, ownership interest, share, stake
To have an interest in an enterprise means to have equity ownership of that enterprise, e.g. by holding shares in a company.
inversión
▲ *an interest in a jointly controlled entity* una inversión en una entidad controlada conjuntamente ▲ *include one's interest in the acquiree in the separate financial statements* incluir una inversión propia en el adquirente en los estados financieros independientes ▲ *interests in joint ventures* inversiones en joint ventures ▲ *the accounting by venturers for interests in joint ventures* la contabilización por los ventures de las inversiones en joint ventures ▲ *the portion of a gain or loss attributable to the equity interests of the other venturers* la parte de una pérdida o ganancia atribuible a las inversiones en patrimonio de otros ventures ▲ *unrelated investors' interests in the associate* inversiones de inversores no relacionados en la asociada

interest and capital repayment
Interest and capital repayment is the regular payment of the amount of interest and principal instalments on a debt.
reembolso de intereses y capital
▲ *an average interest and capital repayment of GBP 10 thousand* un reembolso de intereses y capital medio de 10.000 libras esterlinas

interest and other income US
= other financial income IAS/IFRS, other interest receivable and similar income UK
Interest and other income is an item in the profit and loss account representing interest and other financial revenue earned by an enterprise.
intereses y otros ingresos
= ingresos financieros
NOTE Always plural in Spanish.
▲ *interest and other income for fiscal year 2005* intereses y otros ingresos para el año fiscal 2005 ▲ *interest and other income, net* intereses y otros ingresos, neto ▲ *less interest and other income* menos intereses y otros ingresos ▲ *net interest and other income* intereses y otros ingresos netos
⇛ financials, net

interest cover
Interest cover is a financial ratio that measures the financial strength of an enterprise, defined as operating profit (EBIT,

EBITA or EBITDA) plus interest income divided by interest expenses.

cobertura del interés

= cobertura de intereses, cobertura de los intereses

▲ *interest cover after amortisation and depreciation* cobertura del interés después de amortización y depreciación ▲ *interest cover before amortisation and depreciation* cobertura del interés antes de amortización y depreciación

interest cover ratio UK

= times interest earned ratio US

The interest cover ratio is a financial ratio defined as earnings before interest and tax plus interest income divided by interest expenses that measures an enterprise's financial strength and resilience to interest increases, which is particularly interesting for highly-geared companies.

ratio de cobertura del interés

= interés cover ratio, ratio de cobertura de intereses, ratio de cobertura de los intereses

▲ *a high interest cover ratio* un ratio de cobertura del interés alto ▲ *a low interest cover ratio* un ratio de cobertura del interés bajo ▲ *calculate the interest cover ratio* calcular el ratio de cobertura del interés

interest coverage ratio

→ interest cover ratio

interest element

A loan is often divided into an interest element and a principal element. The interest element consists of the interest accrued over the term of the loan and which has to be paid together with the repayment of principal.

interés

▲ *classify the interest element as an operating activity* clasificar el interés como una actividad de explotación ▲ *interest element of lease payment* interés de pago por alquiler ▲ *separation of the interest element and the spot price of a forward contract* separación del interés y el precio de contado de un contrato de futuros ▲ *the interest element of a lease payment* el interés de un pago por alquiler ▲ *the interest element of the finance cost* el interés del coste financiero

interest expense

An interest expense is an expense incurred by an enterprise in connection with interest-bearing loan capital, i.e. an amount that the borrowing enterprise has to pay to the lender in return for the loan. Interest expense appears as an item in the profit and loss account either separately, as a net amount after offsetting interest income or as part of the aggregate item "net financials".

gasto por interés

= gasto por intereses

▲ *a deductible interest expense* un gasto por interés deducible ▲ *capitalised interest expenses* gastos por intereses capitalizados ▲ *expense interest expenses as incurred* anotar gastos por intereses al devengo ▲ *increased interest expenses* gastos por intereses aumentados ▲ *interest expense and similar charges* gasto por interés y costes similares ▲ *interest expenses before tax* gastos por intereses antes de impuestos ▲ *interest expenses on borrowings* gastos por intereses sobre empréstitos ▲ *interest expenses to group enterprises* gastos por intereses a empresas del grupo ▲ *interest expenses to mortgage credit institutions* gastos por intereses a instituciones de crédito hipotecario ▲ *interest expenses to parent* gastos por intereses a la matriz ▲ *recognise interest expenses as part of the cost* reconocer gastos por intereses como parte del coste ▲ *recognise the amount paid as interest expense over the period of the financing* reconocer la cantidad pagada como gasto por interés durante el periodo de la financiación

interest income UK

= interest revenue IAS/IFRS

Interest income is the interest revenue earned by an enterprise on investments or loans provided. Interest income appears as an item in the profit and loss account either separately, as a net amount after offsetting any interest expenses or as part of the aggregate item "net financials".

ingreso por interés

= ingreso por intereses

▲ *changes in interest income relating to floating rate financial instruments* cambios en ingreso por interés relacionados con instrumentos financieros a interés variable ▲ *elect to have interest income taxed on either a received or receivable basis* elegir recibir ingreso por interés sujeto a impuesto o bien al ser devengado o cobrado ▲ *elimination of intercompany interest income* eliminación del ingreso por interés intragrupo ▲ *interest income after impairment recognition* ingreso por interés después del reconocimiento del deterioro ▲ *interest income from subsidiaries* ingreso por interés de filiales ▲ *realised interest income* ingreso por interés realizado ▲ *the amount of interest income accrued on impaired financial assets* la cantidad de ingreso por interés devengada en activos financieros dañados ▲ *total interest income* total ingreso por intereses ▲ *unrealised interest income* ingreso por interés no realizado

interest paid

Interest paid represents the actual amount of accrued interest due that has been paid.

interés pagado

▲ *the total amount of interest paid during a period* la cantidad de interés pagado total durante un periodo

interest payable

Interest payable is the interest expense of an enterprise related to the cost of loans and borrowings for an accounting period. Interest payable appears as an item in the profit and loss account either separately, as a net amount after offsetting interest receivable or as part of the aggregate item "net financials".

interés a pagar

= intereses a pagar

NOTE Also plural in Spanish accounting texts.

▲ *interest payable and similar charges* intereses a pagar y cargas similares ▲ *interest payable on currency swaps* interés a pagar en swaps de divisas ▲ *net interest payable* interés a pagar neto

interest payable and similar charges UK

= other financial expenses IAS/IFRS

Interest payable and similar charges is an item in the profit and loss account comprising e.g. interest expense related to the cost of loans and borrowings and any currency translation losses for the accounting period.

interés a pagar y cargas similares

= intereses a pagar y carga similares

NOTE Also plural in Spanish accounting texts.

▲ *group interest payable and similar charges* intereses a pagar y cargas similares del grupo ▲ *net interest payable and similar charges* interés neto a pagar y cargas similares

⇛ financials, net

interest rate

= rate of interest

An interest rate is the rate charged by a lender on the principal amount of borrowed money, i.e. the price that a borrower has to pay for borrowing a sum over a specified period of time. An interest rate is expressed as a percentage and may be short-term or long-term. In the economy, interest rates signal the economic conditions and are used by the government or the central bank as a monetary policy instrument.

tipo de interés

▲ *a debt instrument with a variable interest rate* un instrumento de deuda con un tipo de interés variable ▲ *a fixed interest rate* un tipo de interés fijo ▲ *a floating interest rate* un tipo de interés variable ▲ *a loan that bears an off-market interest rate* un préstamo que soporta un tipo de interés fuera de mercado ▲ *a risk-free interest rate* un tipo de interés sin riesgo ▲ *a specified interest rate* un tipo de interés especificado ▲ *an artificially low interest rate* un tipo de interés artificialmente bajo ▲ *an embedded floor or cap on the interest rate on a debt contract* un intervalo máximo o mínimo incluido en el tipo de interés en un contrato de deuda ▲ *an observed interest rate* un tipo de interés observado ▲ *at below-market interest rates* a tipos de interés por debajo del mercado ▲ *current market interest rates* tipos de interés del

mercado actual ▲ *determine at appropriate current interest rates* determinar a tipos de interés corrientes apropiados ▲ *discounted at the interest rate implicit in the lease* descontado al tipo de interés implícito en el arrendamiento ▲ *enter into an interest rate strip* firmar un strip de tipo de interés ▲ *increases in short-term interest rates* aumentos en los tipos de interés a corto plazo ▲ *interest rate collars* collars del tipo de interés ▲ *interest rates used to discount cash flows* tipos de interés utilizado para descontar los flujos de efectivo ▲ *pre-tax interest rate* tipo de interés antes de impuestos ▲ *the contractual interest rate* el tipo de interés contractual ▲ *the fixed interest rate on a hedged item* el tipo de interés fijo en una partida cubierta ▲ *the reported interest rate sensitivity* la sensibilidad del tipo de interés publicado
⇛ interest

interest rate change

Interest rate changes are changes in the level of a given interest rate such as the lending rate, the deposit rate, the repo rate, the fed funds rate or the money-market rate.

cambio en el tipo de interés

▲ *the direct effects of an interest rate change on interest-bearing financial instruments recognised at the balance sheet date* los efectos directos en el cambio en el tipo de interés sobre instrumentos financieros apalancados reconocidos a la fecha del balance ▲ *the impact on operations of an interest rate change* el impacto en operaciones de un cambio en el tipo de interés

interest rate exposure

= interest rate risk, interest-rate exposure

Interest rate exposure is the risk of an enterprise of losses because of changes in interest rates, e.g. decreases in the return on investments because of lower rates and increases in interest payments on loans because of higher rates. Interest rate exposures are required disclosed in the annual report, typically in a special section dealing with risk management, and can be offset by hedging.

exposición al riesgo por tipo de interés

▲ *a fair value hedge of the interest rate exposure of a portfolio of financial liabilities* una cobertura a valor razonable de la exposición al riesgo por tipo de interés de una cartera de pasivos financieros ▲ *an identifiable and separately measurable portion of the interest rate exposure of an interest-bearing liability* una parte identificable y medible separadamente de la exposición al riesgo por tipo de interés de un pasivo apalancado ▲ *the net interest rate exposure* la exposición al riesgo por tipo de interés neta ▲ *the total interest rate exposure of a hedged financial instrument* la exposición al riesgo por tipo de interés total de un instrumento financiero cubierto
⇛ hedging

interest rate future

An interest rate future is a standardised futures contract for the purchase or sale of an underlying asset (e.g. a bond or other debt security) at a fixed agreed price at a fixed future date giving the buyer the right and the obligation to buy or sell. Interest rate futures are typically used for hedging against interest rate fluctuations and not settled by delivery as they are exercised before expiry.

futuros de tipo de interés

= contrato de futuros de tipo de interés, futuros sobre tipo de interés

▲ *enter into an interest rate future* firmar un contrato de futuros de tipo de interés

interest rate hedge

An interest rate hedge is a transaction intending to offset or minimise risk exposure to changes in interest rates. The hedging transaction involves the use of a derivative financial instrument such as an interest rate swap.

cobertura de tipos de interés

= contrato de cobertura del tipo de interés

▲ *enter into an interest rate hedge* firmar un contrato de cobertura de tipos de interés ▲ *interest rate hedge agreements* contratos de cobertura del tipo de interés ▲ *interest rate hedge instruments* instrumentos de cobertura de tipos de interés ▲ *the change in market value of the interest rate hedge* el cambio en el valor de mercado del contrato de cobertura de tipos de interés

interest rate implicit in the lease

IAS/IFRS

Within the context of leases, the interest rate implicit in a lease is the discount rate which, applied at the inception, i.e. the beginning, of a lease term to the minimum lease payments and the unguaranteed residual value of the lease, would cause the resulting total present value to be equal to the fair value of a leased asset, e.g. equipment or property.

tipo de interés implícito en el arrendamiento

= tasa de interés implícita en el arrendamiento

▲ *discount at the interest rate implicit in the lease* descontar el tipo de interés implícito en el arrendamiento

SOURCE IAS 17

interest rate instrument

Interest rate instruments are financial derivatives that are used to hedge interest rate risks. Examples of interest rate instruments are swaps, options and futures.

instrumento de tipo de interés

▲ *deferred gains on interest rate instruments* ganancias diferidas en instrumentos de tipo de interés ▲ *deferred losses on interest rate instruments* pérdidas diferidas en instrumentos de tipo de interés

interest rate risk

= interest risk

Interest rate risk is the risk of loss resulting from adverse interest rate trends. In connection with financial instruments, the interest rate risk is the risk that the fair value or future cash flows of the instrument will fluctuate because of changed market interest rates.

riesgo de tipo de interés

= riesgo de tasa de interés, riesgo por tipo de interés

NOTE The IAS/IFRS term 'riesgo de tasa de interés' is very rare in Spanish accounting texts.

▲ *a fair value hedge of interest rate risk* una cobertura a valor razonable del riesgo de tipo de interés ▲ *a portfolio hedge of interest rate risk* una cobertura del riesgo de tipo de interés de una cartera de inversiones ▲ *calculation of the interest rate risk* cálculo del riesgo de tipo de interés ▲ *cash flow interest rate risk* riesgo de tipo de interés del flujo de efectivo ▲ *disclose interest rate risks* publicar los riesgos de tipo de interés ▲ *fair value interest rate risk* riesgo de tipo de interés a valor razonable ▲ *hedging of the interest rate risk* cobertura del riesgo de tipo de interés ▲ *hedging of the interest rate risk on financial iabilities* cobertura del riesgo de tipo de interés de pasivos financieros ▲ *interest rate risk of fixed-rate liabilities* riesgo de tipo de interés de pasivos a tipo fijo ▲ *interest rate risk of the total portfolio* riesgo de tipo de interés de la cartera de inversiones total ▲ *maintain the entity's existing interest rate risk position* mantener la posición de riesgo de tipo de interés existente de la entidad ▲ *net position with interest rate risk* posición neta con riesgo de tipo de interés ▲ *take interest rate positions to hedge interest rate risks* tomar posiciones de tipo de interés para cubrir los riesgos de tipo de interés ▲ *the level of exposure to interest rate risk* el nivel de exposición al riesgo de tipo de interés

interest rate sensitivity

Interest rate sensitivity is the exposure involving easy and quick reaction to changes in the interest rate level.

sensibilidad del tipo de interés

= sensibilidad de los tipos de interés

▲ *calculate interest rate sensitivity* calcular la sensibilidad de los tipos de interés ▲ *disclose interest rate sensitivity information* publicar información de la sensibilidad del tipo de interés ▲ *the reported interest rate sensitivity* la sensibilidad del tipo de interés publicada

interest rate swap

An interest rate swap is an agreement or a transaction in

which two parties exchange interest payments on the basis of a notional amount of principal, e.g. an enterprise having fixed-rate debt may swap interest payments with an enterprise having floating-rate debt.

swap de tipo de interés
= swap de los tipos de interés, swap de tipos de interés
▲ *a portfolio of interest rate swaps* una cartera de inversión de swaps de tipo de interés ▲ *amortising interest rate swaps* amortizando los swaps de tipos de interés ▲ *an interest rate swap carried at fair value* un swap de los tipos de interés reflejado a valor razonable ▲ *an interest rate swap contingent on a climatic variable such as heating degree days* un swap de tipo de interés contingente en una variable climática tal como días de calor e intensidad ▲ *cross-currency interest rate swap* swap multidivisa de tipos de interés ▲ *currency and interest rate swaps for equity hedging* swaps de divisas y de tipo de interés para cobertura de patrimonio ▲ *the interest rate swap element* el swap de tipos de interés ▲ *use interest rate swaps* utilizar swaps de tipo de interés

interest rate swap contract
An interest rate swap contract is an agreement in which two parties exchange interest payments on the basis of a notional amount of principal, e.g. an enterprise having fixed-rate debt may swap interest payments with an enterprise having floating-rate debt.

contrato de swap de tipo de interés
= contrato de swap de tipos de interés
▲ *enter into an interest swap contract* firmar un contrato de swap de tipos de interés ▲ *terminate an interest rate swap contract* finalizar un contrato de swap de tipo de interés ▲ *the net amount to be paid or received under the interest rate swap contract* la cantidad neta a pagar o recibir según el contrato de swap de tipos de interés
⇛ derivative financial instrument, swap

interest receivable
≠ interest payable
Interest receivable is the interest revenue earned by an enterprise on investments or loans provided. Interest receivable appears as an item in the profit and loss account either separately, as a net amount after offsetting any interest payable or as part of the aggregate item "net financials".

interés a cobrar
= intereses a cobrar
NOTE Also plural in Spanish accounting texts.
▲ *interest receivable and similar income* intereses a cobrar e ingresos similares ▲ *net interest receivable* interés a cobrar neto

interest received
Interest received represents the actual amount of accrued interest paid that has fallen due for payment and is earned on e.g. a bond or other loan.

interés recibido
▲ *interest received etc.* interés recibido etc. ▲ *the tax base of the interest received in advance* la base imponible del interés recibido por adelantado

interest revenue IAS/IFRS
= interest income UK, interest receivable US
Interest revenue is the interest income earned by an enterprise on investments or loans provided. Interest revenue appears as an item in the income statement either separately, as a net amount after offsetting any interest expenses or as part of the aggregate item "net financials".

ingreso por interés
= ingreso de interés, ingreso por intereses
▲ *recognise as interest revenue* reconocer como ingreso por interés
SOURCE IAS 12

interest risk
→ interest rate risk

interest swap
→ interest rate swap

interest yield
Interest yield is the return on an investment. The interest yield on a bond with a nominal interest rate of 10%, bought at a price of 80, is 12.5% (10/80).

rentabilidad de la inversión
= rendimiento de la inversión
▲ *average interest yield* rentabilidad de la inversión media ▲ *calculate the interest yield* calcular la rentabilidad de la inversión ▲ *gross interest yield* rentabilidad de la inversión

bruta ▲ *net interest yield* rentabilidad de la inversión neta

interest-bearing

A debt or a security on which interest accrues is interest-bearing.

con intereses

= que devenga interés

▲ *assumption of interest-bearing liabilities* asunción de pasivos con intereses ▲ *interest-bearing instruments* instrumentos con intereses ▲ *long-term interest-bearing liabilities* pasivos con intereses a largo plazo ▲ *non-current interest-bearing liabilities* pasivos con intereses no corrientes ▲ *the acquisition of an interest-bearing investment* la adquisición de una inversión con intereses ▲ *the current portion of interest-bearing liabilities* la parte corriente de pasivos con intereses ▲ *the direct effects of an interest rate change on interest-bearing financial instruments recognised at the balance sheet date* los efectos directos de un cambio del tipo de interés en instrumentos financieros con intereses reconocidos a la fecha del balance ▲ *the variable interest rate on an interest-bearing liability* el tipo de interés variable en un pasivo con intereses

interest-rate exposure

= interest rate exposure, interest rate risk

Interest-rate exposure is the risk of an enterprise of losses because of changes in interest rates, e.g. decreases in the return on investments because of lower rates and increases in interest payments on loans because of higher rates. Interest rate exposures are required disclosed in the annual report, typically in a special section dealing with risk management and can be offset by hedging.

exposición al riesgo de tipo de interés

= exposición al riesgo por tipo de interés

▲ *hedge the interest-rate exposure* cubrir la exposición al riesgo de tipo de interés

interest-rate hedging

Interest-rate hedging refers to the act of offsetting or reducing risk exposure related to interest rate movements. This may be done by means of different types of financial instruments, such as futures, swaps and options.

NOTE Whereas 'interest-rate hedging' denotes the act, 'interest-rate hedge' denotes the transaction.

cobertura de tipos de interés

▲ *the Group interest rate-hedging policy* la política de cobertura de tipos de interés del Grupo

interest-rate hedging instrument

Interest-rate hedging instruments are financial instruments used to protect against and offset interest-rate exposures typically resulting from future interest-rate changes. Examples of such instruments are futures, options and swaps.

instrumento de cobertura de tipos de interés

▲ *an effective interest-rate hedging instrument* un instrumento de cobertura de tipos de interés efectivo

⇛ financial instrument

interest-rate level

= level of interest rates

The interest-rate level is the level of a given interest rate such as the lending rate, the deposit rate, the repo rate, the fed funds or the money-market rate.

nivel de tipos de interés

▲ *changes in the interest-rate level* cambios en el nivel de tipos de interés ▲ *the general interest-rate level* el nivel de tipos de interés general ▲ *the unusually low interest-rate level* el nivel de tipos de interés inusualmente bajo

interest-rate option

An interest-rate option gives a buyer or a seller the right, but not the obligation, to buy or sell a financial instrument at a fixed price and with a interest rate before expiry of the option. Interest-rate options are typically used for hedging against interest rate fluctuations.

opción sobre el tipo de interés

= opción sobre los tipos de interés

▲ *bonds with embedded interest-rate options* bonos con opciones sobre el tipo de interés incrustados ▲ *European-style interest-rate options* opciones sobre el tipo de interés de estilo europeo

interim

= preliminary

Interim means used or accepted temporarily until a final or complete one is made.

provisional

= a cuenta, interino

▲ *an interim balance sheet* un balance provisional ▲ *an interim statement of changes in equity* estado de cambios en el patrimonio neto provisional ▲ *interim dividend* dividendo a cuenta ▲ *interim financial statements* estados financieros provisionales ▲ *represent an interim step pending the identification of impairment losses* representar un paso provisional pendiente de la identificación de las pérdidas por deterioro

interim accounts UK

= interim financial statements IAS/IFRS, US

≠ full-year accounts

Interim accounts are accounts prepared for periods shorter than a financial year, e.g. half-yearly or quarterly accounts.

estados financieros intermedios

▲ *draw up interim accounts* redactar los estados financieros intermedios ▲ *present interim accounts* presentar los estados financieros intermedios ▲ *publish interim accounts* publicar los estados financieros intermedios ▲ *the preparation of interim accounts* la preparación de los estados financieros intermedios

interim announcement

= interim profit statement

The interim announcement is a financial report which companies submit on the announcement of the interim financial statements on a quarterly or annual basis. Listed companies are generally required by the stock exchange to submit half-yearly interim announcements, and in the USA, companies registered with the Securities and Exchange Commission must also file quarterly interim announcements.

publicación de resultados intermedios

▲ *interim announcement of 31 March 2006* publicación de resultados intermedios a 31 de marzo de 2006 ▲ *publication of an interim announcement* publicación de resultados intermedios

interim certificate

An interim certificate is an official document evidencing title typically to several shares of the same type and issued on a temporary basis by the issuing company to the shareholder. The interim certificate will be replaced by the actual share certificates when the shares have been paid up in full.

certificado provisional

= resguardo provisional

▲ *issue of interim certificates* emisión de certificados provisionales

interim dividend

Interim dividend is dividend declared and paid during the financial year before a company's AGM where the total dividend is proposed by the board of directors and adopted by the shareholders.

dividendo a cuenta

▲ *distribute interim dividend* distribuir el dividendo a cuenta ▲ *pay interim dividend* pagar el dividendo a cuenta

⇛ final dividend

interim entry

An interim entry is a preliminary entry in the bookkeeping accounts of an enterprise.

entrada provisional

▲ *make interim entries* anotar entradas provisionales

interim figure

Interim figures are the results for a financial reporting period shorter than a full financial year, e.g. a quarter or half a year.

cifra provisional

▲ *for reasons of understandability of the interim figures* por razones de comprensibilidad de las cifras provisionales ▲ *release interim figures for the period 1 January 2005 to 31 March 2006* publicar las cifras provisionales para el periodo de 1 de enero del 2005 al 31 de marzo del 2006

interim financial report

An interim financial report is a financial report disclosing financial data, sometimes in a condensed form, for an accounting period shorter than a full financial year, i.e. a quarter, half a year or three quarters.

informe financiero intermedio

▲ *approve an interim financial report* aprobar un informe financiero intermedio ▲ *interim financial reporting* hacer un informe financiero intermedio ▲ *prepare an interim financial report* preparar un informe financiero intermedio ▲ *publish an interim financial report* publicar un informe financiero intermedio ▲ *the amounts reported in the interim financial report for the first six-month period* las cantidades recogidas en el informe financiero intermedio para el primer semestre ▲ *the condensed interim financial report* el informe financiero intermedio abreviado ▲ *the elements of the interim financial report* los elementos del informe financiero intermedio ▲ *the measurement procedures to be followed in an interim financial report* los procedimientos de valoración que se siguen en un informe financiero intermedio ▲ *the minimum contents of an interim financial report* los contenidos mínimos de un informe financiero intermedio ▲ *the notes to an interim financial report* las notas a un informe financiero intermedio

SOURCE IAS 34, paragraph 4

interim financial statements IAS/IFRS, US

= interim accounts UK

≠ full-year financial statements

Interim financial statements are the financial statements prepared by some enterprises for a period shorter than the financial year, e.g. quarterly or half-yearly.

estados financieros intermedios

▲ *complete interim financial statements* completar los estados financieros intermedios ▲ *interim financial statements at 31 March 2005* estados financieros intermedios a 31 de marzo del 2005 ▲ *internal interim financial statements* estados financieros intermedios internos ▲ *prepare interim financial statements* preparar los estados financieros intermedios ▲ *present interim financial statements* presentar los estados financieros intermedios ▲ *publish interim financial statements* publicar los estados financieros intermedios ▲ *the notes to the interim financial statements* las notas a los estados financieros intermedios ▲ *the structure and content of condensed interim financial statements* la estructura y contenido de los estados financieros intermedios abreviados

interim period

An interim period is a financial reporting period of a shorter duration than a full financial year, i.e. a quarter, half a year or three quarters.

periodo intermedio

▲ *additional interim period financial information* información financiera del periodo intermedio adicional ▲ *an amount reported in the interim period* un cantidad anotada en el periodo intermedio ▲ *comparable interim periods* periodos intermedios comparables ▲ *during the interim period* durante el periodo intermedio ▲ *events that are material to an understanding of the current interim period* sucesos que son reales para un entendimiento del periodo intermedio actual ▲ *prior interim periods* periodos intermedios anteriores ▲ *restate the financial statements of prior interim periods of the current financial year* actualizar los estados financieros de los periodos intermedios anteriores del ejercicio actual ▲ *restatement of previously reported interim periods* actualización de los periodos intermedios anotados previamente ▲ *subsequent interim periods* periodos intermedios subsiguientes ▲ *the current interim period* el periodo intermedio actual ▲ *the end of an interim period* el final de un periodo intermedio ▲ *the end of the interim period* al final del periodo intermedio ▲ *the final interim period of the financial year* el periodo intermedio final del año financiero ▲ *the results for each interim period* los resultados para cada periodo intermedio

SOURCE IAS 34, paragraph 4

interim profit

The interim profit is the profit for a financial reporting period shorter than a full financial

year, e.g. a quarter or half a year.
beneficio intermedio
= ganancia intermedia
▲ *interim profit after tax* beneficio intermedio después de impuestos ▲ *interim profit before tax* beneficio intermedio antes de impuestos ▲ *interim profit growth* crecimiento del beneficio intermedio

interim report
An interim report is a financial report prepared by an enterprise, often a listed company, after only part of a full financial year has been completed on a quarterly or a half-yearly basis. The interim report gives the financial highlights and management's review for the interim period on a year-to-date basis and include summary financial statements. Listed companies are generally required by the stock exchange to submit half-yearly interim reports, and in the USA, companies registered with the Securities and Exchange Commission must also file quarterly interim reports.
informe intermedio
▲ *approve an interim report* aprobar un informe intermedio ▲ *information included in an interim report* información incluida en un informe intermedio ▲ *the third quarter interim report* el informe intermedio del tercer trimestre
⇛ annual report

interim results
= half-year results
The interim results appear from the financial statements prepared for a quarter or the first half of an accounting period.
resultados intermedios
NOTE Spanish rules do not require the elaboration and reporting of interim results.
▲ *publication of interim results* publicación de los resultados intermedios

interim results announcement UK
= results announcement UK
The interim results announcement is a financial report which listed companies submits on the announcement of the interim financial statements on a quarterly or annual basis.
anuncio de resultados intermedios
= anuncio de los resultados intermedios
▲ *issue an interim results announcement* emitir un anuncio de resultados intermedios ▲ *publish an interim results announcement* publicar un anuncio de los resultados intermedios
⇛ earnings release, preliminary results announcement

interim statements
→ interim financial statements

intermediate product
Intermediate products are products, typically partly processed, which are transferred between various divisions or units of an organisation for further manufacturing or assembly, or for sale to external customers.
producto intermedio
▲ *a decline in intermediate product sales* un descenso en las ventas de productos intermedios ▲ *determine the price of the intermdiate product* determinar el precio del producto intermedio ▲ *intermediate product pricing* fijar el precio del producto intermedio
⇛ transfer pricing

internal audit
≠ external audit
An internal audit is an audit within an enterprise carried out by auditors employed in the enterprise. Internal auditing includes e.g. monitoring the accuracy and adequacy of the accounting and internal control systems.
auditoría interna
▲ *monitor the effectiveness of the company's internal audit* comprobar la efectividad de la auditoría interna de la empresa ▲ *the internal audit unit* la unidad de auditoría interna

internal auditor
An internal auditor is a person employed by an enterprise to be responsible for and carry out the internal audit. Internal auditing functions include e.g. monitoring the adequacy of the accounting and internal control systems.
auditor interno
▲ *appoint an internal auditor* nombrar un auditor interno
⇛ auditor, external auditor, independent auditor

internal control
Internal controls constitute the system of financial and other controls providing reasonable assurance of compliance with

rules and regulations, efficient operations as well as most efficient use of an entity's assets. Internal controls help minimising errors, fraud and waste.

control interno

▲ *an effective internal control system* un sistema de control interno efectivo ▲ *breaches of internal control policies* rupturas de las políticas de control interno ▲ *material weaknesses in internal control in relation to the financial reporting process* debilidades materiales en el control interno en relación con el proceso de información financiera ▲ *monitor the effectiveness of the company's internal control* examinar la efectividad del control interno de la compañía ▲ *risk management and internal control* gestión del riesgo y control interno

⇛ internal financial control

internal cost

Internal costs are costs already paid, e.g. in the form of wages and salaries, which are now attributed to a particular project or job in order to calculate the internal costs incurred in relation to the project or job for comparison with the costs of alternative externally bought resources.

coste interno

≠ coste externo

▲ *calculate internal costs* calcular los costes internos ▲ *internal costs that are incremental and directly attributable to negotiating and arranging a lease* costes internos marginales y directamente atribuibles a negociación y establecimiento de un alquiler

internal failure cost

Internal failure costs are costs incurred because of defects and deficiencies of manufactured products such as rework, machine repairs or spoilage that are detected prior to delivery to customers.

coste por fallos internos

≠ coste por fallos externos

▲ *increase internal failure costs* aumentar los costes por fallos internos ▲ *reduce internal failure costs* reducir los costes por fallos internos

⇛ appraisal cost, external failure cost, prevention cost

internal financial control UK

Internal financial controls are internal controls that provide reasonable assurance of maintaining an entity's proper accounting records and reliable financial information as well as the safeguarding of assets against unauthorised use or disposition.

control financiero interno

▲ *an effective system of internal financial control* un sistema efectivo de control financiero interno ▲ *exercise internal financial control* ejercitar el control financiero interno

SOURCE Cadbury Report

⇛ internal control

internal financial reporting

= management accounting, managerial accounting US

Internal financial reporting is concerned with the measuring, reporting and provision of accounting information to support the planning and control decisions made by management in a business. Internal financial reporting is often referred to as management accounting.

información financiera interna

= contabilidad de gestión

▲ *a useful tool for internal financial reporting* una herramienta útil para la contabilidad de gestión ▲ *be in charge of internal financial reporting* ser responsable de la información financiera interna ▲ *provide internal financial reporting for the board of directors* ofrecer información financiera interna al consejo de administración

internal growth

= organic growth

≠ external growth, inorganic growth

Internal growth is the organic growth of an enterprise that results from spending internally generated resources to achieve e.g. increased production, penetration on new markets, or development of new products. Organic growth excludes growth via mergers and acquisitions.

crecimiento interno

= crecimiento orgánico

≠ crecimiento externo, crecimiento inorgánico

internal management reporting

Internal management reporting is the financial informa-

tion and accounting data processed and shared within an enterprise, such as budgets, budget analyses, accounting records and other financial reports for internal use.
información de gestión interna
▲ *be responsible for internal management reporting* ser responsable de la información de gestión interna

internal rate of return
= IRR
The internal rate of return is the interest rate or discount factor at which the net present values of the total discounted cash inflows (the return) of an investment project and the total discounted cash outflows (the cost) equals zero. The project is acceptable if the internal rate of return is positive, i.e. equal to or higher than the required rate of return (the hurdle rate).
tasa interna de rentabilidad
= tasa interna de rendimiento, TIR
▲ *an instrument-specific component of the internal rate of return* un componente específico de la tasa interna de rentabilidad ▲ *compute the liability's internal rate of return* calcular la tasa interna de rentabilidad del pasivo
⇛ discount factor, required rate of return

internal rate of return model
= IRR model
The internal rate of return model is a method used for evaluating the profitability of investment projects, i.e. capital budgeting. The model determines the internal rate of return, i.e. the interest rate or discount factor at which the net present values of the total discounted cash inflows (the return) of an investment project and the total discounted cash outflows (the cost) equals zero. The project is acceptable if the internal rate of return is positive, i.e. equal to or higher than the required rate of return (the hurdle rate).
modelo de la tasa interna de rentabilidad
= modelo de la tasa interna de rendimiento, modelo TIR
▲ *a modified internal rate of return model* un modelo de la tasa interna de rentabilidad modificado ▲ *use the internal rate of return model* utilizar el modelo de la tasa interna de rentabilidad
⇛ discount factor

Internal Revenue Service US
= IRS
The Internal Revenue Service is the name of the US federal tax authorities.
Internal Revenue Service
= Agencia Tributaria
▲ *file the forms electronically to the IRS* enviar los ficheros electrónicamente al IRS
⇛ HM Revenue & Customs, income tax law

internally generated goodwill
Internally generated goodwill represents the positive difference between an enterprise's market value and its identifiable carrying amount arising from the own creation of value, rather than in connection with an acquisition. Internally generated goodwill does not represent the cost of any separately identifiable assets and cannot consequently be recognised as an asset.
fondo de comercio generado internamente
▲ *an increase in internally generated goodwill* un aumento en el fondo de comercio generado internamente ▲ *enhance the enterprise's internally generated goodwill* mejorar el fondo de comercio generado internamente de la empresa ▲ *expenditure contributing to internally generated goodwill* gastos que contribuyen al fondo de comercio generado internamente ▲ *replaced by internally generated goodwill* reemplazado por el fondo de comercio generado internamente ▲ *the cost of maintaining the enterprise's internally generated goodwill* el coste de mantenimiento del fondo de comercio generado internamente de la empresa ▲ *the recognition of internally generated goodwill* el reconocimiento del fondo de comercio generado internamente

International Accounting Standard IAS/IFRS
= IAS
International Accounting Standards (IASs) are accounting

guidelines issued by the former International Accounting Standards Committee (IASC). In 2003, the International Accounting Standards Board replaced the IASC and started issuing international accounting standards, now referred to as International Financial Reporting Standards (IFRSs). Some IASs are being updated by the IASB to continue in force while others are withdrawn.

Norma Internacional de Contabilidad

▲ *adopt certain International Accounting Standards* adoptar ciertas Normas Internacionales de Contabilidad ▲ *amendments to other International Accounting Standards* enmiendas a otras Normas Internacionales de Contabilidad ▲ *the application of International Accounting Standards* la aplicación de las Normas Internacionales de Contabilidad

⇛ International Financial Reporting Standard

International Accounting Standards Board IAS/IFRS

= IASB

In 2001, the International Accounting Standards Board (IASB) replaced the International Accounting Standards Committee (IASC) as international standard-issuing organ. In 2003, the IASB started issuing international accounting standards, now referred to as IFRSs. The standards issued by the former IASC are named IASs.

Comité de Normas Internacionales de Contabilidad

▲ *select the members of the International Accounting Standards Board* seleccionar a los miembros del Comité de Normas Internacionales de Contabilidad

International Accounting Standards Committee Foundation

= IASCF

The International Accounting Standards Committee Foundation (IASCF) is the top, not-for-profit corporation overseeing and appointing the members of the International Accounting Standards Board to whom it has delegated the sole responsibility for setting the international accounting standards. The IASCF consists of 19 trustees with diverse geographical and functional background, appointed for a period of three years with the possibility of being renewed once.

Fundación del Comité de Normas Internacionales de Contabilidad

▲ *the administrative office of the International Accounting Standards Committee Foundation* la oficina administrativa de la Fundación del Comité de Normas Internacionales de Contabilidad ▲ *the objectives of the International Accounting Standards Committee Foundation* los objetivos de la Fundación del Comité de Normas Internacionales de Contabilidad

international auditing standard

An international auditing standard is a standard laying down, on an international basis, the basic principles for the scope and procedures that auditors must follow when performing audits of financial reports and statements. The International Standards on Auditing (ISA) have been issued by the International Auditing and Assurance Standards Board (IAASB) under the International Federation of Accountants (IFAC).

norma de auditoría internacional

▲ *carry out an audit based on international auditing standards* llevar a cabo una auditoría basada en las normas de auditoría internacional ▲ *in accordance with international auditing standards* de acuerdo con las normas de auditoría internacional ▲ *the adopted international auditing standards* las normas de auditoría internacional adoptadas ▲ *the carving out of parts of an international auditing standard* la mejora de partes de una norma de auditoría internacional ▲ *the revised international auditing standard* la norma de auditoría internacional revisada

⇛ International Standard on Auditing

International Federation of Accountants

= IFAC

The International Federation of Accountants (IFAC) is an international organisation for national associations of professional accountants. Its objective is to strengthen the accountancy profession internationally and to secure auditing and accountancy services of a uniform and high quality. IFAC has issued a code of ethics for professional accountants.

Federación Internacional de Auditores de Cuentas

▲ *become a member of International Federation of Accountants* llegar a a ser un miembro de la Federación Internacional de Auditores de Cuentas

International Financial Reporting Interpretations Committee

= IFRIC

In 2002, the International Financial Reporting Interpretations Committee (IFRIC) replaced the former Standing Interpretations Committee (SIC). The role of the IFRIC is to prepare interpretations of International Financial Reporting Standards for approval by the IASB and, in the context of the Framework and as appropriate, to clarify and explain issues of financial reporting which are not covered by existing IASs or IFRSs.

Comité de Interpretaciones de las Normas Internacionales de Información Financiera

= IFRIC

▲ *interpretations issued by the International Financial Reporting Interpretations Committee* interpretaciones emitidas por el Comité de Interpretaciones de las Normas Internacionales de Información Financiera

International Financial Reporting Standard IAS/IFRS

= IFRS

International Financial Reporting Standards are issued by the IASB that replaced IASC as the new global standards issuer. IFRS I, First Time Adoption of International Financial Reporting Standards, was issued in June 2003. Some IASs will remain in force until changed or withdrawn; all new standards issued by the IASB are called IFRSs.

Norma Internacional de Información Financiera

= NIIF

▲ *comply with International Financial Reporting Standards* cumplir con las Normas Internacionales de Información Financiera ▲ *first-time adoption of International Financial Reporting Standards* la adopción por vez primera de las Normas Internacionales de Información Financiera ▲ *the date on which the transaction first qualifies for recognition in accordance with International Financial Reporting Standards* la fecha en la que la primera adaptación cumple con los requisitos de reconocimiento de acuerdo con las Normas Internacionales de Información Financiera

⇛ financial reporting standard, International Accounting Standard

International Standard on Auditing IAS/IFRS

= ISA IAS/IFRS

International Standards on Auditing are standards laying down, on an international basis, the basic principles for the scope and procedures that auditors must follow when performing audits of financial reports and statements. The International Standards on Auditing (ISA) have been issued by the International Auditing and Assurance Standards Board (IAASB) under the International Federation of Accountants (IFAC).

Norma Internacional de Auditoría

= NIA

▲ *issue an International Standard on Auditing* emitir una Norma Internacional de Auditoría ▲ *proposed International Standard on Auditing 600* Norma Internacional de Auditoría 600 propuesta

interpret

To interpret is to analyse and explain the meaning of something.

interpretar

▲ *interpret a rule* interpretar una norma ▲ *interpret a statute* interpretar una ley ▲ *interpret a term* interpretar un término ▲ *interpret accounting standards* interpretar las normas contables ▲ *interpret the information contained in the financial statements* interpretar la información contenida en los estados financieros

interpretation

An interpretation is an explanation built on an analysis and understanding of something.

interpretación

▲ *a final interpretation* una interpretación final ▲ *draft interpretation* interpretación provisional ▲ *interpretation of a principle* interpretación de un principio ▲ *interpretation of a treaty* interpretación de un tratado ▲ *interpretation of accounting standards* interpretación de las normas contables ▲ *interpretation of financial statements* interpretación de los estados financieros ▲ *interpretation of rules* interpretación de las normas ▲ *interpretation of statutes* interpretación de las leyes

interpretative communication

An interpretative communication is a document issued by the European Commission providing the interpretation of specific issues.

comunicación interpretativa

▲ *interpretative communication of 20 January 1998* comunicación interpretativa del 20 de enero de 1998 ▲ *publish an interpretative communication* publicar una comunicación interpretativa

intra-group

= intercompany

Intra-group refers to transactions involving or occurring between two or more companies of the same group.

intragrupo

▲ *adjustment for intra-group trade* ajuste por transacciones intragrupo ▲ *elimination of an intra-group receivable* eliminación de una cuenta a cobrar intragrupo ▲ *elimination of intra-group dividend payable* eliminación de un dividendo a pagar intragrupo ▲ *intra-company balances* saldos intragrupo ▲ *intra-company payables* cuentas a pagar intragrupo ▲ *intra-group debt* deuda intragrupo ▲ *intra-group dividends* dividendos intragrupo ▲ *intra-group expenses* gastos intragrupo ▲ *intra-group gains and losses* pérdidas y ganancias intragrupo ▲ *intra-group income* ingresos intragrupo ▲ *intra-group profits* beneficios intragrupo ▲ *intra-group purchased goods* bienes comprados intragrupo ▲ *intra-group receivables* cuentas a cobrar intragrupo ▲ *intra-group sales and purchases* compras y ventas intragrupo ▲ *intra-group shareholdings* participaciones accionariales intragrupo ▲ *intra-group transactions* transacciones intragrupo ▲ *intra-group transfer of enterprise ownership* transferencia intragrupo de la propiedad de la empresa

intra-group debt

= intercompany debt

Intra-group debt refers to amounts due to one company in a group by another in the form of loans, fees or other obligations payable.

deuda intragrupo

▲ *elimination of intra-group debt* eliminación de la deuda intragrupo

intra-group loan

= intercompany loan

An intra-group loan is a loan or other credit extension made by one or more companies in a group to one or more other companies in the same group.

préstamo intragrupo

▲ *fund activities by intra-group loans* financiar actividades con préstamos intragrupo ▲ *proceeds from intra-group loan* ingresos de préstamos intragrupo

intra-group loss

= intercompany loss

An intra-group loss is a loss incurred by a company in a group by selling goods or services to one or more other companies in the same group.

pérdida intragrupo

▲ *changes in intra-group losses* cambios en pérdidas intragrupo

intra-group profit

= intergroup profit

Intra-group profit refers to the profit generated by one company in a group, e.g. by selling goods or services to one or more other companies in the group. When preparing the consolidated financial statements, such profits must be eliminated or adjusted so that they do not appear in the consolidated financial statements.

beneficio intragrupo

▲ *eliminate intra-group profit* eliminar el beneficio intragrupo ▲ *less unrealised intra-group profits* menos beneficios intragrupo no realizados ▲ *un-*

realised intra-group profit beneficio intragrupo no realizado

intra-group receivable

= intercompany receivable

An intra-group receivable is an amount owed by one company to another in the same group, one company having an amount due from the other.

cuenta a cobrar intragrupo

▲ *accounting for intra-group receivables* contabilizando las cuentas a cobrar intragrupo ▲ *interest-bearing intra-group receivables* cuentas a cobrar intragrupo con interés ▲ *total short-term intra-group receivables* total cuentas a cobrar intragrupo a corto

intra-group sales

= intercompany sales

Intra-group sales refer to the turnover generated by one enterprise in a group by selling goods or services to one or more other enterprises in the group. When preparing the consolidated financial statements, intra-group sales must be eliminated or adjusted so that they do not appear in the consolidated financial statements.

ventas intragrupo

▲ *elimination of intra-group sales* eliminación de las ventas intragrupo

intra-group settlement

= intercompany settlement

Intra-group settlement refers to the payment of amounts due to one or more companies in a group by one or more other companies in the same group, e.g. as a result of exchanges of goods or services.

liquidación intragrupo

▲ *management of intra-group settlement* gestión de la liquidación intragrupo

intra-group shareholding

= intercompany shareholding

An intra-group shareholding is a share ownership held by one group company, i.e. parent company or subsidiary, in another company within the same group of companies.

participación accionarial intragrupo

▲ *elimination of intra-group shareholdings* eliminación de las participaciones accionariales intragrupo

intra-group trade

= intercompany trade

Intra-group trade is trade that takes place between companies in a group, e.g. when one company in a group sells goods or services to another company in the same group. When preparing the consolidated financial statements, intra-group trade must be eliminated or adjusted so that it does not appear in the consolidated financial statements.

transacción intragrupo

= actividad comercial intragrupo

▲ *elimination of intra-group trade* eliminación de la transacción intragrupo ▲ *intra-group trade in fixed assets* transacción intragrupo en activos fijos ▲ *intra-group trade in raw materials, consumables and goods for resale* transacción intragrupo en materias primas, insumos y bienes para la reventa

intra-group transaction

= intercompany transaction

An intra-group transaction is a transaction that takes place between companies in a group, e.g. when one company in a group sells goods or services to another company in the same group. When preparing the consolidated financial statements, intra-group transactions must be eliminated or adjusted so that they do not appear in the consolidated financial statements.

transacción intragrupo

= actividad comercial intragrupo

▲ *material intra-group transactions* transacciones intragrupo materiales ▲ *significant intra-group transactions and investments in and balances with group and associated companies and with directors* transacciones intragrupo significativas e inversiones en y saldos con el grupo y asociadas y con directivos

intrinsic value

The intrinsic value is the real value which is inherent in an object and therefore the demand for that object or the current price of it is not relevant. In the context of options, the intrinsic value represents the difference between the exercise price, i.e. the striking price, and the market price, i.e. the current value, of the underlying asset. For a call option it is the value by which the market price exceeds the exercise price, when the option is in-the-money, whereas for a put option, it is the amount by which the exercise price exceeds the market price. The opposite is the case for an option, which is out-of-the-money.

valor intrínseco

▲ *a specified amount of intrinsic value of a share option* una cantidad especificada de valor intrínseco de una opción sobre acciones ▲ *any change in intrinsic value recognised in profit or loss* cualquier cambio en el valor intrínseco reconocido en resultados ▲ *apply the intrinsic value method* aplicar el método del valor intrínseco ▲ *measure the equity instruments at their intrinsic value* calcular los instrumentos de patrimonio neto a su valor intrínseco ▲ *measurements that reflect the intrinsic value of embedded options* cálculos que reflejan el valor intrínseco de las opciones incrustadas ▲ *separation of the intrinsic value and time value of an option contract* separación del valor intrínseco y valor-tiempo de un contrato de opciones ▲ *the intrinsic value of an option to surrender the contract* el valor intrínseco de una opción para cancelar el contrato ▲ *the intrinsic value of the option* el valor intrínseco de la opción ▲ *the total intrinsic value at the end of the period* el valor intrínseco total al final del periodo

⇛ equity value

introduce

To indtroduce means to apply or use something new in an already existing context, for instance to start using a new compensation plan.

introducir

▲ *introduce a bias into the measurement* introducir un sesgo en el cálculo ▲ *introduce a provision in the company's articles of association* introducir una provisión en los artículos de la asociación de la compañía ▲ *introduce new accounting policies* introducir nuevas políticas contables

introduction

An introduction is the application or use of something new in an already existing context.

introducción

▲ *introduction of corporate governance rules* introducción de normas de gobernanza corporativa ▲ *introduction of the Euro* introducción del euro ▲ *past service costs that arose from the introduction of a plan before the acquisition date* costes de servicio pasado que surgieron por la introducción de un plan antes de la fecha de adquisición ▲ *the introduction into IAS 39 of a new hedge accounting method* la introducción en la NIC 39 de una nueva contabilidad de cobertura ▲ *the introduction of an asset-based discount rate* la introducción de un tipo de descuento basado en activos

inventoriable cost US

≠ period cost

Inventoriable costs are product costs attributable to the delivery of a product from supplier to stocks, i.e. purchase or manufacturing costs such as direct materials, labour and freight costs. Inventoriable costs are included in the value of the product and recognised as an asset, i.e. capitalised and added to stocks or other assets, e.g. machinery. On the sale of the product, such costs become costs of sales.

coste inventariable

▲ *the allocation of inventoriable costs* la asignación de los costes inventariables ▲ *the computation of inventoriable costs* el cómputo de los costes inventariables

⇛ product cost

inventories IAS/IFRS, US

= stocks UK

Inventories is an item in the balance sheet under current assets including items that the enterprise holds on stock at the balance sheet date for sale or use in the production process, such as finished goods, raw materials and consumables, work-in-process and merchandise.

inventarios

= existencias

▲ *the amount of inventories* la cuantía de los inventarios ▲ *the cost of inventories* el coste de los inventarios

inventory US, IAS/IFRS

= stock UK

Inventory constitutes the goods on stock in an enterprise, typically including finished goods, goods for resale, raw materials and consumables as well as work-in-process and merchandise. As an item in the balance sheet under current assets the plural form "inventories" applies.

inventario

▲ *accounting for inventories* contabilidad para inventarios ▲ *allocation of costs to inventories* asignación de costes a inventarios ▲ *an item of inventory that is carried at net realisable value* una partida de inventario que se lleva a valor realizable neto ▲ *book inventory* inventario en libros ▲ *changes in inventories of finished goods and work in progress* cambios en inventarios de bienes terminados y trabajo en curso ▲ *cost of inventories* coste de inventarios ▲ *cost of inventories of a service provider* coste de inventarios de un proveedor de servicios ▲ *costs incurred in bringing the inventories to their present location and condition* costes incurridos al traer los inventarios a su localización y condición actual ▲ *determination of the value of inventories* determinación del valor de los inventarios ▲ *inventories of finished goods and merchandise* inventarios de productos terminados y mercaderías ▲ *inventories of work in progress* inventarios de trabajo en curso ▲ *inventories pledged as security for liabilities* inventarios pignorados como garantía de pasivos ▲ *inventory obsolescence* obsolescencia de inventario ▲ *measurement of inventories* medición de inventarios ▲ *obsolescence allowances on inventories* bonificaciones por obsolescencia en inventarios ▲ *purchase inventories on deferred settlement terms* comprar inventarios en condiciones de liquidación diferida ▲ *the accounting policies adopted in measuring inventories* las políticas contables adoptadas al cuantificar inventarios ▲ *the amount of inventories recognised as an expense during the financial year* la cuantía de inventarios reconocidos como un gasto durante el año ▲ *the carrying amount of inventories* el valor contable de los inventarios ▲ *the carrying amount of inventories carried at fair value less costs to sell* el valor contable de inventarios llevado a valor razonable menos gastos de venta ▲ *the costs of conversion of inventories* los costes de conversión de inventarios ▲ *the effect of technological obsolescence on inventories* el efecto de la obsolescencia técnica en inventarios ▲ *the items of inventory that were produced first* las partidas de inventario que se produjeron primero ▲ *the items remaining in inventory at the end of the period* las partidas que permanecen en inventario al final del periodo ▲ *the sales value of the inventory* el valor de ventas del inventario ▲ *write-downs of inventories to net realisable value* eliminación de inventarios a valor realizable neto

inventory buy back

→ inventory buyback

inventory buyback

An inventory buyback takes place when a producer buys back previously sold goods from the inventories of the distributor.

recompra de inventario

▲ *adjust for inventory buyback* ajuste por recompra de inventario

inventory cost

= carrying cost

Inventory costs are costs incurred by holding stock of materials or products for a particular period, typically from time of receipt to time of use in production or sale. Such costs include e.g. storage, insurance and spoilage.

coste de almacenamiento

▲ *a decrease in inventory costs* un descenso en los costes de almacenamiento ▲ *an increase in inventory costs* un aumento en los costes de almacenamiento ▲ *reduce inventory costs* reducir los costes de almacenamiento

⇛ storage cost

inventory management US

= stock management UK

Inventory management comprises activities such as plan-

ning, coordination and control with a view to maintaining appropriate inventories and handling products in line with inventory targets and service requirements.
gestión de inventarios
▲ *effective inventory management* gestión de inventarios efectiva ▲ *improve inventory management* mejorar la gestión de inventarios ▲ *poor inventory management* gestión de inventarios deficiente

inventory reduction US, IAS/IFRS
Inventory reduction is the decrease of finished goods, work-in-process, merchandise or supplies on hand or in transit at a particular point of time.
reducción de existencias
= reducción de inventarios
▲ *achieve a sustainable inventory reduction* conseguir una reducción de inventarios sostenible ▲ *gain from inventory reduction* beneficio por reducción de existencias

inventory turnover US
= stock turnover UK
Inventory turnover is a financial ratio defined as cost of sales divided by average inventory for an accounting period. This ratio measures the efficiency of inventory control.
rotación de existencias
= rotación de inventarios
▲ *a decrease in inventory turnover* un descenso en la rotación de existencias ▲ *an increase in inventory turnover* un aumento en la rotación de existencias ▲ *calculate inventory turnover* calcular la rotación de existencias

inventory turnover time US, IAS/IFRS
Inventory turnover time refers to the period of time that passes before a given volume of goods is turned over, i.e. sold.
periodo de rotación de existencias
= periodo de rotación de inventarios
▲ *adjusted for inventory turnover time* ajustado por periodo de rotación de existencias ▲ *improve inventory turnover time* mejorar el periodo de rotación de existencias ▲ *shorten the inventory turnover time* acortar el periodo de rotación de existencias

inventory value US, IAS/IFRS
Inventory value refers to either the total financial value of the inventory assets or the financial value of a specified part of the inventory assets.
valor de inventarios
= valor de existencias, valor de los inventarios
▲ *eliminate intercompany profit from the inventory value* eliminar el beneficio intragrupo del valor de inventarios ▲ *inventory value of goods purchased within the group* valor de inventarios de los bienes comprados dentro del grupo ▲ *reverse indirect cost from the inventory value* revertir los costes indirectos del valor de los inventarios

inventory write-down US, IAS/IFRS
An inventory write-down is a write-down of the carrying amount as a consequence of a lower recoverable amount.
eliminación de inventarios
= eliminación de existencias, eliminación de los inventarios
▲ *changes in estimate relating to inventory write-downs* cambios en estimaciones relacionadas con eliminaciones de inventario ▲ *make an inventory write-down* realizar una eliminación de inventarios ▲ *recognise and measure losses from inventory write-downs* reconocer y cuantificar las pérdidas procedentes de eliminaciones de inventarios

invest
To invest is to put money, effort, time etc. into something to make a profit or get an advantage, e.g. by buying securities, such as shares and bonds, or property etc. in order to make a profit or to receive interest, or by purchasing materials, machines etc. to produce goods to sell.
invertir
▲ *invest adequately in the maintenance of the operating capacity* invertir de forma adecuada en el mantenimiento de la capacidad de explotación ▲ *invest in shares* invertir en acciones ▲ *invest long-term* invertir a largo ▲ *invest money in an enterprise* invertir dinero en una empresa ▲ *invest short-term* invertir a corto ▲ *invest time and*

money in a project invertir tiempo y dinero en un proyecto

invested capital

= capital employed

Invested capital is defined from the asset side in the balance sheet as non-current intangible and tangible operating assets plus net working capital or from the liability/equity side as equity plus net interest-bearing debt.

capital invertido

▲ *average invested capital* capital invertido medio ▲ *nominal invested capital* capital invertido nominal ▲ *the purchasing power of invested capital* el poder de compra del capital invertido ▲ *total invested capital* total capital invertido

⇛ working capital

investee

An investee is an enterprise subject to investment by another enterprise, the investor. Following the investment, and depending on whether the investor gains direct or indirect controlling or significant influence in the investee, the investee may be related to the investor as a subsidiary or an associate.

participada

▲ *20% of the voting power of the investee* 20% de los derechos de voto de la participada ▲ *an investee that is accounted for under the equity method* una participada que se contabiliza según el método de participación ▲ *distributions from accumulated profits of the investee* distribuciones de beneficios acumulados de la participada ▲ *distributions received from an investee* distribuciones recibidas de una participada ▲ *material transactions between the investor and the investee* transacciones materiales entre el inversor y la participada ▲ *representation on the board of directors of the investee* representación en el consejo de administración de la participada ▲ *the cash flows between the investor and the investee* los flujos de efectivo entre el inversor y la participada ▲ *the financial and operating decisions of the investee* las decisiones financieras y de explotación de la participada ▲ *the investor's share of net assets of the investee* la participación del inversor en los activos netos de la participada ▲ *the investor's share of the results of operations of the investee* la participación del inversor en los resultados de explotación de la participada

investing activity

Investing activities are activities to acquire or dispose of fixed assets and other long-term investments as well as current investments other than cash equivalents.

actividades de inversión

▲ *be specifically identified with investing activities* estar identificado especialmente con las actividades de inversión ▲ *cash flows from investing activities* flujos de efectivo procedentes de actividades de inversión ▲ *net cash used in investing activities* efectivo neto utilizado en actividades de inversión ▲ *the separate disclosure of cash flows arising from investing activities* la publicación por separado de los flujos de efectivo procedentes de las actividades de inversión

SOURCE IAS 7, paragraph 6

investment

1 = contribution

An investment is a commitment or contribution of money or capital in order to earn a financial return.

inversión

▲ *place an investment* colocar una inversión

2 Investments are fixed assets comprising equity interests in or receivables from group enterprises or associates, other investments and participating interests, other receivables, treasury shares and receivables from owners and management. As an item preceded by a Roman numeral in the balance sheet, "investments" appear under fixed assets, with the above elements presented as subitems.

inversión en empresas del grupo y asociadas

= inversión en las empresas del grupo

▲ *cost of an investment* coste de una inversión en las empresas del grupo y asociadas ▲ *investments and other assets* inversiones en empresas del grupo y asociadas y otros activos

3 = equity interest IAS/IFRS, participating interest UK
An investment is an equity interest held by an enterprise in another entity on a long-term basis, typically in the form of a shareholding, for the purpose of securing a contribution to its activities by the exercise of control or significant influence arising from that investment.
inversión en patrimonio
▲ *a reduction in the investment* una reducción en la inversión en patrimonio ▲ *exercise the voting right attaching to the investment* ejercer el derecho de voto unido a la inversión en patrimonio
4 An investment is the parting of a sum of money with a view to obtaining a return or profit in future.
inversión para negociar
= inversión para operar
▲ *a decline in market value of investments* un descenso en el valor de mercado de las inversiones para negociar ▲ *available-for-sale investments* inversiones para negociar disponibles para la venta ▲ *disposal of subsidiaries and long-term investments* enajenación de filiales e inversiones para negociar a largo plazo ▲ *future investment margins* márgenes en inversión para operar futura ▲ *investments accounted for by applying the equity method* inversiones para negociar contabilizadas aplicando el método de participación ▲ *past acquisitions of investments in associates* adquisiciones pasadas de inversiones para negociar en asociadas ▲ *the carrying amount of the investment* el valor contable de la inversión para negociar ▲ *the investment in the legal subsidiary* la inversión para negociar en la filial legal ▲ *the proceeds on the ultimate disposal of the investment* los productos en la enajenación final de la inversión para negociar

investment asset
An investment asset is an asset held by an enterprise with the purpose of gaining a profit and which is not part of the enterprise's production, administration etc.
activo mantenido para negociar
▲ *measure investment assets at fair value* medición de activos mantenidos para negociar a valor razonable ▲ *net interest from investment assets* interés neto procedente de activos mantenidos para negociar ▲ *reserve for fair value of investment assets* reserva a valor razonable de los activos mantenidos para negociar

investment center US
= investment centre UK
An investment center is a division of an enterprise or a managerial responsibility center focusing on financing and capital expenditure.
centro de inversión
▲ *a decentralised investment center* un centro de inversión descentralizado ▲ *operate as an investment center* operar como un centro de inversión

investment centre UK
= investment center US
An investment centre is a division of an enterprise or a managerial responsibility centre focusing on financing and capital expenditure.
centro de inversión
▲ *a decentralised investment centre* un centro de inversión descentralizado ▲ *operate as an investment centre* operar como un centro de inversión

investment company
1 = investment trust UK
≠ unit trust UK
An investment company is a company that manages funds contributed by its shareholders by reinvesting them in a wide range of securities. This diversification ensures that the investment risk is reduced.
compañía inversora
▲ *a listed investment company* una compañía inversora cotizada ▲ *establish an investment company* establecer una compañía inversora

investment income
Investment income is the part of an insurer's income that comes from the interest and dividends on its investments in financial assets, e.g. equities and government bonds, and the return on any other investment, e.g. property, into which it has put its funds.
ingreso financiero
▲ *estimated investment income* ingreso financiero estimado

▲ *investment income such as interest and dividends* ingresos financieros tales como intereses y dividendos

investment of capital

Investment of capital refers to an enterprise's or person's placement of capital by purchasing assets with the purpose of making a profit. Investment of capital includes investments in e.g. land, buildings, plants, shares and subsidiaries.

inversión de capital

= inversión en capital

▲ *an irreversible investment of capital* una inversión de capital irreversible ▲ *control of large investments of capital* control de grandes inversiones de capital ▲ *investments of capital at year-end* inversiones de capital a final de año

⇛ capital investment

investment policy

An investment policy consists of guidelines and procedures for investment decisions of individuals or enterprises with a view to securing a diversified portfolio or mix of assets that minimises risk and maximises return. An investment policy also outlines general rules for the monitoring and evaluation of investment performance.

política inversora

▲ *a description of the investment policies* una descripción de las políticas inversoras ▲ *a statement of investment policy principles* una declaración de los principios de la política inversora

investment portfolio earnings

Investment portfolio earnings comprise the profits on the proprietary investment portfolios of financial institutions.

beneficios de la cartera de inversión

▲ *an increase in investment portfolio earnings* un aumento en los beneficios de la cartera de inversión

⇛ core earnings

investment property

Investment property is property in the form of land or buildings held with the purpose of obtaining a profit from renting and/or proceeds on sale.

inversión inmobiliaria

= propiedad de inversión

NOTE Spanish accountants prefer 'inversión inmobiliaria' to the IAS/IFRS term 'propiedad de inversión'. This IAS term is nonsensical in Spanish.

▲ *a change in the fair value of investment property* un cambio en el valor razonable de la inversión inmobiliaria ▲ *a sale of investment property from a pool of assets* una venta de la inversión inmobiliaria de una agrupación de activos ▲ *a self-constructed investment property* una inversión inmobiliaria de construcción propia ▲ *acquisition of an investment property* adquisición de una inversión inmobiliaria ▲ *disposal of an investment property* eliminación de una inversión inmobiliaria ▲ *future economic benefits that are associated with the investment property* rendimientos económicos futuros que se asocian con la inversión inmobiliaria ▲ *future use as investment property* uso futuro como inversión inmobiliaria ▲ *hold an investment property* mantener una inversión inmobiliaria ▲ *investment property held under a finance lease* inversión inmobiliaria mantenida bajo un arrendamiento financiero ▲ *investment property leased out under an operating lease* inversión inmobiliaria arrendada de acuerdo con un arrendamiento operativo ▲ *investment property linked to liabilities* inversión inmobiliaria unida a pasivos ▲ *lease income on investment property* ingreso por alquiler en inversión inmobiliaria ▲ *measure investment property using the depreciated cost model* cuantificar la inversión inmobiliaria según el modelo del coste amortizado ▲ *measure investment property using the fair value model* medir la inversión inmobiliaria usando el modelo del valor razonable ▲ *property constructed for future use as investment property* edificio construido para uso futuro como inversión inmobiliaria ▲ *qualify as investment property* calificar como inversión inmobiliaria ▲ *synergies between investment property and other assets* sinergías entre la inversión inmobiliaria y otros activos ▲ *the accounting treatment of investment property* el tratamiento contable de la inversión inmobiliaria ▲ *the cost of a purchased investment property* el coste de una inversión inmobiliaria adquirida ▲ *the fair value of an investment property* el valor razonable de una inversión inmobiliaria ▲ *the investment property owner* el propietario de la inversión inmobiliaria ▲ *the nature and characteristics of the investment property* la naturaleza y características de la inversión inmobiliaria ▲ *the present owner of an investment property* el propietario actual de una inversión inmobiliaria ▲ *the residual value of the investment property* el valor residual de la inversión inmobiliaria ▲ *transfer a property from investment property to inventories* transferir un edificio de inversión inmobiliaria a existencias ▲ *transfer from investment property to owner-occupied property* transferir de la inversión inmobiliaria a propiedad de uso propio ▲ *work on an investment property* trabajar en una inversión inmobiliaria

investment return

= investment yield

Investment return is the income on a current basis, e.g. interest and dividends, or the gain on disposal arising from an investment.

rendimiento de la inversión

▲ *investment return for the year* el rendimiento de la inversión para el año ▲ *realised investment returns on a specified pool of assets* rendimientos de la inversión realizados en un conjunto especificado de activos ▲ *together with investment return* junto con el rendimiento de la inversión

investment security

≠ trading security

Investment securities are securities held to maturity rather than for trading and invested for a long term. Examples of investment securities are shares and bonds. In the balance sheet, investment securities are recognised under fixed assets as e.g. financial assets available for sale.

valores de inversión

= cartera de títulos, valores de cartera

▲ *acquisition of investment securities* adquisición de valores de inversión ▲ *disposals of investment securities* enajenaciones de valores de inversión ▲ *gains less losses arising from investment securities* ganancias menos pérdidas procedentes de valores de inversión ▲ *interest income from investment securities* ingresos por intereses procedentes de valores de inversión ▲ *issue an investment security* emitir una cartera de títulos ▲ *rights to investment securities* derechos a valores de inversión

investment trust UK

= investment company

≠ unit trust UK

An investment trust is a company that manages funds contributed by its shareholders by reinvesting them in a wide range of securities. This diversification ensures that the investment risk is reduced.

sociedad de inversión mobiliaria

▲ *establish an investment trust* establecer una sociedad de inversión mobiliaria ▲ *the regulation of investment trusts* la regulación de las sociedades de inversión mobiliaria

investment yield

Investment yield is the return on an investment defined as net income as a percentage of capital value. Examples of investment yields are the dividend yield on a share, i.e. the current dividend as a percentage of the market price, and the bond yield, i.e. the interest on a fixed-rate security as a percentage of the market price.

rentabilidad de la inversión

= rendimiento de la inversión

▲ *a slight increase in the average investment yield* un aumento ligero en la rentabilidad de la inversión media ▲ *calculate the investment yield on bonds* calcular la rentabilidad de la inversión en los bonos ▲ *market-based investment yield* rentabilidad de la inversión basada en el mercado

⇛ investment return

investments in associates IAS/IFRS

"Investments in associates" is an item under non-current as-

sets in the balance sheet referring to equity interests held by a group in associated enterprises. Typically, such investments are recognised at the equity or net asset value of the investees they represent.
inversiones en asociadas
▲ *investments in associates accounted for using the equity method* inversiones en asociadas contabilizadas usando el método de patrimonio neto

investor
An investor is a person, enterprise or association that has made investments in a project in order to make a profit.
inversor
= inversora
NOTE The feminine term 'inversora' can designate a woman investor or a legal entity.
▲ *a potential investor* un inversor potencial ▲ *a present investor* un inversor actual ▲ *a private investor* un inversor privado ▲ *a professional investor* un inversor profesional ▲ *a retail investor* una inversora minorista ▲ *an active investor* un inversor activo ▲ *an institutional investor* un inversor institucional ▲ *equal treatment of investors* tratamiento igualitario de los inversores ▲ *investor events* sucesos del inversor ▲ *investor in a joint venture* inversora en una joint venture ▲ *material transactions between the investor and the investee* transacciones materiales entre la inversora y la participada ▲ *protect the long-term interests of investors* proteger los intereses a largo plazo de los inversores ▲ *recognise directly in the equity of the investor* reconocer directamente en el patrimonio de la inversora ▲ *the income earned by an investor on an investment in an associate* el ingreso devengado por una inversora en una inversión en una asociada ▲ *the information needs of investors* las necesidades de información de los inversores ▲ *the investor entity* la entidad inversora ▲ *the investor's debt or equity instruments* deuda o instrumentos de patrimonio del inversor ▲ *the investor's share of any discontinued operations of associates* la participación de la inversora en cualesquiera operaciones interrumpidas en asociadas ▲ *the investor's share of net assets of the investee* la participación de la inversora en activos netos de la participada ▲ *the investor's share of the profit or loss of the investee* la participación de la inversora en el resultado de la participada ▲ *the profit or loss of the investor* el resultado del inversor ▲ *the ultimate or any intermediate parent of the investor* la matriz última o cualquier intermedia de la inversora

investor information
Investor information is information that is relevant to existing and potential investors, such as historical and current performance indicators, share prices, dividends, a planned raising of new capital, the number of existing investors etc.
información para el inversor
= información para los inversores
▲ *the latest investor information* la información para el inversor más reciente

investor-oriented
If an enterprise is investor-oriented the principal stakeholder is its investors, and the information it releases is made particularly relevant to this group of stakeholders.
orientado al inversor
= orientado a los inversores
▲ *an investor-oriented income statement* una cuenta de resultados orientada al inversor ▲ *an investor-oriented statement* un comunicado orientado a los inversores ▲ *investor-oriented financial and operating data* datos financieros y de explotación orientados al inversor ▲ *investor-oriented financial ratios* ratios financieros orientados al inversor

investor-related
If something is investor-related it is addressed to investors.
relativo al inversor
= relativo a los inversores
▲ *investor-related activities* actividades relativas al inversor ▲ *investor-related financial and operating data* datos financieros y de explotación relativos al inversor ▲ *investor-related information* información relativa a los inversores

invoice[1] *noun*
= bill US
An invoice is a basic document issued by the seller to his customer specifying the goods delivered or services provided, the price charged as well as amount, quality and terms of payment and delivery.
factura
▲ *a receipted invoice* una factura con comprobante ▲ *according to invoice* de acuerdo con la factura ▲ *an invoice for EUR 100* una factura por 100 euros ▲ *consignment invoice* factura dudosa ▲ *invoice date* fecha de la factura ▲ *invoice discounting* factura al descuento ▲ *invoice price* importe de la factura ▲ *invoice value* valor de la factura ▲ *make out an invoice* facturar ▲ *pro-forma invoice* factura pro-forma ▲ *the original invoice amount* la cantidad de la factura original

invoice[2] *verb*
= bill US
To invoice means to prepare an invoice for goods delivered or services provided and send it to a customer.
facturar
▲ *invoice a product* facturar un producto ▲ *invoice in EUR* facturar en euros ▲ *invoice in foreign currency* facturar en divisa extranjera ▲ *invoice sales* facturar ventas ▲ *invoice the customer* facturar al cliente

invoice discounting
Invoice discounting means that an by assigning its sales invoices to a factoring company or invoice discounter, an enterprise can borrow typically 80-90% of its outstanding trade receivables, in this way receiving immediate cash payment. Against a service and a finance charge, the factoring company will administer the collection of the debit balances and when the total outstanding balance has been paid, the enterprise will receive the remaining amount due less the charges.
factura al descuento
▲ *proceeds from invoice discounting* ingresos de factura al descuento

invoiced
= billed US
When something has been invoiced, an invoice has been prepared for it.
facturado
▲ *an invoiced amount* una cantidad facturada ▲ *an invoiced price* un precio facturado ▲ *invoiced expenses* gastos facturados ▲ *invoiced income* ingresos facturados ▲ *invoiced sales for the year* ventas facturadas al año ▲ *the recent acquisition of inventories invoiced in a foreign currency* la adquisición reciente de existencias facturadas en una moneda extranjera

invoicing
Invoicing is the process of preparing invoices for goods delivered or services provided.
facturación
▲ *invoicing department* departamento de facturación ▲ *invoicing of orders* facturación de pedidos ▲ *ready for invoicing* preparado para facturación

invoicing currency
= invoice currency
The currency in which goods or services are denominated and charged in an invoice is called the invoicing currency.
moneda de facturación
▲ *exchange rates of invoicing currencies* tipos de cambio de las monedas de facturación

invoicing on account UK
Invoicing on account implies the invoicing of an amount to be paid on account i.e. as part payment or advance payment of an outstanding amount.
facturación a cuenta
▲ *compare against invoicing on account up to the balance sheet date* comparar frente a la facturación a cuenta hasta la fecha del balance

involve
Involve means to take part in something.
involucrar
= implicar, implicarse, involucrarse
▲ *entities involved in the purchase and sale of unique intangible assets* entidades involucradas en la compraventa de activos intangibles únicos ▲ *involve a qualified actuary in the measurement of all material post-employment benefit obligations* involucrar a un actuario cualificado en la valoración de todas las obligaciones materiales por prestaciones de jubilación ▲ *involve judgements based on*

the latest information available involucrarse en opiniones basadas en la última información disponible

involvement

Involvement means the taking part in something.

participación

▲ *continuing involvement in transferred assets* participación continuada de activos transferidos ▲ *recognise the asset to the extent of the entity's continuing involvement* reconocer el activo hasta la participación continuada de la entidad ▲ *the application of the continuing involvement approach* la aplicación del enfoque de la participación continuada ▲ *the involvement of external assistance* la participación de la asistencia externa

IPO US

= flotation UK, initial public offering US

IPO is the abbreviation for initial public offering, i.e. a company's first offering of shares to the public. Usually an investment bank will assist the company with the IPO and may underwrite the share offering. After the IPO, the shares will be publicly traded on a stock exchange, giving the issuing company the advantage of access to a market for additional capital and providing the shares with a fair market value.

oferta pública inicial

▲ *a successful IPO* una oferta pública inicial ▲ *complete an IPO* completar una oferta pública inicial

IPR&D

IPR&D is the abbreviation for in-process research and development, which refers to research and developmemt projects that have not been completed.

desarrollo e investigación en curso

▲ *accounting for IPR&D* contabilizando el desarrollo e investigación en curso ▲ *excessive IPR&D write-offs* amortizaciones excesivas de desarrollo e investigación en curso ▲ *the acquisition of IPR&D* la adquisición de desarrollo e investigación en curso

IRR

IRR is the abbreviation for internal rate of return, i.e. the interest rate or discount factor at which the net present values of the total discounted cash inflows (the return) of an investment project and the total discounted cash outflows (the cost) equals zero. The project is acceptable if the internal rate of return is positive, i.e. equal to or higher than the required rate of return (the hurdle rate).

TIR

▲ *an IRR of 20%* un TIR del 20% ▲ *compute the liability's IRR* calcular el TIR del pasivo

irreversible

When something is irreversible it is impossible to bring it back to its former condition.

irreversible

▲ *irreversible investments of capital* inversiones de capital irreversibles ▲ *make an irreversible decision* tomar una decisión irreversible

IRS US

IRS is the abbreviation for the Internal Revenue Service, i.e. the US federal tax authorities.

IRS

= agencia tributaria

▲ *submit forms electronically to the IRS* remitir los formularios electrónicamente a la IRS ▲ *the objectives of IRS* los objetivos de la IRS

ISA

1 = International Standard on Auditing IAS/IFRS

ISA is an abbreviation for International Standard on Auditing. The International Standards on Auditing are standards laying down, on an international basis, the basic principles for the scope and procedures that auditors must follow when performing audits of financial reports and statements. The International Standards on Auditing (ISA) have been issued by the International Auditing and Assurance Standards Board (IAASB) under the International Federation of Accountants (IFAC).

NIA

= Norma Internacional de Auditoría

▲ *a draft ISA* un borrador NIA ▲ *issue a revised ISA* emitir una NIA revisada

2 = Individual Savings Account UK

ISA is an abbreviation for Individual Savings Account, a

tax efficient savings account introduced by the UK Government that offers savers tax relief through holding savings invested in cash deposits, shares or life insurance products or a combination of all three types of asset.

cuenta de ahorro individual

▲ *an ISA made up of an investment in shares* una cuenta de ahorro individual compuesta de una inversión en acciones ▲ *transfer an ISA to another bank* transferir una cuenta de ahorro individual a otro banco

issuance

Issuance is the process of making securities available to the public, so that people can buy the securities.

emisión

▲ *issuance of ordinary shares* emisión de acciones ordinarias ▲ *issuances of debt and equity securities* emisiones de deuda y títulos de patrimonio ▲ *shares reserved for issuance under options and sales contracts* acciones reservadas para emisión como opciones y contratos de ventas

issue[1] *noun*

An issue is the process of making securities available to the public, so that people can buy the securities.

emisión

▲ *a fully subscribed issue* una emisión suscrita completamente ▲ *an integral part of the liability issue transaction* una parte integral de la transacción de la emisión de pasivo ▲ *at the time of issue* en el momento de la emisión ▲ *costs that are directly attributable to the issue of a financial asset or financial liability* costes que son directamente atribuibles a la emisión de un activo o pasivo financiero ▲ *issue costs* costes de emisión ▲ *the proceeds from the equity issue* los ingresos procedentes de la emisión de títulos

issue[2] *verb*

To issue means to make securities available to the public, so that people can buy the securities.

emitir

▲ *issue convertible and profit-sharing debt instruments* emitir instrumentos de deuda que devengan intereses convertibles ▲ *issue insurance contracts* emitir contratos de seguros ▲ *issue share options* emitir opciones sobre acciones ▲ *issue shares* emitir acciones ▲ *issue warrants* emitir warrants ▲ *product warranties issued directly by a manufacturer* garantías de productos emitidas directamente por un fabricante ▲ *the entity that issues the equity interests* la entidad que emite las participaciones en el capital

issue date

= date of issue, time of issue

The issue date is the date on which shares, debt instruments, options, warrants, convertible bonds etc. are isusued.

fecha de emisión

= fecha de la emisión

▲ *discount or premium at the issue date* descuento o prima a la fecha de emisión ▲ *mature 25 years from the issue date* vencimiento a los 25 años de la fecha de emisión ▲ *the fair value at the issue date* el valor razonable a la fecha de emisión ▲ *the market price at the issue date* el precio de mercado a la fecha de emisión

issue of bonus shares UK

= scrip issue

An issue of bonus shares is the act of increasing a company's issued capital by issuing additional share certificates for free to its existing shareholders in proportion to their shareholdings, in this way converting accumulated reserves into issued share capital. However, no additional capital is contributed and total equity remains the same; the effect is a reduction of the share price that increases the liquidity of the company's shares in the stock market.

emisión de acciones gratuitas

= emisión de acciones liberadas

▲ *approve the issue of bonus shares* aprobar la emisión de acciones gratuitas ▲ *recommend an issue of bonus shares* recomendar una emisión de acciones gratuitas

issue of shares

= share issue

An issue of shares is the process of making shares available to the public, so that people can buy the shares.

emisión de acciones

▲ *a business combination effected by the issue of shares* una combinación de negocios efectuada mediante la emisión de acciones ▲ *an issue of shares for cash* una emisión de acciones en efectivo ▲ *proceeds received from the issue of shares at fair value* ingresos recibidos de la emisión de acciones a valor razonable

issue price

The issue price is the price of a financial security, such as a share, bond and option, at the date on which it is issued.

precio de emisión

= precio de la emisión

▲ *financial instruments measured on the basis of issue prices* instrumentos financieros medidos a los precios de emisión ▲ *justification of the issue price* justificación del precio de la emisión ▲ *less the issue price* menos el precio de emisión

issued capital

The issued capital of a company is that part of its authorised capital that has actually been issued to shareholders.

capital emitido

▲ *issued capital and reserves attributable to equity holders of the parent* capital emitido y reservas atribuibles a los accionistas de la matriz

⇛ authorised capital, outstanding share, own share

issued share capital

→ issued capital

issuer

An issuer is a legal entity that issues securities, e.g. shares, bonds or derivative financial instruments. Issuers include companies, government entities and investment companies.

emisor

▲ *a contract that exposes the issuer to financial risk* un contrato que expone al emisor a riesgos financieros ▲ *a financial asset that is callable by the issuer* un activo financiero que es exigible por el emisor ▲ *a significant deterioration in the issuer's creditworthiness* un empeoramiento significativo de la solvencia del emisor ▲ *an issuer of a commitment to provide a loan* un emisor de un compromiso para conceder un préstamo ▲ *an issuer of secrurities* un emisor de títulos ▲ *circumstances that are beyond the control of the issuer* circunstancias que se escapan al control del emisor ▲ *on the application of an issuer* en la aplicación de un emisor ▲ *realised investment returns on a specified pool of assets held by the issuer* rendimientos por inversiones realizadas en una combinación específica de activos mantenidos por el emisor ▲ *significant financial difficulty of the issuer* dificultad financiera significativa del emisor ▲ *the legal environment in which the issuer operates* el marco legal en el que opera el emisor

IT audit

= information systems audit, information technology audit

An IT audit is typically an internal audit involving the application of various audit procedures to examine the extent to which the information systems of an enterprise supports its management and financial reporting as well as the information security and IT capacity of the enterprise.

auditoría de los Sistemas de Información

▲ *carry out an IT audit* llevar a cabo una auditoría de los Sistemas de Información ▲ *planning of the IT audit* planificar la auditoría de los Sistemas de Información ▲ *the results of the IT audit* los resultados de la auditoría de los Sistemas de Información

IT capital

IT capital constitutes capital expenditure within the information technology area e.g. communications equipment such as hardware, software, photocopiers and other computer equipment.

inversión en tecnologías de la información

▲ *IT capital investments* inversiones en tecnologías de la información

IT cost

IT costs are expenses incurred that relate to the purchase, maintenance and upgrades of IT equipment such as computers, servers, photocopiers, hardware and software as well as to wages for and training of IT staff.

coste de equipos informáticos

= coste de los equipos de informática

▲ *to slim IT costs* disminuir los costes de los equipos informáticos

item

An item is an entry recognised in the accounting system of an enterprise recording the amount of e.g. an asset, a liability and a financial transaction.

partida

= rúbrica

▲ *a financial item* una partida financiera ▲ *a foreign currency monetary item* una partida monetaria en divisa ▲ *a non-monetary item* una rúbrica no monetaria ▲ *a recognised item* una partida reconocida ▲ *a separate item* una partida separada ▲ *add an item* añadir una partida ▲ *aggregate items* sumar partidas ▲ *an aggregate of items* una suma de partidas ▲ *an extraordinary item* una partida extraordinaria ▲ *any other items* cualesquiera otras partidas ▲ *changes in an item* cambios en una partida ▲ *comparable with the items of the previous year* comparable con las partidas del año anterior ▲ *eligible items* partidas elegibles ▲ *eliminate an item* eliminar una partida ▲ *include an amount directly in an item* incluir una cantidad directamente en una partida ▲ *items below the bottom line* partidas no incluidas en la determinación del beneficio neto ▲ *items in the balance sheet* partidas en el balance ▲ *items in the income statement* partidas en la cuenta de resultados ▲ *items preceded by Arabic numerals* partidas precedidas de números arábigos ▲ *measurement of the elements of the items under equity and liabilities* valoración de los elementos de las partidas debajo de patrimonio neto y pasivos ▲ *state the items separately* anotar las partidas por separado ▲ *the item's underlying substance and economic reality* la naturaleza subyacente y realidad económica de la partida ▲ *unusual items* partidas inusuales

item of expense

= expense item

An item of expense is an item in the income statement that records the amount of a particular expense or cost incurred during the accounting period.

partida de gasto

= partida de gastos

▲ *a main category of items of expense* una categoría principal de partidas de gasto ▲ *all items of expense recognised* todas las partidas de gasto reconocidas ▲ *material items of expense* partidas materiales de gasto

item of income

= income item, revenue item

An item of income is an item in the income statement that records an amount of income generated or earned during the accounting period.

partida de ingreso

= partida de ingresos

▲ *a main category of items of income* una categoría principal de partidas de ingresos ▲ *all items of income recognised* todas las partidas de ingresos reconocidas ▲ *material items of income* partidas materiales de ingresos

item preceded by a Roman numeral

Items preceded by Roman numerals are the items in the balance sheet format marked by Roman numerals, such as intangible assets, tangible assets or investments. These items are sub-items below the principal items, such as fixed assets or current assets, but items above the items preceded by Arabic numerals, such as land and buildings or stocks.

partida precedida por un número romano

▲ *a separate item preceded by a Roman numeral* una partida separada precedida por un número romano

item preceded by an Arabic numeral

Items preceded by Arabic numerals are the lowest-ranking items in the balance sheet format placed below the items preceded by Roman numerals and the principal items. For instance, in the profit and loss account format, the items preceded by Arabic numerals constitute the main items such as turnover, cost of sales, gross profit or loss, operating profit or loss, and profit or loss for the financial year. This applies to the accounts formats required in the UK Companies Act and the Danish Financial Statements Act.

partida precedida por un número arábigo
▲ *a separate item preceded by an Arabic numeral* una partida separada precedida por un número arábigo

item under equity and liabilities
Items under equity and liabilities are the items recognised in the credit side of the balance sheet when presented in the horizontal format.
partida incluida en la columna de patrimonio neto y pasivo
▲ *measurement of the elements of the items under equity and liabilities* medición de los elementos de las partidas incluidas en la columna de patrimonio neto y pasivo

item under financial income and expenses, net
Items under financial income and expenses, net, are accounting items that record interest receivable and payable as well as other income or charges relating to investment and borrowings. In the profit and loss account, the items are aggregated and referred to as "financial income and expenses, net".
partida incluida en la columna de ingresos y gastos

itemised statement
= specification
An itemised statement is a list or record detailing each item included. Examples of itemised statements are price lists, invoices and statements of accounts or costs.
lista detallada de partidas
▲ *an itemised statement of proposed expenditures and estimated revenues* una lista detallada de partidas de gastos propuestos e ingresos estimados ▲ *an itemised statement that lists the total assets and the total liabilities* una lista detallada de partidas que enumera los activos y pasivos totales

J

Japanese Institute of Certified Public Accountants
= JICPA
The Japanese Institute of Certified Public Accountants (JICPA) is the professional accountancy body in Japan. The JICPA issues recommendations on accounting matters. Together with 9 other private-sector accountancy organisations, the JICPA established a private-sector standard-setting authority in 2001, the Financial Accounting Standards Foundation, partly with a view to liaising with the IASB, and partly to transfer rule-making from the public to the private sector and converge Japanese accounting practice towards international practice.
Japanese Institute of Certified Public Accountants
= Instituto Japonés de Auditores de Cuentas
▲ *become a member of the Japanese Institute of Certified Public Accountants* ser miembro del Japanese Institute of Certified Public Accountants ▲ *the major activities of the Japanese Institute of Certified Public Accountants* las actividades principales del Japanese Institute of Certified Public Accountants
⇛ IASB

JIT US,UK
= just-in-time UK, US
JIT is the abbreviation for just-in-time. A just-in-time system is an inventory or production system responding to demand under the JIT philosophy that products are delivered only when required, and units produced or materials ordered on an as-needed basis. In this way stock levels are kept to a minimum, waste is eliminated and inventory investment cut down.
JIT
= just-in-time, justo a tiempo
▲ *JIT production* producción JIT ▲ *JIT supplies* abastecimientos JIT
⇛ kanban

JIT philosophy UK, US
= just-in-time philosophy UK, US
The JIT philosophy is a philosophy to eliminate waste by reducing and eliminating production process time, inventories and time spent on activities that do not add value.
filosofía JIT
= filosofía just-in-time
▲ *the Japanese JIT philosophy* la filosofía japonesa JIT

job
1 A job is the paid work an employee carries out for an employer.
trabajo
= empleo
▲ *job creation scheme* plan de creación de empleo ▲ *job description* descripción del empleo ▲ *job enlargement* ampliación de trabajo ▲ *job enrichment* enriquecimiento laboral ▲ *job security* seguridad laboral ▲ *on the job* en el trabajo
2 A job is an order, a specific task or operation of an enterprise, such as the production of a unit or a series of a product or service.
trabajo
= empleo
▲ *job order* orden de trabajo ▲ *job shop* job shop

job card UK
= labor time ticket US
≠ clock card UK, time card UK
A job card is a card or computer printout that specifies the work to be performed on a particular job. Apart from the job instructions, the card may also record the time to be spent on the job.
tarjeta laboral
▲ *record on a job card* anotar en la tarjeta laboral ▲ *write something on the job card* escribir algo en la tarjeta laboral

job costing
= job-order costing
Job costing is a method for attributing costs to a specific order, operation or job.
sistema de coste por obra o servicio
▲ *internal controls for job costing* controles internos para el sistema de coste por obra o servicio

job record
→ job-cost record

job sheet
→ job-cost sheet

job shop
= job shop production
A job shop is a production process which has different manufacturing processes and handles different batches for each production order. Examples are semi-manufactures and products in the car and electronic components industries.
producción discontinua
= job shop
▲ *job shop costs* costes de producción discontinua ▲ *job shop expenses* gastos de producción discontinua

job shop production
= job shop
Job shop production is a production process which has different manufacturing processes and handles different batches for each production order. Examples are semi-manufactures and products in the car and electronic components industries.
producción discontinua
= job shop, producción job shop
▲ *control job shop production* controlar la producción discontinua ▲ *job shop production of prototype components* producción discontinua de componentes de prototipos

job-cost record
= job record, job sheet, job-cost sheet
A job-cost record is a document in which all costs assigned to an individual job are accumulated from the time the job begins until it is completed.
ficha de coste por obra o servicio
▲ *the job cost record for Job 494* la ficha de coste por obra o servicio para el Trabajo 494

job-cost sheet
= job record, job sheet, job-cost record
A job-cost sheet is a record in which all costs assigned to an individual job are accumulated from the time the job begins until it is completed.
listado de fichas de coste por obra o servicio
▲ *enter on the job-cost sheet* entrar en el listado de fichas de coste por obra o servicio

job-costing system
→ job costing

job-order costing
= job costing
Job-order costing is a method for attributing costs to a specific order, operation, job or batch.
sistema de coste por obra, servicio o pedido
▲ *the flow of costs in job-order costing* el flujo de costes en un sistema de coste por obra, servicio o pedido ▲ *the source documents used in job-order costing* los documentos fuente utilizados en el sistema de coste por obra, servicio o pedido
⇛ hybrid costing system

joint and opening balance sheets
= joint balance sheet for the merger
≠ demerger accounts
Joint and opening balance sheets, i.e. the joint balance sheets of the merging, or combining, enterprises and the opening balance sheet of the continuing enterprise, must be presented in connection with a merger.
balances de fusión y apertura
▲ *fair value joint and opening balance sheets* balances de fusión y apertura a valor razonable ▲ *prepare joint and opening balance sheets* preparar los balances de fusión y apertura

joint control
Joint control refers to a situation where two or more enterprises share the control over specified economic activities pursuant to a contractual agreement to form a joint venture.
control conjunto
▲ *establish joint control over the joint venture* establecer el control conjunto sobre la joint venture ▲ *have joint control over the entity* tener el control conjunto de la entidad ▲ *the date on which the venturer ceases to have joint control over a jointly controlled entity* la fecha en la que el participante en un negocio conjunto deja de tener el control conjunto ▲ *two venturers that share joint control* dos participantes en un negocio conjunto que comparten el control conjunto ▲ *undertake*

an economic activity that is subject to joint control emprender una actividad económica supeditada al control conjunto

joint costs

Joint costs refer to the costs incurred in joint production until the split-off point where the individual products are separated from each other.

costes conjuntos

▲ *allocation of joint costs* distribución de los costes conjuntos ▲ *restrict joint costs* restringir los costes conjuntos ▲ *the joint costs incurred* los costes conjuntos incurridos

⇛ joint production, separable costs, split-off point

joint production

Joint production is production where a single production process results in the simultaneous manufacturing of multiple products. Examples of industries with joint production processes are the food processing, semiconductor and chemical industries.

producción conjunta

▲ *joint production under uncertainty* producción conjunta bajo incertidumbre ▲ *Nash equilibrium of joint production* equilibrio 'Nash' de producción conjunta

⇛ by-product, joint products, main product, split-off point

joint products

Joint products constitute the output from joint production in the form of two or more products with high or limited sales values. Joint products with high sales values are referred to as main products, whereas joint products with positive, but limited, i.e. relatively insignificant sales values constitute by-products. Joint products can only be identified as separate products after the split-off point.

productos conjuntos

▲ *accounting for joint products* contabilizando los productos conjuntos ▲ *allocate common costs to joint products* asignar los costes comunes a los productos conjuntos ▲ *development of joint products* desarrollo de productos conjuntos

⇛ by-product, joint production, main product, split-off point

joint venture

= venture

A joint venture is a strategic contractual agreement between two or more enterprises to jointly undertake specified economic activities. The enterprises jointly control the activities and share risks, profits and losses. A joint venture is typically a short-term relationship relating to one purpose, but it may also be a long-term cooperation or even established as a separate legal entity (jointly controlled enterprise).

joint venture

= negocio conjunto

NOTE Spanish accountants prefer 'joint venture' to the IAS/IFRS term 'negocio conjunto'.

▲ *capital commitments of the venturer in relation to its interests in joint ventures* acuerdos de capital del participante en un negocio conjunto en relación a sus inversiones en joint ventures ▲ *carry out the joint venture activities* llevar a cabo las actividades de la joint venture ▲ *different forms of joint venture* diferentes formas de joint venture ▲ *establish joint control over the joint venture* establecer el control conjunto sobre la joint venture ▲ *form a joint venture* formar una joint venture ▲ *interests in joint ventures* inversiones en joint ventures ▲ *joint ventures in which the entity is a venturer* joint ventures en la que la entidad es una empresa de capital riesgo ▲ *joint ventures of a limited temporal extent* joint ventures de duración temporal limitada ▲ *operators of joint ventures* operaciones de joint ventures ▲ *share of the profit or loss of joint ventures* participar de los resultados de la joint venture ▲ *the activity, duration and reporting obligations of the joint venture* la actividad, duración y obligaciones de información de la joint venture ▲ *the articles or other by-laws of the joint venture* los artículos u otros estatutos de la joint venture ▲ *the board of directors or equivalent governing body of the joint venture* el consejo de administración u órgano de gobierno equivalente de la joint venture

▲ *the joint venture agreement* el acuerdo de joint venture ▲ *the operator or manager of the joint venture* el operador o gestor de la joint venture ▲ *the substance, economic reality and legal form of the joint venture* la naturaleza, realidad económica y forma legal de la joint venture ▲ *transactions between a venturer and a joint venture* transacciones entre una empresa de capital riesgo y una joint venture
⇛ joint control, venturer

joint venture entity
= jointly controlled enterprise
A joint venture entity is an enterprise that is managed jointly and which has been established with the purpose of cooperation. Thus, the participating enterprises in a joint venture entity will often utilize each other's complementary advantages.
entidad en joint venture
= empresa controlada conjuntamente, empresa controlada de forma conjunta
▲ *a 50% participation interest in the joint venture entity* un 50% de participación en la entidad en joint venture ▲ *the entity's share of profits or losses of the joint venture entity* el porcentaje de beneficios o pérdidas de la entidad en joint venture ▲ *the net assets of the joint venture entity* los activos netos de la entidad en joint venture

jointly controlled asset
Jointly controlled assets refer to assets that are jointly owned and controlled by the parties in a joint venture where the joint venture has not been established as a separate legal entity.
activo controlado de forma conjunta
= activo controlado conjuntamente
▲ *the interest in jointly controlled assets* el interés en activos controlados de forma conjunta ▲ *the treatment of jointly controlled assets* el tratamiento de los activos controlados de forma conjunta ▲ *the venturer's share of the jointly controlled asset* la parte de la operación conjunta del activo controlado de forma conjunta ▲ *transfer a jointly controlled asset into a jointly controlled entity* transferir un activo controlado de forma conjunta a una entidad controlada de forma conjunta
⇛ joint venture, jointly controlled operation

jointly controlled enterprise
= jointly controlled entity
A jointly controlled enterprise is a joint venture enterprise, i.e. an enterprise in which two or more venture parties have interests. Pursuant to a contractual agreement, the parties jointly control the economic activities of the enterprise.
empresa controlada de forma conjunta
= empresa controlada conjuntamente, empresa en joint venture
▲ *the company's investment in a jointly controlled enterprise* la inversión de la empresa en una empresa de joint venture ▲ *the company's proportionate share of the jointly controlled enterprise's revenues* la participación proporcional de la empresa en los ingresos de la empresa controlada de forma conjunta
⇛ venturer

jointly controlled entity
= jointly controlled enterprise
A jointly controlled entity is a joint venture entity, i.e. a legal entity in which two or more venture parties have interests. Pursuant to a contractual agreement, the parties jointly control the economic activities of the entity.
entidad controlada de forma conjunta
= entidad controlada conjuntamente, entidad de joint venture
▲ *a venturer with an interest in a jointly controlled entity* un participante en un negocio conjunto con una inversión en una entidad controlada de forma conjunta ▲ *a venturer's share of each of the assets of a jointly controlled entity* una participación del participante en un negocio conjunto en cada uno de los activos de una entidad controlada de forma conjunta ▲ *an interest in a jointly controlled entity* una inversión en una entidad controlada de forma conjunta ▲ *goodwill arising from an interest in a jointly controlled entity* fondo de comercio resultante en una participación en

una entidad controlada de forma conjunta ▲ *investments in jointly controlled entities* inversiones en entidades controladas de forma conjunta ▲ *the date on which the venturer ceases to have joint control over a jointly controlled entity* la fecha en la que el participante en un negocio conjunto deja de tener control conjunto sobre la entidad controlada de forma conjunta ▲ *the venturer's share of net assets of the jointly controlled entity* participación de activos netos de la entidad controlada de forma conjunta por parte del participante en un negocio conjunto ▲ *the venturer's share of the profit or loss of the jointly controlled entity* la participación del participante en un negocio conjunto en los resultados de la entidad controlada de forma conjunta ▲ *transfer a jointly controlled asset into a jointly controlled entity* traspasar un activo controlado conjuntamente a una empresa de joint venture
⇛ joint venture, venturer

jointly controlled operation
Jointly controlled operations refer to the economic activities undertaken by the parties in a joint venture where the joint venture has not been established as a separate legal entity.
operación controlada conjuntamente
= operación controlada de forma conjunta
▲ *the interests in jointly controlled operations* los intereses en las operaciones controladas conjuntamente
⇛ joint venture, jointly controlled asset, venturer

journal
= day book
A journal is a book of account into which transactions are chronologically recorded in double debit and credit entries before being posted to the ledger accounts.
diario
▲ *make an entry in a journal* anotar una entrada en un diario ▲ *record a transaction in a journal* anotar una transacción en un diario
⇛ journal entry, ledger

journal entry
A journal entry is a record of a transaction made in a journal as a credit or a debit entry. Journal entries are next transferred to and posted in a ledger.
entrada en el diario
▲ *make a journal entry* anotar una entrada en el diario
⇛ journal, ledger

just-in-time UK, US
= JIT UK, US
Just-in-time means at the exact time on an as-needed basis and refers to the just-in-time system, which is an inventory or production system responding to demand under the JIT philosophy that products are delivered only when required, and units produced or materials ordered on an as-needed basis. In this way stock levels are kept to a minimum, waste is eliminated and inventory investment cut down.
just-in-time
= JIT, justo a tiempo
▲ *just-in-time data analysis* análisis de datos just-in-time ▲ *just-in-time deliveries* envíos just-in-time ▲ *just-in-time production* producción just-in-time ▲ *just-in-time training* formación just-in-time
⇛ just-in-time inventory system, just-in-time production system, just-in-time system, kanban

just-in-time inventory control system UK, US
→ just-in-time inventory system

just-in-time inventory system UK, US
= just-in-time inventory control system UK, US
A just-in-time inventory system is a demand-pull system responding to demand under the JIT philosophy that products are delivered only when required, and units produced or materials ordered on an as-needed basis. In this way stock levels are kept to a minimum, waste is eliminated and inventory investment cut down.
sistema de inventarios just-in-time
= sistema de inventarios JIT, sistema de inventarios justo a tiempo
▲ *implement a just-in-time inventory system* implementar un sistema de inventarios just-in-

time ▲ *switch to a just-in-time inventory system* cambiarse a un sistema de inventarios just-in-time
⇛ just-in-time, just-in-time production system

just-in-time manufacturing
→ just-in-time production

just-in-time philosophy UK, US
= JIT philosophy UK, US
Just-in-time philosophy is a philosophy to eliminate waste by reducing and eliminating production process time, stocks and time spent on activities that do not add value.
filosofía just-in-time
= filosofía JIT
▲ *the application of the just-in-time philosophy* la aplicación de la filosofía just-in-time
⇛ just-in-time system, kanban, lean management

just-in-time production
= just-in-time manufacturing
Just-in-time production means production responding to demand under the JIT philosophy that parts and materials are purchased only on an as-needed basis in the production process. In this way stock levels are kept to a minimum and waste is avoided.
producción just-in-time
= producción JIT, producción justo a tiempo, fabricación just-in-time
▲ *the implications of just-in-time production* las implicaciones de la producción just-in-time
⇛ just-in-time system

just-in-time production control system UK, US
→ just-in-time production system

just-in-time production system UK, US
= just-in-time production control system UK, US
A just-in-time production system is a demand-pull system responding to demand under the JIT philosophy that parts and materials are purchased only on an as-needed basis in the production process. In this way stock levels are kept to a minimum and waste is avoided.
sistema de producción just-in-time
= sistema de producción JIT, sistema de producción justo a tiempo
▲ *develop a just-in-time production system* desarrollar un sistema de producción just-in-time ▲ *implement a just-in-time production system* implementar un sistema de producción just-in-time
⇛ kanban, lean production

just-in-time purchasing
Just-in-time purchasing relates to the purchase and delivery of materials and finished products so that they arrive in the enterprise exactly at the right time for use in production, resale or distribution.
adquisición just-in-time
▲ *use just-in-time purchasing* utilizar la adquisición just-in-time
⇛ JIT, just-in-time

just-in-time system UK, US
A just-in-time system is a demand-pull inventory or production system responding to demand under the JIT philosophy that products are delivered only when required, and units produced or materials ordered on an as-needed basis. In this way stock levels are kept to a minimum, waste is eliminated and inventory investment cut down.
sistema just-in-time
= sistema JIT, sistema justo a tiempo
▲ *switch to a just-in-time system* cambiarse a un sistema just-in-time ▲ *the implementation of a just-in-time system* la implementación de un sistema just-in-time
⇛ just-in-time, kanban

K

kaizen

Kaizen is a Japanese term which means continuous improvement of performance at every level in an organisation by gradual, small-scale changes with a view to improving existing procedures, systems, products and standards as well as reducing waste.

kaizen

▲ *kaizen budget* presupuesto kaizen

⇛ kaizen costing

kaizen costing

Kaizen costing is a method for minimizing costs in the manufacturing process on a continuous basis.

NOTE "Kaizen" is the Japanese term for "continuous improvement".

sistema de costes kaizen

▲ *prepare a kaizen costing chart* preparar un cuadro de sistema de costes kaizen ▲ *the concept of kaizen costing* el concepto de sistema de costes kaizen

⇛ kaizen

kanban

Kanban is Japanese for card and refers to the production card system applied in the Japanese car industry to indicate the need for additional car parts in the production system. It is related to the just-in-time system also operating on an as-needed basis.

kanban

▲ *use a kanban system* usar un sistema kanban

⇛ just-in-time inventory system, just-in-time production system, just-in-time system

keeping of accounts

= recognition

Keeping of accounts is the process of recognising revenue and expenditure of a defined unit in accounting records to ensure that these disclosures can later form the basis of the financial statements.

llevanza de cuentas

= contabilizar

▲ *entrust the keeping of accounts to an accounting firm* confiar la llevanza de cuentas a una empresa contable

key category

A key category is a main and broadly selected class or group of items with common characteristics or features as compared with other categories.

categoría clave

▲ *key category analysis* análisis de la categoría clave

key figure

A key figure is a figure that is of particular importance in the enterprise's financial statements. Typical key figures are: the revenue for the year, the profit or loss from ordinary operating activities, the net profit or loss for the year, the balance sheet total, investments in property, plant and equipment, equity and any such key figures and financial ratios as are necessary in view of the enterprise's affairs and conditions.

cifra clave

▲ *comparable key figures* cifras claves comparables ▲ *comparative key figures* cifras claves comparativas ▲ *selected key figures* cifras claves seleccionadas

key initiative

A key initiative is an innovative new plan or important action to solve a special issue.

iniciativa clave

▲ *a key initiative for financial year 2005* una iniciativa clave para el año 2005 ▲ *a key initiative this year* una iniciativa clave este año ▲ *a key initiative to support competitiveness* una iniciativa clave para fomentar la competitividad ▲ *as a key initiative for 2006* como una iniciativa clave para el 2006

key success factor

A key success factor is a parameter which is decisive for successful implementation of a goal.

factor clave del éxito

= factor de éxito clave

▲ *represent a key success factor* representar un factor de éxito clave ▲ *the need for a key success factor* la necesidad de un factor clave del éxito

know-how

Know-how is a combination of experience, knowledge and skill acquired by a person or an enterprise concerning the application of appropriate technical processes such as manufacturing.

know-how

= saber hacer

▲ *acquisition of know-how* adquisición de know-how ▲ *amortise know-how* amortizar el know-how ▲ *develop know-how* desarrollar el know-how ▲ *keep know-how secret* mantener el know-how secreto ▲ *know-how obtained from a development activity* know-how resultante de una actividad de desarrollo ▲ *the know-how embodied in the process* el know-how incorporado en el proceso

knowledge

Knowledge is the sum of learning, understanding and experience somebody has obtained about a particular subject.

conocimiento

▲ *acquire knowledge* adquirir conocimiento ▲ *activities aimed at obtaining new knowledge* actividades encaminadas a obtener nuevo conocimiento ▲ *apply new knowledge* aplicar nuevo conocimiento ▲ *collection of new knowledge* adquisición de nuevo conocimiento ▲ *communicate knowledge* comunicar el conocimiento ▲ *development of knowledge* desarrollo del conocimiento ▲ *dissemination of new knowledge* dispersión de nuevo conocimiento ▲ *gain new scientific or technical knowledge and understanding* ganar nuevo conocimiento y comprensión científica o técnica ▲ *have a reasonable knowledge of economic activities and accounting* tener un conocimiento razonable de actividades económicas y de contabilidad ▲ *knowledge exchange* intercambio de conocimiento ▲ *knowledge management* gestión del conocimiento ▲ *knowledge relating to production engineering* conocimiento relativo a la ingeniería de producción ▲ *market knowledge* conocimmiento del mercado ▲ *specific knowledge* conocimiento específico ▲ *the knowledge embodied in the intangible component of the asset* el conocimiento innato en el componente intangible del activo ▲ *the personal knowledge of each employee* el conocimiento personal de cada empleado ▲ *transfer knowledge* traspasar conocimiento

knowledge management

Knowledge management comprises the activities implemented by an enterprise with a view to improving its capacity and ability to develop, share, embed and use knowledge.

gestión del conocimiento

▲ *auditor's statement on supplementary reports on knowledge management* informe del auditor sobre los informes complementarios acerca de la gestión del conocimiento ▲ *coherent knowledge management* gestión del conocimiento coherente ▲ *good knowledge management* buena gestión del conocimiento ▲ *knowledge management initiatives* iniciativas de la gestión del conocimiento ▲ *knowledge management objectives* objetivos de la gestión del conocimiento ▲ *systematic knowledge management* gestión del conocimiento sistemática ▲ *the enterprise's knowledge management strategy* la estrategia de gestión del conocimiento de la empresa

knowledge narrative

A knowledge narrative is a statement in an intellectual capital report of an enterprise which expresses the enterprise's ambition for knowledge management and defines its basic values. By explaining the value of products and services to users, the narrative describes the knowledge resources required to create this value. The narrative is a tale of how this was achieved and reflected in the enterprise's present performance, but also formulates the strategies and know-how needed for the future performance.

narrativa del conocimiento

= narrativa de conocimiento

▲ *knowledge narrative about the purpose and contents of the inte-*

llectual capital report narrativa del conocimiento sobre el propósito y los contenidos del informe de capital intelectual
⇛ intellectual capital report

knowledge resource
= knowledge-based resource
Knowledge resources are intangible resources used by an enterprise comprising the skills and expertise of its employees as well as corporate resources related to procedures, manuals, administrative systems, etc.
recurso del conocimiento
= recurso de conocimiento
▲ *apply knowledge resources* aplicar los recursos del conocimiento ▲ *description of knowledge resources* descripción de los recursos del conocimiento ▲ *develop knowledge resources* desarrollar los recursos del conocimiento ▲ *manage knowledge resources* gestionar los recursos del conocimiento

knowledge sharing
The process of sharing knowledge generated by an organisation with its employees or other organisations is called knowledge sharing.
conocimiento compartido
▲ *IT based knowledge sharing* conocimiento compartido basado en la tecnología de la información ▲ *systematic knowledge sharing* conocimiento compartido sistemático

L

labor time record US
= labor time ticket US
≠ clock card, time card
A labor time record is a ticket that records the time an employee spends on a particular job within total working time.
registro de actividad laboral
= registro de la actividad laboral
▲ *an electronic labor time record* un registro electrónico de actividad laboral ▲ *daily labor time records* registros diarios de actividad laboral

labor time ticket US
= job card UK, labor time record US
≠ clock card, time card
A labor time ticket records the time an employee spends on a particular job within total working time.
registro de dedicación laboral
▲ *prepare labor time tickets* preparar los registros de dedicación laboral

labour cost
Labour costs include wages, social security and pension contributions to employees for an accounting period. The expression can refer either to employees at all levels in an enterprise or to direct labour only.
coste laboral
▲ *average labour cost per worker* coste laboral medio por trabajador ▲ *changes in labour cost* cambios en el coste laboral ▲ *labour cost payable* coste laboral a pagar
⇒ direct labour

labour time record
→ labor-time record

land
1 Land is permanent and immovable property owned by somebody and may include natural resources such as minerals, the sea, forests and agriculture. Together with capital, labour and entrepreneurs, land is one of the factors of production as defined in modern economics.
bien raíz
NOTE Spanish accounting texts prefer the plural 'bienes raíces' to the singular 'bien raíz'.
▲ *defects in title to land* defectos en título a bien raíz ▲ *estates and interests in land* derechos de propiedad sobre bienes raíces ▲ *investments in land* inversiones en bienes raíces ▲ *net operating profit from land* beneficio de explotación neto proveniente de bienes raíces ▲ *operation of land* operación con bienes raíces ▲ *the value of land for tax purposes* el valor de los bienes raíces a efectos fiscales
2 Land is an area of ground or soil used for the location and construction of buildings.
terreno
NOTE Also plural in some Spanish collocations.
▲ *acquisition of land* adquisición de terreno ▲ *an increase in the value of the land on which a building stands* un aumento en el valor del terreno en el que se ha construido un edificio ▲ *land and other property held for resale* terrenos y otras propiedades adquiridos para su reventa ▲ *land held for a currently undetermined future use* terreno para un uso futuro no determinado en la actualidad ▲ *land held for long-term capital appreciation* terreno en propiedad para su revalorización a largo plazo ▲ *the cost of land* el coste de los terrenos

land and buildings UK
Land and buildings is an item under tangible fixed assets in the balance sheet according to the Companies Act 2006 required report format. This item includes immovable property owned by the reporting enterprise.
terrenos y edificios
= terrenos y construcciones
NOTE Always plural in Spanish accountants texts.
▲ *leases of land and of buildings* alquileres de terrenos y edificios ▲ *the fair value of land and buildings* el valor razonable de terrenos y edificios

land value
= site value

The land value states the economic value of land.
valor del terreno
= valor de los terrenos
▲ *an increase in land value* un aumento del valor de los terrenos ▲ *the estimated land value uplift* la revalorización estimada del valor del terreno

language
Language is a communication system consisting of spoken or written words, sounds or signs to enable two or more parties to understand each other in a particular country or region.
lengua
▲ *an official language* una lengua oficial ▲ *different reporting languages of the financial statements* sistemas de lenguas diferentes de los estados financieros ▲ *in a language customary in the sphere of international finance* en una lengua habitual en el ámbito de las finanzas internacionales ▲ *language adaptation* adaptación lingüística ▲ *language qualifications* especificaciones lingüísticas

lapse[1] *noun*
= expiry
Lapse means the termination or failure of a right or privilege through neglect to exercise it within some limit of time, or through failure to do something, e.g. non-payment.
prescripción
= vencimiento
▲ *expose the issuer to lapse risk* exponer al emisor al riesgo de prescripción ▲ *lapse or persistency risk* riesgo de prescripción o persistencia

lapse[2] *verb*
= expire
To lapse means to be terminated, come to a close or to cease because of lapse of time or expiration.
prescribir
= vencer
▲ *potential ordinary shares that are allowed to lapse* acciones ordinarias potenciales a las que se les permite prescribir
⇛ expire

last in, first out
→ LIFO

last-in, first-out
= LIFO
Last-in, first-out (LIFO) is a stock valuation method where the cost of stocks is calculated on the assumption that stock items acquired last are sold first, measuring cost of sales at the most recent costs and closing stocks at the cost of the items earliest purchased.
LIFO
= última entrada, primera salida
▲ *assess on a last-in, first-out basis* valorar según el método LIFO ▲ *use the last-in, first-out method* usar el método LIFO
⇛ first in, first-out

law[1] UK *noun* <no indefinite article, the, no plural>
Law is a system of legal rules in a country or region laid down by a legislative body.
derecho
▲ *a transaction closed or finalised at law* una transacción cerrada o finalizada conforme a derecho ▲ *according to law* conforme a derecho ▲ *applicable law* derecho aplicable ▲ *current English law* derecho inglés vigente ▲ *under US law* según el derecho estadounidense

law[2] US *noun* <a, the, -s>
= statute
A law is a document setting down rules within a specific area and passed by a legislative body.
ley
▲ *according to the law* de acuerdo con la ley ▲ *changes in tax rates or tax laws enacted or announced after the balance sheet date* cambios en los tipos impositivos o leyes impositivas vigentes o previstas para después de la fecha de balance ▲ *comply with local laws* cumplir con las leyes locales ▲ *statutory law* ley estatutaria

law firm
A law firm is an organisation employing attorneys.
bufete
▲ *a corporate law firm* un bufete empresarial ▲ *a leading law firm* un bufete lider ▲ *a partner in a law firm* un socio de un bufete ▲ *an independent law firm* un bufete independiente

lawyer
A lawyer is a person educated in law who gives professional legal advice, draws up legal documents and may represent clients in court.
abogado
▲ *consult a lawyer* consultar a un abogado ▲ *court-assigned*

lawyer abogado de oficio ▲ *lawyer with a right of audience in the Danish Supreme Court* abogado con un derecho de audiencia en el Tribunal Supremo danés ▲ *retain a lawyer* conservar a un abogado ▲ *the company's lawyer* el abogado de la empresa

lay down

To lay down is to stipulate formally and officially.

establecer

▲ *as laid down in the articles* tal y como está establecido en los artículos ▲ *lay down a rule* establecer una norma ▲ *lay down directions for* establecer directrices para

layout of financial statement

= format, reporting format

The layout of a financial statement is the way in which the accounting items are arranged in a particular financial statement such as the balance sheet or the profit and loss account. The financial statements can typically be presented in two different layouts or formats: the account form (horizontal format) and the report form (vertical format).

formato del estado financiero

▲ *introduce a new layout of financial statement* introducir un nuevo formato del estado financiero

LCA

= life cycle assessment

LCA is the abbreviation for life cycle assessment which is an overall evaluation and examination of a product or industrial system over its life cycle, i.e. from raw materials over performance to final disposal, with a view to environmental impacts. The LCA is typically analysed over three stages: inventory (collecting and describing data), interpretation (relating the data to environmental issues) and improvement (changes to reduce any pollution or other environmental damage).

determinación de la vida útil

= determinación de vida útil

▲ *conduct an LCA* llevar a cabo una determinación de la vida útil ▲ *the different phases of an LCA* las diferentes fases para la determinación de la vida útil

LCM method

= lower-of-cost-or-market method

The LCM (lower-of-cost-or-market) method is a method for the measurement of inventory in the balance sheet where the cost and the net realisable value (market value) are determined and the lower value of either is applied.

método del valor menor de mercado o de coste

▲ *use the LCM method* usar el método del valor menor de mercado o de coste ▲ *valued under the LCM method* valorado según el método del valor menor de mercado o de coste

lean manufacturing US

Lean manufacturing means the production using the just-in-time production system to minimise and avoid waste, idle time, defected products and overproduction. Lean manufacturing originated in the US and Japanese car industries.

manufactura esbelta

= manufactura lean, producción esbelta

▲ *the basic principles of lean manufacturing* los principios básicos de la manufactura esbelta

⇛ just-in-time production

lean production UK, US

= lean manufacturing US

Lean production means the manufacturing of products using the just-in-time production system to minimise and avoid waste, idle time, defected products and overproduction. Lean production originated in the US and Japanese car industries.

producción esbelta

= manufactura esbelta, manufactura lean

▲ *implementation of lean production* implementación de la producción esbelta ▲ *the principles of lean production* los principios de la producción esbelta

⇛ just-in-time production, just-in-time system

learning culture

Learning culture is a working environment assuming that employees will engage in training and education to seek further development and learn from experience and errors.

cultura de aprendizaje

= cultura del aprendizaje

▲ *an improved knowledge and learning culture* un conocimiento mejorado y cultura de aprendizaje ▲ *create a learning culture* crear una cultura de aprendizaje

learning curve

A learning curve is a curve showing the improvement rate in acquired skills and experience with practice performance.

curva de aprendizaje

= curva del aprendizaje

▲ *a five stage learning curve* una curva de aprendizaje con cinco tramos ▲ *a steep learning curve* una curva de aprendizaje pronunciada

lease[1] *noun*

1 = lease agreement

A lease is a legal contract under which a person or enterprise (the lessor) owning a specific asset grants another person or enterprise (the lessee) the right to use the asset for a specified period of time in return for periodic lease payments. A lease is classified as either an operating or a finance lease depending on the contractual terms and conditions.

contrato de arrendamiento

= contrato de alquiler

▲ *a non-cancellable lease* un contrato de arrendamiento no cancelable ▲ *cancel a lease* cancelar un contrato de arrendamiento ▲ *enter into a lease* firmar un contrato de arrendamiento ▲ *gross investment in a lease* inversión bruta en un contrato de arrendamiento ▲ *inception of a lease* inicio de un contrato de arrendamiento ▲ *leases of property, plant and equipment* contratos de arrendamiento de edificios, instalaciones y equipos ▲ *net investment in a lease* inversión neta en un contrato de arrendamiento ▲ *renew a lease* renovar un contrato de arrendamiento ▲ *the interest rate implicit in a lease* el tipo de interés implícito en un contrato de arrendamiento ▲ *the subject of the lease* el sujeto del contrato de arrendamiento

2 = lease agreement, lease contract, rental agreement

A lease or lease agreement is a legal contract stipulating the conditions for a lessor's transfer of the right of use, possession and employment of a property to a lessee for a defined period of time in return for payment, i.e. rent.

contrato de arrendamiento

= contrato de alquiler

▲ *enter into a lease* firmar un contrato de arrendamiento ▲ *terminate a lease* finalizar un contrato de arrendamiento

3 A lease is an agreement stipulating the terms and conditions for the right to occupy and use, for a limited number of years, a residential or commercial property belonging to a lessor.

arrendamiento

▲ *depreciate over the lease term* amortizar durante el periodo de arrendamiento

4 The lease of an asset, typically property, is the lending of that asset to a lessee against rent or lease payment for a specified period of time. Depending on the nature of the lease agreement the lease may be in the form of an operating lease, a finance lease or a rental agreement.

arrendamiento

▲ *costs related to the lease out of properties* costes relacionados con el arrendamiento de edificios

lease[2] *verb*

1 To lease is to rent, rent out or let an asset, typically property against payment for a specified time period.

arrendar

▲ *lease operating equipment* arrendar los equipos de explotación ▲ *lease property* arrendar edificios

2 To lease is to grant or be granted the right to use an asset for a specified time period in return for periodic lease payments. Depending on the contractual terms, the lease may be classified as an operating or a finance lease.

arrendar

▲ *contract to lease an asset* contrato para arrendar un activo ▲ *exercise an option to continue to lease the asset* ejercer la opción de continuar arrendando el activo

lease agreement

1 A lease is a legal contract under which a person or enterpri-

se (the lessor) owning a specific asset grants another person or enterprise (the lessee) the right to use the asset for a specified period of time in return for periodic lease payments. A lease is classified as either an operating or a finance lease depending on the contractual terms and conditions.

contrato de arrendamiento

▲ *lease agreements to explore for or use minerals* contratos de arrendamientos para explorar o usar minerales ▲ *the date of the lease agreement* la fecha del contrato de arrendamiento ▲ *the legal form of a lease agreement* la fórmula legal de un contrato de arrendamiento

2 = lease

A lease agreement is a legal contract stipulating the conditions for a lessor's transfer of the right of use, possession and employment of a property to a lessee for a defined period of time in return for payment, i.e. rent.

contrato de arrendamiento

= contrato de alquiler

▲ *enter into a lease agreement* firmar un contrato de arrendamiento ▲ *renew the lease agreement* renovar el contrato de arrendamiento

lease commitment

= lease obligation

Lease commitments refer to the obligations arising from an enterprise's lease of fixed assets under operating and/or finance leases. Under a lease, the enterprise (the lessee) obtains the right to use fixed assets for a specified period against regular lease payments to the lessor.

compromiso de arrendamiento

▲ *amortised interest on the lease commitment* interés amortizado en el compromiso de arrendamiento ▲ *an existing lease commitment* un compromiso de arrendamiento existente ▲ *costs associated with a pre-existing lease commitment of the lessee* costes asociados a un compromiso de arrendamiento preexistente del arrendatario ▲ *operating lease commitments* compromisos de arrendamiento operativo ▲ *rental and lease commitments* compromisos de arrendamiento y alquiler

⇛ finance lease, operating lease

lease expense

= rental expense

Lease expenses are expenses incurred in connection with a lease seen from the point of view of the lessee. The expenses can be calculated for the whole lease term or for each period in which payment is made. Lease expenses may be down payment at the inception of the lease, periodic payments, repair costs, delivery costs etc.

gasto de arrendamiento

= contrato de alquiler

▲ *accounting for lease expenses* contabilizando los gastos de arrendamiento ▲ *lease expense for prior periods* gasto de arrendamiento de ejercicios anteriores ▲ *total lease expenses* total gastos de arrendamiento

lease financing

Lease financing is a means of financing the acquisition of fixed assets such as equipment or cars. Against lease payments to a lessor, a lessee is granted the right to use a particular leased asset for a defined period of time. The use of an asset is financed through fixed lease payments over the period of time rather than through a purchase of that asset for borrowed money. The lease may be financed by the lessor or by an intermediary company such as a financial institution.

arrendamiento financiero

= leasing

▲ *a decrease in lease financing* una disminución de arrendamiento financiero ▲ *an increase in lease financing* un aumento de arrendamiento financiero ▲ *synthetic lease financing* arrendamiento financiero sistético

lease incentive

Lease incentives are incentives provided by the lessor to the lessee in connection with the negotiations for a new or renewed operating lease to make the lessee enter the agreement. Such incentives may consist in the lessor paying an up-front cash amount, reimbursing or covering the costs of the lessee, e.g. relocation costs, or agreeing that the initial lease term be rent-free or at a reduced rent.

incentivo de arrendamiento

▲ *recognise lease incentives as an integral part of the consideration agreed* reconocer incentivos de arrendamiento como parte integral de la consideración acordada ▲ *recognise the benefits of lease incentives received as a reduction of rental expense over the term of the lease* reconocer los beneficios de los incentivos de arrendamiento recibidos como una reducción de los gastos de alquiler durante el plazo del contrato de arrendamiento ▲ *recognise the costs of lease incentives as a reduction in rental income over the term of the lease* reconocer los costos de incentivos de arrendamiento como una reducción en ingresos por concepto de alquileres durante el plazo del contrato de arrendamiento

SOURCE SIC 15, UITF abstract 28

⇛ operating lease

lease payment

= lease rental payment, rent, rental

Lease payments are the periodic payments which a lessor receives from a lessee in pursuance of a lease in return for granting the lessee the right to use the leased asset.

pago de arrendamiento

= alquiler, renta, cuota de arrendamiento

▲ *a reduced lease payment* un pago de arrendamiento reducido ▲ *an average annual lease payment of EUR 1,000* un pago del arrendamiento anual medio de 1.000 euros ▲ *future lease payments* pagos de arrendamiento futuros ▲ *future lease payments receivable* pagos del arrendamiento futuros a cobrar ▲ *lease payment for the year* pago del arrendamiento anual ▲ *lease payments receivable* pagos de arrendamiento a cobrar ▲ *lease payments under an operational lease* pagos de arrendamiento según un arrendamiento operacional ▲ *pay a lease payment* pagar un alquiler ▲ *prepaid lease payment* prepago de la cuota de arrendamiento ▲ *the future aggregate lease payments* los pagos de arrendamiento agregados futuros ▲ *the interest element of the lease payment* el interés del pago por arrendamiento ▲ *the portion of the lease payment that is not fixed in amount* la parte del pago del arrendamiento que no es una cantidad fija ▲ *the present value of the lease payment* el valor actual del pago del arrendamiento ▲ *unavoidable lease payments* pagos de arrendamiento inevitables

lease term

A lease term is the period of interminability for which the lessee has undertaken to lease an asset. If it is reasonably certain at the inception of the lease that the lessee intends to continue to lease the asset for any further periods, with or without further payment, a lease term also includes such periods.

plazo de arrendamiento

▲ *a reduced lease term* un plazo de arrendamiento reducido ▲ *a rent-free lease term* un plazo de arrendamiento libre ▲ *allocate finance income over the lease term* asignar el ingreso financiero durante el plazo de arrendamiento ▲ *at the beginning of the lease term* al inicio del plazo de arrendamiento ▲ *at the commencement of a finance lease term* al comienzo de un plazo de arrendamiento financiero ▲ *at the end of the lease term* al final del plazo de arrendamiento ▲ *by the end of the lease term* al final del plazo de arrendamiento ▲ *charge to the income statement over the lease term* cargo a la cuenta de resultados durante el plazo de arrendamiento ▲ *depreciate over the lease term* amortizar durante el plazo de arrendamiento ▲ *extend the lease term* ampliar el plazo de arrendamiento ▲ *in the initial period of the lease term* en el periodo inicial del plazo de arrendamiento ▲ *recognise on a straight-line basis over the lease term* reconocer según un sistema lineal durante el plazo de arrendamiento ▲ *rent-free lease term* plazo de arrendamiento sin renta ▲ *the minimum payment payable over the lease term* el pago mínimo a pagar durante el plazo de arrendamiento

leaseback

A leaseback is an agreement according to which the seller of a property or other asset leases the sold property or asset from the new owner.

leaseback

= venta con arrendamiento financiero posterior

▲ *disposal by a sale and leaseback* eliminación por venta y leaseback ▲ *sale and leaseback* venta y leaseback

⇛ lease

leased asset

A leased asset is an asset leased and used by an enterprise, the lessee, under an operating lease or a finance lease for a portion of the asset's economic life. Leased assets are typically machinery, equipment, transport means, computer hardware or other movables.

activo arrendado

▲ *acquire legal title to the leased asset* adquirir la titularidad del activo arrendado ▲ *exercise the right to use the leased asset* ejercer el derecho de uso del activo arrendado ▲ *risks and rewards incidental to ownership of a leased asset* riesgos y recompensas incidentales asociados a la propiedad de un activo arrendado ▲ *the depreciation policy for depreciable leased assets* la política de amortización para los activos arrendados amortizables ▲ *the economic benefits of the use of the leased asset* los beneficios económicos del uso del activo arrendado ▲ *the economic life of the entire leased asset* la vida económica del activo arrendado completo ▲ *the fair value of the leased asset* el valor razonable del activo arrendado ▲ *the liabilities for leased assets* los pasivos por activos arrendados ▲ *the residual value of the leased asset* el valor residual del activo arrendado

leasehold

1 = leasehold property

A leasehold is a property that is rented to a lessee for a limited number of years, which gives the lessee the right to occupy and use the property, but not to ownership or title of the property or the land on which it stands.

alquiler

= arrendamiento

▲ *leasehold title* título de alquiler

2 = leasehold interest

A leasehold is a form of property ownership where the lessee has the right to occupy and use a property, belonging to a lessor, for a limited number of years. A leasehold does not include ownership or title to the land on which the property stands.

bien en alquiler

= bien en arrendamiento, bien en propiedad temporal

▲ *acquire the leasehold* adquirir el bien en alquiler ▲ *assign the leasehold* traspasar el bien en alquiler

3 = lease

A leasehold is the right to occupy and use, against payment and for a limited number of years, a residential or commercial property belonging to a lessor.

derecho de alquiler

= derecho de arrendamiento

▲ *a payment made on entering into or acquiring a leasehold* un pago realizado a la entrada o a la adquisición de un derecho de alquiler ▲ *leasehold improvements* mejoras en el derecho de alquiler ▲ *the relative fair values of the leasehold interests in the land element and buildings element of the lease* los valores razonables relativos de los intereses por derecho de alquiler de bienes raíces y edificios del arrendamiento

leasehold improvements

"Leasehold improvements" is an item under tangible fixed assets in the balance sheet that concern expenses attributable to permanent additions or repairs that improve premises rented under a lease for continuous use by an enterprise.

mejoras en bienes arrendados

= mejora en bienes alquilados

▲ *construction-in-progress on leasehold improvements* construcción en curso de mejoras en bienes arrendados ▲ *depreciation of leasehold improvements* amortización de mejoras en bienes arrendados

leasing

Leasing is the activity of borrowing or lending an asset under an operating or a finance lease.

NOTE The term "leasing" refers to the concept and act of leasing. It typically appears in compounds such as "leasing activities" and "leasing company".

leasing

= arrendamiento financiero

▲ *a general description of the lessee's material leasing arrangements* una descripción general del arrendamiento financiero material del arrendatario ▲ *initial direct costs incurred in connection with specific leasing activities* costes directos iniciales incurridos en conexión con actividades de leasing específicas ▲ *negotiating and securing leasing arrangements* negociación y obtención de acuerdos de leasing

⇛ finance lease, operating lease

least-square regression method

US

The least-square regression method measures a cost function objectively, as it is based on statistics rather than human judgment and involves a regression analysis.

método de regresión de mínimos cuadrados

▲ *linear least-square regression method* método de regresión de mínimos cuadrados lineal ▲ *non-linear least-square regression method* método de regresión de mínimos cuadrados no lineal ▲ *use the least-square regression method* utilizar el método de regresión de mínimos cuadrados

⇛ high-low method, visual-fit method

leave

= leave of absence

≠ absenteeism

Leave refers to a defined period of time, paid or unpaid, during which an employee has been allowed to be absent, i.e. stay away from work for legitimate reasons such as birth of a baby, education and sickness.

permiso

= licencia

▲ *educational leave* licencia por estudios ▲ *maternity leave* permiso por maternidad ▲ *parental leave* permiso parental ▲ *paternity leave* permiso por paternidad

leave of absence

= leave

≠ absenteeism

Leave of absence refers to a defined period of time, paid or unpaid, during which an employee has been allowed to be absent, i.e. stay away from work for legitimate reasons such as birth of a baby, education and sickness.

excedencia

= licencia temporal, permiso de ausencia

▲ *apply for leave of absence without pay* solicitar excedencia sin sueldo ▲ *grant leave of absence* conceder excedencia ▲ *paid leave of absence* excedencia pagada

ledger

= general ledger, nominal ledger

A ledger is a book or group of accounts containing accounting records and classifying financial transactions. Today, ledgers are usually stored on computer files that have replaced the old-time binders.

libro mayor

▲ *make an entry in the ledger* realizar una entrada en el libro mayor ▲ *the balance of the ledger* el saldo del libro mayor

⇛ nominal ledger, purchases ledger, sales ledger

ledger account

A ledger account is an account of records in the double-entry bookkeeping system made for transactions relating to a particular activity, such as a debtor or a creditor, and to a type of expense or income.

cuenta del libro mayor

▲ *enter into a ledger account* anotar en la cuenta del libro mayor

legal assistance

When, in the course of his business, a lawyer assists a person or enterprise in connection with legal matters, he is providing legal assistance.

asistencia legal

▲ *have the right to the assistance of a lawyer* tener derecho a la asistencia legal de un abogado ▲ *provide legal assistance* ofrecer asistencia legal

legal expense

Legal expenses are those expenses incurred by a person or enterprise that are attributable to legal assistance.

gasto legal

▲ *incur legal expenses* incurrir en gastos legales ▲ *legal expenses insurance* seguro para gastos legales

legal obligation

A legal obligation is an obligation which must be fulfilled by a person or an enterprise as a result of legislation, case law or a written or oral contract.

obligación legal

▲ *a legal obligation as a result of past events* una obligación legal como un resultado de eventos pasados ▲ *a legal obligation to pay cash* una obligación legal a pagar en efectivo ▲ *give rise to a legal obligation* dar lugar a una obligación legal ▲ *have a legal obligation* tener una obligación legal ▲ *provisions relating to legal obligations* provisiones relativas a obligaciones legales

legal reserve

= statutory reserve

Legal reserves constitute the minimum amount of available funds companies including financial institutions are required to hold according to provisions in law and the articles of association. Legal reserves are typically undistributable reserves recognised in the balance sheet under equity and may comprise various types.

reserva legal

▲ *appropriate to the legal reserve* apropiado a la reserva legal ▲ *the company's legal reserve* reserva legal de la empresa ▲ *transfer to the legal reserve* transferir a la reserva legal

⇛ net revaluation reserve, undistributable reserve

legal risk

A legal risk is the risk that an insufficient legal basis will cause or increase a credit or cash flow risk.

riesgo legal

▲ *assess the legal risks* evaluar los riesgos legales ▲ *be exposed to legal risks* estar expuesto a riesgos legales ▲ *management of legal risks* gestión de riesgos legales ▲ *mitigate any legal risks* mitigar algunos riesgos legales ▲ *potential legal risks* riesgos legales potenciales

legislation

= law

Legislation is the whole or part of the statutes that have been passed by a legislative assembly and which are in force at any given time in a country or region.

legislación

▲ *according to the legislation governing the matter* de acuerdo con la legislación en la materia ▲ *local circumstances or legislation* circunstancias locales o legislación ▲ *take the effect of possible new legislation into consideration* tomar en consideración el efecto de la nueva legislación posible

legitimate

Something that is justified or acceptable according to law is legitimate.

legítimo

▲ *a legitimate claim* una reclamación legítima ▲ *ligitimate expectations* expectativas legítimas

lend

To lend means to transfer assets to a person or enterprise against consideration and, usually, the promise to return the assets.

prestar

▲ *have a commitment to lend funds at a fixed interest rate* tener un compromiso para prestar fondos a un tipo de interés fijo ▲ *lend in foreign currency* prestar en moneda extranjera

lender

A lender is a person, enterprise or other institution that provides loans to others.

prestamista

▲ *an exchange between an existing borrower and lender of debt instruments* un intercambio entre un prestatario y prestamista de instrumentos de deuda existente ▲ *buy back a financial asset at the sale price plus a lender's return* recomprar un activo financiero al precio de venta más la rentabilidad del prestamista ▲ *give lenders security on assets* ofrecer garantías a los prestamistas en activos ▲ *grant the lender the right to convert his claims into investments in the enterprise* conceder al prestamista el derecho a convertir sus reclamaciones en inversiones en la empresa ▲ *observable interest rates charged by lenders* tasas de interés observables cargadas por prestamistas

lending

Lending is the provision of a loan to a borrower.

préstamo

▲ *a securities lending agreement* un acuerdo de préstamo de valores ▲ *a similar securities lending transaction* una transacción de préstamo de valores similar ▲ *repurchase agreements and securities lending* acuerdos de recompra y préstamo de valores ▲ *the asset lent under a securities lending transaction* el activo prestado según una operación de préstamo de valores ▲ *the bank's policy for lending to related parties* la política del banco de préstamo a las partes relacionadas

lending activity

Lending activity is the total amount of loans and advances provided by a lender, usually a financial institution, within a specific period.

préstamos

NOTE Always plural in Spanish accounting texts.

▲ *conduct lending activities* realizar préstamos ▲ *financial institutions' customary lending activities* préstamos habituales de las instituciones financieras ▲ *net amounts of cash receipts and cash payments for deposit or lending activities* cantidades netas de ingresos y pagos en efectivo por depósitos o préstamos

length of service

= years of service

The period of time during which an employee has been employed by an employer is called the length of service.

duración de servicio

= duración del servicio, periodo de servicio, tiempo de servicio

▲ *a level of benefit depending on the length of service* un nivel de prestación dependiendo de la duración de servicio ▲ *average length of service* duración de servicio media ▲ *regardless of the length of service* independientemente de la duración de servicio

less[1] *preposition*

Less means minus or after deducting a certain amount, e.g. profit less tax is profit after tax or net profit.

menos

▲ *measure at fair value less estimated point-of-sale costs* medir a valor razonable menos los costes en el punto de venta estimados ▲ *recognise at fair value less costs to sell* reconocer a valor razonable menos costes para la venta

less[2] *adjective*

"Less" is used before mass nouns.

Less means smaller or fewer when referring to size, amount or value, e.g. less money or less risk.

menos

= menor, inferior

▲ *a price that is less than the fair value of the equity instruments* un precio que es menor que el valor razonable de los instrumentos de patrimonio ▲ *in one year or less* en un año o menos ▲ *less than £10,000* menos de 10.000 libras esterlinas ▲ *own half or less of the voting power* tener la mitad o menos de los derechos de voto

less[3] *adverb*

Less means to a lower degree or not as much, e.g. less expensive or less important.

menos

▲ *less readily available* menos fácilmente disponible ▲ *significantly less risky* significativamente menos arriesgado

lessee

A lessee is a person or enterprise that has entered into a contract to lease an asset, called a lease.

arrendatario

▲ *a lessee's residual value guarantee embedded in a finance lease* un valor residual del arrendatario garantizado incluido en un arrendamiento financiero ▲ *default by the lessee* incumplimiento por parte del arrendatario ▲ *leases in the financial statements of lessees* arrendamientos en los estados financieros de los arrendatarios ▲ *the cost of an item of property, plant and equipment held by a lessee* el coste de una partida de edificios, instalaciones y equipos en poder del arrendatario ▲ *the lessee's incremental borrowing rate* tasa de interés marginal del arrendatario ▲ *the lessee's normal depreciation policy* política de amortización normal del arrendatario ▲ *transfer risks and rights to the lessee* transferir al arrendatario derechos y riesgos ▲ *transfer the right to use an asset to the lessee* transferir al arrendatario el derecho a usar un activo

lessor

A lessor is a person or enterprise who owns an asset and who has entered into a contract to lease out the asset, called a lease, to another person or enterprise, called a lessee.

arrendador

▲ *a manufacturer or dealer lessor* un fabricante o arrendador distribuidor ▲ *any initial direct costs of the lessor* cualesquiera costes directos iniciales del arrendador ▲ *any residual value guaranteed to the lessor* cualquier valor residual garantizado al arrendador ▲ *any unguaranteed residual value accruing to the lessor* cualquier valor residual no garantizado devengado al arrendador ▲ *intermediary lessor* arrendador intermediario ▲ *investment property provided by lessors under operating leases* inversión inmobiliaria aportada por arrendadores según arrendamientos operativos ▲ *leases in the financial statements of lessors* arrendamientos en los estados financieros de los arrendadores ▲ *minimum payments to the lessor* pagos mínimos al arrendador ▲ *the lessee's obligations towards the lessor* obligaciones del arrendatario para con el arrendador ▲ *the lessor's net investment in the lease* inversión neta del arrendador en el arrendamiento

letter of credit

A letter of credit is a contractual document between an exporter or importer and its bank which provides that the bank will pay for goods received.

carta de crédito

= letra de crédito, contrato de crédito

▲ *back to back inland letter of credit* carta de crédito nacional subsidiario ▲ *confirmed letter of credit* carta de crédito confirmada ▲ *irrevocable letter of credit* carta de crédito irrevocable ▲ *revocable letter of credit* carta de crédito revocable ▲ *standby letter of credit* carta de crédito en reserva ▲ *the stipulations of the letter of credit* las estipulaciones de la carta de crédito ▲ *the terms of the letter of credit* los términos de la carta de crédito

letter of demand

A letter of demand is a letter that requests the receiver to do something, for example pay the price for the goods bought.

carta de demanda

▲ *send a letter of demand to the senior management of an enterprise* enviar una carta de demanda a la dirección de una empresa ▲ *the date of the letter of demand* la fecha de la carta de demanda

letter of findings

A letter of findings is a statement of an auditor's opinion about a given issue related to e.g. company law, tax and financial reporting matters, etc.

carta de conclusiones

▲ *a written letter of findings* una carta de conclusiones escrita ▲ *issue a letter of findings* emitir una carta de conclusiones

letter of representation US

A letter of representation is addressed to the certified public accountant by the client and states that the financial statements are the responsibility of management and that management's statements to the auditor during the audit process are true.

carta de representación

▲ *letter of representation certified by the auditor* carta de representación certificada por el auditor

letter of subordination

= letter of postponement, subordination letter

A letter of subordination is a written statement by a creditor to a debtor specifying that the creditor agrees to be repaid after the other creditors have been repaid.

carta de subordinación

▲ *debt subject to a letter of subordination* deuda sujeta a una carta de subordinación ▲ *issue a letter of subordination* emitir una carta de subordinación ▲ *issue a letter of subordination vis-a-vis other creditors* emitir una carta de subordinación respecto a otros acreedores

level of activity

The level of activity is the performance of an enterprise measured in relation to its performance target.

nivel de actividad

▲ *a high level of activity* un nivel de actividad elevado ▲ *a level of activity that falls short of expectations* un nivel de actividad que no supera las expectativas ▲ *an increasing level of activity* un nivel de actividad creciente ▲ *assume an unchanged level of activity* asumir un nivel de actividad sin cambio ▲ *expect a similar level of activity* esperar un nivel de actividad similar ▲ *expect the same high level of activity* espera el mismo nivel de actividad elevado ▲ *reductions in the level of activity* descensos en el nivel de actividad

level of expenses

= level of costs

The level of expenses is a measure of the expenses incurred by an enterprise in total, within a particular geographic area or business area. For instance, if the total expenses incurred in a particular business area are high, this area has a high level of expenses.

nivel de gastos

▲ *a competitive level of expenses* un nivel de gastos competitivo

level of sales

= sales level

The level of sales is a measure of the sales made by an enterprise in total, within a particular geographic area or business area. For instance, if total sales are high, the enterprise has a high level of sales.

nivel de ventas

= nivel de las ventas

▲ *a higher level of sales* un mayor nivel de ventas ▲ *a lower level of sales* un menor nivel de ventas ▲ *maintain the level of sales* mantener el nivel de las ventas

leverage US

Leverage refers to either financial or operating leverage. Financial leverage refers to the relationship between an enterprise's net interest-bearing debt, i.e. loan capital, and its equity. Operating leverage refers to how high the percentage of an enterprise's fixed costs is in relation to total costs.

apalancamiento

= leverage

▲ *high leverage* apalancamiento alto ▲ *low leverage* apalancamiento bajo ▲ *the enterprise's policy on leverage* la política de la empresa sobre el apalancamiento

⇛ contribution margin, financial leverage, operating leverage

leveraged

A leveraged investment is an investment made with borrowed funds, just as a leveraged buyout is the acquisition of the controlling interest in a company through payment with borrowed funds.

apalancado

▲ *a cap or floor leveraged in relation to the host contract* un tope o suelo apalancado en relación al contrato anfitrión ▲ *leveraged acquisition* adquisición apalancada ▲ *leveraged buy-out* compra por apalancamiento

⇛ gearing, leverage

liabilities and equity US

→ equity and liabilities

liabilities and stockholders' equity US

= equity and liabilities IAS/IFRS

Liabilities and stockholders' equity constitute the balance sheet total in the credit side of the balance sheet when presented in the horizontal format and represent the sources of funds for the assets presented in the debit side.

pasivo y patrimonio neto de los accionistas

= patrimonio neto y pasivo

▲ *total liabilities and stockholders' equity* total pasivo y patrimonio neto de los accionistas ▲ *total of all liabilities and stockholders' equity items* el total del pasivo y patrimonio neto de los accionistas

liability[1] *noun* <a, the, liabilities>

Liabilities are present obligations of an enterprise that arise from past events where their settlement is anticipated to result in an outflow from the enterprise of resources that represent economic benefits.

pasivo

▲ *a current liability* un pasivo corriente ▲ *a liability line item* una partida de pasivo ▲ *a liability other than a contingent liabil-*

ity un pasivo diferente a un pasivo contingente ▲ *a long-term liability* un pasivo a largo plazo ▲ *a non-current liability* un pasivo no corriente ▲ *a recognised liability* un pasivo reconocido ▲ *a short-term liability* un pasivo a corto plazo ▲ *an existing liability for restructuring* un pasivo existente por reestructuración ▲ *an integral part of the liability issue transaction* una parte integral de la transacción de emisión del pasivo ▲ *an unconditional right to defer settlement of the liability* un derecho incondicional a diferir la liquidación del pasivo ▲ *assume a liability* asumir un pasivo ▲ *include in the initial measurement of the liability* incluir en el importe inicial del pasivo ▲ *recognise as a separate liability* reconocer como un pasivo independiente ▲ *remove an individual liability from a disposal group classified as held for sale* eliminar un pasivo individual de un grupo clasificado como mantenido para la venta ▲ *ring-fenced liabilities* pasivos delimitados ▲ *settle a liability* liquidar un pasivo ▲ *subordinated liabilities* pasivos subordinados ▲ *the carrying amount of the liability* el valor contable del pasivo

liability[2] *noun* <no indefinite article, the, no plural>

To have liability means to have legal responsibility for payment, damages or injury. A person may incur full, joint or limited liability.

responsabilidad

▲ *assume liability* asumir la responsabilidad ▲ *joint and several liability* responsabilidad conjunta y solidaria ▲ *joint liability* responsabilidad conjunta ▲ *liability for debts and obligations* responsabilidad por deudos y obligaciones ▲ *limited liability* responsabilidad limitada ▲ *personal liability* responsabilidad personal ▲ *proportionate liability* responsabilidad proporcional ▲ *small enterprises with limited liability* pequeñas empresas con responsabilidad limitada ▲ *unlimited liability* responsabilidad ilimitada

liability adequacy test

A liability adequacy test is an assessment of the carrying amounts of an insurer's recognised insurance liabilities as to whether such amounts are sufficient in the light of estimated future cash flows related to the insurer's insurance liabilities. The applied liability adequacy test is to meet certain minimum requirements laid down by IFRS 4, failing this, the deficiency must be recognised in the income statement.

prueba de adecuación del pasivo

= evaluación de suficiencia de pasivo, prueba de adecuación de los pasivos

▲ *apply a liability adequacy test that meets specified minimum requirements* aplicar una prueba de adecuación del pasivo que cumpla los requisitos específicos mínimos ▲ *carry out a liability adequacy test* llevar a cabo una prueba de adecuación del pasivo

SOURCE IFRS 4, Appendix A

liability component

1 The liability component on a convertible bond corresponds to the proceeds that an enterprise would receive for a similar loan without a conversion option at the maturity of the loan. The remaining proceeds correspond to the embedded option part of the loan to convert the bond into an equity instrument, which is the premium that the lender is willing to pay for the embedded option.

componente de pasivo

= componente del pasivo

▲ *derecognise the liability component* dar de baja el componente de pasivo ▲ *the amount of loss relating to the liability component* el importe de la pérdida relacionada con el componente del pasivo ▲ *the effective interest rate on the liability component* el tipo de interés efectivo del componente de pasivo ▲ *the fair value of the liability component* el valor razonable del componente de pasivo

2 ≠ equity component IAS/IFRS

A compound financial instrument is a security which is split into two elements or components: an equity component and a liability component. The liabil-

ity component consists of the amount the issuer is obliged to repay to the holder (i.e. the principal), whereas the equity component represents the residual that results after deduction of the fair value of the liability component from the value of the compound instrument at the issue date. In the financial statements the components are recognised separately in the balance sheet: the liability component as a financial liability and the equity component as an equity instrument under equity. Examples of compound financial instruments are convertible bonds and warrants.
componente de pasivo
≠ componente de patrimonio
▲ *present the liability component and the equity component separately on the balance sheet* presentar el componente de pasivo y patrimonio ▲ *the amount separately determined for the liability component* la cantidad determinada independientemente para el componente de pasivo
SOURCE IAS 32
⇛ compound financial instrument

liability other than provision IAS/IFRS
Liabilities other than provisions include obligations of the enterprise resulting from past transactions and events, that when settled are expected to result in an transfer from the enterprise of resources representing economic benefits, but excludes liabilities that are uncertain in terms of amount or timing (provisions).
pasivo distinto de provisión
= pasivo diferente de provisión
▲ *classify costs as liabilities other than provisions* clasificar costes como pasivos distintos de provisiones

liability to pay tax
→ tax liability

liable
To be liable is to have incurred legal liability for something.
responsable
= sujeto
▲ *be fully liable* ser completamente responsable ▲ *be liable for* ser responsable de ▲ *be liable in damages* ser responsable por daños ▲ *be liable to tax* estar sujeto a impuestos ▲ *be liable to the extent of one's assets* ser responsable hasta el valor de todos sus activos ▲ *be severally liable for all or part of the liabilities of the associate* ser responsable por separado de todas o parte de las obligaciones de la asociada

liable to pay tax
An enterprise or an individual is liable to pay tax because tax is a compulsory levy that must be paid to the tax authorities.
obligado a pagar impuestos
= responsable del pago de impuestos
▲ *be fully liabe to pay tax* ser totalmente responsable del pago de impuestos ▲ *be liable to pay tax* estar obligado a pagar impuestos

LIBOR
= London Interbank Offered Rate Index
LIBOR is the abbreviation of London Interbank Offered Rate, which is the rate of interest charged by banks when they lend money to each other.
LIBOR
NOTE Previous to the Spanish entry into the euro, the Spanish equivalent was MIBOR (Madrid Interbank Offered Rate). The most widely used reference rate in Spain is EURIBOR (European Interbank Offered Rate).
▲ *50 basis points below LIBOR* 50 puntos por debajo del LIBOR ▲ *changes that are attributable to changes in LIBOR* cambios que son atribuibles a los cambios en el LIBOR ▲ *interest at LIBOR minus 100 basis points* interés a LIBOR menos 100 puntos ▲ *six-month LIBOR* LIBOR a seis meses

licence UK
A licence is a permission granted by the holder of intellectual property rights to a person or an enterprise enabling the latter to use these rights in a specified way.
licencia
▲ *a global licence* una licencia global ▲ *acquired licences* licencias adquiridas ▲ *additions of licences* agregaciones de licencias ▲ *amortise expenditure on acquired licences on a straight-line basis over their useful lives* amortizar el gasto por licencias adquiridas de forma lineal a lo largo de su vida útil ▲ *an exclusive licence* una licencia exclusi-

va ▲ *capitalisation of licences* capitalización de licencias ▲ *measure licences at cost* medir licencias al coste ▲ *non-exclusive licence* licencia no exclusiva ▲ *patents and licences* patentes y licencias ▲ *produce under a licence* producir bajo una licencia ▲ *trade mark licence* licencia de marca ▲ *voluntary licence* licencia voluntaria

licence income UK

= licencing income UK, license income US, licensing income US

Licence income refers to the income generated by granting a licence, i.e. it is the payment received by a licence holder for authorising a third party to use specified rights.

ingreso por licencia

= ingreso de licencia

▲ *significant licence income* ingreso por licencia significativo

licencing income UK

= licence income UK, license income US, licensing income US

Licencing income refers to the income generated by granting a licence, i.e. it is the payment received by a licence holder for authorising a third party to use specified rights.

ingreso por licencia

▲ *recognition of licencing income* reconocimiento de ingreso por licencia

license US

A license is a permission granted by the holder of intellectual property rights to a person or an enterprise enabling the latter to use these rights in a specified way.

licencia

▲ *a global license* una licencia global ▲ *acquired licenses* licencias adquiridas ▲ *additions of licenses* agregaciones de licencias ▲ *amortize expenditure on acquired licenses on a straight-line basis over their useful lives* amortizar el gasto por licencias adquiridas de forma lineal a lo largo de su vida útil ▲ *an exclusive license* una licencia exclusiva ▲ *capitalization of licenses* capitalización de licencias ▲ *measure licenses at cost* medir licencias al coste ▲ *non-exclusive license* licencia no exclusiva ▲ *patents and licenses* patentes y licencias ▲ *produce under a license* producir bajo una licencia ▲ *trade mark license* licencia de marca ▲ *voluntary license* licencia voluntaria

license income US

= licence income UK

License income refers to the income generated by granting a license, i.e. it is the payment received by a license holder for authorising a third party to use specified rights.

ingreso por licencia

▲ *a drop in license income* una caída en el ingreso por licencia ▲ *allocation of license income* asignación del ingreso por licencia ▲ *significant license income* ingreso por licencia significativo ▲ *substantial growth in license income* crecimiento sustancial en el ingreso por licencia

licensing agreement

= licence agreement

A licensing agreement is a contract in which permission is granted by the holder of intellectual property rights to a person or an enterprise enabling the latter to use these rights in a specified way.

contrato de licencia

▲ *enter into a licensing agreement* firmar un contrato de licencia ▲ *publish a licensing agreement* publicar un contrato de licencia ▲ *rights under a licensing agreement* derechos de un contrato de licencia

licensing right

A licensing right is the permission granted by the holder of intellectual property rights to a person or an enterprise enabling the latter to use these rights in a specified way.

derecho de licencia

▲ *secure a licensing right* asegurar un derecho de licencia

life

= duration, maturity, maturity period, term

Life is the period of time during which something, for example a financial instrument, is in force.

vida

= periodo, término, vencimiento

▲ *12-month life* 12 meses de vida ▲ *an indefinite life* una vida indefinida ▲ *at the end of the option's life* al final de la vida de la opción ▲ *the expected life of the financial instrument* la vida esperada del instrumento financiero ▲ *the indefinite life of a held-to-maturity investment* la vida indefinida de la inversión mantenida hasta el vencimiento ▲ *the life of the liability* la vida del pasivo ▲ *the remaining life of the held-to-maturity investment* la vida restante de la inversión mantenida hasta el vencimiento ▲ *the risk-free interest rate for the life of the option* el tipo de interés sin riesgo para la vida de la opción ▲ *the weighted average remaining contractual life of the share options* la media ponderada de la vida contractual restante de las opciones sobre acciones

life assurance UK

Life assurance is a type of insurance where a sum of money will be paid on the occurrence of an event that is dependent on the life of a human being.

seguro de vida

▲ *direct life assurance* seguro de vida directo ▲ *post-employment life assurance* seguro de vida para complementar la jubilación ▲ *take out life assurance* hacer un seguro de vida

⇛ life insurance

life assurance company UK

A life assurance company is a company offering insurance that provides for the payment of specified monetary benefits upon death, incapacity or illness. The majority of life insurance companies also offer pension products.

compañía de seguros de vida

▲ *restrictions on the profit of life assurance companies* restricciones en el beneficio de las compañías de seguros de vida

life assurance policy UK

= life policy

A life assurance policy is an insurance contract that provides that a sum of money will be paid on the occurrence of an event that is dependent on the life of a human being.

póliza de seguro de vida

▲ *insurance provisions for life assurance policies where the investment risk is borne by the policyholder* provisiones de las pólizas de seguro de vida en las que el riesgo lo asume el asegurado ▲ *take out a life assurance policy* hacer una póliza de seguro de vida ▲ *write a life assurance policy* suscribir una póliza de seguro de vida

life cycle

1 A life cycle is the entire life of an asset, product or system through all stages, i.e. from raw materials over performance to final disposal or the development stages of an enterprise: start-up, growth, maturity, decline (or renewal).

ciclo de vida

▲ *the product's expected environmental impact over its entire life cycle* el impacto ambiental esperado del producto a lo largo de su ciclo de vida completo ▲ *typical life cycles* ciclos de vida típicos

⇛ life cycle assessment, life-cycle budgeting, product life cycle

2 The life cycle is a demographic segmentation variable dividing consumers into groups according to their life-cycle stages: age, marital status and number of children, which reflects the changing consumer needs of each stage. Other demographic variables include gender, income, social class and lifestyle.

ciclo de vida

▲ *a typical lifecycle for a family* el ciclo de vida típico para una familia ▲ *the life cycle of the segments* el ciclo de vida de los segmentos

life cycle assessment

= LCA, life-cycle analysis

Life cycle assessment (LCA) is an overall evaluation and examination of a product or industrial system over its life cycle, i.e. from raw materials over performance to final disposal, with a view to environmental impacts. The LCA is typically analysed over three stages: inventory (collecting and describing data), interpretation (relating the data to environmental issues) and improvement (changes to reduce any pollution or other environmental damage).

estimación del ciclo de vida

= estimación de vida útil

▲ *carry out a life cycle assessment* llevar a cabo una estimación del ciclo de vida ▲ *the different phases of a life cycle assessment* las

diferentes fases de una estimación del ciclo de vida
⇛ life-cycle budgeting

life insurance
Life insurance is a type of insurance where a sum of money will be paid on the occurrence of an event that is dependent on the life of a human being.
seguro de vida
▲ *a life insurance contract* un contrato de seguro de vida ▲ *post-employment life insurance* seguro de vida para complementar la jubilación ▲ *take out life insurance* hacer un seguro de vida ▲ *whole life insurance for a fixed amount* seguro de vida completo por una cantidad fija

life insurance company
= life insurer
A life insurance company is a company offering insurance that provides for the payment of specified monetary benefits upon death, incapacity or illness. The majority of life insurance companies also offer pension products.
compañía de seguros de vida
= aseguradora, empresa de seguros de vida
▲ *restrictions on the profit of life insurance companies* restricciones en el beneficio de las compañías de seguros de vida
⇛ life insurance enterprise

life insurance contract
A life insurance contract is an insurance contract that provides that a sum of money will be paid on the occurrence of an event that is dependent on the life of a human being.
contrato de seguro de vida
▲ *a life insurance contract in which the insurer bears no significant mortality risk* un contrato de seguro de vida en el que el asegurador no asume riesgos de mortalidad significativos ▲ *a term life insurance contract* un contrato de seguro de vida a término ▲ *an investment-linked life insurance contract* una inversión vinculada a un contrato de seguro de vida ▲ *conclude an individual life insurance contract* celebrar un contrato de seguro de vida individual

life insurance enterprise US
A life insurance enterprise is an enterprise offering insurance that provides for the payment of specified monetary benefits upon death, incapacity or illness. The majority of life insurance companies also offer pension products.
empresa de seguros de vida
= aseguradora, compañía de seguros de vida
▲ *the financial statements of a life insurance enterprise* los estados financieros de una empresa de seguros de vida
⇛ life insurance company

life insurance financial statements
Life insurance financial statements are financial statements prepared by life insurance companies disclosing their operations, earnings and financial position.
estados financieros de la compañía de seguros de vida
▲ *prepare life insurance financial statements* preparar los estados financieros de la compañía de seguros de vida ▲ *the format of life insurance financial statements* el formato de los estados financieros de la compañía de seguros de vida

life insurance obligation
A life insurance obligation is the statistically calculated obligation that insurance companies have on the financial reporting date. The expected mortality can be estimated on the basis of certain factors and thus the insurance company is able to calculate the expected obligation to those customers who have taken out a life insurance policy.
obligación del seguro de vida
= compromiso del seguro de vida, prestación del seguro de vida
▲ *an actuarial calculation and hedge of the life insurance obligations* un cálculo actuarial y cobertura de las obligaciones del seguro de vida

life insurance policy
= life policy
A life insurance policy is an insurance contract that provides that a sum of money will be paid on the occurrence of an event that is dependent on the life of a human being.
póliza de seguro de vida
= póliza del seguro de vida

▲ *take out a life insurance policy* hacer una póliza de seguro de vida ▲ *write a life insurance policy* suscribir una póliza de seguro de vida

life-cycle analysis
= life cycle assessment
A life-cycle analysis is an overall evaluation and examination of a product or industrial system over its life cycle, i.e. from raw materials over performance to final disposal, with a view to environmental impacts. The life cycle is typically analysed over three stages: inventory (collecting and describing data), interpretation (relating the data to environmental issues) and improvement (changes to reduce any pollution or other environmental damage).
análisis del ciclo de vida
▲ *an improved life cycle analysis* un análisis del ciclo de vida mejorado ▲ *conduct a life cycle analysis* dirigir un análisis del ciclo de vida
⇛ life cycle, life-cycle budgeting

life-cycle assessment
= LCA, life cycle assessment
Life-cycle assessment (LCA) is an overall evaluation and examination of a product or industrial system over its life cycle, i.e. from raw materials over performance to final disposal, with a view to environmental impacts. The LCA is typically analysed over three stages: inventory (collecting and describing data), interpretation (relating the data to environmental issues) and improvement (changes to reduce any pollution or other environmental damage).
evaluación del ciclo de vida
▲ *comparison of life-cycle assessments* comparación de las evaluaciones del ciclo de vida ▲ *prepare a life-cycle assessment* preparar una evaluación del ciclo de vida ▲ *the result of a life-cycle assessment* el resultado de una evaluación del ciclo de vida
⇛ life cycle, life-cycle budgeting

life-cycle budgeting
Life-cycle budgeting is the act of preparing a budget for the total revenue and costs of a product over its entire life cycle from the development stage to the customer service implied in selling the last product units.
presupuesto del ciclo de vida
▲ *implement life-cycle budgeting* implementar el presupuesto del ciclo de vida ▲ *use life-cycle budgeting* utilizar el presupuesto del ciclo de vida
⇛ life cycle, life-cycle cost

life-cycle cost
Life-cycle costs refer to the total future costs of a product or an investment over its entire life.
coste del ciclo de vida
▲ *customer life-cycle costs* costes del ciclo de vida del cliente ▲ *minimised life-cycle cost analysis* análisis del coste del ciclo de vida minimizado ▲ *minimised life-cycle costs* costes del ciclo de vida minimizados ▲ *the life-cycle cost minimum to consumers* el coste del ciclo de vida mínimo para consumidores ▲ *the life-cycle cost of the product* el coste del ciclo de vida del producto
⇛ life cycle, life-cycle budgeting

life-cycle costing
Life-cycle costing is a costing method that estimates all costs that are incurred by a product over its entire life as part of the product range of an enterprise.
sistema de costes del ciclo de vida
▲ *full life-cycle costing* sistema de costes del ciclo de vida completo

LIFO
= last-in, first-out
LIFO is the abbreviation for last-in, first-out, which is a stock valuation method where the cost of stocks is calculated on the assumption that goods acquired last are sold first, measuring cost of sales at the most recent costs and closing stocks at the cost of the items earliest purchased.
LIFO
= última entrada, primera salida
▲ *a LIFO basis* un método LIFO ▲ *measure inventories using LIFO* medir inventarios usando el LIFO
⇛ FIFO

LIFO formula
→ LIFO method

LIFO method
= LIFO formula
The LIFO method is a stock valuation method where the cost of stocks is calculated on the assumption that goods acquired last are sold first, measuring cost of sales at the most recent costs and closing stocks at the cost of the items earliest purchased.
método LIFO
▲ *measure inventories using the LIFO method* medir inventarios usando el método LIFO ▲ *use the LIFO method to measure inventory costs* utilizar el método LIFO para medir los costes de inventario
⇛ FIFO method

like-for-like
= LFL
Like-for-like means comparable, typically used about figures for an accounting period which are comparable with similar figures for another accounting period after certain adjustments. For instance like-for-like sales is a measure that refers to current sales in comparison with sales for the previous year excluding effects from any non-recurring items such as sales from new acquisitions.
comparable
▲ *like-for-like sales* ventas comparables
⇛ non-recurring item

limit
= reduce
To limit is to reduce the amount, number etc. of something or to stop something going beyond a particular point.
limitar
= restringir
▲ *limit financial risks* limitar los riesgos financieros ▲ *limit payment under a term life insurance contract* limitar el pago según un contrato de seguro de vida a término ▲ *limit the enterprise's ability to settle net* limitar la responsabilidad de la empresa a la liquidación neta

limitation
= limit, restriction
Limitation means an act of limiting or restricting i.e. the extent of something, or the greatest amount of something that is possible or allowed.
limitación
= límite, restricción
▲ *compulsory limitation* limitación obligatoria ▲ *limitation of amounts resulting from pure lucky-buy negative goodwill* limitación de cantidades resultantes de fondo de comercio negativo atribuibles a la buena suerte ▲ *limitation of net adjustments* limitación de ajustes netos ▲ *limitation of revaluation reserves* limitación de reservas de revalorización ▲ *limitation of revaluation surplus* limitación de excedentes de revalorización ▲ *limitation of value adjustments* limitación de ajustes de valor ▲ *limitation to tax rules* limitación a las normas fiscales ▲ *limitations on retrospective application* limitaciones en aplicación retrospectiva ▲ *limitations on retrospective restatement* limitaciones en reafirmación retrospectiva

limitation of deductibility
A limitation of deductibility is a restriction on the right to deduct incurred expenses for tax purposes.
límite de deducibilidad
▲ *enforce the limitation of deductibility* hacer cumplir el límite de deducibilidad ▲ *fall within the limitation of deductibility* entrar dentro del límite de deducibilidad

limited company
→ limited liability company

limited liability
Limited liability means that the responsibility assumed by e.g. an investor is restricted to a certain limit and amount. The liability of the contributors of capital to a company may be limited by shares or by guarantee, meaning that the contributors are only liable for the company's debt up to an amount corresponding to the value of their shareholding or guarantee.
responsabilidad limitada
▲ *a company with limited liability* una compañía con responsabilidad limitada ▲ *enjoy limited liability* gozar de responsabilidad limitada

limited liability company
= company with a share capital
A limited liability company is a legal entity set up as a company in which the owners are not personally liable for the

company debts, but where their liability is limited to the capital they have contributed. Typically, limited liability companies are companies where the owners' liability is limited by shares, but the liability may also be limited by guarantee where the members have undertaken to contribute with a certain amount guaranteed in case of winding-up.

sociedad de responsabilidad limitada

▲ *be organised as a limited liability company* estar organizada como una sociedad de responsabilidad limitada ▲ *dissolve a limited liability company* disolver una sociedad de responsabilidad limitada ▲ *form a limited liability company* formar una sociedad de responsabilidad limitada

⇛ private limited company, public limited company

limited partner

A limited partner is a partner in a limited partnership whose liability is limited to the extent of his investment.

socio con responsabilidad limitada

▲ *the incoming limited partner* el socio con responsabilidad limitada entrante ▲ *the retiring limited partner* el socio con responsabilidad limitada saliente

limited partnership

A limited partnership is a business organisation with one or more general partners, who manage the business and assume legal debts and obligations, and one or more limited partners, who are liable only to the extent of their investments.

sociedad comanditaria

▲ *be organised as a limited partnership* estar organizada como una sociedad comanditaria

limiting factor

A limiting factor is a parameter which sets narrow limits for activity and performance. A shortage of raw materials or a reduced productive capacity is e.g. a limiting factor which will reduce output and sales.

factor restrictivo

▲ *a major limiting factor* un factor restrictivo relevante ▲ *the greatest limiting factor* el mayor factor restrictivo ▲ *the most important limiting factor* el factor restrictivo más importante

⇛ scarce resource

line item

Line items are entries in the financial statements of an enterprise displaying accounting elements line by line.

rúbrica

= partida contable, rubro

▲ *a line item that is reported in the income statement* una rúbrica que se incluye en el estado de resultados ▲ *a reconciliation to relevant line items on the balance sheet* una conciliación a las rúbricas relevantes en el balance ▲ *a single separate line item within assets* una rúbrica independiente dentro de activos ▲ *additional line items, headings and subtotals* rúbricas adicionales, epígrafes y subtotales ▲ *particular line items in the financial statements* rúbricas concretas en los estados financieros ▲ *the line item in the income statement* la rúbrica en el estado de resultados ▲ *transfer from one line item within equity to another* traspasar de una rúbrica a otra dentro de patrimonio

line of business

= business area, business line, field of operation

A line of business refers to a specific kind of commercial activity engaged in by an enterprise, such as car manufacturing, accounting services or cleaning.

línea de negocio

= área de negocio

▲ *combine the activities in a particular line of business* combinar las actividades en una línea concreta de negocio ▲ *discontinue several products within an ongoing line of business* descartar varios productos dentro de una línea de negocio en funcionamiento ▲ *dispose of a separate major line of business* enajenar una línea de negocio independiente y fundamental ▲ *represent a separate major line of business* representar una línea de negocio independiente y fundamental ▲ *sale or termination of a line of business* venta o terminación de una línea de negocio

line of credit

= credit line

A line of credit is a specified maximum amount of credit extended to a person or an enterprise by a bank or other lending institution usually based on creditworthiness. A line of credit enables the person or enterprise to borrow the entire maximum amount in one borrowing or in several borrowings without having to re-apply each time as long as the maximum amount is not exceeded.
línea de crédito
▲ *committed lines of credit* líneas de crédito comprometidas ▲ *long-term lines of credit* líneas de crédito a largo plazo ▲ *short-term lines of credit* líneas de crédito a corto plazo ▲ *undrawn committed lines of credit* líneas de crédito comprometidas no dispuestas

line-by-line consolidation
= full consolidation
≠ proportionate consolidation
Line-by-line consolidation is a consolidation method where 100% of the assets, liabilities, revenues and expenses of a subsidiary are recognised line-by-line or item for item in the financial statements of the parent company. This is the normal method of consolidation, and it is also used even if the subsidiary is not wholly owned by the parent company.
consolidación global
▲ *the effect of line-by-line consolidation* el efecto de la consolidación global

linear depreciation
→ straight-line depreciation

linear programming
Linear programming is a mathematical technique used to maximise or minimise a linear function of a number of variables subject to multiple constraints.
programación lineal
▲ *solution of linear programming problems* solución de problemas de programación lineal ▲ *use linear programming* utilizar la programación lineal

linear-cost behavior US
= linear-cost behaviour UK
Linear-cost behavior is a cost function where total costs versus a given cost driver or activity can be illustrated as a straight line in a graph or system of coordinates based on the assumption that the costs are either fixed or variable.
comportamiento de coste lineal
▲ *assume linear-cost behavior* suponer comportamiento de coste lineal

linear-cost behaviour UK
= linear-cost behavior US
Linear-cost behaviour is a cost function where total costs versus a given cost driver or activity can be illustrated as a straight line in a graph or system of coordinates based on the assumption that the costs are either fixed or variable.
comportamiento de coste lineal
▲ *assume linear-cost behaviour* suponer comportamiento de coste lineal

liquid
1 ≠ illiquid
To be liquid is to have cash available. A liquid enterprise has a financial status whereby it can quickly convert a significant percentage of assets to cash, has ample financial resources available and is able to pay short-term debts as they fall due.
con liquidez
≠ sin liquidez
▲ *a very liquid company* una empresa con mucha liquidez
2 ≠ illiquid
Liquid means easily convertible into cash and easily bought or sold.
líquido
▲ *a relatively stable and liquid currency* una divisa relativamente estable y líquida ▲ *financial assets that are not traded in active and liquid markets* activos financieros que no se negocian en mercados activos y líquidos ▲ *highly liquid investments that are readily convertible to known amounts of cash* inversiones muy líquidas que se convierten fácilmente en cantidades conocidas de efectivo ▲ *shares that are actively traded in a deep and liquid market* acciones que se negocian activamente en un mercado activo, estable y líquido ▲ *short-term highly liquid investments* inversiones muy líquidas a corto plazo

liquid asset
= quick asset

Liquid assets are cash and assets that can be readily turned into cash such as short-term bank deposits and as such constitute the most current assets of an enterprise, consequently excluding inventories that may prove difficult to sell quickly.

activo líquido

▲ *a portfolio of liquid assets* una cartera de activos líquidos ▲ *short-term liquid assets* activos líquidos a corto plazo ▲ *significant changes in liquid assets* cambios significativos en activos líquidos ▲ *the post-tax return on liquid asset* el rendimiento después de impuestos del activo líquido

liquid ratio

= acid test ratio, quick ratio

The liquid ratio is a financial ratio measuring the liquidity of an enterprise at very short term, defined as current assets excluding stocks less current liabilities, and is a more stringent measure than the current ratio. The ratio should preferably be at least 1:1.

ratio de liquidez

= acid test ratio

▲ *calculate the liquid ratio* calcular el ratio de liquidez ▲ *the average liquid ratio* el ratio medio de liquidez

liquid resource

Liquid resources consist of cash and/or assets readily convertible into cash such as short-term deposits and securities.

recurso líquido

▲ *liquid resource management* gestión del recurso líquido ▲ *movement in liquid resource* movimiento en recurso líquido ▲ *the liquid resource requirements* los requisitos de recurso líquido

⇛ cash and cash equivalents

liquidation

= dissolution, winding-up

A liquidation is the winding-up or dissolution of an enterprise. A liquidation may be solvent (voluntary) or insolvent. An insolvent or compulsory liquidation involves bankruptcy proceedings.

liquidación

= cierre

▲ *dissolution without liquidation* disolución sin liquidación ▲ *enter into liquidation* iniciar la liquidación ▲ *enterprises in the course of liquidation* empresas en proceso de liquidación ▲ *notice of liquidation* notificación de liquidación ▲ *the commencement of the liquidation procedure* el inicio del trámite de liquidación ▲ *the completion of the liquidation procedure* la finalización del trámite de liquidación ▲ *voluntary liquidation* liquidación voluntaria

liquidator

A liquidator is a person who has been appointed to wind up a company.

liquidador

= administrador judicial, síndico

▲ *appoint a liquidator* nombrar un liquidador ▲ *appoint a liquidator by ordinary resolution* nombrar un liquidador por resolución ordinaria ▲ *appoint a provisional liquidator* nombrar un liquidador provisional ▲ *remove a liquidator* quitar a un liquidador

liquidity

Liquidity refers to the immediate availability of sufficient cash to pay short-term debts as they fall due, and of financial resources for investments.

liquidez

▲ *a presentation based on liquidity* una presentación basada en la liquidez ▲ *a presentation of assets and liabilities in increasing or decreasing order of liquidity* una situación de activo y pasivo en orden creciente o decreciente de liquidez ▲ *an assessment of the nature and liquidity of assets* una valoración de la naturaleza y liquidez de los activos ▲ *assessment of the liquidity of the enterprise* valoración de la liquidez de la empresa ▲ *assets classified according to a liquidity presentation* activos clasificados según su estado de liquidez ▲ *classify liabilities in order of their liquidity* clasificar el pasivo según su liquidez ▲ *current liquidity* liquidez corriente ▲ *eliminate excess intercompany liquidity* eliminar el exceso de liquidez intragrupo ▲ *excess liquidity* exceso de liquidez ▲ *generate liquidity* generar liquidez ▲ *list in order of liquidity* ordenar por liquidez ▲ *management and control of li-*

quidity gestión y control de la liquidez ▲ *optimise excess liquidity* optimizar el exceso de liquidez ▲ *presented broadly in order of liquidity* presentada en líneas generales según su liquidez ▲ *procure liquidity* conseguir liquidez ▲ *statutory requirement concerning liquidity* requisito estatutario relativo a la liquidez ▲ *sufficient liquidity* liquidez suficiente

liquidity ratio
A liquidity ratio is a financial ratio that measures the liquidity of an enterprise, i.e. its ability to pay creditors falling due within one year. Liquidity ratios include the current and quick ratios.
ratio de liquidez
▲ *calculate the liquidity ratio* calcular el ratio de liquidez
⇛ current ratio, liquidity test, quick ratio

liquidity risk
Liquidity risk is the risk that an enterprise will have difficulties in providing sufficient funds to pay its debts as they fall due or, in the case of financial instruments, to satisfy financial liabilities.
riesgo de liquidez
▲ *a high liquidity risk* un riesgo de liquidez alto ▲ *a low liquidity risk* un riesgo de liquidez bajo ▲ *affect an entity's exposure to credit and liquidity risk* afectar a la exposición de una entidad al riesgo de crédito y liquidez ▲ *exposed to liquidity risks* expuesto a riesgos de liquidez ▲ *prudent liquidity risk management* gestión prudente del riesgo de liquidez ▲ *reflect the liquidity risks attaching to the assets and liabilities* reflejar los riesgos de liquidez relativos a los activos y pasivos

liquidity test
A liquidity test is a test used for assessing the liquidity of an enterprise. The acid test finds the quick ratio, which is the ratio of the quick or liquid assets (i.e. less stocks) to the current liabilities. If the test includes stocks in the current assets, the test is referred to as the current ratio test.
prueba de liquidez
= test de liquidez
▲ *apply a liquidity test* aplicar una prueba de liquidez
⇛ acid test ratio, current ratio

list
= quote
To list means to officially quote the price of an enterprise's shares or bonds on a stock exchange or other authorised market place, so that they can be freely traded.
cotizar
▲ *become listed on a stock exchange* cotizada en un mercado de valores

listed
= quoted
When an enterprise's shares or bonds are listed it means that they are officially available i.e. bought and sold on a particular stock exchange or other authorised market place.
cotizado
= cotizable
▲ *a commodity futures contract listed for trading on an exchange* un contrato de futuros de materias primas cotizable en bolsa ▲ *a listed company* una compañía cotizada ▲ *a newly listed entity* una entidad cotizada por vez primera ▲ *become listed on a stock exchange* cotizable en un mercado de valores ▲ *form a dual listed corporation* formar una sociedad cotizable en dos mercados ▲ *publicly listed entities* entidades cotizadas en bolsa ▲ *the weighted average cost of capital of a listed entity* el coste de capital medio ponderado de una entidad cotizada

listed company
A listed company is a company that is quoted for trading on an official, organised securities exchange such as a stock exchange or other authorised market place.
NOTE Companies listed on the London Stock Exchange must be public limited companies; in the US, listed corporations are registered with the Securities and Exchange Commission.
compañía cotizada
▲ *newly listed companies* compañías nuevamente cotizadas

listed enterprise
A listed enterprise is an entity whose equity instruments, bonds, other debt instruments or securities are quoted for trading on an official, organised

securities exchange such as a stock exchange or other authorised market place. Therefore, listed enterprises comprise business organisations other than companies such as cooperative societies.

empresa registrada en bolsa

= empresa registrada en la bolsa

▲ *key figures for listed enterprises* cifras clave para las empresas registradas en bolsa ▲ *raise funds for listed enterprises* conseguir fondos para las empresas registradas en bolsa

listing

Listing occurs when an enterprise "goes public" and is admitted to an official list of shares or bonds which can be bought and sold on a particular stock market.

salida a bolsa

▲ *a security eligible for listing* un título elegible para salida a bolsa ▲ *admission to stock exchange listing* admisión para salida a bolsa ▲ *multinational listing* salida a bolsa internacional ▲ *obtaining a stock exchange listing* obteniendo una salida a bolsa

⇛ quotation

listing fee

A listing fee is a fee that enterprises have to pay, usually annually, to the stock exchange or authorised market place on which their shares or bonds are listed.

cuota de cotización

▲ *impose a listing fee on somebody* imponer a alguien una cuota de cotización ▲ *listing fee expenses* gastos de cuota de cotización ▲ *the annual listing fee* la cuota de cotización anual

Listing Rule UK

The Listing Rules are a set of regulations governing the listing of companies on the London Stock Exchange, e.g. there are minimum requirements as to the content and publication of the prospectus on an initial public offering. The Listing Rules also contain continuing obligations of the companies after the listing, e.g. price sensitive information and new share offers must be published. The rules are the responsibility of the Financial Services Authority.

Norma de Cotización

▲ *Listing Rule breach* violación de la Norma de Cotización

loan

= borrowing

A loan is money or other assets borrowed from a person or enterprise for a specified period against the promise to return the money or assets and usually against payment of interest or rent to the owner.

préstamo

▲ *a convertible loan* un préstamo convertible ▲ *a fixed-rate loan* un préstamo a interés fijo ▲ *a floating-rate loan* un préstamo a interés variable ▲ *a loan default* un incumplimiento del préstamo ▲ *a long-term loan* un préstamo a largo plazo ▲ *a mortgage construction loan* un préstamo hipotecario ▲ *a short-term loan* un préstamo a corto plazo ▲ *advance a loan* anticipar un préstamo ▲ *bullet loan* préstamo reembolsable al vencimiento ▲ *consider the age of the loans within the portfolio* considerar el vencimiento de los préstamos dentro de la cartera de inversiones ▲ *contractual cash flows of a loan receivable* flujos de efectivo contractuales de un préstamo a cobrar ▲ *exchange gains on loans* ganancias de cambio en préstamos ▲ *exchange losses on loans* pérdidas de cambio en préstamos ▲ *foreign currency loan* préstamo en moneda extranjera ▲ *forgivable loans* préstamo condonable ▲ *grant a loan* conceder un préstamo ▲ *illegal and uncollectible loans to owners and members of the executive and supervisory boards* préstamos ilegales e incobrables a propietarios y miembros de los consejos de administración y supervisión ▲ *impairment losses on loans and advances* pérdidas por detrioro en préstamos y anticipos ▲ *interest-bearing loans* préstamos que devengan intereses ▲ *interest-only loans* préstamos con periodo de carencia ▲ *loan assets* activos en préstamo ▲ *loan from the ultimate parent* préstamo de la matriz última ▲ *loan repayments received* amortizaciones de préstamos recibidos ▲ *loan sub-participa-*

tion sub-participación en un préstamo ▲ *loans advanced* préstamos anticipados ▲ *loans and advances* préstamos y anticipos ▲ *loans and receivables originated by the enterprise* préstamos y anticipos creados por la empresa ▲ *loans guaranteed by mortgages* préstamos garantizados por hipotecas ▲ *loans receivable and payable* préstamos a cobrar y pagar ▲ *loans to associates* préstamos a asociadas ▲ *loans which have a maturity period of three months or less* préstamos que tienen un periodo de maduración de tres meses o menos ▲ *non-accrual loan* préstamo no devengado ▲ *non-recourse loan* préstamo no reembolsable ▲ *provide loans at below-market interest rates* conceder préstamos con tipos de interés por debajo de los del mercado ▲ *raise new loans* conseguir nuevos préstamos ▲ *raising of loans* obtención de préstamos ▲ *recoveries on loans previously written off* recuperaciones en préstamos previamente eliminados ▲ *refinance existing loans* refinanciar los préstamos existentes ▲ *repay a loan* devolver un préstamo ▲ *secured loans* préstamos asegurados ▲ *syndicated loan* préstamo sindicado ▲ *the basis for writing off uncollectible loans and advances* la base para la eliminación de préstamos y anticipos incobrables ▲ *unsecured loans* préstamos no asegurados

loan agreement

= loan contract

A loan agreement is an agreement between two or more parties about the lending and borrowing of money or other assets. The loan agreement will contain special provisions as to the principal sum or assets, repayment or return, and the loan period.

contrato de préstamo

▲ *a long-term loan agreement* un contrato de préstamo a largo plazo ▲ *blended payments of principal and interest under a loan agreement* pagos conjunto del principal y los intereses en un contrato de préstamo ▲ *enter into a loan agreement* firmar un contrato de préstamo ▲ *long-term bilateral loan agreements* contratos de préstamos bilaterales a largo plazo ▲ *renegotiate a loan agreement* renegociar un contrato de préstamo ▲ *requirements in loan agreements* requisitos en los contratos de préstamo

loan amount

= amount of the loan, loan sum

The loan amount is the sum of money borrowed.

cuantía del préstamo

▲ *aggregate nominal loan amount* cuantía del préstamo nominal total ▲ *the full loan amount outstanding* la cuantía del préstamo total pendiente ▲ *the loan amount outstanding* la cuantía del préstamo pendiente

loan capital

= debt capital

≠ equity

Loan capital is the capital contributed to the enterprise from other sources than the owners, most often by various types of loan.

capital ajeno a largo plazo

= pasivo no corriente, pasivo a largo plazo, financiación ajena a largo plazo

≠ patrimonio neto

▲ *change in loan capital* cambio en el capital ajeno a largo plazo ▲ *cost of loan capital* coste del capital ajeno a largo plazo ▲ *issue of loan capital* emisión de capital ajeno a largo plazo

loan capital financing

Loan capital financing is the contribution of capital to the enterprise from other sources than the owners, most often by various types of loan.

financiación con capital ajeno

= financiación ajena

▲ *the distribution of equity financing and loan capital financing* la distribución de la financiación propia y ajena

loan commitment

= committed credit facility, committed credit line

A loan commitment is a promise by a lender to provide a loan or credit facility to a borrower.

crédito concedido

▲ *an issuer of loan commitments* un emisor de créditos concedidos ▲ *loan commitments that cannot be settled net in cash or another financial instrument* créditos concedidos que no puedan liquidarse en efectivo o en otro instrumento financiero

loan conversion
= refinancing
Loan conversion is the replacement of a loan by another loan on other terms.
reconversión del préstamo
▲ *as a result of the loan conversion* como resultado de la reconversión del préstamo

loan covenant
A loan covenant is a term that the borrower much comply with, otherwise he will be in breach of the loan agreement.
condición del préstamo
= cláusula del préstamo
▲ *according to the loan covenants* según las cláusulas del préstamo ▲ *comply with the loan covenants* cumplir con las condiciones del préstamo ▲ *meet the loan covenants* cumplir las condiciones del préstamo

loan finance
= debt finance, finance by borrowing
Loan finance takes place when an enterprise raises a loan to finance an investment or other activity rather than, for instance, financing it out of internally generated profits.
financiación mediante préstamo
= financiación con préstamo, financiación por préstamo
▲ *long-term loan finance* financiación mediante préstamo a largo plazo ▲ *short-term loan finance* financiación por préstamo a corto plazo

loan financing
= debt financing
Loan financing refers to the loan capital or net interest-bearing debt of an enterprise, i.e. the part of the capital that has not been contributed by owners through equity. Loan financing is borrowed capital and therefore subject to interest payments.
financiación con préstamo
= financiación mediante préstamo
▲ *increase in loan financing* aumento en la financiación con préstamo
⇛ equity, financial gearing

loan note
A loan note is a redeemable debt instrument evidencing an unsecured loan of a fixed amount for a fixed period, typically less than five or ten years, and may be negotiable or non-negotiable. Commercial paper is an example of loan notes.
nota de préstamo
▲ *a convertible loan note* una nota de préstamo convertible ▲ *loan note holder* titular de la nota de préstamo

loan obligation
A loan obligation is the obligation of a borrower to pay instalments and interest on the principal balance to the lender on the due dates for payment.
obligación del préstamo
▲ *collateralised loan obligations* obligaciones del préstamo con garantía prendaría ▲ *default on one's loan obligations* incumplimiento de las obligaciones del préstamo propias

loan portfolio
= portfolio of loans and advances
A loan portfolio is the total of all outstanding loans held by a bank or other lending institution at a given time. A loan portfolio is often segmented according to risk in order to estimate potential losses.
cartera de préstamos
▲ *an increase in the loan portfolio* un aumento en la cartera de préstamos ▲ *buy a loan portfolio* comprar una cartera de préstamos ▲ *refinancing of the loan portfolio to fixed rates* refinanciación de la cartera de préstamos a tipos de interés fijo

loan position
The loan position gives details of the aggregate amount of funds borrowed, i.e. the net interest-bearing debt or outstanding loans of an enterprise at a particular date, and may be determined on a long-term or short-term basis, according to type of loan, in national or foreign currency etc. In an enterprise, the loan position is monitored on a current basis and subject to prudent treasury management.
posición crediticia
▲ *foreign currency loan positions* posiciones crediticias en moneda extranjera

loan stock UK
Loan stock represents a long-term loan of a company, typi-

cally through the issue of lending securities such as debentures or corporate bonds at a fixed rate of interest, usually redeemable on a fixed date.
título de deuda
▲ *conversion of loan stock* conversión del título de deuda ▲ *convertible loan stock* título de deuda convertible ▲ *fixed rate loan stock* título de deuda con interés fijo ▲ *floating rate loan stock* título de deuda con interés variable ▲ *subordinated loan stock* título de deuda subordinado ▲ *unsecured loan stock* título de deuda no garantizado

loan volume
= volume of loans and advances
The loan volume is the aggregate amount of funds borrowed or outstanding loans of an enterprise at a given date or for a given period as measured in national or foreign currency.
volumen de préstamo
= volumen crediticio, volumen de los préstamos
▲ *control of the loan volume* control del volumen de los préstamos

loan-loss provision US
A loan-loss provision is a credit loss expense and allowance for loan impairment deducted from income in the income statement and from loans and allowances under assets in the balance sheet of a bank. The provision represents management's estimate of impairment incurred in the portfolio of loans at the balance sheet date.
provisión por pérdidas en préstamos
▲ *a reduction in the loan-loss provision* una reducción en la provisión por pérdidas en préstamos
⇛ provisioning ratio

loan-to-value limit
= LTV
The loan-to-value limit (LTV) is the percentage relationship between the mortgage loan (cash value) and the property value or purchase price for the property and constitutes the maximum lending limit. The LTV typically differs according to type of property, e.g. an LTV of 80% is seen for residential properties.
porcentaje entre el principal de un préstamo y el valor del activo que lo respalda
= porcentaje entre préstamos valor
▲ *a loan-to-value limit ranging between 40% and 100%* un porcentaje entre el principal de un préstamo y el valor del activo que lo respalda en un intervalo entre el 40% y el 100% ▲ *determine the loan-to-value limit* determinar el porcentaje entre el principal de un préstamo y el valor del activo que lo respalda ▲ *loans exceeding the loan-to-value limit* préstamos que exceden el porcentaje entre el principal de un préstamo y el valor del activo que lo respalda

loan-to-value ratio
The loan-to-value ratio (LTV) shows the proportion between the amount borrowed and the value or cost of a property.
ratio préstamo-valor
▲ *a 95% loan-to-value ratio on new lending* un ratio préstamo-valor del 95% sobre los nuevos préstamos ▲ *the average loan-to-value ratio* el ratio préstamo-valor medio ▲ *the total loan-to-value ratio* el ratio préstamo-valor total ▲ *with a loan-to-value ratio of 100%* con un ratio préstamo-valor del 100%

local currency IAS/IFRS, UK
≠ foreign currency
The local currency of an enterprise is the currency of the primary economic environment and country in which the enterprise carries on business.
moneda nacional
= moneda local
≠ moneda extranjera
▲ *a change in the exchange rate between the reporting currency and the local currency* una modificación en el tipo de cambio entre la moneda de presentación y la moneda nacional ▲ *amounts of local currency held* cantidades mantenidas en moneda nacional ▲ *arrange borrowings substantially in the local currency* formalizar empréstitos principalmente en la moneda nacional ▲ *settle in the local currency* liquidar en la moneda local
⇛ functional currency

lock up
1 A lock up is an investment in assets, e.g. shares, which must be held for a given period of

time during which the assets are not readily transferable.
inversión bloqueada
= inversión inmobilizada
▲ *be subject to a lock up* estar sujeto a una inversión bloqueada
⇛ lock-up agreement

2 With a view to avoiding or discouraging a hostile takeover, the management of a target company may offer a lock up, i.e. an option or a right to a third party - a friendly acquirer - of buying certain assets, e.g. additional equity, in the company on pre-determined terms and conditions.
bloqueo
▲ *enter a lock up* introducir un bloqueo ▲ *sign a lock up* firmar un bloqueo

lock-up agreement
A lock-up agreement is a legally binding contract between a company and its underwriters to the effect that no major shareholders (e.g. management executives, employees or venture capitalists) are allowed to sell any of the company's newly issued shares during a defined time period, typically 180 days up to one year. Such an agreement is typically entered to ensure that the market price of the share will remain stable during the initial trading period.
acuerdo de inmovilización
▲ *enter into a lock-up agreement* firmar un acuerdo de inmovilización ▲ *sign a lock-up agreement* firmar un acuerdo de inmovilización ▲ *the expiration of the lock-up agreement* el vencimiento del acuerdo de inmovilización
⇛ lock up

locked-in cost
= designed-in cost
Locked-in costs are costs related to goods and services not yet incurred by an enterprise that will invariably be incurred at a later time as a consequence of previous decisions made, typically at the design stage.
coste inevitable
▲ *avoid the locked-in costs* eludir los costes inevitables ▲ *reduce long-term locked-in costs* reducir costes inevitables a largo plazo ▲ *spending on locked-in costs* gasto en costes inevitables

London Inter Bank Offered Rate
→ London Interbank Offered Rate

London Inter-Bank Offered Rate
→ London Interbank Offered Rate

London Interbank Offered Rate UK
= LIBOR UK
The London Inter Bank Offered Rate (LIBOR) is the rate of interest charged by banks when they lend money to each other.
London Interbank Offered Rate
= LIBOR, precio del dinero en el mercado interbancario de Londres
▲ *base an interest rate on the London Interbank Offered Rate* establecer un tipo de interés según el London Interbank Offered Rate

long-form audit report
The long form audit report is a report by the auditor(s) for the accounting period under review to the board of directors on the scope and procedures of the audit performed as well as the audit opinion expressed. The report is entered in the auditors' records.
informe completo de auditoría
▲ *prepare a long-form audit report* preparar un informe completo de auditoría

long-lived asset US, IAS/IFRS
= fixed asset UK, long-term asset, non-current asset IAS/IFRS, US
≠ current asset IAS/IFRS, UK, US
Long-lived asset is another term for non-current asset, i.e. an asset that is held by an enterprise for a long-term. Examples of long-lived assets are property, plant and equipment, intangibles and investments.
activo de larga vida
= activo fijo, activo no corriente
▲ *impairment of long-lived assets* deterioro del activo de larga vida ▲ *the carrying amount of the long-lived asset* el valor contable del activo de larga vida ▲ *the retirement of tangible long-lived assets* la retirada de los activos de larga vida tangibles

long-range planning
Long-range planning is the development of an action plan for future operations with a view to achieving defined

goals, typically for a period of five years or longer.

planificación de largo alcance

▲ *coordinate long-range planning* planificación de largo alcance coordinada ▲ *forecasts for long-range planning* previsiones de planificación de largo alcance ▲ *the impact of long-range planning* el impacto de la planificación de largo alcance

long-term UK

For accounting purposes, long-term is typically defined as lasting more than one year.

a largo plazo

▲ *a favourable long-term trend in market prices* una tendencia favorable a largo plazo en los precios de mercado ▲ *a floating-rate long-term debt* una deuda a largo plazo con tipo de interés variable ▲ *a long-term agreement* un acuerdo a largo plazo ▲ *a long-term balance* un saldo a largo plazo ▲ *a long-term debt item* una partida de deuda a largo plazo ▲ *a long-term loan* un préstamo a largo plazo ▲ *a long-term loan agreement* un acuerdo de préstamo a largo plazo ▲ *exceed the long-term average growth rate for the products* superar la tasa de crecimiento medio a largo plazo para los productos ▲ *financial assets of a long-term nature* activos financieros de naturaleza a largo plazo ▲ *financial liabilities that provide financing on a long-term basis* pasivos financieros que aportan financiación a largo plazo ▲ *long-term borrowing* empréstito a largo plazo ▲ *long-term debt* deuda a largo plazo ▲ *long-term employee benefit liabilities* pasivos por prestaciones a empleados a largo plazo ▲ *long-term financing* financiación a largo plazo ▲ *long-term investments* inversiones a largo plazo ▲ *long-term pre-financing* prefinanciación a largo plazo ▲ *long-term receivables* cuentas a cobrar a largo plazo ▲ *refinancing on a long-term basis* refinanciación a largo plazo ▲ *the entity's long-term operations* las operaciones de la empresa a largo plazo

long-term asset

= fixed asset UK, long-lived asset IAS/IFRS, US, non-current asset IAS/IFRS, US

≠ current asset IAS/IFRS, UK, US

Long-term asset is another term for non-current asset, i.e. an asset that is held by an enterprise for a period of more than one year. Examples of long-term assets are property, plant and equipment, intangibles and investments.

activo de larga vida

▲ *acquire long-term assets* adquirir activos de larga vida ▲ *charges for the use of long-term assets of the enterprise* cambios por el uso de los activos de larga vida de la empresa ▲ *construct long-term assets* construir activos de larga vida ▲ *disclose the aggregate amounts of long-term assets* publicar las cantidades totales de los activos de larga vida ▲ *purchase long-term assets* comprar activos de larga vida ▲ *the acquisition and disposal of long-term assets* la adquisición y eliminación de los activos de larga vida

long-term borrowing UK

A long-term borrowing is a loan or credit facility with a term of more than one year.

empréstito a largo plazo

▲ *interest on bank overdrafts and short-term and long-term borrowings* interés sobre los descubiertos bancarios y los empréstitos a corto y largo plazo ▲ *raise long-term borrowings at floating rates* conseguir empréstitos a largo plazo con tipo de interés variable

long-term creditor

= creditor, amount falling due after more than one year GB, UK, long-term debt US

≠ account payable IAS/IFRS, US, short-term creditor US

Long-term creditors are creditors representing amounts that fall due after more than one year.

acreedor a largo plazo

▲ *interest on long term-creditor balances* interés sobre los saldos de los acreedores a largo plazo ▲ *show as a long-term creditor in the balance sheet* mostrar como un acreedor a largo plazo en el balance

long-term debt US, IAS/IFRS

= creditor, amount falling due after more than one year UK, long-term creditor, long-term payable

≠ short-term debt US, IAS/IFRS
Long-term debt is debt with a remaining maturity that exceeds one year.
deuda a largo plazo
≠ deuda a corto plazo
▲ *a floating rate long-term debt* una deuda a largo plazo con tipo de interés variable ▲ *current maturities of long-term debt* vencimientos corrientes de deuda a largo plazo ▲ *increase in long-term debt* aumento de deuda a largo plazo ▲ *other long-term debt* otro tipo de deuda a largo plazo ▲ *principal payments on long-term debt* pagos del principal de la deuda a largo plazo ▲ *reduction of long-term debt* reducción de la deuda a largo plazo

long-term debt obligation US
≠ short-term debt obligation US
A long-term debt obligation is a loan repayable after more than one year. Bonds are examples of long-term debt obligations.
obligación de deuda a largo plazo
▲ *long-term debt obligation maturities* vencimientos de la obligación de deuda a largo plazo

long-term employee benefit IAS/IFRS
= long-term service benefit
≠ short-term employee benefit IAS/IFRS
Long-term employee benefits refer to benefits earned by employees in return for their current and prior services, such as pensions, termination benefits and other benefits, that fall due only after a period of twelve months after the end of the period when the service was rendered.
prestación al empleado a largo plazo
= beneficio al empleado a largo plazo
NOTE Spanish accountants prefer 'prestación' to the IAS/IFRS term 'beneficio' for referring to the benefits earned by employees.
▲ *accounting for other long-term employee benefits* contabilizando otras prestaciones al empleado a largo plazo ▲ *assets held by a long-term employee benefit fund* activos en un fondo de prestaciones al empleado a largo plazo ▲ *long-term employee benefit liabilities* pasivos por prestación al empleado a largo plazo ▲ *long-term employee benefits for key management personnel* prestaciones al empleado a largo plazo para el personal de alta dirección ▲ *other long-term employee benefits* otras prestaciones al empleado a largo plazo ▲ *the measurement of long-term employee benefits* la valoración de las prestaciones al empleado a largo plazo
⇛ short-term employee benefit

long-term investment
≠ short-term investment, trading investment
A long-term investment is an investment in assets not intended disposed of in the immediate future, typically held for three or more years. Long-term investments include investments in bonds, equities, property and other fixed assets, often for pension purposes, as well as a parent company's investment in subsidiaries and associates.
inversión a largo plazo
≠ inversión a corto plazo
▲ *current maturities of long-term investments* vencimientos corrientes de las inversiones a largo plazo ▲ *disposals of long-term investments* venta de las inversiones a largo plazo ▲ *long-term investments carried at cost* inversiones a largo plazo valoradas al coste ▲ *maximize long-term investment return* optimizar la rentabilidad de la inversión a largo plazo
⇛ fixed-asset investment

long-term liability UK, IAS/IFRS
= non-current liability IAS/IFRS, US
≠ current liability IAS/IFRS
A long-term liability is a liability that falls due after more than one year after the balance sheet date. Examples of long-term liabilities are non-current provisions and debt.
pasivo a largo plazo
▲ *an interest-bearing long-term liability* un pasivo a largo plazo que devenga interés ▲ *classify as long-term liabilities* clasificar como pasivos a largo plazo ▲ *recognise as a long-term liability* reconocer como un pasivo a largo plazo

long-term provisions IAS/IFRS
≠ short-term provisions IAS/IFRS
Long-term provisions are non-current liabilities that are uncertain in terms of amount or timing and that concern the financial year or a previous year.
NOTE Long-term provisions are recognised as an item under non-current liabilities in the balance sheet.
provisiones a largo plazo
≠ provisiones a corto plazo
▲ *changes in long-term provisions* cambios en provisiones a largo plazo ▲ *current portion of long-term provisions* parte corriente de las provisiones a largo plazo
⇛ non-current liability

long-term receivable
= non-current receivable
A long-term receivable is a receivable that will not be paid to the enterprise within one year. Long-term receivables are classified as non-current assets.
cuenta a cobrar a largo plazo
▲ *current maturities of long-term receivables* parte corriente de cuentas a cobrar a largo plazo ▲ *current portion of long-term receivables* parte corriente de cuentas a cobrar a largo plazo ▲ *long-term receivables for which adequate collateral exists* cuentas a cobrar a largo plazo para las que existe una garantía prendaria

long-term service benefit
= long-term employee benefit IAS/IFRS
≠ short-term employee benefit IAS/IFRS
Long-term service benefits refer to benefits earned by employees in return for their current and prior services, such as pensions, termination benefits and other benefits, that fall due only after a period of twelve months after the end of the period when the service was rendered.
prestación por servicio a largo plazo
≠ prestación por servicio a corto plazo
▲ *a net obligation in respect of long-term service benefits* una obligación neta con respecto a las prestaciones por servicio a largo plazo ▲ *employees eligible for long-term service benefits* empleados con derecho a prestaciones por servicio a largo plazo ▲ *other long-term service benefits* otras prestaciones por servicio a largo plazo ▲ *the present value of the unfunded obligations for long-term service benefits* el valor actual de las obligaciones no financiadas por prestaciones por servicio a largo plazo
⇛ short-term employee benefit

lose
To lose means that you no longer have something that you previously had.
perder
≠ ganar
▲ *gain or lose tax incentives* ganar o perder incentivos fiscales ▲ *lose an invested amount* perder una cantidad invertida ▲ *lose in importance* perder en importancia ▲ *lose market value* perder valor de mercado

loss
≠ gain, income, profit
A loss is a decrease in economic benefits that arises when expenses exceed revenue, or when a decrease in net assets occur, resulting from a disposal or a fall in value of a fixed asset, or from a non-recurring event such as fire or other damage. A loss for the accounting period arises if an enterprise's total revenue less total expenses is negative.
pérdida
≠ ganancia
▲ *a loss from discontinuing operations* una pérdida de operaciones interrumpidas ▲ *a loss on a trade receivable* una pérdida en una cuenta a cobrar comercial ▲ *a recognised but unrealised gain or loss on an asset* un resultado reconocido pero no realizado en un activo ▲ *a tax loss* una pérdida fiscal ▲ *include changes in their fair value in profit or loss* incluir cambios en su valor razonable en resultados ▲ *increase loss per share from continuing operations* aumentar la pérdida por acción de las operaciones continuas ▲ *the entity's taxable profit or tax loss* el resultado imponible de la entidad ▲ *the financial loss suffered by the deceased's dependants* la pérdida financiera sufrida por los familiares de los fallecidos ▲ *the loss of signifi-*

cant influence la pérdida de influencia significativa
⇛ deficit

loss carry-forward
→ loss carryforward

loss carryforward
A loss carryforward is the transfer of a loss for a particular accounting period to a later accounting period with the purpose of offsetting it against future profits to reduce taxes payable.
pérdida fiscal prospectiva
= traslado de pérdida fiscal a ejercicios futuros
▲ *the potential benefit of income tax loss carryforwards* el beneficio potencial de las pérdidas fiscales prospectivas en el impuesto sobre la renta
⇛ tax loss carryforward

loss of capital
Loss of capital is the loss of equity when the liabilities exceed the assets, and can arise if an enterprise has made a loss for the accounting period that exceeds its retained earnings. Depending on the amount or percentage of capital lost, the management will determine whether the enterprise can continue in operation, whether a capital injection is required or whether the enterprise must be wound up.
pérdida de capital
▲ *a significant loss of capital* una pérdida de capital significativa

loss on curtailment
→ curtailment loss

loss on disposal
≠ gain on disposal
A loss on disposal is the loss suffered by an enterprise on the sale of an asset where the net selling price is lower than the carrying amount of the asset.
pérdida en ventas
= pérdida por venta
≠ ganancia en ventas, ganancia por venta
▲ *after-tax loss on disposal* pérdida en ventas después de impuestos ▲ *determine the gain or loss on disposal* determinar la ganancia o pérdida en ventas ▲ *loss on disposal of discontinued operation* pérdida por venta de operación interrumpida ▲ *loss on disposal of property, plant and equipment* pérdida por venta de edificios, instalaciones y equipos ▲ *loss on disposal of the net investment* pérdida en ventas de la inversión neta ▲ *recognition of any gain or loss on disposal* reconocimiento de cualquier ganancia o pérdida en ventas

loss risk
= loss potential, risk of losses
Loss risk is the risk of suffering a loss because of changes in the assumptions underlying the original calculations.
riesgo de pérdidas
= riesgo de pérdida
▲ *calculate a loss risk* calcular un riesgo de pérdidas ▲ *real, probable loss risk* real, riesgo de pérdidas probable ▲ *the loss risk of a commitment* el riesgo de pérdidas de un compromiso

loss-making
An activity is loss-making when the expenses involved exceed the earnings generated.
generador de pérdidas
▲ *an acquired loss-making long-term contract* un contrato a largo plazo adquirido generador de pérdidas

lower-of-cost-or-market method
= LCM method
The lower-of-cost-or-market method is a method for the measurement of inventory in the balance sheet where the cost and the net realisable value (market value) are determined and the lower value of either is applied.
método del valor más bajo entre el valor de coste o de mercado
▲ *under the lower-of-cost-or-market method* según el método del valor más bajo entre el valor de coste o de mercado ▲ *use the lower-of-cost-or-market method* utilizar el método del valor más bajo entre el valor de coste o de mercado
⇛ FIFO, LIFO

Ltd UK
= private limited company UK
Ltd is the abbreviation for "limited" and is used about a private limited company. Ltd appears after and as part of the firm name.
SL
= sociedad de responsabilidad limitada, SRL, sociedad limitada
▲ *incorporate a company as an Ltd* incorporar una empresa como una SL

LTV
= loan-to-value limit

The LTV is an abbreviation for loan-to-value limit, which is the percentage relationship between the mortgage loan (cash value) and the property value or purchase price for the property and constitutes the maximum lending limit. The LTV typically differs according to type of property, e.g. an LTV of 80% is seen for residential properties.

ratio préstamo-valor

= porcentaje entre el principal de un préstamo y el valor del activo que lo respalda, ratio préstamo, valor

▲ *an LTV ranging between 40% and 100%* un ratio préstamo-valor que se sitúa entre el 40% y el 100% ▲ *determine the LTV* determinar el porcentaje entre el principal de un préstamo y el valor del activo que lo respalda ▲ *loans exceeding the LTV* préstamos que exceden el ratio préstamo-valor

lump sum

A lump sum is a single amount of money paid or payable at once instead of by instalments.

rescate completo

▲ *a lump sum benefit* una prestación de rescate completo ▲ *lump sum upfront payments* rescate completo por adelantado ▲ *make a lump sum cash payment* rescatar completamente en efectivo ▲ *pay a lump sum retirement benefit* pagar un rescate completo por jubilación

⇛ lump sum pension plan

lump sum annuity US

A lump sum annuity is a pension plan contracted with an insurance company under which a lump sum, i.e. one single payment, is made on a defined future date or a series of large instalment payments are made on defined future dates.

pago anual global

lump sum benefit

A lump sum benefit is a benefit payable under a pension scheme or a redundancy scheme in the form of payment by a single amount of money.

prestación de rescate completo

▲ *pay a lump sum benefit* pagar una prestación de rescate completo ▲ *provide a lump sum benefit of 70% payable on retirement for each year of service* aportar una prestación de rescate completo de 70% a pagar en la jubilación por año de servicio

lump sum pension plan

A lump sum pension plan is a pension scheme under which a lump sum is paid to the employee (the member) on retirement at a time agreed in advance, typically when the member has reached an age between 60 and 70.

plan de pensiones de rescate completo

▲ *lump sum pension plan distributions* distribuciones del plan de pensiones de rescate completo ▲ *the impact of partial transition from lump sum pension plan to the defined contribution pension plan* el impacto de la transacción parcial desde un plan de pensiones de rescate completo a uno con aportación definida

⇛ lump sum

M

machine

= machinery

A machine is a technical device using power to perform a certain job, e.g. in the manufacturing process of an enterprise.

máquina

▲ *acquisition of a machine* adquisición de una máquina ▲ *cash flows from continuing use of the machine until its disposal* flujos de efectivo procedentes del uso continuado de la máquina hasta su retirada ▲ *disposal of a machine* enajenación de una máquina ▲ *maintenance of a machine* mantenimiento de una máquina ▲ *order for a machine* pedido de una máquina ▲ *purchase of a machine* adquisición de una máquina ▲ *replace a machine* sustituir una máquina ▲ *revaluation of the cost of a machine* revalorización del coste de una máquina ▲ *revenue generated by using the machine* ingreso generado por el uso de la máquina ▲ *running-in of new machines in the production* funcionamiento de nuevas máquinas en la producción ▲ *the cash-generating unit to which the machine belongs* la unidad generadora de efectivo a la que pertenece la máquina ▲ *the expected remaining useful life of the machine* la vida útil que se prevé de funcionamiento de la máquina ▲ *the machine's fair value less costs to sell* el valor razonable de la máquina menos los costes de venta ▲ *the machine's value in use* el valor en uso de la máquina ▲ *the net selling price of the machine* el precio de venta neto de la máquina ▲ *the recoverable amount of the machine* la cantidad recuperable de la máquina

main product

Main products constitute the output from joint production in the form of joint products with relatively high sales values. Main products can only be identified as separate products after the split-off point.

producto principal

▲ *the main products manufactured* los productos principales fabricados ▲ *the main products sold* los productos principales vendidos

⇛ by-product, joint costs, joint product, joint production, separable costs, split-off point

maintain

To maintain means to keep something in the original shape and condition.

mantener

▲ *maintain a given standard of living* mantener un nivel de vida concreto ▲ *maintain a long-term operating relationship with the enterprise* mantener una relación operativa a largo plazo con la empresa ▲ *maintain and enhance financial performance* mantener y reforzar los resultados financieros ▲ *maintain future economic benefits* mantener futuros beneficios económicos ▲ *maintain or discharge financial liabilities* mantener o eliminar el pasivo financiero ▲ *maintain risk management instruments* mantener instrumentos de gestión de riesgo ▲ *maintain the entity's existing interest rate risk position* mantener la posición de riesgo de tipo de interés existente de la empresa ▲ *maintain the entity's internally generated goodwill* mantener el fondo de comercio generado internamente por la empresa ▲ *maintain the income* mantener la renta ▲ *maintain the operating capability of the enterprise* mantener la capacidad operativa de la empresa

maintenance

Maintenance means keeping something in the original shape and condition, e.g. by repairing it.

mantenimiento

▲ *contractual obligations for future repairs and maintenance* obligaciones contractuales para reparaciones y mantenimiento futuros ▲ *deferred maintenance* mantenimiento diferido ▲ *incur liabilities on the maintenance of intangible resources* devengar pasivos por el mantenimiento de recursos intangibles ▲ *maintenance costs* costes de mantenimiento ▲ *maintenance of a specified amount of earnings for a period* mantenimiento de una cantidad concreta de beneficios para un periodo ▲ *maintenance of assets* mantenimiento de activos ▲ *maintenance of capital equipment* mantenimiento de bienes de capital ▲ *maintenance of machinery* mantenimiento de maquinaria ▲ *maintenance of operating equipment* mantenimiento de bienes de explotación ▲ *maintenance on an ongoing basis* mantenimiento sobre una base continuada ▲ *routine maintenance* mantenimiento rutinario

maintenance cost

= cost of maintenance, maintenance expenditure

Maintenance costs are costs incurred by an enterprise when maintaining and servicing its assets where the assets' future economic benefits are not enhanced. Maintenance costs are recognised in the profit and loss account whereas costs that enhance the future economic benefits of the assets are capitalised.

coste de mantenimiento

= coste del mantenimiento

▲ *a deductible maintenance cost* un coste de mantenimiento deducible ▲ *estimated maintenance costs* costes de mantenimiento estimados ▲ *provision for periodic maintenance costs* provisión para costes de mantenimiento periódicos ▲ *the level of maintenance costs* el nivel de costes de mantenimiento

maintenance expenditure

= maintenance cost UK, maintenance expense US

Maintenance expenditure constitutes costs incurred by an enterprise in connection with repairs and service of its assets to keep them at the normal level of operational capacity. Maintenance expenditure is recognised in the profit and loss account.

gasto de mantenimiento

▲ *repairs and maintenance expenditure on property, plant and equipment* gasto de reparaciones y mantenimiento en edificios, instalaciones y equipos ▲ *the level of future maintenance expenditure* el nivel de gasto de mantenimiento futuro

maintenance expense

= maintenance expenditure

Maintenance expenses constitute costs incurred by an enterprise in connection with repairs and service of its assets to keep them at the normal level of operational capacity. Maintenance expenses are recognised in the profit and loss account.

gasto de mantenimiento

= gasto del mantenimiento

▲ *repairs and maintenance expenses on property, plant and equipment* gastos de reparaciones y mantenimiento en edificios, instalaciones y equipos ▲ *the level of future maintenance expenses* el nivel de gastos de mantenimiento futuros

major shareholder

A major shareholder is a shareholder who owns a certain minimum percentage of voting or non-voting shares in a public limited company. The percentage varies in accordance with specific thresholds set by a country: under the UK Companies Act 2006, the threshold is 3% or more, in Denmark it is stipulated in the Securities Trading Act to be 5% or more. If a shareholding exceeds or falls below the thresholds indicated, the shareholder must notify the issuing company of the change of shareholding structure to meet the requirements for market transparency, market efficiency and investor protection. In the EU Transparency Directive to be implemented in national legislation by EU member countries by 2007, various percentage notification thresholds ranging from 5% to 75% apply.

principal accionista

= accionista mayoritario

▲ *exact ownership interest of major shareholders* inversión exacta de los principales accionistas ▲ *major shareholders of listed companies* principales accionistas de las empresas cotizadas ▲ *requirement for disclosure of major shareholders* exigencia de publicación de los nombres de los principales accionistas

⇛ majority shareholder, minority shareholder

majority interest

= majority holding

A majority interest is the ownership of more than half the contributed capital in an enterprise. Typically, a majority interest refers to the holding of more than 50% of the voting shares in a company.

inversión mayoritaria

▲ *acquire the majority interest in the company* adquirir la inversión mayoritaria de la empresa

majority of shares

A shareholder or a group of shareholders has a majority of shares when the share ownership exceeds 50% of the total shares in a company. This amounts to a controlling interest.

mayoría de acciones

= mayoría de las acciones

▲ *acquire a majority of shares* adquirir una mayoría de acciones

majority owner

→ **majority shareholder** UK

= majority owner, majority stockholder US

≠ minority shareholder

A majority shareholder is an entity or person holding, i.e. controlling, more than 50% of the voting shares of a company.

accionista mayoritario

▲ *dividend payable to majority shareholders* dividendo a pagar a los accionistas mayoritarios

⇛ major shareholder, majority interest, principal shareholder

majority shareholding

= majority holding

A majority shareholding means a quantity of shares in a company totalling more than 50% that is held by a shareholder or a group of shareholders.

inversión mayoritaria

= tenencia de acciones mayoritaria

▲ *hold a majority shareholding* tener una inversión mayoritaria ▲ *transfer a majority shareholding* transferir una inversión mayoritaria

majority stockholder US

= majority shareholder UK

A majority stockholder is an entity or person controlling more than 50% of the voting shares of a company.

accionista mayoritario

▲ *dividend payable to majority stockholders* dividendo a pagar a los accionistas mayoritarios

majority-owned

Majority-owned refers to an enterprise in which another enterprise has a controlling interest, i.e. more than 50% of the voting shares. The financial statements of a majority-owned enterprise must be consolidated with those of the enterprise having a controlling interest.

de participación mayoritaria

= de propiedad mayoritaria

▲ *consolidation of majority-owned subsidiaries* consolidación de filiales de participación mayoritaria ▲ *the annual accounts of our majority-owned subsidiaries* las cuentas anuales de nuestras filiales de participación mayoritaria

make

To make means to carry out, prepare or produce something.

hacer

= llevar a cabo, realizar

▲ *make a deduction for investment losses* realizar una deducción por pérdidas de inversión ▲ *make a proposal* hacer una proposición ▲ *make a setoff* hacer una compensación de deudas ▲ *make a transaction* llevar a cabo una transacción ▲ *make an adjustment of the published results* hacer un ajuste de los resultados publicados ▲ *make intercompany transfers* realizar transferencias interempresariales ▲ *make provisions for* hacer provisiones para ▲ *make value adjustments of securities* realizar ajustes de valor de los títulos

make-or-buy decision

A make-or-buy decision is the decision of whether the components or machines that an enterprise needs for its production are to be produced by the enterprise itself or if they should be bought from an external supplier.

decisión de fabricar o comprar

▲ *the importance of the make-or-buy decision* la importancia de la decisión de fabricar o comprar

managed cost

= discretionary cost UK, US, management cost US, policy cost UK, programmed cost US, programmed fixed cost US

≠ committed cost US, UK
Managed costs are discretionary fixed costs that are determined by and changes because of managerial decisions without any obvious relationship with capacity or production activity. Examples are marketing, training, research and development costs.
coste de administración
= coste de gestión
▲ *adjust managed costs periodically* ajustar los coste de administración periódicamente
⇛ fixed cost

management

1 Management is the direction, running and control of an organisation at different levels or of specifically defined areas.
gestión
▲ *financial management* gestión financiera ▲ *joint management* gestión conjunta ▲ *operational management* gestión operativa ▲ *the appropriate level of management* el nivel apropiado de gestión ▲ *the day-to-day management* la gestión diaria

2 Management is the group of people responsible for directing, running and achieving the objective of an organisation.
NOTE In the UK and the US, the top management consists of a board of directors including both non-executive (outside directors) and executive directors (senior managers).
dirección
▲ *a financial review by management* una revisión financiera por parte de la dirección ▲ *former members of the management* miembros anteriores de la dirección ▲ *management's stewardship of the resources entrusted to it* la administración por la dirección de los recursos a ella confiados ▲ *present members of the management* miembros actuales de la dirección ▲ *remuneration to present and former members of the management* remuneración a los miembros actuales y anteriores de la dirección ▲ *the management's administration of the funds of the enterprise* la administración de los fondos de la empresa por parte de la dirección ▲ *the management's responsibility for the presentation of the annual report* la responsabilidad de la dirección para la presentación del informe anual ▲ *the selection of the management team of the combined entity* la selección del equipo de dirección de la entidad conjunta ▲ *the ultimate management* la dirección última
⇛ board of directors, supervisory board and executive board

management accounting UK

= management control, managerial accounting US
≠ financial accounting
Management accounting is concerned with the measuring, reporting and provision of accounting information to support the planning and control decisions made by management in a business.
contabilidad de gestión
≠ contabilidad financiera
▲ *fundamentals of management accounting* principios de la contabilidad de gestión ▲ *management accounting systems* sistemas de contabilidad de gestión ▲ *strategic management accounting* contabilidad de gestión estratégica

management accounts

Management accounts are accounts prepared by the enterprise for internal use in the decision-making process and allow an enterprise to keep track of its financial performance and to take remedial action should the need arise. Management accounts assist executives in fulfilling organisational objectives.
cuentas de gestión
▲ *prepare management accounts* preparar las cuentas de gestión

management audit

= performance audit
Management audit is a review of the effectiveness of managers in achieving and implementing entity objectives, policies and procedures specified by top management to identify potential weaknesses.
auditoría de gestión
▲ *carry out a management audit* llevar a cabo una auditoría de gestión ▲ *perform a management audit* realizar una auditoría de gestión
⇛ audit

management by exception UK, US

= MBE
Management by exception is concentrating on activities that deviate from the plan and on

ignoring areas that appear to be running according to expectations.
dirección por excepción
= gestión por excepción
▲ *active management by exception* dirección por excepción activa ▲ *facilitate management by exception* facilitar la dirección por excepción ▲ *the need for management by exception* la necesidad de una dirección por excepción

management by objectives
= MBO
Management by objectives is a top-down management principle based on individual employees having their own well-defined objectives for job performance. The objectives are set in cooperation with a superior manager who evaluates the performance.
dirección por objetivos
= gestión por objetivos
▲ *systematic management by objectives* dirección por objetivos sistemática ▲ *the impact of management by objectives* el impacto de la dirección por objetivos

management challenge
In the context of an intellectual capital report, management challenges are the challenges which must be met to further develop, realize and implement an enterprise's basic values and ambition for knowledge management as formulated in the knowledge narrative. Examples of management challenges are determining which existing knowledge resources which need to be strengthened and whether new types of knowledge resources are needed.
desafío de la administración
= desafío de la dirección
▲ *a number of management challenges* un número de desafíos de la administración
⇛ intellectual capital report, knowledge narrative

management commentary IAS/IFRS
A management commentary is part of the financial statements in which the management describes the enterprise's performance and financial condition for the reporting period and its expected development, performance and financial condition.
informe de dirección
= informe de la dirección
▲ *be included in the management commentary* estar incluido en el informe de dirección ▲ *combine the management commentary for the parent and the group* combinar el informe de dirección de la matriz y el grupo ▲ *prepare a management commentary* preparar un informe de dirección ▲ *provide information in the management commentary* aportar información en el informe de la dirección

management control
= management accounting
Management control is the process of accumulating, measuring and reporting accounting data to support the planning and control decisions made by management in an enterprise.
control de gestión
= control de la gestión
▲ *proper management control* control de gestión apropiado

management control system
= cost accounting system, management information system
A management control system is a systematically designed system for retrieval and use of information with a view to supporting and coordinating the overall planning and management decisions in an enterprise so that objectives are achieved and resources efficiently utilised.
sistema de control de gestión
= sistema de control de la gestión
▲ *a comprehensive management control system* un sistema global de control de la gestión ▲ *a computerised management control system* un sistema de control de gestión informatizado

management cost US
= discretionary cost UK, US, managed cost UK, management fixed cost US, policy cost UK, programmed cost US
≠ committed cost US, UK
Management costs are discretionary fixed costs that are determined by and changes because of managerial decisions without any obvious relationship with capacity or production activity. Examples are marketing, training, research and development costs.

coste de gestión
= coste de administración, coste de la administración, coste de la gestión
▲ *calculate management costs* calcular los costes de gestión
▲ *estimate management costs* estimar los costes de gestión
⇛ discretionary cost, discretionary fixed cost, fixed cost

management employee
= executive officer
A management employee is a person employed at management level in an enterprise.
empleado administrativo
▲ *full-time management employees* empleados administrativos a tiempo completo

management information system
= cost accounting system, management control system
A management information system is a systematically designed system for retrieval and use of information with a view to supporting and coordinating the overall planning and management decisions in an enterprise so that objectives are achieved and resources efficiently utilised.
sistema de información de gestión
= sistema de contabilidad de costes, sistema de información de la gestión
▲ *an advanced management information system* un sistema de información de gestión avanzado ▲ *as part of a management information system* como parte de un sistema de información de gestión

management report US
= management's statement, report of management US
The management report is a statement in the annual or interim report of a company that defines management's responsibility for the objectivity and integrity of the financial disclosures. The report states that generally accepted accounting principles have been observed, that the annual report, in all material respects, gives a fair representation of the company's assets, liabilities and equity as well as the results for the year of the company, and that all representations made to the independent auditors are valid and appropriate.
NOTE The management report typically appears in tandem with the auditors' report and makes explicit the distribution of responsibilities between the company's management and the independent auditors.
informe de gestión
= informe de la gestión
▲ *prepare a management report* preparar un informe de gestión
⇛ audit report

management's discussion and analysis US
= management discussion and analysis US, management's discussion and analysis of earnings, MD&A, operating and financial review UK
Management's discussion and analysis (MD&A) is a report that discusses a company's performance and financial condition, focusing on any unusual or infrequent events or significant economic changes and future developments. The MD&A is a requirement of the US Securities and Exchange Commission and must be filed with the SEC annually by companies registered with it.
NOTE In its longer form, the MD&A is referred to as "Management's Discussion and Analysis of Results of Operations and Financial Condition", often using capital initial letters.
debate y análisis de la gestión
▲ *a separate management's discussion and analysis* un debate y análisis de la gestión financiera separada ▲ *provide information in the management's discussion and analysis* ofrecer información en el debate y análisis de la gestión financiera
⇛ management report, Securities and Exchange Commission

management's remuneration
= remuneration to the management
Management's remuneration refers to the payments made to managers in an enterprise for performing the direction, running and control of the enterprise. The remuneration may be related to corporate or individual performance and may be a combination of different types of remuneration, e.g. or-

dinary pay, shares, share options and bonuses.

remuneración de la dirección

= remuneración a la dirección

▲ *disclose management's remuneration* publicar la remuneración de la dirección

manager

A manager is a person who is responsible for the tasks being carried out by his subordinates and for supervising the day-to-day work of an enterprise, a department or a particular responsibility area.

gerente

= director, manager

▲ *appoint a new manager* nombrar un nuevo gerente ▲ *remove the manager* quitar al gerente ▲ *retire as a manager* jubilarse como un gerente ▲ *the manager of the company* el manager de la empresa ▲ *the retiring manager* el gerente saliente

managerial accounting US

= management accounting

≠ financial accounting

Managerial accounting is concerned with the measuring, reporting and provision of accounting information to support the planning and control decisions made by management in a business.

contabilidad de gestión

≠ contabilidad financiera

▲ *apply managerial accounting concepts in practice* poner en práctica los conceptos de la contabilidad de gestión ▲ *the fundamentals of managerial accounting* los fundamentos de la contabilidad de gestión

managerial effort

Managerial efforts are activities which are carried out by a manager to achieve given objectives, and which contribute to delivering efficiency and performance as well as maximising an enterprise's core competencies.

esfuerzo gerencial

▲ *a positive effect on managerial effort* un efecto positivo en el esfuerzo gerencial ▲ *result in an increase in managerial effort* dar lugar a un mayor esfuerzo gerencial

managing director

The managing director is the chief executive of the enterprise and has the overall control of the day-to-bay business in order to ensure the effective implementation of the elements of management.

director general

▲ *appoint a new managing director* nombrar un nuevo director general ▲ *the former managing director* el anterior director general ▲ *the managing director of the company* el director general de la empresa ▲ *the retiring managing director* el director general saliente

mandatory redemption

= compulsory redemption

Mandatory redemption means the unavoidable and enforced exchange for cash of typically shares or bonds by the issuer. Shares that are at a regulatory, legal, taxation or other disadvantage to the issuer or its shareholders may be subject to mandatory redemption.

amortización obligatoria

= cancelación obligatoria, redención obligatoria, rescate obligatorio

▲ *a preference share that provides for mandatory redemption by the issuer* una acción preferencial que prevé una amortización obligatoria por el emisor ▲ *mandatory redemption for a determinable amount* amortización obligatoria por una cantidad a determinar ▲ *mandatory redemption for a fixed amount* amortización obligatoria por una cantidad fijada

⇛ redemption obligation

manufacturing cell

A manufacturing cell groups all the types of an enterprise's production resources which are needed and applied in connection with manufacturing a particular product, e.g. raw materials, manpower, equipment and machines.

célula de fabricación

▲ *a flexible manufacturing cell* una célula de fabricación flexible ▲ *an autonomous manufacturing cell* una célula de fabricación autónoma

manufacturing cost

= manufacturing expense

Manufacturing costs are direct and indirect expenses incurred which related to the manufacturing process in an enterprise. Examples are direct material costs, direct manufacturing labour costs and manufacturing overhead.

coste de producción

= coste de fabricación

▲ *direct manufacturing costs* costes de producción directos ▲ *indirect manufacturing costs* costes de producción indirectos ▲ *recognition of manufacturing costs* reconocimiento de los costes de producción ▲ *the actual manufacturing costs incurred* los costes de producción reales devengados

⇛ manufacturing overhead

manufacturing overhead US

= factory burden US, factory overhead US, indirect manufacturing cost, indirect manufacturing expense US, indirect production cost, indirect production expense US, manufacturing overhead cost, production overhead IAS/IFRS

Manufacturing overheads are costs that are not directly related to the production of goods, i.e. costs for which single products or activities cannot be identified. Examples of manufacturing overheads are indirect labour and materials, rent and insurance of manufacturing units.

coste indirecto de fabricación

▲ *a decrease in manufacturing overhead* un descenso en el coste indirecto de fabricación ▲ *an increase in manufacturing overhead* un aumento en el coste indirecto de fabricación

⇛ manufacturing cost

manufacturing overhead allocated

= manufacturing overhead applied

Manufacturing overhead allocated is a contribution to cover indirect production costs.

costes indirectos de fabricación asignados

= costes indirectos de fabricación aplicados

NOTE Always plural in Spanish accounting texts.

▲ *calculate manufacturing overhead allocated* calcular los costes indirectos de fabricación asignados

manufacturing overhead allocated

= manufacturing overhead applied

Manufacturing overhead allocated constitutes the amount of indirect production costs which via cost-allocation bases have been allocated on cost objects such as orders, products or services.

costes indirectos de fabricación asignados

= costes indirectos de fabricación aplicados

NOTE Always plural in Spanish accounting texts.

▲ *an increase in the manufacturing overhead allocated* un aumento en los costes indirectos de fabricación asignados ▲ *exceed the manufacturing overhead allocated* exceder los costes indirectos de fabricación asignados

manufacturing overhead applied

= manufacturing overhead allocated

Manufacturing overhead applied is a contribution to cover indirect production costs.

costes indirectos de fabricación aplicados

= costes indirectos de fabricación asignados

NOTE Always plural in Spanish accounting texts.

▲ *calculate manufacturing overhead applied* calcular los costes indirectos de fabricación aplicados

manufacturing overhead applied

= manufacturing overhead allocated

Manufacturing overhead applied constitutes the amount of indirect production costs which via cost-allocation bases have been allocated on cost objects such as orders, products or services.

costes indirectos de fabricación aplicados

≠ costes directos de fabricación aplicados

NOTE Always plural in Spanish accounting texts.

▲ *an increase in the manufacturing overhead applied* un aumento en los costes indirectos de fabricación aplicados ▲ *exceed the manufacturing overhead applied* exceder los costes indirectos de fabricación aplicados

manufacturing overhead cost

= factory burden, factory overhead US, factory overhead cost, indirect manufacturing cost, indirect production cost, indirect production expense US,

manufacturing overhead US, production overhead US, IAS/IFRS
Manufacturing overhead costs are costs that are not directly related to the production of goods, i.e. costs for which single products or activities cannot be identified. Examples of manufacturing overhead costs are indirect labour and materials, rent and insurance of manufacturing units.
coste de producción indirecto
= coste de fabricación indirecto
▲ *the actual manufacturing overhead costs* los costes de producción indirectos reales ▲ *variable manufacturing overhead costs* costes de producción indirectos variables
⇛ manufacturing overhead

manufacturing period
The manufacturing period is the time spent for producing a product.
periodo de fabricación
▲ *a long manufacturing period* un periodo de fabricación extenso ▲ *costs relating to the manufacturing period* costes relativos al periodo de fabricación ▲ *the manufacturing period of the non-current asset* el periodo de fabricación del activo no corriente

manufacturing-sector company
A manufacturing-sector company is a company engaged in factory production of machine-made, finished goods from raw materials or components.
empresa del sector manufacturero
▲ *large manufacturing sector companies* grandes empresas del sector manufacturero
⇛ merchandising-sector company, service-sector company

marcom US
= market communications
Marcom is an abbreviation of marketing communications that include an enterprise's external communications activities with a view to marketing their products or services such as direct marketing, sales promotion and advertising, public relations and branding.
comunicaciones de marketing
▲ *a small marcom company* una pequeña empresa de comunicaciones de marketing ▲ *have a marcom background* tener un conocimiento previo de comunicaciones de marketing

margin
A margin is the difference or spread between two amounts/rates/points/lines on a graph etc.
margen
▲ *a margin between different percentage rates* un margen entre diferentes tasas porcentuales ▲ *be subject to regular margin calls* estar sujeto a depósitos de garantía regular ▲ *exceeded the asset's carrying amount by a substantial margin* excedían el valor contable del activo por un margen sustancial ▲ *generate a profit from fluctuations in price or broker-traders' margin* generar un beneficio proveniente de las fluctuaciones en el precio o en el margen de los agentes comerciales ▲ *high-margin products* productos con mucho margen ▲ *interest margin hedge* cobertura del margen de interés ▲ *low-margin products* productos con poco margen
⇛ profit margin

margin deposit
A margin deposit is a particular amount of money required deposited in advance with a broker or dealer by an investor when buying or selling future contracts or other derivative financial instruments as a guarantee of performance.
depósito en garantía
▲ *make a margin deposit* hacer un depósito en garantía

margin of safety UK, US
= safety margin
The margin of safety shows how far sales can fall below budgeted sales before losses occur, i.e. the excess of budgeted or actual sales over the level necessary to break even. The margin of safety is calculated as the budgeted sales in units less the breakeven sales in units.
margen de seguridad
▲ *a significant margin of safety* un margen de seguridad significativo ▲ *an adequate margin of safety* un margen de seguridad adecuado
⇛ margin of safety ratio

margin of safety ratio UK, US
= safety margin ratio

The margin of safety ratio is the safety margin calculated as a ratio and indicates the percentage by which budgeted sales exceed or fall short of the level of sales needed to break even.

ratio de margen de seguridad

= ratio del margen de seguridad, RMS

▲ *calculate the margin of safety ratio* calcular el ratio de margen de seguridad ▲ *determine the margin of safety ratio* determinar el ratio del margen de seguridad

marginal cost

Marginal cost is the additional cost resulting from the production of one extra unit of product or service, or the reduction in cost because of the production of one less unit of product or service.

coste marginal

▲ *long-run marginal costs* costes marginales a largo plazo ▲ *negligible marginal costs* costes marginales insignificantes ▲ *short-run marginal costs* costes marginales a corto plazo

marginal costing

Marginal costing is a cost accounting system in which marginal costs are charged to products (cost units) leaving fixed costs to be charged in full against the total contribution for each accounting period. Marginal costing is used in internal decision-making as it recognises cost behaviour.

sistema de coste marginal

▲ *apply marginal costing* aplicar el sistema de coste marginal ▲ *the use of marginal costing* el uso del sistema de coste marginal

⇛ direct costing, variable costing

marginal income US

= contribution UK, US, marginal revenue UK, unit contribution margin US

Marginal income is the additional income generated from the sale of one additional unit of output, calculated by deducting the variable cost per unit from the unit sales price.

ingreso marginal

▲ *an increase in marginal income* un aumento en el ingreso marginal ▲ *total marginal income* total ingreso marginal

marginal income tax rate

The marginal income tax rate is the tax rate applying to additional income earned. In the progressive tax system, the marginal tax rate is higher than the average tax rate and rises as income increases, resulting in higher tax payable on extra income.

tipo impositivo marginal

▲ *a marginal income tax rate of 50%* un tipo impositivo marginal del 50% ▲ *marginal income tax rate cuts* recortes del tipo impositivo marginal

marginal revenue UK

= contribution UK, US, contribution per unit UK, marginal income US, unit contribution margin US

Marginal revenue is the additional income generated from the sale of one additional unit of output, calculated by deducting the variable cost per unit from the unit sales price.

ingreso marginal

▲ *a monopolist's marginal revenue* un ingreso marginal del monopolista ▲ *calculate marginal revenue* calcular el ingreso marginal ▲ *marginal revenue increases* incrementos del ingreso marginal

mark to market

= mark-to-market

To mark to market is to recognise an investment or other asset by continuous revaluation and adjustment to the current market value in the balance sheet.

ajustar a valor de mercado

▲ *mark to market the derivative instruments* ajustar los instrumentos derivativos a valor de mercado

mark-up

→ markup

mark-up pricing

= cost plus method

Mark-up pricing is a pricing method which seeks to add an appropriate mark-up to the supplier's cost.

fijación del precio mediante la adición del margen de beneficios

▲ *use mark-up pricing* usar la fijación del precio mediante la adición del margen de beneficios

market

A market is a place, whether physical or electronic, where

transactions take place between sellers and buyers, i.e. where goods and services are bought and sold. A market is usually governed by supply and demand which means that the prices of goods and services are determined by the available supply and the number of buyers.

mercado

▲ *a difficult market* un mercado díficil ▲ *a fluctuating market* un mercado fluctuante ▲ *a geographical market* un mercado geográfico ▲ *a homogenous market* un mercado homogéneo ▲ *a volatile market* un mercado volátil ▲ *affected by the thinness of the market* afectado por la inestabilidad del mercado ▲ *an active market* un mercado activo ▲ *an economically comparable market* un mercado económicamente comparable ▲ *consolidate one's position on the market* consolidar su posición en el mercado ▲ *demonstrate the existence of a market* demostrar la existencia de un mercado ▲ *develop a market* desarrollar un mercado ▲ *gain a foothold on a market* asentarse en un mercado ▲ *introduce to the market* introducir en el mercado ▲ *leave a market* dejar un mercado ▲ *the items traded within the market* los artículos comercializados dentro del mercado

market cap

= market capitalisation IAS/IFRS, UK, market capitalization US

Market cap is an abbreviation for market capitalisation, which is defined as the value of a company calculated as the total number of shares outstanding multiplied by the market price for the company's shares.

capitalización bursátil

= capitalización de mercado, valor de mercado del capital emitido

▲ *a decline in the market cap* un disminución en la capitalización bursátil ▲ *companies with a market cap of over $200 million* empresas con una capitalización bursátil superior a los 200 millones de dólares ▲ *two-thirds of total market cap* dos tercios de la capitalización bursátil

market capitalisation IAS/IFRS, UK

= market cap UK, IAS/IFRS, market capitalization US, stock market value US

Market capitalisation is the value of a company calculated as the total number of shares outstanding multiplied by the market price for the company's shares.

capitalización búrsatil

▲ *a high market capitalisation* una alta capitalización bursátil ▲ *a low market capitalisation* una baja capitalización bursátil ▲ *a market capitalisation of USD 200m* una capitalización bursátil por valor de 200 millones de dólares USA ▲ *current market capitalisation* capitalización bursátil actual ▲ *drop in market capitalisation* bajada en la capitalización bursátil ▲ *estimated market capitalisation* capitalización bursátil estimada ▲ *listed market capitalisation* capitalización bursátil oficial ▲ *the latest market capitalisation* la capitalización bursátil final ▲ *the market capitalisation of the enterprise* la capitalización bursátil de la empresa

market capitalization US

= market cap, market capitalisation UK, IAS/IFRS, stock market value US

Market capitalization is the value of a company calculated as the total number of shares outstanding multiplied by the market price for the company's shares.

capitalización bursátil

▲ *a high market capitalization* una capitalización bursátil alta ▲ *a low market capitalization* una capitalización bursátil baja ▲ *a market capitalization of USD 200m* una capitalización bursátil de 200 millones de dólares americanos ▲ *current market capitalization* capitalización bursátil actual ▲ *drop in market capitalization* caída de la capitalización bursátil ▲ *estimated market capitalization* capitalización bursátil estimada ▲ *listed market capitalization* capitalización bursátil cotizada ▲ *the market capitalization of the enterprise* la capitalización bursátil de la empresa

market communications

= marcom US

Market communications include an enterprise's external communications activities with a view to marketing their products or services such as direct marketing, sales promotion and advertising, public relations and branding.

comunicaciones de mercado

▲ *accurate market communications* comunicaciones de mercado precisas

market condition

Market conditions refer to the conditions under which enterprises compete in a market, such as conditions that relate to competition, demand, supply, costs, legislation and distribution.

condición referida al mercado

▲ *adjust to market conditions* ajustar a condiciones de mercado ▲ *changes in market conditions* cambios en las condiciones referidas al mercado ▲ *considering the local market conditions* considerando las condiciones de mercados locales ▲ *determine fair value by reference to the market conditions* determinar el valor razonable con referencia a las condiciones de mercado ▲ *difficult market conditions* condiciones de mercado difíciles ▲ *favourable market conditions* condiciones de mercado favorables ▲ *grants of equity instruments with market conditions* subvenciones de instrumentos de patrimonio con condiciones referidas al mercado ▲ *in the light of current market conditions* a la luz de las condiciones de mercado actuales ▲ *reflect market conditions at the balance sheet date* reflejar condiciones referidas al mercado a la fecha de balance ▲ *the market conditions at the balance sheet date* las condiciones referidas al mercado en la fecha de balance ▲ *these market conditions* estas condiciones referidas al mercado ▲ *unfavourable market conditions* condiciones de mercado desfavorables ▲ *vary with market conditions* variar según las condiciones referidas al mercado

Market Manipulation Directive

The Market Manipulation Directive is a legislative act adopted by the European Parliament and the Council and contains rules to prevent market abuse, i.e. insider trading and market manipulation, when trading in securities admitted for listing or trading on regulated markets within the EU.

Directiva sobre los métodos que constituyen la manipulación del mercado

▲ *the objective of the Market Manipulation Directive* el objetivo de la Directiva sobre los métodos que constituyen la manipulación del mercado ▲ *the scope of the Market Manipulation Directive* el alcance de la Directiva sobre los métodos que constituyen la manipulación del mercado

market price

1 The market price is the price of something offered on an arm's length basis in an open market at a particular time.

precio de mercado

▲ *an observable market price* un precio de mercado observable ▲ *below market price* por debajo del precio de mercado ▲ *changes in market prices* cambios en los precios de mercado ▲ *competitive market prices* precios de mercado competitivos ▲ *current market price per unit of output* precio de mercado actual por unidad de producto ▲ *determine the fair value using market prices* determinar el valor razonable según los precios de mercado ▲ *general market prices for an area or product* precios de mercado generales para un área o producto ▲ *the appropriate market price* el precio de mercado apropiado

⇛ current price

2 The market price is the price quoted by a stock exchange and may be the buying or the selling price of a particular security, or the average price of the buying and selling prices quoted in the market.

precio bursátil

= valor bursátil

▲ *recognise at market price* reconocer a precio bursátil ▲ *the current market price* el precio bursátil actual

⇛ current price

3 The market price is the price in a market such as a stock, commodity or foreign exchange market of a product on a particular date. There may be

a margin between the buying and the selling market prices in which case the market price is quoted as the average between the two prices.

precio de mercado

▲ *changes in market prices* cambios en los precios de mercado

market price issue

A market price issue is an issue of shares at the price quoted in the stock market. The issue may be a re-issue of existing shares to existing shareholders involving the change of nominal value to market value, resulting in a capital increase, or it may be a new issue of additional shares at market price, e.g. employee shares.

emisión a precio de mercado

▲ *relative to the market price issue* relativo a la emisión a precio de mercado

market rate

1 = market exchange rate, market rate of exchange

The market rate of a currency is the value of one currency quoted against another as determined by supply and demand in the foreign exchange market.

tipo de mercado

= tasa de mercado, tipo de interés de mercado

▲ *changes in market rates* cambios en los tipos de mercado

⇛ market price

2 = market interest rate, market rate of interest

In the capital market, the market rate is the current or flat yield on a debt instrument or bond depending on the price determined by the market forces in relation to the coupon rate. When also taking into account the time to maturity, the market rate will correspond to the redemption yield. In the money market, the market rate is a short-term interest rate such as the London Interbank Offered Rate.

tipo de mercado

▲ *a change in the market rate* un cambio en el tipo de mercado ▲ *a commercial market rate* un tipo de mercado comercial ▲ *a rate that is above the market rate of interest* un tipo que está por encima del tipo de interés del mercado ▲ *a rate that is at the market rate of interest* un tipo que está al tipo de interés del mercado ▲ *a rate that is below the market rate of interest* un tipo que está por debajo del tipo de interés del mercado ▲ *adjustment to the market rate of interest* ajuste al tipo de interés del mercado ▲ *as market rates change* como cambio en los tipos de mercado ▲ *at interest rates that are substantially below market rates* a los tipos de interés que están sustancialmente por debajo de los tipos de mercado ▲ *discount at the current market rate of interest* descuento al tipo de interés de mercado actual ▲ *prevailing market rates* tipos de mercado predominantes ▲ *reprice an instrument at market rate of interest* volver a fijar el precio de un instrumento al tipo de interés del mercado ▲ *the current market rate* el tipo de mercado actual ▲ *the effective market rate* el tipo de mercado efectivo

market rent

The market rent is the rent charged on comparable property in the open market.

renta de mercado

▲ *a conservative market rent* una renta de mercado conservadora ▲ *a rent that is substantially lower than the market rent* una renta que es sustancialmente más baja que la renta de mercado ▲ *current market rent* renta de mercado actual ▲ *pay market rent* pagar la renta de mercado

market risk

Market risk is the risk that the value of a financial instrument will change as a result of fluctuations in market prices.

riesgo de mercado

▲ *exposure to market risk under embedded derivatives* exposición al riesgo de mercado bajo instrumentos derivados implícitos ▲ *management of the enterprise's market risks* gestión de los riesgos de mercado de la empresa ▲ *monitoring of market risks* controlando los riesgos de mercado ▲ *the financial market risk* el riesgo de mercado financiero ▲ *transfer the market risk exposure back to the entity* transferir la exposición al riesgo de mercado de nuevo a la empresa

market segment
A market segment is a subset of a total market resulting from a segmentation or division of consumers according to e.g. sex, age, income, occupation, behaviour etc.
segmento de mercado
= segmento del mercado
▲ *high-growth market segments* segmentos del mercado con crecimiento alto ▲ *low-growth market segments* segmentos del mercado con crecimiento bajo ▲ *strategic market segments* segmentos de mercado estratégicos

market share
A market share designates how large a share the sales of an enterprise's products or services constitute in proportion to the total market for the particular products or services in question.
cuota de mercado
▲ *a global market share* una cuota de mercado global ▲ *a significant market share* una cuota de mercado significativa ▲ *an average market share* una cuota de mercado media ▲ *cash market share* cuota de mercado en efectivo ▲ *create a 50% market share* crear una cuota de mercado del 50% ▲ *gain market shares* ganar cuotas de mercado ▲ *improve one's market share* mejorar su cuota de mercado ▲ *increase one's market share* aumentar su cuota de mercado ▲ *market shares on the principal markets* cuotas de mercado en los principales mercados ▲ *regain market shares* volver a ganar cuotas de mercado ▲ *retain one's market shares* retener sus cuotas de mercado ▲ *the current market share* la cuota de mercado actual

market to book ratio US
= market to book value, P/BV, price to book value, price/book value
The market to book ratio is an investment ratio or multiple defined as the share price divided by the book value per share. A market to book ratio exceeding 1 means that the value of the company's shares exceeds that of the equity. This ratio shows how the market values the company and its future.
ratio de valor de mercado a valor en libros
= coeficiente entre capitalización bursátil y patrimonio neto, ratio valor de mercado/valor en libros, razón valor de mercado/valor en libros, valor de mercado a valor en libros, VM/VL
▲ *a decrease in the market to book ratio* una disminución en el ratio de valor de mercado a valor en libros ▲ *a high market to book value* un ratio de valor de mercado a valor en libros alto ▲ *a low market to book value* un ratio de valor de mercado a valor en libros bajo

market to book value
→ market to book ratio

market value
= market price, quoted market price
≠ face value, par value
Market value is the amount obtainable from the sale, or payable on the acquisition, of a financial instrument in an active market in a transaction on an arm's length basis.
valor de mercado
▲ *a declining market value* un valor de mercado a la baja ▲ *acquire shares at market value* adquirir acciones a valor de mercado ▲ *current market values* valores de mercado actuales ▲ *expected market value* valor de mercado previsto ▲ *measure at market value* cuantificar a valor de mercado ▲ *measure securities at market value* cuantificar títulos a valor de mercado ▲ *the aggregate market value of the shares* el valor de mercado agregado de las acciones ▲ *the market value at the balance sheet date* el valor de mercado a la fecha de balance ▲ *the market value of an entity* el valor de mercado de una entidad ▲ *the market value of the liability* el valor de mercado del pasivo ▲ *the market value of treasury shares* el valor de mercado de las acciones propias
⇛ open market value

market value adjusted
To meet the requirement of fair representation in the financial statements, investments including securities are market value adjusted when recognised in the balance sheet, which means that the amount recognised is changed to reflect the current market value

for the accounting period under review, i.e. the price quoted on the relevant stock exchange.

ajustado a valor de mercado

▲ *market value adjusted life insurance* seguro de vida ajustado a valor de mercado ▲ *market value adjusted products* productos ajustados a valor de mercado

market value adjustment

= price adjustment

A market value adjustment implies changing the recognised price of a particular security into another price recognised in the balance sheet. The current recognition at e.g. fair value requires the current market value adjustment of e.g. shares and bonds.

ajuste a valor de mercado

▲ *market value adjustment of investments* ajuste de las inversiones a valor de mercado

market-based

Market-based refers to factors that derive from or are determined by market forces. Prices or the supply or demand of goods and services may be market-based.

basado en el mercado

▲ *a change in the current market-based discount rate* un cambio en el tipo de descuento basado en el mercado actual ▲ *market-based evidence of fair value* pruebas de valor razonable basadas en el mercado

market-related value

The market-related value of e.g. an asset is a value that recognises changes in the fair value of the asset over a time period which is usually five years. The spreading over time reduces the consequences of the financial markets' year-on-year volatility.

NOTE Market-related value is typically used to determine the value of the plan assets of an employee benefit fund.

valor relacionado con el mercado

= valor según las condiciones del mercado, valor según mercado

▲ *a market-related value of $10,000* un valor relacionado con el mercado de 10.000 dólares ▲ *calculate the market-related value* calcular el valor según las condiciones de mercado ▲ *reflected in market-related value* reflejado en el valor según las condiciones de mercado ▲ *the expected future market-related value* el valor relacionado con el mercado futuro previsto ▲ *the use of a market-related value of assets* el uso del valor relacionado con el mercado de los activos

marketable securities US

= other investments UK

Recognised as an item in the balance sheet under current assets, marketable securities constitute investments in the form of readily tradable securities by an enterprise such as shares and bonds.

títulos negociables

▲ *unrealized gain/loss on marketable securities* ganancia/pérdida no realizada en títulos negociables

marketable security US

= marketable instrument

Marketable securities are equity or debt securities that can be bought and sold in an active financial market, such as a stock exchange or other authorised market place, for which a market value can be indicated.

título negociable

= valor negociable

▲ *cash and cash equivalents at beginning of year including marketable securities* efectivo y equivalentes de efectivo a principios de año incluyendo los títulos negociables

⇛ authorised market place, stock exchange

marketing

The activities of an enterprise that are intended to increase the public's attention to its goods and services are collectively referred to as marketing.

marketing

▲ *after proper marketing* después de un marketing adecuado ▲ *clearer focus on marketing* objetivo más claro centrado en el marketing ▲ *create marketing synergies* crear sinergias de marketing ▲ *general overheads incurred by a sales and marketing team* costes indirectos generales incurridos por un equipo de ventas y marketing ▲ *market share and marketing rights* cuota de mercado y derechos de marketing ▲ *the marketing of new products* el marketing de nuevos productos

marketing cost UK

= marketing expense US

Marketing costs are costs attributable to the marketing of the goods and services of an enterprise, such as advertising costs, wages and salaries of sales staff and costs related to promotion material and campaigns.

coste de marketing

= coste del marketing

▲ *low marketing costs* costes de marketing bajos ▲ *the marketing costs incurred* los costes de marketing materializados

⇛ marketing

marketing expense

= marketing cost

Marketing expenses are expenses attributable to the marketing of the goods and services of an enterprise, such as advertising expenses, wages and salaries of sales staff and expenses related to promotion material and campaigns.

gasto de marketing

= gasto en marketing

▲ *a 5% decline in marketing expenses* un bajada del 5% en los gastos de marketing ▲ *an increase in marketing expenses* un aumento en los gastos de marketing ▲ *the marketing expenses incurred* los gastos de marketing devengados

markup

A markup is the difference between the selling price and the total production and distribution costs of a product or service, i.e. the profit. The markup is expressed as a fixed amount or as the percentage relationship of the profit divided by the cost.

margen de beneficios

= margen sobre costes

▲ *a markup of 25%* un margen de beneficios del 25%

master budget

A master budget is the coordinated, aggregate budget of an enterprise for a year, consisting of the operating budget and the financial budget, i.e. the budgeted income statement, balance sheet and cash flow statement.

presupuesto maestro

▲ *prepare a master budget* preparar un presupuesto maestro

master-budget variance

= static-budget variance

A master-budget variance is the difference between the static master budget and the realised budget.

desviación del presupuesto maestro

= variación del presupuesto maestro

▲ *the total master-budget variance* la desviación total del presupuesto maestro

⇛ master budget

matching

Matching is an accounting concept within accrual accounting that implies the recognition of expenses for the same accounting period as the revenue to which they relate rather than when paid in cash.

correlación

▲ *matching costs and revenue* correlación costes e ingresos ▲ *matching of costs and revenue* correlación de costes e ingresos ▲ *matching of revenues and expenses* correlación de ingresos y gastos ▲ *the matching of the maturities and interest rates of assets and liabilities* la correlación de los vencimientos y tipos de interés de activos y pasivos

matching concept

= matching convention, matching principle

The matching concept is one of the fundamental accounting concepts and implies the matching of expenses and revenues within an accounting period, i.e. reporting expenses against the revenues they relate to, so that profit for the period can be determined.

concepto de correlación

= principio de correlación

▲ *be incompatible with the matching concept* ser incompatible con el concepto de correlación ▲ *in compliance with the matching principle* en cumplimiento del concepto de correlación ▲ *the application of the matching concept* la aplicación del concepto de correlación

matching convention

= matching concept, matching principle

The matching convention is one of the fundamental accounting concepts and implies the matching of expenses and revenues within an accounting period, i.e. reporting expenses against the revenues they relate to, so that profit for the period can be determined.

principio de correlación

= concepto de correlación

▲ *apply the matching convention* aplicar el principio de correlación ▲ *under the matching convention* según el principio de correlación

matching principle

= matching concept, matching convention

The matching principle is one of the fundamental accounting concepts and implies the matching of expenses and revenues within an accounting period, i.e. reporting expenses against the revenues they relate to, so that profit for the period can be determined.

principio de correlación

= concepto de correlación

▲ *application of the matching principle* aplicación del principio de correlación ▲ *be incompatible with the matching principle* ser incompatible con el principio de correlación ▲ *consumption under the matching principle* consumo según el principio de correlación ▲ *in compliance with the matching principle* en cumplimiento del principio de correlación ▲ *the matching principle of the transaction-based accounting concept* el principio de correlación del concepto contable basado en la transacción

material[1] *noun* <a, the, -s>

Materials are raw materials or other resources that are processed and become part of the process of manufacturing products and providing services.

material

= materia prima

▲ *abnormal amounts of wasted materials* cantidades excepcionales de materiales malgastados ▲ *acquisition of materials* adquisición de materiales ▲ *consumption of materials* consumo de materiales ▲ *costs of materials* costes de los materiales ▲ *costs of materials used in the construction of an asset* costes de materiales usados en la construcción de un activo ▲ *defects in materials* defectos en los materiales ▲ *direct materials* materiales directos ▲ *direct materials costs* costes de materiales directos ▲ *indirect materials* materiales indirectos ▲ *indirect materials costs* costes de materiales indirectos ▲ *materials made specifically for the contract* materiales fabricados específicamente para cumplir el contrato ▲ *purchase of materials relating to production* adquisición de materiales relacionados con la producción ▲ *surplus materials* materiales sobrantes

material[2] *noun* <no indefinite article, the, no plural>

Material is information that has been processed to meet a specific objective.

material

= documentación

▲ *background material* material previo ▲ *foreign-language material* material en lengua extranjera ▲ *preparation of shareholder material* preparación del material de los accionistas

material[3] *adjective*

= important

Where items or information have been omitted or misstated in the financial statements consequently affecting the decision-making process of the users of the financial statements, such an omission or misstatement is considered material.

relevante

= importante, sustancial, material

▲ *a material obligation for unused compensated absences* una obligación material por ausencias remuneradas no utilizadas ▲ *have a material effect on the financial statements* tener un efecto relevante en los estados financieros ▲ *material amounts of work in progress and receivables* cantidades sustanciales de trabajo en curso y cuentas a cobrar ▲ *material items* partidas relevantes ▲ *material liabilities for malfunctions and breakdowns* responsabilidades materiales por mal funcionamiento y averías ▲ *material terms and conditions relating to assets pledged as collateral* términos y condiciones materiales relativos a los activos pignorados como colaterales ▲ *result in a material impairment loss* dar lugar a pérdida por deterioro sustancial

material financial information

Material financial information constitutes financial and accounting disclosures and data that, if omitted or misstated, might influence the economic decisions of users of such disclosures and data. Whether such information is material depends on the size and nature of the item and an evaluation of the particular conditions.

información financiera relevante

▲ *disclose material financial information* divulgar información financiera relevante ▲ *translation of material financial information into a foreign currency* conversión de la información financiera relevante a una moneda extranjera

⇛ materiality concept

material requirement planning

→ materials requirement planning

materiality

Materiality is a fundamental accounting concept that concerns the judgment of accounting data as important by relative nature and extent. Such data are deemed material if their omission or misstatement may mislead financial statement users.

importancia relativa

= materialidad

NOTE Spanish accountants prefer 'importancia relativa' to the IAS/IFRS term 'materialidad'.

▲ *assessments of materiality* valoraciones de la importancia relativa ▲ *materiality considerations* consideraciones de importancia relativa ▲ *quantified guidance as to materiality* asesoramiento considerado como importancia relativa ▲ *the concept of materiality* el principio de importancia relativa ▲ *the nature and liquidity of assets and their materiality* la naturaleza y liquidez de los activos y su importancia relativa

SOURCE IAS Framework, F 30

materiality concept

= concept of materiality

The materiality concept is one of the fundamental accounting concepts and concerns the judgment of accounting data as important by relative nature and extent. Such data are deemed material if their omission or misstatement may mislead financial statement users.

principio de importancia relativa

= principio de la importancia relativa, principio de materialidad

▲ *apply the materiality concept* aplicar el principio de la importancia relativa ▲ *comply with the materiality concept* cumplir con el principio de importancia relativa

materiality convention

= materiality concept

The materiality convention is one of the fundamental accounting concepts and concerns the judgment of accounting data as important by relative nature and extent. Such data are deemed material if their omission or misstatement may mislead financial statement users.

principio de importancia relativa

= principio de la importancia relativa, principio de materialidad

▲ *apply the materiality convention* aplicar el principio de importancia relativa ▲ *comply with the materiality convention* cumplir con el principio de importancia relativa

materials and supplies US

= raw material and consumables used IAS/IFRS, raw materials and consumables UK

Materials and supplies is an item in the income statement when classified by nature that contains crude or unprocessed materials and auxiliary products applied in production during the accounting period.

materias primas e insumos

= materias primas y suministros

▲ *materials and supplies awaiting use in the production process* materias primas e insumos esperando su uso en el proceso productivo ▲ *the normal levels of materials and supplies* los niveles normales de materias primas y suministros

materials requirement planning

Materials requirement planning is a push-through system, typically computer-based, for calculating requirements for materials, production and stocks of finished goods on the basis of known orders and anticipated demand.

planificación de necesidades de materiales

= planificación de requerimientos de materiales

▲ *software for materials requirement planning* software para la planificación de necesidades de materiales

⇛ just-in-time inventory system, just-in-time production

materials requisition

A materials requisition is a form used within an enterprise containing data of the quantities and types of raw materials or components which are requested procured from stocks or a supplier, and which are needed for production. The requisition records the amount required and is typically used in job-order costing.

requisición de materiales

= pedido de materiales

▲ *fill out a materials requisition* rellenar un impreso de requisición de materiales ▲ *materials requisition form* impreso de pedido de materiales

maturity

1 = life, maturity period, term to maturity

Maturity is the period of time from the creation of a debt until the date on which the principal amount of the debt falls due for payment.

vencimiento

▲ *be based on maturity* basarse en el vencimiento ▲ *classification by maturity* clasificación según el vencimiento ▲ *expected maturity of more than one year* vencimiento previsto superior a un año

2 = maturity date

Maturity is the date of maturity when a liability falls due for payment.

vencimiento

= fecha de vencimiento

▲ *a fixed maturity* una fecha de vencimiento fijada ▲ *at maturity* al vencimiento ▲ *be based on maturity* basarse en la fecha de vencimiento ▲ *classification by maturity* clasificación por vencimiento ▲ *classify liabilities by maturity* clasificar el pasivo por vencimiento ▲ *expected maturity* vencimiento previsto ▲ *pay before maturity* pagar antes del vencimiento

maturity date

The maturity date is the date on which the principal amount of a bond or other debt instrument becomes due and payable.

fecha de vencimiento

= vencimiento

▲ *a fixed maturity date* una fecha de vencimiento fijada ▲ *as from the maturity date* desde la fecha de vencimiento ▲ *disclosures of the maturity date* divulgaciones de la fecha de vencimiento ▲ *information about contractual repricing and maturity dates* información sobre las fechas de vencimiento y revisión de precios contractuales ▲ *the maturity dates of financial assets* las fechas de vencimiento de los activos financieros ▲ *the maturity dates of financial liabilities* las fechas de vencimiento de los pasivos financieros

maturity period

= maturity

The maturity period is the period of time from the creation of a debt until the date on which the principal amount of the debt falls due for payment.

periodo de vencimiento

= vencimiento

▲ *have a maturity period of three months or less* tener un periodo de vencimiento de tres meses o menos

maturity profile

A maturity profile shows the different maturities of e.g. financial instruments divided into duration of years such as <1 year, 1-2 years, 2-5 years, >5 years.

perfil de vencimiento

= perfil del vencimiento

▲ *maturity profile of financial liabilities* perfil del vencimiento de los pasivos financieros ▲ *the maturity profile of debt* el perfil del vencimiento de la deuda

maturity value US

The maturity value of a financial instrument is the amount received on the maturity date. The maturity value is often equal to the face value.

valor de vencimiento

= valor al vencimiento

▲ *determine the maturity value* determinar el valor al vencimiento ▲ *the maturity value of the bond* el valor de vencimiento del bono

MBO

= management by objectives

MBO is an abbreviation for management by objectives, a top-down management principle based on individual employees having their own well-defined objectives for job performance. The objectives are set in cooperation with a superior manager who evaluates the performance.

gestión por objetivos

▲ *implementation of the MBO system* implementación del sistema de gestión por objetivos ▲ *the definition of MBO* la definición de la gestión por objetivos ▲ *the goals of MBO* los objetivos de la gestión por objetivos

MD&A US

= OFR UK, operating and financial review UK

MD&A is the abbreviation for management's discussion and analysis, a report that discusses a company's performance and financial condition, focusing on any unusual or infrequent events or significant economic changes and future developments. The MD&A is a requirement of the US Securities and Exchange Commission and must be filed with the SEC annually by companies registered with it.

debate y análisis de la gestión

▲ *guidance on MD&A disclosure* guía para la publicación del debate y análisis de la gestión ▲ *MD&A disclosure requirements* requisitos para la publicación del debate y análisis de la gestión

mean[1] *noun*

A mean is an arithmetic average obtained by adding two or more amounts and dividing the total by the number of amounts.

promedio

▲ *mean variance* desviación promedio ▲ *the tendency of volatility to revert to its mean* la tendencia de la volatilidad a volver a su promedio

mean[2] *adjective*

Mean is used as an adjective meaning average before a noun, such as number, value or weight.

medio

▲ *mean value* valor medio ▲ *the mean dividend yield of an appropriately comparable peer group* la rentabilidad del dividendo media de un grupo afín muy comparable

measurable

When something is measurable it can be measured, i.e. it is possible to determine or calculate its size or amount.

medible

= evaluable, valorable

▲ *a measurable decrease in the estimated future cash flows* un descenso evaluable en los flujos futuros de efectivo previstos ▲ *a reliably measurable fair value* un valor razonable medible con fiabilidad ▲ *a reliably measurable impact* un impacto medible con fiabilidad ▲ *a separately measurable portion of the interest rate exposure of an interest-bearing asset* una parte medible por separado de la exposición al riesgo del tipo de interés de un activo que devenga intereses ▲ *set out a measurable goal* fijar un objetivo medible

measure

To measure is to determine the value or extent of something.

medir

= evaluar, valorar

▲ *measure a financial liability* medir un pasivo financiero ▲ *measure assets* valorar activos ▲ *measure at amortised cost* medir a coste amortizado ▲ *measure at cost* medir al coste ▲ *measure at fair value* medir a valor razonable ▲ *measure at net realisable value* medir a valor realizable neto ▲ *measure at value in use* medir a valor en uso ▲ *measure costs* medir costes ▲ *measure in accordance with uniform methods* medir conforme a métodos uniformes ▲ *measure individually* medir individualmente ▲ *measure liabilities* valorar pasivos ▲ *measure on the basis of a standard cost method* medir sobre la base de un método de coste estandar ▲ *measure reliably* medir con fiabilidad ▲ *measure revenue* medir ingresos ▲ *measure systematically and consistently* medir sistemáticamente y consistentemente ▲ *measure the carrying amount of intangible assets* medir el valor contable de los activos intangibles ▲ *measure the equity value* medir el valor del patrimonio ▲ *measure under the equity method* medir según el método de participación

measurement[1] IAS/IFRS, US *noun* <a, the, -s>
= appraisal, valuation
Measurement means determining the value of an asset, a liability or other financial statement element to attribute a monetary amount to it on an appropriate measurement basis for recognition in the balance sheet and the profit and loss account.
medición
= evaluación, valoración
▲ *a cost-based measurement of assets and liabilities* una medición de activos y pasivos basada en el coste ▲ *description of any uncertainty connected with measurement* descripción de cualquier incertidumbre en relación con la valoración ▲ *measurement basis* base de valoración ▲ *measurement denominated in Danish kroner or in euro* medición denominada en corona danesa o en euro ▲ *measurement of assets* valoración de activos ▲ *measurement of costs* medición de costes ▲ *measurement of liabilities* valoración de pasivos ▲ *measurement of revenue* medición de ingresos ▲ *measurement on initial recognition* evaluación en un reconocimiento inicial ▲ *measurement under the equity method* valoración según el método de participación ▲ *reliable measurement* medición fiable
⇛ fair value, historical cost

measurement[2] *noun* <no indefinite article, the, no plural>
= valuation
Measurement is the act of calculation or assessment made to estimate or determine the value or amount of something.
medición
= evaluación, valoración
▲ *independent measurement* medición independiente ▲ *methods of measurement* métodos de valoración

measurement attribute IAS/IFRS
= measurement basis
A measurement attribute is a measurement basis used when determining the value or amount of an asset, a liability or other financial statement element. Examples include cost, historical cost, amortised cost, replacement cost, recoverable amount, net realisable value and fair value.
criterio de valoración
▲ *adopt fair value as the measurement attribute* adoptar el valor razonable como criterio de valoración ▲ *the selected measurement attribute* el criterio de valoración seleccionado

measurement basis
= basis of measurement, measurement attribute
A measurement basis is a basis at which elements in the financial statements are quantified, such as assets and liabilities. A measurement basis may be e.g. cost, amortised cost, fair value, etc.
método de valoración
▲ *account for the measurement basis used* explicar el método de valoración usado ▲ *changes in the measurement basis applied* cambios en los métodos de valoración aplicados ▲ *measurement basis for assets and liabilities* método de valoración para activos y pasivos ▲ *on a fair value measurement basis* sobre un método de valoración a valor razonable ▲ *selection of a particular measurement basis* selección de un método de valoración concreto ▲ *the measurement basis or bases used in preparing the financial statements* el método de valoración o métodos usados en la preparación de los estados financieros ▲ *the primary measurement basis* el método de valoración primario ▲ *the use of different measurement bases* el uso de métodos de valoración diferentes

measurement criterion
A measurement criterion is one or multiple standards against which a given variable is measured as a basis for decision-making.
criterio de valoración
▲ *measurement criteria for assets* criterio de valoración para activos ▲ *the measurement citeria*

applied el criterio de valoración aplicado
⇛ measurement attribute

measurement currency
A measurement currency is a currency applied by a reporting enterprise for the measurement of items in the financial statements.
moneda de valoración
= moneda de medición
▲ *an appropriate measurement currency* una moneda de valoración apropiada ▲ *select a measurement currency* seleccionar una moneda de valoración ▲ *translation from measurement currency to presentation currency* conversión de la moneda de valoración a la de presentación

measurement date
The measurement date is the date at which an amount of an asset or a liability is measured for the purposes of recognition in the financial statements. For e.g. equity instruments granted under share-based payments, the measurement date is the date when the fair value of the equity instrument granted is measured, which is the grant date for transactions with employees.
fecha de valoración
= fecha de medición
▲ *at a subsequent measurement date* en una próxima fecha de valoración ▲ *at the measurement date* en la fecha de valoración ▲ *cash flows occurring at the measurement date* flujos de efectivo que ocurren en la fecha de valoración ▲ *measure the fair value of equity instruments granted at the measurement date* medir el valor razonable de los instrumentos de patrimonio concedidos en la fecha de valoración ▲ *on the measurement date* en la fecha de medición

measurement method
= method of measurement
Measurement method is the method applied to determine the amount or quantity of the measurement basis. The method e.g. to find the amount of the fair value of the measurement basis in an ill-functioning market may be expert valuations.
método de valoración
= método de medición
▲ *measurement methods for services and reporting* métodos de valoración para servicios e informes ▲ *the measurement method used* el método de valoración usado ▲ *the value-based measurement methods* los métodos de medición basados en el valor ▲ *uniform measurement methods* métodos de valoración uniformes

Medium Term Note program US
= Medium Term Note programme UK
A Medium Term Note program is a debt or funding scheme used by corporate enterprises that enables the issuer to issue multiple bonds in the form of medium-term notes using the same documentation, in this way avoiding the issuing of documentation for each individual issue. Medium Term Note programs offer enterprises constant cash flows tailored to their specific financing needs. The programs are typically registered with a supervisory authority such as the London Stock Exchange or the Securities and Exchange Commission.
programa de Notas a Medio Plazo
= Medium Term Note Program
▲ *as part of a Medium Term Note program* como parte de un programa de Notas a Medio Plazo ▲ *under the Medium-Term Note program* según el programa de Notas a Medio Plazo
⇛ medium-term note

Medium Term Note programme UK
= Medium Term Note program UK
A Medium Term Note programme is a debt or funding scheme used by corporate enterprises that enables the issuer to issue multiple bonds in the form of medium-term notes using the same documentation, in this way avoiding the issuing of documentation for each individual issue. Medium Term Note programmes offer enterprises constant cash flows tailored to their specific financing needs. The programmes are typically registered with a supervisory authority such as

the London Stock Exchange or the Securities and Exchange Commission.

programa de emisión de renta fija a medio plazo

= Medium Term Note Program

▲ *bonds issued under a Medium Term Note programme* bonos emitidos según un programa de emisión de renta fija a medio plazo ▲ *establish a Medium Term Note programme* establecer un programa de emisión de renta fija a medio plazo

⇛ medium-term note

medium-term note

= MTN

A medium-term note is an unsecured bond issued in a eurocurrency in accordance with standardized loan documentation. Medium-term refers to the life of this type of bond which is typically 3-15 years. An example is the Euro Medium Term Note (EMTN) which is euro-commercial paper issued on the euro bond market. US medium-term notes are corporate debt instruments usually issued at a fixed interest rate with maturities in bands, e.g. 9 months to one year, or 18 months to several years.

nota a medio plazo

= medium-term note, MTN

▲ *issue medium-term notes* emitir notas a medio plazo

⇛ Medium Term Note programme

member

A member is a person registered as one of the owners in an enterprise, e.g. a shareholder in a company.

miembro

▲ *additional payments from members* pagos adicionales de los miembros ▲ *repayments to members* reembolsos a los miembros ▲ *the members of the company* los miembros de la compañía ▲ *the members of the enterprise* los miembros de la empresa

member of the executive board

Members of the executive board are members of the governing body of an enterprise in charge of the day-to-day affairs of the enterprise within the general policy and planning laid down by the supervisory board (i.e. the board of directors). The members will exercise the power and duties under the authority granted by the supervisory board and the articles of association of the enterprise.

miembro del consejo ejecutivo

▲ *a new member of the executive board* un nuevo miembro del consejo ejecutivo ▲ *retirement benefit plan for a member of the executive board* plan de prestación por jubilación para un miembro del consejo ejecutivo

⇛ executive board, supervisory board

member of the executive committee US

Members of the executive committee are members of the governing body of an enterprise in charge of the day-to-day affairs of the enterprise within the general policy and planning laid down by the supervisory board (i.e. the board of directors). The members will exercise the power and duties under the authority granted by the supervisory board and the articles of association of the enterprise.

miembro del consejo ejecutivo

▲ *a new member of the executive committee* un nuevo miembro del consejo ejecutivo ▲ *retirement benefit plan for a member of the executive committee* plan de prestación por jubilación para un miembro del consejo ejecutivo

⇛ executive committee, supervisory board

memorandum of association UK

= certificate of incorporation US

The memorandum of association is a document that contains the regulations governing the external affairs of a company. It is the constitution of the company, and the objects clause specifies the powers of the company.

memorándum de la asociación

▲ *amendment of the memorandum of association* enmienda del memorándum de la asociación ▲ *copy of the memorandum of association* copia del memorándum de la asociación

merchandise US

Merchandise comprises finished goods for resale, i.e. goods bought by an enterprise from a wholesaler for resale to its own customers.

mercadería

= bienes, existencias

▲ *costs for merchandise* costes para bienes para la reventa ▲ *inventories of finished goods and merchandise* inventarios de productos terminados y mercadería ▲ *merchandise purchased by a retailer and held for resale* existencias adquiridas por un minorista y mantenidas para reventa ▲ *sale of merchandise* liquidación de bienes para la reventa ▲ *the cost of merchandise* el coste de bienes para la reventa

merchandise inventories US

= goods for resale UK

Merchandise inventory comprises items of finished goods for resale, i.e. goods bought by an enterprise from a wholesaler for resale to its own customers. Merchandise inventory appears as an item in the balance sheet under current assets.

inventarios de mercancía

= existencias de mercadería

▲ *increase in merchandise inventories* aumentos en los inventarios de mercancía

⇛ finished goods, finished goods and goods for resale

merchandising-sector company

A merchandising-sector company is a company that purchases finished goods and resells them.

empresa del sector comercio

▲ *large merchandising-sector companies* grandes compañías del sector comercio

⇛ manufacturing-sector company, service-sector company

merge

To merge means to combine two or more independent legal entities so that they form one legal entity.

fusionar

= fusionarse

▲ *merge a company into another* fusionarse una compañía con otra ▲ *merge with another company* fusionarse con otra compañía ▲ *merge with transaction-based financial statements* fusionarse con los estados financieros basados en la transacción

merger

= combination

≠ split-off

A merger is a combination of two or more independent legal entities so that they form one legal entity.

fusión

▲ *a legal merger* una fusión legal ▲ *a merger between equals* una fusión entre iguales ▲ *a merger of two equal parties* una fusión entre dos partes iguales ▲ *accounting for mergers* contabilidad para fusiones ▲ *additions relating to mergers* adiciones relacionadas con fusiones ▲ *approve a merger* aprobar una fusión ▲ *change on merger* cambio por fusión ▲ *implement a merger* implementar una fusión ▲ *legal merger* fusión legal ▲ *merger by the acquisition of one or more companies by another* fusión por la adquisición de una o varias compañías por otra ▲ *merger contract* contrato de fusión ▲ *merger costs* costes de fusión ▲ *merger of legal entities* fusión de entidades legales ▲ *prepare a merger* preparar una fusión ▲ *the changes made necessary by the merger* los cambios necesarios para la fusión ▲ *the date on which the merger takes effect* la fecha en que surta efectos la fusión ▲ *the enterprise formed by the merger* la empresa surgida de la fusión ▲ *the nullity of the merger* la nulidad de la fusión

merger accounting UK

= pooling of interests US, uniting of interests IAS/IFRS

≠ acquisition accounting UK, purchase accounting IAS/IFRS, US

Merger accounting is the application of an accounting method used for business combinations if no acquirer or acquired party can be identified. Contrary to acquisition accounting, the assets and liabilities of the merging enterprises are combined at their existing carrying amounts and not at fair value. This method ensures that no enterprise can be identified as the acquirer. This way, no changes of accounting items are made, just as there is no recognition of goodwill or negative goodwill.

método de fusión

= método de adquisición

▲ *abolition of merger accounting* supresión del método de fusión ▲ *account for by using merger accounting* contabilizar usando el

método de fusión ▲ *apply merger accounting to the transfer* aplicar el método de fusión a la transferencia ▲ *prohibit merger accounting* prohibir el método de fusión
⇛ uniting of interests

merger accounting method UK
→ merger method

merger activity
Merger activities refer to actions directly related to a merger and the objective of a merger and include activities such as training of employees, expenses in connection with layoffs, office and production transfer, IT reorganisation etc.
proceso de fusión
▲ *as part of the merger activities* como parte del proceso de fusión

merger agreement
A merger agreement is a contract between two or more enterprises containing the terms on which they have agreed to merge.
acuerdo de fusión
= contrato de fusión
▲ *a part of the merger agreement* una parte del acuerdo de fusión ▲ *according to the merger agreement* de acuerdo con el contrato de fusión ▲ *approve a merger agreement* aprobar un acuerdo de fusión ▲ *as a result of the merger agreement* como un resultado del acuerdo de fusión ▲ *conclude a merger agreement* finalizar un acuerdo de fusión ▲ *the conditions of a merger agreement* las condiciones de un acuerdo de fusión

merger cost
Costs that are associated with the merger of two or more enterprises are called merger costs.
coste de fusión
= coste de la fusión
▲ *incur merger costs* incurrir en costes de fusión ▲ *merger costs after tax* costes de fusión después de impuestos ▲ *merger costs before tax* costes de fusión antes de impuestos ▲ *provide for merger costs* provisionar costes de fusión ▲ *tax on merger costs* impuestos sobre costes de fusión

merger date
The merger date is the date on which the merging enterprises have agreed that the merger shall become effective.
fecha de fusión
= fecha de la fusión
▲ *prior to the merger date* antes de la fecha de fusión ▲ *the merger date chosen* la fecha de fusión elegida ▲ *the period from the merger date to the final approval of the merger* el periodo comprendido desde la fecha de fusión a la aprobación final de la fusión ▲ *the share price at the merger date* el precio de la acción a la fecha de fusión

merger gain
Any gain flowing to the shareholders as a result of a merger is called merger gain.
ganacia de fusión
= ganancia por fusión
▲ *eliminate the merger gain* eliminar la ganancia de fusión

merger goodwill
Merger goodwill is the goodwill arising from mergers that are in reality business combinations where the assets and liabilities of the acquiree are measured at fair value and any merger goodwill arising is initially recognised at cost less impairment losses and must be tested for impairment regularly rather than amortised.
fondo de comercio de la fusión
▲ *determination of merger goodwill* determinación del fondo de comercio de la fusión ▲ *recognise merger goodwill in the balance sheet* reconocer el fondo de comercio de la fusión en el balance ▲ *recognition of merger goodwill* reconocimiento del fondo de comercio de la fusión

merger method UK
= merger accounting method UK, pooling-of-interests method US, uniting-of-interests method IAS/IFRS
≠ acquisition accounting method UK, purchase method IAS/IFRS, US
The merger method is an accounting method used for business combinations if no acquirer or acquired party can be identified. Contrary to the acquisition method, the assets and liabilities of the merging enterprises are combined at their existing carrying amounts and not at fair value.

método de fusión
≠ método de adquisición
▲ *accounted for by the merger method* contabilizado por el método de fusión ▲ *apply the merger method* aplicar el método de fusión ▲ *under the merger method* según el método de fusión

merger provision
Merger provisions are provisions made in connection with a merger.
provisión de fusión
= provisión por fusión
▲ *the initial merger provision* la provisión de fusión inicial

method of accounting
= accounting method, accounting procedure
Methods of accounting are the accounting principles, procedures or tools applied to treat and recognise financial data in the preparation of financial statements, such as methods of depreciation, inventory pricing, income and asset measurement, revenue recognition and accrual accounting.
método de contabilidad
▲ *a method of accounting for an investment* un método de contabilidad para una inversión ▲ *change the method of accounting* cambiar el método de contabilidad ▲ *changed method of accounting* método de contabilidad modificaco ▲ *method of accounting for share trading* método de contabilidad para la cotización de las acciones ▲ *methods of accounting for business combinations* métodos de contabilidad para combinaciones de negocios

method of amortisation UK
= amortisation method, basis of amortisation
The method of amortisation is the policy applied by an enterprise for gradually writing down an intangible asset over its economic life.
método de amortización
▲ *a diminishing balance method of amortisation* un método de amortización constante ▲ *selection of the method of amortisation* selección del método de amortización ▲ *the changed method of amortisation* el método de amortización modificado ▲ *the method of amortisation adopted* el método de amortización adoptado
⇛ method of depreciation, straight-line method

method of amortization US
The method of amortization is the policy applied by an enterprise for gradually writing down an intangible asset over its economic life.
método de amortización
▲ *selection of the method of amortization* selección del método de amortización ▲ *the changed method of amortization* el método de amortización modificado ▲ *the declining balance method of amortization* el método de amortización constante ▲ *the method of amortization adopted* el método de amortización adoptado
⇛ method of amortisation

method of consolidation
A method of consolidation is an accounting method for unifying and adjusting the financial statements of a parent company and its subsidiaries and presenting them as the consolidated financial statements of the group as one single economic entity. Methods of consolidation include full consolidation and proportionate consolidation.
método de consolidación
▲ *alternative methods of consolidation* métodos de consolidación alternativos

method of depreciation
= depreciation method
The method of depreciation is the policy applied by an enterprise for gradually writing down a tangible asset over its useful life.
método de amortización
▲ *selection of the method of depreciation* selección del método de amortización ▲ *the changed method of depreciation* el método de amortización modificado ▲ *the method of depreciation adopted* el método de amortización adoptado ▲ *usage methods of depreciation* métodos de amortización en uso
⇛ method of amortisation

method of recognising income as invoiced
The method of recognising income as invoiced is a method of revenue recognition according to which revenue and the

related costs incurred are recognised in the profit and loss account only when the product, service or contract job has been delivered and invoiced.

método de reconocimiento de ingresos facturados

= método de registro de ingresos facturados

▲ *use of the method of recognising income as invoiced* uso del método de reconocimiento de ingresos facturados ▲ *use the method of recognising income as invoiced* utilizar el método de reconocimiento de ingresos facturados ▲ *use the method of recognising income as invoiced* usar el método de reconocimiento de ingresos facturados

method of recognition

A method of recognition specifies the criteria for including an asset or a liability as an item in the balance sheet, and revenue or expenses as items in the profit and loss account.

método de reconocimiento

= método de registro

▲ *changes in the method of recognition* cambios en el método de reconocimiento ▲ *the method of recognition applied* el método de reconocimiento aplicado

method of revenue recognition

The method of revenue recognition contains the rules and requirements for determining when revenue should be recognised in the financial statements. Revenue should be included in profits when the risks and rewards of ownership have been assumed by another party and it is possible to measure the amount of revenue reliably.

método de reconocimiento de ingresos

= método de reconocimiento de los ingresos, método de reconocimiento del ingreso, método de registro de ingresos

▲ *determination of methods of revenue recognition* determinación de los métodos de reconocimiento de ingresos

mezzanine capital

= mezzanine financing, subordinated debt

Mezzanine capital is unsecured risk capital, characterised as a hybrid form of capital with debt and equity aspects. Normally, it takes the form of subordinated debt and is structured and priced to meet a company's unique situation, as such also referred to as growth capital, as it gives a company a head-start and closes the financing gap between debt and equity.

financiación mezzanine

= deuda subordinada

▲ *provide mezzanine capital* ofrecer financiación mezzanine

minimum lease payment

Minimum lease payments include the periodic payments that a lessee is obliged to make to the lessor under a lease contract as well as any amounts that the lessee or a party related to the lessee guarantees to the lessor.

pago mínimo por arrendamiento

= pago mínimo por el arrendamiento

▲ *estimated future minimum lease payments* pagos mínimos por arrendamiento futuros estimados ▲ *minimum lease payments recorded at the balance sheet date* pagos mínimos por arrendamiento recogidos a la fecha del balance ▲ *reconcile the total minimum lease payments* conciliar los pagos mínimos por arrendamiento ▲ *the aggregate of the minimum lease payments* la agregación de los pagos mínimos por arrendamiento ▲ *the minimum lease payments* los pagos por arrendamiento mínimos ▲ *the minimum lease payments receivable by the lessor* los pagos por arrendamiento mínimos a cobrar por el arrendador ▲ *the present value of total minimum lease payments* el valor actual de los pagos mínimos por arrendamiento totales ▲ *the total of future minimum lease payments* el total de los pagos mínimos por arrendamiento futuros ▲ *total minimum lease payments* total pagos mínimos por arrendamiento ▲ *uncollectible minimum lease payments receivable* pagos mínimos por arrendamiento incobrables

minimum payment

A minimum payment is the smallest payment required for

the acceptable performance of a contractual term or condition.

pago mínimo

▲ *reconcile the minimum payments* conciliar los pagos mínimos ▲ *the present value of the minimum payments* el valor actual de los pagos mínimos ▲ *total minimum payments at the balance sheet date* total pagos mínimos a la fecha del balance

minimum requirement

A minimum requirement refers to the lowest possible or the lowest permissible value, amount, size, extent, degree, etc. of something that must be present before a transaction or some other action may be carried out, accepted or approved. Minimum requirements may be laid down in statutes.

requisito mínimo

▲ *a statutory minimum requirement* un requisito mínimo estatutario ▲ *meet specified minimum requirements* cumplir los requisitos mínimos especificados ▲ *minimum requirements for reporting class B enterprises* requisitos mínimos para informar sobre empresas de clase B ▲ *statutory minimum requirements* requisitos mínimos estatutarios ▲ *the minimum requirement of solvency margin* los requisitos mínimos del margen de solvencia ▲ *the minimum requirements for the content of the annual report* los requisitos mínimos para el contenido del informe anual ▲ *the statutory minimum requirements for the amount of equity* los requisitos mínimos estatutarios para el importe del patrimonio

minor acquisition

= small acquisition

Minor acquisitions are assets acquired at a cost not exceeding a defined value which are expensed in the profit and loss account, i.e. written off in the year of acquisition instead of being recognised under fixed assets and depreciated.

adquisición menor

▲ *a number of minor acquisitions* un número de adquisiciones menores ▲ *exclude minor acquisitions* excluir las adquisiciones menores ▲ *make minor acquisitions* hacer adquisiciones menores

minor asset

= small asset

Minor assets are fixed assets at a cost below a certain value limit, which are fully deductible for tax purposes in the year of acquisition. Minor assets are not depreciated, but expensed on acquisition.

activo menor

▲ *acquisition of minor assets* adquisición de activos menores ▲ *groups of minor assets* grupos de activos menores ▲ *immediate write-off of minor assets* eliminación inmediata de los activos menores ▲ *purchase sums for minor assets* sumas por activos menores

minority

A minority is the smaller part of something or an amount that is less than 50% of the total amount.

minoría

▲ *losses applicable to the minority in a consolidated subsidiary* pérdidas aplicables a la minoría en una filial consolidada ▲ *the minority's proportion of the net fair value of the items* la proporción de la minoría del valor razonable neto de las partidas

⇛ minority interest

minority interest

= non-controlling investment

IAS/IFRS, US

Minority interests are equity investments of less than 50% of the contributed capital in consolidated enterprises owned by parties other than the consolidated enterprises.

participación minoritaria

= accionista minoritario, interés minoritario, inversión minoritaria

NOTE Spanish accountants prefer 'participación minoritaria' to the IAS/IFRS term 'interés minoritario'.

▲ *addition of minority interests* suma de participaciones minoritarias ▲ *adjustment for minority interests* ajuste de los intereses minoritarios ▲ *classification of minority interests* clasificación de intereses minoritarios ▲ *determination of minority interests* determinación de los intereses minoritarios ▲ *divestment of a minority interest* desinversión de una participación minoritaria ▲ *dividend to minority interests* dividendo

para los accionistas minoritarios ▲ *dividends paid to minority interests* dividendos pagados a los intereses minoritarios ▲ *funding from minority interests* financiación procedente de las participaciones minoritarias ▲ *minority interests at beginning of year* participaciones minoritarias al inicio del ejercicio ▲ *minority interests at end of year* participaciones minoritarias al final del ejercicio ▲ *redemption of minority interests* cancelación de participaciones minoritarias ▲ *result before minority interests* resultado antes de intereses minoritarios ▲ *results for the year after tax and minority interests* resultados para el año después de impuestos e intereses minoritarios ▲ *the approval of the owners of the minority interests* la aprobación de los propietarios de las participaciones minoritarias ▲ *the minority interests' equity interests* la inversión de patrimonio de los accionistas minoritarios ▲ *the minority interests' proportionate share of the subsidiaries' equity* el reparto proporcional del patrimonio de las filiales entre los accionistas minoritarios ▲ *the minority interests' share of the equity* el porcentaje del patrimonio de las inversiones minoritarias ▲ *the minority interests' share of the profit or loss* el porcentaje de la pérdida o ganancia de las inversiones minoritarias
⇛ parent's share

minority owner
A minority owner is a person who owns less than 50% of the contributed capital of a company.
propietario minoritario
= accionista minoritario, partícipe minoritario
▲ *dividends to minority owner* dividendos al accionista minoritario ▲ *minority owner's share in net profit or loss* participación del propietario minoritario en los resultados ▲ *other transactions with minority owners* otras transacciones con propietarios minoritarios ▲ *the squeeze-out of the minority owners shares* la exclusión de las acciones de los propietarios minoritarios
⇛ minority shareholder

minority share
= non-controlling interest
A minority share is a non-controlling shareholding held by a minority shareholder, i.e. less than 50% of the total number of shares.
participación minoritaria
= interés minoritario, inversión minoritaria
▲ *hold minority shares* tener participaciones minoritarias ▲ *purchase of minority shares* adquisición de participaciones minoritarias ▲ *sale of minority shares* venta de participaciones minoritarias

minority shareholder
= minority owner, minority stockholder US
≠ majority shareholder
A minority shareholder is a person who owns less than 50% of the voting shares of a company.
accionista minoritario
▲ *at the expense of minority shareholders* a expensas de los accionistas minoritarios ▲ *dividend payable to minority shareholders* dividendo a pagar a los accionistas minoritarios ▲ *minority shareholders' share of equity* parte de patrimonio de los accionistas minoritarios ▲ *minority shareholders' share of extraordinary items* porcentaje de partidas extraordinarias de los accionistas minoritarios ▲ *minority shareholders' share of income from ordinary activities* participación de los accionistas minoritarios en los ingresos de actividades ordinarias ▲ *obtain the approval of minority shareholders* obtener la aprobación de los accionistas minoritarios
⇛ minority owner

minority stockholder US
= minority shareholder UK
A minority stockholder is a person or enterprise that holds a non-controlling interest, i.e. less than 50% of the shares, in a company.
accionista minoritario
≠ accionista mayoritario
▲ *dividend payable to minority stockholders* dividendo a pagar a los accionistas minoritarios ▲ *minority stockholders' share of equity* porcentaje de patrimonio de los accionistas minoritarios ▲ *minority stockholders' sha-*

re of extraordinary items parte de los accionistas minoritarios en las partidas extraordinarias ▲ *minority stockholders' share of income from ordinary activities* parte de los ingresos de las actividades ordinarias de los accionistas minoritarios ▲ *obtain the approval of minority stockholders* obtener la aprobación de los accionistas minoritarios

minutes

Minutes are the official written record of what was said and decided at a meeting.

actas

▲ *board minutes* actas del consejo ▲ *minutes of discussions between the venturers* actas de debates entre los participantes en un negocio conjunto ▲ *minutes of resolution* actas de resolución ▲ *narrative minutes* actas descriptivas

miscellaneous

Miscellaneous means a random assortment of different kinds.

diverso

▲ *miscellaneous assets* activos diversos ▲ *miscellaneous company information* información empresarial variada ▲ *miscellaneous expenses* gastos diversos

misstatement

Misstatement is an expression used in the audit report meaning mistakes in the financial disclosures that are due to errors or fraud.

error

▲ *as a result of misstatements* como un resultado de errores ▲ *change of accounting estimates and misstatements* cambio de estimaciones y errores contables ▲ *free of material misstatement* libre de error material ▲ *material omissions or misstatements of items* omisiones o errores materiales de partidas ▲ *misstatements* errores de contabilidad ▲ *misstatements and omissions* errores y omisiones ▲ *misstatements in the entity's financial statements* errores en los estados financieros de la entidad ▲ *the size and nature of the misstatement* el tamaño y la naturaleza del error

mixed cost UK, US

= semi-fixed cost, semi-variable cost

Mixed costs are costs containing both fixed and variable elements and therefore partly affected by a change in activity level.

coste mixto

▲ *calculate the mixed cost* calcular el coste mixto ▲ *separate a mixed cost into its fixed and variable elements* separar un coste mixto en sus elementos fijos y variables

model financial statements

Model financial statements are illustrative and fictitious financial statements that are prepared, often by accountancy firms, as help and guidance for the drawing up of actual financial statements, e.g. in connection with changed accounting rules such as the transition to IFRS.

estados financieros estándar

= estados financieros estándares, estados financieros modelos

▲ *prepare model financial statements* preparar estados financieros estándar

modest

= moderate

If something is modets it is relatively small, for example an amount or improvement.

discreto

▲ *a modest decrease* un descenso discreto ▲ *a modest increase* un aumento discreto

modified audit report

≠ unmodified audit report

A modified audit report is an audit report that is in some way qualified or includes further information such as an emphasis of matter paragraph.

informe de auditoría modificado

= informe modificado de auditoría

▲ *issue a modified audit report* emitir un informe de auditoría modificado ▲ *the issuance of a modified audit report* la emisión de un informe de auditoría modificado

⇛ adverse opinion, audit report, disclaimer, emphasis of matter paragraph, qualified audit report, qualified opinion

monetary

Monetary means that something relates to or involves money.

monetario

▲ *a monetary amount* una cantidad monetaria ▲ *a monetary*

asset un activo monetario ▲ *a monetary available-for-sale financial asset* un activo financiero monetario disponible para la venta ▲ *a monetary currency transaction* una conversión de divisas monetaria ▲ *a monetary financial instrument* un instrumento financiero monetario ▲ *a monetary item* una partida monetaria ▲ *a monetary liability* un pasivo monetario ▲ *a monetary unit* una unidad monetaria ▲ *a monetary unit of measurement* una unidad de medida monetaria ▲ *gains or losses on the net monetary position* resultados en la posición monetaria neta ▲ *monetary compensation* compensación monetaria ▲ *monetary value* valor monetario ▲ *monetary working capital* capital circulante monetario ▲ *receive monetary compensation from third parties* recibir compensación monetaria de terceras partes

monetary asset

= monetary financial asset
≠ monetary liability
A monetary asset is money or a claim to receive a fixed or determinable amount of money without regard to future prices.

activo monetario

= activo financiero monetario
≠ pasivo monetario
▲ *a non-derivative monetary asset* un activo monetario no derivado ▲ *an intragroup monetary asset* un activo monetario intragrupo ▲ *discount on monetary assets* descuento en activos monetarios ▲ *foreign currency monetary assets* activos monetarios en divisas ▲ *foreign exchange gains and losses on monetary assets* pérdidas y ganancias por tipo de cambio en activos monetarios ▲ *loss from holding monetary assets* pérdida por mantenimiento de activos monetarios ▲ *monetary assets given* activos monetarios entregados ▲ *monetary assets given to equity holders of the acquiree* activos monetarios entregados a los poseedores del patrimonio neto del adquirente ▲ *premium on monetary assets* prima en activos monetarios
⇛ monetary item

monetary balance sheet item

Monetary balance sheet items are monetary items recognised in the balance sheet. Cash, other financial assets and financial liabilities are referred to as monetary items. The definition includes transactions settled at cash amounts that may be fixed or determinable.

partida monetaria del balance

= partida monetaria en el balance
▲ *other monetary balance sheet items* otras partidas monetarias del balance ▲ *remeasurement of monetary balance sheet items* revalorización de las partidas monetarias del balance
⇛ non-monetary item

monetary claim

A monetary claim is a request for payment in money, not in goods or services.

reclamación monetaria

▲ *assignment of monetary claims* cesión de las reclamaciones monetarias ▲ *enforce a monetary claim* ejercutar una reclamación monetaria ▲ *make a monetary claim* hacer una reclamación monetaria ▲ *non-interest bearing monetary claims* reclamaciones monetarias que no devengan intereses ▲ *protect a monetary claim* proteger una reclamación monetaria ▲ *set off a monetary claim* compensar una reclamación monetaria ▲ *the nominal amount of the monetary claim* la cantidad nominal de la reclamación monetaria ▲ *the payment of substantial monetary claims* el pago de reclamaciones monetarias sustanciales ▲ *unwarranted monetary claims* reclamaciones monetarias no garantizadas

monetary financial asset

monetary asset
Monetary financial assets are financial assets with fixed or determinable monetary values without regard to future prices, such as cash and receivables.

activo financiero monetario

= activo monetario
▲ *changes in the fair value of monetary financial assets denominated in a foreign currency* cambios en el valor razonable de los activos financieros monetarios ▲ *collect the value of monetary financial assets* cobrar el valor de los activos financieros monetarios ▲ *discount on monetary financial assets* descuento en activos financieros monetarios ▲ *premium on mo-*

netary financial assets prima en activos financieros monetarios ▲ *the effective yield on a monetary financial asset* el rendimiento efectivo en un activo financiero monetario

monetary financial instrument

Monetary financial instruments are financial assets and financial liabilities that are settled in fixed or determinable amounts of money.

instrumento financiero monetario

▲ *acquisition of monetary financial instruments* adquisición de instrumentos financieros monetarios ▲ *future cash flows associated with a monetary financial instrument* flujos de efectivo futuros asociados a un instrumento financiero monetario ▲ *interest-bearing monetary financial instruments* instrumentos financieros monetarios que devengan intereses ▲ *issuance of monetary financial instruments* emisión de instrumentos financieros monetarios ▲ *purchase of monetary financial instruments* compra de instrumentos financieros monetarios ▲ *the effective yield of a monetary financial instrument* la rentabilidad efectiva de un instrumento financiero monetario

monetary financial liability

= monetary liability

Monetary financial liabilities are financial liabilities with fixed or determinable monetary values without regard to future prices, such as debt.

pasivo financiero monetario

▲ *the effective interest rates for the monetary financial liabilities* los tipos de interés efectivo para los pasivos financieros monetarios ▲ *the net fair values of all monetary financial liabilities* los valores razonables netos de todos los pasivos financieros monetarios

monetary item

≠ non-monetary item

Monetary items are cash or money held as well as assets and liabilities (including provisions) that are settled in fixed or determinable amounts of money. All other assets and liabilities are referred to as non-monetary items.

partida monetaria

▲ *a foreign currency monetary item* una partida monetaria de moneda extranjera ▲ *a hedge of a monetary item* una cobertura de una partida monetaria ▲ *a monetary item that is payable to a foreign operation* una partida monetaria que hay que pagar por una operación extranjera ▲ *a monetary item that is receivable from a foreign operation* una partida monetaria que se recibe de una operación extranjera ▲ *adjustments relating to monetary items* ajustes relativos a las partidas monetarias ▲ *all net monetary items* todas las partidas monetarias netas ▲ *exchange differences on monetary items* diferencias de cambio en partidas monetarias ▲ *intercompany monetary items* partidas monetarias entre empresas ▲ *monetary items qualifying as hedging instruments in a cash flow hedge* partidas monetarias calificadas como instrumentos de cobertura en una cobertura de efectivo ▲ *settlement of monetary items* liquidación de las partidas monetarias ▲ *the foreign currency risk of an intragroup monetary item* el riesgo de moneda extranjera de una partida monetaria intragrupo ▲ *the individual monetary items* las partidas monetarias individuales ▲ *translation of monetary items* conversión de las partidas monetarias

monetary liability

= monetary financial liability

≠ monetary asset

A monetary liability is a promise to pay a fixed or determinable amount of money, the sum of which is unaffected by future prices.

pasivo monetario

▲ *a non-derivative monetary liability* un pasivo monetario no detivativo ▲ *foreign exchange gains and losses on monetary liabilities* ganancias y pérdidas por tipo de cambio en pasivos monetarios ▲ *the translation of monetary liabilities denominated in foreign currencies* una conversión de pasivos monetarios denominados en monedas extranjeras

⇛ monetary item

monetary unit

Monetary unit is a term used about the currency applied in a specific connection, e.g. in the preparation of an enterprise's financial statements, or when referring to the currency of a country.

unidad monetaria

▲ *change the monetary unit applied* cambiar la unidad monetaria aplicada ▲ *make transactions in a monetary unit other than that of the annual report* hacer transacciones en una unidad monetaria diferente de la del informe anual ▲ *the monetary unit applied* la unidad monetaria aplicada ▲ *the monetary unit chosen* la unidad monetaria elegida ▲ *translation from a foreign currency into the monetary unit chosen* conversión de una moneda extranjera en la unidad monetaria elegida ▲ *translation of balance sheet items from a foreign currency into the monetary unit of the annual report* conversión de las partidas del balance de una moneda extranjera en la unidad monetaria del informe anual

monetary unit of measurement

Monetary unit of measurement is a term used about the currency applied in the financial statements of an enterprise.

unidad monetaria de valoración

▲ *change in the monetary unit of measurement* cambio en la unidad monetaria de valoración ▲ *the monetary unit of measurement applied* la unidad monetaria de valoración aplicada

⇛ functional currency, presentation currency

monetary value

Monetary value is the worth of something in money, e.g. a certain currency.

valor monetario

▲ *expected monetary value* valor monetario previsto ▲ *the monetary value of the subscription rights attached to outstanding share options* el valor monetario de los derechos de suscripción vinculados a las opciones sobre acciones pendientes

money market

A money market is a wholesale market, typically a virtual or computerised market, for short-term finance, where highly-liquid debt instruments with maturities ranging from overnight up to one year are traded by financial institutions. Examples of securities traded are treasury bills, certificates of deposit and commercial paper.

mercado monetario

= mercado de dinero

▲ *a foreign money market* un mercado monetario extranjero ▲ *securities normally dealt in on the money market* activos normalmente negociados en el mercado de dinero ▲ *the domestic money market* el mercado monetario nacional

⇛ capital market

money market rate

The money market rate is the interest rate on short-term loans and financial instruments traded in the money market by financial institutions. Examples of money market rates are: the repo rate and LIBOR (UK), the federal funds rate (US) as well as CIBOR.

tipo del mercado monetario

= tipo de mercado monetario

▲ *a drop in money market rates* un descenso en los tipos del mercado monetario ▲ *the short-term money market rates* los tipos del mercado monetario a corto plazo

money purchase plan

→ defined contribution plan

money purchase scheme UK

→ defined contribution plan

mortgage[1] *noun*

hipoteca

A mortgage is a right in property granted to a creditor as security for the repayment of a loan. The debtor keeps the possession of the property and the creditor has a security right in the property.

hipoteca

▲ *a holder of an unsatisfied mortgage* un titular de una hipoteca impagada ▲ *a mortgage construction loan* un préstamo hipotecario ▲ *a prior mortgage* una hipoteca anterior ▲ *create a mortgage* formalizar una hipoteca ▲ *grant a second mortgage* conceder una segunda hipoteca ▲ *grant an advancing mortgage* conceder una hipoteca privilegiada ▲ *loans guaranteed by mortgages* préstamos garantizados con hipotecas ▲ *mort-*

gage by demise hipoteca por subrogación ▲ *mortgage charge* carga hipotecaria ▲ *mortgage of personal property* hipoteca de propiedad personal ▲ *mortgage score* marcador de hipoteca ▲ *mortgage secured on land* hipoteca garantizada con bienes raíces ▲ *mortgage servicing* pago de la hipoteca ▲ *mortgages payable* hipotecas a pagar ▲ *postpone the mortgage* aplazar la hipoteca ▲ *subsequent mortgage* hipoteca siguiente ▲ *the mortgages on the property* las hipotecas sobre los bienes

mortgage[2] *verb*

To mortgage is to provide a legal interest in a property as security for a loan.

hipotecar

▲ *mortgage land* hipotecar el terreno ▲ *mortgage personal property* hipotecar bienes personales ▲ *mortgage the property* hipotecar la propiedad

mortgage bank US

A mortgage bank is a banker specialised in mortgage financing, originating mortgage loans and operating as mortgage agents and intermediaries between borrowers (mortgagors) and lenders (mortgagees) for a fee or commission.

banco hipotecario

▲ *a domestic mortgage bank* un banco hipotecario nacional ▲ *operate a mortgage bank* gestionar un banco hipotecario

⇛ building society

mortgage bond US

= mortgage credit bond

A mortgage bond is a debt instrument secured by a mortgage on real property, conveying the lien on that property from the borrower (the mortgagor) to the lender and bondholder (the mortgagee). Mortgage bonds are issued by mortgage banks that function as intermediaries and specialists in providing mortgage financing.

cédula hipotecaria

= bono hipotecario

▲ *covered mortgage bonds* cédulas hipotecarias cubiertas ▲ *first mortgage bonds* primeros bonos hipotecarios ▲ *long-term mortgage bonds* cédulas hipotecarias a largo plazo ▲ *net proceeds from sale of mortgage bonds* ingreso neto por la venta de cédulas hipotecarias ▲ *the issuance of mortgage bonds* la emisión de cédulas hipotecarias

⇛ covered bond, mortgage, mortgage bank

mortgage debt

= mortgages payable

Mortgage debt is debt representing loans raised for mortgage financing purposes against security on real property.

deuda hipotecaria

▲ *an increase in the enterprise's mortgage debt* un aumento en la deuda hipotecaria de la empresa ▲ *fixed-rate mortgage debt* deuda hipotecaria a tipo fijo

mortgage finance

Mortgage finance is the financing of real property based on the issue of mortgage bonds secured on that property.

financiación hipotecaria

▲ *improved availability of mortgage finance* disponibilidad mejorada de la financiación hipotecaria

mortgage instalment

A mortgage instalment is a periodic repayment paid regularly to settle a mortgage debt.

cuota hipotecaria

= cuota de la hipoteca, letra de la hipoteca

▲ *pay a mortgage instalment* pagar una cuota hipotecaria

mortgage loan

A mortgage loan is a loan granted by a mortgage credit institution or mortgage bank secured upon real property and based on the issuance and subsequent sale of bonds.

préstamo hipotecario

▲ *a nominal mortgage loan* un préstamo hipotecario nominal ▲ *an underlying mortgage loan portfolio* una cartera subyacente de préstamos hipotecarios ▲ *credit risks on mortgage loans* riesgos crediticios de los préstamos hipotecarios ▲ *measurement of mortgage loans at amortised cost* valoración de los préstamos hipotecarios a coste amortizado ▲ *raise mortgage loans secured on real property* conseguir préstamos hipotecarios asegurados con bienes reales ▲ *remortgaging of mortgage loans* volver a hipotecar los préstamos hipotecarios ▲ *repayment of mortgage loans* amortización de los préstamos hipotecarios ▲ *the amount of fixed-rate mortgage loans* la cantidad de préstamos hipotecarios con interés fijo

movement

= change

Movement means a change that brings progress, development or improvement in a situation.

movimiento

= cambio

▲ *cambio in cash and cash equivalents* movimiento en efectivo y equivalentes de efectivo ▲ *movements in market rates of interest* movimientos en los tipos de interés de mercado ▲ *movements in the liability recognised in the balance sheet* movimientos en el pasivo reconocidos en el balance ▲ *movements in the number of share options outstanding* movimientos en el número de opciones sobre acciones pendientes ▲ *movements on the deferred income tax account* movimientos en la cuenta del impuesto sobre beneficio diferido ▲ *movements on the hedging reserve in shareholders' equity* movimientos en la reserva de cobertura en el patrimonio de los accionistas ▲ *significant and volatile movements in fair value* movimientos volátiles y significativos en el valor razonable ▲ *the movements in the allowance account during the period* los movimientos en la cuenta de retribución durante el periodo ▲ *with a presentation of each movement* con una presentación de cada movimiento

movement in capital

Movement in capital is the transfer of capital, e.g. from one investment object to another, such as selling shares and buying bonds.

movimiento de capital

= movimiento del capital

▲ *a substantial movement in capital* un movimiento de capital importante ▲ *reconciliation of movement in capital and reserves* conciliación del movimiento de capital y reservas

moving average

A moving average is an average of prices, e.g. securities, commodity or other sales prices, calculated statistically over a defined period of time for analysis purposes to track trends and developments during that period. Calculated as an average, the resulting figure will be less affected by temporary fluctuations.

media móvil

▲ *a 5-month moving average* una media móvil de 5 meses

multi-employer plan UK, IAS/IFRS

= multi-employer benefit plan IAS/IFRS, multiemployer plan US

A multi-employer plan is an employee benefit plan other than a state plan in which assets contributed by several unrelated employers are pooled for the purpose of providing benefits to employees of the enterprises, irrespective of which enterprise employs the employees in question. Multi-employer plans may be defined contribution plans or defined benefit plans, and employers may participate in more than one multi-employer plan.

plan de pensiones colectivo

▲ *a defined benefit multi-employer plan* un plan de pensiones colectivo de prestación definida ▲ *classify a multi-employer plan as a defined benefit plan* clasificar un plan de pensiones colectivo como un plan de prestación definida ▲ *classify a multi-employer plan as a defined contribution plan* clasificar un plan de pensiones colectivo como un plan de aportación definida ▲ *participate in a multi-employer plan* participar en un plan de pensiones colectivo ▲ *the classification of multi-employer plans* la clasificación de los planes de pensiones colectivos

⇛ defined benefit plan, defined contribution plan

multi-year amortisation

Multi-year amortisation is amortisation provided in respect of intangible assets over a period of many years.

amortización plurianual

▲ *multi-year amortisation of goodwill* amortización plurianual del fondo de comercio

multiemployer plan US *noun*

→ multi-employer plan

multilateral netting

Multilateral netting refers to the offsetting of amounts receivable and amounts payable subject to agreement between more than two parties, typically on an intra-group basis between multinationals, leaving a net balance payable or receivable.

compensación multilateral

▲ *the enforceability of multilateral netting* el cumplimiento de la compensación multilateral ▲ *the validity of multilateral netting* la validez de la compensación multilateral

⇛ bilateral netting, netting agreement

multiple

1 A multiple is a financial ratio where one number is compared with another. Examples are multiples measuring the value of an enterprise's operations based on enterprise value (EV) or shareholders' equity on the basis of the share price.

múltiplo

= múltiple

▲ *earnings multiple* múltiplo de ganancias ▲ *multiple regression* regresión múltiple ▲ *multiple regression analysis* análisis de regresión múltiple

⇛ FCFF, P/BV, P/E

2 = chain store, multiple shop, multiple store

Multiple is short for multiple store. Multiple stores are shops carrying on business under the same firm name in many different places.

cadena

▲ *multiple shop* cadena comercial ▲ *open a new multiple* abrir una nueva cadena

mutual entity

A mutual entity is an entity that is not owned by its shareholders, i.e. investors, but by its members, depositors or policyholders, etc. and may be a joint cooperative enterprise or a mutual insurance company generating economic benefits such as lower costs that are distributed directly to the members, depositors, or policyholders etc. on a pro-rata basis.

entidad de carácter mutualista

= entidad mutualista, mutua

▲ *a business combination involving two mutual entities* una combinación de negocios que implica a dos entidades de carácter mutualista

SOURCE IFRS 3, Appendix A

mutual fund US

= collective investment fund US, unit trust UK

A mutual fund is an open-end investment fund in which contributions from investors are pooled into a portfolio used for reinvesting in assets, typically securities such as shares and bonds. Against a management fee, mutual funds offer investors the advantages of professional investment management as well as diversification. As mutual funds are open-ended, there is no limit to the amount of shares issued by the fund, and investors are able to get their shares redeemed on demand, i.e. bought back by the fund at current net asset value.

fondo de inversión colectiva

▲ *a mutual fund manager* un gestor del fondo de inversión colectiva ▲ *an interest in a mutual fund* una inversión en un fondo de inversión colectiva ▲ *closed-end mutual funds* fondos de inversión colectiva de capital cerrado ▲ *investments in associates held by mutual funds* inversiones en asociadas mantenidas por los fondos de inversión colectiva ▲ *open-ended mutual funds* fondo de inversión colectiva de capital ampliable ▲ *units of an open-ended mutual fund* unidades de un fondo de inversión colectiva de capital ampliable

N

narrative form US
= report form, vertical format UK
≠ horizontal format
The narrative form is a presentation format used in financial statements arranging financial items in one column from top to bottom. For the balance sheet this means that assets are presented above and liabilities and stockholders' equity below. The income statement format starts with sales or revenue as the top line proceeding with additions and deductions of sub-totals to net income as the bottom line.
formato vertical
▲ *present in narrative form* presentar en formato vertical

nature
Nature is the basic qualities and characteristics of something.
naturaleza
▲ *a grouping of assets of similar nature* una agrupación de activos de naturaleza similar ▲ *classify by nature* clasificar por naturaleza ▲ *financial assets of a long-term nature* activos financieros de naturaleza a largo plazo ▲ *items of a dissimilar nature or function* partidas de una naturaleza o función distinta ▲ *of an unusual nature* de una naturaleza inusual ▲ *the amounts, nature and timing of liabilities* las cantidades, naturaleza y vencimiento de los pasivos ▲ *the nature of each activity for which expenditure is incurred* la naturaleza de cada actividad para la cual se incurre en gastos ▲ *the nature of the contingent asset* la naturaleza del activo contingente ▲ *the nature of the enterprise* la naturaleza de la empresa ▲ *the nature of the risk being hedged* la naturaleza del riesgo cubierto

nature of expenditure method
→ classification by nature

NAV
= Net Asset Value
NAV is the abbreviation for net asset value, i.e. measure applying to assets and liabilities that are tradable in a secondary market. The NAV is obtained by adding to shareholders' equity the difference between the carrying amount of assets and liabilities and their objective market value, net of tax and minority interests' share.
valor activo neto
▲ *calculate NAV* calcular el valor activo neto ▲ *NAV calculations* cálculos del valor activo neto

NAVPS
= net asset value per share
NAVPS is the abbreviation for net asset value per share, which is an investment ratio defined as the net asset value, i.e. the adjusted value of the equity per share, divided by number of shares at year-end.
valor neto del activo por acción
▲ *calculate NAVPS* calcular el valor neto del activo por acción ▲ *NAVPS calculations* cálculos del valor neto del activo por acción

NBV
= net book value
NBV is the abbreviation for net book value, which is the value of assets recognised in the balance sheet as the historical cost net of accumulated depreciation or amortisation.
valor en libros neto
= valor contable neto, valor neto según libros
▲ *the NBV of the assets* el valor en libros neto de los activos ▲ *the remaining NBV* el valor en libros neto restante ▲ *use the NBV of an asset to determine its selling price* utilizar el valor en libros neto de un activo para determinar su precio de venta

Nederlands Instituut van Registeraccountants
= Dutch Institute of Auditors, NIVRA
The Nederlands Instituut van Registeraccountants (NIVRA) (or Koninklijk Nederlands Instituut van Registeraccountants) is the main Dutch professional

accountancy body. NIVRA's tasks include advancing the quality of the professional services provided by registeraccountants and being responsible for preparing the guidelines for Dutch accounting principles.

Nederlands Instituut van Registeraccountants

= Instituto de Auditores Holandeses

▲ *become a member of the Nederlands Instituut van Registeraccountants* convertirse en miembro del Nederlands Instituut van Registeraccountants ▲ *the areas of responsibility of the Nederlands Instituut van Registeraccountants* las áreas de responsabilidad del Nederlands Instituut van Registeraccountants

need

A need is something necessary such as a requirement or wish that must to be satisfied.

necesidad

▲ *accommodate the needs of companies, auditors and investors* acomodar las necesidades de empresas, auditores e inversores ▲ *cash needs* necesidades de efectivo ▲ *financial needs* necesidades financieras ▲ *meet the needs of users* satisfacer las necesidades de los usuarios ▲ *relevant to the economic decision-making needs of users* relevante para las necesidades de toma de decisiones económicas de los usuarios ▲ *the needs of the entity to utilise the cash flows* las necesidades de la entidad para utilizar los flujos de efectivo

negative

If something is negative it lacks positive qualities, is harmful, or is less than something else.

negativo

▲ *a negative amount* una cantidad negativa ▲ *a negative balance* un saldo negativo ▲ *a negative development* una evolución negativa ▲ *a negative market value adjustment* un ajuste a valor de mercado negativo ▲ *a negative result* un resultado negativo ▲ *a negative value* un valor negativo ▲ *a possible negative impact on the price of ordinary shares* un posible impacto negativo en el precio de las acciones ordinarias ▲ *derivatives with negative values* derivados con valores negativos ▲ *negative deferred tax* impuesto diferido negativo ▲ *negative economic growth* crecimiento económico negativo ▲ *negative equity* patrimonio negativo ▲ *negative leverage* apalancamiento negativo ▲ *negative market value of derivatives* valor de mercado negativo de derivados ▲ *negative trends* tendencias negativas

negative balance

A negative balance means that liabilities exceed assets.

NOTE If liabilities exceed assets in the balance sheet, a negative equity results.

saldo negativo

▲ *cover a negative balance* cubrir un saldo negativo ▲ *set-off negative balance in subsidiaries* compensar el saldo negativo de las subsidiarias

negative goodwill

≠ goodwill

Negative goodwill arises where the price paid for an acquisition is less than the fair value of its net assets.

fondo de comercio negativo

▲ *deferred tax assets arising from negative goodwill* activos por impuesto diferido provenientes del fondo de comercio negativo ▲ *derecognise negative goodwill* eliminar el fondo de comercio negativo ▲ *measurement of negative goodwill* medición del fondo de comercio negativo ▲ *previously recognised negative goodwill* fondo de comercio negativo reconocido previamente ▲ *recognition of negative goodwill* reconocimiento del fondo de comercio negativo ▲ *the carrying amount of negative goodwill* el valor contable del fondo de comercio negativo

negotiability

Negotiability is the quality that something can be exchanged without any restrictions or conditions, usually for money or money's worth.

negociabilidad

▲ *free negotiability* negociabilidad libre ▲ *restrictions on the negotiability of shares* restricciones a la negociabilidad de acciones ▲ *the free negotiability of shares* la negociabilidad libre de acciones ▲ *the negotiability of bonds* la negociabilidad de bonos ▲ *the negotiability of certifi-*

cates la negociabilidad de certificados ▲ *the negotiability of share options* la negociabilidad de las opciones sobre acciones ▲ *the negotiability of shares* la negociabilidad de acciones

negotiable

If something is negotiable it can be exchanged without any restrictions or conditions, usually for money or money's worth.

negociable

▲ *a freely negotiable bond* un bono negociable libremente ▲ *a freely negotiable share* una acción negocible libremente ▲ *a negotiable dematerialised security* un título no tangible negociable ▲ *a negotiable mortgage* una hipoteca negociable ▲ *a negotiable option* una opción negociable ▲ *a negotiable security* un título negociable

net

Net is used about an amount that remains of a total amount of something, e.g. income, profit or weight, after deduction of another amount, e.g. tax, expenses or packing. Net current assets e.g. are current assets less current liabilities.

neto

▲ *acquisition of investments, net* adquisición de inversiones, neto ▲ *acquisition of other intangible assets as well as property, plant and equipment, net* adquisición de otros activos intangibles así como edificios, instalaciones y equipos, neto ▲ *contract work in progress, net* contrato de trabajo en curso, neto ▲ *currency translation adjustments, net* ajustes por conversión de moneda extranjera, neto ▲ *net assets divested* activos netos desinvertidos ▲ *net cash flow used for investing activities* flujo de efectivo neto usado para actividades de inversión ▲ *net cash flows* flujos de efectivo netos ▲ *net disposable proceeds* productos disponible netos ▲ *net fees and commissions* honorarios y comisiones netas ▲ *net financials* financiaciones netas ▲ *net funding expense* gasto de financiación neto ▲ *net interest* interés neto ▲ *net purchase sum* importe neto de la compra ▲ *net selling price* precio de venta neto ▲ *other operating income, net* otro ingreso de explotación, neto ▲ *settle an amount net* pagar un importe neto ▲ *settle on a net basis* liquidar en una base neta ▲ *tax paid, net* impuesto pagado, neto

net addition

A net addition results when additions exceed disposals. An enterprise may e.g. recognise a net addition of fixed asset investments if it has acquired more subsidiaries than it has disposed of.

incremento neto

▲ *a net addition of distributors* un incremento neto de distribuidores

net amount

A net amount is an amount less any deductions. Net assets e.g. appears after deduction of liabilities, and net income is total income less total expenses for the accounting period.

cantidad neta

▲ *designation of a net amount including assets and liabilities* designación de una cantidad neta que incluye activos y pasivos ▲ *future net amounts* cantidades netas futuras ▲ *the net amount restated to the revalued amount of the asset* la cantidad neta reajustada a la cantidad revalorizada del activo

net asset

Net assets appear after deduction of liabilities from total assets and therefore equal equity.

activo neto

▲ *acquire net assets* adquirir activos netos ▲ *changes in the net assets of the enterprise* cambios en los activos netos de la empresa ▲ *currency translation adjustment of net assets* ajuste de activos netos por conversión de moneda ▲ *dismantle net assets* desmantelar los activos netos ▲ *disposal of the net assets on a piecemeal basis* enajenación de los activos netos gradualmente ▲ *identifiable net assets* activos netos identificables ▲ *net assets acquired* activos netos adquiridos ▲ *net assets available for retirement benefits* activos netos disponibles para prestaciones por jubilación ▲ *net assets exposed to translation risk* activos netos expuestos a riesgo de conversión ▲ *obtain control of the net assets* obtener el control de los activos netos ▲ *obtain control of the net assets of another enterprise* obtener el control de los activos netos de otra empresa ▲ *purchase net assets* comprar activos netos ▲ *sell net assets* vender activos netos ▲ *the carrying amount of the net assets* el valor contable de los activos netos ▲ *the fair value of the group's share of the net assets* el valor razonable del porcentaje de los activos netos del grupo ▲ *the fair value of the net assets* el valor razonable de los activos netos ▲ *the net assets of the acquired enterprise* los activos netos de la empresa adquirida ▲ *the net selling price of the net assets* el precio de venta neto de los activos netos

net asset value[1] *noun* <a, the, -s>
= equity value
Net asset value is the ownership interest in or equity value of a company, typically a subsidiary in a group, i.e. total assets less total liabilities.
NOTE Net asset value is also used as a financial ratio, often calculated on a "per share" basis, also referred to as net asset value or NAV.
valor del patrimonio neto
= valor del activo neto
▲ *calculate the net asset value* calcular el valor del patrimonio neto ▲ *changes in net asset value* cambios en el valor del patrimonio neto ▲ *net asset value attributable to unitholders* valor del patrimonio neto atribuible a los partícipes

net asset value[2] *noun* <a, the, no plural>
= NAV
Net asset value (NAV) is a measure applying to assets and liabilities that are tradable in a secondary market. The NAV is obtained by adding to shareholders' equity the difference between the carrying amount of assets and liabilities and their objective market value, net of tax and minority interests' share.
NOTE Net asset value is also used to refer to the equity value of a company, typically a subsidiary in a group.
valor liquidativo neto
= NAV
▲ *calculate the net asset value* calcular el valor liquidativo neto
⇛ book value per share, net asset value per share

net asset value per share
= NAVPS
Net asset value per share is an investment ratio defined as the net asset value, i.e. the adjusted value of the equity per share, divided by number of shares at year-end.
valor neto por acción
▲ *calculate the net asset value per share* calcular el valor neto por acción ▲ *determine the net asset value per share* determinar el valor neto por acción ▲ *the change in net asset value per share* el cambio en el valor neto por acción ▲ *the change in percentage terms of the net asset value per share* el cambio en términos porcentuales en el valor neto por acción
⇛ book value per share, net asset value

net assets
= shareholders' equity
The net assets of a person or an enterprise appear from the equity and can be assessed by deducting the debts or the liabilities owed to outsiders from the assets. Net assets therefore equal equity.
patrimonio neto
= activos netos
▲ *a change in net assets* un cambio en patrimonio neto ▲ *unrestricted net assets* patrimonio neto sin restricciones

net book value
= amortised cost, depreciated cost, NBV, written-down value
The net book value is the value of assets recognised in the balance sheet as the historical cost net of accumulated depreciation or amortisation.
valor en libros neto
= valor contable neto
▲ *net book value at 31 December 2006 restated* valor en libros neto a 31 de diciembre de 2006 reactualizado ▲ *the net book value of the assets* el valor en libros neto de los activos ▲ *the remaining net book value* el valor en libros neto restante ▲ *use the net book value of an asset to determine its selling price* utilizar el valor en libros neto de un activo para determinar su precio de venta

⇛ book value, net asset value

net carrying value US

→ carrying value

net cash and cash equivalents

The net cash and cash equivalents of an enterprise refer to the amount of cash and short-term, highly liquid investments held less interest-bearing debt.

efectivo y otros activos líquidos equivalentes

▲ *interest-bearing net cash and cash equivalents* intereses por efectivo y otros activos líquidos equivalentes

net cash flow

The net cash flow results after deducting cash outflows for investing activities from cash inflows from operating activities and adding cash inflows from financing activities less dividends.

flujo de efectivo neto

= cash flow neto, flujo de caja neto

▲ *a significant decline in budgeted net cash flows* una disminución significativa en los flujos de efectivo netos presupuestados ▲ *actual net cash flows* flujos de efectivo netos actuales ▲ *expected future net cash flows* flujos de efectivo netos futuros esperados ▲ *expected future net cash flows from the operating activities of the enterprise* flujos de efectivo netos futuros esperados de las actividades de explotación de la empresa ▲ *expected net cash flows* flujos de efectivo netos esperados ▲ *future net cash flows* flujos de efectivo netos futuros ▲ *present value of future net cash flows* valor actual de los flujos de efectivo netos futuros ▲ *the asset's expected contribution to net cash flows* contribución esperada del activo a los flujos de efectivo netos ▲ *the discounted present value of the future net cash flows* el valor actual descontado de los flujos de efectivo netos futuros

⇛ net cash inflow, net cash outflow

net cash inflow

≠ net cash outflow

Net cash inflow is the positive difference between the ingoing and outgoing cash flows in an enterprise during a given accounting period.

entrada neta de efectivo

≠ salida neta de efectivo

▲ *assets expected to generate net cash inflows for the entity* activos con expectativas de generar entradas netas de efectivo para la empresa ▲ *the net cash inflow on sale* la entrada neta de efectivo por venta

⇛ cash flow, net cash flow

net cash outflow

≠ net cash inflow

Net cash outflow is the negative difference between the ingoing and outgoing cash flows in an enterprise during a given accounting period.

salida neta de efectivo

≠ entrada neta de efectivo

▲ *net cash outflows for the asset* salidas netas de efectivo para el activo

⇛ net cash flow

net cost

= net expense

Net costs are total costs less income or revenue. Net financial costs are e.g. financial costs less financial income. In an economic perspective, net costs can be seen as total costs incurred e.g. in a health or environmental project minus the resulting savings of resources.

coste neto

▲ *determination of net costs* determinación de los costes netos

net currency cash flow

A net currency cash flow is a positive or negative cash flow resulting from foreign currency adjustments. The total cash flow effect from positions or investments in several currencies is the net currency cash flow of en enterprise for a given accounting period. The cash flow effect from foreign exchange gains or losses because of currency exposures may be reduced by hedging.

flujo de efectivo en moneda extranjera neto

▲ *budgeted net currency cash flows* flujos de efectivo en moneda extranjera netos presupuestados

net currency exposure

= net currency translation exposure

A net currency exposure shows the currency risk of an enterprise to a given currency, seen as the difference between payment inflows and outflows in that currency or changes in the value of financial instruments denominated in foreign currencies resulting from exchange rate fluctuations. The enterprise may hedge against currency exposures through derivative financial instruments.

exposición neta al riesgo de divisa

▲ *hedge the net currency exposure* cubrir la exposición neta al riesgo de divisa

net currency inflow

≠ net currency outflow

Net currency inflow is the total increase in amounts received by an enterprise measured in currencies other than the presentation currency from one accounting period to the following period.

entrada neta de moneda extranjera

▲ *budgeted net currency inflows* entradas netas de moneda extranjera presupuestadas ▲ *hedge net currency inflows* cubrir las entradas netas de moneda extranjera

net current assets UK

= working capital

Net current assets is an item in the balance sheet appearing as a subtotal after deducting total current assets from total current liabilities. Net current assets are also referred to as working capital.

activos corrientes netos

= capital circulante, fondo de maniobra

▲ *included in net current assets* incluido en activos corrientes netos

⇛ net current liabilities

net current liabilities UK

= working capital

Net current liabilities is an item in the balance sheet appearing as a negative subtotal after deducting total current assets from total current liabilities.

pasivos corrientes netos

= capital circulante

▲ *included in net current liabilities* incluido en pasivos corrientes netos

⇛ net current assets

net debt

= net liabilities

Net debt refers to the total of an enterprise's long-term and short-term borrowings less cash and cash equivalents.

deuda neta

= pasivo neto

▲ *an increase in net debt* un aumento de deuda neta ▲ *movements in net debt* movimientos en deuda neta

net deferred tax asset

≠ net deferred tax liability

A net deferred tax asset is the net amount resulting after offsetting deferred tax assets and liabilities that have arisen in respect of deductible and taxable temporary differences, respectively.

activo neto por impuesto diferido

= activos netod por impuestos diferidos

≠ pasivo neto por impuesto diferido, pasivo neto por impuestos diferidos

▲ *the components of the net deferred tax asset* los componentes del activo neto por impuesto diferido

⇛ deferred tax

net deferred tax liability

≠ net deferred tax asset

A net deferred tax liability is the net amount resulting after offsetting deferred tax assets and liabilities that have arisen in respect of deductible and taxable temporary differences, respectively.

pasivo neto por impuesto diferido

= pasivo neto por impuestos diferidos

≠ activo neto por inpuesto diferido, activo neto por impuestos diferidos

▲ *an increase in net deferred tax liability* un aumento en el pasivo neto por impuestos diferidos ▲ *changes in the net deferred tax liability* cambios en el pasivo neto por impuesto diferido ▲ *net deferred tax liability of $5.3 million* un importe neto por pasivo diferido de 5,3 millones de dólares ▲ *recognise a net deferred tax liability* reconocer un pasivo neto por impuesto diferido ▲ *the cumulative net deferred tax liability* el pasivo neto por impuesto diferido acumulado ▲ *total long-term net deferred tax liability* total pasivo neto a largo plazo por impuesto diferido

⇛ deferred tax

net earnings

= net income US, net profit IAS/IFRS, UK

Net earnings constitute revenue less all expenses for an accounting period, also shown as the bottom line in the income statement.

beneficios netos

= ganancias netas

▲ *future net earnings* beneficios netos futuros ▲ *net earnings from financial transactions* beneficios netos de transacciones financieras

net effect

A net effect is what results after offsetting two transactions or amounts, or after deducting something from something else, e.g. discounts or costs.

efecto neto

▲ *recognition of the net effect in the opening balance sheet* reconocimiento del efecto neto en el balance de apertura ▲ *the net effect of indirectly owned operations* el efecto neto de las operaciones de propiedad indirecta ▲ *total monetary net effect* total efecto neto monetario

net fair value

The net fair value of an asset is the value of that asset after deduction of an amount. For non-current assets held for sale, the net fair value is the fair value less sales costs, also referred to as the net selling price.

valor razonable neto

▲ *any change in the net fair value attributable to the hedged risk* cualquier cambio en el valor razonable neto atribuible al riesgo cubierto ▲ *the net fair value of the identifiable assets acquired* el valor razonable neto de los activos identificables adquiridos ▲ *the net fair value of the right and obligation* el valor razonable neto de los derechos y las obligaciones

net finance cost

Net finance costs arise when finance costs exceed finance income. Net financials comprise e.g. interest, foreign exchange adjustments, capital gains or losses etc.

coste financiero neto

▲ *a decrease in net finance costs* un descenso en los costes financieros netos ▲ *an increase in net finance costs* un aumento en los costes financieros netos ▲ *total net finance costs* total costes financieros netos

net finance income

Net finance income arises when finance income exceeds finance costs. Net financials comprise e.g. interest, foreign exchange adjustments, capital gains or losses etc.

ingreso financiero neto

▲ *a decrease in net finance income* una disminución en el ingreso financiero neto ▲ *an increase in net finance income* un aumento en el ingreso financiero neto

net financial expense

Net financial expenses arise when financial expenses exceed financial income. Net financials comprise e.g. interest, foreign exchange adjustments, capital gains and losses, etc.

gasto financiero neto

▲ *an increase in net financial expense* un aumento en el gasto financiero neto ▲ *total net financial expense* total gasto financiero neto

net financial income

Net financial income arises when financial income exceeds financial expenses. Net financials comprise e.g. interest, foreign exchange adjustments, capital gains or losses etc.

ingreso financiero neto

▲ *total net financial income* total ingreso financiero neto

net financial income or expense

= net financials

Net financial income or expenses is an item in the income statement showing the difference between financial income and financial expenses, i.e. income and expenses in the form of interest, foreign exchange adjustments, capital gains or losses etc.

resultado financiero neto

▲ *current year net financial income or expense* resultado financiero neto del año actual ▲ *include net financial income or expense in the amount* incluir el resultado financiero neto en la cifra

net financials

= financials, net

Net financials result from offsetting financial income and financial expenses.

resultado financiero neto

▲ *currency hedging gain included in net financials* ganancia de cobertura de moneda extranjera incluida en el resultado financiero neto ▲ *net financials and tax* resultado financiero neto e impuestos

⇛ other interest receivable and similar income

net financing

Net financing refers to the net cash flow from operating activities, i.e. the net cash flow generated from an enterprise's activities.

financiamiento neto

▲ *net financing costs* costes de financiamiento neto ▲ *net financing expense* gasto de financiamiento neto ▲ *the company's net financing requirements* requisitos de financiamiento neto de la compañía ▲ *total net financing* total financiamiento neto

net foreign exchange earnings

Net foreign exchange earnings constitute the amount of revenue in foreign exchange exceeding the amount of payments in foreign exchange. Net foreign exchange earnings typically refer to the aggregate earnings from exports in foreign exchange less total imports in foreign exchange of an economy over a given period of time.

ingresos netos en moneda extranjera

= ingresos netos en divisas, ingresos netos por exportaciones

▲ *accounting for net foreign exchange earnings* contabilidad de ingresos netos en moneda extranjera ▲ *accumulated net foreign exchange earnings* ingresos netos en moneda extranjera acumulados ▲ *estimated net foreign exchange earnings* ingresos netos en moneda extranjera estimados ▲ *substantial net foreign exchange earnings* ingresos netos en moneda extranjera sustanciales

net foreign exchange gain

≠ net foreign exchange loss

A net foreign exchange gain is an enterprise's gain after setoff of losses on foreign currency for a particular period or transaction. Foreign exchange gains may be realised or unrealised and arise from foreign exchange adjustments or translations as a result of changes in exchange rates.

beneficio neto en moneda extranjera

= beneficio neto en divisas, ganancia neta en divisas, ganancia neta en moneda extranjera

≠ pérdida meta en moneda extranjera

▲ *operating profit adjusted for net foreign exchange gain* beneficio de explotación ajustado por beneficio neto en moneda extranjera ▲ *realised net foreign exchange gain* beneficio neto en moneda extranjera realizado ▲ *recognise a net foreign exchange gain* reconocer un beneficio neto en moneda extranjera ▲ *unrealised net foreign exchange gain* beneficio neto en moneda extranjera no realizado

net foreign exchange loss

A net foreign exchange loss is an enterprise's loss after setoff of gains on foreign currency for a particular period or transaction. Foreign exchange losses may be realised or unrealised and can result from exchange differences on loans and exchange rate fluctuations.

pérdida neta en moneda extranjera

= pérdida neta en divisas

≠ beneficio neto en moneda extranjera

▲ *net foreign exchange loss on other financial instruments* pérdida neta en moneda extranjera en otros instrumentos financieros ▲ *realised net foreign exchange loss* pérdida neta en moneda extranjera realizada ▲ *recognise a net foreign exchange loss* reconocer una pérdida neta en moneda extranjera ▲ *unrealised net foreign exchnage loss* pérdida neta en moneda extranjera no realizada

net foreign exchange position

The net foreign exchange position is the position in one or more foreign currencies resulting in a currency exposure to an enterprise. The net foreign exchange position is the difference arising after offsetting assets, liabilities and derivative financial instruments in a given foreign currency.

posición neta en moneda extranjera
= pérdida neta en divisas
▲ *determination of the net foreign exchange position* determinación de la posición neta en moneda extranjera ▲ *hedge a net foreign exchange position* cubrir una posición neta en moneda extranjera ▲ *hedging of the net foreign exchange position* cobertura de la posición neta en moneda extranjera ▲ *total net foreign exchange position* total posición neta en moneda extranjera

net gain

A net gain is the positive difference between the original cost of an asset (the carrying amount) and its selling price. For investment assets, the net gain is the difference between the original cost and the proceeds.
NOTE To be compared with a net profit that arises on the sale of an enterprise's products or services as the sales price less the related costs.
beneficio neto
= ganancia neta
▲ *net gain from sale of shares* beneficio neto por venta de acciones ▲ *net gain not recognised in the income statement* beneficio neto no reconocido en el estado de resultados ▲ *net gains from fair value adjustments* beneficios netos por ajustes en el valor razonable

net impairment loss

A net impairment loss arises when impairment losses exceed gains and revaluations on a portfolio of assets.
pérdida neta por deterioro
▲ *net impairment loss on investments* pérdida neta por deterioro en inversiones ▲ *the deduction for the net impairment loss* la deducción por pérdida neta por deterioro ▲ *total net impairment loss of non-current assets* total pérdida neta por deterioro de activos no corrientes
⇛ impairment, impairment loss

net income

1 = net receipts
≠ gross income, gross receipts
Net income is gross income less costs and expenses.
ingreso neto
= renta neta
≠ gasto neto
▲ *estimated future net income* ingreso neto futuro estimado ▲ *estimated net income* ingreso neto estimado ▲ *extraordinary net income* ingreso neto extraordinario ▲ *foreign currency net income* ingreso neto en moneda extranjera ▲ *future net income* ingreso neto futuro ▲ *measure the net income* medir el ingreso neto ▲ *minority interests in the net income of consolidated subsidiaries* intereses minoritarios en el ingreso neto de filiales consolidadas ▲ *net income of a secondary nature* ingreso neto de una naturaleza secundaria ▲ *the nature and amount of items affecting net income* la naturaleza y cantidad de ingreso neto de partidas relacionadas ▲ *the net income attributable to the owners of the parent* el ingreso neto atribuible a los propietarios de la matriz

2 = net profit UK, IAS/IFRS
≠ net loss US, UK, IAS/IFRS
Net income is revenue less all expenses for an accounting period, also shown as the bottom line in the income statement. If negative, it is referred to as net loss.
NOTE In the consolidated income statement, net income is shown as the net income attributable to equity holders of the parent and to minority interests, respectively.
beneficio neto
= ganancia neta
≠ pérdida neta
NOTE Spanish accountants prefer 'beneficio neto' to the IAS term 'ganancia neta'
▲ *adjust one's net income downward* ajustar a la baja los beneficios netos propios ▲ *adjust one's net income upward* ajustar al alza los beneficios netos propios ▲ *appropriation of net income* asignación del beneficio neto ▲ *consolidated net income* beneficios netos consolidados ▲ *minority interests' share of net income* participación de minoritarios en los beneficios netos ▲ *net income after tax* beneficio neto después de impuestos ▲ *net income after tax and minority interests* beneficios netos después de impuestos y minoritarios ▲ *net income before tax* beneficio neto antes de impuestos

▲ *net income for the year as a percentage of average shareowners' equity* beneficio neto para el periodo como un porcentaje de capital propio medio ▲ *net income from property* beneficio neto procedente de bienes raíces ▲ *share of net income* porcentaje de beneficio neto

3 Net income is total amount of income of a person or organisation that remains after deduction of tax, social security contribution and other deductions.
beneficio neto
= ingreso neto
▲ *the calculated net income* el ingreso neto calculado

net income or loss US
Net income or loss shows that amount of income earned by an organisation for an accounting period after deducting all expenses and appears as the bottom line in the profit and loss account. If negative, it is referred to as net loss.
NOTE In the consolidated income statement, net income or loss is shown as the net income or loss attributable to equity holders of the parent and to minority interests, respectively.
resultado neto
▲ *changes in deferred tax relating to the net income or loss* cambios en impuesto diferido relativos al resultado neto

net income or loss for the period IAS/IFRS, US
Net income or loss for the period appears as the bottom line in the income statement and includes all items of revenue, income and expense recognised in the period, unless other accounting treatment has been provided in an accounting standard.
NOTE In the consolidated income statement, net income or loss is shown as the net income or loss attributable to equity holders of the parent and to minority interests, respectively.
resultado neto del periodo
= ganancia o pérdida neta del periodo
▲ *changes in deferred tax relating to the net income or loss for the period* cambios en impuesto diferido relativos al resultado neto del periodo

net interest
Net interest is either net interest receivable or net interest payable. The context or the financial statements will show whether it is one or the other.
interés neto
▲ *net interest from investing activities* interés neto de actividades de inversión ▲ *net interest income* ingreso por interés neto ▲ *the net interest rate exposure* la exposición al riesgo de tipo de interés neto

net interest expense IAS/IFRS, US
Net interest expense is interest charges less interest income.
gasto por interés neto
= gasto financiero neto, resultado financiero negativo
▲ *a decrease in net interest expense* una disminución en el gasto por interés neto ▲ *add back the net interest expense* añadir de nuevo el gasto financiero neto ▲ *after-tax net interest expense* gasto por interés neto después de impuestos ▲ *an increase in net interest expense* un aumento en el gasto por interés neto ▲ *deduct net interest expense* deducir el gasto financiero neto ▲ *other net interest expense* otro gasto por interés neto

net interest income US
Net interest income is interest income less interest charges.
ingreso neto por intereses
= interés neto a cobrar, resultado financiero positivo
▲ *a decrease in net interest income* un decremento en el ingreso neto por intereses ▲ *affect net interest income* afectar al interés neto a cobrar ▲ *an increase in net interest income* un incremento en el ingreso neto por intereses ▲ *net interest income excluding earnings from investment portfolios* interés neto a cobrar excluyendo ingresos de inversión

net interest payable UK, IAS/IFRS
Net interest payable is interest payable less interest receivable.
interés neto a pagar
= interés neto por pagar
▲ *a slight fall in net interest payable* un ligero descenso en el interés neto a pagar

net interest receivable
Net interest receivable is interest receivable less interest payable.
interés neto a cobrar
= ingreso neto por intereses

▲ *a decrease in net interest receivable* un decremento en el ingreso neto por intereses ▲ *affect net interest receivable* afectar al interés neto a cobrar ▲ *an increase in net interest receivable* un incremento en el ingreso neto por intereses ▲ *net interest receivable excluding earnings from investment portfolios* interés neto a cobrar excluyendo ingresos de inversión

net interest-bearing debt

Net interest-bearing debt is interest-bearing debt reduced by interest-bearing financial current assets (cash and securities).

deuda neta que devenga intereses

▲ *reduce one's net interest-bearing debt* reducir la deuda neta que devenga intereses de uno ▲ *total net interest-bearing debt* total deuda neta que devenga intereses

net investment US

For an enterprise, net investments represent the carrying amount of its tangible fixed assets after depreciation and any additions or disposals. In a lease, the net investment constitutes the gross investment after unearned finance income.

inversión neta

▲ *a constant periodic rate of return on the lessor's net investment in the finance lease* un tipo periódico constante de rentabilidad en la inversión neta del arrendador en el arrendamiento financiero ▲ *a zero initial net investment* una inversión neta inicialmente a cero ▲ *dispose of a net investment* enajenar una inversión neta ▲ *hedges of a net investment* coberturas de una inversión neta ▲ *net investment in a foreign operation* inversión neta en una operación en el extranjero ▲ *the investor's net investment in the associate* la inversión neta del inversor en la asociada ▲ *the net investment in the lease* la inversión neta en el arrendamiento

net investment method UK

= closing rate method

The net investment method or closing rate method looks at the investment in a foreign subsidiary as an investment as a whole in the net assets of that enterprise as the name of this method indicates. The financial statements of the foreign subsidiary are translated from their local currencies into the presentation currency of the parent on consolidation. Assets and liabilities are translated at balance-sheet-date exchange rates, whereas profit-and-loss-account items are translated at recognition-date rates, average rates or balance-sheet-date rates.

método de inversión neta

▲ *use the net investment method* utilizar el método de inversión neta

net liability

A net liability arises when a recognised liability exceeds a recognised asset, e.g. in respect of an individual customer or supplier. If an enterprise's net position of total assets and liabilities show total net liabilities, the enterprise will need additional equity contributions to avoid being compulsorily wound up.

pasivo neto

▲ *a net liability of claims* un pasivo neto de reclamaciones ▲ *a reconciliation showing the movements during the period in the net liability* una conciliación que muestra los movimientos durante el periodo en el pasivo neto ▲ *net liability recognised in the balance sheet* pasivo neto reconocido en el balance

net loss

1 ≠ net gain, net profit

A net loss arises when the enterprise's capital losses exceed the capital gains.

pérdida neta

≠ beneficio neto, ganancia neta

▲ *net loss after tax on extraordinary items* pérdida neta después de impuestos en partidas extraordinarias ▲ *net loss not recognised in the income statement* pérdida neta no reconocida en el estado de resultados ▲ *recognise a net loss of GBP 10m* reconocer una pérdida neta de 10 millones de libras esterlinas ▲ *the share of net losses not recognised* la acción con pérdidas netas no reconocidas ▲ *unrealised net losses* pérdidas netas no realizadas ▲ *unrealised net losses on derivatives used for foreign cur-*

rency hedging pérdidas netas no realizadas en derivados utilizados como cobertura de moneda extranjera

2 ≠ net income US, net profit UK, IAS/IFRS

A net loss arises when expenses exceed revenues for a given period. A net loss may also be a previous loss offset in a subsequent profit resulting in a carryforward of the net loss for subsequent offsetting.

pérdida neta

= resultado neto negativo

≠ beneficio neto, ganancia neta

▲ *retax a net loss* volver a gravar una pérdida neta

net operating expense

≠ net operating income

The net operating expenses are the expenses related to the ordinary activities of an enterprise after deduction of operating income.

gasto neto de explotación

≠ ingreso neto de explotación

▲ *a decrease in net operating expenses* un descenso en los gastos netos de explotación ▲ *an increase in net operating expenses* un aumento en los gastos netos de explotación ▲ *other net operating expenses* otros gastos netos de explotación ▲ *total net operating expenses* total gastos netos de explotación

net operating income US

≠ net operating expense

Net operating income is the revenue generated in the ordinary activities of an enterprise after deduction of operating expenses.

ingreso neto de explotación

≠ gasto neto de explotación

NOTE With some Spanish collocations the Spanish term is plural.

▲ *generate net operating income* generar ingresos netos de explotación ▲ *net operating income after tax* ingreso neto de explotación después de impuestos

⇛ operating expense, operating income

net operating profit less adjusted taxes

= NOPLAT

Net operating profit less adjusted taxes (NOPLAT) is a key earnings concept defined as EBITA less taxes on EBITA, i.e. an enterprise's operating profit after taxes that are adjusted to a cash basis, and measures the enterprise's operating profit as it would have been reported if the enterprise had no deferred taxes, no debt or non-operating income and expenses.

EBITA menos impuestos sobre EBITA

= beneficio de explotación neto menos ajustes por impuestos

▲ *calculate net operating profit less adjusted taxes* calcular el EBITA menos impuestos sobre el EBITA ▲ *increase net operating profit less adjusted taxes* aumentar el EBITA menos impuestos sobre el EBITA

net payment

Net payments are in- or outgoing payments after deduction of offsetting amounts such as costs, discounts or refunds related to the payment in question.

pago neto

▲ *discounted net payments* pagos netos con descuentos ▲ *make a single net payment* hacer un único pago neto ▲ *receive a single net payment* recibir un único pago neto

net present value

= NPV

Net present value is the value today of a capital investment or investment project arrived at by deducting the projected cash outflows (costs) from the projected cash inflows (profits) of that investment or project, which have been discounted at a given discount factor, typically the required rate of return. In a choice between alternative investments or projects, the alternative with the highest net present value is the most profitable.

valor actual neto

▲ *a defined benefit obligation with a net present value of 500* una obligación por prestación definida con un valor actual neto de 500 ▲ *reduce the net present value of the obligation by 100* reducir el valor actual neto de la obligación en 100

⇛ discount factor, present value

net present value method

= NPV method

The net present value method is a method for the appraisal of investment alternatives or financing projects. Under this method, all expected future cash inflows and outflows over a period of time are discounted to net present value now. If the net present value exceeds zero, the investment or project is deemed profitable.

método de valor actual neto

= método del valor actual neto

▲ *apply the net present value method* aplicar el método del valor actual neto ▲ *use the net present value method* utilizar el método de valor actual neto

net proceeds

Net proceeds constitute the amount payable to the borrower on the raising of a loan after fees and commission, or the profit from selling assets after costs have been taken away.

ingresos netos de emisión

= valor neto de realización

▲ *the net proceeds accruing to the issuer from the issue* los ingresos netos de emisión que devengan al emisor ▲ *the net proceeds of the loan* los ingresos netos de emisión del préstamo ▲ *the net proceeds received* los ingresos netos de emisión recibidos

net profit UK, IAS/IFRS

= net income

Net profit shows the amount of income earned by an organisation for an accounting period after deducting all expenses, appearing as the bottom line in the profit and loss account.

NOTE In the consolidated profit and loss account, the net profit is shown as the net profit attributable to equity holders of the parent and to minority interests, respectively.

beneficio neto

= ganancia neta

NOTE Spanish accountants prefer 'beneficio neto' to the IAS term 'ganancia neta'

▲ *a computed net profit* un beneficio neto computado ▲ *adjust one's net profit downwards* ajustar a la baja nuestro beneficio neto ▲ *adjust one's net profit upwards* ajustar al alza nuestro beneficio neto ▲ *appropriation of net profit* apropiación del beneficio neto ▲ *consolidated net profit* beneficio neto consolidado ▲ *income arising from distributions from the accumulated net profits* ingreso procedente de la aplicación de beneficios netos acumulados ▲ *minority interests' share of net profit* proporción del beneficio neto correspondiente a los minoritarios ▲ *net profit after tax* beneficio neto después de impuestos ▲ *net profit after tax and minority interests* beneficio neto después de impuestos e intereses de los minoritarios ▲ *net profit before tax* beneficio neto antes de impuestos ▲ *net profit for the year as a percentage of average shareholders' funds* beneficio neto del año como un porcentaje medio ▲ *net profit from land* beneficio neto de bienes raíces ▲ *proportionate net profit* proporcionar beneficio neto ▲ *share of net profit* proporción de beneficio neto

net profit margin

→ return on sales

net profit or loss

Net profit or loss, also referred to as the profit or loss for the period, is the bottom line total in the profit and loss account and includes total revenue, income and expenses recognised in the financial year, unless other accounting treatment has been provided in an accounting standard.

NOTE In the consolidated profit and loss account, the net profit or loss for the period is shown as the net profit or loss attributable to equity holders of the parent and to minority interests, respectively.

resultado neto

▲ *determination of the net profit or loss* determinación del resultado neto ▲ *the net profit or loss for the period* el resultado neto del periodo ▲ *the net profit or loss for the period attributable to ordinary shareholders* el resultado neto del periodo atribuible a los accionistas ordinarios

net profit or loss for the period

IAS/IFRS

Net profit or loss for the period is the bottom line total in the profit and loss account and includes total revenue, income and expenses recognised in the financial year, unless other accounting treatment has been provided in an accounting standard.

NOTE In the consolidated profit and loss account, the net profit or loss for the period is shown as the net profit or loss attributable to equity holders of the parent and to minority interests, respectively.

resultado neto del periodo

▲ *an improvement of the net profit or loss for the period* una mejora en el resultado neto del periodo ▲ *obtain predetermined effects on the net profit or loss for the period* obtener los efectos predeterminados en el resultado neto del periodo ▲ *the determination of net profit or loss for the period* la determinación del resultado neto del periodo ▲ *the disclosure of certain items of net profit or loss for the period* la publicación de ciertas partidas del resultado neto del periodo

net profit or loss for the year UK, IAS/IFRS

= net income or loss for the year, net profit or loss for the period

Net profit or loss for the year is the bottom line total in the profit and loss account and includes total revenue, income and expenses recognised in the financial year, unless other accounting treatment has been provided in an accounting standard.

NOTE In the consolidated profit and loss account, the net profit or loss for the year is shown as the net profit or loss attributable to equity holders of the parent and to minority interests, respectively.

resultado neto del año

▲ *changes in deferred tax relating to the net profit or loss for the year* cambios en el impuesto diferido relacionado con el resultado neto del año

net realisable amount UK, IAS/IFRS

= net realisable value, net realizable amount US, NRV

The net realisable amount or value is the amount expected obtained on the disposal of an asset, less costs of completion and direct selling costs.

cantidad realizable neta

▲ *measure at the lower of cost and net realisable amount* medir al valor más bajo entre el coste y la cantidad realizable neta ▲ *write down to net realisable amount* amortizar a cantidad realizable neta

net realisable value UK, IAS/IFRS

= fair value less costs to sell IAS/IFRS, net realizable value US, NRV

The net realisable value of an asset is the sum of the future cash flows which the asset is expected to generate at the balance sheet date in the ordinary course of business less the selling costs, i.e. the fair value less costs to sell. The net realisable value of a liability is the sum of the future cash flows from the enterprise during the life of the liability.

valor realizable neto

▲ *clear evidence of an increase in net realisable value* prueba clara de un aumento en el valor realizable neto ▲ *estimates of net realisable value* cálculos de valor realizable neto ▲ *evidence of a reduction in the net realisable value of current assets* prueba de una disminución en el valor realizable neto de los activos corrientes ▲ *make a new assessment of net realisable value* hacer una nueva valoración del valor realizable neto ▲ *measure liabilities at net realisable value* medir pasivos a valor realizable neto ▲ *revalue to net realisable value* revalorizar a valor realizable neto ▲ *the net realisable value at the balance sheet date* el valor realizable neto a la fecha de balance ▲ *the revised net realisable value* el valor realizable neto revisado ▲ *write down to net realisable value* eliminar a valor realizable neto ▲ *write-downs of inventories to net realisable value* eliminaciones de inventarios a valor realizable neto

net realizable amount US

= net realisable amount UK, IAS/IFRS, net realisable value, NRV

The net realizable amount or value is the amount expected obtained on the disposal of an asset, less costs of completion and direct selling costs.

cantidad realizable neta

▲ *measure at the lower of cost and net realizable amount* medir al valor más bajo entre el coste y la cantidad realizable neta

▲ *write down to net realizable amount* amortizar a cantidad realizable neta

net realizable value US
= fair value less costs to sell IAS/IFRS, net realisable value UK, IAS/IFRS, NRV
The net realizable value of an asset is the sum of the future cash flows which the asset is expected to generate at the balance sheet date in the ordinary course of business less the selling costs, i.e. the fair value less costs to sell. The net realizable value of a liability is the sum of the future cash flows from the enterprise during the life of the liability.
valor realizable neto
▲ *clear evidence of an increase in net realizable value* prueba clara de un aumento en el valor realizable neto ▲ *estimates of net realizable value* cálculos del valor realizable neto ▲ *evidence of a reduction in the net realizable value of current assets* prueba de una disminución en el valor realizable neto de los activos corrientes ▲ *make a new assessment of net realizable value* hacer una nueva valoración del valor realizable neto ▲ *measure liabilities at net realizable value* valorar pasivos a valor realizable neto ▲ *revalue to net realizable value* revalorizar a valor realizable neto ▲ *the net realizable value at the balance sheet date* el valor realizable neto a la fecha de balance ▲ *the revised net realizable value* el valor realizable neto revisado ▲ *write down to net realizable value* eliminar a valor realizable neto ▲ *write-downs of inventories to net realizable value* eliminaciones de inventarios a valor realizable neto

net receipt
Net receipts are cash inflows generated by a given asset less cash outflows attributable to the same asset.
ingreso neto
▲ *estimated net receipts* ingresos netos estimados ▲ *future net receipts* ingresos netos futuros ▲ *realised net receipts* ingresos netos realizados ▲ *the positive market value of estimated future net receipts* el valor de mercado positivo de ingresos netos futuros estimados ▲ *the timing differences of net receipts* las diferencias temporales de los ingresos netos

net receipts
= net income
≠ gross income, gross receipts
Net receipts are gross receipts less all operating expenses, taxes, and losses, except interest and financial charges on borrowed capital.
ingresos netos
▲ *net receipts from investments* ingresos netos procedentes de inversiones ▲ *net receipts growth* crecimiento de los ingresos netos

net receivable
When an enterprise has a net receivable, this means that the enterprise is owed a higher amount in a currency from another party than the amount owing to that party in the same currency. Furthermore, a net receivable may be due to a customer if the customer has prepaid part of a service not yet rendered.
cuenta a cobrar neta
▲ *adjustment of net receivables* ajuste de las cuentas a cobrar netas ▲ *net receivables recognised* cuentas a cobrar netas reconocidas

net results
= net earnings
Net results refer to the profit or loss of an enterprise for a particular accounting period. However, net results are not an item in the profit and loss account, but an expression used in text sections.
resultados netos
NOTE In Spanish accounting texts, this term can be singular or plural.
▲ *adjust one's net results downwards* ajustar a la baja los beneficios netos propios ▲ *adjust one's net results upwards* ajustar al alza los beneficios netos propios ▲ *consolidated net results* beneficios netos consolidados ▲ *minority interests' share of net results* participación de minoritarios en los beneficios netos ▲ *net results after tax* beneficio neto después de impuestos ▲ *net results after tax and minority interests* beneficios netos después de impuestos y minoritarios ▲ *net results before*

tax beneficio neto antes de impuestos ▲ *net results for the year as a percentage of average equity* beneficio neto para el periodo como un porcentaje de capital propio medio ▲ *net results from real property* beneficio neto procedente de bienes raíces ▲ *share of net results* porcentaje de beneficio neto

net revaluation

Net revaluation refers to the recognition of an increase in the equity value of a parent company's capital and reserves stemming from its equity investments. A net revaluation is calculated as recognised profit plus equity adjustment less expected distributed dividends. The amount resulting from the revaluation is recognised in reserves under the item: "Net revaluation reserve according to the equity method".

revalorización neta

▲ *net revaluation according to the equity method* revalorización neta de acuerdo con el método del valor patrimonial ▲ *net revaluation for the year* revalorización neta del año ▲ *net revaluation of investments in subsidiaries* revalorización neta de las inversiones en filiales ▲ *reserve for net revaluation according to the equity method* reserva por revalorización neta de acuerdo con el método del valor patrimonial ▲ *transfer to reserve for net revaluation according to the equity method* transferir a reserva por revalorización neta de acuerdo con el método del valor patrimonial ▲ *transferred to net revaluation reserve* transferido a reserva por revalorización neta

net revaluation reserve

= reserve for net revaluation

A net revaluation reserve is a reserve in the balance sheet under capital and reserves that contains amounts recognised in respect of the net revaluation of equity investments at equity value.

reserva por revalorización neta

▲ *transfer to the net revaluation reserve* transferir a la reserva por revalorización neta

net revenues US

= net sales, net turnover UK

Net revenues constitute the total sales of products and services etc. over an accounting period relating to the ordinary activities of an enterprise less discounts, returns, VAT and other taxes based on sales revenue. Net revenues appear as the top line item in the profit and loss account.

importe neto de la cifra de negocios

= ventas netas

▲ *adjustment of net revenues* ajuste del importe neto de la cifra de negocios ▲ *combination of net revenues* combinación del importe neto de la cifra de negocios ▲ *consolidated net revenues* importe neto de la cifra de negocios consolidado ▲ *exemption from disclosure of net revenues* exención de publicación del importe neto de la cifra de negocios ▲ *increase net revenues* aumentar el importe neto de la cifra de negocios ▲ *measurement of net revenues* valoración del importe neto de la cifra de negocios ▲ *net revenues and other operating income* ventas netas y otros ingresos de explotación ▲ *net revenues for the year* importe neto de la cifra de negocios del año ▲ *net revenues from the sale of goods and services* importe neto de la cifra de negocios procedente de la venta de bienes y servicios ▲ *net revenues of EUR 10 million* importe neto de la cifra de negocios de 10 millones de euros ▲ *recognition of net revenues* reconocimiento del importe neto de la cifra de negocios ▲ *reduce net revenues* reducir el importe neto de la cifra de negocios ▲ *the distribution of the net revenues on activities* la distribución del importe neto de la cifra de negocios en actividades ▲ *the distribution of the net revenues on geographical markets* la distribución del importe neto de la cifra de negocios en mercados geográficos

net sales

= net revenues, net turnover UK

Net sales can be defined as (1) total sales of an enterprise (turnover) less discounts and any returns made during an accounting period, or (2) the amount resulting after offsetting purchase and sales amounts.

ventas netas
▲ *net sales of forward exchange contracts* ventas netas de contratos de futuros

net selling price
= NSP
The net selling price is the amount obtainable from the sale of an asset in an arm's length transaction between knowledgeable, willing parties, less the costs of disposal.
precio de venta neto
▲ *a single net selling price available for both the assets and the liabilities* un precio de venta neto único disponible tanto para los activos como para los pasivos ▲ *determine the net selling price of goodwill* determinar el precio de venta neto del fondo de comercio ▲ *the higher of an asset's net selling price and its value in use* el mayor de un precio de venta neto de un activo y su valor en uso

net tax asset
Net tax assets arise after deducting tax liabilities from tax assets.
activo neto de impuestos
= activo neto por impuestos
▲ *decrease in net tax assets* decrecimiento en los activos netos por impuestos ▲ *deferred net tax assets* activos netos de impuestos diferidos ▲ *increase in net tax assets* aumento en los activos netos de impuestos

net turnover UK
= net revenues, net sales
Net turnover is the total sales revenue of products and services etc. over an accounting period relating to the ordinary activities of an enterprise less discounts, returns, VAT and other taxes based on sales revenue. Net turnover appears as the top line in the profit and loss account.
ventas netas
= importe neto de las cifras de negocio
▲ *adjustment of net turnover* ajuste del importe neto de la cifra de negocios ▲ *combination of net turnover* combinación del importe neto de la cifra de negocios ▲ *consolidated net turnover* importe neto de la cifra de negocios consolidado ▲ *exemption from disclosure of net turnover* exención de publicación del importe neto de la cifra de negocios ▲ *increase net turnover* aumentar el importe neto de la cifra de negocios ▲ *measurement of net turnover* valoración del importe neto de la cifra de negocios ▲ *net turnover and other operating income* ventas netas y otros ingresos de explotación ▲ *net turnover for the year* importe neto de la cifra de negocios del año ▲ *net turnover from the sale of goods and services* importe neto de la cifra de negocios procedente de la venta de bienes y servicios ▲ *net turnover of EUR 10 million* importe neto de la cifra de negocios de 10 millones de euros ▲ *recognition of net turnover* reconocimiento del importe neto de la cifra de negocios ▲ *reduce net turnover* reducir el importe neto de la cifra de negocios ▲ *the distribution of net turnover on activities* la distribución del importe neto de la cifra de negocios en actividades ▲ *the distribution of the net turnover on geographical markets* la distribución del importe neto de la cifra de negocios en mercados geográficos

net upward adjustment
A net upward adjustment is a revaluation of a given asset for a given period corresponding to the net value increase of that asset.
revalorización neta
▲ *an amount equivalent to the net upward adjustment for the year as a result of changed fair value* una cantidad equivalente a la revalorización neta para el año como resultado del valor razonable modificado ▲ *net upward adjustment of assets* revalorización neta de activos ▲ *the net upward adjustment for the financial year* la revalorización neta para el ejercicio

net value
= net carrying amount
The net value is the value after deducting something, e.g. depreciation, revaluation or selling costs.
valor neto
▲ *book at net value* contabilizar a valor neto

net working capital
= NWC
Net working capital is a key financial figure defined as all

current assets less current liabilities used for the operations of a business. Cash balances as well as taxes and dividends payable are normally not included.
fondo de maniobra neto
▲ *net working capital movement* movimiento del fondo de maniobra neto ▲ *year-end net working capital* fondo de maniobra neto a final de año

net worth
= net assets, owners' equity US
The net worth of an enterprise is equal to total assets less total liabilities, i.e. what the enterprise is worth if if stopped trading.
NOTE In an enterprise, net worth equals equity, whereas net worth for an individual equals personal equity.
patrimonio neto
▲ *exclude an amount from the net worth* excluir una cantidad del patrimonio neto ▲ *include an amount in the net worth* incluir una cantidad en el patrimonio neto

net-present-value method
→ net present value method

netting
Netting refers to the offsetting of amounts receivable and amounts payable subject to agreement between two or more parties, leaving a net balance payable or receivable.
compensación
▲ *contractual netting agreements* acuerdo de compensación contractual ▲ *cross-product netting* compensación multiproducto ▲ *enter into a master netting arrangement* firmar un acuerdo de compensación tipo ▲ *netting agreements with foreign clearing houses and payment systems* acuerdos de compensación con cámaras de compensación extranjeras y sistemas de pago ▲ *netting set* conjunto de compensación ▲ *positive market value after netting* valor de mercado positivo después de compensación ▲ *post-netting total* compensación final total
⇛ netting agreement, offsetting

netting agreement
A netting agreement is an agreement between two (bilateral) or more enterprises (multilateral), typically associates, whereby amounts receivable and payable are offset, leaving a net balance payable or receivable. Netting is typically practised on an intragroup basis by multinationals.
acuerdo de compensación
▲ *conclude a contractual netting agreement* acordar un acuerdo de compensación ▲ *enter into a netting agreement* firmar un acuerdo de compensación

netting off
Netting off means offsetting an asset balance against a liability balance or offsetting expense items against revenue items by deducting one amount from the other. According to the basic assumption of gross presentation in financial reporting, all transactions, value changes and events must be recognised and presented separately and not netted off.
compensar
▲ *no netting off* sin compensar
⇛ gross presentation

neutrality
Neutrality is the lack of partiality. An example is the information contained in financial reporting for which abscence of bias is a necessity in order to present a true and fair view.
neutralidad
▲ *neutrality in the measurement of assets and liabilities* neutralidad en la valoración de activos y pasivos

neutrality concept
= neutrality principle
The neutrality concept is a basic accounting assumption requiring that any change in value must be disclosed in the financial statements irrespective of the effect on equity or income statement, i.e. the disclosures must be free from bias and factual.
principio de uniformidad
▲ *in accordance with the neutrality concept* de acuerdo con el principio de uniformidad ▲ *incompatible with the neutrality concept* incompatible con el principio de uniformidad

new acquisition
A new acquisition refers to an enterprise's purchase or acquisition of assets.
nueva adquisición
▲ *charge new acquisitions to revenue* cargar nuevas adquisi-

ciones a ingresos ▲ *expensed new acquisitions* nuevas adquisiciones imputadas a gastos ▲ *new acquisitions and improvements during the year* nuevas adquisiciones y mejoras durante el año ▲ *new acquisitions with a cost of less than EUR 10,000* nuevas adquisiciones con un coste inferior a 10.000 euros ▲ *other new acquisitions* otras nuevas adquisiciones

new issue

A new issue is a first-time offering of securities such as shares or bonds in the primary market, i.e. the open market for first-time issues, typically a stock exchange. New issues are offered by companies going public to raise new capital by selling shares or bonds to the public for the first time, or by companies already listed on a stock exchange to raise additional capital.

nueva emisión

▲ *new issue of shares for a maximum nominal amount of EUR 5m* nueva emisión de acciones por un valor nominal máximo de 5 millones de euros

⇛ private placing

newly acquired

When an asset of an enterprise is newly acquired, it has been recently obtained by the enterprise.

recientemente adquirida

= adquirida recientemente

▲ *a newly acquired subsidiary* una filial recientemente adquirida ▲ *newly acquired enterprises* empresas adquiridas recientemente

nil-paid

In the context of an issue of rights to subscribe for new shares, "nil paid" means that no payment has to be made by the shareholders to the issuing company for accepting the rights. However, if shareholders choose to exercise the rights, they must pay for the shares on acquisition.

gratuito

▲ *allot shares nil-paid* asignar acciones gratuitas ▲ *issue shares nil-paid* emitir acciones gratuitas ▲ *nil-paid rights* derechos gratuitos

nominal

1 ominal means actual, i.e. not adjusted, e.g. for inflation, but expressed in present money terms. Used about the value of securities, nominal refers to the originally stated value (the face value).

nominal

▲ *estimate future cash flows in nominal terms* estimar flujos de efectivo futuros en términos nominales ▲ *measure at nominal value* medir a valor nominal ▲ *nominal bond rate* tipo de interés nominal del bono ▲ *nominal rate* tasa nominal ▲ *nominal share* el nominal de la acción ▲ *nominal share capital* capital social nominal ▲ *nominal value* valor nominal ▲ *the nominal value of the share* el valor nominal de la acción ▲ *the nominal value of the shareholding* el valor nominal de la participación accionarial

⇛ nominal interest rate, nominal share capital, nominal value

2 A nominal amount is a symbolic, i.e. very small, amount of money paid that is much lower than the amount usually charged or expected in the given circumstances.

simbólico

▲ *an intangible asset acquired for nominal consideration* un activo intangible adquirido por un precio simbólico ▲ *recognise the asset at a nominal amount* reconocer el activo a una cantidad simbólica

nominal common stock US

= authorized capital stock US, nominal share capital UK

The nominal common stock of a corporation represents the total nominal value of all common shares issued. Therefore, the total value of the nominal common stock will usually differ from the market capitalisation.

capital social nominal

▲ *total nominal common stock* total capital social nominal

⇛ market capitalisation, nominal share

nominal interest rate

= coupon rate

The nominal interest rate is the coupon rate on a fixed-interest security such as a bond, expressed as a percentage of the nominal or par value of the security, contrary to the bond yield that relates to the market price.

tipo de interés nominal

▲ *bonds with a nominal interest rate below the effective market rate* bonos con un tipo de interés nominal por debajo del tipo efectivo del mercado

⇛ nominal yield

nominal ledger

= general ledger, ledger

A nominal ledger is a book or group of accounts containing the main accounting records and classifying financial transactions. Today, nominal ledgers are usually stored on computer files that have replaced the old-time binders.

libro mayor

▲ *enter into the nominal ledger* anotar en el libro mayor ▲ *keep a nominal ledger* llevar un libro mayor

⇛ purchases ledger, sales ledger

nominal rate of return

The nominal rate of return includes the rate of return required on an investment plus the risk premium required to cover business risk and any inflation risk.

tasa nominal de retorno

▲ *a nominal rate of return of 5%* una tasa nominal de retorno del 5% ▲ *calculate the nominal rate of return* calcular la tasa nominal de retorno ▲ *the nominal rate of return on an investment* la tasa nominal de retorno de una inversión

⇛ rate of return, real rate of return

nominal share capital

= authorised share capital UK, nominal common stock US

The nominal share capital of a company represents the total nominal value of all ordinary shares issued. Therefore, the total value of the nominal share capital will usually differ from the company's market capitalisation.

capital social nominal

▲ *total nominal share capital* total capital social nominal

⇛ market capitalisation

nominal value

= face value, par value

≠ market value

The nominal value is the par value, face value or stated value of a financial instrument, such as a share or a bond, when it is issued.

valor nominal

= valor a la par

▲ *derivatives with a nominal value exceeding USD 10m* derivados con un valor nominal por encima de los 10 millones de dólares norteamericanos ▲ *measure at nominal value* medir a valor nominal ▲ *recognised nominal value* valor nominal reconocido ▲ *record debt at nominal value* anotar la deuda a valor nominal ▲ *the nominal value of a security* el valor nominal de un título ▲ *the nominal value of the shares* el valor nominal de las acciones

nominal yield

The nominal yield is the rate of return obtained from a fixed-interest bond, i.e. interest, calculated as a percentage of the par value of the bond.

rentabilidad nominal

= rendimiento nominal

▲ *estimate a nominal yield* estimar una rentabilidad nominal ▲ *the bond's nominal yield* la rentabilidad nominal del bono

⇛ nominal interest rate

nomination committee

The nomination committee is a committe set up by the supervisorty board or board of directors. Its main task is to make recommendations to the supervisory board or board of directors with respect to the appointment and removal of directors and executive managers.

comité de candidaturas

▲ *establish a nomination committee* establecer un comité de candidaturas ▲ *set up a nomination board* nombrar un comité de candidaturas ▲ *submit proposals to the nomination committee* remitir las propuestas al comité de candidaturas ▲ *the terms of reference of the nomination committee* los términos de referencia del comité de candidaturas

non-adjusting event

= event after the balance sheet date IAS/IFRS, post balance sheet date event UK

Non-adjusting events are events that occur after the balance sheet date and which will therefore not result in any change in recognised assets or liabilities in the financial statements. Any non-adjusting events that are considered material for the understandability are typically disclosed in the notes. However, events resulting in failure to comply with the going-concern concept will lead to changes in the financial statements.

hechos posteriores a la fecha del balance que no implican ajuste

▲ *adjust for non-adjusting events* ajustar por hechos posteriores a la fecha del balance que no implican ajuste ▲ *material non-adjusting events after the balance sheet date* hechos posteriores a la fecha del balance que no implican ajuste material después de la fecha del balance ▲ *non-adjusting events after the balance sheet date* hechos posteriores a la fecha del balance que no implican ajuste después de la fecha del balance

non-amortisable UK

= non-amortizable US

An asset is non-amortisable when it does not meet the criteria for amortisation whether for accounting or tax purposes.

NOTE The term non-amortisable applies to intangible assets.

no amortizable

▲ *grants related to non-amortisable assets* subvenciones relacionadas con activos no amortizables ▲ *non-amortisable goodwill* el fondo de comercio no amortizable ▲ *recovery of revalued non-amortisable assets* recuperación de activos revalorizados no amortizables ▲ *the carrying amount of a non-amortisable asset* el valor contable de un activo no amortizable ▲ *the non-amortisable part* la parte no amortizable

non-amortised UK

= non-amortized US

Non-amortised assets are intangible assets that have not been amortised, i.e. the cost of the assets has not been systematically allocated over their useful lives; instead the assets may have been stated at cost, revalued carrying amount or carrying amount written down for impairment.

no amortizado

▲ *a non-amortised balance* un saldo no amortizado ▲ *a non-amortised written-down value* un valor eliminado no amortizado ▲ *less non-amortised portion of the revaluation* menos la porción no amortizada de la revalorización

non-amortizable US

= non-amortisable UK

An asset is non-amortizable when it does not meet the criteria for amortization whether for accounting or tax purposes.

NOTE The term non-amortizable applies to intangible assets.

no amortizable

▲ *grants related to non-amortizable assets* subvenciones relacionadas con activos no amortizables ▲ *non-amortizable goodwill* fondo de comercio no amortizable ▲ *recovery of revalued non-amortizable assets* recuperación de activos revalorizados no amortizables ▲ *the carrying amount of a non-amortizable asset* el valor contable de un activo no amortizable ▲ *the non-amortizable part* la parte no amortizable

non-amortized US

= non-amortised UK

Non-amortized assets are intangible assets that have not been amortised, i.e. the cost of the assets has not been systematically allocated over their useful lives; instead the assets may have been stated at cost, revalued carrying amount or carrying amount written down for impairment.

no amortizado

▲ *a non-amortized balance* un saldo no amortizado ▲ *a non-amortized written-down value* un valor eliminado no amortizado ▲ *less non-amortized portion of the revaluation* menos la porción de la revalorización no amortizada

non-audit service

Non-audit services are services other than auditing such as tax consultancy provided by an accountant to an enterprise.

NOTE Under the US Sarbanes-Oxley Act, non-audit services in listed companies are subject to pre-approval by the audit committee of the company's board of directors.

servicio distinto a la auditoría

▲ *accept a non-audit service* aceptar un servicio distinto a la auditoría ▲ *require the disclosure of the fee paid for non-audit services in the notes* requerir la publicación de las tarifas pagadas por servicios distintos a la auditoría en las notas ▲ *the provision of non-audit services to the audit client* la provisión al cliente de la auditoría de servicios distintos a la auditoría ▲ *to commission non-audit services from the auditor* encargar al auditor servicios distintos a la auditoría ▲ *undertake a non-audit service* llevar a cabo un servicio distinto a la auditoría

non-cancellable

Non-cancellable means that an agreement, contract or other arrangement planned or agreed upon cannot be negated or terminated for a stated period of time, except if specific conditions arise that have been specified in advance or if a prohibitive amount is paid.

no cancelable

▲ *a non-cancellable contract* un contrato no cancelable ▲ *future minimum sublease payments expected to be received under non-cancellable subleases* pagos mínimos futuros de subarrendamiento que se espera recibir en virtud de subarriendos no cancelables ▲ *the future minimum lease payments under non-cancellable operating leases* los pagos mínimos futuros por alquiler según los arrendamientos operativos no cancelables

non-cancellable lease

A non-cancellable lease is a lease that cannot be terminated except if an unlikely incidence occurs, if the lessor consents to the cancellation, if the lessee enters into a new agreement with the lessor on the lease of the same or an equivalent asset, or if the lessee pays an additional amount so that, at the inception of the lease, the lease may reasonably be expected to continue.

arrendamiento no cancelable

▲ *a 48-month non-cancellable lease* un arrendamiento no cancelable de 48 meses

non-cancellable period

A non-cancellable period is the stated period of time for which something planned or agreed upon cannot be negated or terminated, unless specific conditions arise that have been specified in advance or if a prohibitive amount is paid.

periodo no cancelable

▲ *lease commitments in the non-cancellable period* compromisos de arrendamiento en el periodo no cancelable

non-cash

A transaction made on a non-cash basis does not involve any cash payment, but is made in kind, i.e. by transferring assets rather than money such as property or shares. For accounting purposes, non-cash expenses are expenses recognised that do not involve any cash payment such as depreciation expenses.

no monetario

▲ *adjust for non-cash operating items* ajustar partidas de explotación no monetarias ▲ *exclusion of non-cash transactions from the cash flow statement* exclusión de transacciones no monetarias en el estado de flujo de efectivo ▲ *identifiable non-cash consideration* consideración no monetaria identificable ▲ *non-cash assets transferred or liabilities assumed* activos no monetarios transferidos o pasivos asumidos ▲ *non-cash operating items* partidas de explotación no monetarias ▲ *non-cash settled options* opciones liquidadas no monetarias ▲ *non-cash transactions* transacciones no monetarias ▲ *principal non-cash transactions* transacciones no monetarias principales ▲ *provide non-cash collateral* proporcionar una garantía no monetaria

non-cash benefit

A non-cash benefit is a benefit that is not paid in money, but in the form of e.g. shares or options.

beneficio no monetario

= ganancia no monetaria

▲ *a non-cash benefit of $0.5 million* un beneficio no monetario de medio millón de dólares ▲ *award a non-cash benefit* conceder un beneficio no monetario ▲ *provide a non-cash benefit* proporcionar un beneficio no monetario ▲ *receipt of a non-cash benefit* comprobante de un beneficio no monetario

non-cash contribution

A non-cash contribution is the contribution of assets other

than cash as payment for shares in connection with a share issue.

aportación no monetaria

= aportación en especie, aportación no dineraria

▲ *by way of non-cash contributions* vía aportaciones no monetarias ▲ *possibility of making non-cash contributions* posibilidad de realizar aportaciones no monetarias ▲ *valuation report on non-cash contributions* informe de valoración de las aportaciones no monetarias

non-commercial

Matters that are not related to or done for commercial purposes are called non-commercial.

no comercial

▲ *a non-commercial operation* una operación no comercial ▲ *non-commercial activities* actividades no comerciales ▲ *non-commercial assets* activos no comerciales ▲ *non-commercial assets* activos no comerciales ▲ *non-commercial financial assets* activos financieros no comerciales ▲ *non-commercial matters* asuntos no comerciales ▲ *non-commercial obligations* obligaciones no comerciales

non-consolidated

Non-consolidated means being separate and not combined with. A non-consolidated company is a separate entity not combined with a group, and its financial statements are not included in the group financial statements.

no consolidado

▲ *non-consolidated entities* entidades no consolidadas ▲ *non-consolidated financial statements* estados financieros no consolidados

non-consolidated subsidiary

≠ consolidated subsidiary

A non-consolidated subsidiary is a subsidiary in which the parent company holds a controlling equity investment but which is not part of group consolidation and whose financial statements are not combined with the group financial statements.

filial no consolidada

= subsidiaria no consolidada

≠ filial consolidada, subsidiaria consolidada

▲ *loan to non-consolidated subsidiary* prestar a una filial no consolidada ▲ *the borrowings of non-consolidated subsidiaries* los empréstitos de las filiales no consolidadas ▲ *transactions with non-consolidated subsidiaries* transacciones con filiales no consolidadas

⇛ group enterprise, subsidiary

non-controllable cost

Non-controllable costs refer to costs of which the level cannot be influenced by the actions and decisions of managers or other persons having responsibilities in the enterprise.

coste no controlable

▲ *a rise in non-controllable costs* una subida en los costes no controlables ▲ *budget responsibility for non-controllable costs* responsabilidad presupuestaria por los costes no controlables ▲ *total non-controllable costs* total costes no controlables

non-controlling interest

= minority share, NCI

A non-controlling interest is a non-controlling shareholding held by a minority shareholder, i.e. less than 50% of the total number of shares.

participación no dominante

▲ *hold non-controlling interests* tener participaciones no dominantes ▲ *purchase of non-controlling interests* adquisición de participaciones no dominantes ▲ *sale of non-controlling interests* venta de participaciones no dominantes

non-controlling investment

= minority interest, NCI

Non-controlling investments are equity investments of less than 50% of the contributed capital in consolidated enterprises owned by parties other than the consolidated enterprises.

inversión no dominante

▲ *addition of non-controlling investments* suma de inversiones no dominantes ▲ *adjustment for non-controlling investments* ajuste por inversiones no dominantes ▲ *classification of non-controlling investments* clasificación de las inversiones no dominantes ▲ *determination of non-controlling investments* determinación de las inversiones no dominantes ▲ *non-controlling investments at beginning of year* inversiones no dominantes al inicio del año ▲ *non-controlling investments at end of year* inversiones no dominantes a final del año ▲ *profit or loss before non-controlling investments* resultados antes de inversiones no dominantes ▲ *results for the year after tax and non-controlling investments* resultados del ejercicio después de impuestos y de inversiones no dominantes

non-core

Non-core means secondary or incidental, e.g. non-core activities are activities that do not belong to the main activities of a business.

secundario

▲ *non-core activity* actividad secundaria ▲ *non-core products* productos secundarios ▲ *non-core services* servicios secundarios

non-core business

Non-core business refers to the activities of an enterprise that generate only minor parts of the sales or revenue, i.e. these activities are not central to the revenue generation and survival of the enterprise.

negocio secundario

▲ *dispose of a non-core business* librarse de un negocio secundario

non-cumulative preference share

≠ cumulative preference share

If a preference share is non-cumulative, the non-payment of preference dividend in one year will not be accumulated and made good in a following year.

acción preferente no acumulativa

▲ *a non-cumulative preference share that is mandatorily redeemable for cash in five years* una acción preferente no acumulativa que es obligatoriamente canjeable por efectivo en cinco años ▲ *the after-tax amount of any preference dividends on non-cumulative preference shares* la cantidad después de impuestos de cualesquiera dividendos preferentes de acciones preferentes no acumulativas

⇛ preference share

non-current

= long-term

≠ current, short-term

Non-current means not expected realised or settled until after 12 months or held for a period beyond 12 months.

no corriente

= a largo plazo

≠ a corto plazo, corriente

▲ *a non-current debt item* una partida de deuda a largo plazo ▲ *non-current borrowing* un préstamo a largo plazo ▲ *non-current marketable securities* valores negociables no corrientes ▲ *non-current maturities of mortgage debt* vencimientos no corrientes de deuda hipotecaria ▲ *non-current receivables* cuentas a cobrar no corrientes ▲ *non-current warranty provisions* provisiones por garantía no corrientes

non-current asset US, IAS/IFRS

= fixed asset UK

≠ current asset

Non-current assets are assets that are intended for permanent ownership or use by the enterprise. Non-current assets may be intangibles, property, plant and equipment, or investments.

activo no corriente

= activo fijo

▲ *a constructed non-current asset* un activo no corriente construido ▲ *a non-current asset that ceases to be classified as held for sale* un activo no corriente que deja de clasificarse como mantenido para la venta ▲ *adjustment to the carrying amount of a non-current asset* ajuste al valor contable de un activo no corriente ▲ *evaluate the financial effects of disposals of non-current assets* evaluar los efectos financieros por eliminaciones de los activos no corrientes ▲ *gains or losses on the remeasurement of a non-current asset* resultado al revalorar uno activo no corriente ▲ *impose conditions on the transfer of a non-current asset* imponer condiciones a la transferencia de un activo no corriente ▲ *non-current assets held for sale* activos no corrientes mantenidos para la venta

non-current liability US, IAS/IFRS

= long-term liability

≠ current liability

Non-current liabilities are liabilities that fall due for payment after more than one year from the balance sheet date.

pasivo no corriente

= pasivo a largo plazo

≠ pasivo a corto plazo, pasivo corriente

▲ *an interest-bearing non-current liability* un pasivo a largo plazo que devenga interés ▲ *present current and non-current liabilities as separate classifications on the face of the balance sheet* presentar pasivos a corto y largo plazo como clasificaciones separadas en el anverso del balance ▲ *recognise as a non-current liability* reconocer como un pasivo a largo plazo

non-deductible IAS/IFRS

Non-deductible is used about deductions disallowed for tax purposes. Certain expenses for instance do not meet the tax criteria for amounts which can be deducted to reduce taxable income.

no deducible

= fiscalmente no deducible, no deducible fiscalmente

▲ *non-deductible capital expenditure* gasto de capital no deducible ▲ *non-deductible expenses* gastos no deducibles ▲ *non-deductible part of the entertainment expenses* parte no deducible de los gastos de representación

non-depreciable

Assets are non-depreciable when they do not meet the criteria for depreciation, whether for accounting or tax purposes. NOTE The term non-depreciable applies to tangible assets.

no amortizable

= no depreciable

▲ *grants related to non-depreciable assets* subvenciones relacionadas con activos no amortizables ▲ *recovery of revalued non-depreciable assets* recuperación de activos revalorizados no amortizables ▲ *the carrying amount of a non-depreciable asset* el valor contable de un activo no amortizable ▲ *the deferred tax liability that arises from the revaluation of a non-depreciable asset* el pasivo por impuestos diferidos que surge de la revalorización de un activo no amortizable ▲ *the non-depreciable part* la parte no amortizable

non-depreciated

Non-depreciated assets are tangible assets that have not been depreciated, i.e. the cost of the assets has not been systematically allocated over their useful lives; instead the assets may have been stated at cost, revalued carrying amount or carrying amount written down for impairment.

no amortizado

▲ *a non-depreciated balance* un saldo no amortizado ▲ *a non-depreciated written-down value* un valor eliminado no amortizado ▲ *less non-depreciated portion of the revaluation* menos la porción no amortizada de la revalorización

non-discounted basis

1 An amount recognised on a non-discounted basis is an amount that has not been measured at present value.

base no descontada

▲ *measure on a non-discounted basis* medir en una base no descontada

2 If a product or a service has been delivered on a non-discounted basis, this means that that product or service was delivered without any discount.

base no descontada

▲ *deliver goods on a non-discounted basis* entregar bienes en una base no descontada

non-distributable reserve

= capital reserve, restricted surplus US, undistributable reserve

≠ distributable reserve, revenue reserve UK, unrestricted earnings US

Non-distributable reserves are reserves that cannot be distributed to shareholders, except if the company is wound up. Non-distributable earnings appear as an item in the balance sheet under equity.

reserva no distribuible

= reserva indisponible

≠ reserva disponible, reserva distribuible

▲ *create a non-distributable reserve* crear una reserva no distribuible ▲ *transfer to a non-distributable reserve* transferir a una reserva no distribuible

non-employee related expense

Non-employee related expenses are expenses that are not related to employee services, such as operating expenses other than labour and advertising, marketing, auditing and property expenses.

gasto no relacionado con personal

= gasto no relacionado con el personal

▲ *the decrease in non-employee related expenses* el descenso en los gastos no relacionados con el personal ▲ *the increase in non-employee related expenses* el aumento en los gastos no relacionados con personal ▲ *the largest single non-employee related expense* el único gasto más grande no relacionado con el personal ▲ *total non-employee related expenses* total gastos no relacionados con personal

non-equity share UK

≠ equity share UK

Non-equity shares are redeemable shares or shares that have limited rights to dividends or to participate in a surplus in a winding-up of a company.

acción no incluida en patrimonio

= acción no incluida en el patrimonio

≠ acción incluida en patrimonio

▲ *classify as non-equity shares* clasificar como acciones no incluidas en patrimonio ▲ *dividends on non-equity shares* dividendos de acciones no incluidas en patrimonio ▲ *redemption of non-equity shares* amortización de acciones no incluidas en patrimonio

SOURCE FRS 4

non-executive director

≠ executive director

A non-executive director refers to a member of a company's board of directors who does not have a position as a manager in the company, i.e. is independent of management and free from any business or other relationship with the company.

director no ejecutivo

▲ *a supervisory board made up solely of non-executive directors* un consejo de supervisión compuesto únicamente por directores no ejecutivos

⇛ remuneration committee

non-financial

Non-financial means not related to finance, profit or money. Non-financial reporting e.g. refers to environmental, ethical or social reporting.

no financiero

▲ *a contract to buy or sell a non-financial item* un contrato para comprar o vender una partida no financiera ▲ *a non-financial obligation* una obligación no financiera ▲ *a non-financial variable* una variable no financiera ▲ *changes in the price of a component of a non-financial asset or non-financial liability* cambios en el precio de un componente de activo o pasivo no financiero ▲ *designation of non-financial items as hedged items* designación de partidas no financieras como partidas cubiertas ▲ *impairment of non-financial assets* deterioro de activos no financieros ▲ *information of a non-financial nature* información de una naturaleza no financiera ▲ *non-financial disclosure* divulgación no financiera ▲ *non-financial indicators* indicadores no financieros ▲ *non-financial reporting* notificación no financiera ▲ *the carrying amount of a non-financial asset or non-financial liability* el valor contable de un activo o pasivo no financiero

non-hedgeable risk

≠ hedgeable risk

Non-hedgeable risks are risks that cannot be effectively neutralised by the purchase or sale of financial instruments.

riesgo sin posibilidad de cobertura

non-monetary

Non-monetary means not involving money or not having any determinable or fixed monetary value. Examples of non-monetary assets are stocks, tangible and intangible assets.

no monetario

= no dinerario

▲ *a non-monetary asset* un activo no monetario ▲ *a non-monetary item* una partida no monetaria ▲ *a non-monetary liability* un pasivo no monetario ▲ *an identifiable non-monetary asset without physical substance* un activo no monetario identificable según su naturaleza física ▲ *non-monetary contributions by venturers* aportaciones no dinerarias de participantes en un negocio conjunto ▲ *non-monetary reward* remuneración no monetaria ▲ *the essential feature of a non-monetary item* la característica esencial de una partida no monetaria

non-monetary asset

Non-monetary assets include all assets that are not cash or monetary amounts to be received. Examples of non-monetary assets are plant and equipment, equity investments, goodwill and trademarks.

activo no monetario

▲ *a non-monetary asset without physical substance* un activo no monetario sin soporte físico ▲ *identifiable non-monetary assets* activos no monetarios identificables ▲ *the average useful lives of the non-monetary assets* la vida útil media de los activos no monetarios ▲ *the effects of changing prices of non-monetary assets* los efectos de las variaciones en los precios de los activos no monetarios ▲ *the fair value of non-monetary assets* el valor razonable de los activos no monetarios ▲ *the tax base of non-monetary assets and liabilities* la base imponible de los activos y pasivos no monetarios ▲ *the value of non-monetary assets* el valor de los activos no monetarios ▲ *transfer of a non-monetary asset* transferir un activo no monetario ▲ *unrealised gains or losses on contributions of non-monetary assets* resultados no realizados por las contribuciones de los activos no monetarios

⇛ monetary asset

non-monetary item

≠ monetary item

Non-monetary items are items that are not classified as monetary items, i.e. assets and liabilities that do not have a fixed or determinable monetary value such as land, buildings, machinery, obligations not payable in money and equity.

partida no monetaria

≠ partida monetaria

▲ *a gain on a non-monetary item recognised directly in equity* una ganancia en una partida no monetaria que se reconoce directamente en patrimonio neto ▲ *items derived from non-monetary items* partidas derivadas de partidas no monetarias ▲ *non-monetary items denominated in a foreign currency* partidas no monetarias denominadas en una moneda extranjera ▲ *non-monetary items that are measured at fair value in a foreign currency* partidas no monetarias que se miden a valor rezonable en una moneda extranjera ▲ *non-monetary items that are measured in terms of historical cost in a foreign currency* partidas no monetarias que se miden en términos de coste histórico en una moneda extranjera ▲ *non-monetary items that are measured on a historical cost basis* partidas no monetarias que se miden en base a un método de coste histórico ▲ *recognise as a non-monetary item* reconocer como una partida no monetaria ▲ *revaluation of a non-monetary item* revalorización de una partida no monetaria

non-operating

Matters that are not related to the ordinary operations of an enterprise are called non-operating.

excepcional

= extraordinario

≠ ordinario

▲ *non-operating activities* actividades excepcionales ▲ *non-operating expenses* gastos excepcionales

non-operating asset

Non-operating assets are assets held for investment purposes, e.g. investment properties.

activo no corriente

▲ *costs associated with non-operating assets* costes asociados con los activos no corrientes ▲ *the book value of non-operating assets* el valor en libro de los activos no corrientes

non-operating exceptional item

A non-operating exceptional item is a material unusual item recognised in the profit and loss account constituting expense or income that is not related to the ordinary activities of an enterprise. The item is exceptional because of its size or incidence.

partida por operaciones excepcionales

= partida para operaciones especiales

▲ *tax on non-operating exceptional items* impuesto en las partidas por operaciones excepcionales

non-profit
= nonprofit, not-for-profit
Non-profit means without the objective of generating a profit and nor operating for commercial purposes. A non-profit organisation is established for e.g. humanitarian, educational or charitable purposes. Consequently, its performance appears from an income and expenditure account (or statement) rather than a profit and loss account and shows a surplus or a deficit rather than a profit or a loss.
sin ánimo de lucro
▲ *a legal entity established as a non-profit organisation* una entidad legal fundada como una organización sin ánimo de lucro ▲ *non-profit bodies* organismos sin ánimo de lucro ▲ *non-profit corporation* corporación sin ánimo de lucro ▲ *non-profit organisation* organización sin ánimo de lucro ▲ *non-profit public bodies* organismos públicos sin ánimo de lucro

non-purchased goodwill
→ internally generated goodwill

non-recognition
Non-recognition refers to the procedure when certain assets, liabilities, income or expenses attributable to transactions made or events occurred are not recognised in the relevant accounting items in the financial statements.
sin reconocimiento
= falta de reconocimiento
▲ *non-recognition of a previously recognised liability* falta de reconocimiento de un pasivo previamente reconocido ▲ *non-recognition of dividends* sin reconocimiento de dividendos ▲ *non-recognition of indirect production costs* sin reconocimiento de costes de producción indirectos

non-recurring cost UK
= non-recurring expense US, one-off expense UK, one-time expense US
≠ non-recurring income
Non-recurring costs are one-time costs, i.e. costs incurred or expected to be incurred only once, being of an infrequent or unusual nature that cannot be attributed to the normal operations of an enterprise. Examples are write-offs and acquisition costs.
coste no recurrente
▲ *include non-recurring costs in* incluir costes no recurrentes en
⇛ non-recurring item

non-recurring event IAS/IFRS
Non-recurring events happen only once. For accounting purposes they may be the acquisition or disposal of assets, write-offs or other one-off items.
evento no recurrente
▲ *an isolated non-recurring event* un evento no recurrente aislado
⇛ non-recurring item, one-off item, one-time item

non-recurring expense US
= non-recurring cost UK, one-off expense UK, one-time expense US
≠ non-recurring income
Non-recurring expenses are one-time expenses, i.e. expenses incurred or expected to be incurred only once, being of an infrequent or unusual nature that cannot be attributed to the normal operations of an enterprise. Examples are write-offs and acquisition costs.
gasto no recurrente
▲ *incur a non-recurring expense* incurrir en un gasto no recurrente
⇛ non-recurring item

non-recurring income
Non-recurring income includes one-time gains that happen only once, being of an infrequent or unusual nature that cannot be attributed to the normal operations of an enterprise such as gains on disposals.
ingreso excepcional
= ingreso extraordinario
▲ *include non-recurring income* incluir el ingreso excepcional en

non-recurring item IAS/IFRS
= one-off item UK, one-time item US
Non-recurring items are items that happen only once, involving significant amounts of a one-time, infrequent or unusual nature that cannot be attributed to the normal operations of an enterprise. For accounting purposes they may be the acquisition or disposal of assets, write-offs or other one-time items.

partida excepcional
= partida extraordinaria
▲ *information on material non-recurring items* información sobre partidas materiales excepcionales ▲ *operating result before non-recurring items* resultado de explotación antes de partidas excepcionales ▲ *provisions for non-recurring items* provisiones para partidas excepcionales
⇛ unusual item

non-tax-deductible
→ non-deductible

non-vesting condition IAS/IFRS
In connection with share-based payments non-vesting conditions are conditions that do not require the provision of services, for example the condition of entering into non-compete clauses in employment contracts, or an external index to reach a specific level.
condición revocable
= condición para la revocabilidad
▲ *satisfy a non-vesting condition* satisfacer una condición revocable
⇛ vesting condition

non-voting
≠ voting
Non-voting shares are shares that do not give their owners the right to vote at the general meetings of shareholders.
sin derecho a voto
▲ *non-voting shares* acciones sin derecho a voto ▲ *the issuing of non-voting preferential shares* la emisión de acciones preferenciales sin derecho a voto

non-voting preference share UK
Non-voting preference shares are shares that do not give their owners the right to vote at the generel meetings of shareholders.
acción preferente sin derecho a voto
▲ *acquire non-voting preference shares in the company* adquirir acciones preferentes sin derecho a voto en la empresa ▲ *the consideration payable per non-voting preference share* la consideración a pagar por acción preferente sin derecho a voto ▲ *the issuing of non-voting preferential shares* la emisión de acciones preferentes sin derecho a voto

noncalendar
A noncalendar period is a period that expires before the end of the calendar year that it replaces and that does not follow the calendar year. For tax purposes, a noncalendar year will typically run at the earliest from 2 April in the year preceding the year that the noncalendar year replaces. For accounting purposes, a noncalendar financial year is an accounting period that does not follow the calendar year, but that has e.g. 30 September as the balance sheet date.
no natural
▲ *a noncalendar accounting period not starting prior to 1 April in the calendar year* un periodo contable no natural que no comienza antes del 1 de abril del año natural ▲ *noncalendar accounting period starting at the earliest on 2 April in the previous calendar year* periodo contable no natural que comienza como muy pronto el 2 de abril del año natural anterior ▲ *noncalendar financial year starting at the earliest on 2 April in the previous calendar year* ejercicio no natural que comienza como muy pronto el 2 de abril del año natural anterior

noncash
→ non-cash

noncurrent asset
→ non-current asset

noncurrent liability
→ non-current liability

nonmonetary asset US
→ non-monetary asset

nonoperating US
→ non-operating

nonprofit
→ non-profit

nonvalue-added costs
Nonvalue-added costs are costs incurred by an enterprise, which do not create value for the enterprise. In case of elimination of a nonvalue-added cost, the customers' perception of the benefits of a product or a service will not be affected in a negative way.
costes sin valor añadido
▲ *a decrease in nonvalue-added costs* un descenso en los costes sin valor añadido ▲ *an increase in nonvalue-added costs* un aumento en los costes sin valor

añadido ▲ *estimate the nonvalue-added costs* estimar los costes sin valor añadido

NOPLAT
= Net Operating Profit Less Adjusted Taxes
NOPLAT is the abbreviation for net operating profit less adjusted taxes (NOPLAT), a key earnings concept defined as EBITA less taxes on EBITA, i.e. an enterprise's operating profit after taxes that are adjusted to a cash basis, and measures the enterprise's operating profit as it would have been reported if the enterprise had no deferred taxes, no debt or non-operating income and expenses.
beneficio neto de explotación menos impuestos ajustados
= NOPLAT
▲ *calculate NOPLAT* calcular el NOPLAT ▲ *improvement of NOPLAT* desarrollo del beneficio neto de explotación menos impuestos ajustados ▲ *included in the calculation of NOPLAT* incluido en el cálculo del beneficio neto de explotación menos impuestos ajustados

normal costing
= normal costing method, normal costing system
Normal costing is a costing method according to which the actual direct costs and the budgeted direct costs are assigned to cost objects.
sistema de costes normal
= sistema de costes estándar
▲ *apply normal costing* aplicar el sistema de costes normal

normal costing method
= normal costing, normal costing system
The normal costing method is a costing method according to which the actual direct costs and the budgeted direct costs are assigned to cost objects.
método de sistema de costes normal
= método de sistema de costes estándar
▲ *apply the normal costing method* aplicar el método de sistema de costes normal

normal costing system
= normal costing, normal costing method
The normal costing system is a costing system according to which the actual direct costs and the budgeted direct costs are assigned to cost objects.
sistema de costes normal
= sistema de costes estándar
▲ *apply the normal costing system* aplicar el sistema de costes normal

normal spoilage
= expected spoilage
Normal spoilage refers to spoilage that is inherent in a specific production process and which may therefore occur even under optimum operating conditions.
deterioro normal
= deterioro previsto
▲ *calculate normal spoilage* calcular el deterioro normal ▲ *costs of normal spoilage* costes del deterioro normal ▲ *take into account normal spoilage* tener en cuenta el deterioro normal ▲ *write off normal spoilage* amortizar el deterioro normal

normal standard
= currently attainable standard
A normal standard is an average standard or level of performance that is normally reached under usual efficient operating conditions allowing for normal breakdowns etc.
norma estándar
▲ *comparison to normal standard* comparación con la norma estándar

normalised earnings
= adjusted earnings
Normalised earnings refer to the earnings from operations seen in isolation, i.e. excluding unusual and one-off items, i.e. non-recurring items, such as the acquisition and disposal of assets that would otherwise distort the trend.
beneficios normalizados
= beneficios ajustados
▲ *growth in normalised earnings* crecimiento en beneficios normalizados ▲ *principles for normalised earnings* principios de los beneficios normalizados

not-for-profit
→ non-profit

note
Notes are explanatory details of the disclosures in the financial statements of which they are an integral part. Some notes are required by accounting legislation or accounting standards,

while others are merely informative.

nota

▲ *a systematic structure of the notes* una estructura sistemática de las notas ▲ *accompanying notes* notas acompañantes ▲ *disclose something in the notes* divulgar algo en las notas ▲ *disclosure in the notes* publicar en las notas ▲ *notes to the balance sheet* notas al balance ▲ *notes to the cash flow statement* notas al estado de flujo de efectivo ▲ *notes to the financial statements* notas a los estados financieros ▲ *notes to the income statement* notas al estado de resultados ▲ *present separately in the notes* presentar por separado en las notas ▲ *refer to the notes* referirse a las notas ▲ *specify an entry in a note* especificar una entrada en una nota ▲ *specify something in the notes* especificar algo en las notas ▲ *vary the ordering of items within the notes* variar el orden de las partidas dentro de las notas

note payable US, IAS/IFRS

= bill payable UK

≠ bill receivable UK, note receivable US, IAS/IFRS

A note payable is a formal written promise to pay money at the maturity date.

efecto a pagar

= pagaré

▲ *bonds and notes payable* bonos y pagarés ▲ *notes payable to former shareholders of acquired companies* efectos a pagar a los accionistas anteriores de las empresas adquiridas ▲ *total notes payable* total efectos a pagar

note receivable US, IAS/IFRS

= bill receivable UK

≠ note payable

A note receivable is a formal written promise to receive money from a debtor at a future date.

efecto a cobrar

= pagaré a cobrar

▲ *notes receivable and payable* efectos a cobrar y a pagar

notes payable UK

= bills payable UK

Notes payable is an item under current liabilities in the balance sheet recognising the bills of exchange written by an enterprise that have to be paid on maturity.

efectos a pagar

▲ *a decrease in notes payable* un descenso en efectos a pagar ▲ *an increase in notes payable* un aumento en efectos a pagar ▲ *foreign notes payable* efectos a pagar extranjeros

notes receivable US

= bills receivable UK

Notes receivable is an item under current assets in the balance sheet recognising the bills of exchange to be received by the enterprise at a future date.

efectos a cobrar

▲ *a decrease in notes receivable* un descenso en efectos a cobrar ▲ *an increase in notes receivable* un aumento en efectos a cobrar ▲ *discount notes receivable* descontar efectos a cobrar ▲ *foreign exchange notes receivable* efectos a cobrar en moneda extranjera

notes section

The notes section is the section with the explanatory notes to the financial statements, i.e. the income statement, the balance sheet and the cash flow statement. The notes to the financial statements are statutory and provide details of the items for the benefit of understandability of users.

sección de notas

▲ *disclose in the notes section* publicar en la sección de notas ▲ *explain in the notes section* explicar en la sección de notas ▲ *see the notes section below* ver la sección de notas a continuación

⇛ understandability

notice

= announcement

A notice is an announcement about something, often written or formal, made to one or more persons.

notificación

= aviso

▲ *at short notice* notificación sin aviso previo ▲ *notice of assessment* notificación de inspección ▲ *notice of dismissal* notificación de despido ▲ *notice of drawing* notificación de libramiento ▲ *notice period* periodo de notificación

notification

Notification is the act of giving notice or official information or a document containing such notice or information.

notificación
= citación
▲ *notification of a capital increase* notificación de un aumento de capital ▲ *notification of claim* notificación de una demanda
⇛ registration

notify
= register
To notify is to inform somebody of something or to register something officially.
notificar
▲ *notify any claims* notificar cualesquiera demandas ▲ *notify the authorities* notificar a las autoridades ▲ *notify the creditor that a third party has assumed the debt obligation* notificar al acreedor que una tercera parte ha asumido la deuda ▲ *notify the shareholders of an intention to redeem the shares* notificar a los accionistas la intención de amortizar las acciones

notional principal amount IAS/IFRS
= notional amount IAS/IFRS
The notional principal amount is the amount (face or similar amount) on which the computation of future payments related to certain derivative financial instruments is based.
importe principal nocional
▲ *calculate floating rate interest amounts by reference to the agreed notional principal amounts* calcular las cantidades a tipo de interés variable haciendo referencia a los importes principales nocionales acordados ▲ *schedule notional principal amounts into all periods until repricing is expected to occur* programar los importes principales nocionales en todos los periodos hasta que ocurra la reactualización de precios esperada ▲ *the notional principal amounts of the outstanding interest rate swap contracts* los importes principales nocionales de los swaps al tipo de interés vigente
SOURCE IAS 32, paragraph 63

notional share
A notional share is a hypothetical or synthetic share. Notional shares are not actual shares, but fictitious shares that may function as the underlying asset for warrants or phantom shares, or shares that represent a bonus awarded as an incentive to management executives or other employees subject to achievement of certain performance goals.
acción nocional
▲ *grants of notional shares* concesiones de acciones nocionales ▲ *the fair value of notional shares granted to employees* el valor razonable de las acciones nocionales concedidas a los empleados ▲ *the growth in value of notional shares* el aumento del valor de las acciones nocionales
⇛ phantom share, warrant

notional value
Within the context of financial instruments such as shares, bonds and financial contracts, the notional value is the underlying or face value of the instrument that underlies, i.e. determines the value of, a derivative financial instrument such as an option or a futures contract, a warrant or a swap.
valor nocional
▲ *the notional value of the company's forward exchange contracts* el valor nocional del acuerdo anticipado de la empresa para intercambio de divisas en una fecha posterior

NPV
= net present value
NPV is the abbreviation for net present value, i.e. the value today of a capital investment or investment project arrived at by deducting the projected cash outflows (costs) from the projected cash inflows (profits) of that investment or project, which have been discounted at a given discount factor, typically the required rate of return. In a choice between alternative investments or projects, the alternative with the highest net present value is the most profitable.
valor actual neto
▲ *a negative NPV* un valor actual neto negativo ▲ *a positive NPV* un valor actual neto positivo ▲ *calculate NPV* calcular el valor actual neto ▲ *NPV calculations* cálculos del valor actual neto ▲ *select the investment with the highest NPV* seleccionar la inversión con el valor actual neto más alto ▲ *the NPV of the project* el valor actual neto del proyecto

NRV

= fair value less costs to sell IAS/IFRS, net realisable value IAS/IFRS, UK, net realizable value US

NRV is the abbreviation for net realisable value, i.e. for an asset the sum of the future cash flows which the asset is expected to generate at the balance sheet date in the ordinary course of business less the selling costs, i.e. the fair value less costs to sell. The net realisable value of a liability is the sum of the future cash flows from the enterprise during the life of the liability.

valor realizable neto

▲ *revalue to NRV* revalorizar a valor realizable neto ▲ *the NRV at the balance sheet date* el valor realizable neto a la fecha de balance ▲ *the revised NRV* el valor realizable neto revisado ▲ *write down to NRV* amortizar a valor realizable neto

numerical

If something is numerical it is expressed in numbers or related to numbers.

numérico

▲ *a numerical reconciliation* una conciliación numérica ▲ *in numerical order* en orden numérico ▲ *numerical information* información numérica ▲ *numerical representations* representaciones numéricas ▲ *numerical statements* estados numéricos ▲ *the numerical part of the financial statements* la parte numérica de los estados financieros

NWC

= net working capital

NWC is the abbreviation for net working capital, i.e. a key financial figure defined as all current assets less current liabilities used for the operations of a business. Cash balances as well as taxes and dividends payable are normally not included.

capital circulante neto

▲ *good NWC management* una buena gestión del capital circulante neto ▲ *the change in NWC* el cambio en el capital circulante neto

O

objective function

An objective function is a mathematical function in the context of linear programming, which either maximises something, e.g. revenue, or minimises something, such as operating expenses.

función objetivo

▲ *a quantified objective function* una función objetivo cuantificada ▲ *the optimal objective function* la función objetivo óptima

objectivity

= verifiability

Objectivity is the accounting concept and requirement that the contents of financial reports are objective and can be checked against independent measures and sources of information.

objetividad

▲ *ensure the objectivity of the financial statements* asegurar la objetividad de los estados financieros ▲ *the objectivity and independence of the external auditor* la objetividad e independencia del auditor externo ▲ *the objectivity of the financial information* la objetividad de la información financiera

⇛ reliability

obligating event

An obligating event is an event that results in a legal or constructive obligation which an enterprise has no realistic alternative but to settle.

suceso que da origen a la obligación

▲ *present obligation as a result of a past obligating event* obligación presente como resultado de un suceso pasado que da origen a la obligación ▲ *there has been no obligating event* no ha habido un suceso que da origen a la obligación ▲ *there is an obligating event* hay un suceso que da origen a la obligación

obligation

An obligation is a duty, commitment, legal responsibility or promise, legal or moral, to comply with certain contractual terms or to meet certain requirements, such as payment, or to otherwise perform or act as expected.

obligación

▲ *a constructive obligation* una obligación constructiva ▲ *a contractual obligation to deliver cash or another financial asset* una obligación contractual para enviar efectivo u otro activo financiero ▲ *a contractual obligation to receive, deliver or exchange financial instruments* una obligación contractual a recibir, enviar o intercambiar instrumentos financieros ▲ *a legal obligation* una obligación legal ▲ *a possible obligation* una posible obligación ▲ *a possible obligation arising from a past event* una posible obligación resultante de un suceso pasado ▲ *a present obligation* una obligación actual ▲ *an obligation to pay guaranteed benefits* una obligación de pagar beneficios garantizados ▲ *assume an obligation* asumir una obligación ▲ *contractual obligations* obligaciones contractuales ▲ *discharge an obligation* pagar una obligación ▲ *measure the amount of the obligation* medir la cuantía de la obligación ▲ *product warranty obligations* obligaciones por garantía del producto ▲ *retirement benefit obligations* obligaciones por jubilación ▲ *rights and obligations under an insurance contract* derechos y obligaciones según un contrato de seguros ▲ *satisfy a contractual obligation* satisfacer una obligación contractual ▲ *settle an obligation* liquidar una deuda ▲ *the present value of the defined benefit obligation* el valor actual de la obligación por prestación definida ▲ *the settlement of employee benefit plan obligations* la liquidación de las obligaciones del plan de pensiones del empleado

SOURCE IAS Framework, F 60

obligation of contribution

An obligation of contribution is an obligation to pay to a third party an amount in full or part compensation for expenses or losses incurred by the third party. Such an obligation may arise under a contract of guarantee.

obligación de contribución

▲ *a potential obligation of contribution* una obligación de contribución potencial ▲ *disclose a significant obligation of contribution* divulgar una obligación de contribución significativa

obligation to make a general offer

= mandatory offer

An obligation to make a general offer occurs when a shareholding is transferred directly or indirectly in a company with one or more share classes accepted for listing on a stock exchange or accepted for trade on an authorised market place. The purchaser then has an obligation to make a general offer, i.e. he must give equal opportunity to all the company's shareholders so that, if the transfer entails achievement of the same status that a parent company has vis-a-vis its subsidiary, the shareholders may dispose of their shares on the same conditions.

obligación de llevar a cabo una oferta global

= oferta obligatoria

▲ *be exempt from the obligation to make a general offer* estar exento de la obligación de llevar a cabo una oferta global

obligation to present financial statements

Accounting requirements define the statutory obligation of enterprices to carry accounts and present an annual report, e.g. the obligation of enterprises covered by the Danish Financial Statements Act.

obligación a presentar estados financieros

▲ *be covered by the obligation to present financial statements* estar cubierto por la obligación a presentar estados financieros

observation

Observation refers to the act of watching something carefully e.g. for auditing purposes, such as an activity, process or procedure, so that an assessment can be made.

observación

▲ *appropriate and regular intervals for price observations* intervalos regulares y apropiados para las observaciones del precio ▲ *daily, weekly or monthly price observations* observaciones del precio diarias, semanales y mensuales ▲ *professional observations* observaciones profesionales

obsolescence

Obsolescence means being out of date and is typically used about stocks where products lose value and suffer from lack of demand because of technology developments and changes in fashion that make them less useful or outdated.

obsolescencia

▲ *a hedge of the risk of obsolescence of a physical asset* una cobertura del riesgo de obsolescencia de un activo físico ▲ *commercial or other types of obsolescence* obsolescencia comercial o de otro tipo ▲ *evidence of obsolescence of or physical damage to an asset* evidencia de obsolescencia de un activo o deterioro físico del mismo ▲ *intangible assets susceptible to technological obsolescence* activos intangibles susceptible de obsolescencia tecnológica ▲ *inventory obsolescence* obsolescencia de los inventarios ▲ *obsolescence allowances on inventories* deducción por obsolescencia de los inventarios ▲ *risk of obsolescence* riesgo de obsolencia ▲ *technical obsolescence* obsolescencia técnica ▲ *technological obsolescence* obsolescencia tecnológica ▲ *write down for obsolescence* devaluación por obsolescencia ▲ *writedown for obsolescence for accounting purposes* amortización por obsolescencia a efectos contables

obstacle

= barrier

An obstacle is a barrier or hindrance that prevents or impedes progress or achievement.

obstáculo

= barrera

▲ *a major obstacle* un obstáculo principal ▲ *practical obstacles* obstáculos prácticos ▲ *remove an obstacle* eliminar un obstáculo

obtain

= provide

To obtain something is to procure or get possession of it.

obtener

= conseguir

▲ *a valuation obtained for investment property* una valoración obtenida por la propiedad en la que se ha invertido ▲ *obtain a loan* conseguir un préstamo ▲ *obtain control of one or more other businesses* obtener control de una o más empresas ▲ *obtain information* obtener información ▲ *obtain ownership* conseguir la titularidad ▲ *obtain the right to the interest cash flows* obtener el derecho a los flujos de efectivo del interés

occur

To occur means to happen or take place, usually unexpectedly or in an unforeseen manner.

ocurrir

= acontecer

▲ *an analysis of events that have occurred* un análisis de los sucesos que han ocurrido ▲ *business combinations that occurred before the date of transition to IFRSs* combinaciones de negocios que ocurrieron antes de la fecha de la transición a las NIIFs ▲ *changes in accounting policies that occur when an entity first adopts IFRSs* cambios en las políticas contables que ocurren cuando una entidad adopta las NIIFs por primera vez ▲ *during the period in which the reverse acquisition occurs* durante el periodo en el que ocurre la adquisición de control

off balance sheet

When assets or liabilities are not recognised inside the balance sheet, but appear below the bottom line, they are off balance sheet.

fuera de balance

▲ *off balance sheet finance* financiación fuera de balance ▲ *off balance sheet items* partidas fuera de balance

off balance sheet item

= off-balance sheet item

An off balance sheet item is a contingent asset or liability that exists at the balance sheet date as a result of past events, but which is recognised below the bottom line of the balance sheet because its existence can only be confirmed by uncertain future events. Examples of off balance sheet items are contingent assets such as tax loss carryforwards, and contingent liabilities such as guarantees.

partida fuera de balance

▲ *commitments arising from off balance sheet items* compromisos surgidos de las partidas fuera de balance ▲ *the expected future earnings from off balance sheet items* los beneficios futuros previstos de las partidas fuera de balance

off-balance sheet

= off balance sheet

When assets or liabilities are not recognised inside the balance sheet, but appear below the bottom line, they are off-balance sheet.

fuera de balance

▲ *off-balance sheet finance* financiación fuera de balance ▲ *off-balance sheet items* partidas fuera de balance

off-balance sheet item

→ off balance sheet item

offer[1] *noun*

1 An offer is an indication of willingness to do or not do something that is capable of being accepted so as to form a contract. In some jurisdictions offers are binding on the offeror when they have reached the addressee, whereas in other jurisdictions offers are not binding on the offeror until they have been accepted.

oferta

▲ *a binding offer* una oferta vinculante ▲ *a mandatory offer* una oferta obligatoria ▲ *make an offer* realizar una oferta

2 An offer is the price at which a seller makes it known that he is willing to sell something.

licitación

▲ *fix an offer* amañar una licitación

offer[2] *verb*

1 To offer is to quote a price for the sale of securities or commodities in an exchange at a specified price or, e.g. in a takeover, to state a price for the purchase of shares from shareholders in a company.

ofrecer

▲ *a rights issue offered to all existing shareholders* una emisión de derechos ofrecida a los accionistas actuales ▲ *offer a loan for subscription* ofrecer un préstamo mediante suscripción ▲ *offer shares for sale* poner acciones a la venta

2 To offer means to give an indication of willingness to do or not do something that is capable of being accepted so as to form a contract.

ofrecer

= ofrecerse

▲ *offer the employees to subscribe for shares* ofrecer a los empleados suscribir acciones ▲ *offer to buy, sell or provide securities* ofrecerse a comprar, vender o aportar títulos

offer for sale

An offer for sale is a method of offering a company's shares to the general public, often an additional amount of shares, and most frequently at a fixed price. An offer for sale may, however, also take place by way of an issue by tender, where investors may bid for a certain amount of shares at or above a set minimum price and shares are allocated to the highest bidders. An offer for sale is typically made through a financial intermediary such as an investment banker.

oferta pública de acciones

= OPA

▲ *an offer for sale at a fixed price* una oferta pública de acciones a un precio fijo ▲ *offer for sale by tender* oferta pública de acciones mediante subasta

offer period

The offer period is the period of time during which an offer is open for acceptance.

periodo de oferta

= duración de la oferta, periodo de la oferta

▲ *a 4-week offer period* un periodo de oferta de cuatro semanas ▲ *expiry of an offer period* caducidad del periodo de oferta ▲ *extend an offer period* ampliar un periodo de oferta ▲ *the mandatory offer period* el periodo obligatorio de la oferta ▲ *the originally fixed offer period* la duración de la oferta fijada originalmente ▲ *the voluntary offer period* la duración optativa de la oferta

offer price UK

≠ bid price

The offer price is the price at which a dealer or market maker is willing to sell a security or commodity on an exchange.

precio de oferta

= precio de la oferta, precio del vendedor, precio pedido

≠ precio del comprador, precio ofrecido

▲ *current offer price* precio de la oferta actual ▲ *fix an offer price* fijar un precio de oferta

offering UK

= offer for sale

An offering is an offer for sale, i.e. subscription, to the public of newly issued securities, typically made by an investment bank or issuing house on behalf of the issuer at a fixed price agreed with the issuer. An offering must be made in compliance with the rules of the stock exchange where the company in question is listed or, for US securities, of the Securities and Exchange Commission.

oferta pública de acciones

▲ *costs of a concurrent offering of some shares and a stock exchange listing of other shares* costes de una oferta pública de acciones concurrentes de algunas acciones y de intercambio de otras acciones cotizadas en el mercado de valores ▲ *offering circular* circular de la oferta pública de acciones ▲ *offering price* precio de la oferta pública de acciones

⇛ private placing

office expense

Office expenses are expenses incurred by an enterprise in the form of consumable office supplies and postage. Typically, office expenses are treated as part of the administrative expenses.

gasto en material de oficina

▲ *ongoing office expenses* los gastos en material de oficina en curso ▲ *the office expenses incurred* los gastos en material de oficina incurridos ▲ *total office expenses* total gastos en material de oficina

office property

= office building

Office property refers to buildings in which the offices of one or more enterprises are situated.

edificio de oficinas

= edificio para oficinas

▲ *factory and office property* fábrica y edificio de oficinas ▲ *the market for office property without special installations* el mercado de edificio de oficinas sin instalaciones especiales

official discount rate

= discount rate

The official discount rate is the interest rate set by a central bank, either as a signal or benchmark rate or as an actual rate charged for short-term loans to banks as a monetary policy tool. The official discount rate typically functions as a reference rate for money-market interest rates.

tasa de descuento oficial

= tipo de descuento oficial

▲ *2 points above the official discount rate* 2 puntos por encima del tipo de descuento oficial ▲ *increase the official discount rate by 1%* aumentar la tasa de descuento oficial un 1% ▲ *lower the official discount rate* bajar la tasa de descuento oficial ▲ *raise the official discount rate* aumentar la tasa de descuento oficial ▲ *reduce the official discount rate by 1%* reducir la tasa de descuento oficial un 1% ▲ *the official discount rate of Danmarks Nationalbank* la tasa de descuento oficial del Danmarks Nationalbank

official list

An official list is a list of all securities traded on a stock exchange's equity, bond or derivatives market that provides information of prices and turnover etc. on a daily basis.

lista oficial

▲ *admitted to the official list* admitido en la lista oficial

offset[1] *noun*

1 = offsetting

An offset is a counterbalancing of one element against another, e.g. where the deduction of one amount from another results in a net balance.

compensación

▲ *a financial asset subject to a legally enforceable right of offset against a financial liability* una activo financiero sujeto a un derecho vinculante de compensación con un pasivo financiero ▲ *designate a written option as an offset to a purchased option* designar una opción escrita como compensación a una opción comprada ▲ *meet the conditions for offset* cumplir las condiciones de compensación

2 = set-off

An offset is an entry that counterbalances in an account whereby a previous entry is reversed and cancelled. Offsets may also be debit entries counterbalancing credit entries in the double-entry bookkeeping system.

compensación

▲ *without offset* sin compensación

offset[2] *verb*

= set off

To offset is to counterbalance one element against another, e.g. to deduct one amount from another leaving a net or zero balance.

compensar

= contrarrestar, equilibrar

▲ *offset a recognised amount* compensar una cantidad reconocida ▲ *offset against cost* compensar contra el coste ▲ *offset against income and expenses* compensar contra ingresos y gastos ▲ *offset consolidated goodwill and negative goodwill* compensar el fondo de comercio consolidado con el fondo de comercio negativo ▲ *offset current tax assets and current tax liabilities* compensar activos por impuesto corriente con pasivos por impuesto corriente ▲ *offset profit and loss* compensar resultados ▲ *offset receivables and payables* compensar las cuentas a cobrar con las cuentas a pagar

offsetting[1] *noun*

= set-off

Offsetting is the counterbalancing of one element against another, e.g. where the deduction of one amount from another results in a net or zero balance.

compensación

▲ *establish restrictive conditions on offsetting* establecer condiciones restrictivas en la compensación ▲ *meet the criteria for offsetting* cumplir los criterios para la compensación ▲ *offsetting criteria* criterios de compensación

⇛ netting

offsetting[2] *adjective*

Offsetting is something that moves in the opposite direction of another specific action/transaction. For instance, it is common to hedge transactions made in foreign currencies, which do not fall due immediately, with an offsetting transaction, thereby counterbalancing the currency risk that exists until payment has been made.

compensatorio

▲ *an offsetting option* una opción compensatoria ▲ *an offsetting tax effect* un efecto impositivo compensatorio ▲ *enter into an offsetting currency transaction* iniciar una transacción monetaria compensatoria ▲ *enter into offsetting contracts* iniciar contratos compensatorios ▲ *offsetting currency transactions* transacciones monetarias compensatorias ▲ *offsetting factors* factores compensatorios ▲ *offsetting forward transaction* transacción anticipada compensatoria ▲ *offsetting payments* pagos compensatorios

OFR UK

= operating and financial review

OFR is an abbreviation for the operating and financial review in a financial report of a company. The OFR is a separate, stand-alone, narrative statement containing the directors' analysis of the company's performance and financial position in the period under review together with an assessment of future developments.

informe de gestión

▲ *a statutory OFR* un informe de gestión estatutario ▲ *non-financial reporting in the OFR* informe no financiero en el informe de gestión ▲ *prepare an OFR* preparar un informe de gestión ▲ *publish an OFR* publicar un informe de gestión ▲ *the contents of the OFR* los contenidos del informe de gestión

OMV

= open market value

OMV is the abbreviation for open market value, which is the value of an asset, typically property, representing the selling value expected obtained in an arm's length transaction, i.e. in the open market.

valor de mercado abierto

= valor en el mercado abierto

▲ *an estimated OMV* un valor de mercado abierto estimado ▲ *difference between cost and OMV* diferencia entre el coste y el valor de mercado abierto ▲ *dividend as a percentage of OMV* dividendo como porcentaje del valor de mercado abierto ▲ *OMV at the balance sheet date* valor de mercado abierto a la fecha de balance ▲ *OMV determined annually by external valuers* valor de mercado abierto determinado anualmente por los evaluadores externos ▲ *recognise at OMV* reconocer a valor de mercado abierto ▲ *revalue to OMV* revalorizar a valor de mercado abierto ▲ *the real OMV* el valor de mercado abierto real

on a half-year basis

On a half-year basis means every six months.

en base semestral

= cada seis meses

on account

Payment on account means paying in advance or paying part of the total amount that needs to be paid.

a cuenta

▲ *a contractual right to receive payments on account* un derecho contractual a recibir pagos a cuenta ▲ *pay on account* pagar a cuenta

on an annual basis

= annualized

To state on an annual basis or annualised is to state e.g. a change which would occur if the movement observed in any period were to continue for exactly 12 months.

en base anual

= anual, anualizado

▲ *calculate something on an annual basis* calcular algo en base anual ▲ *make calculations on an annual basis* hacer cálculos en base anual

on-balance sheet

= recognised in the balance sheet

An on-balance sheet item is an item recognised in the balance sheet either as an asset or as a liability.

en balance

= en el balance

▲ *on-balance sheet loans and advances* préstamos y adelantos en balance

one-off expense UK

= non-recurring cost, non-recurring expense, one-time expense US

≠ non-recurring income

One-off expenses are non-recurring expenses, i.e. expenses incurred or expected to be incurred only once, being of an infrequent or unusual nature that cannot be attributed to the normal operations of an enterprise. Examples are write-offs and acquisition costs.

gasto excepcional

▲ *a number of one-off expenses* un número de gastos excepcionales ▲ *determined without one-off expenses* determinado sin gastos excepcionales ▲ *estimated one-off expenses* gastos excepcionales estimados ▲ *excluding one-off expenses* excluyendo gastos excepcionales ▲ *including one-off expenses* incluyendo gastos excepcionales ▲ *profit from operating activities before estimated one-off expenses* beneficio generado por las actividades de explotación antes de los gastos excepcionales estimados ▲ *total one-off expenses* total gastos excepcionales

⇛ non-recurring item

one-off item UK

= non-recurring item IAS/IFRS, one-time item US

One-off items include significant amounts of a one-time, infrequent or unusual nature that cannot be attributed to the normal operations, such as acquisitions or disposals of activities.

partida excepcional

▲ *adjust for one-off items* ajustar partidas excepcionales ▲ *adjusted for one-off items* ajustado para partidas excepcionales ▲ *minority interests' share of one-off items* acción de partidas excepcionales de los accionistas minoritarios ▲ *net profit or loss for the year excluding one-off items* resultado neto del ejercicio excluyendo partidas excepcionales ▲ *other one-off items* otras partidas excepcionales ▲ *tax relating to one-off items* impuesto relativo a partidas excepcionales ▲ *total one-off items* total partidas excepcionales

one-time expense UK

= non-recurring cost, non-recurring expense, one-off expense UK

≠ non-recurring income

One-time expenses are non-recurring expenses, i.e. expenses incurred or expected to be incurred only once, being of an infrequent or unusual nature that cannot be attributed to the normal operations of an enterprise. Examples are write-offs and acquisition costs.

gasto excepcional

▲ *a number of one-time expenses* un número de gastos excepcionales ▲ *determined without one-time expenses* determinado sin gastos excepcionales ▲ *estimated one-time expenses* gastos excepcionales estimados ▲ *excluding one-time expenses* excluyendo gastos excepcionales ▲ *including one-time expenses* incluyendo gastos excepcionales ▲ *operating income before estimated one-time expenses* beneficio generado por las actividades de explotación antes de los gastos excepcionales estimados ▲ *total one-time expenses* total gastos excepcionales

⇛ non-recurring item

one-time item US

= non-recurring item IAS/IFRS, one-off item UK

One-time items include significant amounts of a one-time, infrequent or unusual nature that cannot be attributed to the normal operations, such as acquisitions or disposals of activities.

partida excepcional

▲ *adjust for one-time items* ajustar partidas excepcionales ▲ *adjusted for one-time items* ajustado para partidas excepcionales ▲ *income tax relating to one-time items* impuesto relativo a partidas excepcionales ▲ *minority interests' share of one-time items* acción de partidas excepcionales de los accionistas minoritarios ▲ *net result excluding one-time items* resultado neto del ejercicio excluyendo partidas excepcionales ▲ *other one-time items* otras partidas excepcionales ▲ *total one-time items* total partidas excepcionales

onerous

Onerous means that the value of unavoidable costs exceeds the value of revenues or benefits, resulting in a loss. 'Onerous' is a term that is often used in connection with unfavourable contracts.

oneroso

= costoso

≠ gratuito, lucrativo

▲ *an onerous contract* un contrato oneroso ▲ *an onerous lease* un alquiler oneroso ▲ *executory contracts that are not onerous* contratos a ejecutar que no sean onerosos ▲ *termination of contracts of the acquiree that have become onerous* finalización de contratos del comprador que han resultado onerosos

onerous contract

An onerous contract is a contract under which the value of unavoidable costs to be incurred by fulfilling the obligations exceeds the value of revenues or benefits to be received.

contrato de carácter oneroso

= contrato oneroso

▲ *be bound by an onerous contract* estar vinculado por un contrato de carácter oneroso ▲ *make a separate provision for an onerous contract* hacer una provisión separada para un contrato de carácter oneroso ▲ *provision for onerous contracts* provisión para contratos de carácter oneroso

ongoing

= continuing

Ongoing means currently happening or continuing.

continuo

▲ *an ongoing change* un cambio continuo ▲ *assess on an ongoing basis* valorar sobre una base continua ▲ *ongoing activities* actividades continuas ▲ *ongoing involvement* implicación continua ▲ *the ongoing operations of the cash-generating unit* las operaciones continuas de la unidad generadora de efectivo

open market value UK

= OMV

Open market value is the value of an asset, typically property, representing the selling value expected obtained in an arm's length transaction, i.e. in the open market.

valor de mercado abierto

= valor en el mercado abierto

▲ *an estimated open market value* un valor de mercado abierto previsto ▲ *carry at open market value* contabilizar a valor de mercado abierto ▲ *difference between cost and open market value* diferencia entre el coste y el valor en el mercado abierto ▲ *dividend as a percentage of open market value* dividendo como un porcentaje de valor de mercado abierto ▲ *measure at open market value* medir a valor de mercado abierto ▲ *open market value at the balance sheet date* valor de mercado abierto a la fecha de balance ▲ *open market value determined annually by external valuers* valor de mercado abierto determinado anualmente por evaluadores externos ▲ *recognise at open market value* reconocer a valor de mercado abierto ▲ *revalue to open market value* revalorizar a valor de mercado abierto ▲ *the real open market value* el valor en el mercado abierto real

⇛ arm's length transaction, fair value

opening

Opening means at the beginning of a period.

inicial

▲ *opening net book amount* valor contable neto inicial ▲ *opening obligation* obligación inicial ▲ *the opening balance of retained earnings* el saldo inicial de los beneficios retenidos ▲ *the opening net investment in the foreign entity* la inversión neta inicial en la entidad extranjera

opening balance

≠ closing balance

The opening balance is the total amount of a debit or credit item at the beginning of an accounting period and reflects the closing balance of the previous accounting period.

saldo de apertura

= saldo inicial

≠ saldo de cierre

▲ *adjust the opening balance of each affected component of equity for the earliest prior period presented* ajustar el saldo de apertura de cada componente de patrimonio afectado al periodo presentado anterior más inicial ▲ *restate the opening balances of assets, liabilities and equity* restablecer los saldos de apertura de activos, pasivos y patrimonio ▲ *the opening balance of retained earnings* el saldo de apertura de los beneficios retenidos ▲ *the opening balance of total operating equipment* el saldo de apertura del equipamiento de explotación total

opening balance sheet

The opening balance sheet is a survey of the assets, liabilities and equity of an enterprise at the time of commencement of its activities.

balance de apertura

= balance inicial

≠ balance de cierre

▲ *an adjustment of the opening balance sheet* un ajuste del balance de apertura ▲ *an audited opening balance sheet* un balance de apertura auditado ▲ *consolidated opening balance sheet* balance de apertura consolidado ▲ *cumulative effect in the opening balance sheet of changes in the accounting policies* efecto acumulativo en el balance de apertura de cambios en las políticas contables ▲ *draft opening balance sheet* borrador de balance de apertura ▲ *opening balance sheet date* fecha de balance de apertura ▲ *opening balance sheet for the acquirer* balance de apertura del adquiriente ▲ *opening balance sheet for the combined enterprise* balance de apertura de la empresa combinada ▲ *opening balance sheet for the enterprise formed by the merger* balance de apertura para la empresa formada por la fusión ▲ *opening balance sheet prepared as at the date of the termination of the bankruptcy proceedings* balance de apertura preparado en la fecha de finalización de los procedimientos de quiebra ▲ *opening balance sheet with accompanying notes* fecha de balance de apertura con notas anexas ▲ *recognition in the opening balance sheet* reconocimiento en la fecha de balance de apertura ▲ *the opening balance sheet for each financial year* el balance de apertura para cada ejercicio

opening IFRS balance sheet

An opening IFRS balance sheet is the balance sheet of an enterprise at the date of transition to the International Financial Reporting Standards.

balance de apertura según NIIF

▲ *each line item in the opening IFRS balance sheet* cada rúbrica en el balance de apertura según NIIF ▲ *prepare an opening IFRS balance sheet at the date of transition to IFRSs* preparar un balance de apertura según NIIF a la fecha de transicción a las NIIFs ▲ *the accounting policies that an enterprise uses in its opening IFRS balance sheet* las políticas contables que usa la empresa en el balance de apertura según NIIF ▲ *the carrying amount of goodwill in the opening IFRS balance sheet* el valor contable del fondo de comercio en el balance de apertura según NIIF

SOURCE IFRS 1, Appendix A

opening inventory US, IAS/IFRS

= opening stock UK

≠ ultimolager

Opening inventory is the balance of inventories at the beginning of an accounting period.

inventario inicial

≠ inventario final

▲ *intercompany profit included in opening inventories* beneficio entre empresas incluido en los inventarios iniciales

opening portfolio

The opening portfolio is the total amount or holding of a certain asset, such as stocks or securities, that is present in an enterprise at the beginning of a new accounting period.

cartera inicial

▲ *3% of the opening portfolio balance* 3% del balance de la cartera inicial ▲ *the opening portfolio of contracts* la cartera inicial de contratos ▲ *the opening portfolio of properties* la cartera inicial de propiedades ▲ *the opening portfolio on 1 January 2006* la cartera inicial a 1 de enero de 2006

opening stock UK

= opening inventory US, IAS/IFRS

Opening stock is the balance of units in stock at the beginning of an accounting period.

inventario inicial

▲ *intercompany profit included in opening stock* beneficio entre empresas incluido en el inventario inicial

operating activities

Operating activities constitute the primary activities of an enterprise in the normal course of business that produce revenue to the enterprise, excluding secondary activities such as investing and financing activities.

actividades de explotación

▲ *profit from operating activities* beneficio por actividades de explotación ▲ *the results of operating activities* los resultados de las actividades de explotación

operating activity

Operating activities refer to an enterprise's main activities as well as other activities that are sources of revenue excluding investing and financing activities.

actividad de explotación

= actividad operativa

NOTE Spanish accountant prefer 'actividad de explotación' to the IAS/IFRS term 'actividad operativa'. "Actividad operativa" is nonsensical in Spanish accounting texts.

▲ *curtail the operating activities of the business* reducir las actividades de explotación del negocio ▲ *liabilities that result from the operating activities of a segment* pasivos procedentes de las actividades de explotación de un segmento ▲ *reporting cash flows from operating activities* publicación de los flujos de caja procedentes de las actividades de explotación ▲ *specifically related to the operating activities of the enterprise* relacionado específicamente con las actividades de explotación de la empresa ▲ *the amount of cash flows arising from operating activities* la cantidad de flujos de efectivo procedente de las actividades de explotación

operating and financial review UK

= directors' report UK, management's discussion and analysis US, management's review, OFR UK

The operating and financial review (OFR) in an annual report of a company is a separate, stand-alone, narrative statement containing the directors' analysis of the company's performance and financial position in the period under review together with an assessment of future developments.

informe de gestión

= informe financiero y de explotación

▲ *a statutory operating and financial review* un informe de gestión estatutario ▲ *prepare an operating and financial review* preparar un informe de gestión ▲ *the information contained in the operating and financial review* la información contenida en el informe de gestión

operating asset

Operating assets are assets related to the operating activities of the enterprise.

activo de explotación

▲ *change in operating assets* cambio en los activos de explotación ▲ *decrease in operating assets* descenso en los activos de explotación ▲ *increase in operating assets* aumento en los activos de explotación ▲ *operating assets shared by two or more segments* activos de explotación compartidos por dos o más segmentos ▲ *sale of operating assets* venta de los activos de explotación ▲ *separate presentation of operating assets* presentación separada de los activos de explotación

operating asset gearing UK

= operating asset leverage US

Operating asset gearing is a financial ratio defined as invested capital excluding goodwill divided by total equity. This ratio shows an enterprise's gearing based on carrying amounts and focuses on operating activities by comparing equity with invested capital and excluding financial assets.

apalancamiento operativo

▲ *high operating asset gearing* apalancamiento operativo alto ▲ *low operating asset gearing* apalancamiento operativo bajo

⇛ operational gearing

operating asset leverage US

= operating asset gearing UK

Operating asset leverage is a financial ratio defined as invested capital excluding goodwill divided by total equity. This ratio shows an enterprise's leverage based on carrying amounts and focuses on operating activities by comparing equity with invested capital and excluding financial assets.

apalancamiento operativo

▲ *high operating asset leverage* apalancamiento operativo alto ▲ *low operating asset gearing* apalancamiento operativo bajo

⇛ operational gearing

operating budget

= production budget, profit plan

An operating budget refers to the part of an enterprise's budget that relates to the main activities of the enterprise, containing e.g. budgets for production costs and volume as well as projections of operating revenues and expenses for an accounting period.

presupuesto operativo

▲ *increase the operating budget* aumentar el presupuesto operativo ▲ *prepare an operating budget* preparar un presupuesto operativo ▲ *reduce the operating budget* reducir el presupuesto operativo

operating cash

Operating cash constitutes an enterprise's amount of cash or net cash inflow from operations, i.e. cash on hand and deposits on current accounts with banks.

efectivo disponible

▲ *an operating cash account* una cantidad de efectivo disponible ▲ *meet operating cash needs* satisfacer las necesidades de efectivo disponible

⇛ operating cash flow

operating cash flow

Operating cash flow shows the increase or decrease in the amount of cash, based on the net in- and outflow of cash stemming from the main operating activities of an enterprise, and appears as the item "cash flow from operating activities" in the cash flow statement.

flujo de efectivo de explotación

= flujo de efectivo operativo

▲ *future operating cash flows* flujos de efectivo de explotación futuros ▲ *information about the specific components of historical operating cash flows* información sobre los componentes específicos de los flujos de efectivo de explotación históricos ▲ *pay dividends out of operating cash flows* pagar dividendos de los flujos de efectivo de explotación

⇛ cash, cash flow statement

operating company

An operating company is a company, e.g. in a group, engaged in day-to-day operations and activities.

empresa operativa

= empresa en funcionamiento

▲ *own an operating company* poseer una empresa operativa

operating cost UK

= operating expense US

≠ operating income US, operating profit UK

Operating costs are the expenses related to the ordinary activities of an enterprise such as sales costs and administrative expenses.

coste ordinario

▲ *a substantial reduction in previously assessed operating costs* una reducción significativa en costes ordinarios previamente evaluados ▲ *accruals for employee and other operating costs* devengos para empleados y otros costes ordinarios ▲ *an allowable operating cost* un coste ordinario deducible ▲ *less operating costs* menos costes ordinarios ▲ *other operating costs* otros costes ordinarios ▲ *the amounts of operating costs applicable to revenues for the period* las cuentas de costes ordinarios imputables a ingresos del periodo

⇛ running cost

operating cost saving

Operating cost savings are reductions or relative decreases in operating costs related to operating activities. Operating costs include cost of sales, payroll as well as maintenance and marketing costs.

ahorro en costes ordinarios

= ahorro en los costes ordinarios

▲ *achieve operating cost savings* lograr ahorros en costes ordinarios ▲ *realise operating cost savings* efectuar ahorros en los costes ordinarios

operating cycle

= working capital cycle

An operating cycle is the time span between the acquisition of materials or services and their cash realisation in terms of revenue from sales.

ciclo de operaciones

= ciclo de funcionamiento

▲ *as part of the normal operating cycle* como parte del ciclo de operaciones normal ▲ *the current operating cycle* el ciclo de operaciones actual ▲ *the nor-*

mal course of the enterprise's operating cycle el curso normal del ciclo de operaciones de la empresa ▲ *the operating cycle of the enterprise* el ciclo de operaciones de la empresa ▲ *within a clearly identifiable operating cycle* dentro de un ciclo de operaciones claramente identificado

operating data

= operating highlight, operational data

Operating data are selected key figures from the profit and loss account, e.g. sales revenue and EBITDA, included in a summary presented in the interim or annual report of an enterprise, in this way providing information at a glance about the enterprise's operating activities and performance, often on a comparative basis for the last five years.

datos operativos

= datos de funcionamiento

▲ *selected financial and operating data* datos operativos y financieros seleccionados

⇛ financial and operating data

operating debt

Operating debt refers to an enterprise's debt related to its operating activities, i.a. trade accounts payable.

deuda operativa

= deuda de funcionamiento

▲ *treat operating debt as a liability* tratar la deuda operativa como pasivo

⇛ trade accounts payable

operating department

= production department

An operating department is a department which creates and adds value to a product or a service and is responsible for operations.

NOTE In a manufacturing enterprise, an operating department is referred to as a production department.

departamento de producción

= departamento operativo

▲ *work in an operating department* trabajar en un departamento de producción

⇛ service department, support department

operating equipment

Operating equipment consists of fixed assets used in business operations.

instalaciones y equipos

NOTE Spanish accountants prefer 'instalaciones y equipos' (always plural) to the IAS/IFRS term 'planta y equipo'.

▲ *a damaged item of operating equipment* una partida dañada de instalaciones y equipos ▲ *delivery of operating equipment* entrega de instalaciones y equipos ▲ *depreciation on operating equipment* depreciación de instalaciones y equipos ▲ *disposal of operating equipment* eliminación de instalaciones y equipos ▲ *fixtures and operating equipment* bienes muebles, instalaciones y equipos ▲ *insurance of operating equipment* seguro de instalaciones y equipos ▲ *maintenance of operating equipment* mantenimiento de instalaciones y equipos ▲ *operating equipment held under finance leases* instalaciones y equipos que aparecen como arrendamientos financieros ▲ *other fixtures and operating equipment* otros bienes muebles, instalaciones y equipos ▲ *production of operating equipment* producción de instalaciones y equipos ▲ *provide for advance depreciation of operating equipment* provisionar por depreciación anticipada de instalaciones y equipos ▲ *the written-down tax value of the operating equipment* el valor impositivo eliminado de instalaciones y equipos ▲ *write-off an item of operating equipment* eliminar una partida de instalaciones y equipos

operating exceptional item UK

An operating exceptional item is a material, unusual item recognised in the profit and loss account constituting expense or revenue related to the ordinary activities of an enterprise. The item is exceptional because of its size or incidence.

partida excepcional de explotación

▲ *tax on operating exceptional items* impuesto sobre partidas excepcionales de explotación ▲ *total operating exceptional items* total partidas excepcionales de explotación

⇛ exceptional item, extraordinary item

operating expense

= operating cost

≠ operating income, operating revenue
Operating expenses are the costs related to the ordinary activities of an enterprise such as selling and administrative expenses.
gasto de explotación
▲ *an allowable operating expense* un gasto de explotación permitido ▲ *direct operating expenses* gastos de explotación directos ▲ *operating expenses, depreciation and amortisation* gastos de explotación, depreciación y amortización ▲ *operating expenses of investment property* gastos de explotación de inmovilizado ▲ *operating expenses related to insurance* gastos de explotación relacionados con el seguro ▲ *other operating expenses* otros gastos de explotación ▲ *other operating expenses payable* otros gastos de explotación a pagar ▲ *the operating expenses applicable to revenue* los gastos de explotación aplicables a ingresos ▲ *total operating expenses* total gastos de explotación ▲ *unrecognised operating expenses* gastos de explotación no reconocidos

operating gearing
Operating gearing refers to how high the percentage of an enterprise's fixed costs is in relation to total costs. Operating gearing also focuses on the ratio of fixed costs to variable costs. If fixed costs increase, operating gearing reduces variable costs, resulting in higher contribution margin, profit and sales volume.
apalancamiento operativo
▲ *companies with high operating gearing* empresas con un apalancamiento operativo elevado

operating highlight
= operating data
Operating highlights are operating key figures from the profit and loss account, e.g. sales revenue and EBITDA, included in a summary presented in the interim or annual report of an enterprise, in this way providing information at a glance about the enterprise's operating activities and performance, often on a comparative basis for the last five years.
cifra de explotación más destacada
= cifra operativa más destacada
▲ *key operating highlight* cifra de explotación más destacada clave

operating income
1 = operating revenue UK, US
≠ operating expense
Operating income is the revenue generated from operations, i.e. in the ordinary activities of an enterprise.
ingreso de explotación
= ingreso operativo
▲ *net revenue and other operating income* ingreso neto y otro ingreso de explotación ▲ *non-recurring operating income* ingreso de explotación no recurrente ▲ *other operating income* otro ingreso de explotación
⇛ net operating income
2 = operating profit
≠ operating loss
Operating income is income from the ordinary operating activities of an enterprise before interest, tax, depreciation and amortisation as presented in the income statement.
ingreso de explotación
= ingreso operativo
▲ *cash flow based operating income* flujo de efectivo basado en el ingreso de explotación
⇛ EBITDA

operating income margin US
= EBITDA margin, operating margin
The operating income margin is a financial ratio calculated as a company's operating profit divided by sales, also referred to as the EBIT or EBITDA margin. This ratio is a measure of the operating profitability of an enterprise.
margen de explotación
= margen EBITDA
▲ *a decrease in the operating income margin* un descenso del margen de explotación ▲ *an increase in the operating income margin* un aumento del margen de explotación ▲ *operating income margin before depreciation and amortization* margen de explotación antes de depreciación y amortización

operating income or loss US
Operating income is the revenue of an enterprise generated from operations, i.e. in the ordinary activities of that enterprise. An operating loss results

when cost of sales and operating expenses are higher than operating revenue.
resultado de explotación
▲ *decrease in operating income or loss* disminución del resultado de explotación ▲ *increase in operating income or loss* aumento del resultado de explotación ▲ *operating income or loss before amortization of goodwill and other intangible assets* resultado de explotación antes de la amortización del fondo de comercio y otros activos intangibles ▲ *show a modest increase in operating income or loss* mostrar un aumento modesto en el resultado de explotación

operating item
Operating items are operating expenses or operating income.
partida de explotación
= partida operativa
▲ *adjusted for non-cash operating items* ajustada las partidas de explotación no monetarias ▲ *adjustment for non-cash operating items* ajuste de partidas de explotación no monetarias ▲ *an operating item that can be attributed or reasonably allocated to a segment* una partida de explotación que se puede atribuir o asignar razonablemente a un segmento ▲ *hedge of operating items* cobertura de partidas de explotación ▲ *non-cash operating items* partidas de explotación no monetarias ▲ *operating items with no effect on cash flow* partidas de explotación sin efecto en el flujo de efectivo

operating lease
= operating lease agreement
≠ capital lease US, finance lease IAS/IFRS, UK
An operating lease is a lease that is not a finance lease, i.e. some of the risks and rewards connected to the ownership of the leased asset remain with the lessor, and the asset is leased for a period which is much shorter than its estimated useful life. Typically, the leased asset and the obligation to pay lease payments are not recognised in the balance sheet of the lessee, but the periodic lease payments are recognised as operating costs in the profit and loss account.
arrendamiento operativo
▲ *assets leased out under operating leases* activos arrendados según arrendamientos operativos ▲ *assets subject to operating leases* activos sujetos a arrendamientos operativos ▲ *biological assets provided by lessors under operating leases* activos biológicos aportados por arrendatarios según arrendamientos operativos ▲ *cancellable operating leases* arrendamientos operativos cancelables ▲ *contractual rights arising under an operating lease* derechos contractuales provenientes de un arrendamiento operativo ▲ *enter into operating leases* llevar a cabo arrendamientos operativos ▲ *investment property provided by lessors under operating leases* inmovilizado aportado por arrendatarios según arrendamientos operativos ▲ *lease income from operating leases* ingreso procedente de arrendamientos operativos ▲ *lease out under an operating lease* arrendar según un arrendamiento operativo ▲ *lease payments under an operating lease* pagos de arrendamiento según un arrendamiento operativo ▲ *minimum lease payments under non-cancellable operating leases* pagos mínimos de arrendamiento según arrendamientos operativos no cancelables ▲ *non-cancellable operating leases* arrendamientos operativos no cancelables ▲ *prepaid or accrued operating lease income* ingreso de arrendamiento operativo devengados o prepagados

operating lease agreement
= operating lease
≠ capital lease US, finance lease IAS/IFRS, UK
An operating lease agreement is a lease that is not a finance lease, i.e. some of the risks and rewards connected to the ownership of the leased asset remain with the lessor, and the asset is leased for a period which is much shorter than its estimated useful life. Typically, the leased asset and the obligation to pay lease payments are not recognised in the balance sheet of the lessee, but the periodic lease payments are recognised as operating costs in the profit and loss account.

contrato de arrendamiento operativo
= acuerdo de arrendaminto operativo
▲ *a cancellable operating lease agreement* un contrato de arrendamiento operativo rescindible ▲ *a non-cancellable operating lease agreement* un contrato de arrendamiento operativo no rescindible ▲ *assets subject to an operating lease agreement* activos sujetos a un contrato de arrendamiento operativo ▲ *at the end of an operating lease agreement* al finalizar el contrato de arrendamiento operativo ▲ *enter into an operating lease agreement* firmar un contrato de arrendamiento operativo ▲ *in accordance with the terms stipulated in the operating lease agreement* de acuerdo con los términos estipulados en el contrato de arrendamiento operativo ▲ *under the terms of the operating lease agreement* según los términos del contrato de arrendamiento operativo

operating leverage US
= operational gearing UK
Operating leverage is a measure of the fixed costs in the operating structure of an enterprise seen by the ratio of fixed costs to total costs. By an increase of fixed costs, operating leverage reduces variable costs, resulting in higher contribution margin, profit and sales volume.
apalancamiento operativo
▲ *degree of operating leverage* grado de apalancamiento operativo

operating loss
An operating loss is the loss on the principal business activities of an enterprise and the amount by which the cost of goods sold and operating expenses exceed operating revenues, presented in the profit and loss account before interest, tax, depreciation and amortisation.
pérdida de explotación
= pérdida operativa
▲ *future operating losses* pérdidas de explotación futuras ▲ *initial operating losses incurred before the asset achieves planned performance* pérdidas de explotación iniciales incurridas antes de que el activo logre los resultados previstos ▲ *operating losses or net cash outflows for the asset* pérdidas de explotación o salidas de efectivo neto del activo
⇛ operating income, operating profit

operating margin
= EBIT margin, EBITDA margin, operating income margin US, operating profit margin UK, profit margin
The operating margin is a financial ratio calculated as a company's operating profit divided by sales, also referred to as the EBIT or EBITDA margin. This ratio is a measure of the operating profitability of an enterprise.
margen de explotación
= margen EBITDA, margen operativo
▲ *an improved operating margin* un margen de explotación mejorado ▲ *calculate the operating margin* calcular el margen de explotación

operating profit UK
= operating income US
≠ operating loss
Operating profit is the profit from the ordinary operating activities of an enterprise before interest, tax, depreciation and amortisation as presented in the profit and loss account.
beneficio de explotación
= resultado positivo de explotación
▲ *cash flow based operating profit* flujo de efectivo basado en el beneficio de explotación ▲ *generate an operating profit* generar un beneficio de explotación ▲ *operating profit* beneficio de explotación
⇛ EBITDA

operating profit margin UK
= operating margin
The operating profit margin is a financial ratio calculated as a company's operating profit divided by sales, also referred to as the EBIT or EBITDA margin. This ratio is a measure of the operating profitability of an enterprise.
margen de explotación
= margen de beneficio de explotación
▲ *a high operating profit margin* un margen de explotación alto ▲ *a low operating profit margin* un margen de explotación bajo ▲ *achieve an operating profit*

margin of at least 20% conseguir un margen de explotación de por los menos el 20% ▲ *calculate the operating profit margin* calcular el margen de explotación ▲ *estimated operating profit margin* margen de explotación estimado ▲ *have an operating profit margin of 10%* tener un margen de explotación del 10% ▲ *increase the operating profit margin* aumentar el margen de explotación

operating profit or loss IAS/IFRS, UK

The operating profit or loss is the profit or loss that arises as a result of the enterprise's principal operations or trading activity.

resultado de explotación

= resultado operativo

NOTE Spanish accountants prefer 'resultado de explotación' to the IAS/IFRS term 'resultado operativo'.

▲ *decrease in operating profit or loss* disminución del resultado de explotación ▲ *entity operating profit or loss from continuing operations* resultado de explotación de la entidad procedente de operaciones continuas ▲ *increase in operating profit or loss* aumento del resultado de explotación ▲ *operating profit or loss before amortisation of goodwill and other intangible assets* resultado de explotación antes de la amortización del fondo de comercio y otros activos intangibles ▲ *operating profit or loss flowing from the asset* resultado de explotación procedente del activo ▲ *show a modest increase in operating profit or loss* mostrar un aumento modesto en el resultado de explotación

operating property US

Operating property is real or personal property owned or leased by a public transportation, communications, power or other utility that contributes to the operation and purpose of the utility.

propiedad en concesión

▲ *an item of operating property* una partida de propiedad en concesión ▲ *assets included in operating property* activos incluidos en propiedad en concesión

operating revenue UK, US

= operating income

≠ operating expense

Operating revenue is the income generated in the ordinary activities of an enterprise.

ingreso de explotación

= ingreso operativo

▲ *operating revenue excluding interest* ingreso de explotación excluyendo el interés ▲ *total operating revenue* total ingreso de explotación

operating review

The operating review is a statement in the annual report of an enterprise containing the management's discussion and interpretation of the performance of the enterprise in the period under review, expectations for the future, financing and risk management, return to shareholders etc.

informe operativo

▲ *prepare an operating review* preparar un informe operativo ▲ *publish an operating review* publicar un informe operativo ▲ *the information contained in the operating review* la información contenida en el informe operativo

⇛ financial review, operating and financial review

operating risk US

Operating risk is the risk of changes in operating profit because of movements in prices and demand as well as changes in operating gearing, i.e. the percentage of fixed costs in relations to variable costs or total costs. To assess this risk, management needs to monitor cost structure and operating gearing.

riesgo operativo

▲ *operating risk control* control del riesgo operativo

operating segment US, IAS/IFRS

An operating segment is a component of an enterprise for which separate financial data are available, that generates revenues and incurs expenses from its business activities, and whose results from operations are reviewed on a current basis by the chief operating decision makers.

segmento operativo

▲ *a component of an operating segment* un componente de un segmento operativo ▲ *a report-*

able operating segment un segmento operativo divulgable ▲ *assess the performance of the operating segment* valorar los resultados del segmento operativo ▲ *identify an operating segment* identificar un segmento operativo ▲ *the total external revenue reported by operating segments* los ingresos externos totales divulgados por segmentos operativos
SOURCE FAS 131, paragraph 10, IFRS 8, paragraph 5

operating unit
An operating unit is a unit in an enterprise responsible for a particular operating activity, e.g. administrative or ancillary services.
unidad operativa
▲ *in close co-operation with the operating units* en estrecha cooperación con las unidades operativas ▲ *integration of operating units* integración de unidades operativas ▲ *separate operating units* separar unidades operativas

operation
The operations of an enterprise consist of business activities such as sales and production as well as the administration of such activities.
operación
▲ *a grouping of assets of similar nature and use in an entity's operations* una agrupación de activos de similar naturaleza y uso en las operaciones de la empresa ▲ *an entity with a history of profitable operations* una empresa con un historial de operaciones rentables ▲ *day-to-day operations* operaciones diarias ▲ *monitor the entity's operations* controlar las operaciones de la empresa ▲ *the design, construction and operation of a pilot plant* el diseño, construcción y operación de una planta piloto ▲ *the ongoing operation of the unit* la operación en curso de la unidad

operation costing
= batch costing
Operation costing is a method or system for calculation of the total costs attributable to a particular job or batch.
sistema de coste por lote

operational
Operational means that something is related to the operations of an enterprise, which consist of business activities such as sales and production as well as the administration of such activities.
operativo
▲ *operational and financial management* gestión operativa y financiera ▲ *operational expenditure* gastos operativos ▲ *operational factors* factores operativos ▲ *operational income adjustment* ajuste en el ingreso operativo ▲ *operational reporting* información operativa

operational audit
An operational audit focuses on the operations of an enterprise rather than on its financial reporting and constitutes the various procedures applied by an internal auditor when examining the processes of the value added generation and management of the enterprise.
auditoría de gestión
= auditoría operativa
▲ *conduct an operational audit* llevar a cabo una auditoría de gestión ▲ *plan the operational audit* planificar la auditoría de gestión

operational data
= operating data
Operational data are selected key figures from the profit and loss account, e.g. sales revenue and EBITDA, included in a summary presented in the interim or annual report of an enterprise, in this way providing information at a glance about the enterprise's operational activities and performance, often on a comparative basis for the last five years.
datos operativos
= datos de explotación
▲ *disclose operational data* revelar los datos operativos ▲ *selected financial and operational data* datos financieros y operativos seleccionados

operational gearing UK
= operating leverage US
Operational gearing refers to how high the percentage of an enterprise's fixed costs is in relation to total costs. Operational gearing also focuses on the ratio of fixed costs to variable costs. If fixed costs increase, operational gearing reduces variable costs, resulting in hig-

her contribution margin, profit and sales volume.
apalancamiento operativo
▲ *a company with high operational gearing* una empresa con un alto apalancamiento operativo ▲ *the benefits of operational gearing* los beneficios del apalancamiento operativo
⇛ operating asset gearing

operational leasing

Operational leasing refers to the act of leasing an asset by means of an operating lease.
arrendamiento operativo
▲ *fixed assets used for operational leasing* activos fijos usados para el arrendamiento operativo

operational management

Operational management refers to the direction, running and control of the operations of an enterprise in order to increase performance and meet stated objectives.
gestión operativa
▲ *an operational management tool* una herramienta de gestión operativa ▲ *effective operational management* gestión operativa efectiva

operational risk

Operational risk is the risk that breakdowns in systems, technology, administrative procedures or other operational factors give rise to or enhance the risk of losses. Other risk types are credit, market or liquidity risk.
riesgo operativo
▲ *economic capital allocated to operational risks* capital económico asignado a riesgos operativos ▲ *hedging of operational risks* cobertura de los riesgos operativos ▲ *management of operational risks* gestión de los riesgos operativos ▲ *model calculations of operational risks within the group* cálculos del modelo de riesgos operativos dentro del grupo ▲ *monitoring of operational risks* control de los riesgos operativos ▲ *reporting of operational risk* divulgación del riesgo operativo ▲ *the business-related operational risk* el riesgo operativo relacionado con el negocio ▲ *the capital to be allocated for operational risks* el capital a asignar a los riesgos operativos

opinion

Opinion refers to the auditor's opinion, i.e. conclusion after having audited the financial statements of an enterprise as expressed in the audit report. The wording is that the financial statements "give a true and fair view" in British English, or "present fairly, in all material respects" in US English if the opinion is unqualified.
opinión
▲ *adverse opinion* opinión adversa ▲ *basis of audit opinion* en opinión de los auditores ▲ *disclaimer of opinion* exención de responsabilidad por opinión ▲ *express an opinion* expresar una opinión

opportunity cost

Opportunity costs constitute the difference between the earnings from the best and the next-best alternatives, i.e. the benefits sacrificed by not choosing the best alternative.
coste de oportunidad
▲ *assess the opportunity costs* evaluar los costes de oportunidad ▲ *future opportunity costs* costes de oportunidad futuros ▲ *total opportunity costs* total costes de oportunidad
⇛ opportunity cost of capital

opportunity cost of capital

Opportunity cost of capital is the anticipated return which is not obtained from one investment opportunity, because another investment opportunity was chosen instead, provided that the investments have the same risk profile for the amount of capital invested.
coste de oportunidad del capital
= coste de oportunidad de capital
▲ *estimate the opportunity cost of capital* estimar el coste de oportunidad del capital ▲ *the project's opportunity cost of capital* el coste de oportunidad del capital del proyecto
⇛ opportunity cost

option

An option is a contract between two parties that gives the acquirer or holder the right, but not the obligation, to buy or sell a given underlying asset, often a security, at a specific price (the exercise price) within a defined period of time. An option to buy is referred to as a call option, whereas an option to sell is a put option. If an option is not exercised, it will lapse on expiry.

opción

▲ *a cash-settled option* una opción liquidada en efectivo ▲ *a non-cash settled option* una opción no liquidada en efectivo ▲ *a surrender or prepayment option embedded in a host debt instrument* una opción de entrega o prepago incluida en un instrumento receptor de deuda ▲ *a written option to buy or sell a non-financial item* una opción establecida para comprar o vender una partida no financiera ▲ *an equity conversion option* una opción de conversión de patrimonio ▲ *be granted an option* ser concedida una opción ▲ *buy an option* comprar una opción ▲ *calculated price per option* precio calculado por opción ▲ *cancel an option* cancelar una opción ▲ *determination of the fair value of an option* determinación del valor razonable de una opción ▲ *dilutive options* opciones diluidas ▲ *exercise a renewal option* ejercer una opción de renovación ▲ *exercise an option* ejercer una opción ▲ *grant an option* conceder una opción ▲ *hedged options* opciones cubiertas ▲ *issue options* emitir opciones ▲ *minimum value of an option* valor mínimo de una opción ▲ *net written options* opciones netas amortizadas ▲ *offsetting option* opción de compensación ▲ *outstanding options* opciones pendientes de pago ▲ *purchased options* opciones adquiridas ▲ *receive an option* recibir una opción ▲ *sell an option* vender una opción ▲ *the actual life of the option* la duración real de la opción ▲ *the estimated life of the option* la duración prevista de la opción ▲ *the exercise price of the option* el precio especificado de la opción ▲ *the expiration date of the option* la fecha de caducidad de la opción ▲ *the expiry of the option* la caducidad de la opción ▲ *the intrinsic value of the option* el valor intrínseco de la opción ▲ *the life of the option* la duración de la opción ▲ *the time value of an option* el valor temporal de una opción ▲ *the value of the option* el valor de la opción ▲ *the value of the option at the time of assignment* el valor de la opción en el periodo de asignación ▲ *the value of the option on the exercise date* el valor de la opción en la fecha especificada ▲ *the vesting period for the options* el periodo de carencia para las opciones

⇛ call option, derivative financial instrument, put option, real option

option to purchase

= purchase option

An option to purchase is a right to buy an asset, usually at a pre-determined price.

opción de compra

▲ *exercise one's option to purchase* ejercer su opción de compra ▲ *have an option to purchase* tener una opción de compra ▲ *the terms of the option to purchase* los términos de la opción de compra

order[1] *noun*

1 In the context of commerce, an order is a –usually written– request for the supply of something, e.g. goods or services, in return for payment.

pedido

▲ *book an order* reservar un pedido ▲ *dispatch an order* enviar un pedido ▲ *execute an order* ejecutar un pedido ▲ *on order* bajo pedido ▲ *order confirmation* confirmación del pedido ▲ *place an order* efectuar un pedido ▲ *placing of orders* efectuar pedidos ▲ *take orders* anotar pedidos

2 An order is an arrangement of things, structured so that one item follows another, usually according to specific criteria.

orden

▲ *in alphabetical order* por orden alfabético ▲ *in order of priority* por orden de prioridad ▲ *order of allocation* orden de asignación ▲ *state separately and in the order stated in the formats* establecer por separado y en el orden establecido en los formatos ▲ *the order of the elements of the annual report* el orden de los elementos del informe anual

order[2] *verb*

1 To order is to require the supply or delivery of goods or services from an enterprise.

pedir

▲ *order a new machine* pedir una máquina nueva ▲ *order for delivery in April* pedir para recibir el envío en abril ▲ *order new products* pedir nuevos productos ▲ *order products from a supplier* pedir productos al proveedor ▲ *the goods or services ordered* los bienes o servicios pedidos

⇛ order book, volume of orders

2 To order is to require or instruct somebody to do something.

ordenar

▲ *order someone to do something* ordenar a alguien que haga algo ▲ *order the goods to be returned* ordenar que se devuelvan los bienes

order book

An order book is a record of the orders which an enterprise has on its order books pending execution.

cartera de pedidos

▲ *a full order book* una cartera de pedidos completa ▲ *a strong order book* una fuerte cartera de pedidos

⇛ order, volume of orders

order intake

The order intake of an enterprise is the number of orders that the enterprise has on its order books and agreed to execute during a certain accounting period. The order intake is an important key figure for valuation of the business potential of an enterprise.

entrada de pedidos

▲ *an increase in order intake* un aumento en la entrada de pedidos ▲ *the order intake for the period* la entrada de pedidos del periodo

⇛ order, volume of orders

order to sell

An order to sell is an order placed with a securities dealer for the sale of equities owned by an investor. Such an order may be executed at current market price or with a certain limit, e.g. a stop limit guaranteeing the investor a certain price or better.

orden de venta

▲ *a realised order to sell* una orden de venta realizada ▲ *a received order to sell* una orden de venta recibida ▲ *an order to sell denominated in foreign currency* una orden de venta fijada en moneda extranjera ▲ *an order to sell in progress* una orden de venta en curso

ordering cost

Ordering costs are costs incurred in connection with the placing or receipt of an order irrespective of its size, but proportionally increasing with the number of orders.

coste por pedido

▲ *a decrease in ordering costs* un descenso en los costes por pedido ▲ *an increase in ordering costs* un aumento en los costes por pedido ▲ *reduce ordering costs* reducir los costes por pedido

⇛ economic order quantity

ordinary activities

Ordinary activities constitute the primary activities of an enterprise in the normal course of business that produce revenue to the enterprise, excluding secondary activities such as investing and financing activities.

actividades ordinarias

▲ *cash flow from ordinary activities* flujo de efectivo procedente de actividades ordinarias ▲ *in the course of ordinary activities* en el curso de las actividades ordinarias ▲ *net profit from continuing ordinary activities* beneficio neto de actividades ordinarias continuadas ▲ *profit or loss from ordinary activities* resultado de las actividades ordinarias ▲ *tax expense related to profit or loss from ordinary activities* impuestos relacionados con el resultado de las actividades ordinarias ▲ *transactions that are clearly distinct from the ordinary activities of the enterprise* transacciones que son claramente diferentes a las actividades ordinarias de la empresa

ordinary activity

An ordinary activity constitutes one of the primary activities of an enterprise in the normal course of business that generates revenue to the enterprise, and excludes any secondary activity such as an investing and financing activity.

actividad ordinaria

▲ *amounts derived from the sale of products falling within the company's ordinary activities* cantidades procedentes de la venta de productos clasificados como actividades ordinarias de la empresa ▲ *as part of an enterprise's ordinary activities* como parte de las actividades ordinarias de una empresa

ordinary amortisation UK
= ordinary amortization US
Ordinary amortisation is the amortisation performed according to a chosen amortisation method on the basis of the amortisable amount.
NOTE The term ordinary amortisation applies to intangible assets.
amortización sistemática
= amortización ordinaria
▲ *ordinary amortisation of goodwill* amortización sistemática del fondo de comercio
⇛ amortisation

ordinary amortization US
= ordinary amortisation UK
Ordinary amortization is the amortization performed according to a chosen amortization method on the basis of the amortizable amount.
NOTE The term ordinary amortization applies to intangible assets.
amortización ordinaria
= amortización sistemática
▲ *ordinary amortization of goodwill* amortización ordinaria del fondo de comercio

ordinary depreciation
Ordinary depreciation is the depreciation charged according to a chosen depreciation method on the basis of the depreciable amount.
NOTE The term ordinary depreciation applies to tangible assets.
amortización ordinaria
▲ *operating profit before ordinary depreciation* beneficio de explotación antes de amortización ordinaria
⇛ depreciation

ordinary dividend
Ordinary dividend is dividend received or paid out on ordinary shares.
dividendo ordinario
▲ *the remaining portion of the ordinary dividend* la parte restante del dividendo ordinario

ordinary expense
Ordinary expenses are expenses that fall within the ordinary activities of the reporting entity and are not extraordinary.
gasto ordinario
▲ *other ordinary expenses* otros gastos ordinarios

ordinary income US
Ordinary income constitutes earnings attributable to the recurring business operations of the enterprise.
ingreso ordinario
= ingreso por actividades ordinarias
▲ *other ordinary income* otro ingreso por actividades ordinarias ▲ *total ordinary income* total ingreso por actividades ordinarias

ordinary loss
An ordinary loss constitutes the negative amount resulting from the recurring business operations contributing to a decrease in net assets.
pérdida ordinaria
▲ *deduct the loss as an ordinary loss* deducir la pérdida como una pérdida ordinaria

ordinary partnership
→ partnership

ordinary share UK
= common share, equity share
Ordinary shares refer to shares which carry full or limited voting rights exercisable e.g. at the Annual General Meeting and which entitle the holder to receive dividends if and when distributed. Ordinary shares represent ownership of the company and are the most common type of shares.
acción ordinaria
▲ *a potential ordinary share* una acción ordinaria potencial ▲ *buy back ordinary shares* recomprar acciones ordinarias ▲ *consolidation of ordinary shares* consolidación de acciones ordinarias ▲ *contingently issuable ordinary shares* acciones ordinarias eventualmente emitibles ▲ *contracts that may be settled in ordinary shares or cash* contratos que se pueden liquidar en acciones ordinarias o en efectivo ▲ *dilutive potential ordinary shares* acciones ordinarias potenciales diluidas ▲ *employee share options with non-vested ordinary shares* las opciones sobre acciones de los empleados sin acciones ordinarias otorgadas ▲ *enterprises*

that are in the process of issuing ordinary shares in public markets empresas que están en proceso de emisión en mercados públicos de acciones ordinarias ▲ *incremental ordinary shares* acciones ordinarias marginales ▲ *major ordinary share transactions* principales transacciones de acciones ordinarias ▲ *ordinary shares issued as part of the cost of a business combination* acciones ordinarias emitidas como parte del coste de una combinación de negocios ▲ *ordinary shares issued for the rendering of services to the entity* acciones ordinarias emitidas por la prestación de servicios a la empresa ▲ *ordinary shares issued in exchange for cash* acciones ordinarias emitidas a cambio de efectivo ▲ *ordinary shares issued in exchange for the settlement of a liability of the entity* acciones ordinarias emitidas a cambio de la liquidación de un pasivo de la entidad ▲ *ordinary shares issued in place of interest or principal on other financial instruments* acciones ordinarias emitidas en lugar de interés o principal en otros instrumentos financieros ▲ *outstanding ordinary shares that are contingently returnable* acciones ordinarias pendientes de pago eventualmente rescatables ▲ *proceeds from the issue of ordinary shares* beneficios de la emisión de acciones ordinarias ▲ *put options on ordinary shares* acciones ordinarias con opciones de venta ▲ *share warrants that are convertible into ordinary shares* warrants de acciones que son convertibles en acciones ordinarias ▲ *the average market price of ordinary shares* el precio medio de mercado de las acciones ordinarias ▲ *the number of ordinary shares issued by the legal parent to the owners of the legal subsidiary* el número de acciones ordinarias emitidas por la matriz legal para los dueños de la filial jurídica ▲ *the weighted average number of ordinary shares outstanding* el número medio ponderado de acciones ordinarias pendientes de pago ▲ *total number of ordinary shares* total número de acciones ordinarias

Ordre des Experts Comptables

= OEC

The Ordre des Experts Comptable (OEC) is the French private-sector professional accountancy body. The government-controlled accountancy body is the Compagnie Nationale des Commissaires aux Comptes of which accountants that audit companies must also be members.

Ordre des Experts Comptables

= Asociación de Expertos Contables de Francia

▲ *become a member of the Ordre des Experts Comptables* ser miembro de la Ordre des Experts Comptables

⇛ Compagnie Nationale des Commissaires aux Comptes

organic growth

= internal growth

Organic growth is the internal growth of an enterprise that results from spending internally generated resources to achieve e.g. increased production, penetration on new markets, or development of new products. Organic growth excludes growth via mergers and acquisitions.

crecimiento orgánico

= crecimiento interno

organisation UK

= organization US

Generally, an organisation means a group of people who work together for the purpose of achieving one or more shared goals. An organisation may be e.g. an enterprise, institution, sports club, school, etc.

organización

▲ *a regulatory organisation* una organización reguladora ▲ *a venture capital organisation* una organización de capital riesgo ▲ *an American organisation* una organización estadounidense ▲ *charitable organisations* organizaciones benéficas ▲ *the employee's level within the organisation* el nivel de los empleados dentro de la organización

organisational capital UK

= organizational capital US

Organisational capital is typically part of an intellectual capital report and refers to the internal structure of an enterprise that is created by its employees, but owned by the enterprise. The internal structure comprises e.g. concepts, patents, computer and other administrative systems.

capital organizacional

▲ *the structure of organisational capital* la estructura del capital organizacional

⇛ customer capital, individual capital, intellectual capital report, structural capital

organization US

= organisation UK

Generally, an organization means a group of people who work together for the purpose of achieving one or more shared goals. An organization may be e.g. an enterprise, institution, sports club, school, etc.

organización

▲ *a regulatory organization* una organización reguladora ▲ *a venture capital organization* una organización de capital riesgo ▲ *an American organization* una organización estadounidense ▲ *charitable organizations* organizaciones benéficas ▲ *the employee's level within the organization* el nivel de los empleados dentro de la organización

organizational capital US

= organisational capital UK

Organizational capital is typically part of an intellectual capital report and refers to the internal structure of an enterprise that is created by its employees, but owned by the enterprise. The internal structure comprises e.g. concepts, patents, computer and other administrative systems.

capital organizacional

▲ *the structure of organizational capital* la estructura del capital organizacional

⇛ customer capital, individual capital, intellectual capital report

original cost

= acquisition cost

The original cost of an asset is the historical cost, i.e. the acquisition cost or production cost initially recognised for that asset in the balance sheet.

coste histórico

= coste inicial

▲ *depreciation based on the asset's original cost* amortización basada en el coste histórico del activo

originated loan

Originated loans are loans, i.e. financial assets other than derivative financial instruments, created or issued by an enterprise rather than acquired or purchased.

NOTE Under the Exposure Draft of Proposed Amendments to IAS 39, 2004, loans included in "loans and receivables" have been redefined to include purchased loans instead of being limited to loans originated by the enterprise.

préstamo original

= préstamo primigenio

▲ *classify as an originated loan* clasificar como un préstamo original

SOURCE Basis for Conclusions on IAS 39: Financial Instruments: Recognition and Measurement

other accounts payable US

= other creditors UK, other payables IAS/IFRS, US

≠ other accounts receivable US, other debtors UK

"Other accounts payable" is an item under liabilities in the balance sheet containing unpaid amounts owed to other parties such as employee costs payable, VAT payable etc.

otras cuentas a pagar

= otras cuentas acreedoras

≠ otras cuentas a cobrar, otras cuentas deudoras

▲ *the current portion of other accounts payable* la parte corriente de otras cuentas a pagar

⇛ trade and other payables

other accounts receivable US

= other debtors UK, other receivables IAS/IFRS, US

≠ other accounts payable US, other creditors UK, other payables IAS/IFRS, US

"Other accounts receivable" is an item under current assets in the balance sheet containing miscellaneous amounts receivable by an enterprise other than those included in trade receivables such as receivables from related parties.

otras cuentas a cobrar

= otras cuentas deudoras

≠ otras cuentas a pagar, otras cuentas acreedoras

▲ *quarterly data for other accounts receivable* datos trimes-

trales por otras cuentas a cobrar ▲ *with the exception of other accounts receivable* con la excepción de otras cuentas a cobrar
⇛ trade accounts receivable

other creditors UK
= other accounts payable US, IAS/IFRS, other payables US, IAS/IFRS
≠ other accounts receivable US, IAS/IFRS, other debtors UK, other receivables IAS/IFRS, US
"Other creditors" is an item under current liabilities in the balance sheet including unpaid amounts owed to other parties such as employee costs payable, VAT payable etc.
otras cuentas acreedoras
= otros acreedores
▲ *included in other creditors* incluido en otras cuentas acreedoras
⇛ creditor

other debtors UK
= other accounts receivable US
≠ other accounts payable US, other creditors
"Other debtors" is an item under current assets in the balance sheet according to the Companies Act 2006 required report format. This item includes miscellaneous amounts receivable by an enterprise other than those included in trade debtors.
otras cuentas deudoras
= otros deudores
▲ *included in other debtors* incluido en otras cuentas deudoras
⇛ trade creditors, trade debtors

other expenses IAS/IFRS
→ other operating expenses

other external charges UK
"Other external charges" is an item in the profit and loss account as presented in the report format classified by nature. This item includes miscellaneous costs attributable to an enteprise's operating activities which may be specified in the notes, such as marketing costs, office expenses and insurance premiums.
otros gastos externos
▲ *materials and other external charges* materiales y otros gastos externos ▲ *raw materials and consumables and other external charges* materias primas, insumos y otros gastos externos

other financial expenses IAS/IFRS
= interest payable and similar charges UK
"Other financial expenses" is an item in the income statement recognising financial expenses for the accounting period of an enterprise such as interest paid, foreign exchange losses and similar expenses, but excluding financial expenses relating to balances with group enterprises, which are disclosed separately.
otros gastos financieros
▲ *interest paid and other financial expenses* intereses pagados y otros gastos financieros
⇛ financials, net, interest payable

other financial income IAS/IFRS
= interest and other income US, other interest receivable and similar income UK
"Other financial income" is an item in the income statement recognising financial income for the accounting period of an enterprise such as interest income from investments, dividends, foreign exchange gains and similar income, but excluding financial income from group enterprises, which are disclosed separately.
otros ingresos financieros
▲ *dividends and other financial income received* dividendos y otros ingresos financieros recibidos ▲ *interest received and other financial income* intereses recibidos y otros ingresos financieros
⇛ financials, net, interest income

other interest receivable and similar income UK
= interest and other income US, other financial income IAS/IFRS
"Other interest receivable and similar income" is an item in the profit and loss account representing interest and other financial revenue earned by an enterprise.
otros intereses a cobrar e ingresos similares
NOTE Always plural in Spanish accounting texts.
▲ *other interest receivable and similar income with a separate indication of that derived from affiliated undertakings* otros inte-

reses a cobrar e ingresos similares con una indicación por separado para los que proceden de las empresas filiales ▲ *the other interest receivable and similar income of £294,000 included in the period* otros intereses a cobrar e ingresos similares de 294.000 libras esterlinas incluidas en el periodo
⇛ financials, net

other investments UK
= marketable securities US
"Other investments" is an item under current assets in the balance sheet according to the Companies Act 2006 required report format. This item includes fixed asset investments in securities such as bonds and other debt instruments as well as equity investments in other companies that are not subsidiaries or associated companies.
otras inversiones
▲ *disposal of long-term assets and other investments* venta de activos a largo plazo y otras inversiones ▲ *proceeds from sale of other investments* ingresos de la venta de otras inversiones

other operating charges UK
"Other operating charges" is an item in the profit and loss account as presented in the report format classified by nature which include expenses that are not related to the ordinary activities of an enterprise such as expenses incurred by the sale of fixed assets, property administration or maintenance expenses.
otros gastos de explotación
= otros gastos operativos
▲ *included in other operating charges* incluido en otros gastos de explotación

other operating expenses IAS/IFRS, US
= other operating costs UK
≠ other operating income IAS/IFRS, other operating revenue
"Other operating expenses" is an item in the profit and loss account as presented in the report format classified by nature which include expenses that are not related to the ordinary activities of an enterprise such as expenses incurred by the sale of fixed assets, property administration or maintenance expenses.
otros gastos de explotación
▲ *differences in other operating expenses* diferencias en otros gastos de explotación

other operating income IAS/IFRS, UK
= other income IAS/IFRS, other operating revenue UK, US
≠ other operating expenses IAS/IFRS, US
"Other operating income" is an item in the profit and loss account as presented in the report format classified by nature which include revenue that is not related to the ordinary activities of an enterprise such as rental revenue, gains on the sale of fixed assets and government grants.
otros ingresos de explotación
▲ *included in other operating income* incluidos en otros ingresos de explotación ▲ *reclassify from shareholders' equity to other opperating income* reclasificar el patrimonio de los accionistas en otros ingresos de explotación

other operating revenue US, UK
= other operating income
"Other operating revenue" is an item in the profit and loss account as presented in the report format classified by nature which include revenue that is not related to the ordinary activities of an enterprise such as rental revenue, gains on the sale of fixed assets and government grants.
otros ingresos de explotación
= otros ingresos operativos
▲ *other operating revenue less discounts* otros ingresos de explotación menos descuentos

other payables IAS/IFRS, US
= other accounts payable US, other creditors UK
≠ other debtors UK, other receivables IAS/IFRS, US
"Other payables" is an item under current liabilities in the balance sheet containing unpaid amounts owed to other parties such as employee costs payable, VAT payable etc.
otras cuentas a pagar
▲ *an increase in other payables* un aumento en otras cuentas a pagar ▲ *trade and other payables* acreedores comerciales y otras cuentas a pagar

other provisions UK

"Other provisions" is an item under provisions for liabilities in the balance sheet according to the Companies Act 2006 required report format. This item includes provisions not classified as provisions for pension and tax liabilities and may include e.g. provisions for warranties.

otras provisiones

▲ *included in other provisions* incluido en otras provisiones ▲ *the provisions shown in the balance sheet under 'Other provisions'* las provisiones mostradas en la hoja de balance en 'Otras provisiones'

other receivables IAS/IFRS, US

= other accounts receivable US, other debtors UK

≠ other creditors UK, other payables IAS/IFRS, US

"Other receivables" is an item under current assets in the balance sheet containing miscellaneous amounts receivable by an enterprise other than those included in trade receivables such as receivables from related parties.

otras cuentas a recibir

= otras cuenta a cobrar

▲ *trade and other receivables* acreedores comerciales y otras cuentas a recibir

⇛ trade receivables

other reserves

1 = other reserves IAS/IFRS

"Other reserves" is one of the items preceded by a Roman numeral under capital and reserves in the balance sheet according to the Companies Act 2006 required report format. The other items preceded by a Roman numeral required under capital and reserves are called up share capital, share premium account and revaluation reserve. Other reserves constitute e.g. reserve for own shares as well as reserves provided for by the articles of association.

otras reservas

▲ *a movement in other reserves* un apunte en otras reservas ▲ *transfers from other reserves* transferencias de otras reservas

⇛ called up share capital, capital and reserves, revaluation reserve, share premium account

2 "Other reserves" is one of the items preceded by an Arabic numeral under capital and reserves in the balance sheet according to the Companies Act 2006 required report format. The other items preceded by an Arabic numeral under other reserves are capital redemption reserve, reserve for own shares and reserves provided for by the articles of association. Other reserves are distributable reserves, representing equity funds which, subject to approval by the annual general meeting, can be applied to cover losses or be distributed to shareholders.

otras reservas

▲ *included in other reserves* incluida en otras reservas

⇛ capital redemption reserve, reserve for own shares, reserves provided for by the articles of association

out-source

→ outsource

out-sourcing

→ outsourcing

outflow

≠ inflow

Outflow is an outgoing movement of cash, funds or other assets from an enterprise.

flujo de salida

▲ *an outflow of cash or other assets of the entity* un flujo de salida de efectivo u otros activos de la entidad ▲ *an outflow of resources embodying economic benefits* un flujo de salida de recursos que incorporan beneficios económicos ▲ *outflow of cash* salida de efectivo ▲ *outflow of funds* salida de fondos

outlay cost

Outlay costs are concrete expenses that result in future cash outflows from an enterprise such as production and start-up costs.

coste desembolsado

▲ *the lowered outlay cost* el coste desembolsado disminuido ▲ *the overall annualised outlay cost* el coste desembolsado total anualizado

outline

An outline is a general description of something, usually including the main points of the subject concerned.

guión

= esquema, líneas generales

▲ *give an outline of something* dar un guión de algo ▲ *prepare an outline* preparar un guión ▲ *the year in outline* el año en líneas generales

outlook

The outlook is a forward-looking statement included as a section of management's review in a interim or annual report of an enterprise expressing management's current expectations, assumptions or forecasts for the financial performance and events in the future accounting period.

previsión

= pronóstico

▲ *a positive outlook* una previsión positiva ▲ *cautious business outlooks* previsiones empresariales prudentes ▲ *negative business outlooks* previsiones empresariales negativas ▲ *the outlook for 2006* la previsión para 2006

output

= production

Output refers to the quantity of products or services which an enterprise is capable of manufacturing, producing or making during a specific time period.

producción

▲ *a significant amount of the output of the asset* una cantidad significativa de la producción del activo ▲ *the estimated amount of output* la cantidad prevista de producción ▲ *the price that the purchaser will pay for the output* el precio que el adquirente pagará por la producción

⇛ productive capacity

output level overhead variance

= denominator-level variance, production-volume variance

The output level overhead variance expresses the difference between the budgeted fixed indirect production costs (overheads) and the fixed indirect production costs (overheads) that have been allocated to the produced units.

variación de los gastos indirectos a nivel de producción

▲ *a favourable output level overhead variance* una variación favorable de los gastos indirectos a nivel de producción ▲ *the output level overhead variance of a period* la variación de los gastos indirectos a nivel de producción de un periodo

output tax UK

= output VAT UK

≠ input tax UK, input VAT UK

Output tax is a value added tax (VAT) that the seller adds to the price of the goods and services he sells. When accounting for VAT to the tax authorities, a VAT-registered enterprise offsets input taxes paid against output taxes charged.

impuesto repercutido

= impuesto sobre las ventas, impuesto sobre ventas

▲ *calculate output tax* calcular el impuesto repercutido ▲ *report output tax* informar del impuesto repercutido ▲ *the difference between the output tax and the input tax* la diferencia entre el IVA repercutido y el IVA soportado

output unit-level cost

Output-unit-level costs are costs incurred each time a unit is produced and include e.g. costs related to direct labour, materials and energy. Such costs will vary with the scope of production.

coste unitario del producto

= coste unitario por producto

▲ *examples of output unit-level costs* ejemplos de costes unitarios del producto ▲ *identify indirect costs as output unit-level costs* identificar los costes indirectos como costes unitarios por producto

output VAT

= output tax

Output VAT is value added tax that the seller adds to the price of the goods and services he sells. When accounting for VAT to the tax authorities, a VAT-registered enterprise offsets input VAT paid against output VAT charged.

IVA repercutido

▲ *an account for output VAT* una cuenta de IVA repercutido ▲ *charge output VAT* cargar el IVA repercutido

⇛ value added tax

output-level variance

= denominator-level variance, production-volume variance

Output-volume variance is the difference between the budgeted fixed indirect production costs (overheads) and the fixed indirect production costs (overheads) that have been allocated to the produced units.

variación del nivel de producción

= variación en el nivel de producción

▲ *a favourable output-level variance* una variación del nivel de producción ▲ *the output-level variance of a period* la variación en el nivel de producción de un periodo

outsource

= out-source

To outsource means to delegate activities that have been carried out internally in the enterprise to external suppliers on a contractual basis.

subcontratar

▲ *outsource a task* subcontratar una tarea ▲ *outsource an activity* subcontratar una actividad ▲ *outsource day-to-day functions* subcontratar las funciones del día a día ▲ *outsource manufacture* subcontratar la producción

outsourcing

= out-sourcing

≠ insourcing

Outsourcing means delegating, on a contractual basis, activities previously carried out internally in the enterprise to external suppliers.

subcontratación

▲ *the general outsourcing of internal audit* la subcontratación general de la auditoría interna

outstanding

An amount, item or claim that has not yet been paid is said to be outstanding.

pendiente

= vigente

▲ *amounts or appropriate proportions of outstanding items* cantidades o proporciones apropiadas de partidas pendientes ▲ *the amount of outstanding assets* la cantidad de activos vigentes ▲ *the principal amount outstanding of the transferred asset* la cantidad principal pendiente del activo transferido ▲ *the reduction of the outstanding liability* la reducción del pasivo vigente

outstanding balance

= balance outstanding

Outstanding balances are amounts owed and payable by one party to another at a given date such as amounts due on a loan or a mortgage or, seen from the creditor's point of view, receivables from debtors.

saldo pendiente

▲ *outstanding balance at 31 December 2005* saldo pendiente a 31 de diciembre de 2005 ▲ *outstanding balance at end of year per grant* saldo pendiente a final de año por subvención ▲ *outstanding balances with other entities in a group* saldos pendientes con otras empresas del grupo ▲ *the amount of outstanding balances* el importe de los saldos pendientes

outstanding debt

An outstanding debt is the part of the principal amount of the debt that still remains to be paid by the debtor.

deuda pendiente

= deuda activa, deuda pendiente de pago

▲ *changes in outstanding debt* cambios en la deuda pendiente ▲ *gross outstanding debt* deuda pendiente bruta

outstanding share UK

Outstanding shares are all issued shares of a company currently held by shareholders not including own shares held by the company itself.

acción en circulación

= capital en circulación

▲ *dilution of outstanding shares* dilución de las acciones en circulación ▲ *fair value of all outstanding shares* valor razonable de todas las acciones en circulación

⇛ issued capital, outstanding stock, own share

outstanding stock US

Outstanding stock is the total issued capital stock of a corporation currently held by stockholders not including treasury stock.

acciones en circulación

= capital en circulación

▲ *dilution of outstanding stock* dilución de las acciones en circulación ▲ *fair value of all outstanding stock* valor razonable de todas las acciones en circulación

⇛ treasury stock

overabsorbed indirect cost

= overallocated indirect cost, overapplied indirect cost

≠ underabsorbed indirect cost, underallocated indirect cost, underapplied indirect cost

Overabsorbed indirect costs refer to the allocation of indirect manufacturing costs for an accounting period to products or orders by an amount that is higher than the actually incurred indirect manufacturing costs for that accounting period.

coste indirecto sobreasignado

▲ *cumulative overabsorbed indirect costs* costes indirectos sobreasignados acumulados

overallocated indirect cost

= overabsorbed indirect cost, overapplied indirect cost

≠ underabsorbed indirect cost, underallocated indirect cost, underapplied indirect cost

Overallocated indirect costs refer to the allocation of indirect manufacturing costs for an accounting period to products or orders by an amount that is higher than the actually incurred indirect manufacturing costs for that accounting period.

coste indirecto sobreasignado

▲ *period-end overallocated indirect costs* costes indirectos sobreasignados de final de periodo

overapplied indirect cost

= overabsorbed indirect cost, overallocated indirect cost

≠ underabsorbed indirect cost, underallocated indirect cost, underapplied indirect cost

Overapplied indirect costs refer to the allocation of indirect manufacturing costs for an accounting period to products or orders by an amount that is higher than the actually incurred indirect manufacturing costs for that accounting period.

coste indirecto sobreasignado

▲ *cumulative overapplied indirect costs* costes indirectos sobreasignados acumulados ▲ *period-end overapplied indirect costs* costes indirectos sobreasignados de final de periodo

overapplied overhead

≠ underapplied overhead

Overapplied overheads refer to allocation of overheads for an accounting period to products or orders by an amount that is higher than the actually incurred overheads for that accounting period.

coste indirecto sobreimputado

▲ *overapplied overhead at the end of a month* coste indirecto sobreimputado al final de un mes ▲ *overapplied overhead for the year* coste indirecto sobreimputado del año

⇛ overallocated indirect cost

overfunded

≠ underfunded

A pension plan is overfunded when the fair value of the plan assets exceed the projected benefit obligation of the plan.

sobrefinanciado

▲ *an overfunded retirement plan* un plan de pensiones sobrefinanciado

⇛ plan asset, projected benefit obligation

overhead

= burden US, indirect cost, overhead cost

Overheads are indirect costs, i.e. costs that are indirectly associated with the units of productions or production processes. Examples are wages, rent, insurance and property taxes. Overheads may be divided into production overheads, administration overheads, distribution overheads etc.

coste indirecto

= gasto indirecto, overhead

▲ *allocation of overheads* asignación de costes indirectos ▲ *attributable overheads* costes indirectos atribuibles ▲ *fixed production overheads* costes indirectos de producción fijados ▲ *future overheads* costes indirectos futuros ▲ *future overheads that can be attributed directly to the use of the asset* costes indirectos futuros que se pueden atribuir directamente al uso del activo ▲ *general overheads* gastos indirectos generales ▲ *non-attributable overheads* costes indirectos no atribuibles ▲ *non-production overheads* gastos indirectos no aplicables a la producción ▲ *overheads that are necessary to generate the asset* costes indirectos que son necesarios para generar el activo ▲ *unallocated overheads* costes indirectos no asignados ▲ *variable production overheads* costes indirectos de producción variables

overhead absorption rate

= overhead recovery rate

Overhead absorption rates are calculated and used in absorption costing for charging and attributing production overhead costs to cost units, i.e. amounts of production.

tasa de absorción de gastos generales

= tasa de absorción de los gastos generales

▲ *a fixed overhead absorption rate* una tasa de absorción de gastos generales fija ▲ *a variable overhead absorption rate* una tasa de absorción de gastos generales variable ▲ *calculate the overhead absorption rate* calcular la tasa de absorción de los gastos generales ▲ *the actual overhead absorption rate* la tasa de absorción de gastos generales actual ▲ *the budgeted overhead absorption rate* la tasa de absorción presupuestada de los gastos generales

⇛ absorption costing, cost unit, full absorption

overhead cost

= indirect cost, overhead, overhead expense US

Overhead costs are indirect costs, i.e. costs that are indirectly associated with the units of productions or production processes. Examples are wages, rent, insurance and property taxes. Overhead costs may be divided into production overheads, administration overheads, distribution overheads etc.

coste indirecto

= overhead

▲ *administration and other general overhead costs* gestión y otros costes indirectos generales ▲ *allocation of overhead costs* asignación de costes indirectos

⇛ fixed production overhead

overhead expenditure

Overhead expenditure constitutes actual indirect costs, i.e. costs that have been incurred and are indirectly associated with the units of productions or production processes. Examples are wages, rent, insurance and property taxes.

gastos indirectos incurridos

NOTE Always plural in Spanish accounting texts.

▲ *administrative and other general overhead expenditure* gastos administrativos y otros gastos indirectos generales incurridos

overhead expense

Overhead expenses are expenses that are not directly related to the production of goods, i.e. expenses for which single products or activities cannot be identified. Examples of overhead expenses are indirect labour and materials, rent and insurance of manufacturing units.

gasto indirecto

▲ *a decrease in overhead expenses* un descenso en los gastos indirectos ▲ *an increase in overhead expenses* un aumento en los gastos indirectos ▲ *reduce overhead expenses* reducir los gastos indirectos ▲ *the actual overhead expenses* los gastos indirectos reales ▲ *the overhead expenses incurred* los gastos indirectos incurridos

overhead recovery rate

= overhead absorption rate

Overhead recovery rates are calculated and used in absorption costing for charging and attributing production overhead costs to cost units, i.e. amounts of production.

índice de recuperación de costes indirectos

= índice de recuperación de los costes indirectos

▲ *a fixed overhead recovery rate* un índice de recuperación de costes indirectos fijo ▲ *a variable overhead recovery rate* un índice variable de recuperación de los costes indirectos ▲ *calculate an overhead recovery rate* calcular un índice de recuperación de costes indirectos

⇛ absorption costing

overnight interest rate

The overnight interest rate is a rate that is reset and adjusted daily as a result of changes in market rates.

tipo de interés a un día

▲ *change the overnight interest rate* cambiar el tipo de interés a un día ▲ *cut the overnight interest rate* recortar el tipo de interés a un día ▲ *raise the overnight interest rate* aumentar el tipo de interés a un día ▲ *the current overnight interest rate* el tipo de interés a un día actual

overseas tax

When an enterprise carries out activities in other countries than in the one in which it is domiciled, it may be liable to pay tax under the laws of these countries, i.e. it is liable to pay overseas tax.

impuesto internacional

▲ *overseas tax liabilities* pasivos por impuesto internacional ▲ *pay overseas tax* pagar el impuesto internacional

overtime premium

An overtime premium is money paid by the enterprise because its employees have worked more hours than agreed or usual.

prima por horas extraordinarias

= prima de las horas extraordinarias

▲ *eligible for overtime premium* derecho a prima por horas extraordinarias ▲ *overtime premium per hour* prima por horas extraordinarias por hora ▲ *statutory overtime premium* prima estatutaria por horas extraordinarias

overview

An overview is a brief description of something omitting details.

visión general

▲ *financial overview* visión general financiera ▲ *overview of group companies* visión general de las empresas del grupo

owe

To owe somebody something means being indebted to somebody, i.e. to be under a legal obligation to pay an amount that has fallen due for payment.

deber

▲ *amounts owed by affiliated undertakings* cantidades debidas por empresas afiliadas ▲ *amounts owed by the company becoming due and payable after more than five years* cantidades debidas por la empresa que vencen y a pagar transcurridos cinco años ▲ *amounts owed to credit institutions* cantidades debidas a instituciones de crédito ▲ *owe an amount* deber una cantidad ▲ *owe someone a duty* deber a alguien un servicio ▲ *pay what you owe* pagar lo que debes

own

= hold

To own is to possess, to hold or have rightfully.

poseer

= tener en propiedad

▲ *equity interests that are not owned, directly or indirectly through subsidiaries, by the parent* inversiones en patrimonio en las filiales que no posee la matriz ni de forma directa ni indirecta ▲ *own foreign enterprises* poseer empresas extranjeras ▲ *own half or less of the voting power of an entity* poseer la mitad o menos de los derechos políticos de una entidad ▲ *own share warrants or equity instruments that are convertible into ordinary shares* poseer warrants sobre acciones o instrumentos de patrimonio que son convertibles en acciones ordinarias ▲ *own shareholdings* poseer acciones

own portfolio

The own portfolio of e.g. a financial institution constitutes its own investment portfolio comprising i.a. equities and bonds.

cartera propia

▲ *management of own portfolio* gestión de la cartera propia ▲ *own portfolio of shares* cartera propia de acciones ▲ *sell shares from the group's own portfolio* vender acciones de la cartera propia del grupo

own share UK

= treasury share IAS/IFRS, US, treasury stock US

Own shares are equity instruments issued by the enterprise itself that have been repurchased and are held by the issuing enterprise itself or, in a group, by a parent or its subsidiaries.

NOTE In the financial statements, the relevant balance sheet items are referred to as "own shares" under assets and "reserve for own shares" under liabilities.

acción propia

▲ *acquire own shares* adquirir acciones propias ▲ *cancel own shares* amortizar acciones propias ▲ *disclosures of own shares* divulgaciones de acciones propias ▲ *dispose of own shares* dar de baja acciones propias ▲ *hold own shares* mantener acciones propias ▲ *purchase of own shares* compra de acciones propias ▲ *realise own shares* liquidar acciones propias ▲ *recognise own shares* reconocer acciones propias ▲ *reserve for own shares* reserva para acciones propias ▲ *sale of own shares* venta de acciones propias

own work capitalised UK

= work performed by the entity and capitalised IAS/IFRS

"Own work capitalised" is an item in the profit and loss account as presented in the report format classified by nature. This item typically includes improvement of buildings and machinery performed by the reporting enterprise's own employees.

trabajos realizados para la empresa capitalizados

NOTE Always plural in Spanish accounting texts.

▲ *adjustments to the value of own work capitalised* ajustes al valor de los trabajos realizados para la empresa capitalizados ▲ *increased income from own work capitalised* ingreso aumentado procedente de trabajos realizados para la empresa capitalizados

owner

An owner is a shareholder in a public limited company, a shareholder in a private limited company or other parties that hold equity investments in an enterprise.

propietario

= accionista

▲ *enter into an agreement of joint control with other owners* acordar el control continuo con otros propietarios ▲ *loans etc. to owners* préstamos, etc. a propietarios ▲ *obtain a relative advantage compared to other owners* obtener una ventaja relativa en relación con otros propietarios ▲ *receivables from owners and management* cuentas a cobrar de propietarios y gestores ▲ *show the capital contributions by owners of the enterprise* mostrar las aportaciones de capital de los accionistas de la empresa ▲ *the owners' respective shares of the profit or loss* las participaciones respectivas de los propietarios en los resultados

owner-occupied property IAS/IFRS

In the context of business property, owner-occupied property is property held for use by the owner enterprise itself, e.g. for administrative, productive or other business purposes.

propiedad ocupada por el dueño

= propiedad ocupada por el propietario, propiedad ocupada por la propiedad

▲ *classify a property as owner-occupied property* clasificar una propiedad como propiedad ocupada por el dueño ▲ *distinguish investment property from owner-occupied property* distinguir la propiedad de inversión de la propiedad ocupada por el dueño ▲ *owner-occupied property awaiting disposal* propiedad ocupada por el propietario pendiente de venta ▲ *transfers to and from inventories and owner-occupied property* se transfiere a y proviene de inventarios y propiedad ocupada por el propietario ▲ *use the land as owner-occupied property* utilizar los bienes raíces como propiedad ocupada por el dueño

SOURCE IAS 40, paragraph 4

owners' equity US

Owners' equity consists of the capital contributed by owners plus retained earnings (reserves), defined as the enterprise's total assets less its total liabilities. Owners' equity represents the claims of owners against the assets of the enterprise.

NOTE "Owners' equity" is used about non-incorporated entities, e.g. sole proprietorships, where corporations apply "shareholders' equity" or "stockholders' equity".

patrimonio de los propietarios

▲ *a description of the nature and purpose of each reserve within owners' equity* una descripción de la naturaleza y propósito de cada reserva dentro del patrimonio de los propietarios ▲ *the components of owners' equity* los componentes del patrimonio de los propietarios ▲ *the movements for the period in owners' equity* los movimientos para el periodo en el patrimonio de los propietarios

⇛ shareholders' equity, stockholders' equity

ownership

= title

Ownership is the proprietary right, in fact and in law, to use, enjoy, transfer or sell property.

propiedad

= titularidad

▲ *a change in ownership* un cambio en la titularidad ▲ *acquire ownership* adquirir el título de la propiedad ▲ *acquisition of ownership* adquisición del título de la propiedad ▲ *active ownership* propiedad activa ▲ *companies with dispersed ownership* empresas con propiedad dispersa ▲ *have ownership of assets* tener el título de propiedad legal sobre activos ▲ *have ownership of something* tener el título de propiedad legal de algo ▲ *legal ownership* título de propiedad legal ▲ *reserve ownership* reservar el título de propiedad ▲ *risks and rewards incident to ownership* riesgos y gratificaciones de la propiedad ▲ *significant risks and rewards of ownership* riesgos y gratificaciones significativos de la propiedad ▲ *the ownership of the customer* la propiedad del cliente ▲ *transfer ownership* transferir el título de propiedad

ownership interest

= equity interest US, IAS/IFRS, investment, share

An ownership interest is a long-term investment in the equity of another enterprise. Depending on the size of the ownership interest, i.e. typically the amount of voting shares held, an investing company acquires a controlling interest or significant influence in the other enterprise.

inversión mayoritaria

= interés mayoritario

▲ *acquisition of ownership interests in other companies* adquisición de inversiones mayoritarias en otras empresas ▲ *allocation of ownership interests* asignación de inversiones mayoritarias ▲ *determine minority interests on the basis of present ownership interests* determinar intereses minoritarios en base a las inversiones mayoritarias actuales ▲ *obtain an ownership interest* obtener una inversión mayoritaria ▲ *the proportion of ownership interest held in jointly controlled entities* la proporción de la inversión mayoritaria en entidades controladas conjuntamente

⇛ controlling interest, participating interest, property interest, significant influence

ownership share

An ownership share represents the amount contributed to the capital of an enterprise by an investor and shows how large the contributed amount is in proportion to the total contributed capital. The ownership share of an investment in a company expresses the number of shares held by an investor compared with the total number of shares issued.

propiedad mayoritaria

= ownership share

▲ *acquisition of ownership shares* adquisición de la propiedad mayoritaria ▲ *dispose of an ownership share* venta de la propiedad mayoritaria

ownership structure

The ownership structure in an enterprise is the composition of the owners of that enterprise. Depending on the number and liability of the owner(s), an enterprise can be classified as a sole proprietorship, a partnership, a limited partnership, a co-operative society or a limited liability company. The ownership structure of a limited company appears from the proportionate distribution of shares on shareholders. In principle, the ownership structure of a listed company will therefore change every time the company's shares are traded. The circle of owners may consist of small-time shareholders, major shareholders, or one principal shareholder, who can be private persons, enterprises, foundations or associations.

estructura mayoritaria

▲ *a new ownership structure* una nueva estructura mayoritaria

⇛ co-operative society, limited liability company, limited partnership, partnership, sole proprietorship

P

p UK

= pence

"p" is an abbreviation for the monetary unit pence.

penique

▲ *a share price increase of 10p* un aumento de 10 peniques en el precio de la acción ▲ *shares issued at 32.17p* acciones emitidas a 32,17 peniques

p.c.

= pc, PC, per cent UK, percent US

p.c. is the abbreviation for per cent. One per cent is one hundredth of an amount.

NOTE "p.c." can also be expressed with the sign "%".

por ciento

▲ *pay interest at the rate of 5 p.c.* pagar el interés al tipo del 5 por ciento

P/BV

= price/book ratio, price/book value

P/BV is the abbreviation for price/book value which is an investment ratio or multiple defined as the share price divided by the book value per share. A price/book value exceeding 1 means that the value of the company's shares exceeds that of the equity. This ratio shows how the market values the company and its future.

precio/valor contable

= precio/valor en libros, ratio precio por valor en libros

▲ *calculate P/BV* calcular el precio/valor contable ▲ *determine P/BV* determinar el precio/valor contable ▲ *high P/BV shares* precio/valor contable de las acciones alto ▲ *low P/BV shares* precio/valor contable de las acciones bajo ▲ *P/BV per share* precio/valor contable por acción

P/CF

= price/cash flow ratio

P/CF is the abbreviation for price/cash flow ratio, which is a financial ratio defined as the market price per share divided by the cash flow per share. As it is related to an enterprise's cash flow, this ratio is used to assess that enterprise's future ability to generate a return in the form of capital gains or dividend distributions.

precio/flujo de efectivo

= precio/cash flow, ratio precio por flujo de efectivo

▲ *calculate P/CF* calcular el precio/flujo de efectivo ▲ *P/CF calculations* cálculos del precio/flujo de efectivo

P/CF ratio

= price/cash flow ratio

The P/CF ratio or price/cash flow ratio is a financial ratio defined as the market price per share divided by the cash flow per share. As it is related to an enterprise's cash flow, this ratio is used to assess that enterprise's future ability to generate a return in the form of capital gains or dividend distributions.

precio/flujo de efectivo por acción

= ratio precio por flujo de efectivo por acción

▲ *absolute P/CF ratio* precio absoluto/flujo de efectivo por acción ▲ *average P/CF ratio* precio medio/flujo de efectivo por acción ▲ *relative P/CF ratio* precio relativo/flujo de efectivo por acción

P/E

= earnings multiple US, multiple US, p/e ratio, PER, price/earnings ratio

P/E is the abbreviation for price/earnings ratio, which is defined as the market price per share divided by earnings per share (EPS). This investment ratio, also referred to as the earnings multiple, compares the market price of an ordinary share with the EPS and is used to analyse the performance potential of a company. A high P/E ratio indicates future earnings growth and signals that investors have high confidence in the company.

PER

= precio/beneficio por acción

▲ *calculate P/E* calcular el PER ▲ *P/E calculations* cálculos del PER

P/E ratio

= earnings multiple US, multiple US, P/E, PER, price/earnings ratio

P/E ratio is the abbreviation for price/earnings ratio, which is defined as the market price per share divided by earnings per share (EPS). This investment ratio, also referred to as the earnings multiple, compares the market price of an ordinary share with the EPS and is used to analyse the performance potential of a company. A high P/E ratio indicates future earnings growth and signals that investors have high confidence in the company.

precio/beneficio

= PER, ratio precio por beneficio, ratio precio-beneficio

▲ *a high P/E ratio* un precio/beneficio alto ▲ *a low P/E ratio* un precio/beneficio bajo ▲ *calculate the P/E ratio* calcular el PER

P/NAV

= price/net asset value

P/NAV is the abbreviation for price/net asset value, which is a financial ratio defined as share price divided by net asset value per share, measuring the value of shareholders' equity by relating the market price per share to its book value.

precio/valor del activo neto por acción

▲ *calculate P/NAV* calcular el precio/valor del activo neto por acción ▲ *P/NAV calculations* cálculos de precio/valor del activo neto por acción

paid

When something, typically money or other consideration, has been given or provided in return for something else, it has been paid.

pagado

▲ *fully paid ordinary shares* acciones ordinarias completamente pagadas ▲ *partly paid shares* acciones parcialmente pagadas ▲ *professional fees paid to accountants* honorarios pagados a los contables ▲ *the amount of cash or cash equivalents paid* la cantidad de efectivo o equivalentes de efectivo pagados ▲ *the amounts that may ultimately be paid* las cantidades que se pueden pagar finalmente ▲ *the fair value of the consideration paid to the preference shareholders* el valor razonable de la contraprestación pagada a los accionistas preferentes

paid up share capital

→ paid-up share capital

paid-in surplus US

= additional paid-in capital US, capital surplus US, share premium UK, IAS/IFRS

Paid-in surplus is a type of reserves under equity representing additional paid-in capital in the form of a premium on issued shares, i.e. amounts contributed in excess of the nominal or stated value to a company.

prima de emisión

▲ *paid-in surplus as at January 1* prima de emisión a 1 de enero ▲ *paid-in surplus during the year* prima de emisión durante el año

paid-up share capital

The paid-up share capital of a company is the part of the issued capital that has actually been paid by shareholders.

capital desembolsado

▲ *amount to 5% of the paid-up share capital* representa el 5% del capital desembolsado ▲ *paid-up share capital less losses incurred* capital desembolsado menos pérdidas incurridas

⇛ issued capital

par

= face value UK, nominal value, par value

≠ market value

Par or par value is the nominal value or stated value of a financial instrument, such as a share or a bond, when it is issued.

valor nominal

= par

▲ *a stated par or principal amount* un valor nominal reflejado o cantidad principal ▲ *agree on the redemption of debt instruments at par* estar de acuerdo con el rescate de los instrumentos de deuda a la par ▲ *ordinary share capital at par* capital en acciones ordinarias a la par ▲ *price above par* precio por encima del valor nominal ▲ *price below par* precio por debajo del valor nominal ▲ *redeem at par* redimir a la par

par value

= face value UK, legal value, par, stated value

≠ market value

Par or par value is the nominal value or stated value of a financial instrument, such as a share or a bond, when it is issued.

valor a la par
= valor nominal
▲ *par value per share* valor a la par por acción ▲ *shares with no par value* acciones sin valor nominal ▲ *the recorded par value of securities* el valor a la par registrado de los títulos

parent
= parent enterprise
A parent is an enterprise that (1) has majority ownership of the voting rights in another enterprise, (2) is an owner and has the right to appoint or remove a majority of the members of the senior management body of the other enterprise, (3) is an owner and has the right to control another enterprise in making operating and financial decisions in accordance with articles of association or an agreement with that enterprise, (4) is an owner and, under an agreement with other owners holds the majority of the voting rights in another enterprise, or (5) holds equity investments in another enterprise and controls that enterprise in making operating and financial decisions.
matriz
= controladora, dominante
NOTE Spanish accountants typically prefer 'matriz' to the IAS/IFRS term 'controladora'.
▲ *a Danish parent* una matriz danesa ▲ *a foreign parent* una matriz extranjera ▲ *a higher-ranking parent* una matriz con un ranking más alto ▲ *a lower-ranking parent* una matriz con un ranking más bajo ▲ *a subsidiary of a parent* una filial de una matriz ▲ *acquire control of the parent* adquirir el control de la matriz ▲ *at least one of the parent's auditors* al menos uno de los auditores de la matriz ▲ *be subject to a parent in a group connection* estar sujeto a una matriz en un grupo ▲ *consolidated financial statements presented by a parent* estados financieros consolidados presentados por una matriz ▲ *equity investments in a parent* instrumentos de patrimonio en una matriz ▲ *interest expenses to parent* gastos por intereses a la matriz ▲ *liabilities vis-à-vis a parent* pasivos en relación a una matriz ▲ *payables to parent* cuantas a pagar a la matriz ▲ *the legal parent* la matriz legal ▲ *the parent's balance sheet date* la fecha del balance de la matriz ▲ *the parent's financial statements* los estados financieros de la matriz ▲ *the parent's transactions with consolidated enterprises* las transacciones de la matriz con sus empresas consolidadas ▲ *the parent's voting rights* los derechos de voto de la matriz ▲ *the senior management of the parent* la dirección senior de la matriz ▲ *the ultimate parent of the group* la matriz última del grupo

parent bank
A parent bank is the parent entity, set up as a company or otherwise, of a banking group, i.e. the company that holds a controlling interest in the subsidiaries of the group.
banco dominante
▲ *the home country of the parent bank* el país de origen del banco dominante
⇛ parent

parent company
A parent company is an enterprise set us as a company that (1) has majority ownership of the voting rights in another enterprise, (2) is an owner and has the right to appoint or remove a majority of the members of the senior management body of the other enterprise, (3) is an owner and has the right to control another enterprise in making operating and financial decisions in accordance with articles of association or an agreement with that enterprise, (4) is an owner and, under an agreement with other owners holds the majority of the voting rights in another enterprise, or (5) holds equity investments in another enterprise and controls that enterprise in making operating and financial decisions.
compañía dominante
= compañía matriz
▲ *parent company and consolidated financial statements* compañía dominante y estados financieros consolidados ▲ *sell a large proportion of production to the parent company* vender una proporción grande de la producción a la compañía dominante

▲ *the home country of the parent company* el país de origen de la compañía dominante
⇛ holding company

parent company accounts UK
= parent's financial statements US
The parent company accounts are the financial statements prepared separately by the parent as a legal entity. Besides, the parent prepares consolidated accounts for the group. For EU companies, the parent's balance sheet is usually presented together with the consolidated accounts, but not always the profit and loss account.
cuentas de la empresa matriz
= estados financieros de la empresa matiz
▲ *notes to the parent company accounts* notas a las cuentas de la empresa matriz ▲ *prepare parent company accounts* preparar las cuentas de la empresa matriz
⇛ consolidated accounts, consolidated financial statements

parent foundation
A parent foundation is a foundation that together with its subsidiaries constitutes a group.
fundación dominante
= fundación matriz
▲ *an operating parent foundation* una fundación dominante en funcionamiento ▲ *the financial statements of the parent foundation* los estados financieros de la fundación dominante

parent undertaking UK
= parent
A parent undertaking is an enterprise that (1) has majority ownership of the voting rights in another enterprise, (2) is an owner and has the right to appoint or remove a majority of the members of the senior management body of the other enterprise, (3) is an owner and has the right to control another enterprise in making operating and financial decisions in accordance with articles of association or an agreement with that enterprise, (4) is an owner and, under an agreement with other owners holds the majority of the voting rights in another enterprise, or (5) holds equity investments in another enterprise and controls that enterprise in making operating and financial decisions.
NOTE A parent undertaking is a parent which may or may not set up as a limited liability company.
empresa dominante
= matriz
▲ *a higher-ranking parent undertaking* una empresa dominante con un ranking más alto ▲ *a lower-ranking parent undertaking* una empresa dominante con un ranking más bajo ▲ *equity investments in a parent undertaking* instrumentos de patrimonio en una empresa dominante ▲ *liabilities vis-à-vis a parent undertaking* pasivos en relación a una empresa dominante ▲ *the senior management of the parent undertaking* la dirección senior de la empresa dominante ▲ *the ultimate parent undertaking of the group* la empresa dominante final del grupo

parent's balance sheet
The parent's balance sheet is a separate balance sheet presented by a parent company of a group together with the consolidated accounts of the group.
balance de la matriz
= balance de la dominante
▲ *recognise assets in the parent's balance sheet* reconocer activos en el balance de la matriz ▲ *remove subsidiaries from a parent's balance sheet* quitar filiales de un balance de la matriz

parent's financial statements IAS/IFRS, US
= parent company accounts UK
The parent's financial statements are the financial statements prepared separately by the parent as a legal entity. Besides, the parent prepares consolidated financial statements for the group. For EU companies, the parent's balance sheet is usually presented together with the consolidated financial statements, but not always the income statement.
estados financieros de la matriz
= estados financieros de la dominante
▲ *notes to the parent's financial statements* notas a los estados financieros de la matriz ▲ *prepare the parent's financial state-*

ments preparar los estados financieros de la matriz
⇛ consolidated financial statements

parent's results
The parent's results are the separate results of the parent entity achieved for the accounting year as disclosed in the parent's profit and loss account and subsequently combined with the results of the subsidiaries to show the group profit or loss in the group accounts.
resultados de la matriz
= resultados de la dominante
▲ *parent's results before income from equity interests in subsidiaries and adjusted for intercompany profits* resultados de la matriz antes de ingresos procedentes de participaciones en filiales e ingresos ajustados por beneficios intragrupo

parent's share
The parent's share is the ownership share of the profit/loss and equity in group subsidiaries that are not wholly owned, i.e. the majority proportion attributable to equity holders of the parent contrary to the minority interests held by outside shareholders.
participación de la matriz
⇛ minority interest

parent-company financial statements US
→ parent's financial statements

parent/subsidiary directive
The parent/subsidiary directive is Council Directive 90/435/EEC of 23 July 1990, and it regulates the common system of taxation applicable in the case of parent companies and subsidiaries of different Member States.
Directiva sobre matrices y filiales
▲ *covered by the parent/subsidiary directive* cubierta por la Directiva sobre matrices y filiales ▲ *the provisions of the parent/subsidiary directive* las disposiciones de la Directiva sobre matrices y filiales

part-time
A part-time employee only works for part of the week.
a tiempo parcial
▲ *on a part-time basis* a tiempo parcial ▲ *work part-time* trabajo a tiempo parcial

part-time employee
A part-time employee is an employee who only works for part of the week.
empleado a tiempo parcial
▲ *the average number of part-time employees* el número medio de empleados a tiempo parcial

partial productivity
Partial productivity is a measure of productivity where the quantity of total produced output is divided by the quantity of a single input used, e.g. labour. If the ratio is high, productivity is high.
productividad parcial
▲ *a decrease in partial productivity* un descenso en la productividad parcial ▲ *an increase in partial productivity* un aumento en la productividad parcial

partially owned
→ partially-owned

partially-owned US, IAS/IFRS
= partly owned UK
≠ wholly owned
A partially-owned company is a company where the ownership is divided between two or more owners each holding a number of shares in the company. Examples of partially-owned companies are subsidiaries and associates where the owners hold different percentages of shares in the company, being either majority or minority shareholders.
propiedad parcial
▲ *a partially-owned subsidiary* una filial de propiedad parcial
SOURCE IAS 28, paragraph 13(c)

participant
A participant is a person who takes part in something, e.g. someone entitled to benefits under a retirement benefit plan either by membership or otherwise.
participante
= partícipe
▲ *a comparison with current fees charged by other market participants* una comparación con los honorarios actuales cargados por otros participantes en la industria ▲ *an insurance policy in the name of a specified plan participant* una política de seguros en el nombre de un participante de un plan específico ▲ *knowledgeable, willing market participants* participantes con

conocimiento del y atracción por el mercado

participating interest UK

= equity interest IAS/IFRS, equity investment IAS/IFRS, investment US

A participating interest is an interest held by an undertaking in the shares of another undertaking on a long-term basis for the purpose of securing a contribution to its activities by the exercise of control or influence arising from or related to that interest.

inversión de control

= participación de control

▲ *exercise the voting right attaching to the participating interest* ejercer el derecho de voto unido a la inversión de control ▲ *foreign participating interests* inversiones de control extranjeras ▲ *hold a participating interest* mantener una participación de control ▲ *hold a participating interest in an enterprise* mantener una inversión de control en una empresa ▲ *income from participating interests* ingresos procedentes de inversiones de control ▲ *participating interest of a temporary nature* inversión de control de una naturaleza temporaria ▲ *participating interests in associates* inversiones de control en asociadas ▲ *participating interests in subsidiaries* inversiones de control en filiales ▲ *the amount of the dividends relating to the participating interest* la cantidad de los dividendos relacionados con la inversión de control ▲ *the book value of a participating interest* el valor en libros de una inversión de control ▲ *the purchase price of the participating interests* el precio de compra de las inversiones de control ▲ *value adjustments in respect of participating interests* ajustes de valor con respecto a las participaciones de control

participating preference share UK

= participating preferred stock US

With a participating preference share the holders are entitled to any ordinary dividend declared in addition to the fixed preference dividend.

acción con derecho a cobro de dividendo preferente

▲ *acquire participating preference shares* adquirir acciones con derecho a cobro de dividendo preferente

participating preferred stock US

= participating preference share UK

Holders of participating preferred stock are entitled to any ordinary dividend declared in addition to the fixed preference dividend.

acción con derecho a cobro de dividendo preferente

▲ *convertible participating preferred stock* acción con derecho a cobro de dividendo preferente convertible

participative budgeting

Participative budgeting is a budgeting process in which involved employees take an active part in the budget preparation.

elaboración participativa del presupuesto

▲ *advantages and disadvantages of participative budgeting* ventajas y desventajas de la elaboración participativa del presupuesto ▲ *the effects of participative budgeting* los efectos de la elaboración participativa del presupuesto

partly owned

= not wholly owned, partially-owned IAS/IFRS, US

≠ wholly owned

Partly owned is used about something of which the ownership is divided between two or more owners, e.g. a company may be owned by several persons or enterprises that each hold a number of shares in the company.

propiedad parcial

▲ *a partly owned company* una empresa de propiedad parcial ▲ *partly owned subsidiaries* filiales de propiedad parcial ▲ *the contribution of the partly owned subsidiaries to consolidated equity* la contribución de las filiales de propiedad parcial al patrimonio consolidado ▲ *the contribution of the partly owned subsidiaries to consolidated profit* la contribución de las filiales de propiedad parcial al beneficio consolidado

partner

A partner is one of the owners of a partnership that has been formed to carry on business with a view to profit.

socio

▲ *the continuing partner* el socio que continua ▲ *the incoming partner* el socio entrante ▲ *the outgoing partner* el socio saliente ▲ *the surviving partner* el socio superviviente

⇛ partnership

partner company

A partner company is a company that cooperates with another company in some activity or towards common goals, typically sharing profits and losses.

empresa partícipe

partnership

= general partnership, ordinary partnership

A partnership is a registered but unincorporated business organisation in which multiple individuals, called general partners, manage the business and are jointly and severally liable for its debts and obligations, whereas other individuals called limited partners have limited liability. A partnership is not a separate legal entity.

sociedad comanditaria

= sociedad en comandita

▲ *a financial partnership* una sociedad en comandita financiera ▲ *articles of partnership* estatutos de la sociedad comanditaria ▲ *competitive parity between corporations and partnerships* paridad competitiva entre corporaciones y sociedades comanditarias ▲ *dissolve a partnership* disolver una sociedad comanditaria ▲ *form a partnership* formar una sociedad comanditaria ▲ *organise an enterprise as a partnership* organizar una empresa como una sociedad comanditaria ▲ *the total external debt of the partnerships* la deuda total externa de las sociedades comanditarias

passing of risk

The passing of risk is the transfer of the risk from the seller to the buyer in connection with the sale of products.

transferencia del riesgo

▲ *the time of the passing of the risk* el momento de la transferencia del riesgo

passive

To be passive is to accept what happens without trying to control or change events or to react to things, or to not take part in making decisions.

pasivo

▲ *a passive investor* un inversor pasivo

past cost

= sunk cost

Past costs are costs which have been incurred at an earlier stage and therefore they are unavoidable and cannot be changed, which makes them irrelevant to decision-making. One example of past costs is the product developments costs of a product for which there is no demand. Such costs cannot influence a decision on new product development activities.

coste pasado

▲ *the amount of past costs* la cantidad de costes pasados

past due

A payment that is past due should already have been made.

en mora

= moroso

▲ *disclose an ageing of financial assets past due* publicar una clasificación de vencimiento de activos financieros en mora ▲ *financial assets that are neither past due nor impaired* activos financieros que no están ni en mora ni deteriorados ▲ *financial assets that are past due but not impaired* activos financieros que están en mora pero no provisionados

past equity method

The past equity method is applied in connection with acquisitions or mergers of enterprises under which an acquiring and an acquired enterprise can be identified. Under this method, no accounting item changes are made in the financial statements of the acquiring enterprise, however, a distribution of increases/decreases in the carrying amounts of assets and liabilities relative to the purchase price is made in the financial statements of the acquired enterprise and any resulting net balance is considered to be goodwill or negative goodwill.

método del valor contable

= método de valor contable

≠ método de adquisición, método de la adquisición

▲ *treat according to the past equity method* tratar de acuerdo con el método del valor contable ▲ *use the past equity method* utilizar el método del valor contable

past service cost

≠ current service cost IAS/IFRS

Past service cost is the change in the value of pension obligations earned by employees in prior accounting periods occurring in the current accounting period as pension benefits are implemented or changed. Past service cost may be positive if new pension benefits are implemented or existing benefits are improved, but it may also be negative if existing benefits are cut down.

coste de servicio pasado

= coste por servicio pasado

≠ coste por servicio actual

▲ *past service cost not yet recognised* coste de servicio pasado no reconocido todavía ▲ *past service cost that arose from benefit changes* coste de servicio pasado procedente de modificaciones en beneficio ▲ *past service cost to be recognised in later periods* coste de servicio pasado a ser imputado en ejercicios posteriores ▲ *recognise past service cost on a straight-line basis* reconocer el coste de servicio pasado según un método lineal ▲ *unrecognised past service cost* coste de servicio pasado no reconocido

SOURCE IAS 19, paragraph 7

patent

= patent right

A patent is the exclusive right to commercially exploit an invention for a specified period.

patente

▲ *acquired concessions, patents, licences, trademarks and similar rights* concesiones, patentes, licencias, marcas registradas y derechos similares adquiridos ▲ *acquired patents* adquirir patentes ▲ *active patents* patentes activas ▲ *additions of patents* sumas de patentes ▲ *amortisation of patents that are used to generate intangible assets* amortización de las patentes que se usan para generar activos intangibles ▲ *amortise acquired patents over periods up to 10 years* amortizar las patentes adquiridas en periodos de hasta diez años ▲ *development of patents* desarrollo de patentes ▲ *evaluate granted patents* evaluar las patentes otorgadas ▲ *infringe a patent* infringir una patente ▲ *infringement of a patent* incumplimiento de una patente ▲ *measure patents at cost* medir patentes al coste ▲ *number of granted patents* número de patentes otorgadas ▲ *number of registered patents with a term of 1 year or longer* número de patentes registradas con uno o más años de vigencia ▲ *patent pending* pendiente de patente ▲ *take out a patent* sacar una patente ▲ *the carrying amount of patents* el valor contable de las patentes

patent cost

Patent costs are those costs that are associated with obtaining a patent for an invention, for instance the costs of applying for the patent.

coste de patente

▲ *R&D expenses excluding patent costs as a percentage of revenue* Los gastos en I + D excluyendo costes de patente como un porcentaje de ingreso

patent right

= patent

A patent right is the exclusive right to commercially exploit an invention for a specified period.

derecho de patente

▲ *acquisition of a patent right* adquisición de un derecho de patente ▲ *holding of patent rights* mantenimiento de los derechos de patente ▲ *infringement of a patent right* incumplimiento de un derecho de patente

pay[1] *noun*

= payment

Pay is something paid for a purpose, especially as a salary or wage.

pago

= remuneración

▲ *pay administration* administración del pago ▲ *pay claim* reclamación del pago ▲ *pay comparability* comparabilidad del pago ▲ *pay policy* política de remuneración

pay[2] *verb*

pagar

1 To pay means to compensate another party for something provided by the other party or for the other party's loss, usually by giving a monetary amount.

pagar

▲ *a contractual obligation to pay cash or another financial asset* una obligación contractual para pagar en efectivo o con otro activo financiero ▲ *ability to pay* capacidad para pager ▲ *an obligation to pay future lease payments* una obligación a pagar los arrendamientos futuros ▲ *an obligation to pay guaranteed benefits* una obligación a pagar los beneficios garantizados ▲ *assume a contractual obligation to pay the cash flows to one or more recipients* asumir una obligación contractual para pagar los flujos de efectivo a uno o más residentes ▲ *pay a contribution* pagar una contribución ▲ *pay contributions into an institution for occupational retirement provision* pagar contribuciones a una institución por obligaciones de jubilación ▲ *pay rent at market rates* pagar la renta a tipos de mercado ▲ *to pay expenses* pagar gastos

2 To pay means to give consideration to employees in return for work performed, e.g. in the form of fixed monetary amounts, bonuses or shares.

remunerar

▲ *pay the employees by way of shares* remunerar a los empleados por medio de acciones

3 When an investment or a project pays, it is profitable, i.e. it returns a profit in the form of e.g. interest, dividend or other yield.

ser rentable

= dar beneficio

▲ *a transaction that pays* una transacción que es rentable

pay interest on

To pay interest on a loan means paying an amount, the price of the loan, calculated as a percentage of the loan determined by the interest rate.

pagar intereses sobre

= pagar intereses de

▲ *pay interest on securities* pagar el interés de los títulos

payable[1] US, IAS/IFRS *noun*

= account payable IAS/IFRS, US, amount payable UK, US, creditor, amount falling due within one year UK

A payable is an amount owed to another party, often due in one year or less, e.g. accounts payable. It is presented as a liability in the balance sheet.

deuda

= cuenta a pagar obligatoria, cantidad a pagar

▲ *a long-term payable* una deuda a largo plazo ▲ *a short-term payable* una deuda a corto plazo ▲ *finance lease payables* deudas de arrendamiento financiero ▲ *non-trade payables* deudas no negociables ▲ *other payables* otras deudas ▲ *payables to mortgage credit institutions* deudas a instituciones de crédito hipotecario ▲ *recognise proposed dividends as a payable* reconocer los dividendos devengados como una deuda ▲ *total payables* total deudas

⇛ accrued expense, short-term debt

payable[2] *adjective*

= due

When an amount or a debt is payable it must be paid, often by a certain date.

pagadero

= a pagar

▲ *accounts and notes payable* cuentas y billetes a pagar ▲ *amount payable* cantidad a pagar ▲ *contingent consideration payable in a business combination* contraprestación contingente pagadera en una combinación de negocios ▲ *corporate income tax payable* impuesto de sociedades a pagar ▲ *dividends payable* dividendos a pagar ▲ *other claims payable* otras reclamaciones a pagar ▲ *payable on demand* pagadero a la demanda ▲ *the amount payable on demand* la cantidad a pagar a la demanda ▲ *the terms of the loans payable* los términos de los préstamos a pagar ▲ *US tax payable* impuesto norteamericano a pagar

payback method

The payback method is a method used in capital budgeting for choosing between various investment products. The number of years required for recovering the projected initial investment is found by dividing the initial investment by the increase in the expected cash flows per year. However, this method disregards the time value of money and any cash flows generated after the initial investment has been recovered.

método del periodo de retorno

▲ *advantages and disadvantages of the payback method* ventajas y desventajas del método del periodo de retorno ▲ *use the payback method* utilizar el método del periodo de retorno

⇛ payback period, payback time

payback period

= payback time, PP

A payback period refers to the period of time it will take to recover the initial monetary amount invested in an asset or project in the form of cost savings or cash inflows resulting from the investment.

periodo de retorno

▲ *a six-year payback period* un periodo de retorno de seis años ▲ *the calculation of a payback period* el cálculo de un periodo de retorno

payback time

= payback period

Payback time is the number of years it will take before an investment has been paid back, i.e. the original amount invested has been covered by cash inflows resulting from the investment.

tiempo de retorno

▲ *a long payback time* un tiempo de retorno largo ▲ *shorten the payback time* acortar el tiempo de retorno

PAYE tax UK

= tax at source UK, withholding tax US, IAS/IFRS

PAYE tax is income tax levied at source under the British PAYE system where an employer withholds and deducts tax from an employee's wages or occupational pension and pays that tax directly to the tax authorities (HM Revenue & Customs) on behalf of the employee.

impuesto en origen

▲ *calculate PAYE tax* calcular el impuesto en origen ▲ *offset against PAYE tax* compensar contra el impuesto en origen

payment

1 = pay

Payment is an amount of money transferred as consideration for services, i.e. remuneration, or the act of paying the amount.

pago

▲ *payment agreement* acuerdo de pago

2 Payment is the transfer of cash from an enterprise at a particular time to a creditor or as consideration for a product or service rendered.

pago

▲ *a cash payment* un pago en efectivo

3 Payment is the transfer of cash to the enterprise from a debtor.

abono

▲ *a voluntary payment* un abono voluntario

4 = provision

Payment is the procurement or provision of consideration in exchange for something.

desembolso

▲ *payment against monetary consideration* desembolso contra contraprestación monetaria

⇛ provision

5 Payment is the act of paying a fee or other consideration for a service rendered.

pago

▲ *make a payment* hacer un pago

6 Payment means the act of paying for something or the actual amount paid.

pago

▲ *any payment made on settlement* cualquier pago hecho a la cancelación ▲ *cash payment* pago en efectivo ▲ *in return for a payment or a series of payments* retorno por un pago o una serie de pagos ▲ *payment for the delivery of goods or services* pago por el envío de bienes o servicios ▲ *the counterparty's right to demand payment in cash* el derecho de la contraparte a demandar el pago en efectivo

7 Payment means the settlement of expenditure.

pago

▲ *full payment of non-accrual loans* pago completo de préstamos no devengados

payment date

= date of payment

The payment date is the date on which payment is made.

fecha de pago

▲ *expected payment date* fecha de pago esperada ▲ *mismatch between the repricing and payment dates* desajuste entre las fechas de pago y de retarificación ▲ *the exchange rate at the payment date* el tipo de cambio a la fecha del pago ▲ *the payment dates of the hedging instruments* las fechas de pago de los instrumentos de cobertura

payment guarantee

A guarantee provided as security for the payment of an obligation is called a payment guarantee.

garantía de pago

▲ *issue a payment guarantee* emitir una garantía de pago ▲ *obtain a payment guarantee* obtener una garantía de pago ▲ *payment guarantees provided* garantías de pago ofrecidas

payment obligation

A payment obligation is an obligation of a person or enterprise to make payment of a specified amount of money on a specified future date to a creditor.

obligación de pago

▲ *long-term payment obligations* obligaciones de pago a largo ▲ *recognise a payment obligation as a liability in the balance sheet* reconocer una obligación de pago como un pasivo en el balance ▲ *short-term payment obligations* obligaciones de pago a corto

payment of interest

Payment of interest must be effected by a borrower in connection with the servicing of a debt. The interest depends on the level of the interest rate on the loan.

pago del interés

= pago de intereses ▲ *defer payment of interest* diferir el pago del interés ▲ *early payment of interest* pago del interés anticipado ▲ *late payment of interest* último pago de intereses ▲ *make a payment of interest* hacer un pago de intereses ▲ *payment of interest and principal* pago del interés y principal ▲ *timely payment of interest* primer pago del interés

payment on account UK

= part payment

Payment on account is part payment e.g. as an instalment of the total amount that needs to be paid, or advance payment made before a product is delivered or a piece of work completed.

pago a cuenta

▲ *current payments on account* pagos a cuenta corrientes

payment service

Payment services refer to the services of transferring funds from payers' accounts to payees' accounts offered by financial institutions or other providers of payment solutions.

servicio de pago

▲ *fee and commission income from payment services* ingreso por tasas y comisiones procedentes de los servicios de pago ▲ *improved payment services* servicios de pago mejorados

payments received on account UK

"Payments received on account" is an item under creditors: amounts falling due within one year or under creditors: amounts falling due after more than one year –depending on whether short-or long-term– in the balance sheet according to the Companies Act 2006 required report format. This item recognised amounts prepaid by customers before delivery of products or services ordered.

pagos recibidos a cuenta

▲ *net of payments received on account* neto de pagos recibidos a cuenta

payments system

A payments system is (1) a system for handling the enterprise's payment transactions and (2) an electronic or a paper-backed mechanism for moving payments and money among financial institutions.

sistema de pagos

▲ *operate a payments system* operar un sistema de pagos

payout ratio US

≠ dividend cover

The payout ratio is an indicator of dividend policy and shows the percentage of profit paid out in dividends to shareholders and is calculated as dividend paid divided by profit attributable to equity holders of the parent multiplied by 100. The reciprocal of this measure is dividend cover. The payout ratio must be seen in connection with other ways of channelling money back to shareholders, e.g. dividend yield and share buybacks.

ratio de distribución de dividendos

= cobertura de dividendo, índice de dividendos a beneficios, índice de dividendos a ganancias

▲ *adopt a payout ratio* adoptar un ratio de distribución de dividendos ▲ *have a high payout ratio* tener un ratio de distribución de dividendos alto ▲ *payout ratio in %* ratio de distribución de dividendos en % ▲ *recommend a payout ratio of 25-30% of the net income for the year* recomendar una cobertura de dividendo del 25-30% del beneficio neto para el año ▲ *set targets for the payout ratio* fijar objetivos para la cobertura de dividendo

⇛ dividend yield, share buyback

payroll

1 A payroll is an employer's record of the total wages and salaries paid in a given period or payable to employees including a list of the employees.

nómina

▲ *be on the company's payroll* estar en la nómina de la empresa ▲ *the company had a large payroll* la compañía tenía muchos empleados ▲ *the company had a long payroll* había muchos empleados en la nómina de la empresa

2 → payroll cost

payroll cost

= cost of labour, payroll

Payroll costs constitute the consideration an employer must give in return for services provided by employees such as wages and salaries or overtime, holiday and sickness pay.

coste laboral

▲ *a significant proportion of total payroll costs* una proporción significativa de costes laborales totales ▲ *a specified percentage of payroll costs* un porcentaje especificado de costes laborales ▲ *change in payroll costs included in inventories* cambios en los costes laborales incluidos en inventarios ▲ *increased payroll costs* costes laborales incrementados ▲ *internal payroll costs* costes laborales internos

payroll fringe cost

Payroll fringe costs constitute an enterprise's costs for fringe benefits, i.e. non-cash benefits which employees are offered apart from their salaries or wages such as a company car, low-cost meals, health plans etc.

coste laboral en especie

▲ *a decrease in payroll fringe costs* un descenso en los costes laborales en especie ▲ *additional payroll fringe costs* costes laborales en especie adicionales ▲ *reduce payroll fringe costs by 10%* reducir los costes laborales en especie en un 10% ▲ *total payroll fringe costs* total costes laborales en especie

payroll liability

Payroll liability is an item in the balance sheet under liabilities showing wages and salaries payable to employees.

remuneración pendiente de pago

= pasivo laboral

▲ *a chart of accounts for payroll liabilities* un esquema de cuentas para las remuneraciones pendientes de pago ▲ *the amount of payroll liabilities* la cuantía de las remuneraciones pendientes de pago

pc

= p.c., PC, per cent

pc is the abbreviation for per cent. One per cent is one hundredth of an amount

por ciento

PC

= p.c., pc, per cent

PC is the abbreviation for per cent. One per cent is one hundredth of an amount.

por ciento

PCF

= price/cash flow

PCF is the abbreviation for price/cash flow, a financial ratio defined as the market price per share divided by the cash flow per share that measures the market's expectations regarding an enterprise's future financial health.

ratio precio/flujo de efectivo

= ratio precio por flujo de efectivo, ratio precio/cash flow

▲ *calculate PCF* calcular el ratio precio/flujo de efectivo ▲ *PCF calculations* cálculos del ratio precio/flujo de efectivo

PE

= PER, price/earnings ratio

PE is an abbreviation for price/earnings ratio or P/E ratio defined as the market price per share divided by EPS.

PER

= precio por beneficio, ratio precio/beneficio por acción

▲ *calculate PE* calcular el PER ▲ *PE calculations* cálculos del PER

peak-load pricing

Peak-load pricing is an enterprise's policy for determining prices involving higher prices to be charged in periods with higher demand from customers for products or services, i.e. peak periods. Peak-load pricing is typically used in the airline industry.

sistema de fijación del precio punta

= sistema de fijación del precio en temporada alta

▲ *systematic peak-load pricing* sistema de fijación sistemática del precio punta

peanut-butter costing US

= cost smoothing

Peanut-butter costing is a costing method according to which resource costs are allocated evenly on all cost objects on the basis of broad averages even though the individual products, services or customers are not equally resource demanding.

sistema de reparto uniforme del coste

= sistema de reparto uniforme de los costes

▲ *use peanut-butter costing* utilizar el sistema de reparto uniforme del coste

peer company

= comparator company

A peer company is an enterprise that is comparable with another enterprise because it operates within the same industry and has more or less the same size, therefore constituting a useful benchmark for analyses of performance and other criteria.

empresa de referencia

▲ *a peer company that is listed* una empresa de referencia que está cotizada ▲ *choice of peer company* elección de una empresa de referencia ▲ *outperform the peer company* mejorar los resultados de la empresa de referencia

⇛ peer group

peer group

A peer group is a number of enterprises or competitors that are comparable because they operate within the same industry and have more or less the same size, therefore constituting a useful benchmark for analyses of performance and other criteria.

grupo de referencia

▲ *an appropriately comparable peer group* un grupo de referencia adecuadamente comparable ▲ *peer group experience* la experiencia del grupo de referencia

pending

Pending means waiting to happen or not yet dealt with or settled.

pendiente de

▲ *pending law suits* pendiente de demandas judiciales ▲ *pending litigation* pendiente de litigio ▲ *pending the identification of impairment losses on individual assets in the group of financial assets* pendiente de la identificación de pérdidas por deterioro de activos individuales en el grupo de activos financieros

pension

= pension benefit

A pension is an amount that is paid regularly to a retired person by the government, a pension fund, an enterprise or a financial institution.

pensión

▲ *be entitled to pension* tener derecho a una pensión ▲ *life-contingent annuities and pensions* pensiones y anualidades de seguros de vida ▲ *pensions and other employee benefits to be paid in cash* pensiones y otras prestaciones a empleados que se pagan en efectivo ▲ *provisions for pensions and other post retirement benefits* provisiones para pensiones y otras prestaciones de jubilación ▲ *the cost of providing pensions* el coste de las pensiones

pension benefit UK, IAS/IFRS

A pension benefit refers to any type of payment to which a retired person or that person's beneficiary is or may become entitled under the terms of a pension plan. Typically, pension benefits are monthly or other periodic payments but may also be lump sums.

prestación de jubilación

= beneficio por retiro, prestación por retiro

NOTE Spanish accountants do not use the IAS/IFRS term

'beneficio' referring to this concept. They always use 'prestación'.

▲ *actuarial present value of promised pension benefits* valor actuarial presente de las prestaciones de jubilación prometidas ▲ *be entitled to a pension benefit* tener derecho a una prestación por jubilación ▲ *funded pension benefits* prestaciones de jubilación provisionadas ▲ *pension benefit costs* costes de la prestación de jubilación

pension benefit plan

= employee benefit plan, post-employment benefit plan IAS/IFRS, retirement benefit plan

A pension benefit plan is an arrangement under which an enterprise provides monetary benefits such as lump sums or periodic payments for its employees on or after retirement.

plan de pensiones

▲ *a supplemental pension benefit plan* un plan de pensiones suplementario ▲ *a tax-qualified pension benefit plan* un plan de pensiones fiscalmente cualificado ▲ *an employee pension benefit plan* un plan de pensiones para los empleados

pension contribution

A pension contribution is a payment made into a pension scheme by the emloyer and the employee.

contribución al plan de pensiones

▲ *annual pension contributions* contribuciones al plan de pensiones anuales ▲ *pension contributions receivable from employers* contribuciones al plan de pensiones procedentes de los empresarios ▲ *pension contributions receivable from members* contribuciones al plan de pensiones procedentes de los partícipes ▲ *pension contributions to defined benefits schemes* contribuciones al plan de pensiones a planes de prestaciones definidas ▲ *pension contributions to defined contributions schemes* contribuciones al plan de pensiones a planes de aportaciones definidas

pension cost

Pension costs are costs which relate to pension benefits to employees and which are incurred by an enterprise due to legislation, collective agreements or under its occupational pension schemes.

coste del plan de pensiones

▲ *accrued pension costs* costes del plan de pensiones devengados ▲ *assess pension costs using the projected unit credit method* evaluar los costes del plan de pensiones utilizando el método de unidad de crédito proyectada

pension fund UK, IAS/IFRS

A pension fund is a separate legal entity containing assets designated to provide payment of pension benefits to employees.

fondo de pensiones

▲ *allocation to the pension fund* asignación al fondo de pensiones

pension obligation

= pension liability

A pension obligation is the obligation of an enterprise to pay benefits to employees on or after retirement under a pension scheme.

obligación por pensiones

▲ *measure the pension obligation as the present value of the estimated future cash outflows* medir la obligación por pensiones al valor actual de los flujos de salida futuros estimados

pension plan

= pension scheme

A pension plan is an arrangement established for the purpose of providing for the payment of pension benefits to employees or their beneficiaries upon retirement. Depending on the type of plan, both employers and employees may contribute.

plan de pensiones

▲ *contributions to defined contribution pension plans* contribuciones a los planes de pensiones de aportaciones definidas ▲ *final salary pension plans* planes de pensiones de salario final ▲ *flat salary pension plans* planes de pensiones de salario fijo

pension provision

A pension provision is an amount set aside for the future payment of pension benefits to employees. The amount is recognised in the balance sheet.

provisión para pensiones

▲ *return on pension provisions* rendimiento de las provisiones para pensiones

pension scheme UK

= post-employment benefit plan IAS/IFRS

A pension scheme is an arrangement with the purpose of providing members with pensions and/or other benefits when they leave service or retire. Pension schemes may provide a pension for dependants of members that are deceased.

plan de pensiones

▲ *compulsory employment-related pension schemes* planes de pensiones relacionados con el empleo obligatorios ▲ *compulsory pension schemes* planes de pensiones obligatorios ▲ *institutions operating occupational pension schemes* las instituciones que gestionan planes de pensiones ocupacionales ▲ *occupational pension scheme* plan de pensiones acupacional ▲ *pension scheme accounting* contabilidad del plan de pensiones ▲ *the financial, technical and other risks associated with the pension scheme* el riesgo financiero, técnico y otros riesgos asociados con el plan de pensiones ▲ *the nature of the pension scheme* la naturaleza del plan de pensiones ▲ *the pension schemes operated by the pension fund* los planes de pensiones gestionados por el fondo de pensiones

pensions and similar obligations UK

"Pensions and similar obligations" is an item under provisions for liabilities in the balance sheet according to the Companies Act 2006 required report format. This item recognises pension liabilities provided for.

pensiones y obligaciones similares

▲ *details of pensions and similar obligations* detalles de pensiones y obligaciones similares ▲ *provisions for pensions and similar obligations* provisiones para pensiones y obligaciones similares

PER

= P/E, price/earnings ratio

PER is an abbreviation for price/earnings ratio or P/E ratio defined as the market price per share divided by earnings per share (EPS). This investment ratio, also referred to as the earnings multiple, compares the market price of an ordinary share with the EPS and is used to analyse the performance potential of a company. A high P/E ratio indicates future earnings growth and signals that investors have high confidence in the company.

PER

= precio por beneficio, ratio precio/beneficio

▲ *the historic PER* el PER histórico ▲ *the prospective PER* el PER prospectivo

per cent

= p.c., pc, PC

One per cent is one hundredth of an amount.

por ciento

▲ *between 70 and 90 per cent of the goods* entre el 70 y el 90 por ciento de los bienes ▲ *less than 10 per cent* menos del 10 por ciento

percent US

= p.c., pc, PC, per cent UK

One percent is one hundredth of an amount.

por ciento

▲ *a 10 percent discount* un descuento del 10 por ciento ▲ *between 70 and 90 percent of the goods* entre el 70 y el 90 por ciento de los bienes ▲ *less than 10 percent* menos del 10 por ciento ▲ *percent of sales* por ciento de ventas

percentage

A percentage is an amount expressed in per cent.

porcentaje

▲ *a percentage change* un cambio de porcentaje ▲ *a statement in percentage terms* un estado en términos de porcentaje ▲ *depreciate assets using a fixed percentage* amortizar activos utilizando un porcentaje fijo ▲ *the percentage of voting equity instruments acquired* el porcentaje de los instrumentos de patrimonio con derecho a voto adquiridos ▲ *the percentage of voting shares acquired* el porcentaje de las acciones con derecho a voto adquiridas ▲ *the performance made as a percentage of the total performance* el resultado medido como un porcentaje del total

percentage of completion method IAS/IFRS

The percentage of completion method is a method of revenue recognition, typically used for long-term contracts, according to which revenues and expenses are recognised in the profit and loss account as the work is done over the term of the contract. When the percentage of completion method is applied, the work in progress is measured at the calculated selling price of the completed proportion of the work and the stage of completion and recognised as such in the balance sheet.

método del porcentaje de realización

▲ *apply the percentage of completion method* aplicar el método del porcentaje de realización ▲ *recognise something on the percentage of completion method* reconocer algo según el método del porcentaje de realización ▲ *requirement of using the percentage of completion method* requisito para la utilización del método del porcentaje de realización ▲ *under the percentage of completion method* según el método del porcentaje de realización ▲ *use the percentage of completion method to determine the appropriate amount of revenue* utilizar el método del porcentaje de realización para determinar la cantidad de ingreso adecuada

⇛ completed-contract method

percentage point

A percentage point is a measure showing the difference between two percentages, e.g. 3 percentage points is the difference between 2% and 5%.

punto porcentual

▲ *a difference of 2 percentage points* una diferencia de 2 puntos porcentuales ▲ *cut interest rates by one-half percentage point from 6.0% to 5.5%* recortar los tipos de interés en medio punto porcentual desde el 6 por ciento al 5,5 por ciento

⇛ basis point

percentage-of-completion method

US, UK

The percentage-of-completion method is a method of revenue recognition, typically used for long-term contracts, according to which revenues and expenses are recognised in the profit and loss account as the work is done over the term of the contract. When the percentage-of-completion method is applied, the work in progress is measured at the calculated selling price of the completed proportion of the work and the stage of completion and recognised as such in the balance sheet.

método del porcentaje de terminación

= método del porcentaje de realización

▲ *under the percentage-of-completion method* según el método del porcentaje de terminación ▲ *use the percentage-of-completion method* utilizar el método del porcentaje de terminación

⇛ completed-contract method

perfect competition

≠ imperfect competition

Perfect competition is a market situation where the individual buyer or seller counts on being able to buy or sell discretionary amounts of a product or service at market price without causing that price to change.

competencia perfecta

▲ *assume perfect competition* presuponer competencia perfecta ▲ *create conditions of perfect competition* crear las condiciones de competencia perfecta ▲ *general equilibrium with perfect competition* equilibrio general en competencia perfecta

perfection standard

= ideal standard

Perfection standards set as their goal peak performance under perfect operating conditions based on existing specifications and equipment and do not allow for defective materials, waste or machine breakdowns. Being extremely difficult to live up to, perfection standards are not favoured by employees who find them demotivating as they set unrealistic benchmarks.

norma ideal

▲ *comply with a perfection standard* cumplir con una norma ideal ▲ *live up to a perfection standard* estar a la altura de una norma ideal ▲ *the old perfection standard* la norma ideal antigua

⇛ currently attainable standard, flexible budget, normal standard

performance

1 Performance is a measure of how effectively a job has been

done and is e.g. an important factor when assessing the total productivity of a system. Financial performance measures look at e.g. economic value added and return on invested capital.

rendimiento

= desempeño

▲ *improve or enhance the asset's performance* mejorar o aumentar el rendimiento del activo ▲ *maintain the asset at its standard of performance* mantener el activo en su estándar de rendimiento ▲ *performance under an option contract* rendimiento según un contrato de opciones ▲ *the economic performance of the asset* el rendimiento económico del activo

⇛ economic value added, ROIC

2 = results

The performance of an enterprise refers to its profit, income or loss for an accounting period. The operating performance can be measured by looking at the EBITA or the return on operating invested capital excluding goodwill.

resultados

NOTE Always plural in Spanish accounting texts.

▲ *assess the performance of the joint venture* evaluar los resultados de la joint venture ▲ *assess the performance of the separate activities of a bank* evaluar los resultados de las actividades separadas de un banco ▲ *disclose the components of financial performance* publicar los componentes de los resultados financieros ▲ *relevant to an understanding of the combined entity's financial performance* relevante para el entendimiento de los resultados financieros de la combinación de negocios ▲ *the financial position and financial performance of the entity* la posición financiera y los resultados financieros de la entidad ▲ *the performance of a specified pool of contracts* los resultados de un conjunto específico de contratos

⇛ EBITA, return on invested capital

performance appraisal

= performance evaluation

A performance appraisal is an appraisal of the performance results achieved by an employee, a department or an enterprise based on a comparison of achieved performance goals and predefined, expected performance goals.

valoración de los resultados

= evaluación de los rendimientos, evaluación de rendimientos, valoración de resultados

▲ *annual performance appraisal* valoración de los resultados anuales ▲ *performance appraisal interview* entrevista para la valoración de los resultados ▲ *the results of the performance appraisal* los resultados de la evaluación de rendimientos

performance audit

= management audit, value for money audit

A performance audit is a review of the effectiveness of managers in achieving and implementing entity objectives, policies and procedures specified by top management to identify potential weaknesses.

auditoría de resultados

= auditoría de actividad, auditoría de los resultados, evaluación de los resultados, evaluación de resultados

▲ *a typical performance audit question* una pregunta típica de auditoría de resultados ▲ *conduct a performance audit* llevar a cabo una auditoría de resultados ▲ *extended performance audit* auditoría de resultados completa ▲ *follow-up performance audit* controlar la auditoría de resultados ▲ *ongoing performance audit* auditoría de resultados en marcha ▲ *the positive outcome of the performance audit* el resultado positivo de la auditoría de la actividad ▲ *the results of our performance audit* los resultados de la auditoría de la actividad

performance evaluation

= performance appraisal

A performance evaluation is an evaluation of the performance results achieved by an employee, a department or an enterprise based on a comparison of achieved performance goals and predefined, expected performance goals.

evaluación de resultados

= evaluación de los resultados, evaluación de los rendimintos, evaluación de rendimientos

▲ *annual performance evaluation* evaluación de resultados anual ▲ *performance evaluation interview* entrevista de evaluación de resultados ▲ *the results of the performance evaluation* los resultados de la evaluación de resultados

performance report US

A performance report gives feedback by comparing results with plans, highlighting variances.

informe de resultados

▲ *prepare a performance report* preparar un informe de resultados ▲ *the annual performance report* el informe de resultados anual

performance-related pay

= merit pay

Performance-related pay takes place when employees or managers are renumerated on the basis of their individual results and performance as well as the resulting positive contributions to the enterprise's results.

retribución por objetivos

= retribución en función de objetivos

▲ *determination of performance-related pay* determinación de la retribución por objetivos

performance-related pay scheme

= merit pay scheme

A performance-related pay scheme is an agreement between an enterprise and its employees or managers under which they are renumerated on the basis of their individual results and performance as well as the resulting positive contributions to the enterprise's results.

plan de retribución por objetivos

= plan de retribución en función de objetivos

▲ *development of performance-related pay schemes* desarrollo de los planes de retribución por objetivos ▲ *implementation of performance-related pay schemes* implementación de los planes de retribución por objetivos ▲ *launch a performance-related pay scheme* lanzar un plan de retribución por objetivos

period

A period is a time span, for accounting purposes understood as the period for which an enterprise prepares its financial statements, e.g. a quarter of a year, half a year or a whole year.

periodo

= ejercicio

▲ *an ownership period of three years* un periodo de propiedad de tres años ▲ *at the beginning and the end of the period* al inicio y final del periodo ▲ *complete a specified period of service* completar un periodo especificado de servicio ▲ *impairment losses recognised in profit or loss during the period* pérdidas por deterioro reconocidas en resultados durante el periodo ▲ *preceding periods* periodos anteriores ▲ *the period covered by the first IFRS financial statements* el periodo abarcado por los primeros estados financieros según NIIFs ▲ *the period over which future economic benefits will be received by the entity* el periodo durante el cual los beneficios económicos futuros serán cobrados por la entidad ▲ *the period over which the entity expects to use the asset* el periodo durante el cual la entidad espera utilizar el activo ▲ *the periods covered by the first financial statements prepared under IASs* los periodos abarcados por los primeros estados financieros preparados según NICs

period between balance sheet dates

The period between balance sheet dates is the period for which an enterprise prepares its balance sheet, running from the opening balance sheet date to the closing balance sheet date at which date total assets, liabilities and equity are shown. The period typically covers a year, half a year or a quarter.

periodo entre las fechas del balance

▲ *the auditor's working conditions during the period between balance sheet dates* las condiciones de trabajo del auditor durante el periodo entre las fechas del balance

period cost

≠ inventoriable cost

Period costs are fixed costs that are charged as incurred on a time basis and not related to output or assets. Examples are selling and marketing costs, depreciation and administrative expenses.

coste periódico

▲ *account for as period costs* contabilizar como costes periódicos ▲ *total period costs* total costes periódicos

period earnings US

→ net income[2]

period of ownership

= ownership period

A period of ownership refers to a period in which a natural or legal person owns or has owned an asset.

periodo de propiedad

▲ *a 3-year period of ownership* un periodo de propiedad de tres años

period of time

= period, span

A period of time is a span of time of a certain length and duration, beginning at a particular time and ending at another time, lasting e.g. one or more minutes, days, months or years.

periodo de tiempo

▲ *a period of time that extends beyond the end of the reporting period* un periodo de tiempo que va más allá del periodo que cubre el informe ▲ *a specified period of time* un periodo de tiempo especificado ▲ *a substantial period of time* un periodo de tiempo sustancial ▲ *for a reasonable period of time* durante un periodo de tiempo razonable

periodic

= periodical

Periodic means recurring or reappearing at regular intervals over a period of time.

periódico

▲ *a constant periodic rate of interest* un tipo de interés periódico constante ▲ *a constant periodic rate of return on the lessor's net investment in the finance lease* una tasa de rendimiento periódica constante de la inversión neta del arrendador del arrendamiento financiero ▲ *a periodic average price* un precio medio periódico ▲ *periodic costs* costes periódicos ▲ *periodic expenses* gastos periódicos ▲ *periodic payments* pagos periódicos ▲ *provide assistance on a periodic basis* ofrecer asistencia de forma periódica ▲ *the amount of the periodic consumption of an asset* la cantidad del consumo periódico de un activo

permanent difference UK

A permanent difference is a difference between an accounting profit or loss and a taxable profit or loss arising because particular income or expenses are non-deductible for tax purposes or tax-exempt. Entertainment expenses are an example of expenses that give rise to a permanent difference.

diferencia permanente

▲ *result in a permanent difference* dar como resultado una diferencia permanente ▲ *treat as a permanent difference* tratar como una diferencia permanente

SOURCE FRS 19, paragraph 2

⇛ temporary difference, timing difference

permanent establishment

A permanent establishment refers to a fixed and permanent place of business through which the operations and activities of an enterprise are wholly or partly carried on. Permanent establishments include head office and other offices, branches, plants and workshops, but the activities must have a certain scope and intensity, which means that e.g. storing facilities and other facilities of a preparatory character are not included. If an enterprise has a permanent establishment in a country, it is liable to pay tax in that country.

establecimiento permanente

▲ *a permanent establishment exists* un establecimiento permanente existe ▲ *alienation of a permanent establishment* alienación de un establecimiento permanente ▲ *allocation of income between a permanent establishment and a head office* asignación de ingresos entre un establecimiento permanente y una oficina principal ▲ *be attributable to the permanent establishment* ser atribuible al establecimiento permanente ▲ *be effectively connected with the permanent establishment* estar efectivamente conectado con el establecimiento permanente ▲ *constitute a permanent establishment* constituir un establecimiento permanente ▲ *determine the business profits of a permanent establishment* determinar los beneficios empresariales de un establecimiento permanente ▲ *have a permanent establishment* tener un establecimiento permanente ▲ *operate through a permanent establishment* operar a través de un establecimiento permanente ▲ *the profits derived from the assets or activities of the permanent establishment* los beneficios derivados de los activos o actividades del establecimiento permanente

perpetual budgeting
= continual budgeting, continuous budgeting
Perpetual budgeting is a budgeting process which is followed-up on a current basis, so that the budget is updated every month or quarter by adding another monthly or quarterly period to the end of the budget ensuring that the budget will always be updated for a minimum of 12 months.
fijación continua del presupuesto
▲ *the purpose of perpetual budgeting* el propósito de la fijación continua del presupuesto

personnel expenses
= employee expense US, staff cost, staff expense
Personnel expenses are the costs of an enterprise relating to salaries, wages, pension costs, uniforms, training etc.
gastos de personal
= gastos del personal
▲ *other personnel expenses* otros gastos de personal ▲ *profit-related personnel expenses* gastos de personal relacionados con beneficios ▲ *specification of personnel expenses* especificación de los gastos del personal

phantom share
Phantom shares constitute a notional or hypothetical amount of shares, representing a bonus awarded as an incentive to management executives and other employees subject to achievement of certain performance goals and/or stock market appreciation of the company's share price. Therefore, phantom shares are not actual shares, but rather a type of compensation that will not involve any loss for the executive or employee.
acción fantasma
= acción ficticia
▲ *phantom shares not involving the issuance of common shares* acciones fantasmas que no implican la emisión de acciones comunes ▲ *taxation of phantom shares* gravación fiscal de las acciones fantasmas
⇛ notional share

phantom stock US
Phantom stock constitutes notional or hypothetical shares of stock, representing a bonus awarded as an incentive to management executives and other employees subject to achievement of certain performance goals and/or stock market appreciation of the company's stock price. Therefore, phantom stock will not confer any ownership in a company, but rather represents a type of compensation that will not involve any loss for the executive or employee.
acción fantasma
= acción ficticia
▲ *cash-settled phantom stock* acción fantasma pagada en efectivo ▲ *taxation of phantom stock* gravación fiscal de las acciones fantasmas

phase out
To phase out means to bring something to an end gradually.
eliminar gradualmente
▲ *phase out a project* eliminar gradualmente un proyecto ▲ *phase out over a period of 5 years* eliminar gradualmente durante un periodo de 5 años

plan asset
Plan assets refer to the assets under a pension plan comprising investments made from contributions as well as returns on such investments and monetary amounts representing contributions paid into the plan.
activo del plan de pensiones
▲ *determine the expected and actual return on plan assets* determinar el rendimiento esperado y actual de los activos del plan de pensiones ▲ *realised and unrealised gains on plan assets* ganancias realizadas y no realizadas en los activos del plan de pensiones ▲ *recognition and measurement of plan assets* reconocimiento y valoración de los activos del plan de pensiones ▲ *return on plan assets* rendimiento en los activos del plan de pensiones ▲ *the fair value of*

plan assets el valor razonable de los activos del plan de pensiones
⇛ plan obligation

plan obligation
A plan obligation is the liability to pay pension or other employee benefits to employees of an enterprise under a pension or other employee benefit plan, e.g. a defined contribution plan, a defined benefit plan or other post-employment benefit plan.
obligación del plan de pensiones
▲ *settle employee benefit plan obligations* pagar las obligaciones del plan de pensiones a los empleados ▲ *the value of plan obligations* el valor de las obligaciones del plan de pensiones ▲ *to discount plan obligations* para descontar las obligaciones del plan de pensiones
⇛ plan asset

plan of reorganisation UK
→ reorganisation plan

plan of reorganization US
→ reorganization plan

plant
= production facilities, production plant
A plant is a production facility consisting of buildings and machinery in which one or more production operations of an enterprise take place, e.g. manufacturing, packaging or labelling.
planta
= instalaciones
▲ *a worn-out plant* una planta vieja ▲ *acquisition of plant* adquisición de instalaciones ▲ *complex pieces of plant* partes complejas de la planta ▲ *construction of plant* construcción de la planta ▲ *costs of moving plant to and from the contract site* costes del traslado de la planta a y desde el sitio del contrato ▲ *damage of plant* daño de la planta ▲ *depreciation and write-downs of plant* amortización y eliminaciones de la planta ▲ *dismantling of plant* desmantelamiento de la planta ▲ *disposal of plant* eliminación de instalaciones ▲ *idle plant* planta ociosa ▲ *investments in plant* inversiones en instalaciones ▲ *lease of plant* arrendamiento de instalaciones ▲ *plant and machinery* instalaciones y maquinaria ▲ *plant capacity* capacidad de la planta ▲ *plant maintenance* mantenimiento de la planta ▲ *shut-down of plant* cierre de la planta ▲ *the normal capacity of the plant* la capacidad normal de la planta
⇛ plant and machinery

plant and equipment US
"Plant and equipment" refers to tangible fixed assets used in business operations.
instalaciones y equipos
= planta y equipo
NOTE Spanish accountants prefer 'instalaciones y equipos' (always plural) to the IAS/IFRS term 'planta y equipo'.
▲ *a damaged item of plant and equipment* una partida dañada de instalaciones y equipos ▲ *delivery of plant and equipment* entrega de instalaciones y equipos ▲ *disposal of plant and equipment* eliminación de instalaciones y equipos ▲ *maintenance of plant and equipment* mantenimiento de instalaciones y equipos ▲ *production of plant and equipment* producción de instalaciones y equipos ▲ *provide for advance depreciation of plant and equipment* provisionar por depreciación anticipada de instalaciones y equipos ▲ *the written-down tax value of the plant and equipment* el valor impositivo eliminado de instalaciones y equipos ▲ *write-off an item of plant and equipment* eliminar una partida de instalaciones y equipos

plant and machinery UK
"Plant and machinery" is an item under fixed assets in the balance sheet according to the Companies Act 2006 required report format.
instalaciones y maquinaria
= planta y maquinaria
NOTE Spanish accountants prefer 'instalaciones y maquinaria' to the IAS/IFRS term 'planta y maquinaria'.
▲ *a damaged item of plant and machinery* una partida dañada de instalaciones y maquinaria ▲ *delivery of plant and machinery* entrega de instalaciones y maquinaria ▲ *disposal of plant and machinery* eliminación de instalaciones y maquinaria ▲ *included in plant and machinery* in-

cluido en instalaciones y maquinaria ▲ *maintenance of plant and machinery* mantenimiento de instalaciones y maquinaria ▲ *production of plant and machinery* producción de instalaciones y maquinaria ▲ *provide for advance depreciation of an item of plant and machinery* provisionar anticipadamente por depreciación de una partida de instalaciones y maquinaria ▲ *the written-down tax value of the plant and machinery* el valor impositivo eliminado de instalaciones y maquinaria ▲ *write-off an item of plant and machinery* eliminar una partida de instalaciones y maquinaria

plant asset US

→ property, plant and equipment

plant manager

= factory manager

A plant manager is responsible for the day-to-day operations and financial performance of a plant or factory.

director de fábrica

▲ *appoint a new plant manager* nombrar un nuevo director de fábrica

PLC UK

= plc UK, public limited company UK

PLC is the abbreviation for public limited company. PLC appears after and as part of the firm name.

NOTE PLC is also seen spelled "plc".

SA

= Sociedad Anónima

▲ *incorporate a company as a PLC* transformar una empresa en SA

plc UK

= PLC UK, public limited company UK

The abbreviation "plc" stands for public limited company, appearing after and as part of the firm name.

NOTE "plc" is also seen spelled "PLC".

SA

= Sociedad Anónima

▲ *incorporate a company as a plc* transformar una empresa en una SA

policy

A policy is a written contract between an insurance company (the insurer) and the policyholder (the insured) specifying the terms of the insurance plan. Under this contract, the insurer accepts a risk and undertakes to indemnify the insured against specific damage, loss or liability resulting from certain events or to pay out compensation to the insured as a result of a certain event.

póliza

▲ *renew a policy* renovar una póliza ▲ *take out a policy* tomar un seguro ▲ *terminate a policy* finalizar una póliza ▲ *with profits policy* con póliza de beneficios

policy cost UK

= discretionary cost US, UK, managed cost UK, management cost US, programmed cost US, programmed fixed cost US

≠ committed cost US, UK

Policy costs are discretionary fixed costs that are determined by and change because of managerial decisions without any obvious relationship with capacity or production activity. Examples are marketing, training, research and development costs.

coste discrecional

≠ coste comprometido

▲ *calculate policy costs* calcular los costes discrecionales ▲ *the estimated policy costs* los costes discrecionales estimados

⇛ fixed cost

policyholder

The policyholder is the party (be it one or more persons, an enterprise or an institution) in an insurance arrangement who has a right to compensation from the insurer should an insured event occur.

tenedor del contrato

= tenedor de la póliza de seguros

▲ *a policyholder's option to surrender an insurance contract for a fixed amount* una opción del tenedor del contrato para rescatar un contrato de seguros por una cantidad fija ▲ *charge the policyholder for future services* cargar al tenedor del contrato por servicios futuros ▲ *compensate the policyholder for a pre-existing risk* compensar al tenedor del contrato por un riesgo pre-existente ▲ *compensation in cash or in kind to policyholders* compensación en efectivo o de

otro tipo a los tenedores del contrato ▲ *direct insurance contracts in which the entity is the policyholder* contratos de seguros directos en los que la entidad es el tenedor del contrato ▲ *guarantee a minimum rate of return to policyholders* garantizar una tasa de rendimiento mínima a los tenedores del contrato ▲ *investments for the benefit for life-assurance policyholders who bear the investment risk* inversiones para la prestación a los tenedores de pólizas de seguro de vida ▲ *reimburse the policyholder* reembolsar al tenedor del contrato ▲ *require an adverse effect on the policyholder* requerir un efecto adverso en el tenedor del contrato ▲ *the death of the policyholder* la muerte del tenedor del contrato
SOURCE IFRS 4, Appendix A

pooling of interests US
= merger accounting UK, uniting of interests IAS/IFRS
≠ acquisition accounting UK, purchase accounting IAS/IFRS
Pooling of interests is a combination of two companies arising from the issue of voting shares by the acquiring company in exchange for those of the acquired company so that all shareholders maintain their proportionate ownership in the combined company.
combinación de intereses
= método de fusión, método de la fusión
≠ método de adquisión, método de la adquisición
▲ *a pooling of interests of two equal parties* una combinación de intereses de dos partícipes iguales ▲ *an ongoing pooling of interests* una combinación de intereses en marcha ▲ *classify a business combination as a pooling of interests* clasificar una combinación de negocios como una combinación de intereses ▲ *the consolidated financial statements for the period in which the pooling of interests occurred* los estados financieros consolidados para el periodo en el que tuvo lugar la combinación de intereses ▲ *the pooling of interests of enterprises* la combinación de intereses de las empresas

pooling of interests method IAS/IFRS, US
→ pooling-of-interests method

pooling-of-interests accounting US, IAS/IFRS
= merger accounting UK, uniting of interests accounting IAS/IFRS
≠ acquisition accounting UK, purchase accounting US, IAS/IFRS
Pooling-of-interests accounting is a method of accounting used for business combinations if no acquirer or acquired party can be identified. Contrary to acquisition accounting, the assets and liabilities of the merging enterprises are combined at their existing carrying amounts and not at fair value. This method ensures that no enterprise can be identified as the acquirer. This way, no changes of accounting items are made, just as there is no recognition of goodwill or negative goodwill.
NOTE The pooling-of-interests method has been replaced by the purchase method of accounting.
método de combinación de intereses
= método de fusión, método de la fusión
≠ método de adquisición, método de la adquisición
▲ *allow pooling-of-interests accounting* permitir el método de combinación de intereses ▲ *application of pooling-of-interests accounting* aplicación del método de combinación de intereses ▲ *wealth effects of pooling-of-interests accounting* efectos riqueza del método de combinación de intereses

pooling-of-interests method US
= merger accounting method UK, merger method UK, uniting-of-interests method IAS/IFRS
≠ acquisition method UK, purchase method IAS/IFRS, US
The pooling-of-interests method is an accounting method applied in the US until 2001 in connection with business combinations. Under this method, all assets and liabilities in the acquired company were recognized at carrying value at the time of combination rather than at fair value and no good-

will was recorded. The acquiring company would issue common stock in exchange for the voting stock of the acquiree.

NOTE The pooling-of-interests method has been replaced by the purchase method of accounting.

método de combinación de intereses

= método de fusión, método de fusión de intereses, método de la combinación de intereses, método de la fusión de intereses, método de la fusión

≠ método de adquisición, método de la adquisición

▲ *allow the pooling-of-interests method* permitir el método de combinación de intereses ▲ *apply the pooling-of-interests method* aplicar el método de combinación de intereses

poorly capitalised UK

A company that is poorly capitalised has a loan capital relative to its equity exceeding the ratio of 4:1. In the case of multinational group companies, a company with an excessive controlled debt, i.e. intragroup loans provided by foreign companies or individuals with a controlling interest in that company, cannot deduct for tax purposes any interest expenses or capital losses relating to the exceeding amount of debt.

pobremente capitalizado

= riesgo de insolvencia

▲ *assess whether the company is poorly capitalised* examinar si la empresa está pobremente capitalizada

⇛ thin capitalisation

population

The population is the complete set of financial data from which an auditor selects sampling units in order to reach a conclusion.

población

▲ *division of the population into subpopulations* división de la población en subpoblaciones

⇛ audit sampling

portfolio

A portfolio is a person's or an enterprise's total holding of securities, loans or other financial assets, debts or liabilities at a given time.

cartera

▲ *a portfolio of fixed-rate assets* una cartera de activos de tipo fijo ▲ *a portfolio of fixed-rate liabilities* una cartera de pasivos a tipo fijo ▲ *a portfolio of forward contracts* una cartera de contrato de futuros ▲ *a portfolio of investment vehicles* una cartera de vehículos de inversión ▲ *a portfolio of licences* una cartera de licencias ▲ *a portfolio of patents* una cartera de patentes ▲ *a portfolio of prepayable loans* una cartera de préstamos pagados por anticipado ▲ *a portfolio of properties in different locations* una cartera de propiedades en diferentes lugares ▲ *a portfolio of qualifications* una cartera de títulos académicos ▲ *a portfolio of receivables* una cartera de deudores ▲ *a portfolio of securities* una cartera de títulos ▲ *accept a portfolio* aceptar una cartera ▲ *be part of a portfolio* integrar una cartera ▲ *buy a portfolio* comprar una cartera ▲ *consider the age of the loans within the portfolio* considerar la duración de los préstamos de la cartera ▲ *sell a portfolio* vender una cartera ▲ *the total held-to-maturity portfolio* el total de la cartera de títulos mantenidos hasta el vencimiento

portfolio hedge

A portfolio hedge is a way of securing a pool of assets or liabilities by ensuring that changes in the fair value of the portfolio are wholly or partly balanced through the use of hedging instruments.

cobertura de la cartera de inversiones

▲ *a portfolio hedge of interest rate risk* una cobertura de la cartera de inversiones contra el riesgo del tipo de interés ▲ *a portfolio hedge that has previously been accounted for as a cash flow hedge* una cobertura de la cartera de inversiones que ha sido previamente contabilizada como una cobertura del flujo de efectivo ▲ *portfolio hedge accounting of core deposits on a fair value measurement basis* cobertura de la cartera de inversiones para contabilizar los depósitos básicos según el método de valoración a valor razonable

▲ *the assets and liabilities included in the portfolio hedge* los activos y pasivos incluidos en la cobertura de la cartera de inversiones

portfolio of liabilities

A portfolio of liabilities is an enterprise's total pool of liabilities. Often, enterprises aim at putting together an optimal and low-cost portfolio of liabilities meant to finance the enterprise in conjunction with its shareholders' funds. An optimal portfolio of liabilities varies from enterprise to enterprise and is very dependent on the liquidity and gearing of the enterprise in different periods.

conjunto de pasivos

= cartera de pasivos

▲ *duration of the portfolio of liabilities* duración del conjunto de pasivos ▲ *include a currency in the portfolio of liabilities* incluir una divisa en el conjunto de pasivos ▲ *the total value of the portfolio of liabilities* el valor total de la cartera de pasivos

⇛ gearing

portfolio of mortgages

A portfolio of mortgages constitutes an enterprise's holding of mortgage deeds.

cartera hipotecaria

▲ *measurement of the enterprise's portfolio of mortgages at amortised cost* medición de la cartera hipotecaria de la empresa a coste amortizado

portfolio of securities

= securities portfolio

A portfolio of securities is a collection of securities held by a person or an enterprise at a given time. An enterprise recognises its portfolio of securities as assets in the balance sheet.

cartera de títulos

▲ *administration of a portfolio of securities* administración de una cartera de títulos ▲ *the return on a portfolio of securities* la rentabilidad de una cartera de títulos

position

1 A position is the placing of an enterprise and its products relative to another or other competing enterprises and their products. In this way, the position will reflect the strengths or weaknesses, opportunities or threats of an enterprise.

posición

▲ *a competitive position* una posición competitiva ▲ *a strategic position* una posición estratégica ▲ *hedge of an identifiable position* cobertura de una posición identificable ▲ *hold a leading position in a market* mantener una posición dominante en un mercado ▲ *strengthen one's position* fortalecer su posición ▲ *weaken one's position* debilitar su posición

2 A position states the extent of a commitment in a market in connection with a portfolio of securities, such as equities, bonds or other financial instruments, currencies or commodities. A position may be long, i.e. the portfolio exceeds the quantity agreed to be sold, it may be short, i.e. the agreed sales exceed the portfolio, or it may be open, i.e. the portfolio is unhedged or unsold. Market rises will be of an advantage to long positions, but at a disadvantage to short or open positions. Also, a position is a measure of the way in which changes in a financial variable (currency or interest) influences an enterprise's value in use or cash flows.

posición

▲ *rated positions* posiciones tasadas ▲ *the gain or loss on the net monetary position* el resultado de la posición monetaria neta ▲ *unrated positions* posiciones no tasadas

3 A position is a job, post or rank of an employee in an enterprise or organisation.

cargo

▲ *a prominent position* un cargo prominente ▲ *an executive position* un cargo ejecutivo ▲ *take up a new position* solicitar un nuevo cargo

positive

When an amount is positive, the value is above zero.

positivo

▲ *a positive balance* un saldo positivo ▲ *a positive cash flow* un flujo de efectivo positivo ▲ *a positive development* un desarrollo positivo ▲ *a positive difference* una diferencia positiva ▲ *a positive effect* un efecto positivo ▲ *a positive equity* un patrimonio positivo ▲ *a positive market value* un valor de mercado positivo ▲ *a positive result* un resultado positivo ▲ *a positive value* un valor positivo ▲ *have positive expectations* tener expectivas positivas ▲ *have the positive intention and ability to hold to maturity* tener la intención y la capacidad positiva de mantener hasta el vencimineto ▲ *positive earnings* beneficios positivos

possession
= holding
Possession is something someone owns or the act of owning, having or controlling e.g. property.
posesión
▲ *possession of an asset* posesión de un activo ▲ *possession of inside information* posesión de información privilegiada ▲ *temporary possession* posesión temporal

post US
= enter, recognise UK, IAS/IFRS, recognize US
To post an item is to recognise an item in the financial statements or to record an entry in an account as a debit or credit item.
anotar
= contabilizar
▲ *post an amount to an account* anotar una cantidad en una cuenta

post balance sheet event US, UK
= event after the balance sheet date IAS/IFRS, US, subsequent event IAS/IFRS, US
Post balance sheet events are those events, both favourable and unfavourable, which occur between the balance sheet date and the date on which the financial statements are approved by the board of directors.
NOTE Events ocurring after the balance sheet date may be adjusting or non-adjusting events, i.e. events evidencing conditions at the balance sheet date or events arising after the balance sheet date, respectively.
acontecimiento posterior a la fecha del balance
▲ *adjust the annual report for post balance sheet events* ajustar el informe anual a los acontecimientos posteriores a la fecha del balance ▲ *adjusting post balance sheet events* ajustando los acontecimientos posteriores a la fecha del balance ▲ *disclosure of post balance sheet events* publicación de los acontecimientos posteriores a la fecha del balance ▲ *non-adjusting post balance sheet events* sin ajustar los acontecimientos posteriores a la fecha del balance
⇛ adjusting event, non-adjusting event

post employment benefit
→ post-employment benefit

post-employment benefit IAS/IFRS
A post-employment benefit refers to any type of payment to which a retired person or that person's beneficiary is or may become entitled under the terms of a pension plan. Typically, pension benefits are monthly or other periodic payments but may also be lump sums.
prestación post-empleo
= beneficio post-empleo
▲ *an increase in the liability for post-employment benefits* un aumento en el pasivo por prestaciones post-empleo ▲ *assets and liabilities arising from post-employment benefits* activos y pasivos que surgen de las prestaciones post-empleo ▲ *determine the ultimate cost of providing post-employment benefits* determinar el coste final de la obligación de prestación post-empleo ▲ *post-employment benefits for key management personnel* prestaciones post-empleo para el personal de alta dirección ▲ *the amount of the post-employment benefits received by the employee* la cantidad de las prestaciones post-empleo recibidas por el empleado

post-employment benefit cost IAS/IFRS
= postretirement benefit cost US, retirement benefit cost UK
Post-employment benefit costs are costs which relate to pension benefits to employees and which are incurred by an enterprise due to legislation, collective agreements or under its occupational pension schemes.
coste por jubilación
= coste por prestaciones definidas post empleo, coste por retiro

NOTE Spanish accountant prefer 'coste por jubilación' or 'coste por retiro' to the IAS/IFRS term 'coste por prestaciones definidas post-empleo'. This term is unnatural Spanish.
▲ *financial components of post-employment benefit costs* componentes financieros de costes por jubilación

post-employment benefit obligation IAS/IFRS
= postemployment benefit obligation, postretirement benefit obligation US, retirement benefit obligation UK
A post-employment benefit obligation is the obligation of an enterprise to pay benefits to employees on or after retirement under a pension scheme.
obligación de prestación post-empleo
= obligación de beneficio post-empleo, obligació de prestación post-empleo
NOTE Spanish accountants prefer 'obligación de prestación post-empleo' to the IAS/IFRS term 'obligación de beneficio post empleo'.
▲ *discount the whole of a post-employment benefit obligation* descontar el total de una obligación de prestación post-empleo ▲ *fund a post-employment benefit obligation* aportar fondos a una obligación de prestación post-empleo ▲ *measure the present value of the post-employment benefit obligations* medir el valor actual de las obligaciones de prestación post-empleo ▲ *the currency and term of the post-employment benefit obligations* la moneda y el término de la obligación de prestación post-empleo ▲ *the measurement of all material post-employment benefit obligations* la valoración del total de las obligaciones materiales de prestación post-empleo

post-employment benefit plan IAS/IFRS
= pension benefit plan, pension scheme UK, postretirement benefit plan US, retirement benefit plan UK
A post-employment benefit plan is an arrangement under which an enterprise provides monetary benefits such as lump sums or periodic payments for its employees on or after retirement.
plan de prestación post-empleo
= plan de beneficio post-empleo, plan de prestaciones post-empleo
NOTE Spanish accountants prefer 'plan de prestación post-empleo' to the IAS/IFRS term 'plan de beneficio post-empleo'.
▲ *a post-employment benefit plan for the benefit of employees of the entity* un plan de prestaciones post-empleo para los empleados de la entidad ▲ *fund a post-employment benefit plan* aportar fondos a un plan de prestaciones post-empleo ▲ *post-employment benefit plans involving insurance contracts* planes de prestación post-empleo que incluyen contratos de seguros ▲ *related party transactions with post-employment benefit plans* relacionado con transacciones al grupo con los planes de prestación post-empleo

post-entry
A post-entry is an adjustment to the balance of an account made in connection with the closing of the accounts before the entry is recognised in the profit and loss account or the balance sheet. Post-entries may occur because of e.g. delayed filing of vouchers and prepayments.
entrada posterior
▲ *electronic post-entry* entrada posterior electrónica ▲ *make a post-entry* hacer una entrada posterior

post-investment audit
= postaudit
A post-investment audit is an evaluation follow-up on an investment project that seeks to determine whether the return on investment is consistent with the expectations.
auditoría posterior a la inversión
▲ *conduct a post-investment audit* llevar a cabo una auditoría posterior a la inversión ▲ *perform a post-investment audit* realizar una auditoría posterior a la inversión ▲ *use a post-investment audit* utilizar una auditoría posterior a la inversión

post-tax profit IAS/IFRS, UK
= income after income tax US, profit after tax UK
≠ income before income tax US, pre-tax profit IAS/IFRS, UK, profit before tax UK, IAS/IFRS
Post-tax profit is the profit of an enterprise for an accounting period after deduction of tax expense.
beneficio después de impuestos
= beneficio después de impuesto, ganancia después de impuestos, ganancia después de impuesto
NOTE Spanish accountant prefer 'beneficio depués de impuestos' to the IAS term 'ganancia después de impuestos'
▲ *the post-tax profit of discontinued operations* el beneficio después de impuestos de las operaciones interrumpidas

post-tax profit or loss
Post-tax profit or loss is the net profit or loss of an enterprise for an accounting period after deduction of tax expense.
resultado después de impuestos
▲ *the post-tax profit or loss of discontinued operations* el resultado después de impuestos de operaciones interrumpidas

postaudit
= post-investment audit
A postaudit is an evaluation follow-up on an investment project that seeks to determine whether the return on investment is consistent with the expectations.
auditoría posterior a la inversión
▲ *conduct a postaudit* llevar a cabo una auditoría posterior a la inversión ▲ *perform a postaudit* realizar una auditoría posterior a la inversión ▲ *use a postaudit* utilizar una auditoría posterior a la inversión

posting error
A posting error occurs when an income or expense item is not recognised correctly in the bookkeeping records or the financial statements.
error de anotación
▲ *make a posting error* hacer un error de anotación

postretirement benefit cost US
= post-employment benefit cost IAS/IFRS, retirement benefit cost UK
Postretirement benefit costs are costs which relate to pension benefits to employees and which are incurred by an enterprise due to legislation, collective agreements or under its occupational pension schemes.
coste por retiro
= coste por jubilación
▲ *net periodic postretirement benefit cost* coste por retiro periódico neto ▲ *offset postretirement benefit cost in the employer's statement of income* compensar el coste por retiro en el estado de resultados del empresario

postretirement benefit expense US
Postretirement benefit expenses are expenses which relate to pension benefits to employees and which are incurred by an enterprise due to legislation, collective agreements or under its occupational pension schemes.
gasto por prestaciones de jubilación
= gasto por prestaciones de retiro
▲ *net postretirement benefit expense* gasto por prestaciones de jubilación neto ▲ *pension and other postretirement benefit expenses* jubilación y otros gastos por prestaciones de jubilación

postretirement benefit obligation US
= post-employment benefit obligation IAS/IFRS, retirement benefit obligation UK
A postretirement benefit obligation is the obligation of an enterprise to pay benefits to employees on or after retirement under a pension scheme.
obligación por prestaciones de jubilación
= obligación por prestaciones de retiro
▲ *accumulated postretirement benefit obligation* obligación por prestaciones de jubilación acumulada ▲ *assume a postretirement benefit obligation* asumir una obligación por prestaciones de jubilación ▲ *the expected postretirement benefit obligation* la obligación por prestaciones de jubilación esperada

postretirement benefit plan US
= post-employment benefit plan IAS/IFRS, retirement benefit plan UK

A postretirement benefit plan is an arrangement under which an enterprise provides monetary benefits such as lump sums or periodic payments for its employees on or after retirement.

plan de pensiones

▲ *amend a postretirement benefit plan* modificar un plan de pensiones ▲ *defined benefit postretirement benefit plans* planes de pensiones de prestación definida

potential ordinary share

A potential ordinary share is a financial instrument or other contract that may give its holder the right to acquire ordinary shares, such as share options and warrants.

acción ordinaria potencial

▲ *a holder of potential ordinary shares* un tenedor de acciones ordinarias potenciales ▲ *antidilutive potential ordinary share* acción ordinaria potencial antidilutiva ▲ *contingent issuable potential ordinary shares* acciones ordinarias potenciales con emisión probable ▲ *conversion of potential ordinary shares* conversión de acciones ordinarias potenciales ▲ *dilutive potential ordinary share* acción ordinaria potencial dilutiva ▲ *issue of potential ordinary shares* emisión de acciones ordinarias potenciales ▲ *potential ordinary shares that are cancelled or allowed to lapse during the period* acciones ordinarias potenciales que se cancelan o amplían su vigencia durante el periodo ▲ *potential ordinary shares that are publicly traded* acciones ordinarias potenciales que se negocian públicamente ▲ *the date of the issue of the potential ordinary shares* la fecha de la emisión de las acciones ordinarias potenciales ▲ *the expenses associated with potential ordinary shares* los gastos asociados con las acciones ordinarias potenciales

power of attorney UK

A power of attorney is a document whereby a person empowers another person to act on his behalf either in general or in specific situations.

poder notarial

= poder

▲ *enduring power of attorney* poder notarial permanente ▲ *general power of attorney* poder notarial general ▲ *irrevocable power of attorney* poder notarial irrevocable ▲ *special power of attorney* poder notarial específico

PPE

PPE is the abbreviation of property, plant and equipment, i.e. physical, non-current assets intended for long-term ownership or use by an enterprise for its operating activities and administration.

edificios, instalaciones y equipos

= inmobilizado material, propiedad, planta y equipo

▲ *an item of PPE* una partida de edificios, instalaciones y equipos ▲ *fair value gains on PPE* ganancias por ajuste a valor razonable de edificios, instalaciones y equipos ▲ *increases in the carrying amount arising on revaluation of PPE* aumentos en el valor contable procedente de una revalorización de edificios, instalaciones y equipos ▲ *proceeds from sale of PPE* ingresos por venta de edificios, instalaciones y equipos ▲ *reclassified and added to PPE* reclasificado y añadido a edificios, instalaciones y equipos ▲ *recognised in cost of PPE* reconocido en el coste de edificios, instalaciones y equipos

⇛ property, plant and equipment

pre-acquisition balance sheet

A pre-acquisition balance sheet is an opening balance sheet that must be prepared for an acquiree at the acquisition date in connection with a business combination.

balance de pre-adquisición

▲ *prepare a pre-acquisition balance sheet* preparar un balance de pre-adquisición

⇛ acquiree

pre-emption right UK

= pre-emptive right US

A pre-emption right is the right of shareholders to be offered any new shares issued by their company, usually at a lower price than the market price. In this way, shareholders can avoid dilution in control or value, as they are able to maintain their percentage share ownership by buying the additionally issued shares.

derecho preferente de suscripción

▲ *an increase of share capital with or without pre-emption rights* un aumento del capital social con o sin derecho preferente de suscripción ▲ *assign a pre-emption right* asignar un derecho preferente de suscripción ▲ *exercise a pre-emption right* ejercer un derecho preferente de suscripción ▲ *exercise of a pre-emption right* ejercicio de un derecho preferente de suscripción ▲ *withdrawal of pre-emption rights* eliminación de los derechos preferentes de suscripción

⇛ rights issue

pre-emptive right US

= pre-emption right UK

A pre-emptive right is the right of shareholders to be offered any new shares issued by their company, usually at a lower price than the market price. In this way, shareholders can avoid dilution in control or value, as they are able to maintain their percentage share ownership by buying the additionally issued shares.

derecho preferente de suscripción

▲ *an increase of capital with or without pre-emptive rights* un aumento de capital social con o sin derechos preferentes de suscripción ▲ *exercise of a pre-emptive right* ejercicio de un derecho preferente de suscripción ▲ *have a pre-emptive right* tener un derecho preferente de suscripción ▲ *withdrawal of pre-emption rights* eliminación de los derechos preferentes de suscripción

pre-tax profit UK, IAS/IFRS

= income before income tax US, profit before tax UK, IAS/IFRS, PTP

≠ income after income tax US, post-tax profit IAS/IFRS

Pre-tax profit is the profit of an enterprise for an accounting period before deduction of tax expense.

beneficio antes de impuestos

= beneficio antes de impuesto, ganancia antes de impuesto, ganancia antes de impuestos

NOTE Spanish accountants prefer 'beneficio antes de impuestos' to the IAS term 'ganacia antes de impuestos'.

▲ *pre-tax profit of discontinued operations* beneficio antes de impuestos de operaciones interrumpidas

pre-tax profit or loss UK, IAS/IFRS

A pre-tax profit or loss is an enterprise's profit or loss for an accounting period before deduction of tax expense.

resultado antes de impuestos

= pérdidas o ganancias antes de impuestos, resultado antes de impuesto

NOTE Spanish accountants prefer 'resultado antes de impuestos' to the IAS/IFRS term 'pérdidas o ganancias antes de impuestos'.

▲ *pre-tax profit or loss from ordinary activities* resultado antes de impuestos de actividades ordinarias ▲ *the revenue, expenses and pre-tax profit or loss of discontinued operations* el ingreso, gastos y resultado antes de impuestos de las operaciones interrumpidas

predatory price

A predatory price is a price which is set below the cost in order to reduce competition or drive competitors out of the market.

precio predatorio

▲ *provide services at predatory prices* ofrecer servicios a precios predatorios

predatory pricing

Predatory pricing means the sale of goods or provision of services, at a price which is below the cost in order to reduce competition or drive competitors out of the market.

fijación de precios predatorios

▲ *allegations of predatory pricing* acusaciones de fijación de precios predatorios ▲ *to ban predatory pricing* eliminar la fijación de precios predatorios

predecessor auditor

≠ incoming auditor

A predecessor auditor is an independent auditor who has stepped down as external auditor for an enterprise, either willingly or by replacement on termination.

auditor anterior

▲ *financial statements audited by a predecessor auditor* estados financieros auditados por un auditor anterior ▲ *review a predecessor auditor's work papers* revisar los papeles de trabajo de un auditor anterior

preference dividend

Preference dividend is the dividend that is received or paid on preference shares.

dividendo preferente

= dividendo preferido

▲ *cumulative preference dividends* dividendos preferentes acumulativos ▲ *the after-tax amount of preference dividends that is deducted from profit or loss* el importe neto de dividendos preferentes que se deduce del resultado ▲ *the amount adjusted for the after-tax amounts of preference dividends* la cantidad ajustada después de impuestos de diviendos preferentes ▲ *the amount of preference dividends for cumulative preference shares* la cantidad de dividendos preferentes para acciones preferentes acumulativas ▲ *the amount of preference dividends that is deducted from the net profit for the year* la cantidad de dividendos preferentes que se deducen del beneficio neto del año

⇛ preference share

preference share

= preferred stock US

A preference share is a share giving the shareholder a preferential right, usually in connection with the distribution of dividend, but often without carrying any voting rights. This type of share may in rare cases be referred to as a C share.

acción preferente

▲ *buy back preference shares outstanding at the balance sheet date* recomprar las acciones preferentes pendientes a la fecha de balance ▲ *convertible preference shares* acciones preferentes convertibles ▲ *cumulative preference shares* acciones preferentes acumulativas ▲ *differences arising on the settlement of preference shares* diferencias que surgen al pagar las acciones preferentes ▲ *dividends on preference shares classified as liabilities* dividendos sobre acciones preferentes clasificados como pasivos ▲ *increasing rate preference shares* aumentando la tasa de las acciones preferentes ▲ *negotiable preference shares* acciones preferentes negociables ▲ *non-cumulative preference shares* acciones preferentes no acumulativas ▲ *non-negotiable preference shares* acciones preferentes no negociables ▲ *preference shares acquired within a short period of their maturity* acciones preferentes adquiridas poco antes de su vencimiento ▲ *preference shares, that are convertible into ordinary shares* acciones preferentes, que se convierten en acciones ordinarias ▲ *preference shares with a specified redemption date* acciones preferentes con una fecha de amortización especifícada ▲ *redeemable preference shares* acciones preferentes amortizables

⇛ B share

preferred dividend US

Preferred dividend is the dividend that is received or paid on preferred stock.

dividendo preferente

▲ *cumulative preferred dividends* dividendos preferentes acumulativos ▲ *the amount of preferred dividends for cumulative preferred stock* la cantidad de dividendos preferentes para acciones preferentes acumulativas ▲ *the amount of preferred dividends that is deducted from the net income for the year* la cantidad de dividendos preferentes que se deducen del beneficio neto del año

⇛ preferred stock

preferred stock US

= preference shares, preferred shares

Preferred stock consists of preferred shares, i.e. shares with a preferential right which are paid dividends at a fixed rate and have preference over common shares for dividend payments. Usually, preferred stock does not carry any voting rights.

acción preferente

▲ *buy back preferred stock outstanding at the balance sheet date* recomprar las acciones preferentes pendientes a la fecha de balance ▲ *convertible preferred stock* acciones preferentes convertibles ▲ *cumulative preferred stock* acciones preferentes acumulativas ▲ *negotiable preferred stock* acciones preferentes negociables ▲ *non-cumulative preferred stock* acciones preferentes no acumulativas ▲ *non-negotiable preferred stock* acciones preferentes no negociables ▲ *preferred stock acquired within a short period of their maturity* acciones preferentes adquiridas poco antes de su vencimiento ▲ *preferred stock with a specified redemption date* acciones preferentes con una fecha de amortización especifícada ▲ *redeemable preferred stock* acciones preferentes amortizables

⇛ B share

preliminary

Preliminary is used about an action to indicate that it precedes another event. The preliminary results for instance are results that are announced before the full report is available.

preliminar

▲ *a preliminary change in capital* un cambio preliminar en el capital ▲ *a preliminary report* un informe preliminar ▲ *a preliminary result* un resultado preliminar ▲ *a preliminary statement* un estado preliminar ▲ *preliminary approval* aprobación preliminar ▲ *preliminary determination of fair values* determinación preliminar a valores razonables ▲ *preliminary injunction* auto preliminar

preliminary announcement of financial statements

= preliminary results announcement UK

A preliminary announcement of financial statements is a statement that listed companies must file with the stock exchange prior to the release of their financial results for a reporting period, such as a quarter, six months or a full year. Apart from summarized financial statements, the announcement typically contains financial information on the period together with an outlook and is a useful tool for analysts and stakeholders.

anuncio preliminar de estados financieros

▲ *as specified in the group preliminary announcement of financial statements No. 01/02 of 6 March 2005* como se especifica en el anuncio preliminar de estados financieros del grupo No. 01/02 del 6 de marzo de 2005 ▲ *decide not to publish a preliminary announcement of financial statements* decidir no publicar un anuncio preliminar de estados financieros ▲ *preliminary announcement of financial statements for 20xx* anuncio preliminar de estados financieros para el 20xx ▲ *preliminary announcement of financial statements for 3 quarters* anuncio preliminar de estados financieros para tres trimestres ▲ *preliminary announcement of financial statements for the period 1 January to 31 December 2005* anuncio preliminar de estados financieros para el periodo comprendido entre el 1 de enero al 31 de diciembre de 2005 ▲ *publication of a preliminary announcement of financial statements* publicación de un anuncio preliminar de estados financieros ▲ *publication of the preliminary announcement of financial statements* publicación del anuncio preliminar de estados financieros

preliminary results UK

= preliminary results announcement UK

The preliminary results is a statement that listed companies must file with the stock exchange prior to the release of their financial results for a reporting period, such as a quarter, six months or a full year. Apart from summarized financial statements, the announcement typically contains financial information on the period together with an outlook and is a useful tool for analysts and stakeholders.

resultados preliminares

▲ *announce the Group's preliminary results* anunciar los resultados preliminares del Grupo ▲ *preliminary results announcement for the year ended 4 April 2006* anuncio de resultados preliminares para el año que finalizó el 4 de abril de 2006 ▲ *prepare the preliminary results* preparar los resultados preliminares

⇛ earnings release, interim results

preliminary results announcement UK

= full year results announcement UK, preliminary results UK, results announcement UK

A preliminary results announcement is a statement that listed companies must file with the stock exchange prior to the release of their financial results for a reporting period, such as a quarter, six months or a full year. Apart from summarized financial statements, the announcement typically contains financial information on the period together with an outlook and is a useful tool for analysts and stakeholders.
anuncio de resultados preliminares
▲ *approve the preliminary results announcement* aprobar el anuncio de resultados preliminares ▲ *preliminary results announcement for the year ended 4 April 2006* anuncio de resultados preliminares para el año que acaba el 4 de abril de 2006
⇛ interim results announcement

premium

1 A premium is the additional price in excess of the market or issue price of a share payable by the purchaser, or the additional amount in excess of the nominal or maturity value of a bond payable by the borrower on redemption of the loan.
prima
▲ *any original issue premium on increasing rate preference shares* cualquier prima de emisión original al aumentar la tasa de acciones preferentes ▲ *any premium* cualquier prima ▲ *compensate investors for purchasing preference shares at a premium* compensar a los inversores por la compra de acciones preferentes con prima ▲ *debt incurred at a premium* deuda incurrida con prima ▲ *debt premiums* primas de deuda ▲ *increase of share capital including premium* aumento del capital social incluyendo la prima ▲ *new issue of shares at a premium* nueva emisión de acciones con prima ▲ *premium on increase of capital* prima sobre el aumento de capital ▲ *premium on increase of contributed capital* prima sobre el aumento del capital aportado ▲ *premium on monetary financial assets* prima en los activos financieros monetarios ▲ *premium on payment* prima en el pago ▲ *premium plus cash consideration* prima más prestación monetaria ▲ *share premium* prima de acción ▲ *the premium over the basic interest rate for credit risk* la prima sobre el tipo de interés básico por riesgo crediticio ▲ *the premium paid for a purchased option* la prima pagada por una opción comprada ▲ *the premium received for a written option or warrant on the entity's own shares* la prima recibida por una opción escrita o warrant sobre las acciones propias de la entidad

2 = insurance premium
The price that the insurer charges for assuming a risk is called the premium or insurance premium. The premium is usually paid by regular instalments over a period of time.
prima
▲ *earned premiums net of reinsurance* primas devengadas netas de reaseguro ▲ *future premiums net of management charges* primas futuras sin costes de gestión ▲ *gross premiums earned* primas brutas devengadas ▲ *gross premiums net of brokerage* primas brutas sin intermediación ▲ *gross premiums written* primas brutas registradas ▲ *individual premiums* primas individuales ▲ *life assurance with return of premiums* seguro de vida con rendimiento de primas ▲ *outward reinsurance premiums* primas de reaseguros externos ▲ *periodic premiums* primas periodicas ▲ *premiums for new business* primas por nuevos negocios ▲ *premiums from bonus contracts* primas de contratos con bonus ▲ *premiums from contracts where the investment risk is borne by the policyholders* primas de contratos donde el riesgo de inversión recae sobre los tenedores de la póliza ▲ *premiums from non-bonus contracts* primas de contratos sin bonus ▲ *premiums received* primas recibidas ▲ *premiums under group contracts* primas según los contratos del grupo ▲ *premiums yet to be written* primas a registrar ▲ *provisions for unearned premiums* provisiones para primas no devengadas ▲ *provisions for unearned premiums and unexpi-*

red risks provisiones para primas no devengadas y riesgos no vencidos ▲ *reinsurance premiums due from ceding insurance companies* vencimiento por cesión de las primas de reaseguro a las aseguradoras ▲ *single premiums* primas únicas ▲ *taxes on premiums* impuesto sobre primas ▲ *the company's portion of total premiums* la posición del total de las primas de la compañía

prepaid
= paid in advance
When payment of an amount has been effected before the due date for payment or received before delivery of goods or services, the amount has been prepaid.
prepagado
= pagado por anticipado
▲ *prepaid expenses* gastos pagados por anticipado ▲ *prepaid funeral plans* planes de defunción pagados por anticipado ▲ *prepaid insurance* seguro prepagado ▲ *prepaid operating lease income* ingresos por arrendamiento operativo prepagados ▲ *prepaid rent* renta prepagada ▲ *prepaid rental* alquiler prepagado ▲ *prepaid subscription* suscripción prepagada

prepaid expense US
= prepayment UK
Prepaid expenses are expenses paid in advance such as insurance, advertising, and rent and which are shown under current assets according to the accruals concept.
gasto anticipado
= gasto pagado por anticipado, gasto prepago
▲ *a separate item of prepaid expenses* una partida separada de gastos anticipados ▲ *classify as prepaid expenses* clasificar como gastos anticipados ▲ *included under prepaid expenses* incluido como gastos anticipados ▲ *prepaid expenses under assets* gastos anticipados colocados como activos
⇛ prepaid expenses and accrued revenue

prepaid expenses US
→ prepaid expense

prepaid expenses and accrued revenue US
= prepayments and accrued income UK, IAS/IFRS
"Prepaid expenses and accrued revenue" is an item recognised according to the accruals concept under current assets in the balance sheet which represents partly payments made at the balance sheet date for goods and services receivable in the following financial years and partly income which has been earned, but not received, in the year under review.
gastos anticipados e ingresos devengados
▲ *other prepaid expenses and accrued revenue* otros gastos anticipados e ingresos devengados
⇛ accrued revenue, prepaid expense

preparation
Preparation is the process of taking the necessary steps to make something ready to fit whatever purpose is intended. When used in connection with i.e. a financial statement, preparation means the act of presenting financial data in written form.
preparación
▲ *preparation of an annual report* preparación de un informe anual ▲ *preparation of an intellectual capital report* preparación de un informe de capital intelectual ▲ *preparation of an interim report* preparación de un informe provisional ▲ *preparation of balance sheet and income statement* preparación del balance y estado de resultados ▲ *preparation of consolidated financial statements* preparación de estados financieros consolidados ▲ *preparation of consolidated financial statements* preparación de estados financieros consolidados ▲ *preparation of estimates of future developments* preparación de las estimaciones de los desarrollos futuros ▲ *preparation of financial statements* preparación de estados financieros

preparation of financial statements
The preparation of financial statements is the compilation of financial data by an enterprise for a particular accounting period to present the financial position and operating results for that period and to meet financial reporting requirements. This preparation ty-

pically includes drafting a balance sheet, income statement, cash flow statement and statement of changes in equity.

preparación de estados financieros

= preparación de los estados financieros

▲ *basis of measurement for the preparation of financial statements* base de valoración para la preparación de estados financieros

prepare

To prepare means to take the necessary steps to make something ready to fit whatever purpose is intended. When used in connection with i.e. financial statements, prepare means to present financial data in written form.

preparar

▲ *consolidated financial statements prepared following a reverse acquisition* estados financieros consolidados preparados de acuerdo con una adquisición invertida ▲ *exemption from preparing consoldated financial statements* exento de preparar estados financieros consolidados ▲ *prepare financial statements on a going concern basis* preparar los estados financieros según el principio de empresa en funcionamiento

preparer of financial statements

A preparer of financial statements is the person or enterprise responsible for drafting and presenting the financial data in the financial statements.

preparador de estados financieros

= preparador de los estados financieros

▲ *the various practical needs of preparers of financial statements* las necesidades prácticas varias de los preparadores de los estados financieros

prepay

= pay in advance

To prepay is to pay for something in advance, e.g. a product or service not yet delivered or provided.

prepagar

= pagar por anticipado

▲ *prepay a loan* prepagar un préstamo ▲ *prepay certain obligations* prepagar ciertas obligaciones

prepayment

1 Under the accruals concept, a prepayment recognised under current assets in the balance sheet is a payment made at the balance sheet date for goods and services receivable in the following financial years.

gasto anticipado

▲ *a separate prepayment* una partida separada de gastos anticipados ▲ *classify expenses as prepayments* clasificar como gastos anticipados ▲ *prepayments under assets* gastos anticipados colocados como activos

⇛ prepayments and accrued income

2 = advance payment

Prepayment refers to an amount of money paid for goods or services in a sales transaction before the due date for payment or before delivery.

anticipo

= entrada

▲ *less payments on account and prepayments* menos pagos en cuenta y anticipos ▲ *receivables and prepayments* cuentas a cobrar y anticipos ▲ *recognise a prepayment as an asset* reconocer un anticipo como un activo

3 Prepayment refers to the act of paying for goods or services before the due date for payment or before delivery.

pago anticipado

▲ *a prepayment option embedded in a host debt contract* una opción de pago anticipado implícita en un contrato de deuda anfitrión ▲ *a substantial prepayment risk* un riesgo por pago anticipado sustancial ▲ *make a prepayment* hacer un pago anticipado

prepayment received

A prepayment received is a payment that has come to hand before the product or the service has been delivered or provided. Under the accruals concept, a prepayment is recognised as deferred income under liabilities, if it has been received in advance of the accounting period in which it is earned.

cobro anticipado

= cobro por anticipado

▲ *prepayments received from customers* cobros por anticipado recibidos de los clientes

⇛ accruals concept, deferred income

prepayments and accrued income
UK, IAS/IFRS
= prepaid expenses and accrued revenue US
Prepayments and accrued income is an item recognised according to the accruals concept under current assets in the balance sheet which represents partly payments made at the balance sheet date for goods and services receivable in the following financial years and partly income which has been earned, but not received, in the year under review.
NOTE In the UK, prepayments and accrued income is an item recognised according to the Companies Act 2006 required report format.
pagos anticipados e ingresos devengados
= gastos anticipados e ingresos devengados
▲ *other prepayments and accrued income* otros pagos anticipados e ingresos devengados
⇛ accruals and deferred income, prepaid expenses

present
= submit
To present is to show, say and explain something or produce it for consideration to others.
presentar
▲ *omit to present the annual report* omitir la presentación del informe anual ▲ *present a proposal* presentar una propuesta ▲ *present comparative information* presentar información comparada ▲ *present data* presentar datos ▲ *present fairly, in all material respects* presentar razonablemente, en todos los aspectos materiales ▲ *present financial statements for previous periods* presentar estados financieros para los periodos anteriores ▲ *present information* presentar información ▲ *present information in narrative form* presentar la información de forma narrativa ▲ *present information in tabular form* presentar la información en forma de tabla ▲ *present the opening IFRS balance sheet in the first IFRS financial statements* presentar la apertura del balance NIIF en los primeros estados financieros NIIF

present value
= discounted value
Present value is the present discounted value, i.e. the current estimate or cash equivalent of future amounts of money such as projected cash flows, as multiplied by a discount factor.
valor actual
▲ *calculated present value* valor actual calculado ▲ *calculation of the present value* cálculo del valor actual ▲ *components of a present value measurement* componentes de una medición a valor actual ▲ *determine liabilities and assets at present value* determinar pasivos y activos a valor actual ▲ *discount provisions to present value* descontar provisiones a valor actual ▲ *increase in the present value* aumento en el valor actual ▲ *measure the present value* medir el valor actual ▲ *present value techniques* técnicas de valor actual ▲ *reconcile to present value* conciliar a valor actual ▲ *the actuarial present value* el valor actual actuarial ▲ *the aggregate present value of the minimum lease payments* el valor actual agregado de los pagos mínimos por arrendamiento ▲ *the lower of fair value and present value of future lease payments* el más bajo entre el valor razonable y el valor actual de los pagos por arrendamiento futuros ▲ *the present value of a defined benefit obligation* el valor actual de una obligación por prestación definida ▲ *the present value of expected dividends* el valor actual de los dividendos esperados ▲ *the present value of funded obligations* el valor actual de las obligaciones financiadas ▲ *the present value of minimum lease payments* el valor actual de los pagos mínimos por arrendamiento ▲ *the present value of the exercise price* el valor actual del precio de compra ▲ *the present value of unfunded obligations* el valor actual de las obligaciones no financiadas
SOURCE IAS Framework, F 100 (d)
⇛ discounted value

presentation
Presentation refers to the act of formally presenting the financial

statements or the way in which the financial statements are prepared and arranged using specific accounting concepts, principles and treatments.

presentación

▲ *a framework for the preparation and presentation of financial statements* un marco para la preparación y presentación de estados financieros ▲ *a review of the presentation of the financial statements* una revisión de la presentación de los estados financieros ▲ *at the time of presentation of the annual report* a la fecha de presentación del informe anual ▲ *financial statements presentation* presentación de estados financieros ▲ *on presentation in accordance with the Danish Financial Statements Act* en la presentación de acuerdo con la Ley danesa de Estados Financieros ▲ *presentation and public announcement of financial statements* presentación y anuncio público de estados financieros ▲ *presentation of a proposal* presentación de una propuesta ▲ *presentation of the annual report* presentación del informe anual ▲ *the basis for presentation of general purpose financial statements* la base de presentación de estados financieros de ámbito general ▲ *the most relevant and reliable presentation* la presentación más relevante y fiable

presentation currency IAS/IFRS

The presentation currency is the measurement currency used by an enterprise for presenting financial statements, and the currency into which financial statements of foreign operations are translated.

NOTE Under IFRS (IAS 21), the former "reporting currency" has been split up in two concepts: "presentation currency" and "functional currency".

moneda de presentación

▲ *translate from the accounting currency into the presentation currency* convertir la moneda contable a la moneda de presentación ▲ *translate the entity's results and financial position into the presentation currency* convertir los resultados de la entidad y la posición financiera a la moneda de presentación ▲ *translation to the presentation currency* conversión a la moneda de presentación ▲ *use of a presentation currency other than the functional currency* uso de una moneda de presentación diferente de la moneda funcional

⇛ functional currency

presentation form of an income statement US, IAS/IFRS

The presentation form of an income statement refers to type of the layout according to which the items are arranged and presented, e.g. the horizontal and the vertical formats.

formato de presentación de un estado de resultados

= formato de presentación de una cuenta de pérdidas y ganancias

▲ *the investor-oriented presentation form of an income statement* el formato de presentación de un estado de resultados orientado al inversor

⇛ horizontal format, vertical format

presentation of profit or loss account UK

The presentation of profit or loss shows the method of presenting the statement of profit of loss, i.e. the financial performance, chosen by an enterprise.

presentación de la cuenta de resultados

= presentación de la cuenta de pérdidas y ganancias

▲ *the investor-oriented presentation form of a profit and loss account* la presentación de la cuenta de resultados orientada al inversor

president US

A president is the chief executive officer (CEO) of a group and as such, he is in charge of the day-to-day management of the group.

presidente

= consero delegado

▲ *be appointed president* ser nombrado presidente del grupo ▲ *take up the position as president* asumir el cargo de presidente del grupo ▲ *the former president* el presidente anterior ▲ *the incoming president* el presidente entrante ▲ *the retiring president* el presidente saliente

prevention cost

Prevention costs are costs incurred to avoid that manufactured products do not comply with specifications such as costs related to process engineering, testing and equipment maintenance.

coste de prevención

▲ *recognise prevention costs* reconocer los costes de prevención ▲ *the prevention costs incurred* los costes de prevención incurridos

⇛ appraisal cost, external failure cost, internal failure cost

previous department cost

= transferred-in cost

Previous department costs are costs previously incurred in the production process by the various departments involved. As the product units move on in the process, the costs related to the units are also transferred to the subsequent department in the production process. In this way, the costs become part of the product unit's direct materials costs, but are still, being separate, referred to as transferred-in costs or previous department costs.

coste transferido

▲ *calculate the previous department costs* calcular los costes transferidos ▲ *the previous department costs for WIP* los costes transferidos por trabajo en curso

previous GAAP

Previous GAAP refers to the generally accepted accounting principles applied by an enterprise prior to its transition to the International Financial Reporting Standards (IFRS).

Principios Contables Generalmente Aceptados anteriores

= PCGA anteriores

NOTE Always plural in Spanish accounting texts.

▲ *a previous GAAP revaluation of an item of property, plant and equipment* una revalorización de una partida de edificios, instalaciones y equipos según los Principios Contables Generalmente Aceptados anteriores ▲ *financial liabilities that were derecognised under previous GAAP* pasivos financieros que fueron eliminados según los Principios Contables Generalmente Aceptados anteriores ▲ *reclassify items recognised under previous GAAP* reclasificar las partidas reconocidas según los Principios Contables Generalmente Aceptados anteriores ▲ *the balance sheet that includes comparative information under previous GAAP* el balance que incluye información comparativa según los Principios Contables Generalmente Aceptados anteriores ▲ *the exchange rate applied under previous GAAP* el tipo de cambio aplicado según los Principios Contables Generalmente Aceptados anteriores ▲ *the transition from previous GAAP to IFRSs* la transición de los Principios Contables Generalmente Aceptados anteriores a las NIIFs

SOURCE IFRS 1, Appendix A

previous year

= prior year

The previous year is the prior year, i.e. the year preceding the current year or year under review.

año anterior

= ejercicio anterior

▲ *previous year adjustment* ajuste de año anterior

price

1 A price is the amount in money terms that a seller requires or a buyer is prepared to pay for a unit of a product, service or production factor.

precio

▲ *a contract price* un precio de contrato ▲ *a pre-determined price* un precio predeterminado ▲ *current prices* precios corrientes ▲ *dispose of an asset at a price close to the fair value* eliminar un activo a un precio cercano al valor razonable ▲ *effect a sale at the best price obtainable* efectuar una venta al mejor precio obtenible ▲ *invoiced price* precio facturado ▲ *non-regulated exercise price* precio de compra no regulado ▲ *pay a price* pagar un precio ▲ *price change* cambio de precio ▲ *price in EUR* precio en euros ▲ *price in USD* precio en dólares norteamericanos ▲ *price per service or product provided* precio por servicio o producto ofrecido

2 A price is the value quoted at a certain time in respect of shares, bonds or units traded in an authorized marketplace, e.g. a stock exchange.

cotización

▲ *a price agreed by a willing buyer and a willing seller in an arm's length transaction* una cotización acordada por un comprador y vendedor interesados en una transacción en condiciones de mercado ▲ *a right to buy a fixed number of the entity's shares for a fixed price* un derecho a comprar un número fijo de las acciones de la entidad a una cotización fijada ▲ *in the absence of a reliable published price* en ausencia de una cotización publicada fiable ▲ *the future prices of the ordinary shares* las cotizaciones futuras de las acciones ordinarias ▲ *the most recent price quote for a corporate bond* la cotización más reciente publicada de un bono corporativo ▲ *the published price at the date of exchange of a quoted equity instrument* la cotización publicada en la fecha de intercambio de un instrumento de patrimonio cotizado

price competition

Price competition arises when suppliers use price reductions or low prices as a competitive tool, attempting to gain market shares. Competition can alternatively be based on marketing or quality.

competencia de precios

= competencia vía precios

▲ *intensified price competition* competencia de precios intensificada ▲ *price competition on financial products* competencia vía precios en los productos financieros ▲ *severe price competition* competencia de precios severa

price determination

1 Price determination is the process whereby prices on goods and services are fixed, e.g. as a function of the production cost, often with an added mark-up. In market economies, prices are typically determined by market forces as a result of the interaction between supply and demand.

determinación del precio

▲ *free price determination* libre determinación de los precios ▲ *general rules on price determination for the renting of houses* reglas generales en la determinación del precio para el alquiler de casas

⇛ cost plus method

2 = determination of price

Price determination is the result of the interaction between supply and demand in financial markets on prices of shares, bonds, currencies etc. Price determination may also refer to the price fixing of companies in connection with their issuance of securities.

fijación del precio

= fijación de los precios

▲ *an uncertain price determination* una fijación incierta de los precios ▲ *price determination of the company's securities* fijación del precio de los títulos de la compañía

price differentiation

= price discrimination

Price differentiation arises when e.g. two enterprises charge different prices for the same product in two or more markets and the price difference is not due to different costs, e.g. transportation costs.

discriminación en el precio

= discriminación en los precios

▲ *illegal price differentiation* discriminación en el precio ilegal ▲ *prohibit price differentiation* prohibir la discriminación en el precio ▲ *the potential for price differentiation* el potencial para la discriminación en los precios

price discrimination

Price discrimination arises when e.g. two enterprises charge different prices for the same product in two or more markets and the price difference is not due to different costs, e.g. transportation costs.

discriminación en el precio

= discriminación en los precios

▲ *illegal price discrimination* discriminación en el precio ilegal ▲ *prohibit price discrimination* prohibir la discriminación en el precio ▲ *the potential for price discrimination* el potencial para la discriminación en los precios

price earnings ratio

→ price/earnings ratio

price elasticity

Price elasticity is the percentage change in volume relative to the percentage change in price and expresses the sensitivity in demand, i.e. sales, to price changes.

elasticidad precio

▲ *calculate price elasticity* calcular la elasticidad precio ▲ *com-*

pute the price elasticity cuantificar la elasticidad precio ▲ *external price elasticity* elasticidad precio externa ▲ *price elasticity of demand* elasticidad precio de la demanda ▲ *price elasticity of supply* elasticidad precio de la oferta ▲ *the price elasticity for the market as a whole* la elasticidad precio para el mercado en su totalidad

price in

= discount, factor in

To price in is to allow for the factual or possible effects of events or announcements in a decision-making process, in a price fixing (typically of shares, bonds etc.), in acquisitions, disposals, investments or other transactions, or in expectations for future developments.

descontar

▲ *price in greater uncertainty* descontar una mayor incertidumbre ▲ *price in interest rate hikes* descontar subidas en los tipos de interés ▲ *price in shareholders' expectations for the company's future performance* descontar expectativas de los accionistas en el futuro de la empresa

price risk

= price exposure

Price risk includes foreign exchange risk and interest rate risk and constitutes the market risk that the values of the asset and liabilities of an enterprise will fluctuate because of outside factors beyond the control of the enterprise, i.e. changes in market prices.

riesgo de precio

▲ *be exposed to price risk* estar expuesto al riesgo de precio ▲ *disclosure of price risks* publicación de los riesgos de precio ▲ *exposure to price risk* exposición al riesgo de precio ▲ *hedge the value of assets and liabilities against price risks* cubrir el valor de los activos y pasivos contra los riesgos de precio ▲ *price risk hedge* cobertura del riesgo de precio ▲ *price risks attaching to shareholdings* riesgos de precio unidos a las participaciones accionariales ▲ *price risks attaching to significant holdings of equity instruments* riesgos de precio unidos a los grupos significativos de instrumentos de patrimonio

SOURCE IAS 32, paragraph 52(a)(iii)

price to book value

→ price/book value

price trend

A price trend refers to the general direction of the development of prices e.g. within a country, region or specific industry.

tendencia del precio

▲ *a favorable price trend* una tendencia del precio favorable ▲ *a negative price trend* una tendencia del precio negativa ▲ *a positive price trend* una tendencia del precio positiva ▲ *the general price trend* la tendencia del precio general

price variance

= input-price variance, rate variance

A price variance is the difference between the budgeted price per unit and the actual purchase or input price per unit of raw materials, semi-manufactures, secondary materials and labour, multiplied by the purchased quantity.

desviación del precio

▲ *direct-labour price variance* desviación del precio en la partida de costes de personal directos ▲ *direct-material price variance* desviación del precio en la partida de costes de materiales directos

⇛ efficiency variance

price-earnings ratio

→ price/earnings ratio

price-recovery component

The price-recovery component calculates the change in operating profit from one accounting period to another which is not attributable to changes in productivity, but only to changes in prices of inputs and outputs.

componente de la recuperación del precio

▲ *an unfavorable price recovery component* un componente de la recuperación del precio desfavorable ▲ *revenue effect of price-recovery component* efecto de los ingresos en el componente de la recuperación del precio

price/book ratio US

= market to book ratio, P/BV, price/book value

The price/book ratio is an investment ratio or multiple defined as the share price divided by the book value per share. A price/book ratio exceeding 1 means that the value of the company's shares exceeds that of the equity. This ratio shows how the market values the company and its future.

ratio precio/valor en libros
= ratio precio-valor contable, ratio precio-valor en libros, ratio precio/valor contable
▲ *price/book ratio per stock* ratio precio/valor en libros por acción

price/book value UK
= market to book value, P/BV, price to book value, price/book ratio
The price/book value is an investment ratio or multiple defined as the share price divided by the book value per share. A price/book value exceeding 1 means that the value of the company's shares exceeds that of the equity. This ratio shows how the market values the company and its future.

ratio precio/valor en libros
= ratio precio por valor en libros, ratio precio-valor en libros
▲ *price/book value per share* ratio precio/valor en libros por acción

price/cash flow
= PCF, price/cash flow ratio
The price/cash flow is a measure of the market's expectations regarding a firm's future financial health. It is calculated by dividing market price per share by cash flow per share.

precio/flujo de efectivo
= precio por flujo de efectivo, precio-flujo de efectivo, ratio precio/flujo de efectivo
▲ *calculate a price/cash flow* calcular un precio por flujo de efectivo ▲ *price/cash flow per share* precio/flujo de efectivo por acción

price/cash flow ratio
= P/CF ratio, PCF, price/cash flow
The price/cash flow ratio is a financial ratio defined as the market price per share divided by the cash flow per share. As it is related to an enterprise's cash flow, this ratio is used to assess that enterprise's future ability to generate a return in the form of capital gains or dividend distributions.

ratio precio/flujo de efectivo
= ratio precio-cash flow, ratio precio-flujo de efectivo, ratio precio/cash flow
▲ *calculate the price/cash flow ratio* calcular el ratio precio/flujo de efectivo ▲ *have a price/cash flow ratio below 15* tiene un ratio precio/flujo de efectivo inferior a 15 ▲ *price/cash flow ratio as of 31 December* ratio precio/flujo de efectivo a 31 de diciembre

price/earnings ratio
= earnings multiple, P/E, P/E ratio, PER
The price/earnings ratio or P/E ratio is defined as the market price per share divided by earnings per share (EPS). This investment ratio, also referred to as the earnings multiple, compares the market price of an ordinary share with the EPS and is used to analyse the performance potential of a company. A high P/E ratio indicates future earnings growth and signals that investors have high confidence in the company.

ratio precio/beneficios
= PER, ratio precio beneficios, ratio precio-beneficios
▲ *calculate the price earnings ratio* calcular el ratio precio beneficios ▲ *historical price-earnings ratio* ratio precio-beneficios histórico ▲ *projected price-earnings ratio* ratio precio-beneficios proyectado

price/net asset value
= P/NAV
Price/net asset value is a financial ratio defined as share price divided by net asset value per share, measuring the value of shareholders' equity by relating the market price per share in relation to its book value.

ratio precio valor contable de la acción
= precio/valor contable de la acción, ratio precio/valor contable de la acción
▲ *calculate price/net asset value* calcular el ratio precio valor contable de la acción ▲ *price/net asset value calculations* cálculo

del ratio precio valor contable de la acción

primary activity

= core activity

≠ secondary activity

A primary activity is a principal activity that is the root cause for the existence of an enterprise and which is its objective.

actividad principal

= actividad primaria

▲ *the primary activities of the group* las actividades principales del grupo

primary financial instrument

Primary financial instruments refer to financial instruments that are not derivative financial instruments. Examples are all types of receivables and payables as well as equity instruments.

instrumento financiero primario

▲ *the financial risks inherent in an underlying primary financial instrument* los riesgos financieros inherentes a un instrumento financiero primario subyacente ▲ *the underlying primary financial instrument* el instrumento financiero primario subyacente

primary insurer

= cedant, ceding company

≠ assuming company, reinsurer

Within the context of reinsurance, a primary insurer is an insurance company that passes on (cedes) the risk to a reinsurer.

aseguradora primaria

▲ *a primary insurer's net contractual rights under a reinsurance contract* derechos contractuales netos de una aseguradora primaria según un contrato de reaseguros ▲ *losses on one or more contracts issued by the primary insurer* pérdidas en uno o más contratos emitidos por la aseguradora primaria ▲ *the primary insurer's accounting policies* las políticas contables de la aseguradora primaria

prime

Prime is a rating used by the credit rating agency Moody's for short-term debt ratings. Prime-1 is the highest quality, after which ranges Prime-2 and Prime-3. Not Prime is lowest on the rating scale and comparable to Speculative Grade on the long-term debt-rating scale.

calificación de solvencia

= prime

prime cost

Prime cost is the total of all costs that directly relate to production including direct materials costs, direct labour costs as well as other direct costs.

coste básico

▲ *5% of prime cost* 5% de coste básico ▲ *accounting for prime costs* contabilizando los costes básicos ▲ *reduce prime costs by 10%* reducir los costes básicos en un 10%

principal[1] *noun*

1 = principal amount

The principal refers to the initial amount of a loan on which interest is charged.

principal

▲ *a right to receive a return of principal* un derecho a recibir una rentabilidad del principal ▲ *blended payments of principal and interest under a loan agreement* pagos combinados de principal e intereses según un acuerdo de préstamo ▲ *default of principal* impago del principal ▲ *index the principal by reference to a commodity price* indizar el principal con referencia al precio de una materia prima ▲ *ordinary shares issued in place of interest or principal on other financial instruments* acciones ordinarias emitidas en el lugar de intereses o principal en otros instrumentos financieros ▲ *principal plus interest at LIBOR minus 100 basis points* principal más intereses al LIBOR menos 100 puntos básicos ▲ *reduced payments of principal* pagos reducidos del principal ▲ *repayment of principal and finance income* amortización del principal e ingresos financieros ▲ *stated rate or amount of interest, dividend or other periodic return on principal* tipo nominal o cuantía del interés, dividendo u otro rendimiento periódico del principal ▲ *the financial asset's original principal* el principal original del activo financiero ▲ *the stated principal* el principal acordado

2 = face value

The principal is the face or par value of a security, typically a

bond, repayable on maturity, on which interest is charged.
nominal
▲ *derivatives with a principal exceeding USD 10m* derivados con un principal por encima de 10 millones de euros ▲ *represent 5.5% of the principal of EUR 2.24m* representar el 5,5% del nominal de 2,24 millones de euros

principal[2] *adjective*
Principal means that something is the most essential or significant, i.e. it ranks first in terms of importance.
básico
▲ *principal place of business* lugar básico del negocio ▲ *the principal characteristics of the financial instruments that are pertinent to their value* las características básicas de los instrumentos financieros que no son pertinentes para su valor ▲ *the principal provisions of the lease* las provisiones básicas del arrendamiento

principal activity
= core business, core business area
Principal activities refer to the activities of an enterprise that generate most of the turnover or revenue, i.e. the enterprise's main products or services.
actividad principal
▲ *a description of the nature of the enterprise's operations and its principal activities* una descripción de la naturaleza de las operaciones de la empresa y sus actividades principales

principal amount
= principal
The principal amount is the original amount borrowed from a lender on which interest is charged, i.e. the original value of a debt.
cantidad principal
= principal
▲ *a principal amount of EUR 1,000* una cantidad principal de 1.000 euros ▲ *average aggregate principal amount* cantidad principal agregada media ▲ *exchange the principal amount for a fixed quantity of oil* cambiar el principal por una cantidad fija de petróleo ▲ *future cash receipts or payments of the principal amount of the instrument* ingresos en efectivo futuros o pagos del principal del instrumento ▲ *nominal principal amount* cantidad principal nominal ▲ *principal amount relating to credit card customers* principal relacionado con las tarjetas de crédito de los clientes ▲ *repayment of the principal amount* devolución del principal ▲ *the agreed, notional principal amount* la cantidad principal nocional, acordada ▲ *the principal amount of bonds* el principal de los bonos ▲ *the principal amount of the asset* el principal del activo

principal item
A principal item is a main item in a financial statement. In the balance sheet, the principal items are the head items above the items preceded by Roman and Arabic numerals, showing elements such as fixed assets, current assets, creditors, provisions and equity.
partida principal
▲ *a separate principal item* una partida principal separada ▲ *present principal items in the income statement* presentar las partidas principales en el estado de resultados ▲ *relevant principal items* partidas principales relevantes

principal shareholder UK, US
= principal stockholder US
A principal shareholder is a person or an enterprise holding 10% or more of the outstanding shares in an enterprise or possessing the power to control or direct the enterprise.
accionista principal
▲ *become a principal shareholder* llegar a ser un accionista principal ▲ *concealed dividend to a principal shareholder* dividendo ocultado a un accionista principal
⇛ major shareholder, majority shareholder

principal stockholder US
A principal stockholder is a person or an enterprise holding 10% or more of the outstanding shares in an enterprise or possessing the power to control or direct the enterprise.
accionista principal
▲ *become a principal stockholder* llegar a ser un accionista principal ▲ *concealed dividend to a principal stockholder* dividendo ocultado a un accionista principal

⇛ principal shareholder

principle of conservatism US

= conservatism convention, prudence UK, IAS/IFRS

The principle of conservatism is an accounting concept implying being prudent in measuring assets and ensuring that uncertainty and risks are adequately disclosed. In the financial statements, revenues are only included when realised, and liabilities are provided for whether certain or uncertain.

principio de prudencia

= principio de conservadurismo, principio de prudencia valorativa

▲ *in conformity with the principle of conservatism* de acuerdo con el principio de prudencia ▲ *one part of the principle of conservatism* una parte del principio de prudencia

principle of determination

The principle of determination is the method applied for determining the measurement bases used in financial statements, e.g. fair value, or used for impairment testing or for assessing the tax base of assets.

principio de valoración

▲ *compatible with the principle of determination* compatible con el principio de valoración ▲ *the principle of determination of the tax base* el principio de valoración de la base impositiva

prior to maturity

Prior to maturity means before maturity or expiry, i.e. before the redemption date or the date when a loan must be repaid.

anterior al vencimiento

▲ *redemption prior to maturity in whole or in part* pago completo o parcial anterior al vencimiento ▲ *sell securities prior to maturity* vender títulos anteriores al vencimiento ▲ *terminate a derivative contract prior to maturity* terminar un contrato de derivados anterior al vencimiento

prior year

= previous year

The prior year is the previous year, i.e. the year preceding the current year or year under review.

ejercicio precedente

= ejercicio anterior

▲ *prior year adjustment* ajuste al ejercicio precedente ▲ *the relevant prior year financial statements* los estados financieros relevantes del ejercicio precedente

prior-year period

Prior-year period refers to the same accounting period of the prior financial year, e.g. if a figure relates to Q1 2006, then the figure of the prior-year period is the one relating to Q1 2005.

periodo correspondiente del ejercicio anterior

▲ *compared to 150 million euros in the prior-year period* comparado con 150 millones de euros en el periodo correspondiente del ejercicio anterior ▲ *the comparable prior-year period* el periodo correspondiente del ejercicio anterior comparable

private company

→ private limited company

private corporation US

1 = closed corporation US, private limited company UK, privately-held company US, privately-held corporation US

≠ public corporation US, public limited company UK, publicly-held company US

A private corporation is a company whose shares are not publicly traded. Usually, private corporations are closely-held, meaning that they have few owners.

empresa no cotizada

= empresa privada no cotizada

▲ *form a private corporation* formar una empresa no cotizada ▲ *the bylaws of the private corporation* los estatutos de la empresa no cotizada ▲ *the charter of the private corporation* el estatuto de la empresa no cotizada

2 ≠ public corporation US

A private corporation is formed to conduct privately-owned business, i.e. by private parties as opposed to government.

empresa privada

= empresa de capital privado

≠ empresa pública

▲ *form a private corporation* formar una empresa de capital privado

private limited company

= Ltd. UK, private company UK

≠ public company UK, public limited company UK
A private limited company is a company that is not allowed to offer its share for sale to the public and for which disclosure requirements are less onerous than for public limited companies.
empresa no cotizada
▲ *form a private limited company* formar una empresa no cotizada ▲ *the articles of association of the private limited company* los artículos de la escritura de constitución de la empresa no cotizada ▲ *the memorandum of association of the private limited company* la escritura de constitución de la empresa no cotizada ▲ *the promoters of a private limited company* los promotores de una empresa no cotizada ▲ *wind up a private limited company* cerrar una empresa no cotizada
⇛ close company

private placement US
= private placing UK
Private placement is the sale of securities, typically shares or bonds, directly to a group of private individuals or institutional investors such as pension funds or insurance companies. The sale usually takes place via an intermediary such as an investment bank. Contrary to a public offering, securities that are privately placed are not available for sale to the general public and do not trade on a stock exchange.
colocación privada
▲ *complete a private placement* completar una colocación privada ▲ *issue shares by private placement* emitir acciones para su colocación privada ▲ *make a private placement* hacer una colocación privada
⇛ institutional investor, offering

private placing UK
= private placement US
Private placing is the sale of securities, typically shares or bonds, directly to a group of private individuals or institutional investors such as pension funds or insurance companies. The sale usually takes place via an intermediary such as an investment bank. Contrary to a public placing, securities that are privately placed are not available for sale to the general public and are not traded on a stock exchange.
colocación privada
▲ *complete a private placing* completar una colocación privada ▲ *issue shares by private placing* emitir acciones para su colocación privada ▲ *make a private placing* hacer una colocación privada
⇛ institutional investor, offering

privately-held company US
= close corporation US, closed corporation US, closely-held corporation US, private corporation US, privately-held corporation US
≠ publicly-held company
A privately-held company is a company whose shares are not publicly traded. Privately-held companies are typically closely-held, meaning that they have few owners.
empresa no cotizada
▲ *found a privately-held company* fundar una empresa no cotizada

privately-held corporation US
→ privately-held company

pro forma
Pro forma figures, results, financial statements etc. are not complete or final, but show what is expected to happen, often based on estimates.
pro forma
▲ *a pro forma balance sheet* un balance pro forma ▲ *additional pro forma comparative information on a restated basis* información comparativa pro forma adicional reformulada ▲ *pro forma invoice* factura pro forma ▲ *the period for which pro forma information is presented* el periodo en el que se presenta la información pro forma ▲ *the presentation of additional pro forma information* la presentación de información pro forma adicional

pro forma comparatives
When an enterprise changes accounting policies, its comparative figures for prior years will not be immediately comparable with the figures presented under the new policies. Therefore, pro forma comparatives based on historical data

are construed and restated to meet the accounting policy changes, in this way ensuring comparability with previous comparative figures.

comparativas pro forma

▲ *additional pro forma comparatives* comparativas pro forma adicionales ▲ *additional pro forma comparatives on a restated basis* comparativas pro forma adicionales reformuladas

pro forma figure

Pro forma figures are budgeted or projected figures, i.e. they are not complete or final, but show what is expected to happen, often based on estimates.

cifra pro forma

▲ *consolidated pro forma figures* cifras pro forma consolidadas

pro forma financial statements

≠ primary financial statements

Pro forma financial statements are financial statements that are budgeted for future accounting periods or prepared on different assumptions than the primary financial statements.

estados financieros pro forma

▲ *prepare pro forma financial statements* preparar los estados financieros pro forma ▲ *release pro forma financial statements* publicar los estados financieros pro forma

pro forma statements

→ pro forma financial statements

pro-forma

→ pro forma

pro-forma financial statements

→ pro forma financial statements

pro-rata allocation

Pro-rata allocation refers to the allocation of revenues or expenses between several groups, units or activities in proportion to their share or usage.

asignación prorrateada

▲ *a reasonable pro-rata allocation* una asignación prorrateada razonable ▲ *pro-rata allocation of goodwill* asignación prorrateada del fondo de comercio

pro-rata consolidation

→ proportionate consolidation

probability

Probability refers to the likelihood that an uncertain event will take place and can be estimated on a scale ranging from 0.0 (not occurring) to 1.0 (certain to occur). A 0.5 probability expresses that there is 50% certainty (or uncertainty) that the event will occur.

probabilidad

▲ *a 90% probability* una probabilidad del 90% ▲ *a minimal probability of material losses for a whole book of contracts* una probabilidad mínima de pérdidas materiales para un conjunto completo de contratos ▲ *an assessment of the probability of losses arising in the future* una valoración de la probabilidad de las pérdidas que puedan surgir en el futuro ▲ *assess the probability of expected future economic benefits* valorar la probabilidad de los beneficios económicos futuros esperados ▲ *subject to the probability criterion for recognition* sujeto al criterio de probabilidad para su reconocimiento ▲ *the probability of loss* la probabilidad de pérdida

probability distribution

Probability distribution is the specification, typically on a curve, showing the probabilities of values and occurrences of a random variable.

distribución de la probabilidad

= distribución de probabilidad

▲ *an associated probability distribution* una distribución de la probabilidad asociada ▲ *give rise to a probability distribution* dar lugar a una distribución de la probabilidad

probable

Probable means that something is likely but not certain to happen or to be true or real.

probable

▲ *a hedged highly probable forecast transaction* una previsión de transacción con cobertura altamente probable ▲ *a probable decline* un descenso probable ▲ *a probable event* un suceso probable ▲ *a probable future economic benefit* un beneficio económico futuro probable ▲ *a probable income* un ingreso probable ▲ *a probable loss* una pérdida probable ▲ *highly probable* altamente probable ▲ *probable future earnings* beneficios futuros probables

SOURCE IFRS 3, Appendix A

problem-solving US

Problem-solving within accounting is the assessment of

courses of action and recommendation of the best course to follow.
solución de problemas
= problem-solving
▲ *creative problem-solving* solución de problemas creativa ▲ *develop problem-solving skills* desarrollar destrezas en la solución de problemas ▲ *problem-solving techniques* técnicas para la solución de problemas

procedure
In a business context, procedures refer to a set of instructions or guidelines that specify how a particular business function or task should be carried out.
procedimiento
▲ *in the normal course of procedure* en el curso normal del procedimiento

proceeds
Proceeds refer to the gain usually in the form of cash that is obtained in connection with a sales transaction or a loan less any costs involved.
ingresos
= cobros, ingresos en efectivo
▲ *any excess of sales proceeds over the carrying amount* cualquier excedente en los ingresos de ventas sobre el valor contable ▲ *expected proceeds* ingresos esperados ▲ *proceeds from borrowings* ingresos de empréstitos ▲ *proceeds from buy-back and sale of treasury shares* ingresos de la recompra y venta de acciones propias ▲ *proceeds from incurring mortgage debt* ingresos procedentes de la deuda hipotecaria ▲ *proceeds from issue of shares* ingresos de la emisión de acciones ▲ *proceeds from long-term borrowings* ingresos procedentes de empréstitos a largo plazo ▲ *proceeds from the issue of convertible debt instruments* ingresos de la emisión de instrumentos de deuda convertibles ▲ *proceeds from the issue of ordinary shares* ingresos de la emisión de acciones ordinarias ▲ *proceeds from the issue of redeemable class A shares* ingresos procedentes de acciones de clase A amortizables ▲ *proceeds from the sale of products and services* ingresos de la venta de productos y servicios ▲ *reduce the proceeds from the equity issue* reducir los ingresos de la emisión de títulos ▲ *the net disposal proceeds* ingresos netos por ventas ▲ *the proceeds on the ultimate disposal of the investment* los ingresos por liquidación de la inversión ▲ *the proceeds received* los ingresos recibidos

process costing
→ process-costing system

process map
A process map is a workflow diagram representing the correlation of activities, cost objects and resources of an enterprise.
mapa de procesos
▲ *create a process map* crear un mapa de procesos

process reengineering
= business process reengineering, reengineering
Process reengineering is a variance method which, based on a well-defined strategy and rethinking, fundamentally and radically renews, adjusts and redesigns the business processes of an enterprise to achieve decisive improvements on critical factors of performance such as costs, quality, service and time.
reingeniería de procesos
▲ *information on process reengineering* información sobre la reingeniería de procesos ▲ *successful process reengineering* reingeniería de procesos exitosa ▲ *the underlying principles for process reengineering* los principios subyacentes para llevar a cabo la reingeniería de procesos

process-costing system
A process-costing system is a system for cost calculation according to which the costs of mass- or series-produced products are determined by accumulating costs for an entire production process and calculating the average unit production costs at each stage of production.
sistema de costes por procesos
▲ *cost flows in a process-costing system* flujos de coste en un sistema de costes por procesos ▲ *the average unit cost in a process-costing system* el coste unitario medio en un sistema de costes por procesos
⇛ hybrid costing system

processing cost
Processing costs are the costs incurred in connection with

the processing of products seen in a wide sense such as payroll costs and production overheads.
coste de procesamiento
▲ *minimise processing costs* minimizar los costes de procesamiento ▲ *unit processing cost* coste de procesamiento unitario

procure
To procure something means to obtain or acquire it.
obtener
▲ *procure raw materials* obtener materias primas

procurement
Procurement means the obtaining or acquisition of something.
procedimiento de contratación
= contratación
▲ *Community law on public procurement* derecho comunitario en el procedimiento de contratación pública ▲ *government procurements* procedimientos de contratación pública ▲ *the procurement of materials* el procedimiento de contratación de materiales ▲ *values of thresholds in the field of public procurement* valores de referencia en el campo del procedimiento de contratación

product
= article, goods
Products are physical objects that are produced or grown with a view to being sold and generating a profit for the person or enterprise selling them.
producto
▲ *a breakthrough for a new product* un avance significativo para un nuevo producto ▲ *a change in the market demand for the product* un cambio en la demanda para el producto ▲ *a credit derivative default product* un producto contra el impago de un crédito derivativo ▲ *an expected purchase or sale of a product* una compra o venta esperada de un producto ▲ *costs of introducing a new product* costes de introducción de un nuevo producto ▲ *objective information about patterns over a product lifecycle* información objetiva sobre modelos a lo largo de la vida de un producto ▲ *product warranties* garantías del producto ▲ *the carrying amount of the main product* el valor contable del producto principal

product
A product is an output with a positive sales value or an output that an enterprise can sell or dispose of without incurring extra costs.
producto
▲ *agricultural products* productos agrícolas ▲ *classification of products by activity* clasificación de productos por actividad ▲ *manufacture a product* fabricar un producto ▲ *product deletion* descatalogación de productos ▲ *product range* gama de productos ▲ *sell products* vender productos

product cost
Product costs are costs directly relating to a specific unit and individual product, comprising both direct and indirect productions costs.
coste del producto
▲ *fixed product costs* costes fijos del producto ▲ *variable product costs* costes variables del producto
⇛ direct cost, indirect production cost

product development cost
Product development costs refer to the costs incurred by an enterprise when carrying out development activities, i.e. when developing new products or production processes or developing further existing products or production processes in order to improve them or enhance their efficiency.
coste de desarrollo del producto
▲ *calculate product development costs* calcular los costes de desarrollo del producto ▲ *product development costs directly related to individual segments* costes de desarrollo del producto relacionados directamente con segmentos individuales ▲ *recognise product development costs as intangible assets are amortised* reconocer costes de desarrollo de productos cuando se amortizan los activos intangibles ▲ *the product development costs incurred* los costes de desarrollo del producto incurridos

product differentiation
Product differentiation refers to an enterprise's efforts to show customers and potential customers how its products differ from other

similar products of its own or from similar, competing products through advertising, packaging or other visible product differences. In this way, the products are distinguished from other products to make them attractive in the eyes of the customers.

diferenciación en el producto

▲ *successful product differentiation* diferenciación en el producto exitosa ▲ *the degree of product differentiation* el grado de diferenciación en el producto ▲ *the need for product differentiation* la necesidad de diferenciación en el producto

product guarantee

= product warranty, warranty

A product guarantee is a legally binding obligation of a producer, seller or distributor vis-à-vis a buyer to replace or repair a sold product if it appears to be defective. A product guarantee is additional to the protection of the buyer under the law and usually, it has to be exercised within a specified period of time after the sale.

garantía del producto

= garantía

▲ *give a product guarantee* dar una garantía del producto ▲ *give product guarantees* dar las garantías del producto ▲ *provisions relating to product guarantees* provisiones relacionadas con las garantías del producto

product liability

Product liability is the legal responsibility of manufacturers and distributors for any injuries or damages resulting from the use of their products.

responsabilidad por daños

▲ *incur product liability* incurrir en responsabilidad por daños ▲ *insurance against product liability* seguro contra responsabilidad por daños

product life cycle US

The product life cycle is the various stages of a product from initial product specification over maturation to its withdrawal from the market. The stages include research, development, introduction, maturity, decline and abandonment.

ciclo de vida del producto

▲ *typical product life cycles for the asset* ciclos de vida del producto típicos del activo

⇛ life cycle assessment, life-cycle budgeting

product mix

= product-mix

A product mix is the allocation, in terms of percentages, of the total product range of an enterprise.

mezcla de productos

▲ *a wide product mix* una mezcla de productos amplia ▲ *expand the product mix* expandir la mezcla de productos ▲ *length of product mix* la amplitud de la mezcla de productos ▲ *rework the product mix* reelaborar la mezcla de productos

product overcosting

≠ product undercosting

The use of simple costing systems, e.g. by allocating costs to different products by averaging, may lead to product overcosting where a product that uses few resources is reported to have a high cost per unit.

sobreimputación de costes al producto

≠ infraimputación de costes al producto

▲ *avoid product overcosting* evitar la sobreimputación de costes al producto ▲ *result in product overcosting* dar como resultado una sobreimputación de costes al producto

product undercosting

≠ product overcosting

The use of simple costing systems, e.g. by allocating costs to different products by averaging, may lead to product undercosting where a product that uses many resources is reported to have a low cost per unit.

infraimputación de costes al producto

≠ sobreimputación de costes al producto

▲ *avoid product undercosting* evitar la infraimputación de costes al producto ▲ *result in product undercosting* dar como resultado una infraimputación de costes al producto

product warranty

= product guarantee

A product warranty is an enterprise's legally binding promise that a product upholds a certain quality and that any product defect occurring under certain conditions and within a specific period of time after purchase will result in repair, replacement or reimbursement.

certificado de garantía

▲ *product warranties issued by another party for goods sold by a retailer* certificados de garantía emitidos por otro participante correspondiente a los bienes vendidos por un minorista ▲ *product warranties issued directly by a retailer* certificados de garantía emitidos directamente por un minorista ▲ *product warranty obligations retained by the seller* obligaciones del certificado de garantía mantenidos por el vendedor

product-cost cross-subsidization

Product-cost cross-subsidization refers to the situation where enterprises deliberately calculate certain costs lower on one or more products or services to calculate higher costs on other products or services. A mobile operator may e.g. decide to charge high call rates, having low sales prices on mobile phones.

producto con coste multicompensado

▲ *evidence of product-cost cross-subsidization* prueba de producto con coste multicompensado ▲ *result in product-cost cross-subsidization* finalizar en un producto con coste multicompensado

product-costing method

A product-costing method is a costing system that seeks to determine the costs attributable to a particular product, unit of production or batch.

método coste-producto

▲ *an accurate product-costing method* un método coste-producto fiable ▲ *choose an alternative product-costing method* eligir un método coste-producto alternativo ▲ *use a product-costing method* utilizar un método coste-producto

product-mix

= product mix

A product-mix is the allocation, in terms of percentages, of the total product range of an enterprise.

mezcla de productos

▲ *a changed product-mix* una mezcla de productos cambiada ▲ *a wide product-mix* una mezcla de productos amplia ▲ *determine the product-mix* determinar la mezcla de productos ▲ *expand the product-mix* expandir la mezcla de productos ▲ *systematic appraisal of the enterprise's product-mix* valoración sistemática de la mezcla de productos de la empresa

product-mix decision

A product-mix decision is the decision made by an enterprise as to which products in which quantities are to enter into its product line in order for the enterprise to maximize its profit.

decisión sobre la gama de productos

▲ *affect the product-mix decision* efectar a la decisión sobre la gama de productos ▲ *product-mix decision criteria* criterios para la decisión sobre la gama de productos ▲ *strategic product-mix decision* decisión sobre la gama de productos estratégica ▲ *the objective of the product-mix decision* el objetivo de la decisión sobre la gama de productos

product-sustaining cost

Product-sustaining costs are costs related to a particular product that are incurred because an enterprise has the product in its product range. Such costs relate to the type of product and are independent of the volume of units produced. Examples are product development costs or marketing costs.

coste por mantenimiento del producto

▲ *an increase in product-sustaining costs* un aumento en los costes por mantenimiento del producto ▲ *high product-sustaining costs* costes elevados por mantenimiento del producto

production

1 Production is the act or process of manufacturing goods, building or growing products, or delivering services performed by an enterprise based on the coordination, acquisition or assembly of resources.

producción

= fabricación

▲ *a competitive production* una producción competitiva ▲ *at the completion of production* al

final de la producción ▲ *changes in the volume of production* cambios en el volumen de producción ▲ *commercial production* producción comercial ▲ *costs directly related to the units of production* costes directamente relacionados con las unidades de producción ▲ *costs that vary with the level of production of the entity* costes que varían con el nivel de producción de la entidad ▲ *periods of abnormally high production* periodos de producción inusualmente alta ▲ *the amortisation of intangible assets used in a production process* la amortización de activos intangibles utilizados en una producción ▲ *the production or supply of goods or services* la producción o suministro de bienes o servicios
⇛ production capacity

2 = output
Production refers to the quantity of products or services which an enterprise is capable of manufacturing, producing or making during a specific time period.
producción
= fabricación
▲ *the estimated amount of production* la cantidad de fabricación estimada ▲ *the price that the purchaser will pay for the production* el precio que el comprador paga por la producción
⇛ productive capacity, productivity

production capacity
= productive capacity
Production capacity refers to the total output or maximum quantity of products or services which an enterprise is capable of manufacturing or producing during a specific time period.
capacidad de producción
= capacidad productiva
▲ *calculated production capacity* capacidad de producción calculada ▲ *excess production capacity* exceso de capacidad de producción ▲ *extension of the production capacity* extensión de la capacidad de producción ▲ *idle production capacity* capacidad de producción ociosa ▲ *increase the production capacity* aumentar la capacidad de producción ▲ *investments in production capacity* inversiones en la capacidad de producción ▲ *physical production capacity* capacidad de producción física ▲ *reach the estimated production capacity* alcanzar la capacidad de producción estimada ▲ *reduce the production capacity* reducir la capacidad de producción ▲ *utilised production capacity* capacidad de producción utilizada
⇛ output, production, productivity

production cost
Production costs are direct and indirect costs that relate to production, i.e. prime costs and production overheads. Production costs may be expressed as the total of all costs relating to production or as per unit of production.
coste de producción
▲ *abnormal amounts of wasted materials, labour or other production costs* cantidades anormales de residuos, personal y otros costes de producción ▲ *allocation of production costs* asignación de costes de producción ▲ *direct production costs* costes de producción directos ▲ *include indirect production costs in the value of inventories* incluir los costes de producción en el valor de inventarios ▲ *increase productions costs* aumentar los costes de producción ▲ *indirect production costs* costes de producción indirectos ▲ *reduce future production costs* reducir los costes de producción futuros ▲ *unallocated production costs* costes de producción no imputados

production department
A production department is a department in a manufacturing enterprise which creates and adds value to a product or a service, i.e. where production takes place.
departamento de producción
▲ *work in a production department* trabajar en un departamento de producción
⇛ service department, support department

production facility
Production facilities refer to buildings, machinery and equipment owned or leased by an enterprise enabling it to carry out its production processes.

instalación productiva
= fábrica
▲ *adaptation of production facilities* adaptación de las instalaciones productivas ▲ *the actual use of the production facilities* el uso actual de las instalaciones productivas ▲ *the normal capacity of the production facilities* la capacidad normal de las instalaciones productivas

production manager
A production manager is a manager in an enterprise whose responsibility is to manage and control the production processes.
director de producción
▲ *appoint a new production manager* nombrar un nuevo director de producción ▲ *the company's production manager* el director de producción de la empresa ▲ *the former production manager* el director de producción anterior ▲ *the retiring production manager* el director de producción saliente

production overhead IAS/IFRS
= factory burden US, factory overhead US, indirect manufacturing cost, indirect manufacturing expense US, indirect production cost, indirect production expense US, manufacturing overhead US, manufacturing overhead cost
Production overheads are costs that are not directly related to the production of goods, i.e. costs for which single products or activities cannot be identified. Examples of production overheads are indirect labour and materials, rent and insurance of manufacturing units.
coste de producción indirecto
▲ *capitalise production overheads* capitalizar los costes de producción indirectos ▲ *compulsory recognition of production overheads* reconocimiento obligatorio de los costes de producción indirectos ▲ *fixed production overheads* costes de producción indirectos fijos ▲ *production overheads that are incurred in converting materials into finished goods* costes de producción indirectos que se incurren al transformar las materias primas en bienes finales ▲ *recognise production overheads* reconocer los costes de producción indirectos ▲ *related production overheads* costes de producción indirectos relacionados ▲ *systematic allocation of production overheads* asignación sistemática de los costes de producción indirectos ▲ *the amount of fixed production overheads* la cuantía de los costes de producción indirectos ▲ *unallocated production overheads* costes de producción indirectos no asignados ▲ *variable production overheads* costes de producción indirectos variables

production wages
Production wages refer to the remuneration paid to employees in the production department directly engaged in the production processes.
salarios de producción
▲ *average production wages* salarios de producción medios ▲ *hourly production wages* salarios de producción por hora

production-denominator level
= denominator level
A production-denominator level is a chosen production level based on e.g. the budgeted sales or the production capacity. The production-denominator level serves as a calculation basis for the rate of fixed indirect production costs used for allocation of these costs on various cost objects.
tasa predeterminada de distribución de costes indirectos de fabricación
= tasa predeterminada de distribución de los costes indirectos de fabricación

production-volume variance
= denominator-level variance, output level overhead variance, output-level variance
Production-volume variance is the difference between the budgeted fixed indirect production costs (overheads) and the fixed indirect production costs (overheads) that have been allocated to the produced units.
variación en la tasa predeterminada de distribución de costes indirectos de fabricación
= variación en la tasa predeterminada de distribución de los costes indirectos de fabricación
▲ *a favourable production-volume variance* una variación en la tasa predeterminada de distribución de costes indirectos de

fabricación favorable ▲ *the production-volume variance of a period* la variación en la tasa predeterminada de distribución de costes indirectos de fabricación de un periodo

productive capacity

= production capacity

Productive capacity refers to the total output or maximum quantity of products or services which an enterprise is capable of manufacturing or producing during a specific time period.

capacidad productiva

= capacidad de producción

▲ *calculated productive capacity* capacidad productiva calculada ▲ *excess productive capacity* exceder la capacidad productiva ▲ *extension of the productive capacity* extensión de la capacidad productiva ▲ *idle productive capacity* capacidad productiva ociosa ▲ *increase the productive capacity* aumentar la capacidad productiva ▲ *investments in productive capacity* inversiones en la capacidad productiva ▲ *physical productive capacity* capacidad productiva física ▲ *reach the estimated productive capacity* alcanzar la capacidad productiva estimada ▲ *reduce the productive capacity* reducir la capacidad productiva ▲ *utilised productive capacity* capacidad productiva utilizada

⇛ output, production, productivity

productivity

Productivity is a measure of the efficiency of production and may be expressed as the amount of output generated by a given amount of input or as the amount of output over a given period of time.

productividad

▲ *closing of a facility to achieve productivity improvements* cierre de una instalación para conseguir mejoras en la productividad ▲ *partial productivity* productividad parcial

productivity component

A productivity component measures the change in costs related to a change in the quantity of inputs between the current and previous periods.

componente de productividad

▲ *adapt the productivity component* adaptar el componente de productividad

professional

Professional used about somebody or something implies relationship to a particular profession or experience that requires special skills, expertise or educational and training background.

profesional

▲ *a professional regulatory body* un órgano regulador profesional ▲ *amounts paid to legal, accounting and other professional advisers* cantidades pagadas a los asesores legales, contables y otros profesionales ▲ *appropriate professional qualifications and experience* cualificaciones y experiencia profesional adecuada ▲ *information covered by professional secrecy* información protegida por el secreto profesional ▲ *insurance against professional liability* seguro de responsabilidad profesional ▲ *professional association* asociación profesional ▲ *professional competence* competencia profesional ▲ *professional education* educación profesional ▲ *professional ethics* ética profesional ▲ *professional fees* honorarios profesionales ▲ *professional fees arising directly from bringing the asset to its working condition* honorarios profesionales directamente procedentes de trasladar el activo a explotación ▲ *professional integrity* integridad profesional ▲ *professional interests* intereses profesionales ▲ *professional secrecy* secreto profesional ▲ *professional standard* norma profesional

profile of returns

A profile of returns shows how future returns on a particular investment are distributed over a certain period of time.

perfil de rendimientos

= cuadro estimativo de rendimientos

▲ *an asymmetric profile of returns* un perfil de rendimientos asimétrico

profit

1 = income US

≠ loss US, UK, IAS/IFRS

For an accounting period, profit constitutes the earnings of an enterprise, i.e. the amount by which revenue exceeds expenses, resulting in increased total assets.

beneficio
= ganancia
▲ *a growing profit* un beneficio creciente ▲ *a specified increase in the entity's profit over a specified period of time* un aumento especificado en el beneficio de la entidad durante un periodo de tiempo especificado ▲ *a specified level of profit to be maintained or achieved in future periods* un nivel de beneficio especificado para ser mantenido o logrado en periodos futuros ▲ *affect accounting profit* afectar al beneficio contable ▲ *distributions from accumulated profits* distribuciones de los beneficios acumulados ▲ *events that occur after the public announcement of profit* sucesos que ocurren después del anuncio público del beneficio ▲ *expected profit* beneficio esperado ▲ *group profit before minority interests* beneficio del grupo antes de los intereses de los accionistas minoritarios ▲ *insufficient profits* beneficios insuficientes ▲ *profit for the year* beneficio del año ▲ *profit from continuing operations attributable to the parent entity* beneficio procedente de operaciones continuas atribuibles a la matriz ▲ *profit from extraordinary items* beneficio de partidas extraordinarias ▲ *profit from ordinary activities before tax* beneficio de actividades ordinarias antes de impuestos ▲ *profit from ordinary operating activities* beneficio de actividades de explotación ordinarias ▲ *the consolidated profit* el beneficio consolidado

2 = gain
A profit is the amount by which the sales price exceeds the costs of products or services sold or the gain obtained on the sale of an asset.
margen
= ganancia
▲ *a reasonable profit* un margen razonable ▲ *eliminate profit* eliminar el margen ▲ *expected profit* margen esperado ▲ *intercompany profit* margen entre empresas ▲ *internal profit* margen interno ▲ *profit on sale* margen de venta ▲ *projected profit* margen proyectado ▲ *unrealised profit* margen no realizado

profit after tax UK
= income after income tax US, post-tax profit IAS/IFRS, UK
≠ income before income tax US, pre-tax profit IAS/IFRS, UK, profit before tax UK, IAS/IFRS
The profit after tax is the profit of an enterprise for an accounting period after deduction of tax expense.
beneficio después de impuestos
▲ *adjusted profit after tax* beneficio después de impuestos ajustado ▲ *Group's share of profit after tax* la proporción del beneficio después de impuestos del grupo ▲ *percentage change in profit after tax* cambio en el porcentaje en el beneficio después de impuestos ▲ *profit after tax before exceptional items* beneficio después de impuestos antes de partidas excepcionales ▲ *reconciliation to profit after tax* conciliación a beneficio después de impuestos

profit and loss account[1] UK
= income statement US, IAS/IFRS, P&L account UK, profit and loss statement UK
The profit and loss account shows income recognised with the deduction of costs recognised resulting in earnings for the period, i.e. the profit or loss for the period.
cuenta de pérdidas y ganancias
= cuenta de resultados, estado de resultados
▲ *aggregate expenses in the profit and loss account* gastos agregados en la cuenta de pérdidas y ganancias ▲ *an item in the profit and loss account* una partida en la cuenta de pérdidas y ganancias ▲ *comparative figures for the profit and loss account* figuras comparativas para la cuenta de pérdidas y ganancias ▲ *format for the profit and loss account* formato para la cuenta de pérdidas y ganancias ▲ *include in the profit and loss account* incluir en la cuenta de pérdidas y ganancias ▲ *notes to the profit and loss account* notas a la cuenta de pérdidas y ganancias ▲ *offsetting in the profit and loss account* compensando en la cuenta de pérdidas y ganancias ▲ *prepare a profit and loss account* preparar una cuen-

ta de pérdidas y ganancias ▲ *present a profit and loss account* presentar una cuenta de pérdidas y ganancias ▲ *present in the profit and loss account* presentar en la cuenta de pérdidas y ganancias ▲ *profit and loss account classified by function* cuenta de pérdidas y ganancias clasificada por función ▲ *profit and loss account classified by type of expenditure* cuenta de pérdidas y ganancias clasificada por tipo de gasto ▲ *profit and loss account in vertical format* cuenta de pérdidas y ganancias en formato vertical ▲ *recognise immediately in the profit and loss account* reconocer inmediatemente en la cuenta de pérdidas y ganancias ▲ *recognition in the profit and loss account* reconocer en la cuenta de pérdidas y ganancias ▲ *the effect on the profit and loss account* el efecto en la cuenta de pérdidas y ganancias ▲ *the predictive value of the profit and loss account* el valor predictivo de la cuenta de pérdidas y ganancias

profit and loss account[2] UK *noun*

= accumulated profit UK, retained earnings IAS/IFRS, US, retained loss, retained profit IAS/IFRS, UK

Profit and loss account is an asset item in the balance sheet under capital and reserves representing the profit and loss reserve or retained earnings transferred from the profit and loss account after deduction of any dividends.

resultado del ejercicio

▲ *the amount of the profit and loss account* la cantidad del resultado del ejercicio

profit and loss account format UK

= income statement format IAS/IFRS, US

A profit and loss account format is a presentation form and layout of a statement of the profit or loss prescribed by legislation or accounting standards, e.g. the UK Companies Act, the Danish Financial Statements Act, IFRS and FASB.

formato de cuenta de pérdidas y ganancias

= formato de la cuenta de pérdidas y ganancias

▲ *items in the profit and loss account format* partidas en el formato de la cuenta de pérdidas y ganancias ▲ *profit and loss account format for groups* formato de la cuenta de pérdidas y ganancias por grupos

⇛ account form, horizontal format, report form, vertical format

profit and loss account item UK

1 = income statement item US, IAS/IFRS, statement of income item US, IAS/IFRS

Profit and loss account items are elements in the profit and loss account such as turnover, cost of sales, gross profit, tax, profit or loss for the financial year etc.

partida de la cuenta de pérdidas y ganancias

▲ *notes to profit and loss account items* notas a las partidas de la cuenta de pérdidas y ganancias

2 = profit and loss account UK, retained earnings US, IAS/IFRS

The profit and loss account item under reserves in the balance sheet is the item where net ordinary as well as extraordinary profits or losses are transferred from the profit and loss account or income statement.

partida de resultados no aplicados

▲ *consolidated profit and loss account item* la partida de resultados no aplicados consolidada ▲ *the breakdown of the profit and loss account item* la distribución de la partida de resultados no aplicados

profit and loss reserve UK

= retained earnings

The profit and loss reserve is an item under equity constituted by net ordinary as well as extraordinary profits or losses transferred from the profit and loss account or income statement.

reserva de beneficios no distribuidos

= reserva de los beneficios no distribuidos

▲ *excluding the profit and loss reserve* excluyendo la reserva de beneficios no distribuidos

profit before tax UK, IAS/IFRS

= income before income tax US, pre-tax profit UK, IAS/IFRS

≠ income after income tax US, post-tax profit IAS/IFRS, profit after tax

Profit before tax is the profit of an enterprise for an accounting period before deduction of tax expense.

beneficio antes de impuestos

= ganancia antes de impuestos

▲ *adjusted profit before tax* beneficio antes de impuestos ajustado ▲ *Group profit before tax* beneficio antes de impuestos del Grupo ▲ *profit before tax and exceptional items* beneficio antes de impuestos y partidas excepcionales

profit center US

= profit centre UK

A profit center is a section, division or other responsibility center of en enterprise to which revenues and costs are traceable. The manager of the center is accountable for revenues and costs and consequently the profitability of that particular center.

centro de resultados

= centro de beneficios

▲ *become a profit center* llegar a ser un centro de beneficios ▲ *function as a profit center* funcionar como un centro de resultados

⇛ responsibility center

profit centre UK

= profit center US

A profit centre is a section, division or other responsibility centre of en enterprise to which revenues and costs are traceable. The manager of the centre is accountable for revenues and costs and consequently the profitability of that particular centre.

centro de resultados

= centro de beneficios

▲ *become a profit centre* llegar a ser un centro de resultados ▲ *function as a profit centre* funcionar como un centro de beneficios

⇛ responsibility centre

profit decline UK

A decline in profits means that company results are poorer seen in relation to previous accounting years.

disminución de beneficios

▲ *profit decline before tax* disminución de beneficios antes de impuestos

profit elimination

Profit elimination is made on consolidation of the financial statements of a parent and its subsidiaries to ensure that any profits from intra-group transactions are ignored in the consolidated profit presented in the consolidated financial statements of a group to ensure that the group is accounted for as a single economic entity.

eliminación de resultados

= eliminación de beneficios

▲ *intercompany profit elimination* eliminación de resultados entre empresas ▲ *the tax effect of unrealized profit elimination* el efecto fiscal de la eliminación de beneficios no realizada

⇛ consolidated financial statements, consolidation

profit from operating activities

= operating income, operating profit

≠ operating loss

Profit from operating activities is the revenue generated from the normal business activities of an enterprise less cost of goods sold and operating expenses, presented before interest, tax, depreciation and amortisation in the profit and loss account.

beneficio por actividades ordinarias

= beneficio de actividades ordinarias, beneficio de explotación

≠ pérdida por actividades ordinarias

▲ *cash flow based profit from operating activities* flujos de efectivo basados en el beneficio por actividades ordinarias

⇛ EBITDA

profit from sale of real property

Profit from sale of real property is the gain realised on disposal of real property, typically the amount that results after deducting the proceeds from the sale, i.e. the sales price less sales costs and fees, from the purchase price of the property in question.

beneficio por la venta de bienes raíces

▲ *capital gains on shares and profits from sale of real property* ganancias de capital en acciones y beneficios por la venta de bienes raíces

⇛ proceeds

profit increase UK

= increase in profits

A profit increase is an improvement of the earnings for the period compared with the earnings for previous periods and means that the profit for the period has been improved.

aumento de beneficios

▲ *a good profit increase* un aumento de beneficios importante

profit margin

= EBITDA margin, operating margin, return on sales, ROS

The profit margin is the difference between the price of a product or service and the cost of producing it. Often applied as a financial ratio calculated as a company's operating profit divided by sales, also referred to as the operating margin.

margen de beneficios

= margen de explotación

▲ *a high profit margin* un alto margen de beneficios ▲ *calculate the profit margin* calcular el margen de beneficios ▲ *constitute a single project with an overall profit margin* constituir un proyecto único con un margen de beneficios completo ▲ *determine the present value of a future profit margin* determinar el valor actual de un margen de beneficios futuro

profit on ordinary activities

= income from ordinary activities

Profit on ordinary activities is the income or loss from the recurring business operations and activities incidental to or arising from these operations, such as investing and financing, contributing to an increase or decrease in net assets.

beneficio de actividades ordinarias

= beneficio por actividades ordinarias

▲ *other profit on ordinary activities* otro beneficio de actividades ordinarias ▲ *total profit on ordinary activities* total beneficio de actividades ordinarias

profit on payments received on account

A profit on payments received on account is the profit that arises when the payments on account to an enterprise exceed the expenses attributable to the account in question.

beneficio por pagos recibidos a cuenta

▲ *recognised profit on payments received on account* beneficio por pagos recibidos a cuenta reconocido ▲ *reverse profit on payments received on account* beneficio contrario por pagos recibidos a cuenta

profit or loss before tax

= pre-tax profit or loss

Profit or loss before tax is the profit or loss of an enterprise for an accounting period before deduction of tax expense.

resultado antes de impuestos

▲ *a proportional share of the profit or loss before tax* una parte proporcional del resultado antes de impuestos ▲ *consolidated profit or loss before tax* resultado consolidado antes de impuestos

profit or loss from ordinary operating activities UK

= income or loss from ordinary operating operations US

Profit or loss from ordinary operating activities is a subtotal derived from the profit and loss account appearing as profit or loss before tax and extraordinary items adjusted for other operating income and expenses as well as interest income and expenses.

resultado procedente de actividades de explotación ordinarias

= resultado procedente de operaciones de explotación ordinarias

profit or loss on ordinary activties UK

The profit or loss on ordinary activities of an enterprise is the profit or loss before extraordinary expenses and may be carried before and after tax.

resultado por actividades ordinarias

= resultado de actividades ordinarias

▲ *estimated profit or loss on ordinary activities* resultado por actividades ordinarias estimado ▲ *profit or loss on ordinary activities after tax* resultado por actividades ordinarias después de impuestos ▲ *tax on profit or loss on ordinary activities* impuesto sobre el resultado por actividades ordinarias

profit plan

= operating budget, production budget

A profit plan or operating budget refers to the part of an enterprise's budget that relates to the main activities of the enterprise, containing e.g. budgets for production costs and volume as well as projections of operating revenues and expenses for an accounting period.

presupuesto de explotación

▲ *annual profit plan* presupuesto de explotación anual ▲ *prepare a profit plan* preparar un presupuesto de explotación ▲ *strategic profit plan* presupuesto de explotación estratégico

profit share

1 A profit share is the share of the earnings for a period distributed as dividends by a company to its shareholders.

participación en beneficios

▲ *average profit share* participación en beneficios media ▲ *performance-related profit share* participación en beneficios relacionada con el rendimiento

2 A profit share is the share of the profit in an enterprise that is attributable to each owner of an enterprise, e.g. a partnership or a company, usually constituting a certain percentage of total earnings. Under profit-sharing schemes, employees can have a share in profits, typically through a share ownership.

beneficio por acción

▲ *a negative profit share* un beneficio por acción negativo ▲ *pre-tax profit share* beneficio por acción antes de impuestos

profit smoothing UK

= income smoothing US

Profit smoothing is the levelling of the profit for the year of an enterprise as a result of the application of different applicable accounting principles.

nivelación de beneficios

▲ *use as a profit smoothing device* utilizar como un instrumento de nivelación de beneficios

profit warning

A profit warning is an announcement made by a public company in advance of its earnings announcement indicating that profits will fall short of previously expected levels.

profit warning

= aviso de menores beneficios

▲ *issue a profit warning* emitir un profits warning

profit-sharing debt instrument

A profit-sharing debt instrument is a participating bond, i.e. a corporate bond that, depending on the terms and type of instrument, besides fixed interest also offers the right to a share in the issuing enterprise's profit when exceeding a certain limit, or a corporate bond with interest payments that are tied to the issuing enterprise's profit.

instrumento de deuda con derecho a la participación en beneficios

▲ *convertible and profit-sharing debt instruments* convertible e instrumentos de deuda con derecho a la participación en beneficios ▲ *issue profit-sharing debt instruments* emitir instrumentos de deuda con derecho a la participación en beneficios

profit-to-sales ratio

→ return on sales

profitability

Profitability is the ability of an enterprise to generate profits and therefore measures the return on invested capital in that enterprise. Various financial ratios measure profitability such as operating margin, EBITA margin, cash flow from operations, return on invested capital, return on equity and financial gearing.

rentabilidad

▲ *a wide range of factors relating to current and expected profitability* un amplio abanico de factores relacionados con la rentabilidad actual y la esperada ▲ *assess the profitability* analizar la rentabilidad ▲ *declining profitability* rentabilidad decreciente ▲ *ensure satisfactory profitability* asegurar una rentabilidad satisfactoria ▲ *falling profitability* rentabilidad decreciente ▲ *high profitability* alta rentabilidad ▲ *improve profitability* mejorar la rentabilidad ▲ *increased profitability* rentabilidad aumentada ▲ *increasing profitability* rentabilidad creciente ▲ *low profitability* baja rentabilidad ▲ *operational profitability* rentabilidad operacional ▲ *reduced profitability* rentabilidad reducida ▲ *set mini-*

mum profitability requirements establecer requisitos de rentabilidad mínimos ▲ *stable profitability* rentabilidad estable
⇛ financial ratio, ROIC

profitable
If an investment or a transaction is profitable, it generates earnings or net profits that exceed all costs related to that investment or transaction.
rentable
▲ *have a history of profitable operations* tener una historia de operaciones rentables ▲ *in a profitable manner* rentable ▲ *profitable growth* crecimiento rentable ▲ *the expectation of profitable operation over the asset's economic life* la expectativa de una operación rentable durante la vida económica del activo

profits warning UK
A profits warning is an announcement from a company that its profit for a particular period of time will be lower than expected.
profits warning
= aviso de menores beneficios
▲ *issue a profits warning* emitir un profits warning

proforma financial statements
→ pro forma financial statements

programmed cost US
= discretionary cost UK, US, managed cost UK, management cost US, policy cost UK, programmed cost US, programmed fixed cost US
≠ committed cost UK, US
Programmed costs are discretionary fixed costs that are determined by and change because of managerial decisions without any obvious relationship with capacity or production activity. Examples are marketing, training, research and development costs.
coste discrecional
≠ coste inevitable
▲ *change the programmed cost* cambiar el coste discrecional
⇛ fixed cost

progress billing US
Progress billings are interim billings in connection with e.g. contract work in progress, typically in connection with long-term construction contracts.
certificación por obra
▲ *amounts of progress billings* cantidades de certificaciones por obra ▲ *compare against progress billings up to the balance sheet date* comparar con las certificaciones por obra hasta la fecha del balance ▲ *less progress billings* menos certificaciones por obra ▲ *the sum of recognised losses and progress billings* la suma de pérdidas reconocidas y de certificaciones por obra

progress payment US
Progress payments are interim payments, i.e. payments on account, for e.g. contract work in progress, typically in connection with long-term construction contracts.
pago a cuenta
▲ *current progress payments* pagos a cuenta corrientes ▲ *progress payments and advances received from customers* pagos a cuenta y anticipos recibidos de clientes ▲ *progress payments received* pagos a cuenta recibidos
⇛ progress billing

progressive
If something is progressive, it increases in percentage terms.
progresivo
= creciente
▲ *a progressive depreciation method* un método de amortización creciente ▲ *progressive depreciation* amortización creciente ▲ *progressive tax* impuesto progresivo ▲ *progressive tax rate structure* estructura fiscal progresiva ▲ *provide for depreciation using a progressive scale* provisionar una amortización utilizando una escala progresiva

progressive amortisation UK, IAS/IFRS
= progressive amortization US
Progressive amortisation is an amortisation method under which amortisation increases proportionally from accounting period to accounting period.
NOTE The term progressive amortisation applies to intangible assets.
amortización creciente
= amortización progresiva
NOTE Spanish accountants prefer 'amortización creciente' to the IAS/IFRS' term 'amortización progresiva'.

▲ *provide for progressive amortisation* provisionar por amortización creciente
⇛ progressive depreciation

progressive amortization US
= progressive amortisation UK, IAS/IFRS
Progressive amortization is an amortization method under which amortization increases proportionally from accounting period to accounting period.
NOTE The term progressive amortization applies to intangible assets.
amortización progresiva
= amortización creciente
▲ *provide for progressive amortization* provisionar la amortización progresiva
⇛ progressive depreciation

progressive depreciation
Progressive depreciation is a depreciation method under which depreciation increases proportionally from accounting period to accounting period.
NOTE The term progressive depreciation applies to tangible assets.
amortización creciente
▲ *provide for progressive depreciation* provisionar por amortización creciente
⇛ progressive amortisation

project cost
Project costs are costs incurred in relation to the execution of a specific project.
coste del proyecto
▲ *determination of project costs* determinación de los costes del proyecto ▲ *the project costs incurred* costes del proyecto incurridos

projected benefit obligation
= PBO
A projected benefit obligation is an estimate of the present value of a pension plan's discounted liabilities at a particular date.
obligación por prestación proyectada
▲ *interest expense of the projected benefit obligation* gesto por intereses de la obligación por prestación proyectada ▲ *the increase in the projected benefit obligation* el aumento en la obligación por prestación proyectada
⇛ accumulated benefit obligation

projected unit credit method
= projected unit method
Within the context of pension plans, the projected unit credit method is a method for calculating the final benefit obligation of a pension plan by measuring benefit entitlements through the allocation of these entitlements to separate units related to individual periods of service.
método de la unidad de crédito proyectada
▲ *use the projected unit credit method to determine the present value of defined benefit obligations* utilizar el método de la unidad de crédito proyectada para determinar el valor actual de las obligaciones del plan de pensiones de prestación definida ▲ *use the projected unit credit method to measure obligations and costs* utilizar el método de la unidad de crédito proyectada para cuantificar las obligaciones
⇛ projected benefit obligation

projected unit method UK
→ projected unit credit method

projection
A projection is a quantitative estimate of the future economic or financial performance of a company, country, or other financial entity based on econometric models and using historical and current data.
proyección
▲ *base cash flow projections on reasonable and supportable assumptions* estimar las proyecciones de flujo de efectivo en supuestos razonables y comprobables ▲ *economic projections* proyecciones económicas ▲ *make projections of future results* hacer proyecciones de los resultados futuros ▲ *projection of future operating cash flows* proyecciones de flujos futuros de efectivo de explotación ▲ *projections of cash inflows from the continuing use of the asset* proyecciones de entradas de flujos de efectivo por el uso continuo del activo ▲ *projections of cash outflows* proyecciones de salidas de flujos de efectivo

promotion expense
Promotion expenses refer to expenses incurred by an enter-

prise when promoting its products or services to generate interest among potential customers. Promotion expenses include expenses for advertising, brochures, exhibitions etc., and constitute a type of marketing expenses.
gasto de promoción
▲ *incur promotion expenses* incurrir en gastos de promoción

property[1] *noun* <a, the, properties>

1 A property means a building or a house.
edificio
= inmueble, propiedad
▲ *invest in real property* inversión en bien raíz ▲ *investments in real property* inversiones en bienes raíces ▲ *net operating income from real property* ingresos de explotación netos procedentes de inmuebles ▲ *operate an internal property fund* operar un fondo de propiedad interna ▲ *property intended for sale in the ordinary course of business* edificio mantenido para la venta en el curso ordinario del negocio ▲ *purchases or sales of property and other assets* compras o ventas de edificios y otros activos ▲ *real property* bien raíz ▲ *real property agency business* agencia de la propiedad inmobiliaria ▲ *real property sales* venta de inmuebles ▲ *the property's purchase price and any directly attributable costs* el precio de compra del edificio y cualesquiera costes directamente atribuibles ▲ *use of a property* uso de un edificio

2 = building
A property is a building.
edificio
= propiedad
▲ *a depreciable property* un edificio amortizable

property[2] *noun* <no indefinite article, the, no plural>
= real property
Property means assets owned by an individual or an enterprise such as land and buildings.
propiedad
= terrenos y construcciones
▲ *a property vendor* un vendedor de propiedad ▲ *a purchase of property* una compra de propiedad ▲ *increasing property prices* precios de la propiedad en aumento ▲ *recently acquired property* propiedad adquirida recientemente

property company
A property company is a company whose primary objective is to own and operate one or more properties in order to buy, sell or rent properties.
inmobiliaria
▲ *the acquisition of property by a property company* la adquisición de edificios por una inmobiliaria

property held for sale
= trading property
Property held for sale is property that has been constructed or acquired with a view to resale within a few years.
propiedad mantenida para la venta
▲ *the carrying amount of the property held for sale* el valor contable de la propiedad mantenida para la venta

property interest
A property interest is an enterprise's or a person's proportionate ownership, i.e. legal, equitable or beneficial interest in a property.
inversión inmobiliaria
▲ *a property interest that is held by a lessee under an operating lease* una inversión inmobiliaria que mantiene un arrendatario baja contrato de arrendamiento operativo ▲ *change the nature of the lessee's property interest* cambiar la naturaleza de la inversión inmobiliaria del arrendatario ▲ *determine the fair value of a property interest* determinar el valor razonable de una inversión inmobiliaria ▲ *eligible property interests* inversiones inmobiliarias elegibles ▲ *the initial cost of a property interest held under a lease* el coste inicial de una inversión inmobiliaria mantenida según un contrato de arrendamiento
⇛ ownership interest

property, plant and equipment
US, IAS/IFRS
= PPE US, IAS/IFRS, tangible asset IAS/IFRS, UK, tangible fixed asset UK
Property, plant and equipment are tangible, i.e. physical, non-current assets intended for long-term ownership or use by

an enterprise for its operating activities and administration. "Property, plant and equipment" is an item under non-current assets in the balance sheet.

edificios, instalaciones y equipos

= inmobilizado material, propiedad, planta y equipo

NOTE Although the Spanish traditional accounting term 'edificios, instalaciones y equipos' (always plural) is common in Spanish accounting texts, the Nuevo Plan General Contable (2007) uses the IAS/IFRS term 'propiedad, planta y equipo' (singular).

▲ *a class of property, plant and equipment* un tipo de edificios, instalaciones y equipos ▲ *a self-constructed item of property, plant and equipment* un elemento autoconstruido incluido en edificios, instalaciones y equipos ▲ *acquisition of property, plant and equipment* adquisición de inmovilizado material ▲ *acquisitions and disposals of items of property, plant and equipment* adquisiciones y enajenaciones de elementos incluidos en edificios, instalaciones y equipos ▲ *an item of property, plant and equipment* una partida de edificios, instalaciones y equipos ▲ *commitments for the purchase of property, plant and equipment* compromisos por la compra de edificios, instalaciones y equipos ▲ *construction of property, plant and equipment* construcción de inmovilizado material ▲ *depreciation of property, plant and equipment used for development activities* depreciación de edificios, instalaciones y equipos utilizados para actividades de desarrollo ▲ *derecognition of items of property, plant and equipment retired or disposed of* anulación de elementos incluidos en edificios, instalaciones y equipos retirados o eliminados de ▲ *fair value gains on property, plant and equipment* ganancias a valor razonable en inmovilizado material ▲ *investments in property, plant and equipment* inversiones en inmovilizado material ▲ *losses arising from sale of property, plant and equipment* pérdidas por venta de inmovilizado material ▲ *measure property, plant and equipment at cost* valoración de edificios, instalaciones y equipos al coste ▲ *prepayments for property, plant and equipment* anticipos por inmovilizado material ▲ *property, plant and equipment classified as held for sale* edificios, instalaciones y equipos clasificados como mantenidos para la venta ▲ *property, plant and equipment held for disposal* edificios, instalaciones y equipos mantenidos para la venta ▲ *property, plant and equipment pledged as security for liabilities* edificios, instalaciones y equipos pignorados como colateral para deudas ▲ *property, plant and equipment retired from active use* edificios, instalaciones y equipos retirados del uso activo ▲ *property, plant and equipment under construction* inmovilizado material en curso ▲ *property, plant and equipment with a limited useful life* inmovilizado material con una vida útil limitada ▲ *purchase of property, plant and equipment* compra de inmovilizado material ▲ *recognition of a loss from the impairment of property, plant and equipment* reconocimiento de una pérdida por deterioro de edificios, instalaciones y equipos ▲ *revaluation of property, plant and equipment* revalorización de inmovilizado material ▲ *revalue property, plant and equipment to fair value* revaluar inmovilizado material a valor razonable ▲ *sale of property, plant and equipment* venta de inmovilizado material ▲ *temporarily idle property, plant and equipment* edificios, instalaciones y equipos temporalmente ociosos ▲ *the carrying amount of property, plant and equipment* el valor contable de inmovilizado material ▲ *the construction or development of an item of property, plant and equipment* la construcción o desarrollo de un elemento incluido en edificios, instalaciones y equipos ▲ *the cost of an item of property, plant and equipment* el coste de un elemento incluido en edificios, instalaciones y equipos ▲ *the gross carrying amount of any fully depreciated property, plant and equipment that is still in use* el valor contable bruto de cualesquiera edificios, instalaciones y equipos totalmente depreciados que todavía están en uso

property portfolio

A property portfolio is the total holdings of properties held by an individual or an enterprise for investment purposes.

cartera de inversión inmobiliaria

▲ *a significant property portfolio* una cartera de inversión inmobiliaria significativa ▲ *revalue the property portfolio on an ongoing basis* revalorizar la cartera de inversión inmobiliaria de acuerdo con el principio de empresa en funcionamiento ▲ *the entire property portfolio* la cartera de inversión inmobiliaria completa

property tax UK

= real estate tax US, real property tax

Property tax is tax levied on real property by local governments, assessed on the property value and charged according to local tax rates. In the UK, tax on property is charged in the form of council tax for residential property and business rates for business property.

impuesto sobre bienes inmuebles

= IBI

▲ *calculate the property tax* calcular el impuesto sobre bienes inmuebles ▲ *collect property tax* recaudar el impuesto sobre bienes inmuebles ▲ *levy property tax* gravar el impuesto sobre bienes inmuebles ▲ *property tax exemption* exención del impuesto sobre bienes inmuebles

proportional

= proportionate

If something is proportional to something else it means that it has a constant relationship in size or degree to something else despite changes in the two objects.

proporcional

▲ *approximately proportional to the overall change in fair value* aproximadamente proporcional al cambio completo en el valor razonable ▲ *the proportional interest in the fair value* el interés proporcional en el valor razonable

proportional consolidation

= proportionate consolidation

Proportional consolidation refers to an accounting method used by entities, typically venture enterprises, in their financial statements for recognising their proportional shares of jointly controlled enterprises. When using this method, the entities consolidate their shares of the assets, liabilities, revenues and expenses of the jointly controlled enterprise in their financial statements.

consolidación proporcional

▲ *application of proportional consolidation* aplicación de la consolidación proporcional ▲ *apply proportional consolidation* aplicar la consolidación proporcional ▲ *be included in the consolidated financial statements by proportional consolidation* estar incluido en los estados financieros consolidados mediante la consolidación proporcional ▲ *discontinue the use of proportional consolidation* descontar el uso de la consolidación proporcional ▲ *exceptions to proportional consolidation* excepciones a la consolidación proporcional ▲ *financial statements in which proportional consolidation is applied* estados financieros en los que la consolidación proporcional se aplica ▲ *include an enterprise in the consolidated financial statements by proportional consolidation* incluir una empresa en los estados financieros consolidados mediante la consolidación proporcional ▲ *proportional consolidation of investments in jointly controlled enterprises* consolidación proporcional de las inversiones en empresas controladas de forma conjunta ▲ *recognise the interest in the jointly controlled entity using proportional consolidation* reconocer la inversión en la entidad controlada conjuntamente utilizando la consolidación proporcional ▲ *use one of the two reporting formats for proportional consolidation* utilizar uno de los dos formatos de información para la consolidación proporcional ▲ *use proportional consolidation* utilizar la consolidación proporcional ▲ *use the line-by-line reporting format for proportional consolidation* utilizar el formato línea a línea para la consolidación proporcional

proportionate

= proportional

If something is proportionate to something else it means that it has a constant relationship in size or degree to something else despite changes in the two objects.

proporcional

▲ *a fully proportionate share of the cash flows from a financial asset* una participación totalmente proporcional de los flujos de efectivo procedentes de un activo financiero ▲ *a proportionate net loss* una pérdida neta proporcional ▲ *a proportionate net profit* un beneficio neto proporcional ▲ *adjustment of the proportionate share* ajuste de la participación proporcional ▲ *elimination of the proportionate share* eliminación de la participación proporcional ▲ *proportionate ownership share* participación proporcional en la propiedad ▲ *recognise on the basis of a proportionate allocation* reconocer según una asignación proporcional ▲ *the proportionate change in the number of ordinary shares outstanding* el cambio proporcional en el número de acciones ordinarias ▲ *the proportionate intrinsic value* el valor intrínseco proporcional ▲ *the proportionate share* la participación proporcional

proportionate consolidation

= pro-rata consolidation, proportional consolidation

≠ full consolidation, line-by-line consolidation

Proportionate consolidation refers to an accounting method used by entities, typically venture enterprises, in their financial statements for recognising their proportionate shares of jointly controlled enterprises. When using this method, the entities consolidate their shares of the assets, liabilities, revenues and expenses of the jointly controlled enterprise in their financial statements.

consolidación proporcional

▲ *application of proportionate consolidation* aplicación de la consolidación proporcional ▲ *apply proportionate consolidation* aplicar la consolidación proporcional ▲ *be included in the consolidated financial statements by proportionate consolidation* estar incluido en los estados financieros consolidados por medio de la consolidación proporcional ▲ *discontinue the use of proportionate consolidation* interrumpir el uso de la consolidación proporcional ▲ *exceptions to proportionate consolidation* excepciones a la consolidación proporcional ▲ *financial statements in which proportionate consolidation is applied* estados financieros en los que se aplica la consolidación proporcional ▲ *include an enterprise in the consolidated financial statements by proportionate consolidation* incluir una empresa en los estados financieros consolidados mediante consolidación proporcional ▲ *proportionate consolidation of investments in jointly controlled enterprises* consolidación proporcional de inventarios en empresas controladas conjuntamente ▲ *recognise the interest in the jointly controlled entity using proportionate consolidation* reconocer la participación en la entidad controlada conjuntamente utilizando la consolidación proporcional ▲ *to report under proportionate consolidation in the financial statements of an enterprise* anotar de acuerdo con la consolidación proporcional en los estados financieros de una empresa ▲ *use one of the two reporting formats for proportionate consolidation* utilizar uno de los dos formatos de anotación para la consolidación proporcional ▲ *use proportionate consolidation* utilizar la consolidación proporcional ▲ *use the line-by-line reporting format for proportionate consolidation* utilizar el formato de anotación línea a línea para la consolidación proporcional

proprietary theory US

= proprietory theory

The proprietary theory is the theory that assets are owned and liabilities are owed by the proprietor(s) as expressed in the equation: assets less liabilities equal equity. The enterprise is the means for the proprietors to generate income as revenues increase equity. As a personal relationship exists between the owner in the role of manager of the enterprise and the owner as a private individual, the theory is particularly relevant for enterprises established as single proprietorships.

teoría de la propiedad

= teoría del propietario

▲ *according to the proprietary theory* de acuerdo con la teoría de la propiedad ▲ *be consistent with proprietary theory* ser consistente con la teoría de la propiedad

⇛ proprietary view

proprietary view

≠ entity concept, entity theory

The proprietary view focuses on the owners of an enterprise rather than on the enterprise itself as a separate entity. The emphasis is therefore on equity defined as assets less liabilities and belonging to the owners, rather than on assets constituting the basis for carrying on the enterprise's operating activities and defined as equal to equity and liabilities.

visión de la propiedad

▲ *use the proprietary view for accounting purposes* utilizar la visión de la propiedad por motivos contables

⇛ proprietary theory

proprietor US

→ sole proprietorship

proprietory theory

= proprietary theory

The proprietory theory is the philosophy that assets are owned and liabilities owed by the proprietor(s) as expressed in the equation: assets less liabilities equal equity. The enterprise is the means for the proprietors to generate income as revenues increase equity. As a personal relationship exists between the owner in the role of manager of the enterprise and the owner as a private individual, the theory is particularly relevant for enterprises established as single proprietorships.

teoría de la propiedad

= teoría del propietario

▲ *according to the proprietory theory* de acuerdo con la teoría de la propiedad ▲ *be consistent with proprietory theory* ser consistente con la teoría de la propiedad

⇛ proprietary view

prorate

To prorate is to allocate something on a pro rata basis, i.e. proportionally. For instance, the deviation that is the consequence of under- or overallocated indirect production costs is prorated on work-in-progress, finished goods and cost of sales.

prorratear

▲ *prorate costs* prorratear costes

⇛ proportional, proportionate

proration

Proration is a distribution of something such as income, expenses or payment on a pro rata basis, i.e. proportionately. An example of proration is the proportional allocation of the deviation resulting from under- or overallocated indirect production costs on work in progress, finished goods and cost of sales.

prorrateo

▲ *automatic proration* prorrateo automático ▲ *full proration of costs* prorrateo completo de costes

⇛ proportional

prospectus

A prospectus is a document prepared when a company wants to invite the public to buy its shares as part of an initial public offering or an increase of its share capital.

folleto de emisión

▲ *a full prospectus* un folleto de emisión completo ▲ *a preliminary prospectus* un folleto de emisión preliminar ▲ *a revised prospectus* un folleto de emisión revisado ▲ *a simplified prospectus* un folleto de emisión simplificado ▲ *approval of a prospectus* aprobación de un folleto de emisión ▲ *European passport for prospectuses* pasaporte europeo para los folletos de emisión ▲ *obligation to prepare a prospectus* obligación de preparar un folleto de emisión ▲ *prepare a prospectus* preparar un folleto de emisión ▲ *publish a prospectus* publicar un folleto de emisión ▲ *supplement to a prospectus* suplemento a un folleto de emisión ▲ *the prospectus in its final form* el folleto de emisión en su formato final

prospectus announcement

A prospectus announcement is advance information to the stock exchange and the public that a company intends to make a public offering for shares. The announcement must be made no later than on the business day before the publication of the prospectus, giving details about where and what time the prospectus can be obtained.

anuncio de publicación del folleto de emisión

▲ *supplementary prospectus announcement* anuncio de publicación del folleto de emisión adicional

Prospectus Directive

The Prospectus Directive is a legislative act adopted by the European Parliament and the Council, and it contains rules to ensure an effective European passport for prospectuses and to ensure a high level of information in order to protect investors when securities are offered to the public or admitted to trading.

Directiva sobre el Folleto de Emisión

▲ *comply with the Prospectus Directive* cumplir con la Directiva sobre el Folleto de Emisión

prospectus requirement

Prospectus requirements are company disclosure requirements laid down by legislation and stock exchange regulation. These requirements are aimed at ensuring that a prospectus prepared by a listed enterprise, which forms the basis of decision of potential investors, gives a true and fair view of the issuer's assets and liabilities, its financial position, performance and expected future development.

requisito del folleto de emisión

▲ *comply with the prospectus requirements* cumplir con los requisitos del folleto de emisión ▲ *prospectus requirements and terms of issue on admission of shares for listing* requisitos del folleto de emisión y las condiciones de emisión para la admisión a cotización de las acciones ▲ *prospectus requirements for issuers of listed shares* requisitos del folleto de emisión para los emisores de las acciones cotizadas

prove

To prove something, such as a statement or data, means to establish the truth or validity of that statement or data by providing documentation that supports it.

probar

▲ *prove something to somebody* probar algo a alguien

provide

1 = obtain, raise

To provide something is to procure or get it.

proporcionar

▲ *expenditure incurred to provide future economic benefits to the entity* gastos incurridos para proporcionar beneficios económicos futuros a la entidad ▲ *financial liabilities that provide financing on a long-term basis* pasivos financieros que proporcionan financiación a largo plazo ▲ *provide a period of grace* proporcionar un periodo de gracia ▲ *provide additional guidance on estimating the discount rate* proporcionar ayuda adicional al estimar el tipo de descuento ▲ *provide assistance to users* proporcionar ayuda a los usuarios ▲ *provide evidence* proporcionar pruebas ▲ *provide information about the financial position of the entity* proporcionar información sobre la posición financiera de la entidad ▲ *provide sufficient evidence of the fair value of another asset* proporcionar pruebas suficientes del valor razonable de otro activo ▲ *provide the most reliable estimate of the fair value of an intangible asset* proporcionar la estimación más fiable del valor razonable de un activo intangible

2 = make a provision

To provide for e.g. future obligations means to set aside an amount as a provision in the financial statements.

provisionar

▲ *restoration costs that have already been provided for* costes de reposición que ya han sido provisionados ▲ *the amount provided* la cantidad provisionada

provide return

To provide return means to create added value and profitability, e.g. in the form of dividend or other return on an investment.

proporcionar rendimiento

▲ *provide return on equity* proporcionar rendimiento al título ▲ *provide returns to the investors* proporcionar rendimientos a los inversores

⇛ return on equity, return on investment

provided

That an amount has been provided means that it has been set aside to cover future liabilities.

provisionada

▲ *the amount provided* la cantidad provisionada

provision

1 A provision is a liability that is uncertain in terms of amount or timing and that concerns the current financial year or a previous financial year.

provisión

▲ *a provision of GBP 100,000* una provisión de 100.000 libras esterlinas ▲ *a specific type of provision* un tipo específico de provisión ▲ *adjust a provision already recognised* ajustar una provisión ya reconocida ▲ *catastrophe provisions* provisiones para catástrofes ▲ *measure a provision* medir una provisión ▲ *other provisions* otras provisiones ▲ *provisions for bonuses and rebates* provisiones para primas y bonificaciones ▲ *provisions for doubtful debts related to the amount of outstanding balances* provisiones para deudas de dudoso cobro hasta la cuantía de los saldos pendientes ▲ *provisions for possible future claims* provisiones para posibles reclamaciones futuras ▲ *provisions for restructuring costs* provisiones para costes de reestructuración ▲ *provisions for unearned premiums* provisiones para primas no devengadas ▲ *provisions made during the year* provisiones hechas durante el año ▲ *provisions used during the year* provisiones utilizadas durante el año ▲ *recognise a provision* reconocer una provisión ▲ *reverse a provision* revertir una provisión ▲ *the carrying amount of the provision for restoration costs* el valor contable de las provisiones para costes de restauración

2 A provision is a condition or statement in an act, an accounting standard, an agreement or other regulatory instrument.

disposición

▲ *a provision in the lease giving the hirer an option to acquire title to the asset* una disposición en el contrato de arrendamiento que da al arrendador una opción para adquirir la titularidad del activo ▲ *an automatic provision to extend the remaining term to maturity of a debt instrument* una disposición automática para extender el término restante hasta el vencimiento de un instrumento de deuda ▲ *contractual provisions* disposiciones contractuales ▲ *the part of the contingent settlement provision that could require settlement in cash or another financial asset* la parte de la disposición para liquidación contingente que pudiera requerir liquidación en efectivo u otro activo financiero

3 Provision is the procurement or supplying of something.

provisión

= suministro

▲ *provision of a non-monetary benefit* provisión de un beneficio no monetario ▲ *provision of essential technical information* provisión de información técnica esencial ▲ *provision of guarantees or collateral* provisión de garantías o colateral ▲ *provision of services* provisión de servicios

provision against offsetting

Provisions against offsetting are rules that disallow that two items or balances are offset in the financial statements. Accounting rules generally require that transactions, events or valuations be recognised and measured separately and not offset, unless it is specifically allowed.

provisión para compensación

▲ *comply with the provision against offsetting* cumplir con la provisión para compensación

SOURCE IAS 1, paragraph 33 et seq.

provision for bad and doubtful debts UK

= allowance for uncollectibles US

Provision for bad and doubtful debts is a provision recognised in the balance sheet because of anticipated default concerning accounts receivable.

provisión para insolvencias y deudores de dudoso cobro

▲ *estimated provisions for bad and doubtful debts* provisiones estimadas para insolvencias y deudores de dudoso cobro ▲ *less provisions for bad and doubtful debts* menos provisiones para insolvencias y deudores de dudoso cobro ▲ *net of provisions for bad and doubtful debts* neto de provisiones para insolvencias y deudores de dudoso cobro

provision for bad debts UK

= allowance for uncollectibles US, provision for uncollectibles US

Provision for bad debts is an amount set aside out of profits in the financial statements, calculated to cover the debts during an accounting period that are not expected to be paid.

provisión para insolvencias

= provisión para incobrables

▲ *a decrease in the provision for bad debts* un descenso en provisión para insolvencias ▲ *an increase in provision for bad debts* un aumento en provisión para insolvencias

provision for future taxes payable

A provision for future taxes payable is an amount set aside under liabilities in the balance sheet to cover taxes that are payable in future periods.

provisión para impuestos futuros a pagar

▲ *make provisions for future taxes payable* provisionar para impuestos futuros a pagar

provision for impairment

A provision for impairment is an allowance made in the financial statements to provide for an anticipated reduction in value or loss of an asset.

provisión por deterioro

▲ *less any provision for impairment* menos cualquier provisión por deterioro ▲ *make a provision for impairment in value of the fixed asset* provisionar por deterioro en el valor del activo fijo ▲ *net provision for impairment in value of intangible assets* provisión neto por deterioro en el valor de los activos intangibles

⇛ impairment, impairment loss

provision for liabilities and charges

A provision for liabilities and charges is a liability that is uncertain in terms of amount or timing and that concerns the current financial year or a previous year.

NOTE When used as an item in the balance sheet, the plural form 'provisions for liabilities and charges' was applied until 2004 when it was replaced by 'provisions for liabilities'.

provisión para riesgos y gastos

▲ *an increase in provision for liabilities and charges* un aumento en la provisión para riesgos y gastos

⇛ provision, provisions for liabilities

provision for restructuring

→ restructuring provision

provision for uncollectibles US

= allowance for uncollectibles US, provision for bad debts UK

Provisions for uncollectibles are amounts set aside out of income in the financial statements, calculated to cover the debts during a fiscal period that are not expected to be paid.

provisión para insolvencias

= provisión para incobrables

▲ *make provisions for uncollectibles* provisionar para insolvencias ▲ *net revenue less provision for uncollectibles* ingreso neto menos provisión para insolvencias

provision of bad debts

→ provision for bad debts

provisioning ratio

The provisioning ratio is a financial ratio defined as total provisions divided by gross lending (i.e. lending before loan-loss provisions) and guarantees. The ratio is used by financial institutions and shows the portfolio quality and loan-loss provisions.

ratio de provisión

▲ *the average provisioning ratio* el ratio de provisión medio ▲ *the variation in the provisio-*

ning ratio la variación en el ratio de provisión
⇛ loan-loss provision

provisions account
= allowance account US
A provisions account is an account under liabilities in the balance sheet where provisions for bad and doubtful debts are recognised.
cuenta de provisiones
▲ *the closing balance of the provisions account* el saldo de cierre de la cuenta de provisiones ▲ *the opening balance on the provisions account* el saldo de apertura de la cuenta de provisiones

provisions for liabilities UK
= provisions US, IAS/IFRS
Provisions for liabilities appear as an item under liabilities in the balance sheet and liabilities that are uncertain in terms of amount or timing and that concern the financial year or a previous year.
provisión para riesgos
▲ *the note on provisions for liabilities* la nota a las provisiones para riesgos

proxy
1 Proxy is the authority given to a person to attend and vote at a general meeting on behalf of a shareholder.
delegación
▲ *proxy voting* votación por delegación ▲ *vote by proxy* votar por delegación
2 = proxy holder
A proxy is a person appointed by a shareholder to attend and vote at a general meeting on behalf of the shareholder.
apoderado
▲ *be present personally or by proxy* estar presente personalmente o por un apoderado

proxy statement
A proxy statement is a document granting authority to a person to attend and vote at a general meeting on behalf of a shareholder.
documento de delegación
▲ *deliver a proxy statement to the shareholders* enviar un documento de delegación a los accionistas ▲ *the current proxy statement* el documento de delegación actual

prudence
= conservatism US
Prudence refers to the prudence concept under which sales revenues should only be recognised when realised, whereas all liabilities which have arisen or are likely to arise should be provided for.
prudencia
= conservadurismo
▲ *eliminate excessive prudence* eliminar la prudencia excesiva ▲ *exercise prudence* ejercer la prudencia ▲ *introduce additional prudence* introducir prudencia adicional ▲ *measure insurance contracts with sufficient prudence* medir los contratos de seguros con prudencia significativa ▲ *on a general basis of prudence* en una base general de prudencia

prudence concept UK/IAS/IFRS
= conservatism US, conservatism convention US, prudence IAS/IFRS, UK
The prudence concept is one of the fundamental accounting concepts under which sales revenues should only be recognised when realised, whereas all liabilities which have arisen or are likely to arise should be provided for.
principio de prudencia
= principio de conservadurismo
▲ *accord with the prudence concept* acorde con el principio de prudencia ▲ *in accordance with the prudence concept* de acuerdo con el principio de prudencia ▲ *one part of the prudence concept* una parte del principio de prudencia ▲ *the application of the prudence concept* la aplicación del principio de prudencia ▲ *under the prudence concept* según el principio de prudencia

prudence convention IAS/IFRS, UK
= conservatism convention US, principle of conservatism US
The prudence convention is one of the fundamental accounting concepts under which sales revenues should only be recognised when realised, whereas all liabilities which have arisen or are likely to arise should be provided for.
principio de prudencia
= principio de conservadurismo
▲ *according to the prudence convention* de acuerdo con el principio de prudencia ▲ *comply with the prudence convention* cumplir con el principio de prudencia

PTP
= pre-tax profit

PTP is an abbreviation for pretax profit, i.e. the profit of an enterprise for an accounting period before deduction of tax expense.

beneficio antes de impuestos

= beneficio bruto

▲ *a 10% increase in PTP* un 10% de aumento en el beneficio antes de impuestos ▲ *calculate the % PTP on sales* calcular el porcentaje de beneficio antes de impuestos en ventas

public authority

Public authorities refer to government bodies and institutions at local, regional or national level which have specific powers or responsibilities or perform specific administrative functions.

gobierno

= administración

▲ *a forgivable loan from a public authority* un préstamo del gobierno condonado

public company

→ public limited company

public corporation

1 = state-owned public limited company DK

A public corporation is a corporation that is owned and managed by the government. In the US, public corporations act as an agency in state administration.

empresa pública

= corporación

▲ *form a public corporation* formar una empresa pública

2 A public corporation is a corporation with many shareholders whose shares are widely held and may be listed and traded on a stock exchange. Owners are found in the general public.

sociedad anónima

▲ *the stock of a public corporation* el capital de una sociedad anónima

public interest entity

Public interest entities are entities that are of significant public relevance because of the nature of their business, their size or their number of employees, in particular companies whose securities are admitted to trading on a regulated market.

entidad de interés público

▲ *non-listed public interest entities* entidades de interés público no cotizadas ▲ *public interest entities which have not issued transferable securities admitted to trading on a regulated market* entidades de interés público que no han emitido títulos negociables admitidos a cotización en un mercado regulado ▲ *require an independent audit committee in public interest entities* exigir un comité de auditoría independiente en las entidades de interés público ▲ *statutory audits in public interest entities* auditorías obligatorias en las entidades de interés público ▲ *strengthen requirements concerning audits in public interest entities* reforzar las obligaciones concernientes con las auditorías de las entidades de interés público ▲ *the audit firms of public interest entities* las firmas de auditoría de las entidades de interés público

public land assessment value

The public land assessment value is the appraisal value of a property, i.e. an estimate of the market value of the property made by a professional valuation officer. The value is determined as a cash value to indicate the market value of the property. The public land assessment value is typically used for tax, sales or mortgaging purposes.

valor de tasación

▲ *disclosures of public land assessment value* publicaciones del valor de tasación

public limited company UK

= plc, PLC, public corporation US, publicly-held company US

≠ private limited company UK, privately-held company US, privately-held corporation US

A public limited company is a registered company that can offer its shares to the public. It must have a specified minimum capital and its owners, the shareholders, are liable to the extent of their contribution. The company's name must end with the words 'public limited company' or the abbreviation plc.

sociedad anónima

= S.A., SA

▲ *a listed public limited company* una sociedad anónima cotizada ▲ *a public limited company registered in England and Wales* una sociedad anónima registrada en Inglaterra y Gales ▲ *found a public limited company* fundar una sociedad anónima ▲ *incorporate a public limited company* incorporar una sociedad anónima

publication

Publication is the act of making data or information public.

publicación

▲ *20 days subsequent to the publication of the annual report* 20 días siguientes a la publicación del informe anual ▲ *a condensed publication* una publicación condensada ▲ *acts whose publication is obligatory* actos cuya publicación es obligatoria ▲ *publication of a preliminary announcement of the financial statements* publicación de anuncio preliminar de los estados financieros ▲ *publication of an environmental report* publicación de un informe medioambiental ▲ *publication of financial ratios* publicación de los ratios financieros ▲ *publication of information* publicación de información ▲ *publication of interim financial statements* publicación de los estados financieros provisionales ▲ *publication of quarterly financial statements* publicación de los estados financieros trimestrales ▲ *publication of the annual report* publicación del informe anual ▲ *publication of the expected results* publicación de los resultados esperados ▲ *publication of the income statement* publicación del estado de ingresos ▲ *publication through the stock exchange* publicación a través del mercado de acciones ▲ *rules on submission and publication* reglas sobre remisión y publicación ▲ *the enterprise's own publication of the annual report* la propia publicación de la empresa del informe anual

publicly-held company US

= public corporation US, public limited company UK, publicly-held corporation US

≠ private limited company US, privately-held company US

A publicly-held company is a company with many shareholders whose shares may be listed and traded on a stock exchange. Owners are found in the general public. In the US, publicly-held companies must file financial statements with the Securities and Exchange Commission.

sociedad anónima

▲ *the stockholders of a publicly-held company* los accionistas de una sociedad anónima

publish

= make public

To publish something means to make it known or available to the public.

publicar

▲ *cause the annual report to be published by the Danish Commerce and Companies Agency* obligar a que el informe anual sea publicado por La Agencia danesa de Sociedades Mercantiles ▲ *publish a correction note* publicar una nota de corrección ▲ *publish a financial calendar* publicar un calendario financiero ▲ *publish a plan* publicar un plan ▲ *publish a stock exchange announcement* publicar un anuncio en el mercado de acciones ▲ *publish an announcement* publicar un anuncio ▲ *publish an annual report* publicar un informe anual ▲ *publish an intellectual capital report* publicar un informe de capital intelectual ▲ *publish information* publicar información

published

= made public

If something has been published, it has been made known or available to the public.

publicado

▲ *a published acquisition* una adquisición publicada ▲ *information published with the financial statements* información publicada con los estados financieros

purchase[1] *noun*

= acquisition

A purchase is an acquisition that is bought, as contrasted with an exchange, a gift or inheritance.

compra

= adquisición

▲ *a concluded purchase* una compra cerrada ▲ *a contract for the purchase or sale of a non-financial item* un contrato para la compra o venta de una partida no financiera ▲ *account for as a purchase* contabilizar como una compra ▲ *commitments for the purchase of property, plant and equipment* compromisos de compra de edificios, instalaciones y equipos ▲ *inventory purchase* compra de inventarios ▲ *major purchases of assets* grandes compras de activos ▲ *purchase and sale during the year* compra y venta durante el año ▲ *purchase of goods or services* compra de bienes y servicios ▲ *purchase of materials* compra de materiales ▲ *purchase of treasury shares* compra de acciones propias ▲ *successive share purchases* compras sucesivas de acciones ▲ *the purchase and sale of unique intangible assets* la compra y la venta de los activos intangibles únicos

purchase[2] *verb*
= acquire, buy
≠ sell
To purchase is to buy or acquire something, usually of a large size or high value.
comprar
= adquirir
≠ vender
▲ *assets and liabilities that the acquirer purchases or assumes* activos y pasivos que el adquirente compra o acepta ▲ *goods purchased for resale* bienes comprados para la reventa ▲ *provisions included in a contract to purchase or sell an asset* provisiones incluidas en un contrato de compra o venta de un activo ▲ *purchase goods or services* comprar bienes o servicios ▲ *purchase inventories on deferred settlement terms* comprar inventarios a plazos ▲ *purchase securities* comprar títulos ▲ *purchase shares* comprar acciones ▲ *purchase treasury shares* comprar acciones propias ▲ *the option to purchase* la opción de comprar

purchase accounting US, IAS/IFRS
= acquisition accounting UK
≠ merger accounting UK, pooling of interests US, uniting of interests IAS/IFRS
Purchase accounting is the application of an accounting method used for business combinations where the identifiable assets and liabilities of the acquired business are recognised in the balance sheet of the acquirer at their fair value at the acquisition date. If the value of the acquired business' net assets is lower than the acquisition cost, this difference is recognised as goodwill.
método de adquisición
▲ *under US GAAP purchase accounting requirements* según los requisitos del método de adquisición defendidos por los PCGA norteamericanos

purchase accounting method US
→ purchase method

purchase consideration
= acquisition cost, purchase price
The purchase consideration is the price paid to buy goods, services, or assets. It equals the list price plus normal incidental costs to acquire the item including preparation, transportation and installation.
condiciones de compra
= precio de compra
▲ *adjustment to the purchase consideration* ajuste a las condiciones de compra ▲ *ordinary shares issued as part of the purchase consideration of a business combination* acciones ordinarias emitidas como parte de las condiciones de compra de una combinación de negocios ▲ *purchase consideration in cash* condiciones de compra en efectivo ▲ *purchase consideration in the form of cash or other monetary assets* condiciones de compra en forma de efectivo u otros activos monetarios

purchase method IAS/IFRS, US
= acquisition accounting method UK, acquisition method UK
≠ merger accounting method UK, merger method UK, pooling-of-interests method US, uniting-of-interests method IAS/IFRS
The purchase method is an accounting method used for business combinations in which the acquirer obtains control over the acquired enterprise. The assets of the acquired enterprise are recorded at fair value at the date of acquisition giving rise to goodwill on consolidation.
método de adquisición
▲ *apply the purchase method* aplicar el método de adquisición ▲ *the date when the appli-*

cation of the purchase method commences la fecha al que se aplica el método de adquisición

purchase price

The purchase price is the amount it costs to buy something.

precio de compra

▲ *distribution of a purchase price on buildings and land* distribución de un precio de compra en edificios y bienes raíces ▲ *hedge of the purchase price* cobertura del precio de compra ▲ *payment of the purchase price* pago del precio de compra ▲ *purchase price plus delivery costs* precio de compra más costes de envio ▲ *the purchase price including import duties and non-refundable purchase taxes* el precio de compra que incluye aranceles e impuestos de compra sin derecho a devolución ▲ *the resolution of purchase price adjustments* la resolución de los ajustes del precio de compra ▲ *total purchase price* total precio de compra

purchase sum

A purchase sum refers to an agreed monetary amount or other consideration given by one or more parties acquiring a specific asset in a sales transaction to one or more other parties selling the asset.

total de la compra

= total compra

▲ *fix a purchase sum* fijar un total de la compra

purchased goodwill UK

= acquired goodwill IAS/IFRS, goodwill on acquisition IAS/IFRS

Purchased goodwill is the goodwill arising from the acquisition of an enterprise or activity, representing the excess price paid over the net assets' fair value. Purchased goodwill is initially recognised at cost less impairment losses and must be tested for impairment regularly, where formerly it used to be capitalised and amortised over the expected economic life, usually a maximum of 20 years.

fondo de comercio adquirido

▲ *adjustments to purchased goodwill* ajustes al fondo de comercio adquirido

purchased supplies

= goods purchased

Purchased supplies constitute the maintenance materials and auxiliary products bought from suppliers by an enterprise.

suministros adquiridos

= insumos adquiridos

▲ *total purchased supplies* total suministros adquiridos

purchases ledger US

= creditors' ledger UK

≠ debtors' ledger UK, sales ledger US

A purchases ledger is a book or group of accounts containing the individual creditors' accounts, i.e. amounts owed to suppliers. The purchases ledger records purchases, payments made and discounts received. Today, purchases ledgers are usually stored on computer files that have replaced the old-time binders.

mayor del comprador

▲ *balances from purchases ledger* saldos del mayor del comprador

purchasing cost

Purchasing costs constitute costs relating to the acquisition of goods, i.e. the amounts paid to suppliers as well as any directly related charges such as transportation costs, transport insurance costs, import levies and excise duties.

coste de adquisición

▲ *administrative purchasing costs* costes de adquisición administrativos ▲ *direct purchasing costs* costes de adquisición directos ▲ *reduce purchasing costs by 10%* reducir los costes de adquisición en un 10% ▲ *total purchasing costs* total costes de adquisición

purchasing manager

A purchasing manager is in charge of the purchase of the materials, equipment etc. that the enterprise needs in its production process.

director de compras

▲ *appoint a new purchasing manager* nombrar un nuevo director de compras ▲ *the former purchasing manager* el anterior director de compras ▲ *the incoming purchasing manager* el director de compras entrante ▲ *the retiring purchasing manager* el director de compras saliente

put option

A put option gives the holder the right, but not the obligation, to sell an underlying asset at an agreed future date at a specified price.

opción de venta

▲ *a convertible debt instrument with an embedded put option feature* un instrumento de deuda convertible con una opción de venta incluida ▲ *a deep out-of-the-money put option* una opción de venta muy fuera de dinero ▲ *a put option obligation* una obligación de una opción de venta ▲ *a put option on an equity instrument* una opción de venta en un instrumento de patrimonio ▲ *a put option written* una opción de venta vendida ▲ *exercise a put option* ejercitar una opción de venta ▲ *have an unconditional put option on an asset* tener una opción de venta incondicional sobre un activo ▲ *purchased put options* opciones de venta compradas ▲ *put options on ordinary shares* opciones de venta en acciones ordinarias ▲ *sell a put option* vender una opción de venta ▲ *the fair value of the put option obligation* el valor razonable de la obligación de la opción de venta ▲ *the obligation under a put option written* la obligación de acuerdo con una opción de venta vendida ▲ *the right under a put option held* el derecho según una opción de venta mantenida ▲ *transfer a put option* transferir una opción de venta ▲ *write a put option* vender una opción de venta ▲ *written put-options* opciones de venta vendidas

puttable financial instrument IAS/IFRS

= puttable instrument IAS/IFRS

A financial instrument that allows the holder to give the instrument back (i.e. put back) to the issuer in exchange for cash or another financial instrument is called a puttable financial instrument.

instrumento financiero con opción de venta

▲ *the classification of puttable financial instruments* la clasificación de los instrumentos financieros con opción de venta ▲ *to issue puttable financial instruments* para emitir instrumentos financieros con opción de venta

SOURCE IAS 32 paragraph 11

⇛ put option

puttable instrument IAS/IFRS

= puttable financial instrument IAS/IFRS

A financial instrument that allows the holder to give the instrument back to the issuer in exchange for cash or another financial instrument is called a puttable instrument.

instrumento con opción de venta

▲ *the classification of puttable instruments* la clasificación de los instrumentos con opción de venta ▲ *to issue puttable instruments* emitir instrumentos con opción de venta

SOURCE IAS 32, paragraph 11

⇛ put option

Q

q.

"q." is the abbreviation for quarter, i.e. one quarter of a year or three months.

NOTE When used together with the relevant quarter, e.g. in financial reports, Q1, Q2, Q3 or Q4 typically applies.

trimestre

▲ *the expected sales for q. 1* las ventas previstas para el primer trimestre

⇛ Q 1/2/3/4 earnings release

Q1

= first-quarter

Q1 is an abbreviation for first-quarter and is used about financial reports, items or statements that relate to the first three months of the accounting year.

NOTE In US accounting the term is "1Q".

primer trimestre

▲ *Q1 interim report* informe provisional del primer trimestre

Q1/2/3/4 earnings release US

A Q1/2/3/4 earnings release is a financial reporting announcement for the first, second, third or forth quarter of a financial year presented to the public and the stock markets by an enterprise on a quarterly or annual basis containing information about earnings and results of operations. Earnings releases usually contain the enterprise's financial highlights, management's interpretation of the period under review together with outlook and expectations as well as summary financial statements.

publicación de los beneficios del 1er/2º/3º/4º trimestre

▲ *publish a Q1 earnings release* dar a conocer la publicación de los beneficios del 1er trimestre

⇛ q.

Q2

= second-quarter

Q2 is an abbreviation for second-quarter and is used about financial reports, items or statements that relate to the 4th, 5th and 6th months of the accounting year.

NOTE In US accounting the term is "2Q".

segundo trimestre

▲ *Q2 interim report* informe provisional del segundo trimestre

Q3

= third-quarter

Q3 is an abbreviation for third-quarter and is used about financial reports, items or statements that relate to the 7th, 8th and 9th months of the accounting year.

NOTE In US accounting the term is "3Q".

tercer trimestre

▲ *Q3 interim report* informe provisional del tercer trimestre

Q4

= fourth-quarter

Q4 is an abbreviation for fourth-quarter and is used about financial reports, items or statements that relate to the last three months of the accounting year.

NOTE In US accounting the term is "4Q".

cuarto trimestre

▲ *Q4 interim report* informe provisional del cuarto trimestre

qualification

1 A qualification is a comment in the audit report limiting the auditor's statement. Qualifications may result from the auditor's disagreement with or failure to receive adequate information from the management, or the lack of appropriate audit evidence.

salvedad

▲ *give rise to qualifications* dar lugar a salvedades ▲ *qualification in the 2005 statement of assurance* salvedad en el estado de aseguramiento de 2005

⇛ qualified audit report, qualified opinion

2 Qualifications are special skills or characteristics enabling persons to perform specific jobs.

cualificación

▲ *appropriate professional qualifications and experience* cualificaciones y experiencia profesionales adecuadas ▲ *the importance of personal qualifications* la importancia de las cualificaciones personales

qualified audit report

≠ unqualified audit report

A qualified audit report is an audit report containing qualifications by the auditor relating to matters that have affected his opinion. Such matters may arise in case of any disagreement with management or limitation of scope that is not sufficiently material to lead to an adverse opinion or disclaimer of opinion. The wording that the financial statements "give a true and fair view" (UK) or "present fairly, in all material respects" (US) is followed by the qualifications "except for" or "subject to".

informe de auditoría con salvedades

≠ informe de auditoría limpio

▲ *issue a qualified audit report* emitir un informe de auditoría con salvedades

⇛ adverse opinion, audit report, modified audit report

qualified opinion

= qualification

A qualified opinion is expressed by an auditor in the audit report in case of any disagreement with management or limitation of scope that is not sufficiently material to lead to an adverse opinion or disclaimer of opinion. The wording that the financial statements "give a true and fair view" (UK) or "present fairly, in all material respects" (US) is followed by the qualifications "except for" or "subject to".

NOTE The expression "qualified opinion" is also used synonymouly with "qualified audit report".

opinión con salvedades

= opinión con salvedad

▲ *give a qualified opinion* dar una opinión con salvedades ▲ *record a qualified opinion* registrar una opinión con salvedades

⇛ audit opinion

qualifying asset

A qualifying asset is an asset that must meet a certain definition to apply in special contexts, such as tax relief. Under IFRS, qualifying assets are assets that - for the accounting treatment of borrowing costs - are only ready for use after a substantial time period, such as investment properties until constructed, intangibles until developed and inventories in progress.

activo cualificado

= activo apto

▲ *acquisition of a qualifying asset* adquisición de un activo cualificado ▲ *construction of a qualifying asset* construcción de un activo cualificado ▲ *expenditures on a qualifying asset* gastos en un activo cualificado ▲ *obtain a particular qualifying asset* obtener un activo cualificado concreto ▲ *production of a qualifying asset* producción de un activo cualificado ▲ *the carrying amount of a qualifying asset* el valor contable de un activo cualificado ▲ *the carrying amount of the qualifying asset* el valor contable del activo cualificado ▲ *the expected ultimate cost of the qualifying asset* el coste último esperado del activo cualificado

SOURCE IAS 23, paragraphs 5 and 6

Qualifying Employee Share Ownership Trust UK

= QUEST UK

A Qualifying Employee Share Ownership Trust is a trust established by a UK company under the requirements of the UK Finance Act 1989, schedule 5, offering special corporation tax relief to the company. The function of the trust is to acquire and distribute shares in the employer's company to the beneficiaries, i.e. employees and former employees of the company establishing the trust.

trust de inversión en acciones de empleados cualificados

= QUEST

▲ *contributions by employers to a Qualifying Employee Share Ownership Trust* contribuciones de los empleados a un trust de inversión en acciones de empleados cualificados ▲ *transfer any shares already held in a Qualifying Employee Share Ownership Trust* transferir cualesquiera acciones ya mantenidas en un trust de inversión en acciones de empleados cualificados

qualifying insurance policy

A qualifying insurance policy is a policy under a defined benefit plan which is issued by a party that is not related to the enterprise offering the plan and of which the proceeds are protected from the enterprise's creditors even in case of bankruptcy.

póliza de seguro apta

= póliza de seguro cualificada, póliza de seguros apta

▲ *account for qualifying insurance policies in the same way as for all other plan assets* contabilizar las pólizas de seguro aptas de la misma forma que el resto de los activos

quality assurance

Quality assurance constitutes the planned and systematic activities required to provide sufficient guarantee that an audit, a product or service complies with a given standard, and to ensure that quality requirements will be met.

aseguramiento de calidad

= aseguramiento de la calidad

▲ *a quality assurance review* una revisión del aseguramiento de la calidad ▲ *a requirement for external quality assurance* un requisito para el aseguramiento de la calidad externo ▲ *an indication of when the last quality assurance review took place* una indicación de cuando tuvo lugar la última revisión del aseguramiento de calidad ▲ *audit firms that are subject to a system of quality assurance* firmas auditoras que están sujetas a un sistema de aseguramiento de la calidad ▲ *quality assurance system* sistema del aseguramiento de calidad ▲ *the competent authorities in charge of quality assurance* las autoridades competentes responsables del aseguramiento de calidad

quality audit

A quality audit is an evaluation of products and processes involving quality assurance procedures and comparison against standards to ensure that such standards have been meet and such products and processes are suitable and effective.

auditoría de calidad

= auditoría de la calidad

▲ *a half-yearly quality audit* una auditoría de calidad semestral ▲ *carry out a quality audit* llevar a cabo una auditoría de calidad ▲ *high quality audits* auditoría de calidad alta

quality control

= quality management

Quality control constitutes the planned and systematic activities and procedures of an enterprise with a view to observing that a particular product or service complies with the requirements for quality, which are e.g. laid down in international quality standards. Audits, for example, must be performed according to professional standards and general principles for auditing financial statements as provided in legislation and e.g. the International Standards on Auditing.

control de calidad

= control de la calidad

▲ *internal quality control of audit firms* control de calidad interno de las auditorías ▲ *systematic quality control* control de calidad sistemático ▲ *the internal quality control system* el sistema de control de calidad interno

⇛ International Standard on Auditing

quality report

A quality report is a quantifiable statement and report on the performance of an enterprise's intangible assets, strengths and opportunities measured against key performance indicators. The enterprise's performance over its whole range of activities are assessed, e.g. using a tool such as the EFQM (European Foundation Quality Management) Business Excellence Model, and areas for improvement are identified.

informe de calidad

= informe de la calidad

▲ *the publication of a quality report* la publicación de un informe de calidad

⇛ Business Excellence Model

quality requirement

Quality requirements refer to legal or other minimum requirements, standards or specifications that must be met before the quality of goods, services or processes can be approved or is acceptable.

requisito de calidad

= requisito de la calidad

▲ *introduce new quality requirements* introducir nuevos requisitos de calidad ▲ *quality requirements of financial reporting information* requisitos de calidad de la información financiera ▲ *satisfy quality requirements* satisfacer los requisitos de calidad ▲ *the general quality requirements* los requisitos de calidad general ▲ *the principal quality requirement of the Danish Financial Statements Act* el requisito de calidad principal de la Ley Danesa de Estados Financieros de la Empresa

quantity discount
= volume discount
A quantity discount is a discount offered to a buyer in relation to the usual prices quoted by a seller if the buyer purchases a number of goods that amounts to a large quantity at the same time or over a specified period.
rappels
= descuentos por grandes cantidades
▲ *allow quantity discounts* conceder descuentos sobre grandes cantidades ▲ *grant quantity discount* conceder rappels ▲ *less quantity discount* menos rappels

quantity variance
= efficiency variance, usage variance
Quantity variance is the difference between the actual quantity used and the budgeted quantity which was expected to be used.
desviación de cantidad
▲ *calculate the quantity variance* calcular la desviación de cantidad ▲ *materials quantity variance* desviación de cantidad en materiales

quarter
= q.
A quarter is one quarter of a year, i.e. a period of three months.
trimestre
▲ *amortisation and depreciation in the quarter* amortización y depreciación en el trimestre ▲ *investments in the quarter* inversiones en el trimestre ▲ *profit for the quarter* beneficio trimestral ▲ *result for the quarter* resultado trimestral ▲ *the first quarter* el primer trimestre ▲ *the fourth quarter* el cuarto trimestre ▲ *the second quarter* el segundo trimestre ▲ *the third quarter* el tercer trimestre

quarterly announcement
The quarterly announcement is the report which listed companies must submit for the first, second, third and fourth quarter concerning the activities and results for the period on the announcement of the interim financial statements.
anuncio de resultados trimestrales
▲ *a published quarterly announcement* un anuncio publicado de resultados trimestrales ▲ *publish a quarterly announcement* publicar un anuncio de resultados trimestrales

quarterly dividend
Quarterly dividend refers to dividend paid to shareholders in relation to a three-month period of the financial year.
dividendo trimestral
▲ *pay quarterly dividend* pagar el dividendo trimestral

quarterly financial statements US, IAS/IFRS
= interim report, quarterly report
Quarterly financial statements are financial statements prepared for three months and included in the quarterly report of an enterprise.
estados financieros trimestrales
▲ *publish quarterly financial statements* publicar los estados financieros trimestrales

quarterly income US
= quarterly profit UK
Quarterly income refers to the income generated by an enterprise for a three-month period, i.e. during a quarter.
ingresos trimestrales
▲ *quarterly income estimates* estimaciones de ingresos trimestrales

quarterly report
= quarterly interim report
A quarterly report is a report prepared for three months.
informe trimestral
▲ *publish a quarterly report* publicar un informe trimestral
⇛ quarterly financial statements

quasi-equity IAS/IFRS
A quasi-equity instrument is a debt instrument with the characteristics of both debt and equity: it is classified as debt,

typically unsecured and of long duration, and may be convertible to equity. Examples of this type include mezzanine debt and subordinated debt. Quasi-equity instruments may also be equity instruments with debt characteristics such as non-equity shares or preference shares.
instrumento financiero compuesto
= instrumento financiero de cuasi-patrimonio, instrumento financiero de cuasipatrimonio
▲ *quasi-equity deferred income tax liabilities* pasivo por impuesto diferido de los instrumentos financieros compuestos
▲ *quasi-equity provisions* provisiones de los instrumentos financieros compuestos

QUEST UK
= Qualifying Employee Share Ownership Trust UK
QUEST is the abbreviation for Qualifying Employee Share Ownership Trust, which is a trust established by a UK company under the requirements of the UK Finance Act 1989, schedule 5, offering special corporation tax relief to the company. The function of the trust is to acquire and distribute shares in the employer's company to the beneficiaries, i.e. employees and former employees of the company establishing the trust.
trust de inversión en acciones de empleados cualificados
= QUEST
▲ *contributions by employers to a QUEST* contribuciones de los empresarios a un trust de inversión en acciones de empleados cualificados ▲ *transfer any shares already held in a QUEST* transferir acciones que ya están en un trust de inversión en acciones de empleados cualificados

quick asset
= liquid asset
Quick assets are cash and other liquid assets that can be readily turned into cash such as short-term bank deposits and as such constitute the most current assets of an enterprise, consequently excluding inventories that may prove difficult to sell quickly.
activo líquido
▲ *a quick asset subtotal* subtotal de un activo líquido ▲ *quick assets at the beginning of the financial year* activos líquidos al inicio del ejercicio financiero

quick ratio
= acid test, acid test ratio, liquid ratio
The quick ratio is a financial ratio measuring the liquidity of an enterprise at very short term, defined as current assets excluding stocks less current liabilities, and is a more stringent measure than the current ratio. The ratio should preferably be at least 1:1.
ratio de liquidez inmediata
= acid test ratio
▲ *calculate the quick ratio* calcular el ratio de liquidez inmediata ▲ *the average quick ratio* el promedio del ratio de liquidez inmediata
⇛ liquidity ratio, liquidity test

quotation
A quotation is the official, quoted price at which the last sale and purchase of a particular security took place.
cotización
▲ *a published price quotation in an active market* un precio publicado de cotización en un mercado activo
⇛ listing

quoted
= listed
When a enterprise's shares or bonds are quoted it means that they are officially available, i.e. bought and sold on a particular stock exchange or other authorised market place.
cotizado
▲ *quoted market prices* precios de mercado cotizados ▲ *quoted market prices in an active market* precios de mercado cotizados en un mercado activo ▲ *the appropriate quoted market price for a liability to be issued* el precio de mercado cotizado apropiado para un pasivo a emitir ▲ *the published price at the date of exchange of a quoted equity instrument* el precio publicado a la fecha de conversión de un instrumento de patrimonio cotizado ▲ *the stock exchange quoted bid price* el precio de oferta cotizado en la bolsa

R

R&D

R&D is the abbreviation for research and development, i.e. the innovative and scientific processes that are carried out and aimed at finding new knowledge and the application of the research findings in practice.

I+D

▲ *maximise the return on R&D assets* maximizar la rentabilidad en los activos de I+D ▲ *R&D activities* actividades de I+D ▲ *R&D costs* costes de I+D ▲ *R&D investment* inversión en I+D

⇛ development, research

R&D expenditure

R&D expenditures are costs related to research and development for an accounting period. Under some accounting rules, certain development (but not research) expenditures may be capitalised and amortised over future periods instead of being written off in the year of expenditure.

gasto en I+D

▲ *a high growth rate of R&D expenditures* un alto índice de crecimiento de los gastos en I+D ▲ *capitalisation of R&D expenditure* capitalización del gasto en I+D ▲ *expense R&D expenditure on intangible assets* el coste del gasto en I+D en activos intangibles ▲ *reduce R&D expenditure growth* reducir el aumento del gasto en I+D ▲ *steady growth in R&D expenditure over recent years* crecimiento paulatino del gasto en I+D en los últimos años ▲ *total R&D expenditures* total gastos en I+D

R&D expense US

= R&D cost UK

R&D expenses are costs related to research and development for an accounting period. Under some accounting rules, certain development (but not research) expenses may be capitalised and amortised over future periods instead of being written off in the year of expenditure.

gasto en I+D

▲ *R&D expenses excluding patent costs* gastos en I+D excluyendo costes de patentes ▲ *the R&D expenses incurred during the year* los gastos en I+D incurridos a lo largo del año

R&D manager

An R&D manager is a manager in charge of the enterprise's research and development activities.

responsable de I+D

= director de I+D

▲ *appoint a new R&D manager* nombrar un nuevo responsable de I+D ▲ *the former R&D manager* el anterior director de I+D ▲ *the incoming R&D manager* el responsable de I+D entrante ▲ *the retiring R&D manager* el responsable de I+D saliente

⇛ R&D

raise

To raise capital or funds means to provide, obtain or collect the capital or funds required for a specific purpose.

obtener

= conseguir

▲ *raise capital* obtener capital ▲ *raise finance for the purposes of the joint venture activity* obtener financiación a efectos de la actividad de la joint venture ▲ *the ability to raise capital* la capacidad para obtener capital

raising

The raising of a loan, money or finances is the procurement of a loan, money or finances.

recaudación

= obtención

▲ *the raising of funds to meet commitments associated with financial instruments* la recaudación de fondos para hacer frente a los compromisos asociados con los instrumentos financieros

raising of additional capital

Raising of additional capital is the increase of the contributed capital or the share capital, e.g. through the issue of new shares or through a capitalisation or bonus issue.

ampliación de capital

▲ *the proposed raising of additional capital* la ampliación de capital propuesta

range

A range means a large number of different things, usually of a similar kind.

serie

= gama, grupo

▲ *a complete range of services* una serie completa de servicios ▲ *a range of numbers* una serie de números ▲ *a range of products* una gama de productos ▲ *a range of services* una serie de servicios ▲ *a range of stakeholders* un grupo de accionistas ▲ *a wide range of competences* una amplia gama de competencias ▲ *the range of estimates within which fair value is highly likely to lie* la serie de estimaciones en las que es posible que se encuentre el valor razonable ▲ *the range of possible outcomes* la serie de resultados posibles ▲ *the range of reasonable fair value estimates* la serie de estimaciones de valor razonable

rate

To rate is to assess the creditworthiness of a person or an enterprise for the purpose of credit granting.

clasificar

▲ *to rate a company* clasificar una compañía

⇛ credit rating

rate at the balance sheet date

The rate at the balance sheet date is the closing spot rate of exchange quoted on the balance sheet date.

tipo a la fecha de balance

▲ *exchange of currencies at the rate at the balance sheet date* cambio de divisas al tipo a la fecha del balance

rate of interest

→ interest rate

rate of return

A rate of return is a measure of the gain or loss from an investment over a specified period of time, i.e. it indicates the profitability of an investment. It is expressed as a percentage and calculated by dividing the income from the investment (typically in the form of dividend, interest, capital gains or losses) by the purchase price or by the current market price.

tasa de rentabilidad

= tasa de rendimiento, tasa de retorno

▲ *a constant periodic rate of return* una tasa de rentabilidad periódica constante ▲ *calculation of the rate of return* cálculo de la tasa de rentabilidad ▲ *equivalent to a rate of return of 5.0%* equivalente a una tasa de rentabilidad del 5% ▲ *market rates of return on investments* tasa de rentabilidad de mercado en inversiones ▲ *project the returns on the assets at an estimated rate of return* proyectar los rendimientos de los activos a una tasa de rentabilidad estimada ▲ *the annualised rate of return* la tasa de rentabilidad anualizada ▲ *the average rate of return* la tasa de rentabilidad media ▲ *the expected rates of return on assets* la tasa de rentabilidad esperada en activos ▲ *the rate of return for the year* la tasa de rentabilidad para el ejercicio ▲ *the rate of return to investors* la tasa de rentabilidad a inversores

⇛ nominal rate of return, real rate of return

rate of return on shareholders' equity

→ return on equity

rate of turnover

The rate of turnover is an activity financial ratio expressing the frequency with which a type of asset of an enterprise is replaced by another asset of the same type within a defined time period. Examples are accounts receivable turnover, inventory turnover, staff turnover and fixed asset turnover.

tasa de rotación

▲ *a decline in the rate of turnover* un descenso de la tasa de rotación

rate of utilisation

The rate of utilisation is a percentage showing the frequency, average capacity or volume of something, typically in relation to another factor such as time.

tasa de utilización

▲ *the technical rate of utilisation* la tasa de utilización técnica

rate variance

= input-price variance

A rate variance is the difference between the budgeted price per unit and the actual purchase or input price per unit of raw materials, semi-manufactures, secondary materials and labour, multiplied by the purchased quantity.

desviación

▲ *a significant rate variance* una desviación significativa ▲ *an insignificant rate variance* una desviación no significativa ▲ *calculate the rate variance* calcular la desviación

rating

A rating is an evaluation of the creditworthiness of an enterprise. It is particularly used about the creditworthiness of an issuer of financial instruments.

rating

= calificación crediticia, calificación de solvencias

▲ *a downgrade in a rating* una degradación en un rating ▲ *a long-term rating* un rating a largo plazo ▲ *a satisfactory rating* un rating satisfactorio ▲ *a short-term rating* un rating a corto plazo ▲ *an external rating* un rating externo ▲ *an internal rating* un rating interno ▲ *award of a rating* adjudicación de un rating ▲ *carry out a rating* ejecutar un rating ▲ *the highest rating obtainable* el rating más alto obtenible

rating agency

→ credit rating agency

ratio analysis

A ratio analysis is an investigation of the financial ratios of one or more enterprises, typically over a minimum period of five years. Ratio analyses are prepared to determine and assess its/their operating earnings trends and financial performance with a view to making comparisons between companies as well as investment recommendations.

análisis de ratios

= análisis de los ratios

▲ *ratio analysis of financial statements* análisis de ratios de los estados financieros ▲ *the use of ratio analysis* el uso del análisis de los ratios

ratio definition

A ratio definition states how a particular financial ratio should be calculated for a specific purpose.

definición de ratio

▲ *present new ratio definitions* presentar nuevas definiciones de ratio

raw material

Raw materials refer to materials and substances in their unprocessed or natural state for the use in production processes to make semi-manufactured or finished products.

materia prima

▲ *convert raw materials into finished goods* convertir las materias primas en productos terminados ▲ *cost of raw materials* coste de las materias primas ▲ *expenses for raw materials* gastos por materias primas ▲ *raw materials and consumables* materias primas e insumos ▲ *raw materials and consumables used* materias primas y consumibles utilizados ▲ *raw materials used* materias primas utilizadas ▲ *the price of a raw material* el precio de una materia prima ▲ *the replacement cost of raw materials* el coste de reposición de las materias primas

raw material and consumables used IAS/IFRS

= materials and supplies US, raw materials and consumables UK

"Raw material and consumables used" is an item in the income statement when classified by nature that contains crude or unprocessed materials and auxiliary products applied in production during the accounting period.

materias primas e insumos utilizados

= materias primas y fungibles utilizados

▲ *disclosure of raw material and consumables used* publicación de materias primas e insumos utilizados ▲ *the cost of raw material and consumables used* el coste de las materias primas e insumos utilizados

raw materials and consumables UK

= materials and supplies US, raw material and consumables used IAS/IFRS

"Raw materials and consumables" is an item in the profit and loss account as presented in the report format classified by nature. This item contains crude or unprocessed materials

and auxiliary products applied in production during the accounting period.
materias primas e insumos
▲ *recognise as an expense for raw materials and consumables* reconocer como un gasto por materias primas e insumos

re-lease[1] *noun* <a, the, -s>
A re-lease is a renewal of a previous lease whose lease term has expired, or the lease of an asset that has been leased previously.
realquiler
▲ *amounts received from re-lease* cantidades recibidas por realquiler

re-lease[2] *verb*
1 To re-lease is to renew a lease to someone, typically when the initial lease term has expired, or to lease out an asset again that was previously leased.
realquilar
▲ *re-lease leased property* realquilar una propiedad alquilada
2 To re-lease is to renew a lease, typically when the initial lease term has expired, or to lease an asset again that was previously leased.
realquilar
= materias primas y fungibles
▲ *release the assets* realquilar los activos

reader of financial statements
A reader of financial statements is the person or enterprise that studies the financial statements to obtain financial reporting information about an enterprise. Financial readers include stakeholders and other interested parties.
analista de estados financieros
= analista de los estados financieros
▲ *the possibility of the reader of financial statements of estimating the future cash flows of the enterprise* la posibilidad del analista de estados financieros de estimar los flujos de efectivo futuros de la empresa

real estate US
= real property
Real estate comprises land, i.e. immovable property, including buildings and other things permanently fixed to the land.
bien raíz
NOTE Spanish accounting texts prefer the plural 'bienes raíces' to the singular 'bien raíz'.
▲ *construction of real estate* construcción de bienes raíces ▲ *net operating income from real estate* beneficio de explotación neto proveniente de bienes raíces ▲ *operation of real estate* operación con bienes raíces ▲ *real estate investments* inversiones en bienes raíces ▲ *rights to real estate* derechos de propiedad sobre bienes raíces ▲ *the value of real estate for tax purposes* el valor de los bienes raíces a efectos fiscales

real estate company US
A real estate company is a company that buys land and buildings in order to sell or rent them.
inmobiliaria
= compañía inmobiliaria
▲ *the acquisition of property by a real estate company* la adquisición de edificios por una inmobiliaria

real estate tax US
= property tax UK, real property tax US, UK
Real estate tax is tax levied on real property, i.e. land and buildings, assessed on the property value and charged according to local tax rates.
impuesto predial
▲ *calculate the real estate tax* calcular el impuesto predial ▲ *collect real estate tax* recaudar el impusto predial ▲ *levy real estate tax* gravar el impuesto predial ▲ *real estate tax exemption* exención del impuesto predial

real interest rate
= real rate of interest
The real interest rate is the rate of interest adjusted for inflation, i.e. not taking into account the inflationary effect. If the inflation rate is 2% and the nominal interest rate is 8%, the real interest rate is 6%.
tipo de interés real
▲ *calculate on the basis of a real interest rate of 1.87%* calcular sobre la base de un tipo de interés real del 1,87% ▲ *use a real interest rate based on a reference date* utilizar un tipo de interés real basado en un dato de referencia
⇛ nominal interest rate

real option
A real option is a right, but not an obligation, which presents

itself in an enterprise's process of carrying on business and involves decision-making. A real option may e.g. be the choice of whether or not to take an investment opportunity or the choice of whether or not to acquire new activities. A real option is not tradeable and should be distinguished from an option which is a financial contract.

opción real

▲ *avail oneself of a real option* hacer uso de una opción real

⇛ option

real property

= real estate US

Real property comprises land, i.e. immovable property, including buildings and other things permanently fixed to the land.

bien raíz

NOTE Spanish accounting texts prefer the plural 'bienes raíces' to the singular 'bien raíz'.

▲ *alienation of real property* enajenación de bienes raíces ▲ *construction of real property* construcción de bienes raíces ▲ *income from real property used for the performance of independent personal services* ingresos provenientes de bienes raíces utilizados para la práctica de servicios personales independientes ▲ *net operating income from real property* beneficio de explotación neto proveniente de bienes raíces ▲ *operation of real property* operación con bienes raíces ▲ *real property investments* inversiones en bienes raíces ▲ *rights to real property* derechos de propiedad sobre bienes raíces ▲ *the value of real property for tax purposes* el valor de los bienes raíces a efectos fiscales

real property tax US, UK

= property tax UK, real estate tax US

Real property tax is tax levied on real property by local governments, assessed on the property value and charged according to local tax rates. In the UK, tax on property is charged in the form of council tax for residential property and business rates for business property.

impuesto sobre bienes raíces

= impuesto sobre los bienes raíces

▲ *calculation of real property tax* cálculo del impuesto sobre los bienes raíces ▲ *collection of real property tax* recaudación del impuesto sobre bienes raíces ▲ *increased real property tax* impuesto sobre bienes raíces aumentado

real rate of interest

→ real interest rate

real rate of return

The real rate of return includes the rate of return required on an investment plus the risk premium required to cover business risk. The real rate of return does not consider any inflation risk.

tasa real de rentabilidad

= tasa real de rendimiento, tasa real de retorno

▲ *a real rate of return of 2.5%* una tasa real de rentabilidad del 2,5% ▲ *earn a positive real rate of return* ganar una tasa real de rentabilidad positiva

⇛ nominal rate of return, rate of return

realisable value UK, IAS/IFRS

= realizable value US

Realisable value is the amount, i.e. cash or cash equivalents, anticipated to be obtained at present on sale of an asset in a fair and orderly market. For accounting purposes, however, the net realisable value is generally applied as it excludes selling costs.

valor realizable

▲ *estimated realisable value* valor realizable previsto ▲ *estimated realisable value of the security provided* valor realizable previsto del activo aportado

SOURCE IFRS Framework, F 100 (c)

⇛ net realisable value

realisation

1 = realization US

Realisation means selling something in return for money and recognising the profit or loss at the time of sale and completion of the transaction.

realización

= liquidación

▲ *information about expected dates of realisation of assets and liabilities* información sobre las fechas previstas para la liquidación de activos y pasivos ▲ *planned realisation* realización prevista ▲ *realisation of the residual value* realización del valor residual ▲ *the realisation of assets in cash or cash equivalents* la realización de activos en efectivo o equivalentes de efectivo ▲ *the realisation of the asset* la liquidación del activo

2 = realization US
Realisation means the achievement of something planned or hoped for.
materialización
= realización
▲ *ensure the realisation of cost reductions* garantizar la materialización de las reducciones de costes

realisation concept
= realisation principle IAS/IFRS, UK
The realisation concept is an accounting principle according to which revenue and liabilities may only be recognised when they can be considered realised, i.e. when a transaction has been agreed on or completed, or when a liability has been settled.
principio de realización
= principio de devengo, principio del devengo
▲ *include gains and losses using the realisation concept* incluir pérdidas y ganancias usando el principio de realización ▲ *the realisation concept provided for in the directive* el principio de realización especificado en la directiva ▲ *use the realisation concept* usar el principio de realización

realisation convention
= realisation concept, realisation principle UK, IAS/IFRS, realization principle US
The realisation convention is an accounting principle according to which revenue and liabilities may only be recognized when they can be considered realized, i.e. when a transaction has been agreed on or completed, or when a liability has been settled.
principio de realización
= principio de devengo, principio de la realización, principio del devengo
▲ *inconsistent with the realisation convention* incompatible con el principio de la realización ▲ *the traditional realisation convention* el principio de realización tradicional

realisation price UK, IAS/IFRS
= realization price US
The realisation price is the price achieved on the sale of an asset.
precio de realización
= principio de la realización
▲ *calculate the realisation price* calcular el precio de realización ▲ *the probable realisation price* el precio probable de la realización

realisation principle UK, IAS/IFRS
= realisation concept, realisation convention, realization principle US
The realisation principle is an accounting principle according to which revenue and liabilities may only be recognised when they can be considered realised, i.e. when a transaction has been agreed on or completed, or when a liability has been settled.
principio de realización
= principio de devengo, principio de la realización, principio del devengo
▲ *include gains and losses using the realisation principle* incluir pérdidas y ganancias usando el principio de realización ▲ *the realisation principle provided for in the directive* el principio de realización especificado en la directiva ▲ *use the realisation principle* usar el principio de la realización

realisation value UK
→ realisable value

realise
1 = realize US
To realise is to achieve something or carry something through.
lograr
= conseguir
▲ *the enterprise's ability to realise its goals* la habilidad de la empresa para lograr sus objetivos

2 = realize US
To realise means to sell something in return for money and recognise the profit or loss at the time of sale and completion of the transaction.
realizar
= materializar
▲ *realise a profit* realizar un beneficio ▲ *realise assets within*

the current operating cycle realizar activos dentro del presente ciclo de explotación ▲ *realise the surplus on the retirement or disposal of the asset* materializar la plusvalía con la retirada o venta del activo ▲ *realised gain* ganancia realizada ▲ *realised loss* pérdida materializada

realised IAS/IFRS, UK
= realized US
≠ unrealised IAS/IFRS, UK, unrealized US
Realised means actually carried out or completed, in financial statements referring to a gain or loss resulting from a change in value of an asset that has been realised by the legal disposal of that asset, whether or not cash has been received.
realizado
= materializado
≠ no materializado, no realizado
▲ *a realised gain* una ganancia realizada ▲ *a realised loss* una pérdida realizada

realizable value US
= realisable value UK, IAS/IFRS
Realizable value is the amount, i.e. cash or cash equivalents, anticipated to be obtained at present on sale of an asset in a fair and orderly market. For accounting purposes, however, the net realizable value is generally applied as it excludes selling expenses.
valor realizable
= valor de realización
▲ *estimated realizable value* valor realizable previsto ▲ *estimated realizable value of the security provided* valor realizable previsto del título aportado
⇛ net realizable value

realization US
1 = realisation UK
Realization means selling something in return for money and recognising the gain or loss at the time of sale and completion of the transaction.
realización
▲ *information about expected dates of realization of assets and liabilities* información sobre fechas previstas de realización de activos y pasivos ▲ *planned realization* realización planificada ▲ *realization of the residual value* realización del valor residual ▲ *the realization of assets in cash or cash equivalents* la realización de activos en efectivo o equivalentes de efectivo ▲ *the realization of the asset* la realización del activo
2 = realisation UK
Realization means the achievement of something planned or hoped for.
logro
▲ *ensure the realization of cost reductions* asegurar el logro de las reducciones de costes

realization price US
= realisation price UK, IAS/IFRS
The realization price is the price achieved on the sale of an asset.
precio de realización
▲ *calculate the realization price* calcular el precio de realización ▲ *the probable realization price* el precio probable de la realización

realization principle US
= realisation concept, realisation convention, realisation principle UK, IAS/IFRS
The realization principle is an accounting principle according to which revenue and liabilities may only be recognized when they can be considered realized, i.e. when a transaction has been agreed on or completed, or when a liability has been settled.
principio de realización
= principio de devengo, principio de la realización, principio del devengo
▲ *include gains and losses using the realization principle* incluir pérdidas y ganancias usando el principio de realización ▲ *the realization principle provided for in the directive* el principio de realización especificado en la directiva ▲ *use the realization principle* utilizar el principio de la realización

realization value US
→ realizable value

realize US
1 = realise UK
To realize is to achieve something or carry something through.
conseguir
= lograr
▲ *the enterprise's ability to realize its goals* la habilidad de la empresa para conseguir sus objetivos
2 = realise UK

To realize means to sell something in return for money and recognise the gain or loss at the time of sale and completion of the transaction.

materializar

= realizar

▲ *realize a profit* materializar un beneficio ▲ *realize assets within the current operating cycle* materializar activos dentro del actual ciclo de explotación ▲ *realize the surplus on the retirement or disposal of the asset* materializar la plusvalía de la retirada o venta del activo ▲ *realized gain* ganancia materializada ▲ *realized loss* pérdida materializada

realized US

= realised UK, IAS/IFRS

≠ unrealised UK, IAS/IFRS, unrealized US

Realized means actually carried out or completed, in financial statements referring to a gain or loss resulting from a change in value of an asset that has been realized by the legal disposal of that asset, whether or not cash has been received.

realizado

≠ no materializado, no realizado

▲ *a realized gain* una ganancia realizada ▲ *a realized loss* una pérdida realizada

realty US

→ real estate

reason

A reason is the cause of something that has occurred and explains why it happened or exists.

motivo

= razón

▲ *by reason of* con motivo de ▲ *disclosure of the reason for using a different presentation currency* divulgación del motivo por el que se usa una moneda de presentación diferente ▲ *the reason for not reclassifying the amounts* el motivo por el que no se reclasifican las cantidades ▲ *the reason for the reclassification* el motivo de la reclasificación ▲ *the reason for using a longer or shorter period* la razón por la que se usa un periodo de tiempo más largo o más corto ▲ *the reasons the published price was not used* los motivos por los que no se usó el precio publicado ▲ *within reason* dentro de lo razonable

reasonable

Something that is reasonable is fair and acceptable.

razonable

▲ *a reasonable approximation of the weighted average* una aproximación razonable de la media ponderada ▲ *a reasonable period for the submission of the annual report* un periodo razonable para la entrega del informe anual ▲ *a reasonable profit* un beneficio razonable ▲ *a reasonable profit allowance* una desgravación de beneficios razonable ▲ *reasonable assurance* aseguramiento razonable ▲ *the variability in the range of reasonable fair value estimates* la variabilidad en la serie de previsiones del valor razonable ▲ *use reasonable and supportable assumptions* usar supuestos razonables y justificables ▲ *within a reasonable time* en un tiempo razonable ▲ *within reasonable limits* dentro de límites razonables

reassess

To reassess something is to reconsider it.

reevaluar

▲ *reassess an internal rating* reevaluar un rating interno ▲ *reassess the depreciation period or the depreciation method* reevaluar el periodo o el método de amortización ▲ *reassess the fair value* reevaluar el valor razonable ▲ *reassess the useful life of an asset as finite rather than indefinite* reevaluar la vida útil de un activo como finita en vez de infinita

reassessment

A reassessment is a revaluation or restatement, often following a renewed examination of something.

reevaluación

▲ *as of the date of reassessment* a la fecha de reevaluación ▲ *make an annual reassessment* hacer una reevaluación anual ▲ *reassessment of embedded derivatives* reevaluación de derivados implícitos ▲ *recognise immediately in profit or loss any excess remaining after the reassessment* reconocer inmediatamente en el resultado cualquier remanente después de la reevaluación ▲ *subsequent reassessment* reevaluación consecutiva ▲ *trigger a reassessment* propiciar una reevaluación

rebuilding cost

= cost of conversion

Rebuilding costs are incurred in connection with the improvement, repair or refurbishment of buildings.

coste de ampliación, renovación y mejora

▲ *estimated rebuilding costs* costes de ampliación, renovación y mejora estimados

⇛ refurbishment

recapture[1] US *noun*

= retaxation DK, UK

Recapture is the inclusion of a previously deducted or excluded amount in gross income or tax liability. Recapture may be applicable to accelerated depreciation, cost recovery, amortisation, and various credits.

reimposición

= regravación

▲ *an amount subject to recapture* una cantidad sujeta a regravación ▲ *recapture in full* reimposición total ▲ *recapture of amortization and depreciation* reimposición de amortización y depreciación ▲ *recapture of foreign losses* reimposición de pérdidas en el extranjero ▲ *recapture of losses in foreign entities participating in joint taxation* reimposición de pérdidas en las entidades extranjeras que participan en la tributación conjunta

recapture[2] US *verb*

= re-tax

To recapture is to include a previously deducted or excluded amount in gross income or tax liability. Recapture may be applicable to accelerated depreciation, cost recovery, amortisation, and various credits.

regravar

= volver a gravar

▲ *recapture a loss* regravar una pérdida ▲ *recapture an amount* regravar una cantidad ▲ *recapture depreciation and amortization* volver a gravar depreciación y amortización ▲ *recapture in full* volver a gravar en su totalidad

recaptured tax amount US

The recaptured tax amount is the amount recognised representing a previously deducted or excluded tax liability amount.

cantidad fiscal regravada

▲ *distribute the recaptured tax amount over a period of 10 years* distribuir la cantidad fiscal regravada en un periodo superior a 10 años

receipt

1 Receipts constitute payments made and money received.

cobro

▲ *scheduled future cash receipts* cobros de caja futuros programados ▲ *the amount and timing of future cash receipts* la cantidad y la planificación de los cobros de caja futuros

2 = voucher

A receipt is a document evidencing that payment has been made and money received.

comprobante

= recibo

▲ *a qualified receipt* un comprobante autorizado ▲ *give a receipt* dar un comprobante ▲ *issue a receipt* emitir un recibo

receivable[1] IAS/IFRS *noun*

= account receivable, amount due UK, amount receivable IAS/IFRS, US

Receivables are claims against third parties, e.g. customers and others for goods, services or amounts of money which are typically due from credit sales.

derecho de cobro

▲ *a current receivable* un derecho de cobro corriente ▲ *a foreign currency receivable* un derecho de cobro en divisa extranjera ▲ *a non-current receivable* un derecho de cobro no corriente ▲ *an intercompany receivable* un derecho de cobro entre empresas ▲ *an unrecognised receivable* un derecho de cobro no reconocido ▲ *foreign currency receivable* derecho de cobro en moneda extranjera ▲ *loans and receivables originated by the enterprise* préstamos y derechos de cobro originados por la empresa ▲ *other receivables* otros derechos de cobro ▲ *receivables from associates* derechos de cobro de asociados ▲ *receivables from credit institutions* derechos de cobro de instituciones crediticias ▲ *receivables from group enterprises* derechos de cobro de las empresas del grupo ▲ *receivables from jo-*

int ventures derechos de cobro de joint ventures ▲ *receivables from owners and management* derechos de cobro de propietarios y dirección ▲ *receivables from public authorities* derechos de cobro de las autoridades públicas ▲ *tax base of a receivable* base imponible de un derecho de cobro ▲ *trade receivables* derechos de cobro comerciales

receivable[2] *adjective*

An amount that is receivable is due for payment, typically in connection with a credit sale.

a cobrar

= adeudado

▲ *a consideration receivable* una consideración a cobrar ▲ *current tax payable and receivable* impuesto corriente a pagar y a cobrar ▲ *dividend receivable* dividendo a cobrar ▲ *formation expenses receivable* gastos de formación a cobrar ▲ *interest and fees receivable* intereses y tasas a cobrar ▲ *tax receivable* impuesto a cobrar

receivables management

Receivables management is an enterprise's application of sound credit and collection policies with a view to minimizing the collection period, i.e. the period of time between sale and collection. Such policies may include cash discounts for prompt payment, defined terms of payment and collection procedures as well as procedures to address the risk of uncollectibles.

gestión de cuentas a cobrar

= gestión de las cuentas a cobrar

▲ *efficient and proactive receivables management* gestión eficiente y activa de cuentas a cobrar ▲ *improve receivables management* mejorar la gestión de las cuentas a cobrar

receive

To receive something is to obtain or get something from another party.

recibir

= cobrar

▲ *a contractual right to receive additional benefits* un derecho contractual a recibir prestaciones adicionales ▲ *receive all amounts due under the terms of the contract* recibir todas las cantidades adeudadas según las condiciones del contrato ▲ *receive compensation for losses from a reinsurer* recibir compensación por pérdidas de una aseguradora ▲ *receive dividends* cobrar dividendos ▲ *the estimate of net cash flows to be received* la estimación de flujos de efectivo netos a recibir

receiving company

The receiving company is the company that gets the assets or liabilities, including any tax losses, or one or more branches of the activity of the transferring company in connection with e.g. a merger or demerger.

empresa receptora

▲ *shareholders of the receiving company* accionistas de la empresa receptora ▲ *shares in the receiving company* acciones en la empresa receptora ▲ *the taxable income of the receiving company* los ingresos imponibles de la empresa receptora ▲ *transfer of activities from the transferring company to the receiving company* traspaso de actividades de la empresa emisora a la receptora

⇛ demerger, merger

reciprocal

The reciprocal is the result derived from the division of 1 by a given quantity. For example, the reciprocal of 5 is 0.2.

recíproco

= inverso

▲ *calculate the reciprocal* calcular el recíproco

reciprocal allocation method

= reciprocal method

The reciprocal allocation method is a cost allocation method which includes all services performed in between service departments in the final cost allocation to the production departments.

método de asignación recíproco

= método de distribución repíproco, mátodo recíproco

▲ *use the reciprocal allocation method* utilizar el método de distribución recíproco

reclassification

Reclassification means transferring an amount from one account to another in a financial statement.

reclasificación

▲ *a reclassification of any amount held in revaluation surplus for investment property* una reclasificación de cualquier cantidad obtenida como plusvalía por revalorización de la inversión inmobiliaria ▲ *disposals and reclassifications* ventas y reclasificaciones ▲ *make a reclassification* reclasificar ▲ *reclassification of inventories* reclasificación de inventarios ▲ *reclassification of inventories purchased within the group* reclasificación de inventarios adquiridos en el grupo ▲ *the nature of the reclassification* la naturaleza de la reclasificación ▲ *the reason for the reclassification* el motivo de la reclasificación

reclassify
= redesignate IAS/IFRS
To reclassify is to move an amount from one account to another in a financial statement.
reclasificar
▲ *reclassify a financial instrument into or out of the fair value through profit or loss category* reclasificar un instrumento financiero a valor razonable o a valor no razonable ▲ *reclassify a foreign entity* reclasificar una entidad extranjera ▲ *reclassify comparative amounts* reclasificar cantidades comparativas ▲ *reclassify into profit or loss the amount that is not expected to be recovered* reclasificar como resultados la cantidad que no se prevé que se recupere ▲ *reclassify some or all of the financial assets* reclasificar parcial o totalmente los activos financieros

recognise UK, IAS/IFRS
= include, recognize US
To recognise an amount or an item in the financial statements is to include that amount or item as an asset or a liability in the balance sheet or as income or expense in the profit and loss account.
reconocer
▲ *obligation to recognise something* obligación a reconocer algo ▲ *omit to recognise* omitir para reconocer ▲ *recognise as separate items* reconocer como partidas independientes ▲ *recognise assets* reconocer activos ▲ *recognise at fair value* reconocer a valor razonable ▲ *recognise at nil value* reconocer a valor cero ▲ *recognise costs* reconocer costes ▲ *recognise directly in equity* reconocer directamente en patrimonio ▲ *recognise immediately* reconocer inmediatamente ▲ *recognise in the balance sheet* reconocer en el balance ▲ *recognise income* reconocer ingresos ▲ *recognise income as earned* reconocer ingresos como ganancias ▲ *recognise liabilities* reconocer pasivos ▲ *recognise on a continuing basis* reconocer de forma continua ▲ *recognise systematically and consistently* reconocer sistemática y consistentemente ▲ *recognise under short-term debt* reconocer según una deuda a corto plazo

recognise as income IAS/IFRS
To recognise as income is to credit an item in the income statement that increases revenues and decreases expenses with a resulting positive effect on the bottom line.
reconocer como ingreso
▲ *an amount that has been recognised as income* una cantidad que se ha reconocido como ingreso ▲ *recognise as income immediately* reconocer como ingreso inmediatamente

recognise immediately UK, IAS/IFRS
= recognize immediately US
To recognise immediately is to enter at once in the profit and loss account or the balance sheet an amount that would otherwise have been recognised over a period or deferred.
reconocer inmediatamente
▲ *recognise immediately in profit or loss after reassessment* reconocer inmediatamente en el resultado después de la reevaluación ▲ *recognise immediately the services received* reconocer inmediatamente los servicios recibidos

recognise in the balance sheet
To recognise an item in the balance sheet means to include this item under assets or liabilities.
reconocer en el balance
▲ *recognise in the balance sheet a pension liability of €500000* reconocer en el balance un pasivo por jubilaciones de 500.000 euros ▲ *recognise in the balance sheet the actuarial gains and losses* reconocer en el balance los resultados actuariales

recognise in the income statement IAS/IFRS
= recognize in the income statement US
To recognise an item in the income statement is to carry an operating item in the income statement.
reconocer en el estado de resultados
▲ *recognise in the income statement the cumulative net loss* reconocer en el estado de resultados la pérdida neta acumulada ▲ *recognise in the income statement the fee income earned over the period* reconocer en el estado de resultados los ingresos por tasas obtenidos durante el periodo

recognise in the profit and loss account UK
When events and transactions are recognised in the profit and loss account of the enterprise they are carried and included in this financial statement as revenue or expenses and impact earnings.
reconocer en la cuenta de pérdidas y ganancias
= reconocer en la cuenta de resultados
▲ *recognise an item in the profit and loss account with a one-year interval* reconocer una partida en la cuenta de pérdidas y ganancias con un intervalo de un año

recognise under equity and liabilities UK, IAS/IFRS
To recognise an item under equity and liabilities is to enter the item in the balance sheet under equity and liabilities. In the horizontal format such an entry is made in the credit side.
reconocer en el patrimonio neto y pasivo
▲ *recognise a payment obligation under equity and liabilities* reconocer una obligación de pago en el patrimonio neto y pasivo

recognise under the accruals concept UK, IAS/IFRS
= recognize under the accruals concept US
To recognise items under the accruals concept is to report revenue and expenses when earned or incurred rather than when received or paid in cash. This involves recognising transactions that relate to the current accounting period in the accounts as "prepayments and accrued income" under assets or as "accruals and deferred income" under liabilities.
reconocer según el principio del devengo
= reconocer según el concepto de devengo, reconocer según el concepto del devengo, reconocer según el principio de devengo

recognised UK, IAS/IFRS
= recognized US
≠ unrecognised IAS/IFRS, UK, unrecognized US
If an amount or an item is recognised in the financial statements, it is carried in the profit and loss account or the balance sheet.
reconocido
▲ *a legal right to set off the recognised amounts* un derecho legal a compensar las cantidades reconocidas ▲ *a recognised financial asset* un activo financiero reconocido ▲ *a recognised financial liability* un pasivo financiero reconocido ▲ *previously recognised goodwill* fondo de comercio previamente reconocido

recognised in the balance sheet
An item recognised in the balance sheet is an item that is included in the balance sheet under assets, equity or liabilities.
reconocido en el balance
▲ *amounts recognised in the balance sheet* cantidades reconocidas en el balance ▲ *goodwill recognised in the balance sheet* fondo de comercio reconocido en el balance ▲ *the amount of deferred tax assets or liabilities recognised in the balance sheet* la cantidad de activos o pasivos fiscales diferidos reconocidos en el balance

recognised in the income statement IAS/IFRS
= recognized in the income statement US
An item recognised in the income statement is an item that is included in the income statement as either revenues or expenses.
reconocido en el estado de resultados
▲ *income recognised in the income statement* ingresos reconoci-

dos en el estado de resultados ▲ *tax recognised in the income statement* impuesto reconocido en el estado de resultados

recognition

Recognition is the recording in the balance sheet or income statement of items relating to assets, liabilities and equity as well as revenues and costs resulting from events and transactions during the financial year. Certain recognition criteria must be met, e.g. it must be probable that the items will result in future economic benefits flowing to or from the enterprise, and they must have a cost or value that can be reliably measured.

reconocimiento

▲ *any uncertainty connected with recognition* cualquier incertidumbre relativa al reconocimiento ▲ *initial recognition* reconocimiento inicial ▲ *measurement on initial recognition* valoración en el reconocimiento inicial ▲ *method of recognition* método de reconocimiento ▲ *on initial recognition* en el reconocimiento inicial ▲ *recognition and measurement* reconocimiento y valoración ▲ *recognition criteria* criterios de reconocimiento ▲ *recognition of assets* reconocimiento de activos ▲ *recognition of costs* reconocimiento de costes ▲ *recognition of income* reconocimiento de ingresos ▲ *recognition of lease payments as an expense* reconocimiento de pagos de alquiler como un gasto ▲ *recognition of liabilities* reconocimiento de pasivos ▲ *unusual matters affecting recognition* temas inusuales que afectan al reconocimiento SOURCE IFRS glossary

recognition criterion

= criterion for recognition

Recognition criteria refer to the criteria that must be met if a specific transaction or event is to be recognised as an item in the financial statements.

criterio de reconocimiento

▲ *disclose the recognition criteria used* divulgar los criterios de reconocimiento empleados

recognition in the income statement US, IAS/IFRS

Recognition in the income statement refers to the process of entering transactions as income or expenses in the income statement.

reconocimiento en el estado de resultados

▲ *deferral of recognition in the income statement* diferimiento del reconocimiento en el estado de resultados

recognition in the profit and loss account UK

Recognition in the profit and loss account refers to the process of entering transactions as revenues or expenses in the profit and loss account.

reconocimiento en la cuenta de pérdidas y ganancias

= reconocimiento en la cuenta de resultados

▲ *deferral of recognition in the profit and loss account* aplazamiento del reconocimiento en la cuenta de pérdidas y ganancias

recognize US

= recognise UK, IAS/IFRS

To recognize an amount or an item in the financial statements is to include that amount or item as an asset or a liability in the balance sheet or as income or expense in the income statement.

reconocer

▲ *obligation to recognize something* obligación de reconocer algo ▲ *omit to recognize* omitir para reconocer ▲ *recognize as separate items* reconocer como partidas independientes ▲ *recognize assets* reconocer activos ▲ *recognize at fair value* reconocer a valor razonable ▲ *recognize at nil value* reconocer a valor cero ▲ *recognize costs* reconocer costes ▲ *recognize directly in equity* reconocer directamente en patrimonio ▲ *recognize immediately* reconocer inmediatamente ▲ *recognize in the balance sheet* reconocer en el balance ▲ *recognize income* reconocer ingresos ▲ *recognize income as earned* reconocer ingresos cuando son efectivos ▲ *recognize liabilities* reconocer pasivos ▲ *recognize on a continuing basis* reconocer de forma continua ▲ *recognize systematically and consistently* reconocer sistemática y consistentemente ▲ *recognize under short-term debt* reconocer bajo deuda a corto plazo

recognize immediately US

= recognise immediately UK, IAS/IFRS

To recognize immediately is to enter at once in the income statement or the balance sheet an amount that would otherwise have been recognized over a period or deferred.

reconocer inmediatamente

▲ *recognize immediately in profit or loss after reassessment* reconocer inmediatamente en los resultados después de la reevaluación ▲ *recognize immediately the services received* reconocer inmediatamente los servicios recibidos

recognize in the income statement US

To recognize in the income statement means to enter a transaction as income or as an expense in the income statement.

reconocer en el estado de resultados

▲ *recognize an item in the income statement with a one-year interval* reconocer una partida en el estado de resultados con un intervalo de un año

recognize under equity and liabilities US

= recognise under equity and liabilities IAS/IFRS, UK

To recognize an item under equity and liabilities is to enter the item in the balance sheet under equity and liabilities. In the horizontal format such an entry is made in the credit side.

reconocer en el patrimonio neto y pasivo

▲ *recognize a payment obligation under equity and liabilities* reconocer una obligación de pago en el patrimonio neto y pasivo

recognize under the accruals concept US

= recognise under the accruals concept IAS/IFRS, UK

To recognize items under the accruals concept is to report revenue and expenses when earned or incurred rather than when received or paid in cash. This involves recognizing transactions that relate to the current fiscal period in the financial statements as the adjusting items: "prepaid expenses and accrued income" under assets or "accrued expenses and deferred income" under liabilities.

reconocer según el concepto del devengo

= reconocer según el concepto de devengo, reconocer según el principio de devengo, reconocer según el principio del devengo

recognized US

= recognised IAS/IFRS, UK

≠ unrecognised UK, IAS/IFRS, unrecognized US

If an amount or an item is recognized in the financial statements, it is carried in the income statement or the balance sheet.

reconocido

▲ *a legal right to set off the recognized amounts* un derecho legal para compensar las cantidades reconocidas ▲ *a recognized financial asset* un activo financiero reconocido ▲ *a recognized financial liability* un pasivo financiero reconocido ▲ *previously recognized goodwill* fondo de comercio previamente reconocido

recognized in the income statement US

= recognised in the income statement UK, IAS/IFRS

An item recognized in the income statement is an item that is included in the income statement as either revenues or expenses.

reconocido en el estado de resultados

▲ *income recognized in the income statement* ingresos reconocidos en el estado de resultados ▲ *tax recognized in the income statement* impuesto reconocido en el estado de resultados

recommend

To recommend is to suggest someone or something as suitable or appropriate.

recomendar

▲ *recommend the use of the equity method* recomendar el uso del método de participación

recommendation

A recommendation is official advice offered or a suggestion that someone or something is suitable for a particular purpose, situation or job.

recomendación

▲ *a general recommendation* una recomendación general

reconcile

To reconcile is to compare two statements, balances or amounts to verify whether they agree.

Amounts recognised in financial statements are e.g. reconciled with vouchers.

conciliar

▲ *reconcile segment revenue to entity revenue from external customers* conciliar los ingresos del segmento con los de la entidad procedentes de clientes externos ▲ *reconcile the opening and closing balances of each element within equity* conciliar los saldos de apertura y cierre de cada elemento de la entidad ▲ *reconcile to entity profit or loss from discontinued operations* conciliar los resultados de la entidad procedentes de operaciones discontinuas

reconciliation

Reconciliation means adjusting the difference between two items (amounts, balances, accounts or statements) so that the figures agree.

conciliación

▲ *a reconciliation of the carrying amount at the beginning and end of the period* una conciliación del valor contable al inicio y final del periodo ▲ *a reconciliation to relevant line items on the balance sheet* una conciliación a partidas relevantes en el balance una a una ▲ *equity reconciliation in column form* conciliación de patrimonio neto en forma de columna ▲ *numerical reconciliation* conciliación numérica ▲ *reconciliation between A and B* conciliación entre A y B ▲ *reconciliation of accounts* conciliación de cuentas ▲ *reconciliation of each class of share capital* conciliación de cada clase de capital social ▲ *reconciliation of movements on intangible assets* conciliación de movimientos en activos intangibles ▲ *reconciliation of opening and closing balances* conciliación de saldos de apertura y cierre ▲ *reconciliation of tax amounts* conciliación de las cuentas fiscales ▲ *reconciliation of the assets and liabilities recognised in the balance sheet* conciliación de los activos y pasivos reconocidos en el balance ▲ *reconciliation of the fair value of the assets* conciliación del valor razonable de los activos ▲ *reconciliation of the movements of the period* conciliación de los movimientos del periodo ▲ *reconciliation of the tax rate for the year* conciliación del tipo impositivo para el año ▲ *reconciliations of changes in insurance liabilities* conciliación de cambios en pasivos por seguros

⇛ restatement

reconciliation method US

= indirect method

≠ direct method

The reconciliation or indirect method is one of two applied methods of preparing the cash flow statement. Under the reconciliation method, the net cash flow from operating activities is reported indirectly by stating as a starting point operating income or profit for the accounting period and next adjusting this amount for, i.e. reconciling it with, the items included in income or profit that have not had any influence on cash in- or outflows, i.e. all accrual or non-cash components.

método indirecto

≠ método directo

▲ *use the reconciliation method* utilizar el método indirecto

SOURCE FAS 95

⇛ cash flow statement

record

= book, recognise

To record an item means to recognise an item as income or expense in the bookkeeping records or the accounts.

registrar

= anotar, reconocer

▲ *record a transaction in the annual report* registrar una transacción en el informe anual ▲ *record an event in the annual report* registrar un suceso en el informe anual ▲ *record initially at cost* registrar inicialmente al coste

recourse

Recourse is the right to demand compensation from the person who has endorsed a negotiable instrument, such as a cheque or a bill of exchange, if the first party liable does not pay.

recurso

▲ *have recourse against the company* poner un recurso contra la compañía ▲ *recourse agreement* acuerdo de no interposición de recurso ▲ *right of recourse* derecho de recurso ▲ *without recourse* sin recurso

recourse guarantee commitment

A recourse guarantee commitment is a commitment by the guarantor to fulfil the obligation of a debtor and pay the creditor if the debtor should be in default.

aval

▲ *recourse guarantee commitments in relation to group enterprises* aval en relación con el grupo

recoverable

Recoverable refers to something that may be regained or repossessed after it has been paid or lost, such as tax or outstanding amounts.

recuperable

▲ *duties and other taxes recoverable by the entity from the taxing authorities* derechos de aduanas y otras tasas recuperable por la entidad procedentes de la agencia tributaria ▲ *the amount recoverable from disposal of the asset* la cantidad recuperable procedente de la eliminación del activo

recoverable amount

The recoverable amount of an asset is the higher of that asset's value in use and its selling price less expected costs of disposal.

valor recuperable

= importe recuperable

▲ *a material decrease in recoverable amount* un descenso material en el valor recuperable ▲ *a previous sensitivity analysis of the recoverable amount* un análisis de sensibilidad previo del valor recuperable ▲ *calculation of the recoverable amount* cálculo del valor recuperable ▲ *determine the recoverable amount* determinar el valor recuperable ▲ *exceed the recoverable amount* exceder el valor recuperable ▲ *fix a recoverable amount* establecer un valor recuperable ▲ *fix a reliable recoverable amount* establecer un valor recuperable fiable ▲ *measure the recoverable amount* medir el valor recuperable ▲ *re-estimate the asset's recoverable amount* recalcular el valor recuperable del activo ▲ *the current recoverable amount determination* la determinación del valor recuperable corriente ▲ *the recoverable amount at the balance sheet date* el valor recuperable a fecha de balance ▲ *the recoverable amount of the revalued asset* el valor recuperable del activo revalorizado ▲ *the total recoverable amount of the assets* el valor recuperable total de los activos ▲ *write down to a lower recoverable amount* amortizar a un valor recuperable más bajo ▲ *write-down to recoverable amount* amortizar a valor recuperable

recovery period

A recovery period refers to the number of years over which an asset can be depreciated.

periodo de amortización

▲ *a recovery period for depreciation* un periodo de amortización por depreciación

recruit

To recruit means to select and hire new staff for the enterprise.

reclutar

▲ *recruit new employees* reclutar nuevos empleados ▲ *recruit qualified advisers* reclutar asesores cualificados

recruitment

Recruitment is the process or business of looking for and selecting new staff for an enterprise.

reclutamiento

▲ *internal recruitment* reclutamiento interno ▲ *recruitment and retention of employees* reclutamiento y mantenimiento de empleados ▲ *recruitment and training* reclutamiento y formación ▲ *recruitment of employees with broad-based experience* reclutamiento de empleados con experiencia ▲ *recruitment of new employees* reclutamiento de nuevos empleados

recurring

= recurrent

≠ non-recurring

When something is recurring it means that it will happen again or repeatedly, i.e. periodically or at regular intervals.

recurrente

▲ *a recurring discussion* una discusión recurrente ▲ *a recurring item of expense* una partida de gasto recurrente ▲ *annually recurring expenses* gastos recurrentes anualmente ▲ *income and expenses of a recurring nature* ingresos y gastos de una naturaleza recurrente

redeem

To redeem means to exchange e.g. a cheque or a share for payment of an amount of money.

amortizar

▲ *entitled to redeem the collateral* con derecho a amortizar la garantía ▲ *exercise the right to redeem* ejercer el derecho de amortización ▲ *have one's shares redeemed* haber amortizado sus acciones ▲ *redeem the financial asset before maturity* amortizar el activo financiero antes del vencimiento ▲ *satisfy an obligation to redeem a preference share* satisfacer una obligación para amortizar una acción preferente ▲ *the shares redeemed* las acciones amortizadas

redemption

= repayment

Redemption is the repayment of the principal amount of a debt or security at or before maturity.

amortización

= cancelación

▲ *a preference share that provides for redemptionon a specific date* una acción preferente que proporciona el derecho de amortización en una fecha específica ▲ *an unconditional right to refuse redemption* un derecho incondicional para rehusar la amortización ▲ *cost payable on redemption* coste a pagar por la amortización ▲ *cumulative redemptions* amortizaciones acumulativas ▲ *demand redemption* demandar la amortización ▲ *gains and losses associated with redemptions of financial liabilities* pérdidas y ganancias asociadas con las amortizaciones de pasivos financieros ▲ *redemption of bonds* amortización de bonos ▲ *the prohibition against redemption* la prohibición contra la amortización ▲ *the redemption of convertible preference shares* la amortización de las acciones preferentes convertibles ▲ *the redemption of ordinary shares outstanding* la amortización de las acciones ordinarias pendientes ▲ *the right to request redemption* el derecho a requerir amortización

redemption amount

A redemption amount is a set price that must be paid by the issuing enterprise to the holder of redeemable securities on redemption.

valor de rescate

▲ *a fixed redemption amount* un valor de rescate fijado ▲ *base on the redemption amount* basarse en el valor de rescate ▲ *the present value of the redemption amount* el valor actual del valor de rescate ▲ *the redemption amount that is payable at the balance sheet date* el valor de rescate que se paga a fecha de balance

⇛ redemption

redemption date

= maturity date

A redemption date is the date on which securities are due to be redeemed by the issuing enterprise.

fecha de amortización

= fecha de la amortización , fecha de vencimiento, fecha del vencimiento

▲ *dividends payable at the discretion of the entity before the redemption date* dividendos a pagar a elección de la entidad antes de la fecha de la amortización ▲ *maturity and redemption date* fecha de vencimiento y amortización

redemption obligation

A redemption obligation is the obligation by a shareholder to redeem his share(s) on demand by the company subject to certain conditions laid down in the company's articles of association, e.g. after a defined period of time or the occurrence of a certain event.

obligación de rescate

= obligación de amortización, obligación de reembolso

▲ *a shareholder subject to a redemption obligation* un accionista sujeto a una obligación de rescate ▲ *the shareholder who has the redemption obligation* el accionista que tiene la obligación de rescate

redemption price

A redemption price is a set price that must be paid by the issuing enterprise to the holder of redeemable shares on redemption.

precio de amortización

= precio de la amortización

▲ *indicate a redemption price* indicar un precio de amortización

redemption right

A redemption right is a right of holders of redeemable shares to require the issuing enterprise to redeem the shares and pay the set redemption price.

derecho de amortización

▲ *exercise a redemption right* ejercer un derecho de amortización ▲ *introduce a redemption right* introducir un derecho de amortización ▲ *redemption right provided in the articles of association* derecho de amortización ofrecido en los estatutos de la asociación

redemption value

The redemption value is the total value at which a loan is repaid. Loans may typically be redeemed at par.

valor de amortización

▲ *a fixed redemption value* un valor de amortización fijado

⇛ par

redesignate IAS/IFRS

= reclassify

To redesignate is to rearrange items from their former classification into new classes of items, e.g. in connection with the application of changed accounting policies.

reclasificar

= reasignar

▲ *redesignate the hedge as a fair value hedge* reclasificar la cobertura como una cobertura a valor razonable

redesignation

A redesignation is a rearrangement of items from their former classification into new classes of items, e.g. in connection with the application of changed accounting policies.

reclasificación

= reasignación

▲ *redesignation of financial assets* reclasificación de activos financieros

reduce

= cut, decrease

To reduce something means making it smaller, i.e. it is decreased in extent, size, scope or number.

reducir

▲ *reduce a difference* reducir una diferencia ▲ *reduce an amount* reducir una cantidad ▲ *reduce commitments* reducir los compromisos ▲ *reduce future production costs* reducir los costes de producción futuros ▲ *reduce the amount of future cash inflows from financial assets* reducir la cantidad de entradas de efectivos futuras procedentes de activos financieros ▲ *reduce the amount of income recognised over the lease term* reducir la cantidad de ingresos reconocidos a lo largo del periodo de arrendamiento ▲ *reduce the carrying amount of goodwill allocated to the unit* reducir el valor contable del fondo de comercio asignado a la unidad ▲ *reduce the perceived misleading aspects of compliance* reducir los aspectos de cumplimiento erróneos percibidos

reduced

When something has been reduced it has been made smaller, i.e. it is decreased in extent or number.

reducido

▲ *a reduced interest rate* un tipo de interés reducido ▲ *catastrophe bonds that provide for reduced payments of principal, interest or both* bonos de catástrofe que ofrecen pagos reducidos del principal e intereses, o ambos ▲ *work reduced hours* trabajo reducido en horas

reducing balance amortisation UK

→ reducing-balance amortisation

reducing balance depreciation UK

→ reducing-balance depreciation

reducing balance method UK

→ reducing-balance method

reducing-balance amortisation UK

= declining-balance amortization US, diminishing-balance amortization UK, IAS/IFRS

≠ straight-line amortisation UK

Reducing-balance amortisation is a method of allocating the cost of an intangible asset over its useful life, in which the amortisation charge for each accounting period in the profit and loss account is based on a percentage of each year's amortisable amount, which means that each year's charge is reduced.

amortización decreciente

▲ *use the reducing-balance amortisation method* utilizar el método de amortización decreciente

⇛ reducing-balance depreciation, reducing-balance method

reducing-balance depreciation UK

= declining-balance depreciation US, declining-balance me-

thod US, diminishing balance method
≠ straight-line depreciation
Reducing-balance depreciation is a method of allocating the cost of a tangible asset over its useful life, in which the depreciation charge for each accounting period in the profit and loss account is based on a percentage of each year's depreciable amount, which means that each year's charge is reduced.
amortización decreciente
▲ *use the reducing-balance depreciation method* utilizar el método de amortización decreciente
⇛ reducing-balance amortisation, reducing-balance method

reducing-balance method UK
= declining-balance method US, diminishing-balance method IAS/IFRS, UK, reducing balance method UK
≠ straight-line method
The reducing-balance method is a method of allocating the cost of a tangible asset or an intangible asset over its useful life, in which the depreciation or amortisation charge for each accounting period in the profit and loss account is based on a percentage of each year's depreciable or amortisable amount, which means that each year's charge is reduced.
método de amortización decreciente
= método de amortización porcentual
▲ *use the reducing-balance method* utilizar el método de amortización decreciente

reduction
= decrease, limitation
A reduction is a cut or decrease of something, resulting in e.g. a smaller amount, size or scope of something.
reducción
▲ *a reduction in earnings per share* una reducción en los beneficios por acción ▲ *a reduction in loss per share* una reducción en pérdida por acción ▲ *a reduction in the cash flows from the asset* una reducción en los flujos de efectivo del activo ▲ *a reduction in the estimated unguaranteed residual value* una reducción en el valor residual no garantizado estimado ▲ *adjustment resulting from a reduction of the corporate income tax rate* ajuste procedente de una reducción del tipo impositivo de los ingresos corporativos ▲ *budget reductions* reducciones presupuestarias ▲ *compensation for a reduction in the value of the assets* compensación por una reducción en el valor de los activos ▲ *recognise the reduction in the carrying amount of the goodwill as an expense* reconocer la reducción en el valor contable del fondo de comercio como un gasto ▲ *reduction of the machinery and equipment balance* reducción del saldo de equipo y maquinaria ▲ *subsequent reductions in a deferred tax liability* reducciones subsiguientes en una deuda fiscal diferida

redundancy payment UK
= severance pay, severance payment, termination benefit IAS/IFRS
Redundancy payment refers to a monetary benefit payable to an employee upon involuntary termination before normal retirement or upon the employee's acceptance of voluntary termination in return for such payment.
indemnización por despido
▲ *make redundancy payments* efectuar indemnizaciones por despido ▲ *measurement of redundancy payments* valoración de las indemnizaciones por despido ▲ *provide redundancy payments* ofrecer indemnizaciones por despido ▲ *provisions for redundancy payments* provisiones para indemnizaciones por despido ▲ *recognise redundancy payments* reconocer indemnizaciones por despido ▲ *redundancy payments falling due more than 1 year after the balance sheet date* indemnizaciones por despido que vencen en el largo plazo ▲ *redundancy payments for key management personnel* indemnizaciones por despido para el personal de alta dirección

reengineering
= business process reengineering
Reengineering is a variance method which, based on a well-defined strategy and rethinking, fundamentally and

radically renews, adjusts and redesigns the business processes of an enterprise to achieve decisive improvements on critical factors of performance such as costs, quality, service and time.

reingeniería

▲ *information on reengineering* información sobre reingeniería ▲ *successful reengineering* reingeniería exitosa ▲ *the underlying principles for reengineering* los principios subyacentes a la reingeniería

reference

A reference is additional information in a text or statement, often in a note, directing the reader to the source of something mentioned or quoted in the text or to additional data on a particular subject.

referencia

▲ *determine fair value by reference to an active market* determinar el valor razonable por referencia a un mercado activo ▲ *recognise revenue by reference to the stage of completion* reconocer ingresos por referencia a la etapa de finalización ▲ *references to the current version of IAS 22* referencias a la versión actual de la NIC 22 ▲ *without direct reference to market conditions* sin referencia directa a las condiciones del mercado

refinance

To refinance is to extend an existing loan by replacing it with a new loan, e.g. with another interest rate and maturity or a changed repayment profile.

refinanciar

▲ *an agreement to refinance or to reschedule payments on a long-term basis* un contrato de refinanciación o de reestructuración de pagos a largo plazo ▲ *refinance an obligation* refinanciar una obligación ▲ *refinance debt instruments* refinanciar los instrumentos de deuda ▲ *refinance existing subordinate debt* refinanciar la deuda subordinada existente

refinancing

Refinancing means extending the maturity date of a loan and/or increasing the amount of existing debt. Also, refinancing may refer to the refunding of a loan by repaying existing debt and obtaining a new loan by issuing new securities, e.g. with a lower interest rate, longer maturity period or lower repayment instalments.

refinanciación

▲ *a binding refinancing agreement* un acuerdo de refinanciación en firme ▲ *refinancing of financial liabilities* refinanciación de pasivos financieros ▲ *refinancing on a long-term basis* refinanciación a largo plazo

refined costing system

A refined costing system reduces the use of broadly averaging costs in the allocation of costs to different products and offers more accurate product cost data. Refined costing systems focus on a more precise measure of the use of resources by cost objects (e.g. jobs, services and products) and the allocation of the cost of indirect resources to different cost objects.

NOTE Activity-based costing is an often-applied refined costing system which identifies individual activities as the fundamental cost objects.

sistema de coste preciso

▲ *use a refined costing system* utilizar un sistema de coste preciso

⇛ activity-based costing, activity-based costing system

reflect

To reflect something means to express, depict or represent something.

reflejar

▲ *reflect future cash outflows or related cost savings* reflejar las salidas de efectivo futuras o ahorros de costes relacionados ▲ *reflect the current market situation* reflejar la situación actual del mercado ▲ *reflect the enterprise's consumption* reflejar el consumo de la empresa ▲ *reflect the interests of the shareholders and the company* reflejar los intereses de los accionistas y de la empresa ▲ *restate comparative information in order to reflect the new accounting policies* incluir nuevamente información comparativa con objeto de reflejar las nuevas políticas contables

refurbishment

Refurbishment involves improvement of buildings or equipment through repair or additions.

mejoras

▲ *carry out refurbishment regularly* llevar a cabo mejoras con regularidad ▲ *charges relating to refurbishment* cambios relacionados con mejoras ▲ *expenditure for refurbishment* gastos por mejoras ▲ *refurbishment costs* costes de mejoras

⇛ conversion

reg. no.

= registration number

"reg. no." is the abbreviation for "registration number", i.e. a number by which something is registered in a record or official list.

nº de registro

= número de registro

▲ *apply for a reg. no.* solicitar un nº de registro ▲ *disclose the reg. no.* publicar el nº de registro ▲ *the enterprise's reg. no.* el nº de registro de la empresa

register

= notify

To register is to record in writing or inform somebody of something officially in writing.

registrar

▲ *fees to register a legal right* tarifas por registrar un derecho legal

register of shareholders UK

= register of members, stock register US

A register of shareholders is a record that contains the names and addresses of the shareholders of a company and lists the number of shares held by each shareholder.

registro de accionistas

= registro de los accionistas

▲ *be entered in the register of shareholders* estar incluido en el registro de accionistas ▲ *copy of the register of shareholders* copia del registro de accionistas ▲ *have one's name recorded in the register of shareholders* tener su nombre anotado en el registro de accionistas ▲ *keep a register of shareholders* mantener un registro de accionistas

⇛ registered share

registered auditor UK

A registered auditor is a chartered certified accountant registered and approved by a recognised, professional accountancy supervisory body, such as the Institute of Chartered Accountants in England and Wales, to carry out audits under the UK Companies Act 1989 on an independent basis.

auditor registrado

▲ *an audit by a registered auditor* una auditoría por un auditor registrado ▲ *an independent registered auditor* un auditor registrado independiente ▲ *signed by a registered auditor* firmado por un auditor registrado ▲ *the registered auditor in charge of the audit* el auditor registrado a cargo de la auditoría

⇛ state-authorised public accountant

registered office UK

Registered office refers to the registered, official address of an enterprise to which official documents must be sent.

domicilio social

▲ *have its registered office in another country* tener su domicilio social en otro país ▲ *have its registered office in Ireland* tener su domicilio social en Irlanda ▲ *the address of the registered office* la dirección del domicilio social

registered share

≠ bearer share

A registered share is a share whose owner or nominee is named on the share certificate and in the share register. Transfer of ownership requires registration, and registered shares are not negotiable.

acción nominativa

≠ acción al portador

▲ *convert bearer shares to registered shares* convertir las acciones al portador en acciones nominativas ▲ *the subscription price of one new registered share* el precio de suscripción de una acción nominativa nueva

registered shareholder UK

= registered stockholder US

A registered shareholder is an owner or nominee whose name is registered as proof of ownership on a share certificate and in the share register of the company in question. It is a legal requirement that registered shares must be registered by name for the owners or nominees to be able to exercise their rights.

accionista nominativo

▲ *contact all registered shareholders* contactar con todos los accionistas nominativos

⇛ bearer share, registered share

registered stockholder US

= registered shareholder UK

A registered stockholder is an owner or nominee whose name is registered as proof of ownership on a stock certificate and in the stock register of the corporation in question. It is a legal requirement that registered stock must be registered by name for the owners or nominees to be able to exercise their rights.

accionista nominativo

▲ *contact all registered stockholders* contactar con todos los accionistas nominativos

registration

Registration is the act of giving notice in writing to an official authority, e.g. submitting company particulars to the companies registry.

inscripción

▲ *registration and other regulatory fees* tarifas por inscripción y otras tarifas obligatorias

⇛ notification

registration number

= reg. no.

The registration number is the number by which something is registered in a record or official list.

número de registro

= nº de registro

▲ *assign a registration number to the enterprise* asignar un número de registro a la empresa ▲ *buy a registration number* comprar un número de registro ▲ *company registration number* número de registro de la compañia ▲ *retain a registration number* mantener un número de registro

regulated market

A regulated market is a trading venue organised under an authorised market operator (such as a stock exchange) where financial instruments are admitted and traded in accordance with certain rules and procedures. As defined under the EU Markets in Financial Instruments Directive (MiFID), a regulated market is a multilateral system authorised and managed by a market operator under the provisions of MiFID, which functions as a venue for third parties with multiple buying and selling interests in financial instruments admitted to trading on the market, with the objective of facilitating the creation of contracts in respect of these instruments.

mercado regulado

▲ *access to regulated markets* acceso a los mercados regulados ▲ *cross-border admission of securities to trading on regulated markets* admisión de títulos multinacionales a cotización en mercados regulados ▲ *debt securities admitted to trading on a regulated market* títulos de deuda admitidos a cotización en un mercado regulado ▲ *have remote access to a regulated market* tener acceso remoto a un mercado regulado ▲ *post-trade transparency requirements for regulated markets* requisitos de transparencia posteriores a la cotización en los mercados regulados ▲ *pre-trade transparency requirements for regulated markets* requisitos de transparencia previos a la cotización en los mercados regulados ▲ *remote members of the regulated market* miembros distantes del mercado regulado ▲ *the management of the regulated market* la dirección del mercado regulado ▲ *the operator of the regulated market* el operador del mercado regulado

regulation

Regulations are legal rules made with the purpose of supplementing primary legislation, i.e. statutes. In the context of European Union law, regulations are part of EU secondary legislation together with directives, decisions, recommendations and opinions. EU Regulations are part of national law in the member countries and take direct effect when created.

regulación

▲ *a draft regulation* un borrador de regulación ▲ *a proposal for a new regulation* una propuesta de nueva regulación ▲ *adopt a regulation* adoptar una regulación ▲ *Commission Regulation (EC) No 2236/2004 of 29 December 2004* Regulación de la Comisión (CE) Nº 2236/2004 de 29 de diciembre de 2004 ▲ *Regulation of the European Parliament and of the Council on the application of international accounting standards* Regulación del Parlamento Europeo y del Consejo sobre la aplicación de las normas internacionales de contabilidad ▲ *the measures provided for in this Regulation* las medidas provistas en esta Regulación

regulatory

= statutory

Something that is regulatory has been laid down in legislation or particular rules and regulations.

reglamentario

▲ *be in compliance with the regulatory framework* cumplir con el marco reglamentario ▲ *legislative, regulatory and administrative or other measures* legislativo, reglamentario y administrativo u otras medidas ▲ *regulatory approval* aprobación reglamentaria ▲ *regulatory capital requirements* requisitos de capital reglamentarios ▲ *regulatory clearance* aprobación reglamentaria ▲ *regulatory powers* poderes reglamentarios ▲ *regulatory price control* control de precios reglamentario ▲ *regulatory requirements* requisitos reglamentarios ▲ *regulatory risk-based capital requirements* requisitos reglamentarios de capital basados en el riesgo ▲ *the regulatory environment* el entorno reglamentario ▲ *the set of regulatory accounts* el conjunto de cuentas reglamentarias

⇛ regulatory rule

regulatory framework

A regulatory framework is a system containing the overall theoretical rules and statutory provisions for a specific legislative area.

marco reglamentario

▲ *conflict with the regulatory framework* conflicto con el marco reglamentario ▲ *establish a regulatory framework* establecer un marco reglamentario ▲ *prohibited by the relevant regulatory framework* prohibido por el marco reglamentario relevante

⇛ regulatory

regulatory rule

Regulatory rules are rules laid down in legislation or regulations.

norma reguladora

▲ *uncertain regulatory rules* normas reguladoras inciertas

reimburse

To reimburse means to refund expenses previously paid by another party, typically on presentation of vouchers. Travelling expenses are e.g. reimbursed when incurred in connection with employment or a particular job.

reembolsar

▲ *reimburse a fee* reembolsar una tarifa ▲ *reimburse amounts paid by the enterprise* reembolsar las cantidades pagadas por la empresa ▲ *reimburse and reward the lessor for its investment and services* reembolsar y recompensar al arrendador por sus inversiones y servicios ▲ *reimburse costs incurred* reembolsar los costes incurridos ▲ *reimburse some or all of the amounts of a provision* reembolsar alguna de las cantidades de una provisión

reimbursement

Reimbursement is payment received or to be received as compensation for expenditure.

reembolso

▲ *a reimbursement related to a provision* un reembolso relacionado con una provisión ▲ *reimbursement of a provision* reembolso de una provisión ▲ *reimbursement of capital* reembolso de capital ▲ *reimbursement of costs incurred* reembolso de los costes incurridos

reinsurance

Reinsurance is an agreement between two insurance companies, typically on an international basis, where one insurance company (the assuming company or reinsurer) agrees to take on the risk or part of the risk of another (the primary or ceding company) against part of the premium on a given policy.

reaseguro

▲ *amounts recoverable under reinsurance* cantidades a recuperar según el reaseguro ▲ *before and after risk mitigation by*

reinsurance antes y después de la mitigación del riesgo mediante un reaseguro ▲ *bonuses and rebates net of reinsurance* bonificaciones y desgravaciones netas por reaseguro ▲ *carry on reinsurance business* continuar con un negocio de reaseguro ▲ *claims incurred net of reinsurance* reclamaciones netas incurridas por reaseguro ▲ *creditors arising out of reinsurance operations* acreedores procedentes de operaciones de reaseguro ▲ *debtors arising out of reinsurance operations* deudores procedentes de operaciones de reaseguro ▲ *earned premiums net of reinsurance* primas netas recibidas de reaseguro ▲ *gains and losses recognised in profit or loss on buying reinsurance* pérdidas y ganancias reconocidas en resultados al contratar el reaseguro ▲ *life insurance provisions net of reinsurance* provisiones netas de seguro de vida por reaseguro ▲ *outward reinsurance premiums* primas de reaseguro de salida ▲ *possible reinsurance recoveries* recuperaciones de reaseguro posibles ▲ *premiums accepted for all reinsurance* primas aceptadas para todos los reaseguros ▲ *reinsurance acceptances* aceptaciones del reaseguro ▲ *reinsurance amount* cuenta de reaseguro ▲ *reinsurance cessions* cesiones de reaseguro ▲ *reinsurance recoveries anticipated* recuperaciones anticipadas de reaseguro ▲ *required solvency margin for a reinsurance undertaking simultaneously conducting non-life and life reinsurance* margen de solvencia requerida a una reaseguradora que hace al tiempo pólizas de vida y no vida ▲ *the pursuit of reinsurance business* el seguimiento del negocio del reaseguro
⇛ cedant

reinsurance amount

Reinsurance amounts cover the actual or estimated amounts that, under contractual reinsurance arrangements, are deducted from the gross amounts of insurance provisions.

cantidad reasegurada

▲ *calculate the reinsurance amount* calcular la cantidad reasegurada

reinsurance asset

When a cedant, i.e. an insurer who passes on the risk to a reinsurer, enters into a reinsurance contract, the cedant acquires certain rights under the contract. Such rights net of obligations are referred to as reinsurance assets.

activo de reaseguro

= activo derivado de reaseguro cedido

NOTE Spanish accountants prefer 'activo de reaseguro' to the IAS/IFRS term 'activo derivado de reaseguro cedido'.

▲ *an event that occurred after initial recognition of the reinsurance asset* un suceso que ocurrió después del reconocimiento inicial del activo de reaseguro ▲ *impairment of reinsurance assets* deterioro de activos de reaseguro ▲ *offset reinsurance assets against the related insurance liabilities* compensar activos de reaseguro contra el seguro relacionado ▲ *reconciliations of changes in reinsurance assets* conciliaciones de cambios en activos de reaseguro

SOURCE IFRS 4, Appendix A

reinsurance contract

A reinsurance contract is a written agreement between two insurance companies where one insurance company (the assuming company) agrees to take on the risk or part of the risk of another (the primary company or cedant) against part of the premium on a given policy.

contrato de reaseguro

▲ *financial reinsurance contracts* contratos de reaseguro financieros ▲ *income or expense from reinsurance contracts* ingreso o gasto de los contratos de reaseguro ▲ *the nature of a reinsurance contract* la naturaleza de un contrato de reaseguro ▲ *the policyholder under a reinsurance contract* el tenedor de la póliza según un contrato de reaseguro ▲ *the quality of a reinsurance contract* la calidad de un contrato de reaseguro

SOURCE IFRS 4, Appendix A

reinsurer

= assuming company
≠ cedant

A reinsurer is an insurance company that agrees to assume the risk or part of the risk of another insurance company, the cedant or ceding company, against part of the premium on a given policy.

reaseguradora

▲ *deposits received from reinsurers* depósitos recibidos de las reaseguradoras ▲ *receive compensation for losses from the reinsurer* recibir compensación por pérdidas de la reaseguradora SOURCE IFRS 4, Appendix A

⇛ reinsurance

relate

To relate to something means to be connected to or attributable to something.

relacionar

= relacionarse

▲ *cash outflows that relate to obligations that have been recognised as liabilities* salidas de efectivo que se relacionan con obligaciones que han sido reconocidas como pasivos ▲ *relate to all operations that have been discontinued by the balance sheet date* relacionar todas las operaciones que han sido abandonadas a la fecha del balance ▲ *relate to something* relacionar con algo ▲ *the corporate assets that relate to the cash-generating unit under review* los activos de corporación que se relacionan con la unidad generadora de efectivo

related

To be related to something means to be connected to or attributable to something.

relacionado

▲ *any related tax effects* cualesquiera efectos fiscales relacionados ▲ *exchange gains and losses related to hedges of the currency risk of a forecast transaction* pérdidas y ganancias por cambio relacionadas con la cobertura por riesgo de divisas en una transacción futura ▲ *the income and related expenses of incidental operations* los ingresos y gastos relacionados de operaciones excepcionales ▲ *the proportionate share of the related accumulated exchange difference* la parte proporcional de la diferencia de cambio acumulada relacionada ▲ *the related cumulative remuneration expense* el gasto acumulado relacionado por remuneración

related company US

= affiliated company

A related company is a company that is linked to another company in the same group in some way. Depending on the parent company interests in it, a related company may be either a subsidiary or an associated company. Two subsidiaries in the same group are related companies.

compañia afiliada

= filial

▲ *merger of related companies* fusión de compañías filiales

⇛ affiliate

related party

Related parties are (1) persons or enterprises that directly or indirectly control, exercise significant influence over, or jointly control the other party or parties when making financial and operating decisions, or (2) several persons or enterprises that are controlled by the same person or enterprise in making financial and operating decisions or (3) members of the board of directors or senior management and their relatives.

parte relacionada

= parte vinculada

▲ *a comprehensive analysis of related party balances* un análisis comprensivo de los saldos de las partes relacionadas ▲ *disclosures of related parties in the annual report* publicaciones de las partes relacionadas en el informe anual ▲ *exchange of assets and services between related parties* cambio de activos y servicios entre partes relacionadas ▲ *identification of outstanding balances between an entity and its related parties* identificación de los saldos pendientes entre una entidad y sus partes relacionadas ▲ *identification of related party relationships and transactions* identificación de las relaciones y transacciones de las partes relacionadas ▲ *payments between the related parties* pagos entre las partes relacionadas ▲ *reacquire own equity instruments from related parties* recomprar los instrumentos de patrimonio propio a las partes relacionadas ▲ *receivables from related parties* cuentas a cobrar procedentes de partes relacionadas ▲ *related party disclosures* publicaciones de partes relacionadas ▲ *the bank's policy for lending to related parties* la política del banco en relación con el préstamo a las partes relacionadas ▲ *transactions between related parties* transacciones entre partes relacionadas

related party relationship

A related party relationship is a connection between parties, typically established by one party exercising direct or indirect control or significant influence over the other with the effect that the parties will share common interests. Examples of related party relationships are parent companies, group enterprises and associates as well as company directors, executives and their relatives.

relación entre partes vinculadas

▲ *a related party relationship affecting the profit or loss and financial position of an entity* una relación entre partes vinculadas que afecta al resultado y a la posición financiera de la entidad ▲ *consider each possible related party relationship* considerar cada posible relación entre partes vinculadas ▲ *disclose the nature of the related party relationship* publicar la naturaleza de la relación entre partes vinculadas ▲ *form a view about the effects of related party relationships on an entity* formar una visión sobre los efectos de las relaciones entre partes vinculadas en una entidad ▲ *identification of related party relationships and transactions* identificación de relaciones y transacciones entre partes vinculadas ▲ *the identification of related party relationships between parents and subsidiaries* la identificación de las relaciones entre partes vinculadas entre matrices y filiales

⇛ related party, related party transaction

related party transaction

≠ arm's length transaction

A related party transaction is a transaction between (1) persons or enterprises, one of which directly or indirectly controls or exercises significant influence over the other party or parties in making financial and operating decisions, or (2) persons or enterprises that are controlled by the same person or enterprise in making financial and operating decisions. Such a transaction is termed a related party transaction whether or not a consideration is paid.

transacción con partes vinculadas

= transacción con partes relacionadas

NOTE Spanish accountants prefer 'transacción con partes vinculadas' to the IAS/IFRS term 'transacción con partes relacionadas'.

▲ *disclosure of related party transactions* publicación de las transacciones con partes vinculadas ▲ *eliminate intragroup related party transactions* eliminar las transacciones intragrupo con partes vinculadas ▲ *enter into related party transactions with equity compensation plans* llevar a cabo transacciones con partes vinculadas con planes de compensación de títulos ▲ *knowledge of related party transactions* conocimiento de las transacciones con partes vinculadas ▲ *related party transactions and outstanding balances with other entities in a group* transacciones con partes vinculadas y saldos pendientes con otras entidades en un grupo ▲ *related party transactions made on terms equivalent to those that prevail in arm's length transactions* transacciones con partes vinculadas hechas en términos equivalentes a aquellas que prevalecen en las transacciones en condiciones de plena competencia ▲ *related party transactions with post-employment benefit plans* transacciones con partes vinculadas con planes de prestación post-empleo ▲ *the effects of related party transactions on the financial statements of the entity* los efectos de las transacciones con partes vinculadas en los estados financieros de la entidad

⇛ arm's length principle

relational capital

Relational capital refers to the value of an enterprise's external relations with other enterprises or persons such as customers, strategic partners or suppliers as well as other stake-

holders and associates, and their loyalty and satisfaction.
capital relacional
▲ *the distinction between relational capital and social capital* la distinción entre capital relacional y capital social

relevance
Relevance is one of the key qualitative characteristics of financial information. Information is relevant if it can influence the economic decisions of users and is timely provided to influence such decisions. Other qualitative characteristics are materiality, reliability, comparability and understandability.
relevancia
▲ *enhance the relevance and reliability of the entity's financial statements* incrementar la relevancia y fiabilidad de los estados financieros de la entidad ▲ *increase the relevance and reliability of the financial statements* aumentar la relevancia y fiabilidad de los estados financieros ▲ *text with EEA relevance* texto con relevancia para el mercado europeo interno ▲ *the relevance, reliability, and comparability over time of financial information* la relevancia, fiabilidad y comparabilidad en el tiempo de la información financiera

relevant costs
≠ relevant revenue
Relevant costs are expected future costs that are influenced by the choice between alternative management decisions.
coste relevante
▲ *calculate relevant costs* calcular los costes relevantes ▲ *determine the relevant costs* determinar los costes relevantes ▲ *total relevant costs* total costes relevantes

relevant range UK, US
The relevant range refers to the activity levels within which assumptions about a specific relationship between costs and the cost driver is valid.
tramo relevante
▲ *within a relevant range* dentro de un tramo relevante

relevant revenue
≠ relevant costs
Relevant revenue refers to expected future revenue that is influenced by the choice between alternative management decisions.
ingreso relevante
▲ *calculate relevant revenue* calcular el ingreso relevante

reliability
Reliability is the accounting concept and requirement that the contents of financial reports are free from material error and bias and that confidence can be placed in them.
fiabilidad
▲ *a high degree of reliability* un alto grado de fiabilidad ▲ *enhance the relevance and reliability of the entity's financial statements* aumentar la relevancia y fiabilidad de los estados financieros de la entidad ▲ *impair the reliability of the information* deteriorar la fiabilidad de la información ▲ *increase the relevance and reliability of the financial statements* aumentar la relevancia y fiabilidad de los estados financieros ▲ *measure with sufficient reliability* medir con fiabilidad suficiente ▲ *the additional reliability that information will bring to the measurement* la fiabilidad adicional que aportará la información a la valoración ▲ *the relevance, reliability and comparability over time of financial information* la relevancia, fiabilidad y comparabilidad a lo largo del tiempo de la información financiera ▲ *the reliability of future cash flows* la fiabilidad de los flujos de efectivo futuros ▲ *the reliability of the annual report* la fiabilidad del informe anual ▲ *the requirement of relevance and reliability* el requisito de relevancia y fiabilidad ▲ *with reasonable reliability* con fiabilidad razonable
⇛ objectivity

reliable
Reliable means trustworthy.
fiable
▲ *a reliable allocation of expenses* una asignación de gastos fiable ▲ *a reliable approximation of the detailed computations* una aproximación fiable de los cálculos detallados ▲ *a reliable determination of expenses incurred* una valoración fiable de los gastos incurridos ▲ *a reliable estimate of obligations* una esti-

mación fiable de las obligaciones ▲ *a reliable statement* un estado fiable ▲ *determine a reliable measurement of the fair value* determinar una valoración fiable del valor razonable ▲ *determine a reliable measurement of the market value* determinar una valoración fiable del valor de mercado ▲ *determine a reliable measurement of the recoverable amount* determinar una valoración fiable de la cantidad a recuperar ▲ *highly reliable information* información altamente fiable ▲ *make a reliable estimate* haber una estimación fiable ▲ *reliable estimates of future cash flows* estimaciones fiables de los flujos de efectivo futuros ▲ *reliable financial forecasts of future cash flows for periods longer than five years* previsiones financieras fiables sobre flujos de efectivo futuros para periodos superiores a cinco años ▲ *reliable information* información fiable ▲ *reliable measurement of a liability* valoración fiable de un pasivo ▲ *the provision of reliable information* la provisión de información fiable ▲ *timely and reliable interim financial reporting* información financiera provisional fiable y en fecha

relieve

To relieve somebody is to assist them by e.g. doing part of their job.

librar

▲ *relieve somebody* librar a alguien ▲ *relieve the debtor of its primary obligation to the creditor* librar al deudor en su obligación primaria con el acreedor ▲ *relieve the enterprise of its responsibility* librar a la empresa de su responsabilidad

reload feature

A reload feature is a feature that triggers the automatic granting of replacement share options in the event of an option holder exercising previously granted option by applying the company's shares instead of cash to achieve satisfaction of the exercise price.

componente de renovación

▲ *options with a reload feature* opciones con un componente de renovación ▲ *reload features that are excluded from the measurement of fair value* componentes de renovación que están excluidos de la valoración de valor razonable ▲ *treatment of a reload feature* tratamiento de un componente de renovación

SOURCE IFRS 2, Appendix A

⇛ reload option

reload option

A reload option is a replacement share option which is granted upon satisfaction of the exercise price of a previous share option by a share already in the holder's possession.

opción de renovación

▲ *account for a reload option as a new option grant* contabilizar una opción de renovación como una concesión de opciones nueva ▲ *grant a reload option* conceder una opción de renovación

SOURCE IFRS 2, Appendix A

⇛ reload feature

remaining

= residual

"Remaining" refers to what is left after everything else has been dealt with, taken away or spent, or about those persons still present after everybody else has left.

restante

▲ *a constant periodic rate of interest on the remaining balance of the liability* una tasa de interés periódica constante en el saldo restante del pasivo ▲ *amortise over the remaining term of the modified liability* amortizar sobre el plazo restante del pasivo modificado ▲ *any remaining gain or loss on the hedging instrument* cualquier resultado restante en el instrumento con cobertura ▲ *extend the remaining term to maturity of a debt instrument* extender el plazo restante hasta el vencimiento de un instrumento de deuda ▲ *recognise immediately in profit or loss any excess remaining after that reassessment* reconocer inmediatamente en resultados cualquier exceso restante después de la reevaluación ▲ *similar remaining maturity* vencimiento restante similar ▲ *the amounts remaining unamortised at the beginning and end of the period* las cantidades restantes no amortizadas al inicio y final del periodo ▲ *the expected pre-*

sent value of all the remaining contractual cash flows el valor actual esperado de todos los flujos de efectivo contractuales restantes ▲ *the expected remaining useful life of the machine* la vida útil restante esperada de la máquina ▲ *the remaining amortisation period of an intangible asset* el periodo de amortización restante de un activo intangible ▲ *the remaining life of the held-to-maturity investment* la vida restante de una inversión mantenida hasta el vencimiento ▲ *the remaining term over which the contractual interest rate is fixed* el plazo restante sobre el que el tipo de interés contractual se fija ▲ *the remaining useful life of the asset* la vida útil restante del activo ▲ *the weighted average remaining contractual life* la vida contractual restante media ponderada

remission of debt

Remission of debt means extinguishment of debt granted by the creditor to the debtor so that the debtor is released from paying the amount owed.

remisión de deuda

= condonación de deuda, condonación de la deuda, remisión de la deuda

▲ *a singular remission of debt* una remisión de deuda singular ▲ *meet the requirements of remission of debt* cumplir los requisitos de condonación de deuda

removal cost

Removal costs are the costs incurred when moving e.g. offices or equipment from one place to another.

coste de traslado

= coste por traslado

▲ *calculate the removal costs* calcular los costes de traslado ▲ *the removal costs incurred* los costes por traslado incurridos

remove

To remove is to take away, eliminate, dispose of or dismiss.

quitar

= eliminar

▲ *power to remove the majority of the members of the board of directors* poder para quitar la mayoría de los miembros del consejo ▲ *remove an individual liability from a disposal group classified as held for sale* quitar un pasivo individual de un grupo de enajenación clasificado como mantenido para su venta ▲ *remove an insurance liability from the balance sheet* quitar un pasivo de seguro del balance ▲ *remove and restore items of property, plant and equipment* quitar y restaurar partidas de edificios, instalaciones y equipos ▲ *remove the majority of the members of the supervisory board from office* eliminar la mayoría del consejo de supervisión ▲ *the amount that was removed from equity and included in profit or loss* la cantidad que fue eliminada del patrimonio neto e incluida en resultados

remuneration

= pay

Remuneration is payment for work, especially in the form of a salary, or financial benefits received as compensation.

remuneración

= pago

▲ *as a part of basic remuneration* como una parte de remuneración básica ▲ *equity instruments granted to employees as part of their remuneration package* instrumentos de patrimonio concedidos a los empleados como parte de su remuneración ▲ *related cumulative remuneration expense* gasto relacionado con la remuneración acumulada ▲ *remuneration for committee work* remuneración por trabajo del comité ▲ *remuneration paid in shares, share options or other equity instruments of the entity* remuneración pagada en acciones, opciones sobre acciones u otros instrumentos de patrimonio de la entidad ▲ *the determination of policy on the remuneration of directors* la determinación de la política sobre la remuneración de los administradores ▲ *the total remuneration and other benefits granted to individual directors* la remuneración total y otras prestaciones concedidas a los administradores

⇛ salary

remuneration committee UK

Remuneration committees are typically found in UK listed companies and consist exclusively of non-executive directors that, independently of management, determine company policy on the remuneration of executive directors. The setting up of remuneration committees was recommended in the Greenbury Report 1995 and later implemented in the Combined Code on Corporate Governance.

comité de remuneraciones

▲ *establish a remuneration committee of at least three members* establecer un comité de remuneraciones de al menos tres miembros ▲ *set up a remuneration committee* constituir un comité de remuneraciones ▲ *the terms of reference of the remuneration committee* los términos de referencia del comité de remuneraciones

⇛ non-executive director, remuneration policy

remuneration of the executive board

Remuneration of the executive board refers to the payments made to managers in an enterprise for performing the direction, running and control of the enterprise. The remuneration may be related to corporate or individual performance goals and may be a combination of different types of remuneration, e.g. ordinary pay, shares, share options and bonuses.

remuneración del consejo de administración

▲ *adjusted for remuneration of the executive board* ajustado a la remuneración del consejo de administración

remuneration of the executive committee US

Remuneration of the executive committee refers to the payments made to managers in an enterprise for performing the direction, running and control of the enterprise. The remuneration may be related to corporate or individual performance goals and may be a combination of different types of remuneration, e.g. ordinary pay, shares, share options and bonuses.

remuneración del consejo de administración

▲ *adjusted for remuneration of the executive committee* ajustado a la remuneración del consejo de administración

remuneration policy UK

Remuneration policy is determined by the remuneration committee in a UK, typically listed, company and sets out company policy on the remuneration of executive directors in line with the Greenbury Report's recommendations. Important policy aspects are how performance is measured and how rewards are related to longer-term company objectives in the light of the company's performance relative to that of peer companies.

política de remuneración

▲ *a clear and comprehensive overview of the enterprise's remuneration policy* una revisión completa y clara de la política de remuneración de la empresa ▲ *determine the remuneration policy* determinar la política de remuneración ▲ *disclose a statement of the remuneration policy of the enterprise* publicar un comunicado de la política de remuneración de la empresa

⇛ remuneration committee

remuneration report UK

A remuneration report is a report issued by the remuneration committee of a UK listed company, in which the committee reports on the remuneration policy applied in the company with a view to determining and accounting for rewards to executive directors in line with the Greenbury Report's recommendations and the principles of good corporate governance as defined in the 1998 Combined Code and the Directors' Remuneration Report Regulations 2002. At the annual general meeting, shareholders may vote on the remuneration report.

informe de remuneraciones

= informe sobre remuneraciones

▲ *an independent remuneration report* un informe de remuneraciones independiente

⇛ remuneration committee, remuneration policy

rendered

When services have been provided or given in return for something, they are considered rendered.

prestado
▲ *consideration paid, payable or provided in exchange for services rendered to the entity* consideración pagada, a pagar u ofrecida a cambio de los servicios prestados a la entidad ▲ *revenue from and allowances for services rendered against payment* ingresos de y bonificaciones por servicios prestados contra pago ▲ *services rendered* servicios prestados ▲ *the services to be rendered by the counterparty as consideration for the equity instruments* los servicios a prestar por la contraparte como consideración por los instrumentos de patrimonio

renewal clause

A renewal clause is a section of an agreement or a contract providing that the agreement or contract can be extended for an additional defined period of time. Examples of contracts containing a renewal clause are leases and employment agreements.

NOTE An automatic renewal clause will extend the term of the contract on expiry if specific action is not taken by the contracting parties.

cláusula de renovación
▲ *disclosure of renewal clauses* publicación de las cláusulas de renovación

rent[1] *noun*

1 = rental
Rent is the amount payable, typically in monthly instalments, by a tenant to the owner for renting and using land, a property or an office.
renta
= ingreso por alquiler
▲ *a contingent rent* una renta contingente ▲ *a rent rebate* una devolución de renta ▲ *a rent which is substantially lower than market rent* una renta que es sustancialmente más baja que la del mercado ▲ *accrued interest and rent* intereses devengados y renta ▲ *contingent rent that is expected to become payable* renta contingente que se espera que se materialice ▲ *monthly rent* renta mensual ▲ *prepaid rent* renta anticipada ▲ *rent receipts* recibos de renta

2 → lease payment

rent[2] *verb*

1 To rent is to lease a property or another asset for a specific period, e.g. under a lease agreement, against the periodic and regular payments of rent or lease payments.
alquilar
▲ *rent a car* alquilar un coche
▲ *rent land* alquilar terreno
⇛ lease

2 = rent out
To rent is to give somebody the right to use a specific asset, typically property, for an agreed period against periodic and regular payments of rent or rental.
alquilar
▲ *rent out property* alquilar propiedad

rental expense

Rental expenses are the total expenses incurred over the entire term of a lease or the expenses incurred for separate periods of a lease, seen from the lessee's point of view. Rental expenses may constitute a down payment on the entering into a lease, or periodic payments, repair costs, delivery costs etc.
gasto por alquiler
= gasto de alquiler
▲ *a pre-paid rental expense* un gasto por alquiler anticipado ▲ *a reduction of rental expense over the lease term* una reducción del gasto por alquiler durante el periodo de arrendamiento ▲ *increase rental expenses* aumentar los gastos por alquiler ▲ *recognise rental expenses in the income statement* reconocer los gastos de alquiler en el estado de resultados ▲ *rental expenses under operational leases* gastos por alquiler en arrendamientos operativos
⇛ lease

rental income

= rent
Rental income refers to income generated by a person or enterprise for renting or leasing property, i.e. for transferring the right to use a specific asset to another party for a specified period of time in return for specified, periodic payments.
ingreso por alquiler
= renta
▲ *a reduction of rental income over the lease term* una reducción del ingreso por alquiler durante el periodo del arrenda-

miento ▲ *accrued rental income* ingreso por alquiler devengado ▲ *rental income from current leases* ingreso por alquiler de arrendamientos actuales ▲ *rental income from future leases* ingreso por alquiler de arrendamientos futuros ▲ *rental income from investment property* ingreso por alquiler de inversiones inmobiliarias

rental obligation

Rental obligation refers to the obligation of a lessee or hirer to pay specified amounts to a lessor or owner to obtain the right to use a specific asset over a given period. Rental obligations are usually recognised in the profit and loss account.

cuota de alquiler

= cuota de arrendamiento

▲ *the corresponding rental obligations net of finance charges* las cuotas de alquiler correspondientes netas de cargas financieras

rental property

A rental property is property owned by an enterprise for lease purposes as opposed to property used by the enterprise for its own purposes. When a property is owned as rental property, it is recognised as investment property and treated for accounting purposes as such.

inversión inmobiliaria

▲ *invest in rental property* invertir en inversión inmobiliaria

renting activity

In a business context, renting activity refers to a person or an enterprise earning a profit by renting out assets.

actividad de renting

▲ *renting activities concerning properties* actividades de renting referidas a propiedades

reorganisation

Reorganisation is the restructuring and rearranging of an enterprise's or a group's operations or finances or part thereof, e.g. for the purpose of making processes more efficient or profitable.

reorganización

= reestructuración

▲ *an investee in legal reorganisation* una participada en la reorganización legal ▲ *bankruptcy or other financial reorganisation* bancarrota u otra reestructuración financiera ▲ *fundamental reorganisations* reorganizaciones fundamentales ▲ *the reorganisation of a group* la reorganización de un grupo

reorganisation plan UK, IAS/IFRS

= reorganization plan UK, US

A reorganisation plan is a plan of restructuring and rearranging an enterprise's or group's operations or finances or part thereof, e.g. for the purpose of making processes more efficient or profitable.

plan de reorganización

▲ *as part of the reorganisation plan* como parte de un plan de reorganización ▲ *prepare a reorganisation plan* preparar un plan de reorganización

reorganization US

= reorganisation UK, IAS/IFRS

Reorganization is the restructuring and rearranging of an enterprise's or a group's operations or finances or part thereof, e.g. for the purpose of making processes more efficient or profitable.

reorganización

= reestructuración

▲ *an investee in legal reorganization* una participada en una reorganización legal ▲ *bankruptcy or other financial reorganization* bancarrota u otra reestructuración financiera ▲ *fundamental reorganizations* reorganizaciones fundamentales ▲ *the reorganization of a group* la reestructuración de un grupo

reorganization plan US

= reorganisation plan UK, IAS/IFRS

A reorganization plan is a plan of restructuring and rearranging an enterprise's or group's operations or finances or part thereof, e.g. for the purpose of making processes more efficient or profitable.

plan de reestructuración

▲ *as part of the reorganization plan* como parte del plan de reestructuración ▲ *prepare a reorganization plan* preparar un plan de reestructuración

repair cost

= cost of repairs

Repair costs are costs incurred that relate to the restoring or refitting of equipment and machinery to the original operating condition. Repair costs are expensed, whereas costs that contribute to improvement of a given asset are considered capital expenditure and are capitalised, i.e. added to the carrying amount of the asset.

coste de reparación

▲ *pay a repair cost* pagar un coste de reparación ▲ *repair costs of property, plant and equipment* costes de reparación de edificios, instalaciones y equipos ▲ *the repair cost of any manufacturing defects that become apparent within the first six months after purchase* el coste de reparación de cualesquiera defectos de fabricación que se manifiesten en los seis meses posteriores a la compra

repatriate

To repatriate is to transfer dividends from foreign companies, capital gains, currency etc. to persons or enterprises in the country of residence.

repatriar

▲ *repatriated as dividend* repatriado como dividendos

repatriation

Repatriation is the transfer of dividends from foreign companies, capital gains, currency etc. to persons or enterprises in the country of residence.

repatriación

▲ *repatriation of dividend* repatriación de dividendos

repay

To repay means to pay or redeem a debt or obligation, or the returning of money received previously.

reembolsar

= amortizar

▲ *repay a debt* reembolsar una deuda ▲ *repay debt outstanding at the balance sheet date* amortizar la deuda pendiente a la fecha de balance ▲ *repay debts* reembolsar deudas ▲ *repay loans or advances* reembolsar préstamos o anticipos ▲ *repay or redeem the financial asset before maturity* amortizar o redimir el activo financiero antes del vencimiento ▲ *repay the compensation in future years* amortizar la deuda en años futuros

repayment

= extinguishment of debt US, redemption, retirement US, UK, settlement

Repayment is the payment or redemption of a debt or obligation, or the returning of money received previously.

reembolso

▲ *date of repayment* fecha de reembolso ▲ *demand immediate repayment* exigir el reembolso inmediato ▲ *early repayment* reembolso anticipado ▲ *extraordinary repayment of a loan* reembolso extraordinario de un préstamo ▲ *net of any principal repayment and amortisation* neto de cualquier reembolso y amortización del principal ▲ *repayment of debt* reembolso de la deuda ▲ *repayment of debt instruments* reembolso de instrumentos de deuda ▲ *repayment of loans or advances* reembolso de préstamos o anticipos ▲ *repayment of principal* reembolso del principal ▲ *repayment of share capital* reembolso del capital social ▲ *repayment of the loan* reembolso del préstamo ▲ *the distribution of dividends and the repayment of capital* la distribución de los dividendos y el reembolso del capital

repayment period

The repayment period is the length of time passing until all principal instalments on a debt have been paid.

periodo de amortización

▲ *a long repayment period* un periodo de amortización largo ▲ *a short repayment period* un periodo de amortización corto ▲ *the actual repayment period* el periodo de amortización actual ▲ *the agreed repayment period* el periodo de amortización acordado ▲ *the maximum repayment period* el periodo de amortización máximo ▲ *the repayment period of the loan* el periodo de amortización del préstamo ▲ *the total repayment period* el periodo de amortización total ▲ *with a 10-year repayment period* con un periodo de amortización de 10 años

repayment profile

The repayment profile shows the distribution of interest payments and principal repayments over the repayment period of a loan. Typically, serial loans offer equal instalment payments over the repayment period, whereas annuity loans provide the option of downward interest adjustments and increasing repayments.

plan de amortización

▲ *a 20-year repayment profile* un plan de amortización a 20 años ▲ *a changed repayment profile* un plan de amortización con cambios ▲ *a declining repayment profile* un plan de amortización decreciente ▲ *a more flexible repayment profile* un plan de amortización más flexible ▲ *a repayment profile of usually up to 25 years* un plan de amortización de normalmente hasta 25 años ▲ *a smooth repayment profile* un plan de amortización suave ▲ *a stipulated repayment profile* un plan de amortización estipulado ▲ *an extended repayment profile* un plan de amortización extendido ▲ *an unchanged repayment profile* un plan de amortización sin cambios ▲ *an uneven repayment profile* un plan de amortización desigual

replace

To replace is to substitute something that has been in use or has been owned for something identical, such as a piece of equipment

reemplazar

= sustituir

▲ *be replaced by* ser reemplazado por ▲ *costs incurred subsequently to replace part of a property* costes incurridos a continuación de sustituir parte de una propiedad ▲ *replace the shares in an existing company with shares in a new company* reemplazar las acciones de una empresa existente con acciones de una nueva

replacement

Replacement refers to the act of substituting something that has been in use or has been owned for something identical, such as a piece of equipment.

reemplazo

= sustitución

▲ *any subsequent purchase or construction of replacement assets* cualquier compra o construcción subsiguiente para el reemplazo de activos ▲ *items of property, plant and equipment restored, purchased or constructed as replacements* partidas de edificios, instalaciones y equipos restaurados, comprados o construidos como sustituciones ▲ *replacement of a damaged old asset by a new asset* reemplazo de un activo viejo dañado por uno nuevo ▲ *require replacement at regular intervals* requiere el reemplazo a intervalos regulares ▲ *the cost of a replacement for part of an intangible asset* el coste de sustitución por parte de un activo intangible ▲ *the replacement of components with shorter lives* el reemplazo de los componentes con vidas más cortas

replacement cost[1] *noun* <a, the, -s>

The replacement cost of an asset is the cost of substituting an asset, measured as the current acquisition cost payable for a similar asset.

coste de reposición

▲ *gross replacement costs* costes de reposición brutos ▲ *net replacement costs* costes de reposición netos ▲ *the value of the shares measured in terms of replacement costs* el valor de las acciones medidas en términos de costes de reposición

replacement cost[2] *noun* <no indefinite article, the, no plural>

The replacement cost of an asset measures the asset's value to be the current acquisition cost payable for a similar asset at the balance sheet date.

coste de sustitución

= coste de la sustitución

▲ *an increase in the replacement cost* un incremento en el coste de sustitución ▲ *current replacement cost* coste de sustitución actual ▲ *derive the replacement cost of an asset from* derivar el coste de sustitución de un activo de ▲ *determination of the replacement cost* determinación del coste de sustitución ▲ *determine the replacement cost* determinar el coste de sustitución ▲ *revalue to replacement cost* revaluar a coste de sustitución ▲ *the additional replacement cost of assets* el coste de sustitución adicional de activos ▲ *the depreciated replacement cost* el coste de sustitución depreciado ▲ *the replacement cost of a specific asset* el coste de sustitución de un activo específico ▲ *use a depreciated replacement cost approach* usar un enfoque de coste de sustitución depreciado

▲ *use replacement cost as the primary measurement basis* utilizar el coste de sustitución como base primaria de medición

repo agreement

A repo agreement is an agreement to sell specific securities and to repurchase the securities at a set price on a specified future date.

acuerdo con pacto de recompra

= contrato con pacto de recompra, contrato de repo, contrato de venta con pacto de recompra, repo

▲ *the life of the repo agreement* la vida del contrato con pacto de recompra

report[1] *noun*

A report is a statement in writing describing, commenting on and/or informing about certain issues or conditions. Examples are financial reports, audit reports and environmental reports.

informe

▲ *a consolidated report* un informe consolidado ▲ *a separate report* un informe separado ▲ *an annual financial report* un informe financiero anual ▲ *an external report* un informe externo ▲ *an interim financial report* un informe financiero provisional ▲ *approve the text of a report* aprobar el texto de un informe ▲ *first quarter report* informe del primer trimestre ▲ *prepare a report* preparar un informe ▲ *publish a report* publicar un informe ▲ *second quarter report* informe del segundo trimestre ▲ *The Danish Accounting Council's Report of 1996 on Revision of the Annual Accounts Act* el informe de 1996 del Consejo de Contabilidad danés sobre la Revisión de la Ley de Cuentas Anuales ▲ *the Nørby Committee's Report on Corporate Governance in Denmark* el Informe del Comité sobre Gobernanza Corporativa en Dinamarca ▲ *third quarter report* informe del tercer trimestre

report[2] *verb*

To report is to give information about or announce something, e.g. the financial performance and position of an enterprise for an accounting period.

informar

▲ *report financial information* informar de aspectos financieros ▲ *report on knowledge resources* informar sobre los recursos del conocimiento ▲ *report the effects of changes in exchange rates in the financial statements* informar sobre los efectos de los cambios en los tipos de cambio en los estados financieros ▲ *report to the public* informar al público ▲ *report to the shareholders* informar a los accionistas

report form US

= narrative form US, vertical format

≠ account form, horizontal format

The report form is a presentation format used in financial statements arranging financial items in one column from top to bottom. For the balance sheet this means that assets are presented above and liabilities and stockholders' equity below. The income statement format starts with sales or revenue as the top line proceeding with additions and deductions of sub-totals to net income as the bottom line.

formato vertical

▲ *balance sheet in report form* balance en formato vertical ▲ *present financial statements in report form* presentar las cuentas en formato vertical

report of the auditors

→ audit report

report of the directors

→ directors' report

reportability

Reportability is the obligation to report certain types of information according to specific rules.

responsabilidad de informar

▲ *meet the criteria for reportability* cumplir los criterios de la responsabilidad de informar

reportable segment

A reportable segment is an operating segment, i.e. a business or geographical segment for which financial data must be reported on a separate basis in the financial statements of an enterprise.

segmento sobre el que debe informarse

▲ *designate a segment as a reportable segment* designar un segmento como un segmento sobre el que debe informarse ▲ *disclose the segment result for each reportable segment* publicar el resultado del segmento de cada segmento sobre el que debe informarse ▲ *identification of reportable segments* identificación de los segmentos sobre los que debe informarse ▲ *identify as a reportable segment* identificar como un segmento sobre el que debe informarse ▲ *segment revenue of reportable segments* ingresos por segmentos de los segmentos sobre los que debe informarse ▲ *the reportable segment to which the asset belongs* el segmento sobre el que debe informarse al que pertenece el activo ▲ *total external revenue attributable to reportable segments* total ingreso externo atribuible a los segmentos sobre los que debe informarse

SOURCE FAS 131, paragraph 71, IAS 14, paragraph 9

reporting

Reporting refers to the submission of a report, i.e. a statement, typically in writing, that provides information of events, evaluation data or results.

elaboración y presentación de informes

= reporting

▲ *evidence available from internal reporting* prueba disponible de elaboración y presentación de informes internos ▲ *extended reporting* elaboración y presentación de informes extendidos ▲ *financial reporting on an ongoing basis* elaboración y presentación de informes financieros sobre el principio de empresa en funcionamiento ▲ *the development of additional reporting systems* el desarrollo de sistemas de elaboración y presentación de informes adicionales ▲ *the reporting structure of an entity* la estructura de la elaboración y presentación de informes de una entidad

⇛ financial reporting

reporting currency

The reporting currency is the measurement currency used by an enterprise for reporting financial statements, and the currency into which financial statements of foreign operations are translated.

NOTE Under IFRS (IAS 21), the former "reporting currency" has been split into two concepts: "presentation currency" and "functional currency".

moneda del informe

= moneda usada en el informe

▲ *change of the reporting currency* cambio de la moneda del informe ▲ *on initial recognition in the reporting currency* reconocimiento inicial en la moneda del informe ▲ *select a reporting currency* seleccionar una moneda del informe ▲ *the reporting currency of the reporting enterprise* la moneda del informe de la empresa que informa ▲ *transactions in the reporting currency* transacciones en la moneda del informe ▲ *translate into the group's reporting currency* convertir a la moneda del informe del grupo ▲ *translation from functional currency into reporting currency* conversión de la moneda funcional en moneda del informe ▲ *translation from the measurement currency into another reporting currency* conversión de la moneda de valoración en otra moneda usada en el informe

⇛ functional currency, presentation currency

reporting date IAS/IFRS

The reporting date is the last date of the latest accounting period for which financial reports and financial statements have been prepared, i.e. the balance sheet date of that period.

fecha de presentación

= fecha de la presentación

▲ *insurance contracts that are not in existence at the reporting date* contratos de seguros que no existen a la fecha de presentación ▲ *the comparative period's reporting date* la fecha de presentación del periodo comparado ▲ *the difference between the reporting date of the subsidiary and that of the parent* la diferencia entre la fecha de presentación de la filial y la de la matriz ▲ *the reporting date for the first IFRS financial statements* la fecha de presentación de los primeros estados financieros NIIF ▲ *the reporting date of the financial statements of a subsidiary* la fecha de presentación

de los estados financieros de una subsidiaria
SOURCE IFRS 1, Appendix A

reporting enterprise
= reporting entity IAS/IFRS, UK
Reporting enterprise refers to the entity, i.e. enterprise or group for which financial statements have been prepared to provide information about its activities and resources.
entidad declarante
= entidad que informa
▲ *an entity that is legally separate from the reporting enterprise* una entidad que es independiente de la entidad declarante ▲ *an integral to the reporting enterprise's operations* una operación integral a las operaciones de la entidad declarante ▲ *incorporation in the financial statements of the reporting enterprise* incorporación en los estados financieros de la entidad declarante ▲ *loans and guarantees granted by the reporting enterprise* préstamos y garantías concedidos por la entidad declarante ▲ *non-transferable financial instruments issued by the reporting enterprise* instrumentos financieros no transferibles emitidos por la entidad declarante ▲ *the reporting currency of the reporting enterprise* la moneda de presentación de la entidad declarante ▲ *the reporting enterprise's investment in a foreign operation* la inversión de la entidad declarante en una operación extranjera ▲ *the tax rate effective in the reporting enterprise's country* el tipo impositivo efectivo en el país de la entidad declarante
SOURCE FAS 52, paragraph 162
⇛ accounting entity, entity

reporting entity IAS/IFRS, UK
= reporting enterprise US
A reporting entity is a separate, independent, economic unit for which financial statements are prepared. Examples of reporting entities are companies or groups.
entidad que informa
= entidad declarante, entidad que elabora los estados financieros
▲ *have a dilutive effect on the basic earnings per share of the reporting entity* tener un efecto dilutivo en los beneficios básicos por acción de la entidad que informa ▲ *identification of the reporting entity* identificación de la entidad que informa ▲ *included in the reporting entity's earnings per share calculations* incluido en los beneficios de la entidad que informa por acción ▲ *purchase of ordinary shares of the reporting entity* compra de acciones ordinarias de la entidad que informa ▲ *the bringing together of separate entities or businesses into one reporting entity* juntar entidades o negocios separados en una entidad que informa ▲ *the presentation currency of the reporting entity* la moneda de presentación de la entidad que informa
SOURCE IFRS 3, Appendix A
⇛ reporting unit

reporting format
= layout of financial statement
A reporting format is the layout and presentation form of a financial statement according to which the items are arranged and presented, e.g. the horizontal and the vertical formats.
formato de información
▲ *an approved alternative reporting format* un formato de información alternativo aprobado ▲ *changes to the reporting format* cambios al formato de información
⇛ horizontal format, vertical format

reporting language
The reporting language is the language used in the financial reporting, e.g. English, German or French.
lengua de elaboración y presentación
▲ *a common reporting language* una lengua de elaboración y presentación común

reporting period
The reporting period is the period for which an enterprise prepares its financial report and/or financial statements, typically a quarter of a year, half a year or a whole year.
periodo de elaboración y presentación
▲ *acquisitions occurring after the beginning of the financial reporting period* adquisiciones que ocurren después del inicio del periodo de elaboración y pre-

sentación financiero ▲ *at the end of the reporting period* al final del periodo de elaboración y presentación ▲ *business combinations effected during the reporting period* combinaciones de negocio efectuadas durante el periodo de elaboración y presentación ▲ *corresponding figures for the previous reporting period* cifras correspondientes al periodo de elaboración y presentación anterior ▲ *performance comparisons between different entities in the same reporting period* comparaciones de las actuaciones de entidades diferentes en el mismo periodo de elaboración y presentación ▲ *the balance sheet at the start of the first IFRS reporting period* el balance al inicio del primer periodo de elaboración y presentación según NIIF ▲ *the length of the reporting period* la duración del periodo de elaboración y presentación ▲ *the profit or loss of consolidated subsidiaries for the reporting period* el resultado del periodo de elaboración y presentación de las filiales consolidadas

reporting procedure

Reporting procedures are the policies applied in an enterprise's internal or external reporting, i.e. presentation and disclosure of information, typically financial data.

procedimiento de elaboración y presentación

▲ *assess the reporting procedures applied* examinar los procedimientos de elaboración y presentación aplicados

⇛ financial reporting

reporting requirement

Reporting requirements are the requirements made to the presentation of financial statements and other financial data, i.e. interim and annual reports. Such requirements are typically laid down in accounting legislation and accounting standards.

requisito de información

▲ *comply with the reporting requirements* cumplir con los requisitos de información ▲ *lay down new reporting requirements* establecer nuevos requisitos de información

reporting unit US

A reporting unit is a separate, independent, economic entity for which financial statements are prepared. It may be a whole organisation or part of one, i.e. an operating segment or a component, which is one level below an operating segment. Examples of reporting units are companies, operating units and divisions.

unidad de información

▲ *the management committee of the reporting unit* el comité de gestión de la unidad de información

SOURCE FAS 142

⇛ reporting entity

representation[1] *noun* <a, the, -s>

1 A representation is a formal or factual statement made by e.g. management, an auditor or a party to a contract.

representación

▲ *false representations* representaciones falsas ▲ *make representations* hacer representaciones ▲ *management representations* representaciones administrativas

2 A representation constitutes a particular format, layout or way in which something is presented, e.g. a plan, data or financial statements.

representación

▲ *a structured representation of the financial position and financial performance of an entity* una representación estructurada de la posición y de los resultados financieros de una entidad

representation[2] *noun* <no indefinite article, the, no plural>

Representation exists when e.g. a person or an enterprise is present or acts officially on behalf of another person or enterprise, i.e. represents that person or enterprise for a particular purpose or in a particular place.

representación

▲ *faithful representation* representación fiel ▲ *legal representation* representación legal ▲ *reliable representation* representación fiable ▲ *representation on the board of directors or equivalent governing body of the investee* representación del inversor en el consejo de administración u órgano de gobierno equivalente ▲ *valid representation* representación válida

reprice IAS/IFRS

To reprice is to substitute the rate of interest with a new rate, e.g. in connection with the roll-over of a loan or the maturity of a financial instrument.

revisar

▲ *financial instruments contracted to be repriced in one month or less after the balance sheet date* instrumentos financieros contratados para ser revisados después de transcurrido un mes o menos de la fecha del balance

repricing date IAS/IFRS

The repricing date is the earlier of two dates: the date when the interest rate is repriced, i.e. reset, to the market rate, or the date on which the item is anticipated to mature. The item typically constitutes a portfolio or whole group of financial assets or liabilities that may be subject to macro hedging for interest rate risk rather than being individually hedged on a loan by loan basis by e.g. interest rate swaps. The international accounting rules IFRS (IAS 39) allow macro hedging subject to certain prerequisites, such as the hedged portfolio being designated on the basis of repricing time periods based on expected repricing dates rather than the contractual dates.

fecha de revisión

= fecha de la revisión

▲ *an explanation of the assumptions made about repricing dates* una explicación de los supuestos hechos acerca de las fechas de revisión ▲ *the contractual repricing dates* las fechas de revisión contractuales ▲ *the estimated repricing dates* las fechas estimadas de la revisión ▲ *the estimated repricing dates of existing assets or liabilities* las fechas de revisión estimadas de activos o pasivos ▲ *the expected repricing date* la fecha de revisión esperada ▲ *the period to the next repricing date* el periodo hasta la nueva fecha de revisión

SOURCE IAS 39, paragraph 81A

⇛ repricing time period

repricing time period IAS/IFRS

A repricing time period is a narrow time period, e.g. three months, identified by an enterprise based on an analysis of repricing dates which are expected, rather than contractual, for its portfolios of financial assets or liabilities. Following the analysis, the amount of assets or liabilities to be designated for hedging is determined by the enterprise. The analysis of the repricing time periods typically involves determining and mapping periods for the occurrence of expected cash flows or allocating notional principal amounts to all periods up to the period of expected repricing.

periodo hasta la fecha de revisión

▲ *3-month repricing time periods* periodos hasta la fecha de revisión de tres meses ▲ *analyse the portfolio into repricing time periods* analizar la cartera en periodos hasta la fecha de revisión ▲ *by expiry of the relevant repricing time period* finalizando el periodo hasta la fecha de revisión relevante ▲ *the duration of repricing time periods* la duración de los periodos hasta la fecha de revisión ▲ *the number of repricing time periods* el número de periodos hasta la fecha de revisión

SOURCE IAS 39, paragraph 81A(a)

⇛ repricing date

repurchase[1] *noun*

= buy-back

A repurchase takes place when an enterprise buys back something it has previously owned and sold. Repurchases typically take place when banks buy back securities sold e.g. to a central bank to borrow funds overnight.

recompra

▲ *a repurchase receivable* una recompra exigible ▲ *an option to repurchase the financial asset at its fair value at the time of repurchase* una opción para recomprar el activo financiero a su valor razonable a la fecha de recompra ▲ *the repurchase of a financial asset shortly after it has been sold* la recompra de un activo financiero poco después de que haya sido vendido ▲ *the repurchase of equity instruments* la recompra de los instrumentos de patrimonio

⇛ repurchase agreement

repurchase[2] *verb*
= buy back
To repurchase is to buy back something previously owned and sold. Banks e.g. repurchase securities when they buy back securities sold to a central bank to borrow funds overnight as part of a repurchase agreement.
recomprar
▲ *a right of first refusal to repurchase the transferred asset at fair value* un derecho de denegación inicial a recomprar el activo transferido a valor razonable ▲ *an obligation to repurchase a fixed number of own shares* una obligación para recomprar un número fijo de acciones propias ▲ *an option giving the transferee the right to repurchase the asset* una opción dada al que transfiere el derecho a recomprar el activo ▲ *repurchase a share at fair value* recomprar una acción a valor razonable ▲ *repurchase preference shares* recomprar acciones preferentes ▲ *repurchase treasury shares* recomprar acciones propias
⇛ repurchase agreement

repurchase agreement
≠ reverse repurchase agreement
A repurchase agreement is a contract under which an enterprise is obliged to buy back a specific asset sold for a specified price in the future. Typically, repurchase agreements involve the selling of government securities that must be bought back at a specific time at a higher price that includes interest.
acuerdo de recompra
= contrato de recompra
▲ *enter into a repurchase agreement* firmar un acuerdo de recompra ▲ *the extent of the repurchase agreement* la extensión del acuerdo de recompra ▲ *the nature of a repurchase agreement* la naturaleza de un acuerdo de recompra

required rate of return
= hurdle rate, RRR
A required rate of return is the return that is considered sufficiently profitable to encourage enterprises and other investors to engage in an investment.
tasa de retorno requerida
▲ *calculation of the required rate of return* cálculo de la tasa de retorno requerida

requirement for notes
The requirement for notes in the financial statements is a requirement by law or accounting standards to supplement items in the financial statements with additional information and details.
requisito de notas en los estados financieros
▲ *comply with the Act's requirements for notes* cumplir con los requisitos de notas en los estados financieros de la Ley

requirement of consistency
The requirement of consistency is one of the fundamental principles required by accounting rules and implies that conformity must exist in accounting treatment from one accounting period to the next and that recognition methods and measurement bases must be applied uniformly to the same category of items.
requisito de uniformidad
▲ *the basic requirement of consistency* el requisito básico de uniformidad

resale
A resale is a transaction where you sell goods that you have bought to someone else.
reventa
▲ *a subsidiary acquired exclusively with a view to resale* una subsidiaria adquirida exclusivamente con vistas a la reventa ▲ *goods purchased and held for resale* bienes comprados y mantenidos para la reventa ▲ *merchandise purchased by a retailer and held for resale* mercancías compradas por un detallista y mantenidas para la reventa

rescind
To rescind something means to end the existence of something so that it is no longer valid or has no longer any effect, e.g. a contract.
rescindir
▲ *rescind a contract* rescindir un contrato

research[1] *noun*
In general, research refers to the innovative, systematic and thorough investigation process, the purpose of which is to discover, develop or revise knowledge, theories and models.

investigación
▲ *engage in research and development* comprometerse en actividades de investigación y desarrollo ▲ *expenditure on research and development* gasto en investigación y desarrollo ▲ *intangible assets arising from research* activos intangibles procedentes de investigación ▲ *research and development* investigación y desarrollo ▲ *research contributions* aportaciones de la investigación ▲ *the latest research* la investigación más reciente ▲ *transfer of research and development* transferencia de investigación y desarrollo
⇛ R&D

research[2] *verb*
To research means to make a systematic and thorough investigation process of which the purpose is to discover, develop or revise knowledge, theories and models.
investigar
▲ *research in new products* investigar en nuevos productos

research activity
Research activity refers to the processes, transactions, functions and other actions of an enterprise, which relate to research.
actividad de investigación
▲ *describe research activities in or for the enterprise* describir las actividades de investigación en la empresa o para la empresa
⇛ R&D

research cost
= research expenditure
Research costs are expenses incurred for research related to certain objectives in an enterprise. Rather than being recognised in the cost of a certain product or project, research costs are typically written off and expensed as incurred.
coste de investigación
▲ *charge research costs as incurred* cargar los costes de investigación cuando ocurran
⇛ R&D

research expenditure
Research expenditure constitutes costs and payments related to a research project.
gasto de investigación
= gasto en investigación
▲ *recognise research expenditure as an expense* reconocer el gasto de investigación como un gasto ▲ *test and research expenditure* prueba y gasto de investigación
⇛ R&D

research finding
= research result
Research findings constitute the results achieved during or after the conclusion of a research project. Research findings are defined in the objectives of the research project and constitute new technical or scientific insight and knowledge.
resultado de la investigación
▲ *disclosure of research findings* publicación de resultados de la investigación ▲ *the application of research findings* la aplicación de los resultados de la investigación ▲ *the applications of the research findings* las aplicaciones de los resultados de la investigación

research phase
A research phase is a distinguishable time period in a course of events during which innovative, systematic and thorough investigation takes place. The purpose of the research phase is to discover, develop or revise knowledge, theories and models.
fase de investigación
▲ *distinguish the research phase from the development phase* distinguir la fase de investigación de la fase de desarrollo ▲ *expenditure incurred in the research phase* gasto incurrido en la fase de investigación ▲ *intangible asset arising from the research phase of an internal project* activo intangible procedente de la fase de investigación de un proyecto interno

research project
A research project is a planned study with a defined objective, a set time frame and financial budget. Research projects are investigations typically initiated by enterprises to achieve new scientific or technical insight and knowledge.
proyecto de investigación
▲ *a 3-year research project* un proyecto de investigación de 3 años ▲ *in-process research projects* proyectos de investigación en marcha

research result
→ research finding

researcher
In general, a researcher is a person who conducts a systematic and thorough investigation process of which the purpose is to discover, develop or revise knowledge, theories and models.
investigador
▲ *an internationally recognised researcher* un investigador reconocido internacionalmente ▲ *the average number of researchers* el número medio de investigadores

reserve
Reserves constitute the part of equity that is not contributed capital representing retained earnings or other surpluses, such as share premium account, revaluation reserve, treasury shares, etc. Reserves may be distributable or undistributable for dividend purposes and must be distinguished from provisions.
reserva
▲ *a description of the nature and purpose of each reserve within equity* una descripción de la naturaleza y finalidad de cada reserva dentro de patrimonio ▲ *a special reserve* una reserva especial ▲ *creation of reserves* creación de reservas ▲ *deduct an amount in a positive reserve* deducir una cantidad en una reserva positiva ▲ *disaggregate reserves into various classes* desagregar las reservas en varias clases ▲ *dissolve a reserve* disolver una reserva ▲ *distributable reserves* reservas disponibles ▲ *eliminate a reserve* eliminar una reserva ▲ *include an amount in a positive reserve* incluir una cantidad en una reserva positiva ▲ *increase a reserve* incrementar una reserva ▲ *issued capital and reserves attributable to equity holders of the parent* capital emitido y reservas atribuibles a los propietarios de la matriz ▲ *net revaluation reserve according to the equity method* valoración neta de la reserva utilizando el método de participación ▲ *other reserves* otras reservas ▲ *reduce a reserve* reducir una reserva ▲ *reserve for fair value of biological assets* reserva por valor razonable de los activos biológicos ▲ *reserve for fair value of investment assets* reserva por el valor razonable de los activos de inversión ▲ *reserve for treasury shares* reserva para acciones propias ▲ *revaluation reserve* reserva de revalorización ▲ *statutory reserve* reserva obligatoria ▲ *tax reserve* reserva fiscal ▲ *the amount of the issuer's reserves* la cuantía de las reservas del emisor ▲ *the reserves that may be used to cover losses* las reservas que pueden usarse para cubrir pérdidas ▲ *transfer an amount to a reserve* transferir una cantidad a una reserva

reserve according to the articles of association UK
= reserve according to the bylaws US, reserves provided for by the articles of association UK, statutory reserve UK
Reserve according to the articles of association is one of the items under capital and reserves in the balance sheet, representing a reserve that must be included according to the articles of association of the reporting company. The articles will typically define the objective and application of such a reserve.
reserva estatutaria

reserve according to the bylaws US
= reserve according to the articles of association UK, reserves provided for by the articles of association UK, statutory reserve UK
Reserve according to the bylaws is one of the items under equity in the balance sheet, representing a reserve that must be included according to the bylaws of the reporting company. The bylaws will typically define the objective and application of such a reserve.
reserva estatutaria

reserve for own shares UK
= capital redemption reserve UK
Reserve for own shares is a non-distributable reserve recognised under equity in the balance sheet that is created when a company buys or redeems its own shares.
reserva para acciones propias
▲ *other movements on reserve for own shares* otros movimientos

en reserva para acciones propias
⇛ own share

reserve fund
= reserve
A reserve fund consists of retained earnings or other reserves for an enterprise's accounting periods that have been transferred to capital and reserves in the balance sheet and as such represents part of shareholders' funds.
reserva
▲ *an undistributable reserve fund* una reserva indisponible ▲ *dividend distribution and reserve funds* distribución del dividendo y reservas ▲ *establish an undistributable reserve fund* establecer una reserva indisponible
⇛ distributable reserves, undistributable reserve

reserves at the beginning of the year
Reserves at the beginning of the year are disclosed in the statement of changes in equity under equity and state the total amount of reserves of an enterprise at the start of the financial year.
reservas al inicio del año
▲ *value adjustment of reserves at the beginning of the year* valorar el ajuste de las reservas al inicio del año

reserves provided for by the articles of association UK
= reserve according to the articles of association UK, reserve according to the bylaws US, statutory reserve
Reserves provided for by the articles of association is one of the items under capital and reserves in the balance sheet according to the Companies Act 2006 reported format, representing reserves that must be included according to the articles of association of the reporting company. The articles will typically define the objective and application of such reserves.
reserva estatutaria
⇛ reserve

residual
= residual amount
A residual is what remains after something has been deducted or taken away. Equity is a residual defined as assets less liabilities.
residual
▲ *represent a residual interest in the net assets of an entity* representar un interés residual en los activos netos de una entidad ▲ *retain the majority of the residual or ownership risks related to the SPE* retener la mayoría del residual o de los riesgos de la propiedad relacionados con la EPE ▲ *the residual cost of the business combination* el coste residual de la combinación de negocios

residual amount
= residual
A residual amount is an amount remaining after something has been deducted or taken away. Equity is a residual amount defined as assets less liabilities.
valor residual
= cantidad residual
▲ *recognise the residual amount* reconocer el valor residual ▲ *the measurement of the residual amount* la cuantificación del valor residual

residual income
= RI
Residual income refers to profit after tax and interest less cost of capital (equity).
ingreso residual
▲ *a constant residual income* un ingreso residual constante ▲ *expected future residual income* ingreso residual futuro esperado ▲ *generate residual income* generar ingreso residual

residual interest[1] *noun* <a, the, -s>
1 The residual interest represents the difference between two values, amounts or other variables. In accounting e.g., the residual interest is the equity which results after deducting total liabilities from total assets, or it may represent goodwill, i.e. the difference in value between the cost and the fair value of assets and liabilities acquired in connection with the acquisition of enterprises.
valor residual
▲ *a right to the residual interest in the assets of the entity in exchange for cash* un derecho al valor residual de los activos de la entidad en un intercambio

por efectivo ▲ *asset recognised for subordination or the residual interest* activo reconocido por subordinación o el valor residual ▲ *retain a residual interest* retener un valor residual

2 A residual interest is an equity investment in a real estate mortgage investment conduit (REMIC), a US corporation, trust or partnership, which issues mortgage-backed securities. Other interests than residual interests in a REMIC are regular interests, which are debt instruments issued to mortgage investors in several classes on the basis of the REMIC's pool of real estate mortgages. A REMIC can issue only one class of residual interests which, as equity interests, will only receive income after payment of interest to holders of regular interests and therefore referred to as 'residual'.

participación residual
= inversión residual

residual interest[2] US *noun* <a, the, no plural>
Residual interest is a return on investment in the form of a type of interest payment via ownership of residual or equity interests in a real estate mortgage investment conduit (REMIC), a US corporation, trust or partnership, which issues mortgage-backed securities. Other shares than residual shares in REMICs are ordinary shares. Under double-tax agreements with the US, non-US residual shareholders are liable to US tax only.

inversión residual
= participación residual

residual item
A residual item is an entry representing a remaining balance of an amount after deducting other items. Equity is a residual item as it constitutes the difference between assets and liabilities recognised in the balance sheet.

partida residual
▲ *assess something as a residual item* valorar algo como una partida residual

residual lease commitment
The residual lease commitment is the outstanding and remaining lease liability relating to a finance lease after payment of the periodic lease payments to date.

opción de compra en el arrendamiento financiero
▲ *the capitalised residual lease commitment* la opción de compra en el arrendamiento financiero capitalizada

residual lease payment
= outstanding lease payment
The residual lease payment is the outstanding amount payable by the lessee to the lessor for the lease term.

pago del valor residual del arrendamiento financiero
▲ *recognise residual lease payments as an expense* reconocer el pago del valor residual del arrendamiento financiero como un gasto
⇛ lease, lease payment, lease term

residual maturity
= remaining life, term to maturity, time to maturity
Residual maturity is the period left until redemption date or the date when a loan must be repaid.

periodo de vigencia
= vigencia
▲ *bonds with a residual maturity greater than one year* bonos con un periodo de vigencia superior a un año ▲ *bonds with a residual maturity of less than 6 months* bonos con un periodo de vigencia de menos de seis meses

residual tax
= tax underpaid, tax underpayment
Residual tax is remaining tax payable owed for a particular tax assessment year.

impuesto residual
▲ *be liable to pay residual tax* estar obligado a pagar el impuesto residual ▲ *provided for a residual tax liability* provisionado para un pasivo de impuesto residual

residual value IAS/IFRS, UK
= salvage value US, scrap value UK
Residual value is the estimated recoverable value of an asset on disposal after depreciation or amortisation at the end of its useful economic life.

valor residual
▲ *a lessee's residual value guarantee embedded in a finance lea-*

se un valor residual del arrendatario con garantía incluida en un arrendamiento financiero ▲ *adjust the residual value* ajustar el valor residual ▲ *an estimate of an asset's residual value* una estimación de un valor residual de un activo ▲ *determine the residual value of the asset* determinar el valor residual del activo ▲ *estimated residual value after the end of the useful life* valor residual estimado después del final de la vida útil ▲ *estimated residual value and useful life* valor residual estimado y vida útil ▲ *realisation of the residual value* realización del valor residual ▲ *review the residual value at least at each financial year-end* analizar el valor residual al menos al cierre de cada ejercicio ▲ *the residual value of an intangible asset with a finite useful life* el valor residual de un activo intangible con una vida útil finita

resource

Resources refer to all items used and needed by an enterprise to produce its goods or provide its services, e.g. labour, raw materials, skills, facilities and equipment.

recurso

▲ *a scarce resource* un recurso escaso ▲ *an identifiable resource* un recurso identificable ▲ *an outflow of resources embodying economic benefits* una salida de recursos que incluyen beneficios económicos ▲ *decisions about the allocation of resources* decisiones sobre la asignación de recursos ▲ *development and extraction of resources* desarrollo y extracción de recursos ▲ *expend resources on the acquisition, development, maintenance or enhancement of intangible resources* gastar recursos en la adquisición, desarrollo, mantenimiento, o mejora de los recursos intangibles ▲ *long-term financial resources* recursos financieros a largo plazo ▲ *obtain the future economic benefits flowing from the underlying resource* obtener los beneficios económicos futuros procedentes del recurso subyacente ▲ *oil, natural gas and similar non-regenerative resources* petróleo, gas natural y recursos no renovables similares ▲ *the availability of adequate technical, financial and other resources* la disponibilidad de recursos adecuados técnicos, financieros y otros ▲ *without a corresponding reduction in resources* sin una reducción correspondiente en recursos

responsibility

Responsibility involves being accountable for or having the duty to be in charge of something, making decisions and judgments, with the implication of being blamed if something goes wrong.

responsabilidad

▲ *assume responsibility* asumir la responsabilidad ▲ *corporate social responsibility* responsabilidad social corporativa ▲ *employee responsibility* responsabilidad del empleado ▲ *environmental responsibility* responsabilidad medioambiental ▲ *legally released from primary responsibility for the liability* legalmente eximido de la responsabilidad primaria por la deuda ▲ *social responsibility* responsabilidad social ▲ *the party assuming primary responsibility* la parte que asume la responsabilidad primaria

responsibility accounting

Responsibility accounting is the identifying and reporting operating data by responsibility centres for which individual managers are responsible and expected to meet certain performance levels and criteria.

contabilidad por áreas de responsabilidad

▲ *form the basis for responsibility accounting* establecer la base para la contabilidad por áreas de responsabilidad ▲ *use responsibility accounting* utilizar la contabilidad por áreas de responsabilidad

responsibility center US

= responsibility centre UK

A responsibility center is a function or unit in an organisation that controls revenue, costs or investments. In accounting systems, examples of responsibility centers are cost, revenue, profit and investment centers.

centro de responsabilidad

▲ *a responsibility center's revenues* ingresos de un centro de responsabilidad ▲ *responsibili-*

ty center budgeting centro de responsabilidad presupuestaria ▲ *the manager of the responsibility center* el gestor del centro de responsabilidad

responsibility centre UK

= responsibility center US

A responsibility centre is a function or unit in an organisation that controls revenue, costs or investments. In accounting systems, examples of responsibility centres are cost, revenue, profit and investment centres.

centro de responsabilidad

▲ *responsibility centre budgeting* centro de responsabilidad presupuestaria ▲ *the manager of the responsibility centre* el gestor del centro de responsabilidad ▲ *tie a user to a responsibility centre* asociar un usurario a un centro de responsabilidad

responsible

To be responsible for an activity means to be in charge of and to have control over the activity.

responsable

▲ *a socially responsible business sector* un sector comercial responsable socialmente ▲ *be responsible for the preparation and presentation of the financial statements* ser responsable de la preparación y presentación de los estados financieros ▲ *responsible for the audit of the financial statements* responsable de la auditoría de los estados financieros ▲ *responsible for the publication of earnings releases* responsable de la publicación de los anuncios de beneficios

restate

To restate means to change the original amount of items in previously prepared financial statements, e.g. to comply with new legislation.

actualizar

▲ *notionally restated* nocionalmente actualizado ▲ *restate comparative information* actualizar la información comparada ▲ *restate financial and operating data* actualizar los datos financieros y de explotación ▲ *restate in accordance with the changed accounting policies* actualizar de acuerdo con las políticas contables modificadas ▲ *restate items* actualizar partidas ▲ *restate proportionately with the change in the gross carrying amount of the asset* actualizar proporcionalmente con el cambio en el valor contable bruto del activo ▲ *restate the comparative information* actualizar la información comparativa ▲ *restate the opening balances of assets, liabilities and equity* actualizar los saldos de apertura de activos, pasivos y patrimonio

restatement

A restatement is a change to a statement or a figure performed to realign it to other or changed rules or principles, such as the restatement of comparative figures in the annual report to changed accounting policies or the restatement of financial statements as presented under IFRS to US GAAP.

actualización

▲ *impracticability in respect of retrospective restatement* no practicable con respecto a la actualización retrospectiva ▲ *limitations on retrospective restatement* limitaciones en la actualización retrospectiva ▲ *make restatements to correct errors retrospectively* hacer actualizaciones para corregir errores de forma retrospectiva ▲ *restatement to US GAAP* actualización a los PCGA norteamericanos ▲ *the amount of the adjustment arising on the restatement* la cuantía del ajuste resultante de la actualización ▲ *the cumulative restatement of assets, liabilities and equity* la actualización acumulativa de activos, pasivos y patrimonio

⇛ reconciliation

restoration

Restoration is the reconstruction, repair or reestablishment of an asset such as a building or a site to its original or former state, structure or condition.

desmantelamiento

▲ *changes in existing restoration and similar liabilities* cambios en desmantelamiento reconocido y otros pasivos similares ▲ *events that change the measurement of an existing restoration liability* sucesos que cambian la valoración de un desmantelamiento reconocido

restoration cost
= cost of restoration
Restoration costs are expenses incurred that are related to the reconstruction, repair or reestablishment of an asset such as a building or a site to its original or former state, structure or condition.
coste de desmantelamiento
= coste del desmantelamiento
▲ *recognition of restoration costs* reconocimiento de los costes de desmantelamiento ▲ *restoration costs on vacating a lease* costes de desmantelamiento por abandonar un arrendamiento ▲ *the carrying amount of the provision for restoration costs* la cantidad contable de la provisión para costes de desmantelamiento ▲ *the present value of the restoration costs* el valor actual de los costes de desmantelamiento

restricted surplus US
= capital reserve UK, non-distributable reserve, undistributable reserve
≠ distributable reserve, revenue reserve UK, unrestricted earnings US
Restricted surplus represents reserves that cannot be distributed to shareholders, except if the company is wound up. Restricted surplus appears as an item in the balance sheet under equity.
reserva indisponible
= plusvalía no distribuible
≠ plusvalía disponible, plusvalía distribuible, reserva disponible
▲ *less the restricted surplus* menos la reserva indisponible ▲ *total restricted surplus as of June 30, 2007* total reserva indisponible hasta el 30 de junio de 2007

restructure
To restructure means that the management of an enterprise alters either the activities or the structure of the enterprise.
reestructurar
▲ *a decision by the executive board or the supervisory board to restructure* una decisión del consejo ejecutivo o del consejo supervisor para reestructurar ▲ *an obligation to restructure* una obligación para reestructurar ▲ *plans to discontinue or restructure the operation to which an asset belongs* planes para abandonar o reestructurar la operación a la que pertenece un activo ▲ *restructure a business segment* reestructurar un segmento de negocio

restructuring
Restructuring refers to the management-controlled reorganisation that alters either the activities or the structure of the enterprise.
reestructuración
▲ *a detailed formal plan for the restructuring* un plan formal detallado de la reestructuración ▲ *a future restructuring to which the entity is not yet committed* una reestructuración futura con la que todavía no está comprometida la entidad ▲ *an existing liability for restructuring* un pasivo existente por reestructuración ▲ *carry out the restructuring* llevar a cabo la reestructuración ▲ *estimated future cash inflows or outflows expected to arise from future restructurings* entradas o salidas de efectivo futuras estimadas que se esperan que aumenten procedentes de reestructuraciones futuras ▲ *provisions for restructurings* provisiones para reestructuraciones ▲ *restructurings of the activities of an entity* reestructuraciones de las actividades de una entidad ▲ *reversals of provisions for the costs of restructuring* reversiones de las provisiones para los costes de reestructuración ▲ *the restructuring of one or more of the combining entities* la reestructuración de una o más de las entidades que se combinan

restructuring charge
Restructuring charges are expenses incurred by an enterprise relating to activities implemented to achieve cost efficiency and increase competitiveness involving changes in the business scope and structure, such as the closing of plants and layoffs of employees.
gasto de reestructuración
= gasto de la reestructuración
▲ *a fourth-quarter restructuring charge* un gasto de reestructuración del cuarto trimestre ▲ *as a result of the restructuring charge* como un resultado del gasto de la reestructuración ▲ *estimated restructuring charges*

gastos de reestructuración estimados

restructuring cost

= cost of restructuring

Restructuring costs are costs that relate to the execution of a restructuring in an enterprise, e.g. in connection with a merger or an acquisition.

coste de reestructuración

= coste de la reestructuración

▲ *estimated restructuring costs* costes de reestructuración estimados ▲ *net of restructuring costs* neto de costes de reestructuración ▲ *other restructuring costs* otros costes de reeestructuración ▲ *provisions for restructuring costs* provisiones para coste de reeestructuración ▲ *restructuring costs incurred* costes de reestructuración incurridos ▲ *restructuring costs relating to enterprises acquired* costes de reestructuración relacionados con empresas adquiridas

restructuring expense

Restructuring expenses are expenses that relate to the execution of a restructuring in an enterprise, e.g. in connection with a merger or an acquisition.

gasto de reestructuración

▲ *reverse restructuring expenses* revertir gastos de reestructuración

restructuring provision

= provision for restructuring

A restructuring provision is a provision in respect of future cash outflows in connection with a restructuring. Certain requirements exist for the timing and size of such a provision.

provisión para reestructuración

= provisión de reestructuración, provisión para la reestructuración

▲ *recognise a restructuring provision* reconocer una provisión para reestructuración ▲ *recognition of a restructuring provision* reconocimiento de una provisión para reestructuración

results

= profit or loss

Results appear after deducting total costs and expenses recognised from total income or profit recognised.

NOTE The term "results" is used in reporting text; as an item in the financial statements such as the profit and loss account, "profit", "loss" or "profit/loss" is used.

resultados

= pérdida o beneficio, pérdidas o beneficios

▲ *present the results and cash flows of the disposal group as discontinued operations* presentar los resultados y flujos de efectivo del grupo eliminado como operaciones abandonadas ▲ *the results and net assets of the legal subsidiary* los resultados y activos netos de la subsidiaria legal ▲ *the results of discontinued operations* los resultados de las operaciones interrumpidas ▲ *the results of operations for the period* los resultados de operaciones del periodo ▲ *translate the results and financial position into the presentation currency* traducir los resultados y la posición financiera a la moneda de presentación

results announcement UK

Results announcements are company notices to the stock exchange, stakeholders and other parties of company performance for a defined accounting period, i.e. full-year, half-year and quarterly results.

anuncio de resultados

▲ *approve the results announcements* aprobar el anuncio de resultados ▲ *the first financial results announcement prepared in accordance with IFRS* el primer anuncio de resultados financieros preparado de acuerdo con las NIFFs

⇛ earnings release, interim results announcement, preliminary results announcement

results in subsidiary

Results in subsidiary refer to the profit or loss of a subsidiary for a financial year. Part of the profit or loss is recognised in the consolidated financial statements depending on the equity interest in the subsidiary.

resultados de la subsidiaria

▲ *the parent's share of the results in subsidiaries* la participación de la matriz en los resultados de las subsidiarias

results of operations

Results of operations constitute the profit or loss generated by an enterprise on its primary activities or trading activities appearing as gross profit less operating expenses or gross loss plus operating expenses, but before interest and tax.

resultados de explotación

▲ *incorporate into the income statement the results of operations of the acquiree* incorporar en el estado de resultados los resultados de explotación de la adquirida ▲ *the results of operations for the period* los resultados de explotación del periodo ▲ *the results of operations of a subsidiary* los resultados de explotación de una subsidiaria ▲ *the results of operations of the component previously presented in discontinued operations* los resultados de explotación del componente previamente presentado como operaciones interrrumpidas ▲ *the results of operations of the group as a whole* los resultados de explotación del grupo como un todo ▲ *the venturer's share of the results of operations of the jointly controlled entity* la participación del participante en un negocio conjunto en los resultados de explotación de la entidad controlada conjuntamente

⇛ operating income, operating loss, operating profit

retail bank

≠ wholesale bank

A retail bank is a financial institution that takes deposits and provides loans besides offering a wide range of services such as mortgages, pensions, and insurance, typically via local branches. Customers are primarily private individuals.

banco comercial

= banco minorista

▲ *a leading retail bank* un banco comercial líder ▲ *acquire a retail bank* adquirir un banco comercial ▲ *large retail banks* grandes bancos comerciales

retail banking

≠ wholesale banking

Retail banking offers a wide range of services such as loans, mortgages, pensions, and insurance as well as providing current accounts and savings accounts typically offered via local branches. Customers are primarily private individuals.

banca minorista

= banca al por menor, banca comercial

≠ banca mayorista

▲ *the outlook for retail banking* la previsión para la banca minorista ▲ *US retail banking* banca minorista norteamericana

Retail Price Index UK

= Consumer Price Index US, CPI US, RPI UK

The Retail Price Index, RPI, is an index showing the rise and fall in prices of consumer goods and services sold in the retail market over a period of time.

Índice de Precios al Consumo

= IPC

▲ *average increase in Retail Price Index* aumento medio en el Índice de Precios al Consumo ▲ *calculated by reference to the UK Retail Prices Index* calculado por referencia al Índice de Precios al Consumo del Reino Unido ▲ *changes in the Retail Prices Index* cambios en el Índice de Precios al Consumo ▲ *the percentage increase of the UK Retail Prices Index* el aumento porcentual del Índice de Precios al Consumo del Reino Unido

retained earnings UK, IAS/IFRS, US

= accumulated profit, retained income US, retained profit IAS/IFRS

Retained earnings are recognised as an item in the balance sheet under capital and reserves and contain profits carried forward from previous years as well as profits transferred from the income statement for the current financial year.

beneficios no distribuidos

= ganancias retenidas

▲ *an adjustment to the opening balance of retained earnings* un ajuste al balance de apertura de los beneficios no distribuidos ▲ *appropriations of retained earnings* apropiaciones de beneficios no distribuidos ▲ *retained earnings as at 1 January* beneficios no distribuidos a 1 de enero ▲ *retained earnings for the year* beneficios del año no distribuidos ▲ *the balance of retained earnings at the beginning of the period* el saldo de beneficios no distribuidos al inicio del periodo ▲ *the retained earnings re-*

cognised in the consolidated financial statements los beneficios no distribuidos reconocidos en los estados financieros consolidados ▲ *transfer directly to retained earnings* transferir directamente a beneficios no distribuidos ▲ *transferred to retained earnings* transferido a beneficios no distribuidos

retained income US

= accumulated profit UK, retained earnings US, retained profit UK, IAS/IFRS

≠ retained loss

Retained income is recognised as an item in the balance sheet under capital and reserves and contain income carried forward from previous years as well as income transferred from the income statement for the current financial year.

beneficio no distribuido

= ganancia no asignada

NOTE Spanish accountants prefer 'beneficio no distribuido' to the IAS/IFRS term 'ganancia no asignada'.

▲ *retained income as at January 1* beneficio no distribuido a 1 de enero ▲ *retained income for the year* beneficio no distribuido del año ▲ *transferred to retained income* transferido a beneficio no distribuido

retained loss UK

≠ retained profit UK

A retained loss refers to the net loss for the year in the profit and loss account as transferred to reserves under equity in the balance sheet thereby reducing retained earnings and total equity.

pérdida no compensada

≠ beneficio no distribuido

▲ *retained loss for the financial year* pérdida no compensada del año financiero

retained profit UK, IAS/IFRS

= accumulated profit UK, retained earnings US

≠ retained loss UK

Retained profit is an item recognised under capital and reserves in the balance sheet that contains undistributed profits carried forward from previous years as well as profit transferred from the profit and loss account for the current financial year and not distributed as dividends.

beneficio no distribuido

= ganancia retenida

NOTE Spanish accountants prefer 'beneficio no distribuido' to the IAS/IFRS term 'ganancia retenida'.

▲ *retained profit for the year* beneficio no distribuido del año ▲ *retained profit or loss* resultado no distribuido

⇛ profit and loss account

retax

To retax is to tax an enterprise or a person again where the provisions for a tax reduction no longer exist.

volver a gravar

= regravar

▲ *retax a loss* regravar una pérdida ▲ *retax amortisation and depreciation* volver a gravar depreciación y amortización ▲ *retax an amount* regravar una cantidad ▲ *retax in full* volver a gravar en su totalidad

retaxable amount

A retaxable amount is the amount on which a person or an enterprise has to pay taxes in case of retaxation, if the preconditions for a tax cut cease to exist.

cantidad imponible reajustable

= valor imponible reajustable

▲ *provisions related to retaxable amounts* provisiones relacionadas con las cantidades imponibles reajustables

retaxation UK

= recapture US

Retaxation is taxation of an enterprise or a person again where the provisions for a tax reduction have ceased to exist.

reimposición

= regravación

▲ *an amount subject to retaxation* una cantidad sujeta a regravación ▲ *retaxation in full* reimposición completa ▲ *retaxation of amortisation and depreciation* reimposición de amortización y depreciación ▲ *retaxation of foreign losses* reimposición de pérdidas en el extranjero ▲ *retaxation of losses in foreign enterprises participating in joint taxation* reimposición de pérdidas en las entidades extranjeras que participan en la tributación conjunta

retaxation rule

A retaxation rule is a provision in the tax regulation indicating where retaxation should take place, typically where the provisions for a tax reduction have ceased to exist.

reglamento de reimposición

= reglamento de regravación

▲ *comply with the retaxation rules* cumplir con los reglamentos de reimposición

retention of title

Retention of title means that the ownership to goods does not pass to the buyer until the buyer has paid the seller in full or has discharged some other obligation under the contract of sale.

retención de la propiedad

▲ *a retention of title clause* una cláusula de retención de la propiedad ▲ *be subject to retention of title* estar sujeto a retención de la propiedad ▲ *retention of title agreement* acuerdo de rentención de la propiedad

retiree benefit expense

Retiree benefit expenses are expenses which relate to pension benefits to retired employees, i.e. retirees, and which are incurred by an enterprise due to legislation, collective agreements or under its occupational pension schemes.

gasto por prestación de jubilación

▲ *liabilities associated with retiree benefit expenses* pasivos asociados con gastos por prestación de jubilación ▲ *other retiree benefit expenses* otros gastos por prestación de jubilación ▲ *the estimated retiree benefit expenses* los gastos estimados por prestación de jubilación

retirement

1 Retirement is the withdrawal from the portfolio of a fixed asset which has been disposed of or scrapped.

eliminación

▲ *a surplus realised on the retirement or disposal of the asset* un superávit realizado a la eliminación o enajenación del activo ▲ *gains or losses arising from the retirement or disposal of investment property* resultados procedentes de la eliminación o enajenación de las propiedades inmobiliarias ▲ *retirement of an item of property, plant and equipment* eliminación de una partida de edificios, instalaciones y equipos

2 extinguishment of debt US, repayment UK

Retirement referring to debt means the repayment of borrowings which may take place before or after maturity by repayment, refunding or conversion of the debt.

cancelación

= conversión, transformación

▲ *a complete retirement of debt* una cancelación de la deuda completa

3 Retirement is the act of permanently withdrawing from employment, usually because of age or ill health.

jubilación

▲ *at the date of retirement* a la fecha de jubilación ▲ *retirement age* edad de jubilación

⇛ retirement benefit, termination

retirement benefit US

A retirement benefit refers to any type of monetary benefit to which a person or that person's beneficiary is or may become entitled on or after retirement under a retirement benefit plan. Typically, retirement benefits are monthly or other periodic payments but may also be lump sums.

prestación de jubilación

= prestación por jubilación

▲ *a curtailment of retirement benefits* un recorte de prestaciones de jubilación ▲ *a description of the retirement benefits promised to participants* una descripción de las prestaciones de jubilación prometidas a los participantes ▲ *actuarial present value of promised retirement benefits* valor actuarial presente de las prestaciones de jubilación prometidas ▲ *be entitled to a retirement benefit* tener derecho a una prestación por jubilación ▲ *enhancement of retirement benefits* mejora de las prestaciones de jubilación ▲ *funded retirement benefits* prestaciones de jubilación provisionadas ▲ *guarantee the payment of retirement benefits* garantizar el pago de las prestaciones de jubilación ▲ *pay a lump-sum retirement benefit* pagar una prestación de jubilación de una sola vez ▲ *retirement benefit costs* costes de la prestación de jubilación ▲ *the age profile of the members entitled to receive retirement benefits* el perfil de edad de los miembros con derecho a percibir prestaciones de jubilación ▲ *the determination of the cost of retirement benefits* la valoración del coste de las prestaciones de jubilación ▲ *the level of retirement benefits in case of cessation of employment* el nivel de las prestaciones de jubilación en caso de pérdida del empleo ▲ *the target level of the retirement benefits* el objetivo a conseguir de las prestaciones de jubilación

retirement benefit cost UK

= post-employment benefit cost IAS/IFRS, postretirement benefit cost US

Retirement benefit costs are costs which relate to pension benefits to employees and which are incurred by an enterprise due to legislation, collective agreements or under its occupational pension schemes.

coste de prestaciones por jubilación

▲ *retirement benefit costs for financial statements covering periods beginning before 1 January 2005* costes de prestaciones por jubilación en estados financieros que cubren los periodos anteriores al 1 de enero de 2005

retirement benefit obligation UK

= post-employment benefit obligation IAS/IFRS, postretirement benefit obligation US

A retirement benefit obligation is the obligation of an enterprise to pay benefits to employees on or after retirement under a pension scheme.

obligación por prestación de jubilación

▲ *retirement benefit obligations reported by defined benefit retirement plans* obligaciones por prestaciones de jubilación incluidas en los planes de prestación definida

retirement benefit plan

= employee benefit plan, pension benefit plan, post-employment benefit plan IAS/IFRS, postretirement benefit plan US

A retirement benefit plan is an arrangement under which an enterprise provides monetary benefits such as lump sums or periodic payments for its employees on or after retirement.

plan de prestaciones por jubilación

= plan de beneficio por retiro

NOTE Spanish accountants prefer 'plan de prestaciones por jubilación' to the IAS/IFRS term 'plan de beneficio por retiro'.

▲ *a favourable retirement benefit plan* un plan de prestaciones por jubilación favorable ▲ *a retirement benefit plan agreement* un acuerdo de plan de prestaciones por jubilación ▲ *a special retirement benefit plan* un plan de prestaciones por jubilación especial ▲ *cancel a retirement benefit plan* cancelar un plan de prestaciones por jubilación ▲ *member of a retirement benefit plan* miembro de un plan de prestaciones por jubilación ▲ *retirement benefit plan investments* inversiones del plan de prestaciones por jubilación ▲ *retirement benefit plan with assets invested with an insurance company* plan de prestaciones por jubilación con activos invertidos con una compañía de seguros ▲ *the present value of the expected payments from a retirement benefit plan* el valor actual de los pagos esperados procedentes de un plan de prestaciones por jubilación ▲ *the report of a retirement benefit plan* el informe de un plan de prestaciones por jubilación ▲ *under the conditions of the retirement benefit plan* según las condiciones del plan de prestaciones por jubilación

retirement benefit scheme

→ retirement benefit plan

retirement fund US

= pension fund UK

A retirement fund is a separate legal entity containing assets designated to provide payment of pension benefits to employees when they retire from service.

fondo de pensiones

▲ *allocation to the retirement fund* asignación al fondo de pensiones ▲ *payment of contributions to a retirement fund* pago de aportaciones a un fondo de pensiones ▲ *repayment of income in the retirement fund* volver a ingresar en el fondo de pensiones ▲ *the fair market value of the group's retirement fund assets* el valor razonable de mercado de los activos del fondo de pensiones del grupo

retroactive

= retrospective

If something is retroactive it has effect backwards in time, i.e. it has an effect on matters that occurred before the retroactive matter was introduced.

retroactivo

= retrospectivo

▲ *full retroactive application* aplicación retroactiva completa

retrospective

If something is retrospective it has effect backwards in time, i.e. it has effect on matters that occurred before the retrospective thing was introduced.

retroactivo

= retrospectivo

▲ *exceptions to retrospective application of IFRSs* excepciones a la aplicación retroactiva de las NIIFs ▲ *impracticability in respect of retrospective application and retrospective restatement* impracticabilidad con respecto a la aplicación y regularización retroactiva ▲ *limited retrospective application* aplicación retroactiva limitada ▲ *make a retrospective restatement to correct an error* hacer una regularización retroactiva para corregir un error ▲ *prohibit retrospective application of IFRSs in some areas* prohibir la aplicación retroactiva de las NIIFs en algunas áreas ▲ *retrospective application* aplicación retroactiva ▲ *retrospective restatement* regularización retroactiva ▲ *the requirement for full retrospective application* el requisito para la aplicación retroactiva completa

return

Return refers to the profit or loss from an investment in securities in the form of dividend or interest income and capital gains or losses.

rendimiento

= rentabilidad, retorno

▲ *a constant periodic rate of return* un tasa de retorno periódica constante ▲ *a constant periodic return* una rentabilidad periódica constante ▲ *provide a return to investors* ofrecer un rendimiento a los inversores ▲ *return after tax* rendimiento después de impuestos ▲ *return before tax* rendimiento antes de impuestos ▲ *return on assets* rendimiento sobre activos ▲ *return on capital* rendimiento del capital ▲ *return on equity* rendimiento de la acción ▲ *return on investment* retorno de la inversión ▲ *return on net assets* rendimiento en activos netos ▲ *return on net operating assets* rendimiento en activos de explotación netos ▲ *return on the securities reserve* rendimiento de la reserva de títulos ▲ *the average rate of return* la tasa de rentabilidad media ▲ *use a discount rate that reflects the estimated return on the insurer's assets* utilizar una tasa de descuento que refleja el rendimiento estimado de los activos del asegurador

return on capital employed

= ROCE

Return on capital employed (ROCE) is defined as return before tax and financing charges divided by net assets (capital employed). ROCE shows the performance regardless of method of financing. Also referred to as return on invested capital (ROIC) or return on net assets (RONA).

rendimiento de capital

= rendimiento de la inversión, rendimiento del capital, rentabilidad del capital

▲ *calculation of the return on capital employed* cálculo del rendimiento de capital ▲ *the consolidated return on capital employed* el rendimiento del capital consolidado

⇛ return on invested capital

return on common equity US

= return on equity, ROE

Return on common equity is a financial profitability ratio defined as profit attributable to holders of common stock for a period as a percentage of average equity. This ratio measures the return on owners' investment in a company and is a variant of the Du-Pont analysis model where ROE is split into three components: profitability, activity and gearing.

coeficiente de rentabilidad de la acción

▲ *calculate return on common equity* calcular el coeficiente de rentabilidad de la acción

return on equity

= ROE

Return on equity (ROE) is a financial profitability ratio defined as profit attributable to ordinary shareholders for a period as a percentage of average equity. This ratio measures the return on owners' investment in a company and is a variant of the Du-Pont analysis model where ROE is split into three components: profitability, activity and gearing.

rentabilidad de los recursos propios

= rentabilidad de recursos propios

▲ *a reduced return on equity* una rentabilidad de los recursos propios reducida ▲ *an increased return on equity* una rentabilidad de los recursos propios aumentada ▲ *return on equity excluding goodwill* rentabilidad de los recursos propios excluyendo el fondo de comercio

return on invested capital

= ROIC

Return on invested capital is a financial profitability and efficiency ratio defined as earnings before interest and tax excluding goodwill write-downs divided by average invested capital excluding goodwill. This ratio expresses a company's ability through its operating activities to generate a return on invested capital and is useful for comparison of the operating performance of various companies. In another version including goodwill, the ratio indicates the company's ability to create shareholder value.

rendimiento de la inversión

= rendimiento de capital, rendimiento del capital, rentabilidad de la inversión

▲ *return on invested capital after tax* rendimiento de la inversión después de impuestos ▲ *return on invested capital before tax* rendimiento de la inversión antes de impuestos

return on investment

= ROI

Return on investment (ROI) is a financial ratio defined as profit before interest and tax divided by capital employed (net assets). ROI is an indicator of the performance of an enterprise.

tasa de retorno de la inversión

= rendimiento del capital invertido, rentabilidad de la inversión

▲ *the measurement of return on investment* la valoración de la tasa de retorno de la inversión

⇛ return on capital employed, return on invested capital

return on risk-weighted assets

= RORWA

Return on risk-weighted assets (RORWA) is a financial ratio related to banking defined as net profit divided by average risk-weighted assets. This ratio measures profitability and also shows a bank's ability to service loan capital.

beneficio neto por activos ponderados por riesgo

= RORWA

▲ *a relatively stable return on risk-weighted assets* un beneficio neto por activos ponderados por riesgo relativamente estable ▲ *changes in quarterly return on risk-weighted assets* cambios en beneficio neto por activos ponderados por riesgo trimestrales ▲ *post-tax return on risk-weighted assets* beneficio neto por activos ponderados por riesgo después de impuestos

return on sales

= operating margin, profit margin, ROS

Return on sales is a profitability ratio, also referred to as the profit margin, which is calculated as operating profit divided by sales. The ratio shows the difference between the sales revenue from a product or service and the cost of producing or providing it.

margen de ventas

= rendimiento sobre ventas, rentabilidad sobre ventas, retorno sobre ventas

▲ *a high return on sales* un margen de ventas alto ▲ *a reduced return on sales* un margen de ventas reducido ▲ *an increased return on sales* un margen de ventas incrementado ▲ *calculate the return on sales* calcular el margen de ventas

return on shares

A return on shares is the profit or dividend obtained on a shareholding, i.e. an investment in a company.

rentabilidad de las acciones

▲ *an annual return on shares of 8.5%* una rentabilidad de las acciones del 8,5% ▲ *negative return on shares* rentabilidad de las acciones negativa ▲ *positive return on shares* rentabilidad de las acciones positiva ▲ *taxation of the return on shares* imposición de la rentabilidad de las acciones ▲ *the average real rate of return on shares* el tipo real medio de rentabilidad de las acciones

return-based

A return-based investment objective or strategy focuses on generating a profit to investors, e.g. creating shareholder value. High returns are typically generated on risk exposures, whereas investments subject to more moderate fluctuations will offer lower returns.

basado en el rendimiento

▲ *a return-based analysis* un análisis basado en el rendimiento

returned product

A returned product is a product that has been returned to the seller.

devolución de ventas

▲ *invoiced sale less returned products* venta facturada menos devolución de ventas

revaluation

1 Revaluation is the adjustment of the carrying amount of an asset or a liability by a write-up or a write-down.

revaluación

▲ *a revaluation decrease* un descenso de la revaluación ▲ *accounting revaluation* revaluación contable ▲ *as a result of revaluation* como un resultado de la revaluación ▲ *increase in the carrying amount arising on revaluation* aumento en el valor contable procedente de la revaluación ▲ *keep revaluations up to date* mantener las revaluaciones actualizadas ▲ *make a revaluation* hacer una revaluación ▲ *revaluation at fair value* revaluación a valor razonable ▲ *revaluation deficits* déficits de la revaluación ▲ *revaluation for tax purposes* revaluación por motivos fiscales ▲ *revaluation of assets and liabilities* revaluación de activos y pasivos ▲ *revaluation of the enterprise acquired* revaluación de la empresa adquirida ▲ *revaluation surplus* superávit de la revaluación ▲ *revaluation surpluses* superávits de la revaluación ▲ *the date of the revaluation* la fecha de la revaluación ▲ *the frequency of revaluations* la frecuencia de las revaluaciones ▲ *time of revaluation* hora de la revaluación

2 Revaluation means writing up and increasing the value, i.e. the carrying amount, of an asset to reflect the fair value or the market value of that asset. Accounting rules differ as to which assets may or may not be revalued.

revalorización

▲ *make revaluations* hacer revalorizaciones

3 = revaluation surplus

A revaluation is the amount by which the carrying amount of an asset is increased.

revalorización

▲ *revaluation of property* revalorización de la propiedad

revaluation reserve UK

= appraisal surplus US, revaluation surplus IAS/IFRS

A revaluation reserve is the amount included in the reserves under equity in the balance sheet representing an unrealised increase in the value of fixed assets, typically property, appearing as the difference between the carrying amounts at the beginning and end of the financial year.

reserva de revalorización

▲ *dissolution of a revaluation reserve* disolución de una reserva de revalorización ▲ *dissolve a revaluation reserve* disolver una reserva de revalorización ▲ *revaluation reserve according to the equity method* reserva de revalorización de acuerdo con el método de participación ▲ *transfer a revaluation reserve to the contributed capital* transferir una reserva de revalorización al capital contribuido

revaluation surplus[1] IAS/IFRS *noun* <a, the, -es>

= appraisal surplus US

Revaluation surplus is the amount by which the carrying amount of an asset is increased when the fair value or market value exceeds the carrying amount. This unrealised increase in value (gain) is recognised in equity under revaluation reserve.

plusvalía por revalorización de activo
= plusvalía por revalorización del activo
▲ *a realised revaluation surplus* una plusvalía por revalorización de activo realizada ▲ *credit an impairment loss directly to equity under the heading revaluation surplus* anotar una pérdida por deterioro directamente a patrimonio en la rúbrica plusvalía por revalorización de activo ▲ *the amount held in revaluation surplus for investment property* la cuantía mantenida en plusvalía por revalorización de activo por inversiones en propiedad ▲ *the amount of the revaluation surplus* la cuantía de la plusvalía por revalorización del activo ▲ *the change in the revaluation surplus arising from a change in the liability* el cambio en la plusvalía por revalorización de activo procedente de una variación en el pasivo ▲ *the cumulative revaluation surplus included in equity* la plusvalía por revalorización de activo acumulativa incluida en patrimonio

revaluation surplus[2] IAS/IFRS *noun*
<a, the, no plural>
= appraisal surplus US, revaluation reserve UK
A revaluation surplus is the amount included in the reserves under equity in the balance sheet representing an unrealised increase in the value of fixed assets, typically property, appearing as the difference between the carrying amounts at the beginning and end of the financial year.
reserva de revalorización
▲ *changes in the revaluation surplus* cambios en la reserva de revalorización

revalue
1 To revalue is to adjust or change the value. Depreciation, amortisation and write-downs for impairment losses contribute to revaluing an asset.
revaluar
▲ *revalue assets* revaluar activos ▲ *revalue assets and liabilities acquired at fair value* revaluar activos y pasivos adquiridos a valor razonable ▲ *revalue assets and liabilities at fair value* revaluar activos y pasivos a valor razonable ▲ *revalue liabilities* revaluar pasivos ▲ *the initial application of a policy to revalue assets in accordance with IAS 16* la aplicación inicial de una política para revaluar activos de acuerdo con la NIC 16
2 = revalue upwards, write up
To revalue is to increase the carrying amount of an asset, such as a tangible asset or a financial asset, i.e. an equity investment.
revalorizar
▲ *to revalue property* revalorizar la propiedad

revenue
1 Revenue constitutes the total sales of products and services over an accounting period relating to the ordinary activities of an enterprise less any discounts, returns, VAT and other taxes based on sales revenue, resulting in an inflow of economic benefits to the enterprise and the consequent increase in its equity. Revenue appears as the top line item in the income statement.
ingreso de actividades ordinarias
= ingreso por actividades ordinarias
▲ *a decline in revenue* un descenso en el ingreso de actividades ordinarias ▲ *achieve revenue of EUR 8bn* lograr un ingreso de actividades ordinarias de 8 millardos de euros ▲ *adjustment of revenue* ajuste del ingreso de actividades ordinarias ▲ *allocate expenses according to revenue* asignar costes de acuerdo con el ingreso de actividades ordinarias ▲ *an increase in revenue* un aumento en el ingreso de actividades ordinarias ▲ *analysis of the enterprise's revenue by currencies* análisis del ingreso de actividades ordinarias por monedas ▲ *combination of revenue* combinación del ingreso de actividades ordinarias ▲ *consolidated revenue* ingreso de actividades ordinarias consolidado ▲ *cyclical revenue* ingreso de actividades ordinarias cíclico ▲ *Danish revenue* ingreso de actividades ordinarias danés ▲ *generate revenue* generar el ingreso de actividades ordinarias ▲ *geographical distribution of revenue* distribución geográfica del ingreso de actividades ordinarias ▲ *impro-*

vement of revenue mejora de ingreso de actividades ordinarias ▲ *increase revenue* aumentar el ingreso de actividades ordinarias ▲ *invoiced revenue* ingreso de actividades ordinarias facturado ▲ *measurement of revenue* valoración del ingreso de actividades ordinarias ▲ *monthly revenue* ingreso de actividades ordinarias mensual ▲ *new products' share of revenue* participación del ingreso de actividades ordinarias de nuevos productos ▲ *operating profit as a percentage of revenue* beneficio de explotación como un porcentaje del ingreso de actividades ordinarias ▲ *recognise revenue by reference to the stage of completion* reconocer el ingreso de actividades ordinarias por referencia a la etapa de finalización ▲ *recognised revenue* ingreso de actividades ordinarias reconocido ▲ *recognition of revenue* reconocimiento del ingreso de actividades ordinarias ▲ *revenue and other operating income* ingreso de actividades ordinarias y otros ingresos de explotación ▲ *revenue for the year* ingreso por actividades ordinarias del año ▲ *revenue from the sale of goods and services* ingreso de actividades ordinarias procedente de la venta de bienes y servicios ▲ *revenue growth* crecimiento del ingreso por actividades ordinarias ▲ *revenue in terms of volume* ingreso de actividades ordinarias en términos de volumen ▲ *revenue of EUR 10 million* ingreso de actividades ordinarias de 10 millones de euros ▲ *revenue per employee* ingreso de actividades ordinarias por empleado ▲ *revenue per unit* ingreso de actividades ordinarias por unidad ▲ *seasonal revenue* ingreso de actividades ordinarias estacional ▲ *the distribution of the revenue on activities* la distribución del ingreso de actividades ordinarias por actividades ▲ *the distribution of the revenue on geographical markets* la distribución del ingreso de actividades ordinarias por mercados geográficos ▲ *the revenue of the combined entity for the period* el ingreso de actividades ordinarias de la entidad combinada para el periodo ▲ *total revenue* total ingreso de actividades ordinarias

⇛ net revenues, net sales, net turnover

2 = income from operations

Revenue is income, typically income attributable to the main and ordinary activities of an enterprise. As such, revenue constitutes an inflow of economic benefits over an accounting period to the enterprise and contributes to equity increases, not including increases attributable to owner contributions.

ingreso

▲ *future revenue* ingreso futuro

revenue account

1 = income and expenditure account, income and expenditure statement

≠ balance sheet

A revenue account is the statement in a non-profit or public sector organisation that corresponds to the profit and loss account or income statement in an enterprise trading for a profit. The revenue account covers a fixed period of time and its balance shows the excess of income over expenditure (or vice versa) instead of a profit or loss.

cuenta de ingresos y gastos

▲ *consolidated revenue account* cuenta de ingresos y gastos consolidada ▲ *prepare a revenue account* preparar una cuenta de ingresos y gastos

⇛ revenue and expenditure account

2 A revenue account records entries and balances concerning the operations of an enterprise. Revenue accounts form the basis of the profit and loss account.

cuenta de ingresos

▲ *reconciliation of revenue accounts* conciliación de las cuentas de ingresos ▲ *revenue accounts in the operating ledger* cuentas de ingresos en el libro mayor

revenue allocation

Revenue allocation is the act of assigning revenues to revenue objects or activities to which they are related, but to which they cannot be directly traced.

asignación de ingresos

▲ *correct revenue allocation* asignación de ingresos correctos ▲ *the methods of revenue alloca-*

tion los métodos de asignación de ingresos

revenue and expenditure account

= revenue account

≠ balance sheet account

A revenue and expenditure account is an income statement account that records revenue and expenditure incurred by an enterprise in its operations.

cuenta de ingresos y gastos

≠ cuenta de balance

▲ *the related revenue and expenditure account* la cuenta de ingresos y gastos relacionada

⇛ income and expenditure account

revenue center US

= revenue centre UK

A revenue center is a division or department within an enterprise which is responsible for the sale of the enterprise's goods or services.

departamento de ventas

▲ *revenue center manager* responsable del departamento de ventas

revenue centre UK

= revenue center US

A revenue centre is a division or department within an enterprise which is responsible for the sale of the enterprise's goods or services.

departamento de ventas

▲ *revenue centre manager* responsable del departamento de ventas

revenue decline

= decline in revenue

A revenue decline is a reduction in revenue during a period compared to previous periods.

descenso de ingresos

= descenso de los ingresos

▲ *a 10% revenue decline* un descenso de los ingresos del 10% ▲ *the fourth straight quarter of revenue decline* el cuarto trimestre seguido de descenso de ingresos

revenue development

Revenue development refers to the changes in the revenue of an enterprise, and the development may be negative, positive, constant, surprising etc.

evolución de los ingresos

▲ *assess the revenue development* examinar la evolución de los ingresos ▲ *revenue development by product group* evolución de los ingresos por grupo de productos ▲ *the revenue development by geographical segment* la evolución de los ingresos por segmentos geográficos

revenue driver

A revenue driver is an operating or other activity in an enterprise that results in revenue growth. Examples are particular products in strong demand, price levels, trade marketing and additional services offered.

generador de ingresos

▲ *a primary revenue driver* un generador de ingresos primario ▲ *a significant revenue driver* un generador de ingresos significativo

revenue growth

= revenue increase, sales growth

Revenue growth refers to an increase in revenue during a period compared to previous periods.

crecimiento de ingresos

= crecimiento de los ingresos, incremento de la facturación

▲ *achieve revenue growth of 24%* conseguir un crecimiento de los ingresos del 24% ▲ *realise substantial revenue growth* constatar un incremento sustancial de facturación

revenue increase

= increase in revenue

An increase in revenue is a rise in total revenue or sales of an enterprise for an accounting period compared with the revenue or the volume of sales for a previous period.

aumento de ingresos

= aumento de facturación, crecimiento de los ingresos

▲ *a reported revenue increase* un aumento de ingresos comunicado ▲ *revenue increase on new products* aumento de ingresos en nuevos productos

revenue item

= income item, item of income

A revenue item is an item in the income statement that records an amount of income generated or earned during the accounting period.

partida de ingresos

▲ *a main category of revenue items* una categoría principal de partidas de ingresos ▲ *all revenue items recognised* todas las partidas de ingresos reconocidas

revenue neutral
The term revenue neutral refers to the situation in which the total turnover of a product or a product line does not change during a specific time period on account of e.g. changes in the tax policy or in the pricing policy of an enterprise.
fiscalmente neutral
▲ *revenue neutral trade* resultado comercial fiscalmente neutral

revenue object
A revenue object is an object such as a division, a customer, or a product for which relevant revenues are desired separately measured.
objeto de ingresos
▲ *a set of revenue objects* un conjunto de objetos de ingresos

revenue recognition
= recognition of revenue
Revenue recognition refers to the process of including realised revenue in the profit and loss account.
reconocimiento de ingresos
= reconocimiento de los ingresos
▲ *cumulative revenue recognition* reconocimiento de los ingresos acumulativos ▲ *provision disallowing revenue recognition of unrealised value increases* disposición que desaconseja el reconocimiento de ingresos de aumentos de valor no realizados ▲ *revenue recognition based on dividends received* reconocimiento de ingresos basado en los dividendos recibidos ▲ *revenue recognition of negative goodwill* reconocimiento de ingresos del fondo de comercio negativo ▲ *revenue recognition of revaluations* reconocimiento de ingresos de revalorizaciones ▲ *revenue recognition on a continuing basis* reconocimiento de los ingresos según el principio de empresa en funcionamiento

revenue reserve UK
= distributable reserve, unrestricted earnings
≠ capital reserve UK, undistributable reserve
Revenue reserve is a reserve representing transfers of profit from the profit and loss account that may be distributed to shareholders. The revenue reserve appears as an item in the balance sheet under equity.
NOTE Revenue reserve is a former UK term which has been replaced by distributable reserves.
reserva disponible
▲ *transfer from or to the revenue reserve* transferencia de o a la reserva disponible

reversal
A reversal is the carryback of a prior transaction or amount recognised, resulting in an elimination of that transaction or amount in a subsequent period.
reversión
= retrocesión
▲ *a reversal of an impairment loss* una reversión de una pérdida por deterioro ▲ *recognition of impairment losses and reversals* reconocimiento de pérdidas por deterioro y reversiones ▲ *reversal due to changes in accounting estimates* reversión debido a cambios en estimaciones contables ▲ *reversal of deferred tax assets written down* reversión de activos por impuestos diferidos eliminados ▲ *reversal of prior amortisation or depreciation* reversión de una amortización o depreciación anterior ▲ *reversals of provisions for the costs of restructuring* reversiones de provisiones para los costes de reconversión ▲ *the amount of reversals of impairment losses recognised in profit or loss* la cantidad de reversiones de pérdidas por deterioro reconocidas en resultados ▲ *the circumstances that led to the reversal of a write-down of inventories* las circunstancias que llevaron a la reversión de una eliminación de inventarios

reverse
= carry back
To reverse means to carry back a prior transaction or amount recognised, which results in an elimination of that transaction or amount in a subsequent period.
revertir
▲ *impairment losses reversed in profit or loss during the period* pérdidas por deterioro revertidas a resultados durante el periodo ▲ *reverse a revaluation* revertir una revalorización ▲ *reverse amortisation or depreciation* revertir la amortización

o la depreciación ▲ *reverse an impairment loss* revertir una pérdida por deterioro ▲ *reverse profit on payments received on account* revertir el beneficio en cantidades entregadas a cuenta ▲ *reverse write-down of goodwill* revertir la eliminación del fondo de comercio

reverse acquisition

A reverse acquisition is an acquisition where an enterprise obtains ownership of the shares of another enterprise, but as part of the exchange transaction issues enough voting shares, as consideration, to allow control of the combined enterprise to pass to the owners of the enterprise whose shares have been acquired.

adquisición inversa

▲ *a reverse acquisition by the legal acquiree* una adquisición inversa por el adquirente legal ▲ *consolidated financial statements prepared following a reverse acquisition* estados financieros consolidados preparados siguiendo una adquisición inversa ▲ *during the period in which the reverse acquisition occurs* durante el periodo en el que la adquisición inversa ocurre ▲ *reverse acquisition accounting* contabilidad de adquisición inversa

reverse repo US

→ reverse repurchase agreement

reverse repo agreement US

→ reverse repurchase agreement

reverse repurchase agreement US

≠ repurchase agreement

A reverse repurchase agreement is an agreement between a buyer (lender) and a seller (borrower) on the purchase and subsequent sale of securities at a fixed price at a fixed date.

acuerdo de recompra inverso

▲ *enter into a reverse repurchase agreement* firmar un acuerdo de recompra inverso ▲ *purchase the collateral securities under a reverse repurchase agreement* comprar los títulos colaterales según un acuerdo de recompra inverso ▲ *the life of the reverse repurchase agreement* la vida del acuerdo de recompra inverso ▲ *the maximum maturity of a reverse repurchase agreement* el vencimiento máximo de un acuerdo de recompra inverso ▲ *the term of a reverse repurchase agreement* el término de un acuerdo de recompra inverso

reverse share split UK

= reverse split, reverse stock split US

≠ share split UK, stock split US

A reverse share split is the opposite of a split, i.e. a procedure whereby the number of outstanding shares in a company is reduced to the effect that the market capitalisation remains the same and consequently the value of each share will increase, which is typically what the company intends to achieve. A reverse share split may be effected as e.g. a 1 for 10 split, which means that a shareholder owning 100 shares will end up holding 10 shares, each with a value that is ten times as high as the value of the shares originally held, but the aggregate value of the shareholding will remain the same.

amortización proporcional de acciones

▲ *decrease as a result of a reverse share split* disminuir como resultado de una amortización proporcional de acciones

reverse split

= reverse share split UK, reverse stock split US

≠ share split UK, stock split US

A reverse split is the opposite of a split, i.e. a procedure whereby the number of outstanding shares in a company is reduced to the effect that the market capitalisation remains the same and consequently the value of each share will increase, which is typically what the company intends to achieve. A reverse split may be effected as e.g. a 1 for 10 split, which means that a shareholder owning 100 shares will end up holding 10 shares, each with a value that is ten times as high as the value of the shares originally held, but the aggregate value of the shareholding will remain the same.

split inverso

= agrupamiento de acciones

▲ *decrease as a result of a reverse split* decremento como un resultado de un split inverso

reverse stock split US
= reverse share split UK, reverse split
≠ share split UK, stock split US
A reverse stock split is the opposite of a split, i.e. a procedure whereby the number of outstanding shares of common stock in a company is reduced to the effect that the market capitalisation remains the same and consequently the value of each share will increase, which is typically what the company intends to achieve. A reverse stock split may be effected as e.g. a 1 for 10 split, which means that a shareholder owning 100 shares will end up holding 10 shares of common stock, each with a value that is ten times as high as the value of the stock originally held, but the aggregate value of the shareholding will remain the same.
split accionarial inverso
= agrupamiento de acciones
▲ *decrease as a result of a reverse stock split* decremento como un resultado de un agrupamiento de acciones

reversing entry
A reversing entry is an accounting entry made to reverse a previous entry at the beginning of an accounting period. Reversing entries are opposite entries that write back, i.e. reverse, adjusting entries made in the previous accounting period such as prepayments or accruals.
asiento de reversión
▲ *reversing entry in equity* asiento de reversión en patrimonio

review[1] *noun*
A review is a formal or official examination.
NOTE For auditing purposes, a review is an examination which is less exhaustive than an audit, and which provides a moderate degree of assurance to interested parties as to the reliability of financial data. By contrast, an audit provides a high degree of assurance.
revisión
▲ *a review of future cash flows* una revisión de flujos de efectivo futuros ▲ *a review of the financial statements* una revisión de los estados financieros ▲ *conduct a review* llevar a cabo una revisión ▲ *review of amortisation period and amortisation method* revisión del periodo y método de amortización ▲ *review of useful life assessment* revisión de la valoración de la vida útil

review[2] *verb*
= analyse, examine
To review is to examine and assess something.
NOTE For auditing purposes, to review is to perform an examination which is less exhaustive than an audit.
revisar
= examinar
▲ *review at least at each financial year-end* revisar al menos al final del ejercicio ▲ *review for impairment* examinar el deterioro ▲ *review the carrying amount of assets* examinar el valor contable de los activos ▲ *review the policies selected by management* examinar las políticas seleccionadas por la dirección

revise
= update
To revise is to reconsider, reevaluate or reexamine with a view to making changes such as corrections and improvements or a general update and restatement.
actualizar
▲ *revise an accounting standard* actualizar una norma contable ▲ *revise an annual report* actualizar un informe anual ▲ *revise an estimate* actualizar una estimación ▲ *revise annual report models* actualizar los modelos de informe anual ▲ *revise statements of accounts* actualizar los estados de cuentas ▲ *revise the estimates of payments or receipts* actualizar las estimaciones de pagos o recibos

revision
= update
Revision is a re-examination, reevaluation or reconsideration that seeks to make changes such as corrections and improvements or a general update and restatement.
actualización
▲ *an extensive revision* una actualización extensiva ▲ *make a revision* hacer una actualización ▲ *revision of accounting standards* actualización de las

normas contables ▲ *revision of information* actualización de información ▲ *revisions to the estimated repricing dates of existing assets* actualizaciones a las fechas de recálculo de precios estimados de los activos existentes

revocation

= withdrawal

Revocation is the act of recalling or terminating a power of attorney or other authority given, cancelling a contract or withdrawing an offer.

revocación

▲ *revocation of a licence* revocación de una licencia ▲ *revocation of a permission* revocación de un permiso

revoke

= call in, withdraw

To revoke is to annul by recalling or rescinding.

revocar

▲ *revoke a licence* revocar una licencia ▲ *revoke a permission* revocar un permiso

revolving credit facility

A revolving credit facility is a loan facility that can be renewed as it is repaid so that it can be used repeatedly.

crédito auto renovable

▲ *a five-year revolving credit facility* un crédito auto renovable a cinco años ▲ *unsecured revolving credit facility* crédito auto renovable no asegurado

reward

≠ risk

A reward is a benefit resulting from something, often seen in connection with risk.

recompensa

▲ *economic rewards* recompensas económicas ▲ *substantially all the significant risks and rewards of ownership of financial assets* sustancialmente todos los riesgos y recompensas de la propiedad de activos financieros ▲ *the risks and rewards incidental to ownership of an asset* los riesgos y recompensas unidos a la propiedad de un activo ▲ *the significant risks and rewards of ownership of the contributed non-monetary assets* los riesgos y recompensas significativos de la propiedad de los activos no monetarios aportados ▲ *the transfer of risks and rewards* la transferencia de riesgos y recompensas

rework

Rework refers to production units that do not adhere to the required quality level and which are therefore repaired so that they may be sold as passable finished products.

reparación de productos defectuosos

= reparación de productos con defectos, reparación de unidades producidas con defectos

▲ *a system for the rework of produced units* un sistema de reparación de unidades producidas con defectos ▲ *estimated rework costs* costes de reparación de productos defectuosos ▲ *rework of previously produced units* reparación de unidades producidas anteriormente con defectos ▲ *the quality of the rework* la calidad de la reparación de productos defectuosos

RI

= residual income

RI is an abbreviation for residual income, which refers to profit after tax and interest less cost of capital (equity).

ingreso residual

▲ *a constant RI* un ingreso residual constante

right

A right is a title or interest in property, usually protected by law.

derecho

▲ *a legal right* un derecho legal ▲ *a temporary right* un derecho temporario ▲ *acquire a right* adquirir un derecho ▲ *exercise a right* ejercer un derecho ▲ *extinguish a right* extinguir un derecho ▲ *forfeit a right* perder un derecho ▲ *have a legal right registered* tener un derecho legal registrado ▲ *have an unconditional right to defer settlement of the liability for at least twelve months after the balance sheet date* tener un derecho incondicional a diferir el pago de la obligación durante al menos doce meses después de la fecha del balance ▲ *internally generated rights* derechos generados internamente ▲ *renew a right* renovar un derecho ▲ *rights and obligations under an insurance contract* derechos y obligaciones según un contrato de seguro ▲ *similar right* derecho similar ▲ *the term of the right* el término del derecho ▲ *waive a right* renunciar un derecho

right of amortisation UK, IAS/IFRS
= right of amortization US
The right of amortisation is the right to allocate the cost of intangible assets over their expected useful lives in a systematic way.
NOTE The term right of amortisation applies to intangible assets.
derecho de amortización
▲ *a tax-related right of amortisation* un derecho de amortización relacionado con impuestos ▲ *statutory limitations on the right of amortisation* limitaciones estatutarias en el derecho de amortización
⇛ right of depreciation

right of amortization US
= right of amortisation IAS/IFRS, UK
The right of amortization is the right to allocate the cost of intangible assets over their expected useful lives in a systematic way.
NOTE The term right of amortization applies to intangible assets.
derecho de amortización
▲ *a tax-related right of amortization* un derecho de amortización relacionado con impuesto ▲ *statutory limitations on the right of amortization* limitaciones estatutarias en el derecho de amortización
⇛ right of depreciation

right of depreciation
The right of depreciation is the right to allocate the cost of tangible assets over their expected useful lives in a systematic way.
NOTE The term right of depreciation applies to tangible assets.
derecho de amortización
▲ *a tax-related right of depreciation* un derecho de amortización relacionado con impuestos ▲ *statutory limitations on the right of depreciation* limitaciones estatutarias en el derecho de amortización
⇛ right of amortisation

right of first refusal
If a potential buyer has a right of first refusal to an item of property, the seller must first offer to sell the item to that buyer before offering it to someone else.
derecho de adquisición preferente
▲ *a mutual right of first refusal* un derecho de adquisición preferente mutual ▲ *repurchase right of first refusal at fair value* recomprar el derecho de adquisición preferente a valor razonable ▲ *retain the right of first refusal to repurchase the transferred asset at fair value* retener el derecho de adquisición preferente para recomprar el activo transferido a valor razonable

right of set-off UK, IAS/IFRS
= right of setoff US, right to set off
A right of set-off is a debtor's legal right, by contract or otherwise, to discharge or eliminate all or part of a debt owed to a creditor by applying against that debt an amount owed by the creditor to the debtor.
derecho de compensación
▲ *a financial asset subject to a legally enforceable right of set-off against a financial liability* un activo financiero sujeto a derecho de compensación legalmente exigible contra un pasivo financiero ▲ *a legal right of set-off* un derecho de compensación legal ▲ *establish the debtor's right of set-off* establecer el derecho de compensación de los deudores ▲ *exercise the right of set-off* ejercer el derecho de compensación ▲ *have a right of set-off* tener un derecho de compensación

right of setoff US
= right of set-off IAS/IFRS, UK, right to set off
A right of setoff is a debtor's legal right, by contract or otherwise, to discharge or eliminate all or part of a debt owed to a creditor by applying against that debt an amount owed by the creditor to the debtor.
derecho de compensación
▲ *a financial asset subject to a legally enforceable right of setoff against a financial liability* un activo financiero sujeto a un derecho de compensación legalmente exigible contra un

pasivo financiero ▲ *a legal right of setoff* un derecho de compensación legal ▲ *establish the debtor's right of setoff* establecer el derecho de compensación del deudor ▲ *exercise the right of setoff* ejercer el derecho de compensación ▲ *have a right of setoff* tener un derecho de compensación

right to deduct

The right to deduct gives taxpayers (both legal and natural persons), a right to deduct certain expenses when calculating taxable income.

derecho a deducir

▲ *full right to deduct* derecho a deducir la totalidad ▲ *grant a right to deduct* permitir un derecho a deducir ▲ *have a right to deduct* tener un derecho a deducir ▲ *lose one's right to deduct* perder su derecho a deducir ▲ *right to deduct an amount* derecho a deducir una cantidad ▲ *right to deduct an expense* derecho a deducir un gasto ▲ *right to deduct insurance premiums* derecho a deducir primas de seguro ▲ *right to deduct interest* derecho a deducir intereses ▲ *right to deduct losses* derecho a deducir pérdidas ▲ *right to deduct royalties* derecho a deducir royalties

rights issue

A rights issue is the issue of additional shares by a company to raise new capital by inviting existing shareholders to purchase (pre-empt) the new shares at a pre-determined price, typically at a discount, i.e. below market price. The offer is made in a certain proportion, e.g. one-for-one, meaning an amount equal to the amount of shares already held. The shareholders may choose to take up the rights offered to them, in this way maintaining the proportion of their shareholding in the company, or they may pass them, which means that the percentage of their shareholding will be reduced.

emisión de derechos

= derechos preferentes de suscripción

▲ *a bonus element in a rights issue to existing shareholders* una prima en una emisión de derechos a los accionistas existentes ▲ *a rights issue offered to all existing shareholders* una emisión de derechos ofrecida a todos los accionistas existentes

⇛ bonus issue, discount, issue of bonus shares, pre-emption right, scrip issue, subscription right

risk[1] *noun*

A risk is the probability that events may turn out differently than expected or predicted.

riesgo

▲ *a business risk* un riesgo empresarial ▲ *a commercial risk* un riesgo comercial ▲ *a financial risk* un riesgo financiero ▲ *a limited risk* un riesgo limitado ▲ *a reasonable adjustment to reflect risk and uncertainty* un ajuste razonable para reflejar el riesgo de incertidumbre ▲ *a special risk* un riesgo especial ▲ *an operational risk* un riesgo operacional ▲ *assess the enterprise's risks and returns* valorar los riesgos y rendimientos de la empresa ▲ *avoidance of a concentration of risks* prevención de una concentración de riesgos ▲ *biometric risks* riesgos biométricos ▲ *changes in risks* cambios en riesgos ▲ *expense risk* riesgo de gasto ▲ *foreseeable risks* riesgos previsibles ▲ *grouping according to risk* agrupamiento respecto al riesgo ▲ *hedge a risk* cubrir un riesgo ▲ *lapse risk* caducar el riesgo ▲ *manage a risk* gestionar un riesgo ▲ *measures to reduce risks* medidas para reducir los riesgos ▲ *minimise the risk of data corruption* minimizar el riesgo de datos erróneos ▲ *mitigate a risk* mitigar un riesgo ▲ *negligible risk* riesgo poco importante ▲ *persistency risk* riesgo persistente ▲ *risk management* gestión del riesgo ▲ *risk mapping* riesgo de duplicidad ▲ *significant risks* riesgos significativos ▲ *special risks apart from any generally occurring risks* riesgos especiales diferentes a cualesquiera riesgos que ocurren generalmente ▲ *substantially all the significant risks and rewards of ownership of financial assets* sustancialmente todos los riesgos y recompensas significativos de la propiedad de los activos financieros ▲ *the risk attaching to a leased asset* el riesgo unido a un activo arrendado ▲ *undertake risks* asumir riesgos

risk[2] *verb*

To risk something means to perform a specific action even though it may have unpleasant or harmful consequences, i.e. the outcome of the action is uncertain. An enterprise may e.g. invest in a specific asset in the hope of receiving a profit even though the investment may result in a loss.

arriesgarse

▲ *risk losing* arriesgarse a perder ▲ *risk suffering damage* arriesgarse a sufrir daños

risk assessment

A risk assessment is an evaluation of the probability of a certain outcome or occurrence of a given action or event, e.g. an investment, a purchase or a sale. The outcome may be success, failure, profit or loss and may, depending on the type of risk, be considered in more detail, and the occurrence or non-occurrence may be mathematically calculated on a quantitative basis.

evaluación del riesgo

▲ *carry out risk assessments* llevar a cabo evaluaciones del riesgo

risk capital

= venture capital

Risk capital refers to capital invested in a start-up or expanding enterprise by an outside party. On the one hand, such investments are usually very risky, but on the other, the investor may get high returns and may sometimes even take part in the management of the enterprise.

capital riesgo

= venture capital

▲ *provide risk capital* proveer capital riesgo ▲ *risk capital in the form of subordinated loan capital* capital riesgo en forma de préstamo subordinado

risk factor

A risk factor is a condition, element, event or action that will result in an undesired situation or adversely affect the outcome of something if realised or taking place.

factor de riesgo

▲ *a major risk factor* un factor de riesgo importante ▲ *financial risk factors* factores de riesgo financiero ▲ *identify risk factors* identificar los factores de riesgo ▲ *offset risk factors* compensar los factores de riesgo ▲ *significant risk factors* factores de riesgo significativos

risk management

Risk management refers to an enterprise's continuing and systematic process of identifying, assessing, controlling and reducing the various types of risks associated with its activities by means of specific practices and analyses. Risk management may involve taking out insurance or using derivative financial instruments.

gestión del riesgo

▲ *contribute to risk management* contribuir a la gestión del riesgo ▲ *describe one's risk management* describir su gestión del riesgo ▲ *evaluate one's risk management* evaluar su gestión del riesgo ▲ *financial risk management* gestión del riesgo financiero ▲ *improved risk management* gestión del riesgo mejorado ▲ *operational risk management* gestión del riesgo operacional ▲ *risk management process* proceso de gestión del riesgo ▲ *risk management strategy* estrategia de gestión del riesgo ▲ *the entity's financial risk management objectives and policies* los objetivos y políticas de la gestión del riesgo financiero de la entidad ▲ *the entity's risk management procedures and objectives* los procedimientos y objetivos de la gestión del riesgo de la entidad

risk management policy

A risk management policy of an enterprise is a course or principle of action for controlling and reducing the various types of risks associated with its activities, including foreign exchange risks and interest rate risks.

política de gestión del riesgo

▲ *adjust one's risk management policies* ajustar sus políticas de gestión del riesgo ▲ *disclose risk management policies* publicar las políticas de gestión del riesgo ▲ *financial risk management policies* políticas de gestión del riesgo financiero

risk management strategy

A risk management strategy of an enterprise is a method or long-term plan for controlling and reducing the various types of risks associated with its activities, including foreign exchange risks and interest rate risks.

estrategia de gestión del riesgo

▲ *describe one's risk management strategies* describir sus estrategias de gestión del riesgo ▲ *the documented risk management strategy for a particular hedging relationship* la estrategia de gestión del riesgo documentada para una relación de cobertura concreta ▲ *the originally documented risk management strategy* la estrategia de gestión del riesgo documentada originalmente

risk margin

The extra compensation charged by an insurer for assuming a risk is called the risk margin.

margen de riesgo

▲ *a low risk margin* un margen de riesgo bajo ▲ *an estimate of the risk margin* una estimación del margen de riesgo ▲ *calibrate the risk margin* valorar el margen de riesgo

⇛ service margin

risk premium

A risk premium constitutes an addition to the transaction price reflecting the risk exposure implied in the transaction. As such, it is part of the return receivable by the investor equal to the difference between the expected rate of return from the investment and the rate of return of a risk-free investment.

prima de riesgo

▲ *a change in the risk premium* un cambio en la prima de riesgo ▲ *demand a higher risk premium* exigir una prima de riesgo más alta ▲ *incorporate the appropriate risk premium* incorporar la prima de riesgo apropiada ▲ *reliable estimates of the risk premium* estimaciones fiables de la prima de riesgo ▲ *the one-year expected risk premium* la prima por riesgo anual esperada

⇛ nominal rate of return, real rate of return

risk profile

A risk profile refers to the level of risk associated with investment in specific assets in comparison with investment in other assets, i.e. a risk profile is a categorisation or class of risk.

perfil de riesgo

= perfil del riesgo

▲ *a conservative risk profile* un perfil de riesgo conservador ▲ *a high risk profile* un perfil de riesgo alto ▲ *a low risk profile* un perfil de riesgo bajo ▲ *a particularly volatile risk profile* un perfil de riesgo muy volátil ▲ *disclose the risk profile* publicar el perfil de riesgo ▲ *evaluation of the risk profile* evaluación del perfil del riesgo ▲ *increase one's risk profile* aumentar su perfil de riesgo ▲ *reduce one's risk profile* reducir su perfil de riesgo ▲ *sensitive risk profiles* perfiles de riesgo sensibles

ROCE

= return on capital employed

ROCE is the abbreviation for return on capital employed, defined as return before tax and financing charges divided by net assets (capital employed). ROCE shows the performance regardless of method of financing and is also referred to as return on invested capital (ROIC) or return on net assets (RONA).

RCE

= rendimiento del capital empleado, rentabilidad del capital empleado

▲ *calculate ROCE* calcular el RCE ▲ *computations of ROCE* cálculos del RCE ▲ *the calculation of ROCE* el cálculo del RCE

⇛ ROIC

ROE

= return on equity

ROE is the abbreviation for return on equity, which is a financial ratio defined as profit attributable to ordinary shareholders for a period as a percentage of average equity. This ratio measures the return on owners' investment in a company and is a variant of the Du-Pont analysis model where ROE is split into three components: profitability, activity and gearing.

coeficiente de rentabilidad de la acción

▲ *a negative ROE* un coeficiente de rentabilidad de la acción negativo ▲ *a positive ROE* un coeficiente de rentabilidad de la acción positivo ▲ *calculate ROE* calcular el coeficiente de rentabilidad de la acción ▲ *pre-tax ROE* coeficiente de rentabilidad de la acción antes de impuestos ▲ *the calculation of ROE* el cálculo del coeficiente de rentabilidad de la acción

ROI

= return on investment

ROI is the abbreviation for return on investment and a financial ratio defined as profit before interest and tax divided by capital employed (net assets). ROI is an indicator of the performance of an enterprise.

tasa de retorno de la inversión

= rentabilidad del capital invertido, rentabilidad de la inversión

▲ *calculate ROI* calcular la tasa de retorno de la inversión ▲ *the calculation of ROI* el cálculo de la tasa de retorno de la inversión

⇛ ROIC

ROIC

= return on invested capital

ROIC is the abbreviation for return on invested capital, a financial profitability and efficiency ratio defined as earnings before interest and tax excluding goodwill write-downs divided by average invested capital excluding goodwill. This ratio expresses a company's ability through its operating activities to generate a return on invested capital and is useful for comparison of the operating performance of various companies. In another version including goodwill, the ratio indicates the company's ability to create shareholder value.

RCI

= rendimiento del capital invertido, rendimiento de capital invertido

▲ *calculate ROIC* calcular el RCI ▲ *measure the return on capital as ROIC* medir la rentabilidad del capital como RCI

rolling budget

= continuous budget

A rolling budget is a budget that is continuously updated, typically on a monthly or quarterly basis, i.e. compared with the bookkeeping records for the previous month or quarter for adjustment if and as required, e.g. because of changed competition, technology development, changes in raw material prices or foreign exchange rates etc. Another monthly or quarterly budget period is added on expiry of the previous period ensuring that an enterprise will always have an updated budget for a minimum of 12 months.

presupuesto rotatorio

= presupuesto continuo

▲ *prepare a three-year rolling budget* preparar un presupuesto rotatorio de tres años

⇛ continual budgeting, master budget

rollover relief UK

Rollover relief means a deferral of capital gains tax on proceeds from sale of business assets in connection with the replacement of those assets.

deducción por reinversión

▲ *grant rollover relief* obtener la deducción por reinversión

RONA

RONA is the abbreviation for return on net assets, a financial ratio measuring profitability defined as operating profit as a percentage of net assets (i.e. assets less current liabilities).

rendimiento sobre activos netos

= RONA

▲ *calculate RONA* calcular el rendimiento sobre activos netos ▲ *RONA calculations* cálculos del rendimiento sobre los activos netos ▲ *the calculation of RONA* el cálculo del rendimiento sobre activos netos

RORWA

= return on risk-weighted assets

RORWA is the abbreviation for return on risk-weighted assets, a financial ratio related to banking defined as net profit divided by average risk-weighted assets. This ratio measures profitability and also shows a bank's ability to service loan capital.

utilidad neta/activos ponderados por riesgo

= utilidad neta por activos ponderados por riesgo

▲ *pre-tax RORWA* utilidad neta/activos ponderados por riesgo antes de impuestos

ROS

= operating margin, profit margin, return on sales

ROS is the abbreviation for return on sales, a profitability ratio also referred to as the profit margin which is calculated as operating profit divided by sales. The ratio shows the difference between the sales revenue from a product or service and the cost of producing or providing it.
margen de ventas
= rendimiento sobre ventas, rentabilidad sobre ventas, retorno sobre ventas
▲ *calculate ROS* calcular el margen de ventas ▲ *ROS calculations* cálculos del margen de ventas

royalty
Royalty is the payment of a sum for the right to use someone else's property or right, usually for the purpose of gain.
royalty
▲ *cash receipts from royalties* recibos de efectivo por royalties ▲ *the beneficial owner of the royalties* el beneficiario de los royalties ▲ *the 'relief from royalty' approach* el enfoque 'libre de royalty'

royalty income
Royalty income is the payment received by an enterprise for having granted someone else the right to use some of its property or rights.
ingreso de royalty
= ingreso por royalty
▲ *rental and royalty income* ingreso de royalty y arrendamiento

RPI UK
= Consumer Price Index US, CPI US, Retail Price Index UK
RPI is an abbreviation for Retail Price Index which is an index showing the rise and fall in prices of consumer goods and services sold in the retail market over a period of time.
IPC
= índice de precios al consumo
▲ *restate for the change in the RPI over the year* recalcular el cambio en el IPC durante el año ▲ *the increase in RPI* el aumento en el IPC

RRR
= hurdle rate, required rate of return
RRR is the abbreviation for required rate of return, i.e. the rate of return that is considered sufficiently profitable to encourage enterprises and other investors to engage in an investment.
tasa de rentabilidad exigida
▲ *calculation of the RRR* cálculo de la tasa de rentabilidad exigida

rules of procedure
The rules of procedure constitute a set of rules specifying how to conduct the business of the board of directors or another governing body of an enterprise.
normas de procedimiento
▲ *adopt rules of procedure* adoptar las normas de procedimiento

run-off profit/loss
In the context of insurance, the run-off profit/loss is the difference between (a) provisions for outstanding claims in the balance sheet at the beginning of the accounting period, adjusted for foreign currency translation differences and discounting effects, and (b) the total amount of claims paid in the accounting period and the part of provisions for outstanding claims attributable to claims that have taken place (but not been notified) in previous accounting periods.
beneficio/pérdida en la liquidación de una aseguradora
= beneficio o pérdida/run-off
▲ *run-off profit/loss for the year* beneficio/pérdida del ejercicio en la liquidación de una aseguradora ▲ *run-off profit/loss, net of reinsurance* beneficio/pérdida en la liquidación de una aseguradora, neto de reaseguro

run-off rate
= run-off margin
In the context of insurance, the run-off rate or margin is calculated as the run-off profit/loss in proportion to the net earned premiums and states the insurance company's amounts paid from provisions for outstanding claims compared with its income.
margen en la liquidación de una aseguradora
= margen run-off, tasa run-off
▲ *a high run-off rate* un margen en la liquidación de una aseguradora alto ▲ *the annualised run-off rate* el margen run-off anualizado

running cost
Running costs are the recurring expenses related to the fixed assets

of an enterprise such as servicing, maintenance, power and fuel costs.
coste corriente
▲ *reduce the running costs* reducir los costes corrientes ▲ *the day-to-day running costs* los costes corrientes del día a día
⇛ operating cost

running-in expense
Running-in expenses are expenses incurred by an enterprise to get an asset, typically productive equipment, ready for operation. Examples are expenses related to test runs and start-up.
gasto de puesta en funcionamiento
▲ *minimise the running-in expenses* minimizar los gastos de puesta en funcionamiento

S

sacrifice
To sacrifice something means to decide not to have it and give it up with the purpose of getting something else.
sacrificar
▲ *sacrifice a benefit* sacrificar un beneficio

safe harbor statement US
= forward-looking statement
A safe harbor statement is a cautionary statement made under the safe harbour rule of the US Securities and Exchange Commission and the Private Securities Litigation Reform Act 1995 by a reporting company. The cautionary statement is made with a view to protecting the company from legal action brought by users claiming to have been misled by the company's earnings releases and annual reports. Typically the outlook section may be subject to risks and uncertainties.
declaración de puerto seguro
= informe de previsión
▲ *describe in detail in the safe habor statement* describir detalladamente en la declaración de puerto seguro
⇛ forward-looking statement

safety margin *noun*
→ margin of safety

safety margin ratio
→ margin of safety ratio

salary
Salary is the fixed, periodic (usually monthly) payment, which an employee receives as consideration for services from the employer under an employment contract.
salario
▲ *adopt a projected salary approach* adoptar un enfoque del salario proyectado ▲ *cash salary and other employment benefits* salario en efectivo y otras prestaciones ▲ *current salary levels* niveles de salario actuales ▲ *failure to incorporate salary projections* fallo a la hora de incorporar las proyecciones salariales ▲ *final salary pension plans* planes de pensiones salariales finales ▲ *fixed salary* salario fijo ▲ *flat salary pension plans* planes de pensiones salariales planos ▲ *increases in benefits attributable to a salary increase* aumentos en prestaciones atribuibles a una subida salarial ▲ *projected salary levels* niveles de salario proyectado ▲ *salary and other expenditure incurred in securing copyrights* salario y otros gastos incurridos al asegurar los derechos de propiedad intelectual ▲ *the estimated final salary payable from the expected retirement date* el salario final estimado a pagar desde la fecha de jubilación esperada ▲ *the expected rates of salary increases* los tipos esperados de aumento salariales
⇛ remuneration, wages and salaries

sale
A sale is a contract under which a seller transfers or agrees to transfer the ownership of property or other assets to a buyer, usually for consideration in money.
venta
▲ *assets held for sale in the ordinary course of business* activos mantenidos para la venta en el curso ordinario del negocio ▲ *'bill and hold' sales* ventas 'facturación sin entrega' ▲ *profit on sale* beneficio en venta ▲ *regular way purchase or sale of a financial asset* compra o venta regular de un activo financiero ▲ *the entity's expected purchase, sale or usage requirements* la compra esperada de la entidad, venta o requisitos de uso ▲ *the estimated costs necessary to make the sale* los costes estimados necesarios para realizar la venta ▲ *the profit or loss resulting from an outright sale of the asset being leased* el resultado procedente de una venta al contado del activo que estaba arrendado ▲ *the sale of inventories after the balance sheet date* la venta de existencias después de la fecha del balance

sale and leaseback
Sale and leaseback is a method of financing applied by an en-

terprise to improve liquidity. The method consists in certain assets, e.g. property, being sold by the enterprise to a finance or leasing company and then later leased by the enterprise from the lessor, i.e. the company that bought the assets.

venta con arrendamiento financiero posterior

= leaseback

▲ *disposal by a sale and leaseback* enajenación por venta con arrendamiento financiero posterior ▲ *sale and leaseback transactions* transacciones de venta con arrendamiento financiero posterior

⇛ sale-and-leaseback transaction

sale of goods

Sale of goods refers to an enterprise's selling of goods to its customers, i.e. the enterprise's transfer of ownership of goods to its customers for a consideration. Sales of goods are recognised in the financial statements.

venta de bienes

▲ *hedge currency risks related to the sale of goods* cubrir los riesgos de cambio relacionados con la venta de bienes ▲ *hedge of the sale of goods* cobertura de la venta de bienes ▲ *income from the sale of goods* ingreso de la venta de bienes ▲ *profit on the sale of goods* beneficio en la venta de bienes ▲ *revenue from the sale of goods* ingreso de la venta de bienes ▲ *sale of goods after the balance sheet date* venta de bienes después de la fecha de balance

sale of shares

A sale of shares is a contract whereby the owner of shares transfers or agrees to transfer the ownership of the shares to a buyer for consideration.

venta de acciones

▲ *shares reserved for issue under options and contracts for the sale of shares* acciones reservadas para emitir de acuerdo con las opciones y los contratos para la venta de acciones ▲ *the profit on the sale of shares* el beneficio en la venta de acciones

sale-and-leaseback transaction

IAS/IFRS, UK

A sale-and-leaseback transaction is a transaction and contractual arrangement in which the owner of an asset sells that asset to a purchaser who then immediately leases back the same asset to the former owner. The lease involved may be an operating or a finance lease.

transacción de venta con arrendamiento posterior

= transacción de venta con arrendamiento financiero posterior, transacción de venta y leaseback

▲ *a sale-and-leaseback transaction resulting in a finance lease* una transacción de venta con arrendamiento posterior que resulta en un arrendamiento financiero ▲ *a sale-and-leaseback transaction resulting in an operating lease* una transacción de venta con arrendamiento financiero posterior que resulta en una operación de alquiler ▲ *the accounting treatment of a sale-and- leaseback transaction* el tratamiento contable de una transacción de venta con arrendamiento posterior ▲ *the terms of the sale-and-leaseback transactions* los términos de las transacciones de venta con arrendamiento posterior

SOURCE IAS 17

⇛ capital lease, finance lease, operating lease

sales

1 "Sales" refers to the volume of products sold in a given accounting period.

ventas

▲ *expected sales* ventas esperadas

2 In compounds, "sales" means "of" or "for" selling as in "sales development".

ventas

▲ *positive sales development* desarrollo de ventas positivo

3 = revenue IAS/IFRS, US, turnover UK

Sales represent the aggregated total of products and/or services sold by an enterprise over a given accounting period, typically a full fiscal year. Sales are recognized as the top line in the income statement.

ventas

▲ *achieve satisfactory sales* lograr ventas satisfactorias ▲ *sales of investment property between pools of assets* ventas de inversiones inmobiliarias entre titulizaciones de activos

sales activity

Sales activities refer to the activities related to selling goods or services commercially, including promotion, taking orders, receiving payment, delivery of goods and provision of services.

actividad de ventas

▲ *refocusing of sales activities* volver a centrarse en las actividades de ventas ▲ *restructuring of sales activities* reestructuración de las actividades de ventas

sales agreement

A sales agreement is an oral or written agreement whereby a seller transfers or agrees to transfer the ownership of property or other assets to a buyer, usually for consideration in money.

contrato de ventas

= acuerdo de ventas

▲ *a binding sales agreement* un contrato de ventas vinculante ▲ *be bound by a binding sales agreement* estar obligado por un contrato de ventas vinculante ▲ *enter into a sales agreement* firmar un contrato de ventas

sales amount

The sales amount is the amount of money that an enterprise will expect to receive as compensation on disposal of an asset.

importe de ventas

= importe de las ventas

▲ *purchase and sales amount* compra e importe de ventas ▲ *the expected sales amount* el importe esperado de las ventas

sales budget

A sales budget is a specification of the plans of an enterprise, indicated in either quantity units or cash, stipulating how the desired sales target can be met.

presupuesto de ventas

▲ *prepare a sales budget* preparar un presupuesto de ventas

sales contract

→ sales agreement

sales decline

A sales decline is a reduction in sales during a period compared to the sales of previous periods.

descenso de ventas

= descenso de las ventas, descenso en ventas

▲ *a sales decline of 6%* un descenso de ventas del 6%

sales director

A sales director is an executive director in charge of the enterprise's sales activities.

director de ventas

▲ *appoint a new sales director* nombrar un nuevo director de ventas ▲ *the former sales director* el anterior director de ventas ▲ *the incoming sales director* el director de ventas entrante ▲ *the retiring sales director* el directos de ventas saliente

sales discount US

= cash discount

A sales discount is a percentage reduction in an invoice amount given in return for cash or quick payment.

descuento por pronto pago

= descuento de pronto pago, descuento por pago al contado

▲ *allow a sales discount* permitir un descuento por pronto pago ▲ *receive a sales discount* obtener un descuento de pronto pago ▲ *sales discounts allowed* descuentos por pronto pago permitidos ▲ *sales discounts received* descuentos por pronto pago recibidos

sales expense

Sales expenses are expenses directly attributable to the sale of products or services, both fixed costs and variable costs such as expenses for storage, packaging, delivery, transportation and promotional materials.

gasto de ventas

= gasto por ventas

▲ *estimated sales expenses* gastos de ventas estimados

sales forecast

A sales forecast is an estimate of the sales volume of an enterprise (calculated in either quantities or cash) under given conditions for a specified period.

previsión de ventas

▲ *prepare a sales forecast* preparar una previsión de ventas

sales gain

= sales proceeds

A sales gain is the seller's profit on a sale of an asset that results as the difference between the sales price less sales costs and the seller's original purchase price of the asset.

beneficio de ventas

= beneficio en las ventas, beneficio en ventas

▲ *a sales gain of 4%* un beneficio de ventas del 4% ▲ *achieve a sales gain* lograr un beneficio en ventas

sales increase

= sales growth

A sales increase represents a relative increase in sales compared with a previous period, e.g. sales for a particular month on a year-over-year basis.

aumento de ventas

= aumento de las ventas, aumento en ventas

▲ *a sales increase of 4%* un aumento de las ventas del 4% ▲ *a stable sales increase* un aumento de ventas estable ▲ *expected sales increase* aumento de ventas esperado ▲ *realise a sales increase* realizar un aumento de ventas

⇛ year-over-year

sales ledger US

= debtors' ledger UK

≠ creditors' ledger UK, purchases ledger US

A sales ledger is a book or group of accounts containing the individual debtors' accounts, i.e. amounts owed by customers. The sales ledger records sales made on credit, amounts received and discounts given. Today, sales ledgers are usually stored on computer files that have replaced the old-time binders.

libro de ventas

= libro mayor de ventas

▲ *enter an amount in the sales ledger* anotar una cantidad en el libro de ventas

sales level

= level of sales

A sales level is a measure of the sales made by an enterprise in total, within a particular geographic area or business area. For instance, if total sales are high, the enterprise has a high sales level.

nivel de ventas

= nivel de las ventas

▲ *a higher sales level* un nivel de ventas más alto ▲ *a lower sales level* un nivel de ventas más bajo ▲ *maintain the sales level* mantener el nivel de las ventas

sales method

= completed-contract method

The sales method or completed-contract method is an accounting method whereby recognition of revenues and related costs in the profit and loss account takes place at the time of completion of the sale and delivery of the product or service in question. For long-term contracts, recognition is subject to completion of the contract and delivery of the product or service in question.

método de ventas

= método de contrato ejecutado

▲ *change from the sales method to the percentage of completion method* cambiar el método de ventas por el método del porcentaje de realización

sales mix UK, US

= sales-mix

The sales mix is the relative proportions or combinations of products that constitute total units sold or total sales in a period.

mezcla de ventas

▲ *a changed sales mix* una mezcla de ventas modificada ▲ *a constant sales mix* una mezcla de ventas constante

⇛ composite unit, sales mix variance

sales mix variance

= sales-mix variance

The sales mix variance is the difference between the budgeted amount for the actual sales mix and the budgeted amount for the budgeted sales mix.

desviación en ventas

= desviación de ventas, desviación en las ventas

▲ *calculate the sales mix variance* calcular la desviación en ventas ▲ *compute the sales mix variance* calcular la desviación en ventas ▲ *total sales mix variance* total desviación en ventas

⇛ sales mix

sales proceeds

Sales proceeds refer to the profit resulting from a sales transaction after deduction of all relevant costs in connection with the transaction.

importe neto de ventas

= ingresos por ventas

▲ *a rent rebate equalling most of the sales proceeds at the end of the lease* una desgravación equivalente a la mayoría del importe neto de ventas al final del arrendamiento ▲ *an excess of sales proceeds over the carrying amount* un exceso del importe neto de ventas sobre el valor contable ▲ *cost and sales proceeds* costes y ventas netas ▲ *purchase and sales proceeds* compras e ingresos netos de ventas ▲ *sales proceeds relating to treasury shares* importe neto de ventas relacionado con acciones propias

sales quantity variance
= sales-quantity variance
Sales quantity variance is the difference between actual sales and budgeted sales, determined in quantities multiplied by the budgeted sales mix and the budgeted sales prices.
desviación en cantidad de ventas
▲ *a favourable sales quantity variance* una desviación favorable en cantidad de ventas ▲ *total sales quantity variance* total desviación en cantidad de ventas
⇛ sales mix, sales volume variance

sales revenue
= revenue IAS/IFRS, US, sales US, turnover UK
Sales revenue is the total revenue generated by the sale of goods and services in connection with the operating activities of an enterprise.
ingresos de ventas
= facturación, ingresos de las ventas, ingresos en ventas, ingresos por ventas
▲ *the difference between the sales revenue and the cost of sale* la diferencia entre los ingresos de ventas y el coste de venta ▲ *the sales revenue recognised at the commencement of the lease term* los ingresos de ventas reconocidos al principio del arrendamiento
SOURCE IAS 17, paragraph 36 (paragraph 44 revised)

sales tax US
Sales tax is a levy imposed on goods and services which are purchased and paid by the end consumer. Sales tax is normally fixed as a percentage of the retail price of a product and in conformity with government laws.
impuesto de ventas
= impuesto por ventas
▲ *calculate sales tax* calcular el impuesto de ventas ▲ *filing a sales tax return* presentación de una devolución del impuesto de ventas ▲ *including sales tax* incluyendo el impuesto de ventas ▲ *sales taxes payable* impuesto de ventas a pagar ▲ *the rate of sales tax applicable* el tipo del impuesto de ventas aplicable
⇛ value added tax, VAT

sales to capital employed ratio UK
→ sales/invested capital

sales turnover
→ sales revenue

sales volume
= volume of sales
The sales volume of an enterprise is the total number of units of products or services sold by that enterprise during a given period.
volumen de ventas
▲ *a lower sales volume* un volumen de ventas menor ▲ *an increase in sales volume* un incremento en el volumen de ventas ▲ *estimated sales volume* volumen de ventas estimado

sales volume variance
= sales-volume variance
Sales volume variance is the difference between actual sales and budgeted sales, assuming that variables such as sales prices, variable and fixed costs are unchanged. This makes the sales volume variance a narrower concept than the sales quantity variance.
desviación en volumen de ventas
= desviación en el volumen de ventas
▲ *calculate the sales volume variance* calcular la desviación en volumen de ventas ▲ *the total sales volume variance* el total de la desviación en volumen de ventas
⇛ sales quantity variance, sales volume

sales-activity variance
A sales-activity variance is a variance that measures realised sales relative to the planned sales target and which is calculated as the actual number of units sold less the budgeted number of units multiplied by the budgeted contribution margin per unit.
desviación en ventas
= desviación en las ventas
▲ *a significant sales-activity variance* una desviación en ventas significativa ▲ *an insignificant sales-activity variance* una des-

viación en ventas insignificante ▲ *calculate the sales-activity variance* calcular la desviación en las ventas

sales-mix
→ sales mix

sales-mix variance
→ sales mix variance

sales-quantity variance
= sales quantity variance
Sales quantity variance is the difference between actual sales and budgeted sales, determined in quantities multiplied by the budgeted sales mix and the budgeted sales prices.
desviación en la cantidad de ventas
▲ *a favourable sales-quantity variance* una desviación favorable en la cantidad de ventas ▲ *total sales-quantity variance* total desviación en la cantidad de ventas

sales-volume variance
= sales volume variance
Sales-volume variance is the difference between actual sales and budgeted sales, assuming that variables such as sales prices, variable and fixed costs are unchanged. This makes the sales volume variance a narrower concept than the sales quantity variance.
desviación en las ventas
= desviación en el volumen de ventas
▲ *provide additional information about the sales-volume variance* ofrecer información adicional sobre la desviación en las ventas

sales/capital employed
→ sales/invested capital

sales/invested capital
= sales to capital employed ratio UK, sales/capital employed UK
Sales/invested capital is a financial ratio measuring an enterprise's efficiency in employing its invested capital as well as its capital intensity. Invested capital may include or exclude goodwill.
ventas por capital invertido
▲ *average annual change in sales/invested capital* cambio anual medio en ventas por capital invertido

salvage value US
= residual value IAS/IFRS, UK, scrap value UK
Salvage value is the estimated recoverable value of a non-current asset on disposal after depreciation or amortisation at the end of its useful life.
valor residual
▲ *exceed the estimated salvage value* exceder el valor residual estimado

sampling unit
A sampling unit is an individual item in a population.
unidad de muestreo
▲ *a primary sampling unit* una unidad de muestreo primaria ▲ *the choice of sampling unit* la elección de la unidad de muestreo ▲ *the most appropriate sampling unit* la unidad de muestreo más adecuada
⇛ audit sampling, population

Sarbanes-Oxley Act US
= SOX US
The Sarbanes-Oxley Act of 2002 was enacted in the US after a series of corporate financial scandals, and its objective is to strengthen corporate governance, restore investor confidence and to combat corporate and accounting fraud. The Act imposes strict requirements on both US and foreign reporting companies listed on US stock exchanges concerning internal controls and procedures for financial reporting, corporate responsibility, codes of ethics and auditor independence. Under the Act a Public Company Oversight Board has been set up, which is responsible for registering, inspecting and disciplining accounting firms.
Ley Sarbanes-Oxley
▲ *be subject to the rules promulgated under the US Sarbanes-Oxley Act of 2002* estar sujeto a las normas promulgadas de acuerdo con la Ley Sarbanes-Oxley de 2002 ▲ *comply with the provisions of the Sarbanes-Oxley Act* cumplir con las estipulaciones de la Ley Sarbanes-Oxley ▲ *in accordance with the Sarbanes-Oxley Act* de acuerdo con la Ley Sarbanes-Oxley ▲ *pursuant to Section 302 of the Sarbanes-Oxley Act* en virtud de la Sección 302 de la Ley Sarbanes-Oxley ▲ *section 404 of the Sarbanes-Oxley Act 2002* sección 404 de la Ley Sarbanes-Oxley 2002
⇛ corporate governance

satisfactory
If something is satisfactory, it is good enough for a particular purpose or in a particular situation and lives up to expectations.
satisfactorio
▲ *a satisfactory development* un desarrollo satisfactorio ▲ *provide a satisfactory basis* ofrecer una base satisfactoria

saving
Saving is an amount of money or number of items that have not been spent or used.
ahorro
▲ *a saving of 5%* un ahorro del 5% ▲ *close a facility to achieve productivity improvements or other cost savings* cerrar una instalación para conseguir aumentos de productividad u otros ahorros de costes ▲ *cost savings* ahorros de costes

scalable US
Something that is scalable has been changed or adjusted according to a standard or to a certain degree.
escalable
▲ *scalable audit approach* enfoque de auditoría escalable

scale-back
A scale-back is a reduction, often made proportionately. In a share buy-back, a scale-back is the proportionate reduction in the amount of shares bought by the company from shareholders in a situation where the company wants to buy shares for a defined monetary value. The company will then scale back the amount of shares tendered by each shareholder on a pro-rata basis.
descenso paulatino
▲ *a scale-back of production* un descenso paulatino de producción

scarce resource
If there is not enough of a resource available, it is referred to as a scarce resource.
recurso escaso
▲ *constrained by a scarce resource* constreñido por un recurso escaso
⇛ limiting factor

schedule
A schedule is a list or inventory of details, often as an explanatory supplement to a deed, will, tax form etc.
anexo
▲ *schedule 1 of the Danish Financial Statements Act* anexo 1 de la Ley danesa de Estados Financieros ▲ *schedule A of the contract* anexo A del contrato
⇛ appendix

scope
= application
Scope means a range of operation, the extent of an activity or an area in which something acts or operates or has power or control.
ámbito
= alcance
▲ *exclusions from the scope of a standard* exclusiones del ámbito de una norma ▲ *intangible assets that are within the scope of another standard* activos intangibles que están dentro del ámbito de otra norma ▲ *leases that are within the scope of IAS 17* arrendamientos que están dentro del ámbito de la NIC 17 ▲ *the scope of the act* el ámbito de la ley ▲ *the scope of the audit* el ámbito de la auditoría ▲ *the scope of the bill* el alcance del proyecto de ley ▲ *the scope of the business undertaken by the entity* el ámbito del negocio emprendido por la entidad

scorekeeping US
Scorekeeping is the accumulation and classification of data.
ordenación de los datos
▲ *budget scorekeeping* ordenación de los datos del presupuesto ▲ *financial scorekeeping* ordenación de los datos financieros

scrap
Scrap is an output that has a limited or no sales value to an enterprise. Scrap constitutes the residual material that remains after a product has been manufactured.
chatarra
▲ *ferrous scrap* chatarra ferrosa ▲ *non-ferrous scrap* chatarra no ferrosa ▲ *remelting of scrap* refundición de chatarra ▲ *sales of waste and scrap materials* venta de residuos y chatarra ▲ *wholesale trade services of waste and scrap* servicios de contratación al por mayor de residuos y chatarra

scrap value UK
= residual value IAS/IFRS, UK, salvage value US

The scrap value is the estimated recoverable value or net realisable value of a fixed asset on disposal after depreciation or amortisation at the end of its useful life.

valor residual

▲ *sell an asset for its scrap value* vender un activo por su valor residual

scrip

In the context of securities, scrip is a subscription receipt, i.e. a temporary certificate issued by a company representing a share of stock in the company.

resguardo provisional

▲ *issue a scrip* emitir un resguardo provisional

⇛ scrip dividend, scrip issue

scrip dividend UK

= share dividend UK, stock dividend US

A scrip dividend is a dividend distributed by way of giving investors scrip, i.e. certificates evidencing ownership of shares or bonds, rather than paying them a share of profit.

dividendo abonado con pagaré

▲ *offer a scrip dividend* ofrecer un dividendo abonado con pagaré ▲ *receive a scrip dividend instead of cash* recibir un dividendo abonado con pagaré en vez de efectivo

⇛ scrip

scrip issue

= bonus issue, capitalisation issue UK, capitalization issue US

A scrip issue is the act of increasing a company's issued capital by issuing additional share certificates for free to its existing shareholders in proportion to their shareholdings, in this way converting accumulated reserves into issued share capital. However, no additional capital is contributed and total equity remains the same; the effect is a reduction of the share price that increases the liquidity of the company's shares in the stock market.

emisión de acciones liberadas

= emisión de acciones gratuitas

▲ *adjusted for scrip issue* ajustado a la emisión de acciones liberadas ▲ *an offer of a scrip issue in lieu of cash dividend* una oferta de una emisión de acciones liberadas en lugar de un dividendo monetario ▲ *receive the dividend by way of scrip issue* recibir el dividendo por medio de una emisión de acciones liberadas

⇛ bonus share, rights issue, scrip

seasonal fluctuation

Seasonal fluctuations are variations that are caused by seasonal influences.

fluctuación estacional

▲ *considerable seasonal fluctuations* fluctuaciones estacionales considerables

SEC US

= Securities and Exchange Commission US

The SEC is an abbreviation for the Securities and Exchange Commission (SEC) is a US federal government agency set up in 1934 that monitors, regulates and supervises US stock exchanges and US as well as foreign companies listed on the stock exchanges. Such companies must register with the SEC, follow SEC regulations and submit regular financial information, e.g. interim and annual reports, to the agency.

SEC

▲ *SEC filing* emisión de un informe de la SEC

secondary activity

Secondary activities are ordinary, recurring activities outside the primary activities of an enterprise such as financial activities, e.g. investments. Operating profit/loss, i.e. the profit/loss on primary activities, together with the profit/loss on secondary activities constitute the profit/loss on ordinary activities.

actividad secundaria

▲ *disposal of secondary activities* enajenación de las actividades secuntarias ▲ *irrespective of any secondary activity* independientemente de cualquier actividad secundaria

⇛ operating profit, profit or loss on ordinary activities

secret reserve

= hidden reserve

Secret reserves are hidden reserves that will not appear

from the balance sheet, i.e. resources that an enterprise accumulates e.g. by recognising assets at understated values. The fair value method of accounting assets seeks to avoid this by measuring assets at current market value.

reserva secreta

= reserva oculta

▲ *constitute a secret reserve* constituir una reserva secreta ▲ *create secret reserves* crear reservas secretas

⇛ fair value method

sector

= industry

A sector comprises all enterprises in a particular area of activity or industry.

sector

▲ *average length of service in the sector* duración media del servicio en el sector ▲ *in the same sector* en el mismo sector ▲ *public sector business entities* entidades empresariales del sector público ▲ *the life expectancy for the sector* la esperanza de vida del sector ▲ *the prospects of the sector* las expectativas del sector ▲ *work in a sector* trabajar en un sector

secure

To secure is to ensure that something will happen or be achieved. To secure a debt means to provide a guarantee that it will be repaid.

asegurar

= garantizar

▲ *secure a high quality* asegurar una calidad alta

Securities and Exchange Commission US

= SEC US

The Securities and Exchange Commission (SEC) is a US federal government agency set up in 1934 that monitors, regulates and supervises US stock exchanges and US as well as foreign companies listed on the stock exchanges. Such companies must register with the SEC, follow SEC regulations and submit regular financial information, e.g. interim and annual reports, to the agency.

Securities and Exchange Commission

NOTE The Spanish equivalent body is the 'Comisión Nacional del Mercado de Valores'.

▲ *the chairman of the Securities and Exchange Commission* el presidente de la Securities and Exchange Commission ▲ *the mission of the Securities and Exchange Commission* la misión de la Securities and Exchange Commission ▲ *the rules issued by the Securities and Exchange Commission* las normas emitidas por la Securities and Exchange Commission

Securities and Investment Board UK

→ Financial Services Authority

securities broker UK

Securities brokers are intermediaries acting as agents for investors in securities transactions. Their function is to match buyers with sellers, a function for which they are paid brokerage commission. Contrary to dealers, brokers do not own the securities they trade.

NOTE If relevant, a securities broker may add to his name "Member of the [name] Stock Exchange".

agente de cambio y bolsa

= broker, operador por cuenta ajena en el mercado financiero

▲ *carry on business as a securities broker* llevar a cabo un negocio como un agente de cambio y bolsa ▲ *licensed securities broker* un agente de cambio y bolsa con licencia

⇛ investment company

securities clearing business

Securities clearing business is the clearing and/or settlement of securities transactions carried out on behalf of a clearing participant. This includes being a party to transactions or otherwise securing the completion of the transactions.

negocio de compraventa de títulos

▲ *facilitate the securities clearing business* facilitar el negocio de compraventa de títulos ▲ *in connection with the securities clearing business* en conexión con el negocio de compraventa de títulos

securities clearing house

A securities clearing house is an organisation that carries out computerised clearing or settlement of securities transactions on behalf of its members.

agencia de compraventa de títulos

▲ *a participant in a securities clearing house* un participante en una agencia de compraventa de títulos

⇛ clearing member

securities dealer

Securities dealers link buyers and sellers in the purchase and sale of securities at a given price. Contrary to securities brokers, dealers act as principals, buying and selling on their own account. Therefore, they hold inventories of securities and make their living by earning the spread between the bid price and the asked price.

agente de cambio y bolsa

= operador por cuenta propia en el mercado financiero

▲ *carry out an inspection visit at the place of business of a securities dealer* llevar a cabo una visita de inspección al lugar de trabajo de un agente de cambio y bolsa ▲ *deprive a securities dealer of his right to keep omnibus accounts* quitar a un agente de cambio y bolsa su derecho a mantener cuentas combinadas

securities market

A securities market is a market in which shares, bonds and other securities are traded.

mercado de títulos

▲ *a fair and transparent securities market* un mercado de títulos fiable y transparente ▲ *enterprises that are in the process of issuing equity or debt securities in public securities markets* empresas que están en proceso de emisión de títulos de patrimonio o deuda en un mercado de títulos público

securities trading

Securities trading is the activity of buying and selling securities, such as shares and bonds, carried out by market makers on their own account or, by dealers or other intermediaries, for the account of others. Trading takes place in the secondary market for securities in circulation and in the primary market for new issues. The trading platform may be the stock exchange trading floor for physical trading or an electronic trading platform for trading online.

compraventa de títulos

= compra venta de los títulos

▲ *Danish Securities Trading Act* Ley danesa de Compraventa de Títulos ▲ *earnings from securities trading* beneficios por compraventa de títulos

securitisation UK, IAS/IFRS

= securitization US

Securitisation refers to a way of obtaining loan financing that involves the creation and issuance by an enterprise of tradeable loan notes or commercial papers on the basis of a pool of non-tradeable assets, such as mortgages, various types of receivables and stocks. This financing technique is an alternative to raising bank loans. Securitisation takes place by a transfer against cash of the assets from the enterprise (the originator) to a special purpose vehicle (the issuer) that finances the transfer by the issue of new debt in the form of tradeable loan notes or commercial paper.

titulización

▲ *a securitisation position* una posición de titulización ▲ *synthetic securitisation exposures* exposiciones sintéticas a la titulización ▲ *the credit quality of a position in a securitisation* la calidad del crédito de una posición en una titulización ▲ *the risks and risk reductions arising from credit institutions' securitisation activities* los riesgos y las reducciones de riesgo procedentes de las actividades de titulización de las instituciones de crédito ▲ *traditional securitisation* titulización tradicional

SOURCE FRS 5, D1-2

securitization US

= securitisation UK, IAS/IFRS

Securitization refers to a way of obtaining loan financing that involves the creation and issuance by an enterprise of tradable loan notes or commercial paper on the basis of a pool of non-tradable assets, such as mortgages, various types of receivables and stocks. This financing technique is an alternative to raising bank loans. Securitization takes place by a transfer against cash of the assets from the enterprise (the originator) to a special purpose vehicle (the issuer) that finances the transfer by the issue of new debt in the form of tradable loan notes or commercial paper.

titulización

▲ *a securitization position* una posición de titulización ▲ *synthetic securitization exposures* exposiciones al riesgo de titulización sintéticas ▲ *the credit quality of a position in a securitization* la calidad del crédito de una posición en una titulización ▲ *the risks and risk reductions arising from credit institutions' securitization activities* los riesgos y las reducciones de riesgo que surgen procedentes de las actividades de titulización de las instituciones de crédito ▲ *traditional securitization* titulización tradicional

security[1] *noun* <a, the, securities>

= financial instrument, instrument

A security is a negotiable claim against the assets or activities of an enterprise in the form of a financial instrument representing a direct ownership right such as a share, an indirect ownership right such as an option, a subscription right or a warrant, or a creditor right such as a bond or a debenture. Equity securities are typically issued by companies and debt securities by enterprises and governmental bodies.

título

▲ *a portfolio of securities* una cartera de títulos ▲ *a securities lending agreement* un acuerdo de cesión de títulos ▲ *debt securities and other fixed-income securities* títulos de deuda y otros títulos de renta fija ▲ *gains less losses arising from dealing securities* beneficios menos pérdidas resultantes de títulos contratados ▲ *gains less losses arising from investment securities* beneficios menos pérdidas resultantes de títulos de inversión ▲ *holders of securities admitted to trading on a regulated market* titulares de valores admitidos a cotización en un mercado regulado ▲ *mortgage-backed securities* títulos respaldados por hipotecas

⇛ bearer security, debt and equity security, financial instrument, registered security

security[2] *noun* <no indefinite article, the, no plural>

1 Security is provided when a person, a bank or other enterprise (the guarantor) gives it for a third party (the principal debtor) in order to assure that the obligations of that third party will be met. Security is typically provided in the form of a guarantee whereby the guarantor assumes liability for the obligations of the debtor in case of default, or in the form of collateral.

seguridad

= garantía

▲ *collateral security provided for Danmarks Nationalbank* seguridad secundaria ofrecida por el Banco Nacional danés ▲ *provide security* proporcionar seguridad

⇛ collateral, fixed charge, floating charge, mortgage

2 Security refers to one or several assets pledged or mortgaged to ensure that a lender (the pledgee or mortgagee) can be satisfied, i.e. paid in full, in case of default by the borrower (the pledgor or mortgagor).

aval

= afianzamiento

▲ *grant security on assets* avalar activos

⇛ collateral, fixed charge, floating charge, mortgage

3 Security is an asset pledged or mortgaged against which a creditor has a legal claim in the event that he is not paid.

fianza

= aval

▲ *acquire shares as security* adquirir acciones como aval ▲ *long-term security* fianza a largo plazo ▲ *property, plant and equipment pledged as security for liabilities* edificios, instalaciones y equipos como fianza de los pasivos ▲ *provide security* aportar aval ▲ *the carrying amounts of intangible assets pledged as security for liabilities* los valores contables de los activos intangibles pignorados como fianza de los pasivos

⇛ collateral, fixed charge, floating charge, mortgage

segment[1] *noun*

A segment is one of several parts, units or sections that together constitute a whole, such as a specific group of customers, a product, line of business or a geographical area.

segmento

▲ *a geographical segment* un segmento geográfico ▲ *a sale of a segment* una venta de un segmento ▲ *allocate costs to segments* asignar costes a los segmentos ▲ *attribute costs to segments* atribuir costes a los segmentos ▲ *disclosure requirements for reporting impairment losses by segment* publicar condiciones para informar de las pérdidas por deterioro por segmento ▲ *goodwill that is directly attributable to a segment* fondo de comercio que se atribuye directamente a un segmento ▲ *the segment in which the non-current asset or disposal group is presented* el segmento en el que el activo no corriente o grupo disponible se presenta

segment[2] *verb* >

To segment means to divide something into separate parts, e.g. an enterprise's revenue by geographical areas or business lines.

segmentar

▲ *to segment a market* segmentar un mercado

segment asset

Segment assets are assets that are used by an operating segment of an enterprise in its operations, and which can be attributed or allocated to that segment.

activo del segmento

▲ *acquire segment assets* adquirir activos del segmento ▲ *depreciation and amortisation of segment assets* depreciación y amortización de los activos del segmento ▲ *measurement of segment assets* medición de los activos del segmento ▲ *the carrying amount of segment assets* el valor contable de los activos del segmento

SOURCE IAS 14, paragraph 16

segment expense

Segment expenses are expenses incurred by an operating segment of an enterprise which relate to its operations and arise from inter-segmental transactions or transactions with external customers, and that can be attributed or allocated to that segment.

gasto del segmento

▲ *cash segment expenses* gastos del segmento monetario ▲ *non-cash segment expenses* gastos del segmento no monetario ▲ *the nature and amount of significant single elements of segment expenses* la naturaleza y cuantía de elementos independientes significativos de gastos del segmento

SOURCE IAS 14, paragraph 16

segment income

1 Segment income is the income that can be attributed or allocated to a specific operating segment of an enterprise as recognised in the income statement of that enterprise, and generated either from inter-segmental transactions or transactions with external customers.

ingreso por segmentos

▲ *other segment income* otros ingresos por segmentos ▲ *segment income before minority interests* ingreso por segmentos antes de intereses minoritarios

2 Segment income is the income from operations before interest and tax that can be attributed or allocated to a specific operating segment of an enterprise as recognised in the income statement of that enterprise, and generated either from inter-segmental transactions or transactions with external customers.

ingreso del segmento

▲ *total segment income* total ingreso del segmento

segment information

Segment information is information in the financial statements about one or more segments, such as business, customer, product or geographical segments. The information may relate to the size, revenue, growth possibilities, etc. of the segments.

información por segmentos

▲ *changes in accounting policies that affect segment information* cambios en las políticas contables que afectan a la información por segmentos ▲ *enhanced segment information* información por segmentos mejorada ▲ *report segment information* publicar la información por segmentos

segment item

An accounting item that relates to the assets, liabilities, re-

venue or expenses of a segment is called a segment item.
partida de los segmentos

segment liability
Segment liabilities constitute the part of a segment's liabilities which have arisen from its operating activities and which can be directly and reasonably related or distributed to the segment, however, not including tax liabilities.
pasivo por segmento
▲ *carrying amount of segment liabilities* valor contable de los pasivos por segmento ▲ *segment liabilities of an entity acquired in a business combination* pasivos por segmento de una entidad adquirida en una combinación de negocios

segment manager IAS/IFRS
A person or group of persons who have the overall responsibility for the financial results, forecasts, operating activities and plans for an operating segment is called segment manager.
gestor de segmento
= administrador de segmento
SOURCE IFRS 8, paragraph 9

segment profit or loss IAS/IFRS
Segment profit or loss refer to the results before adjustments to minority interests generated by a segment of an enterprise resulting after deducting segment expense from segment revenue, i.e. the operating profits generated by the segment.
resultado de los segmentos
= ganancia o pérdida de los segmentos
▲ *amounts allocated to reported segment profit or loss* cantidades asignadas al resultado de los segmentos anotado ▲ *determine reported segment profit or loss* determinar el resultado de los segmentos anotado ▲ *included in the measure of segment profit or loss* incluido en la cuantía del resultado de los segmentos ▲ *information about reported segment profit or loss* información sobre el resultado de los segmentos anotado ▲ *the measurement of segment profit or loss* la valoración del resultado de los segmentos
SOURCE IFRS 8

segment reporting
Segment reporting is the preparation and disclosure of separate financial data by operating segments of an enterprise, typically distributed on geographical or business segments.
información por segmentos
▲ *the accounting policies for segment reporting* las políticas contables para la información por segmentos

segment reporting rule
Segment reporting rules are the requirements determining the disclosure of reportable segments in financial reporting under generally accepted accounting principles and that are typically laid down in accounting standards.
norma de información por segmentos
▲ *comply with the segment reporting rules* cumplir con las normas de información por segmentos ▲ *introduce new segment reporting rules* introducir nuevas normas de información por segmentos
⇛ segment reporting

segment result
Segment results refer to the results before adjustments to minority interests generated by a segment of an enterprise resulting after deducting segment expense from segment revenue, i.e. the operating profits generated by the segment.
resultado del segmento
= resultado por segmento
▲ *restate segment results in prior periods presented in the financial statements* reformular los resultados del segmento en periodos anteriores presentados en los estados financieros ▲ *segment result by business segment* resultado del segmento por segmentos del negocio ▲ *segment result by location of assets* resultado del segmento por localización de activos ▲ *segment result by location of customers* resultado por segmentos por localización de clientes ▲ *segment result for each reportable segment* resultado del segmento por cada segmento de información ▲ *segment result on ordinary activities before financials* resultado por segmentos de actividades ordinarias antes de resultados financieros ▲ *the segment result from continuing operations* el resultado por segmentos de las operaciones continuas ▲ *the segment re-*

sult from discontinued operations el resultado del segmento procedente de las operaciones interrumpidas
SOURCE IAS 14, paragraph 16

segment revenue
Segment revenue is the revenue that can be attributed or allocated to a specific operating segment of an enterprise as recognised in the income statement of that enterprise, and generated either from inter-segmental transactions or transactions with external customers.
ingresos por segmentos
NOTE Always plural in Spanish accounting texts.
▲ *reconcile segment revenue to entity revenue from external customers* conciliar ingresos por segmentos con los ingresos de la entidad provenientes de clientes externos ▲ *segment revenue from external customers* ingresos por segmentos de clientes externos ▲ *segment revenue from transactions with other segments* ingresos por segmentos procedentes de transacciones con otros segmentos ▲ *the majority of the segment revenue* la mayoría de los ingresos por segmentos ▲ *the nature and amount of significant single elements of segment revenue* la naturaleza y cuantía de los elementos independientes significativos de los ingresos por segmentos
SOURCE IAS 14, paragraph 16

segmental accounts UK
Segmental accounts are accounts that show the results for different segments of the enterprise, for instance for customer groups or geographical areas.
cuentas por segmento
▲ *prepare segmental accounts* preparar las cuentas por segmento ▲ *publish segmental accounts* publicar las cuentas por segmento

segmental analysis
A segmental analysis is an analysis of the revenues, profits and assets of the reportable segments of an enterprise, disclosed by geographical area or line of business.
análisis por segmentos
▲ *carry out a segmental analysis* llevar a cabo un análisis por segmentos ▲ *complete a segment analysis* completar un análisis por segmentos

segmental financial statements
US, IAS/IFRS
Segmental financial statements are statements that show the results for different segments of the enterprise, for instance for customer groups or geographical areas.
estados financieros por segmentos
▲ *prepare segmental financial statements* preparar los estados financieros por segmentos ▲ *publish segmental financial statements* publicar los estados financieros por segmentos

segmental information
→ segment information

segmental reporting
→ segment reporting

segmental statement
A segmental statement is an assessment or outline of the size of different segments.
extracto por segmentos
▲ *prepare a segmental statement* preparar un extracto por segmentos

segmentation
Segmentation is the process whereby a large segment is divided into smaller segments on the basis of segment variables.
segmentación
▲ *new bases of segmentation* nuevas bases de segmentación ▲ *primary segmentation* segmentación primaria ▲ *reassessment of the segmentation* revalorización de la segmentación ▲ *secondary segmentation* segmentación secundaria ▲ *segmentation of the net revenue* segmentación de los ingresos netos

sell
To sell means to transfer the ownership of property to a new owner, the buyer, usually against the payment of money.
vender
▲ *be compelled to sell immediately* verse forzado a vender inmediatamente ▲ *be forced to sell* estar obligado a vender ▲ *contracts to buy or sell non-financial items* contratos para comprar o vender partidas no financieras ▲ *enter into binding agreements to sell the assets* firmar acuerdos vinculantes para vender los activos ▲ *sell goods and render services* vender bienes y prestar

servicios ▲ *sell goods in other countries* vender bienes en otros países ▲ *sell the output on an active market* vender el producto en un mercado activo ▲ *the ability to buy or sell a commodity contract for cash* la capacidad para comprar o vender un contrato de materias primas en efectivo ▲ *the practical ability to sell the transferred asset* la capacidad práctica para vender el activo transferido ▲ *the right to sell ordinary shares at a specified price for a given period* el derecho a vender acciones ordinarias a un precio especificado para un periodo concreto

sell off
= dispose of
≠ acquire
To sell off is to divest fixed assets, especially securities, typically quickly and under pressure.
liquidar
▲ *sell off an enterprise* liquidar una empresa ▲ *sell off part of the loan portfolio* liquidar parte de la cartera de préstamos

selling cost UK, IAS/IFRS
= selling expense US
Selling costs are the costs attributable to the sale and distribution of a product or service. Examples include marketing costs, commission to sales representatives and exhibition costs.
coste de venta
▲ *direct selling costs* costes de venta directos ▲ *estimated selling costs* costes de venta estimados ▲ *take selling costs to the income statement* llevar los costes de venta al estado de resultados
⇛ distribution cost

selling expense US
= selling cost UK, IAS/IFRS
Selling expenses are the expenses attributable to the sale and distribution of a product or service. Examples include marketing expenses, commission to sales representatives and exhibition expenses.
gasto de venta
▲ *direct selling expenses* gastos de venta directos ▲ *estimated selling expenses* gastos de venta previstos ▲ *take selling expenses to the income statement* llevar los gastos de venta al estado de resultados

selling price
1 The selling price of an asset is the price obtainable from the sale of that asset at the balance sheet date. The selling price of a liability is the price payable to settle that liability at the balance sheet date.
precio de venta
▲ *an approximate selling price* un precio de venta aproximado
2 = sales amount, sales price
The selling price is the price at which a product or a service is exchanged between a buyer and a seller.
precio de compraventa
▲ *actual selling price* precio de compraventa actual ▲ *selling price of treasury shares* precio de compraventa de acciones propias ▲ *the estimated selling price for the assets of the cash-generating unit* el precio de compraventa estimado de los activos de la unidad generadora de efectivo ▲ *the estimated selling price in the ordinary course of business* el precio de compraventa estimado en el curso ordinario del negocio ▲ *the selling prices of finished goods* los precios de compraventa de productos terminados
3 = offer price
The selling price is the price obtained by the seller when he sells shares, bonds, futures, options, warrants etc.
precio de venta
▲ *the most recently quoted selling price* el precio de venta fijado más recientemente ▲ *the selling price of the instrument to be tendered* el precio de venta del instrumento a subastar

selling profit
= proceeds
The selling profit is the proceeds or gain, usually in the form of cash, obtained in connection with a sales transaction resulting as the difference between the costs incurred by the seller and the selling price obtained on the sale.
beneficio por ventas
▲ *recognise the selling profit* reconocer el beneficio por ventas ▲ *selling profit in excess of cost* beneficio por ventas por encima del coste

selling rate
The selling rate is the price obtained by the seller when he sells foreign currency.

tipo de cambio de venta
▲ *most recently quoted selling rate* tipo de cambio de venta cotizado más recientemente ▲ *official selling rate* tipo de cambio de venta oficial

selling-price variance
= sales price variance
Selling-price variance is the change in revenue because of differences between budgeted or standard prices and the actual sales prices.
desviación en el precio de venta
▲ *an adverse selling-price variance* una desviación adversa en el precio de venta ▲ *average selling-price variance* desviación media en el precio de venta

semi-annual
= biannual, semiannual
Events which are semi-annual, occur or happen twice a year, i.e. every six months.
semestral
= medio año
▲ *carry out semi-annual quality audits* llevar a cabo auditorías semestrales ▲ *semi-annual investor events* inversiones semestrales
⇛ semiannual

semi-fixed cost
= mixed cost UK, US
≠ semi-variable cost UK, US
Semi-fixed costs are costs that have a fixed and a variable element. Telephone costs e.g. have the fixed element of rental and the variable element of number of calls.
coste semi-fijo
≠ coste semi-variable
▲ *a high proportion of semi-fixed costs* una proporción elevada de costes semi-fijos

semi-manufacture
= semi-manufactured product, semi-product
A semi-manufacture is a product at the stage between raw material and finished product (end product), and which is presumed to be subject to further processing.
producto semiterminado
▲ *a decline in sales of semi-manufactures* un descenso en las ventas de productos semiterminados ▲ *produced semi-manufactures* productos semiterminados fabricados ▲ *production and sale of semi-manufactures* producción y venta de productos semiterminados

semi-variable cost UK, US
= mixed cost UK, US, semivariable cost US
≠ semi-fixed cost
Semi-variable costs are costs that have a variable and a fixed element. Telephone costs e.g. have the variable element of number of calls and the fixed element of rental.
coste semi-variable
= coste semivariable
≠ coste semifijo, coste semi-fijo
▲ *total semi-variable costs* total costes semivariables ▲ *treat as semi-variable costs* tratar como costes semi-variables

semiannual
= biannual, semi-annual
Semiannual means half-yearly, i.e. every six months.
semestral
▲ *semiannual interest payments* pagos de interés semestrales
⇛ biannual

semivariable cost US
→ semi-variable cost

senior executive
A senior executive is a high-ranking manager at top-management level in an organisation, such as the chief executive officer, the chief financial officer or the chief operating officer.
ejecutivo senior
▲ *a former senior executive* un ejecutivo senior anterior ▲ *appoint a new senior executive* nombrar un nuevo ejecutivo senior

sensitive
To be sensitive is to be easily affected, i.e. reacting easily to changes. Information which is sensitive needs to be dealt with very carefully and must not be passed on to other parties.
sensible
▲ *a sensitive price* un precio sensible ▲ *a sensitive segmentation* una segmentación sensible ▲ *commercially sensitive information* información comercialmente sensible ▲ *sensitive information* información sensible ▲ *the assumptions to which the unit's recoverable amount is most sensitive* los supuestos a los que es más sensible la cantidad a recuperar de la unidad

sensitivity
Sensitivity shows how quickly or easily e.g. an enterprise is

affected by changes, or its degree of exposure to some source of risk.

sensibilidad

▲ *disclosure of the sensitivity of the measurement* publicación de la sensibilidad de la valoración ▲ *sensitivity to exchange rate changes* sensibilidad a las variaciones en los tipos de cambio ▲ *the sensitivity of carrying amounts to the methods and assumptions underlying the calculation* la sensibilidad de los valores contables a los métodos y supuestos subyacentes al cálculo ▲ *the sensitivity of profit or loss to changes in variables* la sensibilidad de los resultados a los cambios en las variables ▲ *the sensitivity of the information* la sensibilidad de la información

sensitivity analysis

A sensitivity analysis is an analysis used in decision-making processes, which is performed to determine the sensitivity of an outcome to changes in variables. Managers can examine how sensible results are to changes in assumptions or failure to achieve projected data.

análisis de sensibilidad

= análisis de la sensibilidad

▲ *a previous sensitivity analysis of the recoverable amount* un análisis previo de la sensibilidad de la cantidad recuperable ▲ *an interest rate sensitivity analysis* un análisis de la sensibilidad del tipo de interés ▲ *prepare a sensitivity analysis* preparar un análisis de sensibilidad

separable costs

Separable costs are costs incurred after the split-off point in joint production and which are therefore directly attributable to the individual products.

costes separados

▲ *recognise separable costs* reconocer los costes separados ▲ *subtract separable costs* restar los costes separados ▲ *total separable costs* total costes separados

⇛ joint costs, joint production, split-off point

separate

Separate means not related to or integrated in, i.e. independent or individual.

independiente

▲ *a separate financial statement* un estado financiero independiente ▲ *a separate item* una partida independiente ▲ *a separate item under equity* una partida independiente en patrimonio ▲ *a separate management body* un órgano de gestión independiente ▲ *a separate principal item* una partida principal independiente ▲ *a separate statement of changes in equity* un estado independiente de cambios en el patrimonio ▲ *separate annual reports* informes anuales independientes ▲ *state as a separate item* establecer como una partida independiente

⇛ separate entity

separate entity UK

= stand-alone entity US

A separate entity is an enterprise whose activities are not integrated in the activities of the reporting entity and whose financial statements are prepared on an individual basis.

entidad independiente

▲ *business combinations in which separate entities or businesses are brought together to form a joint venture* combinaciones de negocios en las que entidades o empresas independientes se fusionan para formar una joint venture ▲ *pay fixed pension contributions into a separate entity* pagar prestaciones de jubilación fijas a una entidad independiente

⇛ entity concept, reporting unit, separate legal entity

separate legal entity

A separate legal entity is an enterprise or organisation lawfully recognised as a legal person, which means that it has legal personality and the legal capacity to be a party to legal proceedings, enter into a contract, assume obligations and create legal relations.

entidad jurídica independiente

▲ *without regard for the legal boundaries of the separate legal entities* sin considerar las barreras jurídicas de la entidad jurídica independiente

⇛ entity concept, separate entity

separate line item

Separate line items are entries displaying and detailing transactions or events on individual lines in the financial statements of an enterprise thereby meeting the disclosure requirements for detailed information.

rúbrica separada

▲ *a separate line item within liabilities* una rúbrica separada dentro de pasivos ▲ *a single separate line item within assets* una única rúbrica separada dentro de activos ▲ *present as separate line items* presentar como rúbricas separadas ▲ *report as separate line items in the venturer's financial statements* informar como partidas separadas en los estados financieros del participante en un negocio conjunto

separately

When something is done separately, it is done independently, on an individual basis and kept distinct from something else.

independientemente

= por separado

▲ *classify separately* clasificar por separado ▲ *measure the deposit component separately* medir el componente de depósito por separado ▲ *place separately* fijar por separado ▲ *recognise separately* reconocer por separado ▲ *recognise the guaranteed element separately from the discretionary participation feature* reconocer el elemento garantizado independientemente del valor de participación discrecional ▲ *state items separately* establecer partidas por separado ▲ *state something separately in the notes* fijar algo por separado en las notas

sequential allocation method

→ step-down method

sequential tracking

Sequential tracking is a costing method based on the principle that all costs are recorded in the bookkeeping system in the same order as the physical processes occur in the purchasing and production functions. This way, costs can be tracked to the different stages of the production cycle.

rastreo secuencial

= rastreo sincrónico

▲ *use sequential tracking* utilizar el rastreo secuencial

⇛ backflush costing, trigger point

serial loan

A serial loan is a loan repaid by regular, equal repayments over its life.

préstamo de amortización gradual

= préstamo escalonado

▲ *raise a serial loan* conseguir un préstamo de amortización gradual ▲ *service a serial loan* amortizar un préstamo escalonado

service[1] *noun*

A service is a non-material product that consists of labour, human skills or human resources sold with the purpose of making a profit, e.g. delivery, computer, financial or accounting services.

servicio

▲ *a contractual obligation to provide services* una obligación contractual a prestar servicios ▲ *a rendered service* un servicio prestado ▲ *an employee who remains in service for the specified period of service* un empleado que permanece en activo durante un periodo especificado de servicio ▲ *complete a specified period of service* completar un periodo especificado de servicio ▲ *employees and others providing similar services* empleados y otros trabajadores que prestan servicios similares ▲ *fair value of the services received* valor razonable de los servicios recibidos ▲ *fixed-fee service contracts in which the level of service depends on an uncertain event* contratos de servicio con tarifa fija en los que el nivel del servicio depende de un acontecimiento incierto ▲ *parties that have supplied goods or services to the entity* partes que han aportado bienes o servicios a la entidad ▲ *proceeds from the sale of goods and services* ingresos procedentes de la venta de bienes y servicios ▲ *render services* prestar servicios ▲ *revenue associated with a transaction involving the rendering of services* ingresos asociados con una transacción que implica la prestación de servicios ▲ *share options conditional upon completing three years' service* opciones sobre acciones que están condicionadas a la finalización del servicio en tres años ▲ *share-based payment transactions in which an entity acquires or receives goods or services* transacciones con pago basado en acciones en las que una entidad adquiere o recibe bienes o servicios ▲ *the costs of introducing a new service* los costes de introducir un nuevo servicio ▲ *the loss of the ability to charge the policyholder for future services* la pérdida de la capacidad para cargar al titular de la póliza de seguro por servicios futuros ▲ *transactions in which services are received* transacciones en las que se reciben servicios

service[2] *verb*

1 To service means to provide goods or services to customers.
servir
▲ *service the customers of the enterprise* servir a los clientes de la empresa

2 To service a loan means to make interest and principal payments.
amortizar
▲ *to service a debt* amortizar una deuda

service charge

A service charge constitutes expenses for services on sold products where the selling enterprise is obliged to provide after-sales service such as technical help and delivery of spare parts. A service charge may also represent expenses incurred by an enterprise for service on acquired products where after-sales service has not been included in the price.
cargo por servicio
▲ *a service charge of 2%* un cargo por servicio del 2% ▲ *service charges payable* cargos por servicio a pagar ▲ *the proposed service charge* el cargo por servicio propuesto

service cost

1 Service costs are expenses for services on sold products where the selling enterprise is obliged to provide after-sales service such as technical help and delivery of spare parts. A service cost may also represent expenses incurred by an enterprise for service on acquired products where after-sales service has not been included in the price.
coste de garantía
= coste de la garantía
▲ *recognise service costs* reconocer los costes de la garantía ▲ *successive service costs* costes de garantía sucesivos ▲ *the service costs incurred* los costes de garantía incurridos

2 A service cost is a pension cost which may be current or past depending on whether it refers to an increase in the present value of pension obligations as a result of services rendered by employees in the current accounting period or in prior accounting periods.
coste de servicio
▲ *current service cost* coste de servicio actual ▲ *past service cost* coste de servicio pasado
SOURCE IAS 19, paragraph 7
⇛ current service cost, past service cost

service department

= support department
A service department is a department that provides support services for the other departments in an enterprise.
departamento logístico
▲ *assistance from the service department* asistencia por parte del departamento logístico

service margin

The compensation that an insurer charges for providing services other than insurance services is called the service margin.
margen de servicios
⇛ risk margin

service mark

= SM
A service mark is a trademark used about services instead of goods. It may be a logo, picture, name, colour or other symbol. The abbreviation SM is used about service marks.
marca de servicio
= prima por servicios especiales
▲ *a registered service mark* una marca de servicio registrada ▲ *use a service mark* utilizar una marca de servicio
⇛ trademark

service provider

A service provider is a person or enterprise providing services to custumers.
proveedor de servicios
▲ *the service provider has agreed to repair specified equipment after a malfunction* el proveedor de servicios está de acuerdo en reparar el equipo especificado

debido a su mal funcionamiento

service-sector company

A service-sector company is a company engaged in providing services or intangible goods.

empresa del sector servicios

▲ *a large service-sector company* una gran empresa del sector servicios ▲ *foreign-owned service-sector companies* empresas del sector servicios de propiedad extranjera ▲ *the competitiveness of service-sector companies* la competitividad de las empresas del sector servicios

⇛ manufacturing-sector company, merchandising-sector company

set

A set is a group of interconnected or related elements.

conjunto

= serie

▲ *a higher set of rules* un conjunto elevado de reglas ▲ *a set of accounting provisions* un conjunto de provisiones contables ▲ *a set of definitions* un conjunto de definiciones ▲ *a set of established criteria* un conjunto de criterios establecidos ▲ *a set of financial control instruments* un conjunto de instrumentos de control financiero ▲ *a set of initiatives* un conjunto de iniciativas ▲ *a set of management challenges* un conjunto de oportunidades de negocio ▲ *a set of recommendations* un conjunto de recomendaciones ▲ *an internationally known set of accounting rules* un conjunto de reglas contables conocido internacionalmente

set off

= offset

To set off is to counterbalance one element against another, e.g. to deduct one amount from another leaving a net or zero balance.

compensar

▲ *set off an amount* compensar una cantidad

⇛ offsetting

set up

To set up means to arrange, start or establish something.

constituir

= establecer

▲ *set up a committee* constituir un comité

set-off

= contra entry, set-off entry

A set-off is a contra entry in a ledger or an account whereby a previous entry is reversed and cancelled. Set-off entries may also be debit entries offsetting credit entries in the double-entry bookkeeping system.

compensación

▲ *without set-off* sin compensación

⇛ offset, offsetting

set-off entry

→ set-off

settle

To settle is to conclude a transaction, e.g. by delivery, or to pay an outstanding debt or amount owed.

liquidar

= saldar

▲ *a contract that will or may be settled in the entity's own equity instruments* un contrato que se liquidará o puede liquidarse con el propio patrimonio de la empresa ▲ *a derivative that will or may be settled other than by the exchange of a fixed amount of cash* un derivado que se liquidará o puede liquidarse de forma diferente al cambio o a la cantidad fijada de efectivo ▲ *contracts that may be settled in ordinary shares or cash* contratos que se pueden liquidar en acciones ordinarias o en efectivo ▲ *financial instruments and other contracts that may be settled in shares* instrumentos financieros y otros contratos que se pueden liquidar con acciones ▲ *settle a derivative liability by delivery of an unlisted equity instrument* liquidar un pasivo derivado por emisión de un instrumento de patrimonio no cotizado ▲ *settle an asset before maturity* liquidar un activo antes del vencimiento ▲ *settle by issuing equity instruments* liquidar mediante la emisión de instrumentos de patrimonio ▲ *settle current tax assets and liabilities* saldar activos y pasivos por impuesto corriente ▲ *settle in a foreign currency* saldar en una moneda extranjera ▲ *settle in cash* liquidar en efectivo ▲ *settle the amounts on a net basis* saldar las cantidades en una base neta

settlement

Settlement refers to the delivery of an asset or the satisfaction or payment of a liability, e.g. to conclude a transaction or repay a loan.

liquidación

▲ *a cancellation or settlement of the grant of equity instruments* una cancelación o liquidación de la concesión de instrumentos de patrimonio ▲ *differences arising on the settlement of preference shares* diferencias que surgen en la liquidación de acciones preferentes ▲ *elect the settlement alternative with the higher fair value* elegir la liquidación alternativa con el valor razonable más alto ▲ *elect to receive cash on settlement* elegido para recibir la liquidación en efectivo ▲ *issue equity instruments on settlement* emitir instrumentos de patrimonio en efectivo ▲ *long settlement transactions* transacciones con liquidación diferida ▲ *ordinary shares issued in exchange for the settlement of a liability of the entity* acciones ordinarias emitidas a cambio de la liquidación de un pasivo de la entidad ▲ *pay in cash on settlement* pagar la liquidación en efectivo ▲ *settlement of a defined contribution plan* liquidación de un plan de aportación definida ▲ *settlement of an obligation* liquidación de una obligación ▲ *settlement on a net basis* liquidación en una base neta ▲ *short settlement cycle* ciclo de liquidación a corto ▲ *the expected date of recovery and settlement of non-monetary assets and liabilities* la fecha esperada de recuperación y liquidación de activos y pasivos no monetarios ▲ *the settlement of employee benefit plan obligations* la liquidación de las obligaciones del plan de pensiones

⇛ repayment

settlement amount

The settlement amount is the sum of money paid to settle an outstanding account.

finiquito

▲ *cash settlement amounts* finiquito en efectivo ▲ *contractual settlement amounts* finiquitos contractuales

settlement date

The settlement date is the time when cash (for a buyer) or a financial asset, e.g. a security (for a seller) must be delivered in order to complete a securities transaction.

fecha de liquidación

= fecha de la liquidación

▲ *as of the settlement date* a la fecha de la liquidación ▲ *give rise to a fixed price commitment between trade date and settlement date* dar lugar a un compromiso de precio fijo entre la fecha de comercialización y la fecha de liquidación ▲ *recognise at the settlement date* reconocer a la fecha de liquidación ▲ *recognition of purchase and sale as of the settlement date* reconocimiento de compra y venta a la fecha de la liquidación ▲ *regular way purchases and sales of financial assets accounted for at settlement date* compras y ventas regulares de activos financieros contabilizados a la fecha de liquidación ▲ *settlement date accounting* contabilidad a la fecha de liquidación

settlement day

= settlement date

The settlement day is the date when securities and foreign exchange trades are cleared by delivery, payment and transfer of ownership.

fecha de liquidación

= fecha de la liquidación

▲ *as of the settlement day* a partir de la fecha de liquidación ▲ *at the settlement day* a la fecha de la liquidación

settlement gain IAS/IFRS

≠ settlement loss IAS/IFRS

A settlement gain is a gain resulting from any changes in the present value of defined benefit obligations or in the fair value of pension plan assets arising in connection with a reduction of the headcount or total or partial closing down of activities or plans, typically in connection with a restructuring. Such a reduction will lead to a reduction in the pension plan obligation and lower pension plan expenses to be recognised in the financial statements after restating the pension obligations and the plan assets involved on the basis of current actuarial assumptions. A settlement takes place when the legal or constructive obligations for the benefits under the plan are eliminated, e.g. when plan participants receive a lump sum payment in cash instead of keeping the right to received the post-employment benefits originally agreed under the plan.

ganancia por liquidación

≠ pérdida por liquidación

▲ *measure the settlement gain* medir la ganancia por liquidación ▲ *recognise a settlement gain* reconocer una ganancia por liquidación ▲ *the amount of the settlement gain* la cuantía de la ganancia por liquidación

SOURCE IAS 19, paragraphs 109, 111

⇛ curtailment gain, curtailment loss

settlement loss IAS/IFRS

≠ settlement gain IAS/IFRS

A settlement loss is a loss resulting from any changes in the present value of defined benefit obligations or in the fair value of pension plan assets arising in connection with a reduction of the headcount or total or partial closing down of activities or plans, typically in connection with a restructuring. Such a reduction will lead to a reduction in the pension plan obligation and lower pension plan expenses to be recognised in the financial statements after restating the pension obligations and the plan assets involved on the basis of current actuarial assumptions. A settlement takes place when the legal or constructive obligations for the benefits under the plan are eliminated, e.g. when plan participants receive a lump sum payment in cash instead of keeping the right to receive the post-employment benefits originally agreed under the plan.

pérdida por liquidación

≠ ganancia por liquidación

▲ *measure a settlement loss* valorar una pérdida por liquidación ▲ *recognise a settlement loss* reconocer una pérdida por liquidación ▲ *the amount of the settlement loss* la cuantía de la pérdida por liquidación

SOURCE IAS 19, paragraphs 109, 111

⇛ curtailment gain, curtailment loss

settlement price

1 The settlement price is the final price paid for a specific security or financial contract, such as a share, an option or a bond, on the conclusion of the transaction.

valor de amortización

= valor de la amortización

▲ *determination of the settlement price* determinación del valor de la amortización ▲ *settlement price for cash foreign currency purchase* valor de amortización en la compra de moneda extranjera en efectivo ▲ *settlement price for cash foreign currency sale* valor de la amortización en la venta de moneda extranjera en efectivo

2 The settlement price is the final consideration paid, whether in money or otherwise, for a specific asset on the conclusion of a sales transaction.

precio de venta

= precio de la venta

▲ *determine settlement prices* determinar los precios de venta

settlement sum

The settlement sum is the amount of money paid to settle an outstanding account.

cuantía de la liquidación

▲ *determine the settlement sum* determinar la cuantía de la liquidación ▲ *pay the settlement sum* pagar la cuantía de la liquidación

settlement value IAS/IFRS

The settlement value is the amount expected paid in discharge of a liability in the course of normal business operations.

valor de liquidación

= valor de la liquidación, valor de realización

▲ *calculate the settlement value* calcular el valor de liquidación ▲ *the average settlement value* el valor de liquidación medio ▲ *the most probable settlement value* el valor más probable de la liquidación

severance accrual

Severance accrual is the recognition of termination benefit costs that relate to or may arise in future accounting periods as accrued severance liabilities.

devengo por indemnización

▲ *estimated severance accrual at beginning of period* devengo por indemnización estimado al inicio del periodo ▲ *reversal of se-*

verance accrual revocación del devengo por indemnización ▲ *the severance accrual recorded in the second quarter of 2006* el devengo por indemnización anotado en el segundo trimestre de 2006

severance benefit

= dismissal payment, redundancy payment, severance pay, severance payment, termination benefit IAS/IFRS

A severance benefit refers to a monetary benefit payable to an employee upon involuntary termination before normal retirement or upon the employee's acceptance of voluntary termination in return for such benefit.

indemnización por despido

▲ *measurement of severance benefits* valoración de las indemnizaciones de despido ▲ *pay severance benefits* pagar indemnizaciones por despido ▲ *provide severance benefits* ofrecer indemnizaciones por despido ▲ *provisions for severance benefits* provisiones para las indemnizaciones de despido ▲ *recognise severance benefits* reconocer las indemnizaciones por despido ▲ *severance benefits falling due more than 1 year after the balance sheet date* indemnizaciones por despido que vencen después de un año de la fecha de balance ▲ *severance benefits for key management personnel* indemnizaciones por despido para el personal de alta dirección

severance pay

= dismissal payment, redundancy payment, severance benefit, severance payment, termination benefit IAS/IFRS

Severance pay refers to a monetary benefit payable to an employee upon involuntary termination before normal retirement or upon the employee's acceptance of voluntary termination in return for such payment.

indemnización por despido

= indemnización de despido

NOTE The IAS/IFS term 'beneficio por terminación' may lead to confusion considering that this term does not indicate 'involuntary termination'.

▲ *measurement of severance pay* valoración de la indemnización por despido ▲ *pay severance pay* pagar la indemnización por despido ▲ *provide severance pay* ofrecer indemnizaciones por despido ▲ *provisions for severance pay* provisiones para la indemnización de despido ▲ *recognise severance pay* reconocer la indemnización por despido ▲ *severance pay falling due more than 1 year after the balance sheet date* indemnización por despido que vence más de un año después de la fecha del balance ▲ *severance pay for key management personnel* indemnización por despido para el personal de alta dirección

SFAS US

= Statement of Financial Accounting Standards US

SFAS is the abbreviation for Statement of Financial Accounting Standards. SFASs are accounting standards issued by the US Financial Accounting Standards Board to set disclosure requirements and to establish generally accepted accounting principles for companies registered with the Securities and Exchange Commission when preparing their financial statements.

SFAS

= Guía de las Normas de Contabilidad Financiera, Guía de Procedimientos Contables en base a las Normas de Contabilidad Financiera

▲ *issue a new SFAS* emitir un nuevo SFAS ▲ *proposed SFAS* SFAS propuesto ▲ *SFAS No. 123 (revised 2004)* SFAS Nº 123 (revisado en el 2004)

⇛ accounting standard, FRS, IFRS

share[1] *noun*

1 A share is a right of ownership in an incorporated company measured in terms of money. There are different types of shares carrying different rights, e.g. voting rights and rights to dividend.

acción

▲ *a right to buy a fixed number of the entity's shares for a fixed price* un derecho a comprar un número determinado de acciones de la entidad a un precio fijado ▲ *a share with a nominal value of GBP 1* una acción con un valor nominal de 1 libra esterlina ▲ *acquire shares* adquirir acciones ▲ *choose settlement net by exchan-*

ging shares for cash elegir el neto de liquidación mediante acciones que se cambian por efectivo ▲ *contracts for the sale of shares* contratos para la venta de acciones ▲ *costs of a concurrent offering of some shares and a stock exchange listing of other shares* costes de una oferta concurrente de algunas acciones y cotización bursátil de otras acciones ▲ *hold shares* poseer acciones ▲ *holder of A shares* titular de acciones A ▲ *holder of B shares* titular de acciones B ▲ *par value per share* valor a la par por acción ▲ *share call options* opciones de compra de acciones ▲ *successive share purchases* compras sucesivas de acciones ▲ *the number of shares authorised* el número de acciones autorizadas ▲ *the number of shares issued and fully paid* el número de acciones emitidas y desembolsadas totalmente ▲ *the number of shares issued but not fully paid* el número de acciones emitidas con desembolso parcial ▲ *the number of shares outstanding at the beginning and at the end of the period* el número de acciones pendientes de pago al inicio y al final del periodo ▲ *the number of shares reserved for issue under options* el número de acciones reservadas para la emisión según opciones

2 A share is a part or segment of something, e.g. a part of a market.

participación

▲ *a 90% share of all cash flows of a debt instrument* una participación del 90% en todos los flujos de efectivo de un instrumento de deuda ▲ *a fully proportionate share of the cash flows from a financial asset* una participación totalmente proporcional de los flujos de efectivo provenientes de un activo financiero ▲ *determination of the entity's share of the investee's profits or losses* determinación de la participación de la entidad en los resultados de los partícipes ▲ *receive a pro rata share of any dividends or other distributions of equity* recibir una participación prorrateada de cualesquiera dividendos y otras distribuciones del patrimonio ▲ *the investor's share of any discontinued operations of an associate* la participación del inversor en cualquier operación interrumpida de una asociada ▲ *the minority's share of changes in equity* la participación de los minoritarios en los cambios de patrimonio ▲ *the proportionate share of the related accumulated exchange difference* la participación proporcional en la diferencia relativa de cambio acumulado ▲ *the unrecognised share of losses of an associate* la participación no reconocida en las pérdidas de una asociada

share[2] *verb*

To share is to use, apply or divide something or to participate in something with others.

compartir

▲ *operating assets shared by two or more segments* activos de explotación compartidos por dos o más segmentos ▲ *share joint control over a joint venture* compartir el control conjunto de una joint venture

share acquisition

= acquisition of shares

A share acquisition results when a person or an enterprise acquires shares in a company.

adquisición de acciones

▲ *fictitious share acquisitions* adquisiciones ficticias de acciones

share amount

1 A share amount constitutes the total amount of shares held by an investor shown as the aggregate monetary value stated in the currency in which the shares are denominated.

valor de las acciones

= valor accionarial, valor de la inversión en acciones

▲ *the total share amount of the investor* el valor accionarial total del inversor

2 A share amount is the total number of shares, e.g. the amount that an investor holds or intends to purchase, or that constitutes a particular class of shares issued.

número de acciones

▲ *the total share amount* el número de acciones total

share analysis UK

= stock analysis US

A share analysis is an assessment or evaluation of one or more shares for investment purposes.

análisis de valores

= análisis del valor de las acciones

▲ *fundamental share analysis* análisis de valores fundamentales ▲ *technical share analysis* análisis técnico del valor de las acciones

share buy-back IAS/IFRS
= share buyback UK, share repurchase US, IAS/IFRS
A share buy-back is a transaction whereby a company repurchases its own shares from existing shareholders.
rescate de acciones
= recompra de acciones, rescate de las acciones
▲ *enter into a share buy-back arrangement* firmar un acuerdo de rescate de las acciones

share buy-back programme UK
= share buyback programme UK, share repurchase program US, share repurchase programme IAS/IFRS, UK, stock repurchase plan US
A share buy-back programme is a programme authorised by a company's board of directors by which management can buy back a certain amount of the company's own shares in the market during a specified period of time. The effect of a retirement of an amount of the shares is to reduce the number of outstanding shares, resulting in an increase of the market price and the earnings per share.
programa de rescate de acciones
= programa de recompra de acciones
▲ *acquisition in connection with share buy-back programmes* adquisición en conexión con programas de rescate de acciones ▲ *complete a share buy-back programme* completar un programa de rescate de acciones ▲ *launch a share buy-back programme* lanzar un programa de rescate de acciones

share buyback UK
= share buy-back IAS/IFRS, share repurchase IAS/IFRS, US
A share buyback is a transaction whereby a company repurchases its own outstanding shares from existing shareholders.
recompra de acciones
▲ *a share buyback of £41m* una recompra de acciones de 41 millones de libras esterlinas ▲ *a structured share buyback* una recompra de acciones estructurada ▲ *the completed share buyback* la recompra de acciones finalizada ▲ *the planned share buyback* la recompra de acciones planificada

share buyback programme UK
= share buy-back programme UK, share repurchase program US, share repurchase programme UK, stock repurchase plan US
A share buyback programme is a programme authorised by a company's board of directors by which management can buy back a certain amount of the company's own shares in the market during a specified period of time. The effect of a retirement of an amount of the shares is to reduce the number of outstanding shares, resulting in an increase of the market price and the earnings per share.
programa de recompra de acciones
= programa de rescate de acciones
▲ *commence a share buyback programme* comenzar un programa de recompra de acciones ▲ *complete a share buyback programme* completar un programa de recompra de acciones ▲ *launch a share buyback programme* lanzar un programa de recompra de acciones

share capital UK, IAS/IFRS
= common stock US, stock US
Share capital refers to the total amount of capital invested in an enterprise by its shareholders in exchange for shares issued.
capital social
▲ *a minimum of 5% of the voting rights of the share capital* un mínimo del 5% de los derechos de voto del capital social ▲ *amount to a minimum of 5% of the share capital* representar un mínimo del 5% del capital social ▲ *an entity without share capital* una entidad sin capital social ▲ *entities whose share capital is not equity* entidades cuyo capital social no son títulos ▲ *fully paid-up share capital* capital social completamente desembolsado ▲ *increase the company's share capital* aumentar el capital social de la empresa ▲ *increase the share capital*

aumentar el capital social ▲ *issue of share capital* emisión de capital social ▲ *paid-up share capital* capital social desembolsado ▲ *reduce the share capital by EUR 10m* reducir el capital social en 10 millones de euros ▲ *repayment of share capital* reembolso de capital social ▲ *return on share capital* rendimiento del capital social ▲ *the share capital acquired* el capital social suscrito ▲ *the share capital issued* el capital social emitido ▲ *the total nominal share capital* el capital social nominal total
⇛ called up share capital, issued capital, nominal share capital, paid-up share capital

share certificate UK
A share certificate is a document that gives evidence of ownership and other details of the share owned in a company by a particular shareholder.
certificado de acciones
▲ *admit share certificates for listing* admitir a cotización certificados de acciones ▲ *issue share certificates* emitir certificados de acciones ▲ *printing of new share certificates* impresión de los certificados de acciones nuevas ▲ *reprint of old share certificates* reimpresión de los certificados de acciones antiguos

share class UK
= class of shares UK, class of stock US
Share capital may be divided into share classes with different characteristics as determined by the articles of association or bylaws of the company in question. One share class has certain advantages, such as more voting rights, compared with another class of shares.
NOTE In the US, class A shares typically have more voting rights than class B shares, however, in the UK the opposite may be the case.
clase de acciones
▲ *share price per share class* precio de la acción por clase de acción ▲ *shares of the same share class* acciones pertenecientes a la misma clase de acciones

share deal UK
= stock deal US
≠ asset deal
A share deal is a specific structure applied in connection with acquiring a company. In a share deal, the acquisition of a company happens by the buyer taking over or buying the company's shares. The vendor also assumes the liabilities of the company, and therefore share deals are typically more advantageous to the seller than asset deals.
intercambio de acciones
= intercambio de las acciones
▲ *formal approvals of share deals* aprobaciones formales de intercambios de acciones

share in a subsidiary
A share in a subsidiary is an ownership interest held by a parent company.
participación en una subsidiaria
▲ *adjustment for change in the value of the shares in the subsidiary* ajuste por cambio en el valor de las participaciones en una subsidiaria

share incentive plan
= share incentive scheme UK
A share incentive plan is a program involving the awarding of shares, share options or warrants at an especially low price to management executives and other employees in an enterprise subject to achievement of corporate performance goals.
programa de incentivo de acciones
= plan de incentivo de acciones
▲ *a conditional share incentive plan* un programa condicional de incentivo de acciones ▲ *a synthetical share incentive plan* un plan sintético de incentivo de acciones
⇛ employee share ownership plan

share incentive scheme UK
= share incentive plan
A share incentive scheme is a scheme involving the awarding of shares, share options or warrants at an especially low price to management executives and other employees in an enterprise subject to achievement of corporate performance goals.
programa de incentivo de acciones
= plan de incentivo de acciones
▲ *a conditional share incentive scheme* un programa condicional de incentivo de acciones ▲ *a synthetical share incentive*

scheme un plan sintético de incentivo de acciones
⇛ employee share ownership plan

share index
A share index is an index reflecting the composite value of the shares which are included in the index. A share index is often based on shares with one or more common characteristics e.g. companies in the same industry, the same country, or companies whose shares are most frequently traded on a specific market. Price development in a share index is often used as an indicator of the overall price development of shares in the specific industry or market. Examples of share indices are the FTSE 100, the NASDAQ Composite Index, the S&P 500 Index and the OMXC20 (the index for the 20 most traded shares on the Copenhagen Stock Exchange).
índice bursátil
= índice de acciones
▲ *benchmark share index* índice bursátil benchmark ▲ *Danish share indexes* índices bursátiles europeos ▲ *international share indexes* índices de acciones internacionales ▲ *swaps share indexes* índices bursátiles de swaps

share information
Share information is the information relating to the company's shares, and it comprises share price increases or decreases, the number of shares and the market capitalisation of the shares.
información sobre acciones
= información de acciones, información sobre las acciones
▲ *publish reliable share information* publicar información fiable sobre acciones las acciones

share investment
= investment in shares
A share investment consists of the purchase of shares.
inversión en acciones
▲ *a major share investment* una inversión en acciones importante ▲ *a significant share investment* una inversión en acciones significativa

share issue
= equity issue, issue of shares, share offer
A share issue refers either to the authorisation and provision of shares for sale to new or existing shareholders for the purpose of creating share capital or to the distribution of shares to existing shareholders in relation to their shareholdings.
emisión de acciones
▲ *adjust ratios for share issues* ajustar los ratios para las emisiones de acciones ▲ *carry out a share issue* llevar a cabo una emisión de acciones ▲ *cross-border share issues* emisiones de acciones multinacionales ▲ *new shares via share issue* nuevas acciones vía emisión de acciones ▲ *proceeds from share issue* recursos procedentes de la emisión de acciones ▲ *share issue costs* costes de la emisión de acciones
⇛ rights issue

share loss
A share loss is a loss arising on the divestment of one or more shares in a company.
pérdida de acciones
= pérdida en la venta de acciones
▲ *calculate a share loss* calcular una pérdida de acciones ▲ *deductible share losses* pérdidas de acciones deducibles ▲ *deduction for share losses* deducciones por pérdidas de acciones ▲ *large share losses* pérdidas de acciones cuantiosas ▲ *small share losses* pérdidas de acciones de poca cuantía

share market UK
= equity market, stock market US
A share market is a market place where shares are bought and sold, such as a stock exchange or other authorized market place. Trading may be physical and/or computerized.
mercado bursátil
= bolsa, mercado de acciones
▲ *falling share markets* mercados bursátiles a la baja ▲ *share market turbulence* turbulencia en la bolsa ▲ *the Danish share market* el mercado bursátil danés ▲ *the global share markets* los mercados bursátiles globales ▲ *the implicit volatility of the share market* la volatibilidad implícita del mercado de acciones ▲ *the international share markets* los mercados de accio-

nes internacionales ▲ *the trends on the share market* las tendencias en el mercado de títulos ▲ *unsettled share markets* mercados bursátiles a crédito

share of profit or loss UK, IAS/IFRS
A share of profit or loss is the share of earnings attributable to a parent company from an associate or from a non-wholly owned subsidiary.
participación en resultados
= participación en los resultados
▲ *compute the share of profits or losses* calcular la participación en resultados ▲ *the investor's share of profit or loss of the investee* la participación en resultados del inversor en la inversión

share of profit or loss of associates IAS/IFRS
"Share of profit or loss of associates" is an item in the income statement referring to the share of earnings attributable to a parent company from its associated enterprises.
participación en resultados de asociadas
= participación en los resultados de asociadas, participación en los resultados de las asociadas
▲ *include the share of profits or losses of associates in the financial statements* incluir en los estados financieros la participación en los resultados de las asociadas

share offer
= share issue
A share offer refers either to the authorisation and provision of shares for sale to new or existing shareholders for the purpose of creating share capital or to the distribution of shares to existing shareholders in relation to their shareholdings.
oferta de acciones
= emisión de acciones
▲ *adjust ratios for share offers* ajustar ratios para las emisiones de acciones ▲ *carry out a share offer* llevar a cabo una oferta de acciones ▲ *cross-border share offer* oferta de acciones internacional ▲ *new shares via share offer* nuevas acciones vía oferta de acciones ▲ *proceeds from share offers* ingresos procedentes de ofertas de acciones ▲ *share offer costs* costes de las ofertas de acciones

share option UK, IAS/IFRS
= stock option US
A share option is a contract that enables, but not obliges, the holder to buy or sell specific shares at a fixed price within a specified period of time.
opción sobre acciones
= stock option
▲ *a more accurate estimate of the total fair value of the share options granted* una estimación más acertada del valor razonable total de las opciones sobre acciones concedidas ▲ *a net cash-settled share option* una opción sobre acciones pagada en efectivo neto ▲ *a synthetic share option* una opción sobre acciones híbrida ▲ *an automatic grant of additional share options* una concesión automática de opciones sobre acciones adicionales ▲ *cancel a share option* cancelar una opción sobre acciones ▲ *employee share options with fixed or determinable terms* opciones sobre acciones del empleado con términos fijos o a determinar ▲ *exercise a share option* ejercer una stock option ▲ *forfeit a share option* perder el derecho a una opción sobre acciones ▲ *grant share options* conceder opciones sobre acciones ▲ *movements in the number of share options outstanding* cambios en el número de opciones sobre acciones pendientes de pago ▲ *outstanding share options* opciones sobre acciones pendientes de pago ▲ *performance-based share options* opciones sobre acciones basadas en reultados ▲ *receive share options* recibir opciones sobre acciones ▲ *share options exercised* opciones sobre acciones ejecutadas ▲ *share options with relatively short contractual lives* opciones sobre acciones con vidas contractuales relativamente cortas ▲ *the exercise price of the share option* el precio de ejercicio de la opción sobre acciones ▲ *the fair value of the share option* el valor razonable de la opción sobre acciones ▲ *the intrinsic value of the share option* el valor intrínseco de la opción sobre acciones ▲ *the market value of the share option bought* el valor de mercado de la stock option comprada ▲ *the number*

and weighted average exercise prices of share options el número y precios de compra medios ponderados de las opciones sobre acciones ▲ *the number of share options expected to vest* el número de acciones sobre opciones esperadas a que cumplan los plazos para que sean ejecutables ▲ *the recognised intrinsic value of the share option* el valor intrínseco reconocido de la opción sobre acciones ▲ *the share option has expired* la opción sobre acciones ha vencido ▲ *write traded share options* vender opciones sobre acciones cotizadas

⇛ incentive program

share option agreement UK

= stock option agreement US

A share option agreement is a contract giving one of the parties the right, but not the obligation, to buy or sell a fixed amount of shares at a predetermined price within a specified period.

contrato de opción sobre acciones

= contrato de opciones sobre acciones

▲ *enter into a share option agreement* firmar un contrato de opciones sobre acciones ▲ *the employees' share option agreement* el contrato de opción sobre acciones de los empleados

share option plan UK

= share option program US, share option programme UK, share option scheme UK, stock option plan US

A share option plan is an agreement under which management executives and other employees are granted share options as additional compensation or incentive payment supplementing wages and salaries. The employees receive options at a fixed, often favourable price and must exercise them within a specified period after the grant date.

programa de opciones sobre acciones

▲ *treasury shares purchased, sold, issued or cancelled in connection with employee share option plans* acciones propias compradas, vendidas, emitidas o canceladas en relación con el programa de opciones sobre acciones de los empleados

share option program US

= share option plan UK, share option programme UK, share option scheme UK, stock option plan US

A share option program is an agreement under which management executives and other employees are granted share options as additional compensation or incentive payment supplementing wages and salaries. The employees receive options at a fixed, often favourable price and must exercise them within a specified period after the grant date.

programa de opciones sobre acciones

= plan de opciones sobre acciones, programa de opciones de acciones

▲ *a share option program for all employees* un programa de opciones sobre acciones para todos los empleados ▲ *an international share option program* un programa de opciones sobre acciones internacional ▲ *approve a share option program* aprobar un programa de opciones sobre acciones ▲ *commitments under the company's share option program* compromisos según el programa de opciones de acciones de la empresa ▲ *cover of the share option program* cobertura del programa de opciones sobre acciones ▲ *implementation of a share option program* implementación de un programa de opciones sobre acciones ▲ *introduce a share option program* introducir un programa de opciones sobre acciones ▲ *participate in a share option program* participar en un programa de opciones de acciones ▲ *revolving share option program* programa renovable de opciones sobre acciones ▲ *share option program for key employees* programa de opciones sobre acciones para los empleados de alta dirección ▲ *share option program for the company's management* programa de opciones sobre acciones para la dirección de la empresa

share option programme UK

= share option plan UK, share option program US, share option scheme UK, stock option plan US

A share option programme is an agreement under which management executives and other employees are granted share options as additional compensation or incentive payment supplementing wages and salaries. The employees receive options at a fixed, often favourable price and must exercise them within a specified period after the grant date.

programa de opciones sobre acciones

= plan de opciones sobre acciones, programa de opciones de acciones

▲ *a share option programme for all employees* un programa de opciones sobre acciones para todos los empleados ▲ *an international share option programme* un programa de opciones sobre acciones internacional ▲ *approve a share option programme* aprobar un programa de opciones sobre acciones ▲ *commitments under the company's share option programme* compromisos según el programa de opciones sobre acciones de la empresa ▲ *cover of the share option programme* cobertura del programa de opciones sobre acciones ▲ *implementation of a share option programme* implementación de un programa de opciones sobre acciones ▲ *introduce a share option programme* introducir un programa de opciones sobre acciones ▲ *participate in a share option programme* participar en un programa de opciones de acciones ▲ *revolving share option programme* programa renovable de opciones sobre acciones ▲ *share option programme for key employees* programa de opciones sobre acciones para los empleados de alta dirección ▲ *share option programme for the company's management* programa de opciones de acciones para la dirección de la empresa

share option scheme UK

= share option plan UK, share option program US, share option programme UK, stock option plan US

A share option scheme is an agreement under which management executives and other employees are granted share options as additional compensation or incentive payment supplementing wages and salaries. The employees receive options at a fixed, often favourable price and must exercise them within a specified period after the grant date.

programa de opciones sobre acciones

= plan de opciones sobre acciones

▲ *a share option scheme for all employees* un programa de opciones sobre acciones para todos los empleados ▲ *an international share option scheme* un programa de opciones sobre acciones internacional ▲ *approve a share option scheme* aprobar un programa de opciones sobre acciones ▲ *commitments under the company's share option scheme* compromisos de acuerdo con el programa de opciones sobre acciones de la empresa ▲ *cover of the share option scheme* cobertura del programa de opciones sobre acciones ▲ *implementation of a share option scheme* implementación de un programa de opciones sobre acciones ▲ *introduce a share option scheme* introducir un programa de opciones sobre acciones ▲ *participate in a share option scheme* participar en un programa de opciones sobre acciones ▲ *revolving share option scheme* programa de opciones sobre acciones renovable ▲ *share option scheme for key employees* programa de opciones sobre acciones para el personal de alta dirección ▲ *share option scheme for the company's management* programa de opciones sobre acciones para la dirección de la empresa

share premium IAS/IFRS, UK

= additional paid-in capital US, capital surplus US, paid-in surplus US

The share premium is the amount by which the selling price of a share exceeds its nominal or par value. The share premium is transferred to the item "share premium account" under the enterprise's equity in the balance sheet.

prima de emisión

▲ *share premium as at 1 January* prima de emisión a 1 de enero ▲ *share premium during the year* prima de emisión a lo largo del año

share premium account UK

Share premium account is the account to which the premium

must be credited for shares issued at a premium, also used for the item under equity in the balance sheet that represents the additional capital contributed to a company in excess of the nominal or stated value of shares issued.

cuenta de prima de emisión

▲ *appropriations to a share premium account* dotaciones a la cuenta de prima de emisión ▲ *share premium account as at 1 January* cuenta de prima de emisión a partir del 1 de enero

share price

= equity price

A share price is the price of a particular share at which it can be bought or sold at a particular time, typically the price quoted on an authorized marketplace such as a stock exchange.

precio de la acción

▲ *a specified increase in the entity's share price* un aumento especificado en el precio de la acción de la entidad ▲ *dilute the share price* diluir el precio de la acción ▲ *estimate future share prices* estimar los precios de la acción futuros ▲ *fluctuations in share prices* fluctuaciones en los precios de la acción ▲ *movement in share prices* movimiento en los precios de la acción ▲ *regulatory share prices* precios de la acción regulados ▲ *the expected volatility of the share price* la volatibilidad esperada del precio de la acción ▲ *the final share price* el precio de la acción final ▲ *the share price of the day* el precio de la acción del día ▲ *the weighted average share price during the period* el precio de la acción medio ponderado durante el periodo ▲ *year-end share price* precio de la acción a final de año

share price adjustment

A share price adjustment is an adjustment of a share's market value as stated at a given point in time as a result of a change of market price, e.g. on assessing the carrying amount or the tax value of a share. A share price adjustment may result in a capital gain or a capital loss.

ajuste en el precio de la acción

▲ *non-deductible share price adjustments* ajustes no deducibles en el precio de la acción

share price exposure

Share price exposure is the risk of loss due to changes in share prices.

exposición al riesgo del precio de la acción

▲ *compute share price exposure* calcular la exposición al riesgo del precio de la acción ▲ *moderate share price exposure* exposición moderada al riesgo del precio de la acción

share price risk

Share price risk is the risk that share prices may change in future.

riesgo de modificación del precio de la acción

= participación con riesgo de precio

NOTE Spanish accountants prefer 'riesgo de modificación del precio de la acción' to the IAS/IFRS term 'participación con riesgo de precio'. The IAS/IFRS term is nonsensical in Spanish.

▲ *a high share price risk* un riesgo alto de modificación del precio de la acción ▲ *the share price risk measured as VaR (Value-at Risk)* riesgo de modificación del precio de la acción como VaR (Valoración al Riego)

share programme UK

A share programme is an incentive programme involving the awarding of shares, share options or warrants at an especially low price to management executives and other employees in an enterprise subject to achievement of corporate performance goals.

plan de incentivo de acciones

= programa de incentivo de acciones

▲ *a conditional share programme* un programa condicional de incentivo de acciones ▲ *a synthetical share programme* un plan sintético de incentivo de acciones

⇛ employee share ownership plan

share ratio

Share ratios are financial ratios or multiples calculated on the basis of company financial statements with a view to making comparisons between companies in the same industry, as-

sessing the value of companies as well as making investment decisions. Examples of share ratios are earnings per share, cash earnings per share, book value per share, payout ratio, dividend per share, market capitalisation and price/earnings ratio.
ratio de acciones
▲ *calculation of share ratios* cálculo de los ratios de acciones ▲ *comparison of share ratios* comparación de los ratios de acciones ▲ *long-term forecast of share ratios* previsiones a largo plazo de los ratios de acciones

share repurchase US, IAS/IFRS
= share buy-back IAS/IFRS, share buyback UK
A share repurchase is a transaction whereby a company buys back its own outstanding shares from the existing shareholders.
recompra de acciones
= recompensa de las acciones, rescate de acciones
▲ *a share repurchase at fair value* una recompra de acciones a valor razonable ▲ *a share repurchase of $41m* una recompra de acciones de 41 millones de dólares ▲ *a structured share repurchase* una recompra estructurada de las acciones ▲ *the completed share repurchase* la recompra de acciones completada ▲ *the planned share repurchase* la recompra de acciones planificada

share repurchase program US
= share buy-back programme UK, share buyback programme UK, share repurchase programme IAS/IFRS, stock repurchase plan US
A share repurchase program is a program authorised by a company's board of directors by which management can buy back a certain amount of the company's own shares in the market during a specified period of time. The effect of a retirement of an amount of the shares is to reduce the number of outstanding shares, resulting in an increase of the market price and the earnings per share.
plan de recompra de acciones
▲ *commence a share repurchase program* iniciar un plan de recompra de acciones ▲ *complete a share repurchase program* completar un plan de recompra de acciones ▲ *launch a share repurchase program* lanzar un plan de recompra de acciones

share repurchase programme IAS/IFRS, UK
= share buy-back programme UK, IAS/IFRS, share buyback programme UK, share repurchase program US, stock repurchase plan US
A share repurchase programme is a programme authorised by a company's board of directors by which management can buy back a certain amount of the company's own shares in the market during a specified period of time. The effect of a retirement of an amount of the shares is to reduce the number of outstanding shares, resulting in an increase of the market price and the earnings per share.
programa de rescate de acciones
= plan de recompra de las acciones, programa de recompra de acciones, programa de rescate de acciones
▲ *commence a share repurchase programme* iniciar un programa de rescate de acciones ▲ *complete a share repurchase programme* completar un programa de rescate de las acciones ▲ *initiate a share repurchase programme* comenzar un programa de rescate de acciones ▲ *launch a share repurchase programme* lanzar un programa de rescate de acciones

share split UK
= stock split US
A share split refers to an enterprise's division of its existing shares into a larger number of shares with a lower nominal value resulting in a lower share price. A share split does not change the total market value of the enterprise's shares or the shareholdings of the investors.
fraccionamiento del nominal de las acciones
= split
▲ *carry out a share split* llevar a cabo un fraccionamiento del nominal de las acciones ▲ *decrease as a result of a reverse share split* decremento como resultado de un fraccionamiento del nominal de las acciones

▲ *make a share split* hacer un fraccionamiento del nominal de las acciones ▲ *reverse share split* desistir del fraccionamiento del nominal de las acciones
⇛ reverse share split

share subscription
= subscription for shares
A share subscription is the request to purchase shares in a company.
suscripción de acciones
= suscripción de las acciones
▲ *the course of a share subscription process* el curso de un proceso de suscripción de acciones

share trading
= equity trading
Share trading constitutes the purchase or sale of one or more shares.
compraventa de acciones
= compraventa de las acciones
▲ *share trading in the issuer's home market* compraventa de acciones en el mercado nacional del emisor

share-based
If e.g. an instrument, a programme or a financial ratio is "share-based", it means that the instrument, programme or financial ratio has been based on and involves shares or equities.
basado en acciones
▲ *make share-based payments to employees* efectuar pagos basados en acciones a los empleados ▲ *share-based incentive plan* plan de incentivos basado en acciones ▲ *share-based incentives* incentivos basados en acciones ▲ *share-based remuneration expense* gasto por remuneración basada en acciones

share-based payment IAS/IFRS
= stock-based compensation US
Share-based payment is compensation in the form of shares, share options, rights to shares or similar equity instruments for directors, management executives and other employees as well as suppliers as full or part consideration for their services or goods.
NOTE Under IFRS 2, share-based payment transactions are divided into three types: equity-settled, cash-settled or cash- or equity-settled transactions. In equity-settled transactions, the consideration is shares or other equity instruments; in cash-settled transactions, the enterprise provides consideration in an amount based on the price of the enterprise's shares, and for cash- or equity-settled transactions, the consideration is either cash amounts or equity instruments.
pago basado en acciones
▲ *measure the fair value of share-based payment* medir el valor razonable del pago basado en acciones ▲ *recognise share-based payment transactions* reconocer transacciones de pago basado en acciones ▲ *share-based payment transactions* transacciones de pago basado en acciones ▲ *use of share-based payment* uso del pago basado en acciones
SOURCE IFRS 2, paragraph 2

share-based payment arrangement
A share-based payment arrangement is a formal or informal arrangement according to which one or more employees are paid in cash or other assets on the basis of equity securities, e.g. shares, in the company.
acuerdo de pago basado en acciones
= acuerdo de pagos basados en acciones
▲ *agree to a share-based payment arrangement* acordar un acuerdo de pago basado en acciones ▲ *the cancellation of share-based payment arrangements* la cancelación de los acuerdos de pago basado en acciones ▲ *the extent of share-based payment arrangements* la extensión de los acuerdos de pago basado en acciones ▲ *the modification of share-based payment arrangements* las modificación de los acuerdos de pago basado en acciones ▲ *the nature of share-based payment arrangements* la naturaleza de los acuerdos de pago basado en acciones ▲ *the replacement of share-based payment arrangements* la sustitución de los acuerdos de pago basado en acciones ▲ *the specified vesting conditions of a share-based payment arrangement* las condiciones de traspaso especificadas de un acuerdo de pago basado

en acciones ▲ *the total fair value of the share-based payment arrangement* el valor razonable total del acuerdo de pago basado en acciones ▲ *under a share-based payment arrangement* según un acuerdo de pago basado en acciones
SOURCE IFRS 2, Appendix A

share-based payment transaction
IAS/IFRS
A share-based payment transaction is consideration paid by an enterprise in the form of shares, share options or similar equity instruments to employees, suppliers etc. as reimbursement for all or part of their goods and services. A share-based payment transaction also arises if an enterprise incurs liabilities to a supplier by receiving goods or services from that supplier, where the amount of the liabilities depends on the price of shares or similar equity instruments of that enterprise.
transacción con pagos basados en acciones
▲ *current tax arising from share-based payment transactions* impuesto corriente procedente de transacciones con pagos basados en acciones ▲ *deferred tax arising from share-based payment transactions* impuesto diferido procedente de transacciones con pagos basados en acciones ▲ *measure a share-based payment transaction by reference to the fair value of the equity instruments granted* medir una transacción con pagos basados en acciones haciendo referencia al valor razonable de los instrumentos de patrimonio concedidos ▲ *recognise the goods or services received or acquired in a share-based payment transaction* reconocer los bienes o servicios recibidos o adquiridos en una transacción con pagos basados en acciones ▲ *share-based payment transactions in which an entity acquires or receives goods or services* transacciones con pagos basados en acciones en las que una entidad adquiere o recibe bienes o servicios ▲ *share-based payment transactions in which the terms of the arrangement provide the entity with a choice of settlement* transacciones con pagos basados en acciones en las que las condiciones del acuerdo ofrecen a la entidad la elección de liquidación ▲ *share-based payment transactions with cash alternatives* transacciones con pagos basados en acciones con alternativas de efectivo ▲ *undertake a share-based payment transaction* asumir una transacción con pagos basados en acciones
SOURCE IFRS 2, Appendix A

share-price based
An incentive scheme that is share-price based is a plan under which employees will receive additional consideration, e.g. in cash, in amounts based on the market price of an enterprise's shares or on the excess amount of the share price in relation to a fixed amount or index.
basado en el precio de la acción
▲ *share-price based plan* plan basado en el precio de la acción

shareholder
= shareowner US, stockholder US
A person, enterprise or company that owns a share in a company is called a shareholder.
accionista
▲ *a bonus element in a rights issue to existing shareholders* una prima en una emisión de derechos para los accionistas existentes ▲ *a dominant shareholder* un accionista dominante ▲ *a registered shareholder* un accionista registrado ▲ *at the option of the shareholder* a petición del accionista ▲ *become legally obligated to the shareholders* estar obligado de forma legal a los accionistas ▲ *dividends paid to parent shareholders* dividendos pagados a los accionistas de la matriz ▲ *individual shareholder* accionista individual ▲ *institutional shareholder* accionista institucional ▲ *leading shareholders* accionistas dominantes ▲ *on inquiry of a shareholder* a preguntas de un accionista ▲ *shareholders' duties to disclose* deberes de los accionistas a publicar ▲ *the seat or residence of the shareholder* el domicilio o residencia del accionista ▲ *the shareholders of the combining en-*

tities los accionistas de las entidades que se unen

shareholder information

Shareholder information is the information disclosed in the annual report concerning the share capital and shareholders of the company, e.g. the number of shares and their distribution, the price development, the management's holding of shares or the company's holding of own shares.

información al accionista

▲ *the company's shareholder information* la información al accionista de la empresa

shareholders' agreement UK

= shareowner agreement US

A shareholders' agreement is an agreement between two or more shareholders regulating the relationship between the shareholders or their relationship with the company.

acuerdo entre accionistas

= acuerdo entre los accionistas

▲ *disclosures of matters regulated by shareholders' agreements* publicaciones de asuntos regulados por los acuerdos entre accionistas ▲ *enter into a shareholders' agreement* firmar un acuerdo entre accionistas ▲ *prepare a shareholders' agreement* preparar un acuerdo entre accionistas ▲ *there is a shareholders' agreement* hay un acuerdo entre los accionistas

shareholders' equity IAS/IFRS, US

= shareholders' funds UK, stockholders' equity US, total equity IAS/IFRS

Shareholders' equity consists of the capital contributed by owners (shareholders) plus retained earnings (reserves), defined as the company's total assets less its total liabilities. In a group, shareholders' equity is typically distributed on the share of equity attributable to the parent company and the share attributable to minority interests.

NOTE "Shareholders' equity" is used about corporations, where non-incorporated entities apply "owners' equity".

patrimonio neto

▲ *changes in shareholders' equity* cambios en patrimonio neto ▲ *recognise directly in shareholders' equity* reconocer directamente en patrimonio neto ▲ *shareholders' equity at the beginning of the period* patrimonio neto al inicio del periodo ▲ *the consolidated shareholders' equity* el patrimonio neto consolidado ▲ *the opening and closing totals of shareholders' equity of the period* los totales de apertura y cierre de patrimonio neto del periodo

shareholders' funds UK

= shareholders' equity IAS/IFRS, stockholders' equity US, total equity IAS/IFRS

Shareholders' funds consist of the total share capital and reserves of a company, including minority interests, and appear as an item in the balance sheet.

fondos propios

▲ *a change in shareholders' funds* un cambio en los fondos propios ▲ *adjust against shareholders' funds* ajuste contra los fondos propios ▲ *changes in shareholders' funds* cambios en los fondos propios ▲ *recognise directly in shareholders' funds* reconocer directamente en los fondos propios ▲ *reconciliation of movements in shareholders' funds* conciliación de movimientos en los fondos propios ▲ *shareholders' funds at the beginning of the financial year* fondos propios al inicio del ejercicio ▲ *the opening and closing totals of shareholders' funds of the period* los totales de fondos propios al inicio y cierre del periodo

⇛ capital and reserves, owners' equity

shareholders' meeting US

A shareholders' meeting is a meeting of members of a company where they can discuss issues and vote in order to make decisions.

junta general de accionistas

▲ *attend a shareholders' meeting* asistir a una junta general de accionistas ▲ *call a shareholders' meeting* convocar una junta general de accionistas ▲ *hold a shareholders' meeting* celebrar una junta general de accionistas ▲ *notice of shareholders' meeting* notificación de junta general de accionistas ▲ *proposed resolution for the shareholders' meeting* resolución propuesta para la junta general de accionistas ▲ *recommend the annual report for approval by the shareholders' meeting* recomendar el informe anual para su aprobación por la junta general de accionistas ▲ *the approval of the annual report by the shareholders' meeting* la aprobación del informe anual de la junta general de accionistas ▲ *time and place of the shareholders' meeting* hora y lugar de la junta general de accionistas

shareholding

The number of shares held by an entity or an individual at a particular time is referred to as a shareholding.

tenencia de acciones

▲ *a shareholding of 2%* una tenencia de acciones del 2% ▲ *have a shareholding at a similarly low level* tener una tenencia de acciones a un nivel similar bajo ▲ *shareholding at 1 January 2005* tenencia de acciones a 1 de enero de 2005 ▲ *value of shareholding* valor de la tenencia de acciones

shareowner US

= shareholder, stockholder US

A person, enterprise or company that owns a share in a company is called a shareowner.

accionista

▲ *a dominant shareowner* un accionista dominante ▲ *a major shareowner* un accionista principal ▲ *at the option of the shareowner* al deseo del accionista ▲ *leading shareowners* accionistas principales ▲ *the current shareowner* el accionista actual ▲ *the government shareowner* el accionista público

shareowner agreement US

= shareholders' agreement UK

A shareowner agreement is an agreement between two or more shareowners, i.e. shareholders, regulating the relationship between the shareowners or their relationship with the company.

acuerdo entre accionistas

▲ *enter into a shareowner agreement* firmar un acuerdo entre accionistas ▲ *prepare a shareowner agreement* preparar un acuerdo entre accionistas ▲ *there is a shareowner agreement* hay un acuerdo entre los accionistas

shareowners' equity US

= equity, shareholders' funds UK, stockholders' equity US

Shareowners' equity consists of the capital contributed by owners (shareowners) plus retained earnings (reserves), defined as the company's total assets less its total liabilities. In a group, shareowners' equity is typically distributed on the share of equity attributable to the parent company and the share attributable to minority interests.

NOTE "Shareowners' equity" is used about corporations where non-incorporated entities apply "owners' equity".

patrimonio neto

▲ *a change in shareowners' equity* un cambio en el patrimonio neto ▲ *adjust against shareowners' equity* ajustar contra el patrimonio neto ▲ *changes in shareowners' equity* cambios en el patrimonio neto ▲ *recognize directly in shareowners' equity* reconocer directamente en el patrimonio neto ▲ *shareowners' equity at the beginning of the fiscal year* patrimonio neto al inicio del año ▲ *total shareowners' equity* total patrimonio neto

ShareSave UK

ShareSave is a UK savings-related share option scheme offering employees the opportunity of saving for a specified period with an option to buy shares in their company at a fixed price at the end of the savings period.

ShareSave

▲ *options exercised under ShareSave* opciones ejercitadas según ShareSave ▲ *ShareSave plans* planes de ShareSave ▲ *under the employee ShareSave scheme* según el ShareSave de los empleados

short-term

Short-term means relating to or extending over a limited period, usually one year or less.

corto plazo

= a corto

▲ *evidence of a recent actual pattern of short-term profit-taking* prueba de un modelo actual reciente de toma de beneficios a corto plazo ▲ *generate profit from short-term fluctuations in prices* generar beneficio procedente de las fluctuaciones en los precios a corto plazo ▲ *increases in short-term interest rates* aumentos en los tipos de interés a corto plazo ▲ *land held for short-term sale in the ordinary course of business* terreno mantenido para la venta a corto en el curso del negocio ▲ *short-term advances* anticipos a corto plazo ▲ *short-term employee benefits* prestaciones a los empleados a corto plazo ▲ *short-term pre-financing* prefinanciación a corto plazo ▲ *short-term trade receivables and payables* cuentas a cobrar y a pagar a corto plazo

short-term bank deposit

A short-term bank deposit is an amount of money held for a period of up to three months on an account with a bank. Interest may or may not accrue to the account. The deposit may or may not earn interest. Examples of short-term deposit accounts are current accounts and deposit accounts.

depósito bancario a corto plazo

▲ *the effective interest rate on short-term bank deposits* el tipo de interés efectivo de los depósitos bancarios a corto plazo ▲ *the maturity of the short-term bank deposit* el vencimiento del depósito bancario a corto plazo

short-term borrowing

Short-term borrowing refers to a loan or credit facility with a term to maturity of less than one year. In the balance sheet, short-term borrowings appear as an item under current liabilities.

empréstito a corto plazo

▲ *increase in short-term borrowings* aumento en los empréstitos a corto plazo ▲ *the carrying amounts of short-term borrowings* los valores contables de los empréstitos a corto plazo ▲ *total short-term borrowings* total empréstitos a corto plazo

short-term creditor

= account payable IAS/IFRS, US, creditor, amount falling due within one year UK, short-term debt IAS/IFRS, US

≠ long-term creditor

Short-term creditors are creditors representing amounts that fall due within one year.

acreedor a corto plazo

▲ *meet short-term creditor obligations* satisfacer las obligaciones al acreedor a corto plazo

short-term debt US, IAS/IFRS

= account payable US, IAS/IFRS, creditor, amount falling due within one year UK, payable IAS/IFRS, US, short-term creditor

≠ long-term debt US, IAS/IFRS

Short-term debt is an amount owed by an enterprise that falls due within one year, e.g. an amount owed to creditors for goods and services, taxes payable including VAT etc. Short-term debts are recognised under current liabilities in the balance sheet.

deuda a corto plazo

≠ deuda a largo plazo

▲ *changes in short-term debt* cambios en la deuda a corto plazo ▲ *short-term debt owed to credit institutions* deuda a corto plazo contraída con instituciones de crédito

short-term debt obligation US

≠ long-term debt obligation US

A short-term debt obligation is a loan repayable within one year. Examples of short-term debt obligations are commercial paper or the current portion of long-term debt payable within the year.

obligación de deuda a corto plazo

= deuda a corto plazo

≠ obligación de deuda a largo plazo

▲ *meet short-term debt obligations* cumplir las obligaciones de deuda a corto plazo

short-term employee benefit IAS/IFRS

= short-term service benefit

≠ long-term employee benefit IAS/IFRS

Short-term employee benefits refer to benefits earned by employees in return for their current and prior services, such as wages, salaries, bonuses and social security contributions, that fall due within a period of twelve months after the end of the period when the service was rendered.

prestación a los empleados a corto plazo

= beneficio a los empleados a corto plazo

NOTE Spanish accountants prefer 'prestación a los empleados a corto plazo' to the IAS/IFRS term 'beneficio a los empleados a corto plazo'.

▲ *accounting for short-term employee benefits* contabilizando las prestaciones a los empleados a corto plazo ▲ *recognise short-term employee benefits* reconocer las prestaciones a los empleados a corto plazo ▲ *short-term employee benefit obligations* obligaciones por las prestaciones a los empleados a corto plazo ▲ *specific disclosures about short-term employee benefits* publicaciones específicas sobre las prestaciones a los empleados a corto plazo ▲ *the expected cost of short-term employee benefits in the form of compensated absences* el coste esperado de las prestaciones a los empleados a corto plazo en la forma de ausencias compensadas ▲ *the undiscounted amount of short-term employee benefits expected to be paid* la cuantía no descontada de las prestaciones a los empleados a corto plazo

⇛ long-term employee benefit

short-term investment

≠ long-term investment

A short-term investment is an investment in assets that are held for trading, i.e. intended disposed of in the near future, typically within one year. Examples of short-term investments are trading investments.

inversión a corto plazo

▲ *disposals of short-term investments* ventas de inversiones a corto plazo ▲ *maximize short-term investment return* maximizar la rentabilidad de las inversiones a corto plazo

⇛ trading investment

short-term provisions IAS/IFRS

≠ long-term provisions IAS/IFRS

Short-term provisions are current liabilities that are uncertain in terms of amount or timing and that concern the financial year or a previous year. NOTE Short-term provisions are recognised as an item under current liabilities in the balance sheet.

provisiones a corto plazo

▲ *changes in short-term provisions* cambios en provisiones a corto plazo ▲ *other short-term provisions* otras provisiones a corto plazo ▲ *reclassify from long-term to short-term provisions* reclasificar desde provisiones a largo plazo a provisiones a corto plazo

⇛ current liability

short-term receivable

Short-term receivables are claims against third parties, e.g. customers and others for goods, services or amounts of money which are typically due from credit sales. Short-term receivables are classified as current assets in the balance sheet.

cuentas a cobrar a corto plazo

= deudores a corto plazo

≠ acreedores a corto plazo, cuentas a pagar a corto plazo

▲ *cash flows relating to short-term receivables* flujos de efectivo relativos a las cuentas a cobrar a corto plazo ▲ *decrease in short-term receivables* disminución en las cuentas a cobrar a corto plazo ▲ *increase in short-term receivables* incremento en las cuentas a cobrar a corto plazo ▲ *short-term receivables in which the entity guarantees to compensate the transferee for credit losses that are likely to occur* cuentas a cobrar a corto plazo con las que la entidad garantiza compensar al cesionario por pérdidas crediticias que pueden ocurrir con probabilidad ▲ *short-term receivables with no stated interest rate* cuentas a cobrar a corto plazo con un tipo de interés no declarado

show

To show something means to present or give an indication of it.

mostrar

= exhibir, exponer

▲ *omit to show revenue* dejar de mostrar ingresos ▲ *show a balance of USD 100,000* mostrar un saldo de 100.000 dólares norteamericanos ▲ *show a decline* mostrar un declive ▲ *show a loss* mostrar una pérdida ▲ *show a profit* mostrar un beneficio ▲ *show cash and cash equivalents* mostrar efectivo y equivalentes de efectivo ▲ *show cash flows* mostrar flujos de efectivo ▲ *show historical data* mostrar datos históricos ▲ *show separately the effect of each change that has a material effect on the financial statements* mostrar por separado el efecto de cada cambio que tenga un efecto material sobre los estados financieros ▲ *show signs of* mostrar signos de ▲ *show the profit or loss for the year* mostrar el resultado del año

SIC IAS/IFRS

SIC is the abbreviation for the Standing Interpretations Committee which has now been restructured and replaced by IFRIC (the International Financial Reporting Interpretations Committee) in 2002. The role of the SIC was to prepare interpretations of issues relating to International Accounting Standards. SIC interpretations have now been replaced by IFRIC interpretations.

Comité de Interpretaciones de las NIC

▲ *amendments to SIC 32* enmiendas al Comité de Interpretaciones de las NIC 32

SIC decision

= SIC interpretation

A SIC decision is an interpretation of an issue relating to the International Accounting Standards (IASs) by the former Standing Interpretations Committee (SIC), in this way providing guidance on financial reporting issues. SIC was replaced by IFRIC (the International Financial Reporting Interpretations Committee in 2002.

interpretación del Comité de Interpretaciones de las NIC

= interpretación SIC

▲ *according to the relevant SIC decision* de acuerdo con la interpretación relevante del Comité de Interpretaciones de las NIC

⇛ IFRIC, IFRIC interpretation, SIC interpretation

SIC interpretation

= SIC decision

A SIC interpretation is the interpretation of an issue relating to the International Accounting Standards (IASs) provided by the former Standing Interpretations Committee (SIC), in this way providing guidance on financial reporting issues. SIC was replaced by IFRIC (the International Financial Reporting Interpretations Committee in 2002.

interpretación SIC

= interpretación del Comité de Interpretaciones de las NIC

▲ *issue SIC interpretations* emitir interpretaciones SIC ▲ *SIC interpretations on the interpretation of the Standards* interpretaciones SIC en la interpretación de las Normas ▲ *withdraw draft SIC Interpretation D34* anular el borrador de la interpretación SIC D34

⇛ IFRIC

significant

When something is significant, it is considered to have a high level of importance or materiality.

significativo

▲ *a significant change in economic circumstances* un cambio significativo en las circunstancias económicas ▲ *a significant decline in budgeted operating profit* un descenso significativo en el beneficio de explotación presupuestado ▲ *a significant deterioration in the issuer's creditworthiness* un deterioro significativo en la solvencia crediticia del emisor ▲ *a significant increase in the industry's regulatory capital requirements* un aumento significativo en el capital obligatorio de la industria ▲ *a significant part of an item of property, plant and equipment* una parte significativa de una partida de edificios, instalaciones y equipos ▲ *a significant portion of the total contractual benefits* una parte significativa del total de las prestaciones contractuales ▲ *cast significant doubt upon the entity's ability to continue as a going concern* arrojar dudas significativas sobre la capacidad de la empresa para continuar como una empresa en funcionamiento ▲ *enter into significant commitments* firmar compromisos significativos ▲ *life insurance contracts in which the insurer bears no significant mortality risk* contratos de seguros de vida en los que el asegurador no asume riesgo significativo de mortalidad ▲ *operate at a significant loss* operar con una pérdida significativa ▲ *significant changes with a favourable effect on the entity* cambios significativos con un efecto favorable en la entidad ▲ *significant changes with an adverse effect on the entity* cambios significativos con un efecto adverso sobre la entidad ▲ *significant deficiency in internal control* deficiencia significativa en el control interno ▲ *significant factors influencing the negotiations* factores significativos que influyen en las negociaciones ▲ *significant financial difficulty of the issuer or obligor* dificultad financiera significativa del emisor u obligado ▲ *significant insurance risks* riesgos significativos del seguro ▲ *the significant assumptions used to determine fair value* los supuestos significativos utilizados para determinar el valor razonable

significant influence

≠ control, dominant influence

Significant influence refers to the capacity to participate in, but not to control, the financial and operating policy decisions of an enterprise. This capacity may result from a shareholding, an agreement or from legislation.

NOTE An enterprise is presumed to be an associate if another enterprise owns 20-50 per cent of its voting shares, which constitutes significant influence.

influencia significativa

▲ *an interest in the entity that gives the party significant influence over the entity* un interés en la entidad que da a la parte influencia significativa sobre la entidad ▲ *entities under significant influence* entidades bajo influencia significativa ▲ *entities with joint control or significant influence over the entity* entidades con control conjunto o influencia significativa sobre la entidad ▲ *exercise significant influence* ejercer influencia significativa ▲ *from the date when the investor ceases to have significant influence over an associate* desde la fecha en la que el inversor deja de tener influencia significativa sobre una asociada ▲ *gain significant influence* ganar influencia significativa ▲ *gain significant influence by share ownership or agreement* ganar influencia significativa por medio de la propiedad de acciones o acuerdo ▲ *lose significant influence over an investee* perder influencia significativa sobre una participada ▲ *the existence of significant influence by an investor* la existencia de influencia significativa de un inversor

⇛ associate, subsidiary

single proprietorship US

→ sole proprietorship

site

A site is a defined area of land which is suitable for building purposes or on which a building is located.

emplazamiento

= lugar

▲ *a contaminated site* un emplazamiento contaminado ▲ *costs of site dismantlement, removal and restoration* costes de desmantelamiento, retirada y restauración del emplazamiento ▲ *costs of site preparation* costes de preparación del emplazamiento ▲ *restore the site on completion of operations* restaurar el emplazamiento al finalizar las operaciones ▲ *sites used for landfill* emplazamiento utilizado como vertedero ▲ *the costs of dismantling and removing the item and restoring the site on which it is located* los costes de desmantelamiento y de retirada de la partida y de rehabilitación del emplazamiento en el que se asienta

six months

Six months make up half a year.

seis meses

= semestral

▲ *during the first six months of 2005* durante los primeros seis meses de 2005

Six Sigma

Six Sigma is a business development concept the purpose of which is to detect and remedy errors and deficiencies in the processes and product designs of an enterprise. This is done by focusing on customers' needs and on the factors that impact these needs.

Seis Sigma

= Six Sigma

▲ *a Six Sigma project* un proyecto de Seis Sigma ▲ *Six Sigma conversion table* tabla de conversión Seis Sigma ▲ *Six Sigma resources* recursos Seis Sigma ▲ *Six Sigma training* formación Seis Sigma

▲ *the concept of Six Sigma* el concepto de Seis Sigma

six-month period

= half-year period

A six-month period is a period covering a time span of half a year, i.e. six months.

semestre

▲ *the current six-month period* el semestre actual ▲ *the end of the six-month period* el final del semestre ▲ *the past six-month period* el semestre pasado ▲ *the previous six-month period* el semestre anterior

SL method

→ straight-line method

slack

Slack means the flexibility that you have when you change or do something.

laxitud

▲ *budgetary slack* laxitud presupuestaria ▲ *considerable slack* laxitud considerable ▲ *economic slack* laxitud económica

small acquisition

= minor acquisition

Small acquisitions are assets acquired at a cost not exceeding a defined value, which are expensed in the profit and loss account, i.e. written off in the year of acquisition instead of being recognised under fixed assets and depreciated.

pequeña adquisición

▲ *small acquisitions and losses on sale* pequeñas adquisiciones y pérdidas por ventas

smoothing

Smoothing is the levelling of prices, income, wealth or other variables.

estabilización

▲ *smoothing of earnings over interim periods within a financial year* estabilización de los beneficios durante los periodos intercalarios de un año financiero ▲ *smoothing of profits* estabilización de beneficios

⇛ income smoothing, profit smoothing

social

Social is a term relating to human society and the interaction that takes place between people living in it. The term social also relates to the mutual dependence between people in a community and in the context of welfare to the social security schemes provided by this community.

social

▲ *social commitment* compromiso social ▲ *social issues* asuntos sociales ▲ *social responsibility* responsabilidad social ▲ *social responsibility* responsabilidad social ▲ *social security* seguridad social

social bottom line

The social bottom line contains information about knowledge, ethics and social issues.

programa social

▲ *social bottom line objectives* objetivos del programa social

social report

A social report is a statement about the social responsibility, attitude and conduct of an enterprise in relation to employees and people who might otherwise be affected by the enterprise's conduct on the social level (for instance applicants, resigned employees, family, minorities or vulnerable groups in a local community). A social report also includes information about an enterprise's sponsorships, charitable donations and other social activities.

informe social

▲ *publish environmental and social reports* publicar informes medioambientales y sociales

social responsibility

= corporate social responsibility, CSR

Social responsibility or corporate social responsibility is the obligation and awareness of enterprises to employees, stakeholders and the society at large to act in decision-making and business operations in a way that meets the ethical, business, public and legal expectations of society to a business organisation. The focus is on obtaining sustainable development not only economically, but also for social and environmental purposes.

responsabilidad social

▲ *corporate social responsibility* responsabilidad social corporativa

social security IAS/IFRS

Social security is a term covering a range of schemes regulated by public legislation or in some instances administered by private enterprises. Social security is a safety net aiming at providing existential security for a population, and it may comprise health insurance, unemployment compensation, employer's liability insurance, family and maternal benefits, sickness and disability transfers, as well as pensions.

NOTE In the income statement, "social security" is an item recognising the social security costs incurred by the enterprise for its employees.

seguridad social

▲ *other social security costs* otros costes de la seguridad social ▲ *social security contributions payable* contribuciones a pagar por la seguridad social ▲ *social security costs* costes de la seguridad social ▲ *social security costs with separate specification of pensions* costes de la seguridad social con desagregaciones por aportaciones a planes de pensiones

social security contribution

Social security contribution is a tax calculated as a percentage of gross wages and salaries. Social security contributions finance social security schemes.

contribución a la seguridad social

= contribución a seguridad social, cotizaciones a la seguridad social

▲ *gross income after social security contributions* ingreso bruto después de contribuciones a la seguridad social ▲ *pay social security contributions* pagar las contribuciones a la seguridad social ▲ *social security contributions withheld* contribuciones retenidas a seguridad social ▲ *withhold social security contributions* retener las contribuciones a la seguridad social

sole proprietor

→ sole proprietorship

sole proprietorship

= proprietor US, single proprietorship, sole proprietor, sole trader

A sole proprietorship is a type of unincorporated entity owned and operated by a single individual who is personally liable for all debts and obligations of the entity.

empresa individual

▲ *conversion of a sole proprietorship into a limited company* conversión de una empresa individual en una sociedad anónima ▲ *private sole proprietorships* empresas individuales privadas

sole trader

= sole proprietor

A sole trader is a type of unincorporated entity owned and operated by a single individual who is personally liable for all debts and obligations of the entity.

autónomo

= empresario individual

▲ *operate as a sole trader* funcionar como un empresario individual ▲ *private sole traders* empresarios individuales privados

solvency

Solvency refers to the ability of an enterprise to meet its financial obligations as they fall due.

solvencia

▲ *assess the liquidity and solvency of an entity* asegurar la liquidez y la solvencia de una entidad ▲ *the solvency of insurance companies* la solvencia de las compañías de seguros

solvency margin

A solvency margin is a minimum capital adequacy requirement imposed on an enterprise. Some business sectors, such as the banking, insurance and pension sectors, are subject to this requirement. Under the Basle Committee rules of the Bank for International Settlements, the requirement is e.g. that a bank must hold an minimum capital of 8% of the assets.

margen de solvencia

▲ *an adequate available solvency margin* un margen de solvencia disponible adecuado ▲ *required solvency margin for a reinsurance undertaking simultaneously conducting non-life and life reinsurance* margen de solvencia exigido a una reaseguradora que gestiona simultáneamente pólizas de vida y no vida ▲ *solvency margin requirements* requisitos del margen de solvencia ▲ *the available solvency margin* el margen de solvencia disponible ▲ *the required solvency margin* el margen de solvencia requerido

solvency ratio

= equity ratio

The solvency ratio is defined as shareholders' equity at year-end divided by total assets and shows the capital adequacy of an enterprise. The solvency of an enterprise is improved if shareholders' equity increases because of generated profits or repaid debt.

ratio de solvencia

▲ *calculation of the solvency ratio* cálculo del ratio de solvencia

⇛ capital adequacy ratio

solvent

A solvent enterprise is able to meet its financial obligations as they fall due.

solvente

▲ *a solvent company* una compañía solvente ▲ *a solvent entity* una entidad solvente

SORP UK

= Statement of Recommended Practice UK

SORP is the abbreviation for Statement of Recommended Practice. SORPs are non-mandatory documents issued since 1986 by the former Accounting Standards Committee (ASC) or by various bodies for particular industries and franked by the ASC. SORPs are recommendations on accounting practices for specialised industries or sectors and supplement accounting legislation and standards. The successor of the ASC, the Accounting Standards Board, does not issue or frank SORPs.

Documento de Prácticas Recomendadas

▲ *prepared under SORP 2005* preparado según el Documento de Prácticas Recomendadas 2005 ▲ *the main recommendations of the SORP* las principales recomendaciones del Documento de Prácticas Recomendadas

source and application of funds statement

→ statement of source and application of funds

source document

A source document is a document that provides evidence and documentation for certain activities, e.g. transactions that an enterprise is involved in, e.g. an invoice, and therefore constitutes an incorporated part of the bookkeeping records.

documento de origen

▲ *prepare a source document* preparar un documento de origen ▲ *the source document associated with the cost of materials* el documento de origen asociado con el coste de los materiales

⇛ voucher

source of funds

= source of funding

The sources of funds of an enterprise are operating, investing or financing activities that contribute to increasing cash through cash inflows such as profit generated from operations, contributions from owners, raising of loan capital, disposal of fixed assets etc. Sources of funds and uses of funds appear from the cash flow statement.

origen de fondos

= origen de los fondos

▲ *a description of sources of funds* una descripción de los orígenes de los fondos ▲ *the anticipated sources of funds needed to fulfill the commitments* los orígenes de los fondos anticipados necesarios para cumplir los compromisos

⇛ cash flow statement

SOX US

= Sarbanes-Oxley Act US

SOX is an abbreviation for the Sarbanes-Oxley Act which aims to strengthen corporate governance and restore investor confidence.

Ley Sarbanes-Oxley

▲ *meet SOX financial reporting requirements* cumplir los requisitos de información financiera de la Ley Sarbanes-Oxley ▲ *pursuant to SOX 404* en virtud de la Ley 404 Sarbanes-Oxley

⇛ Sarbanes-Oxley Act

SPE IAS/IFRS

= special purpose entity IAS/IFRS

SPE is the abbreviation for special purpose entity. An SPE is an entity, whether incorporated or unincorporated, established by a reporting enterprise with a view to achieving a limited, well-defined purpose.

ECE

= Empresa con Cometido Especial, Empresa con Propósito Especial, EPE

▲ *be exposed to risks incident to the activities of the SPE* estar expuesto a la incidencia de riesgos por las actividades de la ECE ▲ *have control over an SPE* tener el control de una ECE ▲ *impact on the operations of the SPE* impacto en las operaciones de la ECE ▲ *obtain benefits from the SPE's operation* obtener prestaciones por operaciones de la ECE ▲ *obtain the majority of the benefits of the activities of the SPE* obtener la mayoría de las prestaciones de las actividades de la ECE ▲ *own little or none of the SPE's equity* poseer poco o nada del patrimonio de la ECE ▲ *retain the majority of the residual or ownership risks related to the SPE* mantener la mayoría de riesgos de propiedad o residuales relacionados con la ECE ▲ *the predetermination of the activities of the SPE* la predeterminación de las actividades de la ECE

special

If something is special it is unusual or not common.

especial

▲ *a share consolidation combined with a special dividend* una consolidación de acciones con un dividendo especial ▲ *provide for special accounting for regular way contracts* ofrecer contabilidad especial a los contratos regulares ▲ *provide for special treatment for so-called synthetic instruments* ofrecer tratamiento especial a los llamados instrumentos sintéticos

special purpose entity IAS/IFRS

= SPE IAS/IFRS

A special purpose entity is an entity, whether incorporated or unincorporated, established by a reporting enterprise with a view to achieving a limited, well-defined purpose.

entidad con cometido especial

= ECE, empresa con propósito especial, EPE

▲ *the substance of the relationship between the entity and a special purpose entity* la sustancia de la relación entre la entidad y una entidad con cometido especial

SOURCE SIC 12

special purpose financial report UK

≠ general purpose financial report UK

A special purpose financial report contains special, required financial information and is prepared by an enterprise for parties with the authority to obtain that information. Examples include regulatory returns, tax returns and financial reports prepared for bankers.

informe financiero con propósito especial

▲ *audit the attached special purpose financial report* auditar el informe financiero con propósito especial adjunto ▲ *prepare a special purpose financial report* preparar un informe financiero con propósito especial

special shareholders' meeting US

= extraordinary general meeting UK

A special shareholders' meeting is any meeting of the shareholders of a company and its directors that is not an annual general meeting, and its purpose is to discuss and vote on issues that cannot wait to be resolved at the next annual general meeting.

junta general extraordinaria

= junta extraordinaria de accionistas

▲ *call a special shareholders' meeting* convocar una junta general extraordinaria ▲ *hold a special shareholders' meeting* llevar a cabo una junta general extraordinaria ▲ *notice of a special shareholders' meeting* notificación de una junta general extraordinaria ▲ *resolve at a special shareholders' meeting* resolver en una junta general extraordinaria

specific identification

= specific identification method

Specific identification is a method for determining inventory value where the actual cost of a specific product is matched to each unit of output or item sold, such as a car, a work of art such as a piece of jewellery, or another high-cost product.

método de identificación específica de inventarios

= método de identificación específica de los inventarios

▲ *use specific identification* utilizar el método de identificación específica de inventarios

specific price index

A specific price index is an index measuring the changes in

the price level of a specifically defined product, e.g. oil, over a period of time.

índice de precios específico

≠ índice de precios general

▲ *use a specific price index* utilizar un índice de precios específico

⇛ general price index

specification

= breakdown

A specification is a detailed description or a clear statement of something, e.g. a breakdown of amounts on specified items.

anotación

▲ *Specifications to the Annual Report* Anotaciones al Informe Anual

specify

To specify means to define something clearly, to identify it or describe it in detail.

especificar

▲ *a specified proportion of the future economic benefits embodied in the asset* una proporción especificada de los beneficios económicos futuros ▲ *specify disclosures that should be made in financial statements* especificar las publicaciones que deben aparecer en los estados financieros ▲ *specify the financial reporting by an entity when it undertakes a business combination* especificar la información financiera de una entidad cuando lleva a cabo una combinación de negocios ▲ *specify when recoverable amount shall be determined* especificar cuándo se determinará la cantidad a recuperar

split-off

≠ merger

A split-off or partial division is an operation whereby a company transfers, without being dissolved, part of its assets and liabilities in the form of one or more branches of activity to another existing or newly established company (the receiving company). The transferring company's shareholders will, in exchange, receive securities on a pro-rata basis representing the capital of the receiving company.

escisión

= segregación

▲ *a tax-exempt split-off* una escisión exenta fiscalmente

split-off point

= splitoff point

The split-off point is the stage in joint production where the individual products are separated from each other.

punto de escisión

▲ *identify the split-off point* identificar el punto de escisión ▲ *the cost incurred up to the split-off point* el coste incurrido hasta el punto de escisión ▲ *the costs incurred after the split-off point* los costes incurridos después del punto de escisión

⇛ joint costs, joint production, separable costs

splitoff point

→ split-off point

spoilage

Spoilage refers to units of production that do not meet customer requirements and specifications and which are therefore discarded or sold at reduced prices such as clothes or shoes sold as defective products, i.e. "seconds".

desperdicio

= desecho

▲ *a minimum of spoilage* un mínimo de desperdicio ▲ *prevent spoilage* prevenir el desperdicio

⇛ abnormal spoilage, normal spoilage

sponsor[1] *noun*

A person or enterprise that supports an activity, event, education programme etc. financially or otherwise is called a sponsor.

espónsor

= patrocinador

▲ *guaranteed by the sponsor* garantizado por el espónsor

sponsor[2] *verb*

To sponsor an activity, event, education programme etc. means to support it financially or otherwise.

patrocinar

= esponsorizar

▲ *sponsor the training of employees* patrocinar la formación de los empleados

sponsoring

= sponsorship

Sponsoring is the act of supporting organisations, individuals or events, either financially or materially, normally in return for brand recognition or publicity.

patrocinio

= esponsorización

▲ *the sponsoring of art* el patrocinio del arte

sponsorship

= sponsoring

A sponsorship may be support from a person or an organisation, either in financial or material form, to organisations, individuals or events, ordinarily in return for brand recognition or publicity.

patrocinio

= esponsorización

nio local ▲ *a national sponsorship* un patrocinio nacional ▲ *a regional sponsorship* un patrocinio regional ▲ *portfolio of sponsorships* cartera de patrocinios ▲ *sponsorship agreement* contrato de patrocinio ▲ *sponsorship deal* acuerdo de patrocinio

spot market

The spot market is a subcategory of the foreign exchange market. In the spot market, currencies are traded with delivery within two business days, whereas in the forward exchange market, delivery will take place at a future date specified in the relevant forward contract.

mercado al contado

▲ *a global spot market* un mercado al contado global ▲ *spot market pricing* fijación del precio en el mercado al contado ▲ *the price on the spot market* el precio en el mercado al contado ▲ *trade in the spot market* negociar en el mercado al contado

⇛ foreign exchange maket, forward exchange market

spot rate

= current rate of exchange

The spot rate is the the current rate of exchange quoted for delivery now rather than in future.

tipo de cambio al contado

▲ *at the spot rate* al tipo de cambio al contado ▲ *use the spot rate on translation* usar el tipo de cambio al contado en la conversión

spreadsheet

A spreadsheet is a sheet showing accounting figures in cells arranged in rows and columns used for calculation, typically in a computer program such as Excel or Lotus, that allows automatic calculations subject to particular formulas entered by the user.

hoja de cálculo

▲ *the capital asset spreadsheet* la hoja de cálculo de bienes de capital ▲ *use a spreadsheet* usar una hoja de cálculo

SSAP UK

= Statement of Standard Accounting Practice UK

SSAP is the abbreviation for Statement of Standard Accounting Practice. SSAPs are the accounting standards issued pre-1990 by the former UK Accounting Standards Committee. Some SSAPs remain in force, whereas others have been replaced and supplemented by the new Financial Reporting Standards (FRSs) that are issued by the Accounting Standards Board.

SSAP

= Guía de la Práctica Contable

▲ *the issue of a new SSAP* la emisión de un nuevo SSAP ▲ *withdrawal of SSAP 1* retirada del SSAP1

⇛ accounting standard, FRS

stability

Stability refers to the quality of being static and unchanged.

estabilidad

▲ *earnings stability* estabilidad de beneficios ▲ *satisfactory stability* estabilidad satisfactoria ▲ *the stability of the industry in which the asset operates* la estabilidad del sector en el que opera el activo ▲ *the stability of the sector* la estabilidad del sector

staff

Staff refers to the total number of employees in an enterprise and can particularly refer to employees holding staff positions within management, support or services, where employees in line positions work directly with the enterprise's core operating activities.

plantilla

= personal, staff

▲ *a dedicated and competent staff* un personal competente y dedicado ▲ *costs of staff training* costes de formación del personal ▲ *expenditure on training staff to operate the asset* gasto en formación del personal para operar el activo ▲ *increase the staff* aumentar la plantilla ▲ *re-*

duce the staff reducir la plantilla ▲ *staff attrition* reducción de plantilla ▲ *the managerial staff* el personal de gestión

staff cost

= employee cost, employee expense US, personnel expense, staff expense

Staff cost constitutes the costs of an enterprise relating to salaries, wages, pension costs, uniforms, training etc.

coste de personal

= coste del personal

▲ *breakdown of staff costs* clasificación de los costes de personal ▲ *comparatives for staff costs* comparativas para los costes de personal ▲ *disclose staff costs* divulgar los costes de personal ▲ *other staff costs* otros costes de personal ▲ *reductions in staff costs* reducciones en los costes de personal ▲ *staff costs in proportion to total costs* costes de personal en proporción a los costes totales ▲ *staff costs payable* costes de personal a pagar

staff expense

= employee cost, employee expense US, personnel expense, staff cost

Staff expenses are the costs of an enterprise relating to salaries, wages, pension costs, uniforms, training etc.

gasto de personal

= gasto en personal

▲ *other staff expenses* otros gastos en personal ▲ *profit-related staff expenses* gastos de personal relacionados con beneficios ▲ *specification of staff expenses* especificaciones de los gastos de personal

staff group

= group of employees

A staff group is a number of employees in an enterprise carrying out similar jobs. Employees can be divided into those holding staff positions within management, support or services and those holding line positions working directly with the enterprise's core operating activities.

grupo de empleados

▲ *a dedicated staff group* un grupo de empleados comprometidos ▲ *provide training for each staff group* ofrecer formación a cada grupo de empleados

staff turnover UK

= employee turnover US

Staff turnover is a financial ratio measuring the rate of employee replacement in per cent, and it shows whether employees are replaced frequently or whether the headcount is rather stable during a particular accounting period.

facturación por empleado

▲ *a decrease in staff turnover* un decrecimiento en la facturación por empleado ▲ *an increase in staff turnover* un aumento en la facturación por empleado ▲ *high staff turnover* facturación por empleado elevada ▲ *staff turnover rate* tasa de facturación por empleado

stage of completion

The stage of completion is used in connection with project contracts. It is the estimated value of the part of the contract that has been carried out at a specific date, e.g. the reporting date. The stage of completion can be calculated according to different methods depending on the specific situation, e.g. as the relation between the incurred and the estimated expenses of the entire contract.

estado de realización

= estado de ejecución

▲ *a share of the profit based on the stage of completion* una parte del beneficio basada en el estado de realización ▲ *by reference to the stage of completion* por referencia al estado de realización ▲ *determination of the stage of completion* determinación del estado de realización ▲ *measure the stage of completion* medir el estado de realización ▲ *measurement of the stage of completion* valoración del estado de realización ▲ *method for determining the stage of completion* método para determinar el estado de realización ▲ *reach the current stage of completion* alcanzar el estado de realización actual ▲ *the estimated stage of completion* el estado de realización estimado ▲ *the stage of completion at the balance sheet date* el estado de realización a la fecha del balance ▲ *the stage of completion of a construction contract* el estado de realización de un contrato de obra ▲ *the stage of completion of the contract activity* el estado de realización del contrato

stakeholder

Stakeholders constitute a mixed group of individuals with particular interest in a given enterprise including shareholders (owners), employees, creditors, suppliers, customers, financial analysts, potential investors as well as the media, all of whom are typically users of the annual report and the financial statements.

partícipe

= stakeholder

▲ *key stakeholders* partícipes claves ▲ *primary stakeholder* stakeholder primario ▲ *the long-term interest of stakeholders* el interés de los partícipes a largo plazo

stakeholder financial statements

= stakeholder report

Stakeholder financial statements should be seen in the context of the intellectual capital report and report how an enterprise has identified its major stakeholders and created added value to its stakeholders. Stakeholder financial statements are external reports based on a dialogue with the stakeholders and are the responsibility of the enterprise's management.

estados financieros de los partícipes

= estados financieros de los stakeholders, estados financieros para los partícipes, estados financieros para los stakeholders

▲ *issue stakeholder financial statements* emitir los informes financieros de los stakeholders ▲ *prepare stakeholder financial statements* preparar los estados financieros para los stakeholders

stakeholder report

= stakeholder financial statements

A stakeholder report should be seen in the context of the intellectual capital report and reports how an enterprise has identified its major stakeholders and created added value to its stakeholders. Stakeholder reports are external reports based on a dialogue with the stakeholders and are the responsibility of the enterprise's management.

informe de los partícipes

▲ *prepare a stakeholder report* preparar un informe para los stakeholders ▲ *publish a stakeholder report* publicar un informe de los partícipes

stand-alone basis

On a stand-alone basis means on a separate or individual basis.

en base individual

▲ *measure on a stand-alone basis* medir en base individual ▲ *present on a stand-alone basis* presentar en base individual

stand-alone derivative

A stand-alone derivative is a derivative financial instrument that is not an embedded derivative, i.e. it is a separate instrument that is not a component of a hybrid (combined) financial instrument.

derivado individual

▲ *account for as a stand-alone derivative* contabilizar como un derivado individual

stand-alone entity US

= separate entity UK

A stand-alone entity is an enterprise whose activities are not integrated in the activities of the reporting entity and whose financial statements are prepared on an individual basis.

entidad autónoma

▲ *a stand-alone entity preparing financial statements* una entidad autónoma que prepara los estados financieros

standard

A standard is an established level used as a rule or basis for comparison in measuring or judging capacity, quantity, content, value, quality, etc., which helps to ensure that minimum requirements are met.

norma

= standard, regla, normativa

▲ *a US standard* una norma norteamericana ▲ *according to the definition of the standard* de acuerdo con la definición del estándar

standard cost

A standard cost refers to the predetermined cost per unit of a product or service based on the different types of costs incurred when producing goods

or delivering services. The standard cost should be attained, i.e. the actual cost incurred should not differ from the predetermined standard cost.
coste estándar
= sistema de costes estándar
▲ *revalue standard costs on a continuing basis* revaluar los costes estándar en una base continua ▲ *the standard cost method* el método de coste estándar

standard costing
= standard costing method, standard costing system
Standard costing is a costing system that predetermines standard costs for output. Direct costs are related to cost objects by applying standard prices that are multiplied by the standard inputs allowed for actual outputs produced. Indirect production costs are allocated on the basis of the budgeted indirect production cost rate multiplied by the standard inputs (in units) allowed for actual outputs produced.
sistema de coste estándar
▲ *use standard costing* utilizar un sistema de coste estándar
⇛ standard cost

standard costing method
= standard costing, standard costing system
The standard costing method is a costing method that predetermines standard costs for output. Direct costs are related to cost objects by applying standard prices that are multiplied by the standard inputs allowed for actual outputs produced. Indirect production costs are allocated on the basis of the budgeted indirect production cost rate multiplied by the standard inputs (in units) allowed for actual outputs produced.
método de coste estándar
= método de costes estándar
▲ *improvement of the standard costing method* mejora del método de coste estándar ▲ *under the standard costing method* según el método de costes estándar ▲ *use the standard costing method* usar el método de coste estándar
⇛ standard cost

standard costing system
= standard costing, standard costing method
The standard costing system is a costing system that predetermines standard costs for output. Direct costs are related to cost objects by applying standard prices that are multiplied by the standard inputs allowed for actual outputs produced. Indirect production costs are allocated on the basis of the budgeted indirect production cost rate multiplied by the standard inputs (in units) allowed for actual outputs produced.
sistema de coste estándar
= sistema de costes estándar
▲ *a component in the standard costing system* un componente en el sistema de coste estándar ▲ *improvement of the standard costing system* mejora del sistema de coste estándar ▲ *use the standard costing system* usar el sistema de costes estándar
⇛ standard cost

standard deviation
A standard deviation is a deviation from an average at a given measurement. For return on shares, the standard deviation is a risk target that shows how much the return deviates from the average historical return. The wider the standard deviation, the larger the fluctuations have been historically. The historical standard deviations can indicate future return fluctuations.
desviación estándar
▲ *repeatability standard deviation* repetición de la desviación estándar ▲ *standard deviation on monthly observations* desviación estándar en las observaciones mensuales ▲ *the annualised standard deviation* la desviación estándar anualizada ▲ *the standard deviation of the continuously compounded rates of return on the share* la desviación estándar de las tasas de rentabilidad de las acciones compuestas de forma continua

standard input
A standard input is an input quantity specified in advance as the input that is required to produce one unit of the output.
entrada estándar
▲ *select standard input values* seleccionar valores de entrada estándar

standard price

Standard price refers to the price that is normally paid for a particular product in a specific market or to the fixed price of a product quoted in a catalogue, price list, etc.

precio estandar

▲ *charge a standard price* cargar un precio estándar ▲ *the standard price of oil* el precio estándar del petróleo ▲ *the standard price of the product* el precio estándar del producto

standardisation UK, IAS/IFRS

= standardization US

Standardisation is the process of making a process or item of output uniform.

estandarización

▲ *process standardisation* estandarización de procesos ▲ *product standardisation* estandarización de productos

standardise UK, IAS/IFRS

= standardize US

When you standardise something you try to make it uniform within a particular field, product group or in relation to a specific method.

estandarizar

▲ *standardise a process* estandarizar un proceso ▲ *standardised contracts traded on an exchange* estandarizar los contratos negociados en un intercambio

standardization US

= standardisation UK, IAS/IFRS

Standardization is the process of making a process or item of output uniform.

estandarización

▲ *process standardization* estandarización de procesos ▲ *product standardization* estandarización de productos

standardize US

= standardise UK, IAS/IFRS

When you standardize something you try to make it uniform within a particular field, product group or in relation to a specific method.

estandarizar

▲ *standardize a process* estandarizar un proceso ▲ *standardized contracts traded on an exchange* contratos estandarizados negociados en un intercambio

start

To start means to begin.

iniciar

= empezar

▲ *start by* empezar por ▲ *start new operations* iniciar nuevas operaciones ▲ *start to implement the restructuring plan* empezar a implementar el plan de reestructuración

start-up

A start-up refers to the activities involved in the launching of a new business venture, project or enterprise.

lanzamiento

= constitución

▲ *expenditure on start-up activities* gastos por actividades de lanzamiento ▲ *start-up funding* financiación del lanzamiento ▲ *start-up period* periodo de lanzamiento

start-up activity

Start-up activities are activities involved in the launching of a new business venture, project or enterprise.

actividad de lanzamiento

start-up cost

= initial costs

Start-up costs are expenses incurred in connection with the launching of a new enterprise or business project.

coste de lanzamiento

= coste de establecimiento

▲ *incur direct start-up costs* incurrir en costes de lanzamiento directos

state

= recognise

To state is to say or indicate something.

reconocer

▲ *state explicitly* reconocer explícitamente ▲ *state the amount* reconocer la cuantía ▲ *state the main principles* reconocer los principios fundamentales

state tax US

≠ federal tax US

State tax is the income tax levied by certain US state governments on individuals and businesses as opposed to the income tax levied by the US federal government.

impuesto estatal sobre la renta

= impuesto estatal sobre la renta

▲ *calculate the state tax* calcular el impuesto estatal sobre renta ▲ *pay state tax* pagar el impuesto estatal sobre la renta

stated value

= face value, nominal value, par value

≠ market value

The stated value is the par or nominal value of a financial instrument, such as a share or a bond, when it is issued. Stated value is sometimes assigned to shares with no par value for accounting purposes.

valor escrito

= valor nominal

▲ *carry liabilities at stated value* pasivos actuales a valor nominal ▲ *the stated value for a security* el valor escrito de un título ▲ *with a stated value of $1000* con un valor escrito de 1.000 dólares

statement

1 A statement is a written report recording a number of data such as a financial statement.

estado

▲ *a concise statement* un estado conciso ▲ *a detailed statement* un estado detallado ▲ *a separate statement* un estado separado ▲ *statement of changes in equity* estado de cambios en patrimonio ▲ *statement of changes in equity* estado de cambios en patrimonio ▲ *statement of key figures and financial ratios* estado de cifras claves y ratios financieros ▲ *statement of limitations on profits from non-life insurance* estado de las limitaciones en los beneficios procedentes de seguros de no vida ▲ *statement of the assets and liabilities at the time of acquisition* estado de los activos y pasivos en el momento de la adquisición

2 Oral or written information is referred to as a statement.

declaración

▲ *a general statement of the objective of the enterprise* una declaración general del objetivo de la empresa ▲ *the statement by the executive and supervisory boards on the annual report* la declaración de los consejos de supervisión y ejecutivo en el informe anual

statement of accounts

A statement of accounts is a drawing-up or format of a particular type of accounts, e.g. a profit and loss account, a balance sheet, a cash flow statement, or statement of changes in equity.

estado de cuentas

▲ *a separate statement of accounts* un estado de cuentas separado

statement of acquired goodwill

A statement of acquired goodwill is an overview of the amount of goodwill acquired in connection with the acquisition of an enterprise.

estado del fondo de comercio adquirido

▲ *prepare a statement of acquired goodwill* preparar un estado del fondo de comercio adquirido

statement of cash flows US

The statement of cash flows is a statement which, as a minimum, shows the cash flows for the period distributed on operating, investing and financing activities. Furthermore, the statement must show separately any changes in cash and cash equivalents for the financial year and the cash and cash equivalents as at the beginning and end of the period.

NOTE On 6 September 2007, a revised IAS 1 Presentation of Financial Statements has been issued by the IASB and will be effective for accounting periods starting on or after 1 January 2009. The changes include new IFRS titles for the financial statements so that "statement of comprehensive income", "statement of financial position" and "statement of cash flows" will replace the former titles "income statement", "balance sheet" and "cash flow statement".

estado de flujos de efectivo

= estado de cash flow, estado de flujos de caja

▲ *include a statement of cash flows in the financial statements* incluir un estado de flujos de efectivo en los estados financieros ▲ *main items in the consolidated statement of cash flows* partidas principales en el estado de flujos de efectivo consolidado ▲ *notes to the statement of cash flows* notas al estado de flujos de efectivo ▲ *prepare a separate statement of cash flows for the parent company* preparar un estado de flujos de efectivo separado para la matriz ▲ *prepare a statement of cash flows* preparar un estado de flujos de efectivo ▲ *present a consolidated statement of cash flows* presentar un estado de flujos de efectivo consolidado ▲ *present a statement of cash flows* presentar un estado de flujos de efectivo ▲ *present the statement of cash flows according to the direct method* presentar el estado de flujos de efectivo de acuerdo con el método directo ▲ *present the statement of cash flows according to the indirect method* presentar el estado de flujo de efectivo consolidado de acuerdo con el método indirecto ▲ *presentation of the statement of cash flows* presentación del estado de flujos de efectivo ▲ *report in the statement of cash flows* informar en el estado de flujos de efectivo ▲ *statement of cash flows per quarter* estado de flujo de efectivo por trimestre ▲ *statement of cash flows per segment* estado de flujos de efectivo por segmento

statement of changes in equity IAS/IFRS

= statement of movements in equity, statement of stockholders' equity US

A statement of changes in equity is an overview of events during the accounting period, which have influenced equity and thereby the financial position. The statement is included in the annual report and shows the balances at the beginning and end of the period as well as any additions or disposals during the period. The statement may be included as a separate statement or disclosed in a note.

estado de cambios en el patrimonio neto

= estado de cambios en patrimonio neto

▲ *a consolidated statement of changes in equity* un estado de cambios en el patrimonio neto consolidado ▲ *an interim statement of changes in equity* un estado de cambios en el patrimonio neto provisional ▲ *attach a statement of changes in equity* adjuntar un estado de cambios en el patrimonio neto ▲ *commentary on the statement of changes in equity* comentario en el estado de cambios en el patrimonio neto ▲ *disclose in the statement of changes in equity* publicar en el estado de cambios en el patrimonio neto ▲ *prepare a statement of changes in equity* preparar un estado de cambios en el patrimonio neto ▲ *present a statement of changes in equity as a separate component of an enterprise's financial statements* presentar un estado de cambios en el patrimonio neto como un componente separado de los estados financieros de una empresa ▲ *the consolidated statement of changes in equity* el estado de cambios en el patrimonio neto consolidado

statement of changes in financial position US

= funds flow statement UK, statement of source and application of funds UK

A statement of changes in financial position shows the source and application of funds and the changes in an enterprise's working capital for an accounting period. In modern financial reporting, this statement has been replaced by a cash flow statement, as movements in working capital may not give a true and fair view of the liquidity and solvency of an enterprise.

estado de cambios en la posición financiera

= estado de flujo de fondos

▲ *prepare a statement of changes in financial position* preparar un estado de cambios en la posición financiera

statement of comprehensive income IAS/IFRS

A statement of comprehensive income is a financial statement showing the results for the year as well as income and costs recognised directly in equity.

NOTE On 6 September 2007, a revised IAS 1 Presentation of Financial Statements has been issued by the IASB and will be effective for accounting periods starting on or after 1 January 2009. The changes include new IFRS titles for the financial statements so that "statement of comprehensive income", "statement of financial position" and "statement of cash flows" will replace the former titles "income statement", "balance sheet" and "cash flow statement".

estado del resultado global

▲ *prepare a statement of comprehensive income* preparar un estado del resultado global ▲ *the statement of comprehensive income requirement* el requisito del estado del resultado global

statement of directors' responsibilities UK

Under company law in the UK, a statement of directors' responsibilities is required to appear in the annual and interim reports of a company. The statement defines the board of director's responsibility for the objectivity and integrity of the financial disclosures. The directors confirm that accounting legislation, generally accepted accounting principles and articles of association have been observed and that the annual report gives a true and fair view of the assets, liabilities and equity, financial position and results for the year of the company.

NOTE The statement of directors' responsibilities typically appears in tandem with the auditors' report and makes explicit the distribution of responsibilities between the company's directors and the independent auditors.

informe de las responsabilidades de los directores

▲ *statement of directors' responsibilities in respect of the accounts* informe de las responsabilidades de los directores respecto a las cuentas

⇛ auditors' report, statement by the executive and supervisory boards on the annual report

statement of earnings US

→ income statement

Statement of Financial Accounting Standards US

= SFAS US

Statements of Financial Accounting Standards (SFASs) are accounting standards issued by the US Financial Accounting Standards Board to set disclosure requirements and to establish generally accepted accounting principles for companies registered with the Securities and Exchange Commission when preparing their financial statements.

Statement of Financial Accounting Standards

= Estado de Normas de Contabilidad Financiera

▲ *in accordance with Statement of Financial Accounting Standards No. 91* de acuerdo con el Statement of Financial Accounting Standards ▲ *issue a Statement of Financial Accounting Standards* emitir una Statement of Financial Accounting Standards ▲ *proposed Statement of Financial Accounting Standards* Statement of Financial Accounting Standards propuesta ▲ *pursuant to Statement of Financial Accounting Standards No. 71* en virtud del Statement of Financial Accounting Standards Nº 71

⇛ accounting standard, Financial Accounting Standard

statement of financial highlights and key figures

A statement of financial highlights and key figures shows a selection of figures and financial ratios that provide a picture at a glance of the enterprise to stakeholders and are useful for making comparisons between enterprises. Examples are sales, EBITDA margin, EPS and ROIC.

información de cifras financieras relevantes y claves

statement of financial performance UK

A statement of financial performance is a primary financial statement recognising the components relating to a reporting entity's profits, gains and losses. As such it is a general term referring to the profit and loss account and the statement of total recognised gains and losses of an enterprise.

documento de ejecución financiera

▲ *present a single statement of financial performance* presentar un único documento de ejecución financiera ▲ *recognise separately in the statement of financial performance* reconocer por separado en el documento de ejecución financiera

⇛ statement of total recognised gains and losses

statement of financial position US, IAS/IFRS

= balance sheet

The statement of financial position is the balance sheet or state-

ment of an enterprise's assets, equity and liabilities at the end of the accounting period. The statement is a status report estimating the enterprise's assets, equity and liabilities as a snapshot at a certain date.
NOTE On 6 September 2007, a revised IAS 1 Presentation of Financial Statements has been issued by the IASB and will be effective for accounting periods starting on or after 1 January 2009. The changes include new IFRS titles for the financial statements so that "statement of comprehensive income", "statement of financial position" and "statement of cash flows" will replace the former titles "income statement", "balance sheet" and "cash flow statement".
estado de situación financiera
= estado de la situación financiera
▲ *an audited statement of financial position* un estado auditado de situación financiera ▲ *prepare a statement of financial position* preparar un estado de la situación financiera ▲ *recognize in the statement of financial position* reconocer en el estado de la situación financiera ▲ *statement of financial position as at December 31, 2005* estado de situación financiera a 31 de diciembre de 2005

statement of gains and losses UK
= statement of total recognised gains and losses UK, STRGL UK
A statement of gains and losses, also referred to as a statement of total recognised gains and losses, is a primary, separate financial statement required included in the financial statements of UK companies, which recognises gains and losses for the period that are not recognised in the profit and loss account, but result in increases or decreases in equity. The statement combines operating and other financial performance and provides information for the assessment of the company's overall performance and return on investment.
estado de pérdidas y ganancias reconocidas
= estado de ganancias y pérdidas reconocidas, estado de ingresos y gastos reconocidos
▲ *prepare a statement of gains and losses* preparar un estado de pérdidas y ganancias reconocidas ▲ *statement of gains and losses for tax purposes* estado de estado de pérdidas y ganancias reconocidas a efectos fiscales

statement of income
1 → income statement
2 = income tax return UK, tax return IAS/IFRS, US
The statement of income is a taxpayer's annual tax return submitted to the tax authorities showing details of taxable amounts of income, gains and profits and tax-deductible expenses.
declaración de la renta
▲ *prepare a statement of income* preparar una declaración de la renta ▲ *submit a statement of income* remitir una declaración de la renta

statement of movements in equity
= statement of changes in equity IAS/IFRS, statement of stockholders' equity US
A statement of movements in equity is an overview of events during the accounting period that have influenced equity and thereby the financial position. The statement is included in the annual report and shows the balances at the beginning and end of the period as well as any additions or disposals during the period. The statement may be included as a separate statement or disclosed in a note.
estado de cambios en el patrimonio neto
= estado de cambios en patrimonio neto
▲ *a consolidated statement of movements in equity* un estado consolidado de cambios en patrimonio neto ▲ *an interim statement of movements in equity* un estado intermedio de cambios en el patrimonio neto ▲ *attach a statement of movements in equity* adjuntar un estado de cambios en el patrimonio neto ▲ *commentary on the statement of movements in equity* comentario sobre el estado de cambios en patrimonio neto ▲ *disclose in the statement of movements in equity* publicar en el estado de cambios en el patri-

monio neto ▲ *prepare a statement of movements in equity* preparar un estado de cambios en el patrimonio neto ▲ *present a statement of movements in equity as a separate component of an enterprise's financial statements* presentar un estado de cambios en patrimonio neto como un componente independiente de los estados financieros de una empresa ▲ *the consolidated statement of movements in equity* el estado consolidado de cambios en patrimonio neto

statement of operations US
→ income statement

statement of principles UK
→ Statement of Principles

Statement of Principles UK
The Statement of Principles for financial reporting is a conceptual framework issued in 1999 by the Accounting Standards Board in the UK to set out the principles that should underlie the preparation and presentation of general purpose financial statements.
Estado de Principios
▲ *draft Statement of Principles* borrador del Estado de Principios
⇛ Accounting Standards Board, conceptual framework, general purpose financial statements

statement of recognised gains and losses UK
→ statement of total recognised gains and losses

Statement of Recommended Practice UK
= SORP UK
Statements of Recommended Practice (SORPs) are non-mandatory documents issued since 1986 by the former Accounting Standards Committee (ASC) or by various bodies for particular industries and franked by the ASC. SORPs are recommendations on accounting practices for specialised industries or sectors and supplement accounting legislation and standards. The successor of the ASC, the Accounting Standards Board, does not issue or frank SORPs.
Documento de Prácticas Recomendadas
▲ *according to the relevant Statement of Recommended Practice* de acuerdo al Documento de Prácticas Recomendadas relevante ▲ *issue a Statement of Recommended Practice* emitir un Documento de Prácticas Recomendadas
⇛ Accounting Standards Board, Accounting Standards Committee

statement of retained earnings UK
= statement of retained income US
A statement of retained earnings is a statement that details changes in retained earnings over an accounting period resulting from the period's adjustments, dividend distribution, etc. This statement is used when no other changes have occurred in total shareholders' equity during the period in which case a statement of changes in equity must be included.
estado de ingresos no distribuidos
= estado de ingresos retenidos
▲ *consolidated statement of retained earnings* estado de ingresos no distribuidos consolidado

statement of retained income US
= statement of retained earnings UK
A statement of retained income is a statement that details changes in retained income over an accounting period resulting from the period's adjustments, dividend distribution, etc. This statement is used when no other changes have occurred in total shareholders' equity during the period in which case a statement of changes in equity must be included.
estado de ingresos no distribuidos
= estado de ingresos retenidos
▲ *consolidated statement of retained income* estado de ingresos no distribuidos consolidado

statement of source and application of funds UK
= funds flow statement UK, source and application of funds statement UK, statement of changes in financial position US
A statement of source and application of funds shows the

changes in an enterprise's working capital for an accounting period. In modern financial reporting, this statement has been replaced by a cash flow statement, as movements in working capital may not give a true and fair view of the liquidity and solvency of an enterprise.

estado del origen y aplicación de fondos
= estado de cambios en la posición financiera, estado de flujo de fondos
▲ *prepare a statement of source and application of funds* preparar un estado de cambios en la posición financiera

Statement of Standard Accounting Practice UK
= SSAP UK
Statements of Standard Accounting Practice (SSAPs) are the accounting standards issued pre-1990 by the former UK Accounting Standards Committee. Some SSAPs remain in force, whereas others have been replaced and supplemented by the new Financial Reporting Standards (FRSs) that are issued by the Accounting Standards Board.

Statement of Standard Accounting Practice
▲ *the issue of a new Statement of Standard Accounting Practice* la publicación de una nueva Statement of Standard Accounting Practice ▲ *withdrawal of Statement of Standard Accounting Practice 1* retirada de la Statement of Standard Accounting Practice 1
⇛ accounting standard, Financial Reporting Standard

statement of stockholders' equity US
= statement of changes in equity IAS/IFRS, statement of movements in equity
A statement of stockholders' equity is an overview of events during the accounting period that have influenced equity and thereby the financial position. The statement is included in the annual report and shows the balances at the beginning and end of the period as well as any additions or disposals during the period. The statement may be included as a separate statement or disclosed in a note.

estado de cambios en el patrimonio neto
= estado de cambios en patrimonio neto
▲ *a consolidated statement of stockholders' equity* un estado consolidado de cambios en patrimonio neto ▲ *an interim statement of stockholders' equity* un estado intermedio de cambios en el patrimonio neto ▲ *attach a statement of stockholders' equity* adjuntar un estado de cambios en patrimonio neto ▲ *commentary on the statement of stockholders' equity* comentario sobre el estado de cambios en patrimonio neto ▲ *disclose in the statement of stockholders' equity* publicar en el estado de cambios en el patrimonio neto ▲ *prepare a statement of stockholders' equity* preparar un estado de cambios en el patrimonio neto ▲ *present a statement of stockholders' equity as a separate component of an enterprise's financial statements* presentar un estado de cambios en el patrimonio neto como un componente separado de los estados financieros de una empresa ▲ *the consolidated statement of stockholders' equity* el estado consolidado de cambios en el patrimonio neto

statement of total recognised gains and losses UK
= statement of gains and losses UK, STRGL UK
The statement of total recognised gains and losses (STRGL) is a primary, separate financial statement required included in the financial statements of UK companies. The STRGL completes the profit and loss account by recognising any gains and losses for an accounting period that have not been recognised in the profit and loss account but result in increases or decreases in equity. This statement combines operating and other financial performance and provides information for the assessment of the company's overall performance and return on investment for the accounting period in question.

estado de pérdidas y ganancias reconocidas
= estado de ganancias y pérdidas reconocidas, estado de ga-

nancias y pérdidas reconocidas totales, estado de ingresos y gastos reconocidos, estado de pérdidas y ganancias reconocidas totales
▲ *consolidated statement of total recognised gains and losses* estado de pérdidas y ganancias reconocidas totales consolidado
▲ *prepare a statement of total recognised gains and losses* preparar un estado de pérdidas y ganancias reconocidas totales
SOURCE FRS 3
⇛ comprehensive income model

static budget
A static budget is a budget which has been based on a specified and pre-determined production or sales level and which is not subsequently changed during the current budget period.
presupuesto estático
▲ *compare the static budget with actual results* comparar el presupuesto estático con los resultados actuales ▲ *prepare a static budget* preparar un presupuesto estático

static-budget variance
= master-budget variance
A static-budget variance is the difference between an actual, realised, resulting amount and the amount budgeted in the static budget.
desviación en el presupuesto estático
▲ *the computation of a static-budget variance* la valoración de una desviación en el presupuesto estático ▲ *the static-budget variance of operating income* la desviación en el presupuesto estático de ingresos de explotación ▲ *total static-budget variance* total desviación en el presupuesto estático

statutory
1 Something that is statutory has been laid down in a statute, i.e. an act of parliament.
legal
▲ *changes in statutory or regulatory requirements* cambios en los requisitos o regulaciones legales ▲ *income taxes that are created as a result of statutory requirements imposed by governments* los impuestos sobre la renta que se crearon como un resultado de los requisitos legales impuestos por los gobiernos ▲ *statutory requirements* requisitos legales ▲ *statutory restrictions* restricciones legales
2 Something that is statutory has been laid down in regulations of e.g. a particular organisation or enterprise, such as the articles of association of a company.
estatutario
▲ *a vacant statutory position* un puesto estatutario vacante ▲ *statutory constraints* restricciones estatutarias ▲ *statutory provisions* disposiciones estatutarias
⇛ reserves provided for by the articles of association

statutory audit
A statutory audit is an audit of financial statements prescribed by statutes or other regulatory framework.
auditoría legal
▲ *all the persons who are directly involved in the statutory audit* todas las personas que están directamente relacionadas con la auditoría legal ▲ *carry out a statutory audit* llevar a cabo una auditoría legal ▲ *detect, correct and prevent inadequate execution of the statutory audit* detectar, corregir y prevenir la ejecución inadecuada de la auditoría legal ▲ *exert influence on the statutory audit* ejercer influencia en la auditoría legal ▲ *oversight regarding the statutory audit* revisión de la auditoría legal ▲ *perform a statutory audit* realizar una auditoría legal ▲ *persons who are in a position to influence the outcome of the statutory audit* personas que están en una posición para influir en el resultado de la auditoría legal ▲ *quality assurance for the statutory audit* aseguramiento de la calidad de la auditoría legal ▲ *statutory audit of consolidated financial statements* auditoría legal de estados financieros consolidados ▲ *statutory audit services* servicios de auditoría legal ▲ *statutory audit work* trabajo de auditoría legal ▲ *the scope of the statutory audit* el alcance de la auditoría legal

statutory notice
A statutory notice is a notice that one party is required by law to give to another in a particular situation.

aviso reglamentario

▲ *serve a statutory notice on a person* notificar un aviso reglamentario a una persona ▲ *the end of the statutory notice period* el final del periodo del aviso reglamentario

statutory reserve

→ reserves provided for by the articles of association

step acquisition

An acquisition of an enterprise that involves more than one exchange transaction is called step acquisition.

adquisición por fases

= adquisición por etapas

▲ *accounting for the step acquisition* contabilizando la adquisición por fases

step allocation method

→ step-down method

step cost US

= step-function cost UK, stepped cost UK

Step costs are costs that change abruptly at intervals of activity rather than continuous form. The changes occur because resources and their costs come in large and indivisible units.

coste en escalón

= coste discontinuo, coste según actividad, coste semivariable, step cost

▲ *a distinguishing feature of step costs* un rasgo distintivo de los costes en escalón ▲ *step cost increases* aumentos en los costes en escalón

step cost function

= step-cost function

A step cost function is a cost function where costs are constant over various ranges of the level of activity or cost driver, but the costs rise in steps by discrete amounts as the level of activity or cost driver changes from one range to the next.

función de costes en escalón

= función de costes semivariables

▲ *a discrete step cost function* una función discreta de costes en escalón

step-cost function

→ step cost function

step-down allocation method

→ step-down method

step-down method

= sequential allocation method, step allocation method, step-down allocation method

The step-down method allocates costs related to service departments partially and sequentially, i.e. step-by-step, to other service departments and operating departments according to a pre-determined order that recognises the mutual services provided in between the service departments and the number of services rendered.

método de asignación secuencial

▲ *use the step-down method* usar el método de asignación secuencial

⇛ service department

stepped cost UK

= step cost US, step-function cost UK

Stepped costs are costs that change abruptly at intervals of activity rather than continuous form. The changes occur because resources and their costs come in large and indivisible units.

coste discontinuo

= coste en escalón, coste pronunciado

▲ *stepped cost increases* aumentos en los costes discontinuos ▲ *treatment of the stepped cost as a variable cost* tratamiento del coste discontinuo como un coste variable

stipulate

To stipulate means to specify something as an important condition in a contract.

estipular

▲ *as stipulated in the contract* como se estipula en el contrato ▲ *stipulate the return of the assets* estipular el retorno de los activos

stock[1] *noun* <a, the, -s>

1 = inventory US, IAS/IFRS

Stocks are an enterprise's supply of goods for retail sale, raw materials or finished goods. In the balance sheet, stocks are recognised as an item under current assets.

inventario

= stock

▲ *closing stock* inventario de cierre ▲ *opening stock* inventario de apertura

2 A stock is a fixed-interest security issued by a government or a company.

título de renta fija

▲ *to issue stocks* emitir títulos de renta fija

⇛ debenture, loan stock

3 Stock refers to the legal capital of a corporation divided into basically two types of stock of shares: common stock and preferred stock.

acción

= acción de capital

⇛ common stock, share

stock[2] US *noun* <no indefinite article, the, no plural>

Stock is semantically plural, grammatically uncountable singular. To state a given number of shares of stock the terms share(s) or X shares of stock are applied.

= share capital UK, IAS/IFRS, shares UK, IAS/IFRS

Stock refers to two types of shares of capital stock: shares of common stock and shares of preferred stock and constitutes the legal capital of a corporation.

capital

⇛ capital stock, common stock

stock[3] *verb*

To stock is to store a supply of goods or products ready for sale.

almacenar

▲ *to stock goods* almacenar bienes

stock analysis US

= share analysis UK

A stock analysis is an assessment or evaluation of the stock of one or more companies for investment purposes.

análisis de valores

= análisis del valor de las acciones

▲ *fundamental stock analysis* análisis de valores fundamentales ▲ *technical stock analysis* análisis técnico del valor de las acciones

stock buy-back US

= share buy-back UK, share buyback UK, share repurchase IAS/IFRS, US

A stock buy-back is a transaction whereby a company buys back its own outstanding shares from the shareholders.

rescate de acciones

= recompra de acciones, recompra de las acciones

▲ *a stock buy-back at a total market value of USD 3.0m* un rescate de las acciones por un valor de mercado total de 3,0 millones de dólares norteamericanos

⇛ stock buy-back program

stock buy-back program US

A stock buy-back program is a plan authorised by a company's board of directors by which management can buy back a certain amount of the company's own shares in the market during a specified period of time. The effect of a retirement of an amount of the shares is to reduce the number of outstanding shares, resulting in an increase of the market price and the earnings per share.

programa de rescate de acciones

= programa de recompra de acciones

▲ *acquisition in connection with stock buy-back programs* adquisición en conexión con programas de rescate de acciones ▲ *complete a stock buy-back program* completar un programa de rescate de acciones ▲ *launch a stock buy-back program* lanzar un programa de rescate de acciones

stock certificate US

A stock certificate is a document showing the stockholder's ownership in a company, i.e. the number of shares, par value, class of stock, and voting rights.

certificado de acciones

▲ *issue stock certificates* emitir certificados de acciones ▲ *printing of new stock certificates* impresión de los certificados de acciones nuevas ▲ *reprint of old stock certificates* reimpresión de los certificados de acciones antiguos

stock compensation plan US

A stock compensation plan is a formal or informal arrangement under which one or more employees are paid, i.e. rewarded, in the form of shares in the company.

plan de retribución mediante acciones

▲ *expenses incidental to stock compensation plans* gastos por planes de retribución mediante acciones ▲ *general stock compensation plans* planes generales de retribución mediante acciones ▲ *individual stock compensation plans* planes individuales de retribución mediante acciones

stock deal US

= share deal UK

≠ asset deal

A stock deal is a specific structure applied in connection with acquiring a company. In a stock deal, the acquisition of a company happens by the buyer taking over or buying the company's shares. The vendor also assumes the liabilities of the company, and therefore stock deals are typically more advantageous to the seller than asset deals.

intercambio de acciones

= canje de acciones

▲ *formal approvals of stock deals* aprobaciones formales de intercambios de acciones

⇛ asset deal

stock dividend US

= scrip dividend UK, share dividend UK

Stock dividend is the payment of dividend by way of shares rather than cash, expressed as a percentage of the shares already held by the shareholder. By paying stock dividend, a company avoids a drain on liquidity.

dividendo en acciones

▲ *issue stock dividend* emitir un dividendo en acciones ▲ *on a stock dividend issue* en una emisión de un dividendo en acciones ▲ *on a two-for-one stock dividend issue* en una emisión dos por uno de dividendo en acciones ▲ *stock dividend without consideration* dividendo en acciones sin consideración

stock dividend issue US

A stock dividend issue is an issue of a certain percentage of additional shares by a company which is distributed for free to the existing shareholders in proportion to their shareholdings instead of a cash dividend. By a stock dividend issue no extra cash will therefore flow to the company, resulting in an unchanged total amount of equity and market capitalisation and a dilution of the value of each share.

ampliación liberada de capital

= ampliación de capital con cargo a reservas, ampliación de capital gratuita, ampliación de capital liberada, ampliación gratuita de capital

▲ *make a stock dividend issue* efectuar una ampliación liberada de capital

⇛ stock dividend, stock split

stock exchange

A stock exchange is an official, organised securities market for new issues of securities and subsequent physical or electronic trading of shares, bonds, derivative financial instruments and other securities.

mercado de valores

= bolsa, mercado bursatil, mercado de acciones

▲ *be admitted for listing on a stock exchange* estar admitido a cotización en un mercado de valores ▲ *be listed on a stock exchange* estar cotizado en el mercado de valores ▲ *Copenhagen Stock Exchange* El Mercado de Valores de Copenage ▲ *delist a share on a stock exchange* sacar de bolsa una acción ▲ *domestic stock exchange* mercado de valores nacional ▲ *foreign stock exchange* bolsa extranjera ▲ *publish through the stock exchange* publicar a través del mercado de valores ▲ *successive share purchases on a stock exchange* adquisiciones continuas de acciones en un mercado de valores ▲ *the total volume of trade on the stock exchange* el volumen total de negociación en la bolsa

stock exchange announcement

= announcement to the stock exchange

A stock exchange announcement is a notification by listed enterprises of critical information or events that may influence the price formation on the listed securities, such as major increases or reductions in the enterprise's activities, major shareholdings, proposals for acquisitions and management changes. Also, listed enterprises must regularly submit their interim and annual financial reports.

anuncio en bolsa

= anuncio de publicación de resultados, anuncio de publicación del informe de resultados, publicación de resultados

▲ *after the publication of the stock exchange announcement* después de la publicación del informe de resultados ▲ *in a separete stock exchange announcement* en una publicación de resultados separada ▲ *publication through a stock exchange announcement* publicación mediante un informe de resultados ▲ *publish stock exchange announcements* publicar informes de resultados ▲ *stock exchange announcement of 16 April 2005* publicación de resultados del 16 de abril de 2005

⇛ earnings release

stock exchange listing

= stock market listing US

Stock exchange listing is the quotation of an enterprise on a stock exchange and official admission for trading of that enterprise's equity, debt or other securities. Listed enterprises must comply with the listing requirements of the relevant stock exchange such as meeting corporate governance rules and a minimum market capitalisation as well as regularly submitting financial disclosures.

cotización en el mercado de valores

= cotización en el mercado bursátil

▲ *a separate stock exchange listing* una cotización independiente en el mercado de valores ▲ *carry through a stock exchange listing* llevar a cotización en el mercado de valores ▲ *obtain a stock exchange listing* obtener una cotización en el mercado de valores ▲ *plan a stock exchange listing* planificar una cotización en el mercado de valores

stock exchange reporting requirement

Stock exchange reporting requirements are rules for the notification by listed enterprises of critical information that is necessary to ensure a transparent securities market. Such information includes interim and annual financial reports, disclosures of share ownership changes and other critical events.

requisito de información por cambios accionariales

▲ *meet the stock exchange reporting requirements* cumplir los requisitos de información por cambios accionariales

stock goods

Goods that an enterprise has manufactured or bought for resale, but which have not yet been sold, are called stock goods.

inventarios

= existencias, mercaderías

▲ *the quality of stock goods* la calidad de los inventarios

stock index US

A stock index is an index reflecting the composite value of the shares which are included in the index. A stock index is often based on shares with one or more common characteristics e.g. companies in the same industry, the same country, or companies whose shares are most frequently traded on a specific market. Price development in a stock index is often used as an indicator of the overall price development of shares in the specific industry or market. Examples of stock indices are the FTSE 100, the NASDAQ Composite Index, the S&P 500 Index and the OMXC20 (the index for the 20 most traded shares on the Copenhagen Stock Exchange).

índice bursátil

= índice de acciones

▲ *benchmark stock index* índice bursátil benchmark ▲ *European stock indexes* índices bursátiles europeos ▲ *international stock indexes* índices de acciones internacionales ▲ *swaps stock indexes* índices bursátiles de swaps

stock information US

Stock information is any information about the stock, i.e. shares, of the enterprise, including stock price, stock price fluctuations, number of shares issued and the total market cap.

información bursátil

▲ *release stock information* emitir información bursátil

stock management UK

= inventory management US

Stock management comprises activities such as planning, coordination and control with a view to maintaining appropriate inventories and handling products in line with inventory targets and service requirements.

gestión de existencias

= gestión de las existencias

▲ *effective stock management* gestión de existencias efectiva ▲ *improve stock management* mejorar la gestión de existencias ▲ *poor stock management* gestión deficiente de las existencias

stock market US

= equity market, share market UK

A stock market is a market place where shares are bought and sold, such as a stock exchange or other authorized market place. Trading may be physical and/or computerized.

mercado bursátil

= bolsa, mercado de valores, mercado de acciones

▲ *falling stock markets* mercados bursátiles a la baja ▲ *stock market turbulence* turbulencia en la bolsa ▲ *the Danish stock market* el mercado bursátil danés ▲ *the global stock markets* los mercados bursátiles globales ▲ *the implicit volatility of the stock market* la volitibilidad implícita del mercado de acciones ▲ *the international stock markets* los mercados de acciones internacionales ▲ *the trends on the stock market* las tendencias en el mercado de títulos ▲ *unsettled stock markets* mercados bursátiles a crédito

⇛ authorised market place, stock exchange

stock market announcement US

A stock market announcement is a notification by listed enterprises of critical information or events that may influence the price formation on the listed securities, such as major increases or reductions in the enterprise's activities, major shareholdings, proposals for acquisitions and management changes. Also, listed enterprises must regularly submit their interim and annual financial reports.

anuncio en bolsa

= anuncio de publicación de resultados

▲ *release a stock market announcement* hacer público un anuncio en bolsa

stock market listing US

= stock exchange listing

A stock market listing is the quotation of an enterprise on a stock exchange and official admission for trading of that enterprise's equity, debt or other securities. Listed enterprises must comply with the listing requirements of the relevant stock exchange such as meeting corporate governance rules and a minimum market capitalisation as well as regularly submitting financial disclosures.

cotización en el mercado de valores

= cotización en el mercado bursátil

▲ *a separate stock market listing* una cotización independiente en el mercado de valores ▲ *carry through a stock market listing* llevar a cotización en el mercado de valores ▲ *plan a stock market listing* planificar una cotización en el mercado de valores

stock option US

= share option IAS/IFRS, UK

A stock option is a contract that enables, but not obliges, the holder to buy or sell specific shares of stock at a fixed price within a specified period of time.

opción sobre acciones

= stock option

▲ *a synthetic stock option* una opción sobre acciones híbrida ▲ *cancel a stock option* cancelar una opción sobre acciones ▲ *changes in the number of stock options outstanding* cambios en el número de opciones sobre acciones pendientes de pago ▲ *exercise a stock option* ejercer una stock option ▲ *exercise of stock options* ejercicio de opciones sobre acciones ▲ *grant stock options* conceder opciones sobre acciones ▲ *outstanding stock options* opciones sobre acciones pendientes de pago ▲ *receive stock options* recibir opciones sobre acciones ▲ *stock options exercised* opciones sobre acciones ejecutadas ▲ *the exercise price of the stock option* el precio de ejercicio de la opción sobre acciones ▲ *the fair value of the stock option* el valor razonable de la opción sobre acciones ▲ *the intrinsic value of the stock option* el valor intrínseco de la opción sobre acciones ▲ *the market value of the stock option bought* el valor de mercado de la stock option comprada ▲ *the recognized intrinsic value of the stock option* el valor intrínseco reconocido de la opción sobre acciones ▲ *the stock option has expired* la opción sobre acciones ha vencido

stock option agreement US
= share option agreement UK
A stock option agreement is a contract giving one of the parties the right, but not the obligation, to buy or sell a fixed amount of stock at a predetermined price within a specified period.
acuerdo de opciones sobre acciones
▲ *the employees' stock option agreement* el acuerdo de opciones sobre acciones de los empleados

stock option plan US
= share option plan UK, share option program US, share option programme UK, share option scheme UK
A stock option plan is an agreement under which management executives and other employees are granted stock options as additional compensation or incentive payment supplementing wages and salaries. The employees receive options at a fixed, often favourable price and must exercise them within a specified period after the grant date.
plan de opciones sobre acciones
= programa de opciones sobre acciones
▲ *a stock option plan for all employees* un programa de opciones sobre acciones para todos los empleados ▲ *an international stock option plan* un programa de opciones sobre acciones internacional ▲ *approve a stock option plan* aprobar un plan de opciones sobre acciones ▲ *commitments under the company's stock option plan* compromisos de acuerdo con el programa de opciones sobre acciones de la empresa ▲ *cover of the stock option plan* cobertura del programa de opciones sobre acciones ▲ *implementation of a stock option plan* implementación de un programa de opciones sobre acciones ▲ *introduce a stock option plan* introducir un programa de opciones sobre acciones ▲ *participate in a stock option plan* participar en un programa de opciones sobre acciones ▲ *revolving stock option plan* programa de opciones sobre acciones renovable ▲ *stock option plan for key personnel* programa de opciones sobre acciones para el personal de alta dirección ▲ *stock option plan for the company's management* programa de opciones sobre acciones para la dirección de la empresa

stock price US
The stock price is the price of a particular share of stock at which it can be bought or sold at a particular time, typically the price quoted on an authorized marketplace such as a stock exchange.
precio de las acciones
▲ *current stock prices* precio corriente de las accciones ▲ *falling stock prices* precio de las acciones decreciente ▲ *fluctuating stock prices* precio de las acciones fluctuante ▲ *historical stock prices* precio histórico de las acciones ▲ *rising stock prices* precio de las acciones creciente ▲ *the average drop in stock prices* el descenso medio en los precios de las acciones ▲ *the stock price of the day* el precio de las acciones en el día ▲ *withstand a stock price decline* resistir un descenso en el precio de las acciones

stock price decline US
A stock price decline is a fall in the value of and the price quoted for a share on a stock exchange.
descenso del precio de cotización
= caída en el precio de cotización, caída en el precio de la acción
▲ *a substantial stock price decline* un descenso sustancial del precio de cotización ▲ *withstand a stock price decline* resistir una caída en el precio de la acción

stock reduction UK
A stock reduction is a decrease in the number of goods stored by an enterprise compared to a previous level.
reducción de inventarios
= recuducción de existencias
▲ *a 10% stock reduction* una reducción de inventarios del 10% ▲ *stock reduction by sales* reducción de inventarios por ventas

stock register US
= register of shareholders UK

A stock register is an enterprise's record of issued stock certificates containing information about stockholders, shares of stock issued, dates of issuance, cancelled shares of stock, etc.

registro de acciones

▲ *be entered in the stock register* ser introducido en el registro de acciones ▲ *inspection of the stock register* inspección del registro de acciones ▲ *keep the company's stock register* guardar en el registro de acciones de la empresa ▲ *the stock have been entered in the stock register* el título se ha anotado en el registro de acciones

⇛ common stock

stock repurchase US

= share buyback UK

A stock repurchase is a transaction whereby a company buys it own shares from existing stockholders.

recompra de acciones

= recompra de las acciones, rescate de las acciones

▲ *a stock repurchase of $41m* una recompra de acciones de 41 millones de dólares ▲ *a structured stock repurchase* una recompra de acciones estructurada ▲ *the completed stock repurchase* la recompra de acciones completada ▲ *the planned stock repurchase* la recompra de acciones prevista

stock repurchase plan US

= share buy-back programme UK, share buyback programme UK, share repurchase program US, share repurchase programme IAS/IFRS, UK

A stock repurchase plan is a plan authorised by a company's board of directors by which management can buy back a certain amount of the company's own shares in the market during a specified period of time. The effect of a retirement of an amount of the shares is to reduce the number of outstanding shares, resulting in an increase of the market price and the earnings per share.

plan de recompra de acciones

= plan de recompra de las acciones, plan de rescate de acciones

▲ *commence a stock repurchase plan* comenzar un plan de recompra de las acciones ▲ *complete a stock repurchase plan* completar un plan de recompra de acciones ▲ *launch a stock repurchase plan* lanzar un plan de recompra de acciones

stock split US

= share split UK

A stock split refers to an enterprise's division of its existing shares of stock into a larger number of shares of stock with a lower nominal value resulting in a lower stock price. A stock split does not change the total market value of the enterprise's shares of stock or the stockholdings of the investors.

fraccionamiento del nominal de las acciones

= split de acciones

▲ *carry out a stock split* llevar a cabo un fraccionamiento del nominal de las acciones ▲ *decrease as a result of a reverse stock split* decremento como resultado de un fraccionamiento del nominal de las acciones ▲ *make a stock split* hacer un fraccionamiento del nominal de las acciones ▲ *reverse stock split* desistir del fraccionamiento del nominal de las acciones

⇛ stock dividend

stock turnover time UK

Stock turnover time refers to the period of time that passes before a given volume of goods is turned over, i.e. sold.

periodo de rotación de existencias

= periodo de rotación de las existencias

▲ *adjusted for stock turnover time* ajustado por periodo de rotación de existencias

stock write-down UK

= inventory write-down US, IAS/IFRS, stock writedown UK

A stock write-down is a write-down of the carrying amount as a consequence of a lower recoverable amount.

eliminación de inventarios

= eliminación de existencias, eliminación de las existencias, eliminación de los inventarios, liquidació de existencias

▲ *make a stock write-down* realizar una eliminación de inventarios

stock writedown

= inventory write-down US, IAS/IFRS, stock write-down UK

A stock writedown is a writedown of the carrying amount as a consequence of a lower recoverable amount.

eliminación de existencias

▲ *changes in estimate relating to stock writedowns* cambios en la estimación relacionada con las eliminaciones de existencias ▲ *make a stock writedown* hacer una eliminación de las existencias ▲ *recognise and measure losses from stock writedowns* reconocer y valorar pérdidas procedentes de las eliminaciones de existencias

stock-based compensation US

= share-based payment IAS/IFRS

Stock-based compensation is payment to employees in the form of shares of stock or other equity instruments of the employer or of amounts based on the price of the employer's stock. Examples are stock options and stock purchase plans.

retribución basada en acciones

▲ *accounting for stock-based compensation* contabilizar la retribución basada en acciones ▲ *calculate the stock-based compensation expense* calcular el gasto de la retribución basada en acciones ▲ *measure the fair value of stock-based compensation* valorar el valor razonable de la retribución basada en acciones ▲ *recipients of stock-based compensation* receptores de la retribución basada en acciones ▲ *the use of stock-based compensation* el uso de la retribución basada en acciones

stock-out cost

Stock-out costs are costs incurred because of insufficient inventory of particular goods or products in demand. Examples are penalties and lost revenue.

coste de ruptura

▲ *a decrease in stock-out costs* un descenso en los costes de ruptura ▲ *an increase in stock-out costs* un aumento en los costes de ruptura ▲ *reduce stock-out costs by 10%* reducir los costes de ruptura en un 10%

stockbroker US

A stockbroker acts as a middleman between buyers and sellers of stock.

NOTE If relevant, a stockbroker may add to his name "Member of the [name] Stock Exchange".

agente de bolsa

= broker

▲ *licensed stockbrokers* agentes de bolsa titulados ▲ *reputable stockbrokers* agentes de bolsa con buena reputación

stockbroker company

A stockbroker company is a company acting as a middleman between buyers and sellers of securities.

agencia de valores

▲ *contact a stockbroker company* contactar con una agencia de valores

stockholder US

= shareholder, shareowner

A person, enterprise or company that owns shares of stock in a company is called a stockholder.

accionista

▲ *a dominant stockholder* un accionista dominante ▲ *the current stockholder* el accionista actual ▲ *the government stockholder* el accionista público

stockholding US

A stockholding is the number of shares that are held by a person or an enterprise at a specific time.

tenencia de acciones

▲ *a stockholding of 2%* una tenencia de acciones del 2% ▲ *have a stockholding at a similarly low level* tener una tenencia de acciones a un nivel similar bajo ▲ *stockholding at January 1, 2005* tenencia de acciones a 1 de enero de 2005 ▲ *value of stockholding* valor de la tenencia de acciones

stocks UK

= inventories IAS/IFRS, US

Stocks comprise the actual amount of goods on stock of the enterprise at a given point in time. "Stocks" is also an item in the balance sheet under current assets.

existencias

= mercaderías, inventarios, stock

▲ *allocation of costs to stocks* asignación de costes a existencias ▲ *book stocks* reservar existencias ▲ *closing stocks* existencias al cierre ▲ *determination of the value of stocks* determinación del valor de las existencias

storage cost

Storage costs are costs incurred in connection with the warehouse facilities of an enterprise such as employee wages and handling costs.

coste de almacenamiento

▲ *storage costs necessary in the production process* costes de almacenamiento necesario en el proceso productivo

⇛ carrying cost

stores requisition

= materials requisition

A stores requisition is a form used within an enterprise containing data of the quantities and types of raw materials or components which are requested procured from stocks or a supplier, and which are needed for production. The requisition records the amount required and is typically used in job-order costing.

vale de almacen

= documento de solicitud de materiales

▲ *fill out a stores requisition* rellenar un vale de almacen

▲ *stores requisition form* formulario de documento de solicitud de materiales

⇛ job-order costing

straight-line amortisation UK

= straight-line amortization US

≠ declining-balance amortization US, diminishing-balance amortization IAS/IFRS, reducing-balance amortisation UK

Straight-line amortisation refers to an amortisation method under which intangible assets are amortised by a fixed amount in each amortisation period so that the assets are amortised evenly over their estimated useful lives.

NOTE The term straight-line amortisation applies to intangible assets.

amortización lineal

= amortización constante

▲ *use a straight-line amortisation method* utilizar un método de amortización lineal

⇛ straight-line depreciation

straight-line amortization US

= straight-line amortisation UK

≠ declining-balance amortization US

Straight-line amortization refers to an amortization method under which intangible assets are amortized by a fixed amount in each amortization period so that the assets are amortized evenly over their estimated useful life.

NOTE The term straight-line amortization applies to intangible assets.

amortización lineal

= amortización constante

▲ *use a straight-line amortization method* utilizar un método de amortización lineal

⇛ straight-line depreciation

straight-line basis

= straight-line method

Straight-line basis is a method of computing depreciation or amortisation by expensing equal depreciation or amortisation charges for each period in the profit and loss account over the useful life of a fixed asset, because constant benefit from the asset is obtained. Straight-line depreciation or amortisation expense equals cost less residual value divided by life.

NOTE Depreciation is used about tangible assets, and amortisation is used about intangible assets.

método lineal

▲ *depreciation on a straight-line basis* depreciación aplicando un método lineal

⇛ straight-line amortisation, straight-line depreciation, straight-line method

straight-line depreciation

≠ declining-balance depreciation US, diminishing-balance depreciation IAS/IFRS, reducing-balance depreciation UK

Straight-line depreciation is a method of computing depreciation by expensing equal depreciation charges for each period in the profit and loss account over a tangible asset's useful life, because constant benefit from the asset is obtained. Straight-line depreciation expense equals cost less residual value divided by life.

NOTE The term straight-line depreciation applies to tangible assets.

amortización lineal

= amortización constante

▲ *the formula for calculating straight-line depreciation* la fórmula para calcular la amortización lineal

⇛ straight-line amortisation

straight-line method

= straight-line basis

The straight-line method is a method of computing depreciation or amortisation by expensing equal depreciation or amortisation charges for each period in the profit and loss account over the useful life of a fixed asset, because constant benefit from the asset is obtained. Straight-line depreciation or amortisation expense equals cost less residual value divided by life.

NOTE Depreciation is used about tangible assets, and amortisation is used about intangible assets.

método lineal de amortización

= método de amortización lineal

▲ *use the straight-line method* utilizar el método lineal de amortización

strain

If an extra burden is imposed on someone or something that extra burden is called a strain.

tensión

▲ *put a strain on the enterprise* poner en tensión a la empresa

strategic plan

A strategic plan is a plan stipulating how the long-term goals of an enterprise can be achieved.

plan estratégico

▲ *a current strategic plan* un plan estratégico actual ▲ *develop a strategic plan* desarrollar un plan estratégico ▲ *prepare a strategic plan* preparar un plan estratégico

strengthen

To strengthen means to make stronger or improve, e.g. to improve the financial position of the enterprise.

mejorar

= afianzar, consolidar, reforzar

▲ *strengthen competitiveness* mejorar la competitividad ▲ *strengthen our leadership position* mejorar nuestra posición de liderazgo ▲ *strengthen the financial position of the enterprise* mejorar la posición financiera de la empresa

strengthened

If something has been strengthened it has become stronger or improved compared to previously.

mejorado

= afianzado, consolidado, reforzado

▲ *an enterprise with a strenthened position* una empresa con una posición mejorada

strengthening

Strengthening or capital strengthening is the reinforcement of the financial position of an enterprise. It can be obtained through a new issue of shares, which increases the share capital and consequently equity, by repayment of debt or by the conversion of debt to share capital.

mejora

= afianzamiento, consolidación, fortalecimiento

▲ *strengthening of the position of the enterprise* mejora de la posición de la empresa

STRGL UK

= statement of gains and losses UK, statement of total recognised gains and losses UK

STRGL is the abbreviation for the statement of total recognised gains and losses, which is a primary, separate financial statement required included in the financial statements of UK companies. The STRGL completes the profit and loss account by recognising any gains and losses for an accounting period that have not been recognised in the profit and loss account, but result in increases or decreases in equity. The STRGL also combines operating and other financial performance and provides information for the assessment of the company's overall performance and return on investment for the accounting period in question.

estado de pérdidas y ganancias recoconocidas

= estado de ganancias y pérdidas reconocidas, estado de ingresos y gastos reconocidos

▲ *consolidated STRGL* estado consolidado de pérdidas y ganancias reconocidas ▲ *recognise in the STRGL* registrar en el estado de ingresos y gastos reconocidos

strike off

To strike off means to remove or delete something so that it can no longer be seen or registered.

eliminar

= borrar, tachar

▲ *strike a company off the register* eliminar a una empresa del registro

strike price

= exercise price

The strike price is the price at which an option gives the buyer the right to buy or sell the underlying asset.

precio de ejercicio

▲ *a strike price at the market price* un precio de ejercicio al precio de mercado ▲ *at a strike price of* a un precio de ejercicio de ▲ *at strike price* a precio de ejercicio ▲ *options with a strike price of $75 per share* opciones con un precio de ejercicio de 75 dólares por acción

strong

To be strong is to have power or strength that exceeds norms or expectations. Strong can also be used to signify a high level or degree.

irrefutable

▲ *strong evidence that future taxable profit may not be available* pruebas irrefutables de que el beneficio fiscal futuro puede no estar disponible

structural capital

Structural capital is the part of the intellectual capital owned by an enterprise and related to the enterprise's invisible values, capabilities and competitive advantages, i.e. technologies, hardware, software, patents, trademarks, procedures and systems contributing to productivity. Such values are part of the invisible balance sheet as they will not appear from the financial balance sheet. The other part of the invisible balance sheet constitutes individual capital and often also customer capital.

capital estructural

▲ *additional information on structural capital* información adicional sobre capital estructural ▲ *structural capital measurement criteria* criterios de medición del capital estructural

⇛ customer capital, individual capital, intellectual capital, organisational capital

structural rationalisation gain UK

= structural rationalization gain US

A structural rationalisation gain is a gain resulting from a horizontal business combination, i.e. a combination of enterprises operating at the same stage of production or distribution process. The gain arises from a more rational distribution of production between the individual enterprises in the business combination.

ganancia por reorganización estructural

= beneficio por reorganización estructural

▲ *obtain a structural rationalisation gain* obtener una ganancia por reorganización estructural

structural rationalization gain US

= structural rationalisation gain UK

A structural rationalization gain is a gain resulting from a horizontal business combination, i.e. a combination of enterprises operating at the same stage of production or distribution process. The gain arises from a more rational distribution of production between the individual enterprises in the business combination.

ganancia por reorganización estructural

= beneficio por reorganización, estructural

▲ *obtain a structural rationalization gain* obtener una ganancia por reorganización estructural

sub-firm

A sub-firm is a firm that relates to another firm, the suprafirm. In the context of groups, sub-firms typically constitute subsidiaries and their sub-subsidiaries.

subsidiaria

= filial

▲ *hold the majority of votes in the sub-firm* tener la mayoría de votos de la subsidiaria ▲ *the parent's control of the sub-firm* el control de la matriz sobre la filial ▲ *the parent's measurement of investments in the sub-firm* la valoración de la matriz de las inversiones en la filial ▲ *transactions between the parent and the sub-firm* operaciones entre la matriz y la subsidiaria

subcontractor

= subsupplier

A subcontractor is a person or a company who is paid to do

part of the work of another person or company.

subcontrata

▲ *control of subcontractors* control de subcontratas ▲ *payments made to subcontractors in advance of work performed under the subcontract* pagos hechos a las subcontratas antes de realizar el trabajo

subgroup

A subgroup is a group that is part of a large group structure and which cannot be described as an independent group.

subgrupo

▲ *a parent of a subgroup* una matriz de un subgrupo ▲ *a subgroup of a group* un subgrupo de un grupo ▲ *a wholly-owned subgroup* un subgrupo de entera propiedad

subject to

Subject to means dependent on or according to something.

sujeto a

▲ *a financial asset subject to a legally enforceable right of set-off against a financial liability* un activo financiero sujeto a un derecho de obligado cumplimiento de amortización contra un pasivo financiero ▲ *an entity subject to income taxes* una entidad sujeta a impuesto sobre la renta ▲ *assets subject to a fair value put or call option* activos sujetos a una opción de compra o venta a valor razonable ▲ *assets subject to operating leases* activos sujetos a arrendamientos operativos ▲ *be subject to the financial reporting requirements of IFRSs* estar sujeto a los requisitos de información financiera de las NIIFs ▲ *financial assets subject to a master netting arrangement* activos financieros sujetos a un acuerdo de embolsamiento principal ▲ *readily obtainable assets subject to a call option* activos fácilmente obtenibles sujetos a una opción de compra ▲ *shares subject to restrictions on transfer after the vesting date* acciones sujetas a restricciones en la transferencia posterior a la fecha de carencia ▲ *subject to other specified criteria* sujeto a otros criterios especificados ▲ *undertake an economic activity that is subject to joint control* emprender una actividad económica que está sujeta a control conjunto

subject to VAT

Legal and and physical persons carrying on business are subject to VAT which means that they must settle VAT on revenue and file VAT statements with the tax authorities.

sujeto a IVA

▲ *sales subject to VAT* ventas sujetas a IVA ▲ *transactions subject to VAT* operaciones sujetas a IVA

⇛ value added tax

submit

= present

To submit means to present something to someone so that it reaches a wider audience.

entregar

= presentar, remitir

▲ *submit the financial statements to the shareholders for approval* entregar los estados financieros a los accionistas para su aprobación

subordinate[1] *adjective*

To be subordinate means ranking in a lower order or priority than and being junior to other creditors in a claim on assets or to be in a lower or less important position.

subordinado

▲ *a subordinate position* una posición subordinada ▲ *subordinate debt* deuda subordinada ▲ *subordinate loan capital* fondos ajenos subordinados

subordinate[2] *verb*

To subordinate is to rank in a lower order of priority or place in a lower or less important position.

subordinar

▲ *subordinate a mortgage loan* subordinar un préstamo hipotecario

⇛ subordinated debt, subordinated loan capital

subordinate debt

= subordinated debt

Subordinate or subordinated debt is debt that is junior in claim on assets to other debt, and that can only be claimed, in the event of a liquidation, after other debts with a higher claim have been satisfied.

deuda subordinada

▲ *expenses relating to subordinate debt* gastos relativos a deuda subordinada

subordinate loan capital

= subordinated loan capital

Subordinate or subordinated loan capital is capital which

will be repaid only after all other debts and loans have been paid if the borrower gets into financial trouble.

préstamo subordinado

▲ *raising of subordinate loan capital* suscripción de préstamo subordinado

subordinated debt

= subordinate debt, subordinated loan capital

Subordinate or subordinated debt is debt with a subordination agreement which means that creditors who have lent money to an enterprise in the form of subordinated debt will rank after other creditors with respect to receiving settlement of their claim against the enterprise in the event of winding-up or bankruptcy.

deuda subordinada

▲ *included subordinated debt* deuda subordinada incluida ▲ *issue of subordinated debt* emisión de deuda subordinada ▲ *repayment of subordinated debt* refinanciación de la deuda subordinada ▲ *total subordinated debt* total deuda subordinada

subordinated loan capital

→ subordinate loan capital

subordination

Subordination means that a creditor ranks after another creditor or other creditors in the order of priority of creditors.

subordinación

▲ *asset recognised for subordination* activo reconocido para subordinación ▲ *liability covered by the subordination* pasivo cubierto por la subordinación ▲ *special terms for a subordination* términos especiales de una subordinación ▲ *the subordination of retained interest for credit losses* la subordinación del interés retenido para pérdidas crediticias

subscribe

To subscribe is to pay money for a particular purpose, e.g. when applying for shares, or to contract a debt.

suscribir

▲ *subscribe a loan* suscribir un préstamo ▲ *subscribe for a fixed number of non-puttable ordinary shares in the issuing entity* suscribir un número fijo de acciones ordinarias no retornables a la entidad emisora ▲ *the number of shares subscribed* el número de acciones suscritas ▲ *the right to subscribe to the entity's shares at a fixed or determinable price* el derecho de suscripción de las acciones de la entidad a un precio fijado o a determinar

⇛ bind

subscribed capital

The subscribed capital of a company is the part of the company's authorised capital that potential shareholders have subscribed for, i.e. offered to purchase.

capital suscrito

▲ *subscribed capital called but not paid* capital suscrito exigido pero no desembolsado ▲ *subscribed capital or equivalent funds* capital suscrito o fondos equivalentes ▲ *subscribed capital unpaid* capital suscrito no desembolsado

subscriber

= subscriber for shares

A subscriber is a person who offers or agrees to buy shares in a company that is offering its shares to the public.

suscriptor

▲ *prospective subscribers* posibles suscriptores

subscription

Subscription is the act of offering or agreeing to buy shares in a company that is offering its shares to the public.

suscripción

▲ *in public subscription* por suscripción pública

subscription agreement

A subscription agreement is a contract between two parties where the subscriber makes regular pre-payments to an enterprise and in return receives goods or is provided with services on a regular basis.

acuerdo de suscripción

▲ *a favourable subscription agreement* un acuerdo de suscripción favorable

subscription debtor

A subscription debtor is a person or enterprise owing subscription amounts, i.e. amounts paid regularly to an enterprise in accordance with a subscription agreement.

abonado

▲ *subscription debtors outstanding at the year end* abonados

pendientes de pago a final del año
⇛ subscription agreement

subscription income
Subscription income is the income that the enterprise earns by supplying goods or providing services to a subscriber on a regular basis in return for regular pre-payments under a subscription agreement.
ingreso por suscripción
▲ *the invoiced subscription income* el ingreso por suscripción facturado
⇛ subscription agreement

subscription price
The subscription price is the amount payable on the acquisition of, i.e. subscription for, a security.
precio de suscripción
▲ *a fixed subscription price* un precio de suscripción fijo

subscription revenue
Subscription revenue is the part of the total revenue that is attributable to subscription agreements whereby the enterprise supplies goods or provides services to subscribers who make regular pre-payments in return.
ingreso por suscripción
▲ *total subscription revenue* total ingreso por suscripción

subscription right
A subscription right is a privilege granted to existing shareholders to subscribe for shares of an additional issue of shares before it is offered to the public.
derecho de suscripción
▲ *assign a subscription right* asignar un derecho de suscripción ▲ *exercise a subscription right* ejercer un derecho de suscripción ▲ *grant a subscription right* conceder un derecho de suscripción ▲ *granting of a subscription right* concesión de un derecho de suscripción ▲ *notional values of a subscription right* valores nocionales de un derecho de suscripción ▲ *receive consideration for a subscription right* recibir consideración por un derecho de suscripción ▲ *subscription right on raising new capital* derecho de suscripción en la emisión de nuevo capital ▲ *the value of the subscription right* el valor del derecho de suscripción
⇛ rights issue

subsequent adjustment
Subsequent adjustment is the deferred change of a previously estimated amount, e.g. relating to income tax, V.A.T., budgets, wages, subsidies or grants resulting in the receipt or payment of additional amounts.
ajuste posterior
▲ *make a subsequent adjustment to total equity after the vesting date* hacer un ajuste posterior a patrimonio neto total después de la fecha de adjudicación ▲ *subsequent adjustment of fair values initially reported* ajuste posterior del valor razonable inicialmente declarado

subsequent event IAS/IFRS, US
= event after the balance sheet date IAS/IFRS, US, post balance sheet event UK, US
Subsequent events are events that occur after the balance sheet date in the period until the approval of the financial statements.
NOTE Subsequent events may be adjusting or non-adjusting events, i.e. events evidencing conditions at the balance sheet date or events arising after the balance sheet date, respectively.
evento posterior
▲ *material subsequent events* eventos posteriores materiales ▲ *the effects of subsequent events* los efectos de los eventos posteriores
⇛ adjusting event, non-adjusting event

subsidiary IAS/IFRS, US
= subsidiary undertaking UK
An enterprise is a subsidiary if the parent company meets at least one of several requirements. Among these are: that the company holds the majority of the voting rights; that the company has the right to appoint or remove a majority of the members of the senior management body; that the company has the right to control the enterprise in making operating and financial decisions; and that the company is an owner and under an agreement with other owners holds the

majority of the voting rights in the enterprise.

subsidiaria

▲ *a consolidated subsidiary* una subsidiaria consolidada ▲ *a partially-owned subsidiary* una subsidiaria participada en parte ▲ *a subsidiary acquired exclusively with a view to resale* una subsidiaria adquirida exclusivamente con la intención de revender ▲ *a subsidiary previously excluded from consolidation* una subsidiaria previamente excluida de la consolidación ▲ *a subsidiary that has been excluded from the consolidated financial statements of the group* una subsidiaria que ha sido excluida de los estados financieros consolidados del grupo ▲ *a wholly-owned subsidiary* una subsidiaria participada al 100 por 100 ▲ *accounting for investments in subsidiaries in separate financial statements* contabilizando las inversiones en subsidiarias en estados financieros separados ▲ *an investment in a subsidiary* una inversión en una subsidiaria ▲ *minority interests in the profit or loss of consolidated subsidiaries for the reporting period* intereses devengados a los minoritarios en el resultado de subsidiarias consolidadas para el periodo contabilizado ▲ *newly acquired subsidiaries* subsidiarias adquiridas recientemente ▲ *recognise in the subsidiary's individual financial statements* reconocer en los estados financieros individuales de la subsidiaria ▲ *subsidiaries that meet the criteria to be classified as held for sale on acquisition* subsidiarias que cumplen los criterios para ser clasificadas como mantenidas para la venta al producirse la adquisición ▲ *the assets and liabilities of the legal subsidiary* los activos y pasivos de la subsidiaria legal ▲ *the cash flows of a foreign subsidiary* los flujos de efectivo de una subsidiaria extranjera ▲ *the elimination of the intragroup transactions of a subsidiary* la eliminación de las transacciones intragrupo de una subsidiaria ▲ *the legal subsidiary* la subsidiaria legal

⇛ associate, subsidiary company

subsidiary accounts UK

= subsidiary financial statements IAS/IFRS, US

Subsidiary accounts are the independent, detailed records of a subsidiary undertaking's financial affairs presenting the income and expenses for a period as well as the financial position at a particular date. The subsidiary accounts are eventually incorporated in the consolidated accounts.

cuentas subsidiarias

▲ *prepare subsidiary accounts* preparar las cuentas subsidiarias

⇛ consolidated accounts, parent company accounts

subsidiary bank

A subsidiary bank is a subsidiary in a bank group.

sucursal bancaria

▲ *the bank's subsidiary bank* el banco de la sucursal bancaria

⇛ subsidiary

subsidiary company

A company is a subsidiary if the parent company meets at least one of several requirements. Among these are: that the parent holds the majority of the voting rights; that the parent has the right to appoint or remove a majority of the members of the senior management body; that the parent has the right to control the company in making operating and financial decisions; and that the parent is an owner and under an agreement with other owners holds the majority of the voting rights in the company.

NOTE "Company" is used when the subsidiary is set up as a limited liability company. If not, the broader terms "enterprise" or "undertaking" apply.

subsidiaria

= filial

▲ *a wholly owned subsidiary company* una subsidiaria íntegramente participada ▲ *acquisition of subsidiary companies* adquisición de subsidiarias ▲ *shares in subsidiary companies* acciones en subsidiarias

⇛ subsidiary, subsidiary undertaking

subsidiary financial statements IAS/IFRS, US

= subsidiary accounts UK

Subsidiary financial statements are the independent, detailed records of a subsidiary enterprise's financial affairs presenting the income and expenses for a period as well as the financial position at a particular date. The subsidiary financial statements are eventually incorporated in the consolidated financial statements.
estados financieros de la subsidiaria
▲ *prepare subsidiary financial statements* preparar los estados financieros de la subsidiaria
⇛ consolidated financial statements, parent-company financial statements

subsidiary reserve
The subsidiary reserve is a reserve under the enterprise's equity which consists of shares of profit from subsidiaries.
reserva de la subsidiaria
▲ *distribution of profit or loss to subsidiary reserves* distribución de resultados a reservas de la subsidiaria

subsidiary undertaking UK
= subsidiary IAS/IFRS, US
An undertaking is a subsidiary undertaking if the parent company meets at least one of several requirements. Among these are: that the company holds the majority of the voting rights; that the company has the right to appoint or remove a majority of the members of the senior management body; that the company has the right to control the undertaking in making operating and financial decisions; and that the company is an owner and under an agreement with other owners holds the majority of the voting rights in the undertaking.
NOTE "Undertaking" is used in British English meaning "enterprise" in the broad sense of the word, i.e. not referring to any particular type of enterprise.
subsidiaria
= filial
▲ *a wholly-owned subsidiary undertaking* una subsidiaria íntegramente participada ▲ *accounting for subsidiary undertakings* contabilizar subsidiarias ▲ *acquisition of subsidiary undertakings* adquisición de subsidiarias ▲ *disposal of subsidiary undertakings* publicación de subsidiarias ▲ *hold participations in subsidiary undertakings* mantener participaciones en subsidiarias ▲ *subsidiary of a subsidiary undertaking* subsidiaria de una subsidiaria ▲ *the financial statements of the subsidiary undertaking* los estados financieros de la subsidiaria ▲ *the identifiable assets and liabilities of the subsidiary undertaking* los activos y pasivos identificables de la subsidiaria ▲ *winding-up of subsidiary undertakings* cierre de subsidiarias
⇛ subsidiary company

subsidy
A subsidy is a grant, usually in the form of a monetary payment, given to an enterprise by a government or other public sector body for the purpose of supporting the enterprise vis-à-vis competitors or reducing the prices faced by the consumers of the enterprise's goods or services.
subvención
▲ *grant a subsidy* otorgar una subvención ▲ *receive a subsidy* recibir una subvención

substance
= substance over form
Substance, or substance over form, is one of the fundamental accounting concepts under which priority must be given in the presentation of financial statements to the substance of a transaction rather than any legal or other formalities without any real content.
fondo
= sustancia, esencia
▲ *a non-monetary asset without physical substance* un activo no monetario sin sustancia física ▲ *an asset with physical substance* un activo con sustancia física ▲ *evaluate the substance of transactions involving the legal form of a lease* evaluar el fondo de las operaciones que incluyen la forma jurídica de un arrendamiento ▲ *in substance* en esencia ▲ *scenarios that lack commercial substance* escenarios que carecen de sustancia comercial ▲ *the substance of the transaction* el fondo de la transacción

substance over form principle
The substance over form principle is a key accounting concept that implies that the presentation and information in annual reports and financial statements should reflect the economic and financial reality and substance rather than adhere to their legal or technical structure.
principio de la sustancia sobre la forma
= principio de la esencia sobre la forma
NOTE Spanish accountants prefer 'principio de la sustancia sobre la forma' to the IAS/IFRS term 'principio de la esencia sobre la forma'
▲ *comply with the substance over form principle* cumplir con el principio de la sustancia sobre la forma ▲ *in accordance with the substance over form principle* de acuerdo con el principio de la sustancia sobre la forma ▲ *in conformity with the substance over form principle* de conformidad con el principio de la sustancia sobre la forma

subsubsidiary
In some groups a subsidiary may itself be a parent company of one or more subsidiaries; the latter is then referred to as a subsubsidiary or subsubsidiaries.
sub-filial
= subfilial
▲ *hold shares in the subsubsidiary* tener acciones de la sub-filial

subsupplier
= subcontractor
Under provision or delivery of in-house and/or additionally purchased material, a subsupplier produces the complete product or just parts of the product.
subcontratista
▲ *control of subsuppliers* control de subcontratistas ▲ *expenditure relating to subsuppliers* gastos relativos a subcontratistas ▲ *payment to subsuppliers* pago a subcontratistas ▲ *the insurance cover of subsuppliers* la cobertura del seguro de los subcontratistas ▲ *use subsuppliers* usar subcontratistas

subtotal
A subtotal is the total of part of a group of figures or of a section of line items in a financial statement. Examples of subtotals are gross profit, operating profit and profit from ordinary activities in the profit and loss account, where the grand total is the profit for the period.
subtotal
▲ *present subtotals on the face of the balance sheet* presentar subtotales en el anverso del balance ▲ *present subtotals on the face of the income statement* presentar subtotales en el anverso del estado de resultados
⇛ total

subtraction
= deduction
≠ addition
A subtraction is the deduction of an amount from another amount resulting in a reduction of the original amount.
sustracción
= deducción, resta
≠ adición
▲ *a substantial subtraction* una sustracción sustancial ▲ *after the subtraction of a discount of $100* después de la deducción del descuento de 100 dólares ▲ *lead to a subtraction of $10,000* dar lugar a una resta de 10.000 dólares

succession
Succession is the process whereby a person or enterprise takes over the property or rights of another person or enterprise.
sucesión
▲ *incomplete succession* sucesión incompleta

succession concept
The succession concept is the process whereby a person or enterprise takes over the property or rights of another person or enterprise. The succession concept is often used in connection with taxation where a person may take over another person's acquisition cost and thereby defer the taxation that would otherwise have resulted as a consequence of realisation.
concepto de sucesión
▲ *according to the succession concept* de acuerdo con el concepto de sucesión ▲ *comply with*

the succession concept cumplir con el concepto de sucesión

successor auditor
= incoming auditor
≠ predecessor auditor
A successor auditor is a newly appointed, independent, external auditor who did not perform the audit of the financial statements for the previous accounting period and replaces the former auditor.
auditor sucesor
= auditor entrante
≠ auditor anterior, auditor saliente
▲ *a potential successor auditor* un auditor sucesor potencial ▲ *the appointment of the successor auditor* el nombramiento del auditor sucesor ▲ *the results of the successor auditor's review* los resultados de la revisión del auditor sucesor
⇛ audit, auditor

sufficiency
Sufficiency means that the scope or quantity of something, e.g. audit evidence, is adequate.
adecuación
▲ *a high degree of sufficiency* un alto grado de adecuación ▲ *the sufficiency of disclosures* la adecuación de la información

sum
1 = amount, total
A sum is a total amount resulting from adding figures together.
suma
= total
▲ *a discount rate equal to the sum of the benchmark interest rate* una tasa de descuento igual a la suma del tipo de interés benchmark ▲ *the sum of expenditure incurred* la suma del gasto incurrido ▲ *the sum of the carrying amounts assigned to the liability on initial recognition* la suma de los valores contables asignados al pasivo en el reconocimiento inicial ▲ *the sum of the depreciation expense for the asset* el total del gasto por depreciación del activo
2 = amount
A sum is an amount of money.
suma
= cantidad
▲ *a considerable sum* una suma considerable ▲ *a large sum* una gran suma ▲ *an estimated sum* una cantidad estimada ▲ *calculate a sum* calcular una suma ▲ *pay out regular sums for the rest of a policyholder's life* pagar cantidades regulares durante el resto de la vida de un asegurado

summarise
= summarize US
To summarise means to provide a short and concise presentation of the main points of e.g. a plan, project or document without presenting all details.
resumir
▲ *summarised financial information of associates* información financiera resumida de las asociadas

summarize US
= summarise UK, IAS/IFRS
To summarize means to provide a short and concise presentation of the main points of e.g. a plan, project or document without presenting all details.
resumir
▲ *summarized financial information of associates* información financiera resumida de las asociadas

summary
If an annual report or financial statements are characterised as summary, these constitute a simplified or abbreviated version of the complete financial statements or annual report.
resumen
▲ *a summary balance sheet* un balance resumen

sundry
Sundry means miscellaneous and unspecified. In accounting, sundry creditors constitute a mixed bag of amounts payable which have not been separately classified and recognised in individual entries.
diverso
= variado
▲ *sundry costs* costes variados ▲ *sundry creditors* diversos acreedores ▲ *sundry debtors* diversos deudores ▲ *sundry payables* cuentas a pagar diversas ▲ *sundry receivables* diversas cuentas a cobrar ▲ *sundry reserves* reservas variadas ▲ *sundry revenue* ingresos diversos
⇛ various

sunk cost
= past cost

Sunk costs are costs which have been incurred at an earlier stage and therefore they are unavoidable and cannot be changed, which makes them irrelevant to decision-making. One example of sunk costs is the product developments costs of a product for which there is no demand. Such costs cannot influence a decision on new product development activities.

coste hundido

= coste fallido, coste pasado

▲ *the amount of sunk costs* la cantidad de costes hundidos

super variable costing

→ super-variable costing

super-variable costing

= super variable costing, supervariable costing, throughput costing

Super-variable costing is an inventory costing method under which inventory costs only include direct material costs whereas all other product costs are considered operating expenses (period costs). This is based on the assumption that basically, only direct material costs are variable costs, where e.g. direct labour costs are considered fixed costs.

método del coste super-variable

= método del rendimiento de costos

▲ *the rationale behind super-variable costing* la razón de ser del método de coste super-variable ▲ *use super-variable costing* usar el método de coste super-variable

⇛ direct material cost, inventory cost, period cost

superannuation scheme

→ retirement benefit plan

supervariable costing

→ super-variable costing

supervision

Having supervision of something, e.g. an enterprise or an asset, means to have decisive influence on it as well as the authority to obtain the future economic benefits from it. Therefore, a supervising enterprise has the power to control the financial and operating decisions of a supervised enterprise with a view to benefit from its activities.

supervisión

▲ *be under supervision* estar bajo supervisión

supplement[1] *noun*

A supplement is something extra added to something else as an additional or separate part, e.g. an appendix.

suplemento

▲ *a supplement to* un suplemento para ▲ *an application supplement to an IFRS* un suplemento de aplicación a una NIIF

supplement[2] *verb*

To supplement is to add something extra to something.

complementar

▲ *supplement the financial statements with additional disclosures* complementar los estados financieros con divulgaciones adicionales ▲ *supplement the information about contractual repricing and maturity dates* complementar la información sobre la refijación de precios contractuales y fechas de vencimientos ▲ *supplement the statutory disclosures* complementar las publicaciones estatutarias

supplementary

When something is supplementary, it has been added to something else, often constituting a separate part. Large enterprises may e.g. prepare supplementary reports, which are separate reports added to the statutory annual report, such as environmental reports, ethical reports or intellectual capital reports.

complementario

= adiccional, suplementario

▲ *disclose the currency in which the supplementary information is displayed* divulgar la divisa en la que la información adicional se refleja ▲ *disclose the method of translation used to determine the supplementary information* divulgar el método de conversión usado para determinar la información suplementaria ▲ *identify the information as supplementary information* identificar la información como información adicional ▲ *provide fair value information through supplementary disclosures* aportar información sobre el valor razonable por medio de divulgaciones adicionales ▲ *supplementary calculations* cálculos complementarios

supplementary capital
= tier 2 capital
Supplementary capital or tier 2 capital is part of the capital base of banks and consists of revaluation reserve, securities with indefinite maturity and other capital contributions (financing from external sources).
capital suplementario
= tier 2 capital
▲ *approve supplementary capital* aprobar capital suplementario ▲ *calculate the supplementary capital adequacy requirements* calcular los requisitos adecuados del capital suplementario

supplementary report
A supplementary report is a separate, non-statutory report which contains data that follow up on management's review and the financial statements in the annual report and discloses additional relevant matters, e.g. concerning the environment, the enterprise's social responsibility and knowledge as well as ethical objectives. Such reports must give a true and fair view and comply with generally accepted guidelines.
informe adicional
▲ *contents of the supplementary reports* contenidos de los informes adicionales ▲ *disclosures in the supplementary reports* divulgaciones en los informes adicionales ▲ *include supplementary reports* incluir los informes adicionales ▲ *prepare a supplementary report* preparar un informe adicional ▲ *presentation of supplementary reports* presentación de los informes adicionales ▲ *supplementary report on knowledge management* informe adicional sobre gestión del conocimiento ▲ *supplementary reports attached to the annual report* informes adicionales adjuntos al informe anual ▲ *voluntary audit of supplementary reports* auditoria voluntaria de los informes adicionales

supplier
A person or enterprise that provides goods or services to customers in return for payment is called a supplier.
proveedor
▲ *a preferred supplier* un proveedor favorito ▲ *a supplier's warranty agreement* un acuerdo de garantía del proveedor ▲ *accrued unpaid interest to supplier* interés devengado a pagar al proveedor ▲ *customer and supplier relationships* relaciones entre clientes y proveedores

supplies
1 Supplies are consumables, i.e. material goods not directly incorporated into a product. Maintenance materials are a good example of supplies. Supplies appear in the balance sheet item 'materials and supplies' under inventories.
suministros
= insumos
▲ *changes in inventories of finished goods and supplies* cambios en los inventarios de productos terminados y suministros
2 = consumables
Supplies are goods which are bought by companies and used up in administrative work rather than in production.
insumos
= consumibles
▲ *purchase supplies* adquirir insumos ▲ *the cost of supplies* el coste de los insumos

supply of capital
Supply of capital is the increase of capital via equity or loan capital, e.g. by contribution of share capital, withdrawals from overdraft facilities or the raising of loans.
ampliación de capital
▲ *a new supply of capital* una nueva ampliación de capital

support[1] *noun*
Support is help, assistance or funds provided for a particular purpose, project, task, job or e.g. in a decision-making process.
apoyo
= respaldo
▲ *support of reliable information* respaldo de información fiable ▲ *technological and organisational support of knowledge sharing and knowledge development* apoyo organizativo y tecnológico al uso conjunto del conocimiento y a su desarrollo

support[2] *verb*
To support is to assist or help. Information and data may e.g. support decision-making, valuation or other processes in an

enterprise and funds may support e.g. business initiatives.

apoyar

= respaldar

▲ *evidence supporting the amounts and disclosures in the annual report* pruebas que respaldan las cantidades y publicaciones en el informe anual ▲ *evidence to support renewal by the entity without significant cost* pruebas para respaldar la renovación por la entidad sin coste significativo ▲ *support a true and fair view* apoyar una imagen fiel y verdadera ▲ *support capital protection* apoyar la protección del capital ▲ *support financially* apoyar financieramente ▲ *support knowledge sharing* respaldar el uso compartido del conocimiento ▲ *support operational improvements* apoyar mejoras operativas ▲ *support the strategic development* apoyar el desarrollo estratégico ▲ *the reasons supporting the assessment of an indefinite useful life* las razones que apoyan la valoración de una vida útil indefinida

support department

= service department

A support department is a department that provides support services for the other departments in an enterprise.

departamento logístico

▲ *assistance from the support department* asistencia por parte del departamento logístico

surplus

≠ deficit

A surplus arises when one amount exceeds another amount, resulting in a positive amount, e.g. when income exceeds expenditure or exports exceed imports, or when there is an excess amount of something required or expected.

NOTE In a non-profit organisation, a positive bottom line is referred to as a surplus.

plusvalía

≠ déficit

▲ *have a surplus of goods* tener una plusvalía de bienes ▲ *surplus production* producción con plusvalía ▲ *surplus stocks* acciones con plusvalía

⇛ income, profit

surrender

Surrender is the cancellation of a life or similar policy before it has run its full term so that its surrender value can be paid to the policyholder.

renuncia

▲ *a cash surrender option embedded in an insurance contract* una opción de renuncia del pago en efectivo incluida en un contrato de seguros ▲ *surrender charges* costes de renuncia ▲ *waiver on death of charges that would be made on cancellation or surrender* renuncia en caso de muerte de los cargos que se haría sobre la cancelación o rescate

⇛ surrender value

surrender value

The surrender value is the sum of money an insurer will pay to the policyholder in the event that a life or similar policy is cancelled before it has run its full term.

valor de rescate

▲ *a surrender value that varies in response to the change in a financial variable* un valor de rescate que varía en respuesta al cambio de una variable financiera ▲ *the surrender value of the life insurance policy* el valor de rescate de la póliza del seguro de vida

surviving company

A surviving company is the constituent company that, following a merger or consolidation, continues as the parent company for the other constituent companies, or into which one or more other constituent companies are merged, and in which the shareholders of the other merging companies will obtain an interest.

NOTE A constituent company is a company that is a member of a group such as a subsidiary.

empresa superviviente

▲ *the governing body of the surviving company* el órgano de gobierno de la empresa superviviente ▲ *the securities of the surviving company* los títulos de la empresa superviviente ▲ *the stock price of the surviving company* el precio por acción de la empresa superviviente

suspend

To suspend is to bring something to a stop, usually for a short period, e.g. payments.

suspender

▲ *suspend activities* suspender las actividades ▲ *suspend dividend payments* suspender los pagos por dividendo ▲ *suspend payments* suspender pagos ▲ *suspend production* suspender la producción

suspense account

A suspense account is a temporary account for recording debits or credits, e.g. when errors have been detected or transactions have not yet been finalised, until the balances can be entered into the appropriate accounts.

cuenta transitoria

▲ *set up a suspense account* crear una cuenta transitoria ▲ *the balance of the suspense account* el saldo de la cuenta transitoria

suspension of payments

Suspension of payments is the debtor's temporary termination of voluntary payment of debts because of existing or expected insufficiency of funds. In some jurisdictions, court-sanctioned suspension of payments is a legitimate attempt to reorganise the enterprise in order to avoid bankruptcy or winding-up by the court.

suspensión de pagos

▲ *application for suspension of payments* solicitud de suspensión de pagos ▲ *apply for suspension of payments* solicitar la suspensión de pagos ▲ *be in suspension of payments* estar en suspensión de pagos ▲ *file for suspension of payments* declararse en suspensión de pagos

sustainability

Sustainability is the ability to conduct business in a manner that helps preserve resources so that future generations do not suffer from the exhaustion of these resources. When a development is sustainable it can be continued in the same manner for generations without negative impact on the environment or impossibly high costs.

sostenibilidad

▲ *economic sustainability* sostenibilidad económica ▲ *social sustainability* sostenibilidad social ▲ *sustainability in the business strategy* sostenibilidad de la estrategia empresarial

sustainability report

A sustainability report shows the enterprise's impact on economic, social and environmental conditions within a financial year. Sustainability is about leaving environment, the national economy and society as a whole in a sensible and good condition for future generations.

informe de sostenibilidad

▲ *prepare a sustainability report* preparar un informe de sostenibilidad ▲ *publish a sustainability report* publicar un informe de sostenibilidad

sustainable

≠ unsustainable

Something that is strong enough to grow or continue having a positive effect for a long period of time is called sustainable.

sostenible

≠ insostenible

▲ *a sustainable future* un futuro sostenible ▲ *a sustainable regulatory accounting body* un órgano regulador de la contabilidad sostenible ▲ *ensure a sustainable development* asegurar un desarrollo sostenible ▲ *produced in a sustainable manner* producido de una manera sostenible ▲ *sustainable activities* actividades sostenibles ▲ *sustainable development* desarrollo sostenible ▲ *sustainable economy* economía sostenible ▲ *sustainable growth* crecimiento sostenible ▲ *sustainable solutions* soluciones sostenibles ▲ *sustainable use* uso sostenible

Svenska Revisorsamfundet

→ FAR SRS

SWAP

→ swap

swap[1] *noun*

= SWAP, swap contract

A swap is a type of derivative financial instrument, i.e. an agreement between two parties on the exchange of one type of cash payment in relation to a financial instrument for another. A swap may be a currency or an interest rate swap and is agreed on directly between the parties or through an intermediary, such as a bank.

swap

= permuta financiera

▲ *a sale of a financial asset together with a total return swap* una venta de un activo financiero junto con un swap de rentabilidad total ▲ *a swap designated as a cash flow hedge* un

swap designado como una cobertura de flujo de efectivo
▲ *an embedded swap* un swap implícito ▲ *effects of exchange rate changes on loans, equity and swaps* efectos de las fluctuaciones en los tipos de cambio en préstamos, patrimonio y swaps
▲ *enter into swaps* efectuar permutas financieras ▲ *equity swaps* swaps de patrimonio
▲ *insurance swaps* swaps de seguros ▲ *swap trading* negociación de swap ▲ *the fixed rate on a swap* el tipo fijo de un swap
▲ *the notional amount of the swap* el valor nocional del swap
▲ *the variable rate on a swap* el tipo variable de un swap
⇛ derivative financial instrument, interest rate swap

swap[2] *verb*

To swap is to exchange something, e.g. one investment for another or a fixed rate of interest for a variable rate of interest.

permutar

= swap

▲ *to swap back* permutar

swap contract

= swap, SWAP

A swap contract is a type of derivative financial instrument, i.e. an agreement between two parties on the exchange of one type of cash payment in relation to a financial instrument for another. A swap contract may be a currency or an interest rate swap contract and is agreed on directly between the parties or through an intermediary, such as a bank.

contrato de swaps

= contrato de permuta financiera, swap

▲ *an interest rate swap contract* un contrato de swaps de tipo de interés ▲ *enter into a swap contract* efectuar un contrato de swaps

swap rate

The swap rate expresses the difference between the rate at the time of purchase/sale of a currency against another, i.e. the spot rate, and the rate at the time of sale/purchase of the same currency/against the other, i.e. the forward rate. The swap rate is typically expressed as the forward rate at a premium or a discount to the spot rate and takes into consideration the interest rate differential between the two currencies as well as the swap period.

tasa de swap

= tasa de permuta, tasa de permuta financiera

▲ *the difference between the swap rate and the price at the balance sheet date* la diferencia entre la tasa de swap y el precio a la fecha de balance

Swedish Association of Auditors

Swedish Association of Auditors (Svenska Revisorsamfundet - SRS) is a Swedish association for authorised public auditors (auktoriserade revisorer) and approved public auditors (godkända revisorer) who are responsible for auditing in small and medium-sized enterprises. On 1 September 2006, the SRS was combined with FAR, which is a Swedish association for publicly approved and authorised auditors and other highly qualified professionals in the entire accountancy sector in Sweden.

Swedish Association of Auditors

= Asociación Sueca de Auditores

▲ *become a member of the Swedish Association of Auditors* llegar a ser un miembro de la Swedish Association of Auditors

swop[1] *noun*

→ swap

swop[2] *verb*

→ swap

synchronous tracking

Synchronous tracking is a costing method based on the principle that all costs are recorded in the bookkeeping system in the same order as the physical processes occur in the purchasing and production functions. In this way, costs can be tracked to the different stages of the production cycle.

rastreo sincrónico

= rastreo secuestral

▲ *use synchronous tracking* utilizar el rastreo sincrónico

⇛ backflush costing, trigger point

syndicated loan

A syndicated loan is a loan that has been provided by several lenders together.

préstamo sindicado
▲ *drawings on syndicated loans* giros sobre los préstamos sindicados ▲ *the syndicated loan market* el mercado de préstamos sindicados

synergy
Synergy refers to a situation where the combination of two or more assets or processes leads to enhanced combined performance in comparison with the sum of their individual performances. For instance, when two enterprises are merged, they may generate better results than as separate enterprises.
sinergia
▲ *benefit from the synergies of the combination* beneficiarse de las sinergias de la combinación ▲ *create synergies* crear sinergias ▲ *synergies between investment property and other assets* sinergias entre inversiones inmobiliarias y otros activos ▲ *the benefits that result from synergy between the identifiable assets acquired* los beneficios resultantes de la sinergias entre los activos identificables adquiridos

synergy effect
A synergy effect refers to a situation where the combination of two or more assets or processes leads to enhanced combined performance in comparison with the sum of their individual performances. For instance, when two enterprises are merged, they may generate better results than as separate enterprises.
efecto de sinergia
▲ *create a synergy effect* crear un efecto de sinergia

systematic
Systematic refers to actions or processes that are carried out in a uniform way every time in accordance with fixed procedures or plans.
sistemático
▲ *a systematic basis* una base sistemática ▲ *a systematic presentation* una presentación sistemática ▲ *a systematic process* un proceso sistemático ▲ *allocate finance income over the lease term on a systematic and rational basis* asignar ingresos financieros durante el periodo de arrendamiento de forma sistemática y racional ▲ *present notes in a systematic manner* presentar notas de forma sistemática ▲ *provide for systematic amortisation or depreciation of assets over their useful lives* provisionar la amortización o depreciación sistemática de los activos a lo largo de su vida útil ▲ *systematic building of knowledge and competencies* construcción sistemática de conocimiento y competencias ▲ *systematic comparison of performance* comparación sistemática de resultados ▲ *systematic distribution of the amortisation or depreciation basis* distribución sistemática de la base de amortización o depreciación ▲ *systematic quality control* control de calidad sistemático

systematics
Systematics is the science and process of classifying and organising organisms, processes, data etc. into systems.
sistemática
▲ *increased systematics in risk management* sistemática principalmente especializada en gestión de riesgos

systematisation UK
= systematization US
Systematisation is the operation of organising activities and processes into a system.
sistematización
▲ *systematisation of data collection* sistematización en la recopilación de datos ▲ *systematisation of economic risks* sistematización de los riesgos económicos

systematise UK
= systematize US
To systematise is to organise activities and processes into a system.
sistematizar
▲ *systematise data retrieval and reporting* sistematizar la recuperación de datos y su descripción ▲ *systematise the numbers of the intellectual capital report by activities* sistematizar por actividades las cifras del informe de capital intelectual ▲ *systematise the retrieval of information* sistematizar la recuperación de información

systematised UK
= systematized US
When something is systematised, it is arranged, organised

or processed in a uniform way according to a specific system.
sistematizado
▲ *systematised research models* modelos de investigación sistematizados

systematization US
= systematisation UK
Systematization is the operation of organizing activities and processes into a system.
sistematización
▲ *systematization of data collection* sistematización de la recogida de datos ▲ *systematization of economic risks* sistematización de los riesgos económicos

systematize US
= systematise UK
To systematize is to organize activities and processes into a system.
sistematizar
▲ *systematize data retrieval and reporting* sistematizar la recuperación de los datos y la presentación de la información ▲ *systematize the numbers of the intellectual capital report by activities* sistematizar los números del informe del capital intelectual por actividades ▲ *systematize the retrieval of information* sistematizar la recuperación de información

systematized US
= systematised UK
When something is systematized, it is arranged, organized or processed in a uniform way according to a specific system.
sistematizado
▲ *systematized research models* modelos de investigación sistematizados

T

T-account

A T-account is an account in its general form presented in the form of the capital letter 'T'. The title of the account appears above the top line; debits are recorded to the left of the middle line, credits to the right of it.

cuenta T

= cuenta en T

▲ *a separate T-account for output VAT* una cuenta T separada para salida del IVA ▲ *the balance of the T-account* el saldo de la cuenta T ▲ *the VAT T-account* la cuenta T del IVA

take to the profit and loss account UK

To take to the profit and loss account means to recognise an amount as a profit or an expense for the period.

anotar en la cuenta de pérdidas y ganancias

▲ *take the profit or loss of the enterprise to the profit and loss account* anotar el resultado de la empresa en la cuenta de pérdidas y ganancias

taken to the profit and loss account UK

If an amount has been taken to the profit and loss account, that amount has been recognised as a profit or an expense item for the period.

anotado en la cuenta de pérdidas y ganancias

▲ *income taken to the profit and loss account* ingreso anotado en la cuenta de pérdidas y ganancias

takeover bid

A takeover bid refers to an offer to the shareholders of a company to purchase their shares at a specified price –which is generally higher than the listed price– for the purpose of obtaining all of the shares or a controlling interest in the company.

OPA

= oferta pública de adquisición de acciones, oferta pública de compra de acciones

▲ *a failed takeover bid* una OPA fallida ▲ *a takeover bid for the shares of a listed company* una OPA sobre las acciones de una compañía cotizada ▲ *a voluntary takeover bid* una OPA voluntaria ▲ *determination of the price of the takeover bid* determinación del precio de la OPA ▲ *make a takeover bid* hacer una OPA ▲ *mandatory takeover bids* OPAs obligatorias ▲ *the Danish Securities Council's Executive Order on Takeover Bids* la Orden Ejecutiva del Consejo Bursátil danés sobre OPAs

takeover obligation

A takeover obligation is the obligation required by takeover rules, e.g. the EU Takeover Directive, that an acquiring company which has obtained control of another company is obliged to make an offer within four weeks to the minority shareholders to acquire their shares.

obligación del adquirente

▲ *statutory takeover obligation* obligación estatutaria del adquirente

⇛ takeover

tangible asset UK

= PPE US, IAS/IFRS, property, plant and equipment US, IAS/IFRS, tangible fixed asset UK

≠ intangible asset

Tangible assets are physical, fixed assets intended for long-term ownership or use by an enterprise. Examples include land and buildings, plant, machinery and equipment as well as assets in course of construction.

activo tangible

= activo material

▲ *acquisition of tangible assets* adquisición de activos tangibles ▲ *construction of tangible assets* construcción de activos tangibles ▲ *consume a tangible asset* consumir un activo tangible ▲ *depreciation of tangible assets* depreciación de activos tangibles ▲ *fair value gains on tangible assets* ganancias a valor razonable en activos tangibles ▲ *measure tangible assets at cost* medir activos tangibles al coste ▲ *prepayments for tangible assets* pagos anticipados por activos tangibles ▲ *purchase tangi-*

ble assets comprar activos tangibles ▲ *tangible assets in progress* activos tangibles en curso ▲ *tangible assets with a limited useful life* activos tangibles con una vida útil limitada ▲ *the carrying amount of tangible assets* el valor contable de los activos tangibles ▲ *use a tangible asset to develop an intangible asset* usar un activo tangible para desarrollar un activo intangible

tangible fixed asset UK
= PPE US, IAS/IFRS, property, plant and equipment US, IAS/IFRS, tangible asset UK, IAS/IFRS
Tangible fixed assets are physical assets intended for long-term ownership or use by an enterprise. Examples include land and buildings, plant, machinery and equipment as well as assets in course of construction.
inmovilizado material
= activo fijo tangible, edificios, instalaciones y equipos
NOTE 'Inmobilizado material' is always singular in Spanish accounting texts.
▲ *acquisition of tangible fixed assets* adquisición de inmovilizado material ▲ *construction of tangible fixed assets* construcción de inmovilizado material ▲ *fair value gains on tangible fixed assets* ganancias a valor razonable en inmovilizado material ▲ *investments in tangible fixed assets* inversiones en inmovilizado material ▲ *losses arising from sale of tangible fixed assets* pérdidas por venta de inmovilizado material ▲ *measure tangible fixed assets at cost* valoración de edificios, instalaciones y equipos al coste ▲ *prepayments for tangible fixed assets* anticipos por inmovilizado material ▲ *purchase of tangible fixed assets* compra de inmovilizado material ▲ *revaluation of tangible fixed assets* revalorización de inmovilizado material ▲ *revalue tangible fixed assets to fair value* revaluar inmovilizado material a valor razonable ▲ *sale of tangible fixed assets* venta de inmovilizado material ▲ *tangible fixed assets in progress* inmovilizado material en curso ▲ *tangible fixed assets with a limited useful life* inmovilizado material con una vida útil limitada ▲ *the book value of tangible fixed assets* el valor contable del inmovilizado material

target cost
Target costs are costs targeted at a certain, predetermined level or ceiling that in the long run makes it possible for an enterprise to secure competitiveness, thereby achieving its targeted earnings.
coste objetivo
▲ *calculate the target cost* calcular el coste objetivo ▲ *target cost per unit* coste objetivo por unidad

target costing
Target costing is a management control method intended to control the total costs of a product over its life cycle. When this method is applied, the target price of the product is first identified and determined, and the costs are then controlled to meet this target. Target costing is particularly aimed at the product's planning and design phases with a view to ensuring that the choices of product design and production method meet the profitability targets set by the enterprise.
NOTE Target costing is a Japanese management accounting method appropriate for markets with fierce competition.
método del coste objetivo
= método de coste objetivo
▲ *an in-depth analysis of target costing* un análisis en profundidad del método del coste objetivo ▲ *apply target costing* aplicar el método de coste objetivo

target operating income per unit
The target operating income per unit refers to the income per unit set as a profit target by the enterprise on the basis of a targeted sales price. This enables the enterprise to budget for the maximum costs per produced unit.
objetivo de ingresos de explotación por unidad
▲ *achieve the target operating income per unit* conseguir el objetivo de ingresos de explotación por unidad ▲ *calculate the target operating income per unit* calcular el objetivo de ingresos de explotación por unidad

target price
A target price is the price that customers are willing to pay

for a product, and which an enterprise must therefore consider to be the highest possible price. The target price is indicated in market analyses.

precio indicativo

= precio objetivo

▲ *10% below the target price* 10% por debajo del precio indicativo ▲ *lower the target price* bajar el precio indicativo ▲ *raise the target price* aumentar el precio indicativo ▲ *set a target price* establecer un precio indicativo

target rate of return on investment

The target rate of return in investment is the rate of return targeted by an enterprise on a particular investment.

objetivo de tasa de retorno de la inversión

▲ *a specified target rate of return on investment* un objetivo de tasa de retorno de la inversión establecido ▲ *obtain a target rate of return on investment* obtener un objetivo de tasa de retorno de la inversión ▲ *set a target rate of return on investment* establecer un objetivo de tasa de retorno de la inversión

tax[1] *noun*

Tax is a levy imposed by central and local governments on income, profits, assets etc. of individuals and enterprises (direct tax) and on the purchase and sale of goods (indirect tax) to get revenue for public expenditure.

impuesto

▲ *adjustment of tax for previous years* ajuste impositivo de años anteriores ▲ *become subject to pay a tax* estar obligado al pago de impuestoss ▲ *calculated tax on the taxable income for the year* calcular el impuesto sobre la renta imponible anual ▲ *capital gain on shares after tax* dividendos después de impuestos ▲ *capital gain on shares before tax* dividendo antes de impuestos ▲ *collect taxes* recaudar impuestos ▲ *current tax* impuesto corriente ▲ *deductible for tax purposes* deducible por motivos fiscales ▲ *deferred tax* impuesto diferido ▲ *direct taxes* impuestos directos ▲ *estimated tax payable* impuestos estimados a pagar ▲ *expenses not deductible for tax purposes* gastos no deducibles fiscalmente ▲ *extraordinary profit or loss before tax* resultado extraordinario antes de impuestos ▲ *income not subject to tax* renta no sujeta a impuestos ▲ *indirect taxes* impuestos indirectos ▲ *operating profit or loss before financials and tax* resultado operativo antes de impuestos y actividades financieras ▲ *other taxes* otros impuestos ▲ *pay taxes* pagar impuestos ▲ *profit or loss after tax* resultado después de impuestos ▲ *profit or loss before tax* resultado antes de impuestos ▲ *profit or loss before tax and extraordinary items* resultado antes de impuestos y partidas extraordianarias ▲ *profit or loss for the year after tax and minority interests* resultado anual después de impuestos e intereses de los minoritarios ▲ *profit or loss from ordinary activities after tax* resultado de actividades corrientes después de impuestos ▲ *profit or loss from ordinary activities before tax* resultado de actividades ordinarias antes de impuestoss ▲ *provision for taxes payable* provisiones para impuestos a pagar ▲ *share of tax of associates* participación del impuesto de las asociadas ▲ *tax calculated at the rate of 30%* impuesto calculado a la tasa del 30% ▲ *tax for the year* impuesto anual ▲ *tax on extraordinary profit or loss* impuesto sobre resultado extraordinario ▲ *tax on net profit or loss for the year* impuesto sobre el resultado neto anual ▲ *tax on profit or loss from ordinary activities* impuesto sobre resultados de actividades ordinarias ▲ *tax on value added* impuesto sobre el valor añadido ▲ *tax overpaid* impuesto pagado de más ▲ *tax receivable* impuestos a cobrar ▲ *tax refund relating to previous years* devolución de impuestos relacionados con años anteriores ▲ *tax relating to changes in equity* impuestos relacionados con cambios en patrimonio ▲ *tax relating to treasury shares and goodwill* impuestos relacionados con autocartera y fondo de comercio ▲ *tax underpaid* impuesto pagado de menos ▲ *taxes paid during the year* impuestos pagados durante el año ▲ *taxes payable* impuestos a pagar ▲ *the current tax* el impuesto corriente ▲ *the tax on the group's profit before tax* el impuesto sobre el beneficio del grupo antes de impuestos ▲ *the tax taken to the income statement relating to the extraordinary profit or loss for the year* el impuesto llevado al estado de resultados relacionado con el resultado extraordinario anual

tax[2] *verb*

To tax is to impose a levy on the income and profits of individuals and enterprises (direct tax), the purchase and sale of goods (indirect tax), etc. Tax is levied by central and local governments to be used for public spending.

gravar

▲ *tax the profit or loss of the enterprise* gravar el resultado de la empresa

tax accounts

Tax accounts constitute a statement prepared with a view to disclosing the amounts of an enterprise's taxable income and assets to the tax authorities.

cuentas fiscales

= cuentas de impuestos

▲ *prepare tax accounts* preparar las cuentas fiscales ▲ *the measurements of the tax accounts* las mediciones de las cuentas fiscales

tax adjustment

A tax adjustment is a correction to tax amounts calculated e.g. to comply with changed tax rules, transition to new accounting policies or changes in the tax base.

ajuste fiscal

▲ *make a tax adjustment* hacer un ajuste fiscal

tax amount

= tax balance

The tax amount is the tax payable for a particular period, typically a year, to the tax authorities as levied and calculated according to the tax rules and the relevant tax rate.

cuota fiscal

= cuota impositiva

▲ *a current tax amount* una cuota fiscal corriente ▲ *a deferred tax amount* una cuota fiscal diferida ▲ *a reconciliation of tax amounts* una conciliación de las cuotas fiscales ▲ *calculated tax amounts* cuotas fiscales calculadas ▲ *tax amounts paid* cuotas fiscales pagadas

tax assessment

Tax assessment is the determination by the tax authorities of the amount of taxable income and the computation of the tax payable on that income.

liquidación de impuestos

= liquidación fiscal

▲ *change a tax assessment* cambiar una liquidación de impuestos ▲ *have the tax assessment reopened* tener reabierta la liquidación de impuestos

tax assessment notice

A tax assessment notice is a survey of the income and assets of a taxpayer, also showing any residual tax or tax receivable. Tax assessment notices are prepared and submitted to taxpayers by the tax authorities.

notificación de liquidación fiscal

= notificación de liquidación de impuestos

▲ *submit a tax assessment notice* enviar una notificación de liquidación fiscal

tax asset

Tax assets represent income tax recoverable in future accounting periods concerning deductible temporary differences, i.e. negative deferred tax, or carryforwards of unused tax losses or credits.

activo fiscal

▲ *a recognised tax asset* un activo fiscal reconocido ▲ *an unrecognised tax asset* un activo fiscal no reconocido ▲ *capitalisation of tax assets* capitalización de los activos fiscales ▲ *current tax asset* activo fiscal corriente ▲ *deferred tax asset* activo fiscal diferido ▲ *foreign tax assets* activos fiscales extranjeros ▲ *measured tax asset* activo fiscal valorado ▲ *measurement of a deferred tax asset* cuantificación de un activo fiscal diferido ▲ *offset tax assets* compensar los activos fiscales ▲ *revaluation of a tax asset* revalorización de un activo fiscal ▲ *the amount of deferred tax assets* la cuantía de activos fiscales diferidos

tax at source

= PAYE tax, withholding tax

Tax at source is income tax collected at source by e.g. an employer who withholds and deducts the tax from an employee's wages and pays that tax directly to the tax authorities on behalf of the employee.

impuesto en origen

▲ *charge tax at source* cargar impuestos en origen ▲ *withholding of tax at source* retención de impuestos en origen

tax authority

A tax authority is the national or local government department or agency that is in charge of taxation, including assessment and collection, within a country or area.

hacienda

= autoridad fiscal, Hacienda

▲ *comply with the requets of the tax authorities* cumplir con los requisitos de las autoridades fiscales ▲ *the local tax authorities* las haciendas locales

tax avoidance

≠ tax evasion

Tax avoidance is the legal organisation of a taxpayer's affairs to minimise tax liabilities and reduce payment of tax.

evasión legal de impuestos

= reducción legal de la carga impositiva

▲ *a transaction that has as its principal objective tax evasion or tax avoidance* una transacción que tiene como su objetivo principal el fraude fiscal o la evasión legal de impuestos ▲ *distinguish between legal tax avoidance and illegal tax evasion* distinguir entre la evasión legal e ilegal de impuestos

tax base

= value for tax purposes

The tax base is the amount attributed to an asset or a liability on which tax is levied.

base imponible

= base fiscal

NOTE Spanish accountants prefer 'base imponible' to the IAS/IFRS term 'base fiscal'.

▲ *a tax base of nil* una base imponible cero ▲ *adjust the tax base* ajustar la base imponible ▲ *capitalisation of the tax base of a loss* capitalización de la base imponible de una pérdida ▲ *difference between the carrying amount and the tax base* diferencia entre el valor contable y la base imponible ▲ *measurement of the tax base* medición de la base imponible ▲ *tax base of assets and liabilities* base imponible de activos y pasivos ▲ *the appropriate tax base* la base imponible apropiada ▲ *the initial tax base* la base imponible inicial ▲ *the tax base of non-monetary assets and liabilities* la base imponible de activos y pasivos no monetarios ▲ *the tax bases of the identifiable assets acquired* las bases imponibles de los activos identificables adquiridos ▲ *the tax bases of the identifiable assets acquired and liabilities assumed* las bases imponibles de los activos identificables adquiridos y de los pasivos asumidos

SOURCE IAS 12, paragraph 5

tax charge

= tax liability

A tax charge is the calculated tax liability, i.e. the amount owed on taxable profit or income to the tax authorities comprising current and deferred taxes payable.

pasivo por impuestos

= carga fiscal, carga impositiva

▲ *calculate the tax charge* calcular el pasivo por impuestos ▲ *the overall tax charge* la carga impositiva total

⇛ current tax, deferred tax

tax contingency

Tax contingencies are possible tax liabilities, which depend on the occurrence or non-occurrence of particular events and for which no provisions have been made.

contingencia fiscal

▲ *an additional tax contingency* una contingencia fiscal adicional ▲ *the reversal of a tax contingency* la anulación de una contingencia fiscal

tax credit

= income tax credit US

A tax credit is a direct, monetary reduction of the tax liability, i.e. amount of tax payable as opposed to tax relief, tax allowances or tax deductions that are offset against the taxable income. An example of an income tax credit is the offsetting of taxes paid abroad against national taxes payable.

crédito fiscal

▲ *grant a tax credit* conceder un crédito fiscal ▲ *the tax credit granted to resident shareholders*

el crédito fiscal otorgado a los accionistas residentes
⇛ allowance, tax deduction, tax relief

tax credit carryforward
A tax credit carryforward is negative income tax from prior years that can be set off against taxes payable in future years.
crédito fiscal imputado a un ejercicio posterior
▲ *minimum tax credit carryforward* crédito fiscal mínimo imputado a un ejercicio posterior
⇛ carryforward, tax loss carryforward

tax deduction
A tax deduction is a subtraction of expenses incurred from income resulting in a lower taxable income and tax liability.
desgravación fiscal
= deducción fiscal
▲ *measurement of the tax deduction based on the enterprise's share price at the date of exercise* valoración de la desgravación fiscal basada en el precio de la acción de la empresa a la fecha del ejercicio ▲ *obtain a tax deduction* obtener una desgravación fiscal ▲ *receive a tax deduction that relates to remuneration paid in shares* recibir una desgravación fiscal relacionada con la remuneración pagada en acciones ▲ *the amount of the tax deduction* la cantidad de la deducción fiscal ▲ *the estimated future tax deduction* la desgravación fiscal futura estimada
⇛ deduction, tax relief

tax depreciation
= depreciation for tax purposes
≠ accounting depreciation, book depreciation, depreciation for accounting purposes
Tax depreciation is the depreciation allowed for tax purposes of a tangible asset.
depreciación fiscal
▲ *accelerated tax depreciation* depreciación fiscal acelerada ▲ *cumulative tax depreciation* depreciación fiscal acumulativa
⇛ accounting depreciation

tax effect
A tax effect is the tax implications and consequences resulting from decisions made in an enterprise or other factors impacting taxes payable to increase or decrease.
efecto fiscal
▲ *tax effects of all exchange differences* efectos fiscales de todas las diferencias de cambio ▲ *the tax effect of acquisitions* el efecto fiscal de las adquisiciones ▲ *the tax effect of amortisation of goodwill* el efecto fiscal de la amortización del fondo de comercio ▲ *the tax effect of changes in accounting policies* el efecto fiscal de los cambios en las políticas contables ▲ *the tax effect of eliminations* el efecto fiscal de las eliminaciones ▲ *the tax effect of joint taxation* el efecto fiscal de la tributación conjunta ▲ *the tax effect of revaluations* el efecto fiscal de las revalorizaciones ▲ *the tax effect of revaluations of costs* el efecto fiscal de las revalorizaciones de costes ▲ *the tax effects of corrections of prior period errors* los efectos fiscales de las correcciones en el periodo anterior ▲ *total tax effect* total efecto fiscal

tax entity
A tax entity is a unit such as an enterprise which for tax purposes is considered to be a separate, aggregate unit.
entidad fiscal
▲ *elimination within the same legal tax entity* eliminación dentro de la misma entidad fiscal jurídica

tax evasion
≠ tax avoidance
Tax evasion is the illegal misstatement and reduction of tax liabilities to avoid payment of tax.
evasión fiscal
▲ *a transaction that has as its principal objective tax evasion or tax avoidance* una transacción cuyo principal objetivo es la evasión o desgravación fiscal ▲ *distinguish between legal tax avoidance and illegal tax evasion* distinguir entre la desgravación fiscal legal y la evasión fiscal ilegal

tax expense
Tax expense comprises the current and deferred tax liabilities of an enterprise and determines, as a total amount, the enterprise's profit or loss for the accounting period.
gasto por impuesto sobre beneficios
= gasto por el impuesto a las ganancias, gasto por el im-

puesto sobre los beneficios, gasto por impuesto sobre beneficios

NOTE Spanish accountants prefer 'gasto por impuesto sobre beneficios' to the IAS/IFRS term 'gasto por el impuesto a las ganancias'.

▲ *current tax expense* gasto corriente por impuesto sobre beneficios ▲ *deferred tax expense* gasto diferido por impuesto sobre beneficios ▲ *identify a tax expense with investing activities* identificar un gasto por impuesto sobre beneficios con actividades de inversión ▲ *net profit or loss for the year before deducting tax expenses* resultado neto del año antes de deducir los gastos por impuesto sobre beneficios ▲ *reconciliation of the tax expense for the year* conciliación del gasto por el impuesto sobre los beneficios del año ▲ *tax expense for the year* gasto por impuesto sobre los beneficios del año ▲ *tax expense relating to extraordinary items* gasto por impuesto sobre beneficios relacionado con partidas extraordinarias ▲ *tax expense relating to profit or loss from ordinary activities* gasto por impuesto sobre beneficios relacionado con el resultado de las actividades ordinarias ▲ *the amount of tax expense* la cuantía del gasto por impuesto sobre beneficios

SOURCE IAS 12, paragraphs 5 and 6

tax for the year

Tax for the year is the total amount of current tax and deferred tax of an enterprise.

impuesto del año

= impuesto anual, impuesto del ejercicio

▲ *disclosures of current tax for the year and deferred tax* publicaciones del impuesto anual corriente y diferido ▲ *give a true and fair view of tax for the year* dar una imagen fiel y razonable del impuesto del año ▲ *recognition of tax for the year* reconocimiento del impuesto del año ▲ *specification of the tax for the year as current tax and deferred tax* especificaciones del impuesto del año como impuesto corriente y diferido

tax income

Tax income is a tax benefit that arises from the deductible tax losses of an enterprise.

ingreso fiscal

▲ *current tax income* ingresos fiscales corrientes ▲ *deferred tax income* ingresos fiscales diferidos ▲ *recognised tax income* ingresos fiscales reconocidos ▲ *tax income relating to profit or loss from ordinary activities* ingresos fiscales relativos a los resultados de actividades ordinarias ▲ *the amount of tax income* la cantidad de ingresos fiscales

tax legislation

= tax laws

The body of statutes that contains the rules governing taxation within a country or area is referred to as tax legislation.

legislación fiscal

▲ *comply with tax legislation* cumplir con la legislación fiscal ▲ *in conformity with tax legislation* de acuerdo con la legislación fiscal

tax liability

1 = liability to pay tax

Tax liability is the obligation to pay tax.

pasivo fiscal

▲ *be subject to tax liability* estar sujeto a pasivo fiscal ▲ *limited tax liability* pasivo fiscal limitado ▲ *objective tax liability* pasivo fiscal objetivo ▲ *subjective tax liability* pasivo fiscal subjetivo

2 = tax charge

Tax liabilities are amounts owed on taxable profit or income to the tax authorities comprising current tax and deferred tax payable.

pasivo fiscal

▲ *a current tax liability* un pasivo fiscal corriente ▲ *deferred tax liabilities* pasivos fiscales diferidos

⇛ current tax, deferred tax

tax loss

Tax loss is the loss for a period, determined according to tax rules rather than accounting rules, upon which tax is recoverable.

pérdida fiscal

▲ *a tax loss carry-forward* una compensación posterior por pérdida fiscal ▲ *an extraordinary tax loss* una pérdida fiscal extraordinaria ▲ *an unused tax loss* una pérdida fiscal sin aplicar ▲ *deferral of a tax loss* anticipo de una pérdida fiscal ▲ *realise a tax loss* realizar una pérdida fiscal ▲ *recognition of the benefit of tax losses* reconocimiento de un beneficio por pérdidas fiscales ▲ *tax loss carried forward* pérdida fiscal compensada posteriormente ▲ *tax losses that were not recognised by the acquiree before the business combination* pérdidas fiscales que no fueron reconocidas por el adquirente antes de la combinación de negocios

tax loss carryforward

A tax loss carryforward is the transfer of a loss for a particular accounting period to a later accounting period with the purpose of offsetting it against future profits to reduce taxes payable.

pérdida fiscal compensable con beneficios fiscales futuros

▲ *the potential benefit of the acquiree's income tax loss carryforwards* el beneficio potencial de la pérdida fiscal compensable con beneficios fiscales futuros del adquirente

⇛ loss carryforward, tax credit carryforward

tax on profit or loss for the year

The tax on the profit or loss for the year is the current tax payable or recoverable on the taxable profit or loss for the financial year of an enterprise.

impuesto sobre resultados del ejercicio

▲ *current tax on profit or loss for the year* impuestos corrientes sobre resultados del ejercicio

tax payable

Tax payable refers to the amount of tax which an enterprise has to pay on the profit or loss for an accounting period. Current tax payable is recognised in the profit and loss account, whereas deferred tax appears under liabilities in the balance sheet.

impuesto a pagar

▲ *recognition of tax payable* reconocimiento del impuesto a pagar ▲ *taxes payable on foreign operations* impuestos a pagar en operaciones extranjeras

⇛ current tax, deferred tax

tax payment

A tax payment is an amount paid by an enterprise following a tax or charge that has been imposed on the enterprise.

pago fiscal

▲ *a stable tax payment* un pago fiscal estable ▲ *additions, deductions and allowances relating to tax payments* sumas, deducciones y bonificaciones relacionadas con pagos fiscales

tax provision

1 A tax provision is a tax rule prescribed by tax legislation.

disposición fiscal

▲ *become subject to tax provisions* estar sujeto a las disposiciones fiscales ▲ *national tax provision* disposición fiscal nacional

2 = provision for future taxes payable

A tax provision is an amount set aside under liabilities in the balance sheet to cover taxes payable in future periods.

provisión para impuestos

▲ *adjust a tax provision already recognised* ajustar una provisión para impuestos ya reconocida ▲ *measure a tax provision* valorar una provisión para impuestos ▲ *recognise a tax provision* reconocer una provisión para impuestos ▲ *reverse a tax provision* revertir una provisión para impuestos

tax rate

A tax rate is the percentage at which tax is levied on the taxable income or profit, or the tax base of an asset. Tax rates vary for various types of income and groups of tax payers.

tipo impositivo

▲ *a reduction in the tax rate of 1 percentage point* una reducción del tipo impositivo del 1% ▲ *a tax rate of 30%* un tipo impositivo del 30% ▲ *applicable tax rate* tipo impositivo aplicable ▲ *change of the tax rate* cambio del tipo impositivo ▲ *changed tax rate* tipo impositivo modificado ▲ *effective tax rate* tipo impositivo efectivo ▲ *on account tax rate* tipo impositivo a cuenta ▲ *tax rates enacted or substantially enacted by the balance sheet date* tipos impositivos aplicables o sustancialmente aplicables a la fecha del balance ▲ *the marginal tax rates applicable to interest income* los tipos impositivos marginales aplicables a los ingresos por intereses ▲ *the tax rate applicable to the taxable amount derived from the sale of an asset* el tipo impositivo aplicable a la cantidad imponible procedente de la venta de un activo ▲ *the tax rate applicable to undistributed profit* el tipo impositivo aplicable al beneficio no distribuido

tax receivable UK

= income tax receivable US

A tax receivable is an asset for an enterprise and arises because the enterprise has paid too much tax.

impuesto a cobrar

▲ *current tax receivable* impuesto actual a cobrar

tax reconciliation

Tax reconciliation is the calculation in the accounts carried out to substantiate and confirm the current and deferred taxes in the accounts. Thus, the tax reconciliation explains any discrepancy between the enterprise's tax payable and the tax expense in the accounts.

conciliación fiscal

▲ *tax reconciliation in monetary values* conciliación fiscal en valores monetarios ▲ *tax reconciliation in percentages* conciliación fiscal en porcentajes

tax relief

Tax relief is the reduction or saving of taxes payable obtained by allowable deductions from taxable amounts, i.e. taxable income or profit, or by tax exemption relating to particular gains or profits. Tax relief is available by statute, and allowable deductions typically include personal allowances, pension contributions and business losses.

desgravación fiscal

= deducción fiscal

▲ *grant tax relief* otorgar una desgravación fiscal ▲ *the corporation tax relief granted* la desgravación fiscal obtenida por la corporación

⇛ tax deduction

tax return IAS/IFRS, US

= income tax return UK, statement of income

A tax return is a taxpayer's annual statement of income submitted to the tax authorities showing details of taxable amounts of income, gains and profits and tax-deductible expenses.

declaración de la renta

= declaración fiscal, impreso de declaración de la renta

▲ *fill out a tax return* rellenar un impreso de declaración de la renta ▲ *submit the tax return* remitir la declaración de la renta

tax statement

A tax statement is an annual statement of account showing the tax balance from last statement, any amounts paid since, e.g. through the PAYE system, any remaining taxes due to or taxes repayable by the tax authorities for the previous year, any penalties, interest or surcharges due on unpaid taxes, and showing in the bottom line the final tax amount payable.

estado fiscal

▲ *notes to the tax statement* notas al estado fiscal ▲ *prepare a tax statement* preparar un estado fiscal ▲ *submit a tax statement* remitir un estado fiscal

⇛ PAYE tax, tax return

tax year

A tax year is a 12-month period for which income and corporation taxes are calculated. A tax year may be a calendar year, but it may also be another 12-month period; in the UK, for instance, a tax year runs from 6 April to the following 5 April.

año fiscal

▲ *during the tax year* durante el año fiscal ▲ *the previous tax year* el año fiscal anterior

tax-deductible

→ deductible

tax-deductible capital loss account

A tax-deductible capital loss account refers to the capital loss deduction following certain mortgage loans according to which the balance is amortised and reported to the tax authorities during the life of the loan.

cuenta de pérdida de capital fiscalmente deducible

▲ *tax-deductible capital loss account for cash loans* cuenta de pérdida de capital fiscalmente deducible por préstamos en efectivo

tax-exempt

Tax-exempt means free of tax, i.e. not taxed.

fiscalmente exento

▲ *a tax-exempt maintenance grant for operating expenses* una subvención de funcionamiento fiscalmente exenta para gastos de explotación ▲ *reduce the tax-exempt status of interest on the held-to-maturity investments* reducir el tipo de interés fiscalmente exento en las inversiones mantenidas hasta el vencimiento

tax-loss carryforward
→ tax loss carryforward

taxable gain
A taxable gain is a gain on which tax is payable.
beneficio imponible
= beneficio fiscal
▲ *a taxable gain from the sale of property* un beneficio imponible por la venta de la propiedad ▲ *determine the taxable gain* determinar el beneficio imponible

taxable income IAS/IFRS, US
Taxable income is the amount of income of an accounting entity for a period, determined in accordance with the rules governing taxation of the entity, of which taxation for the period will be charged.
base imponible
NOTE Spanish accountants prefer 'base imponible' to the IAS/IFRS term 'base fiscal'.
▲ *a negative taxable income* una base imponible negativa ▲ *computed tax on the taxable income for the year* impuesto calculado sobre la base imponible del año ▲ *taxable income after deductions* base imponible después de deducciones

taxable profit UK
Taxable profit is the profit for a period, determined according to tax rules rather than accounting rules, upon which tax is payable.
resultado fiscal
= resultado impositivo
▲ *computed tax on the taxable profit for the year* impuesto calculado sobre el resultado fiscal del año ▲ *the tax rate applicable to taxable profit* el tipo impositivo aplicable al resultado fiscal
⇛ accounting profit, tax loss

taxable temporary difference IAS/IFRS
≠ deductible temporary difference IAS/IFRS
Taxable temporary differences are temporary differences giving rise to amounts that are taxable in future periods when the carrying amount of an asset or a liability is recovered or settled. Therefore, taxable temporary differences usually result in deferred tax.
diferencia temporaria imponible
▲ *deferred tax liability for a taxable temporary difference* pasivo fiscal diferido por diferencia temporaria imponible ▲ *reversal of existing taxable temporary differences* reversión de las diferencias temporarias imponibles existentes ▲ *sufficient taxable temporary differences* diferencias temporarias imponibles suficientes ▲ *the amount of the taxable temporary difference relating to the goodwill* la cuantía de la diferencia temporaria imponible relacionada con el fondo de comercio
SOURCE IAS 12
⇛ deferred tax

taxation
Taxation constitutes the act or system of charging taxes.
tributación
▲ *deferred for taxation* diferido para tributación ▲ *for legal, taxation or other reasons* por razones legales, fiscales u otras razones ▲ *taxation of foundations and certain associations* la tributación de las fundaciones y de ciertas asociaciones ▲ *taxation of members of investment associations* la tributación de los miembros de las sociedades de inversión ▲ *taxation on fixed assets disposed of* tributación sobre activos fijos eliminados de ▲ *total taxation* total tributación

taxation at source
Taxation at source is the withholding of tax at source, where the payer of typically wages or dividends deducts the tax payable to the relevant tax authorities before payment of the remaining net amount to the recipient.
tributación en origen
▲ *be subject to taxation at source* estar sujeto a tributación en origen ▲ *introduce taxation at source* introducir la tributación en origen
⇛ withholding tax

taxation authority
→ tax authority

taxation of profit from sale of real property
Taxation of profit from sale of real property is the compulsory governmental levy on profits

obtained by a seller on disposal of real property.

impuesto por beneficios en la venta de un bien raíz

= impuesto sobre beneficios en la venta de un bien raíz, impuesto por ganancias en la venta de un bien raíz

▲ *the Danish Act on taxation of profit from sale of real property* la Ley danesa sobre el impuesto por beneficios en la venta de un bien raíz

taxation relief

→ tax relief

taxation rule

Taxation rules are provisions in tax legislation determining tax payable in the form of income tax, corporation tax, VAT or other types of tax. Taxation rules may be national and international - or, in the US, state or federal - rules set by local or central governments.

norma fiscal

▲ *alternative taxation rules* normas fiscales alternativas ▲ *introduce new taxation rules* introducir nuevas normas fiscales

technical provision

= insurance provision

Technical provisions, or insurance provisions, are amounts allocated by an insurance company for the settlement of the company's liabilities in connection with its issued insurance policies.

provisión técnica

▲ *assets covering technical provisions* activos que cubren provisiones técnicas ▲ *cover one's part of the cedant's technical provisions* cubrir su parte de las provisiones técnicas del cedente ▲ *investments of gross technical provisions* inversiones de provisiones técnicas brutas ▲ *non-life technical provisions for claims outstanding* provisiones técnicas de no vida para reclamaciones pendientes ▲ *other technical provisions* otras provisiones técnicas ▲ *reinsurers' share of technical provisions* proporción de provisiones técnicas de los reaseguradores ▲ *technical provisions for life-assurance policies where the investment risk is borne by the policyholders* provisiones técnicas para las pólizas de seguro de vida en las que el riesgo de inversión recae sobre los tenedores de las pólizas ▲ *technical provisions net of reinsurance* provisiones técnicas de reaseguro netas ▲ *the amount of the technical provisions* la cuantía de las provisiones técnicas ▲ *the establishment of adequate technical provisions* el establecimiento de provisiones técnicas adecuadas ▲ *the technical provisions resulting from reinsurance acceptances* las provisiones técnicas procedentes del reaseguro

temporal method

The temporal method is a method used for foreign currency translation when consolidating financial statements of foreign subsidiaries in those of the parent. By this method all amounts are translated at the exchange rates existing at the time of the original transaction underlying them.

método temporal

▲ *use the temporal method* utilizar el método temporal

⇛ closing rate method, current rate method

temporary difference IAS/IFRS, US

Temporary differences include taxable temporary differences or deductible temporary differences and arise as differences between the carrying amounts of assets and liabilities in an enterprise's balance sheet and their tax bases.

diferencia temporaria

≠ diferencia permanente

▲ *accounting for temporary differences* contabilizando las diferencias temporarias ▲ *deductible temporary difference* diferencia temporaria deducible ▲ *determine temporary differences* determinar las diferencias temporarias ▲ *disclose the aggregate amount of the temporary differences* publicar la cantidad agregada de las diferencias temporarias ▲ *future reversal of temporary differences* reversión futura de diferencias temporarias ▲ *give rise to temporary differences* dar lugar al surgimiento de diferencias temporarias ▲ *reversal of the temporary difference* retrocesión de la diferencia temporaria ▲ *reverse temporary differences* revertir las diferencias temporarias ▲ *taxable temporary difference* diferencia temporaria gravable

▲ *underlying temporary differences* diferencias temporarias subyacentes
SOURCE IAS 12, paragraph 5
⇛ deferred tax, permanent difference, timing difference

tender issue

A tender issue is an issue of a portfolio of shares that is offered for sale to the public through a tender offer. Under this method, potential buyers will tender a price, and the shares are sold and allocated to the highest bidders.

oferta pública de acciones

▲ *advantages and disadvantages of a tender issue* ventajas y desventajas de una oferta pública de acciones ▲ *the planned tender issue* la oferta pública de acciones planificada

tender offer

= tender issue

A tender offer an issue of a portfolio of shares that is offered for sale to the public through a tender issue. Under this method, potential buyers will tender a price, and the shares are sold and allocated to the highest bidders.

oferta pública de acciones

▲ *advantages and disadvantages of a tender offer* ventajas y desventajas de una oferta pública de acciones ▲ *the planned tender offer* la oferta pública de acciones prevista

term

1 = life, maturity, period

A term is a period for which something is valid or effective.

plazo

= periodo, término

▲ *12-month term* plazo de 12 meses ▲ *actual term* plazo actual ▲ *expected term* plazo esperado ▲ *in the long term* en el largo plazo ▲ *in the medium term* en el medio plazo ▲ *in the short term* en el corto plazo ▲ *long term* largo plazo ▲ *short term* corto plazo ▲ *term of office* periodo de mandato ▲ *the term of the contract* el término del contrato ▲ *the term of the insurance contract* el término del contrato de seguro ▲ *the term of the loan* el término del préstamo

⇛ term to maturity

2 A term is a stipulation or condition which has been agreed on by the parties to a contract or other legally enforcable document.

término

= cláusula

▲ *a contractual term* una cláusula contractual ▲ *advantageous terms* términos ventajosos ▲ *on the basis of the stated terms of the option feature* en base a los términos manifestados en la opción ▲ *terms that are usual and customary for sales of such assets* cláusulas que son usuales y normales en las ventas de tales activos ▲ *the original or modified terms of the debt instrument* los términos originales o modificados del instrumento de deuda ▲ *uncertainties that arise from the terms of a disposal transaction* incertidumbres que proceden de los términos de una enajenación

⇛ condition

term loan

A term loan is a loan with a fixed life, typically 1-10 years, repayable in regular instalments with interest at a fixed or variable interest rate.

préstamo a plazo

= préstamo a término

▲ *a senior secured term loan* un préstamo a término asegurado senior ▲ *an unsecured term loan* un préstamo a término no asegurado

term of contract

→ contract term

term of the lease

1 The terms of the lease consitute the conditions or stipulations contained in the contract creating a lease.

término del arrendamiento

= condición del arrendamiento, término de arrendamiento

▲ *according to the terms of the lease* de acuerdo con los términos del arrendamiento ▲ *comply with the terms of the lease* cumplir con los términos del arrendamiento ▲ *modify the terms of the lease* modificar los términos del arrendamiento

2 → lease term

term of the loan

The term of the loan is the period for which the loan has been granted and within which the borrower must repay the loan amount.

vigencia del préstamo

▲ *during the term of the loan* durante la vigencia del préstamo

term to maturity
= life, maturity, maturity period, term
The term to maturity is the period of time from the creation of a debt until the date on which the principal amount of the debt falls due for payment.
plazo hasta el vencimiento
= plazo hasta vencimiento, periodo hasta vencimiento
▲ *extend the term to maturity of the debt instrument* aumentar el plazo hasta el vencimiento del instrumento de deuda ▲ *the remaining term to maturity of the debt instrument* el plazo restante hasta el vencimiento del instrumento de deuda ▲ *the term to maturity of the amount to be lent* el plazo hasta el vencimiento de la cantidad a prestar

terminal period
The terminal period is the period exceeding the budget period of an enterprise. It is applied for valuation of an enterprise.
periodo de prórroga
▲ *assets left at end of terminal period* activos abandonados al final del periodo de prórroga ▲ *during the terminal period* durante el periodo de prórroga

terminal value
= horizon value
The terminal value is the total expected value of an investment, e.g. an enterprise, at some point of time in the future, i.e. the present or discounted value of all subsequent cash flows.
valor final
= valor terminal
▲ *calculation of terminal value* cálculo del valor final ▲ *expected terminal value* valor final esperado

terminate
To terminate means to bring an end to something.
terminar
= finalizar
▲ *terminate relations with a trading partner* terminar las relaciones con un socio comercial

termination
1 Termination means withdrawal of an employee from employment, voluntarily or involuntarily, for reasons other than age or illness.
despido
▲ *a lump-sum benefit payable on termination* una indemnización a pagar de una sola vez al despido ▲ *on termination of service* despido por fin de actividad
⇛ retirement
2 Termination is the bringing to an end of something such as an agreement or a contract.
finalización
▲ *expiration or termination of a hedging instrument* expiración o finalización de un instrumento de cobertura ▲ *obligations incurred upon early termination* obligaciones incurridas por finalización anticipada ▲ *termination costs* costes de finalización ▲ *termination of a contract* finalización de un contrato ▲ *the part of the interest payments that the entity would give up upon termination of the contract* la parte de los pagos por intereses que la entidad dejaría de percibir a la finalización del contrato
3 Termination means that something comes to an end or expires, e.g. a contract.
finalización
▲ *termination of contract* finalización del contrato

termination benefit IAS/IFRS
= severance payment
Termination benefit refers to a monetary benefit payable to an employee upon involuntary termination before normal retirement or upon the employee's acceptance of voluntary termination in return for such benefit.
indemnización por despido
= beneficio por terminación, indemnización por cese
NOTE The IAS/IFS term 'beneficio por terminación' may lead to confusion considering that this term does not indicate 'involuntary termination'.
▲ *measurement of termination benefits* valoración de las indemnizaciones por despido ▲ *pay termination benefits* pagar las indemnizaciones por el despido ▲ *provide termination benefits* ofrecer indemnizaciones por despido ▲ *provisions for termination benefits* provisiones para indemnizaciones por despido ▲ *recognise termination benefits* reconocer las indemnizaciones por despido ▲ *termination benefits falling due more than 1 year after the balance sheet date* indemnizaciones por

despido que vencen en el largo plazo ▲ *termination benefits for key management personnel* indemnizaciones por despido para el personal de alta dirección
⇛ dismissal payment

termination of employment
Termination of employment is the removal of an employee from his job with the result that he is no longer employed by the employer.
cese
▲ *upon termination of employment* al cese

The Norwegian Institute of Public Accountants
= DnR
The Norwegian Institute of Public Accountants (DnR) is the professional body for registered public accountants (registrerte revisorer) and state authorised public accountants (statsautoriserte revisorer) in Norway.
Norwegian Institute of Public Accountants
= Instituto Noruego de Auditores Públicos
▲ *membership of The Norwegian Institute of Public Accountants* miembro de la Norwegian Institute of Public Accountants ▲ *the objectives of The Norwegian Institute of Public Accountants* los objetivos de la Norwegian Institute of Public Accountants

the undersigned
The term 'the undersigned' is used to refer to the person who has signed a document.
el abajo firmante
▲ *I, the undersigned, declare that* Yo, el abajo firmante, declaro que

theoretical
When something is theoretical it is based on theory and ideas rather than practice and experience.
teórico
▲ *a theoretical background* un fondo teórico ▲ *a theoretical market value* un valor de mercado teórico ▲ *a theoretical problem* un problema teórico ▲ *a theoretical rate* un tipo teórico ▲ *a theoretical value* un valor teórico ▲ *from a theoretical point of view* desde un punto de vista teórico ▲ *theoretical dilution from warrants* dilución teórica de los warrants ▲ *theoretical ex-rights value per share* valor teórico sin derechos por acción

theory of constraints
= TOC
The theory of constraints (TOC) is a management philosophy which focuses on optimizing the throughput of a concrete production process (constraint or bottleneck) to achieve a higher performance, maximize profits and minimize operating expenses. In management accounting, TOC aims at optimizing the contribution margin per unit of constraining fact, e.g. per machine hour.
teoría de restricciones
= teoría de las restrucciones
▲ *the philosophy behind the theory of constraints* la filosofía que subyace a la teoría de restricciones ▲ *utilise theory of constraints* utilizar la teoría de las restricciones
⇛ throughput accounting, throughput contribution

thin capitalisation IAS/IFRS, UK
Thin capitalisation exists if the loan capital of a company relative to its equity exceeds the ratio of 4:1. In the case of multinational group companies with an excessive controlled debt, i.e. intra-group loans, interest expenses/capital loss on the exceeding amount cannot be deducted for tax purposes. The reason is that returns paid by the company to shareholders on their investments in equity are not deductible, whereas interest payments on debt usually are.
subcapitalización
= capitalización delgada
NOTE Spanish accountants prefer the Spanish term 'subcapitalización' to the IAS/IFRS term 'capitalización delgada'. This literal translation is nonsensical in Spanish.
▲ *legislation governing thin capitalisation* legislación que regula la subcapitalización ▲ *the rules governing thin capitalisation* las normas que regulan la subcapitalización ▲ *thin capitalisation rules* normas de subcapitalización
⇛ double taxation convention

thin capitalization US
= thin capitalisation UK, IAS/IFRS

Thin capitalization exists if the loan capital of a company relative to its equity exceeds the ratio of 4:1. In the case of multinational group companies with an excessive controlled debt, i.e. intra-group loans, interest expenses/capital loss on the exceeding amount cannot be deducted for tax purposes. The reason is that returns paid by the company to shareholders on their investments in equity are not deductible, whereas interest payments on debt usually are.

subcapitalización

= capitalización delgada

NOTE Spanish accountants prefer the Spanish term 'subcapitalización' to the IAS/IFRS term 'capitalización delgada'. This literal translation is nonsensical in Spanish.

▲ *legislation governing thin capitalization* legislación que regula la subcapitalización ▲ *the rules governing thin capitalization* las normas que regulan la subcapitalización ▲ *thin capitalization rules* normas de subcapitalización

third party

A third party is any natural or artificial person who is not directly involved in a particular arrangement such as a contract or an enterprise.

tercera parte

= tercera persona

▲ *a contractual arrangement with a third party* un acuerdo contractual con una tercera parte ▲ *a third party unrelated to the lessor* una tercera parte no relacionada con el arrendador ▲ *an amount due from a third party* una cantidad vencida procedente de una tercera parte ▲ *an issued guarantee of the obligations of a third party* una garantía emitida de las obligaciones de una tercera parte ▲ *compensation from third parties for items of property, plant and equipment* compensación procedente de terceras partes por las partidas de edificios, instalaciones y equipos ▲ *pass on cash flows to unrelated third party investors* trasladar flujos de efectivo a inversores no relacionados con una tercera parte ▲ *third party operator* tercer operador

third-party interest

→ minority interest

thousand

Thousand is a figure, stated in numbers as 1,000.

NOTE Used as a header to a column of figures stated in thousands, the abbreviation '000 is used.

mil

▲ *all amounts in USD thousands* todas las cantidades en miles de dólares norteamericanos ▲ *full thousands* miles totales ▲ *in thousands of euro* en miles de euros ▲ *present information in thousands or millions of units of the presentation currency* presentar información en miles o millones de unidades de la moneda de presentación

throughput accounting

Throughput accounting is a super-variable costing method which limits the possibilities of deferring to future accounting periods the costs in connection with the stockbuilding of work in progress and finished goods. Instead, a throughput contribution is established, calculated as revenue (sales) less direct material costs for units sold. Only direct material costs are treated as variable costs, and all other costs are considered period costs.

contabilidad del rendimiento

= contabilidad de rendimiento

▲ *measure by throughput accounting* medir mediante la contabilidad del rendimiento ▲ *use throughput accounting* utilizar la contabilidad de rendimiento

⇛ theory of constraints, throughput contribution, throughput costing

throughput contribution

The throughput contribution is calculated as sales revenue less direct material costs for units sold.

margen de producción

▲ *increase throughput contribution* incrementar el margen de producción ▲ *maximise throughput contribution* maximizar el margen de producción ▲ *the expected value of the throughput contribution* el valor previsto del margen de producción

⇛ theory of constraints, throughput accounting, throughput costing

throughput costing

= super-variable costing

Throughput costing is an inventory costing method under which inventory costs only include direct material costs whereas all other product costs are considered operating expenses (period costs). This is based on the assumption that basically only direct material costs are variable costs, where e.g. direct labour costs are considered fixed costs.

método de rendimiento de costes

= método de coste supervariable, método de evaluación de costes basado en el rendimiento, throughput costing

▲ *the rationale behind throughput costing* las razones detrás del método de rendimiento de costes ▲ *use throughput costing* utilizar el método de rendimiento de costes

⇛ direct material cost, inventory cost, period cost

throughput time

= cycle time

For manufactured goods, throughput time is the time span in a production process from purchase of raw materials over production to finished product, or, for finished goods or services, the time span from an order is placed to delivery.

tiempo de fabricación

▲ *accounting for throughput time* contabilizar el tiempo de fabricación ▲ *improve throughput time* mejorar el tiempo de fabricación ▲ *reduce throughput time* reducir el tiempo de fabricación

tie up

To tie up e.g. capital and resources is to apply them for a particular investment or project which will make them unavailable for any alternative purposes.

inmovilizar

▲ *tie up funds* inmovilizar fondos

tied-up

When assets or funds are tied-up it means that they are not available for immediate use, but determined for a particular purpose. Funds may e.g. be tied-up in inventories.

inmovilizado

▲ *tied-up funds* fondos inmovilizados

tier I capital

= core capital

Tier 1 capital is the core capital of a bank corresponding to the equity of other enterprises, i.e. share capital, premium on share issues and reserves.

tier 1 capital

= capital básico, core capital

▲ *disclose each component of tier 1 capital* publicar cada componente del capital básico ▲ *instruments eligible for inclusion in tier 1 capital* instrumentos elegibles para su inclusión en el tier 1 capital ▲ *limited to a maximum of 15% of tier 1 capital* limitado a un máximo del 15% del tier 1 capital ▲ *the consolidated bank's tier 1 capital* el tier 1 capital del banco consolidado

⇛ tier 1 capital ratio

tier I capital ratio

= core capital ratio

Tier 1 capital ratio is defined as tier 1 capital divided by total risk-weighted on and off balance sheet items.

ratio de tier 1 capital

= ratio de capital básico, ratio de core capital

▲ *a 4% minimum tier 1 capital ratio* un 4% mínimo del ratio de tier 1 capital

⇛ tier 1 capital

time

= point of time

Time refers to a particular point of time or moment as e.g. shown precisely on a clock by a certain hour, minute and/or second, or to a particular period or span measured in seconds, minutes, hours, days, weeks, months or years.

tiempo

= momento

▲ *at a later time* en un tiempo posterior ▲ *at any time* en cualquier momento ▲ *at the time of initially accounting for the business combination* en el momento de contabilización inicial de la combinación de negocios ▲ *in time* en tiempo ▲ *the comparability of financial statements over time* la comparabilidad de los estados financieros a lo largo del tiempo ▲ *the disposal of assets after a specified time* la enajenación de activos después de un tiempo específicado

time basis

When work is performed or services rendered on a time basis, the amount of time spent is used as a basis for calculating the remuneration, typically by multiplying the time spent in amount of hours by the hourly rate. This system applies e.g. to work that is difficult to measure or where the quality of the work performed takes priority over the quantity.

base temporal

▲ *on a time basis* en una base temporal

time card

= clock card UK

≠ job card UK, labor time ticket US

A time card records the exact time that an employee arrives at and leaves the job by means of a mechanical time clock.

tarjeta de tiempo

▲ *the information that is on the time card* la información contenida en la tarjeta de tiempo ▲ *the top part of a time card* en la parte superior de la tarjeta de tiempo

time frame

A time frame is a specified period of time within which an event will occur or is anticipated to occur.

marco temporal

▲ *a 5-year time frame* un marco temporal de cinco años ▲ *delivery of the asset within the time frame established by convention in the marketplace concerned* publicación del activo dentro del marco temporal establecido por convención en el mercado concerniente ▲ *estimated time frame* marco temporal estimado

time limit

A time limit is a specific period of time within which a specified act must or must not be done.

límite temporal

▲ *a contractual time limit* un límite temporal contractual ▲ *fix a time limit* fijar un límite temporal ▲ *within the time limit indicated* dentro del límite temporal indicado

time of announcement US

The time of announcement is the date when a statement or decision is issued and made known to the authorities or the public, e.g. the date of a stock exchange announcement.

fecha de anuncio

= fecha del anuncio

▲ *at the time of announcement* en la fecha de anuncio

⇛ time of declaration

time of bookkeeping

The time of bookkeeping is the date when revenue, cost, asset or liability items are recognised in the bookkeeping records of an enterprise.

momento de la anotación

= fecha de anotación fecha de la anotación, fecha del registro

▲ *at the time of bookkeeping* en el momento de la anotación

time of construction IAS/IFRS

The time of construction is the time when a product is manufactured or a fixed asset produced or built.

periodo de construcción

= periodo de fabricación

▲ *recognise at the time of construction* reconocer al periodo de fabricación

time of declaration UK

The time of declaration is the date when dividends recommended for distribution by the board of directors are adopted and declared by the annual general meeting.

fecha de anuncio

= fecha del anuncio

▲ *at the time of declaration* en la fecha de anuncio

⇛ time of announcement

time of granting

= grant date

The time of granting is the date when an option, e.g. an employee share option, or another share-based payment arrangement is granted, agreed between an enterprise and an employee or approved, and when the rights under that option or arrangement to cash, assets or equity instruments are conferred to the employee subject to any particular vesting conditions.

fecha de concesión

= fecha de la concesión

▲ *a favourable element at the time of granting* un elemento favorable a la fecha de concesión ▲ *difference at the time of granting* diferencia a la fecha de concesión ▲ *market value at the time of granting of the op-*

tions granted during the year valor de mercado a la fecha de la concesión de las opciones concedidas durante el año ▲ *the quoted price of the share at the time of granting* el valor cotizado de la acción a la fecha de concesión ▲ *the value of an option at the time of granting* el valor de una opción a la fecha de concesión

⇛ share option, share-based payment, vesting condition

time of merger

The time of merger is the effective date of the merger for accounting purposes.

fecha de fusión

= fecha de la fusión

▲ *at the time of merger* a la fecha de la fusión

time of production

The time of production is the time at which a product or asset is produced or manufactured.

periodo de fabricación

▲ *recognise at the time of production* reconocer al periodo de fabricación

time of receipt

The time at which something is received is referred to as the 'time of receipt', and this can be a particular day, hour etc.

fecha de recepción

▲ *fair value at the time of receipt* valor razonable a la fecha de recepción

time of sale

The time of sale is the time at which the sale becomes binding on both the seller and the buyer.

fecha de venta

▲ *carrying amount at the time of sale* valor contable a la fecha de venta ▲ *estimated expenses up to the time of sale* gastos estimados hasta la fecha de venta ▲ *recognition at the time of sale* reconocimiento a la fecha de venta

time of the merger UK

The date on which a merger has been decided on or becomes effective is referred to as the time of the merger.

fecha de la fusión

= fecha de la unión de intereses

▲ *at the time of the merger* a la fecha de la fusión ▲ *determination of the time of the merger* determinación de la fecha de la unión de intereses

time of the pooling of interests US, IAS/IFRS

= time of the uniting of interests IAS/IFRS

The time of the pooling of interests is the time when two entities are combined in one entity.

fecha de la unión de intereses

= fecha de la fusión

▲ *at the time of the pooling of interests* a la fecha de la unión de intereses ▲ *determination of the time of the pooling of interests* determinación de la fecha de la unión de intereses

time of the uniting of interests IAS/IFRS

= time of the pooling of interests IAS/IFRS

The time of the uniting of interests is the time when two entities are combined in one entity.

fecha de la unión de intereses

= fecha de la fusión

▲ *at the time of the uniting of interests* a la fecha de la unión de intereses ▲ *determination of the time of the uniting of interests* determinación de la fecha de la unión de intereses

time to maturity

= remaining life, remaining term, residual maturity, time until expiration

The time to maturity is the period left until redemption date or the date when a loan must be repaid.

periodo de vigencia

= tiempo hasta el vencimiento, tiempo hasta vencimiento

▲ *estimated time to maturity* periodo de vigencia estimado ▲ *the actual time to maturity* el periodo de vigencia actual ▲ *the optimum time to maturity* el periodo de vigencia óptimo ▲ *the remaining time to maturity* el periodo de vigencia restante ▲ *the weighted average time to maturity* el periodo de vigencia medio ponderado

⇛ maturity, term to maturity

time value

In the context of options, the time value is one of the variables in connection with the valuation of options, representing one of two components of the option premium, the other being the intrinsic value. The time value expresses a higher market value of an option compared to its intrinsic value as a result of any time remaining to expiry during which value may be added to the option resulting from a potential rise in the price of the underlying share. Therefore, the option holder may benefit from exercising the option before expiry at a higher premium, as there is also the risk that the option's value will decrease over time.

valor temporal

▲ *a change in the time value* un cambio en el valor temporal ▲ *adjust for the time value of money* ajustar al valor temporal del dinero ▲ *measurements that reflect time value of embedded options* valoraciones que reflejan el valor temporal de las opciones implícitas ▲ *separate the intrinsic value and time value of an option contract* separar el valor intrínseco y el valor temporal de un contrato de opciones ▲ *the time value of an option* el valor temporal de una opción ▲ *the time value of the call option* el valor temporal de la opción de venta

⇛ intrinsic value, time value of money

time value of money

= SWAP

The time value of money takes into consideration aspects of inflation as well as interest earned over time. The value is seen as the discounted present value calculated on the basis of future cash flows, typically exclusive of cash flows from financing activities.

valor del dinero en el tiempo

▲ *a material effect of the time value of money* un efecto material del valor del dinero en el tiempo ▲ *adjust for the time value of money* ajustar al valor del dinero en el tiempo ▲ *current market assessments of the time value of money* valoraciones de mercado actuales del valor del dinero en el tiempo ▲ *due to the time value of money* debido al valor del dinero en el tiempo

SOURCE IAS 36

time-series comparison

A time-series comparison is a comparison of two columns of figures showing their development relative to each other, e.g. an enterprise's return on invested capital over a number of years compared with its revenue development.

comparación de series temporales

▲ *methods used for time-series comparison* métodos usados para la comparación de series temporales

times interest earned ratio US

= interest cover ratio UK

The times interest earned ratio is a financial ratio defined as earnings before interest and tax plus interest income divided by interest expenses, and it measures an enterprise's financial strength and resilience to interest increases, which is particularly interesting for highly-geared companies.

ratio de cobertura del interés

= índice de cobertura de intereses

▲ *calculate the times interest earned ratio* calcular el ratio de cobertura del interés ▲ *determine the times interest earned ratio* determinar el ratio de cobertura del interés ▲ *have a times interest earned ratio of 3.9* tener un ratio de cobertura del interés de 3,9

timing difference UK, IAS/IFRS

Timing differences are differences between an accounting profit and a taxable profit that arise in one accounting period and are reversed in the following period(s).

diferencia temporal

= diferencia temporaria

▲ *temporary differences that are not timing differences* diferencias temporarias que no son diferencias temporales

SOURCE IAS 12, paragraph 1

⇛ deferred tax, permanent difference, temporary difference

title

Title is a person's right of ownership of property.

título de propiedad

= título de la propiedad

▲ *acquire title* adquirir el título de la propiedad ▲ *acquire title to the asset* adquirir el título de propiedad sobre el activo ▲ *acquire title to the asset upon the fulfilment of agreed conditions* adquirir el título de propiedad sobre el activo en el momento de cumplimiento de las condiciones acordadas ▲ *acquisition of title* adquisición del título de la propiedad ▲ *have legal title to assets* tener el título de propiedad legal sobre activos ▲ *have legal title to something* tener el título de propiedad legal de algo ▲ *legal title* título de propiedad legal ▲ *reserve title* reservar el título de propiedad ▲ *restrictions on title* restricciones en el título de propiedad ▲ *retain the legal title to the goods* retener el título de propiedad legal sobre los bienes ▲ *the carrying amounts of intangible assets whose title is restricted* los valores contables de los activos intangibles cuyo título de propiedad está restringido ▲ *the existence and amounts of restrictions on title* la existencia y cuantías de las restricciones en el título de propiedad ▲ *the existence of intangible assets whose title is restricted* la existencia de activos intangibles cuyo título de propiedad está restringido ▲ *transfer title* transferir el título de propiedad ▲ *when legal title passes to the buyer* cuando el título de propiedad pasa al comprador

title insurance

Title insurance refers to insurance that protects lenders and property owners against losses resulting from any unknown errors or legal defects in the title of the bought property.

póliza de seguro

= póliza de seguros

▲ *effect title insurance* póliza de seguro efectiva

TOC

= theory of constraints

TOC is the abbreviation of theory of constraints, a management philosophy which focuses on optimizing the throughput of a concrete production process (constraint or bottleneck) to achieve a higher performance, maximize profits and minimize operating expenses. In management accounting, TOC aims at optimizing the contribution margin per unit of constraining fact, e.g. per machine hour.

teoría de restricciones

= teoría de las restricciones

▲ *the philosophy behind TOC* la filosofía que subyace a la teoría de las restricciones ▲ *utilise TOC* utilizar la teoría de las restricciones

tool

Tools are equipment or instruments applied by enterprises to implement a process, accomplish a goal or solve a task.

herramienta

▲ *a strategic tool* una herramienta estratégica ▲ *a suitable tool* una herramienta adecuada ▲ *a tool of the future* una herramienta del futuro ▲ *a valuable tool* una herramienta valiosa ▲ *an effective measurement tool* una herramienta de valoración efectiva ▲ *computer software for a computer-controlled machine tool* software para una máquina herramienta controlada por ordenador

tools and equipment UK

Tools and equipment is a category of tangible assets comprising immovables and movables, such as office furniture and computers. As an item in the balance sheet, tools and equipment appears under tangible fixed assets.

utillaje y equipo

= herramientas y equipos, utillaje y equipos

▲ *lease of tools and equipment* alquiler de utillaje y equipo ▲ *machinery, tools and equipment* maquinaria, utillaje y equipo ▲ *provide for depreciation on tools and equipment* provisión por depreciación de utillaje y equipo ▲ *purchase of tools and equipment* compra de utillaje y equipo

top line

= revenue IAS/IFRS, sales US, sales revenue, turnover UK

≠ bottom line

The top line refers to the top line item of the income statement, i.e. revenue or sales.

línea superior

≠ línea inferior

▲ *the company performed well both at the top and bottom lines* la empresa operó bien tanto en las líneas superiores como inferiores ▲ *to grow the top and bottom lines* crecer las líneas superiores e inferiores

total[1] *noun*

A total is an aggregate sum or amount, typically appearing as the bottom line of an account or financial statement.

total

▲ *disclose key management personnel compensation in total* publicar el total de la remuneración del personal de alta dirección ▲ *the total of assets classified as held for sale* el total de activos clasificados como mantenidos para la venta ▲ *the total of future minimum lease payments* el total de los pagos mínimos futuros por arrendamiento financiero ▲ *the total of the post-tax profit or loss* el total del resultado después de impuestos

⇛ subtotal

total[2]

= sum

Total means aggregate.

total

= suma

▲ *the entity's total carrying amount of goodwill* el valor contable del fondo de comercio total de la entidad ▲ *the total amount* la cantidad total ▲ *the total impairment loss relating to goodwill* la suma de pérdidas por deterioro relacionadas con el fondo de comercio ▲ *the total profit or loss allocated to each class of equity instrument* el resultado total asignado a cada clase de instrumento de patrimonio ▲ *total business receipts* total recibos comerciales ▲ *total growth* total crecimiento ▲ *total interest margin* total margen de interés ▲ *total market value* total valor de mercado ▲ *total receipts* total recibos ▲ *total revaluation of cost* total revalorización de coste ▲ *total revenue curve* total curva de ingresos

⇛ in total

total[3] *verb*

In US English, it is also correct not to double the final consonant in "total" when the past-tense, past- and present-participle endings are added.

To total is to add up to an aggregate amount.

totalizar

▲ *the costs total EUR 10,000* los costes totalizan 10.000 euros

total assets

The sum of all the assets that are recorded in the assets side of the balance sheet is referred to as total assets.

total activos

= activos totales

▲ *the total assets of the enterprise* los activos totales de la empresa ▲ *total assets of the segment* total activos del segmento

total contribution UK, US

= contribution UK, US, contribution margin US, UK

Total contribution is calculated by multiplying the total number of units sold by the unit contribution margin.

contribución total

▲ *a 10% increase in total contribution* un aumento del 10% en la contribución total

⇛ contribution, contribution margin, unit contribution margin

total debtor balances

The total debtor balances in an enterprise is the total sum of amounts owed to the enterprise by customers, suppliers or other parties.

total saldos deudores

= saldos deudores totales

▲ *1% of the total debtor balances at the balance sheet date* 1% de los saldos deudores totales a la fecha del balance ▲ *an increase in total debtor balances* un aumento en total saldos deudores

total dividend

Total dividend refers either to the aggregate part of the profit of an enterprise distributed to its shareholders or to the aggregate dividend on each share constituted by interim plus final dividend.

dividendo total

= total dividendo

▲ *the total dividend* el dividendo total

total revenue

Total revenue refers to the aggregate revenue for one or more specific periods or to the aggregate revenue of an enterprise consisting of several units.

ingreso total

= total ingreso

▲ *a share of total revenue* una parte del ingreso total ▲ *realise total revenue of EUR 10m* realizar el ingreso total de 10 millones de euros

trace

To trace means to follow items or account postings through

the various accounting records to determine whether proper accounting policies have been observed.

trazar

= perfilar

▲ *trace the costs* trazar los costes

trade account payable

= trade creditor UK, trade payable IAS/IFRS

≠ trade account receivable US, trade debtor UK, trade receivable IAS/IFRS

A trade account payable is an amount owed by an enterprise to a supplier. Trade accounts payable are recognised under current liabilities in the balance sheet.

cuentas comerciales a pagar

= acreedores comerciales

▲ *derecognise a trade account payable* cancelar las cuentas comerciales a pagar

⇛ trade accounts payable

trade accounts payable US

= trade creditors UK, trade payables IAS/IFRS

≠ trade accounts receivable US, trade debtors UK, trade receivables IAS/IFRS

"Trade accounts payable" is an item under current liabilities in the balance sheet comprising amounts owed by an enterprise to suppliers.

cuentas comerciales a pagar

= acreedores comerciales

▲ *changes in trade accounts payable* cambios en cuentas comerciales a pagar ▲ *cost-related trade accounts payable* costes asociados a acreedores comerciales

⇛ trade account payable

trade accounts receivable US

= trade debtors UK, trade receivables IAS/IFRS

≠ trade accounts payable US, trade creditors UK, trade payables IAS/IFRS

"Trade accounts receivable" is an item under current assets in the balance sheet including amounts due from customers of and suppliers to an enterprise.

cuentas comerciales a cobrar

= deudores comerciales

▲ *current trade accounts receivable* cuentas comerciales a cobrar corrientes

trade and other payables IAS/IFRS

"Trade and other payables" is an item under current liabilities in the balance sheet recognising amounts owed by an enterprise to suppliers and other miscellaneous amounts outstanding.

proveedores y otros acreedores

▲ *a decrease in trade and other payables* un descenso en proveedores y otros acreedores ▲ *an increase in trade and other payables* un aumento en proveedores y otros acreedores ▲ *included in trade and other payables* incluido en proveedores y otros acreedores ▲ *total trade and other payables* total proveedores y otros acreedores ▲ *translation of trade and other payables* conversión de proveedores y otros acreedores

⇛ other accounts payable, trade creditors, trade payables

trade conditions

Trade conditions refer to the practice, custom and usage applying to a particular industry or line of business such as the competitive situation, customer types, price sensitivity, marketing strategies etc.

prácticas comerciales

▲ *a change in trade conditions* un cambio en las prácticas comerciales ▲ *existing trade conditions* prácticas comerciales existentes

trade creditor UK

= trade account payable US, trade payable IAS/IFRS

≠ trade account receivable US, trade debtor UK, trade receivable IAS/IFRS

A trade creditor is an amount owed by an enterprise to a supplier. Trade creditors are recognised under current liabilities in the balance sheet.

acreedor comercial

= cuenta comercial a pagar

▲ *a number of new trade creditors* un número de acreedores comerciales nuevos ▲ *an increase in trade creditors* un aumento en acreedores comerciales ▲ *changes in trade creditors* cambios en acreedores comerciales

⇛ trade creditors

trade creditors UK

= accounts payable IAS/IFRS, trade accounts payable US, trade payables IAS/IFRS

≠ trade accounts receivable US, trade debtors UK, trade receivables IAS/IFRS
"Trade creditors" is an item under current liabilities in the balance sheet comprising amounts owed by an enterprise to suppliers.
acreedores comerciales
= cuentas comerciales a pagar
▲ *a decrease in trade creditors* un descenso en acreedores comerciales ▲ *an increase in trade creditors* un aumento en acreedores comerciales ▲ *changes in trade debtors* cambios en acreedores comerciales ▲ *cost-related trade debtors* coste relacionado con acreedores comerciales
⇛ trade creditor

trade date
The trade date is the day on which an enterprise commits itself to buy or sell a financial asset.
fecha de transacción
= fecha de la negociación
▲ *regular way purchases and sales of financial assets accounted for at trade date* compras y ventas regulares de activos financieros contabilizados a fecha de transacción ▲ *the fair value on the trade date* el valor razonable en la fecha de transacción ▲ *the period between the trade date and the settlement date* el periodo comprendido entre la fecha de transacción y la de liquidación ▲ *trade date recognition* reconocimiento de la fecha de transacción ▲ *use trade date accounting* utilizar la contabilidad de la fecha de transacción

trade debtor UK
= trade account receivable US, trade receivable IAS/IFRS
≠ trade account payable US, trade creditor UK, trade payable IAS/IFRS
A trade debtor is a customer or supplier owing money for goods and services to an enterprise. In the balance sheet, trade debtors are recognised under current assets.
deudor comercial
= cuenta comercial a cobrar
▲ *receive future payments from trade debtors* recibir pagos futuros de los deudores comerciales
▲ *value of trade debtors* valor de los deudores comerciales
⇛ trade debtors

trade debtors UK
= trade accounts receivable US, trade receivables IAS/IFRS
≠ trade accounts payable US, trade creditors UK, trade payables IAS/IFRS
"Trade debtors" is an item under current assets in the balance sheet including amounts due from customers of an enterprise.
deudores comerciales
= clientes, cuentas comerciales a cobrar
▲ *a decrease in trade debtors* un descenso en deudores comerciales ▲ *an increase in trade debtors* un aumento en deudores comerciales ▲ *included in trade debtors* incluido en deudores comerciales
⇛ other debtors, trade debtor

trade discount
A trade discount is a retail price reduction offered by wholesalers or manufacturers to retailers or distributors when they buy large quantities.
descuento comercial
▲ *grant a trade discount* otorgar un descuento comercial ▲ *the amount of any trade discounts allowed by the entity* la cantidad de cualesquiera descuentos comerciales permitidos por la entidad ▲ *the purchase price after deducting trade discounts and rebates* el precio de compra después de deducir descuentos comerciales y desgravaciones fiscales

trade mark
→ trademark

trade payable IAS/IFRS
A trade payable is an amount owed by an enterprise to a supplier. Trade payables are recognised under current liabilities in the balance sheet.
acreedor comercial
= cuenta comercial a pagar, proveedores
▲ *short-term trade payables* acreedores comerciales a corto plazo
⇛ trade payables

trade payables IAS/IFRS
= trade accounts payable US, trade creditors UK
≠ trade accounts receivable US, trade debtors UK, trade receivables IAS/IFRS
"Trade payables" is an item under current liabilities in the

balance sheet comprising amounts owed by an enterprise to suppliers.
acreedores comerciales
= cuentas comerciales a pagar, proveedores
▲ *changes in trade payables* cambios en cuentas comerciales a pagar ▲ *cost-related trade payables* costes asociados a acreedores comerciales
⇛ trade payable

trade receivable IAS/IFRS
= trade account receivable US, trade debtor UK
≠ trade account payable US, trade creditor UK, trade payable IAS/IFRS
A trade receivable is an amount due from a customer or a supplier of an enterprise for goods and services. In the balance sheet, trade receivables are recognised under current assets.
deudores comerciales
= cuentas comerciales a cobrar, clientes
▲ *a current trade receivable* un deudor comercial corriente ▲ *a foreign currency trade receivable* un deudor comercial en moneda extranjera ▲ *a non-current trade receivable* un deudor comercial no corriente ▲ *disclosure in the notes about trade receivables* publicar en las notas sobre deudores comerciales ▲ *funds tied up in trade receivables* fondos inmovilizados en deudores comerciales ▲ *short-term trade receivables* deudores comerciales a corto plazo ▲ *trade receivables in consolidated enterprises* deudores comerciales en empresas consolidadas ▲ *trade receivables in subsidiaries* deudores comerciales en subsidiarias
⇛ trade receivables

trade receivables
= trade accounts receivable US, trade debtors UK
≠ trade accounts payable US, trade creditors UK, trade payables IAS/IFRS
"Trade receivables" refers to an item under current assets in the balance sheet including amounts due from customers of or suppliers to an enterprise.
cuentas comerciales a cobrar
= clientes, deudores comerciales
▲ *a decrease in trade receivables* un descenso en cuentas comerciales a cobrar ▲ *an increase in trade receivables* un aumento en cuentas comerciales a cobrar
⇛ trade receivable

trademark
= brand, TM
A trademark is a name, design, symbol or any other feature given to a product or group of products in order to distinguish them from those of other sellers. Trademarks are legally protected and constitute intangible assets in the financial statements of an enterprise.
marca registrada
▲ *a collective trademark* una marca registrada colectiva ▲ *trademark infringement* violación de la marca registrada ▲ *trademark owner* propietario de la marca registrada
⇛ service mark

trademark right
A trademark right is the exclusive right to use a particular trademark in the marketing of products.
derecho de marca registrada
▲ *acquire a trademark right* adquirir un derecho de marca registrada ▲ *acquired trademark rights* derechos de marca registrada adquiridos

trading
Trading is the activity of buying and selling, i.e. exchange of goods and services, between countries, independent parties or group enterprises.
actividad comercial
▲ *cease trading* cesar la actividad comercial ▲ *gains and losses arising on financial instruments held for trading* pérdidas y ganancias que surgen en los instrumentos financieros mantenidos para la actividad comercial ▲ *intercompany profits and losses from trading with associates* pérdidas y ganancias intragrupo procedentes de la actividad comercial con asociadas ▲ *securities admitted to trading on a regulated market* títulos admitidos a cotización en un mercado regulado ▲ *terminate relations with a trading partner* terminar las relaciones con un socio comercial ▲ *trading with associates* actividad comercial con asociados
⇛ securities trading

trading activity
Trading activity is the trade in bonds, currencies, shares etc. The trading activity is often settled by number of transactions or volume of transactions made.
intermediación financiera
= actividad de intermediación financiera
▲ *compute historical volatility for the longest period for which trading activity is available* calcular la volatilidad histórica para el periodo más largo para el que están disponibles los datos de la intermediación financiera ▲ *currency translation adjustment relating to trading activities* ajustes por conversión de moneda relacionados con intermediaciones financieras ▲ *the nature of the trading activity* la naturaleza de la intermediación financiera ▲ *use a liability to fund trading activities* utilizar un pasivo para financiar la intermediación financiera

trading asset
Trading assets are assets on which the enterprise intends to gain a profit in the short term. Derivative financial instruments that have a positive fair value at the balance sheet date must e.g. be classified as trading assets.
activo de inversión
▲ *the company's trading asset portfolio* la cartera de activos de inversión de la empresa

trading book
→ trading portfolio

trading currency
The trading currency is the currency in which a transaction takes place.
moneda comercial
▲ *use the euro as the trading currency* utilizar el euro como moneda comercial

trading day
= business day
A trading day is a day on which financial markets are open for trading, i.e. Monday to Friday excluding holidays.
día hábil
= día laborable
▲ *a calendar of trading days* un calendario de días hábiles ▲ *first trading day excluding dividend* primer día hábil excluyendo dividendo

trading income
Trading income is interest income, commission income or income generated from the trade in financial assets and liabilities, such as financial instruments in the securities market, by an enterprise, typically a financial institution.
ingreso comercial
▲ *decline in trading income* descenso en ingreso comercial ▲ *fluctuating trading income* ingreso comercial fluctuante ▲ *high trading income* ingreso comercial elevado ▲ *low trading income* ingreso comercial bajo ▲ *stable trading income* ingreso comercial estable

trading investment
≠ long-term investment
Trading investments are financial assets acquired with a view to gaining a profit through short-term fluctuations in the market prices of securities, also referred to as financial assets held-for-trading.
inversión mantenida para negociar
= acivo financiero mantenido para negociar
▲ *change in fair value of trading investments* cambio en el valor razonable de las inversiones mantenidas para negociar ▲ *purchases of trading investments* compras de inversiones mantenidas para negociar
⇛ capital investment

trading liability
Trading liabilities are financial liabilities such as investments in the form of financial instruments classified as held for trading, i.e. with the intention of resale within a short term to gain a profit.
pasivo financiero mantenido para negociar
▲ *derivative financial instruments and other trading liabilities* instrumentos financieros derivados y otros pasivos financieros mantenidos para negociar ▲ *recognise a trading liability* reconocer un pasivo financiero mantenido para negociar ▲ *record at fair value as a trading liability* registra a valor razonable como un pasivo financiero mantenido para negociar ▲ *total trading liabilities*

total pasivos financieros mantenidos para negociar

trading partner

A trading partner is a person, business entity or country with whom or which another business entity or country trades with the purpose of buying or selling or both.

socio comercial

▲ *terminate relations with a trading partner* terminar las relaciones con un socio comercial ▲ *the former trading partner* el socio comercial anterior

trading period

A trading period is a defined period of time consisting of a defined number of successive trading days during which transactions involving buying and selling, typically of securities, can be made. To counteract insider dealing, stock exchange trading rules prohibit trading in shares of listed companies around the release of interim and annual results and stipulate defined trading periods when directors and other parties having inside information are permitted to trade.

periodo comercial

▲ *at the beginning of the trading period* al inicio del periodo comercial ▲ *at the end of the trading period* al final del periodo comercial

trading portfolio

= trading book

A trading portfolio consists of financial assets and financial liabilities. The financial assets in a trading portfolio are positions in securities and other financial instruments that are held for trading, and that are primarily subject to market risk. To be included in the trading portfolio of an enterprise the asset/liability must have the main objective of generating income from short-term changes in prices or margin trades. This category may comprise receivables acquired that have not been generated in the course of ordinary operations of the enterprise.

cartera de valores negociables

▲ *be included in a trading portfolio* estar incluido en una cartera de valores negociables ▲ *manage the trading portfolio* gestionar la cartera de valores negociables

trading property

= property held for sale

Trading properties are properties that have been constructed or acquired with a view to resale within a few years.

inversión mantenida para la venta

▲ *the carrying amount of the trading property* el valor contable de la inversión mantenida para la venta ▲ *the cost of the trading property* el coste de la inversión mantenida para la venta ▲ *transfer of property from trading property to investment property* transferencia de edificios de inversión mantenida para la venta a inversión inmobiliaria ▲ *use property as trading property* usar el edificio como inversión mantenida para la venta

trading security UK

≠ investment security

Trading securities are securities that an enterprise has acquired with a view to generating a profit and therefore holds with the intention of selling them within a short term, usually before one year after the acquisition.

título mantenido para la venta

▲ *cash and cash equivalents at beginning of year including trading securities* efectivo y equivalentes de efectivo al inicio del año incluyendo los títulos mantenidos para la venta

training

Training is the process by which a person learns how to do a job and perform the activities associated with the process.

formación

▲ *costs of staff training* costes de la formación del personal ▲ *expenditure on training activities* gastos en actividades de formación ▲ *expenditure on training staff to operate the asset* gastos de formación del personal para poner en funcionamiento el activo ▲ *incremental staff skills leading to future economic benefits from training* incremento de las aptitudes del personal para el futuro, beneficios económicos de la formación ▲ *the expected future economic benefits arising from training* los beneficios económicos futuros esperados derivados de la formación ▲ *top-up training* formación superior ▲ *training manager* director de formación

training and education

Training and education is the process by which a person learns how to do a job and receives instructions with a view to gaining knowledge and developing skills.

formación y educación

▲ *continuous training and education* formación y educación continua

training and education cost

Training and education costs refer to the costs incurred by an enterprise when educating its employees, e.g. by means of supplementary training, courses or retraining programmes.

coste de formación y educación

= coste de formación y reciclaje

▲ *training and education costs per employee* costes de formación y educación por empleado

training and education day

A training and eductaion day is a day on which an employee participates in training or education activities instead of working.

día de formación y educación

▲ *in-house training and education days* días de formación y educación en la empresa ▲ *number of training and education days per employee* número de días de formación y educación por empleado ▲ *out-of-house training and education days* días de educación y formación fuera de la empresa ▲ *training and education days per year* días de formación y educación por año

tranche

A tranche is an instalment of a monetary amount, typically a bank loan, or a stage in a financial transaction, e.g. an issue of securities such as collateralized mortgage obligations or other multi-class securities.

NOTE "Tranche" is French for "slice".

tramo

▲ *a tranche which is economically in a second loss position* un tramo que está económicamente en una posición de pérdida secundaria ▲ *calculate risk-weighted exposure amounts in respect of all tranches in the securitisation* calcular las cantidades por exposición al riesgo promedio con respecto a todos los tramos de la titulización ▲ *different tranches in a securitisation* diferentes tramos en una titulización ▲ *enhancement provided by more junior tranches in the securitisation* mejoras ofrecidas por los tramos más recientes de la titulización ▲ *subordinate tranches in the securitisation* tramos subordinados en la titulización ▲ *the most senior tranche of a securitisation* el tramo más antiguo de una titulización ▲ *the nominal amount of the tranche* la cuantía nominal del tramo ▲ *the subordination of tranches* la subordinación de tramos ▲ *the thickness of the tranche in which the position is held* la espesura del tramo en el que se mantiene la posición ▲ *the tranches junior to or pari passu with the tranche in which the position is held* los tramos recientes a o pari passu con el tramo en el que se mantiene la posición ▲ *transfer a part of the risk of a loan in one or more tranches* transferir una parte del riesgo de un préstamo a uno o más tramos

transaction

A transaction is an event that leads to a change in the assets, liabilities or financial position of an enterprise and which must be recognised in the financial statements.

transacción

▲ *a foreign currency transaction* una transacción en moneda extranjera ▲ *a future transaction* una transacción futura ▲ *a hedged transaction* una transacción cubierta ▲ *a recognised transaction* una transacción reconocida ▲ *a transaction denominated in foreign currency* una transacción denominada en moneda extranjera ▲ *a transaction which generates revenue* una transacción que genera ingresos ▲ *an unrecognised transaction* una transacción no reconocida ▲ *an unsettled transaction* una transacción no pagada ▲ *arm's length transactions* transacciones a valor de mercado ▲ *derivative transactions* transacciones derivadas ▲ *downstream transactions* transacciones descendentes ▲ *elimination of intercompany transactions* eliminación de transacciones entre empresa ▲ *exchange rate prevailing at the date of the transaction* tipo de cambio existente a la fecha de la transacción ▲ *intercompany transactions* transacciones entre empresas ▲ *material transactions* transacciones materiales ▲ *non-cash transactions* transacciones no monetarias ▲ *past transactions* transacciones pasadas ▲ *recent market transactions* transacciones de mercado recientes ▲ *recent prices of actual transactions* precios recientes de transacciones actuales ▲ *related party transactions* transacciones entre partes vinculadas ▲ *settlement of transactions* pago de las transacciones ▲ *the hedged transaction* la transacción cubierta ▲ *transactions among enterprises under joint control* transacciones entre empresas bajo control conjunto ▲ *transactions between consolidated enterprises* transacciones entre empresas consolidadas ▲ *undertake a transaction on adverse terms* llevar a cabo una transacción en términos adversos ▲ *upstream transactions* transacciones ascendentes

transaction cost IAS/IFRS

Transaction costs are incremental costs incurred from an issue, an acquisition or a disposal of a financial asset or liability. Such costs comprise commissions or fees to intermediaries such as brokers or consultants, taxes as well as charges by securities exchanges, but not financing costs or administrative expenses.

coste de transacción

= coste de la transacción

▲ *amortisation of the transaction costs to accounting profit* amortización de los costes de transacción a beneficio contable ▲ *any attributable transaction costs* cualesquiera costes de transacción atribuibles ▲ *capitalised transaction costs* costes de transacción capitalizados ▲ *direct transaction costs* costes directos de la transacción ▲ *external transaction costs* costes de transacción externos ▲ *internal transaction costs* costes internos de la transacción ▲ *less transaction costs* menos costes de transacción ▲ *the proceeds received, net of transaction costs incurred* los ingresos recibidos, neto de costes de transacción incurridos ▲ *the transaction costs of issuing equity instruments* los costes de transacción por emitir instrumentos de patrimonio neto ▲ *transaction costs incurred* costes de transacción incurridos ▲ *unamortised transaction costs* costes de transacción sin amortizar

SOURCE IAS 39, Appendix AG 13, IAS 39, paragraph 9

transaction date

= date of transaction

The transaction date is the day when a transaction, e.g. a purchase or a sale, has been registered to have taken place, and control of the asset traded passes from the seller to the buyer, or, for a contract, the date when a transaction has been agreed.

fecha de transacción

= fecha de la transacción

▲ *a change in the exchange rate between the transaction date and the date of settlement* un cambio en el tipo de conversión entre la fecha de transacción y la de liquidación ▲ *fair value at the transaction date* valor razonable a la fecha de la transacción ▲ *from the transaction date to the balance sheet date* desde la fecha de transacción a la fecha del balance

transaction expense

The costs that are associated with a transaction are referred to as transaction expenses.

gasto de transacción

= gasto de la transacción

▲ *a decrease in transaction expenses* un descenso en los gastos de la transacción ▲ *an increase in transaction expenses* un aumento en los gastos de transacción ▲ *recognise transaction expenses* reconocer los gastos de transacción ▲ *the transaction expenses incurred* los gastos de transacción incurridos

transaction exposure

= transaction risk

Transaction exposure is an enterprise's risk of losses on transactions that remain unsettled at the balance sheet

date if foreign exchange rates move adversely against the reporting currency in the period between the date of transaction and the settlement date.
riesgo de cambio
= riesgo de conversión
▲ *hedge the transaction exposure* cubrir el riesgo de cambio

transaction rate
The transaction rate is the exchange rate applied for the settlement of an enterprise's transactions at the transaction date.
tipo de cambio
= tipo de conversión
▲ *determine by reference to the transaction rate* determinar por referencia al tipo de cambio ▲ *measure at the transaction rate* medir al tipo de cambio ▲ *the most recent transaction rate* el tipo de cambio más reciente
⇛ closing rate

transaction risk
= transaction exposure
Transaction risk is an enterprise's risk of losses on transactions that remain unsettled at the balance sheet date if foreign exchange rates move adversely against the reporting currency in the period between the date of transaction and the settlement date.
riesgo de cambio
= riesgo de conversión
▲ *hedge the transaction risk* cubrir el riesgo de cambio ▲ *net assets with transaction risk* activos netos con riesgo de cambio

transaction-based
= transactions-based
≠ value-based
Financial statements that are transaction-based are prepared on the basis of transactions using the historical cost convention.
basado en transacciones
≠ basado en el valor
▲ *a transaction-based, historical cost accounting model* un modelo contable del coste histórico, basado en transacciones ▲ *the transaction-based accounting model* el modelo contable basado en transacciones ▲ *the transaction-based theory* el método basado en transacciones ▲ *the transaction-based theory of accounting* el principio de la contabilidad basado en transacciones ▲ *transaction-based earnings* beneficios basados en transacciones ▲ *transaction-based financial reporting* información financiera basada en transacciones ▲ *transaction-based financial statements* estados financieros basados en transacciones
⇛ historical cost convention, transaction-based accounts

transaction-based accounts UK
Transaction-based accounts are financial statements prepared on the basis of an enterprise's transactions using the historical cost convention.
cuentas basadas en el precio de adquisición
= cuentas basadas en el precio de la adquisición
▲ *prepare transaction-based accounts* preparar las cuentas basadas en el precio de adquisición ▲ *publish transaction-based accounts* publicar las cuentas basadas en el precio de la adquisición
⇛ historical cost convention

transaction-based financial statements US, IAS/IFRS
Transaction-based financial statements are accounts prepared on the basis of an enterprise's transactions using the historical cost convention.
estados financieros basados en transacciones
▲ *prepare transaction-based financial statements* preparar los estados financieros basados en transacciones ▲ *publish transaction-based financial statements* publicar los estados financieros basados en transacciones
⇛ historical cost convention, value-based financial statements

transfer[1] *noun*
A transfer is a conveyance of something, e.g. an item or an amount, from one place to another or from one person to another.
transferencia
▲ *a portfolio transfer* una transferencia de cartera ▲ *a transfer of resources* una transferencia de recursos ▲ *the transfer of risks and rewards* la transferencia de riesgos y recompensas ▲ *transfer of funds from one company to another* transferencia de fondos de una empresa a otra ▲ *transfer of resources during 2005* transferencia de recursos du-

rante el 2005 ▲ *transfer restrictions* restricciones a la transferencia

transfer[2] *verb*

transferir

1 To transfer is to move something from one place to another, e.g. an amount from one account to another, or to convey something, e.g. property, from one person to another.

traspasar

= transferir

▲ *transfer a risk to a counterparty* traspasar un riesgo a una contraparte ▲ *transfer funds to the parent* traspasar fondos a la matriz ▲ *transfer substantially all the risks and rewards incidental to ownership* traspasar de forma sustancial todos los riesgos y recompensas asociados a la propiedad

2 To transfer is to allocate e.g. earnings not distributed or amounts not distributable to reserves under equity in the balance sheet.

imputar

= llevar

▲ *transfer to the reserve fund* imputar al fondo de reserva

transfer price

Transfer price refers to the price charged for goods, services or rights exchanged between affiliated enterprises.

precio de transferencia

= precio de la transferencia

▲ *a separate evaluation of transfer prices* una evaluación independiente de los precios de transferencia ▲ *internal transfer prices* precios de transferencia internos

transfer pricing

Transfer pricing is the price setting of transfers of goods and services between affiliated, intra-group enterprises. Multinationals may use transfer pricing to move profits to a country with low tax rates with a view to avoid being overtaxed in a country with high tax rates.

método de precios de transferencia

▲ *affected by internal transfer pricing* afectado por el método de precios de transferencia interno

⇛ dual pricing, intercompany profit

transfer to reserves

= appropriation to reserves

Transfers to reserves include profit for the accounting period, which has not been distributed, as well as share premium amounts, or other amounts credited to reserves under equity in the balance sheet.

imputación a reservas

= transferencia a reservas

▲ *annual transfer to reserves* imputación a reservas anual

transferred-in cost

= previous department cost

Transferred-in costs are costs previously incurred in the production process by the various departments involved. As the product units move on in the process, the costs related to the units are also transferred to the subsequent department in the production process. In this way, the costs become part of the product unit's direct materials costs, but are still, being separate, referred to as transferred-in costs or previous department costs.

coste transferido

▲ *calculate the transferred-in costs* calcular los costes transferidos ▲ *the transferred-in costs for WIP* los costes transferidos por trabajos en curso

transition

A transition is a change from one system, form, situation or type to another, e.g. the change from preparing financial statements in accordance with national accounting standards to preparing them in accordance with IFRS.

transición

▲ *the date of transition to IFRSs* la fecha de la transición a las NIIFs ▲ *the transition from previous GAAP to IFRSs* la transición desde los PCGA anteriores a las NIIFs

transition period

= period of transition

The transition period is the time which is spent for completing a transition, a change or move to a different situation.

periodo de transición

▲ *an 18-month transition period* un periodo de transición de 18 meses

transitional

Transitional means transitory and relates to a period of change.

transitorio
▲ *transitional amount* cuenta transitoria ▲ *transitional effect* efecto transitorio ▲ *transitional period* periodo transitorio ▲ *transitional provisions* provisiones transitorias

transitional liability

A transitional liability is an unrecognised defined benefit plan obligation arising on the adoption of a new accounting standard, where the enterprise must determine the present value of that obligation as defined in the new accounting standard. On transition to IFRS, the obligation is determined at present value at the transition date less fair value of any directly related plan assets and any past service costs to be recognised later.

pasivo transitorio
= pasivo transaccional
▲ *an unrecognised part of the transitional liability* una parte no reconocida del pasivo transitorio ▲ *determine the transitional liability* determinar el pasivo transitorio
SOURCE IAS 19
⇛ defined benefit plan

transitional provision

Transitional provisions are rules that apply for a period running after the abolishment of former provisions until new provisions come fully into force. Transitional provisions apply e.g. to financial reporting in connection with the transition to the International Financial Reporting Standards.

disposición transitoria
▲ *specific transitional provisions in individual standards* disposiciones transitorias específicas en las normas individuales ▲ *the transitional provisions in other IFRSs* las disposiciones transitorias en otras NIFFs

transitory item

A transitory item is a debit or credit entry in the accounting system for the current accounting period that is not permanent. A transitory item may relate to the following accounting period.

partida transitoria
▲ *account for as a transitory item* contabilizar como una partida transitoria ▲ *other transitory items* otras partidas transitorias ▲ *purge the income statement of transitory items* eliminar las partidas transitorias del estado de ingresos

translate

To translate means to convert the amount or size of something into another currency or measure, e.g. items in the financial statements may be converted into another currency for the purpose of preparing consolidated financial statements.

convertir
▲ *the resulting translated amounts for non-monetary items* las cantidades convertidas resultantes para las partidas nomonetarias ▲ *translate amounts from the functional currency to the presentation currency* convertir las cantidades desde la moneda funcional a la de presentación ▲ *translate foreign currency items into the functional currency* convertir las partidas en moneda extranjera a la moneda funcional ▲ *translate the financial statements into the presentation currency* convertir los estados financieros a la moneda de presentación

translation

On translation, items recognised in the financial statements of foreign operations in the functional currencies of such operations are changed into the reporting currency of the enterprise.

conversión
= cambio
▲ *apply the translation procedures applicable to the new functional currency prospectively* aplicar los procedimientos de conversión aplicables a la nueva moneda funcional prospectivamente ▲ *the translation of a foreign operation into the presentation currency of the entity* la conversión de una operación en divisas en la moneda de presentación de la entidad ▲ *the translation of cash flows of a foreign operation* la conversión de los flujos de efectivo de una operación extranjera ▲ *the translation of the financial statements into the presentation currency* la conversión de los esta-

dos financieros en la moneda de presentación

translation adjustment

= currency translation adjustment, exchange adjustment, foreign currency adjustment, foreign exchange adjustment

Translation adjustments result from the process of translating financial statements from foreign currencies into the reporting currency of the enterprise, adjusting for exchange differences and applying the appropriate translation method.

ajuste por conversión

= ajuste de conversión, ajuste por la conversión

▲ *translation adjustment at year-end rate* ajuste por conversión al tipo de final de año ▲ *translation adjustment of interest rate and foreign currency swaps* ajuste por la conversión del tipo de interés y swaps de moneda extranjera ▲ *translation adjustment of trading activities* ajuste por conversión de actividades de intermediación financiera ▲ *translation adjustments arising from the translation into Danish kroner* ajustes por conversión procedentes de conversiones en coronas danesas ▲ *translation adjustments of reserves at the beginning of the year* ajustes por conversión de reservas al inicio del año ▲ *unrealised translation adjustments for the year* ajustes por conversión no realizados para el año

translation exposure

= translation risk

Translation exposure is an enterprise's risk of loss if foreign exchange rates move adversely against the reporting currency, affecting assets and liabilities denominated in foreign currencies that are recognised in the financial statements.

riesgo de tipo de cambio

= riesgo de tipo de conversión, riesgo de traslación

▲ *eliminate translation exposure* eliminar el riesgo del tipo de cambio ▲ *hedging of the translation exposure* cobertura del riesgo del tipo de cambio ▲ *minimise the translation exposure* minimizar el riesgo del tipo de cambio ▲ *reduce the translation exposure* reducir el riesgo de tipo de cambio

translation rate

Translation rate refers to the exchange rate that is applied when financial statements or specific financial statement items are translated into another currency.

tipo de conversión

= tipo de cambio

▲ *the translation rate prevailing at the balance sheet date* el tipo de conversión vigente a la fecha del balance

translation reserve

→ foreign currency translation reserve

translation risk

= translation exposure

Translation risk is an enterprise's risk of loss if foreign exchange rates move adversely against the reporting currency, affecting assets and liabilities denominated in foreign currencies that are recognised in the financial statements.

riesgo de conversión

▲ *net assets exposed to translation risk* activos netos expuestos al riesgo de conversión

transparency

Transparency is a concept implying openness, clarity, visibility and understandability, i.e. that something is easy to see through and comprehend. Society expects transparency in e.g. organisations, regulations and administrative processes.

transparencia

▲ *an annual transparency report* un informe de transparencia anual ▲ *computational transparency* transparencia computacional ▲ *ensure proper transparency* asegurar la propia transparencia ▲ *increase transparency and consistency* incrementar la transparencia y la consistencia ▲ *lack of transparency* falta de transparencia ▲ *post-trade transparency requirements for regulated markets* requerimientos de transparencia post-venta para los mercados regulados ▲ *pre-trade transparancy requirements for regulated markets* requerimientos de transparencia pre-venta para los mercados regulados ▲ *the rules governing the transparency of parents* las normas que gobiernan la trans-

parencia de las matrices ▲ *the transparency of parents* la transparencia de las matrices
⇛ clarity, understandability

Transparency Directive
The Transparency Directive is a legislative act adopted by the EU, which contains the minimum requirements for the information, such as financial reports and major shareholding disclosures, submitted by issuers whose securities are admitted to trading on an EU regulated market.
Directiva sobre Transparencia
▲ *according to the Transparency Directive* de acuerdo con la Directiva sobre Transparencia ▲ *in compliance with the Transparency Directive* en cumplimiento de la Directiva sobre Transparencia
⇛ transparency

transparent
When something is transparent it is easy to see through it and understand it.
transparente
▲ *a transparent programme* un programa transparente ▲ *documented in a transparent and clear manner* documentado de una forma clara y transparente ▲ *fiscally transparent* fiscalmente transparente ▲ *less transparent* menos transparente ▲ *sufficiently transparent* suficientemente transparente ▲ *transparent financial reporting* un informe financiero transparente

transport cost
= carriage costs, costs of transportation, transportation expense
Transport costs refer to the costs incurred by an enterprise when transporting or conveying goods or people.
coste de transporte
= coste del transporte
▲ *recognise transport costs* reconocer los costes de transporte ▲ *the transport costs incurred* los costes de transporte incurridos

transportation
Transportation refers to the act of moving goods or people from one location to another, e.g. by train, aircraft, lorry, etc.
transporte
▲ *the transportation industry* la industria del transporte ▲ *transportation expenses* gastos de transporte

transportation expense
= transport cost
Transportation expenses refer to the expenses incurred by an enterprise when transporting or conveying goods or people.
gasto de transporte
= gasto en transporte
▲ *delivery and transportation expenses* gastos de transporte y envío

travelling allowance
= travel allowance
Travelling allowance is reimbursement for expenses incurred by an employee in connection with transport.
dieta de viaje
= viático
▲ *pay travelling allowance* pagar la dieta de viaje ▲ *payment of travelling allowance* pago de la dieta de viaje

travelling expense
Travelling expenses are the expenses incurred by an enterprise in relation to its employees' travelling activities for business purposes, e.g. transportation and accommodation.
gasto de viaje
▲ *an increase in travelleing expenses* un aumento en los gastos de viaje

treasurer US
A treasurer is a manager concerned with the financial matters of an enterprise, e.g. the managing and raising of cash.
tesorero
= responsable de tesorería
▲ *appoint a new treasurer* nombrar un nuevo tesorero ▲ *corporate treasurer* tesorero corporativo ▲ *the incoming treasurer* el tesorero entrante ▲ *the outgoing treasurer* el tesorero saliente ▲ *the retiring treasurer* el tesorero saliente
⇛ controller

treasury
A treasury is a department within an enterprise responsible for the enterprise's main financial operations. The functions of a treasury usually include investment, financing and hedging activities as well as management of cash and bank accounts.
tesorería
▲ *a central treausury* una tesorería central

treasury bond US

= government bond UK

Treasury bonds are interest-bearing securities issued by the US federal government for the purpose of borrowing money. Investment in treasury bonds is regarded as safe.

bono del estado

= bono del tesoro, bono público

▲ *Danish treasury bonds* bonos del estado daneses ▲ *foreign treasury bonds* bonos del estado extranjero ▲ *invest free funds in treasury bonds* invertir los fondos disponibles en bonos del estado ▲ *rating for treasury bonds* rating de los bonos del estado ▲ *the yield of a treasury bond* el rendimiento de un bono del estado

⇛ bond

treasury share IAS/IFRS, US

= own share UK, treasury stock US

A treasury share is a share, i.e. an equity instrument, which has been repurchased and is held by the issuing enterprise. A treasury share may be resold or cancelled. No dividends are paid on treasury shares. Treasury shares are recognised in the balance sheet as a deduction from equity attributable to the equity holders or, on acquisition, as a change in equity.

acción propia

= acción propia en cartera, autocartera

▲ *acquire treasury shares* adquirir acciones propias ▲ *acquisition of treasury shares* adquisición de acciones propias ▲ *cancel treasury shares* cancelar las acciones propias ▲ *disclose the amount of treasury shares held separately* publicar la cantidad de acciones propias mantenidas por separado ▲ *disclosures of treasury shares* publicaciones de acciones propias ▲ *dispose of treasury shares* cesión de acciones propias ▲ *hold treasury shares* mantener las acciones propias ▲ *purchase of treasury shares* compra de acciones propias ▲ *realise treasury shares* realizar acciones propias ▲ *recognise treasury shares* reconocer acciones propias ▲ *reserve for treasury shares* reserva para acciones propias ▲ *sale of treasury shares* venta de acciones propias ▲ *treasury shares issued in connection with employee share option plans* acciones propias emitidas en conexión con los planes de opciones sobre acciones de los empleados

treasury stock US

= own share UK, treasury share IAS/IFRS, US

Treasury stock consists of treasury shares, which are shares issued by a company and later repurchased and held by the company. Treasury stock may be cancelled or resold. No dividends are paid on treasury stock. Treasury stock is recognised in the balance sheet as a deduction from equity attributable to the equity holders or, on acquisition, as a change in equity.

NOTE In the balance sheet, treasury stock is recognised under equity as a non-distributable reserve.

acciones propias

= autocartera, instrumentos de patrimonio propio

▲ *acquisition of treasury stock* adquisición de acciones propias ▲ *cancellation of treasury stock* cancelación de las acciones propias ▲ *disclose treasury stock in the balance sheet* hacer pública las acciones propias en el balance ▲ *disposal of treasury stock* eliminación de la autocartera ▲ *dividends related to treasury stock* dividendos relacionados con las acciones propias ▲ *issuance of treasury stock* emisión de acciones propias ▲ *purchase of treasury stock* compra de acciones propias ▲ *sale of treasury stock* venta de acciones propias ▲ *the acquisition cost of treasury stock* el coste de adquisición de las acciones propias ▲ *write-offs on treasury stock* amortizaciones de acciones propias

treat

To treat is to handle or deal with something according to a particular set of actions or a special procedure.

tratar

▲ *an acquisition of a foreign operation treated prospectively* una adquisición de una operación extranjera tratada prospectivamente ▲ *treat as a separate item* tratar como una partida separada ▲ *treat each exchange tran-*

saction separately tratar cada transacción de cambio por separado ▲ *treat the additional consideration as an adjustment to the cost of the combination* tratar la consideración adicional como un ajuste al coste de la combinación ▲ *treat the adjustment as a revaluation increase or decrease* tratar el ajuste como un aumento o descenso de la reevaluación ▲ *treat the change as a change in an accounting estimate* tratar el cambio como un cambio en una estimación contable ▲ *treat the entire combined contract as a financial asset that is held for trading* tratar el contrato combinado entero como un activo financiero que se mantiene para operar ▲ *treat the land and buildings as a single unit* tratar los terrenos y edificios como una unidad única

treatment

A treatment of something is the handling of something, e.g. a transaction, a plan or a proposal, typically according to a special procedure. Accounting treatment refers to the way assets, liabilities, income and expenses are recognised and measured in the financial statements under the accounting principles and policies applied.

tratamiento

▲ *according to the benchmark treatment* de acuerdo con el tratamiento del índice de referencia ▲ *capitalise in accordance with the permitted capitalisation treatment* capitalizar de acuerdo con el tratamiento permitido de la capitalización ▲ *in accordance with the allowed alternative treatment* de acuerdo con el tratamiento alternativo permitido ▲ *the accounting treatment* el tratamiento contable ▲ *the accounting treatment of portfolio hedging* el tratamiento contable de la cobertura de la cartera de inversiones ▲ *the appropriate treatment for items that are segregated for a specific project* el tratamiento apropiado para las partidas que se segregan para un proyecto concreto ▲ *the treatment of accrued income recognised at year-end* el tratamiento de los ingresos devengados reconocidos a final de año ▲ *treatment of accumulated price adjustments* tratamiento de los ajustes de precios acumulados ▲ *treatment of goodwill* tratamiento del fondo de comercio ▲ *treatment of provisions* tratamiento de las provisiones

⇛ accounting policies, accounting principle

trend

Trend refers to the general direction or tendency of a particular development of something, e.g. the trend in prices.

tendencia

▲ *a downward trend* una tendencia bajista ▲ *a falling trend* una tendencia descendente ▲ *a marked trend* una tendencia de mercado ▲ *a rising trend* una tendencia ascendente ▲ *a trend towards something* una tendencia hacia algo ▲ *affect the trends in share prices* afectar a las tendencias en los precios de las acciones ▲ *an upward trend* una tendencia alcista ▲ *experience a trend* experimentar una tendencia ▲ *identify trends in the enterprise's financial position* identificar las tendencias en la posición financiera de la empresa ▲ *the assessment of trends in financial information for predictive purposes* la evaluación de las tendencias en la información financiera a efectos de predicción ▲ *the global trend* la tendencia global ▲ *trends in share prices* tendencia en los precios de la acción

trial balance

A trial balance shows the debit and credit balances of all ledger accounts at the end of an accounting period. By comparing the total debit balances in the right column with the total credit balances in the left column, it can be verified whether the totals agree, i.e. balance. The trial balance is used for preparing the final accounts for the period.

balance de comprobación

= balance de comprobación de sumas y saldos, balance de sumas y saldos

▲ *prepare a cash flow statement on the basis of a trial balance* preparar un estado de flujo de efectivo según un balance de comprobación ▲ *prepare a trial*

balance preparar un balance de comprobación
⇛ ledger account

trigger point
Trigger points are the stages in the production cycle from the purchase of raw materials to the sale of finished products at which entries are made in the bookkeeping system.
punto de arranque
▲ *change the trigger point* cambiar el punto de arranque ▲ *reach the trigger point* llegar al punto de arranque
⇛ sequential tracking

true and fair override UK
The true and fair override is a sort of escape clause that permits departure from accounting legislation and standards when such departure is needed in the preparation of financial statements to ensure that they give a true and fair view of the financial position of an enterprise.
NOTE The true and fair override originated in British accounting where financial statements have to comply with both the UK Companies Act and accounting standards; where contradiction between these appears, the fair presentation concept requires a company to depart from either the law or from the accounting rules.
excepción al reflejo de imagen fiel
▲ *apply a true and fair override* aplicar una excepción al reflejo de imagen fiel ▲ *use a true and fair override* utilizar una excepción al reflejo de imagen fiel
⇛ true and fair view

true and fair view UK
= fair presentation US, IAS/IFRS
True and fair view refers to the overriding requirement that the financial statements must fairly present, in all material respects, the results and financial position of an enterprise. A true and fair view means that generally accepted accounting principles and conventions have been consistently applied when preparing the financial statements.
imagen fiel
▲ *achieve a true and fair view* conseguir una imagen fiel ▲ *give a qualified opinion as to the true and fair view presented by the annual report* dar una opinión cualificada en cuanto a la imagen fiel en el informe anual ▲ *give a true and fair view* dar una imagen fiel ▲ *information of importance to the true and fair view* la información de importancia para la imagen fiel ▲ *information that is necessary for giving a true and fair view* información que es necesaria para una imagen fiel ▲ *meet the requirement of a true and fair view* cumplir el requisito de imagen fiel ▲ *the general requirement of a true and fair view* el requisito general de una imagen fiel ▲ *the true and fair view of the enterprise's financial position* la imagen fiel de la posición financiera de la empresa

turnover
1 = revenue IAS/IFRS, US, sales US
The turnover is the total sales of an enterprise over an accounting period, i.e. the total revenue for products and services less any trade discounts, VAT, and other taxes based on the revenue. The turnover appears as the top line in the profit and loss account.
facturación
= ventas
▲ *a decline in turnover* un descenso en la facturación ▲ *an increase in turnover* un aumento en la facturación ▲ *cyclical turnover* facturación cíclica ▲ *geographical distribution of turnover* distribución geográfica de las ventas ▲ *invoiced turnover* ventas facturadas ▲ *operating profit as a percentage of turnover* beneficio operativo como un porcentaje de la facturación ▲ *seasonal turnover* facturación estacional ▲ *total turnover* total facturación ▲ *turnover for the year* facturación anual ▲ *turnover in terms of volume* facturación por volumen ▲ *turnover per employee* facturación por empleado ▲ *turnover per unit* facturación por unidad
2 = turnover rate
Turnover means the rate at which something is turned over, e.g. creditors, employees or stocks.

rotación
= renovación
▲ *asset turnover* rotación de activos ▲ *creditor turnover* rotación de acreedores ▲ *debtors' turnover* rotación de deudores ▲ *inventory turnover ratio* ratio de rotación de inventarios ▲ *stock turnover ratio* ratio de rotación de existencias

turnover ratio
= rate of turnover
The turnover ratio is an activity financial ratio expressing the frequency with which a type of asset of an enterprise is replaced by another asset of the same type within a defined time period. Examples are accounts receivable turnover, inventory turnover, staff turnover and fixed asset turnover.
ratio de rotación
= índice de rotación
▲ *a decline in the turnover ratio* una disminución en el ratio de rotación

type of asset
Types of assets refer to the categories of assets recognised in the balance sheet such as fixed assets and current assets.
tipo de activo
▲ *qualify for recognition as some other type of asset* calificar para reconocer como otro tipo de activo ▲ *the types of assets aggregated for the asset's cash-generating unit* los tipos de activos agregados para la unidad generadora de efectivo del activo

type of capital
Type of capital refers to the different sources of finance that is used by an enterprise, i.e. the different types of debt and equity.
tipo de financiación
= clase de financiación
▲ *disclose the types of capital* publicar los tipos de financiación
⇛ debt, equity, financial gearing

type of cost
= cost type
Various types of cost include costs of a uniform nature such as costs for wages and salaries, depreciation and amortisation, impairment, raw materials, interest etc. The profit and loss account may be presented in two formats: classified according to type of cost or according to function.
tipo de coste
▲ *disclose the types of cost* divulgar los tipos de coste
⇛ classified by nature, classified by type of expenditure

type of enterprise
Type of enterprise refers to the legal form of a business organisation and its characteristics as to ownership, liability etc. Types include a sole proprietorship, a limited company, a partnership, or a joint venture.
tipo de empresa
▲ *special rules for particular types of enterprise* normas especiales para determinados tipos de empresa

type of expense
= type of cost
Various types of expenses include expenses of a uniform nature such as costs for wages and salaries, depreciation and amortisation, impairment, raw materials, interest etc. The profit and loss account may be presented in two formats: classified according to type of expense or according to function.
tipo de gasto
= naturaleza del gasto
▲ *disclose the types of expense* publicar los tipos de gasto

type of tax
A type of tax is a particular form of taxation levied at a particular tax rate, e.g. a direct tax such as income tax, corporation tax, inheritance tax and capital gains tax, or an indirect tax such as excise duty or VAT.
tipo de impuesto
▲ *introduce new types of tax* introducir nuevos tipos de impuesto

U

U.S. Bankruptcy Court US
The US Bankruptcy Court has exclusive jurisdiction over bankruptcy cases. Such cases cannot be filed in the state courts, but must be brought before a federal court in one of the 94 federal judicial districts.
U.S. Bankruptcy Court
= Tribunal de Procedimientos Concursales de los Estados Unidos de América
▲ *cases heard by the U.S. Bankruptcy Court* causas vistas por la U.S. Bankruptcy Court

UITF
= Urgent Issues Task Force
UITF is the abbreviation for the Urgent Issues Task Force, which is a sub-committee of the Accounting Standards Board (ASB) and part of the UK accounting standard setting organisation set up in 1990. The UITF assists the ASB in urgent matters where an accounting standard exists, but where unsatisfactory or conflicting interpretations have developed. The UITF operates by seeking a consensus as to the accounting treatment to be adopted.
UITF
= Grupo de Operaciones de Asuntos Urgentes
▲ *objective guidance on interpretation provided by UITF* guía objetiva de interpretación ofrecida por el UITF ▲ *the UITF's proposed guidance on treasury shares* la guía propuesta por el UITF para los títulos del tesoro
⇛ Accounting Standards Board

unallocated
Unallocated means not attributable to, related to, or distributed on several areas, segments, activities etc.
no asignado
▲ *disclose the amount of the unallocated goodwill* publicar la cantidad del fondo de comercio no asignado ▲ *recognise unallocated overheads as an expense in the period in which they are incurred* reconocer los costes indirectos no asignados como un gasto en el periodo en el que se incurren ▲ *unallocated production overheads* costes indirectos de producción no asignados

unallocated cost
Unallocated costs refer to costs that are not related to a particular cost objective, i.e. they cannot be attributed to a specific activity.
coste no asignado
▲ *the book value of the remaining unallocated cost* el valor contable del coste no asignado restante ▲ *the calculation of the percentage of unallocated costs* el cálculo del porcentaje de los costes no asignados

unamortised UK
= unamortized US
Used about an intangible asset, typically goodwill, unamortised means not having been subject to any amortisation. This means that the cost of the asset has been expensed in the year of acquisition and is not systematically allocated over its useful economic life.
no amortizado
= sin amortizar
▲ *the amounts remaining unamortised at the beginning and end of the period* las cantidades que permanecen sin amortizar al principio y final del periodo ▲ *unamortised goodwill* fondo de comercio no amortizado
⇛ amortisation

unamortised cost UK
= unamortized cost US
≠ amortised cost UK, amortized cost US
Unamortised costs refer to the amount of costs of an intangible that remains to be amortised after deduction of accumulated amortisation at a specific date.
coste no amortizado
= coste pendiente de amortizar, coste por amortizar, costo sin amortizar
▲ *at the lower of unamortised cost or net realisable value* a la cantidad más baja que se reconoce como coste no amortizado o valor realizable neto ▲ *less the unamortised cost* menos el coste no amortizado ▲ *treatment of the unamortised cost*

tratamiento del coste no amortizado
⇛ amortised, unamortised

unamortized US
= unamortised UK
When used about an intangible asset, typically goodwill, unamortized means not having been subject to any amortization. This means that the cost of the asset has been expensed in the year of acquisition and is not systematically allocated over its useful economic life.
no amortizado
= sin amortizar
▲ *the amounts remaining unamortized at the beginning and end of the period* las cantidades que permanecen sin amortizar al principio y final del periodo ▲ *unamortized goodwill* fondo de comercio no amortizado
⇛ amortization

unamortized cost US
= unamortised cost UK
≠ amortised cost UK, amortized cost US
Unamortized costs refer to the amount of costs of an intangible that remains to be amortized after deduction of accumulated amortization at a specific date.
coste no amortizado
= coste pendiente de amortizar, coste por amortizar, costo sin amortizar
▲ *at the lower of unamortized cost or net realisable value* a la cantidad más baja que se reconoce como coste no amortizado o valor realizable neto ▲ *less the unamortized cost* menos el coste no amortizado ▲ *treatment of the unamortized cost* tratamiento del coste no amortizado
⇛ amortized, unamortized

unaudited
When something is unaudited, it has neither been critically examined nor compared with a target, a framework, a standard etc.
no auditado
= sin auditar
▲ *an unaudited annual report* un informe anual no auditado ▲ *submit an unaudited annual report* remitir un informe anual no auditado

unavoidable cost
Unavoidable costs are costs that are incurred even though the activity to which they relate is scaled down or discontinued.
coste inevitable
▲ *recognise unavoidable costs* reconocer los costes inevitables

unbundle IAS/IFRS
To unbundle is to recognise the deposit component of an insurance contract separately, i.e. treating it as an individual contract, provided this component can be measured independently of the insurance component.
disociar
▲ *unbundle a contract* disociar un contrato ▲ *unbundle components contained in an insurance contract* disociar los componentes contenidos en un contrato de seguros
SOURCE IFRS 4, Appendix A
⇛ deposit component

unbundling IAS/IFRS
Unbundling is the recognition of deposit components of insurance contracts separately, i.e. the treating of them as individual contracts, provided such components can be measured independently of the insurance components.
disociación
▲ *permit unbundling* permitir la disociación ▲ *prohibit unbundling* prohibir la disociación ▲ *require unbundling* obligar a la disociación ▲ *unbundling of deposit components* disociación de los componentes del depósito
SOURCE IFRS 4, Appendix A

uncalled capital
= capital receivable
The uncalled capital of a company is that part of the issued capital that remains unpaid by shareholders because it has not been called up, i.e. required to be paid.
capital no exigido
= capital a pagar, capital no desembolsado
▲ *make a call on uncalled capital* exigir el capital a pagar ▲ *the uncalled capital of the company* el capital no exigido de la empresa

uncertain
Uncertain means doubtful or not sure and likely to happen or change.
incierto
▲ *a specified uncertain event* un suceso incierto especifícado

▲ *an uncertain future event covered by an insurance contract* un suceso futuro incierto cubierto por un contrato de seguro ▲ *present the uncertain cash flow as if it were a certain cash flow* presentar el flujo de efectivo incierto como si fuera cierto ▲ *the outcome of uncertain circumstances* la salida de circunstancias inciertas ▲ *uncertain future events not wholly within the control of the acquiree* sucesos futuros inciertos que no están completamente dentro del control de la adquirente

uncertainty

Uncertainty relates to matters of which the outcome may be unknown or which may depend on factors and events beyond the control of the enterprise, but which may affect its financial statements.

incertidumbre

▲ *any uncertainty connected with recognition or measurement* cualquier incertidumbre conectada con el reconocimiento o valoración ▲ *information that the uncertainty existed at the last balance sheet date* información de que existía incertidumbre en la fecha final del balance ▲ *key sources of estimation uncertainty* fuentes claves de la estimación de la incertidumbre ▲ *tax uncertainties* incertidumbres fiscales ▲ *the price for bearing the uncertainty inherent in the asset* el precio por soportar la incertidumbre inherente al activo ▲ *the resolution of uncertainties* la resolución de las incertidumbres ▲ *the uncertainties inherent in business activities* las incertidumbres inherentes a las actividades comerciales ▲ *the uncertainty of future cash flows from insurance contracts* la incertidumbre de los flujos de efectivo futuros procedentes de los contratos de seguros ▲ *uncertainties that arise from the terms of the disposal transaction* incertidumbres que surgen de los términos del abandono de la transacción ▲ *uncertainty about the amount of claims payments* incertidumbre sobre la cantidad de reclamaciones de pago

uncertificated security

= book-entry security, dematerialised security

An uncertificated security is a book-entry security that does not exist in a certificated form, but exist as an electronic entry in a register and is issued and tranferred as an uncertificated financial instrument.

título intangible

= anotación en cuenta

▲ *a party to an uncertificated securities transaction* una parte en una transacción de los títulos intangibles ▲ *attachment or enforcement proceedings with respect to uncertificated securities* procedimientos de decomiso o ejecución forzosa con respecto a los títulos intangibles ▲ *collateralisation of uncertificated securities* colateralización de los títulos intangibles ▲ *issue and registration of uncertificated securities* emisión y registro de los títulos intangibles ▲ *multi-tiered holdings of uncertificated securities* holdings muy ramificados con títulos intangibles

unchanged

When something is unchanged, it is unaltered and stays the same.

no modificado

= sin modificar

▲ *an unchanged level* un nivel no modificado ▲ *remain unchanged until the end of the contingency period* permanecer sin modificar hasta el final del periodo de contingencia ▲ *unchanged exchange rates* tipos de cambio no modificados ▲ *value adjustment under unchanged market conditions* ajuste de valor según las condiciones del mercado no modificadas

uncollectible

When a debt is uncollectible it is very unlikely to be paid, and it is consequently a bad debt. Uncollectibles are bad debts.

incobrable

▲ *an expense for impairment losses on uncollectible loans and advances* un gasto por pérdidas por deterioro de préstamos y anticipos incobrables ▲ *the accumulated allowance for uncollectible minimum lease payments receivable* la bonificación acumulada por pagos a cobrar por arrendamiento mínimo incobrables ▲ *write off uncollectible loans and advances* eliminar préstamos y anticipos incobrables

uncontrollable cost

≠ controllable cost

Uncontrollable costs are costs that the management of the relevant responsibility centre cannot influence within a specified period.

coste incontrolable

= coste no controlable

≠ coste controlable

▲ *a decrease in uncontrollable costs* un descenso en los costes incontrolables ▲ *uncontrollable cost increases* aumentos de los costes incontrolables

underabsorbed indirect cost

= underallocated indirect cost, underapplied indirect cost

≠ overabsorbed indirect cost, overallocated indirect cost, overapplied indirect cost

Underabsorbed indirect costs refer to the allocation of indirect manufacturing costs for an accounting period to products or orders by an amount that is lower than the actually incurred indirect manufacturing costs for that accounting period.

coste indirecto no absorbido totalmente

= coste indirecto parcialmente absorbido, coste indirecto sin aplicar completamente

▲ *recognise payroll costs as underabsorbed indirect costs* reconocer los costes de nómina como costes indirectos no absorbidos totalmente

⇛ underapplied overhead

underallocated indirect cost

= underabsorbed indirect cost, underapplied indirect cost

≠ overabsorbed indirect cost, overallocated indirect cost, overapplied indirect cost

Underallocated indirect costs refer to the allocation of indirect manufacturing costs for an accounting period to the account for work in progress by an amount that is lower than the actually incurred indirect manufacturing costs for that accounting period.

coste indirecto no asignado por completo

= coste indirecto parcialmente asignado, coste indirecto sin aplicar completamente

▲ *recognise payroll costs as underallocated indirect costs* reconocer los costes de nómina como costes indirectos no asignados por completo

⇛ underapplied overhead

underapplied indirect cost

= underabsorbed indirect cost, underallocated indirect cost

≠ overabsorbed indirect cost, overallocated indirect cost, overapplied indirect cost

Underapplied indirect costs refer to the allocation of indirect manufacturing costs for an accounting period to products or orders by an amount that is lower than the actually incurred indirect manufacturing costs for that accounting period.

coste indirecto parcialmente aplicado

= coste indirecto absorbido parcialmente, coste indirecto asignado parcialmente, coste indirecto sin aplicar completamente

▲ *recognise payroll costs as underapplied indirect costs* reconocer los costes de nómina como costes indirectos parcialmente aplicado

⇛ underapplied overhead

underapplied overhead

≠ overapplied overhead

Underapplied overheads refer to the allocation of overheads for an accounting period to products or orders by an amount that is lower than the actually incurred overheads for that accounting period.

coste indirecto parcialmente aplicado

▲ *an insignificant amount of underapplied overhead* una cantidad insignificante de coste indirecto parcialmente aplicado ▲ *less underapplied overhead* menos coste indirecto parcialmente aplicado

⇛ underabsorbed indirect cost

underfunded IAS/IFRS

≠ overfunded IAS/IFRS

A pension plan is underfunded when the projected benefit obligations of the plan exceed the fair value of the plan assets.

subfinanciado

= financiado parcialmente, parcialmente financiado

▲ *an underfunded pension plan* un plan de pensiones subfinanciado

⇛ plan asset, projected benefit obligation

underlying

That something is underlying, e.g. an asset, a liability, a risk or another factor or assumption, means that it is the actual, but not immediately obvious basis of something, or forms the basis from which something is derived.

subyacente

▲ *an underlying asset* un activo subyacente ▲ *an underlying cash flow* un flujo de efectivo subyacente ▲ *an underlying cost structure* una estructura de costes subyacente ▲ *an underlying development of costs* un desarrollo de costes subyacentes ▲ *an underlying equity portfolio* una cartera de títulos subyacentes ▲ *an underlying improvement of the operating margin* una mejora subyacente del margen de explotación ▲ *an underlying internally generated intangible asset* un activo intangible subyacente generado internamente ▲ *an underlying liability* un pasivo subyacente ▲ *an underlying market price* un precio de mercado subyacente ▲ *an underlying right* un derecho subyacente ▲ *mitigate the underlying risk exposure* mitigar la exposición al riesgo subyacente ▲ *the cash flows of the underlying transaction* los flujos de efectivo de la transacción subyacente ▲ *the economic effects of the underlying transactions* los efectos económicos de las transacciones subyacentes ▲ *the financial risks inherent in an underlying primary financial instrument* los riesgos financieros inherentes en un instrumento financiero primario subyacente ▲ *the right to control the use of the underlying asset* el derecho a controlar el uso del activo subyacente ▲ *the underlying borrowing* el empréstito subyacente ▲ *the underlying measurement basis* el método de medición subyacente ▲ *the underlying value of the loan at the time of borrowing* el valor subyacente del préstamo en el tiempo del empréstito ▲ *underlying capital resources* recursos de capital subyacentes ▲ *underlying currency risks* riesgos de divisas subyacentes ▲ *underlying temporary differences* diferencias temporarias subyacentes ▲ *underlying value* valor subyacente ▲ *use a derivative to hedge an underlying non-financial variable* usar un derivado para cubrir una variable no financiera subyacente ▲ *volatility on the underlying asset* volatilidad en el activo subyacente

⇛ underlying performance

underlying assumption

= accounting assumption

Underlying assumptions refer to the basic accounting conventions underlying generally accepted accounting principles, such as the going concern assumption that the enterprise will continue in operation for the foreseeable future, the separate entity assumption that the activities and financial statements of an enterprise are separate from those of the owners, the monetary unit assumption that financial disclosures are made and transactions measured in money terms in the financial statements, and the time period assumption that financial reporting is made periodically and on a timely basis.

principio subyacente

= principio contable

▲ *in accordance with the underlying assumptions* de acuerdo con los principios subyacentes

underlying performance

The underlying performance is the performance from operations seen in isolation, i.e. excluding unusual and one-off items such as the acquisition and disposal of assets that would otherwise distort the trend.

actuación subyacente

▲ *changes attributable to the underlying performance* cambios atribuibles a la actuación subyacente ▲ *provide a clear picture of the underlying performance of the group* ofrecer una imagen clara de la actuación subyacente del grupo ▲ *the underlying performance of the business* la actuación subyacente de la empresa

understandability

Understandability is one of the key qualitative characteristics of financial information which means that financial informa-

tion as provided in e.g. financial statements must be comprehensible to users. Other key qualitative characteristics are materiality, relevance, reliability and comparability.
comprensibilidad
▲ *enhance the understandability of the information* aumentar la comprensibilidad de la información ▲ *for reasons of understandability of the interim figures* por razones de comprensibilidad de las cifras provisionales ▲ *the reliability and understandability of the financial statements* la fiabilidad y comprensibilidad de los estados financieros
⇛ clarity, transparency

undertaking
An undertaking is a business enterprise such as a sole trader, limited partnership, company or an economic entity.
empresa
▲ *large and medium-sized undertakings* grandes y medianas empresas ▲ *loans to undertakings with which the company has participating interest* préstamos a empresas con las que la compañía tiene participaciones ▲ *work performed by the undertaking for its own purposes and capitalised* trabajo realizado por la empresa para su propio uso y capitalizado

underwrite
To underwrite is to agree to buy shares or other securities that have not been bought by the public in connection with an issue of those shares etc.
garantizar la suscripción de la emisión
▲ *underwrite a particular financial instrument* garantizar la suscripción de la emisión de un instrumento financiero concreto ▲ *underwrite an issue* garantizar la suscripción de la emisión

underwriting
1 In the context of the new issue of securities, underwriting means providing a guarantee to buy, or find a buyer for, a certain amount or all of the securities issued, or to take up any shares not subscribed for by the public. In this way the underwriter accepts the risk of the issue being undersubscribed against payment of a commission. Underwriters are typically financial institutions such as investment banks or issuing houses.
suscripción garantizada
▲ *services related to underwriting* servicios relacionados con la suscripción garantizada ▲ *underwriting losses* pérdidas por suscripción garantizada ▲ *underwriting of financial instruments* suscripción garantizada de instrumentos financieros
2 In the context of insurance, underwriting is the assuming of risk by an insurer under an agreement (the insurance contract) against payment of a premium by the insured.
reaseguro
▲ *have a high underwriting capacity* tener una capacidad de reaseguro alta ▲ *meet one's underwriting liabilities* cumplir con las obligaciones de reaseguro propias

undistributable reserve
= capital reserve UK, non-distributable reserve, restricted surplus US
≠ distributable reserve, revenue reserve UK, unrestricted earnings US
Undistributable reserves are reserves that cannot be distributed to the shareholders, except if the company is wound up. Undistributable reserves appear as an item in the balance sheet under equity.
reserva indisponible
= reserva no distribuible
≠ reserva disponible, reserva distribuible
▲ *establish an undistributable reserve* establecer una reserva indisponible

unearned finance income
For a finance lease, unearned finance income is the discrepancy between on the one hand the total sum of the minimum lease payments together with any unguaranteed residual value (i.e. the gross investment) and on the other hand the present value of the minimum payments discounted by the interest rate implicit in the lease (i.e. the net investment).
ingreso financiero no devengado
= ingreso financiero no acumulado

▲ *less unearned finance income* menos el ingreso financiero no devengado ▲ *reduce unearned finance income* reducir el ingreso financiero no devengado

unexercisable

When something, e.g. a right or an option, is unexercisable, it means that it is not possible to take advantage of it, i.e. exert the right to buy or sell the option and thereby benefit from it.

no ejercitable

▲ *an unexercisable option* una opción no ejercitable ▲ *the value of unexercisable options* el valor de las opciones no ejercitables

unfavorable variance US

= unfavourable variance UK

An unfavorable variance is a variance between the budgeted amount of e.g. costs or sales and the actual level, which is to the disadvantage of the enterprise.

desviación desfavorable

▲ *an unfavorable variance of $500,000* una desviación desfavorable de 500.000 dólares ▲ *the estimated unfavorable variance* la desviación desfavorable estimada

unfunded

≠ funded

Within the context of pension plans, an enterprise's pension liabilities or obligations, such as employee benefit obligations, are unfunded if they are not covered by any assets. Pension obligations may be wholly or partly funded by contributions paid into a separate fund of assets by employers, and in some cases employees.

no dotado

≠ dotado

▲ *funded and unfunded post-employment benefit obligations* obligaciones por prestaciones de jubilación dotadas y no dotadas ▲ *unfunded defined benefit plans* planes de prestación definida no dotados ▲ *wholly unfunded defined benefit obligations* obligaciones de prestación definida sin dotar completamente

⇛ overfunded, underfunded

unguaranteed residual value IAS/IFRS, UK

An unguaranteed residual value is the part of the residual value of a leased asset which has not been guaranteed in case of a realisation made by the lessor, or which has only been guaranteed by a party associated with the lessor.

valor residual no garantizado

▲ *any unguaranteed residual value accruing to the lessor* cualquier valor residual no garantizado que devenga al arrendatario ▲ *discount the unguaranteed residual value* descontar el valor residual no garantizado ▲ *estimated unguaranteed residual values* valores residuales no garantizados estimados ▲ *including any unguaranteed residual value* incluyendo cualquier valor residual no garantizado ▲ *the estimated unguaranteed residual value* el valor residual no garantizado estimado ▲ *the present value of the unguaranteed residual value* el valor actual del valor residual no garantizado ▲ *unguaranteed residual value at the balance sheet date* valor residual no garantizado a la fecha del balance

unhedged

= uncovered

If a financial risk or transaction is unhedged, it has not been protected or covered, e.g. by a derivative financial instrument.

no cubierto

= sin cubrir

▲ *an unhedged portfolio* una cartera no cubierta

uniform

Uniform means similar or identical in respect of a number of individual things or concepts.

uniforme

▲ *a uniform accounting treatment* un tratamiento contable uniforme ▲ *a uniform method* un método uniforme ▲ *adding together of items of a uniform nature* agrupamiento de partidas de una naturaleza uniforme ▲ *apply something in a uniform manner* aplicar algo de una forma uniforme ▲ *of uniform application* de aplicación uniforme ▲ *use uniform accounting policies for like transactions* utilizar principios contables uniformes para transacciones parecidas ▲ *with uniform contents* con contenidos uniformes

unit

A unit is a single item or part of something such as a unit of output, or a fixed amount or

quantity used applied as a standard, e.g. a monetary unit.
unidad
▲ *a fixed rate per unit of output* un tipo fijo por unidad de producción ▲ *allocate to each unit of production* asignar a cada unidad de producción ▲ *to issue notional units* emitir unidades nocionales ▲ *unit of account* unidad de cuenta
⇛ business unit, cost unit, currency unit, entity

unit contribution margin US
= contribution per unit, marginal income US, marginal revenue UK
The unit contribution margin is the additional income generated from the sale of one additional unit of output, calculated by deducting the variable costs per unit from the unit sales price.
ingreso marginal por unidad
▲ *a constant unit contribution margin* un ingreso marginal por unidad constante ▲ *a unit contribution margin of $200* un ingreso marginal por unidad de 200 dólares ▲ *a weighted average unit contribution margin* un ingreso marginal por unidad medio ponderado
⇛ contribution, contribution margin ratio, total contribution

unit cost
Unit costs are the costs of producing one item such as a product or service.
coste unitario
= coste por unidad
▲ *the calculation of unit costs* el cálculo de los costes unitarios

unit of account
= accounting unit
A unit of account is a measurement unit, typically monetary, used for the purpose of preparing accounts, calculating sums or making comparisons.
unidad de cuenta
▲ *adjustment of the equivalent of the European unit of account in national currency* ajuste del equivalente de la unidad de cuenta europea en moneda nacional ▲ *the European unit of account* la unidad de cuenta europea

unit of measurement
A unit of measurement is a fixed unit used for measuring something. Units of mesurements may be weight, number, time, length etc.
unidad de medida
= unidad de valoración
▲ *a monetary unit of measurement* una unidad de medida monetaria ▲ *the unit of measurement applied* la unidad de medida aplicada

unit trust UK
= collective investment fund US, investment fund, mutual fund US
≠ investment company UK, investment trust UK
A unit trust is an investment organisation that manages and reinvests funds contributed by the unit holders (investors) in a wide range of securities, in this way reducing risk. Unit trusts are open-ended funds, which means that investors may buy and sell units at all times.
fondo de inversión
▲ *a unit of a unit trust* una unidad de un fondo de inversión ▲ *a venture capital organisation, mutual fund, unit trust or similar entity* una organización de capital riesgo, fondo de inversión o entidad similar

uniting of interests IAS/IFRS
= merger accounting, pooling of interests IAS/IFRS, US
≠ acquisition accounting, purchase accounting
Uniting of interests is a combination of two companies arising from the issue of voting shares by the acquiring company in exchange for those of the acquired company so that all shareholders maintain their proportionate ownership in the combined company.
unificación de intereses
▲ *a uniting of interests of two equal parties* una unificación de intereses de dos partes iguales ▲ *classify a business combination as a uniting of interests* clasificar una combinación de negocios como una unificación de intereses ▲ *effect a uniting of interests* efectuar una unificación de intereses ▲ *establishment of a uniting of interests* establecimiento de una unificación de intereses ▲ *expenditure incurred in relation to a uniting of interests* gastos incurridos en relación con una unificación de intereses ▲ *the effects of a business*

combination that is a uniting of interests los efectos de una combinación de negocios que es una unificación de intereses ▲ *the period in which the uniting of interests occurs* el periodo en el que ocurre la unificación de intereses

uniting-of-interests method IAS/IFRS
= merger accounting method UK, merger method UK, pooling-of-interests method US
≠ acquisition method UK, purchase method IAS/IFRS, US
The uniting-of-interests method is a method of accounting for a business combination under which the combining enterprises are treated on an equal basis so that no enterprise can be identified as the acquirer. Under this method, no goodwill is recognised and the enterprises' financial statements for prior financial years are restated as if the enterprises had always been combined.
método de unificación de intereses
= método de fusión
≠ método de adquisición
▲ *apply the uniting-of-interests method* aplicar el método de unificación de intereses

units of production method
= machine-hour method, production-unit method, units-of-production method
The units of production method is a depreciation method under which the depreciable amount is calculated on the basis of the use of productive equipment such as machinery, i.e. the number of units produced. Under this method, the cost of a tangible asset is allocated over its useful life based on the estimated units-of-production capacity. The depreciable amount per unit is calculated by dividing the original cost less the residual value by the projected number of units of production. The depreciable amount will be higher in periods with a large volume of output than in periods with lower output.
NOTE The units of production method is also applied for amortisation of intangible assets, typically in connection with concession contracts.
método de unidades de producción
▲ *apply the units of production method* aplicar el método de unidades de producción ▲ *units of production method of depreciation* método de unidades de producción para amortización
SOURCE IAS 16, paragraph 36

unlisted
= unquoted
The term 'unlisted' is used about securities (i.e. companies) that are not listed for trading on a stock exchange or authorised market place.
no cotizada
▲ *an unlisted bond* un bono no cotizado ▲ *an unlisted company* una empresa no cotizada ▲ *an unlisted enterprise* una empresa no cotizada ▲ *an unlisted entity that regularly issues options or shares to employees* una entidad no cotizada que emite opciones o títulos regularmente para los empleados ▲ *an unlisted equity instrument* un instrumento de patrimonio no cotizado ▲ *an unlisted security* un título no cotizado ▲ *an unlisted share* una acción no cotizada ▲ *an unlisted unit of an investment association* una unidad de una asociación de inversión no cotizada ▲ *unlisted and newly listed entities* entidades no cotizadas y admitidas a cotización recientemente

unqualified audit report
≠ modified audit report
An unqualified audit report is expressed by the auditor when the financial statements give a true and fair view (UK), or present fairly, in all material respects (US), the financial position, operating results and cash flow of a particular enterprise in accordance with generally accepted accounting principles, and no further information, emphasis or matter or modification is required included in the audit report.
informe del editor sin salvedades
= informe del auditor sin reparos
≠ informe del auditor con salvedades
▲ *issue an unqualified audit report* emitir un informe del auditor sin salvedades

⇛ audit report, unmodified audit report

unquoted

= unlisted

The term 'unquoted' is used about securities (i.e. companies) that are not listed for trading on a stock exchange or authorised market place.

no cotizado

▲ *unquoted companies* compañías no cotizadas ▲ *unquoted debt securities* títulos de deuda no cotizados ▲ *unquoted entities* entidades no cotizadas ▲ *unquoted equity instruments* instrumentos de patrimonio no cotizados ▲ *unquoted public companies* sociedades anónimas no cotizadas ▲ *unquoted securities* títulos no cotizados ▲ *unquoted shares* acciones no cotizadas

unrealised

= unrealized US

≠ realised IAS/IFRS, UK, realized US

Unrealised means not actually carried out or completed, e.g. it refers to a gain or loss resulting from a change in value that has been recognised for accounting purposes on an asset, but where the gain or loss has not been realised by the legal disposal of that asset, whether or not cash has been received.

no realizado

= sin realizar

▲ *amortisation of unrealised gains and losses* amortización de pérdidas y ganancias no realizadas ▲ *an unrealised expense* un gasto no realizado ▲ *an unrealised foreign currency gain* una ganancia de divisa no realizada ▲ *an unrealised foreign currency loss* una pérdida de divisa no realizada ▲ *an unrealised gain* una ganancia no realizada ▲ *an unrealised increase in value* un aumento de valor no realizado ▲ *an unrealised intercompany profit* un beneficio entre empresas no realizado ▲ *an unrealised loss* una pérdida no realizada ▲ *an unrealised profit* un beneficio no realizado ▲ *an unrealised value adjustment of financial instruments* un ajuste de valor no realizado de los instrumentos financieros ▲ *unrealised capital gain on investments* ganancia de capital no realizada por inversiones ▲ *unrealised income* ingreso no realizado

unrealised gain UK, IAS/IFRS

= unrealized gain US

An unrealised gain is a gain recognised for accounting purposes because of a change in value on an asset, but which has not been realised by the legal disposal of that asset, whether or not cash has been received.

ganancia no realizada

▲ *recognise the unrealised gains directly in equity* reconocer la ganancia no realizada directamente en patrimonio neto ▲ *recognised but unrealised gains or losses on an asset* ganancias o pérdidas en un activo reconocidas pero no realizadas

unrealised loss UK, IAS/IFRS

= unrealized loss US

An unrealised loss is a loss recognised for accounting purposes because of a change in value on an asset, but which has not been realised by the legal disposal of that asset, whether or not cash has been received.

pérdida no realizada

= pérdida sin realizar

▲ *recognise the unrealised losses directly in equity* reconocer las pérdidas no realizadas directamente en el patrimonio neto ▲ *recognised but unrealised losses on an asset* pérdidas en un activo reconocidas pero no realizadas

unrealized US

= unrealised UK, IAS/IFRS

≠ realised IAS/IFRS, UK, realized US

Unrealized means not actually carried out or completed, e.g. referring to a gain or loss resulting from a change in value that has been recognized for accounting purposes on an asset, but where the gain or loss has not been realized by the legal disposal of that asset, whether or not cash has been received.

no realizado

= sin realizar

≠ realizado

▲ *amortization of unrealized gains and losses* amortización de pérdidas y ganancias no realizadas ▲ *an unrealized expense* un gasto no realizado ▲ *an un-*

realized foreign currency gain una ganancia en moneda extranjera no realizada ▲ *an unrealized foreign currency loss* una pérdida en moneda extranjera no realizada ▲ *an unrealized gain* una ganancia no realizada ▲ *an unrealized increase in value* una revalorización no realizada ▲ *an unrealized intercompany profit* un beneficio interempresarial no realizado ▲ *an unrealized loss* una pérdida no realizada ▲ *an unrealized profit* un beneficio no realizado ▲ *an unrealized value adjustment of financial instruments* un ajuste de valor de los instrumentos financieros no realizado ▲ *unrealized capital gain on investments* ganancia de capital en inversiones no realizada ▲ *unrealized income* ingreso no realizado

unrealized gain US
= unrealised gain IAS/IFRS, UK
An unrealized gain is a gain recognized for accounting purposes because of a change in value on an asset, but which has not been realized by the legal disposal of that asset, whether or not cash has been received.
ganancia no realizada
= ganancia sin realizar
▲ *recognize the unrealized gains directly in equity* reconocer las ganancias no realizadas directamente en el patrimonio neto ▲ *recognized but unrealized gains on an asset* ganancias en un activo reconocidas pero no realizadas

unrealized loss US
= unrealised loss
An unrealized loss is a loss recognized for accounting purposes because of a change in value on an asset, but which has not been realized by the legal disposal of that asset, whether or not cash has been received.
pérdida no realizada
= pérdida sin realizar
▲ *recognize the unrealized losses directly in equity* reconocer las pérdidas no realizadas directamente en el patrimonio neto ▲ *recognized but unrealized losses on an asset* pérdidas en un activo reconocidas pero no realizadas

unrecognised IAS/IFRS, UK
= unrecognized US
≠ recognised IAS/IFRS, UK, recognized US
Unrecognised means not included in any item of the financial statements.
no reconocido
= sin reconocer
▲ *a decrease in the value of the unrecognised deferred tax liability* un descenso en el valor del impuesto diferido no reconocido ▲ *an unrecognised firm commitment* un compromiso en firme no reconocido ▲ *an unrecognised receivable* un cuenta a cobrar no reconocida ▲ *the unrecognised share of losses of an associate* la parte de pérdidas de una filial no reconocida ▲ *unrecognised financial instruments* instrumentos financieros no reconocidos ▲ *unrecognised gains and losses* pérdidas y ganancias no reconocidas ▲ *unrecognised goodwill* fondo de comercio no reconocido ▲ *unrecognised increases in value* incrementos de valor no reconocidos ▲ *unrecognised liabilities* pasivos no reconocidos ▲ *unrecognised resources* recursos no reconocidos ▲ *unrecognised tax assets* activos fiscales no reconocidos ▲ *unrecognised transactions* transacciones no reconocidas

unrecognized US
= unrecognised UK, IAS/IFRS
≠ recognised IAS/IFRS, UK, recognized US
Unrecognized means not included as a separate item in the financial statements or in any item of the financial statements.
no reconocido
= sin reconocer
▲ *a decrease in the value of the unrecognized deferred tax liability* un descenso en el valor del impuesto diferido no reconocido ▲ *an unrecognized firm commitment* un compromiso en firme no reconocido ▲ *an unrecognized receivable* una cuenta a cobrar no reconocida ▲ *the unrecognized share of losses of an associate* la parte no reconocida de pérdidas de una asociada ▲ *unrecognized financial instruments* instrumentos financieros no reconocidos ▲ *unrecognized gains and losses* pérdidas y ga-

nancias no reconocidas ▲ *unrecognized goodwill* fondo de comercio no reconocido ▲ *unrecognized increases in value* incrementos en valor no reconocidos ▲ *unrecognized liabilities* pasivos no reconocidos ▲ *unrecognized resources* recursos no reconocidos ▲ *unrecognized tax assets* activos fiscales no reconocidos ▲ *unrecognized transactions* transacciones no reconocidas

unrecorded expense

An unrecorded expense is an expense that has not been recorded because of lack of an invoice for the expense. One example of an expense that is often unrecorded is a telephone bill.

gasto no registrado

= gasto no contabilizado

▲ *the amount of unrecorded expenses* la cantidad de gastos no registrados

unrecorded revenue

Unrecorded revenue refers to revenue that has not been recorded because of lack of a voucher for the revenue. One example of revenue that is often unrecorded is interest on receivables.

ingreso no registrado

= ingreso no contabilizado

▲ *adjustments for unrecorded revenue* ajustes por ingresos no registrados

unregulated

When an issue is not governed by rules, statutes or standards, it is unregulated.

no regulado

= sin regular

▲ *an unregulated market* un mercado no regulado ▲ *in unregulated areas* en áreas no reguladas

unresolved

When something is unresolved it has not been solved or determined. An unresolved problem or issue is subject to further discussion and no decision has been reached.

no resuelto

= sin resolver

▲ *unresolved uncertainty* incertidumbre no resuelta

unrestricted earnings US

= distributable reserve, revenue reserve UK

≠ capital reserve UK, non-distributable reserve, restricted surplus US, undistributable reserve

Unrestricted earnings are reserves representing transfers of profit from the profit and loss account that may be distributed to shareholders. Unrestricted earnings appear as an item in the balance sheet under equity.

beneficios no distribuidos

= beneficios pendientes de aplicación

▲ *companies with unrestricted earnings* compañías con beneficios no distribuidos ▲ *reinvestment of unrestricted earnings* reinversión de los beneficios no distribuidos

⇛ undistributable reserve

unsatisfactory

= disappointing, not satisfactory

Unsatisfactory means that something does not live up to expectations or does not meet requirements, needs or wishes, e.g. in relation to an enterprise's forecasts, outlooks or stock market announcements.

insatisfactorio

▲ *an unsatisfactory financial year* un año financiero insatisfactorio ▲ *an unsatisfactory result* un resultado insatisfactorio ▲ *unsatisfactory operating efficiency* eficiencia operativa insatisfactoria ▲ *unsatisfactory profitability* rentabilidad insatisfactoria

untaxed

Untaxed means that an amount or income has not been subject to tax.

no tributable

▲ *an untaxed contingency fund* un fondo de contingencia no tributable ▲ *deferred tax related to untaxed contingency funds* impuesto diferido relacionado con fondos de contingencia no tributables

unused capacity

= excess capacity

Unused capacity constitutes the difference between the capacity available and the capacity required to carry out the production necessary for the period in question.

capacidad no utilizada

= capacidad excedente

▲ *a build-up of unused capacity* una acumulación de capacidad no utilizada ▲ *a decrease in unused capacity* un descenso en la capacidad no utilizada ▲ *an increase in unused capacity* un aumento en la capacidad no utilizada ▲ *reduce unused capacity by 10%* reducir la capacidad no utilizada en un 10% ▲ *substantial unused capacity* capacidad sustancial no utilizada

unusual circumstances

Unusual circumstances are non-recurring, special events or transactions occurred during the accounting period under review, which should be disclosed as separate line items in the financial statements. Examples are accounting policy changes, acquisitions or disposals of assets or restructuring charges.

circunstancias inusuales

▲ *description of unusual circumstances* descripción de las circunstancias inusuales ▲ *disclosure of unusual circumstances* publicación de las circunstancias inusuales ▲ *in unusual circumstances* en circunstancias inusuales

⇛ unusual item

unusual item

= non-recurring item, one-off item, one-time item

Unusual items are items of a non-recurring and abnormal nature that concern transactions or events that are unrelated to the ordinary activities of an enterprise. Examples are acquisitions and disposals of fixed assets that - being of a one-time nature - only affect the profit for the accounting period under review.

partida no usual

▲ *recognise and disclose unusual items on the basis of materiality* reconocer y publicar las partidas no usuales en base a su materialidad

⇛ exceptional item, extraordinary item, non-recurring item

unutilised

Unutilised means that something is not used at all or not put to its full use.

no utilizado

= sin utilizar

▲ *an unutilised loss* una pérdida no utilizada

update[1] *noun*

= revision

An update is the change of data to include new and most recent information.

actualización

= puesta al día, revisión

▲ *update of internal compliance procedures* actualización de los procedimientos de comprobación internos

update[2] *verb*

= revise

To update is to add something e.g. to an account, a report or computer software so that it includes new data and the most recent information.

actualizar

= poner al día, revisar

▲ *update annually* actualizar anualmente ▲ *update disclosures* actualizar las publicaciones ▲ *update estimates in the light of experience* revisar las estimaciones a la luz de la evidencia ▲ *update group reporting packages* actualizar los protocolos informativos del grupo ▲ *update on an ongoing basis* actualizar según un método continuo ▲ *update the amounts disclosed for the investments as at the balance sheet date* actualizar las cantidades divulgadas para las inversiones a la fecha del balance ▲ *update the fair value of the assets* actualizar el valor razonable de los activos

upward adjustment

An upward adjustment is an increase of the value of something as a result of changes in events or circumstances.

ajuste al alza

▲ *an upward adjustment of expectations* un ajuste al alza en las expectativas ▲ *an upward adjustment of the expectations for the net profit for the year* un ajuste al alza en las expectativas del beneficio neto del año

Urgent Issues Task Force

= UITF

The Urgent Issues Task Force (UITF) is a sub-committee of the Accounting Standards Board (ASB) and part of the UK accounting standard setting organisation set up in 1990. The UITF assists the ASB in urgent matters where an accounting standard exists, but where unsatisfactory or conflicting interpretations have developed. The UITF operates by seeking a consensus as to the accounting treatment to be adopted.

Urgent Issues Task Force
= Comité Permanente para Asuntos Urgentes
▲ *the members of the Urgent Issues Task Force* los miembros de la Urgent Issues Task Force
⇛ Accounting Standards Board

usage variance
= efficiency variance, quantity variance
Usage variance is the difference between the actual quantity used and the budgeted quantity which was expected to be used.

desviación en cantidad
= variación en cantidad
▲ *the calculation of the usage variance* el cálculo de la desviación en cantidad ▲ *the total usage variance* la desviación en cantidad total

use
= apply
To use something means to employ it for a particular purpose, often in order to achieve something.

utilizar
▲ *use a consistent accounting policy* utilizar una política contable consistente ▲ *use property, plant and equipment during more than one period* utilizar edificios, instalaciones y equipos durante más de un periodo ▲ *use the contractual cash flows over the full contractual term of the financial instrument* utilizar los flujos de efectivo contractuales durante el periodo contractual completo del instrumento financiero ▲ *use the land as owner-occupied property* utilizar el terreno como propiedad ocupada por el propietario ▲ *use the revaluation model* utilizar el modelo de revalorización

use of capital
The use of capital expresses an enterprise's application of invested capital, i.e. the assets and resources of the enterprise acquired for the capital provided by owners and creditors (equity and liabilities). The balance sheet shows the assets, equity and liabilities of the enterprise at the last day of the accounting period.

uso de capital
▲ *an optimal use of capital* un uso de capital óptimo ▲ *control of the use of capital* control del uso de capital ▲ *optimise the use of capital* optimizar el uso de capital
⇛ balance sheet, invested capital

useful life
= useful economic life
Useful life is the period of an asset's economic life during which the asset is expected to be used by an enterprise. Useful life may also be expressed in terms of production or service units.

vida útil
▲ *a limited useful life* una vida útil limitada ▲ *allocation of the depreciable amounts of the assets on a systematic basis over their useful lives* asignación de las cantidades amortizables de los activos de forma sistemática durante sus vidas útiles ▲ *amortisation of an intangible asset with a finite useful life* amortización de un activo intangible con una vida útil finita ▲ *an asset with a long remaining useful life* un activo con una vida útil restante larga ▲ *an unlimited useful life* una vida útil ilimitada ▲ *intangible assets with indefinite useful lives* activos intangibles con vidas útiles indefinidas ▲ *measure the recoverable amount of an intangible asset with an indefinite useful life* medir la cantidad recuperable de un activo intangible con una vida útil indefinida ▲ *the best estimate of the website's useful life* la mejor estimación de la vida útil de la página web ▲ *the change in the useful life assessment from indefinite to finite* el cambio en la estimación de la vida útil de indefinida a limitada ▲ *the determination of useful life for different intangible assets* una determinación de la vida útil de los diferentes activos intangibles ▲ *the expected useful life of the asset* la vida útil esperada del activo
⇛ economic life

usual
When something is usual, it takes place or is done on a regular basis in specific, similar situations.

usual

▲ *a usual term* un término usual

utilisation UK, IAS/IFRS

= utilization US

Utilisation is the act of using something in an effective way or benefiting from something.

utilización

▲ *normal levels of labour, efficiency and capacity utilisation* niveles normales de trabajo, eficiencia y utilización de la capacidad

utilization US

= utilisation UK, IAS/IFRS

Utilization is the act of using something in an effective way or benefiting from something.

utilización

▲ *normal levels of labour and capacity utilization* niveles normales de trabajo, eficiencia y utilización de la capacidad

V

vacation pay US

Vacation pay is a sum of money that is paid to employees while they are on holiday.

paga de vacaciones

= paga por vacaciones

▲ *adjustment of vacation pay payable* ajuste de la paga de vacaciones a pagar ▲ *calculated vacation pay* paga de vacaciones calculada ▲ *payable vacation pay* paga de vacaciones a pagar ▲ *the employer's obligation to pay vacation pay* la obligación del empleador de pagar la paga de vacaciones

vacation pay obligation US

A vacation pay obligation is an employer's obligation to pay vacation pay to the employees in the enterprise.

obligación por paga de vacaciones

= obligación de pagar las vacaciones, obligación de paga de vacaciones

▲ *assess the vacation pay obligation* evaluar la obligación por paga de vacaciones ▲ *provision for vacation pay obligations* provisión para obligaciones por paga de vacaciones

valuable

To be valuable means to have great importance or monetary value.

valioso

▲ *a valuable element* un elemento valioso ▲ *a valuable tool* una herramienta valiosa ▲ *provide a valuable additional perspective* ofrecer una perspectiva adicional valiosa ▲ *sufficiently valuable* suficientemente valioso ▲ *valuable knowledge* conocimiento valioso

valuation UK

= appraisal, measurement

Valuation is the process of measuring and determining the value of an asset, e.g. an enterprise, property or other investment.

valoración

= medición

▲ *a valuation technique* una técnica de valoración ▲ *determine the valuation implications of expected early exercise of options* determinar las implicaciones de la valoración del ejercicio anticipado esperado de opciones ▲ *generally accepted valuation methodologies for pricing financial instruments* metodologías de valoración generalmente aceptadas para calcular el precio de los instrumentos financieros ▲ *independent valuation* valoración independiente ▲ *valuation methods* métodos de valoración

valuation method

= method of valuation

A valuation method is a method that specifies the procedure for measuring and determining the value of an asset or liability.

método de valoración

= método de medición

▲ *accrued benefit valuation method* método de valoración del beneficio devengado

valuation model

A valuation model is a method of calculation applied for the measurement of assets or enterprises in general. The model provides a number of assumptions based on which it is possible to measure the value of a particular asset. The Black-Scholes Option Pricing formula is an example of a valuation model for options.

modelo de valoración

= modelo de medición

▲ *generally accepted valuation models* modelos de valoración generalmente aceptados ▲ *value in use calculated using generally accepted valuation models and techniques* valor en uso calculado utilizando modelos y técnicas de valoración generalmente aceptados

⇛ Black-Scholes formula

valuation report

A valuation report is a written report containing the actual valuation of a specified asset usually made by one or more independent valuation experts.

informe de valoración

= informe de medición

▲ *a valuation report on a merger plan* un informe de valoración de un plan de fusión ▲ *a valuation report on non-cash contributions* un informe de valoración de las contribuciones no monetarias ▲ *prepare a valuation report* preparar un informe de valoración

valuation technique

A valuation technique is a method or process of assessing the value of something.

técnica de valoración

= técnica de medición

▲ *a valuation technique commonly used by market participants* una técnica de valoración utilizada frecuentemente por los participantes del mercado ▲ *a valuation technique that makes maximum use of market inputs* una técnica de valoración que hace el uso máximo de los inputs del mercado ▲ *a valuation technique whose variables include only data from observable markets* una técnica de valoración cuyas variables sólo incluye datos procedentes de mercados controlables ▲ *establish fair value by using a valuation technique* establecer el valor razonable utilizando una técnica de valoración

value

Value is a term used to express the (often monetary) worth of something.

valor

▲ *a drop in value* una caída en el valor ▲ *a negative value* un valor negativo ▲ *a positive value* un valor positivo ▲ *an increase in value* un aumento en el valor ▲ *provisional values* valores provisionales

value added

Value added is the value that is added to a product by an enterprise when products pass through the various stages in the enterprise's production process, constituting the difference between inputs and outputs.

valor añadido

▲ *maximisation of value added* maximización del valor añadido ▲ *the share of the employees in value added* la proporción de los empleados en el valor añadido ▲ *value added statements* estados de valor añadido

value added cost

Value added costs are costs that contribute to the increase of the value, i.e. performance, of a product and make the product preferable to another product seen from a customer's point of view.

coste valor añadido

= coste del valor añadido, coste de valor añadido

▲ *calculate the value added cost* calcular el coste valor añadido ▲ *value added cost per unit of output* coste valor añadido por unidad de producción

value added tax UK

= VAT

Value added tax is a consumption tax that is levied on the value of goods or services when sold. It is often abbreviated VAT.

impuesto sobre el valor añadido

= IVA

▲ *a common system of value added tax* un sistema común del impuesto sobre el valor añadido ▲ *evasion of value added tax* evasión del impuesto sobre el valor añadido ▲ *reduced rates of value added tax* tipos reducidos del impuesto sobre el valor añadido

⇛ input tax, output tax, sales tax, VAT accounts

value adjustment

Value adjustments are changes or corrections to the carrying amount of assets and liabilities in the financial statements to give a true and fair view of their value. Value adjustments arise because of differences between the cost and the fair value or a value previously recognised, e.g. because of depreciation charges, changes in exchange rates or in securities prices.

ajuste de valor

▲ *reversal of value adjustment* reversión del ajuste de valor ▲ *value adjustment for the financial year* ajuste de valor para el año financiero ▲ *value adjustment of assets and liabilities* ajuste de valor de activos y pasivos ▲ *value adjustment of derivatives* ajuste de valor de derivados ▲ *value adjustment of financial assets and liabilities* ajuste de valor de activos y pasivos financieros ▲ *value adjustment of hedging instruments* ajuste de valor de instrumentos de cobertura ▲ *value adjustment of hedging transactions* ajuste de valor de transacciones de cobertura ▲ *value adjustment of investment property* ajuste de valor de inversiones ▲ *value adjustment of revalued property, plant and equipment* ajuste de valor de edificios instalaciones y equipos revalorizados ▲ *value adjustment of share options* ajuste de valor de opciones sobre acciones ▲ *value adjustment on an ongoing basis* ajuste de valor de un modo constante ▲ *value adjustment to fair value* ajuste de valor a valor real

value at the beginning of the year

The value at the beginning of the year is the value of asset and liability items in the balance sheet at the start of an accounting year.

valor al inicio del año

= valor al comienzo del año, valor al principio del año

▲ *adjustment of values at the beginning of the year* ajuste de valores al inicio del año

value chain UK, US

A value chain constitutes the business activities or functions that –seen from the end user's point of view– add value to the product or service produced by an entity.

cadena de valor

▲ *value chain analysis* análisis de la cadena de valor ▲ *value chain management* gestión de la cadena de valor

value creation

Value creation refers to processes, actions or activities that create value for an enterprise whether carried out by the enterprise itself or by another party. The value created may consist in e.g. improved products, improved communication or satisfied customers or employees. These factors may eventually lead to a decrease in costs or to a larger profit.

creación de valor

▲ *economic value creation* creación de valor económico ▲ *ensure value creation* asegurar la creación de valor ▲ *future value creation* creación de valor futuro ▲ *long-term value creation* creación de valor a largo plazo ▲ *short-term value creation* creación de valor a corto plazo ▲ *the enterprise's communication of value creation* la comunicación de la empresa de creación de valor ▲ *value creation for customers* creación de valor para los clientes ▲ *value creation for employees* creación de valor para los empleados ▲ *value creation for shareholders* creación de valor para los accionistas ▲ *value creation for stakeholders* creación de valor para los stakeholders

value engineering

Value engineering is an analysis of products, materials, design and production processes to select the lowest overall costs necessary to achieve the desired function, i.e. performance, and eliminate costs that do not add any value, while ensuring customer satisfaction.

ingeniería de valor

▲ *commission a value engineering study* encargar un estudio de ingeniería de valor ▲ *to use value engineering* para usar la ingeniería de valor

value in use UK, IAS/IFRS

= value-in-use US, VIU IAS/IFRS, UK

Value in use is the current value of an asset seen as the discounted present value of expected cash inflows from continuing use and the proceeds from the ultimate disposal of the asset. For a liability, the value in use is the discounted present value of expected cash outflows during the life of the liability.

valor en uso

▲ *a decrease in the value in use* un descenso en el valor en uso ▲ *a future restructuring on a value in use calculation* una reestructuración futura en un cálculo del valor en uso ▲ *calculate a value in use* calcular un valor en uso ▲ *determination of the value in use of the investment* determinar el valor en uso de la inversión ▲ *determine a value in use* determinar un valor en uso ▲ *estimate the value in use* estimar el valor en uso ▲ *measure at value in use* medir a valor en uso ▲ *the effect of a future res-*

tructuring on a value in use calculation el efecto de una reestructuración futura sobre un valor en uso ▲ *the relevant value in use for the asset or liability* el valor en uso relevante para el activo o pasivo ▲ *the value in use of goodwill* el valor en uso del fondo de comercio
SOURCE IFRS 5, Appendix A

value of claims
When an enterprise satisfies claims for damages it incurs an expense, i.e. it has to pay the value of claims. Sometimes this risk is transferred to an insurance company which therefore has to satisfy the claims.
valor de reclamaciones
▲ *60% of the total value of claims* 60% del valor total de reclamaciones ▲ *the estimate of the value of claims* la estimación del valor de las reclamaciones ▲ *the expected value of claims* el valor esperado de las reclamaciones

value-added cost
→ value added cost

value-adding
A process, an activity, a transaction or an asset is value-adding when it creates value for the enterprise. Value-adding is achieved e.g. by improved communications and products, through satisfied customers and eventually a positive cash flow or less costs.
que añade valor
= que genera valor
▲ *value-adding activities* actividades que añaden valor ▲ *value-adding asset management* gestión del activo que añade valor ▲ *value-adding factors* factores que añaden valor ▲ *value-adding management* gestión que añade valor ▲ *value-adding reporting* presentación de información que añade valor

value-based
Accounting is value-based when the valuation builds on a current and objective value, i.e. market value, fair value or the present value of future cash flows rather than on historical cost. Management is value-based when the focus is on value creation, i.e. maximum shareholder value.
basado en valor
= basado en el valor
▲ *value-based pricing* fijar el precio basado en el valor
⇛ transaction-based

value-based accounting
Value-based accounting implies that measurements of financial data are based on values rather than cost. An asset may e.g. be measured at fair value, value in use or net realisable value rather than at the costs incurred on acquisition or production of that asset.
contabilidad basada en el valor
▲ *change to value-based accounting* cambiar a la contabilidad basada en el valor ▲ *use value-based accounting* utilizar la contabilidad basada en el valor
⇛ transaction-based financial statements

value-based financial reporting
Value-based financial reporting focuses on the balance sheet where profit or loss for the accounting period appears as an increase or decrease in equity (net assets) as seen from the beginning to the end of the period. This approach is based on the accounting equation that equity equals assets less liabilities.
información financiera basada en el valor
▲ *a shift away from transaction-based towards value-based financial reporting* un cambio desde la información financiera basada en la transacción a la información financiera basada en el valor
⇛ transaction-based financial statements, value-based financial statements

value-based financial statements
US, IAS/IFRS
The value-based financial statements aim at measuring the enterprise's assets and liabilities at the balance sheet date at fair value rather than using the historical cost convention.
estados financieros basados en el valor
▲ *prepare value-based financial statements* preparar los estados financieros basados en el valor
⇛ transaction-based financial statements

value-in-use US
= value in use UK, IAS/IFRS

Value-in-use is the current value of an asset seen as the discounted present value of expected cash inflows from continuing use and the proceeds from the ultimate disposal of the asset. For a liability, the value-in-use is the discounted present value of expected cash outflows during the life of the liability.
valor en uso
▲ *a decrease in the value-in-use* un descenso en el valor en uso ▲ *a future restructuring on a value-in-use calculation* una reestructuración futura en un cálculo del valor en uso ▲ *calculate a value-in-use* calcular un valor en uso ▲ *determination of the value-in-use of the investment* determinación del valor en uso de la inversión ▲ *determine a value-in-use* determinar un valor en uso ▲ *estimate the value-in-use* estimar el valor en uso ▲ *measure at value-in-use* medir a valor en uso ▲ *the relevant value-in-use for the asset or liability* el valor en uso relevante para el activo o pasivo ▲ *the value-in-use of goodwill* el valor en uso del fondo de comercio

valuer
A valuer is an external and independent person who calculates the worth of something, e.g. assets and liabilities.
valorador
▲ *a professionally qualified valuer* un valorador cualificado profesionalmente ▲ *a valuation made by an independent valuer* una valoración realizada por un valorador independiente ▲ *an external valuer* un valorador externo ▲ *an independent valuer* un valorador independiente ▲ *an independent valuer* un valorador independiente ▲ *an independent valuer who holds a recognised and relevant professional qualification* un valorador independiente que ostenta una cualificación profesional reconocida y relevante ▲ *obtain the assistance of an external valuer* obtener la ayuda de un valorador externo ▲ *use an external valuer* utilizar un valorador externo

variability
Variability refers to the nature or state of something that may change or of which the level is not uniform due to changes in other factors. For example, the variability of costs denotes that they may vary in relation to e.g. production.
variabilidad
▲ *classification of expenses by nature, function or variability* clasificación de los gastos por naturaleza, función o variabilidad ▲ *general statements about the variability of cash flows* estados generales sobre la variabilidad de los flujos de efectivo ▲ *the variability in the present value of the future net cash flows* la variabilidad en el valor actual de los flujos de efectivo netos futuros ▲ *the variability in the range of reasonable fair value estimates* la variabilidad en la selección de las estimaciones a valor razonable posibles ▲ *the variability of expenses* la variabilidad de los gastos

variable[1] *noun*
A variable is a parameter that is likely to change.
variable
▲ *a demographic variable* una variable demográfica ▲ *a financial variable* una variable financiera ▲ *a non-financial variable* una variable no financiera ▲ *a valid statistical relationship between the two variables* una relación estadística válida entre las dos variables ▲ *an underlying variable* una variable subyacente ▲ *immeasurable variables* variables no medibles ▲ *the sensitivity of profit or loss and equity to changes in variables that have a material effect on them* la sensibilidad del resultado y el patrimonio neto a los cambios en las variables que tienen efecto material sobre ellos

variable[2] *adjective*
When something is variable it is frequently changing in e.g. size, quantity or amount, and is not stable over a period of time.
variable
▲ *a debt instrument with a variable interest rate* un instrumento de deuda con un tipo de interés variable ▲ *a variable payment* un pago variable ▲ *receive a variable number of the entity's own equity instruments* recibir un número variable de

los instrumentos de patrimonio propios de la entidad ▲ *the variable interest rate on an interest-bearing asset or liability* el tipo de interés variable de un activo o pasivo que devengan interés ▲ *variable production overheads that are incurred in converting materials into finished goods* costes indirectos de producción variables en los que se incurren al convertir los materiales en productos terminados

variable budget
= flexible budget
A variable budget is a budget that allows for continuous adjustments depending on the actual cost-driver activities of an enterprise such as the volume of sales or production.
presupuesto variable
▲ *prepare a variable budget* preparar un presupuesto variable

variable cost
≠ fixed cost
A variable cost is a cost that varies in direct proportion to the measure of activity and the changes in the cost-driver level.
coste variable
▲ *negligible variable costs* costes variables insignificantes ▲ *the total variable costs* los costes variables totales
⇛ fixed cost

variable cost percentage US
The variable cost percentage is calculated as total variable costs divided by total sales. This percentage is used by e.g. enterprises selling multiple products, where no single unit prices and unit variable costs are available.
porcentaje de coste variable
▲ *calculate the variable cost percentage* calcular el porcentaje de coste variable ▲ *determine the variable cost percentage* determinar el porcentaje de coste variable

variable cost ratio UK
The variable cost ratio is the total of the variable costs for a period of an enterprise divided by sales, i.e. the variable cost percentage calculated as a ratio.
ratio del coste variable sobre ventas
▲ *calculate the variable cost ratio* calcular la ratio del coste variable sobre ventas
⇛ contribution margin, contribution ratio, variable cost percentage

variable costing
= direct costing
Variable costing is a method for fixing the value of the inventory of an enterprise, which is based on recognition of all direct production costs and variable indirect production costs. The fixed indirect production costs are not included as part of the inventory value, but are considered as period costs.
método del coste variable
= direct costing
▲ *use variable costing* utilizar el método del coste variable ▲ *variable costing profit or loss* resultados del método del coste variable
⇛ full costing

variable overhead efficiency variance
The variable overhead efficiency variance measures how efficiently the cost-allocation base has been applied.
desviación de la eficiencia en la asignación de costes indirectos variables
▲ *recognise the variable overhead efficiency variance as an adjustment of income* reconocer la desviación de la eficiencia en la asignación de costes indirectos variables como un ajuste de ingresos

variable overhead flexible-budget variance
The difference between the actual variable overhead costs incurred and the amount of flexible-budget variable overhead costs is referred to as the variable overhead flexible-budget variance.
desviación en el presupuesto flexible de costes indirectos variables
▲ *calculate the variable overhead flexible-budget variance* calcular la desviación en el presupuesto flexible de costes indirectos variables
⇛ variable overhead spending variance

variable overhead spending variance
The difference between the actual variable overhead amount

incurred and the budgeted variable overhead amount for the actual quantity of output units produced (the cost driver) is referred to as the variable overhead spending variance.

desviación en el gasto de costes indirectos variables

▲ *recognise the variable overhead spending variance as an adjustment of income* reconocer la desviación en el gasto de costes indirectos variables como un ajuste de ingresos

⇛ variable overhead flexible-budget variance

variable production overhead

Variable production overheads are the indirect production costs that change with output, i.e. the volume of activity and different levels of production. Examples are indirect labour and materials.

coste indirecto variable de producción

▲ *recognise variable production overheads* reconocer los costes indirectos variables de producción ▲ *systematic allocation of variable production overheads* asignación sistemática de los costes indirectos variables de producción ▲ *the variable production overheads incurred* los costes indirectos variables de producción incurridos

⇛ fixed production overhead

variable-cost percentage US, UK

→ variable cost percentage

variable-cost percentage

= variable-cost ratio

The variable-cost percentage is a financial ratio calculated by dividing total variable costs by turnover.

porcetaje de costes variables

▲ *calculate the variable-cost percentage* calcular el porcentaje de costes variables ▲ *determine the variable-cost percentage* determinar el porcentaje de costes variables

variable-cost ratio US

→ variable cost ratio

variable-cost ratio

= variable-cost percentage

The variable-cost ratio is a financial ratio calculated by dividing total variable costs by turnover.

ratio de costes variables

▲ *calculate the variable-cost ratio* calcular el ratio de los costes variables ▲ *determine the variable-cost ratio* determinar el ratio de costes variables

variance

Variance is the difference between budgeted, pre-calculated or standard cost and the actual cost.

desviación

▲ *a significant variance* una desviación significativa ▲ *an insignificant variance* una desviación insignificante

variance analysis

A variance analysis is an analysis of the differences between planned and realised data.

análisis de la desviación

= análisis de la varianza

▲ *carry out a variance analysis* llevar a cabo un análisis de la varianza ▲ *quarterly variance analysis* análisis de la desviación trimestral

various

Various used about something means that it exists in a number of different varieties.

variado

= diverso

▲ *financial liabilities maturing within various future time periods* pasivos financieros que vencen en diversos periodos temporales futuros ▲ *incur various costs in issuing own equity instruments* incurrir en costes diversos al emitir instrumentos de patrimonio propios ▲ *the effects of an entity's various activities* los efectos de las actividades variadas de una entidad ▲ *the probabilities of the various outcomes* las probabilidades de las salidas variadas ▲ *the various estimates* las diversas estimaciones ▲ *various products* productos variados

⇛ sundry

VAT UK

= value added tax

VAT is the abbreviation of value added tax, which is a consumption tax that is levied on the value of goods or services when sold.

IVA

= impuesto sobre valor añadido, impuesto sobre el valor añadido

▲ *ex VAT* sin IVA ▲ *inc. VAT* IVA incluido ▲ *input VAT* IVA soportado ▲ *joint registration of VAT* registro conjunto del IVA

▲ *output VAT* IVA repercutido ▲ *state amounts ex VAT* indicar cantidades sin IVA ▲ *the time for payment of VAT* el plazo para el pago del IVA ▲ *VAT and other taxes payable* IVA y otros impuestos a pagar ▲ *without VAT* sin IVA
⇛ input tax, output tax, sales tax

VAT accounts UK
VAT accounts constitute a statement of value added tax payable or receivable on the sale of goods and services with deduction of any VAT paid relating to direct or indirect costs and expenses incurred in the business operations.
cuentas del IVA
= cuentas de IVA
▲ *prepare VAT accounts* preparar las cuentas del IVA

vendor
A vendor is someone who sells something, especially large things and immovable property.
vendedor
▲ *a vendor in a business combination* un vendedor en una combinación de negocios ▲ *the vendor of the land* el vendedor del terreno

venture
= joint venture
'Venture' is an abbreviation of 'joint venture'. A venture is a strategic contractual agreement between two or more enterprises to jointly undertake specified economic activities. The enterprises jointly control the activities and share risks, profits and losses. A venture is typically a short-term relationship relating to one purpose, but it may also be a long-term cooperation or even established as a separate legal entity (jointly controlled enterprise).
joint venture
= negocio conjunto
▲ *a venture capital organisation* una joint venture

venture capital
= risk capital
Venture capital refers to capital invested in a start-up or expanding enterprise by an outside party. On the one hand, such investments are usually very risky, but on the other, the investor may get high returns and may sometimes even take part in the management of the enterprise.
capital riesgo
▲ *a venture capital organisation* una organización de capital riesgo ▲ *provide venture capital* ofrecer capital riesgo

venturer
A venturer refers to one of the enterprises in a joint venture, i.e. a venture party.
participante en un negocio conjunto
= venturer
▲ *a contract between the venturers* un contrato entre los participantes en un negocio conjunto ▲ *a venturer in a jointly controlled entity* un participante en un negocio conjunto en una entidad controlada conjuntamente ▲ *a venturer's share of each of the assets* una participación del participante en un negocio conjunto en cada uno de los activos ▲ *capital contributions by the venturers* aportaciones de capital de los participantes en un negocio conjunto ▲ *change in the venturer's share of net assets of the jointly controlled entity* cambio en la participación patrimonial del participante de la entidad controlada conjuntamente en un negocio conjunto ▲ *consolidated financial statements of the venturer* estados financieros consolidados del participante en un negocio conjunto ▲ *non-monetary contributions by venturers* aportaciones no monetarias de los participantes en un negocio conjunto ▲ *the venturer's debt or equity instruments* los instrumentos de deuda o patrimonio del participante en un negocio conjunto ▲ *the venturer's interest in the jointly controlled entity* la inversión del participante en un negocio conjunto en la entidad controlada conjuntamente ▲ *the voting rights of the venturers* los derechos de voto de los participantes en un negocio conjunto ▲ *transfer funds to the venturer* transferir fondos al participante en un negocio conjunto
⇛ joint control, joint venture, jointly controlled enterprise

verifiability
= objectivity
Verifiability is the accounting concept and requirement that

the contents of financial reports are objective and can be checked against independent measures and sources of information.

verificabilidad

▲ *exact verifiability* verificabilidad exacta ▲ *verifiability in the financial statements* verificabilidad en los estados financieros

⇛ objectivity, reliability

verification

Verification is the confirmation by objective examination of the accuracy of something previously reported.

verificación

▲ *a verification of statements* una verificación de estados

verify

To verify means to confirm or substantiate the accuracy of something.

verificar

▲ *verify invoice calculations* verificar los cálculos de la factura ▲ *verify the accounting data* verificar los datos contables

vertical format

= narrative form US, report form

≠ account form, horizontal format

The vertical format is a presentation form of a financial statement in which the debits and credits are shown in one column one above the other. The profit and loss account is typically presented in the vertical format, with sales or turnover as the top line and profit or loss for the period as the bottom line.

formato vertical

≠ formato horizontal

▲ *balance sheet in vertical format* balance en formato vertical ▲ *present accounts in vertical format* presentar las cuentas en formato vertical

vertical group

≠ horizontal group

A group consisting of enterprises involved in different stages of the production or distribution process of a particular product is called a vertical group.

grupo vertical

≠ grupo horizontal

▲ *a vertical group of companies* un grupo vertical de empresas ▲ *form a new vertical group* formar un grupo vertical ▲ *the formation of a vertical group* la formación de un grupo vertical

vest IAS/IFRS, UK, US

When a fixed right or entitlement to receive compensation, benefits, equity instruments such as share options, or other assets, vests, it accrues to or has been earned by somebody, typically subject to fulfilment of certain conditions such as completion of a defined period of service or meeting certain performance targets. Examples of assets that vest are employee benefits, which vest on retirement or employee share options, which vest, thereby becoming exercisable.

consolidar un derecho

= tener un derecho irrevocable

▲ *an estimate of the number of equity instruments expected to vest* una estimación del número de instrumentos de patrimonio esperados para consolidar un derecho ▲ *repurchase vested equity instruments* recompra de los instrumentos de patrimonio que tienen un derecho irrevocable ▲ *the best available estimate of the number of equity instruments expected to vest* la mejor estimación disponible del número de instrumentos de patrimonio que se espera al consolidar un derecho ▲ *the date when the modified equity instruments vest* la fecha en la que los instrumentos de patrimonio modificados tienen un derecho irrevocable ▲ *the number of equity instruments that vest* el número de instrumentos de patrimonio que tienen un derecho irrevocable ▲ *vest immediately* consolidar un derecho de forma inmediata

SOURCE IFRS 2, Appendix A

vested employee benefit

Vested employee benefits are future or present employee benefits, such as pension benefits, that are not conditional on the employee remaining in employment.

beneficios irrevocables de los empleados

NOTE Always plural in Spanish accounting texts.

▲ *unused vested employee benefits* beneficios irrevocables de los empleados sin usar

vesting

For an employee, vesting means to become eligible or entitled to receive pension benefits or share-based payments after a period of service. At the time when vesting takes place, the pension has been vested.

irrevocabilidad del derecho

= consolidación del derecho

▲ *an acceleration of vesting* una aceleración de la consolidación del derecho ▲ *specified performance conditions attaching to vesting* condiciones de productividad especificadas unidas a la consolidación del derecho ▲ *the target share price upon which vesting is conditioned* el precio objetivo de la acción sobre el que se condiciona la irrevocabilidad del derecho

vesting condition

Vesting conditions are the conditions –typically relating to defined performance targets or periods of service– that must be satisfied according to an equity compensation plan in order for an employee to earn the right to receive cash or obtain shares equating to the agreed amount.

condición para la irrevocabilidad del derecho

= condición para la consolidación del derecho

▲ *failure to satisfy a vesting condition* no satisfacer una condición para la irrevocabilidad del derecho ▲ *market vesting conditions* condiciones del mercado para la irrevocabilidad del derecho ▲ *modify the vesting conditions in a way that is beneficial to the employee* modificar las condiciones para la irrevocabilidad del derecho de forma que sea beneficioso para el empleado ▲ *non-market vesting conditions* condiciones para la irrevocabilidad del derecho diferentes a las del mercado ▲ *provided the specified vesting conditions, if any, are met* si, y sólo si, se cumplen las condiciones para la irrevocabilidad del derecho ▲ *the implications of vesting conditions* las implicaciones de las condiciones para la irrevocabilidad del derecho ▲ *treatment of vesting conditions* tratamiento de las condiciones para la irrevocabilidad del derecho ▲ *vesting conditions that are excluded from the measurement of fair value* las condiciones para la irrevocabilidad del derecho que se excluyen de la medición a valor razonable

SOURCE IFRS 2, Appendix A

⇛ equity compensation plan, non-vesting condition

vesting date

The vesting date is the date when the right to pension benefits or equity compensation can be exercised.

fecha para la irrevocabilidad del derecho

= fecha para la consolidación del derecho

▲ *after vesting date* después de la fecha para la irrevocabilidad del derecho ▲ *on vesting date* en la fecha para la irrevocabilidad del derecho ▲ *subsequent adjustment to total equity after vesting date* ajuste subsiguiente al patrimonio neto total después de la fecha para la irrevocabilidad del derecho ▲ *the period between vesting date and the end of the option's life* el periodo entre la fecha para la irrevocabilidad del derecho y el final de la vida de la opción

vesting period

The vesting period is the period of time before shares are owned unconditionally by an employee in an employee stock option plan. If his/her employment terminates before this period ends, the company can buy back the shares at their original price.

periodo para la consolidación de la concesión

= periodo para la consolidación del derecho, periodo para la irrevocabilidad de la concesión, periodo para la irrevocabilidad del derecho

▲ *a three-year vesting period* un periodo para la consolidación de la concesión de tres años ▲ *entitled to receive dividends during the vesting period* tenía derecho al cobro de dividendos durante el periodo para la consolidación de la concesión ▲ *increase the vesting period* aumentar el periodo para la consolidación de la concesión ▲ *recognise*

over the remainder of the original vesting period reconocer a lo largo de lo que queda del periodo para la consolidación de la concesión original ▲ *reduce the vesting period* reducir el periodo para la consolidación de la concesión ▲ *restrictions on transfer that exist during the vesting period* restricciones existentes a la hora de transferir durante el periodo para la consolidación de la concesión ▲ *the end of the vesting period* el final del periodo para la consolidación de la concesión ▲ *the expected vesting period* el periodo para la consolidación de la concesión esperado ▲ *the length of the vesting period* la duración del periodo para la consolidación de la concesión
SOURCE IFRS 2, Appendix A

vice chairman
= deputy chairman, vice-chairman
A vice chairman is the deputy chairman, i.e. the person next in rank to the chairman.
vicepresidente
▲ *be appointed vice chairman* ser nombrado vicepresidente

vice-chairman
= deputy chairman, vice chairman
A vice-chairman is the deputy chairman e.g. the person next in rank to the chairman.
vicepresidente
▲ *be appointed vice-chairman* ser nombrado vicepresidente

visual-fit method US
The visual-fit method measures cost using all available cost data. The cost analyst draws a straight line through a plot of the cost data; however, being based on human judgment, the fitting of the line to the plotted points and the resulting measurement of the fixed and variable costs are subjective.
método de ajuste visual
= método del ajuste visual
▲ *the reliability of the visual-fit method* la fiabilidad del método del ajuste visual ▲ *using the visual-fit method* utilizando el método de ajuste visual
⇛ high-low method, least-square regression method

VIU IAS/IFRS, UK
= value in use IAS/IFRS, UK
VIU is the abbreviation for value in use, which is the current value of an asset seen as the discounted present value of expected cash inflows from continuing use and the proceeds from the ultimate disposal of the asset. For a liability, the value in use is the discounted present value of expected cash outflows during the life of the liability.
valor en uso
▲ *an asset's VIU* un valor en uso del activo ▲ *calculate the VIU* calcular el valor en uso ▲ *determine the VIU of the investment* determinar el valor en uso de la inversión ▲ *estimate the asset's VIU* estimar el valor en uso del activo
⇛ value in use

volatile
Something that is volatile is subject to frequent changes, e.g. the prices of shares listed on a stock exchange and the value of financial instruments over a period of time.
volátil
▲ *a volatile market* un mercado volátil ▲ *a volatile share* una acción volátil ▲ *exercise options on highly volatile shares* ejercer opciones sobre acciones muy volátiles ▲ *significant and volatile changes in fair value* cambios significativos y volátiles en el valor razonable ▲ *volatile movements in fair value* movimientos volátiles en el valor razonable

volatility
Volatility is a measure of the fluctuation in value of a financial instrument over a given period of time.
volatilidad
= volatibilidad
▲ *a volatility of 14%* una volatilidad del 14 % ▲ *annual volatility* volatilidad anual ▲ *average volatility* volatibilidad media ▲ *determine on the basis of historical volatility* determinar basándose en la volatilidad histórica ▲ *differ from past volatility* diferir de la volatilidad pasada ▲ *expected volatility* volatibilidad esperada ▲ *future volatility* volatilidad futura ▲ *historical volatility* volatilidad histórica ▲ *implied volatility from traded share options on the enterprise's shares* la volatilidad implícita de las opciones sobre acciones negociadas en las acciones de la empresa ▲ *measu-*

re the volatility of a share medir la volatilidad de una acción ▲ *measures of the volatility of actively traded assets* medidas de la volatilidad de los activos negociados activamente ▲ *shares with low volatility* acciones con baja volatilidad ▲ *the expected annualised volatility of a share* la volatilidad anualizada esperada de una acción ▲ *the measure of volatility used in option pricing models* la medida de la acciones con baja volatilidad usada en los modelos de fijación de precios de opciones ▲ *the volatility of currencies* la volatilidad de las monedas ▲ *the volatility of shares* la volatibilidad de las acciones ▲ *the volatility of the fair values of the intangible assets* la volatibilidad de los valores razonables de los activos intangibles

volume of orders

The volume of orders is the total amount of orders that an enterprise has on its order books pending execution.

volumen de órdenes

= volumen de pedidos

▲ *a low volume of orders* un volumen de pedidos bajo ▲ *a significant volume of orders* unos volúmenes de órdenes significativos

⇛ order, order book

voluntary reserve

≠ legal reserve, statutory reserve

A voluntary reserve is a non-statutory reserve under equity consisting of accumulated retained earnings and available for distribution of dividends.

reserva voluntaria

▲ *transfer to the voluntary reserve* traspasar a la reserva voluntaria

vote[1] *noun*

1 A vote is a decision-making by a group of individuals who express their choice or opinion on a particular issue at a meeting or in an election by raising a hand or marking a paper.

voto

= votación

▲ *put to the vote* someter a votación ▲ *the casting of votes* la emisión de votos ▲ *vote by shareholders* votación por los accionistas

2 A vote is an expression of a choice or an opinion at a meeting for or against a proposal or motion, or at an election, by raising a hand or marking a paper.

voto

▲ *50% of the votes cast* 50% de los votos emitidos ▲ *majority of votes* mayoría de votos ▲ *power to cast the majority of votes* poder para emitir la mayoría de los votos ▲ *the casting vote* el voto emitido

vote[2] *verb*

To vote is to express a choice or an opinion at a meeting for or against a proposal or motion, or at an election, by raising a hand or marking a paper.

votar

▲ *vote against a proposal* votar en contra de una propuesta ▲ *vote by a show of hands* votar a mano alzada ▲ *vote by ballot* votar con papeleta ▲ *vote by proxy* votar por representación ▲ *vote down* rechazar mediante votación ▲ *vote on a proposal* votar una propuesta

voting right

Voting right is the legal right of citizens to formally express their opinion at an election as well as the right of a shareholder to vote in person or by proxy in corporate business matters.

derecho de voto

= derecho político

▲ *acquire more than one-half of the voting rights of another combining entity* adquirir más de la mitad de los derechos de voto de otra entidad que se fusiona ▲ *acquire voting rights* adquirir derechos de voto ▲ *amount to a minimum of 5% of the voting rights of the share capital* ascienden a un mínimo del 5% de los derechos de voto del capital social ▲ *concerted exercise of voting rights* ejercicio concertado de los derechos de voto ▲ *differentiation of voting rights* diferenciación de derechos de voto ▲ *dispose of voting rights* venta de derechos de voto ▲ *end the differentiation of voting rights* poner fin a la diferenciación de los derechos de voto ▲ *exercise a voting right* ejercer un derecho de voto ▲ *limit the differentiation of voting rights* limitar la diferenciación de los derechos de voto ▲ *potential voting rights that are currently exercisable or convertible* derechos de voto potenciales que son ejercitables o convertibles en la actualidad ▲ *power over more than half of the voting rights* poder sobre más de la mitad de los derechos de voto ▲ *significant indirect voting rights* derechos de voto indirectos significativos ▲ *temporary transfer for consideration of voting rights* transferir temporalmente la consideración de los derechos de voto ▲ *the total number of shares to which voting rights are attached* el número total de acciones con derechos de voto incluido ▲ *voting rights attached to shares* derechos de voto adjuntados a las acciones

voting share

A voting share refers to the proportional share of the total voting rights in a company owned by a person, enterprise or other shareholder.

porcentaje de voto

= porcentaje de votos

▲ *a voting share of 20%* un porcentaje de voto del 20% ▲ *determination of the voting share* determinación del porcentaje de votos ▲ *disclose the exact voting share* publicar el porcentaje de voto exacto

voucher

= receipt

A voucher is a record of expenditure, disbursement, or completed transaction, e.g. a receipt for the payment of money confirming a book entry.

comprobante

= recibo, vale

▲ *examine the original vouchers* examinar los comprobantes originales ▲ *the vouchers for the accounting period* los comprobantes para el periodo contable

⇛ receipt, source document

W

WACC

= weighted average cost of capital

WACC is the abbreviation for weighted average cost of capital (WACC), which is a measure for the value of enterprises based on a calculation of the cost of capital, i.e. the average cost of equity and cost of debt (loan capital), weighted according to the proportions to total capital and compared with the required rates of return for each part. The WACC is typically used as a discount rate for valuation of enterprises and investment decisions. In the case of a simple debt-equity ratio or capital structure, the WACC is calculated by multiplying the proportion of net interest-bearing debt by the borrowing rate after tax, i.e. borrowers required rate of return, and adding the proportion of equity multiplied by owner's required rate of return.

coste de capital medio ponderado

= coste del capital medio ponderado

▲ *calculate WACC* calcular el coste del capital medio ponderado ▲ *included in the calculation of WACC* incluido en el coste de capital medio ponderado ▲ *pre-tax WACC* coste de capital medio ponderado antes de impuestos ▲ *the use of WACC* el uso del coste de capital medio ponderado

wages and salaries

Wages and salaries constitute the regular compensation offered or remuneration paid by an enterprise to its employees in return for their work and resources. As an item in the profit and loss account under staff costs, "Wages and salaries" include the labour costs of an enterprise for an accounting period.

NOTE Wages and salaries refer partly to wages paid on a weekly basis and partly to salaries paid on a monthly basis.

sueldos y salarios

▲ *increases in wages and salaries* incrementos en sueldos y salarios

⇛ salary

waive

To waive means to give up something that you are entitled to, e.g. to refrain from exercising a legal right.

renunciar

= renunciar a

▲ *waive a right* renunciar a un derecho ▲ *waive an option* renunciar a una opción

waiver

A waiver is the official act of giving up something that you are entitled to, e.g. the act of refraining from exercising a legal right.

renuncia

▲ *waiver of subrogation* renuncia a la subrogación ▲ *waiver on death of charges that would be made on cancellation or surrender* renuncia a la indemnización por fallecimiento que pudiera ejecutarse por cancelación o abandono

warehouse

= storage building

A warehouse is a building used by enterprises to store goods.

almacén

▲ *ex warehouse* franco almacén ▲ *lease of a warehouse* alquiler de un almacén

warehouse facility

= storage facility

A warehouse facility is the right to use a warehouse to store goods, also often understood as the actual warehouse building offering storage facilities.

derecho de depósito

▲ *extension of warehouse facilities* ampliación de los derechos de depósito

warrant

A warrant is a financial instrument entitling the holder to buy a proportionate amount of shares at some specified future date at a specified price, usually a price which is higher than the current market price.

Warrants are traded as securities whose prices reflect the value of the underlying stock. Warrants are offered by companies.

warrant

= derecho de suscripción, opción de compra de acciones

▲ *a debt instrument with detachable share purchase warrants* un instrumento de deuda con warrants de compra de acciones ▲ *exercise a warrant* ejercitar un warrants ▲ *granting of warrants* concesión de warrants ▲ *issue of warrants* emisión de warrants ▲ *the market value of warrants* el valor de mercado de los warrants ▲ *warrants issued by a subsidiary* warrants emitidos por una filial ▲ *warrants to purchase ordinary shares* warrants para comprar acciones ordinarias

⇛ call option, notional share

warrant holder

A warrant holder is a person who is in possession of a warrant.

tenedor de un warrant

▲ *be advantageous to the warrant holder* ser ventajoso para el tenedor de un warrant

warrant programme UK

= warrant program US

A warrant programme is a prospectus for warrants issued by a company, typically as an incentive scheme to reward employees, members of board of directors or management, external consultants or others by granting them warrants to subscribe for shares at a predetermined exercise price.

programa de warrants

▲ *a warrant programme for employees and management* un programa de warrants para los empleados y la dirección ▲ *adopt a warrant programme* adoptar un programa de warrants

warranty

= guarantee UK, guaranty US

A warranty is a promise made by a supplier, manufacturer or seller to give compensation for, or to repair or replace any defective or malfunctioning goods or services delivered subject to defined conditions concerning extent and warranty period.

garantía

▲ *a supplier's warranty agreement* un acuerdo de garantía del oferente ▲ *give 2-year warranties on products* ofrecer 2 años de garantía en los productos ▲ *warranties issued directly by a manufacturer* garantías emitidas directamente por un fabricante ▲ *warranty obligations* obligaciones de garantía

⇛ warranty claim

warranty claim

= guarantee claim UK, guaranty claim US

A warranty claim is a claim submitted by a customer against a seller for damages, compensation or repair because a product is defective or malfunctioning. A warranty claim must be asserted while the product is still under warranty, i.e. within a defined warranty period running from the date of purchase.

reclamación de garantía

▲ *enforcement of a warranty claim* ejecución de una reclamación de garantía ▲ *make a warranty claim* hacer una reclamación de garantía ▲ *the risk of warranty claims* el riesgo de una reclamación de garantía

warranty commitment

= guarantee commitment

A warranty commitment is the obligation to substitute, repair or refund a specified item of goods or services delivered under the terms and conditions of the warranty if the item is defect or not performing or operating properly.

compromiso de garantía

= compromiso de la garantía

▲ *a change in warranty commitments* un cambio en los compromisos de garantía ▲ *an increase in warranty commitments* un aumento en los compromisos de garantía

warranty expense

A warranty expense represents the actual costs incurred by an enterprise, or the costs estimated for the period based on historical patterns, relating to the substitution, repair or refund under a warranty within the warranty period concerning a previously sold product or service. A warranty expense is recognised in the income statement.

coste de garantía
= coste de la garantía, gasto de garantía
▲ *expected future warranty expenses* costes de garantía futuros esperados ▲ *historical warranty expenses* costes de garantía históricos ▲ *incur warranty expenses* incurrir en costes de garantía ▲ *warranty expenses on goods sold* costes de la garantía en los bienes vendidos

warranty obligation
A warranty obligation is the obligation to substitute, repair or refund a specified item of goods or services delivered under the terms and conditions of the warranty if the item is defective and not performing or operating properly.
obligación de garantía
= obligación del certificado de garantía
▲ *product warranty obligations retained by the seller* obligaciones del certificado de garantía mantenidas por el vendedor

warranty provision
A warranty provision is an amount set aside under liabilities in the balance sheet to provide for a known amount in respect of any future claims from customers for repair or replacement of products purchased.
provisión por garantía
= provisión de garantía, provisión para garantía
▲ *a warranty provision for goods sold* provisión por garantía por bienes vendidos

weighted
When something is weighted it means that different importance is given to different factors or components.
ponderado
▲ *a weighted average* una media ponderada ▲ *a weighted cost of capital* un coste ponderado de capital ▲ *a weighted invoicing currency* una moneda de facturación ponderada ▲ *weighted assets* activos ponderados ▲ *weighted average effective interest rate* media ponderada del tipo de interés efectivo ▲ *weighted average number of shares outstanding* número medio ponderado de acciones pendientes ▲ *weighted items* partidas ponderadas

weighted average
A weighted average is an average calculated by taking into account the relative importance of each figure in a data set for which reason it is more heavily influenced by some figures than others.
media ponderada
= promedio ponderado
▲ *the weighted average exercise prices of the share options* la media ponderada de los precios de las opciones sobre acciones del ejercicio ▲ *the weighted average number of ordinary shares outstanding during the financial year* la media ponderada del número de acciones ordinarias pendientes durante el año financiero ▲ *the weighted average of all possible outcomes* la media ponderada de todos los resultados posibles ▲ *the weighted average remaining contractual life* la media ponderada de la vida contractual restante ▲ *weighted average of the cost of similar items at the beginning of a period* la media ponderada del coste de partidas similares al inicio de un periodo

weighted average cost
The weighted average cost is the average cost per unit of stock produced or purchased during a period calculated by dividing the cost of opening stock plus any acquisitions by the total number of units on hand available for sale.
coste medio ponderado
= coste promedio ponderado
NOTE Spanish accountants prefer 'coste medio ponderado' to the IAS/IFRS term 'coste promedio ponderado'.
▲ *calculate the weighted average cost* calcular el coste medio ponderado ▲ *the weighted average cost per unit* el coste medio ponderado por unidad

weighted average cost formula
= weighted average cost method IAS/IFRS
The weighted average cost formula is a stock valuation method used to determine the cost of each unit available for sale at the end of the accounting period by taking the price of similar units at the begin-

ning of an accounting period, e.g. a financial year, and the cost of such units produced or purchased during this period and weigh this by the number of units available for sale. This method is also applied in connection with calculation for tax purposes of profit or loss on disposed shares, where the prices of all shares purchased are added and then divided by the number of shares.

fórmula del coste medio ponderado

= fórcula del coste promedio ponderado

NOTE Spanish accountant prefer 'fórmula del coste medio ponderado' to the IAS/IFRS term 'fórmula del coste promedio ponderado'.

▲ *under the weighted average cost formula* de acuerdo con la fórmula del coste medio ponderado ▲ *use the weighted average cost formula* utilizar la fórmula del coste medio ponderado

weighted average cost of capital

= WACC

The weighted average cost of capital (WACC) is a measure for the value of enterprises based on a calculation of the cost of capital, i.e. the average cost of equity and cost of debt (loan capital), weighted according to the proportions to total capital and compared with the required rates of return for each part. The WACC is typically used as a discount rate for valuation of enterprises and investment decisions. In the case of a simple debt-equity ratio or capital structure, the WACC is calculated by multiplying the proportion of net interest-bearing debt by the borrowing rate after tax, i.e. borrowers required rate of return, and adding the proportion of equity multiplied by owner's required rate of return.

coste medio ponderado del capital

= coste promedio ponderado del capital

NOTE Spanish accountants prefer 'coste medio ponderado del capital' to the IAS/IFRS term 'coste promedio ponderado del capital'.

▲ *the entity's weighted average cost of capital determined by using the Capital Asset Pricing Model* el coste medio ponderado del capital de una empresa determinado por el uso del Modelo de Valoración de Activos de Capital ▲ *the weighted average cost of capital of a listed entity that has a single asset* el coste medio ponderado del capital de una empresa cotizada que sólo tiene un activo único

⇛ debt-equity ratio

weighted-average cost

→ weighted average cost

wholesale bank

≠ retail bank

A wholesale bank is a bank that specialises in doing business with large national and international enterprises, other financial institutions and government departments.

banco mayorista

≠ banco minorista

NOTE In Spain wholesale and retail banks perform similar functions.

▲ *operate as a wholesale bank* operar como un banco mayorista

wholesale banking

≠ retail banking

Wholesale banking constitutes the activities of banks that specialise in doing business with large enterprises, other financial institutions and occasionally wealthy individuals. Examples of wholesale banking activities are investment management, cash management and loan financing.

banca mayorista

▲ *the wholesale banking sector* el sector de la banca mayorista

winding up

Winding up refers to the process of dissolving an enterprise so that it ceases to exist.

liquidación

= cierre

▲ *winding up of an enterprise* cierre de una empresa ▲ *winding up of associates* liquidación de las asociadas ▲ *winding up of subsidiaries* liquidación de las filiales

winding-up

= dissolution, liquidation

Winding-up is the process of dissolving a company so that it ceases to exist.

liquidación

= proceso de cierre

▲ *compulsory winding-up* liquidación obligatoria ▲ *voluntary winding-up* liquidación voluntaria ▲ *winding-up proceedings* procedimientos de liquidación

window dressing US

= creative accounting UK

Window dressing refers to forms of accounting that are intended to present misleadingly optimistic financial statements. This is not illegal as generally accepted accounting principles may be interpreted in different ways, and therefore the establishment of rules in accounting standards and for corporate governance have been established to counteract this practice.

contabilidad creativa

= maquillaje contable

▲ *detect window dressing* detectar la contabilidad creativa

Wirtschaftsprüferkammer

The Wirtschaftsprüferkammer is the state-auditing, government-controlled accountancy body in Germany of which accountants must be members to perform statutory audits. The other professional accountancy body in Germany is the private-sector Institut der Wirtschaftsprüfer.

Wirtschaftsprüferkammer

= Instituto Público Alemán de Auditores de Cuentas

▲ *be a member of Wirtschaftsprüferkammer* ser un miembro del Wirtschaftsprüferkammer

⇛ Institut der Wirtschaftsprüfer

withdraw

1 = draw

≠ deposit

To withdraw is to take cash out of a bank account or from a pension plan, home equity or similar savings, or to extract cash from a credit card.

retirar

= sacar

≠ ingresar, meter

▲ *withdraw money from an account* retirar dinero de una cuenta

2 To withdraw is to take back, remove, retract or stop making available or valid.

retirar

= retirarse

▲ *withdraw a licence* retirar una licencia ▲ *withdraw a plan* retirarse de un plan ▲ *withdraw draft SIC Interpretation D34* retirar el borrador del Comité de Interpretación del Borrador 34 ▲ *withdraw the investment property from use permanently* retirar la propiedad de inversión del uso permanente

withdrawal

1 = drawing

≠ deposit

A withdrawal is the act of removing or taking out funds from a bank account or from a pension plan, home equity or similar savings, or to extract cash from a credit card.

retirada de fondos

≠ ingreso de fondos

▲ *a substantial wihdrawal from the account* una retirada de fondos sustancial de la cuenta ▲ *a withdrawal from a bank account* una retirada de fondos de una cuenta bancaria

2 Withdrawal means the taking back, removal or retraction of an offer, an allegation, support or services, or the stopping of making e.g. products available.

retirada

▲ *withdrawal of IAS 36* retirada de la NIC 36 ▲ *withdrawal of other pronouncements* retirada de otros pronunciamientos

3 ≠ deposit

A withdrawal refers to an amount of money removed or taken out from a bank account.

reintegro

≠ depósito, ingreso en cuenta

▲ *cash withdrawals* reintegros de efectivo

withholding tax

1 = PAYE tax UK, tax at source UK

Withholding tax is income tax that is collected at source at the applicable tax rates and withheld from e.g. an employee's wages by an employer and paid directly to the tax authorities on behalf of the employee.

retención de impuestos en origen

▲ *a compensatory withholding tax of 5%* una retención de impuestos en origen compensatoria del 5% ▲ *be exempt from withholding tax* estar exento de la retención de impuestos en origen ▲ *levy a withholding tax on dividends distributed to the parent* cobrar una retención de impuestos en origen en los dividendos distribuidos a la matriz ▲ *the amount of the withholding tax levied* la cantidad de la retención de impuestos en origen cobrada

2 = coupon tax, dividend tax US
Withholding tax is tax on dividends, interest or other periodic return on investment to non-residents that is deducted at source by the payer who is responsible for paying the tax to the tax authorities on behalf of the recipient.
impuesto por dividendo
▲ *impose a withholding tax of 5%* imponer un impuesto por dividendo del 5% ▲ *net of any withholding tax* neto de cualquier impuesto por dividendo

work[1] *noun*
Work is an activity or a job performed, often - but not necessarily - for payment.
trabajo
▲ *carry out a piece of work* eliminar una parte de trabajo ▲ *ongoing work* trabajo en marcha ▲ *put into work* poner en el trabajo

work[2] *verb*
To work means to undertake an activity - often, but not necessarily, with the object of receiving payment.
trabajar
▲ *work in a line of business* trabajar en una línea de negocios ▲ *work systematically* trabajar sistemáticamente ▲ *work to capacity* trabajar a pleno rendimiento ▲ *work to rule* trabajar a reglamento

work in process US
= goods in process US, work in progress IAS/IFRS, UK, work-in-process US
Work in process refers to unfinished goods, e.g. goods that are still in the process of being manufactured. Work in process is an inventory item under current assets in the balance sheet.
obra en curso
= trabajo en curso
▲ *changes in inventories of finished goods and work in process* cambios en los inventarios de las obras finalizadas y en curso ▲ *work in process arising under construction contracts* obra en curso procedente de contratos de construcción ▲ *work in process being produced by the enterprise* obra en curso en proceso de realización por la empresa ▲ *work in process inventory* inventario de obra en curso

work in progress IAS/IFRS, UK
= goods in process, work in process US, work-in-process US, work-in-progress UK
Work in progress refers to unfinished goods, e.g. goods that are still in the process of being manufactured. Work in progress is an inventory item under current assets in the balance sheet.
obra en curso
= trabajo en curso
▲ *changes in inventories of finished goods and work in progress* cambios en los inventarios de obras terminadas y en curso ▲ *work in progress arising under construction contracts* obra en curso procedente de contratos de construcción ▲ *work in progress being produced by the enterprise* obra en curso en proceso de realización por la empresa ▲ *work in progress inventory* inventario de obra en curso

work performed by the entity and capitalised IAS/IFRS
= own work capitalised UK
"Work performed by the entity and capitalised" is an item in the profit and loss account classified by nature, including e.g. own-produced plant and machinery that has been capitalised, i.e. recognised in the balance sheet under fixed assets.
trabajo realizado por la empresa y capitalizado

work-in-process US
→ work in process

work-in-process inventory US
= work-in-progress stocks UK
A work-in-process inventory is the stock in hand of unfinished goods, i.e. goods that are still in the process of being manufactured.
inventario de obra en curso
= inventario de trabajo en curso
▲ *cut down on work-in-process inventory* recortar el inventario de obra en curso ▲ *maintain work-in-process inventory* mantener el inventario de obra en curso ▲ *minimize work-in-process inventory* minimizar el inventario de obra en curso

work-in-progress UK
→ work in progress

work-in-progress stocks UK
= work-in-process inventory US
Work-in-progress stocks refer to the inventory of unfinished goods, i.e. goods that are still in the process of being manufactured.
inventarios de obra en curso
= existencias de obras en curso
▲ *cut down on work-in-progress stocks* recortar los inventarios de obra en curso ▲ *maintain work-in-progress stocks* mantener los inventarios de obra en curso ▲ *minimise work-in-progress stocks* minimizar los inventarios de obra en curso

worker director UK
= employee board member US, employee director, employee representative
A worker director is a person employed in a company elected and appointed by the employees to serve on the board of directors of the company. Worker directors have the same rights, duties and responsibilities as other board members.
consejero en representación de los trabajadores
▲ *appoint a worker director* nombrar un consejero en representación de los trabajadores ▲ *the new worker director* el nuevo consejero en representación de los trabajadores

working capital
= net current assets
Working capital is defined as the excess of current assets over current liabilities other than provisions, i.e. net current assets.
fondo de maniobra
= capital circulante
▲ *additional working capital* fondo de maniobra adicional ▲ *average working capital* fondo de maniobra medio ▲ *capital tied up in working capital* capital agrupado en el fondo de maniobra ▲ *cash tied up in working capital* efectivo incluido en el fondo de maniobra ▲ *changes in working capital* cambios en el fondo de maniobra ▲ *the net assets that are continuously circulating as working capital* los activos netos que están en continua rotación como fondo de maniobra ▲ *the working capital used in the entity's normal operating cycle* el fondo de maniobra utilizado en el ciclo de operaciones habituales de la entidad ▲ *total working capital* total fondo de maniobra
⇛ capital employed, invested capital

working capital cycle
= operating cycle
The working capital cycle refers to the chain of events and stages in a manufacturing enterprise from the purchase of raw materials over the stages of production (work-in-progress) until the finished goods have been sold and paid for, producing cash to the enterprise. Funds flow through each stage of the cycle.
ciclo del capital circulante
= ciclo de explotación
▲ *improve the working capital cycle* mejorar el ciclo del capital circulante ▲ *the working capital cycle for a manufacturing enterprise* el ciclo del capital circulante de una empresa manufacturera

working capital ratio UK
= current ratio
The working capital ratio is a financial ratio defined as total current assets divided by total current liabilities at balance sheet date. The ratio measures the liquidity of an enterprise, and the higher the ratio is, the more probable it is that the enterprise is able to pay its creditors; however, a ratio that is too high may also indicate poor liquidity management.
ratio de liquidez
▲ *a negative working capital ratio* un ratio de liquidez negativo ▲ *calculate the working capital ratio* calcular el ratio de liquidez
⇛ liquidity ratio, quick ratio

working environment
The working environment comprises the physical and psychological conditions under which people work.
entorno de trabajo
= entorno laboral
▲ *create a good working environment* crear un buen entorno de trabajo ▲ *ensure a good working environment* asegurar un buen

entorno de trabajo ▲ *integrate into the working environment* integrar en el entorno de trabajo ▲ *management of the working environment* gestión del entorno de trabajo ▲ *protection of the working environment* protección del entorno de trabajo

working environment report

A working environment report is a report describing the physical and psychological conditions under which the employees of an enterprise work.

informe del entorno laboral

▲ *prepare a working environment report* preparar un informe del entorno laboral ▲ *publish a working environment report* publicar un informe del entorno laboral ▲ *the annual working environment report* el informe del entorno laboral anual

worldwide income

The worldwide income is a taxpayer's total income from domestic and foreign sources.

ingreso mundial

▲ *calculation of the worldwide income* cálculo del ingreso mundial ▲ *declare the entire worldwide income in the income tax returns* declarar el ingreso mundial completo en los impresos de devolución del impuesto sobre la renta ▲ *tax the enterprise's worldwide income* grabar el ingreso mundial de la empresa ▲ *taxable worldwide income* ingreso mundial grabable ▲ *the total worldwide income* el ingreso mundial total

worldwide income principle

The worldwide income principle is a tax law principle according to which a taxpayer is liable to pay tax on the total domestic and foreign income earned, i.e. irrespective of the origin of the taxable income.

principio del ingreso mundial

▲ *apply the worldwide income principle* aplicar el principio del ingreso mundial ▲ *subject to tax on the basis of worldwide income principle* sujeto al impuesto en base al principio del ingreso mundial ▲ *use the worldwide income principle* utilizar el principio del ingreso mundial

write down

To write down means to adjust downwards and reduce the recorded value of an asset in the financial statements of an enterprise.

minorar

▲ *basis for writing down* base de minoración ▲ *write down a value* minorar un valor ▲ *write down an asset* minorar un activo ▲ *write down for anticipated uncollectibles* minorar por incobrables anticipados ▲ *write down goodwill and other intangible assets* minorar el fondo de comercio y otros activos intangibles ▲ *write down inventories* minorar inventarios ▲ *write down the value of the equity investments* minorar el valor de las inversiones en títulos ▲ *write down to a lower recoverable amount* minorar a una cantidad a cobrar más baja ▲ *write down to net realisable value* minorar a valor realizable neto

write off

To write off is to expense an amount in total.

eliminar

= cancelar, regularizar

▲ *expenditure for reconstruction and improvement written off* gasto por reconstrucción y mejora eliminado ▲ *goodwill written off* fondo de comercio cancelado ▲ *loans and advances written off* préstamos y anticipos cancelados ▲ *operating equipment written off* equipamiento de explotación eliminado ▲ *write off goodwill to equity* regularizar el fondo de comercio a patrimonio neto ▲ *write off minor assets* eliminar activos minoritarios

write off immediately

= write off on acquisition

Writing off immediately means recognising as expense the cost of the asset in full in the profit and loss account in the year of acquisition.

eliminar inmediatamente

▲ *write off an asset immediately* eliminar un activo inmediatamente

write-down

= writedown

A write-down is the recognition in the financial statement of a reduction in the carrying amount of an asset. Write-downs are made for impairment losses on fixed assets or for the decline in value of current assets, e.g. obsolescence of stocks.

minoración

▲ *an impairment loss for any initial or subsequent write-down of the asset* una pérdida por deterioro para cualquier minoración inicial o subsiguiente del activo ▲ *calculation of write-down* cálculo de la minoración ▲ *changes in estimate in the financial year relating to inventory write-downs* cambios en la estimación del año financiero relacionados con minoraciones de inventario ▲ *reverse the amount of the write-down* revertir la cantidad de la minoración ▲ *the amount of the original write-down* la cantidad de la minoración original ▲ *write-down for impairment* minoración por deterioro ▲ *write-downs of inventories to net realisable value* minoraciones de inventarios a valor realizable neto

write-down expense

A write-down expense is a cost incurred by an enterprise in connection with the writing down of an asset.

coste de saneamiento

= coste del saneamiento, gasto por saneamiento

▲ *inventory write-down expense* el coste del saneamiento del inventario ▲ *the current year's write-down expense* el coste de saneamiento del año actual

write-down for obsolescence

Write-down for obsolescence means writing down the value of inventories because the value of the items held in stock or part thereof has been reduced because of technological or market changes.

minoración por obsolescencia

▲ *write-down for obsolescence on inventories* minoración por obsolescencia en inventarios

write-off

= write-off on acquisition

A write-off is the charging to expense in the profit and loss account of an amount representing the entire cost of an asset in the year of acquisition or the removal of an uncollectible asset from the asset side of a balance sheet to record it as a loss or expense in order to reduce or eliminate the value of an asset and thereby reduce profits.

eliminación

= cancelación

▲ *prohibition of write-off on acquisition* prohibición de eliminación en el momento de la adquisición ▲ *write-off of consolidated goodwill to equity* cancelación del fondo de comercio consolidado a patrimonio neto

writeback and capitalisation of asset previously written off

A writeback and capitalisation of an asset previously written off means recognising the value of that asset again and capitalising it in the balance sheet.

reconocimiento y capitalización de activos eliminados anteriormente

writedown

→ write-down

written-down value

= WDV

The written-down value is the value of an asset in an enterprise's financial records after deducting amounts for accounting amortisation and depreciation or, for tax purposes, capital allowances.

valor contable neto

▲ *a negative written-down value* un valor contable neto negativo ▲ *a positive written-down value* un valor contable neto positivo

XBRL US
= eXtensible Business Reporting Language US
XBRL is the abbreviation for eXtensible Business Reporting Language, an XML-based accounting language that facilitates the electronic communication of financial reporting information including the comparison across enterprises.
XBRL
= Lenguaje Extensible de Informes de Negocios
▲ *an XBRL taxonomy* una taxonomía XBRL

Y

year

A year is 12 months or 365 days (in leap years 366 days).

año

= ejercicio

▲ *additions during the year* sumas durante el ejercicio ▲ *complete draft financial statements for the year to 31 December 2005* completar el borrador de los estados financieros para el año hasta el 31 de diciembre de 2005 ▲ *completion of three years' service* finalización del pago de tres años ▲ *deductible at a rate of 20 per cent per year* deducible a una tasa del 20 por ciento anual ▲ *present one year of comparative information* presentar una información comparada de un ejercicio ▲ *the year under review* el ejercicio en revisión

⇛ financial year, fiscal year

year of acquisition

= acquisition year

The year of acquisition is the accounting period, i.e. the financial year, in which an asset has been obtained by an enterprise. In a business combination it is the year when one enterprise (the acquirer) obtains control over the acquired enterprise (the acquiree).

año de adquisición

▲ *at the end of the year of acquisition* al final del año de adquisición ▲ *in the year of acquisition* en el año de adquisición ▲ *the end of the year following the year of acquisition* el final del año siguiente al año de adquisición

year of change

A year of change is the year when a change or amendment has been made.

año de modificación

= año de cambio

▲ *during the year of change* durante el año de modificación

year of disposal

The year of disposal is the accounting period, i.e. the financial year, in which an asset has been sold or otherwise disposed of.

año de enajenación

= ejercicio de enajenación

▲ *submission of the tax return for the year of disposal* propuesta de devolución de impuestos para el año de enajenación

⇛ year of acquisition

year of sale

The year of sale is the accounting period, i.e. the financial year, in which a sale has been completed.

año de venta

= ejercicio de venta

▲ *during the year of sale* durante el año de venta

year of the merger UK

The year of the merger is the year when two entities merge and are combined in one entity.

año de la fusión

= ejercicio de la fusión

▲ *in the year of the merger* en el año de la fusión

⇛ merger

year of the pooling of interests US, IAS/IFRS

The year of the pooling of interests is the year when two entities are combined in one entity.

año de la combinación de intereses

= año de la agrupación de intereses, ejercicio de la combinación de intereses, año de la fusión de intereses

▲ *in the year of the pooling of interests* en el año de la combinación de intereses

year of the uniting of interests IAS/IFRS

The year of the uniting of interests is the year when two entities are combined in one entity.

año de la combinación de intereses

▲ *in the year of the uniting of interests* en el año de la combinación de intereses

year-end

= at the end of

Year-end refers to the final date of an accounting period, i.e. the balance sheet date, typically 31 December.

a fin de año

= a 31 de diciembre

▲ *year-end exposure* exposición al riesgo a 31 de diciembre

year-end balance sheet
= balance sheet at year-end, closing balance sheet
The year-end balance sheet is the balance sheet with all items at the last day in the financial year.
balance de cierre
= balance a 31 de diciembre, balance a fin de ejercicio, balance de fin de año
▲ *prepare a year-end balance sheet* preparar un balance a fin de ejercicio ▲ *release a year-end balance sheet* publicar un balance de cierre ▲ *the year-end balance sheet for the Group* el balance a 31 de diciembre del Grupo

year-end value
The year-end value is the value of assets or liabilities at the balance sheet date of the financial year.
valor de cierre
= valor de fin de año
▲ *disclose year-end values* publicar los valores de cierre
⇛ balance sheet date

year-over-year
Year-over-year refers to a comparison with the same period of time last year. For example, a rise in year-over-year Q3 profit means growth in the profit for the third quarter this year compared with the same period last year.
año a año
▲ *grow three percent year-over-year* crecer un tres por ciento año a año ▲ *year-over-year growth rate* tasa de crecimiento año a año ▲ *year-over-year revenue growth of 20%* crecimiento de los ingresos del 20% año a año

year-to-date
= YTD
Year-to-date (YTD) is the period from the beginning of the financial or calendar year to the present date. YTD is often used in connection with business results.
de uno de enero al día de la fecha
= desde el inicio del ejercicio a la fecha actual
▲ *the year-to-date period* el ejercicio de uno de enero al día de la fecha ▲ *year-to-date financial reporting* publicación de informes financieros de uno de enero al día de la fecha ▲ *year-to-date fluctuations* fluctuaciones de uno de enero al día de la fecha ▲ *year-to-date statement* estado de uno de enero al día de la fecha

yield[1] *noun*
1 The yield is the return on an asset, e.g. the income an investor receives on a capital investment.
rentabilidad
= rendimiento
▲ *a yield curve of interest rates* una curva de rentabilidad de los tipos de interés ▲ *the effective yield on the receivable* la rentabilidad efectiva en la cuenta a cobrar ▲ *the yield on alternative investments* la rentabilidad de las inversiones alternativas ▲ *yield rate* tasa de rendimiento
2 = bond yield
The yield or bond yield is the return received from a fixed-interest bond calculated as the coupon or nominal interest rate as a percentage of the purchase price.
rentabilidad fija
= renta fija
▲ *yield market* mercado de renta fija ▲ *yield spread* diferencial de rentabilidad fija ▲ *yield to maturity* rentabilidad fija al vencimiento

yield[2] *verb*
To yield is to give a return, e.g. on investment.
rentar
▲ *yield a positive return* rentar un rendimiento positivo

yield to maturity
= effective yield
Yield to maturity refers to the internal rate of return on a debt instrument, such as a bond, purchased at a specified price and held until maturity. Yield to maturity is calculated on the basis of the market price, the coupon rate, the time between interest payments and the maturity period.
rentabilidad al vencimiento
= rendimiento del vencimiento
▲ *the yield to maturity on the consideration* la rentabilidad al vencimiento en la consideración

YTD
= year-to-date

YTD is the abbreviation for year-to-date, which is the period from the beginning of the financial or calendar year to the present date. YTD is often used in connection with business results.

de uno de enero al día de la fecha
= desde el inicio del ejercicio a la fecha actual
▲ *YTD financial reporting* publicación de informes financieros de uno de enero al día de la fecha ▲ *YTD fluctuations* fluctuaciones de uno de enero al día de la fecha ▲ *YTD period* periodo de uno de enero al día de la fecha ▲ *YTD statement* estado de uno de enero al día de la fecha

APÉNDICES

Ejemplo: Cuenta de Pérdidas y Ganancias en Inglés Internacional (IFRS) y sus palabras equivalentes en español

Income Statement by function	**Cuenta de resultados (cuenta de pérdidas y ganancias) por función**
1. **Continuing operations** (where appropriate)	1. **Operaciones continuadas** (si es adecuado)
2. **Revenue (Sales)**	2. **Ingresos por ventas**
3. Cost of sales	3. Coste de ventas
4. **Gross profit**	4. **Resultado bruto**
5. Other operating income	5. Otros ingresos de explotación
6. Distribution costs	6. Gastos de distribución
7. Administrative expenses	7. Gastos de administración
8. Other operating expenses	8. Otros gastos de explotación
9. **Operating profit (EBIT)**	9. **Resultado de explotación (EBIT)**
10. Finance costs, net	10. Costes financieros, neto
11. Share of profit from associates after tax	11. Porcentaje de beneficio de filiales después de impuestos
12. **Profit before tax**	12. **Beneficio antes de impuestos (BAI)**
13. Income tax expense	13. Impuesto sobre beneficios
14. **Profit for the period**	14. **Resultado del periodo**
Where appropriate distributed into:	*Distribuido si es apropiado entre:*
15. Profit for the period for continuing operations	15. Resultado del ejercicio por operaciones continuadas
16. **Discontinued operations**	16. **Operaciones interrumpidas**
17. Profit for the period for discontinued operations	17. Resultado del ejercicio de operaciones interrumpidas
18. **Profit for the period**	18. **Resultado del ejercicio**
Attributable to:	Atribuible a:
Equity holders of the parent (profit*)	Matriz (resultado*)
Minority interest	Intereses minoritarios
Earnings per share for profit* during the period	**Dividendo por acción durante el ejercicio**
- basic	- básico
- diluted	- diluido
*profit attributable to equity holders of the parent	* resultado del ejercicio atribuible a la matriz

Income Statement by nature	**Cuenta de resultados (cuenta de pérdidas y ganancias) por naturaleza**
1. **Continuing operations** (where appropriate)	1. **Operaciones continuadas** (si es adecuado)
2. **Revenue (Sales)**	2. **Ingresos por ventas**
3. Other operating income	3. Otros ingresos de explotación
4. Changes in inventories of finished goods and work in progress	4. Variaciones de existencias de productos terminados y en curso de fabricación
5. Work performed by the company and capitalised	5. Trabajos realizados por la empresa para su activo
6. Raw materials and consumables	6. Materias primas y consumibles
7. Employee benefits expense	7. Gastos de personal
8. Other operating expenses	8. Otros gastos de explotación
9. **Earnings before Interest, Tax, Depreciation and Amortisation (EBITDA)**	9. **Resultado antes de intereses, impuestos y amortizaciones (EBITDA)**
10. Depreciation expense	10. Gasto por depreciación
11. Impairment of property, plant and equipment	11. Deterioro del inmovilizado
12. **Earnings before Interest, Tax and Amortisation (EBITDA)**	12. **Resultado antes de intereses, impuestos y amortizaciones (EBITDA)**
13. Amortisation expense	13. Gasto por amortizaciones
14. Impairment of goodwill	14. Deterioro del fondo de comercio
15. **Earnings before Interest and Taxes (EBIT)**	15. **Resultado antes de intereses e impuestos (EBIT)**
16. Finance costs, net	16. Gastos financieros netos
17. Share of profit of associates after tax	17. Participación en beneficios en asociadas después de impuestos
18. **Profit before tax**	18. **Resultado antes de impuestos**
19. Income tax expense	19. Impuestos sobre beneficios
20. **Profit for the period**	20. **Resultado del ejercicio**
Where appropriate distributed into:	*Distribuido si es apropiado entre:*
21. Profit for the period from continuing operations	21. Resultado del ejercicio procedente de operaciones continuadas
22. **Discontinued operations**	22. **Operaciones interrumpidas**
23. Profits for the period from discontinued operations	23. Resultado del ejercicio procedente de operaciones interrumpidas
24. **Profit for the period**	24. **Resultado del ejercicio**
Attributable to:	Aplicable a:
Equity holders of the parent	Matriz
Minority interests	Intereses minoritarios
Earnings per share for profit* during the period	**Dividendo por acción durante el ejercicio**
- basic	- básico
- diluted	- diluido
*profit attributable to equity holders of the parent	* resultado del ejercicio atribuible a la matriz

Consolidated balance sheet	Balance consolidado
1. ASSETS	1. ACTIVO
2. Non-current assets	2. Activo no corriente
3. Property, plant and equipment	3. Inmovilizado material
4. Intangible assets	4. Inmovilizado intangible
5. Goodwill	5. Fondo de comercio
6. Other intangible assets	6. Otros activos intangibles
7. Investments in associates	7. Inversiones en asociadas
8. Deferred income tax assets	8. Activos por impuesto diferido
9. Available-for-sale financial assets	9. Activos financieros mantenidos para la venta
10. Derivative financial instruments	10. Instrumentos financieros derivados
11. Current assets	11. Activo corriente
12. Inventories	12. Existencias
13. Trade receivables	13 Cuentas comerciales a cobrar
14. Other receivables, prepayments and accrued income	14. Otras cuentas a cobrar, anticipos e ingresos diferidos
15. Available-for-sale financial assets	15. Activos financieros mantenidos para la venta
16. Derivative financial instruments	16. Instrumentos financieros derivados
17. Other financial assets at fair value through profit or loss	17. Otros activos financieros a valor razonable
18. Cash and cash equivalents	18. Efectivo y otros activos líquidos equivalentes
19. Total assets	19. Total activo
1. **EQUITY AND LIABILITY**	1. **PATRIMONIO NETO Y PASIVO**
2. **Equity**	2. **Patrimonio neto**
3. Share capital	3. Capital
4. Other reserves	4. Otras reservas
5. Share premium	5. Prima de emisión
6. Treasury shares	6. Acciones propias
7. Fair value adjustments and other reserves	7. Ajustes a valor razonable y otras reservas
8. Retained earnings	8. Beneficios no distribuidos
9. **Total equity attributable to equity holders of the parent**	9. **Total Patrimonio Neto atribuible a los accionistas de la matriz**
10. **Minority interests**	10. **Intereses minoritarios (accionistas minoritarios)**
11. **Total equity**	11. **Total Patrimonio Neto**
12. **Non-current liabilities**	12. **Pasivo no corriente**
13. Long-term borrowings	13. Deudas a largo plazo
14. Derivative financial instruments	14. Instrumentos financieros derivados
15. Deferred income tax liabilities (quasi-equity)	15. Pasivos por impuesto diferido
16. Retirement benefit obligations	16. Obligaciones por prestaciones al personal
17. Other long-term provisions	17. Otras provisiones a largo plazo
18. **Total non-current liabilities**	18. **Total Pasivo no corriente**
19. **Current liabilities**	19. **Pasivo corriente**
20. Trade payables	20. Cuentas comerciales a pagar
21. Other payables, accrued expenses and deferred income	21. Otras cuentas a pagar, gastos diferidos e ingresos anticipados
22. Short-term borrowings	22. Deudas a corto plazo
23. Derivative financial instruments	23. Instrumentos financieros derivados
24. Current portions of long-term borrowings	24. Parte actual de los empréstitos a largo plazo
25. Current income tax liabilities	25. Pasivos por impuesto corriente
26. Short-term provisions	26. Provisiones a corto plazo
27. Total current liabilities	27. Total Pasivo corriente
28. **Total liabilities**	28. **Total Pasivo**
29. **Total equity and liabilities**	29. **Total Patrimonio Neto y Pasivo**

Consolidated Cash Flow Statements for Reporting Companies	Estado de Flujos de Efectivo consolidado para la elaboración y presentación de informes de las empresas
Indirect method	**Método Indirecto**
1. Cash flow from operating activities	1. Flujos de efectivo de las actividades de explotación
2. Cash generated from operations (EBITDA)	2. Efectivo generado por las actividades de explotación antes de intereses e impuestos (EBITDA)
3. Interest paid	3. Intereses pagados
4. Income taxes paid	4. Impuestos sobre el beneficio pagados
5. Net cash from operating activities	5. Flujos netos de efectivo de las actividades de explotación
6. Cash flow from investing activities	6. Flujos de efectivo de las actividades de inversión
7. Acquisition of subsidiary, net of cash acquired	7. Adquisición de subsidiarias, importe neto
8. Purchase of property, plant and equipment (PPE)	8. Compra de inmovilizado material
9. Purchase of intangible assets	9. Compra de inmovilizado intangible
10. Purchase of available-for-sale financial assets	10. Compra activos financieros mantenidos para la venta
11. Loans granted	11. Préstamos garantizados
12. Disposal of subsidiary, net of cash disposed	12. Venta de subsidiarias, importe neto
13. Proceeds from sale of PPE	13. Cobros por venta de inmovilizado material
14. Loan repayments received	14. Cobros por reembolso de préstamos
15. Interest received	15. Cobros de intereses
16. Dividends received	16. Cobros de dividendos
17. Government grants received	17. Cobros de subvenciones
18. Net cash used in investing activities	18. Flujos netos de efectivo de las actividades de inversión
19. Cash flow from financing activities	19. Flujos de efectivo de las actividades de financiación
20. Proceeds from issue of securities	20. Cobros procedentes de la emisión de acciones
21. Purchase of treasury shares	21. Compra de acciones propias
22. Proceeds from borrowings	22. Cobros por emisión de empréstitos
23. Repayments of borrowings	23. Reembolsos de empréstitos
24. Repayment of finance lease liabilities	24. Reembolsos de deudas por arrendamiento financiero
25. Dividends paid to parent shareholders	25. Dividendos pagados a los accionistas mayoritarios
26. Dividends paid to minority interests	26. Dividendos pagados a los accionistas minoritarios
27. Net cash used in financing activities	27. Flujos netos de efectivo de las actividades de financiación
28. Decrease/increase in cash and cash equivalents	28. Disminución/aumento del efectivo y equivalentes
29. Cash and cash equivalents at beginning of period	29. Efectivo y equivalentes al inicio del ejercicio
30. Cash and cash equivalents at end of period	30. Efectivo y equivalentes al final del ejercicio

Ejemplo: Cuenta de Pérdidas y Ganancias en Inglés Británico y sus palabras equivalentes en español

Profit and Loss Account **Format 1**	**Cuenta de Pérdidas y Ganancias** **Formato 1**
1. Turnover 2. Cost of sales 3. Gross profit or loss 4. Distribution costs 5. Administrative expenses 6. Other operating income 7. Income from shares in group undertakings Income from interests in associated undertakings 8. Income from other participating interests 9. Income from other fixed asset investments 10. Other interest receivable and similar income 11. Amounts written off investments 12. Interest payable and similar charges 13. Tax on profit or loss on ordinary activities 14. Profit or loss on ordinary activities after taxation Minority interests 15. Extraordinary income 16. Extraordinary charges 17. Extraordinary profit or loss 18. Tax on extraordinary profit or loss Minority interests 19. Other taxes not shown under the above items 20. Profit or loss for the financial year	1. Facturación 2. Coste de ventas 3. Resultado bruto 4. Costes de distribución 5. Gastos de administración 6. Otros ingresos de explotación 7. Ingresos por participaciones en empresas del grupo y asociadas Ingresos por participaciones en empresas asociadas 8. Ingresos por otras participaciones de capital 9. Ingresos por inversiones inmobiliarias 10. Otros intereses a cobrar e ingresos similares 11. Resultado por eliminación de inversiones 12. Intereses a pagar y otros gastos similares 13. Impuestos sobre resultados de actividades ordinarias 14. Impuestos sobre resultados de actividades ordinarias después de la imposición de intereses minoritarios 15. Ingresos extraordinarios 16. Gastos extraordinarios 17. Resultado extraordinario 18. Impuestos sobre resultados extraordinarios. Intereses minoritarios 19. Otros impuestos no incluidos en las anteriores partidas 20. Resultado del ejercicio

Profit and Loss Account **Format 2**	**Cuenta de Pérdidas y Ganancias** **Formato 2**
1. Turnover	1. Facturación
2. Change in stocks of finished goods and in work in progress	2. Variación de existencias de productos terminados y en curso de fabricación
3. Own work capitalised	3. Trabajos realizados por la empresa para su activo
4. Other operating income	4. Otros ingresos de explotación
5. (a) Raw materials and consumables (b) Other external charges	5. (a) Materias primas y consumibles, (b) Otros gastos externos
6. Staff costs: (a) Wages and salaries (b) Social security costs (c) Other pension costs	6. Gastos de personal (a) Sueldos y salarios (b) Cargas sociales (c) Aportaciones para pensiones
7. (a) Depreciation and other amounts written off tangible and intangible fixed assets (b) Exceptional amounts written off current assets	7. (a) Amortización y otros deterioros de activos fijos materiales e intangibles (b) Deterioros excepcionales de activos corrientes
8. Other operating charges	8. Otros gastos de explotación
9. Income from shares in group undertakings	9. Ingresos por participaciones en empresas del grupo y asociadas
Income from interests in associated undertakings	Ingresos por participaciones en empresas asociadas
10. Income from other participating interests	10. Ingresos por otras participaciones de capital
11. Income from other fixed asset investments	11. Ingresos por inversiones inmobiliarias
12. Other interest receivable and similar income	12. Otros intereses a cobrar e ingresos similares
13. Amounts written off investments	13. Resultado por eliminación de inversiones
14. Interest payable and similar charges	14. Intereses a pagar y otros gastos similares
15. Tax on profit or loss on ordinary activities	15. Impuestos sobre resultados de actividades ordinarias
16. Profit or loss on ordinary activities after taxation Minority interests	16. Impuestos sobre resultados de actividades ordinarias después de la imposición de intereses minoritarios
17. Extraordinary income	17. Ingresos extraordinarios
18. Extraordinary charges	18. Gastos extraordinarios
19. Extraordinary profit or loss	19. Resultado extraordinario
20. Tax on extraordinary profit or loss Minority interests	20. Impuestos sobre resultados extraordinarios. Intereses minoritarios
21. Other taxes not shown under the above items	21. Otros impuestos no incluidos en las anteriores partidas
22. Profit or loss for the financial year	22. Resultado del ejercicio

Balance Sheet **Format 1**	**Balance** **Formato 1**
A Called up share capital not paid	**A Accionistas desembolsos no exigidos**
B Fixed assets	**B Activo fijo (activo no corriente)**
I Intangible assets	*I Inmovilizado inmaterial (activos intangibles)*
1. Development costs	1. Gastos de desarrollo
2. Concessions, patents, licences, trade marks and similar rights and assets	2. Concesiones, patentes, marcas y derechos y activos similares
3. Goodwill	3. Fondo de comercio
4. Payments on account	4. Pagos a cuenta
II Tangible assets	*II Inmovilizado material (Activos tangible)*
1. Land and buildings	1. Terrenos y edificios
2. Plant and machinery	2. Instalaciones y maquinaria
3. Mixtures, fittings, tools and equipment	3. Utillaje, accesorios, herramientas y equipo
4. Payments on account and assets in course of construction	4. Pagos a cuenta y activos en curso de construcción
III Investments	*III Inmovilizado financiero (Inversiones)*
1. Shares in group undertakings	1. Participaciones en empresas del grupo
2. Loans to group undertakings	2. Préstamos a empresas del grupo
3. (a) Interests in associated undertakings (b) Other participating interests	3. (a) Participaciones en empresas asociadas y (b) Otras participaciones
4. Loans to undertakings in which the company has a participating interest	4. Préstamos a empresas asociadas
5. Other investments other than loans	5. Otras inversiones distintas de los préstamos
6. Other loans	6. Otros préstamos
7. Own shares	7. Acciones propias
C Current assets	**C Activo circulante (Activo corriente)**
I Stocks	*I Existencias*
1. Raw materials and consumables	1. Materias primas y consumibles
2. Work in progress	2. Productos en curso
3. Finished goods and goods for resale	3. Productos terminados y bienes disponibles para la venta
4. Payments on account	4. Anticipos a cuenta
II Debtors	*II Deudores*
1. Trade debtors	1. Deudores comerciales
2. Amounts owed by group undertakings	2. Cantidades adeudas por empresas del grupo
3. Amounts owed by undertakings in which the company has a participating interest	3. Cantidades adeudadas por asociadas y empresas con participación significativa
4. Other debtors	4. Otros deudores
5. Called up share capital not paid	5. Accionistas por desembolsos exigidos
6. Prepayments and accrued income	6. Pagos anticipados e ingresos devengados
III Investments	*III Inversiones*
1. Shares in group undertakings	1. Acciones en empresas del grupo
2. Own shares	2. Acciones propias
3. Other investments	3. Otras inversiones
IV Cash at bank and in hand	*IV Efectivo en bancos y caja (Tesorería)*
D Prepayments and accrued income	**D Ajustes por periodificación**
E Creditors: amounts falling due within one year	**E Acreedores a corto plazo (Pasivo exigible a corto plazo)**

1. Debenture loans 2. Bank loans and overdrafts 3. Payments received on account 4. Trade creditors 5. Bills of exchange payable 6. Amounts owed to group undertakings 7. Amounts owed to undertakings in which the company has a participating interest 8. Other creditors including taxation and social security 9. Accruals and deferred income **F Net current assets (liabilities)** **G Total assets less current liabilities** **H Creditors: amounts falling due after more than one year** 1. Debenture loans 2. Bank loans and overdrafts 3. Payments received on account 4. Trade creditors 5. Bills of exchange payable 6. Amounts owed to group undertakings 7. Amounts owed to undertakings in which the company has a participating interest 8. Other creditors including taxation and social security 9. Accruals and deferred income **I Provisions for liabilities and charges** 1. Pensions and similar obligations 2. Taxation, including deferred taxation 3. Other provisions **J Accruals and deferred income** **K Capital and reserves** *I Called up share capital* *II Share premium account* *III Revaluation reserve* *IV Other reserves* 1. Capital redemption reserve 2. Reserve for own shares 3. Reserves provided for by the articles of association 4. Other reserves *V Profit and loss account* Minority interests	1. Préstamos recibidos 2. Préstamos bancarios y descubiertos 3. Pagos recibidos a cuenta 4. Acreedores comerciales 5. Efectos a pagar 6. Cantidades adeudadas a empresas del grupo 7. Cantidades adeudadas a asociadas y empresas con participación significativa 8. Otros acreedores incluidos Hacienda Pública y Seguridad Social 9. Pagos devengados e ingresos diferidos **F. Activo Circulante Neto (Pasivo)** **G. Total activo menos pasivo exigible a corto** **H Acreedores a largo plazo (Pasivo exigible a largo plazo)** 1. Préstamos recibidos 2. Préstamos bancarios y descubiertos 3. Pagos recibidos a cuenta 4. Acreedores comerciales 5. Efectos a pagar 6. Cantidades adeudadas a empresas del grupo 7. Cantidades adeudadas a asociadas y empresas con participación significativa 8. Otros acreedores incluidos Hacienda Pública y Seguridad Social 9. Pagos devengados e ingresos diferidos **I Provisiones para riesgos y gastos** 1. Pensiones y obligaciones similares 2. Impuestos incluyendo impuestos diferidos 3. Otras provisiones **J Ajustes por periodificación** **K Capital y reservas** *I Capital Social* *II Prima de emisión de acciones* *III Reservas de revalorización* *IV Otras reservas* 1. Reserva por capital amortizado 2. Reserva por acciones propias 3. Reserva estatutaria 4. Otras reservas *V Pérdidas y Ganancias* Intereses minoritarios

Ejemplo: Cuenta de Pérdidas y Ganancias en Inglés Norteamericano y sus palabras equivalentes en español

Consolidated Statement of Income	Estado de resultados consolidado
1. **Revenue**	1. **Ingresos**
2. Transmission costs and costs of goods sold	2. Coste de venta y costes de los productos vendidos
3. Other external expenses	3. Otros gastos exteriores
4. Wages, salaries and pension costs	4. Sueldos, salarios y pensiones
5. **Total operating expenses before depreciation, etc.**	5. **Total gastos de explotación antes de depreciaciones, etc.**
6. Other income and expenses	6. Otros ingresos y gastos
7. **Income before depreciation, amortization, and special items**	7. **Resultado antes de amortizaciones, depreciaciones y partidas excepcionales**
8. Depreciation, amortization and impairment losses	8. Depreciación, amortización y pérdidas por deterioro
9. Special items	9. Partidas excepcionales
10. **Operating income**	10. **Resultado de explotación**
11. Income from associates and joint ventures	11. Ingresos de asociadas y joint venture
12. Fair value adjustments	12. Ajustes a valor razonable
13. Financial income	13. Ingresos financieros
14. Financial expenses	14. Gastos financieros
15. **Net financials**	15. **Resultado financiero neto**
16. **Income before income taxes**	16. **Resultado antes de impuestos**
17. Income taxes	17. Impuestos sobre beneficios
18. **Net income from continuing operations**	18. **Resultado neto de operaciones continuadas**
19. Net income from discontinued operations	19. Resultado neto de operaciones interrumpidas
20. **Net income**	20. **Resultado neto**
Attributable to:	**Atribuible a:**
21. Shareholders of the Parent Company	21. Accionistas de la matriz
22. Minority interests	22. Accionistas minoritarios
23. Total	23. Total
EPS (EURO)	**Beneficio por acción (EURO)**
Earnings per share, basic	Beneficio por acción básico
Earnings per share, diluted	Beneficio por acción, diluido
Earnings per share from continuing operations, basic	Beneficio por acción de operaciones continuadas, básico
Earnings per share from continuing operations, diluted	Beneficio por acción de operaciones continuadas, diluido
Earnings per share from discontinued operations, basic	Beneficio por acción de operaciones interrumpidas, básico
Earnings per share from discontinued operations, diluted	Beneficio por acción de operaciones interrumpidas, diluido

Consolidated Balance Sheet at December 31	Balance consolidado a 31 de diciembre
1. **Assets**	1. **Activo**
2. **Non-current assets**	2. **Activo no corriente**
3. Intangible assets	3. Inmovilizado intangible
4. Property, plant and equipment	4. Inmovilizado material
5. Investment in associates and joint ventures	5. Inversiones en asociadas y joint venture
6. Minority passive investments	6. Inversiones minoritarias
7. Deferred tax assets	7. Activos por impuesto diferido
8. Pension assets	8. Activos afectos a planes de pensiones
9. Receivables	9. Cuentas a cobrar
10. Derivative financial instruments	10. Instrumentos financieros derivados
11. Prepaid expenses	11. Gastos anticipados
12. **Total non-current assets**	12. **Total activo no corriente**
13. **Current assets**	13. **Activo corriente**
14. Inventories	14. Existencias
15. Receivables	15. Cuentas a cobrar
16. Income tax receivable	16. Activos por impuesto corriente
17. Derivative financial instruments	17. Instrumentos financieros derivados
18. Prepaid expenses	18. Gastos anticipados
19. Marketable securities	19. Valores negociables
20. Cash	20. Efectivo
21. Assets for sale	21. Activos disponibles para la venta
22. **Total current assets**	22. **Total activo corriente**
23. **Total assets**	23. **Total activo**
1. **Equity and liabilities**	1. **Patrimonio Neto y Pasivo**
2. Common shares	2. Capital Social
3. Reserves	3. Reservas
4. Retained earnings	4. Beneficios no distribuidos
5. Proposed dividends	5. Dividendos a pagar
6. **Equity attributable to Company shareholders**	6. **Patrimonio neto atribuible a accionistas mayoritarios**
7. Minority interests	7. Intereses minoritarios
8. **Total equity**	8. **Total Patrimonio Neto**
9. **Non-current liabilities**	9. **Pasivo no corriente**
10. Deferred tax liabilities	10. Pasivos por impuesto diferido
11. Provisions	11. Provisiones
12. Pension liabilities, etc.	12. Obligaciones por pensiones, etc.
13. Loans	13. Préstamos
14. Derivative financial instruments	14. Instrumentos financieros derivados
15. Deferred income	15. Ingresos diferidos
16. **Total non-current liabilities**	16. **Total pasivo no corriente**
17. **Current liabilities**	17. **Pasivo corriente**
18. Loans	18. Préstamos
19. Trade and other payables	19. Acreedores comerciales y otras cuentas a pagar
20. Income tax payable	20. Pasivo por impuesto corriente
21. Derivative financial instruments	21. Instrumentos financieros derivados
22. Deferred income	22. Ingresos diferidos
23. Provisions	23. Provisiones
24. Liabilities concerning assets held for sale	24. Pasivos vinculados con activos mantenidos para la venta
25. **Total current liabilities**	25. **Total Pasivo corriente**
26. **Total liabilities**	26. **Total Pasivo**
27. **Total equity and liabilities**	27. **Total Patrimonio Neto y Pasivo**

Consolidated Statement of cash flow	Estado de flujos de efectivo consolidado
1. Income before depreciation, amortization and special items	1. Resultado antes de depreciación, amortización y partidas similares
2. Reversal of items without cash flow effects	2. Reversión de partidas sin efecto en los flujos de efectivo
3. Pension contributions	3. Aportaciones al plan de pensiones
4. Payments related to provisions	4. Pagos relacionados con provisiones
5. Cash flow from special items	5. Flujos de efectivo de partidas especiales
6. Change in working capital	6. Cambio en el fondo de maniobra
7. **Cash flow from operating activities before net financials and tax**	7. **Flujos de efectivo de las actividades de explotación antes de intereses e impuestos**
8. Interest received	8. Intereses cobrados
9. Interest paid	9. Intereses pagados
10. Realized currency adjustments	10. Diferencias de cambio
11. **Cash flow from operating activities before tax**	11. **Flujos de efectivo de las actividades de explotación antes de impuestos**
12. Corporate income tax paid	12. Impuestos sobre beneficios pagados por el grupo
13. **Cash flow from operating activities in continuing operations**	13. **Flujos de efectivo de las actividades de explotación por operaciones continuadas**
14. Cash flow from operating activities in discontinued operations	14. Flujos de efectivo de las actividades de explotación por operaciones interrumpidas
15. **Total cash flow from operating activities**	15. **Total flujos de efectivo de las actividades de explotación**
16. Investment in enterprises	16. Inversiones en empresas
17. Investment in property, plant and equipment	17. Inversiones en inmovilizado material
18. Investment in intangible assets	18. Inversiones en inmovilizado intangible
19. Investment in marketable securities	19. Inversiones en valores negociables
20. Investment in other non-current assets	20. Inversiones en otros activos no corrientes
21. Divestment of enterprises	21. Desinversiones en empresas
22. Sale of property, plant and equipment	22. Venta de inmovilizado material
23. Divestment of associates and joint ventures	23. Desinversiones en asociadas y joint ventures
24. Sale of marketable securities	24. Venta de valores negociables
25. Sale of other non-current assets	25. Venta de otros activos no corrientes
26. Change in loans to associates and joint ventures	26. Cambio (variación) en préstamos a asociadas y joint ventures
27. Dividends received from associates and joint ventures	27. Dividendos recibidos de asociadas y joint ventures
28. **Cash flow from investing activities in continuing operations**	28. **Flujos de efectivo de las actividades de inversión de operaciones continuadas**
29. Cash flow from investing activities in discontinued operations	29. Flujos de efectivo de las actividades de inversión de operaciones interrumpidas
30. **Total cash flow from investing activities**	30. **Total flujos de efectivo de las actividades de inversión**
31. Proceeds from long-term loans	31. Cobros de préstamos a largo plazo
32. Repayments of long-term loans	32. Pagos de préstamos a largo plazo
33. Change in short-term bank loans	33. Variación en préstamos bancarios a corto plazo

34. Change in interest-bearing receivables	34. Variación en cuentas a cobrar que devengan intereses
35. Change in minority interests	35. Variación en intereses minoritarios
36. Dividends paid	36. Dividendos pagados
37. Acquisition and disposal of treasury shares, net	37. Adquisiciones y ventas de acciones propias, neto
38. **Cash flow from financing activities in continuing operations**	38. **Flujos de efectivo de las actividades de financiación de operaciones continuadas**
39. Cash flow from financing activities in discontinued operations	39. Flujos de efectivo de las actividades de financiación de operaciones interrumpidas
40. **Total cash flow from financing activities**	40. **Total flujos de efectivo de las actividades de financiación**
41. **Total cash flow**	41. **Total flujos de efectivo**
42. Cash and cash equivalents at January 1	42. Efectivo o equivalentes a 1 de enero
43. **Cash and cash equivalents at December 31**	43. **Efectivo o equivalentes a 31 de diciembre**

FUENTES BIBLIOGRÁFICAS

Las fuentes a las que hemos acudido son las siguientes:

Blake, John/Henry Lunt: *Accounting Standards*. 7th ed. Pearson Education Limited. England 2001.

Drury, Colin: *Management and Cost Accounting*. 6th ed. Thomson Learning, London 2004.

Financial Accounting Standards Board: *Current Text. Accounting Standards as of June 1, 2000. Vols. I-IV.* John Wiley & Cons, Inc., 2000/2001.

Financial Accounting Standards Board: *Current Text. Accounting Standards as of June 1, 2005. Vols I-IV.* John Wiley & Cons, Inc., 2005/2006.

Her Majesty's Stationary Office: *UK Companies Act 2006*.

Horngren, Charles T./Alnoor Bhimani/Srikant M. Datar/George Foster: *Management and Cost Accounting*. 3rd ed. Pearson Education Limited, England 2005.

Horngren, Charles T./Srikant M. Datar/George Foster: *Cost Accounting*. 12th ed. Pearson Prentice Hall, Pearson Education, Inc., New Jersey 2006.

Horngren/Sundem/Stratton: *Introduction to Management Accounting. International Edition*. 13th ed. Pearson Education, Inc., New Jersey 2002.

International Accounting Standards Board: *International Financial Reporting Standards IFRSs*. England 2005.

McLaney, Eddie/ Peter Atrill: *Accounting. An Introduction*. 3rd ed. Pearson Education Limited 2005.

Nobes, Christopher/Robert Parker: *Comparative International Accounting*. 7th ed. Pearson Education Limited. England 2002.

Nobes, Christopher/Robert Parker: *Comparative International Accounting*. 9th ed. Pearson Education Limited. England 2006.

Penman, Stephen A.: *Financial Statement Analysis and Security Valuation*. 2nd ed. McGraw-Hill/Irwin, New York, NY 2004.

Walter Reid/D.R. Myddelton: *The Meaning of Company Accounts*. 8th ed. Gower, England 2005.

Sutton, Tim: *Corporate Financial Accounting and Reporting*. 2nd ed. Pearson Education Limited. England 2004.

The Danish Society of Financial Analysts/the Norwegian Society of Financial Analysts: *Recommendations & Financial Ratios 2005*. Copenhagen 2004.

The Institute of Chartered Accountants in England and Wales: *Accounting Standards 2004/2005*. Wolters-Kluwer (UK) Limited 2004.

European Commission: *The International Accounting Standards*:
http://ec.europa.eu/internal_market/accounting/ias/index_en.htm

Financial Accounting Standards Board, Connecticut, USA: www.fasb.org